KEY EVENTS IN THE LIFE
OF THE HISTORICAL JESUS

Key Events in the Life of the Historical Jesus

A Collaborative Exploration of Context and Coherence

Edited by

Darrell L. Bock and Robert L. Webb

William B. Eerdmans Publishing Company
Grand Rapids, Michigan / Cambridge, U.K.

© 2009 Mohr Siebeck, Tübingen, Germany
All rights reserved

First published 2009 by Mohr Siebeck, Tübingen,
as volume 247 of the Wissenschaftliche Untersuchungen zum Neuen Testament series

This edition published 2010 by
Wm. B. Eerdmans Publishing Co.
2140 Oak Industrial Drive N.E., Grand Rapids, Michigan 49505 /
P.O. Box 163, Cambridge CB3 9PU U.K.

Library of Congress Cataloging-in-Publication Data

Key events in the life of the historical Jesus: a collaborative exploration of context
and coherence / edited by Darrell L. Bock and Robert L. Webb.
p.   cm.
Originally published: Tübingen: Mohr Siebeck, © 2009.
(Wissenschaftliche Untersuchungen zum Neuen Testament, 0512-1604; 247).
Includes bibliographical references and index.
ISBN 978-0-8028-6613-4 (pbk.: alk. paper)
1. Jesus Christ — Historicity. 2. Jesus Christ — Biography.
I. Bock, Darrell L.   II. Webb, Robert L. (Robert Leslie), 1955–
BT303.2.K475   2010
232.9′08 — dc22
2010037719

www.eerdmans.com

Contents

Preface	VII
Subject Outline	IX
1. Introduction to Key Events and Actions in the Life of the Historical Jesus Darrell L. Bock and Robert L. Webb	1
2. The Historical Enterprise and Historical Jesus Research Robert L. Webb	9
3. Jesus' Baptism by John: Its Historicity and Significance Robert L. Webb	95
4. Exorcisms and the Kingdom: Inaugurating the Kingdom of God and Defeating the Kingdom of Satan Craig A. Evans	151
5. Jesus and the Twelve Scot McKnight	181
6. The Authenticity and Significance of Jesus' Table Fellowship with Sinners Craig L. Blomberg	215
7. Jesus and the Synoptic Sabbath Controversies Donald A. Hagner	251
8. Peter's Declaration concerning Jesus' Identity in Caesarea Philippi Michael J. Wilkins	293

9. Jesus' Royal Entry into Jerusalem *Brent Kinman*	383
10. The Temple Incident *Klyne R. Snodgrass*	429
11. The Last Supper *I. Howard Marshall*	481
12. Blasphemy and the Jewish Examination of Jesus *Darrell L. Bock*	589
13. The Roman Examination and Crucifixion of Jesus: Their Historicity and Implications *Robert L. Webb*	669
14. Jesus' Empty Tomb and His Appearance in Jerusalem *Grant R. Osborne*	775
15. Key Events in the Life of the Historical Jesus: A Summary *Darrell L. Bock*	825
List of Contributors	855
Ancient Text Index	857
Modern Author Index	913

Preface

When you work on a project that has spanned more than a decade from start to finish, you never are sure if you will see the end. But in this instance it is not a negative thing, for the meetings of the IBR Jesus Group have been a pleasure from start to finish. Our participants come from three continents, and though separated by geographical distance, close relationships have been built, and friendships have been deepened as a result of our annual gatherings. Our meetings were marked by lively conversation about Jesus, Second Temple Judaism, and historical method. But these times also included wonderful snacks (M&Ms, cake, cookies, and chips) as we worked as well as marvelous evening meals to close our meetings. The closing meal each year became a traditional adjournment to our time together. Nothing quite equals a Brazilian steak house to a bunch of hungry scholars!

We mention this closing meal in particular because of our gratitude to Joe Head, who hosted our annual final meal as well as underwrote, through Bible.org, our annual meetings. His interest in our project has never waned from day one. He has always asked about our progress and cheered us on as we reported our progress each year.

We also want to thank our wives for being willing to join us on two of the occasions in Tübingen and Jerusalem (not bad!), as well as being willing to let us travel away the other times. Their encouragement and support were steadfast and unrelenting throughout the entire project. We thank them!

Finally, special thanks must go to Michael Burer, who volunteered to oversee the production of the final manuscript by making the footnote references consistent stylistically, generating the bibliographies, as well as compiling the indices – and he did the job with a smile! We also appreciate the help of two students who assisted Michael in the indexing process: Curtis Lindsey and Trevor Tarpinian. We wish to acknowledge the use of the academic word-processing program, NotaBene, to make these tasks much easier.

Some people question whether anything meaningful can be accomplished in collaboration. This volume would never have been completed without it – and all the essays are stronger (and longer!) as a result. Those of us in the IBR Jesus group have come to appreciate deeply the value that collegiality can bring to an academic exercise.

August 27, 2009

Darrell L. Bock
Robert L. Webb

Subject Outline

DARRELL L. BOCK and ROBERT L. WEBB
Chapter 1 – Introduction to Key Events and Actions in the Life of
the Historical Jesus 1
Bibliography 7

ROBERT L. WEBB
Chapter 2 – The Historical Enterprise and Historical Jesus Research .. 9
1. Introduction 9
2. Defining History, Historiography, and Historical Method 12
   2.1. Understanding the Term "History" 13
   2.2. Wrestling with Historiography 19
   2.3. Clarifying the Historical Method 32
3. Exploring Historical Explanation, Worldview, and the "Supernatural" .. 39
4. Surveying the Tools and Methods in Historical Jesus Research 54
   4.1. Exploring the Question of Historicity 55
   4.2. Appreciating the Primary Ancient Sources 75
   4.3. Applying Historical Method to Historical Jesus Research 78
5. Conclusion: History, the Historical Jesus, and this Project 82
Bibliography 85

ROBERT L. WEBB
Chapter 3 – Jesus' Baptism by John: Its Historicity and Significance .. 95
1. Introduction 95
2. The Historicity of Jesus' Baptism by John 95
   2.1. An Examination of the Historicity of the Baptism 96
   2.2. An Examination of the Historicity of the Theophany 108
   2.3. Summary 112
3. John and his Baptism in the Context of Second-Temple Judaism 113
   3.1. John's Baptism 113
   3.2. John's Prophetic Proclamation 121

3.3. John's Prophetic Role 126
3.4. John's Life and Death 129

4. Implications of Jesus' Baptism by John for understanding Jesus 132
   4.1. The Turning Point in Jesus' Life 133
   4.2. The Earliest Stage of Jesus' Ministry 135
   4.3. The Ideological Framework for the Earliest Stage of Jesus' Ministry
        and Extrapolations to His Later Ministry 139
   4.4. The Possible Association of the Theophany Narrative
        with Jesus' Baptism 141

5. Conclusion 143

Bibliography 144

CRAIG A. EVANS
Chapter 4 – Exorcisms and the Kingdom: Inaugurating the
Kingdom of God and Defeating the Kingdom of Satan 151

1. Introduction: The Relationship of Kingdom to Jesus' Exorcisms 151

2. The Context Provided by Scriptural Antecedents of the Rule of God 152

3. The Context Provided by Prophecies and Expectations of the Rule of
   God in Second Temple Jewish Literature 157

4. Authenticity and Key Themes of Jesus' Proclamation and Exorcisms in
   Light of Its Context 165
   4.1. The Temptation of Jesus 167
   4.2. Exorcism 168
   4.3. Sending the Twelve 173
   4.4. Healing 174

5. The Significance of Jesus' Proclamation of the Kingdom and Exorcisms 176

Bibliography 176

SCOT MCKNIGHT
Chapter 5 – Jesus and the Twelve 181

1. Introduction 181

2. The Historicity of the Twelve in Jesus' Ministry 181

3. The Twelve in Context 189
   3.1. Background 189
   3.2. The Context of the Hebrew Bible 192
   3.3. The Context of the Dead Sea Scrolls and Pseudepigrapha ... 194
   3.4. Eschatology and the Use of the Word "Tribe" 196

4. Jesus and the Twelve 198
   4.1. The Twelve in the Jesus Traditions 198
   4.2. The Twelve, Jesus, and the Historical Context 205
5. Conclusion 209
Bibliography 209

CRAIG L. BLOMBERG
Chapter 6 – The Authenticity and Significance of Jesus' Table
Fellowship with Sinners 215

1. Introduction: Recent Challenges to an Old Consensus for Authenticity 215
2. On the Background and Historicity of Jesus' Meals with Sinners 217
   2.1. Special Meals in the Hebrew Scriptures 219
   2.2. Sharing a Table in Second-Temple Judaism 222
   2.3. Greco-Roman Symposia 225
3. Jesus' Meals with Sinners: A Search for Background 227
   3.1. More Explicit Texts 227
      3.1.1. Levi's Party (Mark 2:13–17 and parallels) 227
      3.1.2. A Glutton and a Drunkard (Q 7:31–35) 230
      3.1.3. A "Sinner in the City" (Luke 7:36–50) 232
      3.1.4. Zacchaeus Short-Changed? (Luke 19:1–10) 234
   3.2. More Implicit Texts 236
      3.2.1. Tax Collectors and Prostitutes (Matt 21:31b–32) 237
      3.2.2. Feasting in the Wilderness (Mark 6:30–44 and parallels;
             8:1–10 and parallel) 238
      3.2.3. How Not to Win Friends and Influence People (Q 13:28–29) 239
      3.2.4. A Rude Guest (Luke 11:37–54) 240
      3.2.5. A Rude Host and a Reply in Kind (Luke 14:1–24) 241
      3.2.6. Fixing Dinner or Favoring Devotion? (Luke 10:38–42) 242
      3.2.7. A Scandalous Summary (Luke 15:1–2) 242
4. Significance: An Eschatological Symbol of Jesus' Centrality in Bringing
   Holiness 243
Bibliography 244

DONALD A. HAGNER
Chapter 7 – Jesus and the Synoptic Sabbath Controversies 251

1. Introduction 251
2. The Historicity of the Sabbath Controversies 252
   2.1. Methodological issues 252
   2.2. The Synoptic Sabbath-Controversy Texts 255
   2.3. Conclusion concerning the Historicity of the Sabbath Controversies ... 269

3. The Significance of the Sabbath Controversies 271
   3.1. The Jewish Context of Sabbath Observance 271
   3.2. The Significance of the Sabbath Controversies for Understanding Jesus   273

4. Conclusion: Implications for the Historical Jesus 282

5. Postscript 287

Bibliography 288

MICHAEL J. WILKINS
Chapter 8 – Peter's Declaration concerning Jesus' Identity in
Caesarea Philippi 293

1. Introduction 293
   1.1 Peter and Jesus' Identity 293
   1.2. Gospel accounts of Peter's declaration 299
   1.3. The issue of the historicity of Peter's declaration 301

2. The Historicity of Peter's Declaration 304
   2.1. Caesarea Philippi as an unexpected locale for the declaration 309
   2.2. An embarrassing portrait of Peter 313
   2.3. The multiple attestation of Peter's declaration? 316
      2.3.1. John and the Synoptics 316
      2.3.2. Matthew's special material 318
   2.4. Historical Coherence of Peter's declaration with Jesus' mission .. 321
      2.4.1. Jesus' messianic ministry 322
         2.4.1.1. Relationship to John the Baptist 324
         2.4.1.2. Calling and sending the Twelve 326
         2.4.1.3. Acclaimed as Prophet and King 327
      2.4.2. Peter's declaration within Jesus' historical mission 329
         2.4.2.1. The "warning" or "rebuke" to tell no one 332
         2.4.2.2. The view that Jesus rejected Peter's declaration 335
         2.4.2.3. The view that Jesus accepted Peter's declaration, but
                  with qualifications 337
         2.4.2.4. Conclusion to Peter's declaration within Jesus'
                  historical mission 342
      2.4.3. The crucifixion 343
         2.4.3.1. The charge against Jesus 343
         2.4.3.2. The Roman titulus 345
      2.4.4. Conclusion to the criterion of historical coherence 347

3. Peter's Declaration of Jesus in Its Broader Historical Context 349
   3.1. "Messiah" and "messianic" 349
   3.2. Ancient "declarations" 353
      3.2.1. Current ruler: Alexander the Great (336–323 B.C.E.) 355
      3.2.2. Future ruler: Vespasian (69–79 C.E.) 356

3.2.3. Royal pretender: Simon, servant of Herod the Great
 (ca. 4 B. C. E.) 358
3.2.4. Messianic claimant: Simon bar Kochba/Kosiba (132–135 C. E.) . . 360
3.3. Conclusion to the broader historical context 363
4. Conclusion and Significance 365
4.1. The historicity of Peter's declaration 366
4.2. The significance of Peter's declaration 367
   4.2.1. Peter 367
   4.2.2. Jesus' self-understanding 368
   4.2.3. The early church 370

Bibliography 371

BRENT KINMAN
Chapter 9 – Jesus' Royal Entry into Jerusalem 383

1. Introduction 383

2. The Historicity of Jesus' Royal Entry 387
 2.1. The Criterion of Multiple Attestation 387
 2.2. The Criterion of Embarrassment 389
 2.3. The Criterion of Effect 393

3. The Background, Context, and the Event of Jesus' Entry 396
 3.1. Jesus' Actions 396
 3.2. The Disciples' Reactions 405
 3.3. The Size of the Crowd 411
 3.4. The Background of Pilate's Entry 415

4. Conclusion 419

Bibliography 421

KLYNE R. SNODGRASS
Chapter 10 – The Temple Incident 429

1. Introduction 429

2. The Question of Historicity 429

3. The Relationship between the Accounts 439
 3.1. Examining the Various Accounts 439
 3.2. The Synoptic vs. the Johannine Chronology 445

4. What Happened, Where, and under What Circumstances? 447
 4.1. The Scale of the Event 448
 4.2. The Reason for Money Changers 455
 4.3. Corruption in the Temple Practice 455
 4.4. The intention of prohibiting carrying vessels or objects through the
  temple 460

5. The Significance of Jesus' Action in the Temple 462
6. Concluding Reflections 474
Bibliography 476

I. Howard Marshall
Chapter 11 – The Last Supper 481
1. Introduction: The Challenge of the Last Supper 481
2. The Historicity and Background of the Meal 485
   2.1. Approaching the Issue 485
   2.2. An Analysis of the Pericopae preceding the Meal 487
      2.2.1. The Plot against Jesus and the Role of Judas (Mark 14:1–2, 10–11) 487
      2.2.2. Preparation for the Passover Meal (Mark 14:12–16) 489
         2.2.2.1. A Basis in the Hebrew Bible? 490
         2.2.2.2. The Question of a Pre-Marcan Passion Narrative 492
         2.2.2.3. The Content of the Narrative 495
      2.2.3. The Betrayer (Mark 14:17–21) 497
   2.3. The Core Narrative of the Meal Itself (Mark 14:22–25) 504
      2.3.1. General Objections to the Historicity of the Meal 504
         2.3.1.1. The Seminar's Critical Comments on Mark's Version 504
         2.3.1.2. The Seminar's Critical Comments on Matthew's Version . . 505
         2.3.1.3. The Seminar's Critical Comments on Luke's Version 506
         2.3.1.4. Bultmann's objections 507
      2.3.2. Jewish or Pagan Origins and Background of the Meal 507
      2.3.3. Burton L. Mack's Reconstruction of a Hellenistic Origin ... 513
         2.3.3.1. Paul's Aetiological Myth 513
         2.3.3.1. Mark's "Historical" Narrative 514
         2.3.3.2. An Exercise in Imagination 514
         2.3.3.3. Conclusion 515
      2.3.4. The Evidence of the Didache 516
         2.3.4.1. The Uncertainty Surrounding the Interpretation of the Didache 518
         2.3.4.2. The Meal in the Didache 519
         2.3.4.3. Comparing the Didache with Paul's Writing 522
         2.3.4.4. The Didache and the History of Christian Meals 526
      2.3.5. Other Possible Origins of the Church Meals 528
      2.3.6. The Text of Luke concerning the Meal 529
         2.3.6.1. In Favor of the Shorter Text 531
         2.3.6.2. In Favor of the Longer Text 533
      2.3.7. The Nature and Date of the Meal: Paschal or Otherwise 541
         2.3.7.1. Jeremias's Arguments concerning the Nature of the Meal 542
         2.3.7.2. Objections to the Paschal Character of the Meal Itself ... 547
         2.3.7.3. The Issue of the Date of the Meal 549
         2.3.7.4. Alternative Proposals concerning the Date of the Meal ... 551
         2.3.7.5. Evaluating the Alternative Proposals 558

  2.3.8. The Account of the Meal 560
    2.3.8.1. Some General Considerations 562
    2.3.8.2. The Bread Saying 566
    2.3.8.3. The Cup Saying 567
    2.3.8.4. The Command(s) To "Do This" 569
    2.3.8.5. The Statements about Future [Eating and] Drinking 572
  2.3.9. After the Meal 575
    2.3.9.1. Other Sayings 575
    2.3.9.2. The Hallel 575
    2.3.9.3. The Prediction of Peter's Denial 575
3. Historical and Theological Significance of the Last Supper 577
Bibliography 580

Darrell L. Bock
Chapter 12 – Blasphemy and the Jewish Examination of Jesus 589

1. Introduction: The Authenticity of the Event of Jesus' Examination by Jewish Temple Authorities 589
2. The Historicity of the Blasphemy Remark in Jesus' Examination by the Jewish Temple Authorities 592
  2.1. The Issue of Blasphemy in Overview 593
  2.2. The Pastoral Function of the Examination Scene within Mark 597
  2.3. The Setting and the Appeal to Jewish Irregularities:
    A Capital Case with Multiple Violations? 600
  2.4. Potential Sources for the Debate in the Examination 606
  2.5 The "Blasphemy" in the Jewish Examination of Jesus 609
    2.5.1. Option 1: Pronunciation of the Divine Name 610
    2.5.2. Option 2: Being at the Right Hand of God 613
    2.5.3. Option 3: Blasphemy involves how the leaders are addressed 622
    2.5.4 Conclusion on the Nature of the Blasphemy. 625
3. The Potential Authenticity of the Saying 625
  3.1. A Lack of Coherence between the Temple Charge
    and the Rest of the Scene. 626
  3.2. The Issue of "Jewish" Expressions in Mark 14:61–62. 631
  3.3. The Use of Ps 110:1 and Dan 7:13 638
  3.4. Jesus and Apocalyptic Son of Man. 645
  3.5. The Meaning and Relationship of the Titles 652
4. The Significance of Jesus' Examination by the Jewish Temple Authorities .. 656
  4.1 Implications for Method: Importance of Historical Background Work 656
  4.2. Implications for the Historical Jesus from the Jewish Examination
    of Jesus 659
Bibliography 661

ROBERT L. WEBB
Chapter 13 – The Roman Examination and Crucifixion of Jesus: Their Historicity and Implications 669

1. Introduction 669
2. Jesus' Execution by Means of Crucifixion 670
   2.1. The Historicity of Jesus' Execution by Crucifixion 671
      2.1.1. Early Christian references to Jesus' crucifixion 671
      2.1.2. Ancient non-Christian references to Jesus' crucifixion 685
      2.1.3. The criteria of historicity applied to Jesus' execution by crucifixion 689
   2.2. Crucifixion in the Ancient Mediterranean World 695
   2.3. The Historical Significance of Jesus' Execution by Crucifixion 700
3. Jesus' Examination before Rome's Prefect, Pontius Pilate 701
   3.1. The Historicity of Jesus' Trial before Pontius Pilate 702
      3.1.1. Early Christian references to Jesus' examination by Pilate 702
      3.1.2. Ancient non-Christian references to Jesus' examination by Pilate 703
      3.1.3. The criteria of historicity applied to Pilate's examination of Jesus 705
   3.2. The Character of Pontius Pilate's Rule as Prefect of Judea 706
      3.2.1. The Coins Minted by Pilate 707
      3.2.2. The Iconic Standards Incident (ca. 26 C.E.) 714
      3.2.3. The Aqueduct Protest Incident (ca. 27–29 C.E.) 716
      3.2.4. The Galilean Pilgrims Incident (ca. 28–29 C.E.) 717
      3.2.5. The Aniconic Shields Incident (ca. 31–32 C.E.) 719
      3.2.6. The Samaritan Prophet Incident (36 C.E.) 721
      3.2.7. Pilate and the Influence of Sejanus 722
      3.2.8. Conclusion: The Prefecture of Pontius Pilate 724
   3.3. Roman Rule and Capital Crimes in a Roman Province 724
      3.3.1. Roman rule of the Province of Judea 725
      3.3.2. Responsibility for capital crimes in a Roman Province 727
      3.3.3. Roman procedure in a capital situation 730
   3.4. Reconstructing Core Elements in Jesus' Examination by Pontius Pilate 732
      3.4.1. The Jewish priestly authorities as the accusers of Jesus 738
      3.4.2. The nature of the charge(s) against Jesus 740
      3.4.3. Pontius Pilate's verdict concerning Jesus 755
4. Conclusion: The Historical Significance of Jesus' Execution by Crucifixion at the Behest of Pontius Pilate 759
5. Appendix A: Accounts of Jesus' Roman Examination and Crucifixion in Narrative Gospels 761

Bibliography 763

GRANT R. OSBORNE
Chapter 14 – Jesus' Empty Tomb and His Appearance in Jerusalem ... 775

1. Introduction 775

2. The Authenticity of the Resurrection 776
   2.1. The Earliest Resurrection Creedal Statement 776
   2.2. The Empty Tomb 782
   2.3. The Jerusalem Appearance: Luke 24:36–49 = John 20:19–23 791

3. The Context of Resurrection in the Hebrew Bible, Second-Temple
   Judaism, and Hellenism 804

4. The Significance of Jesus' Resurrection 815

5. Conclusion 818

Bibliography 819

DARRELL L. BOCK
Chapter 15 – Key Events in the Life of the Historical Jesus:
A Summary 825

Jesus' Baptism by John the Baptist 827
Exorcisms and the Kingdom of God Versus Kingdom of Satan 828
The Choosing of the Twelve 829
Table Fellowship with Sinners and Outsiders 831
Controversy over the Sabbath with Jewish Leaders 833
Peter's Declaration at Caesarea Philippi 835
Jesus' Entry into Jerusalem 837
Jesus' Action in the Temple 838
Jesus' Last Supper with his Disciples 841
Jesus' Examination Before the Jewish Leadership 842
Jesus' Roman Examination by Pilate and his Crucifixion 845
Jesus' Resurrection as Vindication after a Certain Death 847
Conclusion 850
Bibliography 852

Chapter 1

Introduction to Key Events and Actions in the Life of the Historical Jesus

DARRELL L. BOCK and ROBERT L. WEBB
Co-Conveners of the IBR Jesus Group

The last three decades have seen a renewed interest in historical Jesus research that is marked by new approaches and methods, and which have resulted in an impressive array of new hypotheses.[1] Historical Jesus research is not only alive and well, it is also fascinatingly fruitful. One of the key gains

---

[1] Historical Jesus research is frequently periodized into three quests, with these recent decades considered to be the "Third Quest" (a term coined by N. T. Wright in Stephen Neill and Tom Wright, *The Interpretation of the New Testament, 1861–1986* [2nd ed.; Oxford: Oxford University Press, 1988], 379–403). However, recent discussion has suggested that this schema, while maybe helpful for introducing students to the labyrinth of historical Jesus studies, is too simplistic for scholarly work. For critical discussion, see the chapter, "Secularizing Jesus" in Dale C. Allison, Jr., *Resurrecting Jesus: The Earliest Christian Tradition and Its Interpreters* (New York: T&T Clark, 2005), 1–26, the chapter, "The 'Third Quest' for the Historical Jesus and the Criteria for Authenticity," in Stanley E. Porter, *The Criteria for Authenticity in Historical-Jesus Research: Previous Discussion and New Proposals* (JSNTSup 191; Sheffield: Sheffield Academic Press, 2000), 28–62, and Fernando Bermejo Rubio, "The Fiction of the 'Three Quests': An Argument for Dismantling a Dubious Historiographical Paradigm," *JSHJ* 7 (2009), forthcoming. One should also recall that in raising the emergence of a Third Quest, studies reflecting the "New" or "Second Quest" approaches have not ceased, so that however the schema is presented, today we have differing emphases in basic approach present side by side. There also has been a lively discussion on whether historical Jesus studies have any real value; see the contrasting approach of the essays by Dale C. Allison, Jr. and Francis Watson in Beverly Roberts Gaventa and Richard B. Hays, eds., *Seeking the Identity of Jesus: A Pilgrimage* (Grand Rapids: Eerdmans, 2008). Allison questions the value of the criteria so central to much of our work, preferring the memory of the church and an appeal at a macro level to what he calls recurrent attestation. His questions about how the criteria function with small bits of material is worth pondering. However, he has argued that a coherent, macro portrait is possible and works with an approach that mirrors in many respects his appeal for a more macro concern. The twelve events we have selected all touch on some of the recurrent themes he wishes to affirm. Watson's essay argues for a limited benefit, even necessity, to keeping attention on the historical Jesus in working with the mediated presentation of Jesus the four gospels give us. In the essay by Robert L. Webb in this volume (ch. 2, § 4.1), he proposes that the criteria are insufficient alone, and need to be seen as part of a larger historical method that involves both top-down and bottom-up approaches, of which the criteria form a contributing part.

of recent work has been the careful attention given to Jesus' Second Temple environment as well as an appreciation for how his actions and teaching were set in and addressed a Jewish context.

Precursors include the kind of work done by Joachim Jeremias,[2] who sought to be sure the Jewish roots of Jesus were not lost. George Caird insisted that the right place to start with Jesus was in a backdrop focused on Israel.[3] Martin Hengel also sought roots in the Jewish context, but not at the expense of Greco-Roman concerns, noting how intertwined Hellenism and Judaism had become by Jesus' time.[4]

The historical-Jesus studies presented during the past 30–40 years cover a wide spectrum of approaches. On the one hand we have the work of E. P. Sanders,[5] meticulously working through both a look at key events and themes, while also considering the thrust of Jesus' activity at a more macro-level. On the other, we can consider the approach of Ben Meyer,[6] whose effort concentrates on a synthesis developed out of interaction with key Jewish themes of the Second Temple period. Where Sanders sees a skeleton of events that can confidently be said to reflect Jesus, the other sees the ability to speak comfortably of the aims Jesus had, arguing for a much more rounded portrait. John Meier, in probably the most extensive recent attempt, has been involved in his effort for decades now with the key volumes pulling everything together still awaiting release.[7] His work is a meticulously detailed consideration of key figures and themes that develops a picture at a micro level of detail, while keeping an eye on the big picture. N. T. Wright also has a full study that defends a synthetic model focusing on Jesus speaking to an Israel still in spiritual exile as God returns to His people in victory through the work of Jesus.[8] More recently James D. G. Dunn and Martin Hengel have offered comprehensive accounts, with Dunn emphasizing the flexible nature of the tradition set more in an oral frame, while Hengel has sought to trace a Jesus who focused his presentation on his authority in some type of carefully framed messianic light.[9]

---

[2] Joachim Jeremias, *New Testament Theology: The Proclamation of Jesus* (trans. John Bowden; New York: Scribner, 1971).

[3] G. B. Caird, *Jesus and the Jewish Nation* (Ethel M. Wood Lecture; London: Athlone, 1965).

[4] See his multiple studies on these themes.

[5] E. P. Sanders, *The Historical Figure of Jesus* (London: Penguin, 1993).

[6] Ben F. Meyer, *The Aims of Jesus* (London: SCM, 1979).

[7] Volume 4 of his opus, *A Marginal Jew: Rethinking the Historical Jesus* (4 vols.; ABRL; New York: Doubleday, 1991–2009), was announced as our work was concluding, and this volume will only treat issues tied to Jesus and the Law, as well as the ethical teaching of Jesus.

[8] N. T. Wright, *Jesus and the Victory of God* (vol. 2 of *Christian Origins and the Question of God*; Minneapolis: Fortress, 1996).

[9] James D. G. Dunn, *Jesus Remembered* (vol. 1 of *Christianity in the Making*; Grand

Somewhere in the mix also belong studies that have not abandoned the concern for and emphasis on Hellenistic influence on the tradition, an approach that was a key element of some earlier works (sometimes associated with what was termed the "New Quest") with its effort to sift out the historical Jesus from concerns of emerging church communities of the evangelists. John Dominic Crossan's Jesus reflects the itinerant style of a teacher of wisdom more like a philosopher than any other ancient model, but he also works with an elaborate view of sources that treats all sources at a similar level in terms of historical impact.[10] He spends much valuable time thinking through how Jesus fits into a Hellenistic context, but with less interaction using Second Temple Jewish sources. While the Jesus Seminar made considerable use of Second Temple Jewish sources, they also often spent more time on setting the backdrop for the evangelists' themes out of a Hellenistic context than in a discussion of Second Temple Jewish context. The Seminar came to view Jesus as primarily a teacher of wisdom and aphorisms.[11] This approach was challenged by those who saw Jesus calling Israel back to covenantal faithfulness in a movement that appealed to the need for restoration and looked to the realization of Jewish hopes. So, there has been lively debate on whether Jesus presented himself in a context of Jewish hope about the consummation, often called vaguely the eschatological hope, or whether he was fundamentally wedded to a presentation rooted in wisdom and ethical themes. Other key shorter, comprehensive studies across this spectrum include those by Dale Allison, Bart Ehrman, Paula Fredricksen, Scot McKnight, as well as from a Jewish perspective, including work by David Flusser and Géza Vermès.[12] These shorter studies also gave careful attention to Second Temple context and issues.

Yes, historical Jesus studies is alive and well, and has been for several decades. But it is also somewhat disturbing to observe the diversity in the range of Jesus portraits that have been proposed. Some suggest this diversity

---

Rapids: Eerdmans, 2003–); Martin Hengel and Anna Maria Schwemer, *Jesus und das Judentum* (vol. 1 of *Geschichte des frühen Christentums*; 4 vols.; Tübingen: Mohr Siebeck, 2007–).

[10] John Dominic Crossan, *The Historical Jesus: The Life of a Mediterranean Jewish Peasant* (San Francisco: HarperSanFrancisco, 1991).

[11] Robert W. Funk, et al., *The Five Gospels: The Search for the Authentic Words of Jesus* (New York: Macmillan, 1993).

[12] Dale C. Allison, Jr., *Jesus of Nazareth: Millenarian Prophet* (Minneapolis: Fortress, 1998); Bart D. Ehrman, *Jesus, Apocalyptic Prophet of the New Millennium* (Oxford: Oxford University Press, 1999); Paula Fredriksen, *Jesus of Nazareth, King of the Jews: A Jewish Life and the Emergence of Christianity* (New York: Knopf, 1999); Scot McKnight, *Jesus and His Death: Historiography, the Historical Jesus, and Atonement Theory* (Waco: Baylor University Press, 2005); David Flusser, *Jesus* (2nd ed.; in collaboration with R. Steven Notley; Jerusalem: Magnes, 1997); Géza Vermès, *Jesus the Jew: A Historian's Reading of the Gospels* (London: Collins, 1973).

shows the failure of the quest and its criteria, or at least points to its severe limitations.[13] It is often observed that in seeking to see the historical Jesus down the well of history, one may only be viewing one's own reflection.[14] One of the reasons for this diversity is the complex nature of the study and method itself.[15] It is in this context of both diverse method and debated historical backdrop that the present study emerged.

In the mid-nineteen nineties, Darrell Bock proposed to the Institute for Biblical Research that a team project, a true seminar, be undertaken to study the historical Jesus. Initial discussions took place with Robert Webb, and together we became the co-conveners of the group. We decided after two years of meeting together to proceed. Our plan was that this study group – made up of IBR members with expertise in historical Jesus studies – would work with standard historical-Jesus methods and criteria, and be rooted in a careful look at historiographical questions.[16]

The decision was made to focus our attention on exploring key events and activities in the life of Jesus which met two criteria: a strong case could be made for a judgment of high probability that the core event was historical, and that it was likely significant for understanding Jesus. The goal was to see the extent to which such a study of key events might provide an overall framework for understanding Jesus. Once these key events had been selected, each essay was to do three things: first, it was to set forth a case for the probable historicity of the event using the criteria for authenticity. The focus was to, first, establish the probable historicity of the event's core rather than concerning itself with all of the details. Second, explore the socio-cultural contextual information that contributes to understanding the event in its first-century context. Third, in light of this context, to consider the significance of the event for understanding Jesus. Thus, each study would have both macro and micro concerns, being both analytical and synthetic.

---

[13] So Dale C. Allison, Jr, "The Historians' Jesus and the Church," in *Seeking the Identity of Jesus: A Pilgrimage* (ed. Beverly Roberts Gaventa and Richard B. Hays; Grand Rapids: Eerdmans, 2008), 79–95, especially pp. 79–83.

[14] This observation is often attributed to Albert Schweitzer, but it actually is from George Tyrrell (*Christianity at the Cross-Roads* [1909; repr., London: Allen & Unwin, 1963], 49) who observes concerning Adolf Harnack's *Wesen des Christentums*, "[t]he Christ that Harnack sees, looking back through nineteen centuries of Catholic darkness, is only the reflection of a Liberal Protestant face, seen at the bottom of a deep well." This sometimes trite and frequently-cited view of Jesus studies risks ignoring the fact that people's views of Jesus can and do change as a result of their study. Participating in the discussion and opening oneself up to the hermeneutical spiral can lead to such reassessments.

[15] For discussion in this volume see ch. 2, § 2, which explores why multiple historical representations might be made, and that this is not necessarily a bad or deficient thing.

[16] Besides those who wrote the essays, the group had a few other participants from the IBR. Key among them was Michael H. Burer, who helped us get this manuscript into published form and produced the indices. For further description of the group in terms of historiography, see ch. 2, § 5.

The group would function by assigning each event to a participant who would write a rough draft of the essay. This was then distributed in advance to all members who would then meet to discuss the essay. Each essay was discussed for a full day – paragraph by paragraph and sometimes line by line. Some essays went through multiple drafts and were discussed again for an additional day in a subsequent year. The focus was to discuss the evidence and argumentation to ensure that they were as complete and sound as possible. The process involved extensive discussion and debate which helped to shape and strengthen each essay. Although the group has twelve members, in any given year participants in the discussion ranged from six to nine. Several members were there for a majority of the meetings, so that a line of continuity was maintained throughout our discussions. So in a very real sense this work reflects the input of the group. The collaborative learning experience was very stimulating. Each author, however, remains alone responsible for the views expressed in their particular essay. In other words, the author of each essay had the final call on its contents.

The announcement went out and our first meeting was held in Chicago in 1999. The final meeting was held in Jerusalem in the summer of 2008. In between was another meeting in Chicago, a midway meeting in Tübingen (2005), and the rest of the meetings in Dallas. What started out as the presentation of ten events expanded to address twelve: six in Jesus' earlier ministry at large and six associated with his key, climactic activity in Jerusalem. The first six events were: The baptism by John the Baptist, the exorcisms in relationship to the teaching on the kingdom of God, the choosing of the Twelve, the association with sinners, the Sabbath controversies, and Peter's declaration at Caesarea Philippi. The final six events were the entry into Jerusalem, the temple incident, the last supper, the examination by the Jewish leadership, the examination by Pilate including crucifixion, and the claim of resurrection through the empty tomb and appearance accounts. The studies you see before you are the product of the group's work. Among the team there are differences in particulars, but in general the synthesis set forth is one the team embraces as providing the most coherent understanding of what Jesus did as a historic figure.

Some years more than one event was examined in an elongated schedule for the annual meetings. Literally hours of conversation and interaction are behind each study, including being in the position of looking up primary material, if it was called for, and discussing it, something the advent of computers has made possible.

This published work begins with an essay by Robert L. Webb on history, historiography, and historical method that actually was composed at the end of our work together. This essay opens the book to set the direction of what we sought to do and the issues we consistently faced throughout our meetings. It reflects discussions that regularly came up as individual events were considered and assessed. In other words, this essay was written at the end of our process; it was not written as a guideline at the beginning of it. As noted above, Jesus studies has generated many distinct portraits of Jesus. Webb's examination looks at method and the "forks in the road" choices such method faces, and as such it helps to explain how complex the pursuit of the historical Jesus is and why this variety exists. The essay also helps to show the limits of such an approach, given the nature of our data and our distance from it. This is why our portrait here should be seen as one attempt at putting pieces of a very complex puzzle together.

We write for an audience interested in historical Jesus study, both those who have engaged in it and those who want to get familiar with the range of discussion often tied to it. Such a study concentrates on what it thinks can be demonstrated in a corroborative manner about Jesus. All sources are available for consideration and each is sifted critically. By working with the criteria, our goal was to work with a method that is generally used in such study. We are quite aware that such methods have been subject to important critiques from all sides of the debate, but in many ways these are the best means we have to engage in such a sifting process. Webb's essay summarizes which criteria we used and how we tended to see their importance after we completed our study. It also places the criteria within a larger framework of broad historical method involving both a top-down and bottom-up approach.

The subsequent twelve essays focus on specific events, or in a few cases, key sets of events (i.e., exorcisms in relation to the Kingdom of God, Sabbath controversies, and table fellowship with sinners). A similar structure for the most part appears in each essay proceeding through three concerns: (1) the historicity of the core of the event, (2) the social-cultural contextual information that helps us understand the event, and (3) the significance of the event for understanding the life and ministry of Jesus. In most cases where an event reflects a series of such accounts, a choice was made of a particular event to make the case for the category in question as authentic. This allowed us to focus on the central issues tied to the category.

Darrell L. Bock also has written a concluding essay. This represents the attempt to present a case for the coherence of the portrait that these key events suggest. We think we have shown a compelling case for a path that makes sense for a Jesus rooted historically in the complex cultural backdrop of the Second Temple period. Our study has concentrated on the Jewish context for providing socio-cultural background, as it often sheds significant light on what Jesus was doing.

One of the points expressed consistently in our discussion is the importance of recognizing, taking into account, and making public one's horizon, including one's biases and preunderstanding. Thus, we consider it important to say "where we are coming from" as a group. As the IBR Jesus Group, we are members of the Institute for Biblical Research, which is an academic society specifically for scholars whose disciplines are biblical studies: Hebrew Bible, New Testament and related fields. Its vision is to foster excellence in biblical studies, doing so within a faith commitment. Thus each of us has a commitment to the Christian faith. While some of us would call ourselves "Evangelical Christian," others might prefer "biblically orthodox Christian." Thus, while all are Christians, there is some diversity in out theological viewpoints.

Our hope is that these studies, along with a treatment of the twelve events' coherence, can add to the already vibrant discussion that has been a part of Jesus studies over the last several decades. We see four features of the work as making this study of particular value in assessing Jesus and presenting a portrait of him, not as a final word, but as an introduction to appreciating who Jesus was as an historic figure. These four features are: the group nature of the effort, the study's combining and balancing of analysis and synthesis, its attention to historiographic method and many details of the Second Temple context, along with the study's claim to set a trajectory for considering who Jesus was. These features, as well as the results, made this study a valuable exercise for the participants. We have learned much from one another in the process. So we offer this collection of essays forged in over a decade's reflection on the historical Jesus. Our hope is that our interpretation of these central events provides insight into the central themes of Jesus' life and his aims.

Bibliography

Allison, Dale C., Jr. "The Historians' Jesus and the Church." Pages 79–95 in *Seeking the Identity of Jesus: A Pilgrimage*. Edited by Beverly Roberts Gaventa and Richard B. Hays. Grand Rapids: Eerdmans, 2008.
–. *Jesus of Nazareth: Millenarian Prophet*. Minneapolis: Fortress, 1998.
–. *Resurrecting Jesus: The Earliest Christian Tradition and Its Interpreters*. New York: T&T Clark, 2005.
Bermejo Rubio, Fernando. "The Fiction of the 'Three Quests': An Argument for Dismantling a Dubious Historiographical Paradigm." *JSHJ* 7 (2009).
Caird, G. B. *Jesus and the Jewish Nation*. Ethel M. Wood Lecture. London: Athlone, 1965.
Crossan, John Dominic. *The Historical Jesus: The Life of a Mediterranean Jewish Peasant*. San Francisco: HarperSanFrancisco, 1991.
Dunn, James D. G. *Jesus Remembered*. Vol. 1 of *Christianity in the Making*. Grand Rapids: Eerdmans, 2003–.

Ehrman, Bart D. *Jesus, Apocalyptic Prophet of the New Millennium*. Oxford: Oxford University Press, 1999.
Flusser, David. *Jesus*. 2nd ed. In collaboration with R. Steven Notley. Jerusalem: Magnes, 1997.
Fredriksen, Paula. *Jesus of Nazareth, King of the Jews: A Jewish Life and the Emergence of Christianity*. New York: Knopf, 1999.
Funk, Robert W., Roy W. Hoover, and The Jesus Seminar. *The Five Gospels: The Search for the Authentic Words of Jesus*. New York: Macmillan, 1993.
Gaventa, Beverly Roberts, and Richard B. Hays, eds. *Seeking the Identity of Jesus: A Pilgrimage*. Grand Rapids: Eerdmans, 2008.
Hengel, Martin, and Anna Maria Schwemer. *Jesus und das Judentum*. Vol. 1 of *Geschichte des frühen Christentums*. 4 vols. Tübingen: Mohr Siebeck, 2007–.
Jeremias, Joachim. *New Testament Theology: The Proclamation of Jesus*. Translated by John Bowden. New York: Scribner, 1971.
McKnight, Scot. *Jesus and His Death: Historiography, the Historical Jesus, and Atonement Theory*. Waco: Baylor University Press, 2005.
Meier, John P. *A Marginal Jew: Rethinking the Historical Jesus*. ABRL. New York: Doubleday, 1991–.
Meyer, Ben F. *The Aims of Jesus*. London: SCM, 1979.
Neill, Stephen, and Tom Wright. *The Interpretation of the New Testament, 1861–1986*. 2nd ed. Oxford: Oxford University Press, 1988.
Porter, Stanley E. *The Criteria for Authenticity in Historical-Jesus Research: Previous Discussion and New Proposals*. JSNTSup 191. Sheffield: Sheffield Academic Press, 2000.
Sanders, E. P. *The Historical Figure of Jesus*. London: Penguin, 1993.
Tyrrell, George. *Christianity at the Cross-Roads*. 1909. Repr., London: Allen & Unwin, 1963.
Vermès, Géza. *Jesus the Jew: A Historian's Reading of the Gospels*. London: Collins, 1973.
Wright, N. T. *Jesus and the Victory of God*. Vol. 2 of *Christian Origins and the Question of God*. Minneapolis: Fortress, 1996.

Chapter 2

The Historical Enterprise and Historical Jesus Research

ROBERT L. WEBB

1. Introduction[1]

As historical Jesus research has evolved over the past two and half centuries, one of its basic defining characteristics has been to distinguish the "Christ of faith" from the "Jesus of history." While simplistic, this truism nevertheless aids in clarifying what marks out historical Jesus research from that which preceded it. In the Middle Ages and before, discussion of Jesus was usually in terms that explored the theological significance of "Jesus Christ." If there was any "historical" discussion, it was largely in terms of polemical debates between Christians and those of other faiths over the Christian claims concerning Jesus Christ.[2] The concern was primarily theological, with the twin authorities being the Bible and the Church. A distinction between the "Jesus of history" and the "Christ of faith" was irrelevant in light of this concern and inappropriate in the context of these authorities. This distinction in historical Jesus research was largely developed in association with the Enlightenment, which advocated the role of reason as the basis of authority over against tradition – the political tradition of the State and the religious tradition of the Bible and the Church. Many people today still make no such distinction – when sitting in the pew, it is enough to read the Gospels, for they provide theological answers to questions of faith. For others, however, the development of historical understanding that has arisen in our modern

---

[1] In addition to the members of this collaborative project, I would also like to acknowledge the interaction with and suggestions from a number of others who were not members: Dale C. Allison, James G. Crossley, Philip R. Davies, Lee Martin McDonald, and William J. Webb. Recognizing the diversity of viewpoints represented by these other readers, it will be quite evident that they would not agree with everything in this essay. But I value and appreciate their interaction. It has also been an enjoyable and stimulating process to discuss these issues with my co-chair, Darrell Bock, through the innumerable versions of this essay. We have learned much from each other in the spirit of Prov 27:17.

[2] For examples of such early Christian apologists, see Justin, *Dialogue with Trypho* (second century C.E.) and Origen, *Contra Celsus* (third century C.E.).

context leads to seeking historical answers to historical questions and thus to this distinction between the "Jesus of history" and the "Christ of faith." One is not to be preferred over the other, for both the "Jesus of history" and the "Christ of faith" are equally legitimate subjects of inquiry, but they are using different means to provide answers to different questions.

Most historical Jesus research, while making this distinction, was pursued out of theological interest and was intended to lead to theological conclusions. While the past two and a half centuries have been a quest for the "historical" Jesus, historical Jesus research as a discipline has been in many respects a subset of biblical studies or theology rather than history – to this day a university course on "historical Jesus" is probably taught in a religious or theological studies department rather than the history or classics department. Recently, however, historical Jesus research has been developing a more explicitly historical focus: the larger disciplines of history and philosophy of history are having a greater impact, the cognate disciplines such as cultural anthropology and sociology are being drawn upon, and theologically-driven agendas are viewed as inappropriate to the explicitly historical enterprise of historical Jesus research.[3]

This chapter is intended to complement the accompanying essays in a couple of ways. First, taking the cue from recent historical Jesus studies, this chapter begins with the nature of history, historiography, and historical

---

[3] The history of this past two and a half centuries of historical Jesus research (frequently called "the quest for the historical Jesus") is often divided up into a number of phases. This recent shift to a more explicitly historical focus is often associated with what has been termed the "Third Quest." There are numerous surveys of the history of historical Jesus research; for example, the classic discussion of the eighteenth and nineteenth centuries is Albert Schweitzer, *The Quest of the Historical Jesus: First Complete Edition* (trans. W. Montgomery, et al.; Minneapolis: Fortress, 2001), and for the first half of the twentieth century, see Walter P. Weaver, *The Historical Jesus in the Twentieth Century, 1900–1950* (Harrisburg, PA: Trinity Press International, 1999). For the latter half of the twentieth century, see Mark Allen Powell, *Jesus as a Figure in History: How Modern Historians View the Man from Galilee* (Louisville, KY: Westminster/John Knox, 1998). For a more complete bibliography of such historical surveys, see Craig A. Evans, *Life of Jesus Research: An Annotated Bibliography* (2 ed.; NTTS 24; Leiden: E.J. Brill, 1996). Recently, however, this paradigm of the "three quests" has been called into question. For example, see Stanley E. Porter, *The Criteria for Authenticity in Historical-Jesus Research: Previous Discussion and New Proposals* (JSNTSup 191; Sheffield: Sheffield Academic Press, 2000), 28–62; Dale C. Allison, *Resurrecting Jesus: The Earliest Christian Tradition and Its Interpreters* (London: T&T Clark, 2005), 1–26; Fernando Bermejo Rubio, "The Fiction of the 'Three Quests': An Argument for Dismantling a Dubious Historiographical Paradigm," *JSHJ* 7 (2009): [forthcoming]. It should be noted that a distinction is made here between engaging in historical Jesus research with a theologically-driven agenda or focus, and engaging in it out of theological interest. There should be no problem if a historian has personal interests that lead to professional historical engagement in a research topic, but this interest must not lead to a bias in making historical judgments or providing historical explanations. Aspects of this issue are discussed further in §§ 2.3, 3, and 4 below.

method. Only when these larger issues are appreciated can one understand what historical Jesus research can and should be, and why it has faced some of the difficulties it has. Second, having established this larger context, only then do we turn to issues specific to historical Jesus research. Here I try to provide a road map to the some distinctives of this field. In particular, I identify some "forks in the road" which different scholars take with reference to issues in this field of research. These "forks" help to clarify some of the diversity which may be observed in historical Jesus studies today.

This chapter is intended to be an Introduction – and only that. Each of the sections below could be easily expanded to be a chapter or even a book in length. A cursory examination of the other chapters in this volume demonstrates that this could easily be done! The attempt at brevity in this Introduction is intended to provide the non-specialist reader a survey of some of the foundational principles of historical Jesus research, particularly those which are debated in the discipline today. And for fellow historical-Jesus scholars, this Introduction is intended to convey some of the principles that have guided this project, so that they can place it within the spectrum of this discipline.

It should be noted, however, that the discussions below represent my views on the subject, and they do not necessarily represent all members of this project.[4] We have discussed its contents extensively and they have contributed to shaping my thinking on these matters, but I remain responsible for its contents. It should be noted that this chapter was written at the conclusion of this project, and thus it explores issues that were raised at various points throughout the process, but it never functioned as the guide that preceded the project.

Given the length of this chapter, some guidance at the beginning may help you, the reader, to not get lost, and also so that, if you wish, you might jump ahead to the subjects that are of greater interest to you:

§ 2. Defining History, Historiography, and Historical Method: This section discusses what history is and how is it done. This may appear irrelevant, but these subjects provide the foundation for the historical enterprise. If you do skip ahead over this point, please do return here, for these issues are very important.

§ 3. Historical Explanation, Worldview, and the "Supernatural": In most historical studies, the issues of worldview and the "supernatural" do not arise, but when turning to the subject of Jesus, it must be addressed. So this section provides a bridge between history in general (§ 2) and distinctives in historical Jesus studies (§ 4).

---

[4] For a description of this project and its members, see the preceding "Introduction." See also my own observations in the conclusion to this essay.

§ 4. Tools and Methods in Historical Jesus Research: This section provides an overview of some distinctive tools and methods that are used in historical Jesus research as well as exploring some of the issues that such research raises.

2. Defining History, Historiography, and Historical Method

Those who engage in historical Jesus research, like historians of other subjects and historical periods, study evidence from the past in order to produce a *history* (an account of the results of their research), which they do using a *historical method* (a set of tools and processes used in that research), which in turn arises out of and is based upon a *historiography* (the theoretical principles and perspectives that undergird the historical method used).[5] These are the three interrelated elements in the enterprise: history, historical method, and historiography. All publications of historical Jesus research do the first (i.e., history) using their understanding of the second (i.e., a historical method). Some scholars do discuss explicitly the historical method they use,[6] but relatively rarely does a work on the historical Jesus discuss matters of historiography.[7] One of the reasons for the diversity in

---

[5] The terms "history" and "historiography" are used in different ways in this discipline. I am using the term "historiography" to refer to the underlying philosophical and theoretical principles that guide the historian's method and shape the history produced. This is related to a second meaning of the term, which uses it for a history of history writing. A study of history writing in the past often involves exploring the underlying assumptions being made by the historian in the history produced. Thus, in relation to the previous meaning of the term, historiography can refer to the history of historiography. See the discussion by Peter Novick (*That Noble Dream: The "Objectivity Question" and the American Historical Profession* [Cambridge: Cambridge University Press, 1998], 8 n. 6) who laments the loss of the term "historiology" which could have helped to distinguish these two meanings. On historiography, see Michael Bentley, ed., *Companion to Historiography* (London: Routledge, 1997), who in the "General Introduction: The Project of Historiography" discusses how the inherent relationship between these two meanings of the term developed (xi–xvii), observing that inherent in historiography today is "a prior interest in epistemology" (xiii). See also Arthur Marwick, *The New Nature of History: Knowledge, Evidence, Language* (Chicago: Lyceum Books, 2001), 28–31. This usage is not universal, however. For example, Aviezer Tucker (*Our Knowledge of the Past: A Philosophy of Historiography* [Cambridge: Cambridge University Press, 2004], 1–2) uses the term "historiography" to refer to the historian's representation of the past (for which I use the term "history") and the term "history" refers to the "past events" themselves. Thus he must then use the phrase "philosophy of historiography" for what I mean by "historiography." For a history of historiography, see Ernst Breisach, *Historiography: Ancient, Medieval, and Modern* (2 ed.; Chicago: University of Chicago Press, 1994).

[6] To give only two well-known examples, E. P. Sanders, *Jesus and Judaism* (Philadelphia: Fortress, 1985), 1–22; John Dominic Crossan, *The Historical Jesus: The Life of a Mediterranean Jewish Peasant* (San Francisco: HarperSanFrancisco, 1991), xxvii–xxxiv.

[7] Those scholars who discuss their historiography generally do go on also to discuss

scholars' conclusions concerning the historical Jesus may be traced to differences over historiography and historical method, and even over the nature of history. Thus, to aid discussion in this field, it is incumbent on those who engage in it to present to their readers, if only briefly, their understanding of these matters.

This section examines the broader issues concerning history, historiography, and historical method, and then the following sections consider their application to historical Jesus research in particular. Here we begin with the broader parameters of what constitutes history and then turn to historiography – the theoretical and philosophical underpinnings for doing history. Finally this allows us to consider how these shape historical method. I beg the reader's patience as I try to carefully lay a foundation in which all of these facets are interwoven.

2.1. Understanding the Term "History"

In popular usage today the term "history" is frequently used to refer to what happened in the past. For example, one might make the statement: "The Civil War was a painful time in American history." Here the term "history" is being used to refer to the past itself – the actual events – the actions and activities that took place, and the people who did them. A moment of reflection, however, leads us to realize that we do not have *direct* access to these past events (this will change, of course, when a means of time travel is invented!). For example, in a difference of opinion over some aspect concerning a particular past event, one would have to provide evidence to support one's opinion. But to do so requires that something from that past event survive until the present day. What survives might be a written document or some form of inscription alluding to the event. If no traces[8] have survived until the present, we today would have no access to that past event. In fact, we would know nothing whatsoever about it! If any traces from this past event have survived until the present, in most cases (if not all) these are only partial and fragmentary, but they are all we have to pro-

---

historical method. Well-known examples are John P. Meier, *The Roots of the Problem and the Person* (vol. 1 of *A Marginal Jew: Rethinking the Historical Jesus*; New York: Doubleday, 1991), 4–6, 21–40, and on method see 41–195; N. Thomas Wright, *The New Testament and the People of God* (vol. 1 of *Christian Origins and the Question of God*; Minneapolis: Fortress, 1992), 31–144; James D.G. Dunn, *Jesus Remembered* (vol. 1 of *Christianity in the Making*; Grand Rapids: Eerdmans, 2003), 11–336, esp. 99–136, 327–36.

[8] A variety of terms might be used here, such as "data" or "evidence," but subsequent discussion will show these to be problematic, so I have used "traces," a term also used by Geoffrey R. Elton, *The Practice of History* (2 ed.; afterward by Richard J. Evans; 1967; repr., Oxford: Blackwell, 2002), 8: "Historical study is not the study of the past but the study of present traces of the past." For a longer version of this quotation in light of this discussion, see n. 11 below.

vide access to the past event.⁹ Thus, rather than having direct access to past events, all we really can access today is the surviving traces from the past. The abbreviations PE for "past event" and ST for "surviving traces" will be used throughout this essay to keep this distinction clear. So, a person might think that what they "know" about the past is actually the past event (i.e., PE), but in actuality what one really "knows" is based only on the surviving traces (i.e., ST).Thus, while in popular parlance the term "history" may be used to refer to past events, this usage is problematic and may ultimately be misleading. We need to examine these surviving traces a little more closely.

Surviving traces (i.e., ST) are the material used by the historian. Usually this material consists of written records of past events as reported and recorded by those closely (or not so closely) involved in the events. These written accounts may be based upon oral traditions that have been collected later or an account derived from eyewitnesses of the events. It may even be written by an eyewitness or, to the other extreme, it may have been written by someone who has no real knowledge of the events but has an idea what could have, or should have, happened. Whichever is the case, surviving traces involve the perspectives and interests of the eyewitnesses, the perspectives and interests of those who passed on the traditions, and the perspectives and interests of the person who wrote the written account. So the surviving traces (ST) are hardly "raw" or "objective" data. The nature of these surviving traces is such that they require the later historian to develop a historical method (the tools and processes noted above) to properly handle these surviving traces. So these surviving traces (i.e., ST) are not "history" either, for they are only the "stuff" that has survived from the past – fragmentary, incomplete, and quite possibly biased, and perhaps even contradictory and incorrect.

What modern historians must do is sift through and interpret these surviving traces using the tools and processes of the historical method to come to their understanding of the past event being studied. After completing all the research and analysis, the historian produces an account of his/her understanding of the past event which narrates a description and explanation of it. This we might refer to as a "narrative account" (and we will use the abbreviation NA).¹⁰ Since this is the case, in discussions of history or endeavors to do history it is confusing, if not misleading, to use the term

---

⁹ I have referred here only to written documents and inscriptions (which could include coins), for these are the most common real forms of historical data surviving from the ancient past. With reference to a more recent past, the surviving data might include pictures, films, and other sources. But since the focus of this essay is ultimately on the historical Jesus, the concentration here is on ancient history. Either way, the point being made here does not change.

¹⁰ In using the term narrative account (i.e., NA) I do not distinguish between an individual statement within the narrative account or the total narrative account itself. This

Diagram: Defining "History"

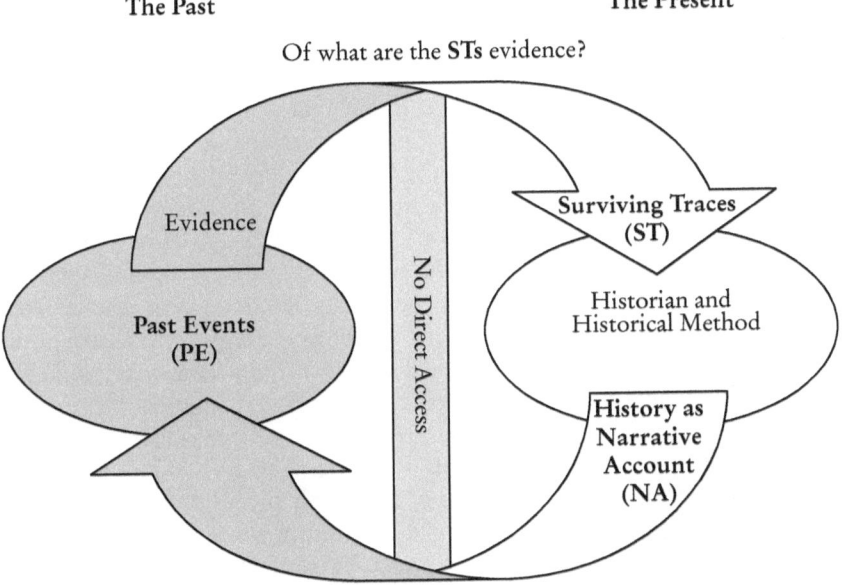

"history" in the sense of either past events (PE) or surviving traces (ST). The term "history" should be reserved for a later historian's narrative account (i.e., NA) of a past event (i.e., PE) that is his/her understanding of that event based upon the interpretation of surviving traces (i.e., ST).[11] Interestingly enough, this understanding of "history" is consistent with the Greek origins of the term, for the Greek noun ἱστορία (cf. the verb ἱστορέω) was *not* used in the sense of "past event," but rather had the sense of "inquiry, examination," and then "knowledge obtained by inquiry," and also "a written record of one's inquiries."[12]

---

distinction will be made later. This language of "narrates a description" will be altered in our discussion of historiography in § 2.2 below.

[11] Geoffrey R. Elton (*The Practice of History*, 8) states: "Historical study is not the study of the past but the study of present traces of the past; if men have said, thought, done or suffered anything of which nothing any longer exists, those things are as though they had never been. The crucial element is the present evidence, not the fact of past existence; and questions for whose answer no material exists are strictly non-questions."

[12] The Greek term was Latinized as *historia*, where its range of meanings is essentially the same as the Greek term. See LSJ 842; P.G.W. Glare, ed., *Oxford Latin Dictionary* (Oxford: Oxford University Press, 1992), 799.

To summarize, "history" is a narrative account (i.e., NA) that we historians write to express an understanding of past events (i.e., PE) based upon our interpretation of the traces (i.e., ST) that have survived from those past events.

An illustration at this point may be helpful: you find a used jigsaw puzzle box for sale (perhaps at a garage sale or in a used store) that says on the side "3,000 pieces." Upon bringing it home you open the box and realize that it only has about 300 pieces in it. You also realize that you have another problem, for the original picture on the top of the box – the one that shows what the picture originally was – has been torn off! You begin to pick out some of the pieces to see if they go together; you might start with all the blue ones. As you look at a particular blue piece, you're not sure whether it should go at the bottom because it represents water, or at the top because it is sky, or perhaps it is a person's shirt and so should go somewhere in the middle. You also notice that the pieces are not all the same size, and so it appears likely that about 50 of these pieces do not even belong to this puzzle at all! How does this illustrate history? A past event (PE) is like the original picture that has been torn off the top of the box and so is no longer accessible. The surviving traces (ST) are the 300 puzzle pieces that are still found within the box. And history (NA) is your attempt to reconstruct what the picture looked like as a whole after you have arranged 250 pieces into some arrangement (remember, you decided 50 pieces did not belong to this puzzle). This illustration is adequate to this point in the discussion, but we will return to it later and observe how in some respects it is deficient.[13]

The definition of history developed thus far is incomplete, for a second component – assumed to this point in the discussion – needs to be made specific. Not all past events (i.e., PE) fall within the purview of history, for the focus of historical inquiry, at least as normally defined and pursued, concerns events in the past involving humans as agents.[14] This actually qualifies

---

[13] Discussion with respect to historical Jesus studies is reserved for the next main section, but since readers will be thinking about the relevance of this discussion, let me make a couple of observations here. With reference to Jesus, the surviving traces, like the puzzle pieces, consist of two basic types: the discrete narrative episodes in the Gospels (i.e., the individual pericopae) and other sources (e.g., Josephus), as well as the overall portraits created by these early authors. In terms of our illusration, it should be pointed out that these earliest portraits are *not* the picture on the front cover of the box, but are rather the earliest surviving attempts to put the puzzle pieces about Jesus together into a coherent picture. Note that the individual Gospel authors handled some of the pieces the same, but they interpreted other pieces differently in the portraits they developed.

[14] Cf. the definition in R. G. Collingwood, *The Idea of History: With Lectures 1926–1928* (rev. ed.; edited with an introduction by Jan van der Dussen; 1946; repr., Oxford: Oxford University Press, 1993), 9–10. He states that history concerns *res gestae* [i. e., "things done"], the attempt to answer questions about human actions done in the past. Elton (*The Practice of History*, 7) states that "[t]he study of history comprehends everything that men have said, thought, done or suffered. That much is commonplace ..." He goes on to note limitations to this definition, similar to some noted here.

the understanding of what is meant by history in two respects. First of all, the focus of history is on the past of *humans* as distinguished from the past of nature.[15] For example, the ice age that shaped the Rocky Mountains is an event (albeit over a long period of time) which has left traces in the present geological record. There was a past event (similar to our PE) and there are surviving traces (similar to our ST). While this was an actual event that happened within the space-time continuum, it is not within the parameters of what constitutes the discipline of history. Keeping in mind that we are using the term "history" *not* to in the sense of past event (i.e., PE) but narrative account (i.e., NA), we can state that the ice age that shaped the Rockies is a past event, but it is not a *historical* event. Rather, this past event is properly the subject of the discipline of geology and is the concern of geologists.[16] Even recent natural events, such as hurricanes, are not a "historical event," *per se*. They are meteorological events, studied by meteorologists and other scientists. However, as a particular natural event has direct impact on human events, actions, and responses, then it does come within the purview of the discipline of history, both as an object of historical study and historical explanation. Take, for example, Hurricane Katrina that hit the American Gulf Coast in 2005 – an examination of this event in terms of the physical factors and weather patterns that led to its original formation and its strength is a meteorological inquiry, and is not really a historical one in the way we are defining history here. However, if Hurricane Katrina is studied in terms of the devastating loss of human life and the socio-economic impact it has had on those who lived in the region, then one is engaged in a historical inquiry.

Secondly, the focus of historical inquiry is on human actions in specific events in the past.[17] In other words, it is concerned not only with past

---

[15] Jonathan Gorman's discussion of history (*Understanding History: An Introduction to Analytical Philosophy of History* [Philosophica 42; Ottawa: University of Ottawa Press, 1992], 69, 75) describes this as "one world, with two kinds of entities in it": nature and humans. They interact with one another within this world, but the means of understanding each is different: "each kind of entity has its associated theory of explanation: for the natural world, covering law theory; and for the world of individual persons, empathetic understanding." Gorman (pp. 78–79) goes on to suggest a third entity within the world beyond these two: "social entities," but since they fundamentally comprise humans in interaction with each other, they are understood in essentially the same manner as individual humans.

[16] This discussion helps to clarify the terms "pre-history" and "pre-historical," which are used to describe events in the past prior to there being any surviving evidence of the impact of these events on humans. This qualification to the term "history" does not prevent someone talking about "the history of the ice age," but such usage reintroduces the confusion discussed above that distinguished history as NA from PE. Furthermore, such usage would not generally be used by historians.

[17] R. G. Collingwood (*Idea of History*, 9) expressed it thus: "What kinds of things does history find out? I answer, *res gestae*: actions of human beings that have been done in the past."

events involving human (as distinct from geology, for example), but it is also concerned with humans as agents of action and thought.[18] Other disciplines may be similar, but their focus is different. For example, archaeology explores the human past through the discovery and interpretation of material remains, but the focus is upon how these material remains help us understand how humans lived rather than explaining specific human events. It is possible that archaeological remains might relate to a particular human event, but the focus of its concerns is what it tells us about human life and practices. But at times archaeology does blend into the discipline of history. For example, if an archaeologist were to uncover in a cave in Palestine the human remains of a man with an iron nail through his feet, and the pottery remains in the cave can be dated to the period of Palestine's Roman occupation prior to 70 C.E., then archaeology considers the date of this crucifixion and the implications these material remains have on understanding Roman crucifixion practices. And if the ossuary in which these bones were discovered had the name Jehoḥanan inscribed on its side, archaeology could link these two pieces of evidence together.[19] But if one were to explore the reasons which led the Romans to crucify this particular man, or to relate it to a particular episode reported by an ancient historian of this period such as Josephus, then one has, strictly speaking, moved from the field of archaeology to that of history. This reveals, of course, how disciplines like archaeology and history overlap and inform one another. This is particularly so when inscriptions are involved, for they are material remains (i.e., archaeology),[20] but they are usually a written record of a human event (i.e., history).

Related disciplines such as anthropology and sociology also study human activity, but their focus is not on specific events in the past but rather on general patterns of human behavior. However, there is not a hard and fast division between these disciplines, for while we can distinguish between na-

---

[18] I include human thought here, for while history involves human event, the term "event" needs to be understood broadly to include the articulation of human ideas, for example.

[19] For the original reports of such, see V. Tzaferis, "Jewish Tombs at and Near Givʿat Ha-Mivtar, Jerusalem," *IEJ* 20 (1970): 18–32; J. Naveh, "The Ossuary Inscriptions from Givʿat Ha-Mivtar," *IEJ* 20 (1970): 33–37; N. Haas, "Anthropological Observations on the Skeletal Remains from Givʿat Ha-Mivtar," *IEJ* 20 (1970): 38–59. For examples of later discussion, see James H. Charlesworth, "Jesus and Jehohanan: An Archaeological Note on Crucifixion," *ExpT* 84 (1972–73): 147–50; J. Zias and E. Sekeles, "The Crucified Man from Givʿat Ha-Mivtar – A Reappraisal," *IEJ* 35 (1985): 22–27.

[20] On material remains, see Anthony Snodgrass, "Archaeology," in *Sources for Ancient History* (ed. Michael Crawford; Cambridge: Cambridge University Press, 1983), 137–84; Charles W. Hedrick Jr., *Ancient History: Monuments and Documents* (Malden, MA and Oxford: Blackwell, 2006), 144–65 (with respect to coins in particular, 126–43).

ture and humans as we did above, we can also distinguish between humans as individuals and humans collectively in "social entities."[21] A social entity may be understood historically in a similar way as can individual humans because a social entity ultimately consists of humans engaging in activities or events. A social entity may be studied in terms of general patterns of human behavior but it may also be viewed more particularly in terms of human events. Thus, in terms of the above example of the crucified Jehoḥanan, one could explore it historically only in terms of an individual historical event. But it can only really be understood when it is contextualized in terms of larger social entities such as Roman crucifixion practices, or Roman practices in governing *humiliores*[22] in their provinces. Thus, while we might clarify that history is the study of "human actions in specific events in the past" as noted above, this does not mean that history is only concerned with individual humans. For history is also concerned with social entities in the past as they exemplify human actions. This could be clarified as "social history."[23]

I am not suggesting hard and fast divisions between these disciplines, but rather distinctions in terms of the core focus of each discipline, and consequently distinctions also in terms of the methods used. Like overlapping circles in a Venn diagram, these disciplines in fact overlap one another, for each can provide evidence for the other, can help other disciplines see evidence in new ways, can lead to asking new questions – all of which ultimately broadens and deepens the understanding of those aspects of human life that are the focus of each discipline.[24]

2.2. Wrestling with Historiography

This discussion thus far has been quite straightforward, but nevertheless necessary for clarification. However, issues become more complex when we turn to placing this relatively basic understanding of history (i.e., history as narrative account, NA) into larger questions concerning one's philosophy

---

[21] See the discussion by Gorman above in n. 15.

[22] That is, those in Roman world who were "low-born," the vast majority of whom would not be Roman citizens but were peasants, commoners, and slaves. This was in contrast to the *honestiores*, the "high-born." See the discussion in this volume in ch. 13, § 2.2.

[23] For discussion see e.g. Miles Fairburn, *Social History: Problems, Strategies, and Methods* (New York: St. Martin's Press, 1999); Larry J. Griffin, *New Methods for Social History* (Cambridge: Cambridge University Press, 1999).

[24] See the discussion of history in relationship to other related disciplines by Elton (*The Practice of History*, 7–11, 21–35). One of the ways that he distinguishes history from these other disciplines is that "[h]istory deals in events, not states; it investigates things that happen and not things that are" (p. 9). I differ from him in that he was more concerned with drawing distinctions between these disciplines, seeing them as "rivals" (p. 21). I see much more overlap and consequently the importance of a healthy working relationship between them.

of history, that is, historiography.[25] Under the influence of the Enlightenment and the development of modern science, history in the nineteenth century was largely understood as "scientific history;" that is, it was viewed as a scientific endeavor that can be pursued using principles of neutrality, objectivity, and value-free observation. The goal, expressed in Ranke's famous dictum, was *"wie es eigentlich gewesen"* – "simply to show how it really was."[26] The historian – the inquiring Subject – is able to stand separate and aloof from the past – the Object – and be totally objective about it. Within the twentieth century however, this understanding was largely overthrown by a variety of historiographic developments, such as the call for an economic or social history (e.g., by Karl Marx and Max Weber), or the emphases of the *Annales* School (especially Lucien Febvre and Marc Bloch). The questions of historiography were concerned with the nature of history, the purpose of doing history, the sources and focus of history, and the possibility of objectivity. Within the second half of the twentieth century the diversity of opinions were represented – at least in English historiographic discussion – by the well-known work of Edward H. Carr (*What is History?*,

---

[25] Due to limitations of space, this discussion must be brief, which unfortunately means having to make generalizations and omissions (over two centuries of historiographic discussion in a few paragraphs!). For discussion of the entire history of historiography, see Breisach, *Historiography: Ancient, Medieval, and Modern*; Bentley, *Companion to Historiography*. For a historiographic survey from the Enlightenment to the present, see Michael Bentley, *Modern Historiography: An Introduction* (London: Routledge, 1999); Joyce Appleby, et al., *Telling the Truth About History* (New York: W. W. Norton, 1994). For a focus on the twentieth century and the transition to the twenty-first, see Georg G. Iggers, *Historiography in the Twentieth Century: From Scientific Objectivity to Postmodern Challenge – with a New Epilogue by the Author* (2 ed.; Middletown, CT: Wesleyan University Press, 2005); Donald R. Kelley, *Frontiers of History: Historical Inquiry in the Twentieth Century* (New Haven, CT: Yale University Press, 2006).

[26] Interestingly, Ranke's statement echoes the statement of Lucian (ca. 120–190 C.E.) in his *How to Write History*: "The historian's sole task is to tell the tale as it happened" (Lucian, *Hist.* 39; Kilburn, LCL). Ranke's point is a statement about the historian's objectivity, but it also stresses that the historian's role is not to judge the past nor to use it to instruct the future. For a discussion of what Ranke intended with this expression, see the Introduction by Georg G. Iggers in Leopold von Ranke, *The Theory and Practice of History* (ed. Georg G. Iggers and Konrad von Moltke; Indianapolis: Bobbs-Merrill, 1973), xix–xx. Some cite Rake's statement with the concluding *"ist"* while others do not. In the one citation that I have been able to locate in Ranke's writing, it states, *"er will bloß sagen, wie es eigentlich gewesen"* – without *"ist."* Leopold Ranke, *Geschichten der romanischen und germanischen Völker von 1494 bis 1535* (Leipzig: Reimer, 1824), vi; see also the reprint edition which included the forwards of both the 1824 and the 1874 editions: Leopold von Ranke, *Fürsten und Völker: Geschichten der romanischen und germanischen Völker von 1494–1514; Die Osmanen und die spanische Monarchie im 16. und 17. Jahrhundert* (ed. Willy Andreas; 1824; repr., Wiesbaden: Emil Vollmer Verlag, 1957), 4. While modern German grammar does, of course, require the finite verb *"ist,"* this statement without *"ist"* should be understood as a grammatical archaism. Since it is von Ranke's dictum, I will leave it as he expressed it.

1962[27]) and Geoffrey R. Elton (*The Practice of History*, 1967[28]).[29] Carr was a relativist who questioned the view of history as merely concerned with objective fact. Historians bring their own ideologies to the examination of the past and to the writing of history. He saw the necessity of using social and economic perspectives (including Marxist historiography), and he believed the results of history should have an impact on the present and the future.[30] Elton, writing a few years after Carr and very much in reaction to him,[31] argued for the possibility as well as the importance of objectivity, that the concern of history is establishing "the true facts," which is studied only out of a concern to understand the past.[32]

There is much that could be explored in the respective views of Carr and Elton, but discussion of historiography has moved well beyond them with the rise of postmodernism, which has brought about a seismic shift in many disciplines, including historiography.[33] So much so, that in its more extreme forms the possibility of doing history itself is called into question. In what is often called the "linguistic turn," the claim is made that history is language

---

[27] Edward Hallett Carr, *What Is History?* (London: Macmillan, 1961).

[28] Elton, *The Practice of History*.

[29] For a brief summary of Carr and Elton, and how they have subsequently been used in subsequent decades of teaching history, see Richard J. Evans, *In Defense of History* (New York: W.W. Norton, 1999), 1–3.

[30] For example, Carr (*What Is History?* 18) states: "By and large, the historian will get the kind of facts he wants. History means interpretation." Later he says, "we can view the past, and achieve our understanding of the past, only through the eyes of the present. The historian is of his own age, and is bound by the conditions of human existence" (p. 19). The historian can, however, also be changed by the process of historical investigation.

[31] Elton frequently castigates Carr with very strong language. For example, Elton (*The Practice of History*, 13) refers to "Mr Carr's somewhat philistine judgement." Elsewhere he alludes to the Marxist historiography of Carr as "in its day a truly remarkable achievement of scientific insight and ill-controlled speculation." Similar rhetorical flourishes may be observed in Elton's description of the *Annales* school as having "lost itself in rhetoric and self-adulation" (p. 122).

[32] Elton states (*The Practice of History*, 59): "Historical method is no more than a recognized and tested way of extracting from what the past has left the true facts and events of that past, and so far as possible their true meaning and interrelation, the whole governed by the first principle of historical understanding, namely that the past must be studied in its own right, for its own sake, and on its own terms." Elton echoes a somewhat Rankean view, an observation strengthened by his statement later in the same paragraph that he has demonstrated "that history can be 'scientifically' studied" (p. 59).

[33] Cf. the comment by Appleby, et al., *Telling the Truth About History*, 3–4: "History has been shaken right down to its scientific and cultural foundations." See also the variety of comments from other historians cited in Evans, *In Defense of History*, 1–8.

Here, as elsewhere, I must paint with a very broad brush. For a presentation of varieties of postmodern historiography, see Keith Jenkins, ed., *The Postmodern History Reader* (London: Routledge, 1997). See also the division of historians into one of three genres of history-writing based on their historiographic position: reconstructionism, constructionism, and deconstructionism in Keith Jenkins and Alun Munslow, eds., *The Nature of History Reader* (London: Routledge, 2004).

and only language, in that it is not about the past but really only about itself, or, as expressed by Jacques Derrida, one of the fathers of postmodernism, "there is nothing outside of the text."[34] In this view, a historical narrative is really only a rhetorical expression of the historian's ideology, and discussions of which historical interpretation is right is an expression of the historian's power. Keith Jenkins, a British popularizer of radical postmodern historiographic thought, explains that

> we recognise today that there never has been, and there never will be, any such thing as a past which is expressive of some sort of essence, whilst the idea that the proper study of history is actually 'own-sakism'[35] is recognised as just the mystifying way in which a bourgeoisie conveniently articulates its own interests as if they belonged to the past itself ... [T]he whole 'modernist' History / history ensemble now appears as a self-referential, problematic expression of 'interests', an ideological-interpretive discourse without any 'real' access to the past as such; unable to engage in any dialogue with 'reality'. In fact, 'history' now appears to be just one more 'expression' in a world of postmodern expressions: which of course is what it is.[36]

In other words, the inquiring Subject has totally engulfed the Object, with the result that any attempt to use language concerning the Object by the Subject is really only self-referential.

This relates to a second issue in a postmodern view of history: It is not that there is no past, but rather that the individual pieces of evidence that have survived from the past (ST) lack context to give them meaning. It is the historian that gives them meaning as they are woven together into a historical narrative. Hayden White, one of the fathers of postmodern historiography, stated: "historical narratives are verbal fictions, the contents of which are as much invented as found and the forms of which have more in common with their counterparts in literature than they have with those in the sciences."[37] Thus, for White, the contents of a historian's historical narrative comprises what she / he has "found" in term of the facts from the past as well as what has been "invented" by the historian in a narrative form which provides a

---

[34] Jacques Derrida, *Of Grammatology* (trans. G. C. Spivak; Baltimore: Johns Hopkins University Press, 1976), 158.

[35] This expression, coined by Keith Jenkins (*On "What Is History?": From Carr and Elton to Rorty and White* [London: Routledge, 1995], 9), is explained earlier on the same page as "studying the past 'objectively and for its own sake' (own-sakism)."

[36] Jenkins, *On "What Is History?"*, 37–38.

[37] Hayden White, *Tropics of Discourse: Essays in Cultural Criticism* (Baltimore: Johns Hopkins University Press, 1978), 82. See also Hayden White, *Metahistory: The Historical Imagination in Nineteenth-Century Europe* (Baltimore: Johns Hopkins University Press, 1973). For a recent summary of his position, see his essay "Literary Theory and Historical Writing" in Hayden White, *Figural Realism: Studies in the Mimesis Effect* (Baltimore: Johns Hopkins University Press, 1999), 1–26.

context and explanation for these facts.³⁸ Keith Jenkins summarizes White's view (along with that of Frank R. Ankersmit – more on him in a moment):

> [W]hilst it is generally the case individual discrete statements (facts) can indeed be checked against the discrete sources to see if the historian's account corresponds to it, the 'picture of the past' cannot be so checked, simply because the statements put together by the historian to form such a picture do not have a picture of their own prior to this assembly for that assembly to then be checked against … What is essential in the writing of historians is not to be found at the level of the individual statement but rather at the level of the picture of the past (in that it is these pictures which, for example, most stimulate historiographical debate and thus determine the way we 'see' the past), then historiography is again as much invented / imagined as found.³⁹

And thus Jenkins concludes:

> Saying true things about the past at the level of statement is easy – anybody can do that – but saying the right things, getting the picture straight, that is not only another story but also an impossible one: you can always get another picture, you can always get another context.⁴⁰

The rise of postmodern historiography has contributed significant insights to the historical enterprise. It recognizes that there is a close relationship between the historian and history (i.e., between the Subject and the Object). All historians interpret and write from their own perspective. The evidence that has survived from the past are "facts" (i.e., ST). While popular parlance uses expressions like "the bare facts," there really is no such thing, for as soon as the historian observes the facts to use them as evidence requires one to view the facts from one's own perspective and choose to interpret them within a particular context. Postmodern historiography also recognizes the narrative structure to history-writing (i.e., NA), and that the historian's explanation and interpretation of the facts and providing causal and explanatory links between them is a contribution made by the historian and thus is "invention." But to "invent" something in this sense *does not mean* that it is fictional and purely imaginary, lacking any relationship with reality or truth,⁴¹ or as Jenkins would claim, that "getting the picture straight"

---

³⁸ White (*Metahistory*, 7, his emphasis) uses the expression "explanation by emplotment" to describe this: "Providing the 'meaning' of a story by identifying the *kind of story* that has been told is called explanation by emplotment. If, in the course of narrating his story, the historian provides it with the plot structure of a Tragedy, he has 'explained' it in one way; if he has structured it as a Comedy, he has 'explained' it another way. Emplotment is the way by with a sequence of events is fashioned into a story is gradually revealed to be a story of a particular kind."

³⁹ Jenkins, *On "What Is History?"*, 21.

⁴⁰ Jenkins, *On "What Is History?"*, 21. Jenkins' dichotomy here between "statement" and "getting the picture straight" is somewhat simplistic. I discuss the matter of "picture" below.

⁴¹ It may be helpful here to be reminded of the sense of "invention" in its classical

is "impossible."[42] There are several ways to respond to Jenkins' form of what might be called "extreme postmodern historiography." It is possible to embrace the strengths of what postmodern historiography can teach us without slipping into total relativism: the "linguistic turn" has shown us much, but we need not end up with language alone. This can be achieved by responding in two ways.[43]

The first response may be found in understanding history as representation. Jenkins called on White and Ankersmit to support his extreme view,[44] but it appears (to me anyway) that he may have misunderstood them, and so a closer look at their views is helpful. White's argument is that the nature of language used in writing history is figurative or poetic rather than literal: it is a "verbal model offered by the historian as a representation and explanation of 'what *really* happened' in the past."[45] He then develops a "tropological" approach that uses the "four basic tropes for the analysis of poetic, or figurative, language: Metaphor, Metonymy, Synecodoche [*sic*], and Irony."[46] In response to those who have differed with him or misunderstood him, White explains:

[T]ropology does not deny the existence of extradiscursive entities or our capacity to refer to and represent them in speech. It does not suggest that everything is language, speech, discourse, or text, only that linguistic referentiality and representation are much more complicated matters than the older, literalist notions of language and discourse make out ...

---

rhetorical sense: There it refers to the rhetor's gathering of the evidence relevant to the case being made and the creation of the various arguments that would support it. On the "invention" of "artificial proofs" Aristotle explains: "As for proofs, some are inartificial, others artificial. By the former I understand all those which have not been furnished by ourselves but were already in existence, such as witnesses, tortures, contracts, and the like; by the latter, all that can be constructed by system and our own efforts. Thus we have only to make use of the former, whereas we must invent the latter" (Aristotle, *Rhet.*, 1.2.2 [LCL, Freese]). Cf. also Aristotle, *Rhet.* 1.2.4; 1.15.1; Cicero, *Inv.* 1.7.9. See also the discussion by Malcom Heath, "Invention," in *Handbook of Classical Rhetoric in the Hellenistic Period 330 B. C.–A. D. 400* (ed. Stanley E. Porter; Leiden: E. J. Brill, 1997), 89–119. This sense of "invention" is closely related to what Collingwood (*Idea of History*, 241–49) called "constructive imagination."

[42] Jenkins, *On "What Is History?"*, 21.

[43] See also the response to these issues by James G. Crossley, "Defining History," in *Writing History, Constructing Religion* (ed. James G. Crossley and Christian Karner; Aldershot, UK: Ashgate, 2005), 9–30.

[44] See other expressions of Jenkins' point of view in Keith Jenkins, *Why History?: Ethics and Postmodernity* (London: Routledge, 1999) and Keith Jenkins, *Re-Thinking History* (with a new preface and conversation with the author by Alun Munslow; London: Routledge, 2003), as well as his introduction in Jenkins and Munslow, *The Nature of History Reader*, 1–18.

[45] White, *Metahistory*, 31, his emphasis.

[46] White, *Metahistory*, 31, which he goes on to explain in 31–38. See also his further development in White, *Tropics of Discourse*, and his summary in the chapter "Literary Theory and Historical Writing" in White, *Figural Realism*, 1–26.

> [T]ropological theory does not collapse the difference between fact and fiction but redefines the relations between them within any given discourse ... Figurative description of real events are not less factual than literalist descriptions; they are factual – or, as I would put it, 'factological' – only in a different way. Tropological theory implies that we must not confuse facts with events.
>
> Events happen, whereas facts are constituted by linguistic description.[47]

And a little later White also states:

> A historical representation can be cast in the mode of a narrative because the tropological nature of language provides that possibility. Therefore, it is absurd to suppose that, because a historical discourse is cast in the mode of a narrative, it must be mythical, fictional, substantially imaginary, or otherwise 'unrealistic' in what it tells us about the world. To suppose that is to indulge in the kind of thinking that results in the belief in contagious magic or guilt by association.[48]

Frank Ankersmit is also helpful, for he presents a similar view, but perhaps does so in language that is a little clearer. If I understand White and Ankersmit correctly, their argument is that, given the nature of the past (i.e., PE that is only accessible through ST that are "found") and the process of the historian providing a narrative of explanation and causation (i.e., history as NA is "invented"), the relationship between history (NA) and the past (PE) is a relationship of *representation* rather than *description*. We may use these terms in popular language virtually interchangeably, but White and Ankersmit are attempting to make a careful distinction between them: In *description* one refers to something and makes a statement about it. For example, if there is such a woman present in the room, one could make the description "this woman has long brown hair."[49] In this description "this woman" is the particular person being referenced, and the attribution "has long brown hair" ascribes a particular quality to her. These two – reference and attribution – are the two distinct elements in a description. Since the woman is in the room, the hearer can see clearly what is meant, view the precise length of the hair and its colour, and so determine whether or not the attribution is true of the referent. In this sense of the term "description," one is not dependent on the description itself for understanding, for the referent is present.

However, Ankersmit distinguishes description from *representation*, for in representation one "'re-present[s]' something by presenting a substitute

---

[47] White, *Figural Realism*, 17–18.
[48] White, *Figural Realism*, 22.
[49] Frank R. Ankersmit (*Historical Representation* [Cultural Memory in the Present; Stanford, CA: Stanford University Press, 2001], 39–40) uses the illustration of "this cat is black." I have altered the illustration so as to later use the illustration of painting a portrait – something more suitable for a woman than a cat.

of this thing in its absence."⁵⁰ In representation the referent is *not* present. So, for example, one could not say "this woman" and point to her, if she were actually absent. But one could still make a similar statement about someone absent, "such-and-such a woman has long brown hair." However, because the woman is absent, all the hearer has are these words that "re-present" her. The hearer may visualize a particular length of hair and a particular shade of brown. But since the woman is not present there is no way to determine whether the verbal "re-presentation" is accurate nor whether the hearer's visualization corresponds with reality. One could even paint a portrait of a woman and "re-present" her with long brown hair. But these representations of the woman with long brown hair, whether by word or portrait – verbal or visual – do not have the two distinct elements of reference and attribution. Rather, they both happen at the same time. As a portrait, the representation exists on its own without the woman being present (in contrast to description, in which the woman was present). Ankersmit's point is that history writing is representation and not description. The past (PE) is absent, and so one cannot "point" or refer to it and make an attribution about of it. Rather, history writing (NA), is understood as representation – it is a "re-presentation" of the past. History as a narrative account (NA), then, is not a description referring to something in the past; rather, it is a representation portraying something about the past.⁵¹

This understanding of history as narrative account (NA) and its relationship to the past itself (i.e., PE) helps us understand and appreciate the contributions of postmodern historiography without being trapped by its extremes. Once one has referred to "this woman" and described her as having long brown hair, the discussion is done. Either her hair is long and brown or it is not, for the woman is present, and a simple comparison of referent and attribution determines the truth or falsity of the description. But one could paint several different portraits representing the same woman with long brown hair. Though each portrait is different, each captures something of the woman. Even though the woman is absent, one could still discuss the relative merits of each portrait. But the issues and criteria are more complex, so that the end result may be that no one portrait is "true" and the others "false" – the kinds of conclusions one could determine with a description.⁵² Similarly, if history as narrative account could refer to the past

---

⁵⁰ Ankersmit, *Historical Representation*, 11.
⁵¹ Ankersmit's argument (*Historical Representation*, 40–41) results in him demonstrating the problem with history writing "referring" to the past, and so encourages replacing the term "reference" with "being about," as I have done here.
⁵² Though, if one of the portraits was of a black cat, then on the basis of certain criteria, the portrait could be judged "false" compared with the other portraits of a woman with brown hair. But, even then, on other criteria, some might argue that such a portrait was

and describe it, then once a description has been made, the matter is – for all intents and purposes – done. But, as discussed earlier, we have no access to the past events themselves (PE), and thus we cannot "refer" to them directly in doing history as narrative account (NA). Rather, in history as narrative account (i.e., history writing) we create representations that portray something about the past events (PE). We can have several different historical representations, and subsequent discussion focuses on the relative merits of each representation, and potentially which representations better re-present the past reality being portrayed.[53] But equally, different historical representations may bring out different features and present different perspectives, so that several different historical representations *may be* equally valid. But this does not mean, on the other hand, that *all* historical representations *are* equally valid, for one representation (NA) may handle the evidence (ST) in sloppy, superficial, incomplete manner, while another representation is careful and complete.

As an aside, and to ensure that we do not misunderstand Ankersmit's discussion of representation, it is important to note that he does not rule out description altogether. For description is possible in history-writing, but only at the level of being able to describe individual pieces of evidence. This is consistent with the discussion above, for as noted, history writing uses the evidence that has survived from the past (i.e., ST). Since this evidence is present and available for all to observe, a historian is able to describe the individual piece of evidence (e.g., "this text states that ..."). All can observe the text and determine quite readily whether or not the description of the piece of surviving evidence is accurate. Thus we can distinguish – as Ankersmit does – "between description (the level of the individual statement) and representation (the level of complete narratives)..."[54]

This discussion helps us realize the weakness of the earlier illustration of the jigsaw puzzle, in which history as narrative account (NA) was illustrated by our attempt to reconstruct what the picture looked like as a whole after you have arranged 250 pieces into some order. It is not enough

---

"true" to some aspect of her character. This demonstrates some of the complexities of representation as compared with description.

[53] As Ankersmit (*Historical Representation*, 41–42) states: "[T]he linguistic turn ... is so essential for a correct understanding of history writing." He observes that discourse contains the two levels of "speaking" and "speaking about" which are fused in historical discussion. "For on the one hand the historical text contains the level of 'speaking' (i.e., the level where the historian describes [my term, 'portrays'] the past in terms of individual statements about historical events, states of affairs, causal links, etc.). But on the other it *also* comprises the level where the discussion takes place about what chunk of language (i.e., what historical text) represents best or corresponds best to some chunk of past reality."

[54] Ankersmit, *Historical Representation*, 54–55.

to describe an individual piece (e.g., "this piece is blue with a bit of brown on one side"), and it is not enough to arrange the pieces into some type of order. Rather, one must create a representation of what the original picture on the front cover might have looked like. Thus, one could make the example of the jigsaw puzzle more complex by explaining that it is not enough to identify and describe the pieces that belong to this particular puzzle, and it is not enough to arrange the 250 pieces into some order (with a lot of blank spaces, for we only have 250 out of a potential 3,000 pieces). What is also required is that one must paint a new picture for the front cover. Different people might paint somewhat different paintings, and one could discuss the relative merits of each painting (i.e., whether it represented a coherent picture) and how they have interpreted the surviving pieces (i.e., described the 250 different pieces). This example helps us distinguish the roles that representation and description have in history writing. But ultimately, the example is still somewhat simplistic, for in the jigsaw puzzle the past reality one is representing is just a two-dimensional picture. In writing a historical narrative (NA), one is actually attempting to create a representation of something far more complex: a chunk of past reality (to use Ankersmit's phrasing) with all the complexities of people and events, causation and explanation, which could be explored from different points of view using different questions. Thus, there may be – even *should* be – many different representations of the same chunk of past reality. And while some may be better than others based on various criteria, still others may be equally valid in their representation as they do so from various perspectives, address different issues, and provide answers to different questions.

A second response that may make it possible to embrace the strengths of what postmodern historiography can teach us without slipping into total relativism is to consider the issue from the perspective of the philosophical stance of critical realism.[55] Expressed somewhat simply, "critical realism …

---

[55] As elsewhere in this section, the discussion here must be brief. The origins of critical realism reach back to the beginning of the twentieth century, but its more recent formulation may be traced to Roy Bhaskar in Britain and a variety of figures in North America, including Bernard Lonergan, whose work explored its relationship to theological thought. Roy Bhaskar coined the term "transcendental realism" with respect to a philosophy of science (Roy Bhaskar, *A Realist Theory of Science* [2 ed.; 1978; repr., Radical Thinkers 29; London: Verso, 2008]) and the term "critical naturalism" with reference to the social sciences (Roy Bhaskar, *The Possibility of Naturalism: A Philosophical Critique of the Contemporary Human Sciences* [3 ed.; London: Routledge, 1998]). But in the work of most who have followed in this philosophical thought, these terms have been combined to form the overarching term "critical realism." Helpful introductions to critical realism include Andrew Collier, *Critical Realism: An Introduction to Roy Bhaskar's Philosophy* (London: Verso, 1994); José López and Garry Potter, eds., *After Postmodernism: An Introduction to Critical Realism* (London: Athlone, 2001). An important collection of essays on critical realism is Margaret Archer, et al., *Critical Realism: Essential Readings* (London: Routledge,

combine[s] and reconcile[s] ontological realism, epistemological relativism and judgmental rationality."⁵⁶ By "ontological realism" is meant that the Object (i.e., the thing observed) is real and exists apart from any observation by the Subject (i.e., the person observing). "Epistemological relativism" recognizes that the Subject observing the Object does so from the Subject's point of view, and so knowledge of the Object is relative to the Subject's perspective and the span of the Subject's horizon. The Subject's horizon provides a context for the Subject to observe and understand the Object. But the Subject's knowledge of the Object does not need to be totally relative, for by "judgmental rationality" the Subject is able to critically engage the Object in dialogue to gain a provisionally better understanding of the Object. Here Hans-Georg Gadamer's discussion of horizons may be helpful, for he observes that engagement between the horizon of the Subject and the horizon of the Object involves the hermeneutical circle in which the Subject engages the Object, but in this process the Object also engages the Subject, and thus the Subject is able to gain a better understanding of the Object through seeking a fusion of these horizons. The understanding that results in the engagement of the Subject and Object in the hermeneutical circle is only provisional, and it is open to expansion and development as the process of the hermeneutical circle is repeated – and thus the better image is that of a "hermeneutical spiral."⁵⁷ In the critical realism of Bernard Lonergan this "judgmental rationality" is understood as a process of experience, initial understanding, and continuing critical judgment.⁵⁸

1998). A helpful discussion of the development of critical realism and its various types, see "Appendix 2: Varieties of Critical Realism" in Donald L. Denton, *Historiography and Hermeneutics in Jesus Studies: An Examination of the Work of John Dominic Crossan and Ben F. Meyer* (JSNTS 262; London: T&T Clark International, 2004), 210–25.

⁵⁶ Archer, et al., *Critical Realism: Essential Readings*, xi, emphasis removed.

⁵⁷ Hans-Georg Gadamer (*Truth and Method* [trans. Barden, et al.; New York: Crossroad, 1984], 167–68, cf. 235–45, 258–74, 325–41) discusses this in terms of the "hermeneutical circle" but his discription is actually of a "spiral," though I am not aware of him actually using this specific term. Others have, of course, pointed out that the term "hermeneutical spiral" more accurately reflects Gadamer's thought, for which see Anthony C. Thiselton, *The Two Horizons: New Testament Hermeneutics and Philosophical Description* (Grand Rapids: Eerdmans, 1980), 104; Grant R. Osborne, *The Hermeneutical Spiral: A Comprehensive Introduction to Biblical Interpretation* (2 ed.; Downers Grove, IL: InterVarsity, 2006), 22, 418–19. For a discussion of the hermeneutical spiral in a variety of fields, see e. g., Lisbet Lindholm, et al., "Clinical Application Research: A Hermeneutical Approach to the Appropriation of Caring Science," *Qualitative Health Research* 16.1 (2006): 137–50; Sherrill A. Conroy, "A Pathway for Interpretive Phenomenology," *International Journal of Qualitative Methods* 2.3 (2003): article 4 (retrieved 14 Feb 2008 from http://www.ualberta.ca/~iiqm/backissues/2_3final/pdf/conroy.pdf). I would understand a full fusion of horizons to be an ideal for which one might strive, but is – at least in the realm of history – a practical impossibility.

⁵⁸ Bernard Lonergan, *Insight: A Study of Human Understanding* (ed. Frederick E. Crowe and Robert M. Doran; vol. 3 of *Collected Works of Bernard Lonergan*; 5 ed.;

What critical realism contributes to historiography is a way to appreciate what postmodernism has brought to these issues without descending into total relativism and self-referentialism. There is an element of relativism, for any historical inquiry of necessity involves the horizon of the historian. And there is a subjective element, for the historical inquiry is dependent upon the narrative context provided by the historian for the evidence and the interpretive judgments that are made in the process. But a critical-realist historian would also claim that (1) in repeated engagements with the evidence of some chunk of past reality from different perspectives, and (2) through dialogue with other historians who also engage the evidence, and (3) through critical self-reflection on the pre-understandings one brings to these engagements, the historian should be able to hermeneutically spiral to a reasonable representation of that chunk of past reality, though still recognizing the provisional and perspectival nature of that representation.[59] How a historian does this is reserved for the discussion in the next section.

I would suggest, then, that the twin principles of understanding history as representation and applying a critical-realist understanding to historiography, allows us to embrace the critique that postmodernism brings to the historical endeavor without having to adopt its totally relativist conclusions. Whether what is being advocated here should be viewed as a "soft-postmodernist" historiography or a "chastened-modernist"[60] historiography will probably depend upon the particular horizon and pre-understanding that each reader brings to these issues, and the presentation that I have made

---

Toronto: University of Toronto, 1992), 296–303. Lonergan (210) refers to this as "one's understanding gradually works round and up a spiral of viewpoints with each one complementing its predecessor ..." See also a summary of his approach in Bernard Lonergan, *Method in Theology* (2 ed.; London: Darton, Longman & Todd, 1973), 3–25, and in Ben F. Meyer, *Critical Realism and the New Testament* (Allison Park, PA: Pickwick, 1989), 1–16. Denton (*Historiography and Hermeneutics*, 83) explains: "Just as the knower is prompted to understand data by his or her questions, the knower is prompted to judgement by a desire to check the answers provided by understanding." On the applicability of Lonergan's work to historiography, see Andrew Beards, "Reversing Historical Skepticism: Bernard Lonergan on the Writing of History," *History and Theory* 33 (1994): 198–219.

I refer here in particular to Bernard Lonergan's expression of critical realism because it is his formulation that has influenced biblical scholars and work in historical Jesus in particular, especially through the work of Ben F. Meyer, for which see Ben F. Meyer, *The Aims of Jesus* (London: SCM, 1979), 16–18; Meyer, *Critical Realism*; Ben F. Meyer, *Reality and Illusion on New Testament Scholarship: A Primer in Critical Realist Hermeneutics* (Collegeville, MN: Michael Glazier, 1994). He in turn has influenced other historical Jesus scholars with reference to critical realism, such as Wright, *The New Testament and the People of God*, 32–46; Scot McKnight, *Jesus and His Death: Historiography, the Historical Jesus, and Atonement Theory* (Waco, TX: Baylor University Press, 2005), 20–22.

[59] For a historiographic discussion of critical realism (though they use the term "practical realism") as a response to the total relativism of radical postmodernism, see Appleby, et al., *Telling the Truth About History*, 247–51.

[60] I was first introduced to this term by McKnight, *Jesus and His Death*, 5 n. 9.

here. Whichever is the case is really secondary, for what matters is whether it has provided a way to mediate between these views and chart a course that allows one to proceed to the task of actually doing history – history as narrative account.

While I think that these twin principles do provide a way to proceed between modernist and radical postmodernist historiography, there is a corollary matter which, while not providing a way to proceed, nevertheless provides a rather devastating critique of the radical postmodernist understanding of historiography, and that is the ethical dilemma of total relativism when different historical narratives are compared. In many cases this might appear irrelevant or even seem odd to bring up, but consider the matter of the Holocaust: if all historical narratives are totally relative and self-referential, then there is no way to evaluate nor differentiate between the "history" provided by a neo-Nazi Holocaust denier and the "history" provided by one who claims to be a Holocaust survivor.[61] On this Michael Shermer and Alex Grobman state: "Ironically, it is with issues such as Holocaust denial that all discussion of historical relativism ends. Ask deconstructionists if they think that the belief the Holocaust happened is as valid as the belief that it did not happen, and the debate quickly screeches to a halt."[62] Similarly, some allege that understanding history writing as representation as argued by Hayden White (and Frank Ankersmit) "promote a debilitating relativism that permits any manipulation of the evidence as long as the account produced is structurally coherent, and thereby allow the kind of perspectivism that permits even a Nazi version of Nazism's history to claim a certain minimal credibility."[63] Such an allegation fundamentally misrepresents the views of historiographers like White and Ankersmit. For example, White calls those who deny the Holocaust "'revisionist' historians," and he states that their "claim is as morally offensive as it is intellectually bewildering."[64]

---

[61] E.g., Elie Wiesel, *Night* (trans. Marion Wiesel; New York: Hill & Wang, 2006).

[62] Michael Shermer and Alex Grobman, *Denying History: Who Says the Holocaust Never Happened and Why Do They Say It?* (Berkeley, CA: University of California Press, 2000), 29.

[63] Hayden White, *The Content of the Form: Narrative Discourse and Historical Representation* (Baltimore: Johns Hopkins University Press, 1987), 76.

[64] White, *Content of the Form*, 76. See his later discussion in Hayden White, "Historical Emplotment and the Problem of Truth," in *Probing the Limits of Representation: Nazism and the 'Final Solution'* (ed. Saul Friedlander; Harvard: Harvard University Press, 1992), 37–53. For Frank Ankersmit's discussion of the Holocaust, see Ankersmit, *Historical Representation*, 160–64, 176–93. See also the other essays in Saul Friedlander, ed., *Probing the Limits of Representation: Nazism and the 'Final Solution'* (Harvard: Harvard University Press, 1992). For a discussion of the ethical constraints of representing the Holocaust, see Hans Kellner, "'Never Again' Is Now," *History and Theory* 33.2 (1994): 127–44. For a survey of the literature on the Holocaust with a discussion of the ethics of interpretation, see Lucy S. Dawidowicz, *The Holocaust and the Historians* (Cambridge, MA: Harvard University Press, 1981).

While both views may *claim* to be representations of historical events in World War II, the twin principles of critical realism and history as representation allow a person to evaluate their respective descriptions of the evidence and consequently *judge* the "revisionist" representation to be a gross mishandling of the evidence and thus a false representation of the past.[65]

2.3. Clarifying the Historical Method

The above discussion has clarified two important elements: what is meant by the term "history" (i.e., historical narrative or NA), and how historiography clarifies the relationship between this narrative account of that chunk of past reality (PE) that the narrative account claims to represent. This discussion has certain implications for one's historical method, that is, the actual process by which the historian investigates the surviving traces (ST) and determines how to use them as evidence to gradually construct and compose the narrative account (NA), and this resulting representation is the historian's attempt to answer certain questions about the past itself (i.e., PE). It is not my intention to provide a detailed description of historical method in general, for there are excellent volumes available for this purpose.[66] Rather, I sketch a brief outline of historical method, but do so highlighting certain implications of the preceding discussion of history and historiography as they bear on historical method. Furthermore, this sketch intends to consider historical method in general; there are some distinctive elements that are relevant to historical Jesus research that will be considered in § 4 below, and § 4.3 applies the method described here to historical Jesus research in particular.

It may be helpful to view the overall historical method to consist of two main phases, preceded by a preliminary stage and followed by a concluding phase. While this will be helpful for descriptive purposes here, it is somewhat artificial, for as we will see, actual practice involves the historian

---

[65] As I reflect on the revisionist "history" (note the quotation marks) of Holocaust deniers, I am struck by the realization that most historical accounts understood as representations (as discussed above) are like the portrait of the woman with long brown hair: portraits as histories may be judged excellent representations or perhaps just fair ones, good portrayals or somewhat biased. But if a historical representation is determined to be blatantly false (i.e., it portrays a man with short, blond hair), this says as much or more about the "historian" who produced it as about the "history" itself.

[66] For helpful, general introductions, see Martha Howell and Walter Prevenier, *From Reliable Sources: An Introduction to Historical Methods* (Ithaca, NY: Cornell University Press, 2001); John Tosh and Seán Lang, *The Pursuit of History: Aims, Methods and New Directions in the Study of Modern History* (4 ed.; London: Pearson Education, 2006). With reference to issues particular to ancient history, see Michael Crawford, ed., *Sources for Ancient History* (Cambridge: Cambridge University Press, 1983); Hedrick Jr., *Ancient History: Monuments and Documents*.

moving back and forth among the stages. Historical method may be viewed as a Gadamerian hermeneutical spiral in which the historian spirals between the phases, and developments in a later phase may (and even should) cause the historian to revise views and judgments produced in an earlier phase. Nevertheless, it is helpful to consider conceptually the phases in research.

The *preliminary phase* actually focuses on the historian. We noted above the importance of the historian being self-aware of his/her horizon and in particular the biases and predispositions of that horizon which shape the questions being brought to the historical enterprise and which influence the evaluations and judgments made, and the contexts and hypotheses preferred. In this preliminary phase, the historian needs to bring such horizon issues to the surface so that they can be taken into account in the subsequent phases of historical research. As Gadamer's hermeneutical circle makes clear: the interpretive process begins with the Subject's own horizon and preunderstanding, and not with the Object.[67]

The *first main phase* involves the historian gathering, interpreting, and evaluating the surviving traces (ST) to determine their function as evidence within a particular context. This phase may be viewed as a dialogical relationship between the historian and these surviving traces. These surviving traces in their initial form might be called "data" or perhaps even "raw data." But using this latter term may be misleading, for while a "raw" datum may exist in and of itself, as soon as the historian proceeds to examine it and relate it to other data, it is no longer "raw," for in the process of observation the historian as Subject observes the Object of necessity from a particular perspective and within the historian's particular horizon. As a result the datum is no longer "raw," for it has already received preliminary processing by the historian.

The dialogical relationship in this phase continues as the historian begins the interpretive processing of these data, which includes several elements. First, for the interpretive process to begin, the historian must provide some kind of context in which to understand the discrete pieces of data. Like the puzzle-assembler who must take the single blue piece of the jigsaw puzzle and provide an initial context (i.e., viewing it as portraying water, or sky, or a shirt), so the historian takes pieces of data and provides an interpretive context for understanding them. As different pieces of data are examined,

---

[67] Gadamer, *Truth and Method*, 235–37. See also the important discussion by Michael Polanyi, *Personal Knowledge: Towards a Post-Critical Philosophy* (Chicago: University of Chicago Press, 1958); Michael Polanyi, *The Tacit Dimension* (Gloucester, MA: Peter Smith, 1983). For discussion from the perspective of biblical hermeneutics at an introductory level, see e.g., Duncan S. Ferguson, *Biblical Hermeneutics: An Introduction* (Louisville: Westminster John Knox, 1986), 6–22; and for an advanced level discussion, see e.g., Thiselton, *Two Horizons*.

different contexts might be considered and abandoned, and then other contexts considered. This consideration of alternative contexts for the data might be viewed as a top-down approach to the data. At a later stage these contextual elements become part of the historian's hypothesis for explaining the data, and they form part of the foundation that informs the historical narrative produced. In situations where the data has already been well worked over by other historians (like World War II or the historical Jesus), this context may be something new that this historian brings to the data which causes it to be viewed in a different light.

Second, the interpretive process also involves the historian bringing questions to the data. How are the data to be understood? In situations where many other historians have already worked with the data, the historian's bringing of new questions to the data can often cause the events concerned to be seen in a new light.

Third, the interpretive process also involves the historian interpreting and evaluating the data in terms of its evidentiary contribution. All data (i.e., STs) are potentially evidence of something, but the question is, *of what* are they evidence? This requires evaluation by the historian. This might be viewed as a bottom-up approach to the data, as discrete pieces of data are evaluated. The puzzle-assembler who has 300 pieces of a puzzle that was originally composed of 3,000 pieces, must make an evaluation whether these remaining 300 pieces even belong to this particular puzzle. Some pieces, for example, might be a different size, and so the puzzle-assembler makes the evaluation that they are not part of this particular puzzle – they belong to a different puzzle altogether. All 300 pieces are "evidence" of *some* puzzle, but the puzzle-assembler must decide whether they are relevant for *this particular* puzzle. In doing history, a datum might be a report that person X said "Y" at event Z. This cannot be taken at face value by the historian, for this ancient datum is just that, a report; that is, it is an ancient *claim* that person X said "Y" at event Z.[68] The claim might be inaccurate at various points: it was not person X but someone else, or "Y" might not accurately represent what was said, or it did not happen at event Z but at another time or place. Alternatively, the claim might be erroneous altogether. For the ancient datum so reported, it is the historian who must evaluate the claims made in it. It is evidence of something, but it is the historian who determines of what it is evidence: whether it is actually evidence for what the ancient datum claims, or that it approximates some aspects but not others, or that it is evidence of something else entirely (e.g., that someone else thought this happened but was mistaken, or that someone else at a later date created this

---

[68] On the matter of engaging reports as a "critical historian," see the discussion later in this section.

report for any of a variety of reasons). In evaluating the evidentiary contribution of data, the historian determines the relevance of the data for the questions under consideration. The historian should provide argumentation and other evidence to support the evaluations made concerning the data so that readers are able to follow the historian's reasoning and observe the evidence, argumentation, and judgments for themselves Thus they are able to determine for themselves whether the historian has handled the evidence in a fair and reasonable manner. This is an element of *description* in history-writing: readers are able to observe the historian's description of discrete data and the evaluation of their evidentiary nature.

One point about this first main phase must be stressed. While three elements have been identified in this phase, they should not be viewed as consecutive steps. Rather, this dialogical relationship between historian and the data is perhaps best modelled by the hermeneutical spiral. First one, then another, and then back again to perhaps reconsider a tentative view established earlier. Thus, it is an ongoing conversation between the top-down considerations of context(s) and the bottom-up evaluation and interpretation of the discrete pieces of data.

The *second main phase* of historical method involves the historian interpreting and explaining the relevant data with hypotheses. Having ascertained in the preceding phase the evidentiary value of the data for the questions the historian is seeking to answer, the historian continues to consider alternative contexts for the data. In the preceding phase contextual information was considered to evaluate the data's evidentiary value, but in this second phase the primary function is to explore alternative hypotheses. Contextual information may also come from considering alternative models derived from cognate disciplines such as cultural anthropology or sociology. As these alternative hypotheses are explored, they are evaluated to determine which hypothesis is preferable for answering the questions being addressed. A preferable hypothesis is one that (a) provides a better explanation of the evidence, and (b) allows for extrapolation that provides a more plausible explanation of the complete historical picture.[69] Returning to the picture-puzzle illustration for a moment, one must keep in mind that one only has 250 relevant pieces for a 3,000 piece jigsaw puzzle. So to repaint the front cover of the puzzle box, one needs to paint a picture (i.e., provide the most plausible hypothesis) that places the 250 pieces appropriately (i.e., explain the evidence) as well as fills in the gaps left blank from the missing 2,750 pieces (i.e., extrapolates to the complete historical picture). This sec-

---

[69] On extrapolation to the larger picture in historical Jesus research, see the interesting discussion by E. P. Sanders and Margaret Davies, *Studying the Synoptic Gospels* (Philadelphia: Trinity Press International, 1989), 335–44, esp. 335–37.

ond main phase is largely the process of the historian gathering together the components and forming the *representation* that the historian is constructing of the chunk of past reality under consideration.

I wish to reiterate at this point, that the two main phases outlined above, while conceptually sequential, are not so in practice. For as one considers other contextual alternatives and alternative explanatory hypotheses, the historian is frequently led to re-evaluate the evidentiary value of the data that were considered in the first main phase: either increasing or decreasing the probability of the authenticity of any one piece of data. At times the historian should also reflect on the preliminary phase as well: to what extent are the preunderstandings and biases of my horizon affecting the judgments and interpretations I am making? This is an application of the hermeneutical spiral, for the historian now knows more about the data and the issues in the investigation, and this may suggest viewing them in a different way.

The *concluding phase* of the historical method is to gather the evidence (i.e., ST), arguments, and hypotheses into a coherent and complete historical narrative that the historian considers the most plausible representation (i.e., NA) of that chunk of past reality being considered (i.e., PE). The historical research has been done; it now needs to written. This narrative account includes (1) *descriptions* of the relevant pieces of data, and (2) the *interpretations* of these data that have produced the conclusions the historian has reached. These descriptions and interpretations also include the contextual material that was used as well as any models from cognate disciplines. The historian uses these descriptions and interpretations to provide a *representation* of the past events in a way that answers the questions the historian has posed and supports the hypotheses the historian has proposed in response.[70] This representation includes (3) *explanations* that relate the data to one another and allow for extrapolation in order to provide a coherent portrait of these past events. Historical explanation is particularly concerned with causality: Why did a particular event happen? What factors led to it happening and to happening in the way it did? What impact did this event have on subsequent events?[71] The representation also includes (4) *evaluations* of

---

[70] Note the use of the terms "description" and then "representation" follow the usage noted in discussing the work of Ankersmit in the preceding discussion in § 2.2 concerning historiography.

[71] For a discussion of causality in contemporary historical explanation, see Howell and Prevenier, *From Reliable Sources*, 119–43. They discuss causality in terms of (a) religious ideology, clericalism, and anticlericalism; (b) social and economic factors; (c) biology and "race"; (d) environment; (e) science, technology, and inventions; (f) power, and (g) public opinion and the mass media. They also explore the role of the individual in causality: Do great men and women make history, or does history make great men and women? (paraphrasing p. 140).

the events. These evaluations may be explicit by considering the events in light of some standard, usually established by the historian. This standard might be an evaluation of the success or failure of a particular event (e.g., a battle), but frequently evaluation involves some type of ethical consideration. Sometimes this may be quite explicit and obvious (e.g., "Hitler's use of death camps is one of the greatest acts of evil perpetrated by one human against others"). But at other times the evaluation may not be so obvious. For example, in the statement "the Allied forces invaded France on DDay to free them from German occupation," the use of the terms "to free" and "occupation" implies an evaluation of the injustice of Germany's actions in France. Another type of evaluation may be more implicit, for historical narratives frequently explore human conflict in one form or another, and such historical narratives frequently provide explanation from the perspective of one of the parties in the conflict. The reference to DDay above is one example. Another example is the "American War of Independence," which is the title used in the United States for this event. But a British perspective could easily refer to it as the "American Colonial Revolt" and explain the events quite differently – from a British perspective. Similarly, when describing events in the first-century Roman province of Judea, events might be represented quite differently if done from the perspective of a Roman governor like Pilate having to deal with a troublesome population in his province or from the perspective of a Jewish peasant having to deal with the heavy-handed rule of a foreigner representing a foreign, pagan power.[72]

While not part of the representation in the historical narrative itself, a complete work should also include (5) *revelation* of the historian. The historian should inform the reader of those preunderstandings and biases that may have affected the judgments and interpretations. Readers can best evaluate the historical representation when they not only have presented to them the evidence, arguments, and hypotheses that contribute to the historical representation, but when they also have an appreciation of the historian who has painted the historical picture.

Basic to all of these phases is an underlying principle of modern historical method: a historian must be a critical historian; that is, a historian must subject all sources to critical inspection.[73] As discussed above, the original sources must be examined and evaluated to determine of what they are actually evidence, and to what extent their descriptions and explanations may be used by the historian in his / her own representation of a particular chunk of

---

[72] See the discussion on the different perspectives of understanding Pilate's verdict in ch. 13, § 3.4.3.
[73] For a classic statement, see Marc Bloch, *The Historian's Craft* (trans. Peter Putnam; New York: Vintage Books, 1953), 79–137.

past reality. No ancient source may be privileged over another based on its origins. In the pre-Enlightenment world, "history" was often understood to be the acceptance of the testimony of a past account, often based upon the authority of the account's author. The Enlightenment, with its emphasis on the autonomy of the human to use reason in exploring the world,[74] transformed this for the historian. This might be called the principle of autonomy for critical investigation.[75] Collingwood explains that

> [S]o far from relying on an authority other than himself, to whose statements his thought must conform, the historian is his own authority and his thought autonomous, self-authorizing, possessed of a criterion to which his so-called authorities must conform and by reference to which they are criticized.[76]

He goes on to state that

> In so far as an historian accepts the testimony of an authority and treats it as historical truth, he obviously forfeits the name of historian; but we have no other name by which to call him.[77]

It is not that testimony is wrong, according to Collingwood, for in practical life we accept the testimony of others all the time, "believing" the testimony to be truthful. But this is not "historical knowledge" until the testimony has been critically examined and evidence is found to provide grounds to use it. In such a case, one "go[es] beyond ... belief" and has historical knowledge:

> As soon as there are such grounds, the case is no longer one of testimony. When testimony is reinforced by evidence, our acceptance of it is no longer the acceptance of testimony as such; it is the affirmation of something based on evidence, that is, historical knowledge.[78]

This principle of critical history is understood to permeate all phases of the historical method, and it perhaps also explains why some self-revelation of the historian helps readers to evaluate a historian's narrative account, allowing the reader to ascertain the extent to which the historian has been a "critical historian."

---

[74] See the discussion by Van A. Harvey, *The Historian and the Believer: The Morality of Historical Knowledge and Christian Belief* (London: SCM, 1967), 38–40, who cites Immanuel Kant's discussion of "What Is Enlightenment?" in Immanuel Kant, *Critique of Practical Reason and Other Writings in Moral Philosophy* (ed. and trans. Lewis W. Beck; Chicago: University of Chicago Press, 1949), 286–92.

[75] Harvey (*Historian and the Believer*, 39–42) refers to this as "the autonomy of the historian."

[76] Collingwood, *Idea of History*, 236.

[77] Collingwood, *Idea of History*, 256.

[78] Collingwood, *Idea of History*, 257.

3. Exploring Historical Explanation, Worldview, and the "Supernatural"

Most discussions of the historical enterprise would be considered complete after having discussed the subjects surveyed in the preceding section: history, historiography, and historical method. However, when the discipline of history is applied to events reported within many religious texts like the Bible, questions concerning history become more complex when descriptions of divine intervention in human events are used as a causal explanation. Such references to divine intervention permeate biblical narratives, from, for example, God's intervention leading to Israel's exodus from Egypt (Exod 3–15), and Jesus' claim to exorcise demons "by the Spirit of God" (Matt 12:28), to the early Christian claim that it was God who raised Jesus from the dead (Acts 2:32; Rom 10:9). To use divine causation as an explanation is to be expected in biblical narratives, for the texts of the Hebrew Bible and the NT are written by authors whose worldview incorporated a God who intervenes in human affairs on behalf of his people and does so for the furtherance of his purposes. These biblical texts are theological, for their interpretation of human events arises out of and promotes this worldview of a God operative in human affairs.[79] To be clear, it is helpful to distinguish between two things here which can become confused in the discussion: there is the event itself that is being described by the biblical author, and there is this author's interpretive explanation of divine causality for that event. Discussion of the possible historicity of an event itself is a distinct matter from discussing the causal explanation provided in the ancient text (i.e., two distinct questions: Did the event happen? What explains why it happened?).

The issue before us is, how should the modern historian handle such descriptions and explanations in primary sources? This is a matter of considerable debate and disagreement in biblical studies, with good and weighty scholars on all sides of the issues. This was also a matter of considerable discussion among those of us involved in the project that produced the essays in this volume. Since this essay is intended to introduce the volume, in this section of this essay I will present three basic alternative views used in biblical studies, rather than arguing for my own view on this matter. This will help the reader understand why there are often differences in historical works in biblical studies, as well as help the reader to sort through the issues from his/her own perspective. These three alternatives are only an attempt to provide a basic paradigm; there may be other views as well as many ways

---

[79] Providing explanations of human events by divine causality is not restricted to the Hebrew Bible or the NT, for it was common through out the ancient Mediterranean world. In his description of that ancient Mediterranean world Collingwood (*Idea of History*, 14) coined the term "theocratic history" for this approach.

to nuance these three. But sketching out these three alternatives introduces the readers to the issues and some of their complexities.

At opposite poles from one another are two approaches. The first we might call the "naturalistic" approach. This approach rejects descriptions and explanations that involve divine causation, because cause and effect within the space-time universe is understood to operate within a closed continuum.[80] This view places history as subject to the scientific paradigm. In our modern context, this approach is often associated with developments arising out of the Enlightenment, but forms of naturalism were also expressed in the ancient Mediterranean world.[81] The opposite pole we might call the "theistic" approach. This approach does not necessarily accept all claims of divine intervention in descriptions and explanations of events. Those who use this approach would critically examine the plausibility of such claims when they are made. In fact, it is quite possible to be quite skeptical of many claims, and yet still be open to the possibility of divine intervention. It is willing not only to consider this possibility as claimed in ancient texts, but also to use divine intervention as an explanation in a historical account of the event. This view does not reject the scientific paradigm, but rather views history as having precedence over science.[82]

---

[80] Note that I am using the term "natural" in a broad, generic sense, perhaps best viewed, somewhat simplistically, as distinct from "supernatural." I am not using the term "natural" in the more limited sense that Collingwood (*Idea of History*, 163) used it to criticize Toynbee's view of history as only biological, wheras Collingwood incorporated human thought as well.

[81] See e.g., the discussion by Cicero in *De natura deorum*. He asks in his introduction, "whether the gods are entirely idle and inactive, taking no part at all in the direction and government of the world, or whether on the contrary all things both were created and kept in motion by them throughout eternity"? And he states, "there are and have been philosophers who hold that the gods exercise no control over human affairs whatever" (*Nat. d.* 1.2–3; Rackham, LCL).

[82] It is helpful to note the relative role that the scientific paradigm plays in each of these views. In the naturalistic approach, science is dominant and so is determinant for how cause and effect operates in history. In the theistic approach, event in history is dominant and so cause and effect may not always function according to science. Perhaps more than any other philosopher, the Italian Marxist Benedetto Croce championed the autonomy of history from science. Distinguishing between real science – the historical moment of the observed event – and its "pseudo concepts" – the universals abstracted from and dependent upon those real events – he argued that since science could not begin to do its work until history had done its, history was ontologically prior. See Benedetto Croce, *History: Its Theory and Practice* (trans. Douglas Ainslie; 1920; repr., New York: Russell & Russell, 1960), 83–107; Benedetto Croce, *History as the Story of Liberty* (trans. Sylvia Sprigge; 1941; repr., New York: Meridian Books, 1955), 25–29, 48–52, 282–91. See also the discussion by Collingwood of "History and Freedom" in Collingwood, *Idea of History*, 315–20, as well as his interaction with the work of Croce (pp. 190–204). The work of Croce has suffered somewhat from neglect, but see the recent collections of essays, some of which wrestle with these issues, in Jack D'Amico, et al., *The Legacy of Benedetto Croce: Contemporary Critical Views* (Toronto: University of Toronto Press, 1999).

The difference between these two poles is not merely a difference of how historical method is understood, but it is, in reality, a difference in ontological worldviews. A naturalistic approach may be (but not necessarily so – more on this below) associated with a worldview that understands the physical, space-time universe to constitute the totality of reality. Whereas a theistic approach, particularly associated with the western religious heritage,[83] arises out of a worldview in which reality includes not only the physical, space-time universe but also a supra-mundane, supernatural world that can and does interact with humans in the physical, space-time universe. This may be illustrated in a Venn diagram portraying two different views of reality: in ontological naturalism the diagram of "reality" consists of a single circle labelled "physical, space-time universe," whereas in the supernaturalist view the diagram of "reality" consists of two overlapping circles, one labelled "physical, space-time universe," and the other "spiritual, supernatural universe."

The difference between these two views is based upon different worldviews. To clarify this difference, I suggest the descriptive names of "ontological naturalistic history" for the historical view of the first pole and "critical theistic history" to identify the latter pole.[84] The difficulty is, of course, that these two worldviews are contradictory. Is there a way forward, or must this ontological difference lead to a methodological impasse?

A third view attempts to find common ground between these two poles by focusing on the commonalities between them rather than on their differences. The first two views both recognize that reality does include the physical, space-time universe, and that cause and effect can be observed operating in both the natural world and the human world. In § 2.1 above we carefully defined the focus of history in two respects: (a) history focuses on the past of humans as distinguished from the past of nature, and (b) history focuses its inquiry on human actions in specific events in the past. One implication

---

[83] This can apply equally to Jewish, Christian, and Islamic traditions. My subsequent discussion will focus on the Judeo-Christian tradition because it is the one I am most familiar with. Furthermore, it is the one that is most relevant to discussion of the historical Jesus which is the focus of this essay and volume.

[84] I use the word "critical" in the term "critical theistic history" to clarify that modern historians of this type can still, as discussed above, be critical and skeptical about claims of divine causation, but be willing to allow critical judgment to persuade them that divine causation may have happened. This stands in contrast to what we might call "naïve theistic history" which either does not or will not critically examine claims of divine causation, but simply accepts them. In the preceding section on historical method, we explored briefly the principle of critical history. For the critical theistic historian, there can be a tension between one's theology and one's historical method. For a Christian, a theistic worldview has at its fundamental core the principle of "belief," and within the Christian tradition, it has the Bible as "testimony." Yet, as a historian he must critically weigh all sources from a historical perspective.

of these two focusing principles is to realize that by definition history is quite focused in this narrow and specific manner. We observed above that the concern of history per se is not the totality of reality even in the natural sphere of the physical, space-time universe. Geology is concerned with the "event" of the formation of the Rocky Mountains, physics is concerned with the "event" of splitting of the atom, and meteorology is concerned with the "event" of the formation of a hurricane. But none of these are the concerns of the discipline of history (though, as seen above in § 2.1 these may impact historical events). Similarly, archaeology is concerned with the "event" of destruction of an ancient village, and sociology and cultural anthropology are concerned with the "event" of human mating rituals. But neither of these are the concerns of the discipline of history either (though as seen above, these may impact historical studies). All of these are "events" within the natural, space-time universe, but they are outside the parameters of history as a discipline. What this demonstrates is that this definitional limitation of what is usually understood to constitute history is not making an ontological statement about the totality of reality; rather, it is recognizing that the modern discipline of history focuses on a particular facet of that reality. For those whose worldview includes a supernatural realm and the possibility of theistic causation in human events, this view of history is limiting. Those who hold this worldview may respond in two different ways: they may define the breadth of history to include the possibility of divine causation (as in the critical theistic view noted above), or they may view this understanding to be a definitional limitation of the modern discipline of history and how it functions, without it being an ontological statement about the nature of reality. This latter view we could call "methodological naturalistic history" – in other words, for the purposes of doing historical work, the historian is methodologically limited to causation within the physical, space-time universe, but this does not limit the historian's personal ontological worldview, just her / his historical method as a historian.

From the perspective of methodological naturalistic history, just as there are related disciplines that concern themselves with other aspects of human life that are beyond the confines of history (like archaeology and cultural anthropology), so there is the related discipline that concerns itself with still another aspect of human life – human existence in relationship to God and the spiritual realm – namely, theology. Just as archaeology and cultural anthropology have distinctive foci as well as distinctive methodological principles in the aspects of human reality with which they are concerned, so also theology has its distinctive focus as well as distinctive methodological principles that govern it as a discipline. A moment ago, the critical theistic historian considered the modern definition of history to be too limiting and an infringement upon his / her worldview, but now the ontological natural-

Diagram: Historical Method and Views of Reality

Ontological Naturalistic History

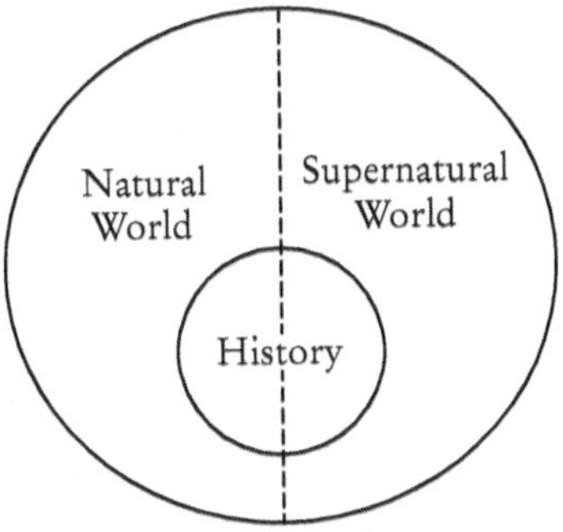

Critical Theistic History

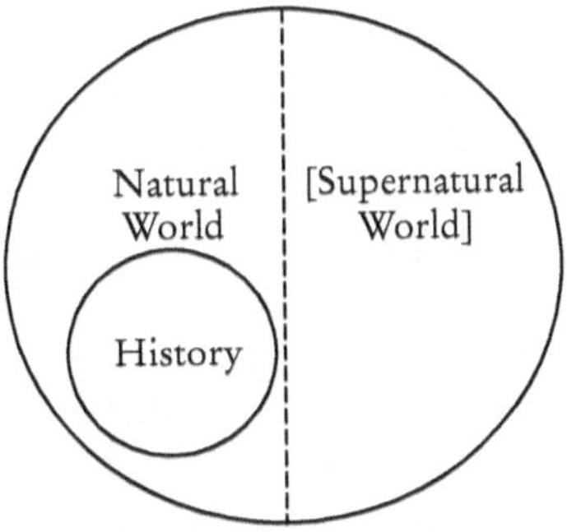

Methodological Naturalistic History

istic historian may feel uncomfortable with allowing for the existence of the discipline of theology as an infringement upon her / his worldview. Both the polar views face ontological tensions with their approaches. Whereas, the methodological naturalistic view attempts to sidestep the issue by focusing on a methodological definition without imposing an ontological viewpoint on history / reality.

In discussions of these matters, Ernst Troeltsch, one of the fathers of modern historical method, is frequently cited, usually his essay, "Über historische und dogmatische Methode in der Theologie" ("Historical and Dogmatic Method in Theology"). It is interesting to note that his concern is not simply historical method, per se, but rather historical method as it relates to the development of theology in distinction to what he terms "dogmatic method." Troeltsch articulates three, now famous, principles of the historical method, which are the "use of criticism, analogy, and correlation."[85] It is this third principle of correlation that is relevant here; he explains that

> there can be no change at one point without some preceding and consequent change elsewhere, so that all historical happening is knit together in a permanent relationship of correlation, inevitably forming a current in which everything is interconnected and each single event is related to all others.[86]

John Macquarrie, commenting on Troeltsch's principle, clarifies how this principle is relevant to the discussion here:

> [t]here is an integral continuity in history, so that everything which happens has to be considered as immanent in the immensely complex causal nexus ... [A]lthough there may be distinctive events and even highly distinctive events, all events are of the same order, and all are explicable in terms of what is immanent in history itself. Thus there can be no divine irruptions or interventions in history.[87]

Troeltsch's principle is important for its description of what constitutes description and explanation in history: it is the cause and effect of correlated events within human existence in the physical world. But what should also be noted is that Troeltsch is not describing history *per se*, but rather he is describing historical method as it relates to theology – in other words, his point here is as much theological and ontological as it is historical. Note in the above quote that he begins with a claim that "there *can be* no change ..."[88] which is an ontological and theological claim as much as it is a statement of historical method. Macquarrie summarizes Troeltsch's somewhat convoluted argument at this point: "[T]here *can be* no divine irruptions or interventions in history. God may indeed be at work in the process, or revealing himself in it, but if so his activity is immanent and continuous. It is not the special or sporadic intervention of a transcendent deity."[89] Tro-

---

[85] Ernst Troeltsch, "Historical and Dogmatic Method in Theology," in *Religion in History* (trans. James Luther Adams and Walter F. Bense; 1898; repr., Fortress Texts in Modern Theology; Minneapolis: Fortress, 1991), 15.

[86] Troeltsch, "Historical and Dogmatic Method in Theology," 14.

[87] John Macquarrie, *Twentieth-Century Religious Thought* (5 ed.; Harrisburg, PA: Trinity Press International, 2002), 142–43.

[88] Troeltsch, "Historical and Dogmatic Method in Theology," 14, my emphasis.

[89] Macquarrie, *Twentieth-Century Religious Thought*, 143, my emphasis. Troeltsch ("Historical and Dogmatic Method in Theology," 19) commented in this regard: "I have the greatest confidence, however, that the implication of the historical method will necessarily lead through the present confusion and derangement of biblical studies to its full and resolute application. Only then will the worst of our fears (regarding apologetics) be lifted from our hearts, and we shall be able to behold with greater detachment and freedom the glory of God in history." Note that for him the "glory of God" will be beheld "in history." In other words, in the natural functioning of history as Troeltsch understood it, God's glory was immanently revealed.

eltsch has stepped beyond the realm of a historian discussing history and is making ontological and theological claims that he then uses to redefine history. In other words, his theological worldview is shaping his historical method. Thus, while Troeltsch's principle is important, it does not really provide a way to adjudicate between the three alternative views presented here, contrary to the way that Troeltsch is often cited to settle this debate.

To summarize, the ontological naturalistic and the critical theistic views of history permit their distinct ontological worldviews to define the type of causation used in historical explanations, whereas the methodological naturalistic view of history attempts to mediate between these two by understanding history as description and explanation of cause and effect of human events within the natural sphere alone, without making ontological claims beyond the natural sphere. The descriptive terms I have suggested for these views are suggested by a similar discussion taking place within the physical sciences, in which the "scientific method" presupposes naturalism: effects in the physical world are studied in terms of their natural causes. Recent discussion within the philosophy of science has debated the distinction between "methodological naturalism" and "ontological naturalism" (or "metaphysical naturalism"). What has been proposed by those who advocate this distinction is that the scientific method can be understood to operate based on "methodological naturalism" – physical phenomena in nature are explained in terms of natural causation without affirming or denying the existence of the supernatural. The claim being made is that the scientific method does not require ontological naturalism – the metaphysical view that denies any reality beyond the physical, space-time universe.[90]

We may explore the issues involved with these three views by observing how historical argumentation functions. As described in § 2.3 above on historical method, the historian evaluates the evidentiary contribution of data and should provide argumentation and other evidence to support the evaluations made. The readers then can follow the historian's reasoning, observe the evidence for themselves, and so determine if the historian's descriptions and evaluations are actually borne out by the evidence provided. Only in

---

[90] According to Ronald L. Numbers ("Science Without God: Natural Laws and Christian Beliefs," in *When Science and Christianity Meet* [ed. David C. Lindberg and Ronald L. Numbers; Chicago: University of Chicago Press, 2003], 266 n. 2) the term "methodological naturalism" was coined by a Christian philosopher, Paul de Vries, who was then a professor at Wheaton College. The paper he presented in the conference in 1983 was subsequently published in Paul de Vries, "Naturalism in the Natural Sciences," *Christian Scholar's Review* 15 (1986): 388–96. For a collection of essays presenting a variety of points of view on this subject, see Robert T. Pennock, ed., *Intelligent Design Creationism and Its Critics: Philosophical, Theological, and Scientific Perspectives* (Cambridge, MA: MIT Press, 2001); see also the essays in David C. Lindberg and Ronald L. Numbers, eds., *When Science and Christianity Meet* (Chicago: University of Chicago Press, 2003).

this manner is the reader ultimately able to evaluate whether the historian's representation of the past events in the created historical narrative is a reasonable representation. In other words, the historian's descriptions and explanations of events and their proposed causes and effects must be open to verification by the reader from observable data interpreted as evidence. Thus there is a necessary empirical element to the historical method.[91]

Such verification of descriptions and explanations is possible in historical representations because the foundation upon which it is built is observable data interpreted and presented as evidence. This observable data is open to all historians and their readers, for these observable data exist within the physical, space-time universe. These data may be extremely diverse, but they have a commonality, as Macquarrie expressed above: "[A]lthough there may be distinctive events and even highly distinctive events, all events are of the same order, and all are explicable in terms of what is immanent ..."[92]

If, however, a person with a theistic worldview were to propose divine causation for a particular human event, this theistic explanation is, by its very nature, an explanation of a different order. This leads to two problems: First, it requires that a reader entertain some form of a theistic worldview before the explanation can evaluated. Second, it introduces a type of argumentation that is wholly different from all others used in historical explanation. As noted a moment ago, the historian's descriptions and explanations of events and their proposed causes and effects must be open to verification by the reader from observable data interpreted and presented as evidence. But by its very nature, introducing a "supernatural" cause for a human event, such causation is beyond the "natural" space-time universe, and thus is not open to verification in the same way that any other "natural" historical description and explanation would be.[93] That is, by definition, what distinguishes "natural" from "supernatural."

It is here that the differences between the views are keenly felt. Take, for example, an ancient text that attributes a human event to divine causation, and consider how each historical view treats it. First, for the ontological naturalistic historian, to evaluate such an explanation requires him/her to

---

[91] For discussions of the evidence and verification in historical explanation, see Patrick Gardiner, *The Nature of Historical Explanation* (Oxford: Oxford University Press, 1961); C. Behan McCullagh, *Justifying Historical Descriptions* (Cambridge: Cambridge University Press, 1984); Evans, *In Defense of History*, 65–87, 111–37.

[92] Macquarrie, *Twentieth-Century Religious Thought*, 163.

[93] Gorman (*Understanding History*, 22) states: "A person who makes a claim to knowledge has to defend it to the satisfaction of others, by appealing to public standards that all can share. Experience, as encapsulated in the language we learned to share in talking about a shared world, is pre-eminently the right kind of thing for this role. Private and privileged sources for knowledge claims, no matter how splendid, are worthless, unless others can be persuaded, by good objective reason, to go along with them."

step outside of who they are and entertain an alternate worldview. Or, this historian rejects the explanation as contrary to her/his worldview, and then either seeks an alternate, natural explanation[94] or else rejects the historicity of the event along with the ancient text's explanation.

Second, the critical theistic historian, on the other hand, is open to the possibility of theistic causation, but equally applies critical faculties to the ancient text's account and explanation. This historian may make the same historical judgments as the ontological naturalistic historian, but not for the same reasons (i.e., reject the ancient text altogether, or provide an alternate, natural explanation). But this historian is willing to entertain the possibility that, if no natural explanation can be found, and yet the evidence for the event itself is strong, then the critical theistic historian's explanation is to attribute the event to divine causation.

Third, the methodological naturalistic historian also applies critical faculties to the ancient text's account, just like the other two historians. And just like the other two historians, this historian may make the same types of judgments: reject the text's claim altogether, or provide an alternate, natural explanation. If, however, no natural explanation can be found, and yet the evidence for the event itself is strong, then this historian can only lay out what they see as the evidence and their evaluation of it, and then say that they have gone as far as they can go as a historian using historical method. For this historian, the argumentation and evidence for "supernatural" causation, because it is of a different order by its very nature, should be understood within the sphere and discipline of theology, which has its own distinct forms of argumentation and evidence. This is not a bifurcation and separation of history and theology; rather, the point is that history has narrow and specific limits, and that history can operate in this way without imposing an ontological judgment on the existence of a supernatural realm.[95] The methodological naturalistic view allows historians who have differing worldviews to participate together in the historical enterprise in spite of their differing worldviews – much in the same manner as scientists can participate in the scientific enterprise yet have differing worldviews. But when

---

[94] E.g., an ancient text might explain a temporary darkening of the sky at noonday to the anger of the gods, but the historian might explain it as being caused by a solar eclipse.

[95] From a theological point of view, theologians can discuss the interaction of the spiritual realm with humans and human events, but the evidence and argumentation for such is of a theological nature. It should be recognized that someone holding to a methodological naturalistic view could do historical work, and then could begin to discuss the spiritual realm and/or theistic causation. But in doing so they have moved from the method and argumentation of history to that of theology, according to their methodological naturalistic view. At times such a move may appear seamless, and this demonstrates the close relationship of theology to history, but they are, nevertheless, distinct.

ontological claims are used in a historical argument to support a historical judgment, the tensions between the views become clear.[96]

Thus, with reference to our example of an ancient text describing a human event *requiring* divine causation, the ontological naturalistic historian might say, "the evidence for this event may appear strong but it cannot have happened, for divine causation does not happen in this physical, space-time universe." The critical theistic historian might say, "the evidence for the event may appear strong, and divine causation can explain this event." The methodological naturalistic historian might say, "the evidence for the event may be strong, but I cannot provide a historical explanation for it." In one sense, the polar views are more satisfying (to themselves), for they are able to go further in their judgments and explanations. But the contradictory nature of their respective worldviews means that these historians easily dismiss the other's work. On the other hand, the mediating view of the methodological naturalistic historian is less satisfying, for its conclusions may be more tentative and explanations are incomplete in certain cases.

To clarify the distinctions being made in this discussion, let us take the example of the resurrection of Jesus. The witness of the NT is that God raised Jesus from the dead (e.g., Acts 2:24, 32; Rom 10:9). The NT does not describe this "event" itself, but rather it provides narratives of an empty tomb (e.g., Mark 16:1–8) and appearances of Jesus (e.g., Luke 24:13–35; 1 Cor 15:4–8), both of which are explained by the explanatory claim that Jesus had been raised from the dead (Mark 16:6; Luke 24:34; 1 Cor 15:4). In terms of the above discussion, these are ancient texts providing accounts in support of an event which they explain as having happened by divine causation.

An ontological naturalistic historian's approach to these ancient accounts is quite obvious: dead people do not rise from the dead; such things do not happen in this physical, space-time universe.[97] There is really nothing

---

[96] The methodological naturalistic view may come to the same historical conclusions as the ontological naturalistic view. Equally, it is possible that the methodological naturalistic view and the critical theistic view may may come to similar conclusions, but what the critical theistic view might identify as causation within history, the methodological naturalistic view would identify it as belonging to the realm of theology.

[97] A example of this point of view, though expressed more eloquently and with more care than this simplistic summary, is Gerd Lüdemann, for which see his earlier works: Gerd Lüdemann, *The Resurrection of Jesus: History, Experience, Theology* (trans. John Bowden; Minneapolis: Fortress, 1994); Gerd Lüdemann, *What Really Happened to Jesus: A Historical Approach to the Resurrection* (trans. John Bowden, in collaboration with Alf Özen; Louisville: Westminster John Knox, 1995). Note that his argument changes somewhat in his most recent work, but his fundamental conclusion remains the same: Gerd Lüdemann, *The Resurrection of Christ: A Historical Inquiry* (Amherst, NY: Prometheus Books, 2004). Other examples of this basic approach include Robert M. Price and Jeffery Jay Lowder, eds., *The Empty Tomb: Jesus Beyond the Grave* (Amherst, NY: Prometheus

further to note with reference to this view, for the ontological perspective of the worldview effectively precludes any other conclusion. This historian would either provide some naturalistic explanation for the empty tomb and appearance stories or reject them all as unhistorical. Unless this historian were to consider a possibility that was outside his / her worldview, there is little communication between the ontological naturalistic historian and the critical theistic historian who might take a different view of these same texts.

The approach of the other two historians – critical theological and the methodological naturalistic – could lead them to the same conclusions as the ontological naturalistic historian: the stories have a natural explanation or the stories as a whole are not historical. These historians can be equally critical, after all, but such conclusions would not based upon ontological worldview premises. To exemplify the distinction between these latter two approaches, consider the views of E. P. Sanders and N. T. Wright on these resurrection texts.

The focus of E. P. Sanders' work has been on the historical Jesus, and for him this work is complete with the discussion of his execution and then the subsequent impact he had on the rise of the early Christian movement. In his earlier work, *Jesus and Judaism* (1985), his brief comment was that "I have no special explanation or rationalization of the resurrection experiences of the disciples."[98] In his later work, *The Historical Figure of Jesus* (1995), he does discuss the resurrection in a concluding chapter which is an "epilogue," because "[t]he resurrection is not, strictly speaking, part of the story of the historical Jesus, but rather belongs to the aftermath of his life."[99] Sanders' discussion of Jesus' resurrection is largely on the tensions within the narratives of the appearance stories and the empty tomb stories. But note that he rejects the possible explanations, suggested by some, that this was either a "deliberate fraud" or "mass hysteria,"[100] and he concludes: "That Jesus' followers (and later Paul) had resurrection experiences is, in my judgment, a fact." In other words, while there are tensions and differences in these accounts, they are evidence of some kind of experience by the disciples. But his next sentence is, "What the reality was that gave rise to the experiences I do not know."[101] Sanders is unwilling to go beyond the limits of what he understands the historical method can provide. As a historian he grants that certain human experiences were historical, but that is as far as

---

Books, 2005); Michael Goulder, "Did Jesus of Nazareth Rise from the Dead?" in *Resurrection: Essays in Honour of Leslie Houlden* (ed. Stephen Barton and Graham Stanton; London: SPCK, 1994), 58–68.

[98] Sanders, *Jesus and Judaism*, 320.
[99] E. P. Sanders, *The Historical Figure of Jesus* (New York: Penguin Books, 1995), 276.
[100] Sanders, *The Historical Figure of Jesus*, 279–80.
[101] Sanders, *The Historical Figure of Jesus*, 280.

he can go *historically*. He is not able to provide a causal explanation for the event. On this matter he explained his approach in his earlier work:

> The relationships between history and theology are very complex ... I have been engaged for some years in the effort to free history and exegesis from the control of theology; that is, from being obligated to come to certain conclusions which are predetermined by theological commitment, and one sees this effort continued here ... I aim to be only a historian and an exegete.[102]

Now, I should draw to the reader's attention that I do not know whether Sanders would consider himself a methodological naturalistic historian as I have defined it. For Sanders has revealed little about his personal beliefs and worldview, apart from his desire to "free history ... from the control of theology" noted above.[103] But Sanders exemplifies the approach of what I've been describing as a methodological naturalist history: the evidence compels him to conclude that the resurrection experiences are not a deliberate fraud – they did happen, but he is unable to provide a natural explanation for them. An event can be affirmed as having taken place with a high degree of historical probability, but one ultimately cannot provide an adequate historical explanation for them. Once one steps beyond this limited and narrow focus, one is ultimately guided by one's metaphysical worldview,[104] as in the critical theistic historian's view.

E. P. Sanders' discussion is limited to a few pages, and this is due largely to his perspective as an historian and his view of the limitations of history. N. T. Wright's discussion in his *The Resurrection of the Son of God* (2003), on the other hand, is an exhaustive treatment of the question. Wright argues in his preliminary methodological discussion that "historical knowledge about the resurrection, of a sort that can be discussed without presupposing Christian faith, cannot be ruled out a priori, even if the resurrection, if acknowledged, would then turn out to offer a differently grounded

---

[102] Sanders, *Jesus and Judaism*, 333–34. He goes on (p. 334) to explain: "But, since I have criticized so many for having their 'history' and 'exegesis' dictated by theology, the reader may well wonder how well 'my' Jesus squares with my theological heritage. I can explain simply: I am a liberal, modern, secularized Protestant, brought up in a church dominated by low christology and the social gospel. I am proud of the things that that religious tradition stands for. I am not bold enough, however, to suppose that Jesus came to establish it, or that he died for the sake of its principles." In the context of his discussion, this last sentence would be, to his mind, making a theological claim for his historical Jesus – a move which he will not make as a historian and exegete.

[103] The one statement Sanders does make is at the conclusion to *Jesus and Judaism*, 334, as he explains: "the reader may well wonder how well 'my' Jesus squares with my theological heritage. I can explain simply: I am a liberal, modern, secularized Protestant, brought up in a church dominated by a low christology and the social gospel."

[104] Cf. the interesting discussion of the limitations of historical method and worldview by Allison, *Resurrecting Jesus*, 337–52. See also his discussion (pp. 269–99) of the paranormal and his own personal experiences with it.

epistemology."¹⁰⁵ His process is to examine how the ancient world understood "life after death" as well as "life *after* 'life after death'," ¹⁰⁶ including the broader ancient Mediterranean world, as well as in the Hebrew Bible and post-biblical Judaism. He turns to examine more specifically how Paul understood resurrection and how other early Christians in the first and second centuries understood it.¹⁰⁷ He then turns to the appearance and empty-tomb narratives. He concludes that the belief of Paul and the early Christians arises from what early Christians had experienced:

> that on the third day after his execution by the Romans, his tomb was empty, and he was found to be alive, appearing on various occasions and in various places both to his followers and to some who, up to that point, had not been his followers or had not believed, convincing them that he was neither a ghost nor a hallucination but that he was truly and bodily raised from the dead.¹⁰⁸

To this point Wright has described early Christian belief and experience. He then moves to summarize this as an historian, of which two points are key: In light of what resurrection meant within Second Temple Judaism, "[t]he other explanations sometimes offered for the emergence of the belief do not possess the same explanatory power," and so he concludes: "It is therefore historically highly probable that Jesus' tomb was indeed empty on the third day after his execution, and that the disciples did indeed encounter him giving every appearance of being well and truly alive."¹⁰⁹ And so he asks, "what explanation can be given for these two phenomena? Is there an alternative to the explanation given by the early Christians themselves?"¹¹⁰ He concludes that the only sufficient and necessary explanation is "[t]he actual bodily resurrection of Jesus (not a mere resuscitation, but a trans-

---

¹⁰⁵ N. Thomas Wright, *The Resurrection of the Son of God* (vol. 3 of *Christian Origins and the Question of God*; Minneapolis: Fortress, 2003), 22. To claim this, Wright discusses (pp. 12–28) objections to the possibility of discussing resurrection historically, but it is unclear how he understands "history" with reference to worldviews. He does define various meanings of "history" (pp. 12–13), of which the final one is "'historical' means not only that which can be demonstrated and written *within the post-Enlightenment worldview*" (p. 13, his emphasis). He goes on to state: "This is what people have often had in mind when they have rejected 'the historical Jesus' (which hereby, of course, comes to mean 'the Jesus that fits the Procrustean bed of a reductionist worldview') in favour of 'the Christ of faith'" (p. 13). It is unclear at this point whether he is accepting or rejecting this approach, and while the subsequent pages (esp. pp. 13–20) address a variety of issues, this point is not clarified. Later as he concludes his discussion, when he states, "This is the point at which we must declare that the matter lies beyond strict historical proof" (p. 694), he appears to indicate that he accepts this view.
¹⁰⁶ See his clarification that resurrection is not post-mortem existence, but rather it is "life *after* 'life after death'," in Wright, *Resurrection*, 30–31.
¹⁰⁷ See the helpful summary in Wright, *Resurrection*, 577–83.
¹⁰⁸ Wright, *Resurrection*, 681.
¹⁰⁹ Wright, *Resurrection*, 686–87; cf. a similar expression of this conclusion in 710.
¹¹⁰ Wright, *Resurrection*, 687.

forming revivification) ..."¹¹¹ For Wright this is "... a bold affront to the principles of post-Enlightenment historical epistemology ..."¹¹² To remain within those historiographic principles is too confining, because for him these raise "worldview-level issues."¹¹³ He recognizes, however, that "[s]aying that 'Jesus of Nazareth was bodily raised from the dead' is not only a self-*involving* statement; it is a self-*committing* statement, going beyond a reordering of one's private world into various levels of commitment to work out the implications."¹¹⁴ Wright then proceeds to discuss the meaning of this historical conclusion in terms of the risen Jesus being the "Son of God."¹¹⁵

Wright exemplifies what I have called critical theistic history. He functions as a critical historian,¹¹⁶ but his interpretation of the evidence ultimately compels him to affirm divine causation for this event, because divine causation provides the best explanation.¹¹⁷

In the field of biblical studies (of which historical Jesus research is usually seen as a subset) this distinction between ontological naturalistic history, methodological naturalistic history, and critical theistic history is a matter of considerable debate.¹¹⁸ In the vast majority of historical inquiries, this

---

¹¹¹ Wright, *Resurrection*, 717, which he argued for in 687–96.
¹¹² Wright, *Resurrection*, 710.
¹¹³ Wright, *Resurrection*, 717; cf. the discussion in 710–18.
¹¹⁴ Wright, *Resurrection*, 717, his emphasis.
¹¹⁵ Wright, *Resurrection*, 719–38.
¹¹⁶ For example, Wright (*Resurrection*, 710) states: "We are left with the secure historical conclusion: the tomb was empty, and various 'meetings' took place not only between Jesus and his followers ... I regard this conclusion as coming in the same sort of category, of historical probability so high as to be virtually certain, as the death of Augustus in AD 14 or the fall of Jerusalem in AD 70." He then states in the following paragraph (p. 710): "It is important to see that we have got this far by following the historical argument, not by invoking any external a priori beliefs."
¹¹⁷ In n. 84 above I distinguished the "critical theistic" history from the "naïve theistic" history. Here is would also want to distinguish the "critical theistic" view from an apologetic approach to these issues, which might use historical arguments in defense of a position. Apologetics as a mode of argumentation in defense of a religious position is entirely appropriate; followers of any religious faith have the right to present arguments in defense of their faith. But an apologist is not functioning as a critical historian any longer, but rather is using history in defense of an already-established apologetic position now being defended. An excellent example of an apologist who uses history in the service of apologetics is William Lane Craig, *Assessing the New Testament Evidence for the Historicity of the Resurrection of Jesus* (SBEC 16; Lewiston, NY: Edwin Mellen, 1989). Thus I would distinguish Wright as a critical theistic historian from Craig as an apologist.
¹¹⁸ Support for ontological naturalistic history may be widely found. See the discussion of Troeltsch, "Historical and Dogmatic Method in Theology", above. More recently, see Philip R. Davies, *Whose Bible Is It Anyway?* (London: T&T Clark, 2004); Philip R. Davies, *Memories of Ancient Israel: An Introduction to Biblical History – Ancient and Modern* (Louisville: Westminster John Knox, 2008). In support of methodological naturalistic history, I cite a couple of scholars whose citation here might surprise some readers. First of all, George Eldon Ladd, a prominent evangelical scholar ("The Problem of History in Contemporary New Testament Interpretation," in *Studia Evangelica*, vol. 5 [ed. Frank

issue probably does not arise. But it does do so with religious texts claiming divine causality for human events, like the early Christian claims about Jesus' resurrection.

Two further points need to be made before this discussion draws to a close, both of which link to discussion in preceding sections. First of all, historical method involves Gadamer's hermeneutical spiral. As a historian investigates surviving evidence, one constructs explanatory hypotheses and tests them against the evidence and the context one has proposed for that evidence. As a historian engages with the evidence and one's hypotheses, spiralling back and forth, it is not only possible that the historian is changed by the spiral, it is virtually certain that the historian is, in fact, changed. Not only does the historian's awareness and knowledge develop, it is also possible that the historian's perspective and values are altered as well. This should not only be allowed, it should be encouraged, for history should contribute to one's growth and development as a human being. The logical extension of this hermeneutical spiral is that it is also possible that an investigation of surviving evidence might also alter one's worldview. One can be pushed

---

L. Cross; TU 103; Berlin: Akademie Verlag, 1968], 99) states: "The critical historian, as historian, cannot talk about God and his acts in the Incarnation, the Resurrection, and the Parousia; for although such events occur within the history of our world, they have to do not merely with the history of men, but with God in history; and for the historian as historian, the subject matter of history ... is man. Therefore the historical-critical method has self-imposed limitations which render it incompetent to interpret redemptive history." Similarly, Bernard Lonergan (*Method in Theology*, 179), who was introduced above in the discussion of critical realism, writing from the perspective of theological method, states: "When things turn out unexpectedly, pious people say, 'Man proposes but God disposes.' The historian is concerned to see how God disposed the matter, not by theological speculation, not by some world-historical dialectic, but through particular human agents." See also the sustained explanation of this point of view in ch. 1, "Faith and History," in Lee Martin McDonald and Stanley E. Porter, *Early Christianity and Its Sacred Literature* (Peabody, MA: Hendrickson, 2000), 1–22, though I understand from personal correspondence with the authors that the view expressed in this chapter represents Lee McDonald more than Stanley Porter. One important scholar arguing for a critical theistic approach to history is Wolfhart Pannenberg, for which see Wolfhart Pannenberg, "Dogmatic Theses on the Doctrine of Revelation," in *Revelation as History* (ed. Wolfhart Pannenberg; trans. David Granskou; New York: Macmillan, 1968), 123–58, esp. 135–39, and on the resurrection in particular, see Wolfhart Pannenberg, *Jesus: God and Man* (trans. Lewis L. Wilkins and Duane A. Priebe; London: SCM, 1968), esp. 88–106 on "Jesus' Resurrection as a Historical Problem." For a more recent discussion, see the argument for an "open historical-critical method" in Paul Rhodes Eddy and Gregory A. Boyd, *The Jesus Legend: A Case for the Historical Reliability of the Synoptic Jesus Tradition* (Grand Rapids: Baker Academic, 2007), 39–90, the chapter on "Miracles and Method: The Historical-Critical Method and the Supernatural." See also Paul S. Minear, *The Bible and the Historian: Breaking the Silence About God in Biblical Studies* (Nashville: Abingdon, 2002), esp. 22–28. See also the variety of views expressed in the essays collected together in C. T. McIntire, ed., *God, History, and Historians: Modern Christian Views of History* (New York: Oxford University Press, 1977).

in worldview directions by the evidence. For example, it is possible that examining the early Christian narratives about the appearances of Jesus and the empty tomb might lead a person to alter her/his worldview and find the Christian explanation as the most probable, and thus adopt some form of theistic worldview. Equally, a person might examine the horrors of the Holocaust which could lead him/her to reject the possibility of a deity and thus to adopt some form of ontological naturalist worldview. The reverse is, of course, possible in each case as well. The dual point is that engaging in the hermeneutical spiral in historical matters can push a person to alter one's worldview with respect to metaphysical matters, but that this does not necessarily alter the definition of what constitutes explanation within history.

Second, we noted above in the discussion of postmodern historiography and of historical method the importance of the historian uncovering his/her own presuppositions and perspectives with respect to the historical matter being examined. This principle becomes patently obvious with respect to the subject of this section. How one evaluates evidence is shaped by many factors, not the least of which is one's worldview with respect to the metaphysical. When such issues come to the fore in surviving evidence, it behooves historians not only to examine critically the evidence but also to reflect on how their own perspectives and worldviews shape that examination – and to inform readers of their historical work what this perspective and worldview is.[119] I do discuss this point with respect to those involved in this project in the concluding section below. At this point I leave it to the reader to weigh these options. Whichever way one leans on this issue, it is helpful to be aware of the methodological and philosophical diversity. And it helps one to appreciate this as one factor contributing to the variety of representations portraying the historical Jesus.

4. Surveying the Tools and Methods in Historical Jesus Research

All of the above discussion concerning history and historical method applies in one way or another to the particular historical investigation of the life of Jesus. There are, however, a few topics that are distinctive to historical Jesus studies, and so they require a brief introduction here. For those who

---

[119] Dale Allison (*Resurrecting Jesus*, 343) states: "it is not merely a question of what the historical arguments are, but of what beliefs and predispositions we bring to those arguments. The truth one discerns behind the texts is largely determined by desires, expectations, and religious and philosophical convictions already to hand. We cannot eschew ourselves. If this is the right conclusion, then we need to scrutinize not just the text but also ourselves."

work in NT studies and historical Jesus research in particular, these are well-known, but they are introduced here for the sake of the non-specialist reader.

4.1. Exploring the Question of Historicity

The issue of "historicity" (sometimes also referred to as "authenticity") is used in historical Jesus studies particularly with reference to the Christian sources that portray him,[120] most notably the Gospels. These Gospels, canonical and extra-canonical, present various portraits of Jesus through accounts of his sayings and teachings as well as his actions and the events in his life. Written by Christians during the first two centuries following the death of Jesus, these primary sources are, first of all, evidence for what early Christians believed about Jesus – or at least by the author and some within the author's immediate audience. Thus, for example, Mark was probably written either shortly before or just after the first Jewish revolt that ended in 70 C.E., and Matthew and Luke are frequently dated as being written in the 80s C.E.. As primary sources written some 40 to 60 years after the events they portray, these three Synoptic Gospels are first and foremost evidence for the beliefs and viewpoints of their authors and some within their respective communities in the 70s and 80s C.E.[121] The question is, to what extent do these accounts of what they believed about Jesus' sayings and events also provide evidence for what they purport to convey, namely, sayings and events from Jesus' life around 30 C.E? In § 2.3, on historical method, we considered one aspect of the historian's interpretive process was evaluating the data in terms of its evidentiary contribution (the bottom-up aspect of the historical method). In the 300 pieces left from a 3,000 piece jigsaw puzzle, the puzzle-assembler must decide if the pieces in the puzzle box actually belong to the particular puzzle being assembled. The Gospels provide data – they are evidence – but of what are they evidence? They do provide evidence for Christian beliefs in the 70s and 80s C.E., but to what extent can the pieces of data also be used as evidence for 30 C.E? This is the question of "historicity" or "authenticity."[122]

The reason for this question is that the traditions contained within the Gospels are understood to have passed through various stages before they came to be written in the Gospels (stages which may be observed in the description in Luke 1:1–4): (1) events stage: eyewitnesses observe an event

---

[120] For discussion of the sources, see § 4.2 below.
[121] The Synoptic Gospels are being used here as examples. The same point could be made with any other Gospel, whether canonical or non-canonical.
[122] "Authenticity" is a historical question. It is distinct from and unrelated to the issue of the "authority" of the Gospels or any particular teaching contained therein for Christian theology.

and/or hear a saying; (2) oral tradition stage: eyewitnesses tell others about what they saw and/or heard who in turn tell others; (3) early collections stage: collections of oral traditions are made based on similarity of the subject material or interest of the collector (these collections may have been oral or written), and (4) Gospel composition stage: the Gospel writers use material from earlier written Gospels, other early collections, and other oral traditions to compose their own Gospel.[123] At any time in this process, it is historically possible and even likely that an event or saying that had been observed or heard was later added to or changed in some way, and it is equally possible that an event or saying was created by someone and inserted into the traditioning process at any stage, whether as an oral tradition, a part of an early collection, or a pericope[124] in a written Gospel. Thus the purpose of the critical methods and criteria are to ascertain the probability of whether or not – and to what extent[125] – something stated in the written Gospels stage can be traced back to the events stage.[126]

---

[123] Often these stages are thought of as separate and discrete (e. g., the events stage is during Jesus' life, 28–30 C. E., and the oral tradition stage begins after his death, etc.). The historical reality was certainly more complex, for these stages overlapped one another. For example, followers of Jesus most likely passed on oral tradition while Jesus was still alive, and the oral traditioning process continued after early collections were made and even after the Gospels were written. And equally, eyewitnesses were still alive during the oral traditioning process (as noted by Richard Bauckham, *Jesus and the Eyewitnesses: The Gospels as Eyewitness Testimony* [Grand Rapids: Eerdmans, 2006]). However, the schema is still helpful, for it shows us the stages in the development that resulted in the writing of the Gospels. Meier, *Roots of the Problem*, 166 and n. 1.

[124] The word "pericope" (pronounced pĕrĭcōpḗ) is a technical term used in Gospel studies for a single unit of material used in a gospel, usually a single saying or a narrative of a single event. These are usually understood to be discrete units that could have been passed on orally independently of one another. For example, the pericope of the parable of the Good Samaritan (Luke 10:25–37), or the pericope of the healing of the leper (Mark 1:40–45).

[125] Whether something can be traced back to the events stage is not simply a matter of "yes" or "no," for a spectrum is possible. For example, a saying of Jesus in a Gospel may be a paraphrase or summary of something Jesus said rather than being *ipsissima verba Jesu* (a Latin expression sometimes used in historical Jesus studies, meaning "the very words of Jesus").

[126] At this point some of my readers may object to this possibility of alteration or addition in the Gospel tradition. It is beyond the confines of this essay to fully defend this point. But a few observations at this point can be made. First of all, what is being described is critical history, one of the principles established above is that a critical historian cannot accept testimony, but must rather subject it to critical investigation. Why? Because of the human propensity to alter or add to human memories and stories. If the possibility or even probability of alteration and addition to the tradition is not granted, then one is not really doing critical history. Second, readers at this point may assume that I am speaking of the four canonical Gospels, or at least the Synoptic Gospels. But I am not, for I am considering the entire traditioning process over the first two centuries. So if I were to ask whether the possibility of alteration or addition applied to the *Gospel of Thomas*, or the *Gospel of Peter*, the answer I would probably receive is, "Yes." From a historical/methodological

Gospel studies generally and historical Jesus studies in particular have developed a number of critical methods and criteria to help the historian evaluate the Gospel data, weighing the probability of whether or not a particular piece of data or part thereof is "historical" or "authentic." The following is intended to provide only a brief description of these critical methods and criteria, and the reader is referred to other, more extended discussions of them.[127] These critical methods and criteria do not all function in the same way, so it is helpful to classify them into three groups: preliminary, primary, and secondary criteria.

Preliminary criteria are the application of certain critical methods to the Gospel texts in a manner which is relevant to historical Jesus concerns and to the application of the primary and secondary criteria. These critical tools are source criticism, redaction criticism, and tradition criticism. Source criticism is concerned with the fourth stage, the Gospel composition stage. It considers the relationship of Christian texts to one another, particularly the question of what earlier texts were used as sources for later texts. While this is most frequently applied to the relationship among the so-called Synoptic Gospels (i.e., Matthew, Mark, and Luke), the question really applies to all the early Christian sources containing Jesus material, including for example, the relationship of the Fourth Gospel to the Synoptics, the relationship of other Gospels such as the *Gospel of Thomas* or the *Gospel of Peter* to other Gospels. Source criticism is relevant to the dating of the sources as well as determining their dependence upon, or independence from, one another.

---

point of view there is no reason to privilege certain sources because they are canonical – this is a category for classifying certain texts as having *theological* authority as sacred texts within Christianity, but this does not grant them any greater *historical* authority (for further discussion of this, see below § 4.2). Certain of these sources may be given greater weight than others due to their relative date, but this is a different matter than their canonical status. Third, this issue is particularly a problem for a person who functions more as a theologian, for whom certain theological presuppositions about the canonical Gospels prevent them from applying standard historical principles to the canonical Gospels that they would to non-canonical Gospels. In such cases the results of scholarly work may better be considered apologetics than critical history (this is not to denigrate apologetics in any way, for all religious traditions have the right to argue in defense of their tradition, but such argumentation should be recognized for what it is: apologetics and not critical history). Fourth, the question of "authenticity" is *only* to determine the probability of whether or not a particular event or saying is historical for its use in a historical representation of the historical Jesus; it does not in any way impinge upon the theological truth of the tradition. Thus, while a critical historian may conclude that a particular event or saying is probably not historical (this is only a statement about 30 C.E.), this same pericope still presents a profound truth about Jesus from a Christian theological perspective.

[127] See the bibliographic references cited in the discussion of each criterion, as well as the bibliography provided by Evans, *Life of Jesus Research: An Annotated Bibliography*, 127–46; Craig A. Evans, *Jesus* (IBR Bibliographies 5; Grand Rapids: Baker, 1992), 52–67; Porter, *Criteria for Authenticity*, 63 n. 1.

Thus the results of source criticism contribute to the criterion of multiple attestation (see below).

With respect to what is known as the "Synoptic Problem"(The relationship between the Synoptic Gospels),[128] the most commonly held position currently by scholars is the Two Source Hypothesis: Matthew and Luke are somewhat later Gospels who each, independently, drew upon two sources. The first source is the earlier Gospel of Mark (e.g., Mark 1:29–31 as the source for both Matt 8:14–15 and Luke 4:38–39). The second source is a text that is not longer extant, referred to as "Q" or the "*Sayings Gospel Q*."[129]

---

[128] For introductions to the Synoptic Problem, see Christopher M. Tuckett, "Synoptic Problem," in *The Anchor Bible Dictionary*, vol. 6 (ed. David N. Freedman; New York: Doubleday, 1992), 263–70; Mark Goodacre, *The Synoptic Problem: A Way Through the Maze* (London: T&T Clark, 2001); Robert H. Stein, *Studying the Synoptic Gospels* (2 ed.; Grand Rapids: Baker Academic, 2001).

[129] It is referred to as "Q" from the German term *Quelle* or "source." It is sometimes called the "*Sayings Gospel Q*" for the majority of its reconstructed content is comprised of sayings material, though there are a few narrative portions in it. The evidence for this Q source is found in those places where Matthew and Luke have material in common but such material is absent in Mark (in other words, Matthew and Luke's source could not be Mark, but this common material points to a common source; e.g., Matt 3:7–10 = Luke 3:7–9). While this hypothesis is the most commonly held among Gospel scholars, they differ over the extent to which this source may be reconstructed from Matthew and Luke and studied as an independent text. For an introductory explanation and defense of the Two Source Hypothesis, see Robert H. Stein, *Studying the Synoptic Gospels* (2 ed.; Grand Rapids: Baker Academic, 2001), 29–169. For a more advanced discussion of Q, see John S. Kloppenborg, *Excavating Q: The History and Setting of the Sayings Gospel* (Edinburgh: T & T Clark, 2000). For a readable reconstruction of Q, see John S. Kloppenborg, et al., *Q – Thomas Reader* (Sonoma, CA: Polebridge, 1990), 3–74. For critical reconstructions of Q, see James M. Robinson, et al., *The Critical Edition of Q* (Hermeneia; Minneapolis: Fortress, 2000), and Harry T. Fleddermann, *Q: A Reconstruction and Commentary* (Biblical Tools and Studies 1; Leuven: Peeters, 2005). It should be noted, however, that not all scholars who hold to the Two Source Hypothesis think that reconstruction of Q is actually possible. And proposals concerning a possible stratigraphy of Q or possible communities of origin are highly debated. In a minority position with reference to the Synoptic Problem, but having some scholarly support, is the Farrer Hypothesis which proposes that Mark was the earliest Gospel, Matthew then used Mark as a source, and finally Luke used both Mark and Matthew as sources. For a defense of the Farrer Hypothesis and a critique of the Two Source Hypothesis, see Mark Goodacre, *The Case Against Q: Studies in Markan Priority and the Synoptic Problem* (Harrisburg, PA: Trinity Press International, 2002); Mark Goodacre and Nicholas Perrin, eds., *Questioning Q: A Multidimensional Critique* (Downers Grove: InterVarsity, 2004). It is referred to as the "Farrer Hypothesis" due to it being founded upon the work of Austin Farrer, for which see Austin Farrer, "On Dispensing with Q," in *Studies in the Gospels: Essays in Memory of R. H. Lightfoot* (ed. D. E. Nineham; Oxford: Blackwell, 1955), 55–88. This view is also associated with the work of Michael D. Goulder, for which see, e.g., Michael D. Goulder, *Luke: A New Paradigm* (2 vols; JSNTSup 20; Sheffield: JSOT Press, 1989). Another minority position is the Griesbach Hypothesis: Matthew was written first, used by Luke, and then Mark is an abbreviation of both Matthew and Luke. This view is first associated with Johann Jacob Griesbach and his *Synopsis Evangeliorum Matthaei, Marci et Lucae*, published in 1776. It is associated more recently with the work of William R. Farmer, for

Most of the scholars involved in this project hold to the Two Source Hypothesis, but they differ over the extent to which they use a reconstructed *Sayings Gospel* Q.

With respect to other source-critical questions, I leave discussion of them to the individual essays in this volume, to be raised as they are relevant.[130]

Redaction criticism is also concerned with the Gospel composition stage, but it examines the ways in which the Gospel writers "redacted" or edited their sources as they creatively composed their Gospels. Observing specific redactions and redactional tendencies in a particular Gospel helps to surface particular theological or pastoral issues and emphases of the individual Evangelist as well as his interests and concerns. Redaction criticism is to a certain extent dependent upon the results of source criticism for examining how a later Evangelist edited an earlier Gospel source, but other redactional observations may be made apart from a particular source-critical hypothesis (e.g., Luke's interest in the issue of the poor). Redaction criticism is frequently used in Gospel studies out of an interest in uncovering a particular Gospel's concerns and interests, as well as providing information to suggest a possible *Sitz im Leben* (i.e., situation in life) for the composition of the Gospel.[131] While the primary focus of redaction criticism is an understanding of these redactional tendencies and what they reveal about the interests of the author, it also helps to distinguish between material that the author has contributed or edited himself from traditional material he has drawn upon.

Often in historical Jesus studies, if something is identified as redactional material contributed by a Gospel author, it is usually discounted as not being historical with reference to Jesus. In many cases this may be appropriate, but sometimes it is applied in a heavy-handed manner that misses the point. As a simple example, it is quite evident that Mark 1:14–15 is a Markan summary, bridging from the ending of John the baptizer's ministry to that of Jesus. Thus, the statement in v. 15 that Jesus came "… saying, 'The time is fulfilled, and the kingdom of God has come near; repent, and believe in the good news'," is probably a Markan redactional creation that was not drawn

---

which see, e.g., William R. Farmer, *The Synoptic Problem: A Critical Analysis* (Macon, GA: Mercer University Press, 1976). For descriptions of these minority views and others, see the introductory discussions in n. 128 above.

[130] For example, on the question of the dependence or independence of the "Jewish-Christian Gospels," see in this volume ch. 3, § 2.1, and on the question of the *Gospel of Thomas* and the *Gospel of Peter*, see ch. 13, § 2.1.1.

[131] For helpful introductions to redaction criticism, see Robert H. Stein, *Studying the Synoptic Gospels* (2 ed.; Grand Rapids: Baker Academic, 2001), 237–79; Norman Perrin, *What Is Redaction Criticism?* (GBS; Philadelphia: Fortress, 1969); Sanders and Davies, *Studying the Synoptic Gospels*, 201–23.

from a source of Jesus' sayings to which Mark had access.[132] To reject v. 15 as "redactional" and thus "not historical" is to miss the point. It may not have been derived from a previously known saying of Jesus reporting *ipsissima verba Jesu* ("the very words of Jesus"), but as a summary of one of the foci and concerns of Jesus' ministry it does provide an excellent historical summary of the *vox Jesu* ("the voice of Jesus").

Tradition criticism is concerned with the second and third stages: the oral tradition and early collections stages. It seeks to identify how the Jesus traditions were shaped by the traditioning process. This also helps to distinguish material that has been received in the process from material that has been reshaped or contributed in the process. The concerns of redaction and tradition criticism are relevant to the question of authenticity, for material that has been identified as reshaped or contributed should be either discounted or at least taken into account in the process of making a judgment concerning the probable historicity of the material.

Primary Criteria are those five criteria the evidence from which should bear the heaviest weight in making a judgment concerning the authenticity of an event or saying, or a particular element within such a pericope. These may be distinguished from secondary criteria as well as dubious criteria that will be discussed later. The relative importance or weight for each of these primary criteria is somewhat subjective among scholars – I have placed them below in an order that makes sense to me, but the more important weighting is to realize the overall weighting to be given to the primary criteria as a group in comparison to the secondary criteria. These criteria can be applied to a pericope as a whole or a particular element within a pericope; thus in the definitions below, I use the term "material" generically to refer to either of these.

(1) Criterion of Multiple Attestation: Material that is found within multiple independent sources (e.g., Mark, Q, Paul, etc.)[133] may be considered more likely to be authentic.[134] The logic of this criterion is that, if the ma-

---

[132] For discussion, see the critical commentaries on Mark.

[133] Some discussions of the criteria combine the criterion of multiple attestation (more than one independent source) and the criterion of multiple forms (more than one literary form), but other discussions separate them. While they are similar, their logic is slightly different, and they function in slightly different ways. Thus I have chosen for the sake of clarity for the non-specialist reader, to separate the discussion into two criteria.

[134] In my definitions of these criteria I had initially worded them "if some condition is met, then the material *is more likely to be authentic.*" But this is actually inaccurate, for either the material is either authentic or not – the event/saying either happened or it did not. The criteria do no impact the authenticity of the event/saying *per se*, rather they impact our judgment or evaluation as historians concerning the probability of its authenticity. Thus the definitions of these criteria have been revised to clarify that it is the historical judgment that is being weighed: "if some condition is met, then the material may be considered/judged more likely to be authentic." For other discussions of this

terial is found in more than one independent source, then it cannot be the creation of any one of these sources, but it must be an earlier tradition used independently by these independent sources. The necessary element in this criterion is the matter of the independence of the sources, and thus this criterion is dependent upon the conclusions drawn from source criticism: is a particular Gospel or source dependent or independent from other Gospels or sources? Source criticism is used most commonly for the question of the relationship between Matthew, Mark, and Luke, but is equally relevant for the question of the dependence or independence of John upon one or more of the Synoptic Gospels, as well as the dependence or independence of other Gospels upon each other, such as the *Gospel of Thomas* or the *Gospel of Peter*. For example, if Mark is viewed as a source for Matthew, then a saying found only in Mark and Matthew would not be viewed as having met the criterion of multiple attestation, for there is really only one source – Mark – with Matthew being dependent upon Mark.

It should also be noted that the criterion of multiple attestation indicates that the material is earlier than the sources in which it is contained, thus making it early material, but this does not *necessarily* mean that it is authentic. A corollary of the earlier explanation of this criterion's logic is the broader principle used in historical method in general as well as historical Jesus research in particular is that the earlier the source (i.e., the closer it is to purported date of what is being claimed) the more likely that it is to be authentic.[135] This criterion is used by some to both raise or lower a judgment concerning authenticity: multiply attested material may be judged as having a greater likelihood of being authentic, whereas singly attested material may be judged as having a lesser likelihood of being authentic. However, if the logic of this criterion is followed carefully, then the latter half of this claim is illogical. Just because a particular event has only one eyewitness and/or chain of transmission, does not make it any less probable than one that has multiple witnesses and chains of transmission. Thus, when evaluating material with this criterion, multiple attestation raises the level of probability because the material has independent corroboration. But single attestation simply means that this material does not benefit from independent corroboration; this does not, by itself, lower the judgment on the mate-

---

criterion, see Sanders and Davies, *Studying the Synoptic Gospels*, 323–30; Meier, *Roots of the Problem*, 174–75; Craig A. Evans, *Jesus and His Contemporaries: Comparative Studies* (AGJU 25; Leiden: E.J. Brill, 1995), 15–18; Porter, *Criteria for Authenticity*, 82–89.

[135] With reference to general historical method on this point, see Howell and Prevenier, *From Reliable Sources*, 69–71. Cf. Evans (*Jesus and His Contemporaries*, 16) who observes that this criterion only demonstrates the antiquity of the tradition (p. 15), nevertheless, "… much of what is multiply attested has often been regarded as authentic, not only because it is multiply attested, but because it often enjoys the support of other criteria."

rial. Viewed comparatively, material benefiting from multiple attestation has a higher probability than singly attested material, but this is only because this criterion has raised the probability of the multiply attested material; it has not lowered the probability of the singly attested material. Furthermore, this criterion cannot be applied simplistically. As noted above, just because a tradition is multiply attested does not mean it is *necessarily* authentic, but more so, just because it is singly attested does not *necessitate* a judgment of inauthenticity.[136] In both cases, all other criteria must be taken into account before a final judgment is made. For example, a tradition might be singly attested and thus have a lower probability of authenticity, but this tradition might not have been used in other sources (thus singly attested) precisely because it was judged by other early Christian authors as being somewhat embarrassing. Thus the application of the criterion of embarrassment in this situation obviates to a considerable extent the judgment based on the tradition being singly attested.[137]

As an example of this criterion raising the judgment of probable authenticity, we may note the core of Jesus' sayings at the last supper are found in Mark 14:22–25 = Matt 26:26–29 = Luke 22:15–20. Assuming the Two Source Hypothesis, this is actually just a single source, for Matthew and Luke are understood to each be dependent upon Mark. Matthew and Luke both reproduce Mark somewhat differently, thus evidencing redactional interests. However, the core of this material is also found in 1 Cor 11:23–25, a letter Paul wrote almost 20 years before Mark was written. And there is no evidence that Mark is dependent upon Paul's letter. Thus for at least a core of elements within this tradition there is multiple attestation – Paul and Mark – and so may be judged as having a greater probability of historicity.[138]

(2) Criterion of Multiple Forms: Material that is found within multiple different forms (e.g., parable, aphorism, conflict story, etc.) of tradition

---

[136] This is a fundamental weakness of the approach by Crossan, *Historical Jesus*, xxvii–xxxiv.

[137] This demonstrates the necessity of all criteria being used together as one weighs the probability of authenticity. See the discussion below. Contrary to this view presented here, John Dominic Crossan (*Historical Jesus*, xxxi–xxxiv) emphasized the criterion of multiple attestation over all others. For example, he states (p. 257): "My methodological discipline in this book forbids the use of single attestations for reconstructing the historical Jesus ..." For a discussion of the problems with Crossan's overemphasis on multiple attestation, see Evans, *Jesus and His Contemporaries*, 16–18.

[138] The issue with reference to this example is somewhat more complex than its simple presentation here, for it could be argued that Luke (written many years after Paul's letter to Corinth) may be aware of the Pauline version of this tradition. Thus there may have been two forms of the tradition: Mark/Matthew and Paul/Luke. But the point being made here is still the same, there are still two independent witnesses to this event. Of course, other criteria come into play in a complete discussion of the probable authenticity of this tradition. For further discussion, see in this volume ch. 11.

may be judged more likely to be authentic.[139] The logic of this criterion is that if a tradition, idea, or theme is found in different types of material, then it is quite early, and thus may be judged more likely to be authentic. This logic is similar to that of the criterion of multiple attestation (and some scholars do combine them into one criterion), but it is really more used with reference to ideas or themes that have the possibility of being found within multiple types of tradition – something that is not possible with the details of a discrete saying or a specific event (and thus it is not quite the same as the criterion of multiple attestation). The logic behind this criterion renders it more appropriate to be used primarily to raise the level of probability. It should be noted, however, that, while this criterion considers the presence of a theme in multiple forms to have greater probability of authenticity, it does not render each individual pericope where that theme is present to be authentic.

As an example of this criterion, consider Jesus' relationship with outsiders, whether "sinners" or "tax collectors," or other types of outcasts. This tradition is found in a variety of events, including Jesus eating with them (e. g., Mark 2:16; Luke 19:1–10), healing them (Mark 1:40–45), and interacting with them (Luke 7:36–50). It is found within pronouncement stories with an aphorism (e. g., Mark 2:15–17), parables (e. g., Luke 14:15–24; 18:9–14), and accusations by Jesus' opponents (Luke 7:34; 15:2). While not all of these may necessarily be authentic (all criteria would need to be applied to each of them), nevertheless, collectively they point to this characteristic of Jesus' activities and teaching having a high probability of being authentic.[140]

(3) Criterion of Dissimilarity: This criterion has developed over time, and a proper understanding of it must take this development into consideration. A classic formulation of the original version of this criterion was by Norman Perrin: "the earliest form of a saying we can reach may be regarded as authentic if it can be shown to be dissimilar to characteristic emphases

---

[139] For discussion of this criterion as distinct from the criterion of multiple attestation, see the original formulation of this criterion by C. H. Dodd, *History and the Gospel* (London: Nisbet & Co., 1938), 91–101; and more recent discussions by Robert H. Stein, "The 'Criteria' for Authenticity," in *Studies of History and Tradition in the Four Gospels* (ed. R.T. France and David Wenham; Gospel Perspectives 1; Sheffield: JSOT Press, 1980), 232–33; M. Eugene Boring, "Criteria of Authenticity: The Lucan Beatitudes as a Test Case," *Forum* 1.4 (1985): 9; Craig A. Evans, "Authenticity Criteria in Life of Jesus Research," *CSR* 19 (1989): 10–11. For discussions of this criterion as part of the criterion of multiple attestation, see Dennis Polkow, "Method and Criteria for Historical Jesus Research," in *Society of Biblical Literature 1987 Seminar Papers* (ed. Kent H. Richard; SBLSP 26; Atlanta: Scholars Press, 1987), 350–51; Sanders and Davies, *Studying the Synoptic Gospels*, 323–30; Meier, *Roots of the Problem*, 174–75; Evans, *Jesus and His Contemporaries*, 15–18.

[140] For further discussion of this theme, see in this volume ch. 6.

both of ancient Judaism *and of* the early Church ..."[141] The emphasis of this criterion as originally formulated was on being dissimilar to both Judaism and early Christianity, and thus was subsequently termed the "criterion of double dissimilarity." The logic behind this criterion is that, if the material is different than traditions in either Judaism and early Christianity, then the origins of the material cannot be traced to either of these sources and so may be viewed as originating from Jesus. This logic is theoretically sound, but the criterion has come under considerable criticism. It is very reasonable to conclude that material that is doubly dissimilar is authentic, but the relatively little material that meets this criterion does not actually result in a "historical Jesus" but rather a "unique Jesus" – a Jesus that had no points of contact with, or influence upon, his environment! It actually produces a "distorted Jesus," for if we know nothing else about Jesus, it is that he was a Jew. Furthermore, our knowledge of Second Temple Judaism and of early Christianity is limited and fragmentary; but one thing that can be said for sure is that both were diverse, so claims of being dissimilar to both is extremely problematic.[142] Finally, as E. P. Sanders states: "We should assume that part of what Jesus said and did became constitutive of Christian preaching, so that elimination of all Christian motifs would result in the elimination of material which also tells us something about Jesus."[143]

These fundamental weaknesses have led to a reworking of both sides of this criterion. First of all, the Jewish side, namely being dissimilar to Judaism, has been set aside – and rightly so. The Christian side, namely being dissimilar to early Christianity, requires nuancing. It can function to both raise and lower the level of probability. In terms of raising the level of probability, if material is discontinuous with early Christianity, then it has a greater likelihood of being authentic. But the opposite cannot be claimed: just because something is continuous with early Christianity, does not necessarily eliminate it from consideration as authentic. It might, however, lower the historian's evaluation of the material's probability of authenticity.

---

[141] Norman Perrin, *Rediscovering the Teaching of Jesus* (London: SCM, 1967), 39, my emphasis. It is sometimes also referred to as the criterion of discontinuity. See also the formulation by Ernst Käsemann in "The Problem of the Historical Jesus," in *Essays on New Testament Themes* (trans. W. J. Montague; SBT 41; London: SCM, 1964), 37.

[142] For this and other criticisms of the criterion of double dissimilarity, see Morna D. Hooker, "On Using the Wrong Tool," *Theology* 75 (1972): 570–81, esp. 574–75; David L. Mealand, "The Dissimilarity Test," *SJT* 31 (1978): 41–50; Tom Holmén, "Doubts About Double Dissimilarity: Restructuring the Main Criterion of Jesus-of-History Research," in *Authenticating the Words of Jesus* (eds Bruce Chilton and Craig A. Evans; NTTS 28.1; Leiden: E. J. Brill, 1999), 47–80; Porter, *Criteria for Authenticity*, 70–76. It should be noted that Norman Perrin did come to realize this weakness in his formulation, as in Norman Perrin, *The New Testament: An Introduction* (New York: Harcourt Brace Jovanovich, 1974), 281–82.

[143] Sanders, *Jesus and Judaism*, 16.

Craig Evans expresses well how this criterion could function to lower the level of probability: "Material cannot be disqualified simply because it is in continuity with the teaching of the early Church, it should be disqualified if it appears to reflect ideas that are inconsistent with the *Sitz im Leben Jesu* [i.e., the situation of Jesus' life]."[144]

An example of this criterion raising the level of probability may be observed in Jesus' saying, "Follow me, and let the dead bury their own dead" (Matt 8:22 = Luke 9:60). From what we know of early Christianity, this saying had little influence, and there is no evidence for Christians neglecting burial practices. The precise meaning of this saying is not relevant to this discussion; suffice it to say, that this saying may be judged as highly probable to be authentic based upon the criterion of dissimilarity.[145] An example of this criterion functioning to lower the level of probability may be observed in Jesus' statement in Matt 16:18, "... and upon this rock I will build my church." The evidence in the Gospels indicate that the focus of Jesus' ministry was upon "the kingdom of God" and not the "church" as it would have been understood by Matthew's audience – a Christian entity distinct from Israel. The term "church" (ἐκκλησία) is only found one other time on the lips of Jesus in the canonical Gospels, also in Matthew (18:15). This suggests the probability that this language is a result of Matthean redaction, and it is quite unlikely that this clause, at least as it is understood in Matt 16:18, is authentic.[146] This is an example of material which is in continuity with early Christian thought but is not in keeping with Jesus' life situation, at least as it is presented in Matthew.[147] It should be noted, that this does not

---

[144] Evans, *Jesus and His Contemporaries*, 21. Cf. Evans, "Authenticity Criteria," 26–27. See also the discussion of this criterion by Sanders and Davies, *Studying the Synoptic Gospels*, 316–23; Meier, *Roots of the Problem*, 171–74.

[145] See the use of this criterion on this text by Sanders and Davies, *Studying the Synoptic Gospels*, 317; cf. Sanders, *Jesus and Judaism*, 252–55. See also the extensive discussion of this text in Martin Hengel, *The Charismatic Leader and His Followers* (trans. James Greig; New York: Crossroad, 1981), 3–15.

[146] John Nolland (*The Gospel of Matthew* [NIGTC; Grand Rapids: Eerdmans, 2005], 667) for example, states: "Difficulty with tracing v. 18 in any form back to the historical Jesus has focussed on the phrase 'my church'. It is doubtful whether Jesus anticipated the emergence of the church as an entity separate from Israel." Cf. the detailed discussion by W. D. Davies and Dale C. Allison, *Commentary on Matthew VIII–XVIII* (vol. 2 of *A Critical and Exegetical Commentary on the Gospel According to Saint Matthew*; ICC; Edinburgh: T&T Clark, 1991), 603–15.

[147] Others argue (e.g., Donald A. Hagner, *Matthew 14–28* [WBC 33B; Dallas, TX: Word Books, 1995], 465–72) that Matthew's "my church" when rendered back into Aramaic could be understood to refer to "my community," alluding to the movement that Jesus was gathering around himself. This gives the phrase a different nuance than would be understood by Matthew's Christian audience, but it also renders it possible for the saying to be rooted in the voice of Jesus. Considering such possibilities are part of how one weighs the evidence using these criteria.

mean that the entire pericope of Matt 16:17–19 should be viewed as inauthentic.[148] Sometimes one may use the criteria on an entire pericope, but at other times, a careful use of them must examine individual elements within the pericope. Note also that in these examples I have used language of raising and lowering levels of probability: "highly probable" with reference to Matt 8:22 = Luke 9:60 and "quite unlikely" to be authentic with reference to the clause in Matt 16:18. All judgments of this nature should be understood on a scale of probabilities: Yes, it is possible in either example to conceive of a way that the opposite could be the case. But historical judgments using the criteria of authenticity are a means of judging which is more probable. This is discussed in greater detail below.

There have been a number of attempts to reformulate this criterion or to largely do away with it altogether. For example, Gerd Theissen and Dagmar Winter proposed the *criterion of historical plausibility*: "[H]istorical plausibility ... reckons with influences of Jesus on early Christianity and his involvement in a Jewish context. Whatever helps to explain the influence of Jesus and at the same time can only have come into being in a Jewish context is historical in the sources."[149] This criterion in effect has two components or "subcriteria." First is the *plausibility of context:* what is attributed to Jesus must be compatible with and plausible within the Jewish context of Palestine in the first half of the first century C.E. Second is the *plausibility of effects:* what is attributed to Jesus must explain Jesus' influence on early Christianity but show "resistance to the general tendencies of early Christianity."[150] This criterion may function both to raise and lower levels of probability.

Similarly, N.T. Wright has proposed that, alongside the traditional criterion of dissimilarity there must be a corollary of a *criterion of double similarity/dissimilarity*: "when something can be seen to be credible (though perhaps deeply subversive) within first-century Judaism, *and* credible as the implied starting point (though not the exact replica) of something in

---

[148] See, e.g., Sanders, *Jesus and Judaism*, 146–47. Ben F. Meyer (*Aims of Jesus*, 193–97) does take it as authentic, but understands its sense and referent quite differently than that implied by Matthew's "Christian" understanding.

[149] Gerd Theissen and Annette Merz, *The Historical Jesus: A Comprehensive Guide* (trans. John Bowden; Minneapolis: Fortress, 1998), 116.

[150] Gerd Theissen and Dagmar Winter, *The Quest for the Plausible Jesus: The Question of Criteria* (trans. M. Eugene Boring; Louisville: Westminster John Knox, 2002), 211. For an interesting discussion of this criterion from a different perspective, see Gerd Theissen, "Historical Scepticism and the Criteria of Jesus Research, or My Attempt to Leap Across Lessing's Yawning Gulf," *SJT* 49 (1996): 147–76. This explanation is an attempt to simplify quite a complex discussion that incorporates not only the traditional criterion of dissimilarity, but also the criteria of multiple attestation and coherence. See this complete work for a full discussion of their proposal. For an assessment of this proposal, see Porter, *Criteria for Authenticity*, 113–22.

later Christianity, there is a strong possibility of our being in touch with the genuine history of Jesus."[151] Wright views this as a way to nuance the criterion of dissimilarity by observing ways in which material may at the same time by both similar and dissimilar. This criterion functions primarily to raise the level of probability of something that might be judged less probable by the less-nuanced criterion of dissimilarity.

Similar to the above two attempts to nuance this criterion, is the *continuum approach*, most closely identified with Tom Holmén. He stresses the importance of a continuum between Judaism – Jesus – Christianity. "By integrating the Jewish context, the teaching of Jesus and the Christian reception history into one account, the continuum perspective seeks to uncover a Jesus who is both fitting within his Jewish context and in a comprehensible relation to early Christian attitudes. Thus, according to this perspective, a historically plausible picture of Jesus is one that can be placed in the Judaism-Christianity continuum."[152]

(4) Criterion of Embarrassment: Material that could have been perceived as embarrassing or problematic for early Christians may be judged as more likely to be authentic.[153] The logic behind this criterion is that it is unlikely that the early Church would have created material that would have been embarrassing to them in some way, particularly if it presented Jesus in an unflattering light or caused problems in discussions with unbelievers or debates with opponents. This criterion only functions to raise the level of probability – material considered embarrassing is more likely to be authentic. The corollary, on the other hand, is not relevant, for it is quite evident that Jesus was in many other senses not only not embarrassing, but attracted a following. The possible weakness of this criterion is determining whether or not a particular matter was *actually* embarrassing or not. It is possible that something might be quite embarrassing to modern cultural or theological sensitivities, but may not have been embarrassing to the early Christians who were handling the traditions concerning Jesus. So what strengthens this criterion is whether or not evidence from first-century Christians can be produced to actually demonstrate that a particular matter was embarrassing.

An example of the criterion of embarrassment is Jesus' crucifixion by the Romans. Reported in numerous sources, both Christian and non-Christian, this end to Jesus' life was a matter of considerable embarrassment to early

---

[151] N. Thomas Wright, *Jesus and the Victory of God* (vol. 2 of *Christian Origins and the Question of God*; Minneapolis: Fortress, 1996), 132, see 131–33.

[152] Tom Holmén, "An Introduction to the Continuum Approach," in *Jesus from Judaism to Christianity: Continuum Approaches to the Historical Jesus* (ed. Tom Holmén; LNTS 352; London: T&T Clark, 2007), 1–2.

[153] For discussion, see Meier, *Roots of the Problem*, 168–71; Evans, *Jesus and His Contemporaries*, 18–19; Porter, *Criteria for Authenticity*, 106–10.

Christians, for it required explanation to both Jewish and Gentile audiences how a crucified Jew could be God's Son and Messiah. That this was actually a matter of some difficulty for the early Church is confirmed by Paul's statement in 1 Cor 1:23 that his proclamation of "Christ crucified" was "a stumbling block to Jews and foolishness to Gentiles."[154]

(5) Criterion of Rejection and Execution: Material that contributes to understanding why Jesus was rejected by Jewish authorities and was executed by Roman authorities may be judged as more likely to be authentic. This logic of this criterion, particularly as formulated by John Meier, focuses attention on "Jesus' violent end at the hands of Jewish and Roman officials and then asks us what historical words and deeds can explain his trial and crucifixion as 'King of the Jews'."[155] Portraits of Jesus that represent him as a kindly, child-loving teacher mouthing pithy sayings simply miss the point. While each element in that portrait are probably correct, they fail to explain in any way why Jesus was also viewed as offensive to some and a threat to others – material that contributes to their explanation and his subsequent rejection and execution should be considered as more likely authentic. This criterion, however, cannot really stand alone, for the early Church was equally concerned with explaining Jesus' rejection and execution, and so this criterion must be weighed along with the others discussed here. In addition to contributing to a judgment on historicity, this criterion also helps to prioritize what material should be judged more significant in the development of a portrait of Jesus. This criterion primarily functions to raise the level of probability, for Jesus certainly said and did many things that did not contribute to his rejection and execution.

An example of this criterion may be observed in its application to Jesus' action in the Temple (Mark 11:15–18). While Jesus' intention in taking this action is debated, it is evident that it contributed to the opposition of the Temple authorities to Jesus and to their decision to have him arrested. Therefore, it is highly probable that Jesus' action in the Temple is historical.[156]

---

[154] For a development of this criterion with reference to Jesus' crucifixion, see in this volume ch. 13.

[155] Meier, *Roots of the Problem*, 177. Cf. a similar discussion by Evans (*Jesus and His Contemporaries*, 13–15) who coins the term "criterion of historical coherence." For Evans, though, the criterion is slightly broader than Meier's formulation; for him the focus is on "the principal features of his life" (p. 13), building upon E. P. Sanders' point (*Jesus and Judaism*, 7) that focus should be upon "the principal puzzles about Jesus, specifically why he attracted attention, why he was executed, and why he was subsequently deified." This led Sanders to formulate his well-known list of eight "almost indisputable facts" (p. 11) about Jesus. Cf. Porter, *Criteria for Authenticity*, 110–13.

[156] For further discussion, see Sanders, *Jesus and Judaism*, 61–76; Craig A. Evans, "Jesus' Action in the Temple and Evidence of Corruption in the First-Century Temple," in *Society of Biblical Literature 1989 Seminar Papers* (ed. David J. Lull; Atlanta: Scholars

Secondary Criteria are those criteria which, for one reason or another, contribute less weight to a judgment concerning the authenticity of a particular piece of tradition. But they nevertheless contribute to an evaluation of authenticity. For the sake of space, these criteria are discussed here only briefly.[157]

(6) Criterion of Coherence: Material that is coherent with (i.e., consistent with) other material already judged probably authentic using the primary criteria may also be considered as possibly or probably authentic.[158] This criterion expands the body of material already established as probably authentic by also including material that may not meet the primary criteria, but nevertheless may be given some weighting of authenticity because it conforms with other material judged authentic. The logic behind this criterion is that sayings and events that are consistent with what has already been judged probably authentic is more likely to also be authentic than material that is not consistent. This criterion is judged to be a secondary one because it is based upon material already established by other criteria, and it is also quite subjective. It is subject not only to how a particular scholar construes what constitutes "coherence," but also subject to what has already been deemed probably authentic. Thus, on a matter as basic as whether or not Jesus' message was eschatologically oriented, this criterion will produce opposite results depending upon what has already been judged as having an eschatological flavor.[159]

(7) Criterion of Aramaic Traces: Material that gives evidence of some use of Aramaic language may be considered more likely to be authentic. The logic behind this criterion is that, while the Gospels are in Greek as are most other historical sources for early Jesus tradition, Jesus spoke primarily Aramaic,[160] and thus one can expect to find traces of Jesus' Aramaic in these

---

Press, 1989), 522–39. See also the discussion in this volume in ch. 10. For other applications of this criterion, see chs. 12 and 13.

[157] Please consult the bibliographic items provided in the footnotes for more extended discussion and examples.

[158] For discussion, see Stein, "Criteria," 250–51; Boring, "Criteria," 17–18; Polkow, "Method and Criteria," 350; Meier, *Roots of the Problem*, 176–77; Evans, *Jesus and His Contemporaries*, 23–24; Porter, *Criteria for Authenticity*, 79–82. See also the earlier discussion by Perrin, *Rediscovering*, 43–45.

[159] For example, consider the difference between Dale Allison's eschatological Jesus vs. Marcus Borg's non-eschatological Jesus: Dale C. Allison, *Jesus of Nazareth: Millenarian Prophet* (Minneapolis: Augsburg Fortress, 1998); Marcus J. Borg, *Jesus, A New Vision: Spirit, Culture, and the Life of Discipleship* (San Francisco: Harper & Row, 1987); Marcus J. Borg, "A Temperate Case for a Non-Eschatological Jesus," *Forum* 2.3 (1986): 81–102; and the debate in Robert J. Miller, ed., *The Apocalyptic Jesus: A Debate* (Sonoma, CA: Polebridge, 2001). With reference to this criterion, see the discussion by Evans, *Jesus and His Contemporaries*, 23–24.

[160] On the issue of Jesus' language(s), see Joseph A. Fitzmyer, "The Languages of Palestine in the First Century A.D.," in *A Wandering Aramean: Collected Aramaic Essays*

Greek renditions of his sayings. While this criterion enjoyed popularity in the past,[161] it has come to be increasingly questioned.[162] There are a number of problems with this criterion, not the least of which is that, while Jesus certainly spoke Aramaic, so did his earliest followers who passed on the Jesus tradition. Thus, the presence of Aramaic or an Aramaic substratum only indicates the origins of those who were using the Aramaic tradition and not that it actually goes back to Jesus. Furthermore, the fact that a saying *can* be translated well into Aramaic does not necessarily demonstrate that Aramaic was its original language.[163] Thus the real value of this criterion becomes somewhat suspect.[164] In the judgment of Meier, it should only be used as a supplementary criterion when other primary criteria also support a judgment of probable authenticity, and perhaps this criterion is better understood to lower the level of probability; in other words, that which is difficult to express in Aramaic is less likely to be authentic.[165] On the other hand, as noted by Evans, we do at times "find Aramaic words and idioms that are foreign to Greek but at home in Aramaic." Thus, it is possible for this secondary criterion to provide support that at least the tradition is early and reflects what one would expect from authentic material.[166]

(8) Criterion of Palestinian Environment: Material that reflects specific Palestinian cultural realities (e.g., customs, procedures, practices of economic, social, and political life in Palestine) may be judged as more likely to

---

(SBLMS 25; Chico, CA: Scholars Press, 1979), 29–56; Joseph A. Fitzmyer, "Methodology in the Study of the Aramaic Substratum of Jesus' Sayings in the New Testament," in *Jésus aux origines de la christologie* (ed. J. Dupont; BETL 40; Gembloux: Duculot, 1975), 73–102; Stanley E. Porter, "Jesus and the Use of Greek in Galilee," in *Studying the Historical Jesus: Evaluations of the State of Current Research* (ed. Bruce Chilton and Craig A. Evans; NTTS 19; Leiden: E.J. Brill, 1994), 123–54.

[161] E.g., Joachim Jeremias, *The Proclamation of Jesus* (vol. 1 of *New Testament Theology*; trans. John Bowden; London: SCM, 1971), 3–37; Matthew Black, *An Aramaic Approach to the Gospels and Acts* (3 ed.; Oxford: Oxford University Press, 1967), as well as the older work by Gustaf Dalman, *The Words of Jesus: Considered in the Light of Post-Biblical Jewish Writings and the Aramaic Language* (trans. D.M. Kay; Edinburgh: T&T Clark, 1902), esp. 1–88.

[162] See e.g., Sanders and Davies, *Studying the Synoptic Gospels*, 333–34.

[163] For these and other difficulties, see Meier, *Roots of the Problem*, 178–80; Sanders and Davies, *Studying the Synoptic Gospels*, 333–34; Porter, *Criteria for Authenticity*, 89–99.

[164] Sanders and Davies (*Studying the Synoptic Gospels*, 333) state that this criterion "appears to us to be useless …"

[165] Meier, *Roots of the Problem*, 179–80. See also the discussion by Evans, *Jesus and His Contemporaries*, 22–23.

[166] Evans, *Life of Jesus Research: An Annotated Bibliography*, 142. An example of an earlier scholar who probably pushed the Aramaic background too far is Jeremias, *Proclamation of Jesus*, 3–37. But see the more recent contribution by Maurice Casey, *An Aramaic Approach to Q: Sources for the Gospels of Matthew and Luke* (SNTSMS 122; Cambridge: Cambridge University Press, 2002); Maurice Casey, *The Solution to the 'Son of Man' Problem* (LNTS 343; London: T&T Clark, 2007).

be authentic.[167] The logic of this criterion is somewhat related to the discussion above concerning the criterion of dissimilarity: Jesus is a product of his Palestinian environment and is addressing audiences in that same environment, and so it is reasonable to presume that Jesus' teaching and lifestyle would reflect this environment. On the other hand, material that does not reflect this environment may be judged less likely to be authentic. While the logic itself is sound, the criterion suffers from some of the same problems as the criterion of Aramaic traces – particularly that many of Jesus' earliest followers also lived in a Palestinian environment, and thus demonstrating Palestinian environment for a particular tradition does not necessitate that it goes back to Jesus. This criterion, however, could be used to complement a judgment based largely upon the primary criteria, for it provides an added confidence that the tradition is early, Palestinian, and what one would expect from the cultural context of a first-century Palestinian Jew.[168] Though it should be noted that this Palestinian context should be demonstrated as specific to Jesus' day; something that is vaguely Jewish or could equally be derived from reading the Hebrew Bible is probably not a candidate for this criterion. The strength of this criterion is, in the judgment of Meier,[169] is to lower the level of probability, for that which does not exhibit Jesus' cultural context is unlikely to be authentic.

I do wish to draw attention to one other possible criterion – a new one which arose in the extensive discussions of the essays in this volume, and that is the criterion of inherent ambiguity.

(9) Criterion of Inherent Ambiguity: Material that could be interpreted in two quite different ways – one positive and one negative – and that would require an explanation to help the audience avoid the negative viewpoint may be considered more likely to be authentic. The logic of this criterion is that it is unlikely that early Christians would create an event in Jesus' life that could be misconstrued negatively without an explanation to present the positive interpretation. In other words, it is more likely that one would create a story that clearly supported one's viewpoint, rather than one that could equally go against one's viewpoint and only supported one's viewpoint with an accompanying explanation. In other words, without explanation and interpretation, the story or event is inherently ambiguous. For example, the event commonly called "the triumphal entry" (Mark 11:1–10) is often rejected as not historical because it appears to be too supportive of a Chris-

---

[167] For discussion see Stein, "Criteria," 236–38, and 248–49 for the negative corrolary; Boring, "Criteria," 10–11; Polkow, "Method and Criteria," 352–53; Meier, *Roots of the Problem*, 180; Evans (*Jesus and His Contemporaries*, 22–23) combines this criterion with the criterion of Aramaic traces.
[168] So Evans, *Jesus and His Contemporaries*, 23.
[169] Meier, *Roots of the Problem*, 180.

tian interpretation of Jesus as messiah. However, the event itself is quite ambiguous, and could equally be viewed in a way quite contrary to Christian interpretation. In other words, the event itself is inherently ambiguous, and only becomes supportive of a Christian viewpoint by added interpretation and explanation. This research project has focused upon events and so it is presented here with that focus; whether it has any application to the sayings of Jesus remains to be seen.

The above criteria of authenticity are the primary ones currently in use today. There are others that have been used in past historical Jesus research, but they have come to be increasingly questioned and so are considered dubious.[170] Others criteria have been proposed, but have not gathered any significant support by others working in the field.[171] This does not necessarily render them unhelpful, but they are beyond the scope of this basic survey. It remains to be seen if the criterion of inherent ambiguity, proposed above, is seen as valid and having value by other historical Jesus scholars.

Several observations should be made concerning the use of these criteria. First of all, they must all be used together. Not all of them will be relevant in all situations, but they should be viewed as functioning collectively to provide the historian with the best judgment concerning a piece of tradition. The corollary to using them together is the realization that they may sometimes be in conflict with one another. Some of the criteria function primarily to raise the level of probability, others primarily to lower it, while still others can function either to raise or lower the level of probability. The net result of this is that in many situations some criteria may pull toward one judgment while others in another direction. This requires the historian to weigh the evidence. But it cannot be stressed enough: weighing the evidence involves using all the criteria together, seeing the issue from various angles.

Second, and arising out of the first, is the realization that the use of these criteria is as much or more art than it is science. The criteria can point in one direction or the other, or both at the same time, each with different strengths and weightings. This requires the historian to have a deft and sensitive manner in handling the weighing of these criteria to arrive at a judgment concerning the authenticity of a particular piece of tradition. There is a subjective element in their use. Using a heavy and rough hand, the historian can push the criteria in one direction or another, and they may be used to justify a preconceived viewpoint. Thus it is important that the historian not only recognize his/her own biases and predispositions but also take these into account, so that the evidence is handled fairly and judiciously, maintaining

---

[170] For a discussion of some dubious criteria, see Meier, *Roots of the Problem*, 178–83; Evans, *Jesus and His Contemporaries*, 24–26.

[171] See, for example, those proposed by Porter, *Criteria for Authenticity*, 126–237.

the integrity and honesty of the historian. The subjectivity must be recognized and accounted for – while total objectivity is an impossible ideal, it is, nevertheless, the goal to which the historian should strive.[172]

Third, given the nature of history and historiography discussed in § 2.1 and 2.2 above, and the manner in which the criteria of authenticity function, one must realize that judgments of authenticity or historicity are matters of greater or lesser probability, as are the explanations and hypotheses built upon them. Certainty – as one assumes in mathematics or hopes for in the sciences – is not realistic or possible in the historical enterprise, and even more so in historical investigations of ancient events. Thus the judicious historian weighs the evidence and provides judgments along a scale of "highly probable" through "possible" to "unlikely."[173] Occasionally a historian might even use terms like "virtually certain" or "most unlikely," but such extreme judgments should probably be reserved for situations in which virtually all the evidence overwhelmingly points in one direction.[174] Otherwise, readers and other historians may in turn judge the historian's judgments as "going beyond the evidence."

Fourth, an issue sometimes discussed with reference to the criteria of authenticity is the matter of burden of proof: Should the burden of proof lie with a scholar who concludes that a piece of tradition is probably not historical, or with the conclusion of probable authenticity? Both positions have been made: burden of proof lies with the historian who concludes a tradition is not authentic (i.e., one should assume authenticity unless demonstrated otherwise),[175] or one who concludes it is authentic (i.e., one should assume

---

[172] For recent discussions of what "objectivity" means and whether or not it is possible in history, see Appleby, et al., *Telling the Truth About History*, 241–70; Novick, *Noble Dream*; Evans, *In Defense of History*, 193–220; Thomas L. Haskell, *Objectivity Is Not Neutrality: Explanatory Schemes in History* (Baltimore: Johns Hopkins University Press, 1998); Eric Hobsbawm, *On History* (New York: New Press, 1997), 124–40.

[173] As an example, in this volume the historicity of Jesus' baptism by John is judged to be "highly probable"; see ch. 3, § 2.1. With respect to the visionary experience, the judgment was that, "it is *probable* that Jesus did at some time experience a prophetic call-vision, and it is *somewhat probable* that it incorporated the elements of divine sonship and spirit anointing. It is *possible* that such a call-vision may have taken place at Jesus' baptism, but there are also problems with their association. It is equally possible that it occurred at some point in time subsequent to the baptism." See also examples in this volume in ch. 11. A classic example of this is Sanders (*Jesus and Judaism*, 11) who begins his study by focusing on those events that are most probable. He identifies eight which he terms "almost indisputable facts."

[174] See the discussion by Sanders and Davies (*Studying the Synoptic Gospels*, 304) of weighing using greater and lesser probabilities, and the examples provided later (312–13).

[175] A classic statement is by Joachim Jeremias (*Proclamation of Jesus*, 37): "[T]he linguistic and stylistic evidence ... shows so much faithfulness towards the tradition of the sayings of Jesus that we are justified in drawing up the following principle of method: In the synoptic tradition it is the inauthenticity, and not the authenticity, of the sayings of

inauthenticity unless demonstrated otherwise).[176] The assumption one way or another is usually based upon prior views concerning the traditioning process that produced the Gospels, or upon theological presuppositions concerning the nature of the canonical Gospels. Given the complexities of the assumptions on both sides of this debate and the ease with which one historian can simply dismiss the work of another historian because of these assumptions, I would suggest that, while both sides of this issue might claim that their position treats the material fairly, both positions do not treat the discipline of history fairly. The handling of evidence and arguments concerning authenticity or inauthenticity should not be built primarily upon assumptions and claims, but built upon the laying out of evidence with argumentation. Thus, I would argue that the burden of proof should lie with historian who is making the case, whether for authenticity or against it. A classic statement of this position was made by Morna Hooker, who states:

> The presuppositions come to the surface when one side declares "The burden of proof is on those who maintain that any of the material is authentic", or when the other asks "Who is more likely to have been creative – Jesus or the Church?" But these are not the real alternatives. All the material comes to us via the Church, and it is likely to have been coloured by the beliefs of those who have handed it on. But the burden of proof, to prove or disprove authenticity, lies neither on one side nor on the other. It is the duty of every scholar who is considering every other saying, to give a reasonable account of all the evidence; for he is not entitled to assume, simply in the absence of contrary evidence, either that a saying is genuine or that it is not.[177]

Take, for example, a discussion of Jesus' sayings concerning the Son of Man, of which one group is frequently called the "coming Son of Man sayings." This particular subset of the Son of Man sayings have an eschatological orientation. In any discussion of Jesus and eschatology, these Gospel sayings are "evidence," but of what are they evidence? Are they evidence of Jesus' own eschatological orientation, or are they evidence of developing eschatological interests in the early Church? Either is theoretically possible (as well as a host of other possibilities), but to assume either based upon *a priori* assumptions is to dismiss prematurely the other possibility. This is not the method of a critical historian, and this is not "fair" to the historical discipline. But it also is not "fair" to the data, for either alternative is possible,

---

Jesus that must be demonstrated." See also Stewart C. Goetz and Craig L. Blomberg, "The Burden of Proof," *JSNT* 11 (1981): 39–63.

[176] A classic statement is by Norman Perrin (*Rediscovering*, 39, emphasis removed): "[W]e have to ask ourselves the question as to whether this saying should now be attributed to the early Church or to the historical Jesus, and the nature of the synoptic tradition is such that the burden of proof will be upon the claim to authenticity."

[177] Hooker, "On Using the Wrong Tool," 580. See also her discussion in Morna D. Hooker, "Christology and Methodology," *NTS* 17 (1970–71): 485. For more recent discussion, see Meier, *Roots of the Problem*, 183 and the literature cited there.

and to assume one position over the other is not "fair" to the evidentiary possibilities of the data.

4.2. Appreciating the Primary Ancient Sources

The intent of this section is not to provide a survey or description of the primary ancient sources; this has been done very well by others. Rather, here I simply highlight a few features about these sources by way of introduction for the non-specialist reader.

First, our knowledge of the ancient Mediterranean world is fragmentary and so very incomplete. The term "traces" in our phrase "surviving traces" (ST) highlights this. Most of what we do know comes to us from the literate minority, and they would have been largely from the elite classes. And so the quantity of data we have for a figure like Jesus – a non-elite – is quite amazing. Yet at the same time, it is also quite evident just how much we do not know. A Gospel like Mark can be read in approximately an hour, and yet it is intended to convey the life of someone who lived for more than 30 years. Thus, the first point to note about our primary ancient sources is that they do not and can not provide historians with answers to everything they might like to know. In the face of surviving traces (ST), a sound historian may often have to say, "We just don't know." On the other hand, what we do have is material considered important for recalling and passing on. There is much we do not have, but what we do have may be considered important.

Second, with reference to Jesus, our primary sources go well beyond the four Gospels in the NT – Matthew through John. These are a number of other early Christian texts that also provide portraits of Jesus, including for example, the *Gospel of Thomas*, the *Gospel of Peter*, the *Gospel of the Hebrews*, as well as numerous others. There are also fragmentary references to Jesus in other Christian texts (often referred to as *agrapha*).[178] While most of our sources for Jesus are early Christian texts, there are also a number of non-Christian sources, both Jewish and Greco-Roman, that refer to Jesus and were written within a century after his death.[179] Most people's first exposure to traditions about Jesus come from the four NT Gospels. They are

---

[178] A helpful introduction and English translation of these texts may be found in E. Hennecke and W. Schneemelcher, eds., *Gospels and Related Writings* (vol. 1 of *New Testament Apocrypha*; rev. ed.; trans. R. McL. Wilson; Louisville: Westminster/John Knox, 1991). With respect to *agrapha*, see F. F. Bruce, *Jesus and Christian Origins Outside the New Testament* (Grand Rapids: Eerdmans, 1974), 82–109; William D. Stoker, *Extracanonical Sayings of Jesus* (SBLRBS 18; Atlanta: Scholars Press, 1989); Robert E. Van Voorst, *Jesus Outside the New Testament: An Introduction to the Ancient Evidence* (Grand Rapids: Eerdmans, 2000), 179–85.

[179] See in this volume, for example, the discussion of some of these in ch. 13, § 2.1.2. For a complete survey, see Van Voorst, *Jesus Outside the New Testament: An Introduction to the Ancient Evidence*, 1–134; see also Craig A. Evans, "Jesus in Non-Christian Sources,"

the most well known, for they are canonical texts, forming part of the Christian scriptures, and thus they are viewed by Christians as authoritative for the formulation of Christian theology about Jesus. For a Christian, whether layperson or theologian, to give preference to the canonical NT Gospels over other early, non-canonical sources is quite appropriate. However, a historian must view these sources differently, for from a historical perspective, one cannot give preference to the NT Gospels just because they are canonical scripture for Christians. A historian, functioning critically,[180] allows all these ancient sources to function on an equal footing. The historian recognizes that these surviving traces are evidence of something, and must render judgments on whether they likely provide evidence for the historical Jesus or more probably provide evidence for later perceptions of Jesus that probably do not reflect the historical Jesus. As a result of this process, the historian may determine that, overall, some sources are more reliable than others and gives them preference. For example, a historian might determining that the Gospel of Mark is probably a more reliable source than the *Gospel of Peter*, but *not* because Mark is canonical scripture and the *Gospel of Peter* is not. Rather, the historian might determine that Mark is an earlier source and appears to have a better awareness of Jesus' Palestinian context than does the *Gospel of Peter*. This, of course, does not mean that the historian then simply accepts everything in Mark and rejects everything from the *Gospel of Peter*. Each individual piece of material from these sources also needs to be examined. The point is, the canonical status of some sources does not mean they are given preferential treatment by the critical historian. All material must be weighed and weighed equally to determine the evidentiary value of the data they contain.

Third, while our knowledge of the ancient Mediterranean world in general or the person of Jesus in particular is partial and fragmentary, it is important for the reader to be aware of the existence of a significant body of material from the ancient world that contributes contextual data in which to place our evidence concerning Jesus. In our discussion above we considered the importance of contextual data for constructing and evaluating various historical hypotheses.[181] This material is derived from both archaeological and literary sources.[182] The archaeological evidence continues to grow.[183]

---

in *Studying the Historical Jesus: Evaluations of the State of Current Research* (ed. Bruce Chilton and Craig A. Evans; NTTS 19; Leiden: E.J. Brill, 1994), 443–78.

[180] For further discussion see § 2.3 on the principle of autonomy for critical investigation.

[181] See above, § 2.3.

[182] A helpful introduction that gathers together this material for a non-specialist reader is Everett Ferguson, *Backgrounds of Early Christianity* (3d ed.; Grand Rapids: Eerdmans, 2003).

[183] See Emil Schürer, *The History of the Jewish People in the Age of Jesus Christ* (ed.

The literary sources[184] include the Hebrew Bible and subsequent versions and translations, Second Temple Jewish literature, including the Apocrypha, Pseudepigrapha,[185] the Dead Sea Scrolls,[186] and the writings of Josephus and Philo,[187] and later Jewish literature, including the Targums[188] and Rabbinic literature.[189] In terms of early Christian literature, these sources, besides the NT, include the NT Apocrypha,[190] the writings of the early Church Fathers,[191] and the Nag Hammadi Library[192] for Gnostic texts. The literature of Greco-Roman authors also provides contextual data for the ancient Mediterranean world.[193] The point of this brief and incomplete survey of ancient material is to draw to the attention of the non-specialist reader this significant body of contextual information that we have for understanding the ancient Mediterranean world. These provide the cultural scripts by

Geza Vermes, et al.; Edinburgh: T & T Clark, 1973–87), and more recently, James H. Charlesworth, ed., *Jesus and Archaeology* (Grand Rapids: Eerdmans, 2006).

[184] For a helpful survey of this literature as well as identification of sources for texts and translations, see Craig A. Evans, *Ancient Texts for New Testament Studies: A Guide to the Background Literature* (Peabody, MA: Hendrickson, 2005).

[185] For English translations, see James H. Charlesworth, ed., *The Old Testament Pseudepigrapha* (2 vols; Garden City, NY: Doubleday, 1983–85).

[186] For texts and English translation, see Florentino García Martínez and Eibert J. C. Tigchelaar, eds., *The Dead Sea Scrolls: Study Edition* (2 vols; Grand Rapids: Eerdmans, 1997–98).

[187] Text and English translation may be found in the Loeb Classical Library.

[188] Translations of the Targums may be found in The Aramaic Bible series published by T&T Clark.

[189] The most convenient translation of the Mishnah remains Herbert Danby, *The Mishnah* (Oxford: Oxford University Press, 1933); for both text and another translation, see Philip Blackman, *Mishnayoth* (7 vols; 2 ed.; New York: Judaica Press, 1983). For the translation of the Tosefta, see Jacob Neusner, trans., *The Tosefta: Translated from the Hebrew with a New Introduction* (2 vols; 1977–86; repr., Peabody, MA: Hendrickson, 2002). The text and translation of the Babylonian Talmud is found in I. Epstein, trans., *Hebrew–English Edition of the Babylonian Talmud* (30 vols; London: Soncino, 1960–90). A recent English translation is by Jacob Neusner, trans., *The Babylonian Talmud: A Translation and Commentary* (22 vols; Peabody, MA: Hendrickson, 2005).

[190] Two recent introductions with English translations are E. Hennecke and W. Schneemelcher, eds., *New Testament Apocrypha* (rev. ed.; 2 vols; trans. R. McL. Wilson; Louisville: Westminster / John Knox, 1991); James K. Elliott, *The Apocryphal New Testament: A Collection of Apocryphal Christian Literature in an English Translation* (Oxford: Oxford University Press, 1993).

[191] The text and translation of the Apostolic Fathers can be found in Bart D. Ehrman, ed. and trans., *The Apostolic Fathers* (2 vols; LCL 24–25; Cambridge, MA: Harvard University Press, 2003). The translations of the early Church Fathers may be found in Alexander Roberts and James Donaldson, eds., *The Ante-Nicene Fathers: Translations of the Writings of the Fathers Down to A.D. 325* (10 vols; 1885; repr., Grand Rapids: Eerdmans, 1979).

[192] A convenient translation is James M. Robinson, ed., *The Nag Hammadi Library in English* (3d ed.; San Francisco: Harper and Row, 1988).

[193] Both original text and English translation of both the Greek and Latin authors may be found in the Loeb Classical Library published by Harvard University Press.

which we can better appreciate how things were understood, how events and actions were viewed and what they would have evoked. Thus, in terms of historical method with reference to the historical Jesus, it is not enough to take one's contextual information from the Gospels only, or even from all the early Jesus traditions. The historian must draw upon this diverse body of evidence to develop a deep and rich appreciation of the ancient Mediterranean world in order to truly understand and interpret the varieties of the Jesus traditions, and ultimately to place Jesus appropriately within his first-century context.[194]

4.3. Applying Historical Method to Historical Jesus Research

In an earlier section we considered historical method in general (§ 2.3). We can now provide a brief sketch of how this applies in particular to historical Jesus research in light of the material considered here, without repeating in detail the preceding discussion.

In historical Jesus research the chunk of past reality (i.e., PE) under consideration is the life and death of Jesus of Nazareth which draws upon surviving traces (i.e., ST) consisting primarily of early Christian Gospels but also other early Christian, Jewish and Greco-Roman sources. By evaluating the evidentiary contribution of these various surviving traces, the historian determines which most probably provide data concerning the historical Jesus. By interpreting these data within a broader context, the historian constructs an historical account (i.e., NA) of how he/she portrays the events under consideration.

The earlier discussion of historical method viewed it conceptually as consisting of two main phases, plus a preliminary and concluding phase. We did observe, though, that the reality of engaging in historical research involves the historian moving back and forth among the phases numerous times in a type of Gadamerian hermeneutical spiral as something in a later phase leads to a reworking of something in an earlier phase.

The preliminary phase focuses on the historian, for we noted above the importance of the historian being self-aware of his/her horizon, and in particular being aware of how the preunderstanding and biases of that horizon might shape the questions brought to the historical endeavor as well as influence the evaluations and judgments made, and the hypotheses preferred. This is absolutely critical when it comes to the field of historical Jesus research, given the deep and pervasive influence that this figure has had – not only in terms of the religious influence and cultural influence through the rise of Christianity and its impact on the development of Western thought,

---

[194] This is one of the emphases of the essays in the rest of this volume: the contextual information that contributes to understanding the event.

but also the social and political events that have subsequently taken place in his name, some for good and others for evil. I think it could safely be argued that no modern historian (at least in the Western world) could realistically engage in historical Jesus research without having had one's personal horizon shaped in some way by "Jesus Christ." In the field of historical Jesus studies, a well-known saying is the danger of seeking the historical Jesus but only seeing one's own reflection at the bottom of the deep well of history.[195] This is a real danger, but it need not be inevitable, if the historian engages in critical self-awareness, and honestly seeks to account for one's biases and preunderstanding in the historical endeavor on the "grounds of personal integrity and honesty towards his or her calling [as a historian]."[196]

The first main phase involves the gathering,[197] interpretation, and evaluation of the data in context. Historical Jesus research requires the interpretation of the surviving evidence within a particular context in order to evaluate the evidentiary contribution of the data. The historian brings contextual information to the data in order to interpret it.[198] Thus, this is both a top-down and bottom-up approach: overall contexts need to be explored as alternative paradigms through which to view the data (i.e., top-down), and the specific data needs to interpreted and evaluated in light of these contexts to determine which is most appropriate for the data and what is the evidentiary contribution of discrete pieces of evidence (i.e., bottom-up). The primary function of the interpretation at this point is to evaluate the data in terms of its evidentiary contribution of the data: how is a particular piece of Jesus tradition to be interpreted in light of the context provided and how probable is it that this particular piece of Jesus tradition goes back to Jesus (or is the product of later tradition or redaction)? This involves the use of the preliminary, primary, and secondary criteria of authenticity discussed

---

[195] While this imagery is often attributed to Albert Schweitzer, it is actually derived from George Tyrrell (*Christianity at the Crossroads* [1909; repr., London: George Allen & Unwin, 1963], 49) who, at the end of his chapter on "The Christ of Liberal Protestantism," states concerning Adolf von Harnack's *Wesen des Christentums* (trans. *What is Christianity?*): "The Christ that Harnack sees, looking aback through nineteen centuries of Catholic darkness, is only a reflection of a Liberal Protestant face, seen at the bottom of a deep well."

[196] Sanders and Davies, *Studying the Synoptic Gospels*, 303.

[197] In many other areas of primary historical research, the gathering of primary data would be a more significant element, and might even be considered a separate phase. But with reference to historical Jesus research the direct primary data has already largely been gathered – until perhaps some new ancient manuscript discovery is made.

[198] Sanders and Davies (*Studying the Synoptic Gospels*, 337), in discussing historical method, state: "We need an overall scheme into which to fit the parts. We need a context. Nothing is known without context." Cf. the earlier discussion of the need for context in the illustration of evaluating the 300 pieces of a 3,000 piece jigsaw puzzle.

above. One's evaluation of evidentiary contribution (i.e., bottom-up) will depend upon the context selected (top-down).[199]

As an example of the relationship between data and context in evaluation, consider Mark 1:8: John the baptizer announced an expected figure who "will baptize you with the Holy Spirit" (πνεύματι ἁγίῳ, lit. "a spirit of holiness"). How do we determine the probable historicity of this being a statement by John the Baptist? If we view this within the context of early Christian proclamation and theology concerning the coming of the Holy Spirit (e.g., Acts 2:33, 38), then our judgment of authenticity would be that this statement in Mark 1:8 is probably not authentic. Rather, it was probably added to this pericope early in the process of Christian traditioning to support Jesus coming in fulfillment of John's prophetic statement and more particularly to support early Christian proclamation of the Holy Spirit's coming as a result of Jesus' death and resurrection. However, another context produces quite a different evaluation. One could place this statement within the context of Second Temple Jewish texts which describe the eschatological expectation of "a spirit of holiness," some of which also link this to the use of water ablutions. More particularly, one could also find this same language being used in the literature of the Qumran Community – a community in existence at the same time as John the Baptist, located just a few kilometers from where John was baptizing.[200] When interpreted within this context, the criteria of authenticity result in quite a different judgment: it is quite probable that John used language expecting "a spirit of holiness," *when interpreted in the context* of Second Temple Jewish eschatological

---

[199] The historical-Jesus scholar, Dale C. Allison, is quite helpful in explaining this point: "we should be looking for something akin to what Thomas Kuhn once called a 'paradigm,' an explanatory model by which to order our data ... The initial task is to create a context, a primary frame of reference, for the Jesus tradition, a context that may assist us in determining both the authenticity of traditions and their interpretation." Allison, *Jesus of Nazareth*, 36, cf. 33–39. See Thomas S. Kuhn, *The Structure of Scientific Revolutions* (3 ed.; Chicago: University of Chicago Press, 1996). See also my discussion of this issue in Robert L. Webb, "Methodological Reflections on John the Baptizer's Influence on Jesus," in *Methodological Approaches to the Historical Jesus: The Second Princeton-Prague Symposium on Jesus Research, Princeton 2007* (James H. Charlesworth; Grand Rapids: Eerdmans, forthcoming). Most recently, Dale C. Allison ("The Historian's Jesus and the Church," in *Seeking the Identity of Jesus: A Pilgrimage* [ed. Beverly Roberts Gaventa and Richard B. Hays; Grand Rapids: Eerdmans, 2008], 79–95) has questioned the value of the criteria of authenticity. I would respond briefly, that dependence upon them exclusively is problematic, but a use of both the top-down and bottom-up approach advocated here provides the best balance for reaching a coherent and probable representation of the historical Jesus – as much as can be achieved historically.

[200] See the discussion of these texts in Robert L. Webb, *John the Baptizer and Prophet: A Socio-Historical Study* (1991; repr., JSNTSup 62; Eugene, OR: Wipf & Stock, 2006), 108–62.

expectation, particularly that associated with sectarian movements in the Judean desert.

The second main phase involves the interpretation and explanation of the data with hypotheses. Having ascertained in the preceding phase which data have evidentiary value for the questions the historian is seeking to answer, the historian continues to consider alternative contexts for the data. In the preceding phase contextual information was considered to evaluate the data's evidentiary value, but in this second phase, the primary function is to explore alternative hypotheses. Contextual information may also come from considering alternative models derived from cognate disciplines such as cultural anthropology or sociology. As these alternative hypotheses are explored, they are evaluated to determine which hypothesis is preferable because (1) it provides a better explanation of the evidence, and (2) it allows for extrapolation that provides a more plausible explanation of the complete historical picture.[201] Keeping in mind that one only has 250 relevant pieces for a 3,000 piece jigsaw puzzle. So to repaint the front cover of the puzzle box, one needs to paint a picture (i.e., provide the most plausible hypothesis) that places the 250 pieces appropriately (i.e., explain the evidence) as well as fills in the gaps left blank from the missing 2,750 pieces (i.e., extrapolates to a complete historical picture). With respect to Jesus research, the primary data which has been judged relevant with some degree of historical probability in the preceding phase continues to be explored in light of larger contexts and hypotheses are explored in order to derive the most plausible hypothesis that provides the larger picture.

As a brief example, consider the description concerning John the Baptist in Mark 1:6, "Now John was clothed with camel's hair, with a leather belt around his waist, and he ate locusts and wild honey." It could be argued that this description has some degree of probability as authentic, but not highly probable. It could be used to provide an overall portrait of the historical John, but perhaps not put too much weight on it. In my own earlier work, I considered this description of his clothing to be a fragmentary piece of evidence that fit within a larger picture in which John has chosen to present himself in continuity with classic Israelite prophetic tradition, but which was also appropriate given the desert locale of his ministry. And his diet was also consistent with this desert motif, functioning as part of a larger picture of John also as an ascetic.[202] This exemplifies two fragmentary pieces of evidence (dress and diet) that I used to extrapolate to a larger picture used to explain who John was: an ascetic prophetic figure. This provided the best

---

[201] On extrapolation to the larger picture in historical Jesus research, see the interesting discussion by Sanders and Davies, *Studying the Synoptic Gospels*, 335–44, esp. 335–37.

[202] See Robert L. Webb, *John the Baptizer and Prophet: A Socio-Historical Study* (1991; repr., JSNTSup 62; Eugene, OR: Wipf & Stock, 2006), 50–55, 360–73.

fit in a desert context in which John was proclaiming a prophetic message. I considered this the most plausible explanatory hypothesis for this fragmentary data. In a subsequent review of this book,[203] it was suggested that I had failed to consider the alternative explanation of a Cynic context. The reviewer was correct – I *had* failed to consider this alternative context, and perhaps I should have. However, as I do so now, I consider it a theoretically possible alternative, but in light of the relative paucity of evidence of a Cynic presence and influence in Palestine, the extent of the evidence for a continuing prophetic tradition in the Judean desert in the first century, and the overall evidence concerning John himself, I consider this theoretically possible explanatory hypothesis to be far less plausible and to have far less explanatory power for an overall picture of John, that I must reject it – but only after considering it in light of the evidence concerning John and the contextual evidence.

The concluding phase of the historical method is to gather the evidence, arguments, and hypotheses into a coherent and complete historical narrative that the historian considers the most plausible representation (i.e., NA) of that chunk of past reality being considered (i.e., PE). At this stage it also behooves the historian to inform the reader of those preunderstandings and biases that may have affected the judgments and interpretations. A reader can best evaluate the historical representation when they not only have presented to them the evidence, arguments, and hypotheses that contribute to the historical representation, but also have an appreciation of the historian who has painted the historical picture.[204]

5. Conclusion: History, the Historical Jesus, and this Project

This wide-ranging essay has tried to gather together a broad perspective on the nature of history, and how historians go about the task of doing history. We have also explored the field of historical Jesus research and linked it to

---

[203] A review that unfortunately I cannot now locate.

[204] One notable example is E. P. Sanders, on which see the quotation in n. 102 above. Another example is Dale Allison (*Resurrecting Jesus*, 343–44), who states near the end of his discussion of the resurrection: "… we need to scrutinize not just the texts but also ourselves. When I do this, I find that I am neither an atheist nor an agnostic … I indeed believe, as best as I can, in the God of Western theism, or rather, in the God of Israel. I also believe that materialistic explanations and this-worldly causalities encompass only part of reality … So my view of things allows me to believe that the crucified Jesus triumphed over death and made this known to his followers, and my personal religious history and current social location – I am a mainstream Protestant who teaches at a Presbyterian seminary – make such a belief congenial." The reader is referred to § 5 below where such a description is provided for those involved in this historical project.

this broader discussion of history. The two-fold goal has been to introduce the non-specialist reader to these disciplines, and to set a context for the essays that follow.

This volume is the result of a decade-long collaborative project by the IBR Jesus Group. Three overarching questions have guided the project: (1) What are the key events in the life of Jesus that we think can be best be demonstrated as being probably historical? (2) In light of the relevant cultural information, what is the significance of each event for understanding the historical Jesus? (3) What is the portrait of Jesus that results from considering these events and their significance? For each of the 12 events selected here, the essay is intended to do three things: present the evidence for the historical probability of the event, lay out the cultural contextual data that helps to understand the event, and explore the historical significance of the event.

When we gathered annually as a group to discuss two or three of these essays, a full day of discussion was allotted to each (with a few being discussed over more than one year). The focus was to discuss the evidence and argumentation to ensure that they were as complete and sound as possible. The process involved extensive discussion and debate which helped to shape and strengthen each essay. The collaborative learning experience was very stimulating! Each author, however, remains alone responsible for the views expressed in their particular essay. (No voting took place, though colored M&Ms were consumed!). We do not all agree with everything in each others' essays, and on some matters there may be strong disagreement. But what we do agree on is the benefit of the process and the merits of these events as core for any discussion of the historical Jesus. Collaboration with adequate time for extensive discussion and debate is a genuine learning and growing experience (in contrast to the typical speed-reading of research papers at the typical academic conference). Thus, it should be pointed out that the authors of the essays to follow in this volume do not all agree with everything that is stated in this introductory essay (which, by the way, did receive a full-day's discussion and extensive internet interaction as well). Thus, for example, in the options laid out in § 3 on "Historical Explanation, Worldview, and the 'Supernatural'," a few members preferred a "methodological naturalistic" understanding of history, while others preferred a "critical theistic" view of history. We did consider initially trying to write a collaborative introduction, but we decided that it would be stronger if written by one person and then have the group interact with it. It should also be noted that this essay was written at the end of the project and not at the beginning. So it is quite possible that there may be some tensions between views expressed in this chapter and particular elements in some of the chapters to follow. Though I suspect that they will be relatively few and not overly significant. This essay functions to provide the reader with a context for understanding the historical endeavor in general and historical Jesus research in particular; it was not written as a guide to the project. It reflects sometimes an appreciation of the limits and tensions we sensed as we pursued the project.

One of the points made a couple of times in the preceding discussion is the importance of recognizing, taking into account, and making publicly available one's horizon including biases and preunderstanding. Thus, we consider it important to inform you, the reader, about "where we are coming from" as a group. As the IBR Jesus Group, we are all members of the Institute for Biblical Research – an academic society specifically for scholars whose disciplines are biblical studies: Hebrew Bible, New Testament, and ancillary fields. Its vision is to foster excellence in biblical studies, doing so within a faith environment. Thus, each of us has a commitment to the Christian faith. Some of us would be comfortable using the term "Evangelical Christian" to describe one's theological stance, while others of us would prefer "biblically orthodox Christian." Thus, while all Christians, there is some diversity in theological viewpoints. Have our particular horizons had an impact on this project? Well, at least in one sense it has, for our interest in the historical Jesus arises – at least partially – from our faith perspective. To what extent has it shaped our arguments and conclusions? Well, we have attempted to take our horizons into account and handle the material with, as E. P. Sanders states in the quotation above, "personal integrity and honesty."[205] Are we successful in the arguments we have made, the hypotheses we have presented, and ultimately at the historical representation we have made? Well, what is presented here is an incomplete portrait of Jesus, for our focus is upon events and not his teaching, and only certain events at that. But what we do offer is a case for these certain events being at the core for understanding Jesus, and that this core provides a coherent view of what he was about. Furthermore, in light of the discussion of historiography above, our claim would be a modest one: this is one (partial) representation in light of the evidence as we have interpreted it. It is certainly not the only one possible, but is it a reasonable and valid representation? Is it perhaps even a compelling representation? We think that it is, but you, the reader, will ultimately be the judge of that.

---

[205] Sanders and Davies, *Studying the Synoptic Gospels*, 303.

Bibliography

Allison, Dale C. "The Historian's Jesus and the Church." Pages 79–95 in *Seeking the Identity of Jesus: A Pilgrimage*. Edited by Beverly Roberts Gaventa and Richard B. Hays. Grand Rapids: Eerdmans, 2008.
–. *Jesus of Nazareth: Millenarian Prophet*. Minneapolis: Augsburg Fortress, 1998.
–. *Resurrecting Jesus: The Earliest Christian Tradition and Its Interpreters*. London: T&T Clark, 2005.
Ankersmit, Frank R. *Historical Representation*. Cultural Memory in the Present. Stanford, CA: Stanford University Press, 2001.
Appleby, Joyce, Lynn Hunt, and Margaret Jacob. *Telling the Truth About History*. New York: W. W. Norton, 1994.
Archer, Margaret, Roy Bhaskar, Andrew Collier, Tony Lawson, and Alan Norrie, eds. *Critical Realism: Essential Readings*. London: Routledge, 1998.
Bauckham, Richard. *Jesus and the Eyewitnesses: The Gospels as Eyewitness Testimony*. Grand Rapids: Eerdmans, 2006.
Beards, Andrew. "Reversing Historical Skepticism: Bernard Lonergan on the Writing of History." *History and Theory* 33 (1994): 198–219.
Bentley, Michael, ed. *Companion to Historiography*. London: Routledge, 1997.
–. *Modern Historiography: An Introduction*. London: Routledge, 1999.
Bermejo Rubio, Fernando. "The Fiction of the 'Three Quests': An Argument for Dismantling a Dubious Historiographical Paradigm." *JSHJ* 7 (2009): [forthcoming].
Bhaskar, Roy. *The Possibility of Naturalism: A Philosophical Critique of the Contemporary Human Sciences*. 3rd ed. London: Routledge, 1998.
–. *A Realist Theory of Science*. 2nd ed. Radical Thinkers 29. London: Verso, 2008.
Black, Matthew. *An Aramaic Approach to the Gospels and Acts*. 3rd ed. Oxford: Oxford University Press, 1967.
Blackman, Philip. *Mishnayoth*. 7 vols. 2nd ed. New York: Judaica Press, 1983.
Bloch, Marc. *The Historian's Craft*. Translated by Peter Putnam. New York: Vintage Books, 1953.
Borg, Marcus J. *Jesus, A New Vision: Spirit, Culture, and the Life of Discipleship*. San Francisco: Harper & Row, 1987.
–. "A Temperate Case for a Non-Eschatological Jesus." *Forum* 2.3 (1986): 81–102.
Boring, M. Eugene. "Criteria of Authenticity: The Lucan Beatitudes as a Test Case." *Forum* 1.4 (1985): 3–38.
Breisach, Ernst. *Historiography: Ancient, Medieval, and Modern*. 2nd ed. Chicago: University of Chicago Press, 1994.
Bruce, F. F. *Jesus and Christian Origins Outside the New Testament*. Grand Rapids: Eerdmans, 1974.
Carr, Edward Hallett. *What Is History?* London: Macmillan, 1961.
Casey, Maurice. *An Aramaic Approach to Q: Sources for the Gospels of Matthew and Luke*. SNTSMS 122. Cambridge: Cambridge University Press, 2002.
–. *The Solution to the 'Son of Man' Problem*. LNTS 343. London: T&T Clark, 2007.
Charlesworth, James H., ed. *Jesus and Archaeology*. Grand Rapids: Eerdmans, 2006.
–, ed. *The Old Testament Pseudepigrapha*. 2 vols. Garden City, NY: Doubleday, 1983–85.

–. "Jesus and Jehohanan: An Archaeological Note on Crucifixion." *ExpT* 84 (1972–73): 147–50.
Collier, Andrew. *Critical Realism: An Introduction to Roy Bhaskar's Philosophy*. London: Verso, 1994.
Collingwood, R. G. *The Idea of History: With Lectures 1926–1928*. Rev. ed. Edited with an introduction by Jan van der Dussen. Oxford: Oxford University Press, 1993.
Conroy, Sherrill A. "A Pathway for Interpretive Phenomenology." *International Journal of Qualitative Methods* 2.3 (2003): article 4 (retrieved 080214 from http://www.ualberta.ca/~iiqm/backissues/2_3final/pdf/conroy.pdf).
Craig, William Lane. *Assessing the New Testament Evidence for the Historicity of the Resurrection of Jesus*. SBEC 16. Lewiston, NY: Edwin Mellen, 1989.
Crawford, Michael, ed. *Sources for Ancient History*. Cambridge: Cambridge University Press, 1983.
Croce, Benedetto. *History as the Story of Liberty*. Translated by Sylvia Sprigge. New York: Meridian Books, 1955.
–. *History: Its Theory and Practice*. Translated by Douglas Ainslie. New York: Russell & Russell, 1960.
Crossan, John Dominic. *The Historical Jesus: The Life of a Mediterranean Jewish Peasant*. San Francisco: HarperSanFrancisco, 1991.
Crossley, James G. "Defining History." Pages 9–30 in *Writing History, Constructing Religion*. Edited by James G. Crossley and Christian Karner. Aldershot, UK: Ashgate, 2005.
–. *Why Christianity Happened: A Sociohistorical Account of Christian Origins (26–50 CE)*. Louisville, KY: Westminster John Knox, 2006.
D'Amico, Jack, Dain A. Trafton, and Massimo Verdicchio, eds. *The Legacy of Benedetto Croce: Contemporary Critical Views*. Toronto: University of Toronto Press, 1999.
Dalman, Gustaf. *The Words of Jesus: Considered in the Light of Post-Biblical Jewish Writings and the Aramaic Language*. Translated by D. M. Kay. Edinburgh: T&T Clark, 1902.
Danby, Herbert. *The Mishnah*. Oxford: Oxford University Press, 1933.
Davies, Philip R. *Memories of Ancient Israel: An Introduction to Biblical History – Ancient and Modern*. Louisville: Westminster John Knox, 2008.
–. *Whose Bible Is It Anyway?* London: T&T Clark, 2004.
Davies, W. D., and Dale C. Allison. *Commentary on Matthew VIII–XVIII*. Vol. 2 of *A Critical and Exegetical Commentary on the Gospel According to Saint Matthew*. ICC. Edinburgh: T&T Clark, 1991.
Dawidowicz, Lucy S. *The Holocaust and the Historians*. Cambridge, MA: Harvard University Press, 1981.
de Vries, Paul. "Naturalism in the Natural Sciences." *Christian Scholar's Review* 15 (1986): 388–96.
Denton, Donald L. *Historiography and Hermeneutics in Jesus Studies: An Examination of the Work of John Dominic Crossan and Ben F. Meyer*. JSNTS 262. London: T&T Clark International, 2004.
Derrida, Jacques. *Of Grammatology*. Translated by G. C. Spivak. Baltimore: Johns Hopkins University Press, 1976.
Dodd, C. H. *History and the Gospel*. London: Nisbet & Co., 1938.

Dunn, James D. G. *Jesus Remembered*. Vol. 1 of *Christianity in the Making*. Grand Rapids: Eerdmans, 2003.
Eddy, Paul Rhodes, and Gregory A. Boyd. *The Jesus Legend: A Case for the Historical Reliability of the Synoptic Jesus Tradition*. Grand Rapids: Baker Academic, 2007.
Ehrman, Bart D., ed. and trans. *The Apostolic Fathers*. 2 vols. LCL 24–25. Cambridge, MA: Harvard University Press, 2003.
Elliott, James K. *The Apocryphal New Testament: A Collection of Apocryphal Christian Literature in an English Translation*. Oxford: Oxford University Press, 1993.
Elton, Geoffrey R. *The Practice of History*. 2nd ed. Afterward by Richard J. Evans. Oxford: Blackwell, 2002.
Epstein, I., trans. *Hebrew–English Edition of the Babylonian Talmud*. 30 vols. London: Soncino, 1960–90.
Evans, Craig A. *Ancient Texts for New Testament Studies: A Guide to the Background Literature*. Peabody, MA: Hendrickson, 2005.
–. "Authenticity Criteria in Life of Jesus Research." *CSR* 19 (1989): 6–31.
–. *Jesus*. IBR Bibliographies 5. Grand Rapids: Baker, 1992.
–. *Jesus and His Contemporaries: Comparative Studies*. AGJU 25. Leiden: E. J. Brill, 1995.
–. "Jesus in Non-Christian Sources." Pages 443–78 in *Studying the Historical Jesus: Evaluations of the State of Current Research*. Edited by Bruce Chilton and Craig A. Evans. NTTS 19. Leiden: E. J. Brill, 1994.
–. "Jesus' Action in the Temple and Evidence of Corruption in the First-Century Temple." Pages 522–39 in *Society of Biblical Literature 1989 Seminar Papers*. Edited by David J. Lull. Atlanta: Scholars Press, 1989.
–. *Life of Jesus Research: An Annotated Bibliography*. 2nd ed. NTTS 24. Leiden: E. J. Brill, 1996.
Evans, Richard J. *In Defense of History*. New York: W. W. Norton, 1999.
Fairburn, Miles, *Social History: Problems, Strategies, and Methods*. New York: St. Martin's Press. 1999.
Farmer, William R. *The Synoptic Problem: A Critical Analysis*. Macon, GA: Mercer University Press, 1976.
Farrer, Austin. "On Dispensing with Q." Pages 55–88 in *Studies in the Gospels: Essays in Memory of R. H. Lightfoot*. Edited by D. E. Nineham. Oxford: Blackwell, 1955.
Ferguson, Duncan S. *Biblical Hermeneutics: An Introduction*. Louisville: Westminster John Knox, 1986.
Ferguson, Everett. *Backgrounds of Early Christianity*. 3d ed. Grand Rapids: Eerdmans, 2003.
Fitzmyer, Joseph A. "The Languages of Palestine in the First Century A.D." Pages 29–56 in *A Wandering Aramean: Collected Aramaic Essays*. SBLMS 25. Chico, CA: Scholars Press, 1979.
–. "Methodology in the Study of the Aramaic Substratum of Jesus' Sayings in the New Testament." Pages 73–102 in *Jésus aux origines de la christologie*. Edited by J. Dupont. BETL 40. Gembloux: Duculot, 1975.
Fleddermann, Harry T. *Q: A Reconstruction and Commentary*. Biblical Tools and Studies 1. Leuven: Peeters, 2005.

Friedlander, Saul, ed. *Probing the Limits of Representation: Nazism and the 'Final Solution'*. Harvard: Harvard University Press, 1992.
Gadamer, Hans-Georg. *Truth and Method*. Translated by Barden, Garrett, and John Cumming. New York: Crossroad, 1984.
García Martínez, Florentino, and Eibert J.C. Tigchelaar, eds. *The Dead Sea Scrolls: Study Edition*. 2 vols. Grand Rapids: Eerdmans, 1997–98.
Gardiner, Patrick. *The Nature of Historical Explanation*. Oxford: Oxford University Press, 1961.
Goetz, Stewart C., and Craig L. Blomberg. "The Burden of Proof." *JSNT* 11 (1981): 39–63.
Goodacre, Mark. *The Case Against Q: Studies in Markan Priority and the Synoptic Problem*. Harrisburg, PA: Trinity Press International, 2002.
–. *The Synoptic Problem: A Way Through the Maze*. London: T&T Clark, 2001.
Goodacre, Mark, and Nicholas Perrin, eds. *Questioning Q: A Multidimensional Critique*. Downers Grove: InterVarsity, 2004.
Gorman, Jonathan. *Understanding History: An Introduction to Analytical Philosophy of History*. Philosophica 42. Ottawa: University of Ottawa Press, 1992.
Goulder, Michael. "Did Jesus of Nazareth Rise from the Dead?" Pages 58–68 in *Resurrection: Essays in Honour of Leslie Houlden*. Edited by Stephen Barton and Graham Stanton. London: SPCK, 1994.
Goulder, Michael D. *Luke: A New Paradigm*. 2 vols. JSNTSup 20. Sheffield: JSOT Press, 1989.
Griffin, Larry J. *New Methods for Social History*. Cambridge: Cambridge University Press, 1999.
Haas, N. "Anthropological Observations on the Skeletal Remains from Givât Ha-Mivtar." *IEJ* 20 (1970): 38–59.
Hagner, Donald A. *Matthew 14–28*. WBC 33B. Dallas, TX: Word Books, 1995.
Harvey, Van A. *The Historian and the Believer: The Morality of Historical Knowledge and Christian Belief*. London: SCM, 1967.
Haskell, Thomas L. *Objectivity Is Not Neutrality: Explanatory Schemes in History*. Baltimore: Johns Hopkins University Press, 1998.
Heath, Malcom. "Invention." Pages 89–119 in *Handbook of Classical Rhetoric in the Hellenistic Period 330 B.C.–A.D. 400*. Edited by Stanley E. Porter. Leiden: E.J. Brill, 1997.
Hedrick Jr., Charles W. *Ancient History: Monuments and Documents*. Malden, MA and Oxford: Blackwell, 2006.
Hengel, Martin. *The Charismatic Leader and His Followers*. Translated by James Greig. New York: Crossroad, 1981.
Hennecke, E., and W. Schneemelcher, eds. *Gospels and Related Writings*. Vol. 1 of *New Testament Apocrypha*. Rev. ed. Translated by R. McL. Wilson. Louisville: Westminster/John Knox, 1991.
–, eds. *New Testament Apocrypha*. Rev. ed. 2 vols. Translated by R. McL. Wilson. Louisville: Westminster/John Knox, 1991.
Hobsbawm, Eric. *On History*. New York: New Press, 1997.
Holmén, Tom. "Doubts About Double Dissimilarity: Restructuring the Main Criterion of Jesus-of-History Research." Pages 47–80 in *Authenticating the Words of Jesus*. Eds Bruce Chilton and Craig A. Evans. NTTS 28.1. Leiden: E.J. Brill, 1999.

—. "An Introduction to the Continuum Approach." Pages 1–16 in *Jesus from Judaism to Christianity: Continuum Approaches to the Historical Jesus.* Edited by Tom Holmén. LNTS 352. London: T&T Clark, 2007.
Hooker, Morna D. "Christology and Methodology." *NTS* 17 (1970–71): 480–487.
—. "On Using the Wrong Tool." *Theology* 75 (1972): 570–81.
Howell, Martha, and Walter Prevenier. *From Reliable Sources: An Introduction to Historical Methods.* Ithaca, NY: Cornell University Press, 2001.
Iggers, Georg G. *Historiography in the Twentieth Century: From Scientific Objectivity to Postmodern Challenge – with a New Epilogue by the Author.* 2nd ed. Middletown, CT: Wesleyan University Press, 2005.
Jenkins, Keith, ed. *The Postmodern History Reader.* London: Routledge, 1997.
—. *On "What Is History?": From Carr and Elton to Rorty and White.* London: Routledge, 1995.
—. *Re-Thinking History.* With a new preface and conversation with the author by Alun Munslow. London: Routledge, 2003.
—. *Why History?: Ethics and Postmodernity.* London: Routledge, 1999.
Jenkins, Keith, and Alun Munslow, eds. *The Nature of History Reader.* London: Routledge, 2004.
Jeremias, Joachim. *The Proclamation of Jesus.* Translated by John Bowden. Vol. 1 of *New Testament Theology.* London: SCM, 1971.
Kant, Immanuel. *Critique of Practical Reason and Other Writings in Moral Philosophy.* Translated and edited by Lewis W. Beck. Chicago: University of Chicago Press, 1949.
Käsemann, Ernst. "The Problem of the Historical Jesus." In *Essays on New Testament Themes.* Translated by W.J. Montague. SBT 41. London: SCM, 1964.
Kelley, Donald R. *Frontiers of History: Historical Inquiry in the Twentieth Century.* New Haven, CT: Yale University Press, 2006.
Kellner, Hans. "'Never Again' Is Now." *History and Theory* 33.2 (1994): 127–44.
Kloppenborg, John S. *Excavating Q: The History and Setting of the Sayings Gospel.* Edinburgh: T & T Clark, 2000.
Kloppenborg, John S., Marvin W. Meyer, Stephen J. Patterson, and Michael G. Steinhauser. *Q – Thomas Reader.* Sonoma, CA: Polebridge, 1990.
Kuhn, Thomas S. *The Structure of Scientific Revolutions.* 3rd ed. Chicago: University of Chicago Press, 1996.
Ladd, George E. "The Problem of History in Contemporary New Testament Interpretation." Pages 88–100 in *Studia Evangelica,* vol. 5. Edited by Frank L. Cross. TU 103. Berlin: Akademie Verlag, 1968.
Lindberg, David C., and Ronald L. Numbers, eds. *When Science and Christianity Meet.* Chicago: University of Chicago Press, 2003.
Lindholm, Lisbet, Anna-Lena Nieminen, Carita Mäkelä, and Sinikka Rantanen-Siljamäki. "Clinical Application Research: A Hermeneutical Approach to the Appropriation of Caring Science." *Qualitative Health Research* 16.1 (2006): 137–50.
Lonergan, Bernard. *Insight: A Study of Human Understanding.* Vol. 3 of *Collected Works of Bernard Lonergan.* 5th ed. Edited by Frederick E. Crowe and Robert M. Doran. Toronto: University of Toronto, 1992.
—. *Method in Theology.* 2nd ed. London: Darton, Longman & Todd, 1973.
López, José, and Garry Potter, eds. *After Postmodernism: An Introduction to Critical Realism.* London: Athlone, 2001.

Lüdemann, Gerd. *The Resurrection of Christ: A Historical Inquiry.* Amherst, NY: Prometheus Books, 2004.
–. *The Resurrection of Jesus: History, Experience, Theology.* Translated by John Bowden. Minneapolis: Fortress, 1994.
–. *What Really Happened to Jesus: A Historical Approach to the Resurrection.* Translated by John Bowden, in collaboration with Alf Özen. Louisville: Westminster John Knox, 1995.
McCullagh, C. Behan. *Justifying Historical Descriptions.* Cambridge: Cambridge University Press, 1984.
McDonald, Lee Martin, and Stanley E. Porter. *Early Christianity and Its Sacred Literature.* Peabody, MA: Hendrickson, 2000.
McIntire, C. T., ed. *God, History, and Historians: Modern Christian Views of History.* New York: Oxford University Press, 1977.
McKnight, Scot. *Jesus and His Death: Historiography, the Historical Jesus, and Atonement Theory.* Waco, TX: Baylor University Press, 2005.
Macquarrie, John. *Twentieth-Century Religious Thought.* 5th ed. Harrisburg, PA: Trinity Press International, 2002.
Marwick, Arthur. *The New Nature of History: Knowledge, Evidence, Language.* Chicago: Lyceum Books, 2001.
Mealand, David L. "The Dissimilarity Test." *SJT* 31 (1978): 41–50.
Meier, John P. *The Roots of the Problem and the Person.* Vol. 1 of *A Marginal Jew: Rethinking the Historical Jesus.* New York: Doubleday, 1991.
Meyer, Ben F. *The Aims of Jesus.* London: SCM, 1979.
–. *Critical Realism and the New Testament.* Allison Park, PA: Pickwick, 1989.
–. *Reality and Illusion on New Testament Scholarship: A Primer in Critical Realist Hermeneutics.* Collegeville, MN: Michael Glazier, 1994.
Miller, Robert J., ed. *The Apocalyptic Jesus: A Debate.* Sonoma, CA: Polebridge, 2001.
Minear, Paul S. *The Bible and the Historian: Breaking the Silence About God in Biblical Studies.* Nashville: Abingdon, 2002.
Naveh, J. "The Ossuary Inscriptions from Givàt Ha-Mivtar." *IEJ* 20 (1970): 33–37.
Neusner, Jacob, trans. *The Babylonian Talmud: A Translation and Commentary.* 22 vols. Peabody, MA: Hendrickson, 2005.
–, trans. *The Tosefta: Translated from the Hebrew with a New Introduction.* 2 vols. Peabody, MA: Hendrickson, 2002.
Nolland, John. *The Gospel of Matthew.* NIGTC. Grand Rapids: Eerdmans, 2005.
Novick, Peter. *That Noble Dream: The "Objectivity Question" and the American Historical Profession.* Cambridge: Cambridge University Press, 1998.
Numbers, Ronald L. "Science Without God: Natural Laws and Christian Beliefs." Pages 265–85 in *When Science and Christianity Meet.* Edited by David C. Lindberg and Ronald L. Numbers. Chicago: University of Chicago Press, 2003.
Osborne, Grant R. *The Hermeneutical Spiral: A Comprehensive Introduction to Biblical Interpretation.* 2nd ed. Downers Grove, IL: InterVarsity, 2006.
Pannenberg, Wolfhart. "Dogmatic Theses on the Doctrine of Revelation." Pages 123–58 in *Revelation as History.* Edited by Wolfhart Pannenberg. Translated by David Granskou. New York: Macmillan, 1968.
–. *Jesus: God and Man.* Translated by Lewis L. Wilkins and Duane A. Priebe. London: SCM, 1968.

Pennock, Robert T., ed. *Intelligent Design Creationism and Its Critics: Philosophical, Theological, and Scientific Perspectives*. Cambridge, MA: MIT Press, 2001.
Perrin, Norman. *The New Testament: An Introduction*. New York: Harcourt Brace Jovanovich, 1974.
–. *Rediscovering the Teaching of Jesus*. London: SCM, 1967.
–. *What Is Redaction Criticism?* GBS. Philadelphia: Fortress, 1969.
Polanyi, Michael. *Personal Knowledge: Towards a Post-Critical Philosophy*. Chicago: University of Chicago Press, 1958.
–. *The Tacit Dimension*. Gloucester, MA: Peter Smith, 1983.
Polkow, Dennis. "Method and Criteria for Historical Jesus Research." Pages 336–56 in *Society of Biblical Literature 1987 Seminar Papers*. Edited by Kent H. Richard. SBLSP 26. Atlanta: Scholars Press, 1987.
Porter, Stanley E. *The Criteria for Authenticity in Historical-Jesus Research: Previous Discussion and New Proposals*. JSNTSup 191. Sheffield: Sheffield Academic Press, 2000.
–. "Jesus and the Use of Greek in Galilee." Pages 123–54 in *Studying the Historical Jesus: Evaluations of the State of Current Research*. Edited by Bruce Chilton and Craig A. Evans. NTTS 19. Leiden: E.J. Brill, 1994.
Powell, Mark Allen. *Jesus as a Figure in History: How Modern Historians View the Man from Galilee*. Louisville, KY: Westminster/John Knox, 1998.
Price, Robert M., and Jeffery Jay Lowder, eds. *The Empty Tomb: Jesus Beyond the Grave*. Amherst, NY: Prometheus Books, 2005.
Ranke, Leopold von. *Geschichten der romanischen und germanischen Völker von 1494 bis 1535*. Leipzig: Reimer, 1824.
Ranke, Leopold von. *Fürsten und Völker: Geschichten der romanischen und germanischen Völker von 1494–1514; Die Osmanen und die spanische Monarchie im 16. und 17. Jahrhundert*. Edited by Willy Andreas. Wiesbaden: Emil Vollmer Verlag, 1957.
–. *The Theory and Practice of History*. Edited by Georg G. Iggers and Konrad von Moltke. Indianapolis: Bobbs-Merrill, 1973.
Roberts, Alexander, and James Donaldson, eds. *The Ante-Nicene Fathers: Translations of the Writings of the Fathers Down to A.D. 325*. 10 vols. Grand Rapids: Eerdmans, 1979.
Robinson, James M., ed. *The Nag Hammadi Library in English*. 3rd ed. San Francisco: Harper and Row, 1988.
Robinson, James M., Paul Hoffmann, and John S. Kloppenborg, eds. *The Critical Edition of Q*. Hermeneia. Minneapolis: Fortress, 2000.
Sanders, E.P. *The Historical Figure of Jesus*. New York: Penguin Books, 1995.
–. *Jesus and Judaism*. Philadelphia: Fortress, 1985.
Sanders, E.P., and Margaret Davies. *Studying the Synoptic Gospels*. Philadelphia: Trinity Press International, 1989.
Schürer, Emil. *The History of the Jewish People in the Age of Jesus Christ*. Edited by Geza Vermes, Fergus Millar, Matthew Black, and Martin Goodman. Edinburgh: T & T Clark, 1973–87.
Schweitzer, Albert. *The Quest of the Historical Jesus: First Complete Edition*. Translated by W. Montgomery, J.R. Coates, Susan Cupitt, and John Bowden. Minneapolis: Fortress, 2001.

Shermer, Michael, and Alex Grobman. *Denying History: Who Says the Holocaust Never Happened and Why Do They Say It?* Berkeley, CA: University of California Press, 2000.
Snodgrass, Anthony. "Archaeology." Pages 137–84 in *Sources for Ancient History.* Edited by Michael Crawford. Cambridge: Cambridge University Press, 1983.
Stein, Robert H. "The 'Criteria' for Authenticity." Pages 225–63 in *Studies of History and Tradition in the Four Gospels.* Edited by R. T. France and David Wenham. Gospel Perspectives 1. Sheffield: JSOT Press, 1980.
–. *Studying the Synoptic Gospels.* 2nd ed. Grand Rapids: Baker Academic, 2001.
Stoker, William D. *Extracanonical Sayings of Jesus.* SBLRBS 18. Atlanta: Scholars Press, 1989.
Theissen, Gerd. "Historical Scepticism and the Criteria of Jesus Research, or My Attempt to Leap Across Lessing's Yawning Gulf." *SJT* 49 (1996): 147–76.
Theissen, Gerd, and Annette Merz. *The Historical Jesus: A Comprehensive Guide.* Translated by John Bowden. Minneapolis: Fortress, 1998.
Theissen, Gerd, and Dagmar Winter. *The Quest for the Plausible Jesus: The Question of Criteria.* Translated by M. Eugene Boring. Louisville: Westminster John Knox, 2002.
Thiselton, Anthony C. *The Two Horizons: New Testament Hermeneutics and Philosophical Description.* Grand Rapids: Eerdmans, 1980.
Tosh, John, and Seán Lang. *The Pursuit of History: Aims, Methods and New Directions in the Study of Modern History.* 4th ed. London: Pearson Education, 2006.
Troeltsch, Ernst. "Historical and Dogmatic Method in Theology." Pages 11–32 in *Religion in History.* Translated by James Luther Adams and Walter F. Bense. Fortress Texts in Modern Theology. Minneapolis: Fortress, 1991.
Tucker, Aviezer. *Our Knowledge of the Past: A Philosophy of Historiography.* Cambridge: Cambridge University Press, 2004.
Tuckett, Christopher M. "Synoptic Problem." Pages 263–70 in vol. 6 of *Anchor Bible Dictionary.* Edited by David N. Freedman. New York: Doubleday, 1992.
Tyrrell, George. *Christianity at the Crossroads.* London: George Allen & Unwin, 1963.
Tzaferis, V. "Jewish Tombs at and Near Givàt Ha-Mivtar, Jerusalem." *IEJ* 20 (1970): 18–32.
Van Voorst, Robert E. *Jesus Outside the New Testament: An Introduction to the Ancient Evidence.* Grand Rapids: Eerdmans, 2000.
Weaver, Walter P. *The Historical Jesus in the Twentieth Century, 1900–1950.* Harrisburg, PA: Trinity Press International, 1999.
Webb, Robert L. *John the Baptizer and Prophet: A Socio-Historical Study.* JSNTSup 62. Eugene, OR: Wipf & Stock, 2006.
–. "Methodological Reflections on John the Baptizer's Influence on Jesus." In *Methodological Approaches to the Historical Jesus: The Second Princeton-Prague Symposium on Jesus Research, Princeton 2007.* Edited by James H. Charlesworth. Grand Rapids: Eerdmans, forthcoming.
White, Hayden. *The Content of the Form: Narrative Discourse and Historical Representation.* Baltimore: Johns Hopkins University Press, 1987.
–. *Figural Realism: Studies in the Mimesis Effect.* Baltimore: Johns Hopkins University Press, 1999.

–. "Historical Emplotment and the Problem of Truth." Pages 37–53 in *Probing the Limits of Representation: Nazism and the 'Final Solution'*. Edited by Saul Friedlander. Harvard: Harvard University Press, 1992.
–. *Metahistory: The Historical Imagination in Nineteenth-Century Europe*. Baltimore: Johns Hopkins University Press, 1973.
–. *Tropics of Discourse: Essays in Cultural Criticism*. Baltimore: Johns Hopkins University Press, 1978.
Wiesel, Elie. *Night*. Translated by Marion Wiesel. New York: Hill & Wang, 2006.
Wright, N. Thomas. *Jesus and the Victory of God*. Vol. 2 of *Christian Origins and the Question of God*. Minneapolis: Fortress, 1996.
–. *The New Testament and the People of God*. Vol. 1 of *Christian Origins and the Question of God*. Minneapolis: Fortress, 1992.
–. *The Resurrection of the Son of God*. Vol. 3 of *Christian Origins and the Question of God*. Minneapolis: Fortress, 2003.
Zias, J., and E. Sekeles. "The Crucified Man from Giv'at Ha-Mivtar – A Reappraisal." *IEJ* 35 (1985): 22–27.

Chapter 3

Jesus' Baptism by John: Its Historicity and Significance[1]

ROBERT L. WEBB

1. Introduction

Many scholars have made the assertion that Jesus was baptized by John,[2] and indeed some have stated that it is one of the surest facts we can know about Jesus. It is surprising, however, that few have fully set out and weighed the arguments surrounding the event.[3] The purpose of this essay is twofold: First, I set out the historical evidence that leads to a conclusion that Jesus' baptism by John is historical. Second, I explore the implications of this event for understanding the historical figure of Jesus.

2. The Historicity of Jesus' Baptism by John

Since the focus of this essay is the historicity of Jesus' being baptized and its significance, we cannot simply make the assertion of historicity; we must weigh the historical evidence and render a historical judgment.

The issue before us is made somewhat more complicated by the fact that in the texts reporting the incident there are actually two events being narrated: the baptism of John by Jesus, and the theophany of the Spirit's descent and the heavenly voice. The two are usually linked in the narratives. For example, Mark 1:9 narrates Jesus' baptism, and 1:10b–11 provides the theophany narrative. Mark 1:10a links these two as taking place one right after the other: "And just as he was coming up out of the water, he saw ..." For

---

[1] This essay is a revised and expanded version of that published as Robert L. Webb, "Jesus' Baptism: Its Historicity and Implications," *BBR* 10 (2000): 261–309.

[2] For example, E. P. Sanders, *Jesus and Judaism* (Philadelphia: Fortress, 1985), 11; John Dominic Crossan, *The Historical Jesus: The Life of a Mediterranean Jewish Peasant* (San Francisco: HarperSanFrancisco, 1991), 234.

[3] A notable exception is John P. Meier, *Mentor, Message, and Miracles* (vol. 2 of *A Marginal Jew: Rethinking the Historical Jesus*; ABRL; New York: Doubleday, 1994), 100–105.

the purposes of our discussion, I begin with an examination of the baptism itself and then turn later to an examination of the theophany, though at times, of course, the two must be addressed together.

2.1. An Examination of the Historicity of the Baptism

The evidence for Jesus' baptism is found in a number of accounts, both canonical and extracanonical. The question immediately arises whether or not any of these sources are independent of each other, and thus whether the criterion of multiple attestation would apply to this event.[4]

The baptism of Jesus is recorded in all three Synoptic Gospels (Mark 1:9–11 = Matt 3:13–17 = Luke 3:21–22):

Matthew 3:13–17	Mark 1:9–11	Luke 3:21–22
[13] Τότε παραγίνεται ὁ Ἰησοῦς ἀπὸ τῆς Γαλιλαίας ἐπὶ τὸν Ἰορδάνην πρὸς τὸν Ἰωάννην τοῦ βαπτισθῆναι ὑπ' αὐτοῦ.	[9a] Καὶ ἐγένετο ἐν ἐκείναις ταῖς ἡμέραις ἦλθεν Ἰησοῦς ἀπὸ Ναζαρὲτ τῆς Γαλιλαίας	[21a] Ἐγένετο δὲ ἐν τῷ βαπτισθῆναι ἅπαντα τὸν λαὸν
[14] ὁ δὲ Ἰωάννης διεκώλυεν αὐτὸν λέγων, Ἐγὼ χρείαν ἔχω ὑπὸ σοῦ βαπτισθῆναι, καὶ σὺ ἔρχῃ πρός με;		
[15] ἀποκριθεὶς δὲ ὁ Ἰησοῦς εἶπεν πρὸς αὐτόν, Ἄφες ἄρτι, οὕτως γὰρ πρέπον ἐστὶν ἡμῖν πληρῶσαι πᾶσαν δικαιοσύνην. τότε ἀφίησιν αὐτόν.		
[16a] βαπτισθεὶς δὲ ὁ Ἰησοῦς εὐθὺς ἀνέβη ἀπὸ τοῦ ὕδατος·	[9b–10a] καὶ ἐβαπτίσθη εἰς τὸν Ἰορδάνην ὑπὸ Ἰωάννου. καὶ εὐθὺς ἀναβαίνων ἐκ τοῦ ὕδατος	[21b] καὶ Ἰησοῦ βαπτισθέντος καὶ προσευχομένου
[16b] καὶ ἰδοὺ ἠνεῴχθησαν [αὐτῷ] οἱ οὐρανοί, καὶ εἶδεν [τὸ] πνεῦμα [τοῦ]	[10b] εἶδεν σχιζομένους τοὺς οὐρανοὺς καὶ τὸ πνεῦμα ὡς περιστερὰν καταβαῖνον εἰς αὐτόν·	[21c–22a] ἀνεῳχθῆναι τὸν οὐρανὸν καὶ καταβῆναι τὸ πνεῦμα τὸ ἅγιον σωματικῷ

---

[4] For a discussion of the criteria of authenticity, in this volume see ch. 2, § 4.1. In the present essay I assume a two-source hypothesis for the Synoptic Gospels. While aware of its problems and alternatives, I find the two-source hypothesis the most plausible, and it continues to find considerable scholarly support. See also in this volume ch. 1, § 4.1. For recent discussion, see Christopher M. Tuckett, *The Contemporary Revival of the Griesbach Hypothesis* (SNTSMS 44; Cambridge: Cambridge University Press, 1983); Robert H. Stein, *The Synoptic Problem: An Introduction* (Grand Rapids: Baker, 1987).

Matthew 3:13–17	Mark 1:9–11	Luke 3:21–22
θεοῦ καταβαῖνον ὡσεὶ περιστερὰν [καὶ] ἐρχόμενον ἐπ' αὐτόν·		εἴδει ὡς περιστερὰν ἐπ' αὐτόν,
17 καὶ ἰδοὺ φωνὴ ἐκ τῶν οὐρανῶν λέγουσα, Οὗτός ἐστιν ὁ υἱός μου ὁ ἀγαπητός, ἐν ᾧ εὐδόκησα.	11 καὶ φωνὴ ἐγένετο ἐκ τῶν οὐρανῶν, Σὺ εἶ ὁ υἱός μου ὁ ἀγαπητός, ἐν σοὶ εὐδόκησα.	22b καὶ φωνὴν ἐξ οὐρανοῦ γενέσθαι, Σὺ εἶ ὁ υἱός μου ὁ ἀγαπητός, ἐν σοὶ εὐδόκησα.
13 Then Jesus came from Galilee to John at the Jordan, to be baptized by him.	In those days Jesus came from Nazareth of Galilee	21a Now when all the people were baptized,
14 John would have prevented him, saying, "I need to be baptized by you, and do you come to me?"		
15 But Jesus answered him, "Let it be so now; for it is proper for us in this way to fulfill all righteousness." Then he consented.		
16a And when Jesus had been baptized, just as he came up from the water,	9b–10a and was baptized by John in the Jordan. And just as he was coming up out of the water,	21b and when Jesus also had been baptized and was praying,
16b suddenly the heavens were opened to him and he saw the Spirit of God descending like a dove and alighting on him.	10b he saw the heavens torn apart and the Spirit descending like a dove on him.	21c–22a the heaven was opened, and the Holy Spirit descended upon him in bodily form like a dove.
17 And a voice from heaven said, "This is my Son, the Beloved, with whom I am well pleased."	11 And a voice came from heaven, "You are my Son, the Beloved; with you I am well pleased."	22b And a voice came from heaven, "You are my Son, the Beloved; with you I am well pleased."

It is quite evident that Matthew and Luke have used Mark in constructing their accounts of Jesus' baptism. This is particularly clear in the theophany portion of the text. The question arises, however, of whether or not Q was also a source for Matthew and Luke. Several lines of evidence support a Q source for Jesus' baptism. First of all, at a few points Matthew and Luke agree with each other's texts against Mark. With respect to the baptism narrative, both Matthew and Luke make the following editorial changes to Mark's text: (1) both drop the reference to John and the Jordan (Matthew does use it earlier in 3:13); (2) both alter Mark's aorist indicative use of the verb βαπτίζω to an aorist participial form (Matthew uses the nominative, while Luke uses the genitive), and (3) both include the name Ἰησοῦς in the statement about Jesus being baptized, whereas Mark had the name earlier in v. 9. With respect to the theophany narrative, Matthew and Luke make several changes as well: (4) Both change Mark's use of the verb σχίζω ("to tear") to the verb ἀνοίγω ("to open"), but they use different forms of the verb: Matthew uses the aorist passive indicative form while Luke uses the aorist passive infinitive. (5) Both change Mark's prepositional phrase εἰς αὐτόν ("on him") to ἐπ' αὐτόν ("onto him"). (6) Both alter Mark's word order τὸ πνεῦμα ὡς περιστερὰν καταβαῖνον ("the Spirit like a dove descended") by shifting the verb καταβαίνω ("to descend") to precede the phrase ὡσ(εὶ) περιστεράν ("like a dove"). So, the Matthew-Luke agreements against Mark include omission of the same words, addition of the same words, alteration of grammatical forms, and alteration of word order. We should note, however, that in three of the six agreements observed above (1, 2, and 4), Matthew and Luke alter Mark's text at the same point, but how they alter the text is only similar, not identical. This renders the evidence not quite as compelling as it otherwise might have been.

A second line of evidence is the text of Q itself,[5] which suggests that the presence of a baptism/theophany pericope is needed from a narrative perspective.[6] The immediately prior pericopae in Q are John's preaching of repentance (Q 3:7–9) and his announcement of a coming figure (Q 3:16–17). The immediately succeeding pericope is Jesus' wilderness temptation (Q 4:1–13). In the temptation pericope, the devil twice inaugurates his temptation with the statement, "If you are the Son of God ..." (Q 4:3, 9). Asking if Jesus was the "Son of God" appears somewhat incongruous unless it is a reference back to the voice in the theophany that stated, "You are my Son ..." If there was no baptism/theophany pericope in Q, then the twin references, "if you are the Son of God ..." appear out of thin air with no antecedent. So, from a narrative perspective, it makes better sense that the devil calls into question the theophanic declaration than that there is a repeated question without a reference. Another narrative piece of evidence is that, without

---

[5] I use the convention of the SBL Q Seminar in citing Q texts by their Lukan reference; e.g., Q 3:16 = Matt 3:11 = Luke 3:16.

[6] The Q source is frequently identified as a "Sayings Gospel," but this is, strictly speaking, not true, at least in an exclusive sense. Several pericopae that are widely recognized as part of Q are narrative material. In addition to Jesus' baptism, three of the more prominent ones are Q 7:1–10 (healing the Centurion's servant); Q 7:18–23 (John's inquiry of Jesus); Q 11:14–23 (the Beelzebul accusation).

the baptism of Jesus, the prior pericopae concerning John the Baptist lack a clear link to the ministry of Jesus. Why begin with John (Q 3:7–9; 3:16–17) if there is no link between John and Jesus at this point in the text?

The above evidence does not lead to certainty, but the weight of the evidence leads me to a conclusion of probability: the text of Q most likely contained an account of Jesus' baptism and the theophany.[7] While this conclusion allows one to claim that an account of the baptism of Jesus probably has at least two independent sources, the fragmentary nature of the evidence precludes a reconstruction of the Q text apart from perhaps a few words.

The Fourth Gospel does not provide an account of the event itself, but it does acknowledge that Jesus' baptism occurred by placing it on the lips of John the Baptist, who is a witness testifying to the event:

John 1:29–34 (Greek)	John 1:29–34 (English)
[29] Τῇ ἐπαύριον βλέπει τὸν Ἰησοῦν ἐρχόμενον πρὸς αὐτόν καὶ λέγει, Ἴδε ὁ ἀμνὸς τοῦ θεοῦ ὁ αἴρων τὴν ἁμαρτίαν τοῦ κόσμου.	[29] The next day he saw Jesus coming toward him and declared, "Here is the Lamb of God who takes away the sin of the world!
[30] οὗτός ἐστιν ὑπὲρ οὗ ἐγὼ εἶπον, Ὀπίσω μου ἔρχεται ἀνὴρ ὃς ἔμπροσθέν μου γέγονεν, ὅτι πρῶτός μου ἦν.	[30] This is he of whom I said, 'After me comes a man who ranks ahead of me because he was before me.'
[31] κἀγὼ οὐκ ᾔδειν αὐτόν, ἀλλ᾽ ἵνα φανερωθῇ τῷ Ἰσραὴλ διὰ τοῦτο ἦλθον ἐγὼ ἐν ὕδατι βαπτίζων.	[31] I myself did not know him; but I came baptizing with water for this reason, that he might be revealed to Israel."
[32] Καὶ ἐμαρτύρησεν Ἰωάννης λέγων ὅτι Τεθέαμαι τὸ πνεῦμα καταβαῖνον ὡς περιστερὰν ἐξ οὐρανοῦ καὶ ἔμεινεν ἐπ᾽ αὐτόν.	[32] And John testified, "I saw the Spirit descending from heaven like a dove, and it remained on him.

---

[7] Scholars of Q differ on this question. For bibliographic references supporting and rejecting this position, see John S. Kloppenborg, *Q Parallels: Synopsis, Critical Notes, and Concordance* (FF; Sonoma, Calif.: Polebridge, 1988), 16, and his more recent discussion in John S. Kloppenborg, *Excavating Q: The History and Setting of the Sayings Gospel* (Edinburgh: T&T Clark, 2000), 93. The International Q Project includes Q 3:21–22 within Q but gives it a probability rating of {C} (as indicated by the verse numbers in double square brackets), for which see James M. Robinson, et al., *The Critical Edition of Q* (Hermeneia; Minneapolis: Fortress, 2000), 18–21. In support of the IQP's position, see James M. Robinson, "The Sayings Gospel Q," in *The Four Gospels 1992: Festschrift Frans Neirynck* (3 vols.; ed. F. Van Segbroeck, et al.; BETL 100; Leuven: Leuven University Press, 1992), 1:361–88, esp. 383–86. See also Meier, *Mentor, Message, and Miracles*, 103. On the other hand, John S. Kloppenborg (*The Formation of Q: Trajectories in Ancient Wisdom Collections* [SAC; Philadelphia: Fortress, 1987], 84–85) does not include the baptismal account in his reconstruction of Q; see also Kloppenborg, *Excavating Q*, 93; Harry T. Fleddermann, *Q: A Reconstruction and Commentary* (Biblical Tools and Studies 1; Leuven: Peeters, 2005), 233–35.

John 1:29-34 (Greek)	John 1:29-34 (English)
³³ κἀγὼ οὐκ ᾔδειν αὐτόν, ἀλλ' ὁ πέμψας με βαπτίζειν ἐν ὕδατι ἐκεῖνός μοι εἶπεν, 'Εφ' ὃν ἂν ἴδῃς τὸ πνεῦμα καταβαῖνον καὶ μένον ἐπ' αὐτόν, οὗτός ἐστιν ὁ βαπτίζων ἐν πνεύματι ἁγίῳ.	³³ I myself did not know him, but the one who sent me to baptize with water said to me, 'He on whom you see the Spirit descend and remain is the one who baptizes with the Holy Spirit.'
³⁴ κἀγὼ ἑώρακα, καὶ μεμαρτύρηκα ὅτι οὗτός ἐστιν ὁ υἱὸς τοῦ θεοῦ.	³⁴ And I myself have seen and have testified that this is the Son of God."

What may be observed in the Evangelist's account is that the baptism is assumed to have occurred (v. 31), and John bears witness to the Spirit's descending like a dove. Interestingly, John does not recount the theophanic voice but, rather, recounts his own divine revelation (v. 33). Instead of the divine voice acknowledging Jesus as "my beloved Son," it is John himself who bears "witness that this is the Son of God" (v. 34b).

It is generally acknowledged that the Fourth Gospel is independent of the Synoptic Gospels.[8] The account of John's witnessing to Jesus based upon his baptism reveals little verbal agreement apart from the phrase τὸ πνεῦμα καταβαῖνον ὡς περιστεράν ("the Spirit descending like a dove," v. 32). It would be difficult to narrate the event without such a stock phrase. Its use here suggests knowledge of the event rather than use of the Synoptic Gospels as a source. This reference to Jesus' baptism in the Fourth Gospel is, therefore, an independent witness to the event.

There are also a few extracanonical references to Jesus' baptism, all of which are in the three fragmentary Gospels known as the Jewish-Christian Gospels.[9] The *Gospel according to the Hebrews* is quoted by Jerome in his

---

[8] For a helpful survey of the debate, see George R. Beasley-Murray, *John* (WBC 36; Waco, Tex.: Word, 1987), xxxv–xxxvii. While most scholars do conclude that the Fourth Gospel is independent of the Synoptics, two scholars who hold to a minority view on the subject are C. K. Barrett and Frans Neirynck.

[9] Of these Jewish-Christian Gospels, the *Gospel according to the Hebrews* is probably the earliest, given it appears to be independent of the canonical Gospels. It is, thus, quite difficult to date, but it is probably first century. The *Gospel according to the Ebionites* and the *Gospel according to the Nazareans*, on the other hand, are most likely dependent upon the Synoptic Gospels and the Gospel of Matthew respectively. These two Gospels are, therefore, later, probably being dated to the first half of the second century. For a discussion of dating and various introductory matters concerning these Gospels, see Wilhelm Schneemelcher and R. McL. Wilson, eds., *New Testament Apocrypha* (rev. ed.; 2 vols.; Louisville: Westminster John Knox, 1990–91), as well as other literature on these Gospels cited in the footnotes below. There are also other extracanonical references to John the Baptist, but they do not refer to Jesus' baptism. These include: Josephus, *Ant.* 18.116–119; *Prot. Jas.* 8:3; 10:2; 12:2–3; 22:3; 23:1–24:4; *PCairo* 2; *Gos. Eb.* 2–3; *Gos. Thom.* 46, 47, 78, 104; cf. *Gos. Thom.* 11, 27, 51. Later traditions concerning John the Baptist may also be found in Gnostic literature, Mandaean literature, and the Slavonic Josephus. See the discussion in Robert L. Webb, *John the Baptizer and Prophet: A Socio-Historical Study* (JSNTSup 62; Sheffield: JSOT Press, 1991), 43–45, 77–78 n. 93.

commentary on Isaiah (on Isa 11:2, *Comm. Isa.* 11:1–3). The fragment containing the reference to Jesus' baptism is cited as *Gos. Heb.* 2:[10]

Gos. Heb. 2 (Latin)	*Gos. Heb.* 2 (English)
... *sed iuxta euangelium quod Hebraeo sermone conscriptum legunt Nazaraei: Descendet super eum omnis fons Spiritus Sancti. Dominus autem spiritus est, et ubi spiritus Domini, ubi libertas ...*	... but according to the Gospel which was written in the Hebrew language and read by the Nazoraeans: The whole fountain of the Holy Spirit came upon him. The Lord is the Spirit and where the Spirit of the Lord is, there is freedom ...
Porro in euangelio cuius supra fecimus mentionem, haec scripta reperimus: Factum est autem cum ascendisset Dominus de aqua, descendit fons omnis Spiritus Sancti, et requieuit super eum, et dixit illi: fili mi, in omnibus prophetis expectabam te, ut uenires, et requiescerem in te. Tu enim es requies mea, tu es filius meus primogenitus, qui regnas in sempiternum.	Further in the Gospel which we mentioned above we find that the following is written: It happened then when the Lord ascended from the water, that the whole fountain of the Holy Spirit descended and rested upon him and said to him: "My son, I expected you among all the prophets that you should come and that I should rest upon you. For you are my rest, you are my first-born son, who shall reign in eternity."

Gos. Heb. 2 alludes to the event of Jesus' baptism with the clause "when the Lord ascended from the water ..." But the emphasis is on the theophany. No mention is made of John the Baptist in the extant text. The theophany consists of the descent of the Spirit without mention of a dove. The voice that speaks in the theophany is the Spirit. There are a few phrases that are similar to the Synoptic accounts: (1) "*Factum est autem cum ascendisset Dominus de aqua*" ("when the Lord ascended from the water"); (2) "*descendit fons omnis Spiritus Sancti*" ("the whole fountain of the Holy Spirit descended"); (3) "*fili mi*" ("my son"). While these phrases are similar, they also manifest differences. The first identifies Jesus as "the Lord." The second adds to the identification of the Spirit the descriptors "the whole fountain" and "Holy." The third is simply a direct address rather than a statement of identity, as it is in the Synoptic Gospels. When *Gos. Heb.* 2 does make a statement of identity, it is considerably expanded beyond that contained in the Synoptic Gospels: "*Tu enim es requies mea, tu es filius meus primogenitus, qui regnas in sempiternum*" ("For you are my rest, you are my first-born son, who shall reign in eternity").

---

[10] This text and translation are cited from A. F. J. Klijn, *Jewish-Christian Gospel Tradition* (VCSup 17; Leiden: Brill, 1992), 98. I have added quotation marks.

While there are similarities between this account in *Gos. Heb.* 2 and the canonical Gospels, they may be explained as stock phrases required to tell the same event. When this observation is combined with the considerable differences between *Gos. Heb.* 2 and the canonical Gospels, we may conclude that there does not appear to be direct dependence upon the canonical Gospels.[11]

Another extracanonical source for Jesus' baptism is the *Gospel according to the Ebionites* which is quoted by Epiphanius (*Panarion* 30.13.7–9). The section relevant to Jesus' baptism is cited as *Gos. Eb.* 4:[12]

Gos. Eb. 4 (Greek)	*Gos. Eb.* 4 (English)
[1] Καὶ μετὰ τὸ εἰπεῖν πολλὰ ἐπιφέρει ὅτι τοῦ λαοῦ βαπτισθέντος ἦλθεν καὶ Ἰησοῦς καὶ ἐβαπτίσθη ὑπὸ τοῦ Ἰωάννου.	[1] And after much is said in the Gospel it continues: After the people had been baptized Jesus also came and was baptized by John.
[2] Καὶ ὡς ἀνῆλθεν ἀπὸ τοῦ ὕδατος, ἠνοίγησαν οἱ οὐρανοὶ καὶ εἶδεν τὸ πνεῦμα τὸ ἅγιον ἐν εἴδει περιστερᾶς, κατελθούσης καὶ εἰσελθούσης εἰς αὐτόν.	[2] And when he ascended from the water the heavens opened and he saw the Holy Spirit in the form of a dove descending and coming to him.
[3] Καὶ φωνὴ ἐκ τοῦ οὐρανοῦ λέγουσα· σύ μου εἶ ὁ υἱὸς ὁ ἀγαπητός, ἐν σοὶ ηὐδόκησα, καὶ πάλιν· ἐγὼ σήμερον γεγέννηκά σε.	[3] And a voice from heaven said: "You are my beloved Son, in you I am well pleased," and next: "This day I have generated you."
[4] Καὶ εὐθὺς περιέλαμψε τὸν τόπον φῶς μέγα. Ὁ ἰδών, φησίν, ὁ Ἰωάννης λέγει αὐτῷ· σὺ τίς εἶ, κύριε (*om.* MS. M);	[4] And suddenly a great light shone about that place. When John saw it, they say, he said to him: "Who are you Lord?"
[5] Καὶ πάλιν φωνὴ ἐξ οὐρανοῦ πρὸς αὐτόν· Οὗτός ἐστιν ὁ υἱός μου ὁ ἀγαπητός, ἐφ' ὃν ηὐδόκησα.	[5] And again a voice came from heaven which said to him: "This is my beloved Son, in whom I am well pleased."
[6] Καὶ τότε, φησίν, ὁ Ἰωάννης προσπεσὼν αὐτῷ ἔλεγεν· Δέομαί σου, κύριε σύ με βάπτισον. Ὁ δὲ ἐκώλυσεν αὐτὸν λέγων· Ἄφες, ὅτι οὕτως ἐστὶ πρέπον πληρωθῆναι πάντα.	[6] After this, it says, John fell down before him and said: "I implore you, Lord, you baptize me." But he refused him and said: "Let it be, since it is necessary that everything will be fulfilled."

---

[11] The independent witness of the *Gospel according to the Hebrews* is maintained by Klijn, *Jewish-Christian Gospel Tradition*, 36–37; Philipp Vielhauer and Georg Strecker, "Jewish-Christian Gospels," in *New Testament Apocrypha* (rev. ed.; 2 vols.; ed. Wilhelm Schneemelcher and R. McL. Wilson; Louisville: Westminster John Knox, 1990–91), 1:172; Ron Cameron, ed., *The Other Gospels: Non-Canonical Gospel Texts* (Philadelphia: Westminster, 1982), 84.

[12] This text and translation are cited from Klijn, *Jewish-Christian Gospel Tradition*, 70. In the translation, I have replaced archaic language with modern equivalents and added quotation marks. I have also added verse numbers to make references easier in the discussion below.

The account of Jesus' baptism in Gos. Eb. 4 is quite similar to those in the Synoptic Gospels. Much of the wording is similar and appears to be dependent upon the Synoptic Gospels, particularly Matthew and Luke. For example, 4:1 appears quite similar to Luke 3:21, which describes the people being baptized and then Jesus is baptized. Furthermore, 4:6 is quite similar to Matt 3:14–15 in recounting John's asking to be baptized by Jesus, but his response is to deny the request with the explanation that it is a fulfillment. What is also of note in *Gos. Eb.* 4 is the repetition of the theophanic voice, once in the second person addressed to Jesus (4:3), and the second time in the third person addressed to John (4:5). This repetition appears to be a conflation of Luke's second-person address by the theophanic voice ("You are … ," 3:22) and Matthew's third person address ("This is … ," 3:17).

These extensive similarities between *Gos. Eb.* 4 and the Synoptic Gospels, and distinctive elements in Matthew and Luke incorporated therein indicate that it is probably dependent upon at least these two Gospels. Therefore, the *Gospel according to the Ebionites* cannot be counted as an independent witness to Jesus' baptism.[13]

A third extracanonical reference that is of interest is recorded in the *Gospel according to the Nazareans*.[14] The relevant fragment is quoted by Jerome in *Pelag.* 3.2. This section is cited as *Gos. Naz.* 2:

Gos. Naz. 2 (Latin)	Gos. Naz. 2 (English)
In Evangelio juxta Hebraeos, quod Chaldaico quidem Syroque sermone sed Habraicis litteris scriptum est, quo utuntur usque hodie Nazareni, secundum Apostolos, sive ut plerique autumnant, juxta Matthaeum, quod et in Caesariensi habetur bibliotheca, narrat historia:	In the Gospel according to the Hebrews which was written in the Chaldaic and Syriac language but with Hebrew letters, and is used up to the present day by the Nazoraeans, I mean that according to the Apostles, or, as many maintain, according to Matthew, which Gospel is also available in the Library of Caesarea, the story runs:
Ecce, mater Domini et fratres ejus dicebant ei: Joannes Baptisma baptizat in remissionem peccatorum: eamus et baptizemur ab eo. Dixit autem eis: Quid peccavi, ut vadem et baptizer ab eo? Nisi forte hoc ipsum quod dixi, ignorantia est.	See, the mother of the Lord and his brothers said to him: "John the Baptist baptizes for the remission of sins, let us go to be baptized by him." He said to them, however: "What sin have I committed that I should go and be baptized by him? Unless perhaps something which I said in ignorance."

---

[13] The dependence of the *Gospel according the the Ebionites* upon the canonical Gospels is held by Klijn, *Jewish-Christian Gospel Tradition*, 38; Vielhauer and Strecker, "Jewish-Christian Gospels," 1:167–68; Cameron, *The Other Gospels*, 103.

[14] An alternative spelling for the name of this Gospel is *Nazoreans*. This text and translation are cited from Klijn, *Jewish-Christian Gospel Tradition*, 102–103. In the translation I have added quotation marks.

In Gos. Naz. 2 Jesus is invited by his mother and brother to join them in being baptized by John. But Jesus refuses because John's baptism is for the forgiveness of sins, and Jesus claims to have committed no sin. A text that denies the event of Jesus' baptism certainly cannot be used as a witness to the event. But it must be included here for two reasons: (1) it is an opposing witness, and (2) it is a valuable witness to the developing Christian response to Jesus' baptism by John. We should also note that scholars differ over whether or not the *Gospel according to the Nazareans* is dependent upon Matthew's Gospel.[15]

From the above examination of the early texts that refer to Jesus' baptism, we may conclude that the criterion of multiple attestation supports the authenticity of this tradition. Three and probably four independent witnesses may be identified: Q 3:21–22 (probable); Mark 1:9–11; John 1:29–34; *Gos. Heb.* 2 (I will count this as four independent witnesses from this point on).[16] A difficulty arises that we should note at this point. While we have several independent witnesses, not all the witnesses give us an account of the event of Jesus' baptism. While Q is probably an independent witness to the fact that Jesus was baptized, no account can be reconstructed. Similarly, the Johannine account does not describe the event itself but, rather, it assumes it. The account in *Gos. Heb.* 2 alludes to the baptism but focuses on the theophany. Thus, while we have four independent witnesses to the *fact* of Jesus being baptized, we really have only one extant *description* of the event, namely Mark 1:9–11.[17]

A second criterion that supports the authenticity of Jesus' baptism by John is the criterion of embarrassment. This criterion holds that material that had the potential to embarrass or cause difficulty for the early church is probably authentic. This is based on the premise that it is unlikely the early church would have created material that would be embarrassing to its claims concerning Jesus.[18]

---

[15] Vielhauer and Strecker ("Jewish-Christian Gospels," 1:154) and Cameron (*The Other Gospels*, 97) conclude that the *Gospel according to the Nazareans* is a secondary expansion of Matthew, whereas Klijn (*Jewish-Christian Gospel Tradition*, 37) concludes that "this Gospel originated in an environment in which traditions used by the Gospel of Matthew were known but that such traditions had a different development."

[16] Crossan's discussion (*The Historical Jesus*, 234) adds Ignatius as another independent witness; see Ign. *Smyrn.* 1:1; Ign. *Eph.* 18:2.

[17] A second issue could also be raised at this point: Is literary independence the same as historical independence? Just because these four sources are independent at a literary level, they are not *necessarily* part of a totally independent historical tradition, for they could still be expressions of the same pre-synoptic stream of tradition. However, since we are limited to the one extant description of the event, this is an issue that can be set aside at this point.

[18] See the discussion of this criterion in this volume in ch. 2, § 4.1; cf. John P. Meier, *The Roots of the Problem and the Person* (vol. 1 of *A Marginal Jew: Rethinking the Historical Jesus*; ABRL; New York: Doubleday, 1991), 168–71.

Mark's account states without equivocation that Jesus was baptized by John (1:9). Two problems are created by such an account: (1) Why does Jesus place himself in the subordinate position to John implied by submitting to his baptism? (2) Why does Jesus submit to a baptism that is "a baptism of repentance for the forgiveness of sins" (Mark 1:4)? Mark's balancing of the baptismal scene (1:9–10a) with the theophany (1:10b–11) is perhaps the only way in which he mitigates the impact of these two problems.

But these two problems are quite clearly issues in the early church, for the developing tradition concerning Jesus and John attempts to deal with the embarrassment caused by them. Luke's account (3:21–22) downplays these two issues by narrating John's arrest (3:19–20) prior to the account of Jesus' baptism. Placing the events in this order has the effect of providing narrative distance between John and Jesus.[19] Furthermore, Luke's account refers to the baptism only in passing, using it to help set the scene for the theophany.[20]

Matthew addresses the problems in quite a different manner. His account adds a verbal exchange between John and Jesus. John evidently recognizes Jesus for who he is,[21] and so he expresses his need to be baptized by Jesus. But Jesus declares that he must be baptized by John "to fulfill all righteousness."[22] Thus Matthew both subordinates John to Jesus and at the same time removes the stigma of a baptism for forgiveness by having the act "fulfill all righteousness."

The Fourth Gospel mitigates these issues in yet another way. It does not narrate the baptism at all. Rather, it only alludes to the baptism in the course of explaining that the purpose of John's baptizing ministry was to identify the Son of God for John the Baptist, in order "that he might be revealed to Israel" (1:32). The basis for John's witness to Jesus is the theophany (descent of the Spirit), and the content of John's witness is what in other texts is the content of the theophanic voice: "I myself did not know

---

[19] While creating some narrative distance, Luke does so to downplay Jesus' baptism by John, not to deny altogether that Jesus was baptized by him. To claim the latter makes too much of Luke's narrative technique here.

[20] The main clause is Ἐγένετο ... ἀνεῳχθῆναι τὸν οὐρανὸν καὶ καταβῆναι τὸ πνεῦμα τὸ ἅγιον. The intervening ἐν τῷ + infinitive phrase and a genitive absolute set the time reference for the theophany. This could be translated literally as "It happened that, when all the people had been baptized, and Jesus had been baptized and was praying, that the heaven opened and the Holy Spirit came down ..."

[21] How John recognizes Jesus in this manner is not explained and is somewhat problematic. In Matthew's Gospel the voice from heaven is not addressed to Jesus (not "you are my Son ...") but to someone else (rather "This is my Son ..."), evidently John and/or the crowds. But the exchange between John and Jesus takes place prior to the declaration of the voice from heaven. So how John has the knowledge to make his request of Jesus is unknown.

[22] Cf. the combination of Luke's and Matthew's emphases in *Gos. Eb.* 4.

him, but the one who sent me to baptize with water said to me, 'He on whom you see the Spirit descend and remain is the one who baptizes with the Holy Spirit.' And I myself have seen and testified that this is the Son of God" (1:33–34).

In *Gos. Heb.* 2 the baptism is not explicitly stated but only implied: "It happened then when the Lord ascended from the water ..." We are not told why he was ascending from the water. The rest of the text expands the theophanic voice, which not only emphasizes Jesus' divine sonship but also states that he came in fulfillment of prophecy.

The text of *Gos. Eb.* 4 does state that "Jesus ... came and was baptized by John" (4:1). But the rest of the text (4:2–6) expands upon the theophany by having the voice speak twice, the first time in the second person (following Mark and Luke) and the second in the third person (following Matthew). Based upon this twofold revelation, John seeks to be baptized by Jesus (also following Matthew). Subservience is emphasized by *Gos. Eb.* 4:6 with the descriptive addition not found in Matthew: "John fell down before him and said, 'I implore you ...'"

Finally, *Gos. Naz.* 2 addresses the problems caused by the baptismal story in yet a different way. It explicitly denies that Jesus was baptized, because he had no need for the forgiveness of sins: "See, the mother of the Lord and his brothers said to him: 'John the Baptist baptizes for the remission of sins, let us go to be baptized by him.' He said to them, however: 'What sin have I committed that I should go and be baptized by him? Unless perhaps something which I said in ignorance.'"

It is quite evident from Mark 1:9–11 through *Gos. Naz.* 2 that there is a developing trajectory in which the baptism by John is downplayed (and then ultimately denied), and the theophany is emphasized. This trajectory reveals the early church's increasing discomfort with Jesus' baptism by John. It is quite unlikely that Jesus' baptism by John was a creation by the early church. Applying the criterion of embarrassment, therefore, Jesus' baptism by John is historically probable.

The two criteria of multiple attestation and embarrassment support the conclusion with a high level of probability that Jesus was baptized by John. This conclusion is widely supported among scholarly circles.[23] But

---

[23] To cite a few particularly influential perspectives: Sanders (*Jesus and Judaism*, 11) lists Jesus' baptism by John as one of the "almost indisputable facts" about the life of Jesus. Crossan (*The Historical Jesus*, 11) concludes that "Jesus' baptism by John is one of the surest things we know about them both." The Jesus Seminar (Robert W. Funk and The Jesus Seminar, *The Acts of Jesus: The Search for the Authentic Deeds of Jesus* [San Francisco: HarperSanFrancisco, 1998], 54) considered the description on Mark 1:9 of Jesus' baptism by John to be worthy of a red vote (77 % red; 18 % pink; 5 % grey; 0 % black; average .91). Cf. W. B. Tatum, *John the Baptist and Jesus: A Report of the Jesus Seminar* (Sonoma, CA: Polebridge, 1994), 148; Meier, *Mentor, Message, and Miracles*, 100–105.

a minority position has been expressed that, while John and Jesus both existed, their paths never crossed – a position most clearly argued by Morton Enslin.[24] He argues that John never baptized Jesus and provides three reasons for this view: (1) The Gospel accounts increasingly reduce "John from an independent prophet ... into a conscious forerunner of Jesus ..."[25] (2) Josephus' description of John the Baptist is different from the Gospels in the reason provided for John's execution, and it lacks any reference to John's announcement of a coming figure (which is the emphasis in the Gospels).[26] (3) John's disciples continued as a viable movement after John had supposedly dramatically identified Jesus as the coming figure.[27]

These three reasons, however, are not adequate to support the claim that Enslin is making. With respect to his first reason, it is evident that the Gospels' interpretation of John as Jesus' forerunner is from a Christian perspective. But, as noted above, the Gospels' presentation of Jesus' baptism by John is also characterized by discomfort that it happened at all. In this instance then, the various Christian attempts to interpret John as Jesus' forerunner is evidence of a historical relationship that needs to be interpreted rather than evidence of a Christian creation. In this light, Enslin's observation supports the historicity of the baptism rather than the reverse.

Enslin's second reason (Josephus' account) has two problems. It is true that Josephus' reason for John's execution by Herod Antipas is different from the Gospels, but his reason does not contradict the Gospels; rather, it complements them. The Gospels view John's arrest and execution from a religious perspective, while Josephus' explanation is socio-political. With the inextricable link in Second Temple Judaism between the religious and the socio-political dimensions of life, the explanations by the Gospels and Josephus are but two sides of a coin.[28] The second element of Enslin's reason is an argument from Josephus' silence about John's proclamation of a coming figure. Not only is an argument from silence questionable, in this instance it fails to appreciate Josephus' own editorial biases, particularly his anti-eschatological and anti-messianic orientation.[29] Since it serves

---

[24] Morton S. Enslin, "John and Jesus," *ZNW* 66 (1975): 1–18. Cf. also Ernst Haenchen, *Der Weg Jesu: Eine Erklärung des Markus-Evangeliums und der kanonischen Parallelen* (2nd ed.; Berlin: De Gruyter, 1968), 58–63; F. Gerald Downing, *Jesus and the Threat of Freedom* (London: SCM, 1987), 154.
[25] Enslin, "John and Jesus," 2–4; quote is from p. 2.
[26] Enslin, "John and Jesus," 5–6.
[27] Enslin, "John and Jesus," 6–7.
[28] For further development, see Webb, *John the Baptizer*, 373–77; Joan E. Taylor, *The Immerser: John the Baptist Within Second Temple Judaism* (Studying the Historical Jesus; Grand Rapids: Eerdmans, 1997), 213–59.
[29] This orientation may be seen, for example, in Josephus' extremely negative portrayal of the various prophetic movements in the Second Temple period, whose eschatological features he scorned (e.g., *J. W.* 2.259; *Ant.* 20.168). Cf. Richard A. Horsley, "Popular

Josephus' purposes to portray John the Baptist positively, he can hardly attribute to John an orientation that Josephus himself strenuously opposed.

Enslin's third argument raises an interesting point, but it is only valid if its premise is true – that John dramatically identified Jesus as the coming figure. This premise is questionable, however, on at least two counts. John's question from prison (Matt 11:2–6 = Luke 7:18–23), which probably has a historical core,[30] portrays John as a disillusioned skeptic, or at best, a hesitant inquirer – hardly one who dramatically announces Jesus' true identity! Second, the identification of Jesus as John's announced figure is more likely due to early Christian theological reflection (e.g., Matt 3:14–15; John 1:29–34).

Enslin's reasons for arguing that John did not baptize Jesus do not hold up under critical reflection. The preliminary conclusion reached above must therefore stand. As a historical event, Jesus' baptism by John is highly probable, to the point of being virtually certain.

We must turn now to the second of the two elements contained in these texts reporting Jesus' baptism by John: the theophany narrative.

2.2. An Examination of the Historicity of the Theophany

The theophany narrative has two components: the descent of the Spirit in the form of a dove and the voice from heaven announcing Jesus "my Son, the Beloved."

The discussion above concerning multiple attestation of the baptismal accounts would also apply to the theophany accounts. The existence of four independent witnesses would support the historicity of the theophany.[31]

Messianic Movements Around the Time of Jesus," *CBQ* 46 (1984): 471–95; Richard A. Horsley and John S. Hanson, *Bandits, Prophets, and Messiahs: Popular Movements in the Time of Jesus* (New Voices in Biblical Studies; Minneapolis: Winston, 1985), 88–134, 160–89; Webb, *John the Baptizer*, 310–12, 333–48.

[30] So Werner G. Kümmel, *Promise and Fulfillment: The Eschatological Message of Jesus* (trans. Dorothea M. Barton; London: SCM, 1958), 110–11; Martin Dibelius, *Die urchristliche Überlieferung von Johannes dem Täufer* (FRLANT 15; Göttingen: Vandenhoeck & Ruprecht, 1911), 33–39; James D. G. Dunn, *Jesus and the Spirit: A Study of the Religious and Charismatic Experience of Jesus and the First Christians as Reflected in the New Testament* (NTL; London: SCM, 1975), 55–60; Joseph A. Fitzmyer, *The Gospel According to Luke I–IX* (AB 28; Garden City: Doubleday, 1981), 662–64; against Maurice Goguel, *Au seuil de l'Évangile: Jean-Baptiste* (Bibliotheque historique; Paris: Payot, 1928), 60–63; Carl H. Kraeling, *John the Baptist* (New York: Scribner, 1951), 130–31; Walter Wink, "Jesus' Reply to John: Matt 11:2–6 // Luke 7:18–23," *Forum* 5 (1989): 121–28. Cf. the discussion in Webb, *John the Baptizer*, 278–82.

[31] It is interesting that Crossan, for whom multiple attestation is a paramount criterion, rejects the theophany out of hand as "theological damage control" (*The Historical Jesus*, 232) and yet maintains that "Jesus' baptism by John is one of the surest things we know about them both" (*The Historical Jesus*, 234).

However, a number of problems arise concerning the historicity of the theophany. First of all, to portray Jesus as endowed with the Spirit and identified as God's Son fits very well with early Christian theological reflection concerning Jesus.[32] Applying the criterion of dissimilarity calls the historicity of the theophany into question.

Second, it also serves the early Christians well from an apologetic perspective to address the problems of Jesus' baptism by John. We saw above that the developing tradition increasingly emphasized the theophany and downplayed the baptism. Even in Mark, where the two items are given more equal weight, the very presence of the theophany immediately succeeding the baptismal account helps to mitigate the difficulties with the baptism. Crossan calls this "theological damage control."[33]

Third, the manner in which the theophany is narrated appears to be a midrash of a number of Hebrew Bible texts, gathered here to provide an initial interpretation of the person of Jesus. For example, the theophanic voice is a combination of Ps 2:7 and Isa 42:1. These texts interpret Jesus as God's son, who is the expected Davidic messiah and the Spirit-anointed servant of Yahweh.[34]

These three points show that the theophany is subject to weighty problems when examined from an historical perspective. However, other observations may be made that mitigate these problems somewhat. The first mitigating factor is that the two components of the theophany encapsulate two key elements of historical Jesus tradition from later in his ministry. First, Jesus attributed his power in ministry to a special endowment of the Spirit, and the presence of the Spirit was evidence that the kingdom was present (e.g., Matt 12:27–28 = Luke 11:19–20; Matt 12:31–32 = Mark 3:28–29 = Luke 12:10; cf. Luke 4:16–21). Second, Jesus speaks of a special relationship with God as his father (e.g., Matt 26:39 = Mark 14:36 = Luke 22:42; Matt 11:25–26 = Luke 10:21; cf. Matt 11:25–27 = Luke 10:21–22). These two components are central to the vocation Jesus articulates and lives,[35] and they

---

[32] In Mark, our earliest usable account (Q being earlier, but it is not sufficiently reconstructable to use separately from Mark), the theophany also functions as the first half of an *inclusio* that frames the Gospel of Mark at a narrative level. The second half of the *inclusio* is the account of Jesus' crucifixion. For discussion see David Ulansey, "The Heavenly Veil Torn: Mark's Cosmic *Inclusio*," *JBL* 110 (1991): 123–25. Cf. Stephen Motyer, "The Rending of the Veil: A Markan Pentecost?" *NTS* 33 (1987): 155–57.

[33] Crossan, *The Historical Jesus*, 232.

[34] Cf. the full elucidation of this midrash by Meier, *Mentor, Message, and Miracles*, 106–7.

[35] The historicity of these two components are widely recognized by scholars, though opinions will differ on specific texts. Dunn, *Jesus and the Spirit*, 11–67; N. T. Wright, *Jesus and the Victory of God* (vol. 2 of *Christian Origins and the Question of God*; Minneapolis: Fortress, 1996), 648–53. Cf. Géza Vermès, *Jesus the Jew: A Historian's Reading of the Gospels* (London: Collins, 1973).

can be placed within the thought world of first-century Judaism without a specifically Christian slant to them. Applying the criterion of coherence[36] to this matter suggests that the content of the theophany could derive from an experience Jesus had.[37] The matter could be expressed more strongly: the presence of the Spirit and a filial relationship with God are experiential in nature rather than conceptual. If Jesus experienced them, then we may ask, "What inaugurated this experience?" A conceptual answer is inadequate; the question requires an experiential answer. In other words, at some point in his early ministry, Jesus had an inaugural experience that formed the basis for the vocation he subsequently articulated and lived.[38]

Another mitigating perspective may be noted from the prophetic nature of Jesus' ministry. If Jesus was perceived by himself and others as a prophet, then it is reasonable to assume that he experienced at some point a prophetic

---

[36] For a description of this criterion, see the discussion in this volume in ch. 2, § 4.1.

[37] Dunn (*Jesus and the Spirit*, 63) states: "it is certain that Jesus believed himself to be empowered by the Spirit and thought of himself as God's son. These convictions must have crystalized at some point in his life. Why should the traditions unanimously fasten on this episode in Jesus' life if they had no reason for making the link and many reasons against it."

[38] Meier (*Mentor, Message, and Miracles*, 108) counters: "To be sure, the narrative encapsulates nicely two main themes of Jesus' preaching and praxis. But what else would we expect from a Christian narrative that sought to supply an initial definition of who Jesus is?" His objection does not, however, address the coherence these two themes have with the ministry of Jesus. In fact, Meier (p. 108) affirms that, prior to beginning his ministry, "Jesus no doubt developed intellectually and experienced existentially these key insights into his relationship with God as his Father and the powerful activity of the spirit manifest in his own life. Indeed, it is possible that the crystallization of these key themes may have had something to do with Jesus' own parting company with John. But to be any more specific about exactly when and how this happened (e. g., at the moment of his baptism) risks going beyond reasonable inference from the data and falling into the psychologizing of Jesus practiced by the old 'liberal lives.'" I beg to differ: affirming the historicity of an experience that has been stated in the text is not "psychologizing" at all. Psychological speculation on *why* he had the experience (e. g., the death of his father at a young age created a need for a "father figure") would be psychologizing, and this should be rejected. Meier, however, throws the baby out with the bathwater on this point. Joel Marcus ("Jesus' Baptismal Vision," *NTS* 41 [1995]: 512–21) in a very interesting paper also calls into question the specific content of the theophany (the descent of the Spirit and the designation of Jesus as God's son). But he goes on to observe that Jesus "possessed a strong sense of prophetic authority ... Such a sense of prophetic authority does not come out of nowhere; it almost demands a radical experience of divine encounter to explain its existence" (p. 513). He suggests that Jesus did, in fact, experience a prophetic call-vision, but proposes that its content was instead another visionary experience that Jesus narrates: "I watched Satan fall from heaven like a flash of lightening" (Luke 10:18). This is certainly a promising suggestion, and worthy of consideration. I would, however, propose that it could just as easily be incorporated as an additional part of Jesus' prophetic call-vision along with the Spirit's descent and the designation as God's son, rather than replacing them.

call-vision. If so, then this theophany could be understood to function as a prophetic call-vision for Jesus.[39]

A third mitigating factor is the presence in the theophany narrative of the description "like a dove" (Matt 3:16 = Mark 1:10 = Luke 3:22; cf John 1:32). Much ink has been spilt discussing the possible origins and significance of this imagery,[40] but none have been entirely satisfactory. This lack of a convincing or obvious background suggests its authenticity according to the criterion of dissimilarity.[41]

One final point needs to be brought into the equation. The sources narrate the baptism and the theophany together, with the latter happening at the occasion of the former. The implication is that Jesus' sense of call to his ministry begins with the theophany experienced at his baptism. The narrative sequence of the Synoptic Gospels would support such a development: Jesus is baptized, receives his prophetic call-vision, and then immediately launches into his public ministry. However, the evidence of the Fourth Gospel presents a different picture: after his baptism, Jesus is part of John's movement and engages in a baptizing ministry in association with John and his ministry. By implication, at some later point in time Jesus does launch out and begin his public ministry as we know it. If so, it is quite possible that a prophetic call-vision may have led to this switch in the direction of his activities, but this would have taken place at a time subsequent to his baptism.[42] In other words, after his baptism, Jesus participates with John in his baptizing ministry, and then later, after a prophetic call-vision, Jesus

---

[39] Cf. Marcus J. Borg, *Jesus, A New Vision: Spirit, Culture, and the Life of Discipleship* (San Francisco: Harper & Row, 1987), 40–42; Wright, *Jesus and the Victory of God*, 536–37; Ben Witherington, III, *The Christology of Jesus* (Minneapolis: Fortress, 1990), 148–49.

[40] A few of the many discussions concerning this issue include Leander E. Keck, "Spirit and the Dove," *NTS* 17 (1970): 41–67; Stephen Gero, "Spirit as a Dove at the Baptism of Jesus," *NovT* 18 (1976): 17–35; Paul Garnet, "The Baptism of Jesus and the Son of Man Idea," *JSNT* 9 (1980): 49–65; Dale C. Allison, Jr., "The Baptism of Jesus and a New Dead Sea Scroll," *Biblical Archaeology Review* 18 (1992): 58–60; Ronnie S. Poon, "The Background to the Dove Imagery in the Story of Jesus' Baptism," *Jian Dao* 3 (1995): 33–49; R. Alastair Campbell, "Jesus and His Baptism," *TynBul* 47 (1996): 191–214; Leif E. Vaage, "Bird-Watching at the Baptism of Jesus: Early Christian Mythmaking in Mark 1:9–11," in *Reimagining Christian Origins: A Colloquium Honoring Burton L. Mack* (ed. Elizabeth A. Castelli and Hal Taussig; Valley Forge, PA: Trinity, 1996), 280–94. See also the survey of alternatives presented by W. D. Davies and Dale C. Allison, Jr., *A Critical and Exegetical Commentary on the Gospel According to Saint Matthew* (3 vols.; ICC; Edinburgh: T&T Clark, 1988–97), 1:331–34.

[41] For discussion of this criterion, see in this volume ch. 2, § 4.1. I am indebted to Craig A. Evans for this suggestion.

[42] For further discussion of the implications of the account in the Fourth Gospel, see below. For an exploration of the temporal separation of the baptism from the prophetic call-vision, see my earlier discussion in Robert L. Webb, "John the Baptist and His Relationship to Jesus," in *Studying the Historical Jesus: Evaluations of the State of Current Research* (ed. Bruce D. Chilton and Craig A. Evans; NTTS 19; Leiden: Brill, 1994), 225–26.

launches out into his own, distinct public ministry as narrated in the Synoptic Gospels. It is quite possible, then, that two temporally separate events were later linked together. This linking could have been done by Jesus in his narration of the events to his disciples (for Jesus' telling them would be the only way they would find out about them), or it is the early Christian witness that has linked the theophany with the baptism, using the former to interpret the latter.

The weighing of this evidence is not easy. My own judgment is that it is *probable* that Jesus did at some time experience a prophetic call-vision, and it is *somewhat probable* that it incorporated the elements of divine sonship and spirit anointing. It is *possible* that such a call-vision may have taken place at Jesus' baptism, but there are also problems with their association. It is equally possible that it occurred at some point in time subsequent to the baptism. The focus of this essay is on Jesus' baptism by John and so, given the prominence of reinterpreting the theophany narrative with Christian theological and apologetic concerns, it is best methodologically to proceed first with examining the significance of Jesus' baptism by John apart from the possible implications of the theophany. And this is how I will proceed below. However, I will conclude with a couple of observations concerning the implications of the theophany for understanding the baptism of Jesus.

2.3. Summary

This investigation of the historicity of the baptism narrative and the associated theophany narrative has led to the following conclusions. First of all, the baptism of Jesus by John is historically very probable or even virtually certain. This conclusion is in agreement with a number of scholars whose judgment is that this is one of the most certain things we can know about Jesus.

On the other hand, the theophany narrative is somewhat problematic. It is probable that Jesus experienced some type of prophetic call-vision at the beginning of his own, distinct ministry. But there are difficulties with this event taking place at the same time as Jesus' baptism, rendering such a temporal placement only a possibility. (They are, however, conceptually associated, for together they form the foundation that launched Jesus' later public ministry.) It is, therefore, methodologically preferable to focus our attention on the significance of Jesus' baptism apart from the possible association with the prophetic call-vision of the theophany narrative. This possible link will be considered briefly later.

Having established the historical probability of Jesus' baptism by John, we must now turn to an examination of the character of John's baptism as well as other elements concerning John.

3. John and his Baptism in the Context of Second-Temple Judaism

Before considering the relationship between John and Jesus, we must consider briefly certain key elements that contribute to our understanding of John.[43] These include John's baptism, his prophetic proclamation, his prophetic role, and other features of his life and death. Since I have discussed elsewhere matters of authenticity and historicity of many of the texts that concern John the Baptist, I do not repeat such discussion here but refer the reader to that earlier work.[44]

3.1. John's Baptism

To understand John, it is most helpful to begin with the feature that is probably most distinctive about him – his baptism. The ritual use of water in ablutions is a widespread religious phenomenon, and it was certainly practiced within first-century Judaism and Christianity. That John performed a water rite identified as a "baptism" is one of the most sure pieces of historical information we possess concerning John.[45] Specific features of John's baptism may be understood within the context of Second Temple Judaism (this is elaborated below), and yet the form and functions of his baptism have features that were distinctive within his context. John was in continuity with his tradition and yet innovative at the same time. The fact that John was given the appellation or nickname "the baptizer" or "the Baptist"[46] suggests that those who give him this nickname recognized that baptism was important to John and that it was also distinctive. For this reason, it is interesting to observe that baptism was not simply something that John performed – it was also something that he preached.[47] He not only called people to repentance and baptism, he also had to explain the significance of his baptism.

Though other forms of ablution were practiced in Second Temple Judaism (e. g., handwashing, footwashing, sprinkling), John's baptism involved bathing, that is, an immersion.[48] This is not surprising, since bathing was

---

[43] This section is a slight revision of part of an earlier essay: Webb, "John the Baptist and His Relationship to Jesus," 187–210. It is used with the permission of the editors.

[44] Webb, *John the Baptizer*.

[45] It is independently attested in several sources: Matt 3:11 = Luke 3:16; Mark 1:4; John 1:25; Josephus, *Ant.* 18.117.

[46] John is so identified in several independent sources; e. g., Matt 11:18 = Luke 7:33; Mark 1:4; *Gos. Thom.* 46; Josephus, *Ant.* 18.117.

[47] Mark 1:4 = Luke 3:6; Josephus, *Ant.* 18.117.

[48] Cf. the expressions ἐν τῷ ... ποταμῷ in Mark 1:5 and ἐκ τοῦ ὕδατος in Mark 1:10, which suggest bathing was the form that John's baptism took. As well, the verb βαπτίζω and the nouns βάπτισμα and βαπτισμός, used of John's baptism, are not the usual terms used for a Jewish ritual bath (exceptions are Mark 7:4; Luke 11:38; Heb 9:10). The

a common form of Jewish ablution.[49] Most descriptions of John's baptism associate it with the Jordan River (e. g., Mark 1:5, 9–10). The use of flowing water (or "living" water) was required in the Hebrew Bible for the most severe forms of uncleanness,[50] and in Second Temple Judaism flowing water or rivers were associated with repentance and forgiveness.[51] In light of this context, John's use of flowing water for his baptism is quite understandable. The particular river associated with John's baptism is the Jordan River. While this may have no significance, it does place John in the wilderness context.[52] Both the wilderness and the Jordan River were important symbols of the Exodus and Conquest in the ideology of prophetic movements of the Second Temple period.[53] Since other features of John's ministry show links with such ideology, John's use of the Jordan River probably does have symbolic significance.[54]

An interesting feature of the form of John's baptism is that it is described as being performed "by John" (ὑπ' αὐτοῦ, Mark 1:5; cf. v. 9), and John himself states, "I baptize ..." (Matt 3:11 = Luke 3:16; Mark 1:8). All evidence in Second Temple Judaism points to Jewish ritual bathing practices being self-administered. John's participation in the act of baptizing, therefore, is probably John's innovation and may have contributed to his nickname, "the baptizer."

How was John's baptism understood to function? The evidence indicates that the answer to this question involves several interrelated functions.

---

verb signifies "to dip" or "to plunge"; BDAG 164–165; LSJ 305–306; Albrecht Oepke, "Βάπτω, κτλ.," *TDNT* 1:529–38. George R. Beasley-Murray, "Baptism, Wash," *NIDNTT* 1:143, points out that the verb λούω is the most common verb used for complete washing or bathing, while νίπτω is used for partial washing, such as handwashing. On these varieties of ablutions in the Hebrew Bible, Second Temple Jewish literature, and the Qumran literature in particular, see the discussion in Webb, *John the Baptizer*, 95–162, and more recently, Jonathan D. Lawrence, *Washing in Water: Trajectories of Ritual Bathing in the Hebrew Bible and Second Temple Literature* (Academia Biblica 23; Atlanta: Society of Biblical Literature, 2006).

[49] E.g., Lev 14–15; 16:4, 24; Sir 34:25 (31:25); Tob (BA) 2:5; Tob (S) 2:9; *T. Levi* 2:3B1–2; 9:11; *Jub.* 21:16a; *As. Mos.* 9.4:13; *Sib. Or.* 4:165; *Apoc. Mos.* 29:11–13; Josephus, *Ag. Ap.* 2.198, 203, 282; *Life* 11–12; *J. W.* 2.129–32, 149–50; *Ant.* 3.263; 18.36–38; Philo, *Spec. Laws* 1.119, 269; *Unchangeable* 7–8; CD 10:10–13; 11:1, 21–22; 1QS 3:4–9; 11QTemple 45:7–10.

[50] Lev 14:5–6, 50–52; 15:13; Num 19:17; Deut 21:4; cf. *m. Miqw.* 1:6–8.

[51] *T. Levi* 2:3B2; *Sib. Or.* 4:165–167; *Apoc. Mos.* 29:11–13. Cf. the discussion of these texts in Webb, *John the Baptizer*, 116–22.

[52] For an examination of the relationship between the Jordan river and the wilderness, see Robert W. Funk, "The Wilderness," *JBL* 78 (1959): 205–14.

[53] E.g., Josephus, *J. W.* 2.259; 2.261–262; *Ant.* 20.97; 20.168. Cf. Richard A. Horsley, "'Like One of the Prophets of Old': Two Types of Popular Prophets at the Time of Jesus," *CBQ* 47 (1985): 457–58; Josef Ernst, *Johannes der Täufer: Interpretation, Geschichte, Wirkungsgeschichte* (BZNW 53; Berlin: De Gruyter, 1989), 278–84; Webb, *John the Baptizer*, 335–39.

[54] Cf. Webb, *John the Baptizer*, 181–83, 360–66.

First, John's baptism was an expression of conversionary repentance – a reorientation of one's life in returning to a relationship with God.[55] This is borne out by the NT phrase βάπτισμα μετανοίας ("a baptism of repentance") used to describe John's baptism (Mark 1:4 = Luke 3:3), and the important role that repentance evidently had in his preaching (Matt 3:8 = Luke 3:8; Matt 3:2; cf. Josephus, *Ant.* 18.117).[56] John preached imminent judgment coming upon all and called people to repentance and baptism. Neither were optional – repentance and its expression in baptism went hand in hand. It was a "repentance–baptism."[57] The practice of "confessing their sins" (Mark 1:5 = Matt 3:6) while being baptized is probably an expression of this close link between the baptism and repentance. The ethical content of John's preaching contributes not only to the message of judgment (e.g., Matt 3:7–10 = Luke 3:7–9) but also to the call to an ethically reoriented life following baptism. Josephus describes John as "one who exhorted the Jews to practice virtue and act with justice toward one another and with piety toward God, and so to gather together by baptism" (Josephus, *Ant.* 18.117; cf. Luke 3:10–14).

Second, for John and those being baptized, baptism was understood to mediate divine forgiveness.[58] In Mark 1:4 = Luke 3:3 John's repentance–baptism is linked with "the forgiveness of sins." In Jewish thought forgiveness of sins was usually associated with repentance (e.g., Isa 55:7) but not with an ablution. According to John, however, it was not only repentance that was required, for baptism and repentance were inextricably linked. It was

---

[55] The term "conversionary" repentance expresses John's continuity with the Hebrew Bible's prophetic call to return (שׁוב) to Yahweh as exemplified in Isa 30:15; Ezek 18:30–32. J. Behm and E. Würthwein, "νοέω, κτλ.," *TDNT* 4:980–99, distinguish between this prophetic emphasis and repentance associated with ritual expressions of penitence such as fasting or sackcloth and ashes. Cf. F. Laubach, et al., "Conversion, Penitence, Repentance, Proselyte," *NIDNTT* 1:353–359; William L. Holladay, *The Root šûbh in the Old Testament* (Leiden: Brill, 1958), 116–57.

[56] Ernst Lohmeyer (*Johannes der Täufer* [vol. 1 of *Das Urchristentum*; Göttingen: Vandenhoeck & Ruprecht, 1932], 68) argues on the basis of the phrase εἰς μετάνοιαν in Matt 3:11 that conversionary repentance is God's act when a person is baptized, but this is unconvincing. The phrase is better understood to be Matthew's redaction, linking repentance to baptism at this point in the text because it had been removed earlier (cf. the use of Mark 1:4 in Matt 3:2). Cf. Ernst, *Johannes der Täufer*, 344.

[57] Robert A. Guelich, *Mark 1–8:26* (WBC 34a; Dallas: Word, 1989), 18–19. The conceptual possibility of linking conversionary repentance with an immersion rite may have been provided by Isa 1:16–17 as well as the example of Naaman in 2 Kgs 5:10, 14–17. The idea is clearly expressed in Second Temple Jewish literature; e.g., 1 QS 3:6–9; *T. Levi* 2:3B; *Sib. Or.* 4:162–70.

[58] This function is described as understood from the perspective of John and his followers. Others may have perceived John's baptism in quite different terms. For example, the Temple hierarchy probably viewed John's baptism as "cheap grace."

repentance-baptism that was essential.⁵⁹ Therefore, the baptism did more than simply symbolize a forgiveness already received on the basis of the repentance alone. Since the baptism was neither optional nor secondary to the forgiveness of sins, the baptism should be understood to mediate the forgiveness in some way.⁶⁰

An interesting implication of this function of baptism is that, since a person was baptized "by John" rather than performing it for themselves, John could be considered a mediator of the forgiveness.⁶¹ The mediatorial role of "the baptizer" in performing baptism to mediate forgiveness is parallel to the mediatorial role of a priest in performing a sacrifice to mediate forgiveness in the sacrificial system (e.g., Lev 5:5–10). This parallel is striking in light of the NT tradition that John came from a rural priestly family (Luke 1:5, 23).⁶²

These first two functions are closely related: John's baptism was an immersion performed by John, through which a person expressed conversionary repentance and received divine forgiveness.

A third function of John's baptism was that it purified from uncleanness. Josephus states that "baptism certainly would appear acceptable to him [i.e., God] if used ... for purification of the body ..." (*Ant.* 18.117). While elements of Josephus' explanation of John's baptism are historically problematic, especially the statement that distinguishes the body and the soul,⁶³ nevertheless, it is quite probable that John's baptism was understood to purify. In the Hebrew Bible and later Jewish thought, the use of immersions was predominantly concerned with cleansing from uncleanness,⁶⁴ so

---

⁵⁹ A relationship between repentance, an immersion, and forgiveness is also expressed in *T. Levi* 2:3B; *Sib. Or.* 4:162–170; 1QS 3:6–9. Cf. the discussion in Webb, *John the Baptizer*, 207–13.

⁶⁰ This interpretation is corroborated by understanding the preposition εἰς in the phrase εἰς ἄφεσιν ἁμαρτιῶν to be expressing the purpose or goal of the repentance-baptism, that is, "with a view to forgiveness of sins." At this point the NT evidence is in tension with Josephus' statement that John's baptism was "not for seeking pardon of certain sins but for purification of the body, because the soul had already been cleansed before by righteousness" (*Ant.* 18.117). For discussion see Webb, *John the Baptizer*, 165–68, 190–92.

⁶¹ Cf. Leonhard Goppelt, *Theology of the New Testament* (2 vols.; trans. John E. Alsup; Grand Rapids: Eerdmans, 1981–82), 1:36; Jürgen Becker, *Johannes der Täufer und Jesus von Nazareth* (BibS(N) 63; Neukirchen-Vluyn: Neukirchener Verlag, 1972), 38–40. This suggests that prophetic symbolism may have played a part in John's role in performing the baptism; cf. George R. Beasley-Murray, *Baptism in the New Testament* (Grand Rapids: Eerdmans, 1962), 43; Charles H.H. Scobie, *John the Baptist* (London: SCM, 1964), 113; Ernst, *Johannes der Täufer*, 332–34.

⁶² See the discussion below in § 3.4.

⁶³ Cf. the discussion in Webb, *John the Baptizer*, 165–68, 194–95.

⁶⁴ In the Hebrew Bible the use of ablutions functioned as part of a larger structure involving cleanness and uncleanness. This structure is not concerned with physical cleanliness but with the status resulting from contact with a source of impurity (e.g., a contagion such as a corpse [Num 19], or discharges [Lev 15]) and the necessary cleansing to restore

that, if John's baptism had nothing to do with cleansing, it would be quite unusual – and no evidence supports such a claim.[65] In the Hebrew Bible it would appear that actual immersions were only used when the contagion (i. e., that which caused the uncleanness) was something physical. But in the Second Temple period, the use of immersions expanded to include cleansing from uncleanness caused by moral contagion also. For example, *Sib. Or.* 4:165–67 contains an exhortation to "wash your whole bodies in perennial rivers. Stretch out your hands to heaven and ask forgiveness for your previous deeds ..."[66] John's use of baptism to cleanse from moral contagion is consistent with this expanded use of immersions in the Second Temple period. It also coheres with John's concern with repentance and forgiveness in conjunction with his baptism.

The state of uncleanness from which John's baptism cleansed would have been considered serious because it was concerned with moral contagion. This may explain why John's baptismal ministry is associated with the Jordan River for, as we observed above, flowing or "living" water was required for cleansing the most serious cases of uncleanness in the Hebrew Bible.[67]

Fourth, John's baptism foreshadowed the ministry of the expected figure that John announced. Matt 3:11 = Luke 3:16 contain John's saying: "I baptize you with water ... he will baptize you with holy spirit and fire" (cf. Mark 1:8; cf. John 1:26–27). The imagery of "holy spirit" and "fire" remove the activities of the expected figure from the realm of a literal water rite, and yet the verb "baptize" is used to characterize his activities. Just as the term "baptize" is used to refer to John's physical activity of baptizing, so it is also

---

to a state of cleanness. Two different forms of contagion may make a person unclean: (1) physical contagion, such as leprosy (Lev 14) or discharges (Lev 15), and (2) moral contagion, such as sexual immorality (Lev 18). These are not two forms of uncleanness but only two types of contagion. The terminology of ablutions is also used metaphorically to refer to cleansing from sin, but an actual immersion does not seem to be in view (e. g., Ps 51:2, 7; Isa 1:16–17; Ezek 16:4, 9). For further discussion see Jacob Neusner, *The Idea of Purity in Ancient Judaism* (SJLA 1; Leiden: Brill, 1973); David P. Wright, *The Disposal of Impurity: Elimination Rites in the Bible and in Hittite and Mesopotamian Literature* (SBLDS 101; Atlanta: Scholars, 1987). Helpful summaries include David P. Wright, "Unclean and Clean," *ABD* 6:729–741; Gordon J. Wenham, *The Book of Leviticus* (NICOT; Grand Rapids: Eerdmans, 1979), 15–29. Cf. Webb, *John the Baptizer*, 96–108. On this subject in general, see the helpful discussion by Jonathan Klawans (*Impurity and Sin in Ancient Judaism* [Oxford: Oxford University Press, 2000]) on this subject generally, and on John the Baptist in particular, see pp. 138–43.

[65] Cf. the parallel between John's baptism and the expected figure's baptism, and the description of the expected figure, who is described in the imagery of the threshing floor as one who will "*clean* the threshing floor" (διακαθαίρω; Matt 3:12 = Luke 3:17).

[66] Cf. *Sib. Or.* 4:162–170; *T. Levi* 2:3B1–14; *Ap. Mos.* 29:11–13; 1QS 3:6–9; 5:13–14. Cf. Webb, *John the Baptizer*, 108–32.

[67] Cf. the emphasis on using rivers or running water with respect to immersions that express repentance in *T. Levi* 2:3B2; *Sib. Or.* 4:165; *Ap. Mos.* 29:12–13.

used metaphorically to refer to the expected figure's activity. This invites a comparison between the functions of their two baptisms. For example, they both cleanse. John's baptism is used to express conversionary repentance and the expected figure's baptism with a holy spirit might be understood to complete the conversion. It also allows for the contrast between the two, with the expected figure being mightier and having a greater baptism.[68] The first announces, anticipates and prepares, while the latter fulfills and completes the process.

This function of John's baptism colors it with an eschatological fervor that coheres closely with the John's announcement of imminent judgment and restoration. John's baptism is the final opportunity to prepare for the eschatological judgment and restoration to be brought by the expected figure.[69]

Fifth, John's baptism functioned as an initiatory rite into the "true Israel." John announced to everyone the necessity of his repentance-baptism to be prepared for the imminent, eschatological judgment and restoration to be carried out by the expected figure. John's baptizing ministry, therefore, created a fundamental distinction between the repentant and the unrepentant, the prepared and the unprepared, those who would receive the expected figure's restoration and those who would be judged. While John called upon individuals to respond, within the context of Second Temple Jewish thought, the effect should be viewed corporately. It was all Israel (i.e., ethnic Israel) that was viewed as facing imminent judgment, and it was only the prepared who would experience the fulfillment of the ancient hopes and promises for restoration (i.e., a remnant, or true Israel). Since repentance-baptism was the necessary rite for preparation and the ones prepared were the group who would be restored, John's baptism was the rite that changed the status of a person from nonmember to member.[70]

The initiatory function of John's baptism has been rejected by some scholars.[71] But two observations may alleviate their objections. First of all,

---

[68] The Hebrew Bible expresses the hope in a greater eschatological ablution in Ezek 36:25–26; cf. Isa 4:4; Joel 3:18; Zech 13:1; 14:8; Mal 3:2–3. Cf. the language used of the Qumran community's own ablutions in 1QS 3:6–9 and the eschatological expectation of a final ablution in 1QS 4:19–22.

[69] Cf. Goppelt, *Theology of the New Testament*, 1:37–38; Ernst, *Johannes der Täufer*, 333.

[70] Cf. Claas Jouco Bleeker, ed., *Initiation; Contributions to the Theme of the Study-Conference of the International Association for the History of Religions Held at Strasburg, September 17th to 22nd 1964* (SHR 10; Leiden: Brill, 1965).

[71] E.g., Becker, *Johannes der Täufer*, 38–40. Ernst (*Johannes der Täufer*, 340) and Goppelt (*Theology of the New Testament*, 1:35) understand John's baptism to create a separation, but fail to recognize the corporate implications of this. Others who reject the interpretation of John's baptism as an initiatory rite include Kraeling, *John the Baptist*, 119–20; Hartwig Thyen, "ΒΑΠΤΙΣΜΑ ΜΕΤΑΝΟΙΑΣ ΕΙΣ ΑΦΕΣΙΝ ΑΜΑΡΤΙΩΝ," in *The Future of Our Religious Past: Essays in Honour of Rudolf Bultmann* (trans. Charles E. Carlston

an initiatory rite does not necessarily need to initiate someone into a closed community, such as the Qumran community for example. An examination of the sectarian groups in Second Temple Judaism reveals a wide variety of group structures. Many of these groups maintained a sectarian identity and yet remained integrated into Jewish life (e.g., the Pharisees, or the early Christian movement).[72] Second, such a view generally focuses on John as only preaching judgment.[73] While this certainly is an emphasis in John's preaching, the evidence indicates that John also announced imminent restoration (e.g., the promise of a holy spirit and the imagery of gathering grain into the granary). In light of Jewish self-understanding as the elect, covenant people of God and a hope for national restoration, John's announcement of restoration as well as judgment would have been understood corporately.

That John's baptism functioned as an initiatory rite is also suggested by Josephus' statement in *Ant.* 18.117: John "exhorted the Jews to practice virtue and act with justice toward one another and with piety toward God, and so to gather together by baptism [βαπτισμῷ συνιέναι]." The verb σύνειμι means "to come together" or "to gather together" with the implication of a common purpose, and the gathering together accomplishes this purpose.[74] Elsewhere, Josephus uses this same verb to describe Jews joining a group or party or the meeting together of such a group. For example, shortly after describing John the Baptist, Josephus uses the same verb in *Ant.* 18.315 to describe two brothers, Asinaeus and Anilaeus, who became armed bandits: "young men of the poorest class gathered together [συνῄεσαν] around them" to form a peasant army.[75] In this statement by Josephus concerning John's preaching, the dative βαπτισμῷ is usually translated "in baptism," "for baptism," or "to baptism," but these expressions do not adequately express the

---

and Robert P. Scharlemann; ed. James M. Robinson; London: SCM, 1971), 132–33, n. 6. Examples of those who support an initiatory function for John's baptism include Scobie, *John the Baptist*, 114–16; Oscar Cullmann, "The Significance of the Qumran Texts for Research Into the Beginnings of Christianity," in *The Scrolls and the New Testament* (ed. Krister Stendahl; London: SCM, 1958), 215; Goguel, *Jean-Baptiste*, 291; Bo Ivar Reicke, "The Historical Setting of John's Baptism," in *Jesus, the Gospels, and the Church: Essays in Honor of William R. Farmer* (ed. E. P. Sanders; Macon: Mercer University Press, 1987), 214–19. Whether an immersion had an initiatory function within the Qumran community is also debated. I have argued elsewhere that 1QS 2:25–3:9; 5:7–15 do support such a function; for discussion and relevant literature, see Webb, *John the Baptizer*, 133–62. Also related is the question of whether Jewish proselyte baptism (an initiatiory rite) predated John's baptism or whether it is in fact a post-70 C.E. phenomenon. The latter position best accounts for the evidence. Cf. Derwood C. Smith, "Jewish Proselyte Baptism and the Baptism of John," *ResQ* 25 (1982): 13–32; Webb, *John the Baptizer*, 122–30.

[72] Cf. Ben F. Meyer, *The Aims of Jesus* (London: SCM, 1979), 233–34.
[73] E.g., Becker, *Johannes der Täufer*, 38–39.
[74] BDAG 968; LSJ 1705; cf. the only NT use of this verb in Luke 8:4.
[75] Cf. σύνειμι in Josephus, *J.W.* 1.129; 4.132. For a discussion of these texts and their relation to στάσις ("strife"), see Webb, *John the Baptizer*, 199–201.

sense of the term in the unusual expression βαπτισμῷ συνιέναι. In light of Josephus' use of this verb, the dative should probably be understood as an instrumental of means: "by means of baptism." John was calling his audience to gather together into some form of group, and baptism was the means by which the group was gathered. From an individual's point of view, baptism was the means by which he/she was "gathered into" or joined the group.[76]

The initiatory function of John's baptism is also implied by John's call to conversionary repentance. In the saying in Matt 3:9 = Luke 3:8 John affirms the covenant promises ("God is able ... to raise up children to Abraham"), but he denies that simply being a member of ethnic Israel is sufficient ("do not presume to say to yourselves, 'We have Abraham as our father'"). For John, then, it is only those who have undergone repentance-baptism who have become the true "children of Abraham."[77]

Sixth, it is also possible that John's baptism functioned, at least implicitly, as a protest against the Temple establishment. It was concluded above that John's baptism mediated divine forgiveness and John, as "baptizer," was the mediator of that forgiveness. We also observed that this had significant parallels to atoning sacrifices of the Temple cult, and thus John's baptism functioned as an alternative to those sacrifices. In Second Temple Judaism, if the Temple was criticized, it was usually the priestly aristocracy's wealth and corruption that was the focus of the criticism.[78] The saying of John in Matt 3:7–10 = Luke 3:7–9 is virtually identical in both Gospels, but the audiences are quite different. Matthew has "Pharisees and Sadducees," while Luke has "crowds." If the Matthean text is a more accurate identification of those addressed in the original audience for the saying,[79] then the pointed rebuke in this text could imply that John was critical of the Temple establishment, especially in light of the close connection between the Sadducees and the Temple.[80]

---

[76] For further development and argumentation, see Webb, *John the Baptizer*, 199–200.

[77] Cf. Luke 1:17, which describes John as one who was "to make ready for the Lord a prepared people." Matthew Black (*The Scrolls and Christian Origins: Studies in the Jewish Background of the New Testament* [BJS 48; New York: Scribner, 1961], 97) compares the self-understanding of the Qumran community and John the Baptist at this point as being the formation of "a new Covenanted Israel" or "the new Israel."

[78] Cf. Craig A. Evans, "Jesus' Action in the Temple and Evidence of Corruption in the First-Century Temple," in *SBL Seminar Papers, 1989* (SBLSP 28; Atlanta: Scholars, 1989), 522–39. An implicit link between criticism of the Temple and the use of immersions for forgiveness may also be observed in the Qumran community's criticism of the Temple, as well as in *Sib. Or.* 4:8, 27–30 (cf. 4:162–170).

[79] For a defense of this position, particularly with respect to the Matthean reference to "Sadducees," see Webb, *John the Baptizer*, 175–78.

[80] For further development of this function, see Webb, *John the Baptizer*, 203–5. Few other scholars recognize this function. Thyen ("ΒΑΠΤΙΣΜΑ," 151) goes no further than to describe John's baptism as "a polemic substitute for temple-sacrifice." Kraeling (*John the Baptist*, 15–27) attributes John's wilderness existence to "some bitter experience"

3.2. John's Prophetic Proclamation

Not only was John perceived to be a "baptizer," he was also understood by many people to be a prophet.[81] In a manner reminiscent of prophets in the Hebrew Bible, John announced imminent judgment, called the people to repentance-baptism, and proclaimed the imminent coming of a figure who would bring judgment and restoration.[82] In the subsequent discussion, we examine John as prophet from two perspectives: the content of his prophetic announcements and the public role of prophet itself.

The most distinctive element of John's prophetic proclamation was his announcement of an expected figure. The NT interprets this figure to be messianic (Luke 3:15) and to have been fulfilled in Jesus. But it is reasonable to ask how John's description might have been understood in light of contemporary Jewish expectation. The texts that describe John's expected figure (Mark 1:7–8; Matt 3:11–12 = Luke 3:16–17) include the following elements in the description: (1) his activities include judgment and restoration; (2) he is coming; (3) he is mighty (i.e., mightier than John); (4) he will baptize with holy spirit[83] and fire, and (5) his judgment and restoration is portrayed using imagery of the threshing floor.

(p. 16) that, as a rural priest, had alienated him from the temple establishment. Cf. Eta Linnemann, "Jesus und der Täufer," in *Festschrift für Ernst Fuchs* (ed. Gerhard Ebeling, et al.; Tübingen: Mohr Siebeck, 1973), 228; Ben Witherington, "Jesus and the Baptist – Two of a Kind," in *SBL Seminar Papers, 1988* (SBLSP 27; Atlanta: Scholars, 1988), 228; and Martin Hengel and Anna Maria Schwemer, *Jesus und das Judentum* (vol. 1 of *Geschichte des frühen Christentums*; 4 vols.; Tübingen: Mohr Siebeck, 2007–), 316–17.

[81] Luke 7:26 = Matt 11:9; Mark 11:32 = Matt 21:26 = Luke 20:6. Josephus' description of John as one "who exhorted the Jews" and had "great persuasiveness with the people" (*Ant.* 18.117, 118) is consistent with the role of prophet. Josephus does not explicitly identify John as a prophet. While he presented John primarily from a positive perspective, Josephus was very negative about those who claimed to be prophets during the Second Temple period, especially those who were popular prophets (i.e., those whose ministry was involved primarily with the common people – the peasants). Cf. Webb, *John the Baptizer*, 307–17, 333–42, esp. 308, n. 4.

[82] John is sometimes characterized as being a prophet of judgment only (e.g., Becker, *Johannes der Täufer*, 38–39), but this characterization ignores the restorative implications of the expected figure baptizing with a holy spirit and of the clause "he will gather the wheat into his granary" (Luke 3:17). Furthermore, it fails to appreciate the prophetic dynamic that the announcement of judgment and call to repentance has as its necessary corollary the hope of some form of restoration or blessing; otherwise the call to repentance is meaningless.

[83] It is sometimes argued that πνεῦμα should be translated "wind" rather than "spirit." For advocates of this view, see Ernest Best, "Spirit-Baptism," *NovT* 4 (1960): 236–43. This is usually argued on the basis that "holy" is a Christian interpolation into John's use of the term πνεῦμα, and that the imagery of wind is implied in John's picture of winnowing at the threshing floor. However, the evidence for the first claim is inadequate, particularly if the term "holy spirit" is understood in light of Jewish description and expectation as "a spirit of holiness." The second point is incorrect, for πνεῦμα is neither mentioned in the picture of the threshing floor, nor is the picture actually describing winnowing at all, and so wind

A survey of the Hebrew Bible and Second Temple Jewish literature reveals a wide variety of expected figures who could be characterized as bringing judgment and restoration (thus satisfying the first element of John's expected figure). These include human agents such as the Davidic or Aaronic Messiah, the eschatological prophet or Elijah-*redivivus*, supernatural figures such as the archangel Michael, Melchizedek, or the Son of Man,[84] and even God himself. Furthermore, the second and third elements describing John's expected figure (coming and mighty) are also used in Second Temple literature to describe each of these expected figures (with the exception of Elijah-*redivivus*, for whom no description as mighty is extant).[85]

With respect to the fourth and fifth elements of John's description of the expected figure, the evidence is not as balanced between the different figures. While, for example, the Davidic Messiah and the Son of Man are each portrayed as *receiving* a spirit,[86] the only figure who is described as *bestowing* a spirit upon others is God. In some texts this spirit is described as "holy," and water/ablution imagery (i.e., similar to "baptize" imagery) is used to describe this bestowal.[87] The use of fire imagery is associated with the judgment brought by Michael/Melchizedek, Elijah-*redivivus*, and possibly the Son of Man,[88] but fire is also used to describe God's judgment, and some of these descriptions also use language associated with water (e.g., "*river* of fire").[89] Threshing-floor imagery, including winnowing, burning

---

is not even implied. For further discussion, see Webb, *John the Baptizer*, 275–77, 295–97; Robert L. Webb, "The Activity of John the Baptist's Expected Figure at the Threshing Floor (Matthew 3.12 = Luke 3.17)," *JSNT* 43 (1991): 103–11.

[84] The figure in Dan 7:14 is described as being "like a son of man" and is not identified by the title "Son of Man." However, *1 En.* 37–71 indicates that by the first century the description of Daniel's human-like figure had been transformed into the title used to describe a supernatural figure of judgment and restoration, at least in one line of interpretation. For discussion of the extensive research into the Son of Man, see Chrys C. Caragounis, *The Son of Man: Vision and Interpretation* (WUNT 38; Tübingen: Mohr Siebeck, 1986), 9–34; Arthur J. Ferch, *The Son of Man in Daniel 7* (Andrews University Seminary Doctoral Dissertation Series 6; Berrien Springs, Mich.: Andrews University Press, 1983), 4–39.

[85] Examples of relevant texts that describe each figure as coming and mighty are provided here; for elaboration and other texts, see Webb, *John the Baptizer*, 219–60. The Davidic Messiah: Zech 9:9; 1QS 9:11; Mic 5:2; *Pss. Sol.* 17:40; the Aaronic Messiah 1QS 9:11; 4QTest 14–20; Michael/Melchizedek: Dan 12:1; 1QM 17:6; cf. 11QMelch; the Son of Man: Dan 7:13; *1 En.* 49:2–3; 52:4, 9; 69:29; Elijah-*redivivus*: Mal 3:2 (cf. 4:5); God: Isa 41:10; *1 En.* 1:3–4, 7–9.

[86] Davidic Messiah: Isa 11:2; *Pss. Sol.* 17:37; the Son of Man: *1 En.* 62:2.

[87] E.g., Ezek 36:26–27; Joel 2:28–29; *Jub.* 1:23; 1QS 4:21. References to a messianic figure bestowing a spirit may be found in *T. Jud.* 24:3 and *T. Levi* 18:11, but these texts are problematic; cf. Webb, *John the Baptizer*, 233–34, n. 61.

[88] Michael/Melchizedek: 11QMelch 3:7; Elijah-*redivivus*: Mal 3:2–3; *Liv. Pro.* 21:3. In *1 En.* 54:6 angels cast the wicked into fire who have evidently been judged by the Son of Man.

[89] E.g., *Sib. Or.* 2:196–97, 203–205, 252–54, 315; 1QH 3:28–31.

chaff, and gathering wheat, is only used to portray God's judgment and restoration,[90] and it is never used to portray the activities of other expected figures.

Since the characteristics and imagery used in John's depiction of his expected figure were drawn from the Jewish scriptures and were "in the air" in Jewish expectation of John's day, it is reasonable to conclude that the elements of John's depiction are consistent with his scriptures and his cultural milieu. The most specific characteristics and imagery in the preceding analysis (ablution language to describe bestowing a holy spirit and a farmer working at a threshing floor) lead us to conclude that John's expected figure was most likely understood to be God himself.[91] However, at least three points cause us to question this initial conclusion. First, John compares this expected figure to himself ("he who is mightier than I," Mark 1:7; Matt 3:11 = Luke 3:16), which would have been considered quite arrogant if the figure was God.[92] Second, John states that this figure wears sandals, that John is unworthy to untie (Mark 1:7; Matt 3:11 = Luke 3:16). While one may speak anthropomorphically of God wearing sandals (cf. Pss 60:8; 108:9), John's statement loses some of its import if in fact John cannot untie the sandals in the first place. Third, John's query from prison concerning Jesus' identity ("Are you the one who is coming [ὁ ἐρχόμενος]?" Matt 11:3 = Luke 7:19) alludes to John's earlier proclamation concerning the mightier one "who is coming after me" (ὁ ὀπίσω μου ἐρχόμενος). By considering the possibility that a human (i.e., Jesus) was his expected figure, John indicated that his expected figure was other than God.

The tension between key features that point to John's expected figure as being God himself and other pieces of evidence that point to a human figure may be partially resolved by observing the relationship between God and other expected figures in Jewish expectation. Each of the other expected fig-

---

[90] E.g., Isa 27:12–13; Jer 13:24; 15:7; Mal 4:1; Wis 5:23.
[91] The identification of John's expected figure as God is supported by Paul G. Bretscher, "Whose Sandals? (Matt 3:11)," *JBL* 86 (1967): 81–87; Hughes, "John the Baptist," 191–219; Thyen, "ΒΑΠΤΙΣΜΑ," 136; Ernst, *Johannes der Täufer*, 50, 305. Alternatively, various scholars have identified John's expected figure with each of the expected figures discussed above with the exception of Michael/Melchizedek. For the Davidic Messiah see Davies and Allison, *Matthew*, 1:313–14; James D.G. Dunn, "Spirit-and-Fire Baptism," *NovT* 14 (1972): 89–92; Scobie, *John the Baptist*, 62–73; for the Aaronic Messiah see Ethelbert Stauffer, *New Testament Theology* (trans. John Marsh; London: SCM, 1955), 24 (cf. Davies and Allison, *Matthew*, 1:313); for the Son of Man see Becker, *Johannes der Täufer*, 34–37; Lohmeyer, *Johannes der Täufer*, 157–60; Kraeling, *John the Baptist*; on Elijah-*redivivus* see Albert Schweitzer, *The Quest of the Historical Jesus: A Critical Study of Its Progress from Reimarus to Wrede* (2nd ed.; trans. W. Montgomery; London: Black, 1911), 372–73; John A.T. Robinson, *Twelve New Testament Studies* (London: SCM, 1962), 28–33; repr. from "Elijah, John and Jesus: An Essay in Detection," *NTS* 4 (1957–58): 263–81.
[92] Kraeling, *John the Baptist*, 54.

ures was understood to bring judgment and restoration as God's agent – it was God's judgment and restoration being carried out by the expected figure. In fact, in some cases the text blends God as the bringer of the judgment and restoration with another expected figure who does it as God's agent. For example, in *Pss. Sol.* 17:1–3 God is the king and savior who will judge and restore his people, and yet in vv. 21–46 God raises up a Davidic Messiah to accomplish the task.[93] In the same way the Hebrew Bible describes God as saving Israel by bringing them out of Egypt and equally of Moses as the one who accomplished it. In such contexts a reference to God identifies a belief in a divine/heavenly prime cause for the judgment or restoration, but a reference to a past human figure or an expected figure identifies a historical/earthly outworking of the same judgment or restoration. Thus, John's expected figure primarily manifests the characteristics of God himself because this was evidently John's focus – that is, on what God was going to do, rather than on who was going to accomplish it or how it would happen in historical/earthly terms. Yet, the other features that point to a figure other than God indicate that John expected God to work through an agent.[94]

John clearly expected judgment (Matt 3:7–10 = Luke 3:7–9),[95] but he did not announce judgment only. The reference to baptizing "with holy spirit and fire" (Matt 3:11 = Luke 3:16; cf. Mark 1:8) might refer to a single activity,[96] but it is better understood to refer to the expected figure bestowing a "holy spirit" as a restorative action on the repentant and the "fire" as an act of judgment on the unrepentant.[97] The two actions are linked, however, for it is one "baptism," which is an act of purging that accomplishes both judgment and restoration. We should note that the expected figure's baptism is not producing these two groups (i.e., the repentant and the unrepentant); it is people's response to John's preaching and baptism that does

---

[93] E.g., Isa 9:2–7; Jer 23:3–4; Ezek 34:22–23; 37:21–24; CD 19:10–11, 15; 11QMelch 2:13; *T. Mos.* 10:2–3. I am indebted to Craig Evans for pointing out this same ambiguity in 4Q451, which refers to both the "Messiah" and the "Lord." But it is ambiguous which one is the "he" who brings the salvation described in the text.

[94] For further discussion, see Webb, *John the Baptizer*, 254–58, 284–88.

[95] On John and judgment see Helmut Merklein, "Die Umkerpredigt bei Johannes dem Täufer und Jesus von Nazaret," *BZ* 25 (1981): 29–46; P. Wolff, "Gericht und Reich Gottes bei Johannes und Jesus," in *Gegenwart und Kommendes Reich: Schülergabe Anton Vogtle Zum 65. Geburtstag* (ed. P. Fiedler and D. Zeller; BBS; Stuttgart: Katholisches Bibelwerk, 1975), 43–49. More recently, see the excellent discussion of John and judgment by Marius Reiser, *Jesus and Judgment: The Eschatological Proclamation in Its Jewish Context* (trans. Linda M. Maloney; Minneapolis: Fortress, 1997), 167–93.

[96] E.g., Dunn, "Spirit-and-Fire Baptism".

[97] Webb, *John the Baptizer*, 289–95. Cf. *Jub.* 1:23; *T. Levi* 2:3B7–8; *Sib. Or.* 4:188–89; 1QS 4:20–21; 1QH 16:12; 17:26. The authenticity of baptizing "with holy spirit" is a matter of considerable debate. For discussion of the alternatives, see Webb, *John the Baptizer*, 272–77.

this. The expected figure's action was to complete the process, bringing each group to their appropriate end – either restoration or judgment.

While the imagery of the farmer at the threshing floor is different from the imagery used in the expected figure's activity of baptism, the sense is similar (Matt 3:12 = Luke 3:17). The burning of chaff in unquenchable fire is a referent to the judgment of the unrepentant, while the statement "he will gather his wheat into the granary" alludes to restoration. This much is quite evident. However, what is frequently misunderstood is the precise activity of the farmer on the threshing floor. Usually, this metaphor is understood to be a farmer winnowing the wheat from the chaff. However, the verb διακαθαίρω does not signify "to winnow," but "to thoroughly purge, clean out,"[98] and the object of the verb is not grain but the threshing floor. Furthermore, the instrument in the farmer's hand, a winnowing shovel (πτύον), is actually used for piling the wheat and chaff and removing them from the winnowing floor, but not for the winnowing itself. The instrument for the act of winnowing itself is a winnowing fork (θρῖναξ).[99] Thus, the activity of John's expected figure being portrayed metaphorically here is *not* the separation of the repentant from the unrepentant (i.e., the wheat from the chaff) but, rather, taking each group to its appropriate end, whether blessing or judgment. As in the preceding discussion concerning the parallels between John's baptism and the expected figure's baptism, so it is implied in this metaphor also: it is the response to John's preaching and baptism that separates the repentant from the unrepentant (i.e., the wheat from the chaff), while the expected figure brings about the final judgment and restoration for these respective groups.

From this discussion we may now glean clues as to what John perceived about the judgment and restoration. First, the time of judgment and restoration is imminent. The mightier one "is coming" (Matt 3:11 = Mark 1:7 = Luke 3:16) and "the axe is already (ἤδη) laid at the root of the trees" (Matt 3:10 = Luke 3:9). Second, the judgment involves the removal of the unrepentant. It is not clear whom John perceived the unrepentant to be. With his baptism functioning as an alternative to the temple sacrifices, one sector of Jewish society that fits this category for John was probably the temple aristocracy. John's ethical and purity concerns, his expectation of restoration, and his criticism of Antipas' second marriage suggest another possible sector was the Roman imperialist powers and the people who supported them. Third, while it is difficult to be more precise about John's perception

---

[98] BDAG 229; LSJ 396.
[99] See *Letters of Alciphron* 2.23:1 for the noun πτύον used with the verb διακαθαίρω to describe the final cleaning of the threshing floor following the winnowing process. For further discussion, see Webb, *John the Baptizer*, 295–300; Webb, "Activity," 103–11.

of the judgment and restoration,[100] we can observe that John is *not* expecting the "end of the world" or the "destruction of the universe." John *does* expect a radical shift in the socio-political and religious life of Israel and the world, but it takes place within the continuity of the space-time universe. We should note that the fire in John's pictures only consumes the unfruitful trees (Matt 3:10 = Luke 3:9) and the chaff (Matt 3:12 = Luke 3:17); the orchard, the wheat, and the threshing floor all remain afterward.[101] The implication is that the unrighteous are removed and the righteous are blessed with a new situation, but one that is in continuity with their present, human existence.

3.3. John's Prophetic Role

Having examined the content of John's prophetic proclamation, we may now turn to the public role of prophet itself.[102] It is sometimes thought

---

[100] This is due to the fragmentary nature of our evidence as well as the observation made earlier, that John focused on the divine/heavenly perspective rather than on the historical/earthly specifics.

[101] This is contrary to those who interpret John in an apocalyptic, "end-of-the-world" framework. Kraeling (*John the Baptist*, 42), for example, states concerning John's view that "judgment has become a cosmic event of such scope and magnitude that it beggars analogy in terms of human experience." The use of "fire" imagery to portray judgment should hardly be used to characterize John the Baptist as an apocalyptic figure. Cf. Becker, *Johannes der Täufer*, 105.

[102] Bruce D. Chilton ("John the Purifier," in *Jesus in Context: Temple, Purity, and Restoration* [by Bruce Chilton and Craig A. Evans; AGJU 39; Leiden: Brill, 1997], 203–20) has recently called into question my analysis of John as prophet. He states that "the irony of the allegedly critical consensus which has emerged is that it so neatly confirms the evaluation of John in the Gospels' presentation" (p. 203). However, the Gospels do *not* *argue* that John is a prophet at all; rather, they assume it. That John was a prophet appears to be widely recognized, and is found in many diverse strands of the tradition. I would suggest instead, that what the Gospels *argue* in their presentation is an *interpretation* of John's prophetic role; namely, that John is the prophetic forerunner of Jesus. This is, in fact, the Gospels' evaluation of John. Chilton's discussion clearly rejects the historicity of this forerunner role as a later Christian interpretation, and I would agree with him in this evaluation. However, in rejecting the prophetic role itself, Chilton fails to distinguish the social role John played in Jewish society as a prophet and the Christian interpretation of that role. In so doing, Chilton throws the baby out with the bathwater. This is consistent with his rejection of any "recoverable message that explains his activity. Historically, his activity is itself as much of his program as we are ever likely to grasp" (p. 219). My own analysis of the traditions concerning John in the Gospels and Josephus is not as skeptical. Chilton's alternative to John as prophet is to portray John as "purifier," alluding to his baptizing activity (p. 212). He notes, however, that John is quite distinct from Bannus, the Qumran community, and other groups (pp. 212–17). His portrayal, dependent on Josephus' statement concerning John, is that "John's baptism was to serve as a ritual of purity following a return to righteousness" (p. 218; cf. pp. 218–19). Chilton's view appears to take Josephus at face value, not considering his biases or hellenizing tendencies. While I concur with Chilton that John's baptism is integral to his program, I think that to portray John's role as "purifier" is to create a unique category just for him. There is no evidence

that the last prophet was Malachi. His book is where the prophetic portion of the Hebrew Bible's canon ended, and some later texts support such a view.[103] Yet numerous figures did in fact arise during the Second Temple period who were believed by their followers to be prophets. Analysis of the social roles of these prophets reveals three different types of prophets: those whose prophetic role also involved being priests, those whose prophetic role also involved functioning as wise persons, and those whose prophetic role involved relating to the common people.[104] These may be identified respectively by the descriptive names clerical prophet,[105] sapiential prophet,[106] and popular prophet (the term "popular" is being used in the sense of that which relates to the populace or common people; one might consider using the term "populist" instead).[107]

While John may have come from a priestly family, he was not a priest while engaged in his prophetic ministry; thus he was not a clerical prophet. Instead, John was a popular prophet. His audience and following appear to have been primarily drawn from the common people – the Judean rural peasantry and the urban poor from Jerusalem.[108]

Examination of other popular prophets during the Second Temple period reveals two sub-types, depending upon whether in their prophetic role they functioned as leaders of prophetic movements or whether they remained lone individuals. I use the nomenclature of "leadership popular prophets"

---

that "purifier" was a socially recognized role within second Temple Judaism. But, a man who has a program, proclaims that program to crowds, and practices a symbolic action as part of that program might just be perceived in what is a socially recognized role in second Temple Judaism – a prophet. And such a perception does not require a Christian presentation at all.

[103] E. g., 1 Macc 9:27; Josephus, *Ag. Ap.* 1.37–41; *t. Soṭah* 13:3.

[104] For further discussion of prophetic typologies and analysis of all three types of prophets, see Webb, *John the Baptizer*, 307–48. For a similar typology, see Horsley, "'Like One of the Prophets of Old'," 435–63; Horsley and Hanson, *Bandits, Prophets, and Messiahs*, 135–89.

[105] Examples of this type of prophet include John Hyrcanus I (Josephus, *J. W.* 1.68–69; *Ant.* 13.282–283, 299–300, 322), and Josephus himself (*J. W.* 3.351–354, 400–402, 406–407; cf. *Life* 1–6). Cf. discussion in Webb, *John the Baptizer*, 317–22; David E. Aune, *Prophecy in Early Christianity and the Ancient Mediterranean World* (Grand Rapids: Eerdmans, 1983), 138–44.

[106] Examples of this type of prophet include those identified as Essenes (Josephus, *J. W.* 2.159), including Judas the Essene (*J. W.* 1.78–80; *Ant.* 13.311–313), Menahem (*Ant.* 15.373–379), Simon (*Ant.* 17.345–347), as well as those identified as Pharisees (*Ant.* 17.41–45), including Samaias (*Ant.* 14.172–176; cf. the name Pollion in *Ant.* 15.3–4). Cf. discussion in Webb, *John the Baptizer*, 321–32; Aune, *Prophecy*, 144–52.

[107] Cf. Webb, *John the Baptizer*, 333–46; Horsley, "'Like One of the Prophets of Old'," 435–63; Horsley and Hanson, *Bandits, Prophets, and Messiahs*, 135–89.

[108] Josephus, *Ant.* 18.118; Matt 3:5 = Mark 1:5; Matt 21:31–32 = Luke 7:29–30; Luke 3:10–14; 3:15, 18; Matt 21:26 = Mark 11:32 = Luke 20:6.

and "solitary popular prophets"[109] to distinguish between these sub-types.[110] Richard A. Horsley and John S. Hanson concluded that John the Baptist was a solitary popular prophet (though they use the nomenclature of "oracular prophet").[111] However, several streams of evidence point to the alternate conclusion, that John was a leadership popular prophet – that is, in his prophetic role, John was the leader of a movement. First of all, as we concluded above, John's baptism functioned as an initiatory rite into the true, remnant Israel.[112] Second, Josephus' description of the crowd that was excited by John's teaching and that led Antipas to fear an outbreak of strife (*Ant.* 18.118) implies a certain amount of group formation. Third, John's perception of imminent judgment and restoration discussed above also implies the formation of a distinctive identity held by those who had been baptized by John. The cumulative effect of this evidence points to the formation of a group. Group formation only implies a distinctive identity by a group of people, manifesting an insider/outsider or "us and them" perspective. This does not necessarily mean they were organized or maintained a separatist communal lifestyle, as did the Qumran community. As the prophet whose proclamation and activities brought about the formation of this group and provided its distinctive self-perception, John constituted the group's leader and is thus best understood to be a leadership popular prophet.[113]

---

[109] Chilton ("John the Purifier," 209, n. 25) criticizes this nomenclature as a "solecism." In so doing, Chilton focuses upon the name only and fails to take into consideration the discussion that the name attempts to encapsulate. Perhaps the suggestion above – using the term "populist" – might alleviate the concern.

[110] Examples of leadership popular prophets include the Samaritan (Josephus, *Ant.* 18.85–87), Theudas (*Ant.* 20.97–98), several unnamed prophets when Felix was procurator (*J. W.* 2.258–260; *Ant.* 20.167–168), the Egyptian (*J. W.* 2.261–263; *Ant.* 20.169–172; Acts 21:38), an unnamed prophet when Festus was procurator (*Ant.* 20.188); cf. also Acts 5:36. Examples of solitary popular prophets include several unnamed prophets during Herod's seige of Jerusalem (*J. W.* 1.347), Joshua ben Hananiah (*J. W.* 6.300–309), one unnamed prophet during the Jewish War (*J. W.* 6.285), and several other unnamed prophets during the Jewish War (*J. W.* 6.286–288). For further discussion, see Horsley, "'Like One of the Prophets of Old'," 435–63; Horsley and Hanson, *Bandits, Prophets, and Messiahs*, 135–89; Webb, *John the Baptizer*, 333–46.

[111] Horsley and Hanson, *Bandits, Prophets, and Messiahs*, 172–73; cf. Horsley, "'Like One of the Prophets of Old'," 450–54.

[112] Horsley and Hanson (*Bandits, Prophets, and Messiahs*, 178) recognize this function: "Baptism in the Jordan was the rite ... by which persons passed into the eschatologically reconstituted community of Israel which would survive God's judgment." Yet they do not appear to realize the implication of this: it was the people's response to John's prophetic proclamation and baptism that formed this "reconstituted community."

[113] For examination of the implications of this in comparison with other leadership popular prophets, see Webb, *John the Baptizer*, 355–77. For an application of sociological theory on social structure and alienation to John in this regard, see Carl R. Kazmierski, "The Stones of Abraham: John the Baptist and the End of Torah (Matt 3,7–10 par. Luke

3.4. John's Life and Death

Having examined his public roles, we conclude this survey of John the Baptist by considering briefly a few other facets of what may be known about him.

In his infancy narrative, Luke recounts the events surrounding the expectation and birth of John into a priestly family in rural Judea (Luke 1:5–25, 39–45, 57–79). Some scholars have proposed that behind Luke 1 stands a source derived from followers of the Baptist, a source that was subsequently Christianized, but others have disputed this claim.[114] Whatever the case, it is widely recognized that using this account for historical purposes is problematic.[115] Nevertheless, John's rural priestly heritage is widely accepted.[116]

Subsequent to the discovery of the Qumran scrolls, speculation raged over whether or not John was himself a member of the Qumran community because of some similarities between their belief system and John's.[117] This speculation was fueled by the intriguing reference concerning John's upbringing in Luke 1:80, that "he was in the wilderness until the day he publicly appeared to Israel." In light of Josephus' description of celibate Essenes who adopted and raised children (*J. W.* 2.120), Luke's statement was interpreted to mean that John was raised in Qumran community. However, concrete evidence of John's membership in the Qumran community is lack-

---

3,7–9)," *Bib* 68 (1987): 22–40, esp. 32–34. Taylor (*The Immerser*, 233) rejects this category for John, saying that "there is no evidence that he predicted that signs and wonders would take place ..." I grant this evidence, but the paradigm I proposed for the various types of prophets, of which leadership popular prophet was one, is based on the social role played by the prophet, not on the type of prophecy uttered.

[114] For discussion and bibliography, see Walter Wink, *John the Baptist in the Gospel Tradition* (SNTSMS 7; London: Cambridge University Press, 1968), 60–72, and more recently, Raymond E. Brown, "Gospel Infancy Narrative Research from 1976 to 1986: Part II (Luke)," *CBQ* 48 (1986): 660–70.

[115] The debate on this issue does not impact the focus of this essay, and so it is not pursued here.

[116] E.g., Paul Hollenbach, "Social Aspects of John the Baptizer's Preaching Mission in the Context of Palestinian Judaism," *ANRW* 2.19.1.852–853; Fitzmyer, *Luke I–IX*, 317; Kraeling, *John the Baptist*, 21–25; Scobie, *John the Baptist*, 55–57; Ernst, *Johannes der Täufer*, 269–72; Richard A. Horsley, *The Liberation of Christmas: The Infancy Narratives in Social Context* (New York: Crossroad, 1989), 91–92.

[117] E.g., W.H. Brownlee, "John the Baptist in the New Light of Ancient Scrolls," in *The Scrolls and the New Testament* (ed. Krister Stendahl; London: SCM, 1958), 33–53; Robinson, *Twelve New Testament Studies*, 11–27; Albert S. Geyser, "The Youth of John the Baptist: A Deduction from the Break in the Parallel Account of the Lucan Infancy Story," *NovT* 1 (1956): 70–75; Otto Betz, "Was John the Baptist an Essene?" *BRev* 6 (1990): 18–25. See also more recently, James H. Charlesworth, "John the Baptizer and the Dead Sea Scrolls," in *The Scrolls and Christian Origins* (ed. James H. Charlesworth; vol. 3 of *The Bible and the Dead Sea Scrolls: The Princeton Symposium on the Dead Sea Scrolls*; Waco: Baylor University Press, 2006), 1–35.

ing. And even if John had been a member at one time, aspects of his teaching are sufficiently different from that found in the Qumran scrolls that one would be forced to conclude that John had broken away from them. Thus while an intriguing hypothesis, it remains speculation.[118]

The NT identifies the locale of John's activities as the wilderness (Matt 3:1 = Mark 1:4 = Luke 3:2; Luke 1:80) and the region around the Jordan river (Matt 3:5–6 = Mark 1:5; Luke 3:3), including the eastern bank of the Jordan (John 1:23; 3:26; 10:40).[119] This location was consistent with John's emphasis on imminent judgment and restoration because it puts him and his audience in touch with important symbols from their past history. The wilderness and the Jordan River were symbols associated with the Exodus and Conquest. It is interesting to observe the parallel between John and other leadership popular prophets on this point. For them, and probably for John also, the Jordan River and the wilderness functioned as reminders of God's redemptive actions taken on their behalf in the past and as symbols of hope in a similar redemption in the imminent future.[120]

John's location also leads us to consider his conflict with Herod Antipas. The accounts in both the NT and Josephus' *Antiquities* place John in direct conflict with Antipas, and they identify Antipas as the one responsible for his arrest and execution. Yet, as tetrarch of Galilee and Perea, Antipas had no jurisdiction over Judea, which was under direct Roman rule. John's locale, however, being the lower Jordan River valley, placed John near Perea and in it when John crossed into the Transjordan. It would have been while he was across the Jordan in Perea that Antipas could have arrested John.

Furthermore, in this location John also would have had contact with the Nabateans, a trading people whose border was less than 20 kilometers to the east and who had a major trade route passing from Nabatea through Perea

---

[118] Cf. the critique by Walter Wink, "John the Baptist and the Gospel," Th.D. diss (New York: Union Theological Seminary, 1963), 75–103; Webb, *John the Baptizer*, 351, n. 4; Robert L. Webb, "John the Baptist," in *Encyclopedia of the Dead Sea Scrolls* (2 vols.; ed. Lawrence H. Schiffman and James C. VanderKam; Oxford: Oxford University Press, 2000), 1:418–21. The discussion by Taylor (*The Immerser*, 15–48) is also helpful.

[119] Willi Marxsen (*Mark the Evangelist* [2nd ed.; trans. James Boyce; Nashville: Abingdon, 1969], 34–38) questioned the historicity of the wilderness tradition, but he did so on the incorrect assumption that "wilderness" and "region around the Jordan" are incompatible references to the same locality. The term ἔρημος ("wilderness") does not necessarily refer to a desert without water – only a uninhabited, uncultivated area. Josephus (*J. W.* 3.515) describes the Jordan river "meandering through a long wilderness area." For further discussion, see Chester Charlton McCown, "The Scene of John's Ministry and Its Relation to the Purpose and Outcome of His Mission," *JBL* 59 (1940): 113–31; Funk, "The Wilderness". On the references to John's locality in the Fourth Gospel, see C. H. Dodd, *Historical Tradition in the Fourth Gospel* (Cambridge: Cambridge University Press, 1963), 236, 279. Cf. also the discussion in Ernst, *Johannes der Täufer*, 278–84.

[120] Josephus, *J. W.* 2.259, 261–262; *Ant.* 20.97, 168. Cf. Horsley, "'Like One of the Prophets of Old'," 457; Webb, *John the Baptizer*, 361–66.

and into Judea. At first John's locale may appear insignificant, but it actually contributes toward understanding the conflict between John and Antipas. The Synoptic Gospels explain that Antipas arrested John for condemning his marriage to Herodias (Matt 14:3–4 = Mark 6:17–18 = Luke 3:19–20), but Josephus explains that Antipas arrested John because "he feared his great persuasiveness with the people might lead to some kind of strife" (*Ant.* 18.118). The wife Antipas had divorced in order to marry Herodias was the daughter of Aretas IV, king of Nabatea. The marriage had been part of a treaty that had provided peace between the Nabateans and the Roman province of Perea. But this divorce was taken as an insult by the Nabatean royal family and later led to war between Aretas and Antipas in which Antipas was defeated and had to be rescued by the Romans (*Ant.* 18.109–125). John's proximity to and contact with the Nabateans rendered his attack on Antipas' new marriage a political threat to the stability of the region.[121] It is interesting to note that Josephus refers to John's arrest and execution by Antipas (*Ant.* 18.116–119) in the context of narrating how Herod's divorce of his first wife precipitated the war between Antipas and Aretas. In other words, his narrative order suggests a link between Herod's divorce and John's arrest; the NT account makes this link explicit.

The explanation of John's conflict with Antipas in the NT is personal and moral (John condemned his marriage) while Josephus' explanation is public and political (Antipas feared strife). While appearing contradictory, these two explanations are actually quite compatible. The NT explains that John condemned Antipas' second marriage because Antipas had married his brother's wife. This action was contrary to the Torah (Lev 18:16) and resulted in impurity (Lev 20:21). Implied in John's condemnation was the charge that the ruler of Galilee and Perea, regions with a large Jewish population, was breaking the Jewish Torah and was therefore unclean. These charges would probably not have greatly concerned Antipas, whose religious persuasions appear to have been minimal at best. But such charges would raise the level of discontent among his Jewish subjects. When this discontent is placed within the context of John's proclamation of judgment and restoration (which would include judgment of Antipas and restoration of faithfulness to the Torah) and his announcement of an expected figure who was coming to bring this judgment and restoration, John's personal attack of Antipas had clear political implications. The implications of the

---

[121] Cf. Kraeling's statement (*John the Baptist*, 90–91, cf. 87–91) that John's rebuke "was not only embarrassing, it was politically explosive. It meant aligning the pious Jewish inhabitants of Peraea with those of Arabic stock against their sovereign and thus fomenting sedition and encouraging insurrection." On this point see also Harold W. Hoehner, *Herod Antipas* (SNTMS 17; Cambridge: Cambridge University Press, 1972), 142–45; Webb, *John the Baptizer*, 366–70.

NT portrayal of John are thus quite consistent with Antipas' fear that John's "great persuasiveness with the people might lead to some kind of strife."[122]

The Roman authorities responded to the rise of leadership popular prophets and their movements with swift and brutal military action, usually resulting in the execution of the leader and the scattering and/or death of the followers.[123] Similarly, John was arrested by Antipas, imprisoned in Machaerus,[124] and later executed.[125] Our sources are silent on whether or not any followers experienced a similar fate.[126]

4. Implications of Jesus' Baptism by John for understanding Jesus

Having ascertained the probability that Jesus was baptized by John, and having established an understanding of John's baptism and other elements of his ministry within the context of first-century Judaism, we are now

---

[122] Cf. Ellis Rivkin, "Locating John the Baptizer in Palestinian Judaism: The Political Dimension," in *SBL Seminar Papers, 1983* (SBLSP 22; Chico, CA: Scholars, 1983), 79–85; Taylor, *The Immerser*, 213–59.

[123] Cf. the references above to these prophets in Josephus' *Antiquities* and *Jewish War*.

[124] The Synoptic Gospels do not state the location of John's arrest and execution. Mark 6 begins with Jesus in Galilee (6:1–2) and then states that Antipas hears of Jesus' ministry (6:14–16). The narrative continues with the lurid account of Antipas' banquet and John's beheading (6:17–29). It is sometimes claimed that Antipas hearing about Jesus in Galilee places John's arrest and execution in Tiberias, the location of Antipas' home in Galilee. But this is an unnecessary assumption based on a rather superficial reading of the text. The record of John's execution is a flashback in Mark's narrative, and it should be treated as such. Mark simply does not state where the banquet and beheading took place (cf. the silence in Matt 14:1–12; Luke 2:18–20). Josephus, on the other hand, states clearly that John was executed at Machaerus (*Ant*. 18.119). Machaerus was located east of the Dead Sea in Antipas' territory. It was an excellent fortification and contained a beautiful palace. Due to its higher altitude it would have been cooler in summer than Tiberias (cf. Josephus, *J. W.* 7.164–177, 186–189). It is an emminently plausible location for John to have been imprisoned and executed, particularly since it is only a few miles from John's location in the lower Jordan River Valley.

[125] On the problems surrounding the NT account of Antipas' banquet and John's beheading, see Hoehner, *Herod Antipas*, 149–71; Joachim Gnilka, "Das Martyrium Johannes' des Täufers (Mark 6,17–29)," in *Orientierung an Jesus: Zur Theologie der Synoptiker: Für Josef Schmid* (Paul Hoffmann; Freiburg: Herder, 1973), 78–92.

[126] Antipas did not, evidently, engage in wholesale execution of John's followers, as the Romans themselves sometimes did with followers of leadership popular prophets. As a client ruler responsible to Rome, Antipas was probably astute enough to realize that such an action would result in an outcry to Rome from his subjects. If this had happened, he might have been deposed in a manner similar to that of his tyrannical brother, Archelaus (cf. Josephus, *J. W.* 2.111; *Ant*. 17.342–44).

ready to bring these two together in order to appreciate the implications of Jesus' baptism by John for our understanding of Jesus.[127]

4.1. The Turning Point in Jesus' Life

Prior to being baptized, Jesus had lived the life of a peasant artisan[128] in the Galilean town of Nazareth. We do not know what led Jesus to make the trek south to where John baptized in the Jordan. For Jesus, being baptized was a turning point in his life – he would never return to that former life. The baptism was the point at which Jesus turned from his former peasant artisan life and turned to a life of ministry. Whether this turning began back in Galilee and was culminated in being baptized, or whether it began with the baptism and the implications were worked out afterwards, is a nuance that we are unable to address for lack of evidence. But whatever is the case, the event of Jesus' baptism is significant as identifying the pinnacle of this turning point.

But the issue of "turning" point has a deeper issue associated with it. Mark describes John's baptism as "a baptism of repentance for the forgiveness of sins" (Mark 1:4b) and when people were baptized, they did so "confessing their sins" (Mark 1:5b). No account, Mark's included, states that Jesus confessed his sins when he was baptized, nor do the accounts specify of what Jesus needed to repent – from what Jesus needed to "turn." As addressed above, the later accounts attempt damage control because of theological problems that this baptism of repentance creates. We must address the historical question that it raises: Of what did Jesus need to repent?

In their attempt to mitigate the potential theological damage that the issue raises, as explored above, our sources are not going to be directly helpful. We are left with three alternatives at this point. First of all, we could simply take the approach found in early Christian Gospels. In the first section of this essay we noted the theological concerns about this issue developing in Matthew through to the *Gospel according to the Nazareans*. However, our historical concerns are different from their theological concerns. From a methodological perspective, a theological presupposition cannot take the place of considering historical questions and their evidence.[129]

---

[127] The focus in this essay is specifically on the implications of Jesus' baptism by John. Elsewhere I have explored other implications of the relationship between John and Jesus; see Webb, "John the Baptist and His Relationship to Jesus," 214–29.

[128] Mark 6:3 identifies Jesus as ὁ τέκτων (cf. Matt 13:55), which identifies one who is a builder, working with wood or stone. To translate this as "carpenter" may be too narrow a designation; thus my use of the term "artisan." See "τέκτων," BDAG 995. The term "peasant" simply identifies Jesus' socially as being of the laboring class.

[129] It is frequently recognized that the conversation between Jesus and John at the baptism in Matt 3:14–15 is Matthew's attempt to mitigate the theological issues raised by

Second, we could make possible inferences about Jesus' state of mind from what we may know about his background and suggest possible sins of which Jesus may have been guilty. This is the approach of Hollenbach. He proposes that, as a carpenter, Jesus was a middle-class artisan upon whom the poor of society depended. Jesus would have seen the abuses this social stratification would have allowed. "[T]hrough John's preaching Jesus discovered that he had participated directly or indirectly in the oppression of the weak members of his society."[130] There are a number of difficulties with Hollenbach's approach, but the two most telling are that it is highly speculative, and it is ultimately an attempt to psychologize about Jesus' state of mind. There is, in fact, no historical evidence of a particular sin for which Jesus needed to repent. The texts are silent.

Third, we could return to the nature of John's baptism and investigate further the character of repentance and confession of sin. This approach is suggested by Meier and proves to be the most helpful way forward on this issue. He points out that

> [c]onfession of sin in ancient Israel did not mean unraveling a lengthy laundry-list of personal peccadilloes, with the result that worship of God was turned into a narcissistic reflection on the self. Confession of sin in ancient Israel was a God-centred act of worship that included praise and thanksgiving. Confession of sin often meant recalling God's gracious deeds for an ungrateful Israel, a humble admission that one was a member of this sinful people, a recounting of the infidelities and apostasies of Israel from early on down to one's own day, and a final resolve to change and be different from one's ancestors.[131]

Meier points to the prayers of confession by Ezra as well the prayers by the initiates into the Qumran community as examples.[132] These prayers of confession are not for personal sins at all but, rather, for Israel's sins as a nation.

This approach is further supported by observing the character of John's message. He was addressing all Israel – that is, Israel as a nation – and calling them to a radical reconstitution of Israel in light of its imminent eschatological future. If this is so, then John was calling for the people to respond to who they were as a nation, not really who they were as individuals. Of course, it was individuals who had to respond, and many could respond out of a personal sense of responsibility for Israel's state. But equally, many of those in Israel – who would be considered faithful – could respond out of a

---

Jesus being baptized according to a baptism of repentance. The passage is questionable historically due to its single attestation and its manifest apologetic concern. Cf. Davies and Allison, *Matthew*, 1:323.

[130] Paul Hollenbach, "The Conversion of Jesus: From Jesus the Baptizer to Jesus the Healer," *ANRW* 2.25.1.199; cf. 198–200.

[131] Meier, *Mentor, Message, and Miracles*, 113–14. See also the recent discussion by Tobias Hägerland, "Jesus and the Rites of Repentance," *NTS* 52 (2006): 166–87.

[132] Ezra 9:6–15; Neh 9:6–37; 1QS 1:18–2:2.

belief in and desire for John's reconstituted Israel.¹³³ Thus, without having to speculate about Jesus' personal state of mind, we can conclude that Jesus did indeed participate in John's baptism, and it was for him a baptism of repentance. Jesus was acknowledging Israel's sin and need to turn around, and he was committing himself to do what he could to bring this about.

4.2. The Earliest Stage of Jesus' Ministry[134]

A second area to be investigated is the implications of Jesus' baptism for appreciating what the earliest stage of Jesus' ministry involved. I am defining this earliest stage as Jesus' ministry *prior to* the arrest of John the Baptist.

Those who were baptized by John became part of John's reconstituted Israel, or in other words, part of John's movement. In so doing, they became identified as followers of John. It would appear that John had two types of followers. First of all, there were those who were baptized and returned to their homes, though they were still part of the reconstituted true / remnant Israel being formed through John's ministry. Second, there were those who were baptized and remained with him to participate more fully in his program and to be taught by him. John had disciples with whom he practiced fasting (Matt 9:14 = Mark 2:18 = Luke 5:33), and whom he had taught to pray, perhaps in some distinctive fashion (Luke 11:1). These disciples were with him (John 1:35; 3:25–26) and were available to serve him (Matt 11:2 = Luke 7:18). Josephus may also have been referring to these disciples when he describes those who gathered around John as those who were "excited to the utmost by listening to his teachings," and "they seemed as if they would do everything which he counselled" (*Ant.* 18.118).[135]

Through his baptism by John, Jesus was not only in agreement with John, he was effectively joining John's movement and becoming a follower of John. In the next section we consider John 3 in greater detail, but it is sufficient at this point to observe that this text suggests that Jesus stayed with John the Baptist for some time. Therefore, of the two types of disciples John had, Jesus was one of those who remained with John to participate fully in his program.[136]

---

[133] With this understanding, I am disagreeing with those scholars interpret John's program as providing purity to people considered unclean, and thus John's baptism had only an individualist focus. E.g., Bruce D. Chilton, *Jesus' Baptism and Jesus' Healing: His Personal Practice of Spirituality* (Harrisburg: Trinity, 1998), 1–29, esp. 28–29; Chilton, "John the Purifier," 218–19; Taylor, *The Immerser*, 49–100.

[134] The material in this section is a revision of a portion out of my earlier work, Webb, "John the Baptist and His Relationship to Jesus," 218–22.

[135] Cf. other references to John's disciples, such as Matt 14:12 = Mark 6:29; Acts 18:25; 19:3–4.

[136] Others who conclude that Jesus was a disciple of John include Maurice Goguel, *The Life of Jesus* (trans. Olive Wyon; New York: Macmillan, 1944), 269–70; Oscar Cullmann,

This conclusion raises at least one important question: Did Jesus participate for a time in John's ministry and movement?[137] The Synoptic Gospels identify the start of Jesus' public ministry as beginning after the arrest of John (Matt 4:12 = Mark 1:14; cf. Luke 3:19; 4:14). But this leaves unexplained why Jesus remained in Judea after being baptized, not returning to Galilee until John's arrest.[138] Data from the Fourth Gospel help to fill in this gap.[139] John 3:22–24 describes Jesus as going with his disciples into the Judean countryside, where he remained with them and baptized.[140] John was also baptizing nearby.

This brief scene could be interpreted in at least three different ways. First, Jesus had a baptizing ministry with his own disciples that was separate and distinct from John's activities.[141] Jesus could even be understood to be competing with John as a rival.[142] Second, Jesus' baptizing ministry may be understood as aligned with John's in such a way that Jesus baptizes under

---

The Early Church: Studies in Early Christian History and Theology (London: SCM, 1956), 177–82; Robinson, *Twelve New Testament Studies*, 39–40; W. R. Farmer, "John the Baptist," *IDB* 2:959; Dodd, *Historical Tradition*, 272–75; Marie-Émile Boismard, "Les traditions johanniques concernant le Baptiste," *RB* 70 (1963): 29; Wink, *John the Baptist*, 38, 55. See also the more recent work of Daniel S. Dapaah, *The Relationship Between John the Baptist and Jesus of Nazareth: A Critical Study* (Lanham, Md.: University Press of America, 2005), 85–118. Josef Ernst ("War Jesus ein Schüler Johannes' des Täufers?" in *Vom Urchristentum zu Jesus: Für Joachim Gnilka* [ed. Hubert Frankemölle and Karl Kertelge; Freiberg: Herder, 1989], 13–33), on the other hand, argues against such a conclusion, but he fails to appreciate the significance of Jesus' baptism by John with respect to this issue.

[137] Two other questions that I've considered elsewhere are: (1) Did Jesus change and move beyond the framework provided by John's ministry and movement, and if so, what produced this change? (2) In what ways is Jesus' later ministry in continuity with John, and in what ways is it different? See my discussion in Webb, "John the Baptist and His Relationship to Jesus," 223–29.

[138] Meyer, *The Aims of Jesus*, 122.

[139] The historical reliability of these traditions concerning the Baptist and Jesus are widely accepted. For discussion see, e.g., Meyer, *The Aims of Jesus*, 122, esp. n. 23; Sanders, *Jesus and Judaism*, 92; Joachim Jeremias, *New Testament Theology: The Proclamation of Jesus* (trans. John Bowden; New York: Scribner, 1971), 45–46; Dodd, *Historical Tradition*, 279–87, 290–93; Linnemann, "Jesus und der Täufer," 219–36, esp. 221–23; Boismard, "Les Traditions Johanniques," 35; Robinson, *Twelve New Testament Studies*, 39–43; Jerome Murphy-O'Connor, "John the Baptist and Jesus: History and Hypotheses," *NTS* 36 (1990): 363; Ernst, *Johannes der Täufer*, 206–10.

[140] The statement in John 4:2 is generally understood to be a later editor's correction of 3:22 (and 4:1) because of the difficulties perceived by having Jesus portrayed as one who baptized. Cf. Raymond E. Brown, *The Gospel According to John I–XII* (AB 29; New York: Doubleday, 1966), 164; Jeremias, *New Testament Theology*, 45–46.

[141] Cf. Sanders, *Jesus and Judaism*, 92; Rudolf Schnackenburg, *The Gospel According to John* (3 vols.; New York: Seabury, 1980–82), 1:410–11.

[142] Wink (*John the Baptist*, 94) suggests rivalry but interprets this to be the results of the portrayal by the fourth Evangelist.

the umbrella of John's baptizing movement.[143] Third, Jesus began baptizing in association with John (as in the second alternative), but gradually they parted company over differences (as implied in the first alternative).[144]

Given the limited data within the Fourth Gospel, choosing between these alternatives is difficult but not impossible. Two preliminary observations may be made to guide the process. We must distinguish historical data contained in this text from what the fourth Evangelist is doing with this material and the narrative framework in which it is now found. Second, our understanding of the relationship between John and Jesus arising out of this text must cohere with what we may deduce from our other sources.

Applying these two observations to the question at hand makes the second alternative the most probable of the three. Separate activities and rivalry (the first alternative) might be implied by the statement that Jesus had his own disciples (John 3:22; cf. 1:35-51) and the complaint about Jesus by John's disciples in John 3:26. However, the reference in 3:22 to Jesus having disciples may be the result of the Evangelist's editorial activity. It makes this text consistent with the larger narrative framework, especially the account in John 1 about John's disciples leaving him to follow Jesus. On the other hand, having disciples *per se* does not preclude Jesus' activities from being part of John's movement. In fact, it is eminently plausible for Jesus to have his own followers and to be baptizing in a separate location and yet to be associated with John's movement.[145] Furthermore, we should observe that any indication of separateness or rivalry in the Fourth Gospel is only between some of their disciples, not between John and Jesus. The Fourth Gospel portrays John in support of Jesus (3:27-30) and Jesus in support of John (4:1-3).

Finally, the statement in the 3:22b-23a makes no distinction between the activities of Jesus and John: Jesus "... was baptizing, and John was also baptizing ..." (... ἐβάπτιζεν. ἦν δὲ καὶ ὁ Ἰωάννης βαπτίζων ...). Jesus had, prior to this point in time, been baptized by John (for the implication of this baptism, see above). Subsequently he held the opinion that John was a prophet, that no one was greater than John (Matt 11:9-11 = Luke 7:26-28), and that John's baptism was from God (Matt 21:24-27 = Mark 11:28-33 = Luke 20:2-8). Jesus' own baptizing ministry, therefore, must be seen in continuity with what precedes it (i.e., his own baptism) and what follows

---

[143] Cf. Meyer, *The Aims of Jesus*, 122; Murphy-O'Connor, "John the Baptist and Jesus," 365; Hollenbach, "Conversion of Jesus," *ANRW* 2.25.1.204-206.

[144] Cf. Scobie, *John the Baptist*, 153-56. Goguel develops an extensive thesis based on this last alternative, but one that suffers from extensive speculation; cf. Goguel, *Jean-Baptiste*, 235-74; Goguel, *The Life of Jesus*, 271-76.

[145] Meyer (*The Aims of Jesus*, 283-84, n. 23) makes this point and cites Anton Fridrichsen: "'the man of God' in the ancient Orient 'is never isolated. He is always the centre of a circle taught by his words and example ...'"

it (i.e., his high opinion of John). Therefore, to read into this text that Jesus was engaging in a baptizing ministry separate from and in opposition to John's movement may be an attempt to preserve a distinctive Jesus similar to the attempt by the Evangelist himself.[146]

Therefore, of the three alternatives listed above, the second alternative is to be preferred over the first. But what about the third alternative, which asserted that Jesus began baptizing in association with John, and later they parted ways in disagreement? This alternative is to be distinguished from *later* differences between Jesus and John as found in the Synoptic Gospels (e.g., Matt 11:16–19 = Luke 7:31–35; see below). The focus of this alternative is the relationship between John and Jesus while both engaged in baptizing ministries. Growing tension and disagreement between them at this point in their ministries is an assertion based primarily on interpreting John 3:25 ("Now a discussion arose between John's disciples and a Jew concerning purification [μετὰ Ἰουδαίου περὶ καθαρισμοῦ]") as a reference to a debate between John's disciples and Jesus or one of Jesus' disciples. This is one possible conclusion given the context. But it could also refer to a more generic debate between members of various religious movements in this wilderness area who emphasized the role of ablutions for purification.[147] In light of the ambiguity of the text, no alternative can command high probability. But perhaps a third alternative is more likely than the others. It is based on observing that the issue of the debate is defined as purification (καθαρισμός). Elsewhere in the Fourth Gospel this term is used for the traditional Jewish rites of cleansing (John 2:6). This usage is reflected in similar contexts in the Synoptic Gospels.[148] But in no other text anywhere is this term used of John's baptism. What is more likely, then, is that the debate concerned a more traditional view of Jewish purification or purification rites versus the way that John's baptism functioned.[149] If so, then it is unlikely that the debate was between John's disciples and Jesus or Jesus' disciples.

Within this broader context of debate (John 3:25), we are introduced to the specific problem that John's disciples had with Jesus (3:26). This next verse states that John's disciples came and complained to John about Jesus. Sometimes the assumption is made that the disciples' complaint about Jesus arose out of the debate in the preceding verse. Charles Scobie, who is a proponent of this interpretation, proposes emending μετὰ Ἰουδαίου to

---

[146] Cf. the Johannine interpretation of John and his baptism in John 1:6–9, 15, 19–42. Wink, *John the Baptist*, 93–95; Webb, *John the Baptizer*, 76–77.

[147] Cf. William B. Badke, "Was Jesus a Discple of John?" *EvQ* 62 (1990): 202.

[148] E.g., Mark 1:44 = Luke 5:14; Luke 2:22; cf. also the use of the related verb, καθαρίζω, in the Synoptic Gospels.

[149] Cf. Brown, *John I–XII*, 151–52.

μετὰ Ἰησοῦ or μετὰ τῶν Ἰησοῦ to support this interpretation.[150] However, while 3:25 may be vague, such ingenious textual emendation remains pure speculation. This view must remain conjectural, as Scobie admits: "we may *conjecture* that Jesus and his disciples were not strict enough [concerning rites of ritual purity] for John's liking."[151] The next pericope (3:26–30) does in fact make specific the nature of the complaint by John's disciples: more people are going to Jesus to be baptized than to John (3:27; cf. 4:1). While this could have given rise to division between the two, this text portrays John and Jesus as refusing to make this an issue (3:27–30; 4:1–3). This is consistent with the portrayal of their relationship in the Synoptic Gospels.

To summarize, Jesus was baptized by John and probably remained with him for some time in the role of disciple. Later, in alignment and participation with John and his movement, Jesus also engaged in a baptizing ministry near John. Although he was still a disciple of John, Jesus perhaps should be viewed at this point as John's right-hand man or protegé.[152] While tensions may have arisen between John's disciples and those around Jesus, the two men viewed themselves as working together. Only later, after the arrest of John, does a shift take place in which Jesus moves beyond the conceptual framework of John's movement in certain respects. Yet Jesus always appears appreciative of the foundation that framework initially provided for him.

4.3. *The Ideological Framework for the Earliest Stage of Jesus' Ministry and Extrapolations to His Later Ministry*

I continue to use the term "earliest stage" to identify the period of Jesus' ministry prior to the arrest of John. By "later ministry" I refer to Jesus' ministry after John's arrest – the ministry that is the focus of the Gospel narratives.[153]

In being baptized by John, Jesus indicated his essential agreement with John's message. Presumably he heard John himself proclaim his message. To summarize the discussion above, John announced that Israel as the people of God had sinned and gone astray, and so they were facing the imminent,

---

[150] Scobie, *John the Baptist*, 154, following Goguel, *The Life of Jesus*, 274, and nineteenth century scholars. Cf. also Schnackenburg, *John*, 1:413.

[151] Scobie, *John the Baptist*, 155, my emphasis. Cf. the rejection of this view by Dodd, *Historical Tradition*, 280, n. 2. The text does manifest a textual problem at this point, but it is only between the singular μετὰ Ἰουδαίου and the plural μετὰ Ἰουδαίων. No textual evidence exists, however, for the emendation.

[152] Murphy-O'Connor ("John the Baptist and Jesus," 363) calls Jesus John's "assistant." Cf. Raymond E. Brown ("Jesus and Elisha," *Perspective* 12 [1971]: 87) who suggests that "Jesus was to the Baptist as Elisha was to Elijah."

[153] Cf. the shift that takes place in Mark 1:14: "Now after John was arrested, Jesus came to Galilee, proclaiming the good news of God ..."

eschatological judgment of God. To be saved from this judgment, the people had to fundamentally change inwardly and outwardly (i. e., repentance understood as conversion), and they had to express this repentance by receiving his baptism. Those who responded with repentance and baptism would be saved from the imminent judgment and would participate in the eschatological reconstitution of the true/remnant Israel, brought about by God's coming representative, whose arrival is imminent.

Jesus, at least at this point in his life, is essentially in agreement with John.[154] While such a conclusion is hardly startling, it does bring with it a number of implications concerning the ideological framework that characterized the beginning of Jesus' ministry. First of all, it implies that Jesus began his ministry with an ideological framework of an eschatology characterized by imminent judgment and restoration. While it is quite plausible that Jesus' eschatology would change and develop beyond this point (and evidence suggests that it probably did), a historical portrait that paints a non-eschatological Jesus[155] is quite implausible, especially in light of the pervasive elements of eschatological thought in the Gospel portraits of the later ministry of Jesus.[156]

Second, it implies that Jesus' ministry began within an ideological framework of re-visioning Israel around a reconstituted true/remnant Israel. Jesus participates in John's baptism in agreement with John's re-visioning of Israel. This suggests that an examination of Jesus' later ministry may reveal a similar concern for reconstituting Israel, but that Jesus' re-visioning may be somewhat different from John's. One example of this concern in the later ministry of Jesus is Jesus' choosing of "the Twelve," symbolic of the twelve

---

[154] Jesus could, of course, at some later point in time change his opinion on some matters and move beyond John. See the discussion below, and Webb, "John the Baptist and His Relationship to Jesus," 226–29.

[155] E. g., Marcus J. Borg, "A Temperate Case for a Non-Eschatological Jesus," in *SBL Seminar Papers, 1986* (SBLSP 25; Atlanta: Scholars, 1986), 521–35; Marcus J. Borg, "Jesus and Eschatology: A Reassessment," in *Images of Jesus Today* (ed. James H. Charlesworth and Walter P. Weaver; Valley Forge: Trinity, 1994), 42–67; Stephen J. Patterson, "The End of Apocalypse: Rethinking the Eschatological Jesus," *ThTo* 52 (1995): 29–48.

[156] For recent defenses of an eschatological Jesus, see Wright, *Jesus and the Victory of God*; Dale C. Allison, Jr., *Jesus of Nazareth: Millenarian Prophet* (Minneapolis: Fortress, 1998). For a critique of a Cynic Jesus, see Hans D. Betz, "Jesus and the Cynics: Survey and Analysis of a Hypothesis," *JR* 74 (1994): 453–75; Paul R. Eddy, "Jesus as Diogenes? Reflections on the Cynic Jesus Thesis," *JBL* 115 (1996): 449–69. See the response by David Seeley, "Jesus and the Cynics Revisited," *JBL* 116 (1997): 704–12. E. P. Sanders (*Jesus and Judaism*, 91–95) put this point in a larger context when he argues convincingly that Jesus must be understood on a trajectory that runs from an eschatologically oriented John the Baptist to an eschatologically oriented early church. Cf. his later articulation of the same point: E. P. Sanders, *The Historical Figure of Jesus* (London: Penguin, 1993), 94–95. See how this is developed in particular by Reiser, *Jesus and Judgment*.

tribes of Israel (Matt 10:1–4 = Mark 3:13–19a = Luke 6:12–16; cf. Mark 6:6b–7 = Luke 9:1–2; Matt 19:28 = Luke 22:28–30).[157]

Third, Jesus' essential agreement with John at the beginning of his ministry implies that judgment and restoration, as well as the re-visioning of Israel, would be effected through divine participation. John articulated God's involvement in two ways: an expected figure and a holy spirit. In Jesus' later ministry the Spirit certainly plays a key role in his thought (e.g., Matt 12:28 = Luke 11:20; Luke 4:18–21).[158] And, of course, the role of an expected figure in Jesus' thought has many entry points for exploration, from the term "Son of Man" to that of "Messiah." Recent scholarly debate has explored the historicity, meaning, and possible implications for Jesus' self-understanding, and further development here is far beyond our scope. The two points to note here are, first of all, that whatever Jesus' views on these matters later in his ministry, they were originally shaped by his involvement with John the Baptist. Second, in his later ministry, Jesus understood that he himself had a role in the judgment and restoration, and re-visioning of Israel, and one way that this self-understanding could be expressed is in relation to John's original expectation. Jesus' response to John's question from prison (Matt 11:2–6 = Luke 7:18–23) suggests a continued relationship with John's expectation and yet clear development beyond it.[159]

What I am arguing here is that it is appropriate to extrapolate from the ideological framework of John's ministry to the earliest stage of Jesus' ministry and then beyond, to later points in Jesus' ministry. This latter extrapolation is appropriate for, in his later ministry, Jesus maintains a high opinion of John (e.g., Matt 11:7–15 = Luke 7:24–30) and defends his own ministry based upon his view that John's baptism was of God (Matt 21:23–27 = Mark 11:27–33 = Luke 20:1–8).

4.4. The Possible Association of the Theophany Narrative with Jesus' Baptism

In the first part of this essay, I concluded that the baptism of Jesus by John is historically *very probable*, to the point of being virtually certain. Also it is *probable* that Jesus did experience at some time a prophetic call-vision, but that there are problems with directly associating the former with the latter, for there is some evidence to suggest that originally they were two separate

---

[157] See the discussion in this volume in ch. 5. Cf. the development of this point by Sanders, *Jesus and Judaism*, 95–106; Allison, *Jesus of Nazareth*, 101–2, 141–45; John P. Meier, "The Circle of the Twelve: Did It Exist During Jesus' Ministry?" *JBL* 116 (1997): 635–72; Robert P. Meye, *Jesus and the Twelve: Discipleship and Revelation in Mark's Gospel* (Grand Rapids: Eerdmans, 1968).

[158] Cf. the classic development by Dunn, *Jesus and the Spirit*.

[159] For further discussion see Webb, *John the Baptizer*, 278–82.

events. If so, then either Jesus told his disciples about his early experiences that brought the two together, or early Christians who used the prophetic call-vision to interpret the baptism. It was, therefore, preferable methodologically to examine Jesus' baptism apart from the possible association with the prophetic call-vision of the theophany narrative.

I should make clear from the earlier discussion that I consider it probable that Jesus did experience some form of prophetic call-vision and that it likely involved the components associated with the theophany narrative. The difficulty was not with the event itself but, rather, with the two events having to take place at the same time and, therefore, the baptism had to be understood in light of the theophany. I did say, however, that we would return to make a couple of brief observations on the baptism *if* it was associated with the theophany, and this is where we now proceed.[160]

First of all, the association of the two impacts the discussion above concerning the implications of Jesus' baptism. For example, it strengthens the first point made above, that Jesus' baptism was the turning point in Jesus' life – from peasant artisan to public ministry. If at his baptism Jesus also experienced a prophetic call-vision, then this event is even more decisive in Jesus' life. As well, the earlier discussion of Jesus baptizing within John's movement portrays Jesus as a disciple of John, working "under John." However, if Jesus experienced the prophetic call-vision at the same time, and if it included the elements of divine sonship and spirit anointing, then the period during which Jesus was baptizing should perhaps be understood as "alongside John."[161]

Second, if the content of the prophetic call-vision included a reference to divine sonship and an experience of the spirit, then the theophany is related conceptually to John's own prophetic announcements. John announced an expected figure who will baptize with a holy spirit and fire. Both elements in the theophany are related: the announcement of divine sonship may be linked to the expected figure that John proclaimed, and the baptizing with a holy spirit may be linked to Jesus' own spirit anointing. At this point, Jesus was not baptizing with a holy spirit; rather, he is himself anointed. Perhaps the implication is that the one who would ultimately baptize others must himself first be baptized by that same spirit.

Third, the prophetic call-vision and its dual elements of divine sonship and spirit anointing can themselves be explored for their implications

---

[160] Some scholars assume the link between the baptism and theophany, and in their discussion of the baptism actually focus almost exclusively on the significance of the theophany. E. g., Campbell, "Jesus and His Baptism".

[161] I am indebted to Darrell Bock for this suggestion. It may be an implication of John 3:30.

for understanding the ministry of Jesus. The announcement of divine sonship could be explored for the implications it would have for the self-understanding of Jesus – his sense of having a special relationship with God as father, and his role within the plans and purposes of God for Israel (whether understood as messianic or otherwise).[162] The divine anointing by the spirit – the action that confirmed and empowered the divine announcement – could be explored for the implications it also has for Jesus' self-understanding. However, with these issues are moving beyond specifically exploring Jesus' baptism itself, which is beyond the scope of this essay.

5. Conclusion

In this essay I have argued that, within the realms of historical probability, Jesus was baptized by John the Baptist. As such, Jesus' baptism was a significant turning point in his life – turning from his former life as a peasant artisan in Nazareth to a life of public ministry. By responding to John's message to the nation of Israel, which called Israel to repent and be baptized, Jesus participated in John's repentance-baptism, acknowledging Israel's need for repentance. As such, Jesus was agreeing with John's vision of a reconstituted Israel – a true / remnant Israel that would be prepared for imminent divine judgment and would participate in God's eschatological restoration and blessing. Jesus thus begins his ministry within an ideological framework marked by this eschatological orientation. For the earliest part of this ministry, Jesus was involved with John and his program. He remained with John as one of his disciples and participated with John in a baptizing ministry.

The theophany narrative, though linked in the texts with Jesus' baptism, may have taken place at a later point in time. Best understood as a prophetic call-vision, this event is also historically likely, but it has less probability than the baptism itself. There is, however, a possibility that it did take place at the same time as Jesus' baptism. If so, it adds new components to the significance of the event, but it does not materially alter the conclusions drawn about the baptism itself as argued in this essay. Nor would the character of the theophany as a prophetic call-vision be materially altered.

---

[162] For example, if the divine announcement ("You are my Son, the Beloved; with you I am well pleased;" Mark 1:11) is understood to combine the images of Messiah (Ps 2:7) and servant of Yahweh (Isa 42:1), this might contribute to explaining why Jesus later radically reinterpreted messiahship to be a suffering figure. See the discussion in the literature of the possible Hebrew Bible texts being alluded to in the divine announcement; e.g. Guelich, *Mark 1–8:26*, 33–34; Davies and Allison, *Matthew*, 1:336–39; Meier, *Mentor, Message, and Miracles*, 106–7.

Jesus' later ministry manifests some differences from as well as developments beyond what has been presented here.[163] But that later ministry also demonstrates significant points of continuity. The later ministry of Jesus must be understood along a trajectory that begins with John the Baptist and ends with the early Church.[164] As such, therefore, Jesus' baptism by John and its implications make a significant contribution to our understanding of the historical Jesus. In other words, John the baptizer provides a foundational and central context for understanding Jesus.

Bibliography

Allison, Dale C., Jr. "The Baptism of Jesus and a New Dead Sea Scroll." *Biblical Archaeology Review* 18 (1992): 58–60.

–. *Jesus of Nazareth: Millenarian Prophet*. Minneapolis: Fortress, 1998.

Aune, David E. *Prophecy in Early Christianity and the Ancient Mediterranean World*. Grand Rapids: Eerdmans, 1983.

Badke, William B. "Was Jesus a Disciple of John?" *EvQ* 62 (1990): 195–204.

Bauer, Walter. *A Greek-English Lexicon of the New Testament and Other Early Christian Literature*. 3rd ed. Revised and edited by Frederick William Danker. Chicago: University of Chicago Press, 2000.

Beasley-Murray, George R. *Baptism in the New Testament*. Grand Rapids: Eerdmans, 1962.

–. "Baptism, Wash." Pages 143–54 in vol. 4 of *New International Dictionary of New Testament Theology*. 4 vols. Edited by Colin Brown. Grand Rapids: Zondervan, 1975–85.

–. *John*. WBC 36. Waco, Tex.: Word, 1987.

Becker, Jürgen. *Johannes der Täufer und Jesus von Nazareth*. BibS(N) 63. Neukirchen-Vluyn: Neukirchener Verlag, 1972.

Behm, J., and E. Würthwein. "νοέω, κτλ." Pages 980–99 in vol. 4 of *Theological Dictionary of the New Testament*. 10 vols. Edited by G. Kittel and Gerhard Friedrich. Translated by Geoffrey W. Bromiley. Grand Rapids: Eerdmans, 1964–76.

Best, Ernest. "Spirit-Baptism." *NovT* 4 (1960): 236–43.

Betz, Hans D. "Jesus and the Cynics: Survey and Analysis of a Hypothesis." *JR* 74 (1994): 453–75.

Betz, Otto. "Was John the Baptist an Essene?" *BRev* 6 (1990): 18–25.

Black, Matthew. *The Scrolls and Christian Origins: Studies in the Jewish Background of the New Testament*. BJS, 48. New York: Scribner, 1961.

Bleeker, Claas Jouco, ed. *Initiation; Contributions to the Theme of the Study-Conference of the International Association for the History of Religions Held at Strasburg, September 17th to 22nd 1964*. SHR 10. Leiden: Brill, 1965.

---

[163] For such a sketch, see Webb, "John the Baptist and His Relationship to Jesus," 223–29.

[164] Hengel and Schwemer (*Jesus und das Judentum*, 322) say the impact of John on Jesus was too great for the tradition to ignore.

Boismard, Marie-Émile. "Les traditions johanniques concernant le Baptiste." *RB* 70 (1963): 5–42.

Borg, Marcus J. *Jesus, A New Vision: Spirit, Culture, and the Life of Discipleship*. San Francisco: Harper & Row, 1987.

—. "Jesus and Eschatology: A Reassessment." Pages 42–67 in *Images of Jesus Today*. Edited by James H. Charlesworth and Walter P. Weaver. Valley Forge: Trinity, 1994.

—. "A Temperate Case for a Non-Eschatological Jesus." Pages 521–35 in *SBL Seminar Papers, 1986*. SBLSP 25. Atlanta: Scholars, 1986.

Bretscher, Paul G. "Whose Sandals? (Matt 3:11)." *JBL* 86 (1967): 81–87.

Brown, Raymond E. *The Gospel According to John I–XII*. AB 29. New York: Doubleday, 1966.

—. "Gospel Infancy Narrative Research from 1976 to 1986: Part II (Luke)." *CBQ* 48 (1986): 660–80.

—. "Jesus and Elisha." *Perspective* 12 (1971): 85–104.

Brownlee, W. H. "John the Baptist in the New Light of Ancient Scrolls." Pages 33–53 in *The Scrolls and the New Testament*. Edited by Krister Stendahl. London: SCM, 1958.

Cameron, Ron, ed. *The Other Gospels: Non-Canonical Gospel Texts*. Philadelphia: Westminster, 1982.

Campbell, R. Alastair. "Jesus and His Baptism." *TynBul* 47 (1996): 191–214.

Caragounis, Chrys C. *The Son of Man: Vision and Interpretation*. WUNT 38. Tübingen: Mohr Siebeck, 1986.

Charlesworth, James H. "John the Baptizer and the Dead Sea Scrolls." Pages 1–35 in *The Scrolls and Christian Origins*. Vol. 3 of *The Bible and the Dead Sea Scrolls: The Princeton Symposium on the Dead Sea Scrolls*. Edited by James H. Charlesworth. Waco: Baylor University Press, 2006.

Chilton, Bruce D. *Jesus' Baptism and Jesus' Healing: His Personal Practice of Spirituality*. Harrisburg: Trinity, 1998.

—. "John the Purifier." Pages 203–20 in *Jesus in Context: Temple, Purity, and Restoration*. By Bruce Chilton and Craig A. Evans. AGJU 39. Leiden: Brill, 1997.

Crossan, John Dominic. *The Historical Jesus: The Life of a Mediterranean Jewish Peasant*. San Francisco: HarperSanFrancisco, 1991.

Cullmann, Oscar. *The Early Church: Studies in Early Christian History and Theology*. London: SCM, 1956.

—. "The Significance of the Qumran Texts for Research Into the Beginnings of Christianity." Pages 18–32 in *The Scrolls and the New Testament*. Edited by Krister Stendahl. London: SCM, 1958.

Dapaah, Daniel S. *The Relationship Between John the Baptist and Jesus of Nazareth: A Critical Study*. Lanham, Md.: University Press of America, 2005.

Davies, W. D., and Dale C. Allison, Jr. *A Critical and Exegetical Commentary on the Gospel According to Saint Matthew*. 3 vols. ICC. Edinburgh: T&T Clark, 1988–97.

Dibelius, Martin. *Die urchristliche Überlieferung von Johannes dem Täufer*. FRLANT 15. Göttingen: Vandenhoeck & Ruprecht, 1911.

Dodd, C. H. *Historical Tradition in the Fourth Gospel*. Cambridge: Cambridge University Press, 1963.

Downing, F. Gerald. *Jesus and the Threat of Freedom*. London: SCM, 1987.

Dunn, James D. G. *Jesus and the Spirit: A Study of the Religious and Charismatic Experience of Jesus and the First Christians as Reflected in the New Testament.* NTL. London: SCM, 1975.

–. "Spirit-and-Fire Baptism." *NovT* 14 (1972): 81–92.

Eddy, Paul R. "Jesus as Diogenes? Reflections on the Cynic Jesus Thesis." *JBL* 115 (1996): 449–69.

Enslin, Morton S. "John and Jesus." *ZNW* 66 (1975): 1–18.

Ernst, Josef. *Johannes der Täufer: Interpretation, Geschichte, Wirkungsgeschichte.* BZNW 53. Berlin: De Gruyter, 1989.

–. "War Jesus ein Schüler Johannes' des Täufers?" Pages 13–33 in *Vom Urchristentum zu Jesus: Für Joachim Gnilka.* Edited by Hubert Frankemölle and Karl Kertelge. Freiberg: Herder, 1989.

Evans, Craig A. "Jesus' Action in the Temple and Evidence of Corruption in the First-Century Temple." Pages 522–39 in *SBL Seminar Papers, 1989.* SBLSP 28. Atlanta: Scholars, 1989.

Farmer, W. R. "John the Baptist." Pages 955–62 in vol. 2 of *The Interpreter's Dictionary of the Bible.* 5 vols. Nashville: Abingdon, 1962.

Ferch, Arthur J. *The Son of Man in Daniel 7.* Andrews University Seminary Doctoral Dissertation Series, 6. Berrien Springs, Mich.: Andrews University Press, 1983.

Fitzmyer, Joseph A. *The Gospel According to Luke I–IX.* AB 28. Garden City: Doubleday, 1981.

Fleddermann, Harry T. *Q: A Reconstruction and Commentary.* Biblical Tools and Studies 1. Leuven: Peeters, 2005.

Funk, Robert W. "The Wilderness." *JBL* 78 (1959): 205–14.

Funk, Robert W., and The Jesus Seminar. *The Acts of Jesus: The Search for the Authentic Deeds of Jesus.* San Francisco: HarperSanFrancisco, 1998.

Garnet, Paul. "The Baptism of Jesus and the Son of Man Idea." *JSNT* 9 (1980): 49–65.

Gero, Stephen. "Spirit as a Dove at the Baptism of Jesus." *NovT* 18 (1976): 17–35.

Geyser, Albert S. "The Youth of John the Baptist: A Deduction from the Break in the Parallel Account of the Lucan Infancy Story." *NovT* 1 (1956): 70–75.

Gnilka, Joachim. "Das Martyrium Johannes' des Täufers (Mark 6,17–29)." Pages 78–92 in *Orientierung an Jesus: Zur Theologie der Synoptiker: Für Josef Schmid.* Paul Hoffmann. Freiburg: Herder, 1973.

Goguel, Maurice. *Au seuil de l'Évangile: Jean-Baptiste.* Bibliotheque historique. Paris: Payot, 1928.

–. *The Life of Jesus.* Translated by Olive Wyon. New York: Macmillan, 1944.

Goppelt, Leonhard. *Theology of the New Testament.* 2 vols. Translated by John E. Alsup. Grand Rapids: Eerdmans, 1981–82.

Guelich, Robert A. *Mark 1–8:26.* WBC 34a. Dallas: Word, 1989.

Haenchen, Ernst. *Der Weg Jesu: Eine Erklärung des Markus-Evangeliums und der kanonischen Parallelen.* 2nd ed. Berlin: De Gruyter, 1968.

Hägerland, Tobias. "Jesus and the Rites of Repentance." *NTS* 52 (2006): 166–87.

Hengel, Martin, and Anna Maria Schwemer. *Jesus und das Judentum.* Vol. 1 of *Geschichte des frühen Christentums.* 4 vols. Tübingen: Mohr Siebeck, 2007–.

Hoehner, Harold W. *Herod Antipas.* SNTMS, 17. Cambridge: Cambridge University Press, 1972.

Holladay, William L. *The Root šûbh in the Old Testament.* Leiden: Brill, 1958.

Hollenbach, Paul. "The Conversion of Jesus: From Jesus the Baptizer to Jesus the Healer." Pages 198–219 in *Aufstieg und Niedergang der römischen Welt: Geschichte und Kultur Roms im Spiegel der neueren Forschung*. Part 2, *Principat*, 25.1. Edited by Hildegard Temporini and Wolfgang Haase. Berlin: De Gruyter, 1982.

—. "Social Aspects of John the Baptizer's Preaching Mission in the Context of Palestinian Judaism." Pages 850–75 in *Aufstieg und Niedergang der römischen Welt: Geschichte und Kultur Roms im Spiegel der neueren Forschung*. Part 2, *Principat*, 19.1. Edited by Hildegard Temporini and Wolfgang Haase. Berlin: De Gruyter, 1979.

Horsley, Richard A. *The Liberation of Christmas: The Infancy Narratives in Social Context*. New York: Crossroad, 1989.

—. "'Like One of the Prophets of Old': Two Types of Popular Prophets at the Time of Jesus." *CBQ* 47 (1985): 435–63.

—. "Popular Messianic Movements Around the Time of Jesus." *CBQ* 46 (1984): 471–95.

Horsley, Richard A., and John S. Hanson. *Bandits, Prophets, and Messiahs: Popular Movements in the Time of Jesus*. New Voices in Biblical Studies. Minneapolis: Winston, 1985.

Jeremias, Joachim. *New Testament Theology: The Proclamation of Jesus*. Translated by John Bowden. New York: Scribner, 1971.

Kazmierski, Carl R. "The Stones of Abraham: John the Baptist and the End of Torah (Matt 3,7–10 par. Luke 3,7–9)." *Bib* 68 (1987): 22–40.

Keck, Leander E. "Spirit and the Dove." *NTS* 17 (1970): 41–67.

Klawans, Jonathan. *Impurity and Sin in Ancient Judaism*. Oxford: Oxford University Press, 2000.

Klijn, A. F. J. *Jewish-Christian Gospel Tradition*. VCSup 17. Leiden: Brill, 1992.

Kloppenborg, John S. *Excavating Q: The History and Setting of the Sayings Gospel*. Edinburgh: T&T Clark, 2000.

—. *The Formation of Q: Trajectories in Ancient Wisdom Collections*. SAC. Philadelphia: Fortress, 1987.

—. *Q Parallels: Synopsis, Critical Notes, and Concordance*. FF. Sonoma, Calif.: Polebridge, 1988.

Kraeling, Carl H. *John the Baptist*. New York: Scribner, 1951.

Kümmel, Werner G. *Promise and Fulfillment: The Eschatological Message of Jesus*. Translated by Dorothea M. Barton. London: SCM, 1958.

Laubach, F., J. Goetzmann, and U. Becker. "Conversion, Penitence, Repentance, Proselyte." Pages 353–62 in vol. 1 of *New International Dictionary of New Testament Theology*. 4 vols. Edited by Colin Brown. Grand Rapids: Zondervan, 1975–85.

Lawrence, Jonathan D. *Washing in Water: Trajectories of Ritual Bathing in the Hebrew Bible and Second Temple Literature*. Academia Biblica 23. Atlanta: Society of Biblical Literature, 2006.

Liddell, Henry George, and Robert Scott, comps. *Greek-English Lexicon*. 9th ed. With a revised supplement 1996, ed. P. G. W. Glare and A. A. Thompson. Edited by Henry Stuart Jones and Roderick McKenzie. Oxford: Clarendon, 1940.

Linnemann, Eta. "Jesus und der Täufer." Pages 219–36 in *Festschrift für Ernst Fuchs*. Edited by Gerhard Ebeling, Eberhard Jüngel, and Gerd Schunack. Tübingen: Mohr Siebeck, 1973.

Lohmeyer, Ernst. *Johannes der Täufer.* Vol. 1 of *Das Urchristentum.* Göttingen: Vandenhoeck & Ruprecht, 1932.
McCown, Chester Charlton. "The Scene of John's Ministry and Its Relation to the Purpose and Outcome of His Mission." *JBL* 59 (1940): 113–31.
Marcus, Joel. "Jesus' Baptismal Vision." *NTS* 41 (1995): 512–21.
Marxsen, Willi. *Mark the Evangelist.* 2nd ed. Translated by James Boyce. Nashville: Abingdon, 1969.
Meier, John P. "The Circle of the Twelve: Did It Exist During Jesus' Ministry?" *JBL* 116 (1997): 635–72.
–. *Mentor, Message, and Miracles.* Vol. 2 of *A Marginal Jew: Rethinking the Historical Jesus.* ABRL. New York: Doubleday, 1994.
–. *The Roots of the Problem and the Person.* Vol. 1 of *A Marginal Jew: Rethinking the Historical Jesus.* ABRL. New York: Doubleday, 1991.
Merklein, Helmut. "Die Umkerpredigt bei Johannes dem Täufer und Jesus von Nazaret." *BZ* 25 (1981): 29–46.
Meye, Robert P. *Jesus and the Twelve: Discipleship and Revelation in Mark's Gospel.* Grand Rapids: Eerdmans, 1968.
Meyer, Ben F. *The Aims of Jesus.* London: SCM, 1979.
Motyer, Stephen. "The Rending of the Veil: A Markan Pentecost?" *NTS* 33 (1987): 155–57.
Murphy-O'Connor, Jerome. "John the Baptist and Jesus: History and Hypotheses." *NTS* 36 (1990): 359–74.
Neusner, Jacob. *The Idea of Purity in Ancient Judaism.* SJLA 1. Leiden: Brill, 1973.
Oepke, Albrecht. "Βάπτω, κτλ." Pages 529–38 in vol. 1 of *Theological Dictionary of the New Testament.* 10 vols. Edited by G. Kittel and Gerhard Friedrich. Translated by Geoffrey W. Bromiley. Grand Rapids: Eerdmans, 1964–76.
Patterson, Stephen J. "The End of Apocalypse: Rethinking the Eschatological Jesus." *ThTo* 52 (1995): 29–48.
Poon, Ronnie S. "The Background to the Dove Imagery in the Story of Jesus' Baptism." *Jian Dao* 3 (1995): 33–49.
Reicke, Bo Ivar. "The Historical Setting of John's Baptism." Pages 209–24 in *Jesus, the Gospels, and the Church: Essays in Honor of William R. Farmer.* Edited by E. P. Sanders. Macon: Mercer University Press, 1987.
Reiser, Marius. *Jesus and Judgment: The Eschatological Proclamation in Its Jewish Context.* Translated by Linda M. Maloney. Minneapolis: Fortress, 1997.
Rivkin, Ellis. "Locating John the Baptizer in Palestinian Judaism: The Political Dimension." Pages 79–85 in *SBL Seminar Papers, 1983.* SBLSP 22. Chico: Scholars, 1983.
Robinson, James M. "The Sayings Gospel Q." Pages 361–88 in vol. 1 of *The Four Gospels 1992: Festschrift Frans Neirynck.* 3 vols. Edited by F. Van Segbroeck, C. M. Tuckett, G. Van Belle, and J. Verheyden. BETL 100. Leuven: Leuven University Press, 1992.
Robinson, James M., Paul Hoffmann, and John S. Kloppenborg, eds. *The Critical Edition of Q.* Hermeneia. Minneapolis: Fortress, 2000.
Robinson, John A. T. "Elijah, John and Jesus: An Essay in Detection." *NTS* 4 (1957–58): 263–81.
–. *Twelve New Testament Studies.* London: SCM, 1962.
Sanders, E. P. *The Historical Figure of Jesus.* London: Penguin, 1993.

–. *Jesus and Judaism*. Philadelphia: Fortress, 1985.
Schnackenburg, Rudolf. *The Gospel According to John*. 3 vols. New York: Seabury, 1980–82.
Schneemelcher, Wilhelm, and R. McL. Wilson, eds. *New Testament Apocrypha*. Rev. ed. 2 vols. Louisville: Westminster John Knox, 1990–91.
Schweitzer, Albert. *The Quest of the Historical Jesus: A Critical Study of Its Progress from Reimarus to Wrede*. 2nd ed. Translated by W. Montgomery. London: Black, 1911.
Scobie, Charles H. H. *John the Baptist*. London: SCM, 1964.
Seeley, David. "Jesus and the Cynics Revisited." *JBL* 116 (1997): 704–12.
Smith, Derwood C. "Jewish Proselyte Baptism and the Baptism of John." *ResQ* 25 (1982): 13–32.
Stauffer, Ethelbert. *New Testament Theology*. Translated by John Marsh. London: SCM, 1955.
Stein, Robert H. *The Synoptic Problem: An Introduction*. Grand Rapids: Baker, 1987.
Tatum, W. B. *John the Baptist and Jesus: A Report of the Jesus Seminar*. Sonoma, CA: Polebridge, 1994.
Taylor, Joan E. *The Immerser: John the Baptist Within Second Temple Judaism*. Studying the Historical Jesus. Grand Rapids: Eerdmans, 1997.
Thyen, Hartwig. "ΒΑΠΤΙΣΜΑ ΜΕΤΑΝΟΙΑΣ ΕΙΣ ΑΦΕΣΙΝ ΑΜΑΡΤΙΩΝ." Pages 131–68 in *The Future of Our Religious Past: Essays in Honour of Rudolf Bultmann*. Edited by James M. Robinson. Translated by Charles E. Carlston and Robert P. Scharlemann. London: SCM, 1971.
Tuckett, Christopher M. *The Contemporary Revival of the Griesbach Hypothesis*. SNTSMS 44. Cambridge: Cambridge University Press, 1983.
Ulansey, David. "The Heavenly Veil Torn: Mark's Cosmic *Inclusio*." *JBL* 110 (1991): 123–25.
Vaage, Leif E. "Bird-Watching at the Baptism of Jesus: Early Christian Mythmaking in Mark 1:9–11." Pages 280–94 in *Reimagining Christian Origins: A Colloquium Honoring Burton L. Mack*. Edited by Elizabeth A. Castelli and Hal Taussig. Valley Forge, PA: Trinity, 1996.
Vermès, Géza. *Jesus the Jew: A Historian's Reading of the Gospels*. London: Collins, 1973.
Vielhauer, Philipp, and Georg Strecker. "Jewish-Christian Gospels." Pages 134–78 in vol. 1 of *New Testament Apocrypha*. Rev. ed. 2 vols. Edited by Wilhelm Schneemelcher and R. McL. Wilson. Louisville: Westminster John Knox, 1990–91.
Webb, Robert L. "The Activity of John the Baptist's Expected Figure at the Threshing Floor (Matthew 3.12 = Luke 3.17)." *JSNT* 43 (1991): 103–11.
–. "Jesus' Baptism: Its Historicity and Implications." *BBR* 10 (2000): 261–309.
–. "John the Baptist." Pages 418–21 in vol. 1 of *Encyclopedia of the Dead Sea Scrolls*. 2 vols. Edited by Lawrence H. Schiffman and James C. VanderKam. Oxford: Oxford University Press, 2000.
–. "John the Baptist and His Relationship to Jesus." Pages 179–229 in *Studying the Historical Jesus: Evaluations of the State of Current Research*. Edited by Bruce D. Chilton and Craig A. Evans. NTTS 19. Leiden: Brill, 1994.
–. *John the Baptizer and Prophet: A Socio-Historical Study*. JSNTSup 62. Sheffield: JSOT Press, 1991.

Wenham, Gordon J. *The Book of Leviticus*. NICOT. Grand Rapids: Eerdmans, 1979.
Wink, Walter. "Jesus' Reply to John: Matt 11:2–6 // Luke 7:18–23." *Forum* 5 (1989): 121–28.
–. "John the Baptist and the Gospel." Th.D. diss. New York: Union Theological Seminary, 1963.
–. *John the Baptist in the Gospel Tradition*. SNTSMS 7. London: Cambridge University Press, 1968.
Witherington, Ben. "Jesus and the Baptist – Two of a Kind." Pages 225–44 in *SBL Seminar Papers, 1988*. SBLSP 27. Atlanta: Scholars, 1988.
Witherington, Ben, III. *The Christology of Jesus*. Minneapolis: Fortress, 1990.
Wolff, P. "Gericht und Reich Gottes bei Johannes und Jesus." Pages 43–49 in *Gegenwart und Kommendes Reich: Schülergabe Anton Vogtle Zum 65. Geburtstag*. Edited by P. Fiedler and D. Zeller. BBS. Stuttgart: Katholisches Bibelwerk, 1975.
Wright, David P. *The Disposal of Impurity: Elimination Rites in the Bible and in Hittite and Mesopotamian Literature*. SBLDS 101. Atlanta: Scholars, 1987.
–. "Unclean and Clean." Pages 729–41 in vol. 6 of *Anchor Bible Dictionary*. 6 vols. Edited by David N. Freedman. New York: Doubleday, 1992.
Wright, N. T. *Jesus and the Victory of God*. Vol. 2 of *Christian Origins and the Question of God*. Minneapolis: Fortress, 1996.

Chapter 4

Exorcisms and the Kingdom: Inaugurating the Kingdom of God and Defeating the Kingdom of Satan[1]

CRAIG A. EVANS

1. Introduction: The Relationship of Kingdom to Jesus' Exorcisms

Jesus proclaims the kingdom of God and casts out demons (Mark 1:15, 23–27, 32–34). That his message is closely bound up with his ministry of exorcism is seen in a striking saying, "If it is by the finger of God that I cast out demons, then the kingdom of God has come upon you" (Luke 11:20), and in his instructions to the disciples to proclaim the kingdom of God and to cast out demons (Matt 10:7–8; Mark 6:7). The present essay is concerned with the relation of the proclamation of the kingdom of God and the exorcisms. It is argued that these elements are closely linked, for the exorcisms demonstrate the reality of the presence of the kingdom (or rule) of God.

There is broad consensus that the central datum of the proclamation of Jesus is the "kingdom of God." Its antecedents, referents, meaning, and context in the teaching and activity of Jesus, however, are much debated. Traditional interpretation has found the roots of Jesus' proclamation in the Scriptures of Israel and its context in the hopes of Israel's restoration. The work of the late George Beasley-Murray and the more recent studies of Bruce Chilton and N. T. Wright, though emphasizing different features, are illustrative and among the better examples.[2]

---

[1] This essay is a revised and expanded version of that published as Craig A. Evans, "Inaugurating the Kingdom of God and Defeating the Kingdom of Satan," *BBR* 15 (2005): 49–75.

[2] George R. Beasley-Murray, *Jesus and the Kingdom of God* (Grand Rapids: Eerdmans, 1986); Bruce D. Chilton, *God in Strength: Jesus' Announcement of the Kingdom* (SNTSU 1; Freistadt: Plöchl, 1979; repr., Biblical Seminar 8; Sheffield: JSOT Press, 1987); Bruce D. Chilton, *A Galilean Rabbi and His Bible: Jesus' Use of the Interpreted Scripture of His Time* (GNS 8; Wilmington: Glazier, 1984); Bruce D. Chilton, *Pure Kingdom: Jesus' Vision of God* (Studying the Historical Jesus; Grand Rapids: Eerdmans, 1996); George Eldon Ladd, *Jesus and the Kingdom: The Eschatology of Biblical Realism* (New York: Harper &

It is also now generally recognized that Jesus was perceived by his contemporaries as an exorcist, and as a successful exorcist at that.[3] This recognition is consistent with a greater openness in current critical study to the importance of miracles in Jesus' ministry[4] and with serious efforts to assess signs and miracles in a Judaic context.[5]

The focus of the present study is on the exorcisms and their relation to Jesus' proclamation of the kingdom. Although the primary purpose is not to explore miracles as such, this study will have relevance for this broader topic. The thesis of the present study is that Jesus' activity of exorcism was an essential component of his proclamation and ministry, clarifying the import of his proclamation and providing tangible evidence of its validity. Three aspects will be treated: (1) the rule of God and its scriptural antecedents, (2) prophecies and expectations concerning the kingdom of God, and (3) Jesus' proclamation and exorcisms in context.

2. The Context Provided by Scriptural Antecedents of the Rule of God

Israel's idea of the kingdom (or rule) of God is rooted in the nation's ancient Scriptures, which depict God as king and warrior. The following texts show God's ruling is important for the concept of kingdom. After the destruction of Pharaoh's army in the sea, Israel proclaims: "The LORD is a warrior; the LORD is his name ... The LORD will reign [יִמְלֹךְ] for ever and ever" (Exod 15:3, 18).[6] A patient and ever-faithful God accompanies wandering Israel: "The LORD their God is with them, and the shout of a king [מֶלֶךְ] is among them" (Num 23:21b). In Deuteronomy the kingship of Yahweh is explicitly acknowledged: "The LORD came from Sinai, and dawned from Seir upon us; he shone forth from Mount Paran, he came from the ten thousands of holy ones, with flaming fire at his right hand ... Thus the LORD became

---

Row, 1964); N. T. Wright, *Jesus and the Victory of God* (vol. 2 of *Christian Origins and the Question of God*; Minneapolis: Fortress, 1996).

[3] See Graham H. Twelftree, *Jesus the Exorcist: A Contribution to the Study of the Historical Jesus* (WUNT 2.54; Tübingen: Mohr [Siebeck], 1993). See also Mary E. Mills, *Human Agents of Cosmic Power in Hellenistic Judaism and the Synoptic Tradition* (JSNTSup 41; Sheffield: JSOT Press, 1990).

[4] The shift in thinking, witnessed especially in some of "Third Quest" scholarship, is documented and evaluated in Craig A. Evans, "Life-of-Jesus Research and the Eclipse of Mythology," *TS* 54 (1993): 3–36.

[5] Eric Eve, *The Jewish Context of Jesus' Miracles* (JSNTSup 231; New York: Sheffield Academic Press, 2002).

[6] See Tremper Longman, III, "God is a Warrior," in *God is a Warrior* (by Tremper Longman, III and Daniel G. Reid; Studies in Old Testament Biblical Theology; Grand Rapids: Zondervan, 1995), 31–47.

king in Jeshurun, when the heads of the people were gathered, all the tribes of Israel together ... The eternal God is your dwelling place, and underneath are the everlasting arms. And he thrust out the enemy before you, and said, 'Destroy'" (Deut 33:2, 5, 27b). Gideon tells Israel: "I will not rule over you, and my son will not rule over you; the LORD will rule [יִמְשֹׁל] over you" (Judg 8:23). Samuel reminds Israel: "And when you saw that Nahash the king of the Ammonites came against you, you said to me, 'No, but a king shall reign over us,' when the LORD your God was your king [מַלְכְּכֶם]" (1 Sam 12:12; cf. 1 Sam 8:7; 10:19).

The prophets also proclaim the kingship and rule of Yahweh. This theme is especially pronounced in Isaiah and grows out of the prophet's vision: "My eyes have seen the King, the LORD of hosts!" (6:5). In the face of grave political danger, Isaiah declares that the "LORD is our judge, the LORD is our ruler, the LORD is our king; he will save us" (33:22). In Second Isaiah this theme is quite pronounced. The Lord is "the King of Jacob" (41:21), and "King of Israel and his Redeemer, the LORD of hosts" (44:6). The eschatological herald of good news is to proclaim to Zion, "Your God reigns [מָלַךְ]" (52:7). According to Isaiah's Little Apocalypse, "on that day the LORD will punish the host of heaven, in heaven, and the kings of the earth, on the earth. They will be gathered together as prisoners in a pit; they will be shut up in a prison ... for the LORD of hosts will reign [מָלַךְ] on Mount Zion and in Jerusalem and before his elders he will manifest his glory" (24:21–23).

Likewise Jeremiah declares that there is none like Yahweh; there is no one who will not fear the "King of the nations" (10:6–7a). Indeed, "among all the wise ones of the nations and in all their kingdoms [מַלְכוּתָם] there is none like" God (10:7b). In contrast to idols of wood, silver, and gold (10:8–9), "the LORD is the true God; he is the living God and the everlasting King [מֶלֶךְ עוֹלָם]" (10:10). According to the vision of the second part of Zechariah, "the LORD will become king over all the earth" (14:9); "every one that survives of all the nations that have come against Jerusalem shall go up year after year to worship the King, the LORD of hosts" (14:16). Indeed, "if any of the families of the earth do not go up to Jerusalem to worship the King, the LORD of hosts, there will be no rain upon them" (14:17). Zephaniah enjoins Israel to fear evil no longer, for the "King of Israel, the LORD, is in your midst" (3:15, 17). Israel need no longer fear her oppressors, for the Lord, "a warrior who gives victory," is among his people (3:16–19).

Perhaps the Psalms, particularly the so-called Enthronement Psalms, offer the most important passages in which God is conceived as Israel's king.[7]

---

[7] See John Gray, *The Biblical Doctrine of the Reign of God* (Edinburgh: T&T Clark, 1979), 20–25; Bruce D. Chilton, "The Kingdom of God in Recent Discussion," in *Study-*

Many times Yahweh is declared king: "The LORD is king [מָלָךְ] for ever and ever; the nations shall perish from his land" (Ps 10:16); or in the words of Ps 24:

> [8] Who is the King of glory [מֶלֶךְ הַכָּבוֹד]? The LORD, strong and mighty, the LORD, mighty in battle! [9] Lift up your heads, O gates! and be lifted up, O ancient doors! that the King of glory may come in. [10] Who is this King of glory? The LORD of hosts, he is the King of glory [מֶלֶךְ הַכָּבוֹד]!

Psalm 47 declares that "the LORD, the Most High, is terrible, a great king over all the earth" (v. 2), enjoining the faithful to "Sing praises to God, sing praises! Sing praises to our King, sing praises! For God is the king of all the earth; sing praises with a psalm!" (vv. 6–7). For other declarations of God as king, see Pss 44:4; 48:2; 68:24; 74:12; 84:3; 93:1; 95:3; 98:6; 99:4; 145:1.

The Psalter also envisions God as enthroned: "The LORD sits enthroned over the flood; the LORD sits enthroned as king for ever" (29:10); and as reigning: "God reigns [מָלַךְ] over the nations; God sits on his holy throne [כִּסֵּא]" (47:8); "The LORD reigns; he is robed in majesty; the LORD is robed, he is girded with strength" (93:1); "The LORD reigns; let the earth rejoice; let the many coastlands be glad!" (97:1); "The LORD reigns; let the peoples tremble! He sits enthroned upon the cherubim; let the earth quake!" (99:1); "The LORD will reign [יִמְלֹךְ] for ever, thy God, O Zion, to all generations" (146:10).

According to the Psalms, God "ordains victories for Jacob" (44:4), "works salvation in the midst of the earth" (74:12), "loves justice" (99:4), and "will judge the peoples with equity" (96:10). Moreover, as king God takes interest in Israel's cultic activity (68:24; 84:3), and as king God regards Mount Zion as his city (48:2). Thus we see that in various ways God is depicted very much as playing the role of king, a king who is enthroned, who rules, who judges, who takes the field as a warrior, who resides in a capital city, and who takes interest in the cultus.

Two other texts from the Hebrew Scriptures make important contributions to ideas of the reign of God. First, in Isaiah we find linkage of God's reign to the "good news" or "gospel" that is to be proclaimed:

> Get you up to a high mountain, O Zion, herald of good news; lift up your voice with strength, O Jerusalem, herald of good news, lift it up, fear not; say to the cities of Judah, "Behold your God!" (Isa 40:9)

> How beautiful upon the mountains are the feet of him who brings good news, who publishes peace, who brings good news of good, who publishes salvation, who says to Zion, "Your God reigns." (Isa 52:7)

---

ing the Historical Jesus: Evaluations of the State of Current Research (ed. Bruce D. Chilton and Craig A. Evans; NTTS 19; Leiden: Brill, 1994), 255–80, esp. 273–74; Chilton, *Pure Kingdom*, 31–42.

The herald of "good news" (בָּשָׂר; LXX: ὁ εὐαγγελιζόμενος) has announced the presence and reign (מָלַךְ; LXX: βασιλεύσει) of God, which in the language of the later Targum is understood as the revelation of the "kingdom of God [מלכותא דאלהא]." The first passage links the good news of God's presence ("Behold your God!") to the injunction to prepare the way of the Lord in the wilderness (cf. Isa 40:3), a motif that reflects the exodus tradition. A way of salvation is being prepared that will lead God's people out of bondage. The second passage further defines the good news, by declaring that Israel's "God reigns" (or "will reign," as it is in the LXX).[8] The association of God's reign with the restoration of Israel is an important point that will have relevance for understanding the context and meaning of Jesus' proclamation of the kingdom.

Second, we find in Daniel several important aspects of the reign of God. Whereas Isaiah speaks of the powerful, saving presence of God, Daniel speaks of the soon triumph of God's kingdom over the evil, oppressive kingdoms that persecute and enslave his people. Daniel's message brings distinctive dynamic, cosmic, and temporal elements.

Daniel's dynamic understanding of "kingdom" (מַלְכוּ/מַלְכוּת) or "dominion" (מִמְשָׁל), whether in reference to God's kingdom or in reference to a human kingdom, is very instructive. Usage suggests that kingdom refers to sphere of influence, capacity to rule (2:37), or even dynasty (2:39–42). There are also important and roughly synonymous features. After his troubling dream of the image, the Babylonian king is told: "You, O king, the king of kings, to whom the God of heaven has given the kingdom, the power, and the might, and the glory ..." (2:37). Parallel to "the kingdom" are "the power" (חִסְנָא), "the might" (תָּקְפָּא), and "the glory" (יְקָרָא). These additional attributes function in an almost epexegetical sense, in that they qualify the significance of "the kingdom." To be given the kingdom, in essence means to be given power, might, and glory (cf. 5:18).

Danielic tradition also brings a cosmic dimension to the idea of kingdom. We are to envision a struggle between the divine kingdom (which overlaps with or is in some sense to be identified with the kingdom of Israel) and the kingdom of evil (which also is to be identified with the succession of human kingdoms that dominated Israel). The idea of opposing forces struggling for dominion is seen in ch. 10, where an angel informs a trembling Daniel:

The prince of the kingdom of Persia withstood me twenty-one days; but Michael, one of the chief princes, came to help me, so I left him there with the prince of the

---

[8] For further discussion of the Isaianic background of kingdom and restoration ideas in the NT, see Craig A. Evans, "From Gospel to Gospel: The Function of Isaiah in the New Testament," in *Writing and Reading the Scroll of Isaiah: Studies of an Interpretive Tradition* (ed. Craig C. Broyles and Craig A. Evans; VTSup 70.1, Formation and Interpretation of Old Testament Literature 1; Leiden: Brill, 1997), 651–91.

kingdom of Persia and came to make you understand what is to befall your people in the latter days. For the vision is for days yet to come. (10:13–14)

The "prince of the kingdom of Persia" is Persia's patron angel. Lying behind this idea is the tradition of angels acting as rulers over the nations, with Yahweh, or his delegate, ruling over Israel. This tradition seems to grow out of Deut 32:8–9 (where the number of "peoples" corresponds to the number of "sons of God"). Ben Sira alludes to it when he says that God "appointed a ruler for every nation, but Israel is the Lord's own portion" (Sir 17:17; cf. *1 En.* 89:59, where we are told of seventy angels, or "shepherds," who represent the seventy Gentile nations). The prince of Persia is probably Satan himself (cf. 1QM 17:5–6, which refers to the "prince of the dominion of wickedness"; see also 4Q225 2 i 9; 2 ii 13–14; 11Q5 19:15, which pleads, "Let Satan have no dominion over me"; 11Q6 4 v 16), while the "prince of the host" in Dan 8:11 is probably Yahweh.

According to Dan 10:13, "Michael, one of the chief princes," came to the aid of the unnamed angel (Gabriel? cf. Dan 9:21–23), who had been delayed three weeks. We probably are to imagine a cosmic battle, in which the host of heaven is engaged in battle with the host of Satan. Michael's arrival made it possible for the angel to reach Daniel. The idea of Michael as Yahweh's representative fighting Satan is attested in Rev 12:7 ("war arose in heaven, Michael and his angels fighting against the dragon; and the dragon and his angels fought"). Although Revelation dates to the end of the first century C.E., the tradition presupposed here is quite old, reaching back to a pre-Christian period.[9]

There is also a temporal element in Daniel's understanding of kingdom. Human kingdoms will come to an end, to be displaced by the everlasting kingdom that God will establish: "And in the days of those kings the God of heaven will set up a kingdom which shall never be destroyed, nor shall its sovereignty be left to another people. It shall break in pieces all these kingdoms and bring them to an end, and it shall stand for ever" (2:44). Every kingdom has been set up by God, including those to be destroyed. Because God established all of the kingdoms, including those that brought the kingdom of Israel (or Judah) to an end, it is within his sovereign power to raise up a final kingdom, which will permanently displace the pagan kingdoms. Israel will once again receive the kingdom (7:18, 27).[10] Daniel lends this tem-

---

[9] For further discussion of the tradition of national angels, see John J. Collins, *Daniel* (Hermeneia; Minneapolis: Fortress, 1993), 374–75.

[10] For further discussion of Daniel's contribution to kingdom ideas in the NT, see Craig A. Evans, "Daniel in the New Testament: Visions of God's Kingdom," in *The Book of Daniel: Composition and Reception* (ed. John J. Collins and Peter W. Flint; VTSup 83.2, Formation and Interpretation of Old Testament Literature 2.2; Leiden: Brill, 2001), 490–527.

poral dimension an element of imminence when he declares that "the time has come; the holy ones have taken possession of the kingdom" (Dan 7:22, *apud* Aramaic and Θ). But this imminence is qualified with the concluding admonition: "But you, Daniel, shut up the words, and seal the book, until the time of the end [קֵץ עֵד־עֵת; Θ: ἕως καιροῦ συντελείας] ..." (12:4; cf. 12:9).

In sum, in Scripture God is understood as king, as ruling over a kingdom (which is understood as his presence and sphere of glory and power). The rule of God is regarded as the content of the "good news," and it is a rule that is anticipated soon, as the grand finale of all human kingdoms. In this sense, this kingdom program is a fresh and new expression of God's rule, distinct from the way he has ruled up to this point. It is also a rule that has and will encounter deadly opposition from Satan – whose name means "opponent" – and his allies. For God's rule to triumph, Satan's rule will have to be shattered.

Thus we have in these scriptural antecedents virtually every element of Jesus' proclamation of the kingdom of God. Before turning to this proclamation and its relationship to exorcism, it will be useful to consider briefly developments in sectarian prophecies and expectations relating to the appearance of the kingdom of God.

3. The Context Provided by Prophecies and Expectations of the Rule of God in Second Temple Jewish Literature

For the purpose of this study the conflict between the kingdoms of Satan and God is of primary interest. Such conflict may be hinted at here and there in other Scriptures, but it is in Daniel that it is made explicit. Several other intertestamental writings make significant contributions to this dimension of the topic. Our discussion will be limited to *Jubilees, 1 Enoch*, the *Testaments of the Twelve Patriarchs*, and the *Testament of Moses*, all of which predate or contain traditions that predate Jesus' ministry.

The book of *Jubilees* offers two relevant passages. The first is found in an eschatological oracle in ch. 23 (i. e., vv. 23b–31).[11] After a period of sin and suffering, Israel "will cry out and call and pray to be saved" (v. 24), but there will be no salvation until they return to the Law, to the way of righteousness (v. 26). Then restoration will begin, gradually, generation by generation, until human life span is one thousand years (v. 27), until old age becomes a thing of the past (v. 28). Then

---

[11] R. H. Charles, *Eschatology: The Doctrine of a Future Life in Israel, Judaism, and Christianity* (2nd ed.; London: A&C Black, 1913), 236–40.

all of their days they will be complete and live in peace and rejoicing and there will be no Satan and no evil (one) who will destroy, because all of their days will be days of blessing and healing. And then the Lord will heal his servants, and they will rise up and see great peace. (vv. 29–30a)

We have here a form of millennial, restorative expectation. The era of sickness, oppression, and short sorrowful lives will give way to an era of longevity, youthfulness, healing, and peace.[12] The oracle of *Jubilees* is at points indebted to Isa 65 (esp. vv. 20, 25, 13 = *Jub.* 23:28–30a) and 66 (esp. v. 14 = *Jub.* 23:30b).[13]

The second passage is part of the recapitulation found in ch. 50, the concluding chapter of *Jubilees*. Harking back to elements of ch. 23, 50:5 sums up:

And jubilees will pass until Israel is purified from all the sin of fornication, and defilement, and uncleanness, and sin and error. And they will dwell in confidence in all the land. And then it will not have any Satan or any evil (one). And the land will be purified from that time and forever.

Satan, or Mastemah (cf. *Jub.* 10:8; 17:15–18:13; 48:2–3, 9–12; 4Q225 2 i 9; ii 13, 14), plays an important role in the book of *Jubilees*. His final defeat is an essential feature in this book's vision of final restoration and bliss. Although *Jubilees* does not explicitly mention the kingdom of God (or the Messiah), its vision of restoration coheres with those visions that do.[14]

In *1 En.* 10 we find a passage that expressly describes the defeat and judgment of Satan (= Aza'el). According to the Greek version:

⁴ καὶ τῷ Ῥαφαὴλ εἶπεν· Δῆσον τὸν Ἀζαὴλ ποσὶν καὶ χερσίν, καὶ βάλε αὐτὸν εἰς τὸ σκότος, καὶ ἄνοιξον τὴν ἔρημον τὴν οὖσαν ἐν τῷ Δαδουὴλ κἀκεῖ βάλε αὐτόν, ⁵ καὶ ὑπόθες αὐτῷ λίθους τραχεῖς καὶ ὀξεῖς καὶ ἐπικάλυψον αὐτῷ τὸ σκότος. καὶ οἰκησάτω ἐκεῖ εἰς τοὺς αἰῶνας, καὶ τὴν ὄψιν αὐτοῦ πώμασον καὶ φῶς μὴ θεωρείτω· ⁶ καὶ ἐν τῇ ἡμέρᾳ [τῆς μεγάλης] τῆς κρίσεως ἀπαχθήσεται εἰς τὸν ἐνπυρισμόν [τοῦ πυρός]

⁴ And to Rafael He said: "Bind Aza'el hand and foot, and cast him into darkness, and open the wilderness which is in Dadou'el and there cast him. ⁵ And put him beneath jagged and sharp stones and hide him in darkness. And let him dwell there forever, and cover his face and let him not see light; ⁶ and in the day of [the great] judgment he shall be led away to the furnace [of fire]."

---

[12] It is has been wondered if "they will rise up" in v. 30 refers to the resurrection. However, this is doubtful (see R. H. Charles, "The Book of Jubilees," *APOT* 2:49, n. 30; George W. E. Nickelsburg, *Resurrection, Immortality, and Eternal Life in Intertestamental Judaism* [HTS 26; Cambridge: Harvard University Press, 1972], 22), and in any case the scenario envisioned in our oracle appears to come about gradually (as in *T. Levi* 18), not suddenly, as is usually the case when resurrection is in view.

[13] Charles, "Jubilees," *APOT* 2:49, n. 28; John C. Endres, *Biblical Interpretation in the Book of Jubilees* (CBQMS 18; Washington, D. C.: Catholic Biblical Association of America, 1987), 58–60. Endres also discusses parallels between *Jub.* 23:24–25 and Isa 63:15–64:1.

[14] See Charles, *Eschatology*, 236–40 (the "messianic era").

We find another reference to the judgment of Aza'el, not preserved in either Greek or Aramaic, but in Ethiopic: "Kings, potentates, dwellers upon the earth: You would have to see my Elect One, how he sits in the throne of glory and judges Azaz'el and all his company, and his army, in the name of the Lord of the Spirits!" (55:4).[15] This Azaz'el (or Aza'el) is related to the scapegoat tradition of Lev 16 and comes to represent in post-biblical literature the chief of the wicked angels, who in some traditions is also understood as a desert demon,[16] which may in part explain the location of Jesus' temptations (Mark 1:12–3; Matt 4:1–11 = Luke 4:1–13) in the desert. Rooted in Gen 6:1–7, Azaz'el is understood as one of the fallen angels (cf. *1 En.* 6:7; 4Q201 3:9; 4Q204 2:26), who stands at their head (cf. 4Q180 1:7), ruling over hell (cf. *Apoc. Ab.* 14:3), and who faces inescapable judgment (cf. *1 En.* 13:1–2). This Azaz'el opposes humanity and all that is good (cf. *Apoc. Ab.* 13:8; 14:4), who as the serpent tempted Adam and Eve (cf. *Apoc. Ab.* 23:6–8).

Although there is some diversity in the Azaz'el traditions, there is agreement in the essential details: Azaz'el is the chief of the fallen angels, who tempts humanity, opposes all that is good, and faces certain judgment, at which time he will be bound and cast into hell. It is very significant that according to Ethiopic *Enoch* 55:4 (of which nothing is extant in Greek or Aramaic), Azaz'el will be judged by God's "Elect One," who will sit on his "throne of glory" and will judge "in the name of the Lord of Spirits" (i.e., God). In context, this Elect One is none other than the "Son of Man" and "Messiah" of the *Similitudes of Enoch* (i.e., *1 En.* 37–71), whose characteristics are heavily influenced by the imagery of Dan 7 (cf. esp. *1 En.* 46:1). Taken together, *1 En.* 10:4–6 and 55:4 envision the judgment of Azaz'el (i.e., Satan) at the time God's Elect One (or Messiah) sits on his throne of glory. Although the kingdom of God is not explicitly mentioned, the enthronement of Messiah (cf. *1 En.* 51:3; 55:4; 61:8), the enthronement of God himself (cf. *1 En.* 62:2–3), and the appearance of kings and governors before the Messiah and before God (cf. *1 En.* 53:5–6; 55:4; 62:9) make it clear that it is indeed the kingdom of God that is in view. When this kingdom is finally realized, then Satan will be judged.

The *Testaments of the Twelve Patriarchs* offer several relevant texts. In the *Testament of Levi* 18:11b–12 we have an interesting text that anticipates the granting of authority to God's people to overpower evil spirits:

---

[15] The discrepancy in the Greek and Ethiopic spellings of Aza'el and Azaz'el reflects the spelling variations in the Hebrew and Aramaic traditions where we find variously עזאזל (in Leviticus) and עזזאל, עשאל, or עסאל (at Qumran).

[16] See Alexander Maurer, "Azazel," in *Encyclopedia of the Dead Sea Scrolls* (2 vols.; ed. Lawrence H. Schiffman and James C. VanderKam; Oxford: Oxford University Press, 2000), 1:70–71.

¹¹ καὶ πνεῦμα ἁγιωσύνης ἔσται ἐπ' αὐτοῖς. ¹² καὶ ὁ Βελιὰρ δεθήσεται ὑπ' αὐτοῦ, καὶ δώσει ἐξουσίαν τοῖς τέκνοις αὐτοῦ τοῦ πατεῖν ἐπὶ τὰ πονηρὰ πνεύματα.

¹¹ The spirit of holiness shall be upon them. ¹² And Beliar shall be bound [δεθήσεται] by him, and he shall grant authority to his children to trample over the wicked spirits.

The binding of Beliar (yet another name for Satan; cf. 2 Cor 6:15)[17] recalls the dominical tradition: "But no one can enter a strong man's house and plunder his goods, unless he first bind [δήσῃ] the strong man; then indeed he may plunder his house" (Mark 3:27). In Mark 5:3 we are told that no one was able to "bind" the Gerasene demoniac, while in Luke 13:16 we are told of a woman whom Satan had "bound" for eighteen years. The trampling over wicked spirits recalls Jesus' promise to his disciples that they have been given the authority to tread upon serpents and scorpions (Luke 10:19).

Graham Twelftree thinks *T. Levi* 18:11b–12 is a Christian interpolation.[18] To be sure, there are signs of Christian editing in *T. Levi* 18 (e.g., "in the water" in v. 7; perhaps also elements in v. 6).[19] But if a Christian composed some or all of this oracle, he did so in a remarkably restrained manner. There is nothing in this passage (with the noted exception) that is distinctively or obviously Christian. The imagery of *T. Levi* 18:11b–12 in all probability is drawn from the Jewish Scriptures. The binding of Satan and his evil allies may be dependent on Isa 24:22–23, while the trampling of Satan probably derives from Gen 3:15 ("he shall bruise his [the serpent's] head") and Ps 91:13 ("you will tread on lion and the adder, the young lion and the serpent you will trample under foot") and the interpretive traditions inspired by these passages.

A similar promise to the righteous is found *T. Naph.* 8:4:

---

[17] In USB⁴ Βελιάρ is read (with no variants mentioned in apparatus). The same reading is given in NA²⁷, but the variants Βελιάν (read by D K), Βελιάβ (read by F G), and Βελιάλ (read by pc lat; Tert) are cited in the apparatus. בליעל (Belial) appears more than one hundred times in the Dead Sea Scrolls (e.g., 1QS 1:18; 2:5, 19; 10:21; 1QM 1:1, 5, 13, 15; 4:2; 11:8; and many more).

[18] Twelftree, *Jesus the Exorcist*, 185. He follows Marinus de Jonge, *The Testaments of the Twelve Patriarchs: A Study of Their Texts, Composition and Origin* (Assen: Van Gorcum, 1953), 89; cf. Matthew Black, "Messiah in the Testament of Levi xviii," *ExpTim* 60 (1949): 322. De Jonge, of course, thinks the *Testaments of the Twelve Patriarchs* are almost entirely a Christian composition. For a review of the debate over the origins of the *Testaments*, see H. Dixon Slingerland, *The Testaments of the Twelve Patriarchs: A Critical History of Research* (SBLMS 21; Missoula, Mont.: Scholars, 1977); Jürgen Becker, *Die Testamente der zwölf Patriarchen* (vol. 3.1 of *Jüdische Schriften aus hellenistisch-römischer Zeit*; Gütersloh: Gütersloher Verlagshaus, 1980), 16–17.

[19] Robert H. Charles, "The Testaments of the Twelve Patriarchs," *APOT* 2:314, and Howard C. Kee, "Testaments of the Twelve Patriarchs," *OTP* 1:795, bracket off this phrase as a Christian interpolation. Charles (pp. 314–15) also brackets off part of v. 5 and the last line of v. 9.

ἐὰν ἐργάσησθε τὸ καλόν, τέκνα μου, εὐλογήσουσιν ὑμᾶς καὶ οἱ ἄνθρωποι καὶ οἱ ἄγγελοι· καὶ θεὸς δοξασθήσεται δι' ὑμῶν ἐν τοῖς ἔθνεσι, καὶ ὁ διάβολος φεύξεται ἀφ' ὑμῶν, καὶ τὰ θηρία φοβηθήσονται ὑμᾶς, καὶ ὁ κύριος ἀγαπήσει ὑμᾶς, καὶ οἱ ἄγγελοι ἀνθέξονται ὑμῶν.

If you achieve the good, my children, humans and angels will bless you; and God will be glorified through you among the gentiles. The devil will flee from you; wild animals will be afraid of you; and the Lord will love you, and the angels will stand by you.

This verse is textually uncertain,[20] but there is nothing about it that compels us to see Christian influence. The phrase "dwelling among humans" in v. 3 is probably an interpolation, but the rest of the oracle is Jewish. The promise that the "devil will flee from you" (ὁ διάβολος φεύξεται ἀφ' ὑμῶν) closely parallels Jas 4:7: "Resist the devil and he will flee from you" (ἀντίστητε δὲ τῷ διαβόλῳ καὶ φεύξεται ἀφ' ὑμῶν). It is more likely that James alludes to (perhaps even quotes) *Naphtali* than that we have another instance of a Christian interpolation. Satan and his evil spirits' fleeing from the righteous is a topos in the *Testaments* that appears in various forms (cf. *T. Dan* 5:1 "Beliar will flee from you [φύγῃ ἀφ' ὑμῶν ὁ Βελιάρ]"; *T. Benj.* 5:2 "If you continue to do good, even the unclean spirits will flee from you [φεύξεται ἀφ' ὑμῶν] and wild animals will fear you"). "Wild animals" (θηρία) are sometimes partners of evil powers (cf. Ps 91; Ezek 34:4, 8 "my sheep have become food for all the wild beasts [θηρίοις], since there was no shepherd," 25). The variety recommends against seeing James as the inspiration of a later Christian interpolation.[21] Satan's flight, the presence of wild animals (θηρία), and the ministrations of angels recall the temptation story (cf. Mark 1:13).

In *T. Jud.* 25:3b we find a promise that Beliar will be cast into eternal fire:

καὶ οὐκ ἔσται ἔτι πνεῦμα πλάνης τοῦ Βελιάρ, ὅτι ἐμβληθήσεται ἐν τῷ πυρὶ εἰς τὸν αἰῶνα.

There shall no more be Beliar's spirit of error, because he will be thrown into eternal fire.

The "spirit of error" (πνεῦμα πλάνης) reminds us of the "deceitful spirits and doctrines of demons" (πνεύμασιν πλάνοις καὶ διδασκαλίαις δαιμονίων) of 1 Tim 4:1 (cf. 1 John 4:6 τὸ πνεῦμα τῆς πλάνης). Being "cast into the fire" (ἐμβληθήσεται ἐν τῷ πυρί) parallels similar expressions in the Gospels (cf. Matt 13:42, 50) and in the book of Revelation (esp. 20:10, 14). Because of

---

[20] See Charles, "The Testaments of the Twelve Patriarchs," 2:339, nn. 4–6.
[21] Note also 1QM 3:5–6 "On the trumpets for their campaigns they shall write, 'The Mighty deeds of God to scatter the enemy and to put all those who hate justice to flight [שונאי] ...'" Although the "enemy" envisioned here is primarily the human variety, it is probable that the demonic enemy was in view as well. They will be scattered and made to flee.

these and other parallels, Twelftree again suspects that we may not have pre-Christian tradition.²² He could be correct, but the lack of distinctively Christian tradition argues against this conclusion. It is more probable that Christianity's references to "spirit of error" and being "cast into fire" are drawn from a rich Jewish eschatological thesaurus. Moreover, the lateness of some of the NT parallels (i.e., in 1 Timothy, 1 John, and Revelation) favors the dependence of these books on the *Testaments*, rather than the reverse. One should note also that much of this language and imagery also appears in the Dead Sea Scrolls, which almost no one thinks are either Christian in origin or edited by Christians.²³

An intriguing passage is found in the *T. Zeb.* 9:8:

καὶ μετὰ ταῦτα ἀνατελεῖ ὑμῖν αὐτὸς ὁ κύριος, φῶς δικαιοσύνης, καὶ ἴασις καὶ εὐσπλαγχνία ἐπὶ ταῖς πτέρυξιν αὐτοῦ. αὐτὸς λυτρώσεται πᾶσαν αἰχμαλωσίαν υἱῶν ἀνθρώπων ἐκ τοῦ Βελιάρ, καὶ πᾶν πνεῦμα πλάνης πατηθήσεται· καὶ ἐπιστρέψει πάντα τὰ ἔθνη εἰς παραζήλωσιν αὐτοῦ, καὶ ὄψεσθε θεὸν ἐν σχήματι ἀνθρώπου ἐν ναῷ, ὃ ἂν ἐκλέξηται κύριος, Ἰερουσαλὴμ ὄνομα αὐτῷ.

And after these things the Lord himself will arise over you, the light of righteousness, with healing and compassion in his wings. He himself will ransom every captive of the sons of men from Beliar, and every spirit of error will be trampled down. He will turn all nations to being zealous for him.²⁴ And you will see [God in human form [in the Temple],] that which the Lord may choose: Jerusalem is its name.

Not only do we have a Christian interpolation (set off in brackets), but the ms evidence is diverse. Some mss omit most of the middle section of this passage; others read the last sentence differently. Whatever the original reading may have been, what is the origin of "He himself will ransom every captive of the sons of men from Beliar, and every spirit of error will be trampled down"? Charles thinks it is pre-Christian; so does Kee.²⁵ Twelftree, however, once again doubts the pre-Christian origin of the material, arguing that "every spirit of error will be trampled down" is drawn from some of the NT passages considered above (esp. Luke 10:19–20).²⁶ Perhaps this is so, but for the reasons given above (and in the notes), it is concluded that this

---

²² Twelftree, *Jesus the Exorcist*, 186.
²³ On spirit of deceit and the like, see 1QS 4:9 "the spirit of falsehood result in ... cruel deceit and fraud" (= 4Q257 5:7); 1QH 9:22 "a spirit of error." For judgment in fire, see 1QS 4:13 "for all eternity, with a shameful extinction in the fire of Hell's outer darkness" (= 4Q257 5:12); 1QH 4:13 "fire [shall burn] in Sheol below"; 1QH 14:18–19; 4Q185 1–2 i 9 "flames of fire they mete out judgment"; 4Q429 4 i 6; 4Q491 8–10 line 15 "as a fire bur]ning in the dark places of the damned. Let it bu[rn] the damned of Sheol"; 11Q13 3:7 "[they] destroyed Belial by fire."
²⁴ Or "All the nations will turn to zeal for him."
²⁵ Charles, "Testaments," *APOT* 2:331, n. 8 ("a Jewish expansion"); Kee, "Testaments," *OTP* 1:807. Kee brackets off "God in human form" and omits "in the Temple."
²⁶ Twelftree, *Jesus the Exorcist*, 186–87. So also Becker, *Die Testamente*, 90.

material (with the exception of what has been set off in brackets) is probably of non-Christian origin.

For our purposes, the value of this passage lies in the contrasting juxtaposition of ransoming those held captive by Beliar (cf. Mark 3:26–27), on the one hand, and trampling "every spirit of error," on the other. Once again we have the paradigm of Satan's decline, upon the advent of God's reign, even if some of this specific language is not employed.

Finally, we may consider *T. Dan* 5:10–11:

¹⁰ καὶ ἀνατελεῖ ὑμῖν ἐκ τῆς φυλῆς Ἰούδα καὶ Λευὶ τὸ σωτήριον κυρίου· καὶ αὐτὸς ποιήσει πρὸς τὸν Βελιὰρ πόλεμον, καὶ τὴν ἐκδίκησιν τοῦ νίκους δώσει πατράσιν ἡμῶν. καὶ τὴν αἰχμαλωσίαν λάβῃ ἀπὸ τοῦ Βελιάρ, ψυχὰς ἁγίων, καὶ ἐπιστρέψει καρδίας ἀπειθεῖς πρὸς κύριον, καὶ δώσει τοῖς ἐπικαλουμένοις αὐτὸν εἰρήνην αἰώνιον. ¹¹ καὶ τὴν αἰχμαλωσίαν λάβῃ ἀπὸ τοῦ Βελιάρ, ψυχὰς ἁγίων, καὶ ἐπιστρέψει καρδίας ἀπειθεῖς πρὸς κύριον, καὶ δώσει τοῖς ἐπικαλουμένοις αὐτὸν εἰρήνην αἰώνιον. καὶ τὴν αἰχμαλωσίαν λάβῃ ἀπὸ τοῦ Βελιάρ, ψυχὰς ἁγίων, καὶ ἐπιστρέψει καρδίας ἀπειθεῖς πρὸς κύριον, καὶ δώσει τοῖς ἐπικαλουμένοις αὐτὸν εἰρήνην αἰώνιον.

¹⁰ And there shall arise for you from the tribe of Judah and (the tribe of) Levi the Lord's salvation. He will make war against Beliar; he will grant the vengeance of victory as our goal. ¹¹ And he shall take from Beliar the captives, the souls of the saints; and he shall turn the hearts of the disobedient ones to the Lord.

Twelftree doubts that "He will make war against Beliar," etc. is pre-Christian material.[27] He cites de Jonge with approval, who notes apparent tension between the implied plural of "from the tribe of Judah and (the tribe of) Levi" and the explicit singular of "he will make war against Beliar; he will grant the vengeance," etc.[28] But Kee rightly remarks that what is envisioned is "the Lord's salvation" (regardless of the role of the figures raised up from the tribes of Judah and Levi). It is God himself that is the singular subject of "he will make war against Beliar."[29] This is not some clumsy Christian interpolation.

The result of this war against Beliar and the freeing of captives (again, cf. Mark 3:26–27) is paradise regained: "the saints shall refresh themselves in Eden; the righteous shall rejoice in the New Jerusalem," etc. (*T. Dan* 5:12–13). Although the kingdom of God is not explicitly mentioned, the oracle does go on to say that "the Holy One of Israel will rule over them in humility and poverty, and he who trusts in him shall reign in truth in the heavens" (5:13b). The hope of restoration is expressed in the context of most of the passages from the *Testaments* that have been considered. The patriarchs will be resurrected (*T. Jud.* 25:1–2) and the righteous will rejoice

---

[27] Twelftree, *Jesus the Exorcist*, 187.
[28] De Jonge (*Testaments*, 87) sees this as a Christian passage.
[29] Kee, "Testaments," *OTP* 1:809, n. d. God "is the agent of all that follows." So also Becker, *Die Testamente*, 95.

and be vindicated (*T. Levi* 18:13–14; *T. Jud.* 25:4–5; *T. Zeb.* 9:7–9). The twin aspects of the demise and judgment of Satan, on the one hand, and the advent and consummation of the reign of God, on the other, are almost a commonplace.

Finally, we must consider a very significant passage from the *Testament* (or *Assumption*) *of Moses*.

Et tunc parebit regnum illius in omni creatura illius.
Et tunc Zabulus finem habebit,
et tristitia[m] cum eo adducetur. (10:1)

And then his kingdom will appear in his whole creation.
And then the Devil will have an end,
And sorro[w] will be led away with him.

Here again we find juxtaposed the complementary ideas of the advent of God's rule (the antecedent of "his" in the first line is God) and the demise of Satan. This text is especially important, for evidently it was composed c. 30 C.E., or at about the time Jesus was a public figure.[30] This text links the oppressive administration of the high priesthood and the corruption of the Herodian princes to the time of tribulation that immediately precedes the advent of God's rule and the collapse of Satan's rule. No other text offers a closer template, over against the outline of Jesus' eschatology may be compared.[31]

To summarize what has been learned in sections 1 and 2 above, we find in the Scriptural antecedents the confession that God is king, that he is enthroned, and that he will bring judgment in behalf of his people. According to Isaiah, the reign of God is the "good news" that is to be proclaimed and stands at the center of Israel's hopes of redemption and restoration.[32] According to Daniel, the kingdom of God is locked in a struggle with the kingdom of Satan. God's rule will eventually prevail, and his kingdom, which in some sense is the kingdom of Israel, will be an eternal kingdom. The triumph of God's kingdom will lead to the destruction of Satan's kingdom.

In the later prophecies and expectations of the intertestamental writings the spiritual dimension of the kingdom hope is intensified. In this respect,

---

[30] For this date, see J. Priest, "Testament of Moses," in *Old Testament Pseudepigrapha* (2 vols.; ed. James H. Charlesworth; New York: Doubleday, 1983–85), 1:920–21. Priest argues for a first century date, likely in the first three decades.

[31] For further examination of *T. Mos.* 10, see my discussion in Craig A. Evans, "Jesus' Exorcisms and Proclamation of the Kingdom of God in the Light of the Testaments," in *The Changing Face of Judaism, Christianity, and Other Greco-Roman Religions in Antiquity* (ed. Ian H. Henderson and Gerbern S. Oegema; Studien zu den Jüdischen Schriften aus hellenistisch-römischer Zeit 2; Gütersloh: Gütersloher Verlagshaus, 2006), 210–33.

[32] For a collection of studies that consider this theme, see James M. Scott, ed., *Restoration: Old Testament, Jewish, and Christian Perspectives* (Supplements to the Journal for the Study of Judaism 72; Leiden: Brill, 2001).

these prophecies and expectations parallel, and in some instances may even grow out of, the Danielic tradition. Satan and his allies will be imprisoned or destroyed, no longer able to afflict the righteous. The righteous will live in peace and will experience the blessings of God's benevolent rule.

It is in the light of these traditions that the proclamation of Jesus and the attendant exorcisms should be understood. This is not to say, however, that Jesus' proclamation of the rule of God introduces nothing new. These materials provide a backdrop that Jesus and his contemporaries knew and presupposed. Familiarity with these traditions will enable us to see more clearly in what ways Jesus' message was similar to or different from the teachings and expectations of his contemporaries.

4. Authenticity and Key Themes of Jesus' Proclamation and Exorcisms in Light of Its Context

Jesus speaks of the kingdom of God in many contexts: in public and private teaching, often with parables, in public calls for repentance, in acts of wonder and exorcism, and in his commissioning and sending of apostles. That Jesus' proclamation of the kingdom of God was understood to portend Israel's restoration, with profound implications for society and ruling powers, is clearly seen in the request for a sign (Mark 8:11–13) and in Jesus' crucifixion as "king of the Jews" (Mark 15:26). The request for a sign is especially important, for it suggests that at least some of his contemporaries, including those who were not numbered among his following, associated Jesus' proclamation of the kingdom with the revolutionary messages of other men, who proffered "signs" (as in the case of Theudas in the 40's or the unnamed Jewish man from Egypt in the 50's). The signs of these men were based on major events of salvation, such as crossing the Jordan River (Joshua 4) or conquering the Promised Land (Joshua 6). Their proclamations and promises prompted deadly police action.[33] Jesus' proclamation and activity would likely have been viewed, at least generally, in this light.

We have in Mark 1:14–15 a summary of Jesus' kingdom proclamation. We begin with it:

¹⁴ Now after John was arrested, Jesus came into Galilee, preaching the gospel of God [κηρύσσων τὸ εὐαγγέλιον τοῦ θεοῦ], ¹⁵ and saying, "The time is fulfilled, and the kingdom of God is at hand; repent, and believe in the gospel [πεπλήρωται ὁ καιρὸς καὶ ἤγγικεν ἡ βασιλεία τοῦ θεοῦ· μετανοεῖτε καὶ πιστεύετε ἐν τῷ εὐαγγελίῳ]."

---

[33] Theudas promises to divide the Jordan, as part of the re-entering and re-conquering of the Promised Land (cf. Josephus, *Ant.* 20.97–98), while the Egyptian Jew promised that the walls of Jerusalem would collapse, enabling his following to enter the city, probably on analogy with Joshua's conquest of Jericho (cf. Josephus, *Ant.* 20.169–170).

Two major components of this proclamation appear to reflect elements from Daniel and Isaiah. First, Jesus' proclamation seems to reflect the perspective of Dan 7, as seen in the following (with parallels to the Gospel tradition underlined):

Dan 7:22 Θ   καὶ ὁ καιρὸς ἔφθασεν καὶ τὴν βασιλείαν κατέσχον οἱ ἅγιοι
Dan 7:22 ar   קדישין ומלכותא החסנו וזמנא מטה
Mark 1:15   πεπλήρωται ὁ καιρὸς καὶ ἤγγικεν ἡ βασιλεία τοῦ θεοῦ
Matt 12:28 = Luke 11:20 ἔφθασεν ἐφ' ὑμᾶς ἡ βασιλεία τοῦ θεοῦ[34]

Daniel's "the time has arrived and the saints have gained the kingdom" (as seen esp. in Θ) closely corresponds to Jesus' statements that "the time is fulfilled" and "the kingdom of God has come" (both ἔφθασεν and ἤγγικεν may translate מְטָה).

Second, Isaiah's "gospel," namely that God is present (Isa 40:9) and that God is king (Isa 52:7), is probably what lies behind the words: "the kingdom of God is at hand." This is likely so because of the verbal coherence between the Aramaic paraphrase of these passages and Jesus' proclamation. "Behold, your God" (הִנֵּה אֱלֹהֵיכֶם) in Isa 40:9 and "Your God reigns" (מָלַךְ אֱלֹהָיִךְ) in Isa 52:7 are rendered in the Aramaic as follows:

Tg. Isa. 40:9: "The kingdom of your (pl.) God [אתגליאת מלכותא דאלהכון] is revealed!"
Tg. Isa. 52:7: "The kingdom of your (sg.) God [אתגליאת מלכותא דאלהיך] is revealed!"

This is not the place to argue for Jesus' familiarity with the emerging Aramaic paraphrase and interpretation of Isaiah, for that has been done ably elsewhere.[35] It is enough to observe the contribution that Isaiah has made to Jesus' proclamation (e.g., Isa 61:1–2 in Matt 11:5; Luke 7:22 "the poor have good news preached to them"). It is probably not coincidental that Jesus' colleague John the Baptist was associated with Isaiah 40 (specifically with reference to v. 3, where the voice calls for the preparation of the way of the Lord),[36] a passage that also speaks of the good news (in v. 9).

These succinct traditions of Jesus' proclamation derive from Mark and Q, which are early and reliable sources of dominical tradition. Here there is no mention of Satan, evil spirits, or the cosmic struggle depicted in Daniel

---

[34] See also Dan 4:21(24): "This is the interpretation, O king: It is a decree of the Most High, which has come upon [מְטָה עַל; Θ: ἔφθασεν ἐπί] my lord the king."

[35] Bruce D. Chilton, "Regnum Dei Deus Est," *SJT* 31 (1978): 261–70; Chilton, *A Galilean Rabbi*, 57–67.

[36] On Isa 40:3 in John and Qumran, see James H. Charlesworth, "Intertextuality: Isaiah 40:3 and the Serek Ha-Yahad," in *The Quest for Context and Meaning: Studies in Biblical Intertextuality in Honor of James A. Sanders* (ed. Craig A. Evans and Shemaryahu Talmon; Biblical Interpretation Series 28; Leiden: Brill, 1997), 197–224; Joan E. Taylor, *The Immerser: John the Baptist Within Second Temple Judaism* (Studying the Historical Jesus; Grand Rapids: Eerdmans, 1997), 25–29. John's arrest and execution cohere with a message based on a text of national renewal, such as we have in Isaiah 40.

and in other intertestamental traditions, but these elements do appear elsewhere in the dominical tradition concerned with the kingdom of God. We may review this material under four heads: (1) temptation, (2) exorcism, (3) sending the twelve, and (4) healing.

4.1. The Temptation of Jesus

The temptation tradition is multiply attested, appearing in both Mark and Q. Mark's account is the simplest, saying only in 1:12–13 that

¹² Καὶ εὐθὺς τὸ πνεῦμα αὐτὸν ἐκβάλλει εἰς τὴν ἔρημον. ¹³ καὶ ἦν ἐν τῇ ἐρήμῳ τεσσεράκοντα ἡμέρας πειραζόμενος ὑπὸ τοῦ σατανᾶ, καὶ ἦν μετὰ τῶν θηρίων, καὶ οἱ ἄγγελοι διηκόνουν αὐτῷ.

¹² The Spirit immediately drove him out into the wilderness. ¹³ And he was in the wilderness forty days, tempted by Satan; and he was with the wild animals; and the angels ministered to him.

This text alludes to some of the themes observed above. The antithesis between the Spirit (of God – "Holy Spirit," according to Luke 4:1) and Satan is clearly seen. Although not expressly stated, "being tempted by Satan" is surely to be understood as an attack, an attempt either to discredit or perhaps even to destroy Jesus. The presence of "wild animals" (θηρία) is interesting, immediately recalling *T. Naph.* 8:4b: "The devil will flee from you; wild animals [θηρία] will be afraid of you, and the angels will stand by you." This parallel suggests that the wild animals are Satan's allies (perhaps representative of demons?), who are then countered by angels. Thus we have the Spirit of God versus Satan, angels versus wild animals, and Jesus at the center of the conflict. Although the evangelist Mark makes very little of it, the story of the temptation bears important witness to the magnitude of the conflict that Jesus' mission is about to provoke.

The Q tradition (Matt 4:1–11 = Luke 4:1–13) provides a tripartite form of the temptation that personalizes the confrontation between Jesus and Satan. In two of the temptations, Jesus is invited to demonstrate his divine sonship ("command these stones to become bread"; "throw yourself down") and in one, Jesus is invited to worship Satan himself. This temptation (it is the third temptation in Matthew, but the second in Luke) highlights the antithetical nature of the struggle. Will Jesus worship Satan, or will he worship God?[37] Although Q provides details Mark lacks, this event coheres with the kingdom versus Satan theme in such a way as to suggest its core authenticity and is an event finding itself stubbornly deposited in a largely sayings tradition, pointing to the event's roots reflecting an early tradition.

---

[37] This polarity is seen in Jesus' rebuke of Simon Peter: "Get behind me, Satan! For you are not thinking the thoughts of God, but the thoughts of people" (Mark 8:33).

Following the temptation, at least according to the Markan narrative sequence, Jesus begins to proclaim the kingdom of God (Mark 1:14–15). Having accepted God's rule for himself, Jesus has begun to proclaim the rule of God for all of Israel. By remaining loyal to God, Jesus remains qualified, as God's "son" (Mark 1:11), to proclaim God's kingdom.

4.2. Exorcism

We shall trace examples from Mark, Q, and material special to Luke, so again the theme is multiply attested. The Markan passage does not explicitly refer to the kingdom of God, but the reference to the kingdom of Satan justifies its inclusion. Responding to the charge that he "is possessed by Beelzebul, and by the prince of demons he casts out the demons" (Mark 3:22), Jesus says:

²³ Καὶ προσκαλεσάμενος αὐτοὺς ἐν παραβολαῖς ἔλεγεν αὐτοῖς· πῶς δύναται σατανᾶς σατανᾶν ἐκβάλλειν; ²⁴ καὶ ἐὰν βασιλεία ἐφ' ἑαυτὴν μερισθῇ, οὐ δύναται σταθῆναι ἡ βασιλεία ἐκείνη· ²⁵ καὶ ἐὰν οἰκία ἐφ' ἑαυτὴν μερισθῇ, οὐ δυνήσεται ἡ οἰκία ἐκείνη σταθῆναι. ²⁶ καὶ εἰ ὁ σατανᾶς ἀνέστη ἐφ' ἑαυτὸν καὶ ἐμερίσθη, οὐ δύναται στῆναι ἀλλὰ τέλος ἔχει. ²⁷ ἀλλ' οὐ δύναται οὐδεὶς εἰς τὴν οἰκίαν τοῦ ἰσχυροῦ εἰσελθὼν τὰ σκεύη αὐτοῦ διαρπάσαι, ἐὰν μὴ πρῶτον τὸν ἰσχυρὸν δήσῃ, καὶ τότε τὴν οἰκίαν αὐτοῦ διαρπάσει.

²³ And he called them to him, and said to them in parables, "How can Satan cast out Satan? ²⁴ If a kingdom is divided against itself, that kingdom cannot stand. ²⁵ And if a house is divided against itself, that house will not be able to stand. ²⁶ And if Satan has risen up against himself and is divided, he cannot stand, but is coming to an end. ²⁷ But no one can enter a strong man's house and plunder his goods, unless he first binds the strong man; then indeed he may plunder his house." (3:23–27)

Comparing a divided Satan to a divided kingdom strongly implies that Jesus understands his great foe as the head of a kingdom that, by further implication, opposes God's kingdom. The reference to Beelzebul as the "prince of demons" supports this interpretation.[38] Moreover, the statement that a divided Satan "is coming to an end" (τέλος ἔχει, lit. "has an end") matches exactly the Latin wording in *T. Mos.* 10:1: "And then his kingdom will appear in his whole creation. And then the Devil will have an end [*finem habebit*]." This important parallel suggests that Jesus understood that two kingdoms are at war, and that, as one stronger than the "strong man" (cf. Mark 1:7, where John foretells the coming of one "stronger" than he), he has bound (δήσῃ) Satan and is now plundering his house, that is, liberating his hostages – those oppressed through demonic possession and illness.

---

[38] See *T. Sol.* 3:6 "I am Beelzebul, the ruler of demons." On this epithet, see Wolfgang Herrmann, "Baal Zebub," *DDD* 154–56.

Probably related to the idea of binding the strong man and plundering his house is the interesting vision of Satan's fall from heaven, found only in the Lukan Gospel:

¹⁷ Ὑπέστρεψαν δὲ οἱ ἑβδομήκοντα [δύο] μετὰ χαρᾶς λέγοντες· κύριε, καὶ τὰ δαιμόνια ὑποτάσσεται ἡμῖν ἐν τῷ ὀνόματί σου. ¹⁸ εἶπεν δὲ αὐτοῖς· ἐθεώρουν τὸν σατανᾶν ὡς ἀστραπὴν ἐκ τοῦ οὐρανοῦ πεσόντα. ¹⁹ ἰδοὺ δέδωκα ὑμῖν τὴν ἐξουσίαν τοῦ πατεῖν ἐπάνω ὄφεων καὶ σκορπίων, καὶ ἐπὶ πᾶσαν τὴν δύναμιν τοῦ ἐχθροῦ, καὶ οὐδὲν ὑμᾶς οὐ μὴ ἀδικήσῃ.

¹⁷ The seventy returned with joy, saying, "Lord, even the demons are subject to us in your name!" ¹⁸ And he said to them, "I saw Satan fall like lightning from heaven. ¹⁹ Behold, I have given you authority to tread upon serpents and scorpions, and over all the power of the enemy; and nothing shall hurt you. (10:17–19)

In this material, Satan is seen as having fallen from heaven, implying his defeat and loss of heavenly access and powers.[39] He has been bound and he has fallen from heaven. The description of Satan's falling from heaven "like lightning" (ὡς ἀστραπὴν ἐκ τοῦ οὐρανοῦ πεσόντα) has led some to think the saying alludes to Isa 14:12: "How you are fallen from heaven [ἐξέπεσεν ἐκ τοῦ οὐρανοῦ], O Day Star, son of Dawn! How you are cut down to the ground, you who laid the nations low!"[40] Interestingly, "above the stars of God I will set my throne" in MT Isa 14:13 becomes "above the people of God I will set the throne of my kingdom" in the Aramaic. If this passage and the Aramaic tradition that later emerged lie behind Jesus' statement, then again we find the idea that Satan's kingdom is in a state of collapse and that he is losing his power over God's people. As mentioned above, the statement that Jesus has given his disciples "authority to tread upon serpents and scorpions, and over all the power of the enemy" probably alludes to Ps 91:13 and perhaps to *T. Levi* 18:12.

Perhaps the most important text for our concerns is found in Luke 11:19–20, a tradition that combines Q material with the accusation narrated in Mark 3:22–27. The text reads as follows:

---

[39] Dietrich Rusam ("Sah Jesus wirklich den Satan vom Himmel fallen [Lk 10.18]? Auf der Suche nach einem neuen Differenzkriterium," *NTS* 50 [2004]: 87–105) rightly calls attention to Luke's redaction in 10:18. Indeed, the whole of 10:17–20 gives evidence of the evangelist's hand, but there is no compelling reason for assigning the declaration, "I saw Satan fall like lightning from heaven," to post-Easter tradition. It is more likely that something was there to redact than that this entire scene was created. This scene coheres with the emphasis on cosmic battle we see in all of these texts. On Satan's fall from heaven, one should see *L. A. E.* 12:1; *2 En.* 29:5; *T. Sol.* 20:16–17.

[40] A.P. Tàrrech, "Lc 10,18: La Visió de la Caiguda de Satanàs," *Revista Catalana de Teologia* 3 (1978): 217–43; I. Howard Marshall, *The Gospel of Luke* (NIGTC 3; Grand Rapids: Eerdmans, 1978), 428–29. In later traditions (e. g., *Mek.* on Exod 15:1 [*Shirata* 2]; *Exod. Rab.* 8:2 [on Exod 7:1]; *Song Rab.* 8:14 § 1), Isa 14:12 is sometimes understood as a reference to Satan's (or his agent's) fall from heaven.

¹⁹ εἰ δὲ ἐγὼ ἐν Βεελζεβοὺλ ἐκβάλλω τὰ δαιμόνια, οἱ υἱοὶ ὑμῶν ἐν τίνι ἐκβάλλουσιν; διὰ τοῦτο αὐτοὶ ὑμῶν κριταὶ ἔσονται. ²⁰ εἰ δὲ ἐν δακτύλῳ θεοῦ [ἐγὼ] ἐκβάλλω τὰ δαιμόνια, ἄρα ἔφθασεν ἐφ' ὑμᾶς ἡ βασιλεία τοῦ θεοῦ.

¹⁹ And if I cast out demons by Beelzebul, by whom do your sons cast them out? Therefore they shall be your judges. ²⁰ But if it is by the finger of God that I cast out demons, then the kingdom of God has come upon you.

This passage is important because it directly links exorcism to the proclamation of the kingdom of God. Casting out demons is seen as proof that the kingdom of God has come. It shows that, as Twelftree says, "the exorcisms themselves are the coming of the kingdom."[41]

Verse 19 replies to the charge that Jesus "casts out demons by Beelzebul, the prince of demons" (Luke 11:15). This accusation closely resembles the one found in Mark 3:22 ("He is possessed by Beelzebul, and by the prince of demons he casts out the demons"). The evangelist Luke draws upon his Markan source at this point, pulling together elements from Mark 3, as well as the request for a sign in Mark 8:11–13 (cf. Luke 11:16: "while others, to test him, sought from him a sign from heaven"). As the narrative unfolds, the Lukan evangelist will also make use of material from Q.[42] Thus, the synthetic nature of the composition complicates the question of original context. It is quite possible that the saying in v. 20 derives from a different context, though more will be said on this below.[43]

Verse 20 parallels Matt 12:28 almost verbatim, and in all probability has been drawn from Q:

εἰ δὲ ἐν πνεύματι θεοῦ ἐγὼ ἐκβάλλω τὰ δαιμόνια, ἄρα ἔφθασεν ἐφ' ὑμᾶς ἡ βασιλεία τοῦ θεοῦ.

But if it is by the Spirit of God that I cast out demons, then the kingdom of God has come upon you.

The only difference is Matthew's ἐν πνεύματι in place of Luke's ἐν δακτύλῳ. Most scholars of late think "Spirit of God" is original and that Luke replaced it with "finger of God."[44] It must be admitted that the Lukan evangelist's use of "hand of God" (cf. Luke 1:66; Acts 4:30; and elsewhere) offers

---

[41] Twelftree, *Jesus the Exorcist*, 170.

[42] See the discussion in Joseph A. Fitzmyer, *The Gospel According to Luke X–XXIV* (AB 28a; Garden City: Doubleday, 1985), 917–18; John Nolland, *Luke 9:21–18:34* (WBC 35b; Dallas: Word, 1993), 635.

[43] The parallel saying in Matt 12:28 also seems to be out of its original context, being coupled – somewhat at cross-purposes – with 12:27 ("by whom do your sons cast out" demons), implying that the exorcisms of others (and probably not the disciples) may just as clearly demonstrate the presence of the kingdom of God as Jesus' exorcisms. Surely Jesus did not think this. Either the sayings of vv. 27 and 28 were uttered in different contexts, or they related to one another in a different way.

[44] For summary of arguments and bibliography, see Nolland, *Luke 9:21–18:34*, 639.

a measure of support for this position. But given his interest in the Spirit, the evangelist likely would not replace "Spirit of God."[45] Accordingly, I am still inclined to view "finger of God" as original and "Spirit of God" as Matthean redaction, intended to clarify the meaning of the expression and avoid an anthropomorphism.

Many have accepted Matt 12:28 = Luke 11:20, along with other related texts (such as Mark 3:27), as a genuine saying of Jesus.[46] Among other things, the authenticity of the saying virtually guarantees the historicity of Jesus' ministry of exorcism – at least as he and his contemporaries would have understood exorcism.[47] But equally important is the light that this saying may shed on Jesus' understanding of his exorcisms (and of his other acts of power), especially if the Lukan form of the saying is accepted.

---

[45] One thinks of Matt 7:11 = Luke 11:13, where in the former God gives "good things to those who ask him," while in the latter God gives "the Holy Spirit to those who ask him." In this case, it is probable that the Lukan evangelist replaced Q's "good things" with "the Holy Spirit." So Fitzmyer, *Luke X–XXIV*, 915–16; W. D. Davies and Dale C. Allison, Jr., *A Critical and Exegetical Commentary on the Gospel According to Saint Matthew* (3 vols.; ICC; Edinburgh: T&T Clark, 1988–97), 1:684; and many others. (One should compare also Luke 4:1, where "the Holy Spirit" augments "the Spirit" in Mark 1:12; or Luke 3:22, where "Holy" is added to "Spirit" in Mark 1:10.) Why would this evangelist, with his evident interest in the Holy Spirit *in the immediate context* substitute ἐν δακτύλῳ θεοῦ for ἐν πνεύματι θεοῦ? For further discussion, see Davies and Allison, *Matthew*, 2:340; Martin Hengel, "Der Finger und die Herrschaft Gottes in Lk 11,20," in *La Main de Dieu – Die Hand Gottes* (ed. Ren Kieffer and Jan Bergman; WUNT 94; Tübingen: Mohr Siebeck, 1997), 87–106, esp. 101–2 (avoidance of anthropomorphism); and James M. Robinson, et al., *The Critical Edition of Q* (Hermeneia; Minneapolis: Fortress, 2000), 232–33. The Matthean evangelist himself adds reference to the Spirit in 1:18, 20; 12:18, 32.

[46] Rudolf Bultmann, *The History of the Synoptic Tradition* (trans. John Marsh; Oxford: Blackwell, 1972), 13–14; Rudolf Bultmann, "Ist die Apokalyptic die Mutter der christlichen Theologie? Eine Auseinandersetzung mit Ernst Käsemann," in *Apophoreta: Festschrift für Ernst Haenchen zu seinem siebzigsten Geburtstag am 10. Dezember 1964* (ed. W. Eltester and F. H. Kettler; BZNW 30; Berlin: Töpelmann, 1964), 64–69, esp. p. 65: "I cannot be persuaded that Luke 6:20–21; 10:23–24; 11:20; Mark 2:18–19; 3:27; and Matt 11:5 are post-Easter community formulations" (author's translation). Also Vincent Taylor, *The Formation of the Gospel Tradition* (2nd ed.; London: Macmillan, 1935), 120; James D. G. Dunn, "Matthew 12:28/Luke 11:20 – A Word of Jesus?" in *Eschatology and the New Testament: Festschrift for George R. Beasley-Murray* (ed. W. Hulitt Gloer; Peabody: Hendrickson, 1988), 29–49; James D. G. Dunn, *Jesus Remembered* (vol. 1 of *Christianity in the Making*; Grand Rapids: Eerdmans, 2003–xx), 458–60. The Jesus Seminar also gives Luke 11:20 a *pink* rating, indicating the belief that the saying approximates something Jesus actually said; cf. Robert W. Funk, et al., *The Five Gospels: The Search for the Authentic Words of Jesus* (New York: Macmillan, 1993), 329–30. The editors comment that Luke's "by the finger of God" is more primitive than Matthew's "by the Spirit of God" (p. 330).

[47] See Rudolf Bultmann, *Jesus and the Word* (trans. Louise Pettibone Smith and Erminie Huntress; New York: Scribner, 1934), 28, 173–74: "But there can be no doubt that Jesus did the kind of deeds which were miracles to his mind and to the minds of his contemporaries, that is, deeds which were attributed to a supernatural, divine cause; undoubtedly he healed the sick and cast out demons ... he obviously himself understood his miracles as a sign of the imminence of the Kingdom of God."

The claim to cast out demons "by the finger of God" in all probability alludes to Exod 8:15 (Eng. v. 19),[48] however the Lukan evangelist himself may have understood and applied its idiom. The Exodus context is fascinating:

[14] The magicians tried by their secret arts to bring forth gnats, but they could not. So there were gnats on man and beast. [15] And the magicians said to Pharaoh, "This is the finger of God [אֶצְבַּע אֱלֹהִים הִוא/δάκτυλος θεοῦ ἐστιν τοῦτο]." But Pharaoh's heart was hardened, and he would not listen to them; as the LORD had said.

This passage mirrors in an interesting way Jesus' saying, "if it is by the finger of God that I cast out demons, then the kingdom of God has come upon you." Because the Exodus context involves hard-heartedness and true and false miracle workers, that is, those who perform wonders with the aid of God (i.e., Moses and Aaron) and those who perform wonders with the aid of false gods (or demons) and gimmickry (i.e., Pharaoh's magicians), it may be, after all, that Jesus' saying in its original setting was part of a controversy, as we have it in Matt 12:22–32, Luke 11:14–23, or Mark 3:22–30. Exodus 8 says nothing about demons, but in rabbinic tradition the passage came to be understood that way: "As soon as the magicians realised that they were not able to produce gnats, they recognised that the deeds were those of God and not demons [שֵׁדִים]. They no longer claimed to compare themselves with Moses in producing the plagues" (*Exod. Rab.* 10.7 [on Exod 8:15]).[49]

Exodus 7–10 repeatedly refers to the signs (אֹתֹת/σημεῖα) that Moses performed before Pharaoh, yet Pharaoh's heart remained hard and unbelieving. In the Lukan setting (i.e., 11:16) "others, testing him, sought from him a sign [σημεῖον] from heaven." We seem to have a collocation of parallel ideas in Exodus and in the dominical tradition – the phrase "finger of God," performing miracles/signs, viewing antagonists or protagonists as false, reference to the demonic (explicit in the Gospels, explicit in later Jewish interpretation), conflict between two spheres of power (or kingdoms). If so, then it suggests that Jesus appealed to the famous contest between Moses and the magicians of Pharaoh. Jesus asserts that he casts out demons "by the finger of God," not "by Beelzebul, the prince of demons." This com-

---

[48] Fitzmyer, *Luke X–XXIV*, 922: "Jesus' words allude to the story of the third plague in Exod 8:15." See also Hengel, "Der Finger und die Herrschaft Gottes in Lk 11,20," 91, 97–99. There is an ostracon of uncertain date and provenance, in which one adjures "by the finger of god" (κατὰ τοῦ δακτύλου τοῦ θεοῦ) that one Hor not open his mouth and speak with one Hatros. For discussion, see Adolf Deissmann, *Light from the Ancient East* (trans. Lionel R. M. Strachan; New York: Doran, 1927), 305–6 and pl. 56.
[49] The translation is based on S. M. Lehrman, *Exodus* (ed. H. Freedman and Maurice Simon; vol. 3 of *Midrash Rabbah*; 3rd ed.; 10 vols.; London: Soncino, 1983), 136. Lehrman translates "the deeds were those of God and not witchcraft." However, שֵׁד (or שֵׁיד) is normally understood as "demon" (cf. *Jastrow, Dictionary* 1523–24). שֵׁדִים is translated with δαιμόνια in the LXX (cf. Deut 32:17; Ps 105[6]:37).

parison may have typological meaning, implying that the power of God at work in Jesus' ministry is commensurate to the power of God at work in the great deliverance from Egypt long ago. Just as God dismantled the kingly authority of Pharaoh and his gods (or demons) and transferred his people under his own authority, so now in Jesus' ministry Satan's kingdom is being dismantled and Israel is being invited to embrace divine rule.

The ease with which Jesus casts out demons (cf. Mark 1:27: "With authority he commands even the unclean spirits, and they obey him!") constitutes *prima facie* evidence that indeed "the kingdom of God has come upon" the people Jesus addresses. But in what sense does Jesus mean "come upon" (ἔφθασεν ἐπί)? Nolland rightly wonders if the allusion to Exod 8:15(19) is threatening, in the sense of "overtaking" someone.[50] For example, in 1 Thess 2:16 Paul says, "wrath has finally come upon them" (ἔφθασεν δὲ ἐπ' αὐτοὺς ἡ ὀργὴ εἰς τέλος)," which evidently alludes to *T. Levi* 6:11: ἔφθασεν δὲ ἡ ὀργὴ κυρίου ἐπ' αὐτοὺς εἰς τέλος (see also Eccl 8:14). Nolland could be correct, for it is odd that Jesus says "the kingdom has come upon *you*" (with emphasis added). Why not say "upon us"? Does Jesus mean to distinguish between himself and his following, on the one hand, and those who disbelieve and oppose his proclamation, on the other? Is he suggesting that his critics oppose God and face judgment, just as surely as did Pharaoh and his magicians?

We cannot answer these intriguing questions with certainty. Perhaps Jesus has simply argued that his exorcisms offer clear proof of the truth of his proclamation of the kingdom: the kingdom of God has indeed arrived. But Jesus may have threatened his critics with the judgmental aspect of the kingdom (as seen also in the preaching of John the Baptist; cf. Mark 1:7–8; Matt 3:7–12; Luke 3:7–9, 15–17): the exorcisms demonstrate that the rule of God (as opposed to the perverse rule of wicked men) has finally overtaken those who reject his authority. It is time to repent and accept God's rule.

4.3. Sending the Twelve

Conflict with Satan and the proclamation of the kingdom of God are found together in the teaching relating to the sending of the Twelve.[51] The Markan and Matthean forms of the tradition should be studied together:

---

[50] Nolland, *Luke 9:21–18:34*, 640.
[51] The appointment of the twelve is rightly linked to covenant renewal and eschatological restoration in ch. 5 in this volume (cf. the earlier version, Scot McKnight, "Jesus and the Twelve," *BBR* 11 [2001]: 203–31). See also John P. Meier, "Jesus, the Twelve and the Restoration of Israel," in *Restoration: Old Testament, Jewish, and Christian Perspectives* (ed. James M. Scott; Supplements to the Journal for the Study of Judaism 72; Leiden: Brill, 2001), 365–404.

⁷ And he called to him the twelve, and began to send them out two by two, and gave them authority over the unclean spirits [ἐξουσίαν τῶν πνευμάτων τῶν ἀκαθάρτων]... ¹² So they went out and preached that men should repent. ¹³ And they cast out many demons [δαιμόνια πολλὰ ἐξέβαλλον], and anointed with oil many that were sick and healed them. (Mark 6:7–13)

⁷ "And preach as you go, saying, 'The kingdom of heaven is at hand [ἤγγικεν ἡ βασιλεία τῶν οὐρανῶν].' ⁸ Heal the sick, raise the dead, cleanse lepers, cast out demons [δαιμόνια ἐκβάλλετε] ..." (Matt 10:7–8 = Luke 9:1–2)

According to Mark's version, Jesus gave the twelve "authority over unclean spirits" and then they "went out and preached that men should repent." The evangelist makes no mention of proclaiming the arrival of the kingdom of God. But surely that is to be understood as part of the preaching of repentance (as it is in Mark 1:15). This element is present in the Matthean version of the commissioning of the twelve. Jesus commands the twelve to preach that "the kingdom of heaven is at hand" and to "cast out demons." Although Matthean editing is present (such as substituting "heaven" for "God"), the combination of healing, exorcism, and proclaiming the kingdom of God in the Lukan version of the discourse (cf. 9:1–2; 10:9, 11) suggests that this collocation is traditional[52] and that Mark's version is abridged.

4.4. Healing

Healing in general is part of the demonstration of the powerful presence of God and his rule, not only because it was part of the eschatological promise of Isaiah (cf. Isa 26:19; 35:5–6; 61:1–2 in Matt 11:5 = Luke 7:22; 4:16–30; and in 4Q521), but because there is evidence that some of the healings were linked in various ways to exorcism, or at least to the demonic world. We see this in the healing of Simon Peter's mother-in-law, where Jesus is said to have "rebuked the fever" (Luke 4:39), as though a sentient being was responsible for the fever.[53] This text is from the Marcan tradition (Mark 1:30–31; Matt 8:14–15). Of course, many times exorcism and healing are mentioned together (e.g., Matt 10:1, 8; Mark 1:34; 6:13; Luke 9:1). But there is one episode in particular that is quite illustrative from Luke's sources. With reference to the woman who was bent over and unable to straighten, in Luke 13:16 Jesus asks:

And ought not this woman, a daughter of Abraham whom Satan bound [ἣν ἔδησεν ὁ σατανᾶς] for eighteen years, be loosed from this bond [οὐκ ἔδει λυθῆναι ἀπὸ τοῦ δεσμοῦ τούτου] on the sabbath day?"

---

[52] Davies and Allison, *Matthew*, 2:170: "Q's missionary discourse contained the command to preach the nearness of the kingdom."

[53] On this, see John Nolland, *Luke 1–9:20* (WBC 35a; Dallas: Word, 1989), 211–12.

This episode illustrates graphically what Jesus describes parabolically in Mark 3:27. Until Jesus' appearance and the proclamation and powerful demonstration of the kingdom (or rule) of God, the children of Abraham were in bondage, in some cases literally "bound" by Satan. But Jesus has bound Satan and may now set at liberty his captives, or as he said to the infirm woman: "You are freed [ἀπολέλυσαι] from your infirmity" (Luke 13:12). What Satan had bound (δέω), Jesus has now loosed (λύω).

This contrasting terminology opens up a potentially new interpretation of an old, familiar saying, forms of which appear in two places in Matthew:

δώσω σοι τὰς κλεῖδας τῆς βασιλείας τῶν οὐρανῶν, καὶ ὃ ἐὰν δήσῃς ἐπὶ τῆς γῆς ἔσται δεδεμένον ἐν τοῖς οὐρανοῖς, καὶ ὃ ἐὰν λύσῃς ἐπὶ τῆς γῆς ἔσται λελυμένον ἐν τοῖς οὐρανοῖς.

I will give you the keys of the kingdom of heaven, and whatever you bind on earth shall be bound in heaven, and whatever you loose on earth shall be loosed in heaven." (Matt 16:19)

Ἀμὴν λέγω ὑμῖν· ὅσα ἐὰν δήσητε ἐπὶ τῆς γῆς ἔσται δεδεμένα ἐν οὐρανῷ, καὶ ὅσα ἐὰν λύσητε ἐπὶ τῆς γῆς ἔσται λελυμένα ἐν οὐρανῷ.

Truly, I say to you, whatever you bind on earth shall be bound in heaven, and whatever you loose on earth shall be loosed in heaven. (Matt 18:18)

Although there is nothing about the Matthean contexts to suggest exorcism or conflict with spiritual powers,[54] it is possible that the original meaning of this saying had exorcism in view. This is suggested not only because of the juxtaposition of δέω and λύω in Luke 13:16, but because other texts speak of the "binding" of Satan, where δέω is employed: καὶ ὁ Βελιὰρ δεθήσεται ὑπ᾽ αὐτοῦ, καὶ δώσει ἐξουσίαν τοῖς τέκνοις αὐτοῦ (*T. Levi* 18:12). "Beliar shall be bound by" the coming deliverer and "he will give authority to his children," just as surely as Jesus "will give" to Peter "the keys" (i.e., authority) to "bind" or "loose." One also thinks of the binding of the demon Asmodeus in Tobit: "And Raphael was sent to heal the two of them ... and to bind [δῆσαι] Asmodeus the evil demon" (3:17); "the demon ... fled to the remotest parts of Egypt, and the angel bound [ἔδησεν] him" (8:3).[55]

---

[54] Davies and Allison (*Matthew*, 2:638) rightly conclude that in the Matthean context, the saying on binding and loosing is to be understood in terms of the rabbinic notion of deciding what is forbidden and what is permitted.

[55] See also the various texts in the *Testament of Solomon*: "King Solomon, I brought the demon to you just as you commanded me; observe how he is standing bound [δεδεμένος] in front of the gates outside" (1:14); "[Beelzeboul] brought me the evil demon Asmodeus, bound [δεδεμένον]" (5:1); "I, Solomon ... bound [δεσμεύσας] him with greater care" (5:6); "I ordered her to be bound [δεσμευθῆναι] by the hair and to be hung up in front of the Temple that all those sons of Israel who pass through and see might glorify the God of Israel who has given me this authority [ἐξουσίαν]" (13:7).

5. The Significance of Jesus' Proclamation of the Kingdom and Exorcisms

In sum, there is a significant body of material that documents and illustrates in various ways the linkage of Jesus' announcement of the powerful presence of God's rule with the dismantling of Satan's kingdom. Perhaps the most important evidence outside of the NT itself is the pseudepigraphal *Testament of Moses*, which may very well have been composed in Palestine at about the time of Jesus' ministry. Not only does this document juxtapose the advent of the divine kingdom and the downfall of Satan, it also depicts an eschatological scenario that corresponds at important points with the scenario envisioned by Jesus.

This eschatological focus coheres nicely with what other essays on John the Baptist and the choosing of the Twelve show. These core events dealing with the heart of Jesus' ministry show that Jesus' ministry was rooted in eschatological hope tied to the promised rule of God. Jesus was more than a teacher of wisdom. The kingdom and his central role in its arrival were a core element of his teaching. They presented Jesus as a figure invested with authority whose presence meant God was at work bringing eschatological promise to reality.[56] In addition, the struggle to bring the kingdom to earth was defined in cosmic terms; the battle for the kingdom was not primarily presented in human political terms.

The surviving literature from Palestine of late antiquity clarifies important aspects of Jewish eschatology, in the light of which Jesus' proclamation of the kingdom and his ministry of exorcism would have been interpreted. In short, for Jesus and his following the exorcisms offered dramatic proof of the defeat and retreat of Satan's kingdom in the face of the advancing rule of God.

Bibliography

Beasley-Murray, George R. *Jesus and the Kingdom of God*. Grand Rapids: Eerdmans, 1986.

Becker, Jürgen. *Die Testamente der zwölf Patriarchen*. Vol. 3.1 of *Jüdische Schriften aus hellenistisch-römischer Zeit*. Gütersloh: Gütersloher Verlagshaus, 1980.

Black, Matthew. "Messiah in the Testament of Levi xviii." *ExpTim* 60 (1949): 321–22.

Bultmann, Rudolf. *The History of the Synoptic Tradition*. Translated by John Marsh. Oxford: Blackwell, 1972.

---

[56] Other essays in this volume will point to parallel examples of authority associated with Jesus' actions.

–. "Ist die Apokalyptic die Mutter der christlichen Theologie? Eine Auseinandersetzung mit Ernst Käsemann." Pages 64–69 in *Apophoreta: Festschrift für Ernst Haenchen zu seinem siebzigsten Geburtstag am 10. Dezember 1964*. Edited by W. Eltester and F. H. Kettler. BZNW 30. Berlin: Töpelmann, 1964.

–. *Jesus and the Word*. Translated by Louise Pettibone Smith and Erminie Huntress. New York: Scribner, 1934.

Charles, R. H. *Eschatology: The Doctrine of a Future Life in Israel, Judaism, and Christianity*. 2nd ed. London: A&C Black, 1913.

– "The Book of Jubilees." Pages 1–82 in vol. 2 of *The Apocrypha and Pseudepigrapha of the Old Testament*. 2 vols. Edited by Robert H. Charles. Oxford: Clarendon, 1913.

–. "The Testaments of the Twelve Patriarchs." Pages 282–367 in vol. 2 of *The Apocrypha and Pseudepigrapha of the Old Testament*. 2 vols. Edited by Robert H. Charles. Oxford: Clarendon, 1913.

Charlesworth, James H. "Intertextuality: Isaiah 40:3 and the Serek Ha-Yahad." Pages 197–224 in *The Quest for Context and Meaning: Studies in Biblical Intertextuality in Honor of James A. Sanders*. Edited by Craig A. Evans and Shemaryahu Talmon. Biblical Interpretation Series, 28. Leiden: Brill, 1997.

Chilton, Bruce D. *A Galilean Rabbi and His Bible: Jesus' Use of the Interpreted Scripture of His Time*. GNS 8. Wilmington: Glazier, 1984.

–. *God in Strength: Jesus' Announcement of the Kingdom*. SNTSU 1. Freistadt: Plöchl, 1979. Repr., Biblical Seminar 8; Sheffield: JSOT Press, 1987.

–. "The Kingdom of God in Recent Discussion." Pages 255–80 in *Studying the Historical Jesus: Evaluations of the State of Current Research*. Edited by Bruce D. Chilton and Craig A. Evans. NTTS 19. Leiden: Brill, 1994.

–. *Pure Kingdom: Jesus' Vision of God*. Studying the Historical Jesus. Grand Rapids: Eerdmans, 1996.

–. "Regnum Dei Deus Est." *SJT* 31 (1978): 261–70.

Collins, John J. *Daniel*. Hermeneia. Minneapolis: Fortress, 1993.

Davies, W. D., and Dale C. Allison, Jr. *A Critical and Exegetical Commentary on the Gospel According to Saint Matthew*. 3 vols. ICC. Edinburgh: T&T Clark, 1988–97.

de Jonge, Marinus. *The Testaments of the Twelve Patriarchs: A Study of Their Texts, Composition and Origin*. Assen: Van Gorcum, 1953.

Deissmann, Adolf. *Light from the Ancient East*. Translated by Lionel R. M. Strachan. New York: Doran, 1927.

Dunn, James D. G. *Jesus Remembered*. Vol. 1 of *Christianity in the Making*. Grand Rapids: Eerdmans, 2003–.

–. "Matthew 12:28/Luke 11:20 – A Word of Jesus?" Pages 29–49 in *Eschatology and the New Testament: Festschrift for George R. Beasley-Murray*. Edited by W. Hulitt Gloer. Peabody: Hendrickson, 1988.

Endres, John C. *Biblical Interpretation in the Book of Jubilees*. CBQMS 18. Washington, D. C.: Catholic Biblical Association of America, 1987.

Evans, Craig A. "Daniel in the New Testament: Visions of God's Kingdom." Pages 490–527 in *The Book of Daniel: Composition and Reception*. Edited by John J. Collins and Peter W. Flint. VTSup 83.2. Formation and Interpretation of Old Testament Literature 2.2. Leiden: Brill, 2001.

—. "From Gospel to Gospel: The Function of Isaiah in the New Testament." Pages 651–91 in *Writing and Reading the Scroll of Isaiah: Studies of an Interpretive Tradition*. Edited by Craig C. Broyles and Craig A. Evans. VTSup 70.1. Formation and Interpretation of Old Testament Literature 1. Leiden: Brill, 1997.

—. "Inaugurating the Kingdom of God and Defeating the Kingdom of Satan." *BBR* 15 (2005): 49–75.

—. "Jesus' Exorcisms and Proclamation of the Kingdom of God in the Light of the Testaments." Pages 210–33 in *The Changing Face of Judaism, Christianity, and Other Greco-Roman Religions in Antiquity*. Edited by Ian H. Henderson and Gerbern S. Oegema. Studien zu den Jüdischen Schriften aus hellenistisch-römischer Zeit, 2. Gütersloh: Gütersloher Verlagshaus, 2006.

—. "Life-of-Jesus Research and the Eclipse of Mythology." *TS* 54 (1993): 3–36.

Eve, Eric. *The Jewish Context of Jesus' Miracles*. JSNTSup 231. New York: Sheffield Academic Press, 2002.

Fitzmyer, Joseph A. *The Gospel According to Luke X–XXIV*. AB 28a. Garden City: Doubleday, 1985.

Funk, Robert W., Roy W. Hoover, and The Jesus Seminar. *The Five Gospels: The Search for the Authentic Words of Jesus*. New York: Macmillan, 1993.

Gray, John. *The Biblical Doctrine of the Reign of God*. Edinburgh: T&T Clark, 1979.

Hengel, Martin. "Der Finger und die Herrschaft Gottes in Lk 11,20." In *La Main de Dieu – Die Hand Gottes*. Edited by Ren Kieffer and Jan Bergman. WUNT 94. Tübingen: Mohr Siebeck, 1997.

Herrmann, Wolfgang. "Baal Zebub." Pages 154–56 in *Dictionary of Deities and Demons in the Bible*. 2nd ed. Edited by Karel van der Toorn, Bob Becking, and Pieter W. van der Horst. Leiden: Brill, 1999.

Jastrow, Marcus. *A Dictionary of the Targumim, the Talmud Babli and Yerushalmi, and the Midrashic Literature*. New York: Judaica Press, 1982.

Kee, Howard C. "Testaments of the Twelve Patriarchs." Pages 775–828 in vol. 1 of *Old Testament Pseudepigrapha*. 2 vols. Edited by James H. Charlesworth. New York: Doubleday, 1983–85.

Ladd, George Eldon. *Jesus and the Kingdom: The Eschatology of Biblical Realism*. New York: Harper & Row, 1964.

Lehrman, S. M. *Exodus*. Vol. 3 of *Midrash Rabbah*. 3rd ed. 10 vols. Edited by H. Freedman and Maurice Simon. London: Soncino, 1983.

Longman, Tremper, III. "God is a Warrior." Pages 31–47 in *God is a Warrior*. By Tremper Longman, III and Daniel G. Reid. Studies in Old Testament Biblical Theology. Grand Rapids: Zondervan, 1995.

McKnight, Scot. "Jesus and the Twelve." *BBR* 11 (2001): 203–31.

Marshall, I. Howard. *The Gospel of Luke*. NIGTC 3. Grand Rapids: Eerdmans, 1978.

Maurer, Alexander. "Azazel." Pages 70–71 in vol. 1 of *Encyclopedia of the Dead Sea Scrolls*. 2 vols. Edited by Lawrence H. Schiffman and James C. VanderKam. Oxford: Oxford University Press, 2000.

Meier, John P. "Jesus, the Twelve and the Restoration of Israel." Pages 365–404 in *Restoration: Old Testament, Jewish, and Christian Perspectives*. Edited by James M. Scott. Supplements to the Journal for the Study of Judaism, 72. Leiden: Brill, 2001.

Mills, Mary E. *Human Agents of Cosmic Power in Hellenistic Judaism and the Synoptic Tradition*. JSNTSup 41. Sheffield: JSOT Press, 1990.
Nickelsburg, George W. E. *Resurrection, Immortality, and Eternal Life in Intertestamental Judaism*. HTS 26. Cambridge: Harvard University Press, 1972.
Nolland, John. *Luke 1–9:20*. WBC 35a. Dallas: Word, 1989.
–. *Luke 9:21–18:34*. WBC 35b. Dallas: Word, 1993.
Priest, J. "Testament of Moses." Pages 919–34 in vol. 1 of *Old Testament Pseudepigrapha*. 2 vols. Edited by James H. Charlesworth. New York: Doubleday, 1983–85.
Robinson, James M., Paul Hoffmann, and John S. Kloppenborg, eds. *The Critical Edition of Q*. Hermeneia. Minneapolis: Fortress, 2000.
Rusam, Dietrich. "Sah Jesus wirklich den Satan vom Himmel fallen (Lk 10.18)? Auf der Suche nach einem neuen Differenzkriterium." *NTS* 50 (2004): 87–105.
Scott, James M., ed. *Restoration: Old Testament, Jewish, and Christian Perspectives*. JSJSup 72. Leiden: Brill, 2001.
Slingerland, H. Dixon. *The Testaments of the Twelve Patriarchs: A Critical History of Research*. SBLMS 21. Missoula, Mont.: Scholars, 1977.
Taylor, Joan E. *The Immerser: John the Baptist Within Second Temple Judaism*. Studying the Historical Jesus. Grand Rapids: Eerdmans, 1997.
Taylor, Vincent. *The Formation of the Gospel Tradition*. 2nd ed. London: Macmillan, 1935.
Tàrrech, A. P. "Lc 10,18: La Visió de la Caiguda de Satanàs." *Revista Catalana de Teologia* 3 (1978): 217–43.
Twelftree, Graham H. *Jesus the Exorcist: A Contribution to the Study of the Historical Jesus*. WUNT 2.54. Tübingen: Mohr [Siebeck], 1993.
Wright, N. T. *Jesus and the Victory of God*. Vol. 2 of *Christian Origins and the Question of God*. Minneapolis: Fortress, 1996.

Chapter 5

Jesus and the Twelve[1]

SCOT MCKNIGHT

1. Introduction

Without overstating the case, we can affirm today that Jesus scholarship has come to this confident conclusion (among others): the number "twelve" signifies a category already in existence during the life of Jesus, and most scholars think that Jesus chose the number "twelve" with fundamental intention. Which intention, or which set of factors shaped this intention, however, has not yet been confidently concluded. It is the purpose of this essay to assess once again the arguments for the historicity of the Twelve and then to suggest why it was that Jesus selected twelve.

2. The Historicity of the Twelve in Jesus' Ministry

The list of the twelve names appears in Mark 3:16–19; Matt 10:2–4; Luke 6:14–16; and Acts 1:13; such a listing of a famous teacher's pupils is known also in rabbinic Judaism (*m. ʾAbot* 2:8–14; compare the list of Jesus' supposed disciples in *b. Sanh.* 43a).[2] Apart from one irregularity[3] and some

---

[1] This essay is a revised and expanded version of that published as Scot McKnight, "Jesus and the Twelve," *BBR* 11 (2001): 203–31.

[2] The intention and emphasis of each text are noteworthy: the mishnaic text elaborates on each in the direction of piety and describes the legacy of each disciple (the good qualities of each disciple of Yohanan b. Zakkai, their response to the meaning of "the straight path" and "the bad road," and their three memorable sayings); the text of the Babylonian Talmud discredits Jesus, his disciples, and the emerging church by the absence of favorable witness for Jesus and by exegesis, which also confirms execution for each of the named disciples of Jesus (which names are Matthai, Nakai, Nezer, Buni, and Todah), only one or two (Matthai and Todah [Thaddaeus?]) of which appears to be in the Christian list. The lists of the disciples in the earliest Jesus traditions are stark and nearly absent of commentary; their intentions appear to be nothing more than a list in order to know who are the authentic Tradents of the Jesus tradition.

[3] The one irregularity is Thaddaeus or Judas ben Jacob (Jude son of James). Most conclude that Simon "the Zealot" and Simon "the Cananean" are the same person. However,

minor differences in order, which I shall not explore here, the names are solidly consistent and grouped in fours:

Mark	Matthew	Luke	Acts
Simon Peter	Simon Peter	Simon Peter	Peter
James b. Zebedee	Andrew	Andrew	John
John b. Zebedee	James b. Zebedee	James b. Zebedee	James b. Zebedee
Andrew	John b. Zebedee	John b. Zebedee	Andrew
Philip	Philip	Philip	Philip
Bartholomew	Bartholomew	Bartholomew	Thomas
Matthew	Thomas	Matthew	Bartholomew
Thomas	Matthew	Thomas	Matthew
James b. Alphaeus	James b. Alphaeus	James b. Alphaeus	James b. Alphaeus
Thaddaeus	Thaddaeus	Simon the Zealot	Simon the Zealot
Simon the Cananean	Simon the Cananean	Jude b. James	Jude b. James
Judas Iscariot	Judas Iscariot	Judas Iscariot	

Apart from this evidence, the following traditions mention the Twelve: Mark mentions a separate "ordination" (Mark 3:13–15; compare with Luke 6:13); the group is occasionally described as being with Jesus, in whose presence they are instructed (4:10; 9:35; 10:32; 11:11; 14:17); and Judas is designated "one of the Twelve" (14:10, 43; compare with Matt 26:14; Luke 22:3; John 6:71). In addition, the Q tradition underscores the special role that the Twelve will have in the future Kingdom as judges (Matt 19:28 = Luke 22:30). The later Evangelists confirm these impressions: Matthew paints the Twelve onto his canvas as recipients of Jesus' instruction (for example, Matt 11:1; 20:17; 26:20), and the same is done by Luke (8:1; 18:31) and John (6:67, 70). John identifies Thomas, alias Didymus, as one of the Twelve (20:24). It is not the purpose of this essay to examine the historicity of each of these traditions but instead to assess the reliability of Jesus' having a specially designated Twelve and to see if this number provides insight into the mission of Jesus.

The most complete analysis of the historicity of the Twelve is by John P. Meier, whose study forms a survey of research, a response to the major

---

E. P. Sanders leads these differences to a different conclusion: see his *The Historical Figure of Jesus* (London: Penguin, 1993), 120–22. His arguments are not without serious merit but will not be the focus of this study. See here N. T. Wright, *Jesus and the Victory of God* (vol. 2 of *Christian Origins and the Question of God*; Minneapolis: Fortress, 1996), 300, n. 214.

critical studies,⁴ as well as a consensus-building programmatic statement.⁵ One of the first papers I wrote in preparation for a Ph.D. dissertation on Matthew's presentation of the missionary discourse was a study of the intention of Jesus in the mission of the Twelve. More than a decade later, Meier's study summarizes the arguments, and these arguments have not changed substantively. In the case of Meier, we encounter characteristic thoroughness and special emphasis given to criteria.⁶ I shall reexamine these

---

⁴ In particular, see Philipp Vielhauer, *Aufsätze zum Neuen Testament* (TB 31; Munich: Kaiser, 1965), 55–91; Gunter Klein, *Die zwölf Apostel: Ursprung und Gehalt einer Idee* (FRLANT 77; Göttingen: Vandenhoeck & Ruprecht, 1961); Walter Schmithals, *The Office of Apostle in the Early Church* (trans. John E. Steely; Nashville: Abingdon, 1969), 67–87, 231–88.

⁵ John P. Meier, "The Circle of the Twelve: Did It Exist During Jesus' Ministry?" *JBL* 116 (1997): 635–72; updated and expanded in John P. Meier, *Companions and Competitors* (vol. 3 of *A Marginal Jew: Rethinking the Historical Jesus*; ABRL; New York: Doubleday, 2001), 125–285; see also E. P. Sanders, *Jesus and Judaism* (Philadelphia: Fortress, 1985), 98–106, where he states that the historicity of the Twelve is "the weakest item in the list" of his facts about Jesus (p. 101). For further studies, see Jacques Dupont, "Le nom d'apôtres a-t-il été donné aux douze par Jésus?" *OrSyr* 1 (1956): 267–90, 425–44 (Jesus established the Twelve but the word "apostle" is later); Béda Rigaux, "Die 'Zwölf'" in Geschichte und Kerygma," in *Der historische Jesus und der kerygmatische Christus: Beiträge zum Christusverständnis in Forschung und Verkündigung* (ed. Helmut Ristow and Karl Matthiae; Berlin: Evangelische, 1960), 468–86; Béda Rigaux, "The Twelve Apostles," *Concilium* 34 (1968): 5–15; Robert P. Meye, *Jesus and the Twelve: Discipleship and Revelation in Mark's Gospel* (Grand Rapids: Eerdmans, 1968), 192–209; Wolfgang Trilling, "Zur Entstehung des Zwölferkreises: Eine geschichtskritische Überlegung," in *Die Kirche des Anfangs: für Heinz Schürmann* (ed. Rudolf Schnackenburg, et al.; Freiburg: Herder, 1977), 201–22 (who opts for pre-Markan, and therefore probably authentic, tradition in Mark 3:14a, 16a and for substance in the inclusion of Judas as well as in the tradition in 1 Cor 15:5 and the term "eleven"; Matt 19:28 is inconclusive); Ben F. Meyer, *The Aims of Jesus* (London: SCM, 1979), 154, n. 82; Jürgen Becker, *Jesus of Nazareth* (trans. James E. Crouch; Berlin: De Gruyter, 1998), 27–28; Heinz O. Guenther, *The Footprints of Jesus' Twelve in Early Christian Traditions: A Study in the Meaning of Religious Symbolism* (AOS 7.7; Berne: Lang, 1985). In what follows I will not catalog views on the historicity, since the arguments and evidence are summarized with exhaustive thoroughness by Meier.

⁶ Ancient evidence does not easily submit to the supposedly impartial and scientific criteria established by modern Jesus historians. Any reading of modern scholarship finds a plethora of compelling arguments used to establish solid historical evidence; only sometimes do these arguments follow the lines of the criteria. Three modern examples, each using historical judgment with considerable *élan* but without being tied to the criteria, are Sanders, *Jesus and Judaism*; Wright, *Jesus and the Victory of God*; and Paula Fredriksen, *Jesus of Nazareth, King of the Jews: A Jewish Life and the Emergence of Christianity* (New York: Knopf, 1999). Of the three, it is the latter that shows methodological tension in that Fredriksen uses dissimilarity along with an argument, working backwards, that if Paul and a Jesus tradition both have something there is good reason to believe it is historically probable. This is really a variation on multiple attestation. Historians have to live with methodological tension, since historiography is not laboratory science. A good bibliographic entry into criteria research can be seen in Craig A. Evans, *Jesus* (IBR Bibliographies 5; Grand Rapids: Baker, 1992), 52–67; see also his more exhaustive volume, *Life of Jesus Research: An Annotated Bibliography* (2nd ed.; NTTS 24; Leiden: Brill, 1996).

arguments and then add, by way of confirmation, a final explanatory argument for the historicity of the Twelve.

Before I do this, I wish to give a response to the recent conclusion of the Jesus Seminar regarding the viability of a special group called "the Twelve" during the life of Jesus. Their conclusion is that "there was general agreement among the Fellows that the number 'twelve' in connection with an inner circle of disciples is a fiction."[7] Four arguments are advanced: first, *sources*. The presence of the Twelve in Q is acknowledged but assigned to the later (third) stage of the evolution of Q; the category "twelve" is not found in the *Gospel of Thomas*, it does not appear in the body of the *Didache*, and is absent from Clement's letter to Corinth and Ignatius's letters. Second, *Sachkritik*: the Twelve are connected to the "eschatological self-consciousness of the Christian community," and this eschatological outlook is a later Christian retrojection onto the Jesus traditions. Here we see the role that theology, in particular the noneschatological Jesus, plays in determining what is history. Third, *redaction criticism*: it is argued that the number "twelve" appears in "Mark's editorial work rather than in the body of the anecdotes," and the use of "twelve" including Judas "must also be regarded as a fabrication if the figure of Judas is a fiction, as many scholars think."[8] Fourth, *problems with the lists*: the inconsistencies in the lists (Mark, Luke, and John's lists of names) suggest that the category "twelve" is more symbolic than it is historical.

The arguments presented above would require fuller retort than is possible in this amount of space but, because what follows below is a defense of the Twelve during the lifetime of Jesus, I can limit my comments. To begin with, denying an imminent eschatology to Jesus bifurcates Jesus scholarship today, but there is hardly a consensus for a noneschatological Jesus. The most important and eloquent proponent of the noneschatological viewpoint, who also maintains an independent line from the one found in the Funk orientation of the Jesus Seminar, is Marcus Borg.[9] On the other hand, the major studies of the present generation have had a decidedly eschatological Jesus – and I think here of Ben F. Meyer, E. P. Sanders, John P. Meier,

---

One example of the complexity of argument and artful skill and judgment needed by a modern historian concerned with reconstructing an ancient, myth-overladen life is J. C. Holt, *Robin Hood* (London: Thames and Hudson, 1982). For further discussion of criteria in this volume, see ch. 2, § 4.1.

[7] Robert W. Funk and The Jesus Seminar, *The Acts of Jesus: The Search for the Authentic Deeds of Jesus* (San Francisco: HarperSanFrancisco, 1998), 71.

[8] Funk and Seminar, *The Acts of Jesus*, 71.

[9] See Marcus J. Borg, *Jesus, A New Vision: Spirit, Culture, and the Life of Discipleship* (San Francisco: Harper & Row, 1987); see also his essays, "A Temperate Case for a Non-eschatological Jesus" and "Jesus and Eschatology: Current Reflections," in his *Jesus in Contemporary Scholarship* (Valley Forge: Trinity, 1994), 47–68, 69–96.

N. T. Wright, and Dale C. Allison.[10] The argument of the Jesus Seminar here also wobbles on too confident of a judgment on the supposed layers of the Q tradition for, as many would argue, if we are not able to judge the various stages of evolution in the Q tradition, then the Twelve in Matt 19:28 = Luke 22:30 may well be at the root of the Q tradition.[11] In other words, for starters, if we endorse an eschatological Jesus and think Q is hardly capable of clear and compelling dissection by modern scholarship, then the Twelve may go back to Jesus. The arguments for this theory are noteworthy and encompass the criticisms of the Jesus Seminar, and to these I now turn.

First, *multiple attestation* suggests that the Twelve emerged in the lifetime of Jesus as special companions and men who were sent out on a mission to extend the ministry of Jesus. As is seen in the lists above, the Twelve are attested in three Gospels and Acts. It is almost certain that Matthew and Luke are dependent on Mark, but two points serve to show independence: (a) the variations of the lists even while dependent; (b) the variation within Luke–Acts. Some have argued from these variations that Matthew and Luke each had access to a pre-Markan tradition list of the Twelve names; Meier contends that Luke 6:14–16 may derive from L. The lists indicate then, at least, a single tradition (Mark) that was picked up with editing by later Evangelists; it is possible that the variations can be explained by a pre-Markan tradition or an L tradition.

More importantly, the term "twelve" is found in various strata of the Jesus traditions as well as different forms (meeting the criteria established in the community of scholarship), indicating at least a historical core to the number, even if the precise names are not clearly identifiable. Mark (3:14; 4:10; 6:7; 9:35; 10:32; 11:11; 14:10, 17, 20, 43), Q (Matt 19:28 = Luke 22:30),[12] perhaps "L" (Luke 8:1–3),[13] John (6:67, 70, 71; 20:24), and Paul (1 Cor 15:3–5) all indicate the presence of the Twelve during the life of Jesus. "In addition to multiple attestation of *sources*," says Meier, "these texts also give us multiple attestation of *forms*: the Twelve are mentioned in narrative (Mark, John), sayings (Q, John), a catalogue-like list (Mark, probably L),[14]

---

[10] My own study fits into the same category; cf. Scot McKnight, *A New Vision for Israel: The Teachings of Jesus in National Context* (Grand Rapids: Eerdmans, 1999), 120–55. In addition, many of the essays in this volume make the case for an eschatological Jesus, starting with the treatment and significance of John the Baptist, for which see ch. 3.

[11] Dale C. Allison, Jr., *The Jesus Tradition in Q* (Harrisburg: Trinity, 1997), 35–36, for instance, contends that it is possible that Q 22:28–30 ended Q¹ as well.

[12] For the historicity of this text, see the discussion below in § 4.1.

[13] On this, see John Nolland, *Luke 1–9:20* (WBC 35a; Dallas: Word, 1989), 364, 365–67.

[14] Since some of the divergences between Mark and Luke can be explained as Lukan stylistic improvements (e. g., keeping the brothers together in group one of the list or changing Simon "the Cananaean" to "the Zealot"), it is possible that Luke's list is simply Mark's with some redaction. However, Luke (varying from the Markan-Matthean tradition) has "Jude ben James" in both his Gospel and the Acts (cf. John 14:22). The differ-

and a creedal formula (1 Cor 15:3–5). In light of this broad spread of both sources and forms, suggestions that the Twelve arose only in the early days of the church must be judged pure conjecture with no real support in the NT texts."[15]

Second, using an argument that I consider logic rather than criteriological science,[16] I would say that there are *elements of tension* in the emerging Jesus traditions that suggest the Twelve emerged from the time of Jesus. Meier calls this the "criterion of embarrassment."[17] Judas is called "one of the Twelve" (for example, in Mark 14:43) and, so the argument goes, early Christians would not have made that kind of stuff up! There is no plausible context in the early church for inventing a betrayer if there was not one;

---

ences between Luke's list and Acts' can be best explained as Lukan redaction rather than use of sources, though the variations in the second block of names are not easy to unravel. As a result, Meier ("The Circle of the Twelve," 650–52) contends, probably accurately, that Luke had access to an "L" tradition with a list of the disciples.

[15] Meier, "The Circle of the Twelve," 663. Meier in his discussion of the Twelve in *Companions and Competitors*, 128–47, argues that multiple attestation, embarrassment and the general flow of the tradition all favor the idea that Jesus was responsible for the creation of the Twelve. Meier also argues that the idea that one of the Twelve betrayed Jesus meets the criterion of embarrassment and challenges the idea that one should reject the whole of the Passion Narrative as a later fabrication. This detail also counters the claim that the Passion was the compilation of events built around creations from Jewish scriptural prophecies (*Companions and Competitors*, 145–46). Also Michael F. Bird, *Jesus and the Origins of the Gentile Mission* (LNTS 331; London: T&T Clark, 2007), 33–35, notes that the criteria of multiple attestation and embarrassment support the authenticity of the Twelve. Bird places Jesus in the context of the Jewish restoration movement, supports the eschatological conception of such a role for the Twelve as Sanders and Jeremias contend, and sees the restoration initiated in the Twelve in ways similar to 1QS 8:1 with its twelve lay people representing the twelve tribes and three priests representing the Levitical clans. The signs of Jesus' ministry supports the claim that the restoration has started (Luke 7:18–23 = Matt 11:2–6).

[16] I still consider the hermeneutical discussion by Meyer (*The Aims of Jesus*, 23–110) to be the finest explanation to date of Jesus study criteria (indexes). However, analysis of ancient texts frequently forces historians to transcend or to work outside such categories. In particular, as can be seen in some recent studies of Jesus (including those of E. P. Sanders, N. T. Wright, J. D. Crossan, P. Fredriksen, as well as my own recent offering), operating from the "mission" or "focus" of the life of Jesus may yield better results than from criteria and sayings. If certain "facts" are established (e.g., that Jesus was put to death on a political charge, that he announced the imminent arrival of the Kingdom, et al.), then how are we to construe Jesus' life and his intentions? My *New Vision for Israel* is less concerned with establishing which sayings are authentic than with expounding traditionally-interpreted sayings in light of a reconfiguration of his mission as a mission to Israel. In many cases, the traditional interpretation, considered by some to be inauthentic because of that interpretation (e.g., his perception of his own death), yields to a more accurate historical perception of a particular (and, therefore, becomes as plausibly authentic as it becomes less traditional theologically). Few of my reviewers have seen this. The present collection of essays also pursues such a coherence within the tradition providing a similar kind of reconfiguration.

[17] Meier, "The Circle of the Twelve," 663–70.

and, *mutatis mutandis*, there is no reason to make the betrayer one of the Twelve if there was not a betrayer.[18] Why would someone create trouble for himself if he were making things up? Further, the crucifixion of Jesus and the betrayal by Judas are indissolubly connected and are in fact correlates: see 1 Cor 15:3–5 and John 17:12.[19] Since it is clear that the early church most likely would not have invented Judas, a close associate who betrayed Jesus, as a *Fundament* of the story about Jesus, and since he is included among the Twelve, it is probable that the Twelve emerged from the time of Jesus and Judas.[20] In the quotable words of Dom Crossan: "He is too bad to be false."[21]

Third, the *fluctuating and fading tradition history of the Twelve in the NT* suggests an early arrival as well as an early departure of the Twelve.[22] Meier states this argument clearly: "If the group of the Twelve had arisen in the early days of the church [rather than during the life of Jesus] and, for whatever reason, reached such prominence that its presence ... was massively retrojected into the Gospel traditions, *one would have expected that the history of the first Christian generation would be replete with examples of the Twelve's powerful presence and activity in the church.*"[23] First, we know so little about some of the Twelve that one must question the theory that they were invented wholesale. Why not use other names that are known, and why use persons who seem to have negligible influence? Second, why do the Twelve appear so infrequently in the NT? Apart from the Jesus traditions, they hardly emerge: in the pre-Pauline creedal formula (1 Cor 15:3–5), in Acts not after 6:2,[24] and only once in Revelation (21:14). If they were invented as authoritative figures to function at some institutional level, we are led to ask what institution this might have been and why they are not shown meeting this need?

---

[18] So William Klassen, *Judas: Betrayer or Friend of Jesus?* (Minneapolis: Fortress, 1996), 34–38.

[19] So Meier, "The Circle of the Twelve," 665. Meier thinks the traditions develop here: from Mark 15:24 to John 13:18; Matt 27:9–10; and Acts 1:16, 20. He also counters the proposals of Vielhauer, Klein, Schmithals, and Crossan (pp. 667–70).

[20] John Dominic Crossan, *Who Killed Jesus?: Exposing the Roots of Anti-Semitism in the Gospel Story of the Death of Jesus* (San Francisco: HarperSanFrancisco, 1995), finds treachery on the part of Judas far more likely than the inclusion of Judas in the Twelve or than of his death as described in early Christianity (pp. 71–75).

[21] Crossan, *Who Killed Jesus?: Exposing the Roots of Anti-Semitism in the Gospel Story of the Death of Jesus*, 71.

[22] See Rigaux, "The Twelve Apostles"; Jürgen Roloff, *Apostolat, Verkündigung, Kirche: Ursprung, Inhalt und Funktion des kirchlichen Apostelamtes nach Paulus, Lukas und den Pastoralbriefen* (Gütersloh: Mohn, 1965), 138–68.

[23] Meier, "The Circle of the Twelve," 670 (italics mine).

[24] Even the ultimate cameo appearance of Matthias may suggest the disappearance of a former member (Acts 1:20–26). And, as was asked by members of our discussion, why not Barnabas? or James? or Paul? Why choose someone who is otherwise completely unknown? Such a record may well indicate memory of a transient, unknown figure.

The facts press us to this conclusion: the Twelve emerged in the life of Jesus and then were virtually dropped as a functioning institution. Two considerations support this view: (1) the problems in the lists suggest that the names were either unknown, or the figures were a distant memory (they were names only remembered for "their *twelveness*,"[25] leading Sanders to the view of the "historicity of a symbol"[26]); (2) the expectations established by Jesus for the future role of the Twelve in judging the twelve tribes of Israel, in some form of "restoration" (Matt 19:28 = Luke 22:28–30), were for interpreters gradually marginalized or at least deemphasized by other views of the future for God's people. The earthly life of Jesus, then, had a genuine focus on the Twelve; time, changes, social relocations, alternative leadership developments, and the charismatic power of key figures such as Peter and Paul simply eclipsed the institution of the Twelve. At the beginning, there were the Twelve; by the middle of the first century, they were history – but they were indeed just that. And what was this history all about? Why did Jesus choose Twelve? Before we answer this question, one other supporting argument for the Twelve may be offered.

Fourth, *the encapsulation theory of conversion suggests that close followers would be historically likely.* I do not mean by this that Jesus chose only twelve because of encapsulation theory. Instead, I am suggesting that a close group of associates is likely to have emerged among converts to Jesus and that "twelve," as a mere symbol for close associates, is thereby suggested – even if the specific number is not implied in the argument. Recent research in conversion, most clearly presented by Lewis R. Rambo,[27] shows that all religious conversions take shape in a pattern that permits individual variations of considerable magnitude. Rambo himself presents a consensus-like report of the following stages: context, crisis, quest, encounter (with an advocate) and interaction, commitment (involving surrender and testimony), and consequences. Our concern here is with the encounter: this is the point at which an *encapsulation* process takes place, the point at which the potential convert is initiated into and exposed to a new self-contained world of meaning. Encapsulation is the process of shielding in order for conversion to take place effectively; it may involve physical, but certainly involves social and ideological, encapsulation. In this encapsulation process

---

[25] See G. B. Caird, *New Testament Theology* (ed. L. D. Hurst; Oxford: Clarendon Press, 1994), 382.

[26] Sanders, *Jesus and Judaism*, 101. The following is only slightly overstated by Sanders: "The twelve disciples are in one way like the seven hills of Rome: they are a little hard to find, although the idea is very old" (p. 102).

[27] Lewis R. Rambo, *Understanding Religious Conversion* (New Haven: Yale University Press, 1993), 103–8; see also Arthur L. Greil and David R. Rudy, "Social Cocoons: Encapsulation and Identity Transformation Organizations," *Sociological Inquiry* 54 (1984): 260–78.

there are four dimensions of influence: relationships, rituals, rhetoric, and roles. A convert's identity is reshaped through some form of encapsulation.

If this can be assumed, and I believe Rambo's model of conversion is a compelling presentation of years of research (both clinical research and research into the history of scholarship), a simple conclusion follows: it is highly likely, in fact, nearly certain, that Jesus *isolated* some of his followers and *encapsulated* them in order to lead them into a complete conversion. It follows then that there was a special group of Jesus' followers. That they were called "the Twelve" is not confirmed by encapsulation theory, but that there would have been some close associates is nearly certain. At a general level of religious experience, here thinking of conversion to Jesus' vision for Israel, it is highly probable that there would have been a few men who were considered the "closest" associates of Jesus, and we have every reason therefore to look for such a group in the earliest Jesus traditions. This conclusion can be confirmed by evidence both in Judaism (John the Baptist had disciples) and in the wider Mediterranean world (see, for example, the Epistle of Socrates and the Socratics).[28]

To conclude, it is highly probable, then, that Jesus had a special group of followers, designated during his lifetime as the Twelve. These twelve men are found in a variety of forms scattered throughout the early Jesus traditions; their presence creates tension within the traditions themselves; the history of the early Jesus and Christian traditions reveals an echo of a now-distant institution in the Jesus materials; and, on general religious grounds, it is likely that Jesus had a group of closest associates. What is the significance of such a group of Twelve followers?

3. The Twelve in Context

3.1. Background

Now that we have established the tradition of the Twelve as reliably going back to the very life of Jesus, it remains for us to ask how the term "twelve" has been interpreted by scholars who see the tradition as reliable and how it might be interpreted if a wider lens is used to encompass even more ancient Jewish evidence.

Apart from an occasional study or two, the *reason* for choosing precisely twelve has not been investigated as much as the historicity of the Twelve. In fact, most scholars fight hard to win an argument for the historical reliability of traditions about the Twelve and then simply conclude: historical,

---

[28] E.g., *Ep.* 28.11. Found in Abraham J. Malherbe, ed., *The Cynic Epistles: A Study Edition* (SBLSBS 12; Missoula, Mont.: Scholars, 1977), 292.

therefore *eschatological*. In the words of Albert Schweitzer, "Primitive theology is simply a theology of the future, with no interest in history!"[29] In short, most scholars conclude that the choice of twelve was symbolic[30] but had only one motive: *to inaugurate the restoration and reunification of the twelve tribes as promised in ancient Jewish traditions, most notably in Isaiah and Ezekiel*.[31] Jeremias expresses this position well: "That Jesus chose precisely twelve men to serve as messengers indicates that he had a particular programme in mind ... The *twelve messengers* correspond to the twelve tribes of Israel (Matt. 19.28 par. Luke 22.29f); they represent the eschatological community of salvation."[32] Or, in the words of E. P. Sanders, "an eschatological miracle, a decisive act by God to redeem his people."[33]

If the majority focus on the number "twelve" as an eschatological image – with some emphasizing a claim on the whole nation[34] or emphasizing that Jesus' vision was for the nation (in contrast to simply individual redemption for the remnant: for example, 1 Kgs 19:18; Isa 7:3, 9; 8:16–20; 10:21; 28:16; 37:31; 42:19; 43:10,12; Jer 3:16; 23:3; 30:8–9; 31:10; Ezek

---

[29] Albert Schweitzer, *The Quest of the Historical Jesus: A Critical Study of Its Progress from Reimarus to Wrede* (trans. W. Montgomery; Baltimore: Johns Hopkins University Press, 1998), 344 (an edition that unfortunately fails to mention the translator and lacks the important introduction by James M. Robinson, which was translated for the German edition!). German edition, p. 394. Further, p. 351 (ET): "Eschatology is simply 'dogmatic history' – history as moulded by theological beliefs – which breaks in upon the natural course of history and abrogates it" (German, p. 403). In this context, Schweitzer sees the twelve "as those who are destined to hurl the firebrand into the world, and are afterwards ... to be his associates in ruling and judging it" (p. 371).

[30] This has been thoroughly explored by Heinz Schürmann in the study "Der Jüngerkreis Jesu als Zeichen für Israel (und als Urbild des kirchlichen Rätestandes)"; see his *Jesus, Gestalt und Geheimnis: Gesammelte Beiträge* (ed. Klaus Scholtissek; Paderborn: Bonifatius, 1994), 64–84. A study devoted to Jesus is his "Die Symbolhandlungen Jesu als eschatologische Erfüllungszeichen. Eine Rückfrage nach dem irdischen Jesus," pp. 136–56 in the same text.

[31] Joachim Jeremias, *New Testament Theology: The Proclamation of Jesus* (trans. John Bowden; New York: Scribner, 1971), 234–35 (though the eschatological twelve embodies a universal salvation, pp. 245–47); Meyer (*The Aims of Jesus*, 153–54), who cites only the evidence given by Jeremias (who refers to his own earlier work); Sanders, *Jesus and Judaism*, 104; Joachim Gnilka, *Jesus of Nazareth: Message and History* (trans. Siegfried S. Schatzmann; Peabody, Mass.: Hendrickson, 1997), 183; Caird, *New Testament Theology*, 173, 382–83 (cf. G. B. Caird, *Jesus and the Jewish Nation* [Ethel M. Wood Lecture; London: Athlone, 1965], 8–9, 20–21); Gerd Theissen and Annette Merz, *Der historische Jesus: Ein Lehrbuch* (2nd ed.; Göttingen: Vandenhoeck & Ruprecht, 1997), 200–201; Wright, *Jesus and the Victory of God*, 300 (who has that deft British "of course").

[32] Jeremias, *New Testament Theology*, 234. Inclusion of Gentiles cannot be established on the basis of the number "twelve"; nor does the term "restoration" lead in that direction. Gentile inclusion must be established on the grounds of other evidence. "Twelve" may be a claim on *all* Israel but not more than Israel.

[33] Sanders, *Historical Figure*, 120; see also p. 185.

[34] E. g., Sanders, *Historical Figure*, 107 (also Sanders, *Jesus and Judaism*, 104).

34:15–16; Mic 4:6–7; 7:18–19; Amos 5:15; Zeph 3:12),[35] – others, without denying the eschatological dimension, center on the Twelve as a nucleus of the remnant or as leaders of a new movement within Israel. Here the focus becomes more *ecclesial*, referring to leadership of a new movement shaped by the various quests for holiness within first-century Judaism.[36] A combination of the two above views, extending the view of those who emphasize the *ecclesial* dimension, suggests both a continuity and a discontinuity: the old Israel now fulfilled.[37] No one speaks more completely for this view than Jürgen Roloff: "Jesus dokumentiert also in der Berufung der Zwölf seinen Herrscheranspruch über das endzeitliche Israel. Zugleich aber bleibt es nicht beim bloßen Anspruch: im Akt der Berufung konzipiert er dieses neue Gottesvolk in einer Weise, die zugleich zeichenhaft und real ist."[38] In this view of the Twelve, we have christology,[39] eschatology, ecclesiology, and symbolic action.

Finally, others have suggested that the term "twelve" is to be interpreted more simply: as no more than a claim on the nation *as a whole*.[40] In other words, "twelve" was a symbol,[41] a *general evocation* of all Israel, rather

---

[35] Gnilka, *Jesus of Nazareth*, 183; see the more complete study of this in Gerd Theissen, "Gruppenmessianismus: Überlegungen zum Ursprung der Kirche in Jüngerkreis Jesu," in *Volk Gottes, Gemeinde und Gesellschaft* (ed. Ingo Baldermann, et al.; Jahrbuch für biblische Theologie 7; Neukirchen-Vluyn: Neukirchener, 1992), 101–23; Ben F. Meyer, "Jesus and the Remnant of Israel," *JBL* 84 (1965): 123–30; Meyer, *The Aims of Jesus*, 115–28, 132–37, 153–54, 210–19; R. Newton Flew, *Jesus and His Church: A Study of the Idea of the Ecclesia in the New Testament.* (2nd ed.; London: Epworth, 1943), 17–98.

[36] The heaviest emphasis given to the *ecclesial* dimension can be seen in A. M. Farrer, "The Ministry in the New Testament," in *The Apostolic Ministry: Essays on the History and the Doctrine of the Episcopacy* (Kenneth E. Kirk; London: Hodder & Stoughton, 1946), 113–82, esp. pp. 119–33. A good balance can be found in, among others, Wright, *Jesus and the Victory of God*, 299–300, 430–31; David Flusser, *Judaism and the Origins of Christianity* (Jerusalem: Magnes, 1988), 173–85; Roloff, *Apostolat, Verkündigung, Kirche*, 138–68 (explores "twelve" in the context of the development of the ecclesiological development of the apostolate).

[37] See C. F. D. Moule, *The Birth of the New Testament* (3rd ed.; BNTC; London: Black, 1981), 54; Rigaux, "Die 'Zwölf'," 482–86; Rudolf Schnackenburg, *God's Rule and Kingdom* (trans. John Murray; New York: Herder, 1963), 215–34; Schürmann, *Jesus, Gestalt und Geheimnis*, 145–46.

[38] Roloff, *Apostolat, Verkündigung, Kirche*, 146. English Translation: "Thus in summoning the Twelve, Jesus documents his claim to rule the eschatological Israel. However, this is not merely a claim: in the act of summoning he presents a concept of God's chosen people in a manner which is both symbolic and real."

[39] Roloff (*Apostolat, Verkündigung, Kirche*, 147, n. 37) states: "Der Zwölferkreis der Erdentage ist gerade keine heilsmächtige Realität in sich selbst, sondern ist Gefäß und Werkzeug für das gegenwärtige Wirken Jesu." ("The earthly Circle of the Twelve is not in itself a reality of salvific power; it is a vessel and a tool for the current ministry of Jesus.")

[40] E. g., Werner Georg Kümmel, "Jesus und die Anfänge der Kirche," *ST* 7 (1953): 1–27.

[41] The most important recent study on Jesus' symbolic actions is by Morna D. Hooker, *The Signs of a Prophet: The Prophetic Actions of Jesus* (Harrisburg: Trinity, 1997), here

than an embodiment of a *specific* hope for restoring Israel by reuniting the twelve tribes.⁴² The only way to arbitrate this disparity of viewpoints is to examine the evidence once again. In studying this issue, I was surprised how frequently influential pieces of research seem not to examine the breadth of data about the concept "twelve" in ancient Judaism. In particular, the almost knee-jerk impulse to favor the eschatological perception of why Jesus' choice of twelve is in need of serious reconsideration. While it is easy to truck out evidence of an eschatological orientation, a fuller grasp of the evidence permits a broader (and more historically-nuanced) interpretation.⁴³

3.2. The Context of the Hebrew Bible

If we follow the biblical story line without attempting to reconstruct a critical history of either the term "twelve" (שְׁנֵים עָשָׂר and so on) or the term "tribes" (שְׁבָטִים) – if we read the story as a first-century Jew probably would have done – the following points are notable. First, the "story" of the Twelve begins not with Jacob but Ishmael, whom Elohim promises that he will make "fertile and exceedingly numerous. He shall be the father of twelve chieftains, and I will make of him a great nation" (Gen 17:20, נְשִׂיאִם; compare 25:12–18). But, as the text reads, "My covenant I will maintain with Isaac" (17:21).

Second, the predominant use of "twelve" is for the sons of Jacob/Israel (35:22–26; Sir 44:23–45:1). The sense of the "twelve sons of Israel" as heads of the twelve tribes moves from a physical literality (the actual sons of Israel and a real tribal interest; see Gen 42:13, 32; 49:28; Tob 1:4; 4:12; 5:9–14; Add Esth 14:5) to a representation for the *descendants* (the twelve tribes) and *hereditary representatives* (twelve tribal princes/chieftains, and so on). So: Moses sets up an altar at the foot of Sinai with twelve pillars "for the twelve tribes of Israel" (Exod 24:4); Moses finds "chieftains" and "heads" (Num 1:5–16) who will help him take a census of the whole house of Israel (see 1:44); Moses sends twelve to reconnoiter the land that was promised to Israel (Deut 1:22–23); and upon entry into the land beyond the Jordan and after its reconstitution, the "twelve" play a major role (see Josh 4:2, 3, 8, 9, 20; 18:24; 19:15; 21:7, 40). Much later Ezra offers twelve goats to purify Israel, the whole of Israel, "according to the number of the tribes of

---

p. 39, where she sees the Twelve as an eschatological embodiment of Jesus' intention. See also Scot McKnight, "Jesus and Prophetic Actions," *BBR* 10 (2000): 197–232.

⁴² Some arguing for historicity are unclear regarding specific intention on the part of Jesus: e.g., C.G. Montefiore, *The Synoptic Gospels* (2nd ed.; 2 vols.; London: Macmillan, 1927), 1:88. Others see his intention as a broad claim on all Israel: e.g., Becker, *Jesus of Nazareth*, 28.

⁴³ E.P. Sanders (*Jesus and Judaism*, 98) speaks for many: "that 'twelve' would necessarily mean 'restoration.'"

Israel" (Ezra 6:17). The same reference to the twelve tribes is found in the later tradition of 1 Esdras (5:1, 4; 8:54) and, of course, the original tribal structure becomes the foundation for the emergence of the *Testaments of the Twelve Patriarchs*.

A feature of this tribal use of "twelve" is the regular use of twelve objects as an embodiment of the twelve tribes of Israel: twelve pillars (Exod 24:4); twelve stones on the breastplate (39:14; compare with Sir 45:11); twelve bowls (Num 7:84); twelve bulls, rams, lambs, goats (7:87; 1 Esd 7:8; 8:65–66); twelve staffs (Num 17:17[2]); cutting a prostitute into twelve pieces, one for each tribe (Judg 19:29); and Ahijah's cutting of the robe into twelve pieces, ten for Jeroboam, when the kingdom was split (1 Kgs 11:30–31; see also *Jos. Asen.* 5:6).

Third, an important feature of the term "twelve" is its *association with covenant establishment and renewal*. Whenever "twelve" is mentioned in the Hebrew Bible, one naturally thinks of Israel's sons and their successors. Inasmuch as Israel's tribes are tied into a sacrificial cult, there will be evidence for the entirety of Israel being represented vicariously in sacrifices (for example, Exod 24:4; Num 7:87). More importantly, when the children of Israel are about to enter into the land, an event that will be in fulfillment of a covenant promise given to Abraham (Gen 12; 15), a *covenant renewal*, is enacted and the number "twelve" plays a central role in the renewal. Joshua is instructed by Yahweh to select twelve men, "one from each tribe" (Josh 4:1), who are to pick up twelve stones from the middle of the Jordan where the priests are standing and to deposit them where they spend the night (4:3). These stones are to become an *iconic* catalyst to tell the story of how the waters of the Jordan were cut off by God because of the "Ark of the Lord's Covenant," and they are to be a "memorial for all time" (4:7). In addition, Joshua himself sets up a small altar of twelve stones at the feet of the priests who are supporting the Ark of the Covenant, "and they have remained there to this day" (4:9b). When they encamp at Gilgal, Joshua sets up twelve stones as a memorial (4:20). Eventually, the tribes are assigned twelve cities (see, for example, 18:24; 19:15; 21:7, 38). To my knowledge, few have looked to Joshua[44] for a background to Jesus' choice of twelve as I shall do below; entering into this discussion now is what the great American humorist James Thurber called a "flashforwards"!

Fourth, we ought to observe the frequency with which *twelve are selected to represent the nation*. In Num 1:44 we find that there is one "chieftain" for each ancestral house, twelve total; in 31:5 twelve thousand, one thousand per tribe, are chosen; to reconnoiter the land, one man per tribe is selected (Deut 1:23); later, Joshua is instructed by Yahweh to select one man per

---

[44] See discussion in McKnight, "Jesus and Prophetic Actions".

tribe on two different occasions (Josh 3:12; 4:2; compare with a similar use in 1 Esd 5:1, 4; 8:54). When the myth of the translation of (portions of) the Hebrew Bible into Greek is elaborated in the *Letter of Aristeas,* the tribes and the number "twelve" emerge: six translators from each tribe (35–51).

3.3. The Context of the Dead Sea Scrolls and Pseudepigrapha

An important extension of this fourth sense of representatives can be seen in the Dead Sea Scrolls' attention to *twelve leaders,* and here the eschatological nature of the community and its fundamental beliefs enter the picture to give these twelve leaders both an *ecclesial* and an eschatological function. The evidence is neither unambiguous nor abundant, though a possible historical trajectory has been traced in the insightful essay of William Horbury.[45] More importantly, in the use of twelve with a leadership role at roughly the time of Jesus, as well as in a particular community with eschatological orientations, we find a significant parallel to the presence of twelve in the vision of Jesus.[46] Examples of use of the number at Qumran follow:

1QS 8:1: "In the Community council (there shall be) *twelve* men and three priests."[47] Their task? To be perfect in the whole revelation, to implement the truth, to practice "unassuming behaviour of one to another" (8:2), to preserve faithful commitment to the Law in the land to atone for sin, and to walk with one another in light of the revelation (8:3). 1Q28a 11–22 (also called 1QSa, or *Rule of the Congregation*):

At [a ses]sion of the men of renown, [those summoned to] the gathering of the community council, when [God] begets the Messiah with them ... After, [the Mess]iah of Israel shall [enter] and before him shall sit the *heads* of the th[ousands of Israel, each] one according to his dignity, according to [his] po[sition] in their camps and according to their marches. And all the *heads* of the cl[ans of the congre]gation with the wise [men ...] shall sit before them.

While the number "twelve" does not appear here, one might suppose that precisely twelve "heads" are in mind for at least one of the above-italicized words. Their "sitting" here refers to a holy convocation of the leadership for judgment or for a meal (see lines 17–22).

4Q159 (*Ordinances*ª) frgs. 2–4:3–4: "And [... te]n men and two priests, and they shall be judged by these *twelve*." These twelve, which include

---

[45] William Horbury, "The Twelve and the Phylarchs," *NTS* 32 (1986): 503–27.

[46] Cf. Flusser, *Judaism and the Origins of Christianity,* 173–85. Flusser contends that the origins of the Twelve for Jesus can be traced to the Qumran material, which also has a substantive parallel in the book of Revelation.

[47] For each citation from the Scrolls, I have used the translation of Florentino García Martínez and Eibert J. C. Tigchelaar, *The Dead Sea Scrolls Study Edition* (2 vols.; Grand Rapids: Eerdmans, 1997).

two priests, are assigned judgment over capital offenses (line 5). 1QM (*Milḥamah*, or *War Scroll*) 2:1–3:

¹ They shall arrange the chiefs (ראשי) of the priests behind the High Priest and of his second (in rank), *twelve* chiefs (ראשים שנים עשר) to serve ² in perpetuity before God. And the twenty-six chiefs of the divisions shall serve in their divisions and after them the chiefs of the levites to serve always, *twelve*, one ³ per tribe. And the chiefs of their divisions shall each serve in his place. The chiefs of the tribes, and after them the fathers of the congregation, shall take their positions in the gates of the sanctuary in perpetuity.

Here we have twelve priests serving before God eternally, twelve (additional?) levites, and twelve (more?) chiefs / tribal princes.[48] 4Q164 (pIsaᵈ) 4–6: "Its interpretation [of 'I will place all your battlements of rubies' from Isa 54:12] concerns the *twelve* [chiefs of the priests who] illuminate with the judgment of the Urim and Thummim [... without] any from among them missing, like the sun in all its light."[49] This duodecimal "council" (line 2), similar to the council in 1QM 8:1, is composed of priests and laity, and these twelve function along with "heads of the tribes" (line 7; twelve in number, of course). We have here then a council of some sort, composed of twenty-four, a priestly, oracular judicial body (see Ezek 48:31; Rev 21:12–14, 19–21).

We find an even more intriguing piece of evidence in 11Q19 (*Temple Scrollᵃ*) 57:11–14: "And *twelve* princes (נשיא) of his [the eschatological king] people shall be with him, and *twelve* priests and *twelve* levites, who shall sit together with him for judgment and for the law." With the ideal king, we have here a council of thirty-seven, both priestly and tribal, exercising judgment (see 11Q19 576, 11–12; 11Q13 [*Melchizedek*]; compare with *1 En.* 45:3; 51:3; 61:8; 62:1–2).[50] The theme of judgment pervades the scrolls when it comes to the "twelve."

Outside the scrolls, the interesting prediction of *T. Ab.* 13:6, a second-century C.E. text, suggests a Jewish motif of "judgment by twelve": "And at the second Parousia they will be judged by the twelve tribes of Israel" (Sanders, *OTP*). Other texts confirm this: *T. Jud.* 25:1–2: "And after this Abraham, Isaac, and Jacob will be resurrected to life and I and my brothers will be chiefs (wielding) our scepter in Israel: Levi, the first ..." *T. Benj.* 10:7: "Then shall we also be raised, each of us over our tribe, and we shall prostrate ourselves before the heavenly king."

To summarize, the number "twelve" in the biblical story denotes the tribes of Israel, the descendants of Jacob, who became Israel. "Twelve" thus

---

[48] So Horbury, "The Twelve and the Phylarchs," 511. See further in 1QM 3:14; 5:1–2.

[49] For this text, see esp. Joseph M. Baumgarten, "Duodecimal Courts of Qumran, Revelation, and the Sanhedrin," *JBL* 95 (1976): 59–78, esp. the restored text on p. 60.

[50] Numbers of judges in the Sanhedrin, for instance, were debated; see *m. Sanh.* 1:6; see also 4:3.

defines "biblical" Israel, pre-captivity Israel, as a tribal-based community with its roots in God's redemptive acts under Abraham, Israel, Moses, and Joshua. Further, the number "twelve" becomes a central feature of the conquest of the land and, in particular, of the crossing of the Jordan and the reestablishment of the covenant in connection with this major act of Yahweh, as he fights for his people in granting the land he has promised. In Israel's tribal arrangement, twelve men are regularly selected, just as twelve objects are sometimes put forward, to embody the entirety of the nation in some ritual enactment. These twelve function vicariously.

One negative conclusion is immediately noticeable for Jesus studies: I have found *no instance of "twelve" functioning eschatologically in the Hebrew Bible*, although the term does function eschatologically in the unfolding Jewish tradition. This means that an eschatological connotation will rarely exhaust the intentions of later writers who use the tradition of the number "twelve."

3.4. Eschatology and the Use of the Word "Tribe"

For eschatological connotations we must turn to other evidence, including the term "tribe." In so doing, I shall present data that envision a regathering of the "tribes" of Israel (combining the lost Northern tribes with the two and one-half tribes extant [Judah, Benjamin, half-Levi]) in an eschatological act of God to reunite the sons of Israel and preserve them from disaster (*T. Zeb.* 9:1–3; *2 Bar.* 1:2; 62:5; 77:19; 78:1). Reunification of the tribes is an "ideal state of affairs."[51]

Besides a fairly common use of the word "tribe" (for example, Num 33:54; Deut 1:13; 16:18; 1 Sam 15:17; 1 Kgs 11:31–32; Ps 78:55), there are several eschatological instances, some with a priestly orientation: (1) clearly Isa 11:11–12: "In that day, my Lord will apply his hand again to redeeming the other part of his people from Assyria ... He will hold up a signal to the nations and assemble the banished of Israel and gather the dispersed of Judah from the four corners of the earth" (compare with 27:13); (2) possibly Isa 49:6: "Is it too little that you should be my servant in that I raise up the tribes of Jacob and restore the survivors of Israel?"; (3) perhaps Isa 63:17: "Relent for the sake of your servants, the tribes that are your very own!"; (4) Jer 3:18; 29:14; 30:3; 31:7–10; 32:36–41: Jeremiah, who at times is absorbed with Ephraim, also clearly expects a reunification of the twelve tribes in the land, a restoring of the fortunes of Israel and Judah, because "Ephraim is my firstborn" (31:9); (5) clearly Ezek 36:8–11; 37:19: "Thus says the Lord God: I am going to take the stick of Joseph – which is in the hand of Ephraim – and of the tribes of Israel associated with him, and I will

---

[51] Gnilka, *Jesus of Nazareth*, 183.

place the stick of Judah upon it and make them into one stick; they shall be joined in my hand" (see 32:36–41); (6) also Ezek 47:13: "These shall be boundaries of the land that you shall allot to the twelve tribes of Israel" (compare with 47:21; 48:1, 19, 23, 29, 31); (7) at the foundation of this hope for restoration perhaps lies Amos 9:14: "I will restore my people Israel";[52] and, finally, (8) we can note the following texts: Mic 2:12; 4:6–7; Zeph 3:19–20; Zech 10:8–10.

Outside the canonical texts, this notion of a restoration of the twelve tribes, regathering the dispersed from both exiles, finds "widespread"[53] expression, most notably in Sir 36 and probably in 48:10; 36:13, 16: "Gather all the tribes of Jacob, and give them their inheritance, as at the beginning." And these tribes will gather in "Jerusalem" (36:18) and "Zion" (36:19), proving Yahweh's prophets trustworthy (36:21). One thinks also of the implicit vision of *Pss. Sol.* 11 and 17:26–34: here we find the land divided into tribes once more (compare with 8:28–32; 11:2; 17:44). Tob 14:7 anticipates exiled Israelites returning, as do 2 Macc 1:27–28; 2:18; *T. Levi* 16:6; *T. Ash.* 7:7; *T. Benj.* 9:2; *Jub.* 1:15; *2 Bar.* 77:5–6; 78, especially v. 7; 1QM; 11Q19 18:14–16; 57:5–6; 59:1–13 (theme of covenant renewal); compare with 4Q252 3:1–14; 4Q504 (DibHamª); 4Q508 (*Festival Prayers*ᵇ) frg. 2:2 ("the time of the return," שוב); Jos. Asen. 5:6.

The vision of a restored twelve tribes occupying the land emerges most explicitly in the Hebrew Bible under the priestly hand of Ezekiel; Isaiah's words evoke the restoration of the twelve tribes, but his vision hardly focuses on such an image. In short, the expectation of the twelve tribes' being restored, as in former days, is one significant crystallizing shape of future expectation in the evidence of the Hebrew Bible. Later traditions unfold these formative visions. However, what we do have in the Bible is a covenantal and selectional emphasis on the concept "twelve" when it expresses the ancient establishment of God's people as heirs to Jacob.

To contend, on the other hand, that "twelve" means "eschatological restoration" is to suggest a higher correlation than the evidence permits. To contend that Jesus must have meant "eschatological reunification of the twelve tribes" because he used twelve disciples may find support in some texts, such as in Isaiah, Ezekiel, and Sir 36, but is the evidence so uniformly monodirectional? I think not. When the Jesus traditions are seen in this context, a new appreciation for what Jesus meant in choosing twelve emerges.

---

[52] Cf. Francis I. Andersen and David Noel Freedman, *Amos* (AB 24a; New York: Doubleday, 1989), 893.

[53] Sanders, *Jesus and Judaism*, 96; he cites further evidence on pp. 96–98. On the theme of exile, see now the important edited collection of James M. Scott, ed., *Exile: Old Testament, Jewish, and Christian Conceptions* (Supplements to the Journal for the Study of Judaism 56; Leiden: Brill, 1997).

If these several strands – especially a covenantal emphasis emerging from the Jordan River texts of Joshua with an ecclesial dimension at the front and an eschatological hope in the future of Ezekiel at the back – represent the fuller picture out of which choosing twelve would have emerged and been understood by contemporary Jews, it is only by examining the evidence of the Jesus traditions themselves that we will be permitted a more nuanced grasp of what Jesus meant to evoke when he chose the Twelve.

4. Jesus and the Twelve

We have established that there is solid evidence and there are persuasive arguments for contending that Jesus used "twelve" for a special group of his followers (even if a name or two is not probative). If we could gather a larger cluster of texts around the Twelve, we might establish with more precision the intention of Jesus in choosing twelve. The evidence is not abundant, but there are a few significant segments to analyze: (1) general descriptions of the Twelve, (2) the choosing and sending of the Twelve, and (3) the Q tradition about the Twelve as future "judges" of the twelve tribes.

4.1. The Twelve in the Jesus Traditions

First, I consider the following segment to be possible information about the Twelve, harder to prove historical because this kind of evidence is isolated and sometimes fraught with tradition-critical complexities. Nonetheless, it is reasonable because it is coherent with the fact that Jesus did associate himself especially with a group of twelve disciples.[54] For instance, when Mark 4:10 tells us that Jesus was alone after telling several parables and that ἠρώτων αὐτὸν οἱ περὶ αὐτὸν σὺν τοῖς δώδεκα τὰς παραβολάς, we are dealing with narrative information (these are Mark's words) that is also reasonable and coherent information: that is, if Jesus did gather the Twelve and did tell parables, it is reasonable that the Twelve were with him many times (see 3:14)[55] as well as that they asked him the meaning of his parables. Other pieces of evidence, in my judgment, belong in this segment: that the Twelve

---

[54] In this essay I will not examine the various other terms used for the followers of Jesus, such as *apostles* and *disciples*. The issues here are (1) church development and (2) redactional perspective of the Evangelists. Early redaction critics of Mark saw most of these references as Markan redaction; cf, e.g. Trilling, "Zur Entstehung Des Zwölferkreises," 201–10; Roloff, *Apostolat, Verkündigung, Kirche*, 140–45 ("Mk hat den Zwölferapostolat gekannt," p. 143); Gnilka, *Jesus of Nazareth*, 182. For fuller study, compare Meier, "The Circle of the Twelve," 636–42; Francis H. Agnew, "The Origin of the NT Apostle-Concept: A Review of Research," *JBL* 105 (1986): 75–96.

[55] On which text, see Roloff, *Apostolat, Verkündigung, Kirche*, 145–48.

were urged to make themselves servants (Mark 9:35 D) and to accept the fate of their teacher (10:32–34 = Matt 20:17–19; Luke 18:31–34; compare with John 6:67); that they Twelve were with him during his last week (Mark 11:11; 14:17–20 = Matt 26:20–25; Luke 22:14 [ἀπόστολοι]; 22:21–23 [omits "twelve"]). If one thinks Jesus actually fed a large multitude miraculously, it is only slightly possible that the twelve baskets remaining reflect this group's presence (see Mark 6:43 = Matt 14:20; Luke 9:17; compare with Luke 9:12, where δώδεκα is used).

I consider all this information both possible and reasonable; if Jesus did isolate the Twelve, it is highly likely that they did these kinds of things with Jesus and heard from Jesus about following him. However, what we learn here about the Twelve is negligible: that they heard Jesus' interpretation of various parables, that they were warned of his fate and that they would have to endure a trial themselves, and that they were with him during the last week and heard his words on those special occasions. This kind of information tells us more about discipleship than it does about why Jesus chose the Twelve. If anything, it tells us that the Twelve were more than a symbol but, instead, an actual part of the outworking of Jesus' vision of the kingdom, which he believed was presently entering history as his still, small voice.

Second, that Jesus sent out the Twelve opens up another segment of information that intersects with the data about the number "twelve" in ancient Judaism.[56] The fundamental texts are found in Mark 3:14; Matt 10:1; Luke 6:13 and Mark 6:7–13, 30; Matt 9:35–11:1; Luke 9:1– 6, 10; 10:1–12; the texts appear to relate a threefold process: an early call and designation; a mission of the Twelve; a subsequent mission of the 70/72.[57] It is entirely probable

---

[56] If the "two-by-two" mission is genuine memory, it is less likely that it was mutual support (cf. Eccl 4:9–12; Gen 2:18) than a form of providing an additional witness (cf. Deut 17:6; 19:15; John 8:17; 2 Cor 13:1; 1 Tim 5:19; Heb 10:28; as well as Acts 8:14; 13:2; 15:27, 36–40; 17:14; 19:22; 1 Cor 9:6; cf. also *Jos. Asen.* 3:2). See Joachim Jeremias, "Paarweise Sendung im Neuen Testament," in *New Testament Essays. Studies in Memory of Thomas Walter Manson, 1893–1958* (ed. A.J.B. Higgins; Manchester: Manchester University Press, 1959), 136–43; David Daube, "Responsibilities of Master and Disciples in the Gospels," *NTS* 19 (1972): 1–15. From another angle, see John Dominic Crossan (*The Historical Jesus: The Life of a Mediterranean Jewish Peasant* [San Francisco: HarperSanFrancisco, 1991], 333–37), who proposes a plausible *Sitz im Leben* for the notion of "healed healers."

[57] For my own study of these texts, see Scot McKnight, "New Shepherds for Israel – Matthew 9:35–11:1: An Historical and Critical Study of Matthew 9:35–11:1," Ph.D., diss. (Nottingham: University of Nottingham, 1986); subsequent studies include Risto Uro, *Sheep Among the Wolves: A Study on the Mission Instructions of Q* (AASF 47; Helsinki: Suomalainen Tiedeakatemia, 1987); Dorothy Jean Weaver, *Matthew's Missionary Discourse: A Literary Critical Analysis* (JSNTSup 38; Sheffield: Sheffield Academic Press, 1990); Eung Chun Park, *The Mission Discourse in Matthew's Interpretation* (WUNT 2.81; Tübingen: Mohr Siebeck, 1995), 9–31 (a spotty survey of scholarship). These four dissertations are each concerned with the mission at the level of church tradition and redactional theology; they shall be left to the side except when tradition- critical remarks are apposite.

that Matthew has conflated Mark with Q, along with other traditions;[58] it is possible that Luke's mission of the 70 is a conflation of the sources available to him, although others think Jesus may well have sent out disciples more than one time.[59] Few have disputed that Jesus sent out some of his followers – probably the Twelve – mostly because the story is found in separate traditions (Mark 6:7–13; Luke 10:1–16; Matt 9:35–11:1 has residual elements from M; some see L traditions in Luke 10:1–16; see also 22:35). The act itself is coherent with the substantive content of why Jesus chose twelve: to evoke the restoration of the twelve tribes not only must there be twelve but they must be its leaders.[60] T. W. Manson spoke for many when he said and, like Melchizedek, still speaks: "The mission of the disciples is one of the best-attested facts in the life of Jesus."[61]

See also Allison, *The Jesus Tradition in Q*, 104–19; Paul Hoffmann, *Studien zur Theologie der Logienquelle* (NTAbh 8; Münster: Aschendorff, 1972), 236–355; Heinz Schürmann, "Mt 10, 5b–6 und die Vorgeschichte des synoptischen Aussendungsberichtes," in *Neutestamentliche Aufsätze: Festschrift für Prof. Josef Schmid zum 70. Geburtstag* (ed. Josef Blinzler; Regensburg: Pustet, 1963), 270–82 (who contends there was a single messianic mission, found now in the remnants of Luke 10:1; Matt 10:5–6; Luke 10:8–12 [Matt 10:5–6 was originally between Luke 10:7 and 10:8] this mission was "eine letzte große Anfrage an Israel vor dem Ende"; Schürmann, *Jesus, Gestalt und Geheimnis*, 146). I am unpersuaded that the mission can be accurately described as a "symbolic action" or even as an "eschatologische Erfüllungszeichen," though the shaking off of dust can be so designated (cf. Mark 10:11; *contra* Schürmann, *Jesus, Gestalt und Geheimnis*, 146).

[58] E. g., Jacques Dupont, "'Vous n'aurez pas achevé les villes d'israël avant que le fils de l'homme ne vienne'," *NovT* 2 (1958): 229; T. W. Manson, *The Sayings of Jesus: As Recorded in the Gospels According to St. Matthew and St. Luke* (London: SCM, 1949), 73–74; Ferdinand Hahn, *Mission in the New Testament* (trans. Frank Clarke; SBT 47; London: SCM, 1965), 42–43 (but cf. p. 46).

[59] On this, see esp. Paul Hoffmann, "Lk 10:5–11 in der Instruktionsrede der Logienquelle," in *Evangelisch Katholischer Kommentar: Vorarbeiten* (Neukirchen-Vluyn: Neukirchener Verlag, 1971), 3:38–39.

[60] Meier, "The Circle of the Twelve," 657. At some level, then, the notion of sending twelve coheres with the term "apostle," though recent research has shown the term to be less derived from the Hebrew *šālîaḥ*, even though substantively related: cf. Agnew, "Apostle-Concept". See also Robert W. Herron, "The Origin of the New Testament Apostolate," *WTJ* 45 (1983): 101–31. A foundational text, though not often discussed in the literature, remains Isa 61:1–11.

[61] Manson, *Sayings of Jesus*, 73. Sanders (*Jesus and Judaism*, 103) states: "In particular, apart from what we learn from the symbolic nature of the number twelve, we do not know Jesus' purpose in calling them. Mark 3.14 says that it was for them 'to be with him', and that has recently been taken to be a plain statement of fact. [Here he refers to Eduard Schweizer's 1968 book on Jesus.] But Mark cannot have known what was in Jesus' mind." Two points: (1) Being with Jesus is so obviously historical it cannot be contested – what else do disciples do but accompany their master? Sanders is overly sceptical here. I do not question that some German scholarship has grossly overinterpreted "being with him" into a neat ecclesiological formula. (2) I am unsure what Sanders means by "cannot" when it comes to Mark's knowledge – does he mean some kind of psychological knowledge? In which case, Sanders' scepticism is justified. Or does he mean he cannot know Jesus' intention or another person's intention? If so, Sanders is again overly sceptical. The ancient tra-

Without extensive exegesis of each text or a detailing of the tradition history, the following observations are pertinent:

First, the Twelve are not physical descendants of each of the twelve tribes: they are a symbolic representation of the twelve tribes. Jesus is obviously not using "twelve" in the sense of a literal, physical fulfillment of the prophetic hope of the reunification of the tribes, for this hope has every indication of being physical. His intention here is to embody the hope of either representing Israel in a covenant renewal or representing reunification symbolically in his chosen twelve followers.[62] This very action of Jesus is not without significance for his understanding of what he is doing and how he sees Israel's history coming to its fulfillment.

Second, the Twelve are restricted to a Galilean / Israelite mission and are prevented from extending their mission to either Gentiles or Samaritans (Matt 10:5–6).[63] The restriction by Jesus emerges from a complex historical-missionary situation[64] and involves several critically-debated Jesus traditions (Mark 7:24–30 = Matt 15:21–28; Mark 5:1–20 = Matt 8:28–34; Luke

---

dition of Peter's connection to Mark may not be that far from historical reality. The actions of Jesus in gathering disciples to be with him and of sending them out (if they were sent out) surely imply that Jesus wanted them with him and that he wanted them to spread the Kingdom. These assertions of Jesus' intention can be exaggerated in significance; but they need not be. On knowing another's intentions, the classic study remains G. E. M. Anscombe, *Intention* (2nd ed.; Library of Philosophy and Logic; Oxford: Blackwell, 1979).

[62] While the terms "restoration" and "reunification [of the twelve tribes]" may be properly distinguished, with the former being the more general Jewish expectation and the latter a special dimension of this larger expectation on the part of some, at times the terms are also nearly synonymous: those expecting a reunification of the twelve tribes certainly also had in mind this action of God as part of the larger restoration. "Restoration" is a good term for describing Jewish eschatology as well as the particular slant that Jesus gives to this hope when he uses the term "Kingdom." N. T. Wright is not alone in being asked why Jesus does not use the term "restoration"; the answer to this question is that Jesus thought the term "Kingdom" was a better term expressing the complex of factors that scholars today call "restoration." When Jesus uses "Kingdom," he has in mind the fulfillment of the Jewish expectations that involved the restoration of Israel.

[63] This text has only occasionally been questioned with respect to authenticity. The Jesus Seminar, for instance, found a Jesus who was more universal in orientation, so it assigned the saying to a Judaizing branch of earliest Christianity. But, the saying is Matthean neither in style or substance (except for the parallel at 15:24), and it leaves us with a Jesus somewhat incongenial to the Church's mission. That is, on the basis of criteria, it is fundamentally dissimilar to earliest Christianity. On this, W. D. Davies and Dale C. Allison, Jr., *A Critical and Exegetical Commentary on the Gospel According to Saint Matthew* (3 vols.; ICC; Edinburgh: T&T Clark, 1988–97), 2:168–69.

[64] On this, see Scot McKnight, *A Light Among the Gentiles: Jewish Missionary Activity in the Second Temple Period* (Minneapolis: Fortress, 1991). That there was some kind of "crisis" in Galilee is rarely held today; cf. F. Mußner, "Gab es eine 'galiläische Krise'?" in *Orientierung an Jesus: Zur Theologie der Synoptiker* (ed. P. Hoffmann; Freiburg: Herder, 1973), 238–52; Hugh Montefiore, "Revolt in the Desert? (Mark vi. 30ff)," *NTS* 8 (1962): 135–41.

8:26–39; Mark 11:15–19 = Matt 21:12–13;[65] Luke 19:45–48; Mark 12:1–12 = Matt 21:33–46; Luke 20:9–10; Mark 13:10 and 14:9 = Matt 10:18; 24:14; 26:13; Q: Luke 7:1–10 = Matt 8:5–13; Luke 7:18–23 = Matt 11:2–6; Luke 14:34–35 = Matt 5:13–16; Luke 4:16–30; Matt 7:6).

In summary, the following are noteworthy: (1) Jesus had no mission to the Gentiles; his mission was directed toward Israel because his mission was about the restoration of Israel as it realized its covenant expectations and hopes; (2) the eschatology of Jesus leads one to think of his mission as being an urgent call to repentance in light of the coming judgment of God on a disobedient nation;[66] (3) Gentile inclusion is by way of exception and permission to enter rather than the direct result of an intentional, inclusive mission; (4) Gentile inclusion is primarily an eschatological phenomenon as a result of God's direct intervention in history, and this places Gentiles in the final judgment (for example, Mark 12:1–12 and parallels);[67] (5) along these salvation-historical lines, then, one can argue that Jesus' universalism is the consequence of his particularism: a mission to Israel embraces an eventual impact for the entire creation.[68] Just as Isaiah's vision begins with Israel and erupts into a universal praise (Isa 61:1–11) and just as Israel is to become a light to the nations (49:4–7), so Jesus restricts his mission to Israel because Israel's restoration impacts the world. In the words of T. W. Manson, "a transformed Israel would transform the world."[69]

Third, the mission of the Twelve was fundamentally the same mission that Jesus had, and this means that the Twelve's mission was to extend the mission of Jesus into the various villages of Galilee (Israel).[70] If the "authorization" of the Twelve is less demonstrable (see Mark 3:15; 6:7 = Matt 10:1; Luke 9:1), what the Twelve were commissioned to do[71] becomes potential

---

[65] See Craig A. Evans, "From 'House of Prayer' to 'Cave of Robbers': Jesus' Prophetic Criticism of the Temple Establishment," in *The Quest for Context and Meaning: Studies in Biblical Intertextuality in Honor of James A. Sanders* (ed. Craig A. Evans and Shemaryahu Talmon; Biblical Interpretation Series 28; Leiden: Brill, 1997), 417–42.

[66] On this, see McKnight, *A New Vision for Israel*, 1–15, et passim; Caird, *New Testament Theology*, 361; see also Vincent Taylor, "The Life and Ministry of Jesus," in *The Interpreter's Bible* (12 vols.; Nashville: Abingdon, 1951), 7:125–26.

[67] On which, see Klyne Snodgrass, *The Parable of the Wicked Tenants: An Inquiry Into Parable Interpretation* (WUNT 27; Tübingen: Mohr Siebeck, 1983).

[68] On this, cf. David Bosch, *Die Heidenmission in der Zukunftsschau Jesu: Eine Untersuchung zur Eschatologie der synoptischen Evangelien* (ATANT 36; Zürich: Zwingli, 1959), 132; T. W. Manson, *Only to the House of Israel? Jesus and the Non-Jews* (FBBS 9; Philadelphia: Fortress, 1955). That the same applies to the restriction from entering Samaritan territory can be found in John 4:4–42.

[69] Manson, *Only to the House of Israel? Jesus and the Non-Jews*, 24.

[70] See Schürmann, *Jesus, Gestalt und Geheimnis*, 70–72; Crossan, *The Historical Jesus*, 333–37.

[71] Cf. here Eduardo Arens, *The ηλθον-Sayings in the Synoptic Tradition: A Historico-Critical Investigation* (OBO 10; Freiburg: Universitätsverlag, 1976). Among other things,

information – and, since authorization is typically Jewish, the Twelve become at least ipso facto authorized. And what were they commissioned to do? (a) extend the Kingdom of God and its peace: see the Q tradition in Luke 10:5–6 (peace is perhaps a Lukan redaction); 10:9, 11; (b) the Twelve were "enabled" to perform Kingdom miracles, such as exorcism (Mark 6:7 = Matt 10:1; Luke 9:1; compare with Mark 3:27; Luke 10:18; 11:20 = Matt 12:28),[72] healing the sick (Matt 10:1 = Luke 9:1; 10:9),[73] and announcing the arrival of the Kingdom[74] – in short, they were "fishers of men" (Mark 1:16–20 = Matt 4:18–22); (c) Matthew's specific instructions betray a redactional hand designed to portray the mission of the Twelve as identical to Jesus' actions in Matt 8:1–9:34; (d) their means of subsistence was identical to Jesus': trust in God for provisions through the hospitality of others (see Q: Luke 9:58 = Matt 8:20; Luke 11:3 = Matt 6:11; Luke 12:22–31 = Matt 6:25–34; here Mark 6:8–11 = Matt 10:9–15; Luke 9:3–5; 10:4–12).[75]

The implication seems fairly straightforward: they were to be a radical sign[76] of the Kingdom's power by finding support through local sympathizers. This mission of Jesus and its extension through the ministries of his followers now gain support from the recently published Dead Sea Scroll

---

the bare facts as discerned by Arens show that Jesus had a "vocation-consciousness" (*Sendungsbewusstsein*) rather than a "self-consciousness" (*Selbstbewusstsein*); see p. 339.

[72] See esp. Graham H. Twelftree, *Jesus the Exorcist: A Contribution to the Study of the Historical Jesus* (WUNT 2.54; Tübingen: Mohr [Siebeck], 1993); John P. Meier, *Mentor, Message, and Miracles* (vol. 2 of *A Marginal Jew: Rethinking the Historical Jesus*; ABRL; New York: Doubleday, 1994), 398–506; W. Manson, "Principalities and Powers: The Spiritual Background of the Work of Jesus in the Synoptic Gospels," *Bulletin for the Society of New Testament Studies* 3 (1952): 7–17; McKnight, *A New Vision for Israel*, 107–10.

[73] Cf. Becker, *Jesus of Nazareth*, 211–33; Leonhard Goppelt, *Theology of the New Testament* (2 vols.; trans. John E. Alsup; Grand Rapids: Eerdmans, 1981–82), 1:139–57; Reginald H. Fuller, *The Mission and Achievement of Jesus: An Examination of the Presuppositions of New Testament Theology* (SBT 12; London: SCM, 1954), 35–43; Johannes Hempel, *Heilung als Symbol und Wirklichkeit im biblischen Schrifttum* (NAWG 3; Göttingen: Vandenhoeck & Ruprecht, 1958), 237–314 (esp. pp. 271–91); Michael L. Brown, *Israel's Divine Healer* (Studies in Old Testament Biblical Theology; Grand Rapids: Zondervan, 1995).

[74] It is at this juncture that the *Tradent* role of the Twelve becomes fundamental, even if its later ecclesiological dimensions need to be relinquished. Cf., e.g., Roloff, *Apostolat, Verkündigung, Kirche*, 166; Rainer Riesner, *Jesus als Lehrer: Eine Untersuchung zum Ursprung der Evangelien-Überlieferung* (WUNT 2.7; Tübingen: Mohr Siebeck, 1981), 481–87; Moule, *The Birth of the New Testament*, 225–37, who connects the Twelve to the process of canonization.

[75] Details are imprecise (e.g., bag, sandals or no sandals? staff or no staff?) but the general impression is strong that Jesus restricted his missioners' provisions. In general, see the important study of Walter Lewis Liefeld, "The Wandering Preacher as a Social Figure in the Roman Empire," Ph.D. diss. (New York: Columbia University, 1967), 245–71; cf. *m. Ber.* 4:5; *m. Roš Haš.* 2:9.

[76] Cf. Norman Perrin, *Rediscovering the Teaching of Jesus* (New York: Harper & Row, 1967), 142–45.

4Q521 frg. 2, col. 2, as emerging from an existing Jewish hope. Here the messianic ministry, largely realizing the hopes of Isaiah 61, includes the very things early Jesus traditions attribute to Jesus: among other things, the Lord will call the righteous by name, renew the faithful, aid and preach good news to the poor, give an eternal Kingdom to the pious, free prisoners, give sight to the blind, straighten out the twisted, and raise the dead.

A third segment of information emerges from a close scrutiny of the Q tradition in Luke 22:28–30 = Matt 19:28 that the Twelve will judge the twelve tribes of Israel.[77] (1) The tradition-critical history of this logion is notoriously complex, revealing only potential redactional features of each Evangelist,[78] though the Matthean context perhaps has more to speak for it.[79] The eschatology of this Q logion anchors it into the very life of Jesus, not only because it is indisputably Jewish and uncharacteristic of earliest Christian history (Judas will be judging?), but also because its shape is entirely Jewish and coherent with Jesus' vision (dissimilar at a substantive level).[80] (2) Matthew may duplicate the term δώδεκα but, in so doing, adds no new information; perhaps it is Luke who has omitted the term.[81] (3) A secure feature of the early Q tradition is the following: κρίνοντες τὰς δώδεκα φυλὰς τοῦ Ἰσραήλ. This clause provides valuable information concerning why Jesus, distinct from the Twelve as the Son of Man in judgment (see Matt 25:31; 26:64; 1 En. 62:5; 69:29), appointed twelve special leaders.[82] The term "judging" may mean either determinative judgment in an executive, judicial

---

[77] See George R. Beasley-Murray, *Jesus and the Kingdom of God* (Grand Rapids: Eerdmans, 1986), 273–77; Meier, "The Circle of the Twelve," 653–59; Johannes Friedrich, *Gott im Bruder? Eine methodenkritische Untersuchung von Redaktion, Überlieferung und Traditionen in Mt 25,31–46* (Calwer Theologische Monographien 7; Stuttgart: Calwer Verlag, 1977), 53–56.

[78] For example, παλιγγενεσία could be Matthean redaction; but the term is hard to count in Matthew's arsenal, since it is found in the NT only one other time (Titus 3:5).

[79] The Lukan context preceding this *logion* concerns the *defection* of Judas (Luke 22:21–23); this context is less likely than Matthew's. See Davies and Allison, *Matthew*, 3:55, for summary conclusions. It is possible, however, to read Luke's context as a reaffirmation of Jesus' authority in spite of betrayal, in which case, the balance is again even. A conspectus of judgments on this *logion*'s status in Q can be found in John S. Kloppenborg, *Q Parallels: Synopsis, Critical Notes, and Concordance* (FF; Sonoma, Calif.: Polebridge, 1988), 202. For a less-confident judgment on the historicity of the *logion*, see Trilling, "Zur Entstehung Des Zwölferkreises," 213–20; for a more positive assessment, see Rigaux, "Die 'Zwölf'," 476–77.

[80] So, e.g., Meier, "The Circle of the Twelve," 657–58. For the broader picture, see McKnight, *A New Vision for Israel*, 120–55.

[81] So John Nolland, *Luke 18:35–24:53* (WBC 35c; Dallas: Word, 1993), 1066.

[82] That the christology of the twelve judging is Son of Man christology was pointed out long ago. See, e.g., Roloff, *Apostolat, Verkündigung, Kirche*, 149–50. Paul believed saints would judge the world (1 Cor 6:2–3) and in the Apocalypse the victor is promised a seat with the Son of Man (1:13), on his throne (3:21; 20:4), which is the place of judgment. On this, cf. Albert S. Geyser, "The Twelve Tribes in Revelation: Judean and Judeo-Christian

sense (salvation or damnation; see Dan 7:9, 19–28; 1 En. 95:3; Pss. Sol. 17:28; 1QH 4:22), even in a witnessing sense (Isa 24:23; see also 3:14); or rulership and establishing justice (see Matt 2:6; 20:20–21; Judg 3:10; Ps 2:10; Dan 9:12; 1 Macc 9:73; 11Q19 56:20). For our context, it is not necessary to argue the pros and cons of each. I adhere to the latter meaning largely because of the book of Judges, Psalms (for example, 10:18; 35; 76:9; 82:1–4; 103:6), Isa 42:1; 49:6, and the Qumranic evidence cited above, where we set the Twelve in historical context.[83] In each case the Twelve are appointed to a leadership role in the final Kingdom,[84] where they will exercise rule/judgment over the twelve tribes of Israel.[85] Thus, while in the sending tradition no evidence exists for a fulfillment of the literal expectation for the reunification of the twelve tribes, in this logion we see such an expectation.

4.2. The Twelve, Jesus, and the Historical Context

The historical context for the Twelve, if drawn from our previous discussion of the ancient evidence about "twelve," suggests the following: First, the Twelve sent by Jesus could conceivably correspond to the ancient custom of twelve representatives; however, in every case of twelve representatives,

---

Apocalypticism," *NTS* 28 (1982): 388–99. Each of these traditions may well derive from the Q tradition.

[83] Ingo Broer, "Das Ringen der Gemeinde um Israel: Exegetischer Versuch über Mt 19, 28," in *Jesus und der Menschensohn: für Anton Vögtle* (ed. Rudolf Pesch and Rudolf Schnackenburg; Freiburg im Breisgau: Herder, 1975), 148–65; Trilling, "Zur Entstehung Des Zwölferkreises"; E.J. Kissane, "A Forgotten Interpretation of Mt 19:28," *ITQ* 17 (1921): 359–66; Beasley-Murray, *Jesus and the Kingdom of God*, 275–76; Nolland, *Luke 18:35–24:53*, 1067 (ruling); Davies and Allison, *Matthew*, 3:55–56; Roloff, *Apostolat, Verkündigung, Kirche*, 149; Richard A. Horsley, *Jesus and the Spiral of Violence: Popular Jewish Resistance in Roman Palestine* (San Francisco: Harper & Row, 1987), 201–8. Flusser (*Judaism and the Origins of Christianity*, 173–85) connects judging to the stones of the Urim and Thummim and finds confirmation in Rev 21:14, 19–20. The absence of a priestly emphasis in the Jesus traditions speaks against this theory. His lines of thought continue throughout David Flusser, *Jesus* (2nd ed.; in collaboration with R. Steven Notley; Jerusalem: Magnes, 1997). See also Richard A. Horsley and Jonathan A. Draper, *Whoever Hears You Hears Me: Prophets, Performance, and Tradition in Q* (Harrisburg: Trinity, 1999), 262–63.

[84] The use in Matthew of the Greek term παλιγγενεσία has generated significant debate: (1) it is possible to find a Semitic foundation for such a Greek term (cf. 1QS 4:25); (2) it seems probable, however, that the term is a Matthean expression; (3) it is entirely reasonable to think Jesus could have said something that gave rise to such a translation; (4) it is remotely possible that Jesus suggested the restoration of the twelve tribes; (5) it is most likely that the term describes an era (cf. Josephus, *Ant.* 11.66; cf. Beasley-Murray, *Jesus and the Kingdom of God*, 275 and n. 235). On the term, see Fred W. Burnett, "Παλιγγενεσία In Matt 19:28: A Window on the Matthean Community?" *JSNT* 17 (1983): 60–72; J. Duncan M. Derrett, "Palingenesia (Matthew 19:28)," *JSNT* 20 (1984): 51–58; David C. Sim, "The Meaning of παλιγγενεσία in Matthew 19.28," *JSNT* 50 (1993): 3–12.

[85] Cf. Jeremias, *New Testament Theology*, 272; Broer, "Das Ringen," 158–59; *contra* Kissane, "A Forgotten Interpretation," 361–66.

those who are chosen represent each and every tribe (for example, Num 1:44; Deut 1:23; Josh 3:12; 4:2, 3, 8; 1 Esd 5:1, 4; 8:54). What I am suggesting here is that this background for the use of "twelve" by Jesus does not appear to be paramount. Jesus chose the Twelve to embody all of Israel but not to represent each tribe. The parallel to the Qumran community's leadership is more apposite here: a nonliteral fulfillment of the reunification of the twelve tribes or a simple reutilization of the ancient twelve patriarchal ideal drives the choice of twelve as leaders in these texts and, in the case of Jesus, with no priestly emphasis. In the words of Beda Rigaux:

Alles, was man daraus folgern kann [e. g., the parallel with Qumran], ist, dass in den letzten Jahrhunderten des Judentums ein Klima entstanden war, in dem die Geschichte Israels eine betont theologische und messianische Bedeutung erhielt. Man ging zurück auf Adam, auf Henoch, auf die Patriarchen, um sie zu Offenbarern der Geheimnisse Gottes zu machen. Israel war das Zentrum der göttlichen Sorge.[86]

Second, the Twelve being sent by Jesus correspond in potentially suggestive ways with the Covenant renewal and the ancient story of crossing the Jordan, entering into and capturing the land by the strong hand of Joshua (see Josh 4:1, 3, 7, 9, 20). Just as tribal representatives of ancient Israelites were to go throughout the land to capture it for Yahweh and then to "rule" over that land, so the Twelve sent by Jesus were to go throughout the land (esp. Galilee and then beyond) and declare the Kingdom so that the nation could be reclaimed for Yahweh's covenant. Just as twelve tribal leaders formed the ancient leadership, so with Jesus the leadership comprised twelve men. It is possible that the "judging" of the Twelve was originally set in a Covenant reminder context: Luke 22:29–30 connects the two concepts, as has been argued by Heinz Schürmann and Rudolf Otto.[87]

This connection of the Twelve with the covenant ideal can be strengthened by appealing to the foundational event of Jesus' mission: the baptism by John in the Jordan.[88] The connections I draw here are of varying degrees of probability but, together, are suggestive that the Twelve were connected

---

[86] Rigaux, "Die 'Zwölf'," 483. English translation: "The only conclusion to be reached from this (e. g., the parallel with Qumran), is that in the last centuries of Judaism a climate developed in which the history of Israel attained a decidedly theological and Messianic significance. Adam, Enoch and the patriarchs were drawn on in order to make them into revelators of the God's secrets. Israel was the center of divine attention."

[87] See Beasley-Murray, *Jesus and the Kingdom of God*, 276–77.

[88] See esp. Robert L. Webb, "Jesus' Baptism: Its Historicity and Implications," *BBR* 10 (2000): 261–309; Robert L. Webb, "John's Baptizing Activity in the Context of First-Century Judaism," *Forum* 1 (1999): 99–123 (though I would distance myself from use of the view that proselytes were baptized upon conversion in first-century Judaism); Robert L. Webb, "Josephus on John the Baptist: Jewish Antiquities 18.116–119," *Forum* 2 (1999): 141–68. Webb's discussion is updated in this volume in ch. 3.

to covenant renewal. As I have stated in another context,[89] this baptism (1) took place in the Jordan, and (2) probably the baptisands entered the water from the other side of the Jordan and, only after the baptism, reentered the land as a symbolic "action" of covenant renewal, purification, and conquest.[90] The second observation can be gleaned from the following: John exposed Herod, who was tetrarch of Galilee and Perea (Mark 6:8, 17–29; compare with Luke 13:31–33); John was imprisoned in Machaerus (Josephus, Ant. 18.116–119); Jesus' response to John's query "Are you the one who is to come, or do we wait for another?" shows serious connections with Qumran (see Matt 11:2–6 and 4Q521, frgs. 2, 4; esp. 2.1, 6–8, 12–13); the Gospel of John connects John's ministry to Perea (see John 1:28; 3:26; 10:40). Thus, it is indeed plausible that John's ministry was Transjordanian (Perean) and evoked a symbolic action of entering into the land of Israel from the Transjordan similar to the entry of the generation of Moses and Joshua. When these observations are juxtaposed in the same paragraph, they suggest that the Twelve were at least shaped by Jesus' knowledge of the covenant renewal traditions of Joshua. We can place somewhere in this mixture the plausible connection of John with Qumran and the role that twelve (see above) played there as a possible genesis for Jesus' use of "twelve."[91] While this grouping is eschatological, it is equally covenantal. The covenantal, however, shapes the eschatological.

Here then are the suggestive details:

The baptism evoked the entry into the land in ancient history (Josh 3:1–4:18); the use of twelve stones can be plausibly connected to Jesus' choice of twelve (Josh 4:1–10). When John declared vociferously that God is able "from these stones" (Luke 3:8 = Matt 3:9) to raise up children for Abraham, this was perhaps what turned Jesus from disciple into prophet. Part of his task was to make the stones declare the glory of God's covenant with Abraham.

The mission of the Twelve was an attempt to spread the message throughout the land and, if any vision was involved on the part of Jesus, then the hope was to gain the land and its people for the Kingdom of God. This evocational context emerged from the Jewish hope to restore the land, to reunify the tribes, and to reestablish the covenant.

---

[89] Scot McKnight, "Jesus' New Vision Within Judaism," in *Who Was Jesus? A Jewish-Christian Dialogue* (ed. Paul Copan and Craig A. Evans; Louisville: Westminster John Knox, 2001), 73–96.

[90] Cf. Robert L. Webb, *John the Baptizer and Prophet: A Socio-Historical Study* (JSNTSup 62; Sheffield: JSOT Press, 1991), 360–66 (who sketches this interpretation admirably); Colin Brown, "What Was John the Baptist Doing?" *BBR* 7 (1997): 37–49; see also McKnight, "Jesus and Prophetic Actions".

[91] Schürmann (*Jesus, Gestalt und Geheimnis*, 31–44) has argued, however, that dimensions of Jesus' vision were in place prior to the baptism; cf., e.g., "Jesu Aufbruch zum Jordan: Beginn der ureigenen Basileia-Verkündigung Jesu."

Third, there are solid grounds for contending that Jesus envisioned a reunification of the twelve tribes that would take place in the land of Israel. This is only implied, I am suggesting, in the choice and sending of the Twelve, but it is firmly assumed in the Q tradition in Luke 22:30 = Matt 19:28 and probably in a text otherwise not studied here – namely, Luke 13:28–30 = Matt 8:11–12 (compare with Ps 107:2–3; Isa 43:5–6; Pss. Sol. 11:2–3).[92]

Fourth, it is implied in all that precedes that Jesus' choice of the Twelve to embody his covenantal and eschatological vision implies a political vision, a vision for the nation, and this in some ecclesial sense. Jesus thinks the current leadership is in need of replacement; his twelve special followers are to be that new "nation" (Matt 21:43). To embody his vision in these Twelve is heady political stuff. The evidence considered here does not go as far as G. W. Buchanan did, or even as far as R. A. Horsley did, in attempting to reconstruct a political Jesus.[93] However, the evidence clearly implies that Jesus had a design for the nation; his vision was not yet the world. It also points to a self understanding about his own sense of authority that other events in this volume also indicate.

This political design clearly implies negative critique of the establishment. It would take us wide of the mark here to consider whether Jesus' critique of the leadership in the form of his choice of the Twelve is primarily targeted at the Pharisees or the Sadducees, but the evidence does imply a trenchant dissatisfaction with what is going on in Jerusalem and, no doubt, through Jerusalem, in Galilee. His vision is grand enough to critique the entire leadership. While I am not convinced that this critique of the establishment emerges because Jesus is a Galilean, as was mentioned so suggestively by G. Vermes,[94] Jesus' childhood region certainly does not frown on such grandiose plans for the nation. His critique is solid: anti-Pharisee, anti-Sadducee, and anti-Roman (what else can the disparaging words of Luke 7:24–35 = Matt 11:7–19 mean?). Jesus envisions a new leadership for the entire nation, and this means that the entire establishment must be swept clean, a veritable coup d'état, with his Twelve as the new shepherds for those who would then be lost in Israel.

---

[92] See esp. Allison, *The Jesus Tradition in Q*, 176–91, who single-handedly disputes the consensus that this text is speaking of Gentile inclusion in the Kingdom.

[93] George Wesley Buchanan, *Jesus, the King and His Kingdom* (Macon, Ga.: Mercer University Press, 1984); Horsley, *Jesus and the Spiral of Violence*.

[94] Géza Vermès, *Jesus the Jew: A Historian's Reading of the Gospels* (London: Collins, 1973).

5. Conclusion

Jesus' sending out the Twelve shows little parallel with the expectation of the reunification of the twelve tribes.[95] Instead, the connotations of his choice and sending out of the Twelve show more significant parallels with Qumran leadership, T. Jud. 25:1–2, and T. Benj. 10:7, and covenant reestablishment as found in Joshua 4. His expectation of the reunification of the twelve tribes in the land does emerge in the Q tradition (Luke 22:30 = Matt 19:28; Luke 13:28–30 = Matt 8:11–12), and his Twelve were to function in a leadership rule in that Kingdom. There is significant evidence for us to think that Jesus had in mind a restored Israel – twelve new leaders, the land under control, a pure Temple, and a radically obedient Israel. The two themes of covenant and eschatology that swirl around the number "twelve" form a combined witness to the centrality of Jesus' vision for Israel: salvation-historical fulfillment – that is, covenant reestablishment – in his mission's inauguration of the Kingdom and the embodiment of leadership in his twelve special leaders, who will rule and liberate the twelve tribes of Israel in the Kingdom.

Bibliography

Agnew, Francis H. "The Origin of the NT Apostle-Concept: A Review of Research." *JBL* 105 (1986): 75–96.

Allison, Dale C., Jr. *The Jesus Tradition in Q.* Harrisburg: Trinity, 1997.

Andersen, Francis I., and David Noel Freedman. *Amos.* AB 24a. New York: Doubleday, 1989.

Anscombe, G. E. M. *Intention.* 2nd ed. Library of Philosophy and Logic. Oxford: Blackwell, 1979.

Arens, Eduardo. *The ηλθον-Sayings in the Synoptic Tradition: A Historico-Critical Investigation.* OBO 10. Freiburg: Universitätsverlag, 1976.

---

[95] I am nuancing in what sense one should speak of Jesus' act as eschatological. Compare the view of Meier, *Companions and Competitors*, 153, who argues that Jesus looked for a complete Israel in a complete kingdom of God and says, "It is within this overarching hope for the regathering in the end time of *all* Israel, all twelve tribes, that Jesus' choice of an inner circle of twelve disciples must be understood" [italics original]. For Meier, Jesus' act fits into the eschatology of the regathering of the tribes, Jesus' understanding of being the end time prophet like Elijah, and reflects an effort designed to set in motion this regathering. However, Sean Freyne sees things differently. He also sees Jesus as acting in an Elijah-like manner but as not being interested in territorial concerns; see his *Jesus, a Jewish Galilean: A New Reading of the Jesus Story* (London: T&T Clark, 2004), 118–20, 135. Finally, Bird, *Gentile Mission*, 38–39, sees a mixture of a call to reform the entire nation and the calling of a remnant in Jesus' action, a nucleus of the eschatological community, as Bird cites and agrees with my argument in an earlier version of this study: McKnight, "Jesus and the Twelve," 223.

Baumgarten, Joseph M. "Duodecimal Courts of Qumran, Revelation, and the Sanhedrin." *JBL* 95 (1976): 59–78.
Beasley-Murray, George R. *Jesus and the Kingdom of God.* Grand Rapids: Eerdmans, 1986.
Becker, Jürgen. *Jesus of Nazareth.* Translated by James E. Crouch. Berlin: De Gruyter, 1998.
Bird, Michael F. *Jesus and the Origins of the Gentile Mission.* LNTS 331. London: T&T Clark, 2007.
Borg, Marcus J. *Jesus, A New Vision: Spirit, Culture, and the Life of Discipleship.* San Francisco: Harper & Row, 1987.
–. *Jesus in Contemporary Scholarship.* Valley Forge: Trinity, 1994.
Bosch, David. *Die Heidenmission in der Zukunftsschau Jesu: Eine Untersuchung zur Eschatologie der synoptischen Evangelien.* ATANT 36. Zürich: Zwingli, 1959.
Broer, Ingo. "Das Ringen der Gemeinde um Israel: Exegetischer Versuch über Mt 19, 28." Pages 148–65 in *Jesus und der Menschensohn: für Anton Vögtle.* Edited by Rudolf Pesch and Rudolf Schnackenburg. Freiburg im Breisgau: Herder, 1975.
Brown, Colin. "What Was John the Baptist Doing?" *BBR* 7 (1997): 37–49.
Brown, Michael L. *Israel's Divine Healer.* Studies in Old Testament Biblical Theology. Grand Rapids: Zondervan, 1995.
Buchanan, George Wesley. *Jesus, the King and His Kingdom.* Macon, Ga.: Mercer University Press, 1984.
Burnett, Fred W. "Παλιγγενεσία In Matt 19:28: A Window on the Matthean Community?" *JSNT* 17 (1983): 60–72.
Caird, G. B. *Jesus and the Jewish Nation.* Ethel M. Wood Lecture. London: Athlone, 1965.
–. *New Testament Theology.* Edited by L. D. Hurst. Oxford: Clarendon Press, 1994.
Crossan, John Dominic. *The Historical Jesus: The Life of a Mediterranean Jewish Peasant.* San Francisco: HarperSanFrancisco, 1991.
–. *Who Killed Jesus?: Exposing the Roots of Anti-Semitism in the Gospel Story of the Death of Jesus.* San Francisco: HarperSanFrancisco, 1995.
Daube, David. "Responsibilities of Master and Disciples in the Gospels." *NTS* 19 (1972): 1–15.
Davies, W. D., and Dale C. Allison, Jr. *A Critical and Exegetical Commentary on the Gospel According to Saint Matthew.* 3 vols. ICC. Edinburgh: T&T Clark, 1988–97.
Derrett, J. Duncan M. "Palingenesia (Matthew 19:28)." *JSNT* 20 (1984): 51–58.
Dupont, Jacques. "Le nom d'apôtres a-t-il été donné aux douze par Jésus?" *OrSyr* 1 (1956): 267–90, 425–44.
–. "'Vous n'aurez pas achevé les villes d'Israël avant que le fils de l'homme ne vienne.'" *NovT* 2 (1958): 228–44.
Evans, Craig A. "From 'House of Prayer' to 'Cave of Robbers': Jesus' Prophetic Criticism of the Temple Establishment." Pages 417–42 in *The Quest for Context and Meaning: Studies in Biblical Intertextuality in Honor of James A. Sanders.* Edited by Craig A. Evans and Shemaryahu Talmon. Biblical Interpretation Series, 28. Leiden: Brill, 1997.
–. *Jesus.* IBR Bibliographies 5. Grand Rapids: Baker, 1992.
–. *Life of Jesus Research: An Annotated Bibliography.* 2nd ed. NTTS 24. Leiden: Brill, 1996.

Farrer, A. M. "The Ministry in the New Testament." Pages 113–82 in *The Apostolic Ministry: Essays on the History and the Doctrine of the Episcopacy*. Kenneth E. Kirk. London: Hodder & Stoughton, 1946.

Flew, R. Newton. *Jesus and His Church: A Study of the Idea of the Ecclesia in the New Testament*. 2nd ed. London: Epworth, 1943.

Flusser, David. *Jesus*. 2nd ed. In collaboration with R. Steven Notley. Jerusalem: Magnes, 1997.

–. *Judaism and the Origins of Christianity*. Jerusalem: Magnes, 1988.

Fredriksen, Paula. *Jesus of Nazareth, King of the Jews: A Jewish Life and the Emergence of Christianity*. New York: Knopf, 1999.

Freyne, Sean. *Jesus, a Jewish Galilean: A New Reading of the Jesus Story*. London: T&T Clark, 2004.

Friedrich, Johannes. *Gott im Bruder? Eine methodenkritische Untersuchung von Redaktion, Überlieferung und Traditionen in Mt 25,31–46*. Calwer Theologische Monographien 7. Stuttgart: Calwer Verlag, 1977.

Fuller, Reginald H. *The Mission and Achievement of Jesus: An Examination of the Presuppositions of New Testament Theology*. SBT 12. London: SCM, 1954.

Funk, Robert W., and The Jesus Seminar. *The Acts of Jesus: The Search for the Authentic Deeds of Jesus*. San Francisco: HarperSanFrancisco, 1998.

García Martínez, Florentino, and Eibert J. C. Tigchelaar. *The Dead Sea Scrolls Study Edition*. 2 vols. Grand Rapids: Eerdmans, 1997.

Geyser, Albert S. "The Twelve Tribes in Revelation: Judean and Judeo-Christian Apocalypticism." *NTS* 28 (1982): 388–99.

Gnilka, Joachim. *Jesus of Nazareth: Message and History*. Translated by Siegfried S. Schatzmann. Peabody, Mass.: Hendrickson, 1997.

Goppelt, Leonhard. *Theology of the New Testament*. 2 vols. Translated by John E. Alsup. Grand Rapids: Eerdmans, 1981–82.

Greil, Arthur L., and David R. Rudy. "Social Cocoons: Encapsulation and Identity Transformation Organizations." *Sociological Inquiry* 54 (1984): 260–78.

Guenther, Heinz O. *The Footprints of Jesus' Twelve in Early Christian Traditions: A Study in the Meaning of Religious Symbolism*. AOS 7.7. Berne: Lang, 1985.

Hahn, Ferdinand. *Mission in the New Testament*. Translated by Frank Clarke. SBT 47. London: SCM, 1965.

Hempel, Johannes. *Heilung als Symbol und Wirklichkeit im biblischen Schrifttum*. NAWG 3. Göttingen: Vandenhoeck & Ruprecht, 1958.

Herron, Robert W. "The Origin of the New Testament Apostolate." *WTJ* 45 (1983): 101–31.

Hoffmann, Paul. "Lk 10:5–11 in der Instruktionsrede der Logienquelle." Pages 37–53 in vol. 3 of *Evangelisch Katholischer Kommentar: Vorarbeiten*. Neukirchen-Vluyn: Neukirchener Verlag, 1971.

–. *Studien zur Theologie der Logienquelle*. NTAbh 8. Münster: Aschendorff, 1972.

Hooker, Morna D. *The Signs of a Prophet: The Prophetic Actions of Jesus*. Harrisburg: Trinity, 1997.

Horbury, William. "The Twelve and the Phylarchs." *NTS* 32 (1986): 503–27.

Horsley, Richard A. *Jesus and the Spiral of Violence: Popular Jewish Resistance in Roman Palestine*. San Francisco: Harper & Row, 1987.

Horsley, Richard A., and Jonathan A. Draper. *Whoever Hears You Hears Me: Prophets, Performance, and Tradition in Q*. Harrisburg: Trinity, 1999.

Jeremias, Joachim. *New Testament Theology: The Proclamation of Jesus*. Translated by John Bowden. New York: Scribner, 1971.

–. "Paarweise Sendung im Neuen Testament." Pages 136–43 in *New Testament Essays. Studies in Memory of Thomas Walter Manson, 1893–1958*. Edited by A.J.B. Higgins. Manchester: Manchester University Press, 1959.

Kissane, E.J. "A Forgotten Interpretation of Mt 19:28." *ITQ* 17 (1921): 359–66.

Klassen, William. *Judas: Betrayer or Friend of Jesus?* Minneapolis: Fortress, 1996.

Klein, Gunter. *Die zwölf Apostel: Ursprung und Gehalt einer Idee*. FRLANT 77. Göttingen: Vandenhoeck & Ruprecht, 1961.

Kloppenborg, John S. *Q Parallels: Synopsis, Critical Notes, and Concordance*. FF. Sonoma, Calif.: Polebridge, 1988.

Kümmel, Werner Georg. "Jesus und die Anfänge der Kirche." *ST* 7 (1953): 1–27.

Liefeld, Walter Lewis. "The Wandering Preacher as a Social Figure in the Roman Empire." Ph.D. diss. New York: Columbia University, 1967.

McKnight, Scot. "Jesus and Prophetic Actions." *BBR* 10 (2000): 197–232.

–. "Jesus and the Twelve." *BBR* 11 (2001): 203–31.

–. "Jesus' New Vision Within Judaism." Pages 73–96 in *Who Was Jesus? a Jewish-Christian Dialogue*. Edited by Paul Copan and Craig A. Evans. Louisville: Westminster John Knox, 2001.

–. *A Light Among the Gentiles: Jewish Missionary Activity in the Second Temple Period*. Minneapolis: Fortress, 1991.

–. "New Shepherds for Israel – Matthew 9:35–11:1: An Historical and Critical Study of Matthew 9:35–11:1." Ph.D., diss. Nottingham: University of Nottingham, 1986.

–. *A New Vision for Israel: The Teachings of Jesus in National Context*. Grand Rapids: Eerdmans, 1999.

Malherbe, Abraham J., ed. *The Cynic Epistles: A Study Edition*. SBLSBS 12. Missoula, Mont.: Scholars, 1977.

Manson, T.W. *Only to the House of Israel? Jesus and the Non-Jews*. FBBS 9. Philadelphia: Fortress, 1955.

–. *The Sayings of Jesus: As Recorded in the Gospels According to St. Matthew and St. Luke*. London: SCM, 1949.

Manson, W. "Principalities and Powers: The Spiritual Background of the Work of Jesus in the Synoptic Gospels." *Bulletin for the Society of New Testament Studies* 3 (1952): 7–17.

Meier, John P. "The Circle of the Twelve: Did It Exist During Jesus' Ministry?" *JBL* 116 (1997): 635–72.

–. *Companions and Competitors*. Vol. 3 of *A Marginal Jew: Rethinking the Historical Jesus*. ABRL. New York: Doubleday, 2001.

–. *Mentor, Message, and Miracles*. Vol. 2 of *A Marginal Jew: Rethinking the Historical Jesus*. ABRL. New York: Doubleday, 1994.

Meye, Robert P. *Jesus and the Twelve: Discipleship and Revelation in Mark's Gospel*. Grand Rapids: Eerdmans, 1968.

Meyer, Ben F. *The Aims of Jesus*. London: SCM, 1979.

–. "Jesus and the Remnant of Israel." *JBL* 84 (1965): 123–30.

Montefiore, C.G. *The Synoptic Gospels*. 2nd ed. 2 vols. London: Macmillan, 1927.

Montefiore, Hugh. "Revolt in the Desert? (Mark vi. 30ff)." *NTS* 8 (1962): 135–41.

Moule, C. F. D. *The Birth of the New Testament*. 3rd ed. BNTC. London: Black, 1981.
Mußner, F. "Gab es eine 'galiläische Krise'?" Pages 238–52 in *Orientierung an Jesus: Zur Theologie der Synoptiker*. Edited by P. Hoffmann. Freiburg: Herder, 1973.
Nolland, John. *Luke 18:35–24:53*. WBC 35c. Dallas: Word, 1993.
–. *Luke 1–9:20*. WBC 35a. Dallas: Word, 1989.
Park, Eung Chun. *The Mission Discourse in Matthew's Interpretation*. WUNT 2.81. Tübingen: Mohr Siebeck, 1995.
Perrin, Norman. *Rediscovering the Teaching of Jesus*. New York: Harper & Row, 1967.
Rambo, Lewis R. *Understanding Religious Conversion*. New Haven: Yale University Press, 1993.
Riesner, Rainer. *Jesus als Lehrer: Eine Untersuchung zum Ursprung der Evangelien-Überlieferung*. WUNT 2.7. Tübingen: Mohr Siebeck, 1981.
Rigaux, Béda. "The Twelve Apostles." *Concilium* 34 (1968): 5–15.
–. "Die 'Zwölf' in Geschichte und Kerygma." Pages 468–86 in *Der historische Jesus und der kerygmatische Christus: Beiträge zum Christusverständnis in Forschung und Verkündigung*. Edited by Helmut Ristow and Karl Matthiae. Berlin: Evangelische, 1960.
Roloff, Jürgen. *Apostolat, Verkündigung, Kirche: Ursprung, Inhalt und Funktion des kirchlichen Apostelamtes nach Paulus, Lukas und den Pastoralbriefen*. Gütersloh: Mohn, 1965.
Sanders, E. P. *The Historical Figure of Jesus*. London: Penguin, 1993.
–. *Jesus and Judaism*. Philadelphia: Fortress, 1985.
Schmithals, Walter. *The Office of Apostle in the Early Church*. Translated by John E. Steely. Nashville: Abingdon, 1969.
Schnackenburg, Rudolf. *God's Rule and Kingdom*. Translated by John Murray. New York: Herder, 1963.
Schürmann, Heinz. *Jesus, Gestalt und Geheimnis: Gesammelte Beiträge*. Edited by Klaus Scholtissek. Paderborn: Bonifatius, 1994.
–. "Mt 10, 5b–6 und die Vorgeschichte des synoptischen Aussendungsberichtes." Pages 270–82 in *Neutestamentliche Aufsätze: Festschrift für Prof. Josef Schmid zum 70. Geburtstag*. Edited by Josef Blinzler. Regensburg: Pustet, 1963.
Schweitzer, Albert. *The Quest of the Historical Jesus: A Critical Study of Its Progress from Reimarus to Wrede*. Translated by W. Montgomery. Baltimore: Johns Hopkins University Press, 1998.
Scott, James M., ed. *Exile: Old Testament, Jewish, and Christian Conceptions*. Supplements to the Journal for the Study of Judaism, 56. Leiden: Brill, 1997.
Sim, David C. "The Meaning of παλιγγενεσία in Matthew 19.28." *JSNT* 50 (1993): 3–12.
Snodgrass, Klyne. *The Parable of the Wicked Tenants: An Inquiry Into Parable Interpretation*. WUNT 27. Tübingen: Mohr Siebeck, 1983.
Taylor, Vincent. "The Life and Ministry of Jesus." Pages 114–44 in vol. 7 of *The Interpreter's Bible*. 12 vols. Nashville: Abingdon, 1951.
Theissen, Gerd. "Gruppenmessianismus: Überlegungen zum Ursprung der Kirche in Jüngerkreis Jesu." Pages 101–23 in *Volk Gottes, Gemeinde und Gesellschaft*. Edited by Ingo Baldermann, Ernst Dassmann, and Ottmar Fuchs. Jahrbuch für biblische Theologie, 7. Neukirchen-Vluyn: Neukirchener, 1992.

Theissen, Gerd, and Annette Merz. *Der historische Jesus: Ein Lehrbuch*. 2nd ed. Göttingen: Vandenhoeck & Ruprecht, 1997.

Trilling, Wolfgang. "Zur Entstehung des Zwölferkreises: Eine geschichtskritische Überlegung." Pages 201–22 in *Die Kirche des Anfangs: für Heinz Schürmann*. Edited by Rudolf Schnackenburg, Josef Ernst, and Joachim Wanke. Freiburg: Herder, 1977.

Twelftree, Graham H. *Jesus the Exorcist: A Contribution to the Study of the Historical Jesus*. WUNT 2.54. Tübingen: Mohr [Siebeck], 1993.

Uro, Risto. *Sheep Among the Wolves: A Study on the Mission Instructions of Q*. AASF 47. Helsinki: Suomalainen Tiedeakatemia, 1987.

Vermès, Géza. *Jesus the Jew: A Historian's Reading of the Gospels*. London: Collins, 1973.

Vielhauer, Philipp. *Aufsätze zum Neuen Testament*. TB 31. Munich: Kaiser, 1965.

Weaver, Dorothy Jean. *Matthew's Missionary Discourse: A Literary Critical Analysis*. JSNTSup 38. Sheffield: Sheffield Academic Press, 1990.

Webb, Robert L. "Jesus' Baptism: Its Historicity and Implications." *BBR* 10 (2000): 261–309.

–. *John the Baptizer and Prophet: A Socio-Historical Study*. JSNTSup 62. Sheffield: JSOT Press, 1991.

–. "John's Baptizing Activity in the Context of First-Century Judaism." *Forum* 1 (1999): 99–123.

–. "Josephus on John the Baptist: Jewish Antiquities 18.116–119." *Forum* 2 (1999): 141–68.

Wright, N. T. *Jesus and the Victory of God*. Vol. 2 of *Christian Origins and the Question of God*. Minneapolis: Fortress, 1996.

Chapter 6

The Authenticity and Significance of Jesus' Table Fellowship with Sinners

CRAIG L. BLOMBERG

1. Introduction: Recent Challenges to an Old Consensus for Authenticity[1]

In many ways, an examination of Jesus' meals and associations involves a quest for their proper background.[2] Do Jesus' associations evoke the Greco-Roman context of symposia with the appropriate ethical implications? Or is a preferable background to be found in meals of fellowship and hope tied to eschatological implications in Second Temple Jewish thought? Were those at the table really part of the social and moral fringe? These issues of background relate directly to questions about authenticity. So this study of table fellowship in Jesus' public ministry pursues their background and authenticity together before setting out the significance of the results.

Until quite recently, a broad cross-section of NT scholars agreed that Jesus' intimate association over meals with the notoriously wicked of his world formed one of the most historically reliable motifs in the canonical Gospels.[3] Barely over a decade ago, János Bolyki could devote an entire

---

[1] I would like to thank the IBR Jesus Group for their invaluable comments and interaction with me in June 2006 on an earlier draft of this essay. I must similarly thank my research assistant during the 2006–7 school year, Scott Moore, for tracking down a large number of supplementary sources, both ancient and modern, that those comments necessitated, and to Jonathan Waits, my research assistant during the 2007–8 school year, for doing the same on a much smaller scale after additional requests for different kinds of revisions came in from this volume's editors.

[2] This essay has a significant tradition history, building on both my previous book (Craig L. Blomberg, *Contagious Holiness: Jesus' Meals with Sinners* [New Studies in Biblical Theology; Downers Grove: InterVarsity, 2005]) and article (Craig L. Blomberg, "Jesus, Sinners, and Table Fellowship," *BBR* 19 [2009]: 35–62) on similar topics. My mandate here, however, has been to turn the latter into a shorter piece, completely updated, and focusing strictly on the twin issues of authenticity and meaning as it relates to meals tied to Jesus' public ministry.

[3] Cf., e.g., the agreement between John Dominic Crossan (*The Historical Jesus: The Life of a Mediterranean Jewish Peasant* [San Francisco: HarperSanFrancisco, 1991], 344) and N. T. Wright (*Jesus and the Victory of God* [vol. 2 of *Christian Origins and the Ques-*

monograph to the topic of Jesus' table fellowship and argue for the centrality of the overall motif to the agenda of the historical Jesus as well as for the authenticity of a substantial core of a majority of the passages illustrating the practice.[4] In 2003, however, Dennis Smith published a substantial work challenging this consensus. Building on a number of his own previous studies, as well as the German volume of Matthias Klinghardt, Smith became convinced that the Gospel writers portray the festive meals that Jesus enjoys as Greco-Roman symposia, and that these portraits largely reflect the redactional innovations of the Evangelists rather than the activity of the historical Jesus.[5] Kathleen Corley, in books released in 1993 and 2002, has envisioned Jesus fraternizing with friends at public meals, but has denied that they included literal tax collectors and prostitutes.[6] Instead, she argued, this language reflects conventional labeling or vilification, particularly of the "new Roman women" who increasingly joined their husbands at public banquets against older social conventions.[7] Thus we should not envision Jesus associating with the most notoriously wicked of his society, as E. P. Sanders has so famously claimed.[8]

Both Smith and Corley view the symposium format as having so permeated the first-century Roman empire that even Jews in Israel would have adopted it for their celebrations. Where Smith and Klinghardt reject the historicity of Jesus' meal scenes, they do so not because of their depiction as symposia, but because they detect layers of tradition and redaction in the relevant pericopae and a consistent Lukan literary and theological emphasis on Jesus eating with sinners. Neither of these arguments withstands close

---

tion of God; Minneapolis: Fortress, 1996], 149), prominent scholars better known for their disagreements on issues related to the historical Jesus.

[4] János Bolyki, *Jesu Tischgemeinschaften* (WUNT 96; Tübingen: Mohr Siebeck, 1998).

[5] Dennis E. Smith, *From Symposium to Eucharist: The Banquet in the Early Christian World* (Minneapolis: Fortress, 2003), and his earlier writings cited therein; Matthias Klinghardt, *Gemeinschaftsmahl und Mahlgemeinschaft: Soziologie und Liturgie frühchristlicher Mahlfeiern* (Texte und Arbeiten zum neutestamentlichen Zeitalter; Tübingen: Francke Verlag, 1996).

[6] Kathleen E. Corley, *Private Women, Public Meals: Social Conflict in the Synoptic Tradition* (Peabody: Hendrickson, 1993), 92; Kathleen E. Corley, *Women and the Historical Jesus: Feminist Myths of Christian Origins* (Santa Rosa: Polebridge, 2002), 52.

[7] Corley, *Private Women, Public Meals*, 59–62. One wonders, though, how relevant a social development more prominent in the Western than in the Eastern "half" of the Roman empire, and predominantly limited to the upper classes, would be for Jesus and outcasts in Israel.

[8] E. P. Sanders, *Jesus and Judaism* (Philadelphia: Fortress, 1985), 174–99. Sanders rejected the earlier consensus that "sinners" were simply those who did not follow the more scrupulous purity laws of the Pharisees, arguing instead that they were actually the flagrantly immoral in Israel. For a more sweeping rejection of the authenticity of Jesus' acceptance of one key category of sinners, the tax collectors, see William O. Walker, Jr., "Jesus and the Tax Collectors," *JBL* 97 (1978): 221–38. For a brief rebuttal of his arguments, see Blomberg, *Contagious Holiness*, 27.

scrutiny,[9] but other related issues remain unresolved. Were symposia as pervasive as these writers claim? Would Jesus have participated in what often degenerated into little more than drinking parties? If not, and if this *is* how the Evangelists portray Jesus, then must we reject the historicity of the relevant texts, even if for slightly different reasons than Smith and Klinghardt? How do we adjudicate between Corley and Sanders? And what of Sanders' claim that Jesus often accepted sinners *without* calling them to repentance?[10]

2. On the Background and Historicity of Jesus' Meals with Sinners

Appropriate criteria of authenticity become crucial at this juncture. The old quartet of dissimilarity, multiple attestation, Palestinian environment and coherence can still be employed *positively* to support historicity, but only Palestinian environment makes sense when used *negatively* to exclude material which does not fit it.[11] As derivatives of multiple attestation and dissimilarity, the criteria of multiple forms and embarrassment, respectively, may also support the trustworthiness of a tradition, and John Meier stresses the inclusion of a criterion of "rejection and execution" (i.e., what explains Jesus' crucifixion) as well.[12] An even more promising approach, especially given the tension between dissimilarity and Palestinian environment, emerges with what Wright calls the criterion of "double similarity and dissimilarity"[13] or what Gerd Theissen, Annette Merz and Dagmar Winter term the "criterion of historical plausibility" (*Plausibilitätskriterium*).[14]

---

[9] Identifying redactional traits or persistent literary emphases enables one to discover what a given evangelist stresses and in what fashion, but neither selection nor stylization has any necessary bearing on authenticity. See, e. g., Joel B. Green, "Which Conversation Shall We Have? History, Historicism and Historical Narrative in Theological Interpretation: A Response to Peter van Inwagen," in *Behind the Text: History and Biblical Interpretation* (Craig Bartholomew, et al.; Scripture and Hermeneutics Series 4; Carlisle: Paternoster; Grand Rapids: Zondervan, 2003), 141–50.

[10] Sanders, *Jesus and Judaism*, 200–211. *Contra* which, see Bruce D. Chilton, "Jesus and the Repentance of E. P. Sanders," *TynBul* 39 (1988): 1–18.

[11] See already Robert H. Stein, "The 'Criteria' for Authenticity," in *Studies of History and Tradition in the Four Gospels* (ed. R. T. France and David Wenham; Gospel Perspectives 1; Sheffield: JSOT Press, 1980), 225–63.

[12] For all of these points, see John P. Meier, *The Roots of the Problem and the Person* (vol. 1 of *A Marginal Jew: Rethinking the Historical Jesus*; ABRL; New York: Doubleday, 1991), 167–77. See also the discussion of the criteria in this volume in ch. 2, § 4.1.

[13] Wright, *Jesus and the Victory of God*, 131–33.

[14] Gerd Theissen and Annette Merz, *The Historical Jesus: A Comprehensive Guide* (trans. John Bowden; Minneapolis: Fortress, 1998), 115–18; Gerd Theissen and Dagmar Winter, *The Quest for the Plausible Jesus: The Question of Criteria* (trans. M. Eugene Boring; Louisville: Westminster John Knox, 2002).

Supporters of this four-part criterion argue that when a given element or episode of the Gospel tradition simultaneously (a) fits credibly into a first-third-of-the-first-century Palestinian Jewish context, while nevertheless (b) reflecting some practice that sharply distinguished it from conventional Judaism, and (c) continues to influence subsequent Christian thought a little, (d) without being a dominant later motif, then we have a powerful case for authenticity. It is unlikely that any typical Jew or Christian would have made up this motif, falsely attributing it to Jesus.

Tom Holmén has replied that only (b) and (d), corresponding to the older dissimilarity criterion, prove valuable, because the more an item corresponds to a Jewish context or a later Christian emphasis, the more likely someone other than Jesus could have created it.[15] To some degree, this is true, but the argument fails to distinguish between degrees of correspondence and therefore between degrees of probability that an element of the Gospel tradition does not stem from Jesus himself. Stanley Porter critiques Theissen's employment of his version of double similarity and double dissimilarity as insufficiently disentangled from the older quartet of criteria and as very subjectively employed.[16] The former problem, however, is not inherent in the method itself, while the latter has been minimized in Wright's work, which Porter does not discuss. Of course, there will be some subjectivity with using most of the criteria, but double similarity and double dissimilarity still appears to represent a significant advance on or supplement to the older methodology.

How then do Jesus' meals fare when measured against this four-pronged standard? We may dispense with the latter two prongs – (c) and (d) – comparatively quickly. The requisite continuity and discontinuity with later Christianity comes into play at once. Jesus' followers continued to eat together (Acts 2:42, 46; 20:7–12; Jude 12) and looked forward to the coming Messianic banquet or wedding feast of the Lamb (Rev 19:7–9). Sharing meals with "outsiders" at times remained a key to breaking down barriers, most notably between Jews and Gentiles. The lengthy Cornelius narrative in Acts (10:1–11:18) proves paradigmatic in this respect (cf. also Acts 16:34; 27:33–36). On the other hand, ordinary meals, even festive ones, soon gave way to the celebration of the Lord's Supper as the focal point of Christian

---

[15] See esp. Tom Holmén, "Doubts About Double Dissimilarity: Restructuring the Main Criterion of Jesus-of-History Research," in *Authenticating the Words of Jesus* (ed. Bruce D. Chilton and Craig A. Evans; NTTS 28.1; Leiden: Brill, 1999), 47–80.

[16] Stanley E. Porter, *The Criteria for Authenticity in Historical-Jesus Research: Previous Discussion and New Proposals* (JSNTSup 191; Sheffield: Sheffield Academic Press, 2000), 116–22. Porter himself helpfully suggests three new criteria – "Greek language and its content," "Greek textual variance," and "discourse features," but by his own admission each of these applies only to a small minority of the Gospel tradition.

table fellowship.¹⁷ Building on Jesus' own appropriation of the Passover meal at his Last Supper,¹⁸ Jesus' followers came to view the memorializing of his death via bread and wine as one of the central elements of worship (1 Cor 10:14–22, 11:17–34; Heb 13:10). They also developed criteria for excluding certain kinds of unrepentant sinners from this table (1 Cor 11:27–32; *Did.* 9:5, 10:6, 14:2). Other non-ritual and / or fully inclusive meals recede in significance.¹⁹ Thus it is highly unlikely that Christians a generation or more after Jesus' lifetime, based on later church practice, would have invented as a major motif in their portrait of the historical Jesus his countercultural association with the outcast in the intimacy of table fellowship.

2.1. Special Meals in the Hebrew Scriptures

But what of similarity and dissimilarity with pre-Christian Judaism, including a Judaism supposedly permeated by Greco-Roman symposium revelry? Here the issues become more complex and require more detailed scrutiny. The Hebrew Scriptures present a diverse array of special meals. In the Pentateuch alone, we encounter a varied menu: meals for ratifying covenants with God and people (Gen 26:30–31, 31:54; Exod 18:12, 24:9–11), festivities for weddings and other family milestones (Gen 24:54, 29:22–23, 43:24–34), banquets to celebrate military victories (Gen 14:18), and meals in the context of extending hospitality to strangers (Exod 2:20). Genesis 18:1–8, in which Abraham thereby entertains angels "unawares," with its unusually lavish provisions, becomes a model for considerable later Jewish and Christian emulation.²⁰ In the Exodus, the Passover ritual is born (Exod 12); in the wilderness God provides manna from heaven (Exod 16), a miracle which Jews later believe will be replicated by the Messiah (see esp. *2 Bar.* 29:5–8; cf. Philo, *Names* 44–45; Sir 24:19–23). The Promised Land will flow "with milk and honey" (Num 13:27),²¹ while sacrificial meals will accompany the forgiveness of sins wherever the Tabernacle is erected (Lev 1–7). But one

---

¹⁷ On which, see especially ch. 11 in this volume.

¹⁸ This imagery was present whether or not the meal was celebrated on the day of the first, main meal of that year's Passover festival. See Scot McKnight, *Jesus and His Death: Historiography, the Historical Jesus, and Atonement Theory* (Waco: Baylor University Press, 2005), 275–92.

¹⁹ Bolyki, *Jesu Tischgemeinschaften*, 222–28; cf. Andrew McGowan, "Naming the Feast: The *Agapē* and the Diversity of Early Christian Meals," in *Studia Patristica: Papers Presented at the Twelfth International Conference on Patristic Studies Held in Oxford, 1995* (ed. Elizabeth A. Livingstone; StPatr 29–33; Leuven: Peeters, 1997), 2:314–18.

²⁰ Andrew E. Arterbury, *Entertaining Angels: Early Christian Hospitality in Its Mediterranean Setting* (New Testament Monographs; Sheffield: Sheffield Phoenix, 2005), 59–71.

²¹ For a complete list of references, see Timothy R. Ashley, *The Book of Numbers* (NICOT; Grand Rapids: Eerdmans, 1993), 239, n. 18.

exclusivist note is sounded. Leviticus 11 introduces the dietary laws that will separate the Israelites from all the peoples surrounding them, reminding all nations of their role as God's uniquely chosen people. Here barriers begin to emerge, establishing boundaries between Jews and Gentiles, particularly in the context of meals (cf. esp. Deut 14:2). As Gene Schramm elaborates, "the effects of practicing kashruth, from a socio-religious standpoint, are clear: the strictures of kashruth make social intercourse between the practicing Jew and the outside world possible only on the basis of a one-sided relationship, and that is on the terms of the one who observes kashruth."[22]

In the historical books (or Former Prophets), a broad cross-section of these different kinds of meals reappears (e.g., Judg 6:21, 14:10; 1 Sam 1:3–8; 1 Kgs 8, 13). During the monarchies, ceremonial feasting accompanies the anointing of kings (1 Sam 9:12–24; 1 Kgs 1:9–10), while new miraculous feeding miracles occur (1 Kgs 17:1–6, 7–24; 2 Kgs 4:38–41, 42–44). NT writers will later present remarkably close counterparts to some of these passages in the context of ministry (see esp. Luke 7:11–17; Mark 6:30–44 and parallels), but with enough differences and other earmarks of authenticity to belie the claim that they were merely created on the basis of parallels from the Hebrew scriptures.[23] More than just expressions of hospitality, meals increasingly establish networks of human allegiance, so that treachery against those with whom one has eaten proves all the more heinous (1 Kgs 13, 18:19). A unique text that cuts against this grain appears in 2 Kgs 6:15–23. After Elisha traps the blinded Arameans in battle and leads them to Samaria, he rebukes the king's desire to kill them and commands instead that food and water be set before them "so that they may eat and drink and go back to their master" (v. 22). This results in a great banquet and the temporary end of raiding parties from the north. Here appears key background material for Jesus' later parable of the Good Samaritan (Luke 10:27–35). Second Chronicles 28:8–15 offers a similar gesture of good will against prisoners of war. At the same time, nothing in either text suggests that any of the Israelites actually ate *with* their enemies.[24]

---

[22] Gene Schramm, "Meal Customs: Jewish Dietary Laws," *ABD* 4:650. Cf. John E. Hartley, *Leviticus* (WBC 4; Dallas: Word, 1992), 163. *Kashrut* is the Hebrew term for "fitness," historically predating the word *kosher* (which is first known from the Talmud) to refer to anything that was ritually pure or clean, especially food. See Geoffrey Wigoder, et al., *The New Encyclopedia of Judaism* (New York: New York University Press, 2002), 214–16, 464, s.v. "Dietary Laws," and "Kosher" respectively.

[23] See Craig L. Blomberg, "The Miracles as Parables," in *Miracles of Jesus* (ed. David Wenham and Craig L. Blomberg; Gospel Perspectives 6; Sheffield: JSOT Press, 1986; repr., Eugene, Or.: Wipf &Stock, 2003), 327–59.

[24] Indeed, in the former passage, T.R. Hobbs (*2 Kings* [WBC 13; Waco: Word, 1985], 78) suspects that Elijah was "more intent upon embarrassing his foes with kindness than sparing them for purely humanitarian reasons."

The Latter Prophets introduce two new, diametrically opposite kinds of banquets. Due to syncretistic influences from the surrounding nations, some Israelites begin to participate in the debauched *marzeah*[25] festivals. Marvin Pope sufficiently captures the spirit of this feast with his definition: "a social and religious institution which included families, owned property, houses for meetings and vineyards for wine supply, was associated with specific deities, and met periodically, perhaps monthly, to celebrate for several days at a stretch with food and drink and sometimes, if not regularly, with sacral sexual orgies."[26] Texts like Amos 4:1, 6:4–7; Jer 16:5; Isa 28:1–9; Hos 4:16–19, 7:1–16; and Ezek 8:7–13, 39:17–20 probably represent prophetic lambastes against such practices in Israel. More edifying are passages that prophesy a coming eschatological, perhaps even Messianic, banquet, beginning with Isa 25:6–9. On the one hand, the prophet stresses that the Lord will prepare this feast of choice meats and fine wines "for all peoples" (v. 6). On the other hand, he immediately adds that Moab, representative of God's enemies, will be trampled down (vv. 10–12). The vision is not only of the salvation of *Israel* and all who join themselves to her, but also of the destruction of her opponents (chs. 26–27).[27] A solitary text bucks the overall trend and again forms the background for a "parable" of Jesus. Isaiah 58:6–12 promises restoration and renewal to the recalcitrant Israelites if they share their food with the hungry, provide the poor wanderer with shelter, clothe the naked and satisfy the needs of the oppressed (cf. Matt 25:31–46). But the end of v. 7 makes it difficult to demonstrate that Isaiah has anyone beyond the people of Israel in view when he explains that they should not "turn away from their own flesh and blood."[28]

The Writings, as with their contents more generally, prove the most amorphous of the three major divisions of the HB with respect to shared meals. Meals of all kinds abound in the Psalms.[29] Particularly famous is Ps

---

[25] The Hebrew root probably meant either "to gather together" or "to cry aloud." See Heinz-Josef Fabry, "מַרְזֵחַ marzēaḥ," *TDOT* 9:10–11.

[26] Marvin H. Pope, "A Divine Banquet at Ugarit," in *The Use of the Old Testament in the New and Other Essays: Studies in Honor of William Franklin Stinespring* (ed. James M. Efird; Durham: Duke, 1972), 193. Cf., in detail, John L. McLaughlin, *The Marzeah in the Prophetic Literature: References and Allusions in Light of the Extra-Biblical Evidence* (VTSup 86; Leiden: Brill, 2001); more briefly, Stefan Schorch, "Die Propheten und der Karneval: Marzeach – Maioumas – Maimuna," *VT* 53 (2003): 397–415.

[27] Walter Brueggemann (*Isaiah* [2 vols.; Westminster Bible Companion; Louisville: Westminster John Knox, 1998], 200) restates these twin emphases: "The work of this God is both positive and negative. The positive is a welcoming feast that signifies the new governance of abundance and well-being. The negative is the elimination of that which threatens and precludes festivals of generosity."

[28] Cf. William H. Brownlee, *Ezekiel 1–19* (WBC 28; Waco: Word, 1986), 78; Iain Duguid, *Ezekiel* (NIV Application Commentary; Grand Rapids: Zondervan, 1999), 91.

[29] For the fullest study, see Stephen A. Reed, "Food in the Psalms," Ph.D. Diss. (Claremont: Claremont Graduate School, 1987).

23, which includes the metaphor of God preparing a table for the shepherd in the presence of his enemies (v. 5). His cup overflows, but it is clear that he is not sharing his bounty with his enemies, but being provided for and protected in their midst. Psalm 41:9 offers a typological backdrop for Judas' betrayal of Jesus (see esp. John 13:18), as "David's" close friend whom he trusted enough to share his bread with him "has lifted up his heel against" him. Job calls down curses on himself if it is not true that he shared bread with the needy (Job 31:17). Ecclesiastes, of course, includes the best of dining as one of the vanities of this life that by itself proves meaningless; while the Song of Songs compares sexual love to an earthly feast. In the right contexts, the satisfaction of both bodily appetites remains beautiful. Contrasting banquets and menus reappear in Daniel and Esther, too, both to save God's people and to judge her enemies. Analogous to 2 Kgs 6:22–23, Prov 25:21–22 commands the Israelite, "If your enemies are hungry, give them food to eat; if they are thirsty, give them water to drink. In doing this, you will heap burning coals on their heads, and the Lord will reward you." Yet even here we are probably not meant to imagine actual table fellowship among enemies, and the second sentence suggests that the acts of kindness are intended to shame them into repentance. R.N. Whybray observes that "these verses are concerned with the harmony and well-being of the local community, which ought to override the selfish interests and feuds of individuals. *Love* of enemies, however, is not prescribed."[30]

2.2. Sharing a Table in Second-Temple Judaism

If shared meals narrated in the HB typically marked off close friends or co-religionists from outsiders, even while acknowledging an ideal age in which the ground-rules would differ, the Second Temple period saw Judaism develop an even clearer nationalist or ethnocentrist emphasis. One might assign a large swath of teaching to the category of avoiding ritual impurity, including that which accrued through table fellowship with those who did not follow the laws of *kashrut*.[31] A huge quantity of traditions on this topic appears in the rabbinica, but this corpus always raises questions, some of

---

[30] R.N. Whybray, *Proverbs* (NCB; London: Pickering; Grand Rapids: Eerdmans, 1994), 367.

[31] In addition to the Levitical dietary laws, *kashrut* came to include regulations concerning ritual handwashing, surfaces on which and containers in which food was served, priestly and Levitical gifts, the land, produce used for tithes, utensils, stoves, ovens, seats, beds and human bodies. See Christine Hayes, "Purity and Impurity, Ritual," in *Encyclopaedia Judaica* (2nd ed., 22 vols.; ed. Fred Skolnik and Michael Berenbaum; Detroit: Macmillan; Jerusalem: Keter, 2007), 16:746–56; Gedalyahu Alon, *Jews, Judaism and the Classical World: Studies in Jewish History in the Times of the Second Temple and Talmud* (Jerusalem: Magnes, 1977), 146–73; and the ancient sources cited in both.

them unanswerable, about the date of the origins of the traditions prior to their written forms in the early Christian period. Because we have plenty of material to work with in the unambiguously pre-Christian Second-Temple Jewish literature, for this section we will limit ourselves to this corpus for data.[32]

Within Second Temple wisdom literature, Sirach extends the dangers of eating with the wicked, enunciated in the biblical book of Proverbs, to include dining with another person's spouse (9:9), the powerful (13:8–13), and the stingy (14:10). The extensive focus in Sir 31:12–32:2 on drinking wine in moderation rather than excess, if not a response to symposia, at least continues the warnings against *marzeoth*.[33] Tobit proves exemplary in commending almsgiving to the poor and needy, but 4:17 shows that, even in a context of enjoining charitable giving, feeding the hungry and clothing the naked, one can read, "but give none [of your bread] to sinners." The whole plot line of the book of Judith turns on its heroine's insistence that God was about to judge his people at the hands of the Assyrians for breaking his dietary laws, which is why (she claims) she is defecting to the enemy. Instead, her obedience to those same laws allows her to bring her own "lunch bag," which turns out to be her vehicle for hiding the severed head of the Assyrian commander, Holofernes, after she slays him when he thinks he is going to seduce her (Jdt 10:5, 10–13; 12:5–20; 13:6–11)! The Additions to Esther revise the canonical text so that where the queen originally does eat of the king's food, some of which was not "kosher," now she does not (see esp. 14:17). The books of the Maccabees, finally, repeatedly highlight the faithful Jews' refusal to eat unclean food even when they had to die at the hands of the Seleucid rulers as the consequence (1 Macc 1:62–63; 2 Macc 6:18–7:42; 3 Macc 3:2–5; 4 Macc 5–18).

In other Second Temple literature one finds the *Letter of Aristeas* with its classic and expansive justification of the Jewish purity laws.[34] *Jubilees* 22:16 has God explicitly command Jacob, "separate yourself from the gentiles, and do not eat with them, and do not perform deeds like theirs. And do not become associates of theirs, because their deeds are defiled, and all of

---

[32] Thus we will lay to one side a consideration of the Pharisaic groups known as *haburot* or *haberim*, known only from the rabbinic literature. For the key debate about their nature, see Jacob Neusner, "Two Pictures of the Pharisees: Philosophical Circle or Eating Club," *AThR* 64 (1982): 525–38.

[33] See further Hans V. Kieweler, "Benehmen bei Tisch," in *Der Einzelne und seine Gemeinschaft bei Ben Sira* (ed. Renate Egger-Wenzel and Ingrid Krammer; BZAW 270; Berlin: De Gruyter, 1998), 191–215.

[34] This pagan banquet may in fact be portrayed as a symposium. But the upshot of its discourse section is to demonstrate the differences between Jewish and Gentile practices and the superiority of the former. Cf. further Sandra R. Shimoff, "Banquets: The Limits of Hellenization," *JSJ* 27 (1996): 440–52, esp. 445.

their ways are contaminated, and despicable, and abominable."[35] *Joseph and Aseneth* depicts the two young people's initial refusal to be given to each other in marriage in large part because of their respective religions' incompatible laws concerning table fellowship. Once Aseneth converts to Judaism and agrees to keep a "kosher" house, the wedding can proceed. Other Second Temple texts expand on the vision of an eschatological or Messianic banquet in the future.[36] In *1 En.* 62:14, the righteous will eat with the Son of Man forever. In *2 En.* 42:5, the righteous dead can look forward to "dinner with delightful enjoyments and riches that cannot be measured, and joy and happiness in eternal light and life." In *2 Bar.* 29:3–4, "the Anointed One will begin to be revealed." Then "Behemoth will reveal itself from its place and Leviathan will come from the sea, the two great monsters which I created on the fifth day of creation and which I shall have kept until that time. And they will be nourishment for all who are left."

The Dead Sea Scrolls likewise develop the twin themes of avoiding impurity and anticipating a Messianic banquet.[37] All participants at the Qumran community's communal meals had to remain in a state of ritual purity (1QS 5:13); some texts insist on purification baths before every meal (4Q513, 4Q514). Just as the unrighteous may not eat these Essenes' fare, neither may the sectarians sell their food to the Gentiles (CD 12:8–10) or eat any impure food themselves (12:11–15), including even items that Gentiles have merely touched (4QMMT 6–11)! Both the *Rule of the Community* and the *Damascus Document* stress separation from all kinds of sinners (e.g., 1QS 5:2, 10–11, 14–18; CD 6:14–18). Even the Qumran hymns regularly warn against the danger of sin and sinners (e.g., 1QH 7:21–23; 10:10–11, 31–36; 12:7–21, etc.), with one passage closely parallel to the appropriation of Ps 41:9 in John 13:18: "[all those who have ea]ten my bread have lifted their heel against me, and all those joined to my Council have mocked me with wicked lips" (1QH 13:23b–24). That such betrayal occurred by those who had shared table fellowship made it that much more traitorous. By the time one reaches the War Scroll, full-fledged enmity exists between the sectarians and the Gentiles on almost every page, with the ultimate goal the extermination of "the sons of darkness." The sectarians then looked forward to a joyous Messianic banquet, but conspicuously absent are any other peoples

---

[35] Interestingly, in the larger context of this passage it becomes clear that it is the ritual impurity more than the immoral behavior of the Gentiles that defiles them. Cf. Bolyki, *Jesu Tischgemeinschaften*, 197.

[36] Cf. further John F. Priest, "A Note on the Messianic Banquet," in *The Messiah: Developments in Early Judaism and Christianity* (ed. James H. Charlesworth; Minneapolis: Fortress, 1992), 222–38.

[37] See, respectively, Michael Newton, *The Concept of Purity at Qumran and in the Letters of Paul* (SNTSMS 53; Cambridge: Cambridge University Press, 1985); and Lawrence H. Schiffman, "Communal Meals at Qumran," *RevQ* 10 (1979): 45–56.

or any other kinds of Jews. Even in the Age to Come, the dinner proceeds according to a carefully monitored agenda of actions, beginning with those highest in the hierarchy and most ritually pure (1QSa 2:17–22).[38]

Second Temple Judaism thus, in many respects, saw the drawing of even sharper boundaries between pious Jews and unclean outsiders. Table fellowship could create intimate friendship, so it was increasingly reserved for those a person deemed the right kind of companions – who ate the right kinds of food. The Dead Sea sectarians were clearly the most extreme outgrowth of this trend, but it was by no means limited to them. Basic to the rationale behind this behavior was the conviction that the power of the unclean to defile the clean far outstripped the ability of the clean to sanctify the unholy.[39]

2.3. Greco-Roman Symposia

Walter Burkert defines a quite different kind of meal with deep roots in the history of Hellenistic culture.

> The symposium is an organization of all-male groups, aristocratic and egalitarian at the same time, which affirm their identity through ceremonialized drinking. Prolonged drinking is separate from the meal proper; there is wine mixed in a krater for equal distribution; the participants, adorned with wreaths, lie on couches. The symposium has private, political, and cultural dimensions: it is the place of *euphrosyne* [good cheer], of music, poetry, and other forms of entertainment; it is bound up with sexuality, especially homosexuality; it guarantees the social control of the *polis* [city] by the aristocrats. It is a dominating social form in Greek civilization from Homer onwards and well beyond the Hellenistic period.[40]

Fairly homogenous groupings of people typically characterized such gatherings; their egalitarian nature usually was limited to a certain group of peers. Special banqueting halls were reserved for these gathering; reclining typically took place on cushions arranged to form a square-shaped U. Originally a part of pre-classical Greek village communal meals and special gatherings to prepare soldiers for battle, the symposium became in classical days "highly valued" and "widely practiced at many levels ... as occasions

---

[38] Cf. further Lawrence H. Schiffman, "Non-Jews in the Dead Sea Scrolls," in *The Quest for Context and Meaning: Studies in Biblical Intertextuality in Honor of James A. Sanders* (ed. Craig A. Evans and Shemaryahu Talmon; Biblical Interpretation Series 28; Leiden: Brill, 1997), 153–71; Aharon Shemesh, "The Origins of the Laws of Separatism: Qumran Literature and Rabbinic Halacha," *RevQ* 18 (1997): 223–41.

[39] See further Blomberg, *Contagious Holiness*, 65–86, and the primary and secondary literature there cited.

[40] Walter Burkert, "Oriental Symposia: Contrasts and Parallels," in *Dining in a Classical Context* (ed. William J. Slater; Ann Arbor: University of Michigan Press, 1991), 7.

for philosophical, political, and moral discussions and their reflections in poetic and prose literature."[41]

In the classical period, the most famous and restrained form of symposia were narrated by Plato (*Symposium*) and Xenophon (also *Symposium*). The participation of Socrates and other philosophers led to the post-meal time entertainment portion of the symposium largely limited to refined, intellectual discourse. In later times Plutarch would include among his list of acceptable topics for conversation whether or not the host should arrange the seating of his guests, why places at table acquired degrees of honor, why it was the custom to invite many guests to a wedding banquet but not a good idea to do so for ordinary symposia, whether or not the music of flute girls afforded appropriate after-dinner entertainment, and whether or not it was good to deliberate over wine (*Mor.* 1.615, 1.619, 4.666, 5.678, 7.710, 7.714). But these were the exceptions, not the norm, even in the classical age.

During the Hellenistic period, symposia increasingly deteriorated into showcases of gluttony and drunkenness (Athenaeus, *Deipn.* 614a–615a). One example occurs even in Plato's *Symposium* 223B: "So Agathon was getting up in order to seat himself by Socrates, when suddenly a great crowd of revelers arrived at the door, which they found just opened for some one who was going out. They marched straight into the party and seated themselves: the whole place was in an uproar and, losing all order, they were forced to drink a vast amount of wine." Eventually, Greek and Roman writers would compose satires about the symposia, attesting to their notoriety (Petronius, *Satyricon*; Juvenal, *Sat.* 5; Martial, *Epigr.* 60).

The Roman *cena* or *convivium* was at times a bit less hedonistic,[42] not least because of the controversial first-century participation of the "new Roman women"[43] (somewhat liberated wives in well-to-do families who accompanied their husbands to dinner), whose presence did away with the courtesans previously provided for the sexual favors of the otherwise all-male diners. But these symposia never became as prominent and, even when celebrants did not become totally inebriated or engaged in public sex, drinking and merriment remained the primary purpose of the gatherings.[44] As we turn to the Gospels, we will have to inquire if there really are any signs

---

[41] Nicholas R. E. Fisher, "Greek Associations, Symposia, and Clubs," in *Civilization of the Ancient Mediterranean: Greece and Rome* (3 vols.; ed. Michael R. Grant and M. Rachel Kitzinger; New York: Scribner, 1988), 2:1167.

[42] Nicholas R. E. Fisher, "Roman Associations, Dinner Parties and Clubs," in *Civilization of the Ancient Mediterranean: Greece and Rome* (3 vols.; ed. Michael R. Grant and M. Rachel Kitzinger; New York: Scribner, 1988), 1199–1225.

[43] On which, see esp. Bruce W. Winter, *Roman Wives, Roman Widows: The Appearance of New Women and the Pauline Communities* (Grand Rapids: Eerdmans, 2003).

[44] Cf. esp. Francois Lissarrague, *The Aesthetics of the Greek Banquet: Images of Wine and Ritual* (trans. Andrew Szegedy-Maszak; Princeton: Princeton University Press, 1990).

to confirm the claims that Jesus' meals with sinners are being portrayed as symposia.

3. Jesus' Meals with Sinners: A Search for Background

Twelve passages in the Synoptic Gospels potentially merit attention under this heading. Space precludes a full-fledged analysis of each of them, so we will focus on the most detailed and relevant passages at greater length and pass very rapidly over the rest. We will proceed from episodes most explicitly depicting Jesus dining with the most notorious sinners and outcasts of his society to those which have a more implicit bearing on our topic. We will also move through the key passages roughly in an order that progresses from those with the strongest cases for authenticity to those that are not quite as secure. With the vast majority of scholars, we will assume Markan priority and, more tentatively, some form of the Q-hypothesis.[45] The texts in this section come from Mark, Q, and L, so the theme is multiply attested. In the following section texts are also present from M. We shall note points of coherence as we proceed through the texts.

3.1. More Explicit Texts

3.1.1. Levi's Party (Mark 2:13–17 and parallels)

On form-critical grounds, the climactic saying (v. 17) of this pronouncement story becomes the most demonstrably historical core of the passage.[46] While there are many settings in which calling sinners rather than the righteous could apply, the immediate context of a group of tax collectors and their friends fits aptly.[47] These were the toll collectors or revenue contractors of their day, Jewish middlemen working for the Roman *publicani* and viewed by many other Jews as traitors to their nation. To the extent that they made a decent living for themselves skimming extra profits off the top of their take, they would have formed part of the "up and out" (even if not

---

[45] See further Craig L. Blomberg, "The Synoptic Problem: Where We Stand at the Start of a New Century," in *Rethinking the Synoptic Problem* (ed. David A. Black and David Beck; Grand Rapids: Baker, 2001), 17–40. On Q, see Darrell L. Bock, "Questions About Q," in *Rethinking the Synoptic Problem* (ed. David A. Black and David Beck; Grand Rapids: Baker, 2001), 41–64. Bock's essay supports the presence of Q, but questions whether we can be sure it was a single written source.

[46] See throughout Arland J. Hultgren, *Jesus and His Adversaries: The Form and Function of the Conflict Stories in the Synoptic Tradition* (Minneapolis: Augsburg, 1979).

[47] *Contra* Rudolf Bultmann (*History of the Synoptic Tradition* [Oxford: Blackwell, 1963; repr., Peabody: Hendrickson, 1994], 18) who deduced that the loose connection between v. 17 and v. 15 meant that the latter was a "story" created to fit the former.

"down and out") from the standpoint of the orthodox Jewish leadership. Many self-respecting Pharisees and scribes would not have associated with them in table fellowship as Jesus is described as doing (*b. Bek.* 31a, *t. Demai* 3:4).[48] Yet there is nothing anachronistic or out of place in the episode that could not have happened in his day. The juxtaposition of "tax collectors" with the generalized term "sinners" shows the paradigmatic nature of that occupation as representing immorality and treason against Israel, not to mention the resulting ritual impurity.[49] In the Jewish literature,

> Tax collectors were grouped with murderers and robbers. To avoid loss, one could deceive a tax collector. The word of a tax gatherer could not be trusted, nor could his oath be believed. As a consequence, he could not testify in a court of law or hold a communal office. Money in the pocket of a tax collector was considered stolen property.[50]

A tax collector, grateful for Jesus' calling him, would have naturally reciprocated by offering hospitality.[51] Subsequent Pharisaic criticism does not require the Jewish leaders to have been eavesdropping on the banquet, though the open-air courtyards of many homes might have made it possible for them to do so had they so desired (cf. *b. Taʿan.* 23ab).[52] The early church was scarcely known for its high tolerance of the most notoriously sinful of their society, so discontinuity with subsequent Christianity likewise emerges. Still, this is not a portrait, as in Sanders' reconstruction of the historical Jesus, in which Christ accepts sinners without any hint of repentance. Mark 2:15b explicitly declares that "there were many who *followed* him," employing a verb regularly used in the Synoptics for discipleship, of at least some tentative or initial form, including as recently as in Mark 1:20.[53] So there is continuity with the early church as well. Multiple attestation and

---

[48] When we lack unambiguous pre-Christian Jewish documentation of various practices, we will cite the oldest relevant rabbinic literature, recognizing that if the traditions behind the documentation do not go back to Jesus' time in oral form, then the points they support may need to be modified.

[49] For all of these points, see Fritz Herrenbrück, *Jesus und die Zöllner: historische und neutestamentlich-exegetische Untersuchungen* (WUNT 2.41; Tübingen: Mohr, 1990), esp. 231–34. *M. Ṭehar.* 7:6 begins, "If taxgatherers entered a house [all that is within it] becomes unclean."

[50] Frank Stern, *A Rabbi Looks at Jesus' Parables* (Lanham: Rowman, 2006), 141, citing *m. Ned.* 3:4, *m. B. Qam.* 10:1–2, *m. Ṭehar.* 7:6, among others.

[51] This makes unlikely the view that one or more of the Evangelists envision Jesus hosting Levi and his friends at *Jesus'* place of lodging. Rightly, David M. May, "Mark 2:15: The Home of Jesus or Levi?" *NTS* 39 (1993): 147–49.

[52] Robert H. Gundry, *Mark: A Commentary on His Apology for the Cross* (Grand Rapids: Eerdmans, 1993), 129. Cf. R. K. Harrison, "House," *NIDBA* 244. *Contra* many (e. g., Adela Yarbro Collins, *Mark* [Hermeneia; Minneapolis: Fortress, 2007], 192–93) who have argued that such a scene would have proved unlikely.

[53] Indeed, in the Gospels ἀκολουθέω is used exclusively for Jesus' disciples and never for his opponents. See James R. Edwards, *The Gospel According to Mark* (Pillar New

multiple forms both reinforce authenticity, as the Q-parable of the children in the marketplace (Matt 1:16–19; Luke 7:31–35) generalizes to depict Jesus' frequent involvement in such table fellowship.

If ever there were a context in the Gospels where we might expect Hellenistic influence in general or the appearance of a symposium in particular, it would be with a meal involving well-to-do turncoats working for Rome. And just possibly that is what we are meant to envision. But Mark offers no actual positive signs of this kind of meal. The verbs for dining in v. 15 come from the verbs κατάκειμαι and συνανάκειμαι, which mean "reclining" and "reclining together with," respectively. But first-century Judaism had come to embrace reclining at table for a variety of festive meals, not just symposia, and at times these verbs and their cognates did not refer to a literal posture at all, but merely to dining (e.g., *m. Ber.* 6:5, *m. Neg.* 13:9, *Prot. Jas.* 18:2). For whatever reason, καθίζω, the standard term for sitting, though found 48 times in the NT, *never* appears in the context of table fellowship, even though we know that Jews regularly sat for ordinary meals.[54] So nothing can be inferred about the nature of a given meal simply from the presence of verbs that in other contexts sometimes referred to literal reclining.[55] Indeed, R. T. France suspects that Mark saw in this special meal "a symbol of the messianic banquet," but with a guest list that was "not at all what most Jews would have expected."[56]

What *is* striking is that Jesus favors these moral outcasts with his presence, rather than becoming contaminated by them, a feature not found in conventional symposia *or* Jewish feasting.[57] Indeed, v. 17 suggests that he is in the process of trying spiritually to cleanse the unclean, just like a medical doctor attempts to bring physical healing to a patient. Matthew 9:13a ("I desire

---

Testament Commentary; Grand Rapids: Eerdmans, 2002), 81. Cf. Dieter Lührmann, *Das Markusevangelium* (Tübingen: Mohr, 1987), 59.

[54] Indeed, its only occurrence in the context of any form of eating appears in 1 Cor 10:7, where it reproduces the LXX translation of Exod 32:6.

[55] This point cannot be stressed too much, because many who support the symposium hypothesis often infer the presence of such a meal from the use of these and related verbs alone. For the wider use of reclining, see Hugo Blümner, *The Home Life of the Ancient Greeks* (trans. Alice Zimmern; 1893; repr., Whitefish, Mont.: Kessinger, 2007), 203; Shemuel Safrai, "Home and Family," in *The Jewish People in the First Century: Historical Geography, Political History, Social, Cultural and Religious Life and Institutions* (ed. Shemuel Safrai and Menahem Stern; vol. 2, section 1 of *Compendia Rerum Iudaicarum ad Novum Testamentum*; Assen: Van Gorcum, 1976), 736; David Noy, "The Sixth Hour is the Mealtime for Scholars: Jewish Meals in the Roman World," in *Meals in a Social Context: Aspects of the Communal Meal in the Hellenistic and Roman World* (ed. Inge Nielsen and Hanne S. Nielsen; Aarhus: Aarhus University Press, 1998), 138.

[56] R. T. France, *The Gospel of Mark* (NIGTC; Grand Rapids: Eerdmans, 2002), 131.

[57] Cf. Joel Marcus, *Mark 1–8* (AB 27; New York: Doubleday, 2000), 231: "Jesus is not defiled by his contact with impurity but instead vanquishes it through the eschatological power active in him."

mercy and not sacrifice") provides a plausible, scriptural motive for such an objective. Eugene Boring summarizes, "To become a follower of Jesus is to be incorporated into an inclusive group that eats and drinks together in an atmosphere of celebration."[58] This holds true even if, as many have argued, vv. 14 and/or 15 were brought together with vv. 16 and/or 17 together or individually, at some stage of the text's tradition history,[59] because the main points enumerated here all emerge from within v. 15.

3.1.2. A Glutton and a Drunkard (Q 7:31–35)

The little parable of the children in the marketplace appears in similar contexts in both Matthew and Luke – chapters in which Jesus is commenting on John the Baptist and comparing himself to his forerunner. The wording is extremely similar in both Gospels, making a reconstruction of the probable Q-form relatively straightforward. Most would prefer Luke's "children" to Matthew's more theologically motivated "deeds" as what originally would vindicate Wisdom in the last line of the account.[60] The parity in the treatments of John and Jesus, both in the parable proper and in the appended logia, could suggest that the two individuals were on a par with each other.[61] Early Christianity, eager to exalt Jesus and play down John, would not likely have invented such parity. Nor would they have readily characterized Jesus as a "glutton and a drunkard."[62] At the same time, despite this caricature of his behavior, the generalization does go on accurately to portray Jesus as a "friend of tax collectors and 'sinners,'" cohering closely with the specific example of banqueting with Levi and his associates, which we have already discussed.[63] The expression also passes the test of "embarrassment" with flying colors. In terms of continuity and discontinuity with Judaism, even the accurate portions of this depiction of Jesus – eating and drinking with sinners and their unclean food (or hands, or utensils, etc.) – go beyond what many upstanding religious teachers would have found appropriate (cf.,

---

[58] M. Eugene Boring, *Mark* (NTL; Louisville: Westminster John Knox, 2006), 81.

[59] So, e. g., Karl Kertelge, *Markusevangelium* (NEchtB 2; Würzburg: Echter, 1994), 33.

[60] So, e. g., James M. Robinson, et al., *The Critical Edition of Q* (Hermeneia; Minneapolis: Fortress, 2000), 140–48.

[61] Craig L. Blomberg, *Interpreting the Parables* (Downers Grove: InterVarsity, 1990), 210; Howard C. Kee, "Jesus: A Glutton and a Drunkard," *NTS* 42 (1996): 383.

[62] John Nolland, *Luke 1–9:20* (WBC 35a; Dallas: Word, 1989), 346.

[63] See esp. Mary J. Marshall, "Jesus: Glutton and Drunkard?" *JSHJ* 3 (2005): 47–60. Dale C. Allison, Jr. (*Jesus of Nazareth: Millenarian Prophet* [Minneapolis: Fortress, 1998], 104–5, 172–72) thinks John and Jesus are paired more because of their similarities, but this loses the dynamic of the parable – the children won't play games on either end of the spectrum. He rightly labels the parable's portrait of Jesus a caricature, but caricatures typically start with and then exaggerate an element of truth, rather than pointing to the opposite of that truth! For the kind of asceticism that Jesus here eschews, see *Gos. Thom.* 27.

e. g., *m. Ṭehar.* 2:2, *b. Soṭah* 22a, *t. Mak.* 3:7, *t. Demai* 2:2, 11, 15; 2:20–3:10; not to mention numerous Qumran texts already cited above).[64] Yet the theme of the overall and ultimate rejection of both spokesmen for God by the majority of the Jewish populace, and by their leadership in particular, closely matches the historical realities of first century attitudes about separation, and official reactions to claims made to have independent authority, that no one disputes.[65] Even the novel interpretation of Thomas Phillips, which reads the closing line as conventional Greco-Roman wisdom still on the lips of John's and Jesus' critics,[66] ably illustrates a counter-cultural reaction to typical attitudes. Such a reading perfectly satisfies the criteria of continuity and discontinuity with contemporary backgrounds.

The more one focuses on the "tax collectors and 'sinners'," the more one can make the case that Hellenistic influence may have led these outcasts to host various symposia. "Playing the flute" *does* recall one of the common forms of entertainment at these Greco-Roman banquets (Plato, *Symp.* 176E, Xen., *Symp.* 2.1, Plut. *Mor.* 7.710–11). But flute players also regularly accompanied Jewish wedding feasts (and therefore presumably the eschatological banquet that Revelation would later call the "wedding feast of the Lamb" as well), so there is no way to narrow down the kinds of "partying" in view here. Nor need we choose between Smith and Corley, who see merely unjustified slander, and the majority who insist that Jesus did fraternize with his society's disreputable. As Rudolf Schnackenburg determines, "Underlying the reproach are Jesus' meals with 'tax collectors and sinners' (see [Matt] 9:10). The crass expressions used reflect denunciations in leading Jewish circles and are actually traceable to Jesus' days on earth."[67] That God's wisdom will be justified despite Jesus' unconventional practices suggests that his "partying" does not render him impure. He does not shun the unclean and includes even the most morally impure among those with whom he is willing to associate.[68]

---

[64] See the texts cited in the discussion in § 2.2. Israel Abrahams, *Studies in Pharisaism and the Gospels* (Library of Biblical Studies; 1924; repr., New York: Ktav, 1967), 55. For these and related references, see Jacob Neusner, "The Fellowship (חבורה) in the Second Jewish Commonwealth," *HTR* 53 (1960): 125–42.

[65] "Result: vv. 16–19d *may* indeed come from Jesus" (Ulrich Luz, *Matthew 8–20* [trans. James E. Crouch; Hermeneia; Minneapolis: Fortress, 2001], 148).

[66] Thomas E. Phillips, "'Will the Wise Person Get Drunk?' The Background of the Human Wisdom in Luke 7:35 and Matthew 11:19," *JBL* 127 (2008): 385–96.

[67] Rudolf Schnackenburg, *The Gospel of Matthew* (trans. Robert R. Barr; Grand Rapids: Eerdmans, 2002), 107.

[68] Jonathan Klawans (*Impurity and Sin in Ancient Judaism* [Oxford: Oxford University Press, 2000]) thoroughly discusses ritual and moral impurity in the various strands of ancient Jewish literature, concluding that a stricter separation of the two arose in the rabbinic eras than before and that John the Baptist and Jesus refused to compartmentalize the two but greatly prioritized the latter.

3.1.3. A "Sinner in the City" (Luke 7:36–50)

Jesus' compassion for outcasts of many different kinds – women, lepers, other sick persons, Samaritans, Gentiles, and the poor – forms a major emphasis within Luke's writing. So we cannot argue that the specific pericopae of Jesus' meals with sinners in this Gospel fail to fit the Evangelist's redactional tendencies. But there are plenty of other signs of authenticity that emerge. In this passage, we find a woman who appears at a banquet hosted by Simon the Pharisee. Despite noteworthy parallels with the account of Jesus' anointing by Mary of Bethany (Matt 26:6–13; Mark 14:3–9; John 12:1–8), this passage should probably be viewed as a separate event.[69] But the criterion of multiple forms, even though not multiple attestation, is still satisfied. Alternately, a fair cross-section of those interpreters who believe that one original event lies behind all four of these accounts finds the Lucan version overall the most primitive. Then one could appeal to multiple attestation in support of authenticity, especially when Mark, John and Luke are viewed as largely independent developments of that one generating event.[70]

The unnamed woman here is never called a prostitute *per se*, but rather one who was viewed "in the city" as a "sinner." Theoretically, she could have been "the wife of someone with a dishonorable occupation," "a woman in debt," "an adulteress," or a person who was ill, disabled or in regular contact with Gentiles. Still, prostitution was the most probable "occupation" from which she would have incurred this stigma.[71] Obviously, the woman is not a formal courtesan, as regularly encountered in symposia. No self-respecting Pharisee would plan that kind of banquet.[72] Nor does Luke describe her with any of the standard terms for a *professional* prostitute – πόρνη, κοινή, πανκοινή, or ἑταίρα. The woman, moreover, engages in none of the other activities that symposia "escorts" typically

---

[69] See esp. I. Howard Marshall, *The Gospel of Luke* (NIGTC 3; Grand Rapids: Eerdmans, 1978), 304–7. Cf. Nolland, *Luke 1–9:20*, 352. For a classic example of how one can bypass this debate, assuming (rather than demonstrating) that Luke dramatically altered Mark, and logically derive quite different conclusions, see J. Patrick Mullen, *Dining with Pharisees* (Interfaces; Collegeville, Minn.: Liturgical, 2004).

[70] As, e. g., in Robert Holst ("The One Anointing of Jesus: Another Application of the Form-Critical Method," *JBL* 95 [1976]: 435–46), who determined that the narrative of the woman's act was best preserved in Luke, that the actual responses by Jesus and others was more literally preserved in Mark and John, but that the theological intention of Jesus' final declarations was best brought out, again, by Luke.

[71] Barbara E. Reid, "'Do You See This Woman?' Luke 7:36–50 as a Paradigm for Feminist Hermeneutics," *BR* 40 (1995): 43; cf. Darrell L. Bock, *Luke* (2 vols.; Baker Exegetical Commentary on the New Testament 3a–b; Grand Rapids: Baker, 1994–96), 1:695.

[72] Stuart L. Love, "Women and Men at Hellenistic Symposia Meals in Luke," in *Modeling Early Christianity: Social-Scientific Studies of the New Testament in Context* (ed. Philip F. Esler; London: Routledge, 1995), 206.

performed – drinking, reclining, dancing, playing music, and the like.[73] But her behavior remains scandalous. Joel Green affirms that "letting her hair down in this setting would have been on a par with appearing topless in public, for example. She would have appeared to be fondling Jesus' feet, like a prostitute or slave girl accustomed to providing sexual favors."[74] The portrait remained shocking for Jew and Christian alike.

But then is it even credible in an early first-century Galilean Jewish setting? Those who see a symposium here liken the woman to the stock figure of an uninvited guest who can disrupt the banquet in various ways. But these figures differed from the prostitutes; they provided entertainment or participated in the philosophical debates. It is better to follow Charles Cosgrove, who demonstrates that the woman's unbound hair, in and of itself, would not always have been as scandalous as Green suggests,[75] even if the total package of her behavior proves highly suggestive. Moreover, this woman most likely had prior knowledge that Jesus would be present at this gathering.[76] Jesus declares her behavior to represent pure love that flowed from saving faith (vv. 47–50); her sins "have already been forgiven" (the perfect passive ἀφέωνται – vv. 47, 48).[77] The imagery of the forgiveness of debts in the little parable of vv. 41–43 could suggest the background of the Jewish year of Jubilee (Lev 25:8–55).[78] Her desire to "crash" this party and lavish her thanks on Jesus then becomes perfectly understandable. Her ability to do so stems from the access the public had to the open courtyards or to the open doors in more formal banqueting rooms (recall above, § 2.3 and 3.1.1). As the guests reclined, their feet would have extended out from the cushions so that an "intruder" would have encountered that part of their body first. Though admittedly speculative, John Nolland's reconstruction shows one plausible way the subsequent set of events could have unfolded:

> The accidental fall of tears on feet begins a chain reaction: with nothing at hand to remove the offending tears, the woman makes use of her let-down hair; the intimate proximity thereby created leads to a release of affectionate gratitude expressed in kissing the feet which have just been cleaned from the dust of journey in this unique and probably unintended manner; and the anointing perfume, no doubt intended for

---

[73] Reid, "'Do You See This Woman?'," 44–45. Cf. François Bovon, *Luke 1* (trans. Christine M. Thomas; Hermeneia; Minneapolis: Fortress, 2002), 293.

[74] Joel B. Green, *The Gospel of Luke* (NICNT; Grand Rapids: Eerdmans, 1997), 310.

[75] Charles H. Cosgrove, "A Woman's Unbound Hair in the Greco-Roman World, with Special Reference to the Story of the 'Sinful Woman' in Luke 7:36–50," *JBL* 124 (2005): 675–92.

[76] John J. Kilgallen, "Forgiveness of Sins (Luke 7:36–50)," *NovT* 40 (1998): 108.

[77] John J. Kilgallen, "Faith and Forgiveness: Luke 7,36–50," *RB* 112 (2005): 372–84.

[78] Sharon H. Ringe, *Jesus, Liberation, and the Biblical Jubilee: Images for Ethics and Christology* (OBT; Philadelphia: Fortress, 1985), 66–71.

the head (since only this has a place in Jewish custom) but finding no ready access thereto, is spent upon that part of Jesus' body with which the woman has already made intimate contact.[79]

Luke wants the tears themselves to be understood as reflecting "repentant sorrow for her sinfulness," given the consistent meaning of κλαίω earlier in his narrative (6:21, 25; 7:13, 32),[80] which makes her acceptance by the dinner guests more imaginable. The comparatively gentle rebuke of Simon the Pharisee implied by the parable in which he is likened to a less indebted sinner who has nevertheless had his sins forgiven, too, further bespeaks authenticity. Thus the passage scandalizes Jewish and early Christian sensibilities, while fitting into an early period in Jesus' ministry in an intelligible Jewish context when hostilities against the Jewish leaders had not yet escalated.[81] Yet, according to the moral intuitions of many Jews *and* Christians, Jesus' allowing this potentially sexual advance implicated him in outright sin, not merely ritual impurity.[82] From Luke's perspective, however, he remains sinless and she becomes ritually and spiritually whole.[83] He also shows his authority to make judgments about what sin and forgiveness are, an idea running through several of these scenes, including the next one.

3.1.4. Zacchaeus Short-Changed? (Luke 19:1–10)

Only Zacchaeus among the tax collectors in the Gospels is called an ἀρχιτελώνης (a *chief* toll collector). Even without Luke's explicit adjective (v. 2), therefore, we should have imagined him to be "rich," in part at least due to an even greater degree of extortionary earnings than his subordinates amassed. Jesus' actions would have thus shocked his onlookers all the more.[84] Before hearing any word that could reflect Zacchaeus' state of mind or heart, Jesus invites himself to this man's home for dinner. He is thereby requesting the conventional hospitality owed to traveling strangers, but without showing the least concern for Zacchaeus' perpetual ritual impurity

---

[79] Nolland, *Luke 1–9:20*, 354–55. Similarly, Marshall, *Luke*, 308–9.

[80] John P. Heil, *The Meal Scenes in Luke-Acts: An Audience-Oriented Approach* (SBLMS 52; Atlanta: Society of Biblical Literature, 1999), 46.

[81] A similar line of reasoning is adopted by Kathleen E. Corley, "The Anointing of Jesus in the Synoptic Tradition: An Argument for Authenticity," *JSHJ* 1 (2003): 61–72. In keeping with her earlier work, however, Corley insists that the woman was a respectable person, not a notoriously sinful one like a prostitute.

[82] Louise Schottroff's argument from silence (*The Parables of Jesus* [Minneapolis: Fortress, 2006], 147) that the woman does not necessarily give up her sinful lifestyle seems weak, especially in light of Jesus' frequent calls to repentance elsewhere.

[83] Cf. Thorsten Moritz, "Dinner Talk and Ideology in Luke: The Role of the Sinners," *EuroJTh* 5 (1996): 57.

[84] "To stay in such a person's home was tantamount to sharing in his sin" (Marshall, *Luke*, 697).

due to his immoral and traitorous lifestyle. Perhaps for that very reason, Zacchaeus is so humbled that, when the entourage has reached his home, he announces that he is giving half of his goods to the poor and restoring fourfold to those whom he has defrauded – good signs of genuine repentance (v. 8; cf. John the Baptist's charge to tax collectors in 3:13, unpacking his call to repentance in 3:2; around the maximum the law advised for recompense from stealing, Exod 22:1). Jesus' holiness, not Zacchaeus' past immorality, has rubbed off on his counterpart.

This "reverse contagion" clearly satisfies the two dissimilarity portions of the criterion of historical plausibility. The realism of a chief tax collector having defrauded his countrymen in this fashion coheres with the ancient reputation attached to toll collectors. Whether in the Latin West or the Greek East, whether in pre- or post-Christian Judaism, τελῶναι are regularly grouped with other notorious criminals or sinners, and most commonly thieves and smugglers.[85] Luke's use of the passage to epitomize the heart of Jesus' ministry – to seek and to save the lost (v. 10) – coheres with early Christianity as well. Zacchaeus must repent, but the way Jesus elicits this response is by taking the initiative to associate with him in ways guaranteed to bring down the wrath of the conservative religious insiders, indeed, of much of the populace as a whole. The scene has been re-enacted countless times in church history by those who have attempted to emulate Jesus in this respect. All four prongs of the double dissimilarity and similarity criterion are thus again satisfied.[86]

A common, recent objection to this interpretation indeed demonstrates how hard it is for many to accept such countercultural behavior on Jesus' part. Perhaps Zacchaeus is *not* repenting in this passage; perhaps his declaration in v. 8 is a *vindication* of his typical behavior. The present tenses (δίδωμι and ἀποδίδωμι) by themselves read more naturally as ongoing, current actions, not as futurist presents promising what Zacchaeus will do in the near future.[87] But this interpretation founders on the first-class condition of v. 8b ("if I have defrauded anyone"). While first-class (real) conditions do not necessarily express true statements, they do present them from the

---

[85] Herrenbrück, *Jesus und die Zöllner*, 72–89, and the texts there printed. See, e. g., Demosth. 21.133, Diog. Laertius, 4.46, Poll. 6.128, Xenon. 3.390, Yalq 1.182, among others. Of those J. Gibson ("Hoi Telōnai Kai Hai Pornai," *JTS* 32 [1981]: 430, n. 1) notes, see esp. *Toh.* 7:6, *Derek Erez* 2 and *Ned.* 3:4.

[86] From a more conventional form-critical perspective, see François Bovon (*Das Evangelium nach Lukas* [3 vols.; EKKNT 3; Düsseldorf: Benziger; Neukirchen-Vluyn: Neukirchener Verlag, 1989–2001], 3:271), who, even after stripping away what he believes to be more recent tradition-historical layers, finds a core passage here of Jesus dining with the historical Zacchaeus.

[87] See esp. Alan C. Mitchell, "Zacchaeus Revisited: Luke 19:8 as a Defense," *Bib* 71 (1990): 153–76.

viewpoint of the speaker or writer as not introducing any doubt.[88] If Luke wanted to portray Zacchaeus as promising to restore fourfold anything he has defrauded without believing that he had in fact defrauded anyone, Luke would have used at least a third-class (hypothetical) condition. The "today" of v. 9 reinforces this observation. Had v. 8 reflected Zacchaeus' regular practices, there would be no reason to announce that salvation had arrived at his house on this particular day. Nor would Jesus' role have been that of seeking and saving the lost (v. 10), merely of pointing out and helping to facilitate the public recognition of one who was already saved, though perhaps not widely recognized as such.[89] The declaration here points to Jesus' authority to pronounce who can be forgiven in the new era he brings.

The only meal in this passage is the one implied, though never narrated, by Zacchaeus' acceptance of the obligation to host Jesus as an overnight lodger in his home. So we can scarcely speak of anything that would point us toward a symposium format. As a wealthy employee of Rome, we might imagine that if ever there were a setting in which a Gospel character were used to such banquets it would be here. But we are told nothing that would positively move us in the direction of this interpretation. Indeed, the only hint we get, if it is even that, as to other meals that Luke might have had in mind, comes with his inclusion of Jesus' statement that "this man, too, is a son of Abraham," an expression that acknowledges his ethnic and religious connection to the house of Israel, whatever his recent involvement with Hellenistic culture has been. What is more, Luke may hear an echo of Jesus' teaching about the eschatological banquet, when "sons" of the kingdom are thrown out as Gentiles come to feast at table with Abraham and the other patriarchs (Q 13:28–29; see below, § 3.2.3).

3.2. More Implicit Texts

In these more implicit texts, we see the repetition of common themes about open hospitality and inclusiveness present in the explicit texts. We also observe the presentation of themes reflective of the imagery of the messianic banquet.

---

[88] Grammarians often use the expression "assumed true for the sake of argument." Slightly more nuanced and to be preferred is "assertion for the sake of argument." See Stanley E. Porter, *Verbal Apsect in the Greek of the New Testament with Reference to Tense and Mood* (Studies in Biblical Greek 1; New York: Peter Lang, 1989), 294.

[89] For similar and related arguments, see Robert H. Stein, *Luke* (NAC 24; Nashville: Broadman, 1992), 466–67.

3.2.1. Tax Collectors and Prostitutes (Matt 21:31b–32)

A refrain which could have stood in either "Q" or "M" forms the conclusion to Matthew's parable of the two sons.[90] Following the form-critical dictum that parables did not originally have concluding explanations or applications, this verse and a half has often been assigned to later redaction. But this "law of tradition" proves highly improbable; rabbinical parables regularly ended with similar explanations.[91] The language is pre-Matthean[92] and coheres with the picture already unfolding in the previously treated passages. As Arland Hultgren concludes, "The fact that believing John is so strongly emphasized twice (21:32a,c), thereby putting a very high estimate upon him, casts doubt on whether the saying was created within a Christian community. It must have originated in the earliest stratum of the tradition, reflecting the attitude of Jesus himself."[93]

This is the only place in the NT where tax collectors are paired not with other "sinners" more generally but with "prostitutes." Perhaps some of this language is generalized slander applicable to other professions, too, but Luke 7:36–50 shows that we dare not deny the probable reference to literal harlots as well. The combination of these otherwise unrelated occupations probably stems from the fact that prostitutes in the Roman empire were often licensed, so that they could be taxed, and the tax collectors would be responsible for gathering that revenue (cf., e.g., Cicero, *Verr.* II.1.39.101; Dio Chrysostom, *4 Regn.* 97.98, *1 Serv. lib.* 14; Plutarch, *Apoph. lac.* 236 B-C).[94] Thus there is compatibility with earliest Christianity and the Judaism of its day. But apparently few in either religion dared emulate Jesus' scandalous disregard for appearances in dining with these overtly immoral groups, so neither Jew nor Christian is likely to have made up such a description of Jesus.[95] That the previously immoral enter the kingdom "ahead" of the chief priests and elders of the people leaves the door open for the latter to

---

[90] Matthew's parable of the "Two Sons" has usually been viewed as independent tradition, but at times it has been treated as a drastic abbreviation of Luke 15:11–32.

[91] Cf. esp. David Stern, "Rhetoric and Midrash: The Case of the Mashal," *Prooftexts* 1 (1981): 261–91. For numerous examples, see Robert M. Johnston and Harvey K. McArthur, *They Also Taught in Parables: Rabbinic Parables from the First Centuries of the Christian Era* (Grand Rapids: Zondervan, 1990).

[92] Joachim Jeremias, *The Parables of Jesus* (3rd ed.; trans. S. H. Hooke; London: SCM, 1972), 80–81.

[93] Arland J. Hultgren, *The Parables of Jesus: A Commentary* (The Bible in Its World; Grand Rapids: Eerdmans, 2000), 223; following M. Dibelius, W. Wink and N. Perrin.

[94] Corley, *Private Women, Public Meals*, 40, and the primary and secondary literature there cited. Cf. also Gibson, "Hoi Telōnai Kai Hai Pornai," 430.

[95] Gal 2:11–15 involved eating "only" with *Gentile* Christians, not the immoral, yet note even here how quickly the Judaizers were able to convince everyone except Paul to abandon the practice.

enter as well, an aperture not likely made available by a later editor.[96] But it will require repentance (like the ultimately obedient son's change of heart in the parable – v. 29), which shows that Jesus was not just accepting the tax collectors and prostitutes without laying down any conditions for their acceptability before God. Thus we have seen continuity with Judaism, discontinuity with Judaism, discontinuity with Christianity and continuity with Christianity, in that order. No explicit meal appears here, but to the extent that "entering the kingdom" often suggested an eschatological banquet,[97] such a festive occasion may well lie in the background.

3.2.2. Feasting in the Wilderness (Mark 6:30–44 and parallels; 8:1–10 and parallel)

As I first demonstrated over twenty years ago, the core of the Markan version of the feeding of the 5000 is most likely authentic, not least because it closely matches the core parabolic teaching of the historical Jesus (cf. Matt 7:7–9 and parallel, 13:33 and parallel; Luke 11:5–8, and 14:16–24; cf. also Matt 6:11 and parallel).[98] Here we may add further rationale. I take there to have been two separate feeding incidents,[99] but even if one generative event has produced the distinct pericopae in Mark, our points here remain unaffected. Jesus providing bread in the wilderness represents precisely what many Jews had come to expect the Messiah to do, re-enacting the miracle of the provision of supernatural sustenance in Moses' day (recall *2 Bar.* 29:5–8). We have also seen the background from the Hebrew Scriptures to the miraculous provision of bread enabling Elisha to feed a large number of people out of a small number of loaves with abundant leftovers in 2 Kgs 4:42–44. But here Jesus feeds so many in such a remote place that the people could hardly have obeyed the purity laws of the day. Indeed, in so heterogeneous a crowd of "peasants" from Galilee, many present may have been considered more permanently unclean.[100] The requisite continuity with

---

[96] Blomberg, *Interpreting the Parables*, 187.

[97] Joel Marcus, "Entering Into the Kingly Power of God," *JBL* 107 (1988): 667–68.

[98] Blomberg, "The Miracles as Parables," 337–40.

[99] There is good reason to see it as a deliberately intended mirror image of its predecessor, by Mark and/or Jesus himself, demonstrating Jesus to be the "bread of life" for a primarily Gentile audience in the way he had already revealed himself to a primarily Jewish audience. See J. Knackstedt, "Die beiden Brotvermehrungen im Evangelium," *NTS* 10 (1964): 309–35. Cf. Robert A. Guelich, *Mark 1–8:26* (WBC 34a; Dallas: Word, 1989), 409; France, *Mark*, 306–7; R. Alan Culpepper, *Mark* (Smyth & Helwys Bible Commentary; Macon: Smyth & Helwys, 2007), 208.

[100] As Wilson C.K. Poon ("Superabundant Table Fellowship in the Kingdom: The Feeding of the Five Thousand and the Meal Motif in Luke," *ExpTim* 114 [2003]: 228) elaborates, "The good news of God's unconditional acceptance of sinners is *materially fulfilled* by Jesus' table fellowship with all kinds of 'undesirables' without regard to the meal conventions of the Pharisees." Cf. Green, *Luke*, 365.

messianic hope and discontinuity with issues of cleanliness in conventional Judaism again appears.

Intriguingly, Mark actually identifies the groups into which the crowd divides as *symposia* (Mark 6:39). This is the only NT occurrence of this word. But there is nothing in the context to suggest Mark viewed the gathering as a collection of formal drinking parties, and it is difficult to see how the distributive plural (sitting down "by companies") could make much sense as a form of dividing the crowd if a Greco-Roman festive banquet were implied! Tellingly, both Matthew and Luke omit the term in their versions of the event; Luke, the Hellenist, would surely have preserved if not clarified the reference were it a more specific kind of shared meal. Indeed, the arrangement of the people, also described as comprising "groups of hundreds and fifties" (Mark 6:40) much more clearly calls to mind the Jewish background of the division of the children of Israel during their wilderness wanderings into similarly sized companies (cf. Exod 18:25; Num 31:14; and, among the Essenes, 1QS 2:21–22 and CD 13:1). As elsewhere in the Gospels, a new Moses (and a new Elisha) has appeared, reenacting the ministries of the Moses and Elisha of old.[101] Verses 39–40 do make reference to "reclining," but again the verbs need not indicate a literal posture, and we cannot be meant to imagine the thousands leaning back on couches that they brought with them into the wilderness![102] The heterogeneity of the crowd further distinguishes the gathering from a symposium. If there is any allusion to a banquet, it would be to the coming Jewish Messianic banquet, not to any Greco-Roman form of dining.[103] If Eucharistic significance is present, especially in Matthew and Luke, it more likely reflects redactional overlay that does not jeopardize the authenticity of the oldest core of the passage.[104]

3.2.3. *How Not to Win Friends and Influence People (Q 13:28–29)*

Matthew's and Luke's versions of these sayings appear in quite different contexts and in different sequences (Matt 8:11–12; Luke 13:28–29). Still,

---

[101] Cf. esp. Marcus, *Mark 1–8*, 410. On these portraits of the eschatological prophet at the core of authentic historical Jesus material, see Wright, *Jesus and the Victory of God*, 147–97.

[102] Cf. Bock, *Luke*, 1:832.

[103] William L. Lane, *The Gospel According to Mark* (NICNT; Grand Rapids: Eerdmans, 1974), 232–33; Edwards, *Mark*, 192.

[104] Peter-Ben Smit, *Fellowship and Food in the Kingdom: Eschatological Meals and Scenes of Utopian Abundance in the New Testament* (WUNT 2.234; Tübingen: Mohr Siebeck, 2008), 72–73. But the language of thanking God, breaking bread and distirbuting here is so conventional with accounts of ordinary Jewish meals that even the redactional layers may not be as Eucharistic as has often been alleged. See esp. Klaus Berger, *Manna, Mehl und Sauerteig* (Stuttgart: Quell, 1993), 99, 152, and the literature there cited (cf., e.g., *b. Ber.* 39b and 47a.)

the common core of both versions is the contrast between people from throughout the nations taking their place at the eschatological banquet with the Jewish patriarchs, while many "subjects of the kingdom" (ethnic Jews) are evicted.[105] Here we do not have an account of Jesus actually eating with the outcast during his lifetime but his prediction of an unexpected guest list at the great supper over which he will one day preside. The inclusion of Gentiles fits early Christian hope, while the exclusion of many Jews (presumably including some among Jesus' audience) distinguishes these logia from more conventional Jewish expectation (e.g., Isa 66:15–21; *Pss. Sol.* 17:22–31; *2 Bar.* 72:2–6; *t. Sanh.* 13:2).[106] At the same time, Matthew's model of love for an enemy of one's people and his household (in this case the military officer representing the occupying foreign armies) proved little easier for Christians than Jews to emulate, while Luke's context of the closed door appears to exclude lawless "Christian" believers, a theme that cuts against the grain of the universal emphasis of early Christian mission. Simply eating and drinking with Jesus is no guarantee of salvation. Moreover, nothing distinctively related to a symposium appears, nor does the presence of Gentiles defile the Jews, for all are made pure in the age to come.

3.2.4. A Rude Guest (Luke 11:37–54)

In this text, Jesus snubs his Pharisaic host, by refusing to perform the expected ritual of ceremonial handwashing/purification before the meal. Compounding that insult, which was seemingly unprovoked, he then turns on at least some of the other guests and berates them for their hypocrisy in stressing external purity while masking internal filth of various forms.[107] This then launches him on a tirade with numerous woes against the worst practices of various Pharisees and scribes,[108] woes which implicitly call their listeners to a "profound repentance."[109] What early Christian, desiring to exalt Jesus, would have invented a story of him behaving in so rude a fashion? Yet his invective does cohere with the criticisms that do emerge without any moderating elements at a later date.

---

[105] See Schnackenburg, *Matthew*, 82.

[106] Davies and Allison (*A Critical and Exegetical Commentary on the Gospel According to Saint Matthew* [3 vols.; ICC; Edinburgh: T&T Clark, 1988–97], 2:27–29) argue, against almost everyone, that Q's portrayal of Jesus' teaching has *not* Gentiles *but* a restored Israel in view. See, however the excellent, point-by-point responses, along with other arguments for authenticity, in Michael F. Bird, *Jesus and the Origins of the Gentile Mission* (LNTS 331; London: T&T Clark, 2007), 83–93.

[107] Cf. James L. Resseguie, *Spiritual Landscape: Images of the Spiritual Life in the Gospel of Luke* (Peabody: Hendrickson, 2004), 73–76.

[108] Cf. Green, *Luke*, 470. Cf. C. F. Evans, *Saint Luke* (TPINTC; London: SCM; Philadelphia: Trinity, 1990), 503.

[109] Heil, *The Meal Scenes*, 92.

As for coherence with Jewish background, E. Springs Steele has claimed that we must envision a Hellenistic symposium here – based on the elements of a host notable for his wealth or wisdom, a chief guest, other invitees from the social elite, and a gradual reversal of the honor or identity of the guests, triggered by a *fait divers* (in this case the host's amazement at Jesus' failure to wash his hands).[110] But the truly distinctive elements of a symposium – a clear separation of the meal from the discourse, the invocation of God or the gods, the pouring of a libation, and emphasis on drinking, levity and other forms of entertainment – are all missing. The meal remains thoroughly Jewish; the setting and activity, credible. No "down and outs" explicitly appear, but, contrary to all expectation, the Jewish leaders present are implicitly lumped with such marginalized as the tax collectors as "up and outs." Their lack of deeds befitting true repentance, however, shows that they, rather than those they criticize, are the truly unclean.[111]

3.2.5. *A Rude Host and a Reply in Kind (Luke 14:1–24)*

In another Pharisaic banquet setting, a man with dropsy suddenly appears in front of Jesus, on the Sabbath no less, as if to test his very reputation for defying *halakah* through his healing ministry (vv. 2–6).[112] In response, Jesus attacks the entire convention of seating oneself according to perceived position or rank and of inviting only those guests who can reciprocate on some other occasion (vv. 7–14).[113] His follow-up parable reinforces this point by showing how God will not tolerate those who refuse his invitation, when their excuses remain flimsy and hypocritical,[114] but will nevertheless fill his "banquet table," by finding replacement guests from the highways and byways (vv. 16–24).

---

[110] E. Springs Steele, "Luke 11:37–54 – a Modified Hellenistic Symposium?" *JBL* 103 (1984): 379–94.

[111] Cf. Green, *Luke*, 470–71: "Jesus' deviant behavior might have led to his negative valuation, a possibility Luke circumvents by referring to Jesus as 'Lord' and by reasserting Jesus' capacity and mission, prophesied by Simeon, to make known the inner thoughts of others (2:35). In a remarkable turn of events, then, the one whose behavior seems deviant is acknowledged to Luke's audience as Lord, and the Lord classifies those whose behaviors apparently have not transgressed the boundaries of socio-religious propriety as 'fools.'"

[112] Bock, *Luke*, 2:1256–57.

[113] Very similar teaching on voluntarily seating oneself at a lower place than one thinks one deserves, to increase the chances of later promotion rather than demotion, is later attributed to Simeon ben 'Azzai in *Lev. Rab.* 1:5 and appears in an anonymous saying in *'Abot R. Nat.* 25. See Joseph A. Fitzmyer, *The Gospel According to Luke X–XXIV* (AB 28a; Garden City: Doubleday, 1985), 1046–47.

[114] On which, see esp. Kenneth E. Bailey, *Through Peasant Eyes: More Lucan Parables, Their Culture and Style* (Grand Rapids: Eerdmans, 1980), 95–99.

Thus the entire scenario fits a credible early first-century Jewish context, Jesus' teaching builds on Prov 25:6–7,[115] even while his rebuke so radically and bluntly rejects the etiquette of the setting that no ordinary Jew would likely have invented it. The concern for the sick, the poor and the person of low "estate" coheres with important early Christian emphases, but Jesus' rudeness would no doubt have been substantially moderated by subsequent Christians concerned more to honor and glorify him than to portray him as so thoroughly discourteous and subversive.[116] To the extent that Luke's focus remains on Jesus' critique of this form of meal, one should agree with Willi Braun in identifying the scene as an *anti*-symposium.[117] As in Luke 11, the sinners with whom Jesus dines turn out to be the religious leaders, not the social riff-raff. Too close association with *them* potentially defiles a person, rather than table fellowship with the poor, crippled, lame or blind!

3.2.6. *Fixing Dinner or Favoring Devotion? (Luke 10:38–42)*

At first glance, the inclusion of this pericope seems inappropriate, since there are no explicit sinners or actual meal involved. Still, the hospitality extended to travelers of this kind necessarily implied a nice dinner and overnight lodging.[118] Mary's behavior was sufficiently countercultural that Jews then and Christians ever since have often found it inappropriate, despite its general coherence with a Jewish setting and with subsequent Christian trajectories in the direction of greater opportunities for women in religious contexts.[119]

3.2.7. *A Scandalous Summary (Luke 15:1–2)*

These two verses form Luke's redactional introduction to and summary of Jesus' message for "tax collectors and sinners" (recall above, § 3.2.1), as epitomized by the three parables of the lost sheep, coin and sons in vv. 3–32. Given that vv. 1–2 form a different literary subgenre than our passages thus far have comprised, the criterion of multiple forms comes into play to sup-

---

[115] J. Duncan M. Derrett, "Choosing the Lowest Seat: Lk 14,7–11," *Estudios Bíblicos*, 60 (2002): 147–68.

[116] Cf. Green, *Luke*, 550.

[117] Willi Braun, "Symposium or Anti-Symposium? Reflections on Luke 14:1–24," *TJT* 8 (1992): 70–84; Willi Braun, *Feasting and Social Rhetoric in Luke 14* (SNTSMS 85; Cambridge: Cambridge University Press, 1995).

[118] Arterbury, *Entertaining Angels*, 15–93. More specifically, "Martha extends to Jesus the kind of hospitality, which implies a meal, that he instructed his disciples to depend upon while on their missionary journeys (9:3–4; 10:7–8)" (Heil, *The Meal Scenes*, 69).

[119] See esp. Esther Yue L. Ng, *Reconstructing Christian Origins? The Feminist Theology of Elisabeth Schüssler Fiorenza: An Evaluation* (Paternoster Biblical and Theological Monographs; Carlisle: Paternoster, 2002).

port the authenticity of Jesus' table fellowship with sinners. The parables in general, and those of Luke 15 in particular, are widely recognized as authentic, even by the old dissimilarity criterion;[120] they satisfy the double similarity and dissimilarity criterion even better. To the extent that the introduction aptly encapsulates their message, it forms an important historical justification for generalizing from the behavior depicted in the parables to a key component of Jesus' ministry itself.[121] He has come to call sinners, even those who have "fallen" as far as the prodigal son. But repentance is explicitly in view in each of the parables, so it will not do to deny that Jesus called sinners to mend their ways. If the banquet with the fatted calf points to anything other than a joyous Jewish dinner, it is the eschatological banquet and not a Hellenistic symposium that is intimated.[122] And if anyone is in danger of rendering others morally or ritually impure, it is the overly critical religious leaders, not the notorious sinners and outcasts of society.

4. Significance: An Eschatological Symbol of Jesus' Centrality in Bringing Holiness

To varying degrees, all of the Synoptic meal scenes in which Jesus fellowships at table with sinners demonstrate the fourfold combination of intelligibility in their Jewish context and continuity with some aspect of early Christianity, along with significant divergence from conventional Jewish belief or practice and typical early Christian thought and behavior. The criteria of multiple attestation, multiple forms, embarrassment and coherence also are regularly satisfied. The meals do not closely resemble Greco-Roman symposia, so potential objections to authenticity that such portraits could raise do not apply. It is highly probable that Jesus ate in more egalitarian, non-symposiastic (i.e., less hierarchical and exclusive) fashion with the outcast of his society, even if one questions the authenticity of an individual text or two and even after one strips away the more obvious redactional accretions to the various passages surveyed. Double dissimilarity and multiple attestation support the authenticity of the core fact of these scenes. Jesus associated with tax collectors and sinners – those on the fringe of first century Jewish society. A careful examination of the cultural background also points to the eschatological meal as supplying the key context for what Jesus does.

---

[120] See esp. Jeremias, *The Parables of Jesus*, 128–36. Cf. Hultgren, *The Parables of Jesus: A Commentary*, 46–91.
[121] Bovon (*Lukas*, 3:21) speaks of this kind of table fellowship as "einem Test, einem Kriterium, einem Schibboleth" of whether the church stands or falls.
[122] The slaughter of one special, large animal could make one think of the role of Behemoth in *2 Bar.* 29.

So when one probes the significance of these meals, one finds repeated hints that Jesus is foreshadowing the eschatological banquet at which he, the key eschatological figure, will partake in radically inclusive fashion with his followers gathered from all the people groups on the planet. This eschatological thrust fits what we have seen in other essays in this collection. Whether one thinks of the setting John the Baptizer invokes, the point of Jesus choosing twelve, the signs indicated by exorcisms, or the significance of Sabbath activity, these actions point to the eschatological thrust of Jesus' activity. Indeed, one could speak of these meals as enacted prophecy or symbolic of the arrived kingdom's surprising inclusions. But this is no "brokerless" kingdom, as in Crossan's depictions,[123] for Jesus himself is the crucial "broker."[124] What makes the meal significant is his presence, as well as his remarks explaining the significance of who is included and why. Nor does this inclusivism imply universalism. There are surprising exclusions as well. Not everyone is saved, and no one is saved apart from repentance and faith in Jesus. These scenes are significant not merely because they are meals of acceptance, but because they are meals with Jesus showing authority about why such acceptance is present (Luke 7:36–50; 19:1–10). The dissimilar nature of the meal with Jewish expectations requires explanation. Jesus' authority in an eschatological context is the basis for the newly revealed inclusiveness. So precisely to enhance the possibilities of genuine repentance for those alienated by standard Jewish separationism and to show the results of the new way he brings, Jesus "mixes it up" with the notorious and the riff-raff of his world. Scarcely fearing that he will be morally or ritually defiled by them, in many instances he winds up leading them to God and to true ceremonial and spiritual wholeness. Or to put it more succinctly, holiness not impurity turns out to be the most contagious.[125]

Bibliography

Abrahams, Israel. *Studies in Pharisaism and the Gospels*. Library of Biblical Studies. 1924. Repr., New York: Ktav, 1967.
Allison, Dale C., Jr. *Jesus of Nazareth: Millenarian Prophet*. Minneapolis: Fortress, 1998.
Alon, Gedalyahu. *Jews, Judaism and the Classical World: Studies in Jewish History in the Times of the Second Temple and Talmud*. Jerusalem: Magnes, 1977.

---

[123] Crossan, *The Historical Jesus*, 225.
[124] John P. Meier, *Companions and Competitors* (vol. 3 of *A Marginal Jew: Rethinking the Historical Jesus*; ABRL; New York: Doubleday, 2001), 125–97.
[125] Cf. Scot McKnight, *The Jesus Creed: Loving God, Loving Others* (Brewster: Paraclete, 2004), 159–60.

Arterbury, Andrew E. *Entertaining Angels: Early Christian Hospitality in Its Mediterranean Setting*. New Testament Monographs. Sheffield: Sheffield Phoenix, 2005.
Ashley, Timothy R. *The Book of Numbers*. NICOT. Grand Rapids: Eerdmans, 1993.
Bailey, Kenneth E. *Through Peasant Eyes: More Lucan Parables, Their Culture and Style*. Grand Rapids: Eerdmans, 1980.
Berger, Klaus. *Manna, Mehl und Sauerteig*. Stuttgart: Quell, 1993.
Bird, Michael F. *Jesus and the Origins of the Gentile Mission*. LNTS 331. London: T&T Clark, 2007.
Blomberg, Craig L. *Contagious Holiness: Jesus' Meals with Sinners*. New Studies in Biblical Theology. Downers Grove: InterVarsity, 2005.
–. *Interpreting the Parables*. Downers Grove: InterVarsity, 1990.
–. "Jesus, Sinners and Table Fellowship." *BBR* 19 (2009): 35–62.
–. "The Miracles as Parables." Pages 327–59 in *Miracles of Jesus*. Edited by David Wenham and Craig L. Blomberg. Gospel Perspectives, 6. Sheffield: JSOT Press, 1986. Repr., Eugene, Or.: Wipf &Stock, 2003.
–. "The Synoptic Problem: Where We Stand at the Start of a New Century." Pages 17–40 in *Rethinking the Synoptic Problem*. Edited by David A. Black and David Beck. Grand Rapids: Baker, 2001.
Blümner, Hugo. *The Home Life of the Ancient Greeks*. Translated by Alice Zimmern. 1893. Repr., Whitefish, Mont.: Kessinger, 2007.
Bock, Darrell L. *Luke*. 2 vols. Baker Exegetical Commentary on the New Testament, 3a–b. Grand Rapids: Baker, 1994–96.
–. "Questions About Q." Pages 41–64 in *Rethinking the Synoptic Problem*. Edited by David A. Black and David Beck. Grand Rapids: Baker, 2001.
Bolyki, János. *Jesu Tischgemeinschaften*. WUNT 96. Tübingen: Mohr Siebeck, 1998.
Boring, M. Eugene. *Mark*. NTL. Louisville: Westminster John Knox, 2006.
Bovon, François. *Das Evangelium nach Lukas*. 3 vols. EKKNT 3. Düsseldorf: Benziger; Neukirchen-Vluyn: Neukirchener Verlag, 1989–2001.
–. *Luke 1*. Translated by Christine M. Thomas. Hermeneia. Minneapolis: Fortress, 2002.
Braun, Willi. *Feasting and Social Rhetoric in Luke 14*. SNTSMS 85. Cambridge: Cambridge University Press, 1995.
–. "Symposium or Anti-Symposium? Reflections on Luke 14:1–24." *TJT* 8 (1992): 70–84.
Brownlee, William H. *Ezekiel 1–19*. WBC 28. Waco: Word, 1986.
Brueggemann, Walter. *Isaiah*. 2 vols. Westminster Bible Companion. Louisville: Westminster John Knox, 1998.
Bultmann, Rudolf. *History of the Synoptic Tradition*. Oxford: Blackwell, 1963. Repr., Peabody: Hendrickson, 1994.
Burkert, Walter. "Oriental Symposia: Contrasts and Parallels." Pages 7–24 in *Dining in a Classical Context*. Edited by William J. Slater. Ann Arbor: University of Michigan Press, 1991.
Chilton, Bruce D. "Jesus and the Repentance of E. P. Sanders." *TynBul* 39 (1988): 1–18.
Collins, Adela Yarbro. *Mark*. Hermeneia. Minneapolis: Fortress, 2007.
Corley, Kathleen E. "The Anointing of Jesus in the Synoptic Tradition: An Argument for Authenticity." *JSHJ* 1 (2003): 61–72.

–. *Private Women, Public Meals: Social Conflict in the Synoptic Tradition.* Peabody: Hendrickson, 1993.

–. *Women and the Historical Jesus: Feminist Myths of Christian Origins.* Santa Rosa: Polebridge, 2002.

Cosgrove, Charles H. "A Woman's Unbound Hair in the Greco-Roman World, with Special Reference to the Story of the 'Sinful Woman' in Luke 7:36–50." *JBL* 124 (2005): 675–92.

Crossan, John Dominic. *The Historical Jesus: The Life of a Mediterranean Jewish Peasant.* San Francisco: HarperSanFrancisco, 1991.

Culpepper, R. Alan. *Mark.* Smyth & Helwys Bible Commentary. Macon: Smyth & Helwys, 2007.

Davies, W. D., and Dale C. Allison, Jr. *A Critical and Exegetical Commentary on the Gospel According to Saint Matthew.* 3 vols. ICC. Edinburgh: T&T Clark, 1988–97.

Derrett, J. Duncan M. "Choosing the Lowest Seat: Lk 14,7–11." *Estudios Bíblicos,* 60 (2002): 147–68.

Duguid, Iain. *Ezekiel.* NIV Application Commentary. Grand Rapids: Zondervan, 1999.

Edwards, James R. *The Gospel According to Mark.* Pillar New Testament Commentary. Grand Rapids: Eerdmans, 2002.

Evans, C. F. *Saint Luke.* TPINTC. London: SCM; Philadelphia: Trinity, 1990.

Fabry, H.-J. "מַרְזֵחַ marzēaḥ." Pages 10–15 in vol. 9 of *Theological Dictionary of the Old Testament.* 17 vols. Edited by G. Johannes Botterweck, Helmer Ringgren, and Heinz-Josef Fabry. Translated by John T. Willis, David E. Green, and Douglas W. Stott. Grand Rapids: Eerdmans, 1974–2006.

Fisher, Nicholas R. E. "Greek Associations, Symposia, and Clubs." Pages 1167–97 in *Civilization of the Ancient Mediterranean: Greece and Rome.* 3 vols. Edited by Michael R. Grant and M. Rachel Kitzinger. New York: Scribner, 1988.

–. "Roman Associations, Dinner Parties and Clubs." Pages 1199–1225 in *Civilization of the Ancient Mediterranean: Greece and Rome.* 3 vols. Edited by Michael R. Grant, and M. Rachel Kitzinger. New York: Scribner, 1988.

Fitzmyer, Joseph A. *The Gospel According to Luke X–XXIV.* AB 28a. Garden City: Doubleday, 1985.

France, R. T. *The Gospel of Mark.* NIGTC. Grand Rapids: Eerdmans, 2002.

Gibson, J. "Hoi Telōnai Kai Hai Pornai." *JTS* 32 (1981): 429–33.

Green, Joel B. *The Gospel of Luke.* NICNT. Grand Rapids: Eerdmans, 1997.

–. "Which Conversation Shall We Have? History, Historicism and Historical Narrative in Theological Interpretation: A Response to Peter van Inwagen." Pages 141–50 in *Behind the Text: History and Biblical Interpretation.* Craig Bartholomew, C. Stephen Evans, Mary Healy, and Murray Rae. Scripture and Hermeneutics Series, 4. Carlisle: Paternoster; Grand Rapids: Zondervan, 2003.

Guelich, Robert A. *Mark 1–8:26.* WBC 34a. Dallas: Word, 1989.

Gundry, Robert H. *Mark: A Commentary on His Apology for the Cross.* Grand Rapids: Eerdmans, 1993.

Harrison, R. K. "House." Pages 243–44 in *The New International Dictionary of Biblical Archaeology.* Edited by Edward M. Blaiklock and R. K. Harrison. Grand Rapids: Zondervan, 1983.

Hartley, John E. *Leviticus.* WBC 4. Dallas: Word, 1992.

Hayes, Christine. "Purity and Impurity, Ritual." Pages 746–56 in vol. 16 of *Encyclopaedia Judaica*. 2nd ed., 22 vols. Edited by Fred Skolnik and Michael Berenbaum. Detroit: Macmillan; Jerusalem: Keter, 2007.
Heil, John P. *The Meal Scenes in Luke-Acts: An Audience-Oriented Approach*. SBLMS 52. Atlanta: Society of Biblical Literature, 1999.
Herrenbrück, Fritz. *Jesus und die Zöllner: historische und neutestamentlich-exegetische Untersuchungen*. WUNT 2.41. Tübingen: Mohr, 1990.
Hobbs, T. R. *2 Kings*. WBC 13. Waco: Word, 1985.
Holmén, Tom. "Doubts About Double Dissimilarity: Restructuring the Main Criterion of Jesus-of-History Research." Pages 47–80 in *Authenticating the Words of Jesus*. Edited by Bruce D. Chilton and Craig A. Evans. NTTS 28.1. Leiden: Brill, 1999.
Holst, Robert. "The One Anointing of Jesus: Another Application of the Form-Critical Method." *JBL* 95 (1976): 435–46.
Hultgren, Arland J. *Jesus and His Adversaries: The Form and Function of the Conflict Stories in the Synoptic Tradition*. Minneapolis: Augsburg, 1979.
–. *The Parables of Jesus: A Commentary*. The Bible in Its World. Grand Rapids: Eerdmans, 2000.
Jeremias, Joachim. *The Parables of Jesus*. 3rd ed. Translated by S. H. Hooke. London: SCM, 1972.
Johnston, Robert M., and Harvey K. McArthur. *They Also Taught in Parables: Rabbinic Parables from the First Centuries of the Christian Era*. Grand Rapids: Zondervan, 1990.
Kee, Howard C. "Jesus: A Glutton and a Drunkard." *NTS* 42 (1996): 374–93.
Kertelge, Karl. *Markusevangelium*. NEchtB 2. Würzburg: Echter, 1994.
Kieweler, Hans V. "Benehmen bei Tisch." Pages 191–215 in *Der Einzelne und seine Gemeinschaft bei Ben Sira*. Edited by Renate Egger-Wenzel and Ingrid Krammer. BZAW 270. Berlin: De Gruyter, 1998.
Kilgallen, John J. "Faith and Forgiveness: Luke 7,36–50." *RB* 112 (2005): 372–84.
–. "Forgiveness of Sins (Luke 7:36–50)." *NovT* 40 (1998): 105–16.
Klawans, Jonathan. *Impurity and Sin in Ancient Judaism*. Oxford: Oxford University Press, 2000.
Klinghardt, Matthias. *Gemeinschaftsmahl und Mahlgemeinschaft: Soziologie und Liturgie frühchristlicher Mahlfeiern*. Texte und Arbeiten zum neutestamentlichen Zeitalter. Tübingen: Francke Verlag, 1996.
Knackstedt, J. "Die beiden Brotvermehrungen im Evangelium." *NTS* 10 (1964): 309–35.
Lane, William L. *The Gospel According to Mark*. NICNT. Grand Rapids: Eerdmans, 1974.
Lissarrague, Francois. *The Aesthetics of the Greek Banquet: Images of Wine and Ritual*. Translated by Andrew Szegedy-Maszak. Princeton: Princeton University Press, 1990.
Love, Stuart L. "Women and Men at Hellenistic Symposia Meals in Luke." Pages 198–212 in *Modeling Early Christianity: Social-Scientific Studies of the New Testament in Context*. Edited by Philip F. Esler. London: Routledge, 1995.
Lührmann, Dieter. *Das Markusevangelium*. Tübingen: Mohr, 1987.
Luz, Ulrich. *Matthew 8–20*. Translated by James E. Crouch. Hermeneia. Minneapolis: Fortress, 2001.

McGowan, Andrew. "Naming the Feast: The *Agapē* and the Diversity of Early Christian Meals." Pages 314–18 in vol. 2 of *Studia Patristica: Papers Presented at the Twelfth International Conference on Patristic Studies Held in Oxford, 1995*. Edited by Elizabeth A. Livingstone. StPatr, 29–33. Leuven: Peeters, 1997.

McKnight, Scot. *Jesus and His Death: Historiography, the Historical Jesus, and Atonement Theory*. Waco: Baylor University Press, 2005.

–. *The Jesus Creed: Loving God, Loving Others*. Brewster: Paraclete, 2004.

McLaughlin, John L. *The Marzeah in the Prophetic Literature: References and Allusions in Light of the Extra-Biblical Evidence*. VTSup 86. Leiden: Brill, 2001.

Marcus, Joel. "Entering Into the Kingly Power of God." *JBL* 107 (1988): 663–75.

–. *Mark 1–8*. AB 27. New York: Doubleday, 2000.

Marshall, I. Howard. *The Gospel of Luke*. NIGTC 3. Grand Rapids: Eerdmans, 1978.

Marshall, Mary J. "Jesus: Glutton and Drunkard?" *JSHJ* 3 (2005): 47–60.

May, David M. "Mark 2:15: The Home of Jesus or Levi?" *NTS* 39 (1993): 147–49.

Meier, John P. *Companions and Competitors*. Vol. 3 of *A Marginal Jew: Rethinking the Historical Jesus*. ABRL. New York: Doubleday, 2001.

–. *The Roots of the Problem and the Person*. Vol. 1 of *A Marginal Jew: Rethinking the Historical Jesus*. ABRL. New York: Doubleday, 1991.

Mitchell, Alan C. "Zacchaeus Revisited: Luke 19:8 as a Defense." *Bib* 71 (1990): 153–76.

Moritz, Thorsten. "Dinner Talk and Ideology in Luke: The Role of the Sinners." *EuroJTh* 5 (1996): 47–69.

Mullen, J. Patrick. *Dining with Pharisees*. Interfaces. Collegeville, Minn.: Liturgical, 2004.

Neusner, Jacob. "The Fellowship (חבורה) in the Second Jewish Commonwealth." *HTR* 53 (1960): 125–42.

–. "Two Pictures of the Pharisees: Philosophical Circle or Eating Club." *AThR* 64 (1982): 525–38.

Newton, Michael. *The Concept of Purity at Qumran and in the Letters of Paul*. SNTSMS 53. Cambridge: Cambridge University Press, 1985.

Ng, Esther Yue L. *Reconstructing Christian Origins? The Feminist Theology of Elisabeth Schüssler Fiorenza: An Evaluation*. Paternoster Biblical and Theological Monographs. Carlisle: Paternoster, 2002.

Nolland, John. *Luke 1–9:20*. WBC 35a. Dallas: Word, 1989.

Noy, David. "The Sixth Hour is the Mealtime for Scholars: Jewish Meals in the Roman World." Pages 134–44 in *Meals in a Social Context: Aspects of the Communal Meal in the Hellenistic and Roman World*. Edited by Inge Nielsen and Hanne S. Nielsen. Aarhus: Aarhus University Press, 1998.

Poon, Wilson C. K. "Superabundant Table Fellowship in the Kingdom: The Feeding of the Five Thousand and the Meal Motif in Luke." *ExpTim* 114 (2003): 224–30.

Pope, Marvin H. "A Divine Banquet at Ugarit." Pages 170–203 in *The Use of the Old Testament in the New and Other Essays: Studies in Honor of William Franklin Stinespring*. Edited by James M. Efird. Durham: Duke, 1972.

Porter, Stanley E. *Verbal Aspect in the Greek of the New Testament with Reference to Tense and Mood*. Studies in Biblical Greek, 1. New York: Peter Lang, 1989.

–. *The Criteria for Authenticity in Historical-Jesus Research: Previous Discussion and New Proposals*. JSNTSup 191. Sheffield: Sheffield Academic Press, 2000.

Priest, John F. "A Note on the Messianic Banquet." Pages 222–38 in *The Messiah: Developments in Early Judaism and Christianity*. Edited by James H. Charlesworth. Minneapolis: Fortress, 1992.
Reed, Stephen A. "Food in the Psalms." Ph.D. Diss. Claremont: Claremont Graduate School, 1987.
Reid, Barbara E. "'Do You See This Woman?' Luke 7:36–50 as a Paradigm for Feminist Hermeneutics." *BR* 40 (1995): 37–49.
Resseguie, James L. *Spiritual Landscape: Images of the Spiritual Life in the Gospel of Luke*. Peabody: Hendrickson, 2004.
Ringe, Sharon H. *Jesus, Liberation, and the Biblical Jubilee: Images for Ethics and Christology*. OBT. Philadelphia: Fortress, 1985.
Robinson, James M., Paul Hoffmann, and John S. Kloppenborg, eds. *The Critical Edition of Q*. Hermeneia. Minneapolis: Fortress, 2000.
Safrai, Shemuel. "Home and Family." Pages 728–833 in *The Jewish People in the First Century: Historical Geography, Political History, Social, Cultural and Religious Life and Institutions*. Vol. 2, section 1 of *Compendia Rerum Iudaicarum ad Novum Testamentum*. Edited by Shemuel Safrai and Menahem Stern. Assen: Van Gorcum, 1976.
Sanders, E. P. *Jesus and Judaism*. Philadelphia: Fortress, 1985.
Schiffman, Lawrence H. "Communal Meals at Qumran." *RevQ* 10 (1979): 45–56.
–. "Non-Jews in the Dead Sea Scrolls." Pages 153–71 in *The Quest for Context and Meaning: Studies in Biblical Intertextuality in Honor of James A. Sanders*. Edited by Craig A. Evans and Shemaryahu Talmon. Biblical Interpretation Series, 28. Leiden: Brill, 1997.
Schnackenburg, Rudolf. *The Gospel of Matthew*. Translated by Robert R. Barr. Grand Rapids: Eerdmans, 2002.
Schorch, Stefan. "Die Propheten und der Karneval: Marzeach – Maioumas – Maimuna." *VT* 53 (2003): 397–415.
Schottroff, Louise. *The Parables of Jesus*. Minneapolis: Fortress, 2006.
Schramm, Gene. "Meal Customs: Jewish Dietary Laws." Pages 648–50 in vol. 4 of *Anchor Bible Dictionary*. 6 vols. Edited by David N. Freedman. New York: Doubleday, 1992.
Shemesh, Aharon. "The Origins of the Laws of Separatism: Qumran Literature and Rabbinic Halacha." *RevQ* 18 (1997): 223–41.
Shimoff, Sandra R. "Banquets: The Limits of Hellenization." *JSJ* 27 (1996): 440–52.
Smit, Peter-Ben. *Fellowship and Food in the Kingdom: Eschatological Meals and Scenes of Utopian Abundance in the New Testament*. WUNT 2.234. Tübingen: Mohr Siebeck, 2008.
Smith, Dennis E. *From Symposium to Eucharist: The Banquet in the Early Christian World*. Minneapolis: Fortress, 2003.
Steele, E. Springs. "Luke 11:37–54 – a Modified Hellenistic Symposium?" *JBL* 103 (1984): 379–94.
Stein, Robert H. "The 'Criteria' for Authenticity." Pages 225–63 in *Studies of History and Tradition in the Four Gospels*. Edited by R. T. France and David Wenham. Gospel Perspectives, 1. Sheffield: JSOT Press, 1980.
–. *Luke*. NAC, 24. Nashville: Broadman, 1992.
Stern, David. "Rhetoric and Midrash: The Case of the Mashal." *Prooftexts* 1 (1981): 261–91.

Stern, Frank. *A Rabbi Looks at Jesus' Parables*. Lanham: Rowman, 2006.
Theissen, Gerd, and Annette Merz. *The Historical Jesus: A Comprehensive Guide*. Translated by John Bowden. Minneapolis: Fortress, 1998.
Theissen, Gerd, and Dagmar Winter. *The Quest for the Plausible Jesus: The Question of Criteria*. Translated by M. Eugene Boring. Louisville: Westminster John Knox, 2002.
Thomas E. Phillips. "'Will the Wise Person Get Drunk?' The Background of the Human Wisdom in Luke 7:35 and Matthew 11:19." *JBL* 127 (2008): 385–96.
Walker, William O., Jr. "Jesus and the Tax Collectors." *JBL* 97 (1978): 221–38.
Whybray, R. N. *Proverbs*. NCB. London: Pickering; Grand Rapids: Eerdmans, 1994.
Wigoder, Geoffrey, Fred Skolnik, and Shmuel Himelstein, eds. *The New Encyclopedia of Judaism*. New York: New York University Press, 2002.
Winter, Bruce W. *Roman Wives, Roman Widows: The Appearance of New Women and the Pauline Communities*. Grand Rapids: Eerdmans, 2003.
Wright, N. T. *Jesus and the Victory of God*. Vol. 2 of *Christian Origins and the Question of God*. Minneapolis: Fortress, 1996.

Chapter 7

Jesus and the Synoptic Sabbath Controversies

DONALD A. HAGNER

1. Introduction

One of the ongoing, intractable questions in Gospel scholarship concerns the attitude of Jesus to the law of Moses. Is Jesus loyal to the law and observant of it, does he violate it and cancel it out, or does he somehow transcend it by penetrating to its essence? One aspect of that larger question, in a microcosm, is the issue of Jesus and the Sabbath. In a large and important study of the Sabbath,[1] Lutz Doering reviews the options under six headings: (1) Jesus was against the Sabbath commandment; (2) Jesus was against only the Pharisaic halakah and not the Sabbath commandment itself; (3) Jesus was not fundamentally against the Sabbath commandment, but only against its universal and inflexible application; (4) the free stance of Jesus vis-à-vis the Sabbath is marked by the eschatological stamp of his teaching and work; (5) Jesus does not view the law as a rigid ordinance, but in terms of its intent (this, Doering notes, can be combined with 3 or 4); and (6) Jesus lived in full conformity to the Sabbath praxis of the day.[2] Doering does not note which of these he prefers, but from his total presentation it would seem to be 5 together with either 3 or 4, or perhaps both.

The present essay discusses the historicity and significance of the synoptic Sabbath controversies. In the first part we look at the historical question with some attention to the redactional activity of the evangelists. In the second part we look at the problem of Jesus and the Sabbath as it can be understood within the theological framework of the person of Jesus, his message and his work.

---

[1] Lutz Doering, *Schabbat: Sabbathalacha und -praxis im antiken Judentum und Urchristentum* (Texte und Studien zum antiken Judentum 78; Tübingen: Mohr Siebeck, 1999).

[2] Doering, *Schabbat*, 399–400.

2. The Historicity of the Sabbath Controversies

2.1. Methodological issues

Questions of methodology have only become more complicated as the years have passed. In a relatively recent article, John P. Meier, who has been busy for some years now with his monumental historical Jesus project,[3] advocates a heightened methodological sensitivity in the area of Jesus and the law.[4] Meier calls attention to two large problems.

First, there is the problem, usually glossed over, of knowing the actual extent, status and stability of the written Torah in the time of Jesus.[5] Meier points, for example, to the instability of the text of Scripture in the first century. He notes further that despite the veneration of the law, it was not uncommon for the laws to be rewritten (cf. *Jub.* 2:25–33, which prohibits preparing food or drink on the Sabbath, and carrying anything in or out of the house; see too *Jub.* 50:1–13). He also indicates how laws that are not actually in Torah were often nevertheless attributed to Torah. Since the example Meier presents here concerns the Sabbath, we must look more closely at this. Meier reminds us that although the Mosaic law forbids work on the Sabbath, nowhere does the written Torah specify the nature of work, for example, by any extensive list of forbidden activities. An illustration of the difficulty can be seen in the lack of clarity concerning whether Israelite soldiers were allowed to fight on the Sabbath. Whereas in earlier generations they apparently did fight on the Sabbath, during the time of the Maccabean revolt some refused to do so (cf. 1 Macc 2:27–38). Others, however, allowed that *defensive* action was permissible on the Sabbath (see Josephus, *Ant.* 14.63, who presents as "the law" what earlier he presented as an *ad hoc* decision of Mattathias [*Ant.* 12.277]).

Similarly, Meier points out, both Josephus and Philo hold "that Moses *commanded* in the *written* Law that Jews should study the Torah ... and / or to attend the synagogue ... on the Sabbath,"[6] although, of course, no such commandments are to be found in the Scriptures. Meier's point is simply that it is sometimes difficult to pin down what "the law" really

---

[3] John P. Meier, *A Marginal Jew: Rethinking the Historical Jesus* (ABRL; New York: Doubleday, 1991–), three volumes to date. In the fourth volume Meier promises to deal in detail with the "enigma" of Jesus and the law; see John P. Meier, *Law and Love* (vol. 4 of *A Marginal Jew: Rethinking the Historical Jesus*; ABRL; New Haven: Yale University Press, 2009).

[4] John P Meier, "The Historical Jesus and the Historical Law: Some Problems Within the Problem," *CBQ* 65 (2003): 52–79.

[5] Meier, "The Historical Jesus and the Historical Law," 55–67.

[6] Meier, "The Historical Jesus and the Historical Law," 63.

said in the first century. Thus he asks, "Jesus and the Law – but what was the Law?"[7]

The second problem mentioned by Meier is more familiar to scholars. Here the issue concerns the difficulty of knowing exactly what specific interpretive traditions concerning the meaning of the Sabbath might have influenced Jesus' approach to the Torah.[8] In Meier's words, "deciding *which* interpretive traditions Jesus presupposes, embraces, or rejects seems at times nigh impossible."[9] Here Meier focuses on divorce rather than the Sabbath. He indicates, for example, that it now seems, contrary to the earlier view, that the Qumran documents do not forbid divorce. Further, Meier concludes that using the disputes between the houses of Shammai and Hillel concerning the grounds for divorce as the background for understanding the teaching of Jesus is anachronistic.[10] We have long known of the difficulty of using later rabbinic materials to throw light upon the New Testament. Now Meier calls attention to the wider problem of the difficulty of using all such background materials with any real degree of confidence.

Meier's concluding warning is appropriate: "Both the historical Jesus and the historical Law are problematic quantities, containing problems within problems. Anyone trying to construct a path through this maze should first post a road sign: Proceed with caution."[11] It would be hard to fault such a statement. At the same time, however, since Meier's article stems from his historical Jesus project, it is perhaps excessively stringent, almost minimalist, having in mind the highest possible degree of certitude, rather than the probable historical knowledge that might otherwise suffice. But as with practically all historical knowledge, here varying degrees of probability would seem to be all that is available to us.

In volume 2 of *A Marginal Jew*, Meier repeatedly came to the decision of *non liquet* (not clear) for the historicity of various healing pericopae (although as we shall see, he now suggests that he will come to a more firmly negative conclusion in volume 4). On this point Meier earlier wrote:

It may turn out that, because of the lack of data, no clear decision can be made one way or the other in most or even all of the cases [referring to stories that lack multiple attestation]. This decision should not be viewed as a diplomatic way of saying the accounts do not go back in some form to the historical Jesus, anymore than it should be taken as a covert judgment of historicity. *Non liquet* means *non liquet*, no more, no less. Often both liberal and conservative scholars are understandably unhappy

---

[7] Meier, "The Historical Jesus and the Historical Law," 67.
[8] Meier, "The Historical Jesus and the Historical Law," 67–79.
[9] Meier, "The Historical Jesus and the Historical Law," 67.
[10] Meier, "The Historical Jesus and the Historical Law," 74, 76.
[11] Meier, "The Historical Jesus and the Historical Law," 79.

with a decision not to decide, but sometimes the fragmentary state of our sources leaves us no other option.[12]

Meier calls the designation *non liquet* a "frustrating judgment." I find it not a little amusing, despite Meier's caveat, that the Jesus Seminar takes *non liquet* as consistently supporting their negative conclusions.[13] In fact, however, *non liquet* hardly prohibits a positive conclusion. In the end, the issue comes down to degrees of probability, and most importantly where the burden of proof resides. One's a priori inclination becomes a crucially important factor in deciding for or against historicity.[14]

As with virtually all the Gospel materials, so too with regard to the Sabbath controversies, the typical tests for authenticity naturally come into play. The three well-known criteria, dissimilarity, multiple attestation, and coherence, can, to be sure, be useful at times. They are nevertheless not without their problems, as has frequently been pointed out.[15] Extremely problematic, on the other hand, is the insistence of some that the burden of proof always lies with those who would accept an element of the tradition as authentic. Such a view cripples the possibility of historical knowledge so fundamentally that it is unrealistic and counterproductive, to say the least. There is something very wrong with a methodological approach that produces an empty cipher.[16] The burden of proof here must remain with those who would deny historical authenticity to the materials we have.[17] Peter Stuhlmacher makes the point well: "When one treats the gospel tradition not with a finally uncritical, flat-out doubt, but with an appropriate 'critical sympathy' (W. G. Kümmel), it is appropriate to proceed methodologically not from its historical unbelievability, but from its believability."[18] Given

---

[12] John P. Meier, *Mentor, Message, and Miracles* (vol. 2 of *A Marginal Jew: Rethinking the Historical Jesus*; ABRL; New York: Doubleday, 1994), 706–7.

[13] Robert W. Funk, et al., *The Five Gospels: The Search for the Authentic Words of Jesus* (New York: Macmillan, 1993), 49–50.

[14] See further the discussion in this volume in ch. 2, § 4.1.

[15] See especially Stanley E. Porter, *The Criteria for Authenticity in Historical-Jesus Research: Previous Discussion and New Proposals* (JSNTSup 191; Sheffield: Sheffield Academic Press, 2000); Gerd Theissen and Dagmar Winter, *The Quest for the Plausible Jesus: The Question of Criteria* (trans. M. Eugene Boring; Louisville: Westminster John Knox, 2002); discussion and bibliography in Craig A. Evans, *Life of Jesus Research: An Annotated Bibliography* (2nd ed.; NTTS 24; Leiden: Brill, 1996), 132–34, 136–38, 139–41.

[16] Thus Bo Ivar Reicke, "Incarnation and Exaltation: The Historic Jesus and the Kerygmatic Christ," *Int* 16 (1962): 156–68.

[17] See Stewart C. Goetz and Craig L. Blomberg, "The Burden of Proof," *JSNT* 11 (1981): 39–63.

[18] Peter Stuhlmacher, *Biblische Theologie des Neuen Testaments* (2 vols.; Göttingen: Vandenhoeck & Ruprecht, 1992), 1:45; the entire sentence is italicized in the original. For the opposite view, see Doering, *Schabbat*, 407: "It must therefore be firmly held that *the burden of proof lies upon the assertion of authenticity*" (italics original).

how admittedly little we often have available, no other approach can be fair to the documents we possess.

A preliminary observation is in order here. We have a variety of witnesses that should encourage a positive inclination toward the historicity of the Sabbath-controversy passages. The Sabbath-controversy passages are represented in several strands of historical material, and thus pass the test of multiple attestation. The incident of the plucking of the grain on the Sabbath is found in all three Synoptics. That Jesus healed on the Sabbath is even more solidly attested in our sources. In addition to the tradition found in Luke's special material, we also have evidence from the Gospel of John: the healing of the paralyzed man at the pool of Bethesda (John 5:1–47; defended in 7:19–24); the healing of the man who was blind from birth (John 9:1–41). There is also evidence in non-biblical material that the Sabbath was a subject of the greatest importance (e.g. Qumran, Josephus, Gospel of Thomas) that points to the likelihood that Jesus ran into trouble on this matter. Furthermore, there is no evidence that the Sabbath was an actual problem in the early church, and thus there is little reason to believe that the Sabbath-controversy stories are the creation of the early church.

2.2. *The Synoptic Sabbath-Controversy Texts*

How much debate is there concerning the historicity of the synoptic Sabbath- controversy narratives? We shall now look at the several passages one by one.

The disciples' plucking of the grain on the Sabbath (Mark 2:23–28 = Matt 12:1–8 = Luke 6:1–5) presents the first challenge. The three accounts agree closely, with typical variations, except for two major differences: (1) the Matthean insertion (Matt 12:5–7): "Or have you not read in the law how on the Sabbath the priests in the temple profane the Sabbath, and are guiltless? I tell you, something greater than the temple is here. And if you had known what this means, 'I desire mercy, and not sacrifice,' you would not have condemned the guiltless;" and (2) Matthew's and Luke's omission of the Markan logion: "The Sabbath was made for man, not man for the Sabbath" (Mark 2:27).

The conclusions of the Jesus Seminar on these texts are mixed. For the Markan pericope they put some of Jesus' words in pink ("Jesus probably said something like this"), namely (their translation): "The Sabbath day was created for Adam and Eve, not Adam and Eve for the Sabbath day. So the son of Adam lords it even over the Sabbath day" (Mark 2:27–28). They think that these logia are "aphoristic" and "memorable" and that they "could have circulated independently." As for the story itself, on the other hand, they conclude–without supporting argument–that "the narrative context in which this saying is preserved may well be the invention of the community." As for the other words of Jesus (Mark 2:25–26), they "are an integral part of the story and so never circulated independently. As a consequence, they tell us nothing about what Jesus may have said."[19] The logion "The son of Adam lords it over the Sabbath day," which is given a rating of pink in Mark, is given a lower rating (gray means "Jesus did not say this, but the ideas contained in it are close to his own") in the parallels in Matt 12:8 and Luke 6:5. The reason for this is that according to the Seminar, Matthew and Luke, by eliminating the first logion and presenting only the second logion, show that they understand the latter christologically, i.e. as referring to the apocalyptic Son of Man. But this for the Seminar indicates a misunderstanding, since they take the second logion, like the first, to refer merely to human beings. Mark too understood the second logion to refer to the apocalyptic Son of Man, "but he nevertheless preserves the original parallelism, which makes it possible to recover Jesus' meaning."[20] Why Jesus cannot have been referring to *himself* as the apocalyptic Son of Man is not argued, but simply assumed.

The Seminar takes Mark 2:25–26 to be "a Christian scribal insertion," for the reason that it was the tendency of Christians "to buttress their position by reference to the scriptures." On the other hand, it is alleged that "Jesus was apparently not given to this practice."[21] How such a conclusion can be drawn when Jesus admittedly justifies his action on the Sabbath by an appeal to Gen 1:26 and Ps 8:4–8,[22] in material designated pink, is left unexplained.

Laudably, the Jesus Seminar has modified its views on the historicity of this pericope to some extent. To begin with, they said "the narrative context in which this saying is preserved may well be the invention of the community."[23] On the other hand, in their subsequent volume on Acts, they conclude: "the story paints a picture of typical activities" and not "a single scene."[24] Yet, remarkably, "The Fellows think that the practice of Jesus and the disciples and the objection of the Pharisees has some basis in fact."[25] The Seminar puts the additional material found in Matt 12:5–7 in black without comment, following a general bias against the historicity of M material.

---

[19] Funk, et al., *The Five Gospels*, 50. The Jesus Seminar is rather more conservative in their conclusions on this passage in Robert W. Funk and The Jesus Seminar, *The Acts of Jesus: The Search for the Authentic Deeds of Jesus* (San Francisco: HarperSanFrancisco, 1998).
[20] Funk, et al., *The Five Gospels*, 183.
[21] Funk and Seminar, *The Acts of Jesus*, 68.
[22] See Funk, et al., *The Five Gospels*, 49 and 183.
[23] Funk, et al., *The Five Gospels*, 49.
[24] Funk and Seminar, *The Acts of Jesus*, 68.
[25] Funk and Seminar, *The Acts of Jesus*, 284.

In advance of what will appear in vol. 4, Meier has decided against the historicity of the plucking of grain on the Sabbath incident, for the following reasons: (1) the presence of the Pharisees in the grainfield "strains credibility";[26] (2) the question of the distance traveled to the grainfield; (3) the distortion and misrepresentation of the story in 1 Sam 21; (4) the irrelevance of that story, which does not mention the Sabbath.

Others, of course, have challenged the historicity of our passage.[27] One reason for this is the widespread belief that the passage is composite, with its component parts put together initially by Mark or perhaps already in the tradition used by Mark.[28] The fact that Mark 2:27–28 is introduced afresh with the words καὶ ἔλεγεν αὐτοῖς, suggests to many that these two logia may stem from elsewhere in the tradition and were attached to the present passage.[29] Alternatively, some conclude that these verses originally followed v. 24, and that it is vv. 25–26, introduced with καὶ λέγει αὐτοῖς, that have been inserted into the pericope.[30] A further issue is that 2:28 is regarded by many as a later addition to v. 27. Meier concludes that vv. 27–28 "were added secondarily, either at the same time or in separate stages."[31]

Even as cautious a scholar as C. E. B. Cranfield regards v. 28 as probably an addition to the story. He doubts that Jesus would have used a messianic title like Son of Man in reference to himself, and concludes that "the most probable explanation seems to be that this verse is a Christian comment–either Mark's own or an exegetical comment already attached to v. 27 in the tradition he used."[32] Eduard Schweizer concludes that "this story appears to be fictitious," wondering where the Pharisees come from, why they do not

---

[26] John P. Meier, "The Historical Jesus and the Plucking of the Grain on the Sabbath," *CBQ* 66 (2004): 573.

[27] Doering (*Schabbat*, 408–32), for example, comes to very similar conclusions as the Seminar.

[28] For full discussion, see Frans Neirynck, "Jesus and the Sabbath: Some Observations on Mark ii,27," in *Jésus aux origines de la christologie* (ed. Jacques Dupont; BETL 40; Louvain: Louvain University Press, 1989), 227–70.

[29] A view held by scholars as diverse as Rudolf Bultmann, *The History of the Synoptic Tradition* (trans. John Marsh; New York: Harper & Row, 1963), 16, and William L. Lane, *The Gospel of Mark* (NICNT; Grand Rapids: Eerdmans, 1974), 118–19; cf. Robert A. Guelich, *Mark 1–8:26* (WBC 34a; Dallas: Word, 1989), 120. Vincent Taylor (*The Gospel According to St. Mark* [2nd ed.; London: Macmillan, 1966], 218) writes: "There can be little doubt that the sayings have been added, either by Mark or an earlier compiler, from a sayings collection."

[30] E.g., Morna D. Hooker, *A Commentary on the Gospel According to St. Mark* (BNTC; London: A&C Black, 1991), 104.

[31] Meier, "The Plucking of the Grain," 572. Meier notes, however, that this conclusion leaves open the question whether the two logia go back to the historical Jesus.

[32] C. E. B. Cranfield, *The Gospel According to Saint Mark* (CGTC; Cambridge: Cambridge University Press, 1959), 118.

fault the disciples for walking beyond the allowed distance on the Sabbath, and also noting that the story lacks a specific setting (when and where).[33]

What can be said in response to the arguments against the historicity of this pericope? We may begin by noting that we probably have evidence of multiple attestation in this pericope. Theissen and Merz have noted that the large number of "minor agreements" between Matthew and Luke against Mark argue for the existence of a parallel tradition.[34] There is furthermore the coherence of the Sabbath-healing stories with the present narrative, which together point to the problematic non-observance of the Sabbath on the part of Jesus, thus increasing its historical plausibility.

It should be made clear that the story can be essentially historical even if the passage as we have it is composite. Thus, even if vv. 27–28 were added, or vv. 25–26 inserted, from another context, the story can still have happened more or less as recounted. All claims concerning the pre-history of the pericope, however, are necessarily speculative. As R. Gundry puts it, listing no fewer than eight options for the Markan passage, "the woods are full of mutually destructive theories regarding stages of tradition-history leading up to the present pericope."[35]

Let us begin with Meier's first two objections, raised earlier by Schweitzer and others. Is it realistic to imagine Pharisees in the grainfields spying on Jesus? Why is this thought to be so improbable? With their suspicions more than aroused (cf. Mark 2:7, 16; 3:6) there is every reason to think that the Pharisees could well have been interested in seeing what Jesus might be up to on that Sabbath, and hence with other curious onlookers have walked along behind the disciples (cf. Mark 1:28, 37, 45). But why, secondly, was there no charge concerning walking beyond the accepted limit (a distance of no more than approximately a half a mile[36])? There is in the text no indication that the limit had been exceeded.[37] Jesus and his disciples may well

---

[33] Eduard Schweizer, *The Good News According to Mark* (trans. H. Donald; Richmond: John Knox, 1970), 70. Cf. Adela Yarbro Collins, *Mark* (Hermeneia; Minneapolis: Fortress, 2007), 201, who concludes that the passage represents "the sort of debate [Jesus] may well have engaged in and the manner of his argumentation."

[34] Gerd Theissen and Annette Merz, *The Historical Jesus: A Comprehensive Guide* (trans. John Bowden; Minneapolis: Fortress, 1998), 367–68.

[35] Robert H. Gundry, *Mark: A Commentary on His Apology for the Cross* (Grand Rapids: Eerdmans, 1993), 148.

[36] See CD 10:20–22, "No-one is to walk in the field to do the work which he wishes [on] the Sabbath. He is not to walk more than one thousand cubits outside the city." Cf. Josephus, *Ant.* 13.252; m. ʿErub. 4:3 ff.

[37] "The incidental question as to traveling on the Sabbath does not arise, for in the Gospels this aspect is ignored, and we must suppose that the disciples had not engaged on a long journey, for such a proceeding would constitute an entire breach with the spirit of the Sabbath rest." Israel Abrahams, *Studies in Pharisaism and the Gospels* (Library of Biblical Studies; 1924; repr., New York: Ktav, 1967), 134.

have been just beyond the border of the town,[38] on "a Sabbath afternoon stroll [more] than a missionary expedition."[39] In agreement with this, there is no indication in Mark (unlike Matt 12:1) that the disciples were hungry.

Meier's other observations concerning the use of the story in 1 Sam 21 raise difficult points to be sure. It seems to me, however, that Meier demands a school-room exactitude here that is unnecessary for the argument to work. First, although David's men are not with him at that precise moment, according to 1 Sam 21:2–3. David refers to them in the words "I have made an appointment with the young men for such and such a place. Now then, what do you have at hand?" Clearly the bread is for him and his hungry men whom he will shortly meet. This seems obvious from the text of 1 Sam 21. Thus it is hardly necessary to conclude that the question of the high priest "Why are you alone, and no one with you?" "directly and blatantly contradicts what Jesus claims the text says."[40] This is to approach the text in a woodenly literal way. But is the text of 1 Sam 21 really distorted or misrepresented here? Mark nowhere uses plural verbs to say that "they" went into the house of God; the verb "went in" (εἰσῆλθεν) is singular, referring to David.[41] Mark says, furthermore, that David gave it (ἔδωκεν) to those who were with him. And why cannot they have eaten the bread later? Why must the loaves have been eaten then and there, as Meier seems to insist?

But there are further issues. The passage of scripture to which Jesus appeals does not refer at all to the Sabbath. So how does it serve as a defense for the actions of Jesus' disciples? The argument is not direct, but analogical. The point is that the dictates of the law, here eating bread that only the priests were allowed to eat, but including the Sabbath commandment by implication, can be transcended by a matter of greater importance. Even if the Sabbath were mentioned in the story of David, the argument would not work, at least in Mark, where there is not so much as a mention that the disciples were hungry (Matthew does add this point to make the case more convincing), let alone in mortal danger, which might have justified acting in this way on the Sabbath.

Finally, there is the issue of the mistaken reference to the high priest as not Ahimelech (as in 1 Sam 21), but Abiathar. Meier admits that in some

---

[38] See the interesting statement in *m. Soṭah* 4:3: In a discussion of the Sabbath limit, it is said that "The one thousand cubits are the outskirts [of the city] and the two thousand cubits are the [surrounding] fields and vineyards."

[39] So D. A. Carson, "Jesus and the Sabbath in the Four Gospels," in *From Sabbath to Lord's Day: A Biblical, Historical and Theological Investigation* (ed. D. A. Carson; Grand Rapids: Zondervan, 1982), 61.

[40] Meier, "The Plucking of the Grain," 575.

[41] Meier ("The Plucking of the Grain," 574) is therefore not strictly correct when he says that "Jesus claims that David had companions with him when he came to the priest at Nob." That is an inference and not stated in Mark's text.

Hebrew Bible texts there seems to be a confusion between the son and the father, although there is no evidence available to us regarding such a variant specifically for the 1 Samuel text. Mark's reading here, understandably omitted by Matthew and Luke, may simply be an example of this confusion. In any event, it hardly seems fair to make this confusion of names, really a minor point and found in other texts, a determining factor in whether Jesus spoke these words.[42]

Some twenty years ago Maurice Casey mounted a very interesting defense of the historicity of the pericope, based on a reconstruction of the underlying Aramaic and an examination of the cultural background of the episode.[43] Casey regards the story as an example of *Peah*, i.e., plucking of grain that had been left on the border of the field for the poor (Lev 19:9; 23:22). Although Mark does not say so, the clear implication, according to Casey, is that the disciples were hungry (this making more appropriate the analogy of David and his men eating the bread of the presence). Given the disturbing actions of Jesus, e.g., already in Mark healing on the Sabbath and eating with tax-collectors and sinners, "the probability that some Pharisees would come and observe him early in the ministry is extremely strong."[44]

Casey regards Mark 2:23–28 as coherent argumentation. "We should not find Jesus' argument incoherent, and the Marcan narrative a mosaic of separate pieces, on the ground that the argument does not follow an analytical mode foreign to the environment in which the argument was produced."[45] While Casey may have overstated his case, he concludes "the whole narrative has an excellent *Sitz im Leben* in the life of Jesus. The early church cannot have created it."[46] It is important to note here, however, that the logic of Casey's argument depends on his taking Mark 2:28 in a non-christological sense. If that verse is taken as referring to Christ, then Casey would not accept its historicity. We shall return to this problem below.

It seems clear that the introductory formula at the beginning of Mark 2:27, καὶ ἔλεγεν αὐτοῖς, need not be taken as introducing material from an-

---

[42] Meier's conclusion ("The Plucking of the Grain," 578) seems to me overstated, unnecessary, and unfair: "the recounting of the incident of David and Ahimelech shows both a glaring ignorance of what the OT text actually says and a striking inability to construct a convincing argument from the story."

[43] Maurice Casey, "Culture and Historicity: The Plucking of the Grain (Mark 2:23–28)," *NTS* 34 (1988): 1–23. See also chapter 4, "Two Sabbath Controversies: Mark 2:23–3:6" in Casey's book, *Aramaic Sources of Mark's Gospel* (SNTSMS 102; Cambridge: Cambridge University Press, 1998), 138–92.

[44] Casey, "The Plucking of the Grain," 5.

[45] Casey, "The Plucking of the Grain," 11.

[46] Casey, "The Plucking of the Grain," 20. The same statement is found in his book (*Aramaic Sources*, 166).

other context.⁴⁷ It can equally well mark a new aspect of material being presented at the same occasion. Noting this phenomenon at Mark 6:10, 7:9 and 9:1, Gundry concludes "we do not have convincing evidence to suppose that in 2:27 the phrase indicates the importation of sayings into a pericope that lacked them before."⁴⁸ Gundry points out that the insertion of the phrase prevents the misunderstanding of v. 28 as an editorial comment rather than a saying of Jesus; but it had to be put at the beginning of v. 27 because of the subordinating conjunction ὥστε at the beginning of v. 28. "Mark wants this saying [v. 28] to be understood as spoken by Jesus."⁴⁹ Also worth noting here is E. Lohse's opinion, who after considering the evidence concludes that 2:27 "als echtes Jesuswort anzusehen ist."⁵⁰

Gundry astutely comments that it would be strange for a later redactor to have added the argument from the OT in Mark 2:25–26, especially when no OT arguments are used in the context, and especially when the passage about David and his men does not specifically refer to the Sabbath. The additional fact that this support is haggadic (from a story) rather than halakhic (from a legal stipulation), as would be required in legal disputes,⁵¹ further "increases the chances of originality and authenticity."⁵²

Finally, we may note five points mentioned by R. Pesch in support of the historicity of this pericope: (1) the presence of similar passages concerning Jesus and the Sabbath in special Luke and in John, and the irrelevance to early church interests of plucking grain on the Sabbath; (2) Jesus and the disciples were poor itinerants; (3) the plausibility of Jesus being held responsible for the disciples' conduct; (4) Jesus also uses scripture in other conflict stories; and (5) Jesus knew himself to be on a mission and compares himself to David again in Mark 12:25–27.⁵³

---

⁴⁷ For its review of the discussion, F. Neirynck's article ("Jesus and the Sabbath: Some Observations on Mark ii,27") is indispensable.

⁴⁸ Gundry, *Mark*, 143.

⁴⁹ Gundry, *Mark*, 144.

⁵⁰ Eduard Lohse, "Jesu Worte über den Sabbat," in *Judentum, Urchristentum, Kirche: Festschrift für Joachim Jeremias* (2nd ed.; ed. Walther Eltester; Berlin: Töpelmann, 1964), 85.

⁵¹ See D. M. Cohn-Sherbok, "An Analysis of Jesus' Arguments Concerning the Plucking of Grain on the Sabbath," *JSNT* (1979): 31–41.

⁵² Gundry, *Mark*, 148. Note Gundry's earlier comment: "To argue that because the scriptural argument in vv 25–26 is not Christological it comes from Jesus rather than from the church wrongly posits that only non-Christological statements are historically acceptable on his lips. To argue that because the scriptural argument is not eschatological it comes from the church rather than from Jesus wrongly posits that only eschatological statements are historically acceptable on his lips. Easy formulas do not decide historical questions" (p. 146).

⁵³ Rudolf Pesch, *Das Markusevangelium* (2 vols.; HTKNT 2; Freiburg im Breisgau: Herder, 1977), 1:183. W. D. Davies and Dale C. Allison (*A Critical and Exegetical Com-

If one accepts the essential historicity of Mark 2:23–28 and thus of Matt 12:1–4, what about the M tradition in Matt 12:5–7? The majority of scholars take these verses as originating from the evangelist or at least leave it an open question. The evangelist, it is commonly argued, may have regarded the argument of 12:3–4 as unconvincing, and made the addition to strengthen the case, modeling vv. 5–7 on vv. 3–4. It is, of course, impossible to disprove this hypothesis. Another plausible hypothesis, however, is that Jesus also spoke vv. 5–7 and that this material was preserved in an oral tradition available to Matthew. It coheres beautifully with the preceding verses, and if Jesus presented the first illustration, it is also possible that he presented the second in parallel form. Furthermore, the quotation of Hos 6:6 here can well come from Jesus, in the same way that its first occurrence probably goes back to the historical Jesus, as clearly does the pericope in which it occurs, 9:12–13. Here again the initial bias one assumes regarding the historicity of the gospel tradition, whether negative or positive, will largely determine the conclusion to which one is attracted.

There are thus good arguments for taking the pericope as essentially historical,[54] despite the objections that some have raised.[55]

The second main Synoptic Sabbath controversy concerns the healing of the man with the withered hand (Mark 3:1–6 = Matt 12:9–14 = Luke 6:6–11). Again the three synoptic accounts are remarkably similar. The only major difference between them is found in Matthew's addition of the question, "What man of you, if he has only one sheep and it falls into a pit on the Sabbath, will not lay hold of it and lift it out? Of how much more value is a man than a sheep" (Matt 12:11–12a). This material is not found in Mark, but almost the same question occurs in Luke's story of the Sabbath healing of the man with dropsy (Luke 14:5), thus raising the level of historical probability.

Jesus' words in this passage are not authentic according to the Jesus Seminar. Words like "Get up here in front of everybody" and "Hold out your hand," they reject as words that would not have been remembered. Also

---

mentary on the Gospel According to Saint Matthew [3 vols.; ICC; Edinburgh: T&T Clark, 1988–97], 2:305) accept this validity of these points in defense of the parallel Matt 12:1–8.

[54] For a listing of those who defend the historicity of the story, see Yong-Eui Yang, *Jesus and the Sabbath in Matthew's Gospel* (JSNTSup 139; Sheffield: Sheffield Academic Press, 1997), 165, n. 112.

[55] William R. G. Loader (*Jesus' Attitude Towards the Law: A Study of the Gospels* [WUNT 2.97; Tübingen: Mohr Siebeck, 1997], 52–53), in a long excursus on the tradition of Mark 2:1–3:6 and the historical Jesus, although coming to somewhat conservative conclusions, adjudges only "possibility" for 2:23–28. He accepts the contention of Sanders and Vermes that the Pharisees would not have been bothered by any of Jesus' activity on the Sabbath, and that therefore if any history underlies these pericopes the opposition must have come from some "extremist" group.

attributed to the evangelist is the thought-provoking question (Mark 3:4), ignored in their comments, "On the Sabbath day is it permitted to do good or to do evil, to save life or to destroy it?" While apparently rejecting the historicity of the story, they do at least concede that "the story suggests ... that Jesus did engage in controversy regarding the Sabbath observance."[56]

As noted above, the Matthean parallel has these additional words: "If you had only a single sheep, and it fell into a ditch on the Sabbath day, wouldn't you grab on to it, and pull it out? A person is worth considerably more than a sheep. So, it is permitted to do good on the Sabbath day" (Matt 12:11–12, the Seminar's translation). These the Seminar puts in gray because they believe that "in its present form" it was "formulated by the evangelist." They add, however, that "the content of the saying is believed to be reminiscent of Jesus' teaching."[57] The Lukan parallel (Luke 6:6–11) gets the same negative verdict given to the Markan passage.

The doubt of the Seminar concerning Mark 3:1–6 begins with v. 6 and works backwards. "The plot against Jesus described in v. 6 is widely regarded as a Markan fiction. Nothing in the way Jesus treats the withered hand would have called for an attempt on his life."[58] Their argument then proceeds as follows:

If the plot is a Markan invention, then the authenticity of the saying in v. 4 becomes problematic: the rhetorical question Jesus proposes is designed for this particular story. It sets up the option of saving life, in this case, the hand of the man, or destroying life–Jesus' own. Moreover, the rhetorical query is a typical way of responding to the charge in v. 2. In short, it is difficult to isolate any elements in the story that are not part of Mark's compositional scheme that climaxes in the plot of v. 6.[59]

They remark further that since Jesus performs no overt action other than to ask the man to hold out his hand, the Pharisees would not have found anything objectionable in what he did and that they would not have thought that Jesus violated the Sabbath. Hence, "The response on the part of the Pharisees is trumped up by the storyteller."[60] Finally, since the story does not follow the form of the typical healing narrative, Jesus here taking the initiative himself, this leads to the "suspicion that the story was created to support growing christological interests in the Christian community."[61]

---

[56] Funk, et al., *The Five Gospels*, 50. Doering (*Schabbat*, 445) makes the same proposal.
[57] Funk, et al., *The Five Gospels*, 184.
[58] Funk and Seminar, *The Acts of Jesus*, 69.
[59] Funk and Seminar, *The Acts of Jesus*, 69: "Considering the gravity of these problems, gray [= possible, but unreliable] was a generous designation."
[60] Funk and Seminar, *The Acts of Jesus*, 69.
[61] Funk and Seminar, *The Acts of Jesus*, 69.

In vol. 2 of his *Marginal Jew*, Meier also expresses his doubts concerning this passage. As with the Seminar, he begins with doubt about the authenticity of Mark 3:6 and works backwards:

> If, then, we consider 3:6 not to reflect one precise event in the actual ministry of the historical Jesus in A.D. 28–30, this raises serious questions about the historicity of the rhetorical question in 3:4 and hence of the form of the dispute as it now appears in Mark 3:1–6. But what is Mark 3:1–6 without the element of the dispute story? Once one unravels 3:6, which in turn unravels 3:4, one wonders what is left of the ball of yarn that is 3:1–6.[62]

His conclusion is, "I do not think that the Sabbath controversy, as presented in Mark 3:1–6, goes back to a historical event in Jesus' ministry." But at the same time he is fair enough to admit that it cannot be proved that the narrative is unhistorical, and he finally concludes that "the historicity of the miracle story in Mark 3:1–6 is best left in the limbo-category of not clear (*non liquet*)."[63]

In his more recent article on the plucking of grain on the Sabbath, discussed above, Meier indicates that he has now moved more firmly in the direction of rejecting the historicity of this and other pericopae involving healing on the Sabbath. The reason: "I hope to show in volume 4 that there is no solid evidence that in the early first century A.D. Palestinian Jews of any stripe would have considered healing a violation of the Sabbath; if this opinion is correct, then my decision of *non liquet* would have to be revised in the direction of 'not historical.'"[64] The question of whether healing on the Sabbath would have been a problem for first-century Jews will be discussed below.

In responding to the objections raised concerning the historicity of this passage, we must first address the questions surrounding v. 6. It is, of course, quite possible that this verse is a redactional addition, placed here as the culmination of the chain of controversy passages that begins in 2:1. Mark (or someone before him) has apparently gathered together controversy stories for their cumulative impact.[65] It is unlikely that the plot to kill Jesus arose just from this particular healing on the Sabbath. But when Jesus repeatedly acted toward the Sabbath with a pretentious authority,[66] doing so in the

---

[62] Meier, *Mentor, Message, and Miracles*, 731, n. 16.
[63] Meier, *Mentor, Message, and Miracles*, 683–84.
[64] Meier, "The Plucking of the Grain," 561, n. 2.
[65] Hooker (*St. Mark*, 108) states, "It may be that a more accurate historical presentation of the material would have spread the conflict stories out through the ministry of Jesus but, by placing them together in the early stages of his gospel, Mark emphasizes the implacable opposition of official Judaism to Jesus and explains–at a human level–his final rejection."
[66] Christian Dietzfelbinger, "Vom Sinn der Sabbatheilungen Jesu," *EvT* 38 (1978): 287.

context of his proclamation of the dawning of the Kingdom, he would easily have been regarded as a dangerous threat.

R. A. Guelich regards v. 6 as part of the passage, arguing that (1) since the passage does not fit the form-critical category for a healing pericope (it is more a pronouncement story), it is illegitimate to eliminate v. 6 on form-critical grounds; (2) the fact that καὶ ἐξέρχεσθαι is favored by Mark hardly means that the entire verse is redactional; and (3) Mark may have chosen to put this pericope here precisely because he wanted to conclude this section with the point made in v. 6.[67]

Even if one concludes that v. 6 *is* redactional, however, it hardly follows that the passage unravels and is necessarily unhistorical, *pace* Meier and the Seminar. The reason they think it does is the result of a questionable interpretation of v. 4. They take the words about doing harm and killing on the Sabbath to refer the Pharisees' and Herodians' plot to do away with Jesus. According to this view, the choice is not between two things Jesus may do, but rather between what Jesus may do (good; save life) and what his enemies are contemplating doing (harm; kill). Thus v. 4 needs the statement of v. 6. It is exegetically more likely, however, that the words are to be understood as Jesus' own choice between healing and not healing. Not to heal is thus taken as harming and in effect killing.[68] If this view is taken, then v. 4 is not absolutely dependent upon v. 6 to make good sense.

The flat statement of the Seminar that the words of Jesus in this pericope would not have been remembered is simply biased opinion. The words "Come here" (the Greek is more striking: ἔγειρε εἰς τὸ μέσον, literally "rise up in the midst [of the crowd]") and "Stretch out your hand," are exactly the kind of vivid words that would leave an indelible impression upon anyone who witnessed the event (cf. Mark 5:41). More significant is the question, "On the Sabbath day is it permitted to do good or to do evil, to save life or to destroy it?" Contrary to the Seminar's opinion, the question is both striking and memorable. Lohse concludes: "Also in this word Jesus himself speaks, not first the community."[69] Pesch concludes "the text is an

---

He argues that the story of Mark 3:1–6 represents in stylized form a number of Sabbath healings performed by Jesus.

[67] Guelich, *Mark 1–8:26*, 132. Gundry (*Mark*, 156) also supports "the originality and authenticity" of v. 6. Why, he asks, would the evangelist create this reference to the Pharisees and Herodians plotting against Jesus when neither have a role to play in his account of the passion narrative?

[68] Thus, e. g., Schweizer, Cranfield, Guelich, Hooker. For the opposite view, see Taylor, Lane, Gundry.

[69] Lohse, "Jesu Worte über den Sabbat," 85. So too, Matt. 12:11–12 (cf. Luke 14:5) is, according to Lohse "ein echtes Jesuswort" (p. 87); Dietzfelbinger ("Vom Sinn der Sabbatheilungen Jesu," 288) concludes the same.

important and reliable source for the work, self-understanding, and influence (antagonism against) of Jesus."[70]

It may be argued that since healing on the Sabbath was not an issue in the early church, it is unlikely that this story would have been created to meet a pressing need.[71] All in all, it seems fair to conclude with Guelich that "there seems to be no solid evidence for disputing the historical roots of this story in Jesus' ministry."[72] Supporting the historicity of the logion of Jesus in Matt 12:11, are the presupposition of "Jewish sentiment," the language typical of Jesus ("which one of you"), its consistency with other Sabbath controversy stories, and its similarity to the tendency of Jesus elsewhere to exalt mercy over the typical understanding of holiness.[73]

There are two further Sabbath-controversy passages, found only in Luke. In the first of these a woman with a bent-over back is healed on the Sabbath (Luke 13:10–17). Justifying his deed, Jesus is recorded as saying (Luke 13:15–16): "You hypocrites! Does not each of you on the Sabbath untie his ox or his ass from the manger, and lead it away to water it? And ought not this woman, a daughter of Abraham whom Satan bound for eighteen years, be loosed from this bond on the Sabbath day?" The Seminar regards these words as apparently "created by Luke specifically for this story." They add the unsupported and dogmatic conclusion: "They were not among the remembered sayings of Jesus transmitted orally before the gospels were written."[74] As for the story itself, they conclude:

> It seemed entirely probable to the members of the Seminar that Jesus was faced with a confrontation on a Sabbath after healing someone's non-life-threatening condition ... They also thought it probable that Jesus questioned Sabbath regulations and that he occasionally failed to observe them. However, they did not think the story of the afflicted woman supported these probabilities, except as a remote fictive memory.[75]

They support their conclusion by noting the pericope's "Lukan vocabulary, style, and themes," noting further that Luke here "indulges his proclivity to

---

[70] Pesch, *Das Markusevangelium*, 1:195. Pesch calls attention to the antiquity and semitisms of the text, as well as the parallels in other gospel traditions.

[71] Sven-Olav Bäck, *Jesus of Nazareth and the Sabbath Commandment* (Åbo: Åbo Akademi University Press, 1995), 85: "If a 'community problem' is reflected in the story, it is a problem otherwise unknown."

[72] Guelich, *Mark 1–8:26*, 132. Lohse ("Jesu Worte über den Sabbat," 84) too gives strong affirmation: "Unter allen in den Evangelien erzählten Sabbatgeschichten könnte die Perikope Mc 3 1–5 am ehesten eine Situation im Wirken des historischen Jesus wiedergeben." Casey (*Aramaic Sources*, 192) also finds the natural *Sitz im Leben* of the passage to be "in the life of Jesus."

[73] Davies and Allison, *Matthew*, 2:316–17.

[74] Funk, et al., *The Five Gospels*, 346. But how can they possibly *know* this, one wonders?

[75] Funk and Seminar, *The Acts of Jesus*, 319. Is not the bias of the Seminar showing in these remarks?

imitate the Greek scriptures (LXX)," and that "this was the principle reason for the black designation."[76]

The second Lukan pericope (Luke 14:1–6) refers to the Sabbath healing of a man with dropsy. Here we get both questions (from Jesus), "Is it lawful to heal on the Sabbath, or not?" and "Which of you, having a son or an ox that has fallen into a well, will not immediately pull him out on a Sabbath day?" The Jesus Seminar rejects the authenticity of the first, on the grounds that it is not "memorable" and "portrays Jesus as initiating a discussion of a fine legal point," but gives the second a gray color "on the grounds that it reflects Jesus' view on the question of Sabbath observance, but only in a general way."[77]

The Seminar's justification for the black vote given to the story is expressed in the following words:

In this case the setting in the house of a Pharisee is most likely a Lukan contrivance. The appearance of the patient at a dinner party, as noted earlier, is unmotivated. Taking the initiative in both the cure and the debate is unusual for Jesus, who normally only responds when questioned or addressed and who functions as a healer only when requested. These abnormalities, plus the fact that the story exhibits other traces of Luke's style, suggested a black vote.[78]

At this point we find a conclusive statement concerning Jesus and the Sabbath that is worth quoting in full:

The Seminar took polls on several general questions about Jesus' concern with matters of Sabbath observance. The Fellows agreed by an overwhelming margin that Jesus probably did not engage in debates on fine points of law, nor did he initiate discussion or debate about Sabbath observance. On the other hand, the Fellows strongly agreed that Jesus did engage in activities that suggested he had little concern for Sabbath observance. His actions did provoke those who were concerned about such regulations and their response must have involved him in arguments about proper Sabbath observance.[79]

It is hardly obvious why Jesus would not have initiated discussion about the Sabbath if in fact he engaged in activities that suggested he had little concern for observing the Sabbath. These tensions suggest that the Seminar's position is not as well thought out as it might be. And as is so often the case, what they set forth as the opinion of "scholarship" turns out to be the opinion of a relatively small representation of scholars, while those who differ are studiously ignored.

---

[76] Funk and Seminar, *The Acts of Jesus*, 319.
[77] Funk, et al., *The Five Gospels*, 350. Again, is this anything more than subjective opinion?
[78] Funk and Seminar, *The Acts of Jesus*, 321.
[79] Funk, et al., *The Five Gospels*, 350.

The Seminar seems to have an a priori bias against the two Lukan pericopes because they represent L tradition. There can be no question but that the passages reveal Lukan redaction, but that should not prejudice the historical question. Meier also calls attention to the points made by the Seminar against Luke 13:10–17. At the same time, however, he calls attention to details that "may at least point to pre-Lucan tradition," namely the absence of Pharisees and the specific "eighteen years" that the woman had suffered. "These concrete details may point to pre-Lucan tradition and even to tradition stemming from the historical Jesus, but they hardly prove the case."[80] Meier nevertheless concluded that the question of the historicity of the pericope remains unclear (*non liquet*). As we have seen, however, he will conclude against the historicity of the passage in his volume 4. Joseph Fitzmyer's conclusion is more positive: "The story itself probably reflects one of the real-life situations of Jesus' own ministry: a cure and debate over the Sabbath in Stage I of the gospel tradition."[81]

Meier's treatment of Luke 14:1–6 parallels that of Luke 13:10–17. Here too Meier notes "signs of heavy Lucan redaction."[82] Again we may ask why this fact disqualifies a story from being historical.[83] Indeed, Meier himself makes the following observation:

> Still, the question of historicity is not so easily settled. Luke 14:1–6 does have characteristics that mark it off from all other stories of healing on the Sabbath: the healing takes place in the house of a Pharisee, not in a synagogue, and in the context of a meal. Dropsy as the ailment cured is unparalleled in the rest of the Bible. Jesus heals not with a word but with a touch. No opposition to Jesus is voiced, Jesus' reaction to his adversaries is not as fierce as elsewhere, and no hostile action is planned against Jesus. Thus, the question of Luke 14:1–6 being a mere variant of other stories of healing on the Sabbath is not such an open-and-shut case as might first appear.[84]

Although Lohse regards the story as an example of Gemeindebildung, the logion of 14:5 "muß zum ältesten Bestand der Logienüberlieferung gerechnet werden" ("must be reckoned with the oldest form of the logia

---

[80] Meier, *Mentor, Message, and Miracles*, 2:684.

[81] Joseph A. Fitzmyer, *The Gospel According to Luke X–XXIV* (AB 28a; Garden City: Doubleday, 1985), 1011. For a detailed response to "difficulties" bearing on the authenticity of the passage, see John Nolland, *Luke 9:21–18:34* (WBC 35b; Dallas: Word, 1993), 722–23.

[82] Meier, *Mentor, Message, and Miracles*, 711. He notes the opinion of Busse that the story is a Lukan creation, and Bultmann's opinion that it is a variant of the story of the healing of the man with the withered hand in Mark 3:1–6.

[83] Fitzmyer (*Luke X–XXIV*, 1039) astutely observes: "It is not clear, however, how such [Lukan] expressions would argue for the episode as a community-formation (*Gemeindebildung*), as several commentators (E. Lohse, J. Roloff) would have it."

[84] Meier, *Mentor, Message, and Miracles*, 2:711. But again volume 4 promises to take a more negative slant on the historicity question.

tradition").⁸⁵ John Nolland, admitting Luke's hand in the formation of the passage, and calling attention to the transferring of motifs from one Sabbath-healing pericope to another in the transmission of the tradition, points to the oddity of the reference to dropsy, if it does not stem from tradition, and concludes that "Luke had an additional Sabbath-healing account at his disposal here, even if its visibility is finally minimal in the present account."⁸⁶

2.3. Conclusion concerning the Historicity of the Sabbath Controversies

The conclusions of capable scholars who oppose, and those who support, the historicity of the synoptic Sabbath-controversy passages reveal, if nothing else, the endemic difficulty of the question. Of course one cannot decide pro or con by counting the number of scholars on one side or the other. One can indeed weigh the arguments, but opinions will still differ. One may be tempted to throw one's hands up in despair. What does seem finally to emerge is one indisputable fact: the crucially determinative role that is played by one's predisposition to the question. This should not be surprising in a day when we are learning that there is no truly "objective" or "neutral" knowledge and that *every* position necessarily begins from some kind of "faith" basis. This does not excuse us from doing our homework well. Nor does it mean that we accept everything blindly and uncritically, "by faith," so to speak. But we are made freshly aware of the difficulty of the historical enterprise.

Must we then give up on the whole question of truth? Not at all. While we may not often be able to adjudicate, or "prove," individual points, in my opinion only a view that places the burden of proof upon those who deny the historicity of the tradition, rather than upon those who affirm it, can arrive at a satisfactory explanation of the gospel materials. In the same way, only those who approach these materials with faith in their essential truthfulness, will be able to make convincing coherence of the Jesus of the NT – something a highly skeptical view can hardly do. The strange paradox, then, is that there is no more helpful tool for the Gospel interpreter than faith in the truthfulness of the Gospels themselves.⁸⁷

---

⁸⁵ Lohse, "Jesu Worte über den Sabbat," 81. Matthew Black (Matthew Black, "Aramaic Spoken by Christ and Luke 14:5," *Journal of Theological Studies* n. s. 1 [1950]: 60–62) finds wordplay in an Aramaic substratum of this logion. This suggestion, however, is challenged by Fitzmyer, *Luke X–XXIV*, 1042.

⁸⁶ Nolland, *Luke 9:21–18:34*, 745.

⁸⁷ Among options offered in the interesting discussion of Theissen and Merz, I find myself most attracted to what they call "orientation on the biblical picture of Jesus." Their comments on this orientation seem appealing: "All historical reconstructions of Jesus are surrounded with an aura of hypothesis. Why should we not prefer the biblical picture of Jesus to these constructs of scholarly imagination, confident that it is an effect of the

To conclude this part of our essay: contrary to the skepticism of the Jesus Seminar and other scholars, a strong case can be made for the historicity of the Sabbath-controversy passages. As with all historical argument, we necessarily deal with degrees of probability rather than absolute certitude. But the evidence warrants acceptance of these accounts as highly probable, trustworthy history.[88]

The fact that the evangelists are active in composing their narratives and that they make redactional changes of their sources does not necessitate a negative conclusion concerning the basic historical character of their narratives. We have redacted traditions, interpreted stories, we have Jesus presented from a post-resurrection perspective, we have *ipsissima vox* and not the verbatim Aramaic words of Jesus – all of these things are true, but they hardly need to be thought of as undermining the essential historical character of our Gospels.

It is *a priori* extremely unlikely that Jesus could come with his revolutionary message about the dawning of the Kingdom of God and never speak of his relation to something as common as the question of Sabbath observance. This was an exceptionally important matter to first-century Judaism. The Pharisees, as self-appointed guardians of the law, would have been deeply concerned about Jesus, even to the point of plotting his death. "The Sabbath was therefore the chief, almost the sole, safeguard against the lapse of Jews into the beliefs and practices of their pagan neighbours, and to take away this safeguard meant the end of Judaism. The Pharisees believed they were fighting for the very existence of Israel."[89] In answer to the claim of Sanders concerning the incredibility of the idea that the Pharisees would want to put Jesus to death for the healing in Mark 3:1–6, Casey makes the following five points: (1) there is an common, unjustified assumption that the relation between Jesus and his opponents must be the as that between other Jewish groups who differed concerning the interpretation of the law; (2) this assumption goes against our primary sources; (3) the Pharisees would have needed to defend their interpretation of the law against that of Jesus:

---

historical Jesus? Do we not have the 'real Jesus' in the picture which he has produced?" See *The Historical Jesus*, 119.

[88] In a similar vein, Theissen and Merz, *The Historical Jesus*, 367: "A comparison with other Sabbath conflicts in primitive Christianity and Judaism shows that these conflicts are not just fictitious scenes."

[89] G.B. Caird, *New Testament Theology* (ed. L.D. Hurst; Oxford: Clarendon Press, 1994), 386–87; Dietzfelbinger, "Vom Sinn der Sabbatheilungen Jesu," 291: "Wer den Sabbat nicht hält, hindert Israel daran, Israel zu sein." ("Whoever does not observe the Sabbath is preventing Israel from being Israel.") James D.G. Dunn, speaking of Mark 2:23–28, says that "For Jesus to show such disregard for Israel's covenanted obligation was tantamount to denying Israel's election and abrogating the covenant." See his article "Mark 2.1–3.6: A Bridge Between Jesus and Paul on the Question of the Law," *NTS* 30 (1984): 402.

(4) after Jesus' death the split between the Jews and the Christians points to the truth of the earlier conflict between Jesus and the Pharisees; (5) the circumstances of the ministry of Jesus were altogether exceptional.[90]

That these Sabbath-controversy passages have the ring of truth to them will be further evident from the discussion of their theological import that now follows.

3. The Significance of the Sabbath Controversies

It is now time to look at the Sabbath controversies to determine their significance for understanding Jesus, his authority, and his attitude toward the law. After a brief treatment of the Hebrew Bible and Jewish background on Sabbath observance, we will look at each episode for its significance.

3.1. The Jewish Context of Sabbath Observance

There is little need to provide as background a full survey of the Sabbath in the Hebrew Bible, Second Temple and Rabbinic Judaisms,[91] but some preliminary observations are in order. Of foundational importance, of course, is the initial Sabbath commandment:

> Remember the Sabbath day, to keep it holy. Six days you shall labor, and do all your work; but the seventh day is a Sabbath to the Lord your God; in it you shall not do any work, you, or your son, or your daughter, your manservant, or your maidservant, or your cattle, or the sojourner who is within your gates; for in six days the Lord made heaven and earth, the sea, and all that is in them, and rested the seventh day; therefore the Lord blessed the Sabbath day and hallowed it (Exod 20:8–11; cf. Deut 5:12–15).

The elaborate nature of this initial statement of the commandment already indicates its importance. The commandment touches the total household, even the animals and the sojourners. To observe the Sabbath furthermore means to imitate the Creator (Gen 2:2–3). The Sabbath is "to the Lord your God" and a "hallowed" day. To mention only two texts, one can see the importance of the Sabbath in Num 15:32–36 (with which contrast the Western text addition to Luke 6:4) and, for the Second Temple period, *Jub.* 2:17–21: "The weekly Sabbath is for Judaism a sign of election, for no people apart

---

[90] Casey, *Aramaic Sources*, 190.
[91] See George Foot Moore, *Judaism in the First Centuries of the Christian Era: The Age of Tannaim* (3 vols.; 1930; repr., New York: Schocken, 1971), 2:21–39; Emil Schürer, *The History of the Jewish People in the Age of Jesus Christ (175 B. C. – A. D. 135)* (new English ed.; 3 vols.; ed. Geza Vermes, et al.; Edinburgh: T&T Clark, 1973–87), 2:467–75; Eduard Lohse, "σάββατον," *TDNT* 7:2–20; E. P. Sanders, *Jewish Law from Jesus to the Mishnah: Five Studies* (London: SCM, 1990), 6–23. For the rabbinic material, see Str-B 1:610–30.

from Israel has sanctified God in keeping the Sabbath."[92] The Sabbath day is extended to the concept of the sabbatical year with its concern for the poor and oppressed (Lev 25–26; Deut 15:1–8). It is easily understandable why the Sabbath became so important for the Jews and indeed one of the key identity markers of Judaism.[93]

While it is abundantly clear that the Sabbath is to be observed by the avoidance of work, a question not easily answered is how "work" is to be defined. Precisely this question explains the growth of the Sabbath halakah. There was no scarcity of opinion concerning what did and what did not constitute violation of the Sabbath commandment. The rabbis themselves recognized this: "The rules about the Sabbath, Festal-offerings, and Sacrilege are as mountains hanging by a hair, for [teaching of] Scripture [thereon] is scanty and the rules many" (m. Ḥag. 1:8). The 39 forbidden classes of work listed in m. Šabb. 7:1–2 were only a start on the question. This key text reads:

> The generative categories of acts of labor [prohibited on the Sabbath] are forty less one: he who sows, ploughs, reaps, binds sheaves, threshes, winnows, selects [fit from unfit produce or crops], grinds, sifts, kneads, bakes; he who shears wool, washes it, beats it, dyes it; spins, weaves, makes two loops, weaves two threads, separates two threads; ties, unties, sews two stitches, tears in order to sew two stitches; he who traps a deer, slaughters it, flays it, salts it, cures its hide, scrapes it, and cuts it up; he who writes two letters, erases two letters in order to write two letters; he who builds, tears down; he who puts out a fire, kindles a fire; he who hits with a hammer; he who transports an object from one domain to another – lo, these are the forty generative acts of labor less one.[94]

The entirety of the tractate Šabbat and its supplement ʿErubin indicate the industry of the rabbis and the multitudinous opinions and disputes on the subject (one may also think of the attention given to strict observance of the Sabbath in the Qumran scrolls, the Damascus Document and Jubilees).[95] Despite all of this labor devoted to the understanding of the Sabbath commandment, perfect obedience to the Sabbath remained an elusive goal. If Israel could but successfully keep two Sabbaths, it was argued, then the Messiah would come (b. Šabb. 118b; Targum Yerushalmi II on Exod 20).

---

[92] Lohse, TDNT 7:8.

[93] Cf. the concern for observance of the Sabbath in the early post-exilic period (Neh 13:15–22). On the seriousness of violation of the Sabbath, cf. Num 15:30–36. For the connection between the covenant and the Sabbath, see Exod 31:16–17; Isa 56:6.

[94] Citation is from Jacob Neusner, The Mishnah: A New Translation (New Haven: Yale University Press, 1988). The citation lacks his formatting.

[95] Abrahams, Studies in Pharisaism and the Gospels, 131: "The exact limits within which the early halacha permitted the infringement of the Sabbath law are not easily defined, for no subject is more intricate than the history of the principle of the subordination of Sabbatarian rigidity."

Amid the sheer amount and bewildering nature of the Sabbath halakah as developed in the Second Temple period and in post-70 Judaism, and reflected in Mishna and Talmud, a couple of points need to be made, since they bear on the synoptic controversies. All would have agreed that the Sabbath was a gift of God to Israel, and that it was made for human welfare, though few perhaps would have drawn the conclusions from this notion that Jesus did. There was a fair amount of agreement as to what was not allowed on the Sabbath: "a wide consensus governed the practice of most of the inhabitants of Jewish Palestine. Not doing one's regular work, not lighting a fire, not starting on a journey–all these must have been standard."[96] So too there seems to have been a common conviction that, while cures of minor ailments were not allowed, the Sabbath law had to give way in cases of danger to life: "Any case in which there is a *possibility* that life is in danger thrusts aside the Sabbath law" (*m. Yoma* 8:6; *t. Šabb.* 15:16). With this background in mind, we turn again to our passages.

3.2. The Significance of the Sabbath Controversies for Understanding Jesus

In the controversy concerning the plucking of grain on the Sabbath, the Pharisees accuse Jesus' disciples of "doing what is not lawful on the Sabbath" (Mark 2:24). What is the standard by which this judgment is made? Does the action of the disciples for which Jesus is questioned, and correctly held responsible,[97] violate only the Pharisees' halakah (i.e., oral Torah) or the written Torah itself? The scriptures, of course, prohibit work on the Sabbath, and further specify that work on the Sabbath is to be avoided "even in ploughing time and in harvest time" (Exod 34:21). One might think at first sight that Deut 23:25 would be pertinent here: "When you go into your neighbor's standing grain, you may pluck the ears with your hand, but you shall not put a sickle to your neighbor's standing grain." While this takes care of the moral problem of eating another's grain, however, it says nothing about such activity on the Sabbath. This implicit identification of the impropriety of harvesting on the Sabbath is made explicit in the just cited *m. Šabb.* 7:1–2, where among the 39 classes of forbidden work on the Sabbath includes reaping and threshing (rubbing the grain in the hands [Luke 6:1] could technically be defined as the latter).[98]

---

[96] Sanders, *Jewish Law from Jesus to the Mishnah*, 16.
[97] On this, see David Daube, "Responsibilities of Master and Disciples in the Gospels," *NTS* 19 (1972): 1–15.
[98] It has often been noted that there is no problem caused by the disciples eating grain from another's grainfield since that is allowed in Deut 23:25. Ulrich Luz (*Matthew 8–20* [trans. James E. Crouch; Hermeneia; Minneapolis: Fortress, 2001], 181) notes a germane but late Talmudic text (*b. Šabb.* 1:28a): "One may pinch with the hand and eat but not with a tool; one may crush and eat something …with the fingertips." Theissen and Merz

It is clear that Jesus allows his disciples to violate the Torah as understood and interpreted by the Pharisaic halakah.⁹⁹ Although it *is* in the end a matter of interpretation, and Jesus makes no frontal attack on the Torah itself, at the same time the question is how Jesus handles himself in this situation and whether he displays a sovereignty in understanding the Torah quite different from the approach of the Pharisees. "What is alarming in the story is Jesus' *indifferent attitude* towards the accusation of having violated the Sabbath."¹⁰⁰ It is more than a battle of interpretations, however, as we will see.

The cogency of the argument from the story of David and his men eating the bread of the presence has been much debated. Is the story really a suitable parallel to what Jesus allows his disciples to do? Some have indicated that a point from halakah, rather than a historical anecdote (haggadah), is required to counter the Pharisees' objection.¹⁰¹ But allowing that exception, there is no reference to the Sabbath in the record of 1 Sam 21:1–7.¹⁰² A further problem is that David's men may have been in dire need (at the point of starvation–so the Pharisees would have thought), whereas the disciples appear to be having a snack. Mark and Luke say nothing about the disciples even being hungry; only Matthew adds the point to strengthen the parallel and make the argument more cogent (Matt 12:1).

According to the Gospels, David's infringement appears to have been that he and his men ate bread that only the priests had the right to eat (Lev 24:9). David and his men violated the letter of Torah (the account is in 1 Sam 21:1–6). Is Jesus' citing of this narrative a tacit admission that he and his

---

(*The Historical Jesus*, 368) call attention to the following in Philo (*Moses* 2.22), speaking of the Sabbath: "For it is not permitted to cut any shoot or branch, or even a leaf, or to pluck any fruit whatsoever."

⁹⁹ Given *m. Šabb.* 7:1–2, quoted above, I fail to see how Loader (*Jesus' Attitude*, 52) can say "There is no law or law interpretation known to us which Jesus' disciples would be contravening." The idea that the infringement was that the disciples were making a path (ὁδὸν ποιεῖν, Mark 2:23), as, e.g., Hooker suggests (*St. Mark*, 102), seems highly improbable.

¹⁰⁰ Tom Holmén, *Jesus and Jewish Covenant Thinking* (Biblical Interpretation Series 55; Leiden: Brill, 2001), 102.

¹⁰¹ Cohn-Sherbok, "An Analysis of Jesus' Arguments"; David Daube, *The New Testament and Rabbinic Judaism* (JLCRS 2; London: University of London, Athlone Press, 1956), 67–71. Matthew's added defense, about the priests violating the Sabbath in their work (Matt 12:5), *does* meet the technical requirement, as Daube points out: "There is nothing *haggadhic* about this. The argument is of a kind which no student of *halakha* could lightly dismiss" (p. 71). For a similar approach, cf. John Mark Hicks, "The Sabbath Controversy in Matthew: An Exegesis of Matthew 12:1–14," *ResQ* 27 (1984): 79–91.

¹⁰² There is, however, an apparently early rabbinic tradition that the incident took place on a Sabbath (*b.Menaḥ.* 95b; *Yal.* on 1 Sam 21:5).

disciples have also violated the letter of the law?[103] Matthew's added second justification (12:5) would seem to imply the same thing: "Or have you not read in the law how on the Sabbath the priests in the temple profane the Sabbath, and are guiltless?"[104]

What is the validating parallel principle at work here? Is it mere hunger? Is it being on a divinely ordained mission? Is it Davidic typology,[105] with the Son of David in view? It seems clear that even if it is not technically correct by rabbinic standards,[106] we have a species of a fortiori (*qal wahomer*) argument here. That is made explicit by the unique and utterly astonishing statement of Jesus in Matthew that "something greater than the temple is here" (Matt 12:6) – and it is in this statement that we clearly move off of rabbinic ground. If the priests are allowed technically to violate the Sabbath in the service of God,[107] how much more may the Sabbath be violated by the greater reality of the Messiah and his disciples in the service of the dawning Kingdom of God.[108] Matthew's addition of Hos 6:6 makes the further point that mercy takes precedence over strict observance of the letter of the law. Again, the meeting of human need, which is a core element of the dawning Kingdom, must supersede technical Sabbath observance. Matthew concludes that if the Pharisees had known the meaning of Hos 6:6, they "would not have condemned the guiltless" (using the same word [ἀναίτιος] that is used of the temple priests who work on the Sabbath). Despite the technical violation of the Sabbath law by his disciples, Jesus and his disciples remain without guilt.

What starts out in Matthew as an argument over the interpretation of the Sabbath commandment ends up on another level involving the dramatic newness of christology and mission. That, however, is Matthew's unique handling of the passage. What about Mark and Luke? All three Synoptic

---

[103] Stephen Westerholm, *Jesus and Scribal Authority* (ConBNT 10; Lund: Gleerup, 1978), 98: "His action is not brought in line with Torah, but cited as a biblical example where the letter of Torah is broken. No Pharisaic argument, this!"

[104] Cf. *b. Šabb.* 132.b: "Temple service takes precedence over the Sabbath." See too *m. ʿErub.* 10:11–15; *m. Pesaḥ.* 6:1–2. In John 7:22–23 (as in *m. Šabb.* 18:3; 19:1–6) the command to circumcise on the eighth day takes precedence over the Sabbath.

[105] Thus Yang, *Jesus and the Sabbath*, 176–77.

[106] Thus Cohn-Sherbok, "An Analysis of Jesus' Arguments," 31–41.

[107] Etan Levine ("Sabbath Controversy According to Matthew," *NTS* 22 [1976]: 480–83) argues that what was in view was the Pharisees' allowance of reaping the first sheaves, or ʿomer offering, on the Sabbath (see *m. Menaḥ.* 10:1). This seems only a remote possibility. As Yang (*Jesus and the Sabbath*, 179) points out, Matthew has "have you not read in the law," and that the violation of the Sabbath takes place "in the temple," not the fields.

[108] As Loader (*Jesus' Attitude*, 203) rightly says, these arguments in Matthew "bring to expression a christology which has been assumed throughout." Yang (*Jesus and the Sabbath*, 181), however, draws too much out of the temple allusion at this point in the narrative when he concludes "The role and authority of the temple as the focus of God's presence thus is transferred to and fulfilled by Jesus."

witnesses end the pericope with the important christological statement: "The Son of man is lord of the Sabbath." Mark has an emphatic καί, "even the Sabbath." Here the astounding statement is made that Jesus is κύριος, and κύριος even of the Sabbath. This is no ordinary teacher or healer who has the temerity to violate accepted norms of Sabbath activity. He strides through the Synoptic tradition as one who has no parallel and whose unique authority is not a derived authority. But as we have seen, some have argued that in Mark the statement is not to be taken as a reference to Jesus, but to son of man in the sense of "humanity." The reasoning is that the preceding verse in Mark (Mark 2:27), omitted by both Matthew and Luke, refers to humans and not to Jesus: "The Sabbath was made for man, not man for the Sabbath." Then, by synonymous parallelism, "son of man" in the next line is also meant to refer to humankind, and not to Jesus himself, and so the logion of Mark 2:28 was not originally christological.[109]

Mark 2:27 does refer to humans, and similar things were said by the rabbis.[110] The Sabbath was made for the sake of human beings, and not vice versa. Does it follow, however, that man is the lord of the Sabbath? This would seem to be very unlikely.[111] Though the rabbis may have accepted that the Sabbath was made for man, they did not interpret this fact in the way that Jesus did. They took it mainly to mean that when a life was in danger, then and only then, could the Sabbath restrictions be lifted. Jesus does not attack the Torah or its authority in this episode. Rather, as in all the Sabbath controversies, he unhesitatingly cuts through to the underlying intent of Torah (as in Matt 5:17–48). The sovereign freedom with which Jesus interprets the Sabbath law is inseparable from his unique identity as the Agent of God's redemptive rule. As Son of Man, he is Lord of the Sabbath.[112]

As we have seen, there are several instances in the Synoptic Gospels of healings performed by Jesus on the Sabbath. The first one in Mark is the exorcism of an unclean spirit on the Sabbath (Mark 1:21–28). The focus of this story, however, is solely on the power of Jesus over the demonic, and the fact that the exorcism was done on a Sabbath, although noted, causes

---

[109] T.W. Manson ("Mark ii.27f," in *Coniectanea Neotestamentica 11* [Lund: Gleerup, 1947], 138–46) has argued–implausibly, in my opinion–that in both verses a corporate Son of Man (=the nation of Israel) is in view.

[110] Thus, *b. Yoma* 85b, speaking of the Sabbath, "For it is holy unto you [Exod 31:14]. That is, it is committed into your hands, not you into its hands." Also, the Midrash, *Mek.* 109b on Exod 31:14: "The Sabbath is delivered unto you, and you are not delivered to the Sabbath."

[111] Cranfield (*Saint Mark*, 118) quotes the words of Rawlinson, "Our Lord would not have been likely to say that 'man' was 'lord of the Sabbath,' which had been instituted by God." Similarly, Bäck, *Jesus of Nazareth and the Sabbath Commandment*, 93.

[112] Lohse, *TDNT* 7:22: "In this originally independent saying the Christian community is confessing Jesus, the Son of Man, who as the *kyrios* decides concerning the applying or transcending of the Sabbath. In His lordship Sabbath casuistry comes to an end."

no Sabbath controversy.[113] But the careful reader will have noticed the reference to the Sabbath and hence be prepared for the Sabbath controversies that follow in the narrative. Immediately after the episode of the plucking of grain on the Sabbath, comes the story of the healing of the withered hand (Mark 3:1–6 and parr.). Now, with the preceding infringements of the Sabbath in mind, the Pharisees lie in wait for Jesus "to see whether he would heal him on the Sabbath, so that they might accuse him" (Mark 3:2).

As we have already had occasion to note, healing on the Sabbath was allowed only in those instances where life was threatened. "Whenever there is doubt whether life is in danger this overrides the Sabbath" (*m. Yoma* 8:6). The rabbinic response to Jesus in this instance would surely have been that the man could have waited till the following day to be healed (cf. Luke 13:14: "But the ruler of the synagogue, indignant because Jesus had healed on the Sabbath, said to the people, 'There are six days on which work ought to be done; come on those days and be healed, and not on the Sabbath day.'"). Jesus, on the other hand, regards human need *of any kind* as justifying remedial action on the Sabbath.[114] In a way that cuts straight across the nomistic casuistry of the Pharisees, and with an unmatched authority, Jesus puts priority on the reality of human need rather than on an overstress of the Sabbath itself. He does not do away with the usefulness of observing the Sabbath, but only with an observance that hinders a human being from experiencing wholeness and well-being.[115]

Thus Jesus says to his critics, "Is it lawful on the Sabbath to do good or to do harm, to save life or to kill?" (Mark 3:4). This *mashal* means, at the least, that healing is in keeping with a proper understanding of the Sabbath law. The key would then be what was said in Mark 2:27, "the Sabbath was made for man, not man for the Sabbath." The Sabbath was made for the man with the withered hand, and thus he deserved to be healed on it.[116] But probably more is to be seen here. Eschatological and christological[117] perspectives hover in the background. Jesus, the eschatological Son of Man, not only presents the correct understanding of the Sabbath commandment, as in the

---

[113] For this theme, see in this volume ch. 4.

[114] So Abrahams, *Studies in Pharisaism and the Gospels*, 134: "All things considered, it would seem that Jesus differed fundamentally from the Pharisees in that he asserted a general right to abrogate the Sabbath law for man's ordinary convenience, while the Rabbis limited the license to cases of danger to life." Is it not an understatement of human suffering, however, to regard those healed as merely inconvenienced?

[115] Thus rightly, Berndt Schaller, *Fundamenta Judaica: Studien zum antiken Judentum und zum Neuen Testament* (ed. Lutz Doering and Annette Steudel; SUNT 25; Göttingen: Vandenhoeck & Ruprecht, 2001).

[116] Hooker (*St. Mark*, 107) states, "To delay healing for a day is to deny the Torah's true intention, which is the glory of God and the benefit of man."

[117] Loader (*Jesus' Attitude*, 36) rightly says that the christological statement of 2:28 functions also for the present pericope.

preceding pericope, but also brings the Kingdom of God in his ministry. Part and parcel of that Kingdom is the overcoming of evil and suffering.[118] To refrain from healing the man would have been to contradict the greater reality that Jesus was all about. And, given that the Sabbath became itself a foreshadowing of the time of salvation (*Zohar* on Gen 48a: "The Sabbath is a mirror of the world to come"),[119] far from being an activity to avoid, it was especially appropriate to heal on the Sabbath.[120]

This too would appear to be the explanation of the reference to doing harm and to killing. As Cranfield puts it, "To omit to do the good which one could do to someone in need is to do evil."[121] Although, as we have seen, the words do not necessarily refer to those who plot the death of Jesus (Mark 3:6), there is obvious irony in the fact that they apparently did do their plotting on the Sabbath.[122]

---

[118] Bäck (*Jesus of Nazareth and the Sabbath Commandment*, 161–78) rightly places the whole discussion in the context of Jesus' announcement of the dawning of the Kingdom of God.

[119] Further texts are in Str-B 4.2:839–40. Robert Goldenberg ("The Place of the Sabbath in Rabbinic Judaism," in *The Sabbath in Jewish and Christian Traditions* [ed. Tamara Cohn Eskenazi, et al.; New York: Crossroad, 1991], 43) writes: "Through the lens of the Sabbath we can glimpse the Jewish vision of eternity." Thus Lohse, *TDNT* 7:8: "The day of the rest which the patriarchs celebrated grants a foretaste already of eternal glory, which will be an unending Sabbath." See too Harald Riesenfeld, *The Gospel Tradition* (trans. E. Margaret Rowley and Robert A. Kraft; Philadelphia: Fortress, 1970), 114–15. Even the verb used to refer to the restoration of the man's hand, ἀποκαθίστημι, possibly is an intentional allusion to eschatological restoration (cf. the use of the word in reference to Elijah, Mark 9:12; Matt 17:11).

[120] So too Doering, *Schabbat*, 456: "Immerhin ist aber die Interpretation sehr wahrscheinlich, *daß Leid und Krankheit* nach Jesu Auffassung *nicht mit dem Charakter des Sabbats vereinbar sind*, der von dem Rückverweis auf die Schöpfermacht Gottes und wohl auch von der Vorausschau auf die Endzeit bestimmt ist. Das bedeutet aber, daß Jesus am Sabbat, einem Tag, an dem Gott dem Menschen ohnehin in besonderer Weise zugewandt ist und an dem Mensch in diese Nähe in Ruhe, Freude und Lobpreis feiert – daß Jesus also an diesem Tag *auch heilen muß*" (italics original). ("At least it is a very probable interpretation that according to Jesus *suffering and illness* are not compatible with the character of the Sabbath, which is determined by referring back to the creative power of God and the foreshadowing of the time of salvation. This does however mean that on the Sabbath, a day on which God is focused on human beings in any case in a particular way and on which human beings celebrate in peace, joy and praise, Jesus *has to heal* on this day.") See too, Schaller, *Fundamenta Judaica*, 146.

[121] Cranfield, *Saint Mark*, 120. Cranfield adds that failing to do good is to break the Sixth Commandment, and quotes Calvin: "There is little difference between manslaughter and the conduct of him who does not concern himself about relieving a person in distress." Cf. Schweizer, *The Good News According to Mark*, 75: "Failure to do good is the same as doing evil; failure to save a life is the same as destroying it." So too Guelich, *Mark 1–8:26*, 136: "If 'to do good' / 'to save a life' meant to heal, then 'to do evil' / 'to take a life' meant not to heal and thus deprive this one of the benefits of God's restoring power." Against this explanation, see Carson, "Jesus and the Sabbath," 69–70.

[122] The idea that "killing" here refers to self-defense on the Sabbath (thus Theissen and

The special Matthean logion (Matt 12:11-12), "What man of you, if he has one sheep and it falls into a pit on the Sabbath, will not lay hold of it and lift it out? Of how much more value is a man than a sheep!" again prioritizes human need over strict obedience to the law.[123] With this *a fortiori* argument in mind,[124] Matthew changes Mark's question into a declarative statement: "So it is lawful to do good on the Sabbath" (Matt 12:12). The reference to "mercy" in Hos 6:6, so recently quoted (in Matt 12:7), is also applicable here.

There are those who deny that this healing narrative involves any violation of the Sabbath. Géza Vermès, following David Flusser, states that "Speech could not be construed as 'work' infringing the law governing the Jewish day of rest."[125] But unless one simply denies any historical basis whatsoever to these narratives, the healings performed by Jesus *were* regarded by the Pharisees as violating their halakah, and hence the Sabbath. Theissen and Merz make the following correct observation: "the fact that [the healings] took place only through words (as in Mark 3.1 ff.) does not in itself make them a permissible action. Of course words were allowed on the Sabbath. But so too was eating and drinking–however, not when both exclusively served a therapeutic purpose."[126] If Jesus were regarded as a healer, furthermore, then any kind of healing by his agency whatsoever would probably have been regarded as work. Holmén's observation is also telling: "If healing is not work, we do not know why Jesus would compare it to pulling an ox, child and/or a sheep out from a well or a pit."[127]

In this passage we again encounter christological and eschatological motifs. Again it is Jesus, the Lord of the Sabbath (as in the immediately prior verse in all three Synoptics), who with incomparable authority interprets the meaning of the Sabbath and performs a sovereign act of healing. "In 2:23-28 and 3:1-6 he bends the letter of the Sabbath law because he is an es-

---

Merz, *The Historical Jesus*, 369) is implausible and breaks the parallelism of the passage, in particular being incompatible with the words "to do evil."

[123] Not all would have agreed that an animal could be pulled out of a pit on the Sabbath. According to the rabbis, an animal in a pit on the Sabbath could be provided food and comfort, but could not be pulled out (*b. Šabb.* 128b). The Essenes also prohibited pulling an animal out of a pit on the Sabbath (CD 11:13-14; cf. 4Q251 2:5-6).

[124] Yang (*Jesus and the Sabbath*, 204) emphasizes that this argument is far from rabbinic or halachic since the argument does not find its basis in Torah, but is "proclamatory again rather than explanatory and therefore provocative rather than persuasive."

[125] Géza Vermès, *Jesus the Jew: A Historian's Reading of the Gospels* (London: Collins, 1973). Cf. David Flusser, *Jesus* (trans. Ronald Walls; New York: Herder & Herder, 1969), 49. In his *The Religion of Jesus the Jew* (Minneapolis: Fortress, 1993), 23, Vermès concludes that "The whole debate seems to be, however, a storm in a tea-cup since none of the Sabbath cures of Jesus entailed 'work', but were effected by word of mouth, or at most, by the laying on of hands or other simple physical contact." For the same view, see E. P. Sanders, *Jesus and Judaism* (Philadelphia: Fortress, 1985), 266.

[126] Theissen and Merz, *The Historical Jesus*, 368.

[127] Holmén, *Jesus and Jewish Covenant Thinking*, 104.

chatological figure, the Son of Man, and therefore the lord of the Sabbath."[128] As in the preceding passage, the question ultimately concerns not halakah but the person and work of Jesus. Luke is the only Synoptic writer to note here that Jesus "himself knew their reasonings" (Luke 6:8), namely that they wanted to bring accusation against him. Jesus will nevertheless heal on the Sabbath both because there is no better day to bring wholeness than the Sabbath (with its intention to benefit humanity and its eschatological anticipation) and because the salvation in the fullest sense, including healing, is an indispensable part of the Kingdom that he brings in his person and ministry.[129]

We may deal much more briefly with the healings in Luke 13:10–17 and 14:1–6, calling attention only to the distinctive aspects of these pericopae.

The story of the healing of the woman with the bent over back (Luke 13:10–17) has four distinctives. First, here alone in the synoptic healing narratives (cf. John 9:6, where Jesus makes clay with spittle and applies it to the blind man's eyes–the one instance of clear "work" in connection with a Sabbath healing) do we find Jesus doing something physically, namely laying hands on the woman (Luke 13:13). It is therefore perhaps easier to regard this healing as involving work, but it is hard to think of this as very significant, since it seems from the other narratives as though healing *of any kind* could be thought of as involving a kind of "work."

Second, as we have seen, here alone among the healing narratives do we encounter the Jewish rationale about these matters, articulated by the indignant ruler of the synagogue where the healing took place: "There are six days on which work ought to be done; come on those days and be healed, and not on the Sabbath day" (Luke 13:14). The objection[130] would apply to all the Sabbath healings performed by Jesus. That is, in none of the stories is the recipient of the healing in such desperate straits that the healing could not have been delayed until the next day. The reason Jesus heals on the Sabbath, as we have seen, is not the result of a different halakah, or a dispute about halachic matters, but the result of transcendent concerns having to do with his person and mission.

Third, only in this pericope does Jesus refer to his opponents as "hypocrites," apparently because their regard for the plight of animals on the Sabbath is greater that for that of suffering human beings: "Does not each of you on the Sabbath untie his ox or his ass from the manger, and lead it away to water it?" (Luke 13:15). This example, unique to Luke (cf. the example

---

[128] Joel Marcus, *Mark 1–8* (AB 27; New York: Doubleday, 2000), 214.

[129] Schaller, *Fundamenta Judaica*, 146.

[130] Cf. *m. Šabb.* 19:1: "R. Akiba laid down a general rule: Any act of work that can be done on the eve of Sabbath does not override the Sabbath ..." The same statement is found in *m. Menaḥ.* 11:3; cf. *m. Pesaḥ.* 6:2.

in Luke 14:5), cannot be paralleled exactly in Jewish writings.[131] C. G. Montefiore notes that the rabbis would never have allowed cruelty to animals and that oxen require daily watering.[132] He adds that the woman could have waited another day.

Fourth, and for our purposes most important, Jesus describes the infirmity of the woman as the result of being "bound" by Satan (Luke 13:16). Healings in the Gospel accounts are the result of a cosmic battle with eschatological implications, with the power of Satan necessarily yielding to the power of the Kingdom brought by Jesus.[133] Again, then, since the Sabbath is a foreshadowing of the coming eschatological reality, wherein all human woes, suffering, sickness, and death, are done away with, not only may the work of the Kingdom be done on the Sabbath–there is in fact *no better day* for the meeting of human need. It is the mission of Jesus to bring the rule of God, and eschatological salvation is about the well-being of all who are oppressed.[134]

The second Sabbath healing unique to Luke concerns the man with dropsy who turns up at the dinner party in the Pharisee's house (14:1–6). There is little further to say about this pericope, which bears some similarity to other Sabbath-healing narratives we have examined (esp. Matt 12:9–14). Reminiscent of Matt 12:11 is the question of Luke 14:5: "Which of you, having a son or an ox that has fallen into a well, will not immediately pull him out on a Sabbath day?"[135] The rhetorical question again points to the propriety of doing good on the Sabbath, and answers the question of 14:3: "Is it lawful to heal on the Sabbath or not?" The silence of the Pharisees is twice remarked upon (14:4, 6), and indeed the Pharisees never speak in this pericope. They are mute before the authority of Jesus.[136] That the man

---

[131] Tying and loosing knots are among the prohibited works in *m. Šabb.* 7:2. On the movement of animals for the purpose of drinking, see *m. ʿErub.* 2:1–4.

[132] C. G. Montefiore, *The Synoptic Gospels* (2nd ed.; 2 vols.; London: Macmillan, 1927), 2:501.

[133] See Eric Eve, *The Jewish Context of Jesus' Miracles* (JSNTSup 231; New York: Sheffield Academic Press, 2002), 373–75. In this volume, Craig Evans' essay treats this theme in more detail; see in particular, ch. 4, § 3.

[134] According to Doering (*Schabbat*, 467), Luke presents "eine Intepretation der Heilung im Sinne der Königsherrschaft Gottes, dazu die Darstellung der Hoheit Jesu." Cf. Paul-Gerhard Klumbies, "Die Sabbatheilungen Jesu nach Markus und Lukas," in *Jesus Rede von Gott und ihre Nachgeschichte im frühen Christentum: Beiträge zur Verkündigung Jesu und zum Kerygma der Kirche* (ed. Dietrich-Alex Koch, et al.; Gütersloh: Mohn, 1989), 176.

[135] It is not surprising to find that some mss (א, K, L, f^1, f^{13}, 33 and others) have ὄνος, "ass," in place of υἱός, "son" (D has πρόβατον, "sheep"; cf. the Matthean parallel). The fact that υἱός is the harder reading and found in 𝔓⁴⁵ and 𝔓⁷⁵, as well as in A (which also includes the article), B, and the Textus Receptus, makes it easily the preferred reading.

[136] Klumbies, "Die Sabbatheilungen Jesu," 175.

should be healed on the Sabbath is again implicitly connected with the identity and mission of Jesus.[137]

4. Conclusion: Implications for the Historical Jesus

We are now in a position to draw some final conclusions about our subject. If we return to the options listed by Doering mentioned at the beginning of this essay, we may say the following. The first and last options, the two extremes, we can dismiss out of hand. It is widely agreed that Jesus did not oppose the Sabbath commandment,[138] either in principle or in actuality[139] and it is equally clear from the material before us that he did not fully conform to the Sabbath observance of his day. Jesus certainly did not overthrow, but neither did he abide by, the Sabbath commandment itself. Jesus in fact seems remarkably indifferent to the law. Tom Holmén notes that Jesus does not deny the accusations that he has transgressed the Sabbath, and is altogether remarkably indifferent about the Sabbath: "he simply was not particularly concerned about keeping the commandment."[140] At the least, one must say that, as "Lord of the Sabbath," Jesus was in some sense able to transcend the Sabbath commandment. It is worth noting that in his response to the man who wanted to inherit eternal life, Jesus refers to keeping the commandments, but the Sabbath is not among the ones he specifically mentions

---

[137] Cf. Dietzfelbinger, "Vom Sinn der Sabbatheilungen Jesu," 297–98.

[138] For a convincing argument that the early Christian communities "took for granted the legitimacy of the Sabbath," see Herold Weiss, "The Sabbath in the Synoptic Gospels," *JSNT* 38 (1990): 13–27, here 22.

[139] One notable exception is Willy Rordorf, *Sunday: The History of the Day of Rest and Worship in the Earliest Centuries of the Christian Church*. (trans. A. A. K. Graham; Philadelphia: Westminster, 1968), 63: "It is a misunderstanding to hold that Jesus did not attack the Sabbath commandment itself, but only the casuistical refinements of the Pharisees." A few lines later he can say "this commandment enslaved human beings"; cf. pp. 77–79. Cf. C. G. Montefiore (2nd ed., 1:cxxxv), against most other recent Jewish scholars: "His teaching about divorce, about the Sabbath, about clean and unclean, was in the spirit of the Prophets, but not in strict accordance with the letter of the Law ... Jesus, too, though less fervently than his Rabbinical opponents, professed to believe, and did actually believe, in the divineness of the Law. But his impassioned prophetic attitude drove him on to action and to teaching which were in violation of the Law." For a strong statement that Jesus did away with the Sabbath commandment, see Leonhard Goppelt, *Theology of the New Testament* (2 vols.; trans. John E. Alsup; Grand Rapids: Eerdmans, 1981–82), 1:92–95.

[140] Holmén, *Jesus and Jewish Covenant Thinking*, 105. On this same page he states, "Hence, regardless of which side one takes, it cannot be argued, *on the basis of all or any deliberatively chosen part of the extant evidence*, that Jesus was particularly interested in keeping the Sabbath" (italics original).

(Mark 10:17–22 and parallels). The primary consideration is to "come and follow me."[141]

There is, on the other hand, some truth in each of Doering's four remaining options. The second states that Jesus was not against the Sabbath, but only against a halachic approach to the Sabbath commandment. One of the most obvious things about the Synoptic Sabbath- controversy passages is that Jesus does not take a halachic approach to the Sabbath.[142] He does present arguments in defense of his conduct or that of his disciples, but they are not really halachic and they fall short of being convincing at the halachic level. In fact, the argument is not conducted at the halachic level at all. H. Riesenfeld correctly concludes "there is nothing to indicate that on any occasion he wanted to take part in the discussion of Jewish law on its own level ... as a matter of fact Jesus did not dispute about details."[143] This is an important point. Jesus raises the Sabbath question to an entirely new level.

To be sure, Jesus is the definitive interpreter of the law and hence of the Sabbath. The truth in Doering's third option is that Jesus does oppose a universal and inflexible application of the Sabbath law. The reason for this is what Doering refers to in his fifth option, namely that Jesus does not approach the law as an ordinance, but in terms of its intent. This is why the logion of Mark 2:27 is so very important: "The Sabbath was made for man, not man for the Sabbath." In good Jewish form, Jesus penetrates to the essence of the Sabbath, by going back to its foundation in Genesis. In so doing, he simultaneously alludes to the eschatological reality anticipated by the Sabbath. The Sabbath is meant for the mercy (cf. the quotation of Hos 6:6 in Matt 12:7), wholeness, and well-being that comes with salvation. The Sabbath commandment must therefore give way to, and not have the effect of annulling (as in the Pharisaic halakah), the Sabbath's true purpose

---

[141] The contrast with *Gos. Thom.* 27 could not be greater: "If you do not keep the Sabbath (as) Sabbath, you will not see the Father."

[142] Loader, *Jesus' Attitude*, 521: "One of the problems in approaching the traditions is that they do not portray Jesus as a formal interpreter of the Law ... Much of Jesus' instruction in Mark, and doubtless, therefore, the Markan tradition was about mission, his own and that of his disciples." Christoph Hinz ("Jesus und der Sabbat," *KD* 19 [1973]: 95) makes a similar observation: "Die Heilungen Jesu aber nehmen keine kasuistischen Ausnahmebestimmungen zur Entschuldigung in Anspruch, sondern sie wollen geradezu provozieren, das Verständnis vom Sinn des Sabbats entlarven." See too Westerholm, *Jesus and Scribal Authority*. For the view, however, that Jesus offers his own Sabbath halakah in place of that of the Pharisees, see Markus Bockmuehl, "Halakha and Ethics in the Jesus Tradition," in *Early Christian Thought in Its Jewish Context* (J. Barclay and J. Sweet; Cambridge: Cambridge University Press, 1996), 264–78; and along the same line, Phillip Sigal, *The Halakah of Jesus of Nazareth According to the Gospel of Matthew* (Lanham, MD: University Press of America, 1986), 119–53.

[143] Riesenfeld, *The Gospel Tradition*, 118. Cf. Doering, *Schabbat*, 477: "Er bestimmt den Sabbat *seinem Wesen nach nicht primär durch die Regulierung der Arbeitsruhe, sondern durch die Gottesherrschaft*" (italics original).

and significance. Yang therefore rightly refers to Jesus as "the recoverer and fulfiller of God's original and ultimate will for the Sabbath."[144]

It is Doering's fourth option that comes the closest to the truth: the free stance of Jesus toward the Sabbath is a result of the eschatological stamp of his teaching and work.[145] It is in a fundamental sense about the meaning of Jesus and his mission. This, however, falls just short of recognizing the determinative factor, *the person of Jesus* – for, of course, his teaching and work cannot adequately be understood without coming to grips with his personal identity. This has been pointed to already by the texts we have examined, most impressively in the two logia: "the Son of man is lord even of the Sabbath" (Mark 2:28; Matt 12:8; Luke 6:5); and "I tell you, something greater than the temple is here" (Matt 12:6).[146]

At issue in the Sabbath question is more than a matter of whose interpretation of the Torah is most convincing or authoritative. It is a much larger and more important matter: the dawning of the Kingdom of God,[147] and especially the identity of Jesus[148] and his definitive authority. "The Sabbath incident in Mark 6:1–6 then makes clear what has been the case all along; it is not Jesus' healings on the Sabbath that are the cause of offense but the claims that He makes for Himself."[149] As Robert Banks puts it, "What Jesus, in

---

[144] Yang, *Jesus and the Sabbath*, 225.

[145] Loader, *Jesus' Attitude*, 523: "The eschatological teaching of Jesus entails both a claim to fulfilment in the present and a focus on final future reversal in the time when God's reign is fully established. It forms an important context for understanding his attitude towards the Law."

[146] Jacob Neusner, "Practice: Jesus and Torah," in *Judaism in the New Testament: Practices and Beliefs* (by Bruce D. Chilton and Jacob Neusner; London: Routledge, 1995), 142: "When, therefore, Jesus says that something greater than the Temple is here, he can only mean, he and his disciples may do on the Sabbath what they do because they stand in the place of the priests in the Temple: the holy place has shifted, now being formed by the circle made up of the master and his disciples."

[147] Dietzfelbinger, "Vom Sinn der Sabbatheilungen Jesu," 295: "Von dieser Verkündigung der anbrechenden Gottesherrschaft her ist nun auch Jesu Reden über den Sabbat und sein Verhalten am Sabbat zu interpretieren. Sein Reden und Handeln am Sabbat ist Teil seiner Verkündigung." ("Jesus' speeches about the Sabbath and his behavior on the Sabbath are to be interpreted on the basis of this proclamation of the dawning of the Kingdom of God. His comments and his actions on the Sabbath are a part of the proclamation.")

[148] Daniel J. Harrington ("Sabbath Tensions: Matthew 12:1–14 and Other New Testament Texts," in *The Sabbath in Jewish and Christian Traditions* [ed. Tamara Cohn Eskenazi, et al.; New York: Crossroad, 1991], 53) rightly concludes that Matthew "breaks out of the Jewish debate by giving the two stories a christological dimension."

[149] Andrew T. Lincoln, "From Sabbath to Lord's Day: A Biblical and Theological Perspective," in *From Sabbath to Lord's Day: A Biblical, Historical and Theological Investigation* (ed. D. A. Carson; Grand Rapids: Zondervan, 1982), 360. It is this, more than anything, that causes the Jewish authorities to take action against Jesus. From at least 1:21 onwards in Mark the striking and unique authority of Jesus is in view (2:1–3:6 may well be a pre-formed unit taken up by Mark). This is the answer to the argument that the Phari-

fact, takes up, however, is not a particular orientation towards the Sabbath law, but the demand that the Sabbath be orientated towards, interpreted by, and obeyed in accordance with, his own person and work."[150]

This is why the discussions of Abrahams, Vermes and Sanders,[151] all of whom try to fit Jesus' approach to the Sabbath within a straightforward Jewish framework, are unconvincing. None of them can manage to explain the hostile reaction of the Jewish authorities, and hence they must severely edit the narratives or deny their historicity.

By contrast, the maverick Jacob Neusner, who will have nothing of the standard Jewish reclamation of Jesus, captures the main point in his discussion of the Sabbath in Matthew:

> At issue in the Sabbath is neither keeping nor breaking this one of the Ten Commandments. At issue here as everywhere else is the person of Jesus himself, in Christian language, Jesus Christ. What matters most of all is the simple statement, no one knows the Father except the Son, and anyone to whom the Son chooses to reveal him. There, startling and scarcely a consequence of anything said before or afterward, stands the centerpiece of the Sabbath-teaching: my yoke is easy, I give you rest, the son of man is lord of the Sabbath indeed, because the son of man is now Israel's Sabbath ... Christ now stands on the mountain, he now takes the place of Torah.[152]

As we indicated at the beginning, the question of Jesus and the Sabbath is a part of the larger question of Jesus and the law. In the much-discussed latter issue one must also in the end deal with the personal identity of Jesus and his unique mission. This focus on Jesus' authority is something several of the essays in this volume highlight as a point of coherence among these key events. With regard to the Sabbath, Jesus stands as the supremely authoritative interpreter of the law. The result is that, as with the Sabbath, Jesus is

---

sees would not have wanted to do away with Jesus because of his actions on the Sabbath. Cf. Darrell L. Bock, *Jesus According to Scripture: Restoring the Portrait From the Gospels* (Grand Rapids: Baker, 2002), 608: "the opposition to Jesus did not surface on the basis of this one set of Sabbath actions only."

[150] Robert Banks, *Jesus and the Law in the Synoptic Tradition* (SNTSMS 28; Cambridge: Cambridge University Press, 1975), 131. Similarly Bock, *Jesus According to Scripture*, 118: "In the end, all the controversies force a choice about who Jesus is." Cf. Hinz, "Jesus und der Sabbat," 98.

[151] In light of the Gospel materials we have looked at, it is difficult to see how Sanders (*Jewish Law from Jesus to the Mishnah*, 23) can say: "I conclude, then, that the synoptic Jesus behaved on the Sabbath in a way which fell inside the range of current debate about it, and well inside the range of permitted behaviour ... Other Jews disagreed about equally substantial issues. The synoptic stories show that any possible transgression on the part of Jesus or his followers was minor and would have been seen as such by even the strictest groups." Cf. Vermès, *The Religion of Jesus the Jew*, 22–24; *Jesus the Jew*, 36; Abrahams, *Studies in Pharisaism and the Gospels*, 1:131.

[152] Jacob Neusner, *A Rabbi Talks with Jesus: An Intermillennial, Interfaith Exchange* (New York: Doubleday, 1993), 72–73; see too his essay "Practice: Jesus and Torah".

able in remarkable ways to transcend the law. The law and the righteousness that is the goal of the law are upheld, but in innovative ways that deviate from the conventions of the Pharisees. When all is said and done, one must conclude with Robert Banks that what we must come to terms with "is not so much his relationship to the Law ... as how the Law now stands in relationship to Jesus as the one whose teaching and practice transcend it and fulfil it and to whom all attention must now be directed."[153]

Did Jesus break with the Sabbath? Our answer must be: at one level, technically, perhaps yes. In a deeper sense, however, Jesus protects the true meaning of the Sabbath, and so ultimately the answer is no.[154] As we have repeatedly pointed out, however, the issue involves something radically different from Jesus presenting an alternative Sabbath halakah in rivalry with the Pharisees. Bäck rightly concludes "In short, he does not move in the sphere of Torah, but is independent of it."[155] A correct understanding of the matter necessarily involves recognition of the determinative importance of messianic fulfillment in all that Jesus does and says–in short, matters of christology and eschatology. Here, as always in the NT, newness does not replace the old, but rather the old is taken up and fulfilled in the new.[156] Fulfillment involves newness. "Placed in a messianic setting the Sabbath was transformed so that it entirely pointed forward to a new order for the life of man."[157] According to Matt 5:17, Jesus cautions against the wrong conclusion: "Think not that I have come to abolish the law and the prophets; I have come not to abolish them but to fulfill them." The messianic Son of Man, who brings the eschatological fulfillment of the Kingdom of God, as the Lord of the Sabbath, interprets the Sabbath in accord with its original intention–a day created by God for the experiencing of health, wholeness, and joy, a day which by its very nature therefore points toward and anticipates the salvation from sin and suffering that he now brings to the world.

---

[153] Banks, *Jesus and the Law in the Synoptic Tradition*, 251–52.

[154] Lohse, *TDNT* 7:22: "The absolute obligation of the commandment is thus challenged, though its validity is not contested in principle." Cf. T. W. Manson, "Jesus, Paul, and the Law," in *Judaism and Christianity* (3 vols.; ed. E. I. J. Rosenthal; London: Sheldon, 1937), 3:129: "He did not hesitate to break through [the Law's] restrictions in the interest of His own task; ... He reserved the right to criticize freely, not only the oral tradition and the scribal decisions, but even the written Torah itself. We can see this clearly enough if we take a single example–the Sabbath law."

[155] Bäck, *Jesus of Nazareth and the Sabbath Commandment*, 192.

[156] Yang (*Jesus and the Sabbath*, 306) captures the tension well: "Jesus' fulfilment of the Sabbath, like that of other laws, has the elements of both 'continuity' and 'discontinuity' in the sense that the Sabbath is no longer the same after Jesus' fulfilment but is transcended by that fulfilment."

[157] Riesenfeld, *The Gospel Tradition*, 117. On p. 120 Riesenfeld speaks of the "eschatological actualizing of the symbolic content of the Sabbath."

5. Postscript

Just prior to the printing of the present essay, the fourth volume of John P. Meier's masterly treatment of the historical Jesus, devoted to the consideration of Jesus and the law, appeared.[158] The importance of this work necessitates a few comments, however inadequate. On the historical issue per se of the sabbath healings, Meier, as promised, is more negative than in his discussion of miracles contained in volume two. In volume two, where the three narratives were assessed as miracle stories, as we saw above, the verdict was *non liquet* (not clear); Meier now argues that the Synoptic controversy stories of healing on the sabbath cannot be historical: "in all four Gospels, we have not a single narrative of a sabbath dispute occasioned by a healing that probably goes back to the historical Jesus" (p. 259). The reason for this shift in opinion rests on Meier's discovery that there is no evidence in pre-70 C.E. Jewish literature that healing on the sabbath was forbidden. Here a determinative conclusion depends on the weakest form of reasoning: the argument from silence. Meier readily admits that he is arguing from silence, but regards the universal, widespread silence "a metaphorical shout" (p. 255). Nevertheless, should a precarious argument from silence be allowed to become the decisive pivot that determines a historical conclusion? Against the admitted multiple attestation of the Synoptic healing stories, Meier is reduced to saying "sometimes a brief inspection employing the criterion of multiple attestation can be deceiving" (p. 253). Thus even when the evidence satisfies a major criterion of authenticity, a positive conclusion must give way to other considerations. Meier also continues to deny the historicity of the narrative concerning plucking grain on the sabbath. Although he concludes positively concerning the historicity of the logion in Mark 2:27, he denies the authenticity of 2:28, regarding it as necessarily a later christological comment. Oddly enough, Meier accepts the historicity of what he takes to be the halakic type sayings associated with the sabbath controversy stories (on the grounds of multiple attestation) while denying the historicity of the narratives themselves! He simply isolates them from their context.

On the issue of Jesus and the law, Meier has fully collapsed the Jesus of the Gospels into Jesus the halakic Jew. "All questers for the historical Jesus should repeat the following mantra even in their sleep: the historical Jesus is the halakic Jesus" (p. 297). But the evidence for this conclusion, so important to Meier, is extremely flimsy, i.e. the few elements of halakic-type argumentation found in the sabbath controversy stories. Are these really sufficient evidence to warrant the conclusion that Jesus was fundamentally

---

[158] Meier, *Law and Love*.

halakic? Meier has to suppose that there was much more of this material that simply did not come into the Gospels. Above all for Meier, Jesus must be made to fit more or less comfortably into the first century Palestinian Jewish context (but then why the hostility of the Pharisees?). In actuality, history is full of the surprising and unexpected. But not for Meier the historian. Strict historical criteria can allow for no surprises. The telescoped narratives of the Synoptics (much more was spoken and done than is recorded), freely edited by the evangelists, can easily be deconstructed as Meier does.

Most disappointingly, Meier demeans the "Christian depiction of Jesus." But this depiction of Jesus does more justice to the Gospels as historical documents than Meier's reconstruction. Meier's sense of the "historical probabilities," which cannot but remain debatable, becomes the truth over against the Gospels. It is worth remembering that "the quest of the historical Jesus" is a misnomer. It is not a search that can bring us the real Jesus (although that often seems to be the implication), but rather a search that provides what necessarily and finally must remain an artificial construct. The fact remains that the historical method, strictly practiced à la Meier, is ill-equipped to deal with the uniqueness represented by the story of Jesus.

Bibliography

Abrahams, Israel. *Studies in Pharisaism and the Gospels*. Library of Biblical Studies. 1924. Repr., New York: Ktav, 1967.

Banks, Robert. *Jesus and the Law in the Synoptic Tradition*. SNTSMS 28. Cambridge: Cambridge University Press, 1975.

Bäck, Sven-Olav. *Jesus of Nazareth and the Sabbath Commandment*. Åbo: Åbo Akademi University Press, 1995.

Black, Matthew. "Aramaic Spoken by Christ and Luke 14:5." *Journal of Theological Studies* n. s. 1 (1950): 60–62.

Bock, Darrell L. *Jesus According to Scripture: Restoring the Portrait From the Gospels*. Grand Rapids: Baker, 2002.

Bockmuehl, Markus. "Halakha and Ethics in the Jesus Tradition." Pages 264–78 in *Early Christian Thought in Its Jewish Context*. J. Barclay and J. Sweet. Cambridge: Cambridge University Press, 1996.

Bultmann, Rudolf. *The History of the Synoptic Tradition*. Translated by John Marsh. New York: Harper & Row, 1963.

Caird, G. B. *New Testament Theology*. Edited by L. D. Hurst. Oxford: Clarendon Press, 1994.

Carson, D. A. "Jesus and the Sabbath in the Four Gospels." Pages 58–97 in *From Sabbath to Lord's Day: A Biblical, Historical and Theological Investigation*. Edited by D. A. Carson. Grand Rapids: Zondervan, 1982.

Casey, Maurice. *Aramaic Sources of Mark's Gospel*. SNTSMS 102. Cambridge: Cambridge University Press, 1998.

–. "Culture and Historicity: The Plucking of the Grain (Mark 2:23–28)." *NTS* 34 (1988): 1–23.
Cohn-Sherbok, D. M. "An Analysis of Jesus' Arguments Concerning the Plucking of Grain on the Sabbath." *JSNT* (1979), 31–41.
Collins, Adela Yarbro. *Mark*. Hermeneia. Minneapolis: Fortress, 2007.
Cranfield, C. E. B. *The Gospel According to Saint Mark*. CGTC. Cambridge: Cambridge University Press, 1959.
Daube, David. *The New Testament and Rabbinic Judaism*. JLCRS 2. London: University of London, Athlone Press, 1956.
–. "Responsibilities of Master and Disciples in the Gospels." *NTS* 19 (1972): 1–15.
Davies, W. D., and Dale C. Allison, Jr. *A Critical and Exegetical Commentary on the Gospel According to Saint Matthew*. 3 vols. ICC. Edinburgh: T&T Clark, 1988–97.
Dietzfelbinger, Christian. "Vom Sinn der Sabbatheilungen Jesu." *EvT* 38 (1978): 281–98.
Doering, Lutz. *Schabbat: Sabbathalacha und -praxis im antiken Judentum und Urchristentum*. Texte und Studien zum antiken Judentum, 78. Tübingen: Mohr Siebeck, 1999.
Dunn, James D. G. "Mark 2.1–3.6: A Bridge Between Jesus and Paul on the Question of the Law." *NTS* 30 (1984): 395–415.
Evans, Craig A. *Life of Jesus Research: An Annotated Bibliography*. 2nd ed. NTTS 24. Leiden: Brill, 1996.
Eve, Eric. *The Jewish Context of Jesus' Miracles*. JSNTSup 231. New York: Sheffield Academic Press, 2002.
Fitzmyer, Joseph A. *The Gospel According to Luke X–XXIV*. AB 28a. Garden City: Doubleday, 1985.
Flusser, David. *Jesus*. Translated by Ronald Walls. New York: Herder & Herder, 1969.
Funk, Robert W., and The Jesus Seminar. *The Acts of Jesus: The Search for the Authentic Deeds of Jesus*. San Francisco: HarperSanFrancisco, 1998.
Funk, Robert W., Roy W. Hoover, and The Jesus Seminar. *The Five Gospels: The Search for the Authentic Words of Jesus*. New York: Macmillan, 1993.
Goetz, Stewart C., and Craig L. Blomberg. "The Burden of Proof." *JSNT* 11 (1981): 39–63.
Goldenberg, Robert. "The Place of the Sabbath in Rabbinic Judaism." Pages 31–44 in *The Sabbath in Jewish and Christian Traditions*. Edited by Tamara Cohn Eskenazi, Daniel J. Harrington, and William H. Shea. New York: Crossroad, 1991.
Goppelt, Leonhard. *Theology of the New Testament*. 2 vols. Translated by John E. Alsup. Grand Rapids: Eerdmans, 1981–82.
Guelich, Robert A. *Mark 1–8:26*. WBC 34a. Dallas: Word, 1989.
Gundry, Robert H. *Mark: A Commentary on His Apology for the Cross*. Grand Rapids: Eerdmans, 1993.
Harrington, Daniel J. "Sabbath Tensions: Matthew 12:1–14 and Other New Testament Texts." Pages 45–56 in *The Sabbath in Jewish and Christian Traditions*. Edited by Tamara Cohn Eskenazi, Daniel J. Harrington, and William H. Shea. New York: Crossroad, 1991.
Hicks, John Mark. "The Sabbath Controversy in Matthew: An Exegesis of Matthew 12:1–14." *ResQ* 27 (1984): 79–91.

Hinz, Christoph. "Jesus und der Sabbat." *KD* 19 (1973): 91–108.
Holmén, Tom. *Jesus and Jewish Covenant Thinking*. Biblical Interpretation Series, 55. Leiden: Brill, 2001.
Hooker, Morna D. *A Commentary on the Gospel According to St. Mark*. BNTC. London: A&C Black, 1991.
Klumbies, Paul-Gerhard. "Die Sabbatheilungen Jesu nach Markus und Lukas." Pages 165–78 in *Jesus Rede von Gott und ihre Nachgeschichte im frühen Christentum: Beiträge zur Verkündigung Jesu und zum Kerygma der Kirche*. Edited by Dietrich-Alex Koch, Gerhard Sellin, and Andreas Lindemann. Gütersloh: Mohn, 1989.
Lane, William L. *The Gospel of Mark*. NICNT. Grand Rapids: Eerdmans, 1974.
Levine, Etan. "Sabbath Controversy According to Matthew." *NTS* 22 (1976): 480–83.
Lincoln, Andrew T. "From Sabbath to Lord's Day: A Biblical and Theological Perspective." Pages 344–412 in *From Sabbath to Lord's Day: A Biblical, Historical and Theological Investigation*. Edited by D. A. Carson. Grand Rapids: Zondervan, 1982.
Loader, William R. G. *Jesus' Attitude Towards the Law: A Study of the Gospels*. WUNT 2.97. Tübingen: Mohr Siebeck, 1997.
Lohse, Eduard. "Jesu Worte über den Sabbat." Pages 79–89 in *Judentum, Urchristentum, Kirche: Festschrift für Joachim Jeremias*. 2nd ed. Edited by Walther Eltester. Berlin: Töpelmann, 1964.
–. "σάββατον." Pages 2–20 in vol. 7 of *Theological Dictionary of the New Testament*. 10 vols. Edited by G. Kittel and Gerhard Friedrich. Translated by Geoffrey W. Bromiley. Grand Rapids: Eerdmans, 1964–76.
Luz, Ulrich. *Matthew 8–20*. Translated by James E. Crouch. Hermeneia. Minneapolis: Fortress, 2001.
Manson, T. W. "Jesus, Paul, and the Law." Pages 125–41 in vol. 3 of *Judaism and Christianity*. 3 vols. Edited by E. I. J. Rosenthal. London: Sheldon, 1937.
–. "Mark ii.27 f." Pages 138–46 in *Coniectanea Neotestamentica 11*. Lund: Gleerup, 1947.
Marcus, Joel. *Mark 1–8*. AB 27. New York: Doubleday, 2000.
Meier, John P. "The Historical Jesus and the Historical Law: Some Problems Within the Problem." *CBQ* 65 (2003): 52–79.
–. "The Historical Jesus and the Plucking of the Grain on the Sabbath." *CBQ* 66 (2004): 561–81.
–. *Law and Love*. Vol. 4 of *A Marginal Jew: Rethinking the Historical Jesus*. ABRL. New Haven: Yale University Press, 2009.
–. *A Marginal Jew: Rethinking the Historical Jesus*. ABRL. New York: Doubleday, 1991–.
–. *Mentor, Message, and Miracles*. Vol. 2 of *A Marginal Jew: Rethinking the Historical Jesus*. ABRL. New York: Doubleday, 1994.
Montefiore, C. G. *The Synoptic Gospels*. 2nd ed. 2 vols. London: Macmillan, 1927.
Moore, George Foot. *Judaism in the First Centuries of the Christian Era: The Age of Tannaim*. 3 vols. 1930. Repr., New York: Schocken, 1971.
Neirynck, Frans. "Jesus and the Sabbath: Some Observations on Mark ii,27." Pages 227–70 in *Jésus aux origines de la christologie*. Edited by Jacques Dupont. BETL 40. Louvain: Louvain University Press, 1989.

Neusner, Jacob. *The Mishnah: A New Translation*. New Haven: Yale University Press, 1988.
–. "Practice: Jesus and Torah." Pages 135–44 in *Judaism in the New Testament: Practices and Beliefs*. By Bruce D. Chilton and Jacob Neusner. London: Routledge, 1995.
–. *A Rabbi Talks with Jesus: An Intermillennial, Interfaith Exchange*. New York: Doubleday, 1993.
Nolland, John. *Luke 9:21–18:34*. WBC 35b. Dallas: Word, 1993.
Pesch, Rudolf. *Das Markusevangelium*. 2 vols. HTKNT 2. Freiburg im Breisgau: Herder, 1977.
Porter, Stanley E. *The Criteria for Authenticity in Historical-Jesus Research: Previous Discussion and New Proposals*. JSNTSup 191. Sheffield: Sheffield Academic Press, 2000.
Reicke, Bo Ivar. "Incarnation and Exaltation: The Historic Jesus and the Kerygmatic Christ." *Int* 16 (1962): 156–68.
Riesenfeld, Harald. *The Gospel Tradition*. Translated by E. Margaret Rowley and Robert A. Kraft. Philadelphia: Fortress, 1970.
Rordorf, Willy. *Sunday: The History of the Day of Rest and Worship in the Earliest Centuries of the Christian Church*. Translated by A. A. K. Graham. Philadelphia: Westminster, 1968.
Sanders, E. P. *Jesus and Judaism*. Philadelphia: Fortress, 1985.
–. *Jewish Law from Jesus to the Mishnah: Five Studies*. London: SCM, 1990.
Schaller, Berndt. *Fundamenta Judaica: Studien zum antiken Judentum und zum Neuen Testament*. Edited by Lutz Doering and Annette Steudel. SUNT 25. Göttingen: Vandenhoeck & Ruprecht, 2001.
Schürer, Emil. *The History of the Jewish People in the Age of Jesus Christ (175 B. C. – A. D. 135)*. New English ed. 3 vols. Edited by Geza Vermes, Fergus Millar, and Matthew Black. Edinburgh: T&T Clark, 1973–87.
Schweizer, Eduard. *The Good News According to Mark*. Translated by H. Donald. Richmond: John Knox, 1970.
Sigal, Phillip. *The Halakah of Jesus of Nazareth According to the Gospel of Matthew*. Lanham, MD: University Press of America, 1986.
Strack, Hermann L., and Paul Billerbeck. *Kommentar zum Neuen Testament aus Talmud und Midrasch*. 6 vols. Munich: Beck, 1922–61.
Stuhlmacher, Peter. *Biblische Theologie des Neuen Testaments*. 2 vols. Göttingen: Vandenhoeck & Ruprecht, 1992.
Taylor, Vincent. *The Gospel According to St. Mark*. 2nd ed. London: Macmillan, 1966.
Theissen, Gerd, and Annette Merz. *The Historical Jesus: A Comprehensive Guide*. Translated by John Bowden. Minneapolis: Fortress, 1998.
Theissen, Gerd, and Dagmar Winter. *The Quest for the Plausible Jesus: The Question of Criteria*. Translated by M. Eugene Boring. Louisville: Westminster John Knox, 2002.
Vermès, Géza. *Jesus the Jew: A Historian's Reading of the Gospels*. London: Collins, 1973.
–. *The Religion of Jesus the Jew*. Minneapolis: Fortress, 1993.
Weiss, Herold. "The Sabbath in the Synoptic Gospels." *JSNT* 38 (1990): 13–27.

Westerholm, Stephen. *Jesus and Scribal Authority*. ConBNT 10. Lund: Gleerup, 1978.

Yang, Yong-Eui. *Jesus and the Sabbath in Matthew's Gospel*. JSNTSup 139. Sheffield: Sheffield Academic Press, 1997.

Chapter 8

Peter's Declaration concerning Jesus' Identity in Caesarea Philippi

MICHAEL J. WILKINS

1. Introduction

1.1 Peter and Jesus' Identity

In this essay we examine Peter's declaration regarding Jesus' identity.[1] It is the testimony of one of the Twelve – even as a spokesperson for the Twelve – of his master's identity as Messiah. This incident comes after Peter and the Twelve have witnessed the collective events performed by Jesus to that point in his ministry. Those events combine to give an understanding of Jesus' identity. So at this critical turning point in Jesus' historical ministry, Peter's declaration reveals what Jesus' closest followers understood about him. And Jesus' response to Peter provides insights to Jesus' self-understanding.

This study is somewhat distinctive in that it examines an event in which one of Jesus' followers testifies to his understanding of Jesus' identity based upon the preceding events in Jesus' mission. The other studies primarily examine events performed by Jesus. However, the present study somewhat mirrors a later study that examines an event, the Jewish inquiry, in which one of Jesus' opponents inquires of Jesus about his reported identity as Messiah. This comes after having heard reports of the collective events performed by Jesus throughout his ministry. The high priest's exclamation of blasphemy at Jesus' response also provides insights to Jesus' self-understanding.[2]

Therefore, our examination of the historicity of Peter's declaration complements the prior studies of the events of Jesus' Galilean ministry because they provide the context for understanding Peter's declaration.[3] The studies

---

[1] Peter's statement is regularly referred to as his "confession." However, since "confession" has religious implications, I have chosen the more neutral term "declaration" to guide our study of the historical nature of his statement.

[2] See in this volume ch. 12.

[3] The events of Jesus' Galilean ministry include (1) Jesus' baptism; (2) choosing the

of the events of Jesus' final week in Jerusalem provide additional context for understanding the high priest's inquiry and his exclamation of blasphemy.[4]

In this essay we follow the three-part organization that is the common to most of the studies in this volume. The first part examines the issues at stake in the study of Peter's declaration and the arguments for the historicity of the event, applying to the event the traditionally-used criteria of authenticity. The second part examines the historical context, especially declaration data from the Jewish and/or Greco-Roman context that will enable us to understand further the meaning of Peter's declaration. The third part explores the implications of the event, especially the meaning of the declaration and its significance for understanding Jesus' self-consciousness.

The accounts of Peter's declaration include several controversial and debated topics, including issues related to Messianism, the so-called "Messianic secret," the title "Son of Man," and the transition to Jesus' prediction of his suffering. Since these issues are complex and the literature on each is massive, we will examine them only to the degree that they impinge on our central topic, Peter's declaration concerning Jesus. The important pericope units tied to this event follow:

Peter's Declaration[5]

Matthew 16:13–20	Mark 8:27–30	Luke 9:18–21	John 6:66–69
		¹⁸Καὶ ἐγένετο ἐν τῷ εἶναι αὐτὸν προσευχόμενον κατὰ μόνας	⁶⁶Ἐκ τούτου πολλοὶ [ἐκ] τῶν μαθητῶν αὐτοῦ ἀπῆλθον εἰς τὰ ὀπίσω καὶ οὐκέτι μετ' αὐτοῦ περιεπάτουν.
¹³Ἐλθὼν δὲ ὁ Ἰησοῦς εἰς τὰ μέρη Καισαρείας τῆς Φιλίππου	²⁷Καὶ ἐξῆλθεν ὁ Ἰησοῦς καὶ οἱ μαθηταὶ αὐτοῦ εἰς τὰς κώμας Καισαρείας τῆς Φιλίππου·	συνῆσαν αὐτῷ οἱ μαθηταί,	
ἠρώτα τοὺς μαθητὰς αὐτοῦ λέγων· τίνα λέγουσιν οἱ ἄνθρωποι εἶναι τὸν υἱὸν τοῦ ἀνθρώπου;	καὶ ἐν τῇ ὁδῷ ἐπηρώτα τοὺς μαθητὰς αὐτοῦ λέγων αὐτοῖς· τίνα με λέγουσιν οἱ ἄνθρωποι εἶναι;	καὶ ἐπηρώτησεν αὐτοὺς λέγων· τίνα με λέγουσιν οἱ ὄχλοι εἶναι;	⁶⁷εἶπεν οὖν ὁ Ἰησοῦς τοῖς δώδεκα· μὴ καὶ ὑμεῖς θέλετε ὑπάγειν;

Twelve; (3) Jesus' exorcisms; (4) Sabbath controversies; (5) table fellowship/sinners; (6) Peter's declaration of Jesus.

[4] The events of Jesus' final week in Jerusalem include (1) Jesus' climactic entry to Jerusalem, (2) the Temple incident, (3) the Last Supper, (4) the Jewish trial, (5) the Roman examination and crucifixion, (6) the resurrection.

[5] Adapted from Kurt Aland, ed., *Synopsis Quattuor Evangeliorum* (Stuttgart: Deutsche Bibelstiftung, 1976), 229–31, § 158.

Matthew 16:13–20	Mark 8:27–30	Luke 9:18–21	John 6:66–69
¹⁴ οἱ δὲ εἶπαν· οἱ μὲν Ἰωάννην τὸν βαπτιστήν, ἄλλοι δὲ Ἠλίαν, ἕτεροι δὲ Ἰερεμίαν ἢ ἕνα τῶν προφητῶν.	²⁸ οἱ δὲ εἶπαν αὐτῷ λέγοντες [ὅτι] Ἰωάννην τὸν βαπτιστήν, καὶ ἄλλοι Ἠλίαν, ἄλλοι δὲ ὅτι εἷς τῶν προφητῶν.	¹⁹ οἱ δὲ ἀποκριθέντες εἶπαν· Ἰωάννην τὸν βαπτιστήν, ἄλλοι δὲ Ἠλίαν, ἄλλοι δὲ ὅτι προφήτης τις τῶν ἀρχαίων ἀνέστη.	
¹⁵ λέγει αὐτοῖς· ὑμεῖς δὲ τίνα με λέγετε εἶναι;	²⁹ καὶ αὐτὸς ἐπηρώτα αὐτούς· ὑμεῖς δὲ τίνα με λέγετε εἶναι;	²⁰ εἶπεν δὲ αὐτοῖς· ὑμεῖς δὲ τίνα με λέγετε εἶναι;	
¹⁶ ἀποκριθεὶς δὲ Σίμων Πέτρος εἶπεν·	ἀποκριθεὶς ὁ Πέτρος λέγει αὐτῷ·	Πέτρος δὲ ἀποκριθεὶς εἶπεν·	⁶⁸ ἀπεκρίθη αὐτῷ Σίμων Πέτρος· κύριε, πρὸς τίνα ἀπελευσόμεθα; ῥήματα ζωῆς αἰωνίου ἔχεις, ⁶⁹
σὺ εἶ ὁ χριστὸς ὁ υἱὸς τοῦ θεοῦ τοῦ ζῶντος.	σὺ εἶ ὁ χριστός.	τὸν χριστὸν τοῦ θεοῦ.	καὶ ἡμεῖς πεπιστεύκαμεν καὶ ἐγνώκαμεν ὅτι σὺ εἶ ὁ ἅγιος τοῦ θεοῦ.
¹⁷ ἀποκριθεὶς δὲ ὁ Ἰησοῦς εἶπεν αὐτῷ· μακάριος εἶ, Σίμων Βαριωνᾶ, (... 17b–19⁶)			
²⁰ τότε διεστείλατο τοῖς μαθηταῖς ἵνα μηδενὶ εἴπωσιν ὅτι αὐτός ἐστιν ὁ χριστός.	³⁰ καὶ ἐπετίμησεν αὐτοῖς ἵνα μηδενὶ λέγωσιν περὶ αὐτοῦ.	²¹ ὁ δὲ ἐπιτιμήσας αὐτοῖς παρήγγειλεν μηδενὶ λέγειν τοῦτο	

---

[6] Matt 16:17b–19: ὅτι σὰρξ καὶ αἷμα οὐκ ἀπεκάλυψέν σοι ἀλλ' ὁ πατήρ μου ὁ ἐν τοῖς οὐρανοῖς. ¹⁸ κἀγὼ δέ σοι λέγω ὅτι σὺ εἶ Πέτρος, καὶ ἐπὶ ταύτῃ τῇ πέτρᾳ οἰκοδομήσω μου τὴν ἐκκλησίαν καὶ πύλαι ᾅδου οὐ κατισχύσουσιν αὐτῆς. ¹⁹ δώσω σοι τὰς κλεῖδας τῆς βασιλείας τῶν οὐρανῶν, καὶ ὃ ἐὰν δήσῃς ἐπὶ τῆς γῆς ἔσται δεδεμένον ἐν τοῖς οὐρανοῖς, καὶ ὃ ἐὰν λύσῃς ἐπὶ τῆς γῆς ἔσται λελυμένον ἐν τοῖς οὐρανοῖς.

Peter's Declaration (NRSV)

Matthew 16:13–20	Mark 8:27–30	Luke 9:18–21	John 6:66–69
¹³ Now when Jesus came into the district of Caesarea Philippi,	²⁷ Jesus went on with his disciples to the villages of Caesarea Philippi;	¹⁸ Once when Jesus was praying alone, with only the disciples near him,	⁶⁶ Because of this many of his disciples turned back and no longer went about with him.
He asked his disciples, "Who do people say that the Son of Man is?"	on the way he asked his disciples, "Who do people say that I am?"	he asked them, "Who do the crowds say that I am?"	⁶⁷ So Jesus asked the twelve, "Do you also wish to go away?"
¹⁴ And they said, "Some say John the Baptist, but others Elijah, and still others Jeremiah or one of the prophets."	²⁸ And they answered him, "John the Baptist; and others, Elijah; and still others, one of the prophets."	¹⁹ They answered, "John the Baptist; but others, Elijah; and still others, that one of the ancient prophets has arisen."	
¹⁵ He said to them, "But who do you say that I am?"	²⁹ He asked them, "But who do you say that I am?"	²⁰ He said to them, "But who do you say that I am?"	
¹⁶ Simon Peter answered,	Peter answered him,	Peter answered,	⁶⁸ Simon Peter answered him, "Lord, to whom can we go? You have words of eternal life. ⁶⁹ We have come to believe and know that
"You are the Messiah, the Son of the living God."	"You are the Messiah."	"The Messiah of God."	you are the Holy One of God."
¹⁷ And Jesus answered him, "Blessed are you, Simon			

Matthew 16:13–20	Mark 8:27–30	Luke 9:18–21	John 6:66–69
son of Jonah! (... 17b–19⁷) ²⁰ Then he sternly ordered the disciples not to tell anyone that he was the Messiah.	³⁰ And he sternly ordered them not to tell anyone about him.	²¹ He sternly ordered and commanded them not to tell anyone,	

Jesus Foretells His Passion

Matthew 16:21–23	Mark 8:31–33	Luke 9:22	John 6:70–71
²¹Ἀπὸ τότε ἤρξατο ὁ Ἰησοῦς δεικνύειν τοῖς μαθηταῖς αὐτοῦ ὅτι δεῖ αὐτὸν εἰς Ἱεροσόλυμα ἀπελθεῖν καὶ πολλὰ παθεῖν	³¹ Καὶ ἤρξατο διδάσκειν αὐτοὺς ὅτι δεῖ τὸν υἱὸν τοῦ ἀνθρώπου πολλὰ παθεῖν καὶ ἀποδοκιμασθῆναι ὑπὸ τῶν πρεσβυτέ- ρων καὶ	²² εἰπὼν ὅτι δεῖ τὸν υἱὸν τοῦ ἀνθρώπου πολλὰ παθεῖν καὶ ἀποδοκιμασθῆναι ἀπὸ τῶν πρεσβυτέρων καὶ	⁷⁰ ἀπεκρίθη αὐτοῖς ὁ Ἰησοῦς· οὐκ ἐγὼ ὑμᾶς τοὺς δώδεκα ἐξελεξάμην;
ἀπὸ τῶν πρεσβυτέρων καὶ ἀρχιερέων καὶ γραμματέων καὶ ἀποκτανθῆναι καὶ τῇ τρίτῃ ἡμέρᾳ ἐγερθῆναι.	τῶν ἀρχιερέων καὶ τῶν γραμματέων καὶ ἀποκτανθῆναι καὶ μετὰ τρεῖς ἡμέρας ἀναστῆναι·	ἀρχιερέων καὶ γραμματέων καὶ ἀποκτανθῆναι καὶ Τῇ τρίτῃ ἡμέρᾳ ἐγερθῆναι.	
²² καὶ προσλαβόμενος αὐτὸν ὁ Πέτρος ἤρξατο ἐπιτιμᾶν αὐτῷ λέγων· ἵλεώς σοι, κύριε· οὐ μὴ ἔσται σοι τοῦτο.	³² καὶ παρρησίᾳ τὸν λόγον ἐλάλει. καὶ προσλαβόμενος ὁ Πέτρος αὐτὸν ἤρξατο ἐπιτιμᾶν αὐτῷ.		

---

⁷ Matt 16:17b–19: "For flesh and blood has not revealed this to you, but my Father in heaven. ¹⁸ And I tell you, you are Peter, and on this rock I will build my church, and the gates of Hades will not prevail against it. ¹⁹ I will give you the keys of the kingdom of heaven, and whatever you bind on earth will be bound in heaven, and whatever you loose on earth will be loosed in heaven."

Matthew 16:21–23	Mark 8:31–33	Luke 9:22	John 6:70–71
²³ ὁ δὲ στραφεὶς εἶπεν τῷ Πέτρῳ· ὕπαγε ὀπίσω μου, σατανᾶ· σκάνδαλον εἶ ἐμοῦ, ὅτι οὐ φρονεῖς τὰ τοῦ θεοῦ ἀλλὰ τὰ τῶν ἀνθρώπων.	³³ ὁ δὲ ἐπιστραφεὶς καὶ ἰδὼν τοὺς μαθητὰς αὐτοῦ ἐπετίμησεν Πέτρῳ καὶ λέγει· ὕπαγε ὀπίσω μου, σατανᾶ, ὅτι οὐ φρονεῖς τὰ τοῦ θεοῦ ἀλλὰ τὰ τῶν ἀνθρώπων.		καὶ ἐξ ὑμῶν εἷς διάβολός ἐστιν. ⁷¹ ἔλεγεν δὲ τὸν Ἰούδαν Σίμωνος Ἰσκαριώτου· οὗτος γὰρ ἔμελλεν παραδιδόναι αὐτόν, εἷς ἐκ τῶν δώδεκα.

Jesus Foretells His Passion

Matthew 16:21–23	Mark 8:31–33	Luke 9:22	John 6:70–71
²¹ From that time on, Jesus began to show his disciples that he must go to Jerusalem and undergo great suffering at the hands of the elders and chief priests and scribes, and be killed, and on the third day be raised. ²² And Peter took him aside and began to rebuke him, saying, "God forbid it, Lord! This must never happen to you." ²³ But he turned and said to Peter, "Get behind me, Satan! You are a stumbling block to me; for you	³¹ Then he began to teach them that the Son of Man must undergo great suffering, and be rejected by the elders, the chief priests, and the scribes, and be killed, and after three days rise again. ³²He said all this quite openly. And Peter took him aside and began to rebuke him. ³³ But turning and looking at his disciples, he rebuked Peter and said, "Get behind me, Satan!	²² saying, "The Son of Man must undergo great suffering, and be rejected by the elders, chief priests, and scribes, and be killed, and on the third day be raised."	⁷⁰ Jesus answered them, "Did I not choose you, the twelve? Yet one of you is a devil."⁷¹ He was speaking of Judas son of Simon Iscariot, for he, though one

Matthew 16:21–23	Mark 8:31–33	Luke 9:22	John 6:70–71
are setting your mind not on divine things but on human things."	For you are setting your mind not on divine things but on human things."		of the twelve, was going to betray him.

1.2. Gospel accounts of Peter's declaration

Peter's declaration of Jesus' identity occurs in some form in all four Gospels (see the synopsis above). There is significant difference in wording and context between the Synoptics and John, although all depict Peter declaring his conviction or allegiance when Jesus asks the disciples about their understanding of his identity or commitment to him.[8]

Mark gives the core of the declaration, "You are the Christ" (Mark 8:29; σὺ εἶ ὁ χριστός[9]). Neither Matthew's variation, "You are the Christ, the Son of the living God" (Matt 16:16; σὺ εἶ ὁ χριστὸς ὁ υἱὸς τοῦ θεοῦ τοῦ ζῶντος) nor Luke's, "the Christ of God" (Luke 9:20; ὸν χριστὸν τοῦ θεοῦ) alter the basic point found in Mark, although the distinctives of their accounts are instructive, which we will examine below. The expression ὁ χριστός is "the anointed [one]." The Greek translates the Hebrew מָשִׁיחַ, although the transliteration μεσσίας also sometimes occurs in the Gospels (John 1:41; 4:25). John's account has Peter exclaiming about Jesus, "you are the Holy One of God" (John 6:68–69; σὺ εἶ ὁ ἅγιος τοῦ θεοῦ).

Mark (8:27–30) records Jesus leading his disciples out of Galilee into the predominantly Gentile area of Caesarea Philippi, northeast of the Sea of Galilee. Jesus queries his disciples about the general, public opinion of his identity (8:27). The disciples reply with various identities: John the Baptist, Elijah, or one of the prophets (8:28). Jesus then presses them to give their own opinion of his identity. Peter replies for the group to say, "You are the Christ" (8:29). Jesus firmly commands them not to tell anyone about him (8:30). Then he gives his first passion prediction (8:31), at which point Peter takes Jesus aside and begins to rebuke him (8:32). Jesus looks at the disciples and tells Peter, "Get behind me, Satan" (8:33).

Luke (9:18–20) is similar to Mark with his brevity, but with a number of differences. There is no reference to traveling in Caesarea Philippi. The nearest previous reference to location had Jesus withdrawing with his disciples to Bethsaida, the city on the northeast corner of the Sea of Galilee

---

[8] For an overview of the accounts, see John P. Meier, *Companions and Competitors* (vol. 3 of *A Marginal Jew: Rethinking the Historical Jesus*; ABRL; New York: Doubleday, 2001), 226.

[9] ℵ L *pc* r¹ add ὁ υἱὸς τοῦ θεοῦ and W *f*¹³ *pc* b sy^p sa^mss have ὁ υἱὸς τοῦ θεοῦ τοῦ ζῶντος. These readings are due to the influence of Matt 16:16.

(9:10). Luke records that it is now a scene of prayer (9:18). Similar to Mark, Jesus asks for the public's opinion of his identity and the disciples reply with the names of John the Baptist and Elijah. They also include the opinion that one of the ancient prophets had arisen (9:19). When queried about their understanding of his identity, Peter again replies for the group, but with a lengthened declaration, "... the Christ of God" (9:20). With heightened emphasis, Jesus sternly ordered and commanded the disciples not to tell anyone (9:21). This flows into the passion prediction (9:22). Significantly, Luke does not have the interchange between Peter and Jesus.

Matthew's account (16:13–20) has an expanded scene and declaration. The scene is Caesarea Philippi, but Jesus' query asks for public opinion of the identity of "the Son of Man" (16:13). The disciples' reply includes among the names found in Mark and Luke a reference to the prophet Jeremiah (16:14). As spokesperson, now *Simon* Peter responds with an expanded declaration, "You are the Christ, the Son of the living God" (16:16). Therefore, in the Matthean pericope occur three key titles, Son of Man, Messiah, and Son of God. One significant difference between the accounts is Matthew's well-known, but unique, record of Jesus' response to Peter's declaration. In three strophes, Jesus points out that the declaration was a result of the blessing of divine revelation (16:17), he declares that Peter will be the foundational rock of the future Hades-resistant church that Jesus will build (16:18), and he predicts the role that Peter will play in the use of the keys to provide or restrict access to the kingdom of heaven (16:19). Significantly, Matthew records that Jesus still concludes the scene by ordering the disciples to silence, but makes explicit that they are not to tell anyone that he was the Messiah (16:20). Then Jesus gives his first passion prediction (16:21), at which Peter takes Jesus aside and begins to rebuke him, saying it is not appropriate for him (16:22). Jesus then says to Peter, "Get behind me, Satan" (8:33).

The fourth Gospel (6:67–69) records a Petrine declaration that is quite different than that found in the Synoptics. The nearest stated location is in a synagogue in Capernaum in Galilee (6:59), not Caesarea Philippi. Jesus has finished a discourse on the bread of life, which included shocking references to eating his flesh and drinking his blood (6:35–58). This produces a crisis when many of Jesus' disciples are offended at his teaching (6:60–61). Jesus reveals that from the beginning they had never believed (6:64). Then these many disciples withdraw and no longer follow him, indicating that they are no longer Jesus' disciples. In the middle of this crisis, Jesus turns to the Twelve, now mentioned for the first time in John's Gospel, to question them whether they also want to leave him (6:67). Simon Peter answers for the group with elevated wording, "Lord, to whom can we go? You have the words of eternal life. We have come to believe and know that you are the Holy One of God" (6:68–69). "Holy One of God" may have messianic overtones, similar to the reference to "the Holy Messiah" (מ[שיח הקודש) in a Hebrew liturgical fragment (1Q30 f1:2) and "the holy anointed ones" (<במשיחי> הקודש) in CD 6:1.[10] Rather than the warning to silence as found in the Synoptics, Jesus responds with a dire declaration that although he had chosen the Twelve, one of them is a devil (6:70). A Johannine aside indicates that it is Judas who would betray Jesus (6:71).

The wording of the declaration between the Synoptics and John is strikingly different. The Johannine version gives an expanded statement of Jesus' identity as "Lord" (κύριε), a declaration of abandonment to Jesus as the one who solely has words of eternal life, and a combination of belief and knowledge in Jesus' identity as "the Holy One of God."[11]

The strikingly unique and yet strikingly common materials in the Gospels' accounts of Peter's declaration has lead to different conclusions regarding the traditions behind them. We discuss this below when examining the criteria for authenticity and their application to this incident. This comingling of unique and common materials has led also to diverse scholarly conclusions regarding the historicity of Peter's declaration.

1.3. The issue of the historicity of Peter's declaration

Peter's declaration has long been a benchmark for ascertaining the apostles' understanding of Jesus' identity and also for understanding Jesus' own self-understanding.[12] But from early in the twentieth century up to recent years, modern scholars have subjected Peter's declaration to critical examination, and many have declared it not to be an historical event. The latter contend that the incident is a classic example of the distinction between the *Jesus of history* and the *Christ of faith*.[13] They contend that the Jesus of history that we find in the Synoptic Gospels never explicitly called himself Messiah, and he silenced those who tried to give him messianic status (Mark 1:24–25; 8:29–30). Jesus knew that he was a special agent of God, but he did not claim that he was anything other than a prophet like John the Baptist.

They further contend that the Jesus that is depicted in the rest of the NT is the Christ of faith. The hopes of Jesus' mission were utterly devastated

---

[10] See Craig A. Evans, *Jesus and His Contemporaries: Comparative Studies* (AGJU 25; Leiden: Brill, 1995), 91.

[11] Variants have ὁ Χριστὸς ὁ ἅγιος τοῦ θεοῦ ($\mathfrak{P}^{66}$) and ὁ Χριστὸς ὁ υἱὸς τοῦ θεοῦ τοῦ ζῶντος ($C^3 \Theta^*$), which are considered assimilations from the Synoptics. Cf. George R. Beasley-Murray, *John* (2nd ed.; WBC 36; Nashville: Nelson, 1999), 85.

[12] Donald A. Hagner (*Matthew 14–28* [WBC 33b; Dallas: Word, 1995], 465) points out that relatively few scholars in the history of scholarship denied the historicity of Peter's declaration itself.

[13] First coined by Martin Kähler in 1896. See his *The So-Called Historical Jesus and the Historic, Biblical Christ* (trans. Carl E. Braaten; Philadelphia: Fortress, 1964).

with his execution at the hands of the Roman authorities. But soon the followers of Jesus began to believe that Jesus' mission was not dead, because it was alive in their minds and hearts. It was as though Jesus himself was still alive. And if his mission was not dead, then he really was not only the Messiah of Israel, but also the Messiah of all the nations. Jesus was still alive in their minds and hearts and was more exalted than ever, and by faith the early followers declared that he was the Christ, the Messiah, who is the very Son of God (Acts 9:22; cf. Rom 1:3–4; Col 1:13–16).[14]

So, many modern critics contend that when the authors of the Gospels wrote the story of Jesus' life, they did so from the perspective of faith that Jesus was the Christ, but with the recognition that the Jesus of history did not make that claim, nor did he understand himself to be such. When we find evidence of these kinds of claims in the Gospels, they are understood to be the Gospel writers interpolating later beliefs back into Jesus' ministry.[15]

Rudolf Bultmann viewed the incident as a legend of faith, a retrojection of the church's belief in the resurrection back into the Gospel accounts. He concludes that, "The scene of *Peter's Confession* (Mk. 8:27–30) ... is an Easter-story projected backward into Jesus' life-time, just like the story of the Transfiguration (Mk. 9:2–8)."[16] Hans Conzelmann rejected any note of historicity in the declaration: "... any assumption of a historical nucleus makes the texts incomprehensible. The scene is not a story, but a piece of christological reflection given the form of a story. Peter utters the creed of the community, 'You are the Messiah.'"[17]

---

[14] This view is sketched out clearly by Bart D. Ehrman, *The New Testament: An Historical Introduction to the Early Christian Writings* (3rd ed.; Oxford: Oxford University Press, 2004), 275–84. He concludes: "By the end of the first century, Christians in some circles had already proclaimed that Jesus was himself divine, that he existed prior to his birth, that he created the world, and all that is in it, and that he came into the world on a divine mission as God himself. This a far cry from the humble beginnings of Jesus as an apocalyptic prophet" (p. 282).

[15] E. g., Ehrman, *The New Testament*, 275–85; Helmut Koester, *From Jesus to the Gospels: Interpreting the New Testament in Its Context* (Minneapolis: Fortress, 2007), 203–5; Raymond Martin, *The Elusive Messiah: A Philosophical Overview of the Quest for the Historical Jesus* (Boulder: Westview, 1999), 3–45.

[16] Rudolf Bultmann, *Theology of the New Testament* (trans. Kendrick Grobel; 2 vols.; New York: Scribner, 1951–55), 1:26; cf. Rudolf Bultmann, *The History of the Synoptic Tradition* (trans. John Marsh; New York: Harper & Row, 1963), 257–59. Followed for example by Günther Bornkamm, *Jesus of Nazareth* (trans. Irene McLuskey, et al.; Minneapolis: Fortress, 1995), 169–78, and Maria Horstmann, *Studien Zur Markinischen Christologie: Mk 8,27–9,13 Als Zugang Zum Christusbild Des Zweiten Evangeliums* (NTAbh 6; Münster: Aschendorff, 1969), 12–18.

[17] Hans Conzelmann, *An Outline of the Theology of the New Testament* (trans. John Bowden; NTL; London: SCM, 1969), 130.

This is similar to the more recent view of Robert Funk and the Fellows of the Jesus Seminar, who unhesitatingly indicate that the episode is largely or entirely fictive. In their view this is "... a stylized scene shaped by Christian motifs."[18] They indicate that the declaration is the creation of the storyteller in the early Christian movement. Peter may well have been the first to confess that Jesus was the Anointed, but it was most probably after the Easter event. The Caesarean declaration narrative, as well as other stories that provide a narrative frame for his later post-Easter declaration, are the product, in all likelihood, of the later Christian imagination. It is quite likely that the two events actually coincided – i. e., Peter had his Easter vision *and* came to the conclusion that Jesus was Messiah at the same time. In their distinctive color-coding of Gospels material, the Fellows of the Jesus Seminar gave the incident a "black" reading, which indicates, "I would not include this narrative information in the primary database for determining who Jesus was," or "This information is improbable. It does not fit verifiable evidence; it is largely or entirely fictive."[19]

Burton Mack likewise contends that Peter's declaration, linked with the later actions of Jesus in the temple cleansing, is theological fiction. He maintains that, "Mark's fiction of an anti-temple messiahship (a contradiction in terms) could have worked only after the temple had already been destroyed. The Gospel theme must therefore be a post 70 c. e. fabrication. Before that time the scenario would have appeared ridiculous."[20]

However, there is a wide spectrum of scholars who regard the incident of Peter's declaration as historical. For example, Jewish scholar Joseph Klausner long ago recognized the historical character of Peter's declaration of Jesus' messianic identity, which leads him to state, "... to deny this would make the whole history of Christianity incomprehensible."[21] C. E. B. Cranfield states, "We conclude that in these verses we are near to the personal reminiscence of Peter and have before us a section based on sound historical tradition."[22] James D. G. Dunn is not so conclusive, but states, "Over all the probability must be deemed quite high that in Mark 8:27–30 pars. we see

---

[18] Robert W. Funk and The Jesus Seminar, *The Acts of Jesus: The Search for the Authentic Deeds of Jesus* (San Francisco: HarperSanFrancisco, 1998), 104.

[19] Funk and Seminar, *The Acts of Jesus*, 36–37.

[20] Burton L. Mack, *A Myth of Innocence: Mark and Christian Origins* (Philadelphia: Fortress, 1988), 282–83. He surmises that after the failed Jewish War of the late sixties Mark fabricated the incident of Peter's declaration and the Passion prediction after the destruction of the Temple in 70 C. E. in part to counter enthusiasm for messianic uprisings after the tragic events of the failed Jewish War.

[21] Joseph Klausner, *Jesus of Nazareth: His Life, Times, and Teaching* (trans. Herbert Danby; New York: Macmillan, 1945), 300.

[22] C. E. B. Cranfield, *The Gospel According to Saint Mark* (CGTC; Cambridge: Cambridge University Press, 1959), 267.

recalled an episode within the mission of Jesus in which the issue of Jesus' messiahship was raised."[23] Somewhat less tentative, Raymond E. Brown states, "If we were to judge that the confession itself is not implausible historically, it would suggest that Jesus' followers hailed him as the Messiah during his lifetime and that he did not deny such a designation even if he thought it involved misunderstanding."[24]

The range of views regarding the historicity of Peter's declaration is wide. I will argue in this essay that the incident is historical, with pastoral and theological dimensions, and that the evangelists presented a plausible recounting of Peter's declaration within the developing ministry of Jesus.[25]

We now turn to address the various problems that are raised regarding the historicity of the declaration and then evaluate the pericope in the light of the evidence for its historicity. The primary questions explored are: At some point in his public ministry, did Peter, as spokesman for the other disciples, make a striking declaration regarding Jesus' identity? What did he, and they, mean by it? What led them to see Jesus in this light? And further, what did Jesus himself think, at that stage, about the matter?[26]

2. The Historicity of Peter's Declaration

Several problems have been raised regarding the historicity of Peter's declaration. However, based upon a careful examination of the incident, the view that the incident is historical and reliable has much more to commend it than does the view that the declaration scene is a piece of fiction. In this section we employ several of the criteria for authenticity used generally by Jesus scholars as a means of weighing the evidence. Although these criteria

---

[23] James D. G. Dunn, *Jesus Remembered* (vol. 1 of *Christianity in the Making*; Grand Rapids: Eerdmans, 2003–), 645.

[24] Raymond E. Brown, *An Introduction to New Testament Christology* (New York: Paulist, 1994), 75.

[25] Hugh Anderson holds a somewhat mediating position, suggesting that the story contains some historical basis, but it is largely created by the evangelist with theological or pastoral motivations: "... the Evangelist thought of the section first and foremost less as a faithful account of the past than as a word in season, or indeed a sermon, to the Church of his own day: in short that his interests were rather less historical than expository." Cf. Hugh Anderson, *The Gospel of Mark* (NCB; London: Oliphants, 1976), 208. Most scholars would agree that the evangelists included within their motivation for writing a concern to address the theological and pastoral needs of his community. But such a motivation does not necessitate excluding the historical dimension of the text. I contend here that the evangelists presented a credible historical accounting of the incident that includes their theological perspectives.

[26] Cf. Meier, *Companions and Competitors*, 226; N. T. Wright, *Jesus and the Victory of God* (vol. 2 of *Christian Origins and the Question of God*; Minneapolis: Fortress, 1996), 529.

have been discussed more fully in the introductory essay to this volume,[27] a brief overview is helpful to the discussion in this essay of Peter's declaration.

In recent years the criteria themselves have been subject to evaluation,[28] especially the well-known criterion of dissimilarity, which in years past has been understood by some scholars to be the most important among the criteria.[29] Although at present there does not appear to be any real consensus as to the priority and effectiveness of the various criteria, some important developments have occurred recently, especially with reference to *historical* criteria.[30]

Gerd Theissen and Dagmar Winter subjected the criteria – especially multiple attestation, dissimilarity, and coherence – to evaluation. They concluded that the real criteria of authenticity are to be found only in the criterion of dissimilarity and the criterion of coherence, and of the two, the

---

[27] For further discussion in this volume, see ch. 2, § 4.1.

[28] E. g., Ben F. Meyer, *The Aims of Jesus* (London: SCM, 1979), 76–94, for the philosophical issues; Robert H. Stein, "The 'Criteria' for Authenticity," in *Studies of History and Tradition in the Four Gospels* (ed. R. T. France and David Wenham; Gospel Perspectives 1; Sheffield: JSOT Press, 1980), 225–63; Craig A. Evans, "Authenticity Criteria in Life of Jesus Research," *Christian Scholar's Review* 19 (1989): 6–31; Dennis Polkow, "Method and Criteria for Historical Research," in *SBL Seminar Papers*, 1987 (SBLSP 26; Atlanta: Scholars, 1987), 336–56; Stanley E. Porter, *The Criteria for Authenticity in Historical-Jesus Research: Previous Discussion and New Proposals* (JSNTSup 191; Sheffield: Sheffield Academic Press, 2000); Joel Willitts, "Presuppositions and Procedures in the Study of the 'Historical Jesus': Or, Why I Decided Not to be a 'Historical Jesus' Scholar," *JSHJ* 3 (2005): 61–108.

[29] Two of the leading advocates of the principle of this criterion were Bultmann, *History*, 205, and Ernst Käsemann, *Essays on New Testament Themes* (trans. W. J. Montague; SBT 41; Naperville: Allenson, 1964), 15–47, which was given more formal expression in Norman Perrin, *Rediscovering the Teaching of Jesus* (New York: Harper & Row, 1967), 39–43. For critiques of the use of this criterion, see Morna D. Hooker, "Christology and Methodology," *NTS* 17 (1970–71): 480–87; Morna D. Hooker, "On Using the Wrong Tool," *Theology* 75 (1972): 570–81; Reginald H. Fuller, "The Criterion of Dissimilarity: The Wrong Tool?" in *Christological Perspectives: Essays in Honor of Harvey K. McArthur* (ed. Robert F. Berkey and Sarah A. Edwards; New York: Pilgrim, 1982), 42–48; M. Eugene Boring, "The Historical-Critical Method's 'Criteria of Authenticity': The Beatitudes in Q and Thomas as a Test Case," in *The Historical Jesus and the Rejected Gospels* (ed. Charles W. Hedrick; Semeia 44; Atlanta: Scholars, 1988), 9–44; Nils Alstrup Dahl, *Jesus the Christ: The Historical Origins of Christological Doctrine* (ed. Donald H. Juel; Minneapolis: Fortress, 1991), 402, who calls for the "criterion of similarity"; Tom Holmén, "Doubts About Double Dissimilarity: Restructuring the Main Criterion of Jesus-of-History Research," in *Authenticating the Words of Jesus* (ed. Bruce D. Chilton and Craig A. Evans; NTTS 28.1; Leiden: Brill, 1999), 47–80.

[30] See James H. Charlesworth, *The Historical Jesus: An Essential Guide* (Nashville: Abingdon, 2008), 15–32; Scot McKnight, "Jesus of Nazareth," in *The Face of New Testament Studies: A Survey of Recent Research* (ed. Scot McKnight and Grant R. Osborne; Grand Rapids: Baker, 2004), 153–62.

criterion of dissimilarity is the more important in historical Jesus research.[31] After highlighting the difficulties of this criterion when used solely as a dual negative in distinguishing the historical Jesus from the post-Easter Christian community and from Judaism and the Jewish environment,[32] they proposed a reformulation of the criterion of dissimilarity to form a more wholistic "criterion of historical plausibility," which they believe more realistically addresses the plausibility of "context" within Judaism and the plausibility of "consequence" in relation to the early church.[33]

Also contending for a more comprehensive understanding of the historical Jesus within the historical context are two other prominent Jesus scholars, John Meier and Craig Evans. Both have articulated the criteria that they employ and have given the criteria a relative ranking in effectiveness in attempting to evaluate the authenticity of events and sayings of Jesus. Below is a comparative listing and relative ranking of the criteria that they use.

John P. Meier[34]	Craig A. Evans[35]
Primary Criteria	*Valid Criteria*
1) Embarrassment	1) Historical Coherence
2) Discontinuity	2) Multiple Attestation
3) Multiple Attestation	3) Embarrassment
4) Coherence	4) Dissimilarity
5) Rejection and execution	5) Semitisms and Palestinian Background
	6) Coherence

John P. Meier	Craig A. Evans
Secondary (or Dubious) Criteria	*Dubious Criteria*
6) Traces of Aramaic	7) Least distinctive features
7) Palestinian Environment	8) Vividness of Narration
8) Vividness of Narration	9) Proleptic eschatology
9) Tendencies of the Developing Synoptic Tradition	
10) Historical Presumption	

---

[31] Gerd Theissen and Dagmar Winter, *The Quest for the Plausible Jesus: The Question of Criteria* (trans. M. Eugene Boring; Louisville: Westminster John Knox, 2002), 1–18.

[32] Theissen and Winter, *The Quest for the Plausible Jesus*, 19–26.

[33] Theissen and Winter, *The Quest for the Plausible Jesus*, 24–26, 172–225. A similar approach is taken in Tom Holmén, ed., *Jesus from Judaism to Christianity: Continuum Approaches to the Historical Jesus* (LNTS 352; London: T&T Clark, 2007).

[34] John P. Meier, *The Roots of the Problem and the Person* (vol. 1 of *A Marginal Jew: Rethinking the Historical Jesus*; ABRL; New York: Doubleday, 1991), 167–95.

[35] Evans, *Jesus and His Contemporaries*, 1–49; esp. 13–26.

At many points Meier and Evans employ the criteria similarly, although they use different terminology and somewhat different definitions to describe them. One difference is how they have assigned a different relative value to each criterion in establishing authenticity of events and sayings of Jesus.

In particular is the primacy that Evans assigns to the criterion of "historical coherence." In his view, data that coheres with the historical circumstances and the principal features of Jesus' life should be given precedence. In this he follows the programmatic lead of E. P. Sanders, who suggests that we may expect authentic material "… to explain historically some of the principal puzzles about Jesus, specifically why he attracted attention, why he was executed, and why he was subsequently deified."[36] This is in line with Meier's criterion of "rejection and execution," which Evans considers to be is the most important feature to consider when evaluating the authenticity of any other incident of Jesus' life and mission.[37] Although Meier assigns the criterion of rejection and execution the fifth and final spot in the list of his "primary" criteria, he also considers it one of the most important. Unlike the other four, he contends that this criterion looks to one of the most striking things about Jesus' earthly life, which was his violent death, and attempts to understand the whole of Jesus' life in the light of that final event.[38] While Meier and Evans formulate this criterion differently,[39] it is instructive that it has risen to such prominence among Jesus scholars.

In this study we will follow this lead in the use of this criterion in the light of the proposed criterion of historical plausibility proposed by Theissen and Winter. The assumption of the fact of Jesus' execution at the hands of the Jewish and Roman authorities lies at the base of a network of coherent facts, and any specific action or word of Jesus that is coherent with this historical scenario is potentially authentic.[40] This is especially crucial in understanding how Peter's declaration coheres historically with the developing mission of Jesus, how it coheres with the charges against Jesus by the Jewish leaders, and how it ultimately points to Jesus' execution at the hands of the Roman authorities.

---

[36] E. P. Sanders, *Jesus and Judaism* (Philadelphia: Fortress, 1985), 7; Sanders makes this point in defense of Morton Smith's efforts to establish historical facts in *Jesus the Magician* (San Francisco: Harper & Row, 1978); cf. Sanders, *Jesus and Judaism*, 5–7.
[37] Evans, *Jesus and His Contemporaries*, 14.
[38] Meier, *The Roots of the Problem and the Person*, 177.
[39] For a comparison of the methods of Meier and Evans, see Porter, *Criteria for Authenticity*, 110–13.
[40] Meier, *The Roots of the Problem and the Person*, 177; Evans, *Jesus and His Contemporaries*, 13–15; cf. Porter, *Criteria for Authenticity*, 112.

Combining Sanders' well-known list of "almost indisputable facts" with what Evans calls a few "highly probable events" results in the following:[41]

Sanders – "almost indisputable facts"
1. Jesus was baptized by John the Baptist
2. Jesus was a Galilean who preached and healed.
3. Jesus called disciples and spoke of there being twelve.
4. Jesus confined his activity to Israel.
5. Jesus engaged in a controversy about the Temple.
6. Jesus was crucified outside Jerusalem by the Roman authorities.
7. After his death Jesus' followers continued as an identifiable movement.
8. At least some Jews persecuted at least parts of the new movement, and it appears that this persecution endured at least to a time near the end of Paul's career.

Evans – "highly probable details"
9. Jesus was viewed by the public as a prophet.
10. Jesus' Temple controversy involved criticism of the ruling priests.
11. The Romans crucified Jesus as "king of the Jews."

Evans contends that many of the sayings of Jesus, and by extension many other events in Jesus' ministry, cohere with the above historical elements, often either explaining them or being explained by them.[42]

We will see in the discussion to follow that this is especially true in the incident of Peter's declaration of Jesus. The various criteria for authenticity will be employed as they are relevant to our analysis of the pericope, which then will be evaluated in the light of the criterion of historical coherence. We will use Mark's basic narrative and compare it to the other Gospels where appropriate. We will undertake an examination of the Markan Petrine declaration pericope by employing the following primary criteria – Palestinian environment, Embarrassment, Multiple Attestation, Historical Coherence – which will lead to the conclusion that the Gospel writers recorded an historically authentic account of Peter's declaration that Jesus was the Christ / Messiah, and its authenticity affirms Jesus' self-identity as the Messiah of Israel, *but* a very different kind of Messiah than even Peter expected.

---

[41] Sanders, *Jesus and Judaism*, 11; Evans, *Jesus and His Contemporaries*, 15. One can easily see that four of the twelve key event essays in this study reflect this list. The group's contention is that coherence and a judicious use of the key criteria can extend significantly the content of this list.

[42] Evans, *Jesus and His Contemporaries*, 15. This is similar to the extensive work of N. T. Wright with the criterion of coherence in finding explanation for historical data within the "story" of Judaism and of Jesus, which lends itself to the use of the criterion of double similarity and dissimilarity; cf. Wright, *Jesus and the Victory of God*, 83–89, 131–32.

2.1. Caesarea Philippi as an unexpected locale for the declaration

Mark tells us that Peter's declaration took place in Caesarea Philippi in "the villages of Caesarea Philippi." This is an odd expression, for the reader might have expected "the region of Caesarea Philippi" after the pattern found earlier (cf. Mark 5:1, 17; 7:24, 31; 8:10). Matthew likewise finds Jesus traveling to the northern regions of Caesarea Philippi, while Luke leaves out any geographical markers, after he records that Jesus most recently withdraws to the city of Bethsaida, also like Caesarea Philippi under the tetrarchy of Herod Philip.

The criterion that Evans entitles "Semitisms and Palestinian background" is helpful here. This criterion indicates that if the text of the Gospels describes events or concepts – e.g., customs, beliefs, or social and political conditions – distinctive to early first-century Palestine before the loss of Land and Temple after the destruction of Jerusalem in 70 C.E., then one need not look to the later, more Hellenistic church for its origin.[43]

During the Hellenistic occupation following the conquest of the region by Alexander the Great, a sanctuary to the god Pan was built in a grotto on the main source of the Jordan River, with the nearby town taking the name Paneas, the shrine being called Panion (or Paneas; the modern city of Banias), a scenic town at the foot of Mount Hermon, rising some 1700 feet higher and 25 miles north of the Sea of Galilee, and 30 miles inland from the Mediterranean Sea.[44] Herod Philip, son of Herod the Great, ruled this region and developed near the site a sizeable town, which he renamed Caesarea-Philippi[45] in honor of Caesar Augustus, but carrying his own name (Philippi, i.e., "of Philip") to distinguish it from the larger and more influential Caesarea Maritima on the Mediterranean coast (Acts 8:40).[46]

This narrative setting in Caesarea Philippi directs some scholars on form-critical considerations to suggest that the event is a Markan creation. Bultmann declares that the place-name does not give to the narrative a historical character, since it belongs to the preceding material. He contends that Mark consistently adds geographical editorial references at the beginning and end of stories, so the reference to Bethsaida in 8:22a initiates the story, which

---

[43] Evans, *Jesus and His Contemporaries*, 22–23; Charlesworth, *The Historical Jesus*, 25; cf. Meier, *The Roots of the Problem and the Person*, 180.

[44] When the Seleucid ruler Antiochus III conquered Ptolemy V (200 B.C.E.), Paneas/Panion was the scene of one of the most decisive battles, which brought Palestine under Seleucid rule.

[45] Josephus *Ant.* 18.28; *J.W.* 2.168. Both names reflect Philip's Roman backing.

[46] See Seán Freyne, *Galilee, from Alexander the Great to Hadrian, 323 B.C.E. to 135 C.E.: A Study of Second Temple Judaism* (Studies in Judaism and Christianity in Antiquity. 5; Wilmington: Glazier, 1980), 13–14, 32, 43, 52, n. 28, 136–37, 272. Also, John Kutsko, "Caesarea Philippi," *ABD* 1:803.

corresponds to the concluding reference to Caesarea Philippi in 8:27. Adela Collins suggests that Mark created the itinerary in Caesarea Philippi for symbolic reasons as an appropriate setting for revelation.[47] Peter's confession and the latter transfiguration provide a narrative frame that are based on traditions about the appearance of the risen Jesus to Peter. Peter's later post-Easter declaration is the product, in all likelihood, of the later Christian imagination.[48] Others suggest that this largely pagan setting provides a convenient theological contrast for the evangelists to demonstrate that Jesus was superior to the celebrated pagan deity Pan.[49] Since Jesus elsewhere does not appear as a religious activist attacking foreign religions or religious icons, the story is probably a creation of the Gospel writers.[50] And Collins suggests that Mark places Peter at Caesarea Philippi to make the further point "... for those aware of the imperial cult practiced there that *Jesus* is the agent of the supreme deity, not the emperor."[51]

Answering these objections to historicity, others counter that the scene "... bears the marks of a witness not far from the events described."[52] While Mark regularly introduces a new section with a geographical reference (e. g., Mark 9:2, 30; 10:1, 46; 11:1, 12, 15, 27), he does not always conclude these sections with a geographical reference (10:1, 17), and the evangelist never employs specific locales in his transitions (cf. 1:21; 2:1; 3:1, 20; 5:1; 6:16; 7:24).[53] It is possible, therefore, that Mark 8:22a and 8:27a introduce their respective pericopae without giving a geographical conclusion. Further, the sequence together of ἐξῆλθεν ... ἐν τῇ ὁδῷ ("he went on ... on the way") emphasizes a new beginning, perhaps from the perspective of a Galilean narrator,[54] and v. 27b calls for an introductory statement, since Mark does not begin a dialogue referring to ἐν τῇ ὁδῷ ("on the way") without identifying the locality (cf. 10:32 and 8:27) or the context to which the "dialogue on the way" belongs (cf. 2:23; 9:33; 10:17). Lastly, while μαθηταί ("disciples")

---

[47] Adela Yarbro Collins, *Mark* (Hermeneia; Minneapolis: Fortress, 2007), 400.

[48] Bultmann, *History*, 64–65, 257; followed by George W. E. Nickelsburg, "Enoch, Levi, and Peter: Recipients of Revelation in Upper Galilee," *JBL* 100 (1981): 575–600, esp. 599.

[49] On the worship of Pan, see Vassilios Tzaferis, "Cults and Deities Worshipped at Caesarea Philippi-Banias," in *Priests, Prophets, and Scribes: Essays on the Formation and Heritage of Second Temple Judaism in Honour of Joseph Blenkinsopp* (ed. Eugene Ulrich, et al.; JSOTSup 149; Sheffield: JSOT Press, 1992), 190–201.

[50] John J. Rousseau and Rami Arav, *Jesus and His World: An Archaeological and Cultural Dictionary* (Minneapolis: Fortress, 1995), 35.

[51] Collins, *Mark*, 401.

[52] C. S. Mann, *Mark* (AB 27; Garden City: Doubleday, 1986), 339.

[53] Rudolf Pesch, *Das Markusevangelium* (2 vols.; HTKNT 2; Freiburg im Breisgau: Herder, 1977), 1:417.

[54] Pesch, *Das Markusevangelium*, 2:30; Hans F. Bayer, *Jesus' Predictions of Vindication and Resurrection: The Provenance, Meaning, and Correlation of the Synoptic Predictions* (WUNT 2.20; Tübingen: Mohr Siebeck, 1986), 155.

in 8:27a is repeated in 8:27b, the geographical reference introduces a new section rather than concludes the preceding one.⁵⁵

We noted earlier that this tradition that Peter's declaration took place in Caesarea Philippi in "the villages of Caesarea Philippi" (τὰς κώμας Καισαρείας τῆς Φιλίππου) presents an odd expression, for the reader might have expected "the region of Caesarea Philippi" after the pattern found earlier (5:1, 17; 7:24, 31; 8:10).⁵⁶ But Mark's expression strikes a strong note of reminiscence. Associating the declaration with this Gentile place strikes a chord of an actual memory of an event in an unexpected locale. There is little evidence for a tendency in Palestinian Jewish-Christian circles to add to the tradition a reference to a city outside of Palestine.⁵⁷ Although the mention of villages links this pericope with the preceding one, which had its setting in a village (8:22–26), the awkwardness of the expression as a whole, the unexpectedness of the reference to Caesarea of Philippi, and moving in this northerly direction that is the opposite direction from Jerusalem, to which the following materials point, argue for the historicity for the topographical setting.⁵⁸

As to the supposition that this is a resurrection scene projected back to the earthly ministry of Jesus, no other resurrection appearance to any of the twelve is recorded as taking place so far north or outside Galilee. There is no indication why the disciples would have been in that territory following Jesus' crucifixion, and alternately, there is no reasonable explanation for a resurrection appearance to be attributed to that gentile region.⁵⁹

Mark's record of Jesus leaving Jewish Galilee to go to the largely pagan area outside of upper Galilee in Caesarea Philippi sounds a plausible historical note. Josephus reports an incident in which correct borders was of concern to some Jews living in the region of Caesarea Philippi (Josephus, *Life* 74–75; *J.W.* 2.592), and hints that Syria was regarded as part of the land of Israel (Josephus, *J.W.* 7.43). Later rabbinic debates may also give

---

⁵⁵ Bayer, *Jesus' Predictions*, 154; Dunn, *Jesus Remembered*, 644–45.

⁵⁶ Matthew has "into the parts (εἰς τὰ μέρη) of Caesarea Philippi," focusing on the villages that would be included in the larger district, as he did in 15:21; cf. BDAG 633; W. D. Davies and Dale C. Allison, Jr., *A Critical and Exegetical Commentary on the Gospel According to Saint Matthew* (3 vols.; ICC; Edinburgh: T&T Clark, 1988–97), 2:616.

⁵⁷ Bayer, *Jesus' Predictions*, 155; Craig A. Evans, *Mark 8:27–16:20* (WBC 34b; Nashville: Nelson, 2001), 10, 13.

⁵⁸ E. g., Vincent Taylor, *The Gospel According to St. Mark* (2nd ed.; London: Macmillan, 1966), 374; Bayer, *Jesus' Predictions*, 155; Mann, *Mark*, 339; Robert H. Gundry, *Mark: A Commentary on His Apology for the Cross* (Grand Rapids: Eerdmans, 1993), 425–26; Evans, *Mark*, 10, 13; Dunn, *Jesus Remembered*, 644–45: "There are several indications that Mark has been able to draw on a well-rooted memory, with the variations between the Synoptists characteristic of performance flexibility"; cf. Davies and Allison, *Matthew*, 2:612.

⁵⁹ Dunn, *Jesus Remembered*, 644–45.

evidence that there were Jews living in Syria in the early first century. Debates regarding tithing indicate that the discrepancy between the actual and ideal borders of the land of Israel was a live one in the first century (*m. Ḥal.* 4:11: "He that owns land in Syria is as one that owns land in the outskirts of Jerusalem").

According to the evangelists, Jesus' travels, especially toward the latter part of his mission, took him through different sub-regions of Galilee – towards the coastal plain (Mark 7:24–29), across the lake to the Golan area (Mark 5:1–19) and upper Galilee (Mark 7:24–29), each politically, culturally and religiously diverse. Mark specifies that Jesus visits the "villages" of Caesarea Philippi, not the city itself, which may imply that Jesus did not envision himself becoming embroiled in the political and religious debates of the city. Mark meticulously suggests that Jesus operated within the orbit of the cities of the pagan regions ("region of Tyre," 7:24; "country of the Gerasenes," 5:1; "in the region of the Decapolis," 7:31; "the villages around Caesarea Philippi," 8:27), but he does not mention any ministry *within* any of the cities mentioned.[60] This may indicate that Jews living in these primarily pagan regions lived mainly in the villages, not the cities, and Jesus ministered among them, which is in keeping with his primary concern for "the lost sheep of the house of Israel" (Matt 10:5–6; 15:24). One plausible view of this presentation in terms of the historical Jesus is that he covered all regions of the northern part of the inherited land of Israel, inspired by his ideas and hopes of Jewish restoration eschatology.[61]

Another plausible, and complementary, explanation for Jesus leading his disciples to Caesarea Philippi is the growing turmoil in the region of Galilee under the jurisdiction of Herod Antipas. When Antipas had John the Baptist beheaded, Jesus took his disciples – who had just returned from a mission tour in Galilee – away to a place alone, which Luke indicates is Bethsaida, outside of Antipas' rule (Mark 6:32; Luke 9:10). Since Jesus was increasingly becoming known also to Antipas (6:14), he probably realized that he himself may be facing danger. Mark cites Jesus' movement in and out of Galilee during this time (Tyre and Sidon, 7:24; Decapolis, 7:31; Dalmanutha, 8:10), finally going to Bethsaida (8:22) and then to Caesarea Philippi (8:27) into the tetrarchy of Philip. In the relative safety away from Antipas' reach, Jesus had time alone with his disciples as he faced the next critical phase of his ministry.[62] This will be explored more fully below.

---

[60] Sean Freyne, *Jesus, a Jewish Galilean: A New Reading of the Jesus Story* (London: T&T Clark, 2004), 40, 55–57, 76–77.

[61] Freyne, *Jesus, a Jewish Galilean*, 40, 55–57, 76–77.

[62] Cf. Markus Bockmuehl, *This Jesus: Martyr, Lord, Messiah* (Edinburgh: T&T Clark, 1994), 85–87.

Therefore, the criterion of Palestinian background satisfactorily supports the historical authenticity of this declaration pericope. The Markan text describes events and concepts that were distinctive to early first-century Palestine, so we need not look to later Hellenistic explanations for its origin.

2.2. An embarrassing portrait of Peter

A second criterion may be even more helpful. The criterion of embarrassment has the task to isolate Gospel material that would not have been invented by the early church, since the saying or event would have created embarrassment or theological difficulties for the church, its leaders, and for the evangelist himself.[63] As Meier says, "The point of the criterion is that the early church would hardly have gone out of its way to create material that only embarrassed its creator or weakened its position in arguments with opponents."[64]

The criterion of embarrassment authenticates the Petrine declaration incident in a significant way. After Peter makes his declaration, Jesus' response is one at first of silence, and then he commands Peter and the others to tell no one.[65] Then in the sequel, which is firmly tied to the declaration by each of the Synoptics,[66] Jesus gives his first passion prediction, with Matthew and Mark also recording a dramatic interchange between Jesus and Peter that results from the prediction. Peter responds to the prediction by rebuking Jesus, and at this, Jesus turns and rebukes Peter, saying, in identical language in both Mark and Matthew, "Get behind me, Satan!" (ὕπαγε ὀπίσω μου, σατανᾶ) (cf. Mark 8:33; Matt 16:23).

This has been recognized by many scholars as a classic case for the use of the criterion of embarrassment, because if Mark or the early church had created the declaration scene in order to elevate Peter, why would they disgrace Peter with a story about his opposition to Jesus' passion prediction?[67]

---

[63] For discussion see Meier, *The Roots of the Problem and the Person*, 168–71; Evans, *Jesus and His Contemporaries*, 18–19.

[64] Meier, *The Roots of the Problem and the Person*, 168. See in this volume also the discussion of this criterion in ch. 2, § 4.1.

[65] We will consider this so-called "Messianic secret" below under the criterion of historical coherence.

[66] The connection from the declaration scene to the passion prediction scene is most pronounced in Luke, but also notable in Mark. The auxiliary verb ἤρξατο ("began") is used habitually by Mark and forestalls treating it as a signpost of a new main section beginning with 8:31, which is supported by it being used again almost immediately for Peter's rebuke in 8:32b; Gundry, *Mark*, 445; cf. Timothy Wiarda, *Peter in the Gospels: Pattern, Personality, and Relationship* (WUNT 2.127; Tübingen: Mohr Siebeck, 2000), 34–45.

[67] E.g., Taylor, *St. Mark*, 375; I. Howard Marshall, *The Origins of New Testament Christology* (Issues in Contemporary Theology; Downers Grove: InterVarsity, 1976), 95; Meier, *Companions and Competitors*, 236–38; Evans, *Mark*, 10; Dunn, *Jesus Remembered*, 645; Robert H. Stein, *Mark* (BECNT; Grand Rapids: Baker, 2008), 395–96.

Whatever had been gained by the declaration proper was lost in Jesus calling him Satan.

There were tensions between the apostles in the decades of the early church, and we can see differences between Paul and Peter, especially when addressing the difficult issues of circumcision and Jewish-Gentile relations. Built upon this is the well-known theory of Ferdinand Baur and the Tübingen school of a much-divided early church made up of a Petrine, Palestinian, Jewish-Christian wing versus a Pauline circle of Hellenistic Christianity.[68] According to this theory, although both wings acknowledge that Peter played an important role at the start of the early church through his vision and declaration of Jesus, they view Peter differently as the church has expanded. As we noted above, those who advocate this theory find in Matthew's version of the declaration an old Aramaic tradition formulated in the Palestinian church and representing Peter's experience of Easter. The saying in 16:17–19 was the original ending to the episode of Peter's declaration. On this theory, Peter's statement of faith became a creative model for others (cf. the statements of faith made by Peter and Mary in John 6:68–69; 11:27).[69] The declaration narrative helps to explain Peter's place of priority in 1 Corinthians 15:3b–5. Since Peter is the first to come to the conviction that Jesus is the Anointed, the Messiah, he henceforth holds a pre-eminent or privileged position among the disciples. Peter's position is reinforced when he becomes the first to have a vision of the risen Jesus (1 Cor 15:5; Luke 24:34).[70] It is then proposed that Mark omitted the special Matthean saying of Jesus to Peter because it represented the Petrine, Palestinian, Jewish-Christian point of view. Once Jesus' saying was omitted, Mark – representing the Pauline circle of Hellenistic Christianity – inserted a different polemical ending consisting of the instruction to be silent and the Passion-prophecy.[71] Although Peter declared Jesus as Messiah, from Mark's perspective he was no hero. Matthew is the evangelist who elevates Peter.[72]

---

[68] First advanced by Ferdinand C. Baur, "Die Christuspartei in der korinthischen Gemeinde, der Gegensatz des petrinischen und paulinischen Christentums in der ältesten Kirche, der Apostel Petrus in Rom," *Tübinger Zeitschrift Für Theologie* 5 (1831): 61–206. Now the theory is championed by Michael D. Goulder, *St. Paul Versus St. Peter: A Tale of Two Missions* (Louisville: Westminster John Knox, 1994).

[69] Robert W. Funk, et al., *The Five Gospels: The Search for the Authentic Words of Jesus* (New York: Macmillan, 1993), 75.

[70] David Catchpole, "The 'Triumphal' Entry," in *Jesus and the Politics of His Day* (ed. E. Bammel and C. F. D. Moule; Cambridge: Cambridge University Press, 1984), 319–34, esp. 328; see also Funk, et al., *The Five Gospels*, 207; Funk and Seminar, *The Acts of Jesus*, 303.

[71] Bultmann, *History*, 258–59.

[72] See Goulder, *St. Paul Versus St. Peter*, 16–23, 99–106. The evidence for the current thesis by Goulder is found in several points of comparison, the most important as follows: (1) Mark narrates that Peter gives Jesus the merely human title "Christ (8:29)," whereas Matthew adds a divine element, "the Son of the living God" (16:16). (2) Mark

This theory correctly points to the serious confrontation between Peter and Paul as recorded in Galatians 2, and Matthew's Gospel was likely addressed to the church at Antioch, precisely the location of the confrontation. In the *Kerygmata Petrou* (H II 16–17), one of the later Pseudo-Clementines, we also find confrontation between Peter and Paul.[73]

However, it is not at all certain that Matthew has Paul in view anywhere else in his Gospel,[74] and there is even less evidence for a continuing conflict between Peter and Paul, much less such a radical division in the church. It is further difficult to imagine that there emerged in that period such a rebuke of the one who was regarded on all sides as the first disciple of Jesus. It is very difficult to imagine that anyone would go so far as to create the allegedly pure fiction that would brand Peter as Satan, and harder still to imagine that it would have found a permanent place in the tradition and acceptance as part of it. Meier contends that it is not simply Christians of later centuries who have felt the embarrassment – Luke, who often seeks to spare Peter in his narrative, drops the whole incident of Peter's rebuke of Jesus and Jesus' rebuke of Peter.[75] Such a hard statement must surely have arisen from this historical incident.[76] We will engage a full explanation of the incident below, but we can contend here that Peter undoubtedly did not recognize that suffering was to be involved in the messianic office of Jesus that he had just declared, and his attempt to deter Jesus from that destiny was nothing less than a satanic temptation.

The evangelists did not shrink from recording an incident that is embarrassing to Peter, the leader of the Twelve apostles, which adds credibility to their intentions to record incidents the way that they occurred. So Peter is commended for his God-inspired declaration that Jesus is the Christ/Messiah, and in Matthew is designated to play a primary leadership role in

---

gives Peter no credit at all for his declaration and is met only with the command to silence (8:30), whereas Matthew acclaims Peter with Jesus' beatitude for God's revelation and his pronouncement of his role in the church (16:17–19). (3) Mark makes it clear that Peter has only begun on the road to understanding the necessity of Jesus' suffering (8:31), while Matthew separates this from Peter's triumph with the enigmatic, "From that time ..." (16:21). (4) Mark records that even though Jesus explains these things "plainly," he emphasizes that Peter *rebukes* Jesus (8:31), whereas in Matthew it is tempered by the addition of a gentle "God forbid, Lord!" (16:22).

[73] See Georg Strecker, "The Pseudo-Clementines: Kerygmata Petrou," in *New Testament Apocrypha* (rev. ed.; 2 vols.; ed. Wilhelm Schneemelcher and R. McL. Wilson; Louisville: Westminster John Knox, 1990–91), 2:535–36.

[74] Some suggest 5:19 and 13:25, but this is highly unlikely (cf. e.g., Hagner, *Matthew 14–28*, 109).

[75] Meier, *Companions and Competitors*, 277, n. 97.

[76] Cf. Taylor, *St. Mark*, 375; Marshall, *The Origins of New Testament Christology*, 95, n. 14; Leonhard Goppelt, *Theology of the New Testament* (2 vols.; trans. John E. Alsup; Grand Rapids: Eerdmans, 1981–82), 1:170; Davies and Allison, *Matthew*, 2:651–55; Meier, *Companions and Competitors*, 236–38; Evans, *Mark*, 10.

the establishment of the church. However, when Jesus reveals an aspect of his messianic ministry, suffering and dying, that is incongruent with Peter's still-developing conception, he is declared by Jesus to be a Satan-inspired hindrance to Jesus' fuller messianic mission. The historical credibility of the evangelists' record of this incident is heightened by their willingness to include material that is embarrassing to Peter.

2.3. The multiple attestation of Peter's declaration?

As noted above, the similarities between the Synoptic and Johannine accounts has lead some scholars to contend that John is either dependent on the Synoptics or that he gives an account of a separate incident. In that case we have only one tradition behind the Synoptic account. For others, they understand John's account of Peter's declaration to be a parallel, independent tradition, opening the possibility of multiple attestation.

Further, for some the similarities of the Synoptic accounts of Peter's declaration indicate a common tradition behind them. For others, the special material in Matthew's account regarding Jesus' response to Peter's declaration leads to the supposition that we have two sources behind the scene, with the further possibility of multiple attestation of the event.

We will consider first the relationship of the Synoptics to John.

2.3.1. John and the Synoptics

Many consider the Johannine account to be independent but equivalent to that in the Synoptics, which indicates multiple attestation. Pheme Perkins contends, "Multiple attestation and historical plausibility make it possible to defend the claim that the confession of Peter is not entirely a post-Resurrection episode."[77] Within that view, some propose that the fourth evangelist drew upon Mark directly.[78] Others reason that the Johannine account draws upon traditions parallel to the Synoptics rather than drawing upon them directly, such as in a pre-Markan tradition.[79] Similarly, others suggest

---

[77] Pheme Perkins, *Peter: Apostle for the Whole Church* (Minneapolis: Fortress, 2000), 29–31.

[78] E. g., C. K. Barrett, *The Gospel According to St. John* (2nd ed.; Philadelphia: Westminster, 1958), 306–7; suggested by Kevin Quast, *Peter and the Beloved Disciple: Figures for a Community in Crisis* (JSNTSup 32; Sheffield: JSOT Press, 1989), 43; Thomas L. Brodie, *The Quest for the Origin of John's Gospel: A Source-Oriented Approach* (Oxford: Oxford University Press, 1993), 81.

[79] E. g., Rudolf Schnackenburg, *The Gospel According to John* (3 vols.; New York: Seabury, 1980–82), 2:75–78; Barnabas Lindars, *The Gospel of John* (ed. Barnabas Lindars; NCB; London: Oliphants, 1972), 275–76; Goppelt, *Theology of the New Testament*, 1:169; Beasley-Murray, *John*, 87–88; Gail R. O'Day, "The Gospel of John: Introduction, Commentary, and Reflections," in *The New Interpreter's Bible* (12 vols.; Nashville: Abingdon, 1995), 9:611; Paul N. Anderson, *The Christology of the Fourth Gospel: Its Unity and*

that there was an independent source close to Matthew's special tradition that John drew upon at several places in his narrative.[80] Dunn suggests that, "John's account also recalls a turning point (in Galilee) which drew a declaration from Peter (John 6:69). Since there is no literary interdependence between the two versions, the probability is that both attest a memory of some such event and the diversity of the ways it was handled in different streams of oral performances."[81] Raymond Brown likewise contends for an independent tradition, in which case Peter declares Jesus as "the Holy One of God," not as the Messiah, indicating that "the holy one" may be broadly equivalent to the Messiah.[82]

On the other hand, others contend that Peter's declaration in John's Gospel is a separate incident, perhaps an authentic reminiscence of an all-but-forgotten tradition in the crisis of Jesus' ministry. As such it reflects developing faith and knowledge in Peter's and the other disciples' understanding of Jesus' identity.[83] Among the points set forth in support of this view are: (1) The location differs: in the Synoptics the location is Caesarea Philippi, while in John the nearest geographical notation is Capernaum (John 6:59). (2) Jesus' question to the disciples differs: in the Synoptics the question regards their understanding of Jesus' identity, while in John's account Jesus questions them about their allegiance to him, whether they will stay with him or leave. (3) The crisis differs: in the Synoptics it is a crisis of messianic identity, while in John it is a crisis brought on by other disciples who have abandoned their discipleship to Jesus. (4) The declaration differs: in the Synoptics the declaration is that Jesus is the "Messiah," while in John it is the recognition that Jesus alone has words of eternal life as the "Holy One of God." (5) The one identified as the opponent is different: in the Synoptics Peter is rebuked as Satan for attempting to stop Jesus from the cross, whereas in John it is Judas who is a devil for his future betrayal.

It is quite difficult to make a judgment whether or not we have multiple attestation of Peter's declaration. The Johannine and Synoptic accounts are quite unique, which favors separate incidents, but they are so similar in their

---

Disunity in the Light of John 6 (WUNT 2.78; Tübingen: Mohr Siebeck, 1996), 226; Dunn, *Jesus Remembered*, 645; Perkins, *Peter*, 29–31; F. Lapham, *Peter: The Myth, the Man and the Writings: A Study of Early Petrine Text and Tradition* (JSNTSup 239; London: Sheffield, 2003), 8; Andreas J. Köstenberger, *John* (BECNT; Grand Rapids: Baker, 2004), 221.

[80] Offered as a significant possibility by Raymond E. Brown, *The Gospel According to John I–XII* (AB 29; New York: Doubleday, 1966), 301–2; Meier, *Companions and Competitors*, 273, n. 78; Davies and Allison, *Matthew*, 2:608; Francis J. Moloney, "The Fourth Gospel and the Jesus of History," *NTS* 46 (2000): 42–58.

[81] Dunn, *Jesus Remembered*, 645.

[82] Brown, *New Testament Christology*, 78–79.

[83] E.g., C. H. Dodd, *Historical Tradition in the Fourth Gospel* (Cambridge: Cambridge University Press, 1963), 220–22; Leon Morris, *The Gospel According to John* (NICNT; Grand Rapids: Eerdmans, 1995), 343–44, n. 161.

broad contours that it is difficult to defend the plausibility of Peter making two different historical declarations within such a relatively short period of time. On the other hand, while the similarity of the accounts favors independent traditions of the same event, they are so different in their details that it is difficult to defend how traditions regarding such a significant declaration from this leading apostle could circulate without an attempt from the apostolic community to bring congruence to them. This would favor two accounts of two separate declarations.

The arguments for multiple attestation are significant, which would strongly support the historicity of Peter's declaration. Nonetheless, the significant differences between the accounts cause me to lean somewhat reluctantly toward understanding them to be two separate historical incidents. Although source relationships cannot be discussed here fully, the majority position is that the Synoptics have some configuration of dependency, which means that among them there is only one independent source for the core of the story. If the focus were to broaden, so that we allow some sort of declaration that Peter addresses to Jesus at a critical moment in his public ministry, then we could use John 6:66–71 as a separate witness. However, at that point "we could no longer speak of Peter's confession of faith in Jesus precisely as the Messiah; both the location and the content of the confession in John's Gospel are different."[84]

As we will discuss below, and is supported by our previous discussion of the Palestinian environment, apparently the tradition carried two turning points, one in Galilee and one in Caesarea Philippi, and the incident in the Fourth Gospel appears to be an independent tradition of a separate declaration. The declaration of Peter in John's account appears to be an earlier declaration, which in some way prepares for his later declaration in Caesarea Philippi.[85]

On the basis of this judgment, the criterion of multiple attestation cannot be invoked for independent traditions in John and the Synoptics of one declaration by Peter.

2.3.2. Matthew's special material

The case for the authenticity of Matt 16:17–19 has a bearing on our study if the saying reflects a tradition that was independent of Mark. In that situation it would indicate multiple attestation to Peter's declaration.

---

[84] Meier, *The Roots of the Problem and the Person*, 189, n. 27. This seems to contradict his later statement, "... multiple attestation of sources does make it likely that, at some pivotal moment in the public ministry, Peter made a profession of faith in Jesus" (Meier, *Companions and Competitors*, 237). But by the latter it appears that Meier is contending for the authenticity of the event in its broadest conception.

[85] See also Davies and Allison, *Matthew*, 2:612.

Many scholars doubt the authenticity of Matthew's material in 16:17–19 because it is missing in Mark's and Luke's accounts and because it contains many items that appear to be anachronistic reflections of a later period (e. g., the primacy granted to Peter in office and authority, the appearance of the word ἐκκλησία ["church"], and the security of the church). On this basis, Jesus' saying is considered to have been created by Matthew, although there are significant variations of views among scholars. Some consider the saying to be a Matthean midrashic embroidery[86] or a legend or tradition created by the Matthean church to counteract a Pauline party.[87] Several consider the saying to be a Matthean redaction reflecting an incident originally in the context of the Last Supper in conjunction with Jesus' words to Peter (22:31–32),[88] or finding its source in the traditions of the post-resurrection appearances to Peter,[89] or a Matthean attempt to exalt Peter after his death,[90] or to authenticate the Gentile church's existence and its foundation in the declaration of Peter.[91] Still others have suggested that Matt 18:18 was originally a Christian prophetic saying that circulated in the Matthean community as a saying of Jesus, and that 16:19 derived from that saying.[92]

In a different direction, but still denying authenticity, some have proposed that Jesus' saying was an old Aramaic tradition formulated in the Palestinian church and represents Peter's experience of Easter. The saying

---

[86] Michael D. Goulder, *Midrash and Lection in Matthew: The Speaker's Lectures in Biblical Studies, 1969–71* (London: SPCK, 1974), 386–87; Francis Wright Beare, *The Gospel According to Matthew* (San Francisco: Harper & Row, 1982), 353–54; Robert H. Gundry, *Matthew: A Commentary on His Handbook for a Mixed Church Under Persecution* (2nd ed.; Grand Rapids: Eerdmans, 1994), 330–36.

[87] T. W. Manson, *The Sayings of Jesus* (1937; repr., Grand Rapids: Eerdmans, 1979), 203–4; Funk, et al., *The Five Gospels*, 207.

[88] Oscar Cullmann, *Peter: Disciple – Apostle – Martyr: A Historical and Theological Study* (2nd ed.; trans. Floyd V. Filson; Philadelphia: Westminster, 1962), 190–92.

[89] E. g., G. D. Kilpatrick, *The Origins of the Gospel According to St. Matthew* (Oxford: Clarendon, 1950), 39–40; Werner Georg Kümmel, *The Theology of the New Testament According to Its Major Witnesses: Jesus-Paul-John* (trans. John E. Steely; Nashville: Abingdon, 1973), 129; Christoph Kähler, "Zur Form- und Traditionsgeschichte von Matth. XVI. 17–19," *NTS* 23 (1977): 36–58; Raymond E. Brown, et al., *Peter in the New Testament* (Minneapolis: Augsburg, 1973), 85; Goppelt, *Theology of the New Testament*, 1:213.

[90] Günther Bornkamm, "End-Expectation and Church in Matthew," in *Tradition and Interpretation in Matthew* (trans. Percy Scott; by Günther Bornkamm, et al.; NTL; Philadelphia: Westminster, 1963), 47–48, and Bornkamm, *Jesus of Nazareth*, 186–88; Hans Conzelmann, *History of Primitive Christianity* (trans. John E. Steely; Nashville: Abingdon, 1973), 155.

[91] Ulrich Luz, *Matthew 8–20* (trans. James E. Crouch; Hermeneia; Minneapolis: Fortress, 2001), 354–60.

[92] M. Eugene Boring, *The Continuing Voice of Jesus: Christian Prophecy and the Gospel Tradition* (Louisville: Westminster John Knox, 1991), 252–53, and M. Eugene Boring, "The Gospel of Matthew: Introduction, Commentary, and Reflections," in *The New Interpreter's Bible* (12 vols.; Nashville: Abingdon, 1995), 8:344.

was the original ending to the episode of Peter's declaration, which Mark omitted because it represented the Petrine Palestinian Jewish-Christian point of view. Once Jesus' saying was omitted, Mark – representing the Pauline circle of Hellenistic Christianity – inserted a different polemical ending consisting of the instruction to be silent and the Passion-prophecy.[93]

Others have argued for the authenticity of Jesus' saying to Peter, suggesting that it represents a more primitive tradition than the parallels in Mark and Luke, whether this represents special material included in the declaration by Matthew,[94] or was material omitted by Mark in favor of making Peter's declaration strictly functional to his Christology.[95] The case for authenticity is based at the least upon the appearance of the several criteria.

Some have pointed to various Semitisms: e.g., Peter is called μακάριος ("blessed," אַשְׁרֵי), Σίμων Βαριωνᾶ ("Simon son of Jonah"), and is the subject of the Aramaic wordplay on כֵּיפָא ("rock"). Other proposed Semitisms are found in the expression for humans as "flesh and blood," the expression "the gates of Hades," and the figurative language of "binding and loosing."[96]

Others have pointed to the criterion of consistency or coherence: Several features in 16:17–19 are consistent with the teaching and actions of Jesus elsewhere in the Synoptics; e.g., the use of beatitudes, the use of ἐκκλησία as a reference to the new community of God that Jesus gathered through his invitation to the kingdom of God and the calling of the twelve, and the reference to Peter's name.[97] Further, Jesus' statement about building a future community is consistent with his ministry of selecting the twelve disciples, teaching them, and commissioning them point to a future role for them.[98]

The criterion of dissimilarity has also been invoked by others: A promise such as this cannot be traced back to Judaism, and certain elements of the narrative are not distinctly Christian figures of speech, such as "gates of Hades," "keys of the kingdom of heaven," and "bind and loose."[99]

---

[93] Bultmann, *History*, 258–59.

[94] E.g., D.A. Carson, "Matthew," in *The Expositor's Bible Commentary* (ed. Frank E. Gaebelein; Grand Rapids: Zondervan, 1984), 8:366–74; Davies and Allison, *Matthew*, 2:606–15; Hagner, *Matthew 14–28*, 466. Martin Hengel has a mixed perspective, in that he argues that the nickname *Cephas* goes back to Jesus, but that the wordplay Peter-rock arose immediately after Easter, and that the saying itself looks back over the whole career of Peter; Martin Hengel, *Der unterschätzte Petrus: zwei Studien* (Tübingen: Mohr Siebeck, 2006), esp. 1–21.

[95] Meyer, *The Aims of Jesus*, 189.

[96] See Meyer, *The Aims of Jesus*, 193–95; Davies and Allison, *Matthew*, 2:604–7; Hagner, *Matthew 14–28*, 466.

[97] Davies and Allison, *Matthew*, 2:611; Hagner, *Matthew 14–28*, 465, 469–72.

[98] For further discussion see in this volume ch. 5; cf. Hagner, *Matthew 14–28*, 465–66.

[99] See Davies and Allison, *Matthew*, 2:612. For further discussion, see Michael J. Wilkins, *The Concept of Disciple in Matthew's Gospel: As Reflected in the Use of the Term Μαθητής* (NovTSup 59; Leiden: Brill, 1988), 173–216.

And while mixing the criteria differently, other criteria may have bearing: Pierre Bonnard suggests that these verses (1) cohere to the totality of the Matthean Christ; (2) are confirmed by the role that Peter plays in the first days of the Christian community; and (3) can demand that their content be applied to the Christ of the Gospels.[100]

Therefore, in my judgment the case for authenticity is stronger. If so, this impacts our study differently, depending on one's view of the sources. If this is special material that Matthew has included in his Markan source, it should be considered as a dominical saying that reflects on Peter's declaration. However, we do not then have multiple attestation of the declaration. If the larger declaration scene, including the dominical saying, are independent of Mark, then we have multiple attestation for the declaration scene generally, but not 16:17–19.[101]

Given the complexity of the issues, and not wishing to build this study on one particular source theory, I will not include the dominical saying in the study of the declaration. Instead I will focus on the declaration as found in Mark's Gospel, and will not consider the Matthean version as a separate and independent source. This should not affect the central focus of this study, since this is an inquiry into the authenticity of Peter's declaration, not Jesus' saying. In that sense, even those who deny the authenticity of Jesus' saying to Peter will be able to profit from the rest of our study. However, for those who accept its authenticity the pericope adds corroborative value to this study.

Therefore, without including John's declaration or Matthew's special material, we do not have multiple attestation for Peter's declaration.

2.4. *Historical Coherence of Peter's declaration with Jesus' mission*

Next, and perhaps most importantly, the evangelists' accounts of Peter's declaration demonstrate authenticity because the incident has coherence historically with both the developing messianic ministry of Jesus and the final events of Jesus' life that led to his crucifixion. We noted above that the

---

[100] Pierre Bonnard, *L'Évangile Selon Saint Matthieu* (CNT 2.1; Geneva: Labor et Fides, 1992), 242.

[101] See Porter, *Criteria for Authenticity*, 181–209, who invokes a further criterion of Greek Textual Variance when examining Jesus' sayings. On his view, it is plausible that the entire declaration scene is independent and prior to Mark, which allows him to consider the textual variants between the versions. He finds two clusters of words; the first is Jesus' question to his disciples regarding the people's understanding of his identity, and the second is Jesus' question to the disciples about their opinion. Because of his view of independent traditions in Matthew and Mark, it is probable that we have the words of Jesus captured fairly certainly, because there are textual lexical variants but no changes in meaning. On the same basis, since the second cluster is exactly the same, it indicates virtual certainty of capturing the words of Jesus. Again, this is all based on the independency and priority of the Matthean declaration scene.

criterion that is lauded today as being perhaps of the most value is that of *historical coherence*, which looks at the larger pattern of Jesus' historical circumstances and the principal features of his life to see if other incidents cohere with it historically. Evans advances the criterion in the following way: "Material that coheres with what we know of Jesus' historical circumstances and the principal features of his life should be given top priority." This criterion especially asks what words and activities fit in with and explain Jesus' trial and crucifixion as "king of the Jews," which is "the single most important feature that must be taken into account in any work that wishes to be taken seriously."[102] This criterion looks at the whole of Jesus' life and attempts to understand it in the light of Jesus' violent death. As Meier states, "A Jesus whose words and activities did not threaten or alienate people, especially powerful people, is not the historical Jesus."[103]

This is an important criterion for our study of Peter's declaration. The assumption of Jesus' execution at the hands of the Jewish and Roman authorities lies at the base of a network of coherent facts, and since the words and activities in the declaration scene tightly cohere with this historical scenario, they are candidates for being considered authentic.[104] I will seek to demonstrate in this section that Jesus was recognized as a messianic figure by his followers, but of a sort that had to be more fully informed by Jesus. Many of the same features that led his followers to acclaim him as Messiah also led the Roman authorities to crucify him as a messianic claimant, but of a different sort than he actually was. So the Messianic movement that developed after his death was directed by Jesus' intentions as the Messiah who suffered for his people. We will first look at several incidents in Jesus' life leading up to Peter's declaration incident to evaluate how the declaration coheres with what precedes it. Then we will look at incidents that follow the declaration incident to see how those events cohere with Jesus' developing mission.

2.4.1. Jesus' messianic ministry

It is widely accepted by scholars that Jesus was crucified as "king of the Jews," as we will see shortly, but how does that comport with the declaration of him as Christ/Messiah? Was there evidence in his earlier ministry that people considered Jesus to be a kingly Messiah? Martin Hengel advances the opinion that, "If Jesus was arrested, delivered to Pilate, and crucified in Jerusalem as a messianic pretender, then this pretension must also have been apparent in his activity prior to the final conflict in

---

[102] Evans, *Jesus and His Contemporaries*, 13–14. See also in this volume ch. 2, § 4.1.
[103] Meier, *The Roots of the Problem and the Person*, 177.
[104] Meier, *The Roots of the Problem and the Person*, 177; Evans, *Jesus and His Contemporaries*, 13–15; cf. Porter, *Criteria for Authenticity*, 112.

Jerusalem."[105] So, the messianic identity must be grounded in some way before his crucifixion.[106] Yet there is little in the Gospel portrait of Jesus that accords with the first century Jewish expectation of a militant messiah. What in Jesus' ministry could have led to such charges?

We will examine messianic concepts current in Jesus' environment a bit more fully in the next section, but here we acknowledge some basic issues adopted by a wide range of scholarly opinion. (1) The term and title "Messiah" in the Hebrew Bible comes from the Hebrew מָשִׁיחַ, "anointed," and primarily refers to a present political and religious leader who is appointed by God and the nation through a symbolic "anointing," and was applied predominantly to a king, but also to a priest, and occasionally to a prophet. The Greek expression ὁ χριστός "the anointed [one]" translates the Hebrew, although the transliteration μεσσίας also sometimes occurs in the Gospels (John 1:41; 4:25). (2) Of the many factions in Judaism, each group that entertained a messianic hope interpreted "Messiah" in the light of its historical experiences and interpretations of Scripture. (3) Diverse interpretations of common traditions were entertained by different groups, so that there were diverse religious streams within Second Temple Judaism.[107] While some of this may be debated, it provides a starting point for understanding Jesus' ministry in the light of current messianic studies.

It is into this environment that Jesus initiated and conducted his ministry. The Gospel tradition finds Jesus noticeably reticent to claim messianic status, which makes sense when we understand the above issues. The use of a messianic title could confuse rather than clarify, because a messianic claim by Jesus would be understood initially by any person in the light of his or her interpretative stream of Judaism. Whatever it was that characterized Jesus' own self-perception of his messianic status in his ministry, given the diversity of messianic hopes within Judaism we should expect to find that people responded differently to him according to their perceptions. And such is the case. Peter Stuhlmacher notes that there is an important factor in the Synoptic tradition that within Jesus' ministry people soon began to part company over him, and the division had to do primarily with their messianic expectations and how Jesus fit within them.[108] Three instances stand out.

---

[105] Martin Hengel, *Studies in Early Christology* (Edinburgh: T&T Clark, 1995), 58.

[106] John J. Collins, *The Scepter and the Star: The Messiahs of the Dead Sea Scrolls and Other Ancient Literature* (ABRL; New York: Doubleday, 1995), 204.

[107] While there was vigorous debate, these were among the consensus issues of the First Princeton Symposium on Judaism and Christian Origins; cf. James H. Charlesworth, ed., *The Messiah: Developments in Earliest Judaism and Christianity* (Minneapolis: Fortress, 1992), xv.

[108] Peter Stuhlmacher, "My Experience with Biblical Theology," in *Biblical Theology: Retrospect and Prospect* (ed. Scott J. Hafemann; Downers Grove: InterVarsity, 2002), 177–79.

2.4.1.1. Relationship to John the Baptist

From establishing Jesus' essential agreement with John the Baptist's message and ministry,[109] Robert Webb arrives at a number of implications concerning the ideological framework that characterized the beginning of Jesus' ministry. First, Jesus began his ministry with an eschatological framework that was characterized by imminent judgment and restoration. Second, Jesus began his ministry within an ideological framework of re-visioning Israel around a reconstituted true/remnant Israel. Third, judgment and restoration and the re-visioning of Israel would be effected through divine participation, especially through an expected figure and spirit. From Jesus' early ideological framework that is consonant with John's, it is appropriate to extrapolate to later points in Jesus' ministry, because he continues to maintain a high opinion of John (e. g., Matt 11:7–15; Luke 7:24–30) and he defends his own ministry based upon the fact that John's baptism was of God (cf. Matt 21:25–27; Mark 11:27–33; Luke 20:1–8).[110]

Jesus' activities that derived from this ideological framework would evoke from people very different perceptions of him. Those who focused upon activities in his ministry that implied imminent judgment and restoration may have considered him to be God's eschatological prophetic messenger, perhaps along the lines of an anticipated prophet like Moses or Elijah.[111] Others who focused upon activities related to the re-visioning of Israel around a reconstituted true/remnant Israel, especially through an expected figure and spirit, may well have evoked hopes of a Davidic Messiah.[112]

John himself appears to be conflicted. He preached of imminent eschatological judgment. Large crowds had gathered to the fiery preacher, and the gathering took on very different appearances. From a religious perspective, the presence of the crowds connoted a spiritual revival of repentance. But from a political perspective the crowds were perceived as a threat of sedition. Either way, John ended up imprisoned. The Gospels took more of a

---

[109] Robert L. Webb, "Jesus' Baptism: Its Historicity and Implications," *BBR* 10 (2000): 261–309, which is the first of the essays in this project; for the updated version in this volume see ch. 3. Webb has concluded the following about John's message: John announced that Israel as the people of God had gone astray and were facing the imminent, eschatological judgment of God. The people had to change fundamentally both inwardly and outwardly (i. e., repentance understood as conversion) in order to be saved from the coming judgment. Receiving John's baptism was the way of expressing this repentance. Those who responded with repentance and baptism would be saved from the imminent judgment. They would participate in the eschatological reconstitution of the true/remnant Israel, which would be brought about by God's coming representative, whose arrival was imminent. See also his discussion in Robert L. Webb, *John the Baptizer and Prophet: A Socio-Historical Study* (JSNTSup 62; Sheffield: JSOT Press, 1991).

[110] See in this volume ch. 3, § 4.3.

[111] E. g., Deut 18:18; Mal 3:1; 4:5; 1 Macc 14:41; 11QMelchizedek 2:18–20; CD 2:12.

[112] E. g., *Pss. Sol.* 17, 18; 4QpIs^a; 4QWar Scroll [4Q285].

moral and spiritual perspective of John's arrest, pointing to his accusations that Antipas has engaged in an "unlawful" marriage to Herodias, his half-brother's wife (Matt 14:4; Mark 6:18; Luke 3:19). Josephus took a soldier's and politician's perspective of the arrest and execution of John, indicating that Antipas executed him because he feared that the enthusiasm of his followers would lead to sedition.[113]

John's expectation of imminent eschatological judgment led to his imprisonment, not what he may have expected would have occurred if Jesus truly was the One who would initiate these events. So from prison he questioned Jesus about his identity as the Coming One (Matt 11:2–3; Luke 7:18–20). Jesus responded that in his ministry of healing and preaching the good news John should draw an appropriate conclusion regarding whether he was the Coming One (Matt 11:2–6; Luke 7:21–23). It is in this type of text that we may find a clue to Jesus' identity, which speaks of him as the one anointed with the Spirit, whose mission heralded the kingdom (cf. Luke 4:16–23; cf. Isa 35:5–6).[114]

The much discussed *Messianic Apocalypse* (4Q521) from Qumran has a significant parallel to Jesus' answer to John, and it also has a reference to a Messiah. This messianic ministry includes the very things that are said of Jesus:

> [1] [for the heav]ens and the earth will listen to his Messiah, [2] [and all] that is in them will not turn away from the holy precepts. [3] Be encouraged, you who are seeking the Lord in his service! *Blank* [4] Will you not, perhaps, encounter the Lord in it, all those who hope in their heart? [5] For the Lord will observe the devout, and call the just by name, [6] and upon the poor he will place his spirit, and the faithful he will renew with his strength. [7] For he will honour the devout upon the throne of eternal royalty, [8] freeing prisoners, giving sight to the blind, straightening out the twisted. [9] Ever shall I cling to those who hope. In his mercy he will jud[ge,] [10] and from no-one shall the fruit [of] good [deeds] be delayed, [11] and the Lord will perform marvelous acts such as have not existed, just as he sa[id] [12] for he will heal the badly wounded and will

---

[113] Josephus writes, "When others too joined the crowds about him, because they were aroused to the highest degree by his sermons, Herod became alarmed. Eloquence that had so great an effect on mankind might lead to some form of sedition, for it looked as if they would be guided by John in everything that they did. Herod decided therefore that it would be much better to strike first and be rid of him before his work led to an uprising, than to wait for an upheaval, get involved in a difficult situation and see his mistake" (Josephus, *Ant.* 18.116–119; Feldman, LCL). Cf. Craig A. Evans, "Josephus on John the Baptist and Other Jewish Prophets of Deliverance," in *The Historical Jesus in Context* (ed. Amy-Jill Levine, et al.; Princeton Readings in Religions; Princeton: Princeton University Press, 2006), 55–57. See also the discussion in Webb, *John the Baptizer*.

[114] Christopher Rowland, *Christian Origins: An Account of the Setting and Character of the Most Important Messianic Sect of Judaism* (2nd ed.; London: SPCK, 2002), 177–78; François Bovon, *Luke 1* (trans. Christine M. Thomas; Hermeneia; Minneapolis: Fortress, 2002), 277–88.

make the dead live, he will proclaim good news to the meek, ¹³ give lavishly [to the need]y, lead the exiled and enrich the hungry. (4Q521.1–13)¹¹⁵

Although there is some interchange of identity within the text, apparently it is the Lord who will call the righteous by name, heal the wounded, give life to the dead, and preach good news to the poor. But the mention of the Messiah indicates that God acts through an agent. John Collins suggests that it is quite likely these works were considered "works of the messiah," as well as of God, before the Gospels. The works in question are typical of what is attributed to Jesus in the Gospels, so this text strengthens the case that the appellation "anointed" or "messiah" could have been attached to him because of his words and deeds.¹¹⁶ Although Collins does not consider the "messiah" in 4Q521 to be perceptively royal, it may overstate the case to say that he is only to be regarded as a prophet like the "anointed" speaker in Isaiah 61.¹¹⁷ Florentino Martínez presents evidence that the simple title "Messiah" here was used as a reference to the "davidic Messiah."¹¹⁸ Prophetic and royal messianic activity can look strikingly similar.

With the parallel to the activity of the apocalyptic Messiah in 4Q521, it is not difficult to see why Jesus is explicitly regarded in the Gospels as a prophet (Mark 6:4, 15; John 6:14), and in that sense "anointed," but his authority in exercising the power of the kingdom of God may well have begun to lead the people to understand that his ministry included a royal dimension.

2.4.1.2. Calling and sending the Twelve

Jesus carried on, and furthered, John's prophetic announcement of the arrival of the kingdom of God, but in doing so he called and sent out the Twelve on a mission. This was a statement of hope of restoration or reunification to national Israel, but it was also a threat of judgment to those who did not repent. In his preaching of the arrival of the kingdom of God, Jesus linked his anointing by the Spirit with his miraculous ministry as a demonstration that the kingdom had arrived in his ministry and that he was operating with

---

[115] Florentino García Martínez, ed., *The Dead Sea Scrolls Translated: The Qumran Texts in English* (2nd; trans. Wilfred G. E. Watson; Leiden: Brill, 1996), 394.
[116] Collins, *The Scepter and the Star*, 205.
[117] Collins, *The Scepter and the Star*, 205–6.
[118] Florentino García Martínez, "Messianic Hopes in the Qumran Writings," in *The People of the Dead Sea Scrolls: Their Writings, Beliefs and Practices* (trans. Wilfred G. E. Watson; ed. Florentino García Martínez and Julio Trebolle Barrera; Leiden: Brill, 1995), 168–69. He suggests that the two-fold reference to the "devout," the *ḥasidim* whom "the Lord will observe" (4Q521:5) and whom he will honor "upon the throne of eternal royalty" (4Q521:7), which frame the references from Ps 146, are an indication that the eschatological salvation that the Lord achieves in the age of his Messiah is limited to the members of the eschatological congregation. That would suggest a "davidic Messiah."

divine authority (cf. Matt 12:28; Luke 11:20). The mission of the Twelve was to spread this message with the hope to gain the land and its people for the kingdom of God. With this calling and sending, this mission implies a politically royal dimension, because it is a vision for the nation. The Twelve represent the new leadership that is needed to replace the failing religious leadership of Israel. Later Jesus will declare that the kingdom will be taken away from the leadership of Israel and given to the nation producing the fruits of it (cf. Matt 21:43). This does not make him into a primarily political Jesus,[119] but the national dimension in the light of the announcement of the kingdom of God and the calling and sending of the Twelve is significant, and probably could not be ignored by the leadership of Israel.[120] It is not hard to imagine that at least the beginnings of accusations were forming that Jesus was a threat to the national security with his vision of establishing the kingdom of God, however misguided those accusations may have been.

2.4.1.3. Acclaimed as Prophet and King

In one scene, when Jesus preached, healed and worked great miracles, it elicited responses acclaiming him as "the prophet who is to come into the world." But Jesus rejects this acclaim because it included a frenzied desire to make him king (John 6:14–15). Jesus is here connected with the tradition that regarded Moses as a king as well as a prophet.[121] The Johannine interpretation of this event is that Jesus is portrayed as eschewing the popular understandings of leadership.[122] The historicity of the event has been doubted on the basis that if the crowds attached political connotations to the incident, word might have reached Antipas, who would then have viewed Jesus as a political threat.[123] Yet, in the whole context of Jesus'

---

[119] As in Richard A. Horsley, *Jesus and the Spiral of Violence: Popular Jewish Resistance in Roman Palestine* (San Francisco: Harper & Row, 1987). In part 3, chapters 6–10, Horsley discusses the nature of Jesus' social revolution with the inauguration of his understanding of the kingdom of God. For a more prophetic orientation, see Richard A. Horsley, *Hearing the Whole Story: The Politics of Plot in Mark's Gospel* (Louisville: Westminster John Knox, 2001), 250–53.

[120] See on this Scot McKnight, "Jesus and the Twelve," *BBR* 11 (2001): 203–31, which has been revised in this volume as ch. 5.

[121] Cf. Deut 18:18; 33:5; 4QTest (175) 5–8. As prophet, perhaps 1QRule of the Community 9.11.1; as king see Josephus *Ant.* 4.327; Wayne A. Meeks, *The Prophet-King. Moses Traditions and the Johannine Christology* (NovTSup 14; Leiden: Brill, 1967), 318–19 and passim; Anderson, *Christology*, 177; Craig S. Keener, *The Gospel of John* (2 vols.; Peabody: Hendrickson, 2003), 1:670.

[122] Anderson, *Christology*, 177. Of the sixteen times that the term βασιλεύς ("king") occurs in John's Gospel, it never is used by Jesus to refer to himself. See also Paul N. Anderson, "Why This Study is Needed, And Why It is Needed Now," in *John, Jesus, and History, Volume 1: Critical Appraisals of Critical Views* (ed. Paul N. Anderson, et al.; SBLSymS 44; Atlanta: SBL, 2007), 23, n. 20, 56–57.

[123] Freyne, *Galilee*, 143; Schnackenburg, *John*, 2:18–20.

ministry he was viewed as a threat to the religious establishment, and after Antipas executed John the Baptist he had already taken notice of Jesus for his widespread ministry (Matt 14:1–12; Mark 6:14–29; Luke 9:7–9). And all of the Synoptics indicate that in response to the news of John the Baptist's execution, Jesus withdrew from Galilee, almost certainly because of Antipas' attention to him.[124]

Although the Synoptic tradition contains no explicit parallel to this particular popular move to have Jesus claim a kingly role, they do show evidence that there was a popular expectation that Jesus was initiating something revolutionary with his message of the arrival of God's kingdom.[125] Luke records Jesus' later recognition that the crowds "... supposed that the kingdom of God was to appear immediately" (Luke 19:11) and that Jesus' followers had an expectation of redemption for Israel: "... we had hoped that he was the one to redeem Israel" (Luke 24:21).

In the light of the growing anxieties of Antipas regarding Jesus, it is probable that there were incidents in which the people's mistaken expectations of Jesus' mission prompted them to act. And John may have had special information behind his narrative.[126] Raymond Brown asserts, "... we believe that in these verses John has given us an item of correct historical information. The ministry of miracles in Galilee culminating in the multiplication (which in John, as in Mark, is the last miracle of the Galilee ministry) aroused a popular fervor that created a danger of an uprising which would give authorities, lay and religious, a chance to arrest Jesus legally."[127] He goes on to suggest that the age of the Johannine material may be judged by the contrary tendency to remove material from the Gospels that might give substance to the Jewish charge that Jesus was a dangerous political figure. If John was written when persecution of Christians under Domitian at the end of the century was all too real, "... then the invention of the information in vss. 14–15 seems out of the question."[128]

In Palestine in the first century, wilderness prophets who promised signs like Moses' usually gained large followings. These groups often hailed their leaders as a prophet or deliverer, and they were often interpreted as political insurrectionists (e.g., Josephus *J. W.* 2.261–263; *Ant* 17.273–274; 20.97–98, 169–171). In that time of varied messianic expectations, it is not hard to imagine that the lines between prophetic and royal hope became blurred

---

[124] Matt 14:13; cf., Mark 6:31–32; Luke 9:10.
[125] For messianic expectations generally in Galilee at the time of Jesus, and the connection to the historical Jesus, see Sean Freyne, "A Galilean Messiah?" *ST* 55 (2001): 198–218.
[126] Dodd, *Historical Tradition*, 213–15, 221–22; Brown, *John I–XII*, 249–50; Lindars, *John*, 244; D. A. Carson, *The Gospel According to John* (Grand Rapids: Eerdmans, 1991), 271–73; Beasley-Murray, *John*, 88–89; Keener, *John*, 1:669–71.
[127] Brown, *John I–XII*, 249–50.
[128] Brown, *John I–XII*, 250.

among some of the people. It is therefore likely that at least some among the crowd understood Jesus in this potentially political light,[129] especially when Jesus' own preaching and activity – focused on the kingdom of God – could arouse pent-up hopes for the return of the Davidic glories. It is a matter of history that Jesus rejects the popular, earthly kingship that the people desire, even leading to his passion, but also that his preaching and activities connected him as God's agent with respect to the arrival of God's kingdom.[130] Nonetheless, even though Jesus rejects attempts to make him into a political / militaristic king, misconceptions of his mission would eventually lead to his execution by the Romans as the "king of the Jews."[131]

2.4.2. *Peter's declaration within Jesus' historical mission*

In the preceding section I reached two conclusions regarding John 6 that are important for the historical context of the declaration scene in the Synoptics. The first conclusion regarded the feeding of the five thousand incident, especially the people's acclaim for Jesus and Jesus' response (John 6:14–15). I concluded that the incident has historical support, which indicates that Jesus rejected the popular, earthly kingship that many among the crowd were intent on foisting upon him. This crowd had misunderstood Jesus' activities, which caused them to mistake Jesus' identity and intentions. They desired an earthly kingship, which Jesus avoided. Nonetheless, his popularity among the people was noticed by the ruling authorities, especially Herod Antipas, who increasingly viewed Jesus as a political threat.

The second conclusion was related to the declaration by Peter in John's Gospel (John 6:67–72). Based upon the dissimilarities between the incident in John and the declaration incident in the Synoptics, I concluded that they were probably separate declaration scenes. That leads to the further implication that we have two declaration incidents by Peter. Peter's declaration in John's Gospel is one of personal and corporate commitment of Peter and the Twelve to Jesus, and stands in stark contrast to the "many disciples" who forsake their commitment to Jesus and abandon him at a crisis of unbelief (John 6:60–66). These disciples who left Jesus may have been disappointed by his avoidance of the kingly role the crowds wanted him to take (John 6:14–15).[132] So Peter's declaration also stands in contrast

---

[129] Cf. Anderson, *Christology*, 177–79; Keener, *John*, 1:670–71.

[130] Lindars, *John*, 244; cf. C.F.D. Moule, *The Origin of Christology* (Cambridge: Cambridge University Press, 1977), 2–4; cf. Ulrich Wilckens, *Gechichte des Wirkens Jesu in Galiläa* (vol. 1, Part 1 of *Theolgie des Neuen Testaments*; 2nd ed.; Neukirchen-Vluyn: Neukirchener Verlag, 2005), 24–53; ministry in Jerusalem, 54–123.

[131] See the discussion of this charge in this volume in ch. 13, § 3.4.2.

[132] See Dodd, *Historical Tradition*, 213–15, 221–22; Carson, *John*, 300; Beasley-Murray, *John*, 88–89, 97; Keener, *John*, 1:669–71.

to the crowd that wants to foist their own desires upon Jesus and have him be their prophet-king (John 6:14–15). Peter declares that he and the Twelve have committed themselves to Jesus alone for his words of eternal life, and that they have come to believe and to know that he is the "Holy One of God" (John 6:68–69). We noted above that "Holy One of God" may have messianic overtones, similar to the reference to "the Holy Messiah" (מ[שיח הקודש) in a Hebrew liturgical fragment (1Q30 f1:2) and "the holy anointed ones" (<במשיחי> הקודש) in CD 6:1.[133] In the Hebrew Bible the title "Holy One of God" is applied to persons consecrated to God, such as Aaron (Ps 106:16), Elisha (2 Kgs 4:9), and Samson (Judg 16:17). It is not clear from the Gospel texts if "Holy One" has a messianic connotation, but as "The Holy One" was especially a title for God himself in the Hebrew Bible (e. g., 2 Kgs 19:22; Job 6:10; Isa 1:4, etc.) and in early Judaism (e. g. *1 En.* 1:3; 10:1, etc.), it seems to function so for John.[134] The closest parallel elsewhere in John is when Jesus speaks of himself as "the one whom the Father has sanctified [ἡγίασεν; or "made holy"] and sent into the world" (John 10:36).[135] In the Synoptics the title "Holy One of God" only occurs once, in the reference to Jesus as professed by an unclean spirit (Mark 1:24), although it is somewhat similar in form to "Messiah of God" in Luke's account of Peter's declaration of Jesus (Luke 9:20). In the book of Acts the early church praises God for "your holy servant Jesus [τὸν ἅγιον παῖδά σου Ἰησοῦν], whom you anointed [ἔχρισας]" (Acts 4:27).

Jesus does not respond to Peter's declaration, instead speaking of the betrayer Judas (John 6:70–71), which implies that he accepts Peter's declaration. At the least, Peter's declaration is an advance over the crowd's deficient commitment in their frenzy to have Jesus be their prophet-king, and the deficient commitment of discipleship of the many who abandon Jesus.[136] At the most, Peter's declaration here is a statement of unwavering commitment to Jesus and indication that he is increasingly aware of a messianic status for Jesus. Apparently Jesus and the Twelve are still in Galilee, which implies that the declaration in John precedes chronologically the declaration in the Synoptics.

These conclusions set the context for Peter's declaration in Caesarea Philippi. This is a crisis time for Jesus' ministry. He has rejected the crowd's desire for him to be a mainly political prophet-king whose goal is to threaten Rome (John 6:14–15). Many of his own disciples have abandoned

---

[133] See Evans, *Jesus and His Contemporaries*, 91; cf. Keener, *John*, 1:697.

[134] Evans, *Jesus and His Contemporaries*, 91.

[135] Brown, *John I–XII*, 298.

[136] William R. Domeris ("The Confession of Peter According to John 6:69," *TynBul* 44 [1993]: 155–67) contends that the title intentionally confronts the crowd's misguided messianic expectations.

him because discipleship to him was not what they had anticipated (cf. John 6:60–66). John the Baptist has been executed, and Jesus is coming to the attention of Antipas, who may have heard of the crowds' acclaim for him to be prophet-king. Luke reports that certain Pharisees advised Jesus to leave immediately because Antipas wanted to kill him (Luke 13:31–33). Jesus begins to withdraw from Galilee to the relatively safer Caesarea Philippi (Mark 6:14–31).

There are dangerous currents swirling that associate Jesus with a form of seditious messianic kingdom, but far different than the kind of kingdom that he has been preaching. This marks a significant turning point, and provides a reason for testing the loyalty and understanding of the disciples.[137] Asking who the people understand him to be is preparatory to asking the disciples who they consider him to be. The people consider Jesus to be a prophetic figure – John the Baptist, Elijah, Jeremiah (in Matthew), or one of the other prophets. This is consistent with the crowd that had acclaimed Jesus to be the prophet, whom they wanted to be king (John 6:14–15).

But this is not enough for Jesus. He wants to know who the disciples themselves think him to be. Peter speaks for the other disciples, "You are the Christ / Messiah" (Mark 8:29; Matthew and Mark agree in substance). What we know elsewhere of Peter's character and the way in which he is a prominent counterpart to Jesus for good and for bad strikes a note of historical coherence and reminiscence.[138] In the Jewish tradition we find messianic recognition offered by followers that was not advanced by the candidates themselves. We saw this tendency in the acclamation of the crowd in Galilee and will see it again below in Simon ben Kosiba). Such pronouncements by followers seem to be presupposed here.[139]

The bare statement "the Messiah" is un-interpreted. What did Peter mean? The context may provide clues. Peter's declaration is tightly connected in each of the Synoptics with Jesus' command to tell no one, the first

---

[137] Davies and Allison, *Matthew*, 2:612; Bockmuehl, *This Jesus*, 85–87. On the turning point related to the arrest of John the Baptist, see James D. Tabor, "'Are You the One?': The Textual Dynamics of Messianic Self-Identity," in *Knowing the End from the Beginning: The Prophetic, the Apocalyptic and Their Relationship* (Lester L. Grabbe and Robert D. Haak; JSPSup 46; London: T&T Clark, 2003), 179–89. Another explanation may be that the disciples would have had chances of gathering the kind of information concerning which Jesus queries them, which he would not have had himself, because they could mingle with the crowds unnoticed, something he couldn't do; cf. Cranfield, *Saint Mark*, 268.

[138] Reinhard Feldmeier, "The Portrayal of Peter in the Synoptic Gospels," in *The Gospel and the Gospels* (trans. John Vriend; ed. Peter Stuhlmacher; Grand Rapids: Eerdmans, 1991), 252–56; similarly Martin Hengel, *The Four Gospels and the One Gospel of Jesus Christ: An Investigation of the Collection and Origin of the Canonical Gospels* (trans. John Bowden; Harrisburg: Trinity, 2000), 83–85.

[139] Dunn, *Jesus Remembered*, 645; Evans, *Mark*, 9. There is in Jewish tradition other evidence of leaders who took the claim for themselves. See § 3 below.

of Jesus' passion predictions, and a dramatic interchange between Jesus and Peter (in Mark and Matthew).[140]

2.4.2.1. The "warning" or "rebuke" to tell no one

We do not get a clear affirmation or negation from Jesus in response to Peter's declaration. Instead, Jesus issues a stern warning or command to them (ἐπετίμησεν αὐτοῖς) not to tell anyone about him (Mark 8:30). The word ἐπιτιμάω is also used by Mark and Matthew to describe Peter's warning or rebuke of Jesus for giving the passion prediction (Mark 8:32; Matt 16:22) and by Mark to describe Jesus' warning or rebuke of Peter as Satan (Mark 8:33). Importantly, this is the same verb Mark uses to describe Jesus' response when the demons acknowledge him as Son of God (3:12). On other occasions Jesus had admonished people to be silent (using ἐπιτιμάω only in 1:25; 3:12), but it is only here that the warning to be silent is directed to the specific title "Messiah," which Matthew makes explicit (Matt 16:20). The command to silence disappears from Mark after the transfiguration scene (9:9).

The warning to be silent is the root of the well-known theory of the "Messianic secret" proposed by William Wrede over a hundred years ago. Wrede proposed that Jesus' command to keep his Messianic identity secret is a subtle Markan explanation, adapted from the developing Christian tradition, of why the early church saw Jesus as Messiah even though nobody had thought of him in that way during his lifetime. He proposed that the earliest traditions about Jesus' life were non-messianic, although following Easter the church came to believe that Jesus was the Messiah. Wrede contended that Mark has the purpose to demonstrate that Jesus kept his Messianic identity secret until after the resurrection. Wrede states, "Our conclusion is that *during his earthly life Jesus' messiahship is absolutely a secret and is supposed to be such; no one apart from the confidants of Jesus is supposed*

---

[140] The simple connection from the declaration scene to the passion prediction scene is most pronounced in Luke, but also notable in Mark. The auxiliary verb ἤρξατο ("began") is used habitually by Mark and forestalls treating it as a signpost of a new main section beginning with 8:31, which is supported by it being used again almost immediately for Peter's rebuke in 8:32b; cf. Gundry, *Mark*, 445. The auxiliary also occurs in the transition in Matt 16:21, connected with the signpost "from that time, he began" (Ἀπὸ τότε ἤρξατο). This phrase occurs earlier in Matt 4:17, and has been seen as a key to the structure of Matthew's Gospel, suggesting that Matthew uses it to divide the Gospel into three primary sections: 1:1–4:16; 4:17–16:20; and 16:21–28:20; cf. Jack Dean Kingsbury, *Matthew: Structure, Christology, Kingdom* (Philadelphia: Fortress, 1975); David R. Bauer, *The Structure of Matthew's Gospel: A Study in Literary Design* (JSNTSup 31; Sheffield: Almond, 1988). Its appearance marks a crucial transition in the narrative, but its use with the auxiliary demonstrates that the preceding declaration scene prompted, and is intimately connected with, the passion scene; cf. Hagner, *Matthew 14–28*, 477; Davies and Allison, *Matthew*, 2:653–55.

to learn about it; with the resurrection, however, its disclosure ensues. This is in fact the crucial idea, the underlying point of Mark's entire approach."[141] For the declaration scene Wrede emphasizes: "I would go further and assert that *a historical motive is really absolutely out of the question; or, to put it positively, that the idea of the messianic secret is a theological idea.*"[142]

The discussion of this theory continues to this day, although Wrede himself appears to have had doubts about his thesis only a few years after he penned his famous work, and only two years before his death. In a little discussed letter, he indicated that he was more than previously inclined to believe that Jesus thought of himself as chosen to be the Messiah. Upon further reflection he considered it remarkable to suggest that those who worshipped him as such received into their religious belief something that previously had an entirely different meaning.[143]

And that is where the discussion centers, at least in part, today. The primary deficiency of this theory is that it has polarized Mark's purposes regarding history and theology. Many current scholars have called Wrede's original thesis into question precisely at that point.[144] Scholars today attempt to understand how Mark could hold theological beliefs about Jesus that had matured over the years, while he attempted at the same time to record events as they occurred in Jesus' historical ministry. The attempts vary, but they seem to be in line with the way that Wrede had begun to shift in his thinking – the Christ of the church's faith had continuity in some way with the Jesus that operated in history. Mark writes with theological

---

[141] William Wrede, *The Messianic Secret* (trans. J. C. G. Greig; London: Clarke, 1971), 68 (his emphasis).

[142] Wrede, *The Messianic Secret*, 67 (his emphasis); so also Funk and Seminar, *The Acts of Jesus*, 103–4.

[143] My gist of the excerpt cited by Martin Hengel and Anna Maria Schwemer from a previously unpublished letter from Wrede to Adolf von Harnack in 1905: "Ich bin geneigter als früher zu glauben, daß Jesus selbst sich als zum Messias ausersehen betrachtet hat. Damit war gewiß notwendig gegeben, daß sie, die ihn als solchen verehrten, ein Moment in ihre Religion aufnahmen, was nicht zu seiner Religion gehörte, res[spektive] dort eine ganz andere Bedeutung hatte." ("I am more disposed than I used to be to believe that Jesus saw himself as the chosen Messiah. Thus it was implied that those who worshipped him as such accepted an element in their religion which was not part of his religion and which had a completely different significance in his religion.") Martin Hengel and Anna Maria Schwemer, *Der messianische Anspruch Jesu und die Anfänge der Christologie: Vier Studien* (WUNT 138; Tübingen: Mohr Siebeck, 2001), ix.

[144] Wright, *Jesus and the Victory of God*, 529. For a survey of much of the 20th century, see James L. Blevins, *The Messianic Secret in Markan Research, 1901–1976* (Washington, D. C.: University Press of America, 1981). For a critical analysis in Mark's Gospel, see Heikki Räisänen, *The "Messianic Secret" in Mark's Gospel* (trans. Christopher Tuckett; Studies of the New Testament and Its World; Edinburgh: T&T Clark, 1990). For a critique of Wrede by a leading Jesus scholar, see James H. Charlesworth, "From Messianology to Christology: Problems and Prospects," in *The Messiah: Developments in Earliest Judaism and Christianity* (ed. James H. Charlesworth; Minneapolis: Fortress, 1992), 33–35.

conviction and with historical sensitivities.¹⁴⁵ Mark's theological intentions regarding the silence commands can be seen in the various contexts in which they occur, which are primarily within editorial material.¹⁴⁶ But within each of those contexts we find plausible historical reflection by Mark as he roots those commands to silence within the historical ministry of Jesus.¹⁴⁷

And that is what we find in the command to silence following Peter's declaration. I argue here that the command to silence coheres historically with Peter's declaration. Yet in what way? What did Jesus mean by the warning? Was it a rebuke of Peter for making the declaration, or was it a form of affirmation? Did Jesus' warning to silence imply that he was rejecting Peter's declaration, or did it imply that he accepted it? There are significant arguments for either position, but I will argue here that Jesus accepted Peter's declaration, but he did so with certain qualifications. Those outside would hear in the title certain aspects that he did not accept as being representative of his identity as Messiah. So the use of the title Messiah needed qualification for those outside. Jesus accepted certain aspects of the declaration that correctly identified the kind of Messiah that he was establishing himself to be, but the use of the title needed qualification for those inside, so that they would understand the expanded concept of Messiah that Jesus was revealing himself to be.

This is the most plausible explanation of Jesus' command to silence in that it most closely coheres with the developing historical messianic mission that Jesus has been advancing. Jesus is indeed Messiah, but not exactly the way that Peter understands him to be in his declaration. We will demonstrate that to be the case, after we first look at the claims of those who maintain that Jesus rejected Peter's declaration.

---

[145] For discussion from those whose scholarly analyses span the spectrum from a Markan theological insertion to a Markan historical reflection, see Christopher Tuckett, ed., *The Messianic Secret* (IRT 1; Philadelphia: Fortress, 1983). See also on the editorial and literary side, Meier, *Companions and Competitors*, 236; Joel Marcus, *Mark 1–8* (AB 27; New York: Doubleday, 2000), 525–27, and on the historical-reflection side, see Martin Hengel, *Studies in the Gospel of Mark* (trans. John Bowden; Philadelphia: Fortress, 1985), 41–45; R. T. France, *The Gospel of Mark* (NIGTC; Grand Rapids: Eerdmans, 2002), 330–31.

[146] Mark 1:25, silencing a demon calling "the Holy One of God"; 1:34, silencing the demon who knew him; 3:12, silencing unclean spirits who called him "Son of God"; 5:43, silencing the disciples from telling others that he had raised the girl from the dead; 7:36, silencing the man healed of deafness from telling others; 8:26, preventing the man healed of blindness from going to his village, 8:30, silencing the disciples from telling of Peter's declaration of Jesus as Messiah; 9:9, silencing the disciples from telling anyone about the transfiguration, until after the Son of Man is raised from the dead.

[147] E. g., Taylor, *St. Mark*, 122–24; James D. G. Dunn, "The Messianic Secret in Mark," in *The Messianic Secret* (ed. Christopher Tuckett; IRT 1; Philadelphia: Fortress, 1983), 116–31; Brown, *New Testament Christology*, 74, n. 99; James R. Edwards, *The Gospel According to Mark* (Pillar New Testament Commentary; Grand Rapids: Eerdmans, 2002), 63–65.

2.4.2.2. The view that Jesus rejected Peter's declaration

On the one hand is the view that Jesus' command to be silent is a direct rebuke and rejection of Peter's declaration. This is a broadly held view, with a primary consideration being that since Jesus did not explicitly use the title to refer to himself, when it was applied to him by others he rejected it.[148] One explanation is that Jesus rejects Peter's declaration because it only identifies him as *theios aner*, a divine man working miracles and demonstrating divine power, and that Jesus substitutes his own teaching about the suffering Son of man.[149] Others go in a different direction and conjecture that if the command to silence and the Passion predictions are removed as redactional, a vestige of rejection is found in Jesus' rebuke of Peter as Satan.[150] Over half a century ago Sigmund Mowinckel set a trajectory for this view as he concludes that Jesus rejects Peter's declaration because it represents a "national Jewish Messianic idea" that was territorial, political, and this worldly. This was the conception of Messiah to which his disciples clung, but it was the temptation of Satan. Jesus rejects this idea because the new conception of a savior, which Jesus created, is expressed in the Son of Man.[151] An additional view suggests Jesus rejected Peter's declaration because no human or angel was empowered to make such a divine declaration. According to one tradi-

---

[148] E.g., Bultmann, *Theology*, 1:26–32; Reginald H. Fuller, *The Foundations of New Testament Christology* (New York: Scribner, 1965), 109; Ferdinand Hahn, *The Titles of Jesus in Christology; Their History in Early Christianity* (trans. Harold Knight and George Ogg; London: Lutterworth, 1969), 157–58, 223–28; Erich Dinkler, "Peter's Confession and the 'Satan' Saying: The Problem of Jesus' Messiahship," in *The Future of Our Religious Past: Essays in Honour of Rudolf Bultmann* (trans. Charles E. Carlston and Robert P. Scharlemann; ed. James M. Robinson; New York: Harper & Row, 1971), 169–202; Géza Vermès, *Jesus the Jew: A Historian's Reading of the Gospels* (London: Collins, 1973), 149; William L. Lane, *The Gospel of Mark* (NICNT; Grand Rapids: Eerdmans, 1974), 291–92; Charlesworth, "From Messianology to Christology: Problems and Prospects," 12; Gerd Theissen and Annette Merz, *The Historical Jesus: A Comprehensive Guide* (trans. John Bowden; Minneapolis: Fortress, 1998), 539; Francis J. Moloney, *The Gospel of Mark: A Commentary* (Peabody: Hendrickson, 2002), 166–67.

[149] Theodore J. Weeden, *Mark – Traditions in Conflict* (Philadelphia: Fortress, 1971), 64–67.

[150] E.g., Fuller, *The Foundations of New Testament Christology*, 109: "Jesus rejects Messiahship as a merely human and even diabolical temptation." Similarly, see Walter Wink, *Engaging the Powers: Discernment and Resistance in a World of Domination* (Minneapolis: Fortress, 1992), 356–63; Ched Myers, et al., *"Say to This Mountain": Mark's Story of Discipleship* (Maryknoll: Orbis, 1996), 100–102.

[151] Sigmund Mowinckel, *He That Cometh: The Messiah Concept in the Old Testament and Later Judaism* (1956; repr., Grand Rapids: Eerdmans, 2005), 450. Among others, followed at least in part by Joseph A. Fitzmyer, *The One Who is to Come* (Grand Rapids: Eerdmans, 2007), 140.

tion, only God can disclose who is the Messiah (e.g., *Pss. Sol.* 17; 4 Ezra 13:52).[152]

The following problems surface for the view that Jesus rejected Peter's declaration.

(1) Structure. The incorrect ideas of the people (Mark 8:27) are set over against the view of the disciples (8:29a). The preparatory questions show that Jesus expects the right answer. His basic direct silence indicates they have replied with the correct answer.

(2) Usage. No passage in Mark's Gospel (or others) suggests that the Christ title is in any way questionable. The title can be used side by side with "son of the Blessed One" and then "Son of Man" (cf. 14:61). Nothing in the usage of the title points to an alleged inherent militaristic meaning (cf. 15:32).

(3) Silence corrects content. Further, the silence command occurs in the following Transfiguration incident when the disciples are forbidden to tell of seeing the glory of the Son of God, following which is talk about the Son of Man (9:7–9), as in the declaration scene. It would be strange to have two commands to silence come in reference to opposite intentions without the author signaling a switch. This parallels the commands to the demons because they knew Jesus (1:34), which becomes clear that they had correct content (3:11). The warning to be silent here implies that Peter got the content of Jesus' messianic identity right, to that point.

(4) Change of titles. There are two issues at stake here: (a) the interchangeable use of the titles, and the fact that (b) warning does not imply rejection. If it could be demonstrated that the titles Messiah and Son of Man were sharply contrasted, it could lead to an understanding that Jesus rejects the Messiah title. However, that is not the case.

(a) Mark prefers "Son of God" at points (cf. 3:11; 15:39; and the use of "Son" in 5:7; 14:61; cf. 1:11; 9:7), and the association as Son is linked with Son of Man (cf. 8:38 with Luke 12:8). However, as noted above, the title Messiah can be used side by side with "son of the Blessed One" and then "Son of Man" (cf. 14:61).

(b) Mark seems to use the titles somewhat interchangeably, which indicates that there is no rejection of the title Messiah in 8:29 when Mark changes to the title Son of Man in 8:31. If rejection were intended in the declaration scene, then we might expect that to be the case in the following scenes when Son of Man replaces a prior title. But in the transfiguration story, the Beloved Son title (9:7) is replaced by the Son of Man title in the following discussion (9:9). If change of title to Son of Man there implies

---

[152] Offered as a possibility by Charlesworth, "From Messianology to Christology: Problems and Prospects," 12, n. 25.

rejection, it would imply a correction of a saying of God, something we cannot envision Mark doing.[153]

2.4.2.3. The view that Jesus accepted Peter's declaration, but with qualifications

On the other hand is the view that Jesus' command to silence implies that he accepted Peter's declaration. Ben Meyer states, "Jesus' reserve did not in any case signify that the conclusion drawn by Peter was mistaken."[154] But we should nuance Meyer's statement to include that Peter's declaration was correct as far as it went, but it needed qualifying. A nuanced view, which is the one held by the majority of scholars, is that Jesus accepted Peter's declaration that he is the Messiah, but he commanded him and the rest of the Twelve to be silent for two overlapping reasons: (1) the title "Messiah" still carries with it among the people, and Jesus' enemies, connotations that Jesus rejects. (2) although Peter is largely correct in what he declares Jesus to be, he does not yet know the full nature of Jesus as Messiah. We will now unpack both of those.

2.4.2.3.1. Jesus commands silence because of the people's and his enemies' misperceptions. In the first place, Peter and the Twelve are not to broadcast the declaration to those outside. The crowds of people, who have been pressing to be near Jesus, may incorrectly perceive the declaration. If Jesus had gained such notoriety because of the widespread belief that he was a prophet, the reaction could be uncontrolled if they mistook the use of the title to be a declaration of an earthly kingship.[155] Jesus also needed to exercise caution because of the potential reaction of the religious and political leadership. If they heard Jesus' disciples publicly broadcasting that Jesus was the Messiah, they may perceive it to be a threat to their earthly institutions. Jesus has seen the gathering opposition to his developing messianic mission, which is largely misunderstood by his opponents. N.T. Wright notes on this dual misunderstanding of those outside:

---

[153] Räisänen, *The "Messianic Secret"*, 178–81; Christopher M. Tuckett, *Christology and the New Testament: Jesus and His Earliest Followers* (Louisville: Westminster John Knox, 2001), 111–12; Larry W. Hurtado, *Lord Jesus Christ: Devotion to Jesus in Earliest Christianity* (Grand Rapids: Eerdmans, 2003), 289–90; I. Howard Marshall, *New Testament Theology: Many Witnesses, One Gospel* (Downers Grove: InterVarsity, 2004), 82–88.
[154] Ben F. Meyer, "Jesus Christ," *ABD* 3:788.
[155] Evans, *Mark*, 9; Eckhard J. Schnabel, "The Silence of Jesus: The Galilean Rabbi Who Was More Than a Prophet," in *Authenticating the Words of Jesus* (ed. Bruce D. Chilton and Craig A. Evans; NTTS 28.1; Leiden: Brill, 1999), 207–9; Rowland, *Christian Origins*, 176; Petr Pokorný, *The Genesis of Christology: Foundations for a Theology of the New Testament* (trans. Marcus Lefébure; Edinburgh: T&T Clark, 1987), 38–45.

Once Jesus was thought of as a potential or would-be Messiah, the movement would swiftly attract attention of the wrong sort. Herod had already heard about Jesus, and reckoned he was a prophet of sorts. If he had known more, he might not have been content with merely 'hoping to see him' (Luke 23:8; cf. Matt 14:1 f. / Mark 6:14–16/ Luke 9:7–9; Luke 13:31 f.). We have already seen that Jesus spoke about Herod, and about John and himself in relation to Herod, in ways which implied an awareness that he was making a claim which Herod would find threatening.[156]

Jesus accepted the private use of the title to identify him, but commanded silence because those outside who could easily misunderstand the true meaning and intent of the use of the title.[157] That misperception requires qualification.[158]

2.4.2.3.2. Jesus commands silence because Peter and the Twelve do not yet know the full nature of Jesus as Messiah. But the command to silence also implies a qualification to those inside. Although Peter is largely correct in what he declares Jesus to be, he does not yet know the full nature of Jesus' messianic ministry. Jesus accepts Peter's declaration, but the warning to the disciples not to tell anyone about his messianic identity implies that there are qualifications to that acceptance.[159] The declaration held for Peter to that point in his discipleship the fullest understanding of Jesus' identity possible. He and the other disciples had been privy to the developing disclosure of Jesus' identity through his words and deeds. Peter has declared his unqualified commitment to Jesus as the Holy One of God, and he and the disciples have believed on him for eternal life (John 6:68–69). The declaration in John's Gospel is accurate, and Jesus accepts it, especially in contrast to the popular assessment of Jesus as prophet only. Jesus is "anointed" as one standing at the hub of God's promised kingdom program. These are the elements that plausibly are also included in Peter's declaration in Caesarea Philippi

---

[156] Wright, *Jesus and the Victory of God*, 529–30; see also 495–97.

[157] Narry F. Santos, *Slave of All: The Paradox of Authority and Servanthood in the Gospel of Mark* (JSNTSup 237; London: Sheffield, 2003), 150–56.

[158] Marshall, *The Origins of New Testament Christology*, 28; Mann, *Mark*, 341–42; Donald Guthrie, *New Testament Theology* (Downers Grove: InterVarsity, 1981), 240–41; Meyer, "Jesus Christ," 3:787; Morna D. Hooker, *A Commentary on the Gospel According to St. Mark* (BNTC; London: A&C Black, 1991), 201; Gundry, *Mark*, 427–28; France, *Mark*, 330–31; Evans, *Mark*, 15–16; Ben Witherington, III, *The Gospel of Mark: A Socio-Rhetorical Commentary* (Grand Rapids: Eerdmans, 2001), 240; Hurtado, *Lord Jesus Christ*, 289. Similarly, but from a post-Easter perspective of the disciples, see Suzanne Watts Henderson, *Christology and Discipleship in the Gospel of Mark* (SNTSMS 135; Cambridge: Cambridge University Press, 2006), 247–49.

[159] An indication of acceptance is that Matthew can have Jesus' positive response to Peter's declaration followed by the warning. It does not contradict the Matthean beatitude and pronouncement regarding Peter; see Davies and Allison, *Matthew*, 2:641; Leon Morris, *The Gospel According to Matthew* (Pillar New Testament Commentary; Grand Rapids: Eerdmans, 1992), 427.

that Jesus accepts. This in itself goes far beyond the popular and religious opponents' conceptions of Jesus' identity as prophet or military Messiah.

So the declaration in Caesarea Philippi requires qualification. Jesus quickly gives the passion prediction to carry further the disciples' understanding of his identity and mission. Peter's reaction indicates that he has not at all understood the cross in Jesus' messianic ministry and attempts to hinder him, which prompts Jesus' rebuke of him. We noted earlier that rebuke is the same verb that Mark uses to describe Jesus' response when the demons acknowledge him as Son of God (3:12). These are accurate titles for Mark, but need an appropriate time, context and witness to their essential meanings.[160] The declaration carried a realistic mixture of inaccuracy and accuracy, which explains Peter's next presumptuous actions. Raymond Brown states, "If we were to judge that the confession itself is not implausible historically, it would suggest that Jesus' followers hailed him as the Messiah during his lifetime and that he did not deny such a designation even if he thought it involved misunderstanding."[161] Mark would not imply that the title Messiah is wholly wrong and to be rejected because he uses it in the title to his Gospel.

Although we do not have a record of Jesus explicitly applying that title to himself,[162] it could be countered that Jesus never rejects the title – neither in the trial before the high priest nor before Peter and the disciples in Caesarea Philippi. In the command to silence, Jesus merely forbids Peter and the disciples to betray the secret.[163] The ensuing repudiation of Peter as Satan is because of his reaction to the passion-prediction. The messianic secret stems from the eschatological secret of Jesus himself, and his conduct. Martin Hengel states, "... the messianic 'mystery' originates in the 'mystery' of Jesus."[164] He goes on to explain how this is shown in Jesus' use of "Son of Man," which he understands to express the perfection of his mes-

---

[160] Pheme Perkins, "The Gospel of Mark: Introduction, Commentary, and Reflections," in *The New Interpreter's Bible* (12 vols.; Nashville: Abingdon, 1995), 8:623.

[161] Brown, *New Testament Christology*, 75. Similarly, T. W. Manson, *The Servant-Messiah: A Study of the Public Ministry of Jesus* (1953; repr., Grand Rapids: Baker, 1977), 71–72; Taylor, *St. Mark*, 374–80; Ralph P. Martin, *Mark: Evangelist and Theologian* (Grand Rapids: Zondervan, 1972), 129–30; Meyer, "Jesus Christ," 3:788; Edwards, *Mark*, 252.

[162] Note however that Jesus apparently uses Χριστός twice as a self-reference, but the ambiguity of reference makes them beyond our purposes here; "For truly I tell you, whoever gives you a cup of water to drink because you bear the name of Christ will by no means lose the reward" (Mark 9:41) and "Nor are you to be called instructors, for you have one instructor, the Messiah" (Matt 23:10).

[163] Hengel, *Studies in Early Christology*, 58. For a condensed and somewhat updated version, see Martin Hengel, "Jesus, The Messiah of Israel: The Debate About the 'Messianic Mission' of Jesus," in *Authenticating the Activities of Jesus* (ed. Bruce D. Chilton and Craig A. Evans; NTTS 28.2; Leiden: Brill, 1999), 324–49, esp. 341–44.

[164] Hengel, *Studies in Early Christology*, 59.

sianic ministry. "Messiah" was a title that could be understood differently by different groups within Judaism, and it represented Jesus' intentions only as his ministry introduces and expounds just what was fitting for the God-elected 'Anointed.' He is the Messiah that is more fully revealed in the Son of Man sayings.[165]

The expression "Son of Man" has been subject to weighty examination in the past century,[166] and debate continues to the present, both in full-length monographs[167] and in summary overviews.[168] One general conclusion is that the expression was not a fixed, formal title in Judaism early in the first century. The expression would have struck a relatively ambiguous chord with the majority of the people. It could evoke usage in Ezekiel, where God refers to the prophet with the expression "son of man" over ninety times

---

[165] Hengel, *Studies in Early Christology*, 59–63.

[166] For an historical overview, see Delbert Burkett, *The Son of Man Debate: A History and Evaluation* (SNTSMS 107; Cambridge: Cambridge University Press, 1999).

[167] Major studies include: Morna D. Hooker, *The Son of Man in Mark: A Study of the Background of the Term "Son of Man" and Its Use in St. Mark's Gospel* (London: SPCK, 1967); Frederick Houk Borsch, *The Son of Man in Myth and History* (NTL; Philadelphia: Westminster, 1967); A. J. B. Higgins, *The Son of Man in the Teaching of Jesus* (SNTSMS 39; Cambridge: Cambridge University Press, 1980); Seyoon Kim, *The "Son of Man" as the Son of God* (WUNT 30; Tübingen: Mohr Siebeck, 1983); Barnabas Lindars, *Jesus, Son of Man: A Fresh Examination of the Son of Man Sayings in the Gospels in the Light of Recent Research* (Grand Rapids: Eerdmans, 1983); Mogens Müller, *The Expression "Son of Man" and the Development of Christology: A History of Interpretation* (Copenhagen International Seminar; London: Equinox, 2008); Chrys C. Caragounis, *The Son of Man: Vision and Interpretation* (WUNT 38; Tübingen: Mohr Siebeck, 1986); Volker Hampel, *Menschensohn und historischer Jesus: ein Rätselwort als Schlüssel zum messianischen Selbstverständnis Jesu* (Neukirchen-Vluyn: Neukirchener Verlag, 1990); Douglas R. A. Hare, *The Son of Man Tradition* (Minneapolis: Fortress, 1990); Anton Vögtle, *Die "Gretchenfrage" des Menschensohn-Problems: Bilanz und Perspective* (QD 152; Freiburg im Breisgau: Herder, 1994); Burkett, *The Son of Man Debate: A History and Evaluation*; Dieter Sänger, *Gottessohn und Menschensohn: exegetische Studien zu zwei Paradigmen biblischer Intertextualität* (Biblisch-theologische Studien 67; Neukirchen-Vluyn: Neukirchener, 2004); Maurice Casey, *The Solution to the 'Son of Man' Problem* (LNTS 343; London: T&T Clark, 2007).

[168] Helpful overviews and summaries from diverse perspectives are: Géza Vermès, "The Use of בר נשא / בר נש in Jewish Aramaic," in *An Aramaic Approach to the Gospels and Acts* (3rd ed.; ed. Matthew Black; Oxford: Clarendon, 1967), 310– 30; Joseph A. Fitzmyer, *A Wandering Aramean: Collected Aramaic Essays* (SBLMS 25; Missoula, Mont.: Scholars, 1979), 143–61; Darrell L. Bock, "The Son of Man in Luke 5:24," *BBR* 1 (1991): 109–21; Robert H. Stein, *The Method and Message of Jesus' Teachings* (rev. ed.; Louisville: Westminster John Knox, 1994), 135–51; David Flusser, *Jesus* (2nd ed.; in collaboration with R. Steven Notley; Jerusalem: Magnes, 1997), 124–33; Marinus de Jonge, *God's Final Envoy: Early Christology and Jesus' Own View of His Mission* (Grand Rapids: Eerdmans, 1998), 86–94; Dunn, *Jesus Remembered*, 724–61; Thomas Kazen, "The Coming Son of Man Revisited," *JSHJ* 5 (2007): 155–74; Thomas Kazen, "Son of Man as Kingdom Imagery: Jesus Between Corporate Symbol and Individual Redeemer Figure," in *Jesus from Judaism to Christianity: Continuum Approaches to the Historical Jesus* (ed. Tom Holmén; LNTS 352; London: T&T Clark, 2007), 87–108.

(e.g., Ezek 2:1, 3, 6, 8, etc.; cf. Dan 8:17), pointing to Ezekiel's frailty as a human before the mighty God revealed in the vision.[169] But the expression "Son of Man" was also used in Daniel's prophecy to refer to a glorified Sovereign, the apocalyptic figure who rules forever with the Ancient of Days (Dan 7:13–14). This latter sense of the expression found its way into use in Judaism (cf. *1 Enoch* and *2 Esd* 13 [or *4 Ezra* 13]). But the expression was not widely used.

For many scholars the use of the expression by Jesus as recorded in the Gospels indicates an idiom, either as a circumlocution for "I" or as an indirect expression with the force of "some person," and the former appears to have more current support.[170] With such a general ambiguity, it became for Jesus a convenient vehicle as a cipher that he could fill with content and he could also use to define and to convey his messianic identity. It did not have popular associations attached to it, such as were attached to titles like "Messiah," or "Son of David," or even "Son of God." Instead, Jesus can reveal his identity by referring to himself with the expression.[171] With a general three-fold progression, Jesus uses the expression to clarify who he is and what is his ministry. (1) The Son of Man is humble (e.g., Matt 8:20; Luke 9:58). (2) The Son of Man will suffer and die (e.g., Mark 8:27; 31 = Matt 16:13, 27–28 = Luke 9:18; 22). (3) The Son of Man is the returning, exalted, glorious king and judge (Mark 13:26 = Matt 24:30 = Luke 21:27). The saying most important for this study is Jesus' reference to himself as one who will suffer and die.[172]

We have seen that Jesus' messianic mission was not always understood because of the misperceptions and faulty expectations of the people, the religious leaders, and even his own disciples. So here Jesus qualifies Peter's declaration of his identity to include a significant expansion: he will be a suffering and dying Messiah. Jesus has seen the gathering opposition to his mission, and it is obvious to him that he will be arrested and put to death,

---

[169] Leslie C. Allen, *Ezekiel 1–19* (WBC 29; Dallas: Word, 1994), 38.

[170] Vermès, "The Use of בר נש/בר נשא in Jewish Aramaic," 31–330; cf. the historical overviews by Casey, *The Solution to the 'Son of Man' Problem*, 1–55.

[171] No one else uses the expression to refer to Jesus, and in the rest of the NT the title is used of him only once (Acts 7:56), except for three OT references or quotations (Heb 2:6 = Ps 8:5; Rev 1:13 and 14:14 = Dan 7:13). In every instance except two the title is found only on the lips of Jesus, but even in these it should be noted that the audience used this title because he had previously used it as a self-designation (John 12:23), and the angel is simply repeating Jesus' own words (Luke 24:7). See Dunn, *Jesus Remembered*, 737–39. On both the Markan literary and Jesus' historical usage, see Harry L. Chronis, "To Reveal and to Conceal: A Literary-Critical Perspective on 'the Son of Man' in Mark," *NTS* 51 (2005): 459–81, esp. 476–81.

[172] For discussion and defense of the authenticity of the saying, see Casey, *The Solution to the 'Son of Man' Problem*, 200–211.

as has his forerunner, John the Baptist.¹⁷³ At the end, after he has used the sufficiently ambiguous expression "Son of Man" to clarify his identity and ministry, as he uses it for the last time at his trial before Caiaphas and the Sanhedrin, it was clear that he is claiming to the Messiah of Israel (cf. 26:63–68).¹⁷⁴

Therefore, the qualification to those inside is that in confessing Jesus as Messiah, a central place must be given to the suffering of the cross and vindication through the resurrection. Jesus accepts Peter's declaration, which must now be supplemented with explicit teaching regarding the future suffering.¹⁷⁵ That Peter did not fully understand the suffering is indicated by his bumbling efforts to guide Jesus. However, the necessity of the cross demands that Jesus see any attempt to deter him as a diabolical temptation. Peter is still learning more fully that Jesus will be a crucified Messiah.

2.4.2.4. Conclusion to Peter's declaration within Jesus' historical mission

Jesus does not warn the disciples to be silent about Peter's declaration of his identity because he considered it incorrect. Jesus accepted the declaration, but he did so with two qualifications. We noted above that Jesus wisely expressed caution in the public declaration of the title Messiah because of the enthusiasm of some of the crowds who may mistake the use of the title to be a declaration that Jesus was establishing a militaristic kingship. Jesus also expressed caution because some of the religious and political establishment will likewise misunderstand its meaning and heighten their opposition to him. But Jesus did not reject the title Messiah as declared by Peter and the disciples.

The second qualification was related to content. We established that Peter's declaration was accurate to a degree, but it needed amplification to include the unique nature of Jesus' messianic identity as one who will suffer. Jesus is not a political or militaristic conquering Messiah, but a suffering Messiah.

---

¹⁷³ While he questions the authenticity of some of the Son of Man sayings, Tuckett indicates that this is one of the clearest uses of the expression; see Christopher Tuckett, "The Son of Man and Daniel 7: Inclusive Aspects of Early Christologies," in *Christian Origins: Worship, Belief, and Society* (ed. Kieran J. O'Mahony; JSNTSup 241; London: Sheffield, 2003), 184. See also James D. G. Dunn, "'Are You the Messiah?': Is the Crux of Mark 14.61–62 Resolvable?" in *Christology, Controversy and Community: New Testament Essays in Honour of David R. Catchpole* (David G. Horrell and Christopher M. Tuckett; NovTSupp 99; Brill: Leiden, 2000), 1–22, esp. 12.

¹⁷⁴ E. g., Birger Gerhardsson, "The Christology of Matthew," in *Who Do You Say That I Am? Essays on Christology: In Honor of Jack Dean Kingsbury* (ed. Mark Allan Powell and David R. Bauer; Louisville: Westminster John Knox, 1999), 20–21.

¹⁷⁵ Collins, *Mark*, 402–5.

It remains now to see Peter's declaration in the light of the final stages of Jesus' earthly mission to see how they cohere historically.

2.4.3. The crucifixion

The historicity of Jesus' crucifixion is largely unquestioned, and its relationship to our study of Peter's declaration is crucial. In his trend-setting investigation of the historical Jesus, E. P. Sanders begins his analysis of the death of Jesus with this statement: "We should begin our study with two firm facts before us: Jesus was executed by the Romans as would-be 'king of the Jews', and his disciples subsequently formed a messianic movement which was not based on the hope of military victory."[176] Paula Fredriksen likewise tops her list of the "facts" that we can know about Jesus with his crucifixion. She states, "The single most solid fact about Jesus' life is his death: he was executed by the Roman prefect Pilate, on or around Passover, in the manner Rome reserved particularly for political insurrections, namely, crucifixion."[177]

Even those who are skeptical of the overall historicity of the Passion narratives largely do not deny the fact of Jesus' crucifixion. For example, regarding the Temple incident as a reason for Jesus' crucifixion, John Dominic Crossan states, "... I think the symbolic destruction was but the logical extension of the miracle and table conjunction, of open healing and open eating; I think that it actually happened and, *if* it happened at Passover, *could* easily have led to arrest and execution."[178] While he is tentative regarding the why of the crucifixion, he concludes confidently, "My point, then, is not that there is the slightest doubt about the *fact* of Jesus' crucifixion under Pontius Pilate."[179]

2.4.3.1. The charge against Jesus

Jesus came to be regarded as a threat both to the religious establishment of Israel and to the political leaders representing Rome, leading to his execution. Roman execution by crucifixion at that time as a form of capital punishment had to be based on charges of serious crimes against the state and high treason. Martin Hengel states that "... it was a religious-political punishment, with the emphasis falling on the political side; however, the

---

[176] Sanders, *Jesus and Judaism*, 294.
[177] Paula Fredriksen, *Jesus of Nazareth, King of the Jews: A Jewish Life and the Emergence of Christianity* (New York: Knopf, 1999), 8.
[178] John Dominic Crossan, *The Historical Jesus: The Life of a Mediterranean Jewish Peasant* (San Francisco: HarperSanFrancisco, 1991), 360; his emphasis.
[179] Crossan, *The Historical Jesus*, 375; his emphasis. For a more detailed presentation of the evidence and argumentation in support of the crucifixion, see in this volume ch. 13, § 2.

two aspects cannot yet be separated in the ancient world."[180] At the center of the charges in the Gospel narratives made against Jesus were "messianic" accusations of the royal-militaristic sort, which became the basis of his execution.[181]

The Gospels agree that the Romans crucified Jesus between two men who were convicted of serious crimes (Matt 27:38; Mark 15:27; Luke 23:35; John 19:18). They are bandits or robbers (λῃσταί), which indicates that they were social activists engaged in pre-political, organized rebellion.[182] This same term occurred earlier when Jesus chided those who came to arrest him in Gethsemane, as though he was an armed insurrectionist (Matt 26:55). This is also the same term that describes Barabbas (John 18:40). Pilate apparently has been rounding up, arresting, and convicting people who were stirring the people to insurrection. The two crucified on either side of Jesus may have been involved with acts of assassination or violence against the Roman occupation. Had the people not selected Barabbas over Jesus, Barabbas probably would have been crucified there with these compatriots in revolution. But instead, Jesus, falsely accused of treasonous crimes, receives a rebel's execution. A cogent explanation for this is that Jesus was charged by the Romans with being a regal pretender as a threat against the state.[183]

The Jewish religious leadership charged Jesus with a very different kind of messianic charge – blasphemy. In response to the high priest's question, "Are you the Messiah, the Son of the Blessed One?," Jesus states, "I am; and 'you will see the Son of Man seated at the right hand of the Power,' and 'coming with the clouds of heaven'" (Mark 14:61–62). Jesus' claim was immediately understood by the Jewish religious leadership as blasphemy – "... a false claim that equates Jesus in a unique way with God and that reflects an arrogant disrespect toward the one true God."[184] With

---

[180] Martin Hengel, *Crucifixion in the Ancient World and the Folly of the Message of the Cross* (Philadelphia: Fortress, 1977), 46.

[181] Mark 15:1–26; Luke 23:1, 32–38; Matt 27:11–14, 20–23, 37; John 18:33–37; 19:12. Two of the events to be treated in detail in essays to follow deal with the Jewish examination of Jesus and Jesus' crucifixion under Pilate. Much of what is summarized here is treated in detail in these subsequent studies, for which in this volume see chs. 12 and 13.

[182] Cf. Richard A. Horsley and John S. Hanson, *Bandits, Prophets, and Messiahs: Popular Movements in the Time of Jesus* (New Voices in Biblical Studies; Minneapolis: Winston, 1985), 48.

[183] E. g., Dahl, *Jesus the Christ*, 39–40; followed by Hurtado, *Lord Jesus Christ*, 56–57. Contra James McLaren, *Why Jesus Died: An Historian's Perspective* (LNTS 356; London: T&T Clark, 2008), who argues for Jesus' death being an isolated, individual execution precipitated by his singular criminal activity in the Temple incident.

[184] Darrell L. Bock, *Blasphemy and Exaltation in Judaism and the Final Examination of Jesus* (WUNT 2.106; Tübingen: Mohr Siebeck, 1998), 203. This discussion as it relates to Mark 14 is updated in this volume in ch. 12.

Jesus' following and popularity, he is perceived by the Jewish leaders as a threat to Israel.[185]

When the Jewish leaders deliver Jesus to the Roman officials they present the charges in political terms that would motivate them also to charge Jesus. Pilate's first question to Jesus was, "Are you the king of the Jews?" (Mark 15:2). Both the Jewish leaders and the Roman officials recognized that Jesus was being taken by his followers as a messianic figure.[186] Messianic followers would certainly be regarded as a threat to both the Jewish religious establishment and the Roman political / military rule, whatever they both would have understood by way of the "messianic" charge. So Jesus now "... ran afoul of both Jewish and Roman authorities and was taken to be deeply offensive on both religious and political grounds ... And execution by crucifixion indicates a clear intent to humiliate and eliminate an offender by the strongest measure in Roman judicial usage."[187] Crucifixion became what they believed would be the cruel and convenient, final and ultimate, deterrent to both the Jewish leaders' and the Roman politicians' perceptions of Jesus' messianic threat.[188]

2.4.3.2. *The Roman titulus*

The titulus inscriptions of the four Gospel accounts are uniform in their testimony to the core charge against Jesus.

This is Jesus the king of the Jews (Matt 27:37)
The king of the Jews (Mark 15:26)
This is the king of the Jews (Luke 23:38)
Jesus of Nazareth the king of the Jews (John 19:19)

The inscription title that is identically common to all of the Gospels is "The king of the Jews" (ὁ βασιλεὺς τῶν Ἰουδαίων),[189] which indicates that it is firmly fixed in the tradition. This calls us back to the Roman trial, where the question was posed by Pilate to Jesus, "Are you the king of the Jews?" (Mark 15:2). Rather than being a secondary expansion parallel to 15:3–5,[190] the question more probably was formulated in view of what will later become the titulus inscription. The title also occurs in the Barab-

---

[185] Goppelt, *Theology of the New Testament*, 1:169, states, "... it remains an established fact that Jesus was suspected of wanting to present himself as the Christ, i.e., the King of salvation, and was therefore condemned to death."

[186] Hurtado, *Lord Jesus Christ*, 56.

[187] Hurtado, *Lord Jesus Christ*, 57.

[188] For a more extensive discussion of the *titulus* and the expression "king of the Jews," see in this volume ch. 13, § 3.4.2.

[189] Οὗτός ἐστιν Ἰησοῦς ὁ βασιλεὺς τῶν Ἰουδαίων (Matt 27:37); ὁ βασιλεὺς τῶν Ἰουδαίων (Mark 15:26); ὁ βασιλεὺς τῶν Ἰουδαίων οὗτος (Luke 23:38); Ἰησοῦς ὁ Ναζωραῖος ὁ βασιλεὺς τῶν Ἰουδαίων (John 19:19).

[190] So Bultmann, *History*, 170–72, 284.

bas episode and in the scene where the soldiers do mock homage to Jesus, and it is presupposed in the reviling of the crucified (15:9, 12, 16–20). This presentation in Mark's passion narrative is confirmed by the fact that the crucifixion of Jesus as "king of the Jews" is also a chief motif of the Johannine narrative, which on the whole is not dependent on the Synoptics (John 18:33 ff., 19:1–3, 12–15, 19–22). The motif is very old. Pilate formulates the title on the cross in order to annoy the Jews, but with the inscription in the three primary languages (Latin, Greek and Hebrew; cf. John 19:19), it is a universal proclamation that the one crucified is the "king of the Jews."[191]

The charge against Jesus did not require his own messianic claim, but can in principle be accounted for on the basis of the messianic claims and hopes of Jesus' followers, and then the settled conviction of the authorities that his activities prompted the basis of the charge against him.[192] Whatever it was that Jesus claimed for himself in his teachings or public actions, the governing authorities found their own good reasons to crucify him, and that had to do with the fear that he was being taken by his followers as a messianic figure, which could lead to trouble with Rome (cf. the sentiments of Caiaphas in John 11:49–50; and the Qumran text 11Q Temple Scroll 64:6–13). That is consistent with the Gospel narratives that make the royal-messianic charge the basis of his execution. Nils Dahl declares, "Since the central place of the name 'Messiah' cannot be explained from the preaching of Jesus, there remains only one possibility: the title 'Messiah' was inseparably connected with the name of Jesus because Jesus was condemned and crucified as a messianic pretender."[193] The Gospels are agreed that Jesus was crucified with others condemned of serious crimes, and from what we know of Roman crucifixion, it was a form of capital punishment for those crimes.[194] Larry Hurtado concludes, "… Jesus' execution had to have been based on one or more charges of a very serious nature, perhaps involving a threat to public order, which would certainly correspond to a perceived royal-messianic claim, whether made by him or his followers."[195]

---

[191] Dahl, *Jesus the Christ*, 34, 36–37; Hengel, *Studies in Early Christology*, 54.

[192] Lynn H. Cohick, "Jesus as King of the Jews," in *Who Do My Opponents Say I Am?: An Investigation of the Accusations Against Jesus* (ed. Scot McKnight and Joseph Modica; LNTS 327; London: T&T Clark, 2008), 111–32.

[193] Dahl, *Jesus the Christ*, 40. Similarly Scot McKnight, "Calling Jesus *Mamzer*," *JSHJ* 1 (2003): 76: "The titulus of the crucifixion narrative reflects what is most likely a historical accusation against Jesus (cf. Mk 15:2, 9, 12, 16–20, 26, 32), at least during the last week of his life, no doubt the beginnings at least of rumbles and murmurs after hearing Jesus speak so consistently of the imminent arrival of the kingdom of heavens (Mk 1:15). Some Jews thought Jesus presumptuously claimed to be 'king of the Jews.'"

[194] Hengel, *Crucifixion*, 33–38.

[195] Hurtado, *Lord Jesus Christ*, 57.

There is a striking anomaly of the messianic claims of Jesus by his followers. His crucifixion as "king of the Jews" cannot be doubted. The claims to Davidic kingship also figure prominently in early Christian sources. For Paul, the title *Christos*, messiah, is treated as a virtual name. And it is unlikely that Jesus' followers would have given him such a politically inflammatory title if it had no basis in his life, which on the level of political embarrassment speaks for the authenticity of the material. So, the messianic identity must be grounded in some way before his crucifixion.[196] Yet there is little in the Gospel portraits of Jesus that accords with the Jewish expectation of a militant messiah. What in Jesus' ministry could have resulted in such charges? This leads to our conclusions regarding the historical coherence of Jesus' messianic ministry, the declaration by Peter that Jesus is Messiah, and Jesus' crucifixion.

2.4.4. Conclusion to the criterion of historical coherence

Peter's declaration that Jesus is the Christ / Messiah coheres clearly with the broader historical portrait of Jesus' unique messianic ministry and his crucifixion as the king of the Jews. Peter rightly declares that Jesus' true identity is that of the Christ / Messiah, because it coheres with what Peter had seen Jesus developing in his messianic ministry. Yet Jesus instructs Peter and the others not to broadcast that declaration (cf. Matt 16:20; Mark 8:30; Luke 9:21). Jesus does not warn the disciples to be silent because he considered it incorrect. Jesus accepted the declaration, but he did so with two qualifications.

In the first place, Jesus expressed caution in the public use of the title Messiah / Christ because the crowds, the religious establishment, and the Roman government will mistakenly assume that Jesus was establishing a political or militaristic kingship. But Jesus did not reject the title Messiah as declared by Peter. Peter's understanding is that Jesus is a different kind of Messiah than many of the crowds desired for Jesus to be. We find evidence that there was at least on one occasion a movement to make Jesus king (John 6:14–15). Peter's understanding also contrasts to a primarily prophetic view of Jesus as the pericope itself indicates (cf. Mark 8:27–28). Peter's understanding of Jesus is also quite different than the kind of Messiah the religious leaders were threatened that Jesus might become. Antipas executed John the Baptist at least in part because he feared that the enthusiasm of followers would lead to sedition (Josephus, *Ant.* 18.116–119). And now he was looking with alarm at the rising enthusiasm of the crowds around John's successor, Jesus, who continued the talk of the arrival of a kingdom.

---

[196] Collins, *The Scepter and the Star*, 204.

In the second place, Jesus accepts Peter's declaration, but he will need to clarify to Peter and the Twelve that he was a different kind of Messiah than even they understood him to be. Peter has a particular understanding of Jesus as the Messiah, which includes him being the Holy One of God (John 6:68–69). But it did not include a clear understanding of the necessity of the cross, which would remain a mystery until the resurrection. So Jesus reveals that suffering and dying were included in his messianic ministry (Mark 8:31). This is a historical inevitability in the light of the religious and political opposition. Peter only partially understood Jesus' intent in his messianic ministry, because when Jesus revealed this aspect of his messianic mission, Peter wanted to deter him and force Jesus into his own conception of Messiah (Mark 8:32). But such deterrence was not from God, and Peter is declared to be a tool of Satan in that move (8:33). Jesus is Messiah, but he is to be a suffering and dying and raised Messiah, something that even his closest followers could not yet fully grasp.

The crowds' expectations will be stimulated and then dashed with the events involving Jesus' symbolic entry into Jerusalem, the temple incident, and the Jewish and Roman trials, and they will prefer to preserve a more militant leader like Barabbas. The religious leaders will be convinced that Jesus is a messianic blasphemer, which will cause them to take Jesus to the Roman leaders with charges that he has incited the people with his messianic pretensions.[197] And the Romans will have Jesus crucified as "king of the Jews," a title that coheres with the external form of Peter's declaration, but not with the internal meaning increasingly understood by Peter.

There were widely-varied messianic expectations found in Judaism at the time of Jesus' ministry. Jesus deflected any attempts by those around him to conform to their expectations, and instead carefully articulated and demonstrated the ways he was the Messiah. Although the arrival of the kingdom of God in the person of Jesus was not one involving armies and weapons of war, it nonetheless was misunderstood by the common people, the religious authorities, and the political and military regime to the extent that it resulted in his execution.

The criterion of historical coherence establishes the authenticity of Peter's declaration of Jesus as Messiah within his overall historical mission and crucifixion. Peter has a growing recognition of Jesus' unique messianic ministry, which surpasses the crowds' understanding. Yet it was not fully developed. Jesus understands the swelling historical inevitability of his ar-

---

[197] Meyer, "Jesus Christ," 3:786–88; Tuckett, *Christology and the New Testament*, 210–13; Dunn, *Jesus Remembered*, 645; Wright, *Jesus and the Victory of God*, 530: "Jesus ... had some redefinitions of 'Messiahship' in mind; but he accepted the title itself. If he had not, his action in the Temple, and the riddles which surrounded it, would remain inexplicable."

rest and execution, which will be in accord with the prophetic inevitability of his sacrificial death.

The collective testimony of the criteria of Semitisms and Palestinian background, Embarrassment, and Historical Coherence present convincing evidence that Peter's declaration of Jesus as the Messiah is historical.

3. Peter's Declaration of Jesus in Its Broader Historical Context

In this section we undertake an examination of Peter's declaration within its broader historical context. We will look first at modern attempts to define "messiah" and "messianic" and how Jesus' mission fits within those definitions. There were many prophetic and royal messianic movements in the ancient world, and significantly so in the Jewish milieu. As noted above, the variety of messianic figures in early Jewish expectation belies a single messianic expectation.[198] Then we will look at various other "declarations" found in ancient texts. The following questions guide this section: Who would have been called "messiah" or "king" in the ancient world? Who would have made a declaration similar to Peter's? Is it historically plausible that Jesus would have been called "messiah" or "king" in the historical setting of the time?

3.1. "Messiah" and "messianic"

The absolute form "the Messiah," without an accompanying genitive or possessive pronoun, occurs rarely and primarily in late first century C.E. texts (*1 En.* 48:10; 52:4; *2 Bar* 30:1; 70:9; *4 Ezra* 7:28, 29; 12:32).[199] When it does occur, it usually refers to the eschatological Davidic king. A royal Messiah, the *māšîaḥ* of Israel, representing the royal line of David, and a priestly Messiah, the *māšîaḥ* of Aaron, representing the high-priestly house, with the former subject to the latter, are mentioned in both the Dead Sea Scrolls[200]

---

[198] Charlesworth, "From Messianology to Christology: Problems and Prospects," 3–35; Jacob Neusner, et al., *Judaisms and Their Messiahs at the Turn of the Christian Era* (Cambridge: Cambridge University Press, 1987), passim; Collins, *The Scepter and the Star*, 195–209.

[199] See S. Talmon, "The Concepts of *Māšîaḥ* and Messianism in Early Judaism," in *The Messiah: Developments in Earliest Judaism and Christianity* (ed. Charlesworth. James H.; Minneapolis: Fortress, 1992), 79–115; Marinus de Jonge, "The Earliest Christian Use of *Christos*: Some Suggestions," *NTS* 32 (1986): 321–43, which draws upon his earlier article, Marinus de Jonge, "The Use of the Word 'Anointed' in the Time of Jesus," *NovT* 8 (1966): 132–48.

[200] 1QS 9:10–11; 1QSa 12–13; cf. CD 12:22–23; 13:20–22; 19:9–11 [7:20–21]; 20:1; Talmon, "*Māšîaḥ* and Messianism," 104–5.

and the *Testaments of the Twelve Patriarchs*.[201] Prophets also could be called "Yahweh's anointed" or "anointed ones."[202] The Messiah is mentioned only twice in the Mishnah (*m. Soṭah* 9:9–15 and *m. Ber.* 1:5) and those texts do not make dominant the hope for the restoration of the past glories of the Davidic dynasty nor actively look for a victory over history.[203] The latter passage connects the Exodus from Egypt with "the days of the messiah" as a guiding historical-theological concept.[204]

One of the distinctive features of late second Temple Judaism that separated the various sects is that they tended to focus on one strand of messianic expectation, sometimes to the exclusion of other strands. For example, many focused on scriptural statements of a kingly conqueror who would sit on David's throne (e. g., 2 Sam 7:11–16). Some focused on statements of a great prophet like Moses who would give the authoritative interpretation of God's Law (Deut 18:15–18). Still others looked at scriptural priestly passages and expected a mysterious figure like Melchizedek to have a messianic function (Gen 14:18–20; Ps 110:4). However, we do find evidence that at least some in Israel held these strands at once in tension. A trilogy of messianic proof-texts in a single document from the Qumran community speaks first of an eschatological prophet like Moses (4QTestimonia 1–8; cf. Deut 5:28–29; 18:18–19), then of a departing kingly star and an arising kingly scepter from Israel who will crush their enemies (4QTestimonia 9–13; cf. Num 24:15–17), and finally of a priestly figure like Levi whom Moses blessed (4QTestimonia 14–22; cf. Deut 33:8–11).[205] However, this probably is an indication that the Qumran community expected more than one messiah. A famous passage in the Rule of the Community awaits the arrival of a complex of messianic figures: "… until the prophet comes, and the Messiahs of Israel and of Aaron" (1QRule of the Community [1QS] 9:11).[206]

The relative scarcity of explicit use of the term "messiah" in ancient texts has led to extended debate within current scholarship regarding what texts can appropriately be called "messianic." This has broad implications for messianic studies generally, but also for understanding of Peter's declara-

---

[201] *T. Reu.* 6:5–12; *T. Levi* 18:2–9; David E. Aune, "Christian Prophecy and the Messianic Status of Jesus," in *The Messiah: Developments in Earliest Judaism and Christianity* (ed. James H. Charlesworth; Minneapolis: Fortress, 1992), 409.

[202] Ps 105:15; CD 2:12; 6:1; 1QWar Scroll [1QM] 11:7–8; 11QMelch 18.

[203] See Jacob Neusner, *Messiah in Context: Israel's History and Destiny in Formative Judaism* (Philadelphia: Fortress, 1984), 26–30, 37–38.

[204] Baruch M. Bokser, "Messianism, The Exodus Pattern, and Early Rabbinic Judaism," in *The Messiah: Developments in Earliest Judaism and Christianity* (ed. James H. Charlesworth; Minneapolis: Fortress, 1992), 241–43, following David Daube, *The Exodus Pattern in the Bible* (London: Faber and Faber, 1963), 31–34.

[205] See Géza G. Xeravits, *King, Priest, Prophet: Positive Eschatological Protagonists of the Qumran Library* (STDJ 47; Leiden: Brill, 2003).

[206] For discussion, see Collins, *The Scepter and the Star*, 74–101.

tion. Andrew Chester has surveyed the literature and proposes a helpful taxonomy of four basic positions regarding which ancient texts should be taken into consideration when defining "messiah" and "messianic."[207]

(1) *"Minimalist" Definition.* The minimalist position contends that only those texts that specifically use the term "messiah" (or its equivalent in the language of the text) should be used when deriving definitions of who is to be regarded as a messiah and what is called messianic.[208] The advantage of this position is that it avoids a loose and general portrayal of messianism and focuses on explicit messianic texts. However, the drawback is that this position excludes a substantial range and number of texts that are generally acknowledged as messianic even though the term "messiah" is absent. Also, terms other than "messiah" to designate historical figures may be of real significance for understanding the nature of a messianic developed hope.[209] For example, texts that refer to an eschatological "prophet" or "judge" may not include the term "messiah," but are widely considered to be messianic.

(2) *"Messiah" as an Extended Category.* The second position argues that texts that can be considered messianic are those where the figure denoted is specifically designated as "messiah" elsewhere within the same text and where there is a context of eschatological deliverance.[210] Hence, the "man" who arises from the sea in 4 Ezra 13:3–14:9 is understood to be the Messiah, because 4 Ezra is the work of one author, and the "man" is elsewhere clearly identified with the figure elsewhere designated "messiah." This position requires that the term "messiah" must occur, but it is an advance over the first view in that it need not occur in every passage. The category is further extended in that it includes an element of eschatological deliverance that broadens the scope of messianism. The advantage of this position is that it helps avoid reading into texts a messianic nature that may not have been intended and it includes an eschatological element. However, the drawback to this position, like the first, is that it unnecessarily limits what texts can be called messianic by requiring the term "messiah" be present, and it restricts messianic expectation to a rigid eschatological orientation.[211] For example,

---

[207] Andrew Chester, *Messiah and Exaltation: Jewish Messianic and Visionary Traditions and New Testament Christology* (WUNT 207; Tübingen: Mohr Siebeck, 2007), 193.

[208] Representatives of this position are Charlesworth, "From Messianology to Christology: Problems and Prospects," 3–35, and de Jonge, "The Earliest Christian Use of *Christos*: Some Suggestions", which draws upon his earlier article, "The Use of the Word 'Anointed' in the Time of Jesus".

[209] Chester, *Messiah and Exaltation*, 194–95.

[210] Chester, *Messiah and Exaltation*, 196. Chester names John J. Collins ("He Shall Not Judge by What His Eyes See," *DSD* 2 [1995]: 145–46, esp. 146) as representative of this position, although he acknowledges that Collins varies in his writings on this definition.

[211] Chester, *Messiah and Exaltation*, 197–98.

historical figures who are designated "messiah" in the Qumran texts would be excluded because they are not connected with the "end-time."

(3) *Messiah as an Agent of Final Deliverance.* A third position focuses on the crucial criterion that "messiah" should be understood as the agent of eschatological divine deliverance, whether or not he is designated "messiah" or "anointed" in the particular text in question.[212] Here the advance is that the term "messiah" is not itself the decisive criterion. This recognizes that messianic expectations broadened in first century C.E. Judaism to include eschatological deliverance in figures not specifically connected with the terms משיח or χριστός. The example is given of the "righteous Branch" in Jer 23:5–6, who can reasonably be called "messianic" even though the specific term "messiah" does not occur. It denotes an ideal, future Davidic king, who in later tradition is called "messiah." The difficulty with this position is that in some marginal cases it is not always readily apparent whether the figure in question is genuinely messianic or not. Chester expresses preference for this third position.[213]

(4) *Messiah as Future Ruler.* The final position in this taxonomy understands the messiah as a ruler that is coming in the future, but not necessarily the eschatological future.[214] The "future" in many texts is often thought of as very near, so that a present leader, such as Zerubbabel, John Hyrcanus, or bar Kochba, was seen as a messiah. Thus the movements surrounding these present rulers were considered messianic. The advantage of this definition is that the Hebrew Bible expresses considerable hope for future royal figures, but the expectation is not always specifically eschatological. The disadvantage of this approach is that Jewish hope in the first century C.E. developed clear eschatological connotations.

To conclude, Chester's definition of the third position in this taxonomy is helpful in understanding the concept of "messiah" within first century C.E. Jewish messianic expectations: "... a messiah is a figure who acts as the agent of the final divine deliverance, whether or not he is specifically designated as 'messiah' or 'anointed.'"[215] A common theme in early Jewish texts from just before or during the first century C.E. is that Messiah would come to judge and/or destroy the wicked (*Pss. Sol.* 17–18; *4 Ezra* 12; *2 Bar.* 40:72), deliver God's people (*Pss. Sol.* 17; *4 Ezra* 12), and reign in a blessed kingdom (*Pss. Sol.* 17). Given the fact that messianism arose in Israel in the context of

---

[212] Chester, *Messiah and Exaltation*, 196. Here Chester cites J. Collins once again as representing this position, and he contends that this is much more representative of J. Collins' view than the above position; cf. Collins, *The Scepter and the Star*, 11–14.

[213] Chester, *Messiah and Exaltation*, 201.

[214] Chester, *Messiah and Exaltation*, 201–2, who cites William Horbury, *Jewish Messianism and the Cult of Christ* (London: SCM, 1998), 6–7, as the clearest representative of this definition.

[215] Chester, *Messiah and Exaltation*, 201.

exile, alienation and oppression during the Second Temple period, it is not surprising to find this common theme.[216]

Although Jesus did not refer to himself with the explicit term Messiah / Christ, we have seen that the nature of his mission was messianic: he was associated with the eschatological prophet, John the Baptist; he announced the arrival of the kingdom of God; he called the Twelve and sent them to Israel as a warning of eschatological judgment. However, Jesus' messianic ministry was misinterpreted by the crowds to mean that he was the eschatological prophet / king who was the agent of divine political / militaristic deliverance. And ironically, Jesus was executed by the Romans as "king of the Jews" because he was misperceived as stirring the crowds to rebellion.

Although Jesus accepts Peter's declaration that he is the Messiah, he qualifies the use of the title to include the kind of Messiah that he intended to be, not precisely what Peter expected him to be.

3.2. Ancient "declarations"

Peter's declaration fits within, yet differs from broader first century messianic hopes, and it likewise fits within, yet differs from other declarations that we find in the ancient Mediterranean world. In this ancient world a special connection was thought to exist between kings and the divine world. The conceptual ideology of the king could be accorded either through divine quality or descent, or else he could be regarded as divinely chosen or elected. Therefore, sacral legitimation of the rule of the king, especially for those who were usurpers, was considered essential and played a significant role in divine authorization of the ideal future savior-king.[217] One means of sacral legitimation was prophetic or oracular recognition of the king as one divinely ordained to rule. It provided both supernaturally guaranteed identification and divine legitimation for individuals of singular importance, and it was an important feature of ancient coronation rituals and ancient kingship ideologies.

Sacral legitimation was important for Jewish revolutionary figures in the first century C. E., especially in the light of the longing for the restoration of the Davidic throne by God's "anointed." Josephus points to an "ambiguous oracle" that was a major factor in stirring up the people's messianic expectations (*J. W.* 6.312–314[218]), which most likely was an allusion to the scriptural

---

[216] Ben Witherington, III, *The Many Faces of the Christ: The Christologies of the New Testament and Beyond* (Crossroad Companions to the New Testament; New York: Crossroad, 1998), 15.

[217] Aune, "Christian Prophecy," 411.

[218] "But what more than all else incited them to the war was an ambiguous oracle, likewise found in their sacred scriptures, to the effect that at that time one from their country would become ruler of the world. This they understood to mean someone of their own

oracle found in Num 24:17: "a star shall come out of Jacob, and a scepter shall rise out of Israel." In the context where he mentions the "ambiguous oracle" Josephus tells us that one of the omens that incited the Jewish people to revolt was a "star" (ἄστρον) in the sky (*J. W.* 6.289). Eschatological expectations were afire in first-century Palestine with the belief that prophecy was in the process of fulfillment, and several of the leaders of Israel's revolutionary movements can correctly be called messianic figures, with the belief that they were "anointed" for the task of liberating and restoring Israel.[219]

Most of the early movements within Judaism appear to have been initiated by ambitious individuals who gathered a group around them, either intentionally or through their charisma or vision. The movements came in three broad revolutionary waves, although there was revolutionary activity throughout.[220] We find within these movements at least two individuals whose followers, for a variety of reasons, acclaimed them as a messianic or kingly leader/deliverer (e. g., Simon, a servant of king Herod, and Simon bar Kochba). These recognition oracles served to legitimate for the followers that the one they were following was authorized by God to lead the people.

We now look at accounts in the broader Mediterranean world of the oracular legitimation. We start with a declaration made to a current ruler, Alexander the Great, and then turn to a future ruler, Vespasian. We also will briefly examine the oracular legitimation of two Jewish revolutionaries, Simon, servant of Herod, and Simon, bar Kochba. We will see that the scriptural oracle of Num 24:17 is quite likely a prominent point of reference as sacral legitimation in Josephus' own prophecy of Vespasian's future rule, in the fervor of those who follow the earlier revolutionary figure Simon, and in the later rise of bar Kochba.

---

race, and many of their wise men went astray in their interpretation of it. The oracle, however, in reality signified the sovereignty of Vespasian, who was proclaimed Emperor on Jewish soil" (Thackeray, LCL).

[219] Martin Hengel, *The Zealots: Investigations Into the Freedom Movement in the Period from Herod I Until 70 A. D.* (2d ed.; Edinburgh: T&T Clark, 1989), 290–302; Horsley and Hanson, *Bandits, Prophets, and Messiahs*, 88–134, esp. 88–110; Evans, *Jesus and His Contemporaries*, 53–81; esp. 53–58.

[220] These movements can be broadly subsumed under the categories of *prophetic* (e. g., the Samaritan; Theudas; the Egyptian; Jesus, son of Hananiah) or *royal* (e. g., Judas, son of Hezekiah; Menahem; Simon son of Giora). The first wave, in 4 B.C.E. came with the death of king Herod, and included: Judas, son of Ezekiah; Simon, servant of Herod; Athronges, the shepherd. The second wave, from 66–70 C. E., came with the Jewish revolt against Rome, and included: John of Gischala; Jesus, son of Hananiah; Menahem; and Simon, son of Giora). The third wave, from 132–135 C. E., came with the final revolt against Rome, and was led by Simon bar Kochba. See Horsley and Hanson, *Bandits, Prophets, and Messiahs*, 118–27.

3.2.1. Current ruler: Alexander the Great (336–323 B. C. E.)

"You are the son of Zeus."

An example of sacral legitimation of a current ruler is found in an oracle directed to Alexander the Great. The authentication of Alexander the Great as ruler over the many formerly independent kingdoms was thought to be secured through sacral legitimation. He appealed to his divine descent as legitimating his attempt to unify these kingdoms by the imposition of Hellenistic language and culture. Oracles revealing Alexander's divine status are recorded by Callisthenes, the official eyewitness historian and propagandist of Alexander's expedition (preserved in a fragment of a lost work in Strabo, *Geography*, 17.1.43). The most famous were reportedly pronounced by an Egyptian prophet at the oracle of Zeus-Ammon on the Oasis of Siway, the oracle of Apollo at Didyma, and the prophetess Athenais. Nothing further is known of the latter oracles, but fragmentary versions of Alexander's visit to Siwah have been preserved.[221] These fragmentary versions allow for at least a partial historical reconstruction of the incident.[222]

Alexander had recently conquered Egypt, which made him the successor to the pharaohs. He journeyed to the Libyan Oracle of Ammon, which was well-respected in Greece, ranked in importance only after the sanctuaries of Zeus at Olympia and the sanctuary of Zeus in Dodona. The priest of Ammon, identified with Zeus, greeted Alexander as "son of Zeus."[223] Alexander entered the Adyton, the innermost shrine of shrine of Amun, a privilege usually reserved exclusively for the priests, while his entourage was allowed to enter only the front court. Alexander posed questions to the oracle, but he never revealed either his questions or the answers he received. However, Callisthenes, doubtless with Alexander's approval, turned the priest's greeting into an oracular announcement of Alexander's divine sonship.[224]

---

[221] Cf. Arrian, *Campaigns of Alexander (Anabasis)* 3.3–4; Plutarch, *Alexander* 27.5–11; Diodorus Siculus, *Library of History* 17.49.2–51; Quintus Curtius Rufus, *Life of Alexander the Great* 4.25–4.

[222] See the overview in A. B. Bosworth, "Alexander and Ammon," in *Greece and the Eastern Mediterranean in Ancient History and Prehistory: Studies Presented to Fritz Schachermeyer on the Occasion of His Eightieth Birthday* (ed. K. H. Kinzl; New York: De Gruyter, 1977), 51–75.

[223] Strabo, *Geographica* 17.1.43. Plutarch (*Alexander* 27.9) recounts a rationalizing tradition in which historians before him had challenged the accuracy of the alleged proclamation of Alexander as son of Zeus and had suggested that the priest of Ammon, who was not fluent in Greek, gave a slip in his greeting: "... some say the prophet, wishing to show his friendliness by addressing him with 'O paidion,' or *O my son*, in his foreign pronunciation ended the words with "s" instead of "n," and said, 'O paidios,' and that Alexander was pleased at the slip in pronunciation, and a story became current that the god had addressed him with 'O pai Dios,' or *O son of Zeus*" (Perrin, LCL).

[224] Aune, "Christian Prophecy," 412.

The many popular accounts of Alexander's visit to Siwah repeat and amplify Callisthenes' account of an oracular recognition of Alexander's divine status as a son of Zeus.[225]

3.2.2. Future ruler: Vespasian (69–79 C.E.)

"You are Caesar ... and emperor"

An example of sacral legitimation of a future ruler is found in a prophecy directed to Vespasian. Vespasian had no hereditary claim to rule Rome as Caesar. He needed not only political but sacral legitimation of his authority to rule. Just two years before he was acclaimed by the people as the new ruler to replace Nero, he received a prophecy from the Jewish general Josephus that he would soon be Caesar.

Josephus was the military commander of Galilee during the Jewish wars that began in 66 C.E. when zealots ousted the Roman procurator and set up a revolutionary government in Jerusalem. Josephus fortified the towns of the north against the approaching Roman army. In the spring of 67 C.E, the Romans under the command of Vespasian arrived in Galilee and quickly destroyed the Jewish resistance in Galilee. Josephus held the fortress of Jotapata for forty-seven days, but with the fall of the city he and forty others of the Jewish resistance took refuge in a nearby cave (*J. W.* 3.341–42). After several days Josephus was about to surrender, because he recalled nightly dreams in which God had foretold him the fate of the Jews and the destinies of the Roman sovereigns (*J. W.* 3.351). Although by law a Jewish general was supposed to die with his men (*J. W.* 3.400), Josephus felt that he had a divine mission to announce to the world the future fortunes of his Roman captors (*J. W.* 3.137–38, 354). But the others voted to commit suicide rather than surrender. Josephus argued the immorality of suicide on the basis that it represented impiety towards God who created them (*J. W.* 3.362–83), but he finally agreed to their wish. However, Josephus contrived a plan whereby they would draw lots, and each person would kill the person who preceded him in the lottery. Josephus contrived to draw the last lot, and as one of the two remaining, convinced his intended victim to surrender to the Romans (*J. W.* 3.387–91).

Led in chains before Vespasian, Josephus requested a private audience, which Vespasian granted, but also allowed Titus, his son, and two of his friends to remain.[226] Josephus was now on a mission from God, and he told

---

[225] Cf. Aune, "Christian Prophecy," 412; Bosworth, "Alexander and Ammon," 74–75.

[226] When the prophecy was uttered is debated, but Josephus' account (*J. W.* 3.392) and that of Suetonius (*The Deified Vespasian* 5.7) imply that it was soon after the surrender; see Seth Schwartz, *Josephus and Judaean Politics* (Columbia Studies in the Classical Tradition 18; Leiden: Brill, 1990), 4–5, and n. 9.

Vespasian about the prophetic dreams he had received from God concerning the general's future rule. Assuming the role of a prophet, Josephus addressed the general:

> You imagine, Vespasian, that in the person of Josephus you have taken a mere captive; but I come to you as a messenger of greater destinies. Had I not been sent on this errand by God, I knew the law of the Jews and how it becomes a general to die. To Nero do you send me? Why then? Think you that [Nero and] those who before your accession succeed him will continue? You will be Caesar, Vespasian, you will be emperor, you and your son here. Bind me then yet more securely in chains and keep me for yourself; for you, Caesar, are master not of me only, but of land and sea and the whole human race. For myself, I ask to be punished by stricter custody, if I have dared to trifle with the words of God (*J. W.* 3.400–403; Thackeray, LCL).

Just a few months later some of the legions in Europe revolted against Nero's rule, his own elite troops conspired against him, and Nero committed suicide on June 9, 68 C. E. The following turbulent year witnessed three Roman generals (Galba, Otho, Vitellius) seize power in rapid succession, but in December 69 C. E., in keeping with Josephus' prediction, the people of Rome acclaimed Vespasian as emperor, ratifying the acclamation of his own troops (*J. W.* 4.655).

At first Vespasian did not believe the prophecy, because he thought that Josephus was being duplicitous. But as told later by Josephus, Vespasian gradually changed his mind and began to believe in the prophecy, because God gradually led his thought to the power he would gain, and because he found that Josephus had proved himself to be a reliable, trustworthy prophet in other matters (*J. W.* 3.404–407). Josephus had remained a prisoner in the Roman camp, but when Vespasian became emperor he released Josephus from prison. From that time on, Josephus attached himself to the Roman cause, adopted the name Flavius (Vespasian's family name), accompanied his patron to Alexandria, and there married for the third time (Josephus' first wife had been lost at the siege of Jotapata, and his second had deserted him in Judaea). Following the fall of Jerusalem and the destruction of the Temple, Josephus took up residence in Rome, where he devoted the remainder of his life to literary pursuits under imperial patronage.

Josephus' actions have been subject to scrutiny throughout history. Some have accused him of later concocting the story of the prophecy to preclude questions about his actions in the war where he avoided dying with his troops. A similar prediction was later attributed to rabbi Yohanan ben Zakkai, who fled Jerusalem during the revolt and worked out a deal with the Roman authorities to establish a school at Yavneh/Jamnia (*b. Giṭ* 56a–b; *'Abot R. Nat.* 4:5). That remarkable prophecy also has been suspected by some of masking less noble pleading for survival. The suggestion is then made that Josephus invented the episode in the interest of justifying his behavior, and that rabbinic tradition borrowed the device to exonerate Rabbi Yohanan.[227] However, in recent years a moderating position has dominated, in which Josephus is not completely exonerated from his self-justification, but his consistent claim to having prophetic gifts is given due regard.[228]

Josephus' prophecy became famous in Rome, likely because of the new emperor's propaganda efforts. Vespasian had no hereditary claim to rule and needed legitimation.[229] Several Roman authors of the time point to signs and wonders that appeared at the time of Vespasian's ascension, and Josephus' prophecy is listed among them (e.g., Suetonius, *Vespasian* 4–5; Dio Cassius 65.1.4). These accounts amplify Josephus' prophecy as an oracular recognition of Vespasian's status as Caesar.

3.2.3. *Royal pretender: Simon, servant of Herod the Great (ca. 4 B.C.E.)*

"He was declared to be a king"

Josephus records that at least one royal pretender – Simon, the servant of Herod the Great – elevated himself to the status of "king" through his own ambitions. But there is evidence that he was placed in that role also by his followers.

Following the death of Herod the Great, crowds of people swarmed into Jerusalem for the Passover celebrations and pressed Archelaus, Herod's son and heir apparent, to relieve the tax burdens and release the many political prisoners still chained in various Herodian fortresses. The anxious response from Archelaus was to send in the army, which massacred thousands of the worshiping pilgrims. Shortly afterward Archelaus left for Rome to advance his claim for appointment as Herod's successor. The countryside of Israel virtually exploded in revolt, and these revolts took the form of messianic movements. Josephus focused on three movements: the one led by Simon, another led by Judas son of the brigand-chief Ezekias (*Ant.* 17.271–72), and one led by Athronges the shepherd.[230]

---

[227] E.g., Abraham Schalit, "Josephus Flavius," in *Encyclopaedia Judaica* (2nd ed., 22 vols.; ed. Fred Skolnik and Michael Berenbaum; Detroit: Macmillan; Jerusalem: Keter, 2007), 11:435–42. This was especially the perspective in Josephus research from the time before World War 2. For discussion, see Per Bilde, *Flavius Josephus Between Jerusalem and Rome: His Life, His Works and Their Importance* (JSPSup 2; Sheffield: JSOT Press, 1988), 52.

[228] Bilde, *Flavius Josephus Between Jerusalem and Rome: His Life, His Works and Their Importance*, 52–60. See also Steve Mason, *Josephus and the New Testament* (Peabody: Hendrickson, 1992), 45–51, 72. For discussion of Josephus' overall intentions, see Shaye J.D. Cohen, *Josephus in Galilee and Rome: His Vita and Development as a Historian* (Columbia Studies in the Classical Tradition 8; Leiden: Brill, 1979), esp. 228–31.

[229] Cf. Tessa Rajak, *Josephus: The Historian and His Society* (London: Duckworth, 1983).

[230] Horsley and Hanson, *Bandits, Prophets, and Messiahs*, 111.

Several important points characterized these messianic movements that had royal pretenders at their head. (1) They are centered on a charismatic king. (2) The royal pretenders were all from humble his origins. (3) The participants in the messianic movements were primarily peasants, and the revolts mostly occurred in the various country districts in contrast with the Jerusalem metropolis. (4) The movements appear to be somewhat organized, at the least into what could be called "armed bands" for military purposes. (5) The principal goal of the movements was to restore the traditional ideals of a free and egalitarian Jewish society by overthrowing Herodian and Roman domination.[231]

Simon was among those who took a leadership role in those uprisings. The acclaim of the people for his leadership acted as legitimation of his qualifications, especially as his qualifications were so much in contrast to the current Herodian and Roman leaders. The intimate connection between an anti-Roman movement of pronounced popular character and messianic leadership also characterizes the period of the Great Revolt seventy years later in the movements surrounding such leaders as Menahem leader of the Sicarii and Simon bar Giora.[232] Simon had been a servant of king Herod, and because he was handsome, tall, and strong he had great personal confidence in his abilities to succeed. Simon took advantage of the chaotic conditions following the death of Herod and the departure of Archelaus to Rome and dared to place the "diadem" on his head, which was the equivalent of declaring himself to be king in the absence of Archelaus. Josephus then narrates, "... having got together a body of men, he was himself also acclaimed king by them in their madness, and he rated himself worthy of this beyond anyone else" (Josephus, *Ant.* 17.274; Marcus, LCL).

The term "diadem" (διάδημα) by the Hellenistic period had become a virtual synonym for kingship, and Josephus not only uses it with reference to Simon and Athronges, but also among others Antiochus IV Epiphanes, Demetrius I Soter, Aristobulus I, Hyrcanus II, and Herod the Great. Apparently Josephus was quite familiar with the distinctively Jewish messianic language, but he carefully avoids expressions such as "branch" or "son of

---

[231] Cf. Horsley and Hanson, *Bandits, Prophets, and Messiahs*, 114–17; Shemuel Safrai and Menahem Stern, eds., *The Jewish People in the First Century: Historical Geography, Political History, Social, Cultural and Religious Life and Institutions* (ed. Shemuel Safrai and Menahem Stern; vol. 1, section 1 of *Compendia Rerum Iudaicarum ad Novum Testamentum*; Assen: Van Gorcum, 1974), 280–83. For a discussion of the distinction between popular and elite forms of messianism with respect to Simon, see Sean Freyne, "The Herodian Period," in *Redemption and Resistance: The Messianic Hopes of Jews and Christians in Antiquity* (ed. Markus Bockmuehl and James Carleton Paget; London: T&T Clark, 2007), 29–61, esp. 36–37.

[232] Safrai and Stern, *The Jewish People in the First Century*, 280–81.

David" and "messiah."²³³ On the other hand, he does not hesitate to use language of "kingship." Josephus, hardly sympathetic to messianic movements because of his Roman sponsorship,²³⁴ seems to imply that the movement was driven by a revolutionary spirit rashly pursuing Jewish independency. His descriptions of the motivating forces of the people, such as "... he was himself also proclaimed king by them in their madness" and "... most of the Peraeans, who were disorganized and fighting with more recklessness than science" (*Ant.* 17.276), and "... such was the great madness that settled upon the nation because they had not king" (*Ant.* 17.277), seem to imply a revolutionary motivation that was admirable for its nationalistic fervor, but unthinking in the light of the power of Rome.²³⁵ This is a movement that fanatically pursues Jewish nationalistic independency, regardless of how hopeless it seems from a reasoned perspective. Josephus seems to suggest that the movement was "... fired by (divine) inspiration, or a special spirit."²³⁶

These people, and the one that they designate to lead them, were not simply pursuing independency. Rather, in the light of their history as the people of God, they believed that God was leading them to establish once again his kingdom among them. The declaration and adoption of the royal title leads to the conjecture that it was linked with eschatological expectations.²³⁷ The rush to proclaim Simon king was provoked by a political/religious fervor. But the pursuit of divine legitimation by the acclaim resulted in the beheading of Simon by Gratus, one of Herod's commanders, and most of the movement being slaughtered (*Ant.* 17.276).

3.2.4. *Messianic claimant: Simon bar Kochba / Kosiba (132–135 C.E.)*

"This is the king, the Messiah."

Some one hundred and thirty years after the revolts of 4 B.C.E., and some sixty years after the great revolt of 66–70 C.E., the Jews again rebelled against Roman rule. Simon bar Kochba, the leader of the renewed third wave of the rebellion against Rome, is acclaimed by Rabbi Akiba as Messiah in response to bar Kochba's impressive deeds in the rebellion.²³⁸ The aged and revered religious leader's stature acted as a powerful legitimation

---

²³³ Chester, *Messiah and Exaltation*, 197; Horsley and Hanson, *Bandits, Prophets, and Messiahs*, 114.
²³⁴ Cf. Evans, "Josephus on John the Baptist and Other Jewish Prophets of Deliverance," 55–63. On Josephus and his general relationship to his Roman audience, see also Helen Bond, *Pontius Pilate in History and Interpretation* (SNTSMS 100; Cambridge: Cambridge University Press, 1999), 49–93.
²³⁵ Safrai and Stern, *The Jewish People in the First Century*, 280–81.
²³⁶ Horsley and Hanson, *Bandits, Prophets, and Messiahs*, 114.
²³⁷ Safrai and Stern, *The Jewish People in the First Century*, 280.
²³⁸ Cf. Collins, *The Scepter and the Star*, 202–4; Evans, *Jesus and His Contemporaries*, 210; Horsley and Hanson, *Bandits, Prophets, and Messiahs*, 127–31.

of bar Kochba's leadership role among the peasantry, although not among the majority of the rabbis.[239]

The Roman emperor Hadrian (117–138 C.E.), during a tour of the east that included Jerusalem (ca. 128–132 C.E.), decided upon enforcing the policy of hellenization to align the Jews more directly with the empire. He banned circumcision, built a new pagan city, Aelia, on the ruins of Jerusalem, and erected a temple to Jupiter Capitolinus over the ruins of the Jewish temple. This outrage recalled the desecrations enacted centuries earlier by Antiochus IV Ephiphanes (ca. 167 B.C.E.). Enraged, the Jews rebelled in 132 C.E. in much the same way that they had against Antiochus (164 B.C.E.), and their revolt had a scope, power, and destructive consequences at least as violent as that of the time of the revolt against Vespasian in 66–70 C.E. At the head of the rebellion in 132 C.E. was Simon bar Kosiba. He was reputedly of Davidic descent and had a wildly enthusiastic following among the people. Tineius Rufus was governor of Judea at the time of the uprising, but he and his troops were no match for the revolutionaries. With bar Kosiba at the lead, the revolutionaries swept victoriously through Palestine and beyond its frontiers.[240]

As bar Kosiba won battle after battle, eschatological messianic expectations flamed. Of the many popular messianic movements in Palestine from the death of Herod the Great in 4 B.C.E. up to the revolt led by bar Kosiba, "... it was only bar Kosiba who apparently made an explicit messianic claim."[241] And his claim was publicly recognized and announced by Rabbi Akiba, who alluded to the leader's messianic status by saying, "This is the king, the Messiah."[242] This is the typical form of a recognition oracle.[243] The full recounting is found in *y. Taʿan.* 4:8 [68d 48–51]:

> ¹Rabbi Simeon ben Yoḥai taught: "Rabbi Aqiba, my master, used to interpret the passage, ²"a star shall go forth from Jacob" [Num 24:17] thus: Kozeba goes forth from Jacob." ³When Rabbi Aqiba saw Bar Kochba [Kozeba], he said, "This is the king, the Messiah."

In referring to bar Kosiba as bar Kochba, "son of a star," Akiba indicated Simon's messianic status by an allusion to the prophecy of Num 24:17, which was considered a messianic prophecy. Elsewhere we gain insight to Akiba's fuller messianology as he interprets the plural "thrones" of Dan 7:9

---

[239] Emil Schürer, *The History of the Jewish People in the Age of Jesus Christ (175 B.C. – A.D. 135)* (new English ed.; 3 vols.; ed. Geza Vermes, et al.; Edinburgh: T&T Clark, 1973–87), 1:544.

[240] Schürer, *History*, 1:540–49.

[241] Aune, "Christian Prophecy," 407.

[242] Schürer, *History*, 1:543.

[243] Joseph A. Fitzmyer, *Essays on the Semitic Background of the New Testament* (Missoula: Scholars, 1974), 314–15.

and how he speculates on other messianic characteristics.[244] Craig Evans concludes that Akiba entertained wide messianic expectations that included predictions of when Messiah would appear, what signs would attend his approach, and how long his rule would endure. Those expectations coalesced in what Akiba saw occurring in Kosiba's exploits. The latter expectation, that Messiah's rule would have a certain length, leads to the conclusion that Akiba thought of a Messiah who was fully human, but who sat on a throne next to the throne of God.[245] This is a high messianology, which drew cries of blasphemy from later rabbis.[246]

The title that bar Kosiba preferred, according to numismatic and papyrological evidence, was not Messiah, but *Nasi* ("prince"), a traditional title of the Israelite king. He struck his own coins with the inscriptions, "Prince of Israel" and "Year 1 of the liberty of Jerusalem."[247] And with the application of the Balaam oracle to Simon bar Kosiba, Rabbi Akiba created the expression by which bar Kosiba's messianic movement became known to subsequent (Christian) history: bar Kochba = Son of the Star.[248]

Although the peasantry rallied around Rabbi Akiba's declaration of bar Kosiba's messianic identity, most of the rabbis denied it. In the same rabbinic passage that records Akiba's declaration, a contrary rabbi's declaration occurs: "⁴Rabbi Yoḥanan ben Torta answered him: 'Aqiba, grass will grow out on your cheeks and the Son of David will still not have come'" (*y. Taʿan.* 4:8 [68d 48–51]. And latter rabbinic writings refer to bar Kochba as bar Koziba, Son of the Lie = Liar,[249] which was probably invented by his opponents, and those of Akiba, especially in recognition of the failure of the supposed messianic uprising and its disastrous consequences.[250]

And for Christians, their recognition of bar Kochba's claim and Rabbi Akiba's declaration prevented them from participating in the revolution, because they understood the messianic nature of the movement and were unable to participate in it without denying their Messiah. Justin and Eusebius claim that Christians were severely persecuted by bar Kochba because they would not participate in his messianic revolution.[251]

---

[244] Cf. *b. Sanh.* 38b = *b. Ḥag.* 14a and *Midr. Tanḥ.* B on Lev 19:1–2 (*Qedošin* § 1); cited in Evans, *Jesus and His Contemporaries*, 204–7.

[245] Evans, *Jesus and His Contemporaries*, 210.

[246] Evans, *Jesus and His Contemporaries*, 207.

[247] Schürer, *History*, 1:543–44; Aune, "Christian Prophecy," 407.

[248] Horsley and Hanson, *Bandits, Prophets, and Messiahs*, 134, n. 31.

[249] E. g., *Lam. Rab.* 2:4 reads: "R. Johanan said: Rabbi used to expound *There shall step forth a star* (kokab) *out of Jacob* (Num. XXIV, 17), thus: read not '*kokab* but *kozab* (lie)"; cf. *y. Taʿan.* 4:8 [68d 48–51].

[250] Cf. Schürer, *History*, 1:543–44, n. 131.

[251] Justin 1 *Apology* 31:6; Eusebius, *Chronicon*, cited in Schürer, *History*, 1:545, n. 141. See also Richard A. Horsley, "Jesus and Judaism: Christian Perspectives," in *Eusebius,*

Things at first went so well with bar Kochba's revolt that Hadrian himself came from Rome to Palestine to quell the uprising. He summoned the governor of Britain, Gaius Julius Severus, to his aid with 35,000 men of the 10th Legion. Severus gradually wore down and constricted the rebels' area of operation and retook Jerusalem. Cassius Dio narrates:

> Severus did not venture to attack his opponents in the open at any one point, in view of their numbers and their desperation, but by intercepting small groups, thanks to the number of his soldiers and his under-officers, and by depriving them of food and shutting them up, he was able, rather slowly, to be sure, but with comparatively little danger, to crush, exhaust and exterminate them. Very few of them in fact survived. (Cassius Dio, *Hist. Rom.* 69.13.1–3)

In 135 C.E., bar Kochba was killed at Bether, the strong mountain fort not far from Jerusalem. Judaea was desolated, the remnant of the Jewish population annihilated or exiled, and Jerusalem barred to Jews from the time forward (cf. Cassius Dio, *Hist. Rom.* 69.12.1–14.3). The city was turned into a Roman colony with the name Aelia Capitolina. The original plan of Hadrian to hellenize Jerusalem was implemented, despite the messianic uprising surrounding bar Kochba.[252]

Rabbi Akiba's oracular declaration of the messianic identity of Simon bar Kochba was in response to bar Kochba's own claim and his impressive deeds in the rebellion. Akiba's declaration was based on his own very full messianic expectation. The aged and revered religious leader's stature acted as a powerful legitimation of bar Kochba's leadership role. But in later rabbinic texts Akiba is said to have changed his mind about bar Kochba's messianic status. This quite well could have been because he had become disillusioned by the failure of bar Kochba's messianic movement.[253]

3.3. Conclusion to the broader historical context

The discussion of which ancient texts should be allowed when pursuing an understanding of who is Messiah and what is messianic in the ancient world yielded the following definition: "... a messiah is a figure who acts as the agent of the final divine deliverance, whether or not he is specifically designated as 'messiah' or 'anointed.'"[254] Although Jesus did not refer to himself as "messiah" because he avoided the varied messianic expectations found in the ancient world, his mission was messianic. And various means served

---

Christianity, and Judaism (ed. Harold W. Attridge and Gohei Hata; StPB; Leiden: Brill, 1992), 53–79, esp. 54–61.

[252] Schürer, *History*, 1:549–52; Horsley and Hanson, *Bandits, Prophets, and Messiahs*, 127–31.

[253] Evans, *Jesus and His Contemporaries*, 209–10. Evans suggests that it also could have been that later rabbis changed Akiba's mind for him in the various texts.

[254] Chester, *Messiah and Exaltation*, 201.

to legitimate Jesus' messianic ministry and message. The confirmation by the eschatological prophet John the Baptist, Jesus' proclamation of the imminent arrival of the kingdom of God, the miracle tradition, the calling and sending of Twelve apostles with an eschatological message of judgment, and his prophetic/messianic actions (e.g., climactic entry to Jerusalem; the temple incident), all constituted forms of legitimation.[255] Another type of legitimation was Peter's declaration, which has the form and the function of a recognition oracle, with similarities, yet stark differences, to others in the ancient world.[256]

It was not unusual in the ancient world for people to express their understanding of a great leader's identity. And it was not unusual for rulers to accept, and even at times to seek, legitimation of their royal status and reign. Peter's declaration in Caesarea Philippi that Jesus was the "Messiah" was oracular legitimation of what Jesus was demonstrating in his messianic mission, even thought the declaration needed nuancing by Jesus. The exclamation by the priest of Ammon that Alexander the Great was the son of Zeus and Josephus' prophecy that Vespasian would be crowned king go in different directions. Jesus qualified Peter's declaration to fit his own messianic identity, whereas both Alexander and Vespasian apparently manipulated the circumstances to fit their aspirations.

The scriptural oracle of Num 24:17 is a prominent point of reference as sacral legitimation in Josephus' prophecy of Vespasian's future rule, and also figures prominently in the fervor of the people to follow the revolutionary figure Simon, and in the leadership role of bar Kochba in the later revolution.

Jesus and his movement occurred only some thirty years after the messianic movement of Simon and the other mass uprisings. These messianic movements occurred in all three principle areas of Jewish settlement in Palestine (Judah, Galilee, Perea).[257] Several of these earlier mass movements were composed of Jewish peasants who had rallied around the leadership of charismatic figures viewed as anointed kings of the Jews. And these peasants came from villages that were associated with Jesus' own movement – Bethlehem, Sephoris, Emmaus. Bethlehem, the village of Jesus' birth, had suffered under Herod's suspicion of an alternative king being born there (Matt 2:16–18). The city of Sephoris, burned and its inhabitants sold into slavery in 4 B.C.E., was just a few miles north of Jesus' home

---

[255] See above under our discussion of Peter's declaration and the criterion of historical coherence.
[256] Aune, "Christian Prophecy," 412–13.
[257] Freyne, "A Galilean Messiah?" 199–205.

village Nazareth.[258] And the town of Emmaus, the location of one of the resurrection appearances according to the Gospel tradition (Luke 24:13–32), had been destroyed by the Romans in retaliation for another mass messianic movement a little more than a generation prior to the beginning of Jesus' own messianic movement.[259] Jesus' movement would have been readily compared to the earlier messianic movements that were still fresh in the minds of the Jewish peasants.[260]

The incident when the crowds clamored for Simon the revolutionary to be king sounds strikingly similar to the later rush by the crowd to come and take Jesus by force to make him king (John 6:14–15). But Jesus would have nothing of that crowds' misguided fervor, because he was motivated by a different agenda for the kingdom of God: to accept his fate to die for the people as their suffering Servant, regardless of any attempts, even by Peter, to deter him and force him into another agenda (Mark 8:31–33).

Akiba's declaration bears similarity to Peter's in the surface declaration that a popular leader who had rallied great crowds was Messiah. Peter declares Jesus to be Messiah because of the great miracles that he has seen him perform, and also because of the overall messianic mission that he has seen unfold in Jesus' ministry. But in a different direction than Akiba, Peter will come to an expanded understanding of Jesus' identity as Messiah as one who will not establish a political/militaristic kingdom, but who will establish one that is based in his suffering and dying and rising.

Peter's declaration fits within the concept of oracular legitimation in the ancient world, but departs significantly in the light of Peter's developing understanding of Jesus' identity, and Jesus' own self-understanding.

4. Conclusion and Significance

The purpose of this essay was to provide a fresh assessment of the historicity and significance of Peter's declaration at Caesarea Philippi of Jesus' identity. In this final section we will summarize the arguments made earlier for the historicity of the incident, and then we will sketch out the significance, including the meaning of the declaration for Peter, for Jesus' own self-understanding, and the implications for the early church.

---

[258] See Richard A. Horsley, *Archaeology, History, and Society in Galilee: The Social Context of Jesus and the Rabbis* (Valley Forge: Trinity, 1996), 44–65.
[259] Safrai and Stern, *The Jewish People in the First Century*, 280.
[260] Richard A. Horsley, *Galilee: History, Politics, People* (Valley Forge: Trinity, 1995), 268–71.

4.1. The historicity of Peter's declaration

Several criteria lead to the conclusion that the Gospel writers recorded an historically authentic account of Peter's declaration that Jesus was the Christ/Messiah.

First, Caesarea Philippi is an unexpected locale for the declaration, which attests to the credibility of the evangelists' record. Associating the declaration with this Gentile region strikes a chord of an actual memory of an event in an unexpected locale. The record of Jesus' leaving Jewish Galilee to go to the Jews living in the villages in the largely pagan area outside of upper Galilee in Caesarea Philippi sounds a plausible historical note. Jesus covered all regions of the northern part of the inherited land of Israel, inspired by his ideas and hopes of Jewish restoration eschatology. Further, Caesarea Philippi is outside the jurisdiction of Herod Antipas, who had recently executed John the Baptist, and who was increasingly viewing Jesus also as a threat to the security of his realm. The criterion of Palestinian background satisfactorily supports the historical authenticity of this declaration pericope. The Markan text describes events and concepts that were distinctive to early first-century Palestine.

Second, the evangelists did not avoid recording an incident that is embarrassing to Peter, the leader of the Twelve apostles, which adds credibility to their intentions to record incidents the way that they occurred. Although Peter is commended for his declaration that Jesus is the Christ/Messiah, when Jesus reveals an aspect of his messianic ministry, suffering and dying, that is incongruent with Peter's still-developing conception, he is declared by Jesus to be a Satan-inspired hindrance to Jesus' fuller messianic mission. The historical credibility of the evangelists' record of this incident is heightened by their willingness to include material that is embarrassing to Peter, a high leader of the early church.

Third, and perhaps most importantly, the evangelists' accounts of Peter's declaration demonstrate authenticity because the incident has coherence historically with both the developing messianic ministry of Jesus and the final events of Jesus' life that led to his crucifixion. As to the former, the developing messianic ministry of Jesus was seen in the following ways. (1) In his relationship to the eschatological prophet John the Baptist, Jesus is also explicitly regarded as a prophet (Mark 6:4, 15; John 6:14). But his authority in exercising the power of the kingdom of God leads to the understanding that his ministry included a royal dimension, and in that sense he was "anointed" by God not only as a prophet, but as a king. (2) By calling and sending out the Twelve on a mission to Israel, Jesus issues a statement of hope of restoration or reunification to national Israel, but also a threat of judgment to those who did not repent. The calling and sending implies a royal dimension, because it is a vision for the nation as he established the kingdom of God, and the Twelve represent the new leadership that is needed to replace the failing religious leadership of Israel. (3) On at least one occasion the crowd acclaim him as "the prophet who is to come into the world," but Jesus rejects the acclaim because it included a frenzied desire to make him king (John 6:14–15). Jesus is here connected with the tradition that regarded Moses as a king as well as a prophet. The crowd understood Jesus in a potentially political light, which aroused pent-up hopes for the return of the Davidic glories. Although Jesus consistently rejected the popular, earthly kingship that the people desire, misconceptions of his messianic mission would eventually lead to his execution by the Romans as the "King of the Jews."

At this point in Jesus' developing messianic ministry, Peter makes his momentous declaration that Jesus is the Christ / Messiah. He has recognized Jesus' intention to be God's agent as Messiah in establishing the kingdom of God. Yet Peter is silenced by Jesus, not because he is incorrect, but because the title "Messiah" still carries with it among the people, and Jesus' enemies, political / militaristic connotations that Jesus rejects. Also, although Peter is largely correct in declaring Jesus to be the Messiah, he does not yet know the full nature of his messianic nature, which Jesus clarifies to include suffering and dying.

Peter's declaration coheres historically with what he has seen developing in the messianic mission of Jesus, and also coheres with what Jesus sees in the gathering opposition to his messianic mission. As Jesus approaches the final week of his life, the events involving his symbolic royal entry into Jerusalem and the authoritative temple incident combine to have Jesus arrested, and the religious leaders will be convinced that he is a messianic blasphemer. In turn, this will cause them to take Jesus to the Roman leaders with charges that he has incited the people with his messianic pretensions. And the Romans will have Jesus crucified as "King of the Jews," a title that coheres with the external form of Peter's declaration, but not with the internal meaning that Jesus increasingly revealed to Peter to include suffering and dying.

4.2. The significance of Peter's declaration

These collective criteria lead to the conclusion that the Gospel writers recorded an historically authentic account of Peter's declaration that Jesus was the Christ / Messiah. This leads us to consider the significance of the declaration for Peter, for Jesus' self-understanding, and for the early church.

4.2.1. Peter

Peter recognized in Jesus' mission that he was the Messiah who was anointed in the baptism by John, who announced the arrival of the kingdom of

God, which was divinely legitimated in the miracles and exorcisms, and was demonstrated in sending out the Twelve with a message to Israel of hope and judgment. Peter also recognized that Jesus rejected popular acclaim as the prophet-king. In this Peter had come to an understanding that Jesus was quite different than what many in Israel hoped for in Messiah. Peter saw that Jesus was not only an eschatological prophet, but that he was also Israel's anticipated royal Messiah. This prophetic, yet royal mission of Jesus elicited from Peter his declaration that Jesus is indeed the Messiah.[261] Peter and the others are silenced by Jesus, because the title Messiah still carries with it among the people political / militaristic connotations that Jesus rejects. The people largely want that kind of Messiah, so Jesus warns against fueling their misguided eagerness to crown him king, as the crowds had done with Simon the servant of Herod some thirty years earlier, and as they will do some hundred years later with Simon bar Kochba.

Establishing the historicity of Peter's declaration also has significant implications for understanding the historical disciples of Jesus. Peter *did* come to understand the messianic identity of Jesus during his lifetime. It is partial to be sure, because he had not yet understood the necessity of suffering and dying. That lends plausibility to Peter's later actions, because his partial understanding led him to attempt to deter Jesus from his fate, it led him to watchlessness and fearful denial at the time of Jesus' greatest need, and it led to cowardly abandonment while Jesus endured his crucifixion.[262]

Nonetheless, as Peter declares Jesus to be Messiah, he opens himself to the schooling of Jesus and later history as he comes to a much more complete understanding of what messiahship meant for Jesus.

4.2.2. *Jesus' self-understanding*

If Peter understood Jesus to be Messiah, does that mean that Jesus also had that understanding of his own identity? Several secure strands of tradition lead to an affirmative answer to that question.

First, we noted above that when John the Baptist asks from prison if he is "the one who is to come," Jesus answers with allusions to Isaiah 35:5–6 and 61:1–2 (Matt 11:2–6; Luke 7:18–22). The *Messianic Apocalypse* fragment from Qumran (4Q521) contains parallel allusions to the passages from Isaiah and understands them as the works of Messiah. This leads to the supported conclusion that Jesus has answered John in the affirmative, that yes, he is the coming One, the Messiah. Jesus knows that he is doing the works

---

[261] de Jonge, *God's Final Envoy*, 10, passim.
[262] See Brown, *New Testament Christology*, 74–75.

of the Messiah.²⁶³ Jesus' messianic consciousness is revealed as he speaks of himself as the one anointed with the Spirit, whose mission heralded the kingdom, and it is in this sense that we may say that Jesus saw himself as the anointed one.²⁶⁴

Second, Jesus rejected the idea of a political / militaristic messiahship and in his teaching focused on the arrival of the kingdom of God as a matter of producing internal righteousness that affects external righteous deeds (e. g., Matt 5:20; 6:1; 15:17–20). In this way he was defining his identity as the Messiah. There was broad variation in messianic expectations among first-century Jews of a royal figure who would accomplish the rescuing purposes of Israel's God. The category of messiahship had not been fully crystallized, so Jesus had the space to construct his own creative variation out of previously uncombined elements.²⁶⁵ For example, in the *Psalms of Solomon* there was an expressed hope that Messiah would "... gather a holy people whom he will lead in righteousness," and "... he will be a righteous king over them, taught by God" (*Pss. Sol.* 17:26, 30, 32). Jesus intensifies this extant messianic idea in his notion of the kingdom of God, which speaks to the intentional shaping of his messianic identity.²⁶⁶

Third, the evangelists' pericope regarding Peter's declaration, focusing attention on the identity of the person of Jesus himself, seems alien to the rest of the authentic Gospel material, where Jesus consistently points away from himself (at least implicitly) to refer to God. As Jesus accepts the title, but then qualifies it with the Son of Man statement, he refashions the conception of messiahship for Peter and the other disciples. This points to Jesus' self-understanding of his messianic identity.²⁶⁷ It also points to this conversation as a special moment in Jesus' teaching to his disciples, something its use in the tradition also suggests with its role as a turning point in the ministry of Jesus.

Fourth, we have demonstrated that Jesus carried out a messianic mission by his baptism by John, by announcing the arrival of the kingdom of God, by sending out the Twelve to announce hope and judgment to the nation of Israel, by doing the deeds of the coming One, by accepted Peter's declara-

---

²⁶³ Cf. Evans, *Jesus and His Contemporaries*, 437–56; Ben Witherington, III, *The Christology of Jesus* (Minneapolis: Fortress, 1990), 233, 267–68.

²⁶⁴ Rowland, *Christian Origins*, 177–78.

²⁶⁵ N. T. Wright, "Theology, History and Jesus: A Response to Maurice Casey and Clive Marsh," *JSNT* 69 (1998): 105–12, esp. 111.

²⁶⁶ For discussion of the tension between messianic expectations that focused on resistance and / or redemption, and how Jesus seemingly balanced both, see Markus Bockmuehl, "Resistance and Redemption in the Jesus Tradition," in *Redemption and Resistance: The Messianic Hopes of Jews and Christians in Antiquity* (ed. Markus Bockmuehl and James Carleton Paget; London: T&T Clark, 2007), 65–77.

²⁶⁷ Tuckett, *Christology and the New Testament*, 210–13.

tion that he was the Messiah, with qualification, and by his final week of royal entry to Jerusalem and the Temple incident.²⁶⁸ On that basis we conclude that Jesus intended to be understood as, and he understood himself to be, the Messiah.

4.2.3. The early church

Virtually without question it is acknowledged that the early church used the term Messiah to refer to Jesus. Our study concludes that what accounts for that usage is at least threefold: (1) Peter's and the other disciples' recognition of Jesus' messianic identity during his earthly mission; (2) Jesus' revelation of his messianic identity in his mission; (3) The titulus declaring that Jesus was executed as king of the Jews.²⁶⁹ The significance of Peter's declaration at Caesarea Philippi is that Jesus was understood to be, and was declared to be, the anticipated Christ / Messiah during his earthly ministry. It also recognizes that Jesus accepted the title Christ / Messiah, but only when used according to his unique messianic identity and mission. This also emphasizes that Jesus understood himself to be the anticipated Christ / Messiah, who uniquely focuses on the establishment of the kingdom of God for all people

This is what the early church understood in confessing Jesus as the Christ. Peter's declaration of a title was only the beginnings of understanding Jesus' identity. It later came to be a much more complete confession for the early church. He was the anointed One who announced the arrival of the kingdom of God, but he is also the crucified One, the resurrected One, and now they believed the exalted and glorified One. All of these elements became associated with the title, and now the name, of Jesus as the Christ. So a scarlet thread runs through Jesus' revelation of his identity in his messianic mission. It grew out of Jesus' ministry activity. It was affirmed in Peter's first articulation of Jesus' identity with his declaration at Caesarea Philippi. It was demonstrated through the report of Jesus' final ministry in Jerusalem and his passion. It culminates for the early church in the declaration and

---

²⁶⁸ Focus on Jesus as eschatological prophet has been a helpful major concern of recent scholarship. The present study moves to examine Jesus also as a royal, eschatological Messiah. Recent study further focuses upon the Temple incident as an indication of Jesus' self-understanding as Israel's long-awaited, eschatological high-priest, which is addressed in this volume in ch. 10. For other discussions see Anna Maria Schwemer, "Jesus Christus als Prophet, König und Priester: Das *munus triplex* und die frühe Christologie," in *Der messianische Anspruch Jesu und die Anfänge der Christologie: Vier Studien* (by Martin Hengel and Anna Maria Schwemer; WUNT 2.138; Tübingen: Mohr Siebeck, 2001), 165–230; Crispin H. T. Fletcher-Louis, "Jesus as the High Priestly Messiah: Part 1," *JSHJ* 4 (2006): 155–75; and Crispin H. T. Fletcher-Louis, "Jesus as the High Priestly Messiah: Part 2," *JSHJ* 5 (2007): 57–79.

²⁶⁹ Cf. Tuckett, *Christology and the New Testament*, 212–13; Brown, *New Testament Christology*, 74–75.

confession of Jesus as the Christ.[270] The so-called distinction between the Jesus of history and the Christ of faith is an unhelpful divide.[271] Jesus is the Christ of history *and* the Christ of faith.

Bibliography

Aland, Kurt, ed. *Synopsis Quattuor Evangeliorum*. Stuttgart: Deutsche Bibelstiftung, 1976.
Allen, Leslie C. *Ezekiel 1–19*. WBC 29. Dallas: Word, 1994.
Anderson, Hugh. *The Gospel of Mark*. NCB. London: Oliphants, 1976.
Anderson, Paul N. *The Christology of the Fourth Gospel: Its Unity and Disunity in the Light of John 6*. WUNT 2.78. Tübingen: Mohr Siebeck, 1996.
–. "Why This Study is Needed, And Why It is Needed Now." Pages 13–70 in *John, Jesus, and History, Volume 1: Critical Appraisals of Critical Views*. Edited by Paul N. Anderson, Felix Just, and Tom Thatcher. SBLSymS 44. Atlanta: SBL, 2007.
Aune, David E. "Christian Prophecy and the Messianic Status of Jesus." Pages 404–22 in *The Messiah: Developments in Earliest Judaism and Christianity*. Edited by James H. Charlesworth. Minneapolis: Fortress, 1992.
Barrett, C. K. *The Gospel According to St. John*. 2nd ed. Philadelphia: Westminster, 1958.
Bauer, David R. *The Structure of Matthew's Gospel: A Study in Literary Design*. JSNTSup 31. Sheffield: Almond, 1988.
Bauer, Walter. *A Greek-English Lexicon of the New Testament and Other Early Christian Literature*. 3rd ed. Revised and edited by Frederick William Danker. Chicago: University of Chicago Press, 2000.
Baur, Ferdinand C. "Die Christuspartei in der korinthischen Gemeinde, der Gegensatz des petrinischen und paulinischen Christenhums in der ältesten Kirch, der Apostel Petrus in Rom." *Tübinger Zeitschrift Für Theologie* 5 (1831): 61–206.
Bayer, Hans F. *Jesus' Predictions of Vindication and Resurrection: The Provenance, Meaning, and Correlation of the Synoptic Predictions*. WUNT 2.20. Tübingen: Mohr Siebeck, 1986.
Beare, Francis Wright. *The Gospel According to Matthew*. San Francisco: Harper & Row, 1982.
Beasley-Murray, George R. *John*. 2nd ed. WBC 36. Nashville: Nelson, 1999.
Bilde, Per. *Flavius Josephus Between Jerusalem and Rome: His Life, His Works and Their Importance*. JSPSup 2. Sheffield: JSOT Press, 1988.
Blevins, James L. *The Messianic Secret in Markan Research, 1901–1976*. Washington, D.C.: University Press of America, 1981.
Bock, Darrell L. *Blasphemy and Exaltation in Judaism and the Final Examination of Jesus*. WUNT 2.106. Tübingen: Mohr Siebeck, 1998.

---

[270] Peter Stuhlmacher, "The Messianic Son of Man: Jesus' Claim to Deity," in *The Historical Jesus in Recent Research* (ed. James D.G. Dunn and Scot McKnight; Sources for Biblical and Theological Study; Winona Lake: Eisenbrauns, 2005), 325–44, esp. 327–333.

[271] For an overview of this unhelpful divide, see James D.G. Dunn, *A New Perspective on Jesus: What the Quest for the Historical Jesus Missed* (Grand Rapids: Baker, 2005), 15–34.

–. "The Son of Man in Luke 5:24." *BBR* 1 (1991): 109–21.
Bockmuehl, Markus. "Resistance and Redemption in the Jesus Tradition." Pages 65–77 in *Redemption and Resistance: The Messianic Hopes of Jews and Christians in Antiquity*. Edited by Markus Bockmuehl and James Carleton Paget. London: T&T Clark, 2007.
–. *This Jesus: Martyr, Lord, Messiah*. Edinburgh: T&T Clark, 1994.
Bokser, Baruch M. "Messianism, The Exodus Pattern, and Early Rabbinic Judaism." Pages 239–58 in *The Messiah: Developments in Earliest Judaism and Christianity*. Edited by James H. Charlesworth. Minneapolis: Fortress, 1992.
Bond, Helen. *Pontius Pilate in History and Interpretation*. SNTSMS 100. Cambridge: Cambridge University Press, 1999.
Bonnard, Pierre. *L'Évangile Selon Saint Matthieu*. CNT 2.1. Geneva: Labor et Fides, 1992.
Boring, M. Eugene. *The Continuing Voice of Jesus: Christian Prophecy and the Gospel Tradition*. Louisville: Westminster John Knox, 1991.
–. "The Gospel of Matthew: Introduction, Commentary, and Reflections." Pages 87–505 in vol. 8 of *The New Interpreter's Bible*. 12 vols. Nashville: Abingdon, 1995.
–. "The Historical-Critical Method's 'Criteria of Authenticity': The Beatitudes in Q and Thomas as a Test Case." Pages 9–44 in *The Historical Jesus and the Rejected Gospels*. Edited by Charles W. Hedrick. Semeia 44. Atlanta: Scholars, 1988.
Bornkamm, Günther. "End-Expectation and Church in Matthew." Pages 15–51 in *Tradition and Interpretation in Matthew*. Translated by Percy Scott. By Günther Bornkamm, Gerhard Barth, and Heinz Joachim Held. NTL. Philadelphia: Westminster, 1963.
–. *Jesus of Nazareth*. Translated by Irene McLuskey, Fraser McLuskey, and James M. Robinson. Minneapolis: Fortress, 1995.
Borsch, Frederick Houk. *The Son of Man in Myth and History*. NTL. Philadelphia: Westminster, 1967.
Bosworth, A. B. "Alexander and Ammon." Pages 51–75 in *Greece and the Eastern Mediterranean in Ancient History and Prehistory: Studies Presented to Fritz Schachermeyer on the Occasion of His Eightieth Birthday*. Edited by K. H. Kinzl. New York: De Gruyter, 1977.
Bovon, François. *Luke 1*. Translated by Christine M. Thomas. Hermeneia. Minneapolis: Fortress, 2002.
Brodie, Thomas L. *The Quest for the Origin of John's Gospel: A Source-Oriented Approach*. Oxford: Oxford University Press, 1993.
Brown, Raymond E. *The Gospel According to John I–XII*. AB 29. New York: Doubleday, 1966.
–. *An Introduction to New Testament Christology*. New York: Paulist, 1994.
Brown, Raymond E., Karl P. Donfried, and John Reumann, eds. *Peter in the New Testament*. Minneapolis: Augsburg, 1973.
Bultmann, Rudolf. *The History of the Synoptic Tradition*. Translated by John Marsh. New York: Harper & Row, 1963.
–. *Theology of the New Testament*. Translated by Kendrick Grobel. 2 vols. New York: Scribner, 1951–55.
Burkett, Delbert. *The Son of Man Debate: A History and Evaluation*. SNTSMS 107. Cambridge: Cambridge University Press, 1999.

Caragounis, Chrys C. *The Son of Man: Vision and Interpretation*. WUNT 38. Tübingen: Mohr Siebeck, 1986.
Carson, D. A. *The Gospel According to John*. Grand Rapids: Eerdmans, 1991.
—. "Matthew." Pages 1–599 in vol. 8 of *The Expositor's Bible Commentary*. Edited by Frank E. Gaebelein. Grand Rapids: Zondervan, 1984.
Casey, Maurice. *The Solution to the 'Son of Man' Problem*. LNTS 343. London: T&T Clark, 2007.
Catchpole, David. "The 'Triumphal' Entry." Pages 319–34 in *Jesus and the Politics of His Day*. Edited by Ernst Bammel and C. F. D. Moule. Cambridge: Cambridge University Press, 1984.
Charlesworth, James H., ed. *The Messiah: Developments in Earliest Judaism and Christianity*. Minneapolis: Fortress, 1992.
—. "From Messianology to Christology: Problems and Prospects." Pages 3–35 in *The Messiah: Developments in Earliest Judaism and Christianity*. Edited by James H. Charlesworth. Minneapolis: Fortress, 1992.
—. *The Historical Jesus: An Essential Guide*. Nashville: Abingdon, 2008.
Chester, Andrew. *Messiah and Exaltation: Jewish Messianic and Visionary Traditions and New Testament Christology*. WUNT 207. Tübingen: Mohr Siebeck, 2007.
Chronis, Harry L. "To Reveal and to Conceal: A Literary-Critical Perspective on 'the Son of Man' in Mark." *NTS* 51 (2005): 459–81.
Cohen, Shaye J. D. *Josephus in Galilee and Rome: His Vita and Development as a Historian*. Columbia Studies in the Classical Tradition, 8. Leiden: Brill, 1979.
Cohick, Lynn H. "Jesus as King of the Jews." Pages 111–32 in *Who Do My Opponents Say I Am?: An Investigation of the Accusations Against Jesus*. Edited by Scot McKnight and Joseph Modica. LNTS 327. London: T&T Clark, 2008.
Collins, Adela Yarbro. *Mark*. Hermeneia. Minneapolis: Fortress, 2007.
Collins, John J. "He Shall Not Judge by What His Eyes See." *DSD* 2 (1995): 145–64.
—. *The Scepter and the Star: The Messiahs of the Dead Sea Scrolls and Other Ancient Literature*. ABRL. New York: Doubleday, 1995.
Conzelmann, Hans. *History of Primitive Christianity*. Translated by John E. Steely. Nashville: Abingdon, 1973.
—. *An Outline of the Theology of the New Testament*. Translated by John Bowden. NTL. London: SCM, 1969.
Cranfield, C. E. B. *The Gospel According to Saint Mark*. CGTC. Cambridge: Cambridge University Press, 1959.
Crossan, John Dominic. *The Historical Jesus: The Life of a Mediterranean Jewish Peasant*. San Francisco: HarperSanFrancisco, 1991.
Cullmann, Oscar. *Peter: Disciple – Apostle – Martyr: A Historical and Theological Study*. 2nd ed. Translated by Floyd V. Filson. Philadelphia: Westminster, 1962.
Dahl, Nils Alstrup. *Jesus the Christ: The Historical Origins of Christological Doctrine*. Edited by Donald H. Juel. Minneapolis: Fortress, 1991.
Daube, David. *The Exodus Pattern in the Bible*. London: Faber and Faber, 1963.
Davies, W. D., and Dale C. Allison, Jr. *A Critical and Exegetical Commentary on the Gospel According to Saint Matthew*. 3 vols. ICC. Edinburgh: T&T Clark, 1988–97.
de Jonge, Marinus. "The Earliest Christian Use of *Christos*: Some Suggestions." *NTS* 32 (1986): 321–43.
—. *God's Final Envoy: Early Christology and Jesus' Own View of His Mission*. Grand Rapids: Eerdmans, 1998.

–. "The Use of the Word 'Anointed' in the Time of Jesus." *NovT* 8 (1966): 132–48.
Dinkler, Erich. "Peter's Confession and the 'Satan' Saying: The Problem of Jesus' Messiahship." Pages 169–202 in *The Future of Our Religious Past: Essays in Honour of Rudolf Bultmann*. Edited by James M. Robinson. Translated by Charles E. Carlston and Robert P. Scharlemann. New York: Harper & Row, 1971.
Dodd, C.H. *Historical Tradition in the Fourth Gospel*. Cambridge: Cambridge University Press, 1963.
Domeris, William R. "The Confession of Peter According to John 6:69." *TynBul* 44 (1993): 155–67.
Dunn, James D.G. "'Are You the Messiah?': Is the Crux of Mark 14.61–62 Resolvable?" Pages 1–22 in *Christology, Controversy and Community: New Testament Essays in Honour of David R. Catchpole*. David G. Horrell and Christopher M. Tuckett. NovTSupp 99. Brill: Leiden, 2000.
–. *Jesus Remembered*. Vol. 1 of *Christianity in the Making*. Grand Rapids: Eerdmans, 2003–.
–. "The Messianic Secret in Mark." Pages 116–31 in *The Messianic Secret*. Edited by Christopher Tuckett. IRT, 1. Philadelphia: Fortress, 1983.
–. *A New Perspective on Jesus: What the Quest for the Historical Jesus Missed*. Grand Rapids: Baker, 2005.
Edwards, James R. *The Gospel According to Mark*. Pillar New Testament Commentary. Grand Rapids: Eerdmans, 2002.
Ehrman, Bart D. *The New Testament: An Historical Introduction to the Early Christian Writings*. 3rd ed. Oxford: Oxford University Press, 2004.
Evans, Craig A. "Authenticity Criteria in Life of Jesus Research." *Christian Scholar's Review* 19 (1989): 6–31.
–. *Jesus and His Contemporaries: Comparative Studies*. AGJU 25. Leiden: Brill, 1995.
–. "Josephus on John the Baptist and Other Jewish Prophets of Deliverance." Pages 55–63 in *The Historical Jesus in Context*. Edited by Amy-Jill Levine, Dale C. Allison, Jr., and John Dominic Crossan. Princeton Readings in Religions. Princeton: Princeton University Press, 2006.
–. *Mark 8:27–16:20*. WBC 34b. Nashville: Nelson, 2001.
Feldmeier, Reinhard. "The Portrayal of Peter in the Synoptic Gospels." Pages 252–56 in *The Gospel and the Gospels*. Edited by Peter Stuhlmacher. Translated by John Vriend. Grand Rapids: Eerdmans, 1991.
Fitzmyer, Joseph A. *Essays on the Semitic Background of the New Testament*. Missoula: Scholars, 1974.
–. *The One Who is to Come*. Grand Rapids: Eerdmans, 2007.
–. *A Wandering Aramean: Collected Aramaic Essays*. SBLMS 25. Missoula, Mont.: Scholars, 1979.
Fletcher-Louis, Crispin H.T. "Jesus as the High Priestly Messiah: Part 1." *JSHJ* 4 (2006): 155–75.
–. "Jesus as the High Priestly Messiah: Part 2." *JSHJ* 5 (2007): 57–79.
Flusser, David. *Jesus*. 2nd ed. In collaboration with R. Steven Notley. Jerusalem: Magnes, 1997.
France, R.T. *The Gospel of Mark*. NIGTC. Grand Rapids: Eerdmans, 2002.
Fredriksen, Paula. *Jesus of Nazareth, King of the Jews: A Jewish Life and the Emergence of Christianity*. New York: Knopf, 1999.

Freyne, Sean. "A Galilean Messiah?" *ST* 55 (2001): 198–218.
–. "The Herodian Period." Pages 29–61 in *Redemption and Resistance: The Messianic Hopes of Jews and Christians in Antiquity*. Edited by Markus Bockmuehl and James Carleton Paget. London: T&T Clark, 2007.
–. *Jesus, a Jewish Galilean: A New Reading of the Jesus Story*. London: T&T Clark, 2004.
–. *Galilee, from Alexander the Great to Hadrian, 323 B. C. E. to 135 C. E.: A Study of Second Temple Judaism*. Studies in Judaism and Christianity in Antiquity. 5. Wilmington: Glazier, 1980.
Fuller, Reginald H. "The Criterion of Dissimilarity: The Wrong Tool?" Pages 44–53 in *Christological Perspectives: Essays in Honor of Harvey K. McArthur*. Edited by Robert F. Berkey and Sarah A. Edwards. New York: Pilgrim, 1982.
–. *The Foundations of New Testament Christology*. New York: Scribner, 1965.
Funk, Robert W., and The Jesus Seminar. *The Acts of Jesus: The Search for the Authentic Deeds of Jesus*. San Francisco: HarperSanFrancisco, 1998.
Funk, Robert W., Roy W. Hoover, and The Jesus Seminar. *The Five Gospels: The Search for the Authentic Words of Jesus*. New York: Macmillan, 1993.
García Martínez, Florentino, ed. *The Dead Sea Scrolls Translated: The Qumran Texts in English*. 2nd. Translated by Wilfred G. E. Watson. Leiden: Brill, 1996.
–. "Messianic Hopes in the Qumran Writings." Pages 159–89 in *The People of the Dead Sea Scrolls: Their Writings, Beliefs and Practices*. Edited by Florentino García Martínez and Julio Trebolle Barrera. Translated by Wilfred G. E. Watson. Leiden: Brill, 1995.
Gerhardsson, Birger. "The Christology of Matthew." Pages 14–32 in *Who Do You Say That I Am? Essays on Christology: In Honor of Jack Dean Kingsbury*. Edited by Mark Allan Powell and David R. Bauer. Louisville: Westminster John Knox, 1999.
Goppelt, Leonhard. *Theology of the New Testament*. 2 vols. Translated by John E. Alsup. Grand Rapids: Eerdmans, 1981–82.
Goulder, Michael D. *Midrash and Lection in Matthew: The Speaker's Lectures in Biblical Studies, 1969–71*. London: SPCK, 1974.
–. *St. Paul Versus St. Peter: A Tale of Two Missions*. Louisville: Westminster John Knox, 1994.
Gundry, Robert H. *Mark: A Commentary on His Apology for the Cross*. Grand Rapids: Eerdmans, 1993.
–. *Matthew: A Commentary on His Handbook for a Mixed Church Under Persecution*. 2nd ed. Grand Rapids: Eerdmans, 1994.
Guthrie, Donald. *New Testament Theology*. Downers Grove: InterVarsity, 1981.
Hagner, Donald A. *Matthew 14–28*. WBC 33b. Dallas: Word, 1995.
Hahn, Ferdinand. *The Titles of Jesus in Christology; Their History in Early Christianity*. Translated by Harold Knight and George Ogg. London: Lutterworth, 1969.
Hampel, Volker. *Menschensohn und historischer Jesus: ein Rätselwort als Schlüssel zum messianischen Selbstverständnis Jesu*. Neukirchen-Vluyn: Neukirchener Verlag, 1990.
Hare, Douglas R. A. *The Son of Man Tradition*. Minneapolis: Fortress, 1990.
Henderson, Suzanne Watts. *Christology and Discipleship in the Gospel of Mark*. SNTSMS 135. Cambridge: Cambridge University Press, 2006.

Hengel, Martin. *Crucifixion in the Ancient World and the Folly of the Message of the Cross*. Philadelphia: Fortress, 1977.

–. *The Four Gospels and the One Gospel of Jesus Christ: An Investigation of the Collection and Origin of the Canonical Gospels*. Translated by John Bowden. Harrisburg: Trinity, 2000.

–. "Jesus, The Messiah of Israel: The Debate About the 'Messianic Mission' of Jesus." Pages 324–49 in *Authenticating the Activities of Jesus*. Edited by Bruce D. Chilton and Craig A. Evans. NTTS 28.2. Leiden: Brill, 1999.

–. *Studies in Early Christology*. Edinburgh: T&T Clark, 1995.

–. *Studies in the Gospel of Mark*. Translated by John Bowden. Philadelphia: Fortress, 1985.

–. *Der unterschätzte Petrus: zwei Studien*. Tübingen: Mohr Siebeck, 2006.

–. *The Zealots: Investigations Into the Freedom Movement in the Period from Herod I Until 70 A. D.* 2d ed. Edinburgh: T&T Clark, 1989.

Hengel, Martin, and Anna Maria Schwemer. *Der messianische Anspruch Jesu und die Anfänge der Christologie: Vier Studien*. WUNT 2.138. Tübingen: Mohr Siebeck, 2001.

Higgins, A. J. B. *The Son of Man in the Teaching of Jesus*. SNTSMS 39. Cambridge: Cambridge University Press, 1980.

Holmén, Tom, ed. *Jesus from Judaism to Christianity: Continuum Approaches to the Historical Jesus*. LNTS 352. London: T&T Clark, 2007.

–. "Doubts About Double Dissimilarity: Restructuring the Main Criterion of Jesus-of-History Research." Pages 47–80 in *Authenticating the Words of Jesus*. Edited by Bruce D. Chilton and Craig A. Evans. NTTS 28.1. Leiden: Brill, 1999.

Hooker, Morna D. "Christology and Methodology." *NTS* 17 (1970–71): 480–87.

–. *A Commentary on the Gospel According to St. Mark*. BNTC. London: A&C Black, 1991.

–. "On Using the Wrong Tool." *Theology* 75 (1972): 570–81.

–. *The Son of Man in Mark: A Study of the Background of the Term "Son of Man" and Its Use in St. Mark's Gospel*. London: SPCK, 1967.

Horbury, William. *Jewish Messianism and the Cult of Christ*. London: SCM, 1998.

Horsley, Richard A. *Archaeology, History, and Society in Galilee: The Social Context of Jesus and the Rabbis*. Valley Forge: Trinity, 1996.

–. *Galilee: History, Politics, People*. Valley Forge: Trinity, 1995.

–. *Hearing the Whole Story: The Politics of Plot in Mark's Gospel*. Louisville: Westminster John Knox, 2001.

–. "Jesus and Judaism: Christian Perspectives." Pages 53–79 in *Eusebius, Christianity, and Judaism*. Edited by Harold W. Attridge and Gohei Hata. StPB. Leiden: Brill, 1992.

–. *Jesus and the Spiral of Violence: Popular Jewish Resistance in Roman Palestine*. San Francisco: Harper & Row, 1987.

Horsley, Richard A., and John S. Hanson. *Bandits, Prophets, and Messiahs: Popular Movements in the Time of Jesus*. New Voices in Biblical Studies. Minneapolis: Winston, 1985.

Horstmann, Maria. *Studien zur markinischen Christologie: Mk 8,27–9,13 als Zugang zum Christusbild des zweiten Evangeliums*. NTAbh 6. Münster: Aschendorff, 1969.

Hurtado, Larry W. *Lord Jesus Christ: Devotion to Jesus in Earliest Christianity.* Grand Rapids: Eerdmans, 2003.
Kazen, Thomas. "The Coming Son of Man Revisited." *JSHJ* 5 (2007): 155–74.
–. "Son of Man as Kingdom Imagery: Jesus Between Corporate Symbol and Individual Redeemer Figure." Pages 87–108 in *Jesus from Judaism to Christianity: Continuum Approaches to the Historical Jesus.* Edited by Tom Holmén. LNTS 352. London: T&T Clark, 2007.
Kähler, Christoph. "Zur Form- und Traditionsgeschichte von Matth. XVI. 17–19." *NTS* 23 (1977): 36–58.
Kähler, Martin. *The So-Called Historical Jesus and the Historic, Biblical Christ.* Translated by Carl E. Braaten. Philadelphia: Fortress, 1964.
Käsemann, Ernst. *Essays on New Testament Themes.* Trans. W.J. Montague. SBT 41. Naperville: Allenson, 1964.
Keener, Craig S. *The Gospel of John.* 2 vols. Peabody: Hendrickson, 2003.
Kilpatrick, G.D. *The Origins of the Gospel According to St. Matthew.* Oxford: Clarendon, 1950.
Kim, Seyoon. *The "Son of Man" as the Son of God.* WUNT 30. Tübingen: Mohr Siebeck, 1983.
Kingsbury, Jack Dean. *Matthew: Structure, Christology, Kingdom.* Philadelphia: Fortress, 1975.
Klausner, Joseph. *Jesus of Nazareth: His Life, Times, and Teaching.* Translated by Herbert Danby. New York: Macmillan, 1945.
Koester, Helmut. *From Jesus to the Gospels: Interpreting the New Testament in Its Context.* Minneapolis: Fortress, 2007.
Köstenberger, Andreas J. *John.* BECNT. Grand Rapids: Baker, 2004.
Kutsko, John. "Caesarea Philippi." Page 803 in vol. 1 of *Anchor Bible Dictionary.* 6 vols. Edited by David N. Freedman. New York: Doubleday, 1992.
Kümmel, Werner Georg. *The Theology of the New Testament According to Its Major Witnesses: Jesus-Paul-John.* Translated by John E. Steely. Nashville: Abingdon, 1973.
Lane, William L. *The Gospel of Mark.* NICNT. Grand Rapids: Eerdmans, 1974.
Lapham, F. *Peter: The Myth, the Man and the Writings: A Study of Early Petrine Text and Tradition.* JSNTSup 239. London: Sheffield, 2003.
Lindars, Barnabas. *The Gospel of John.* Edited by Barnabas Lindars. NCB. London: Oliphants, 1972.
–. *Jesus, Son of Man: A Fresh Examination of the Son of Man Sayings in the Gospels in the Light of Recent Research.* Grand Rapids: Eerdmans, 1983.
Luz, Ulrich. *Matthew 8–20.* Translated by James E. Crouch. Hermeneia. Minneapolis: Fortress, 2001.
Mack, Burton L. *A Myth of Innocence: Mark and Christian Origins.* Philadelphia: Fortress, 1988.
McKnight, Scot. "Calling Jesus *Mamzer.*" *JSHJ* 1 (2003): 73–103.
–. "Jesus and the Twelve." *BBR* 11 (2001): 203–31.
–. "Jesus of Nazareth." Pages 149–76 in *The Face of New Testament Studies: A Survey of Recent Research.* Edited by Scot McKnight and Grant R. Osborne. Grand Rapids: Baker, 2004.
McLaren, James. *Why Jesus Died: An Historian's Perspective.* LNTS 356. London: T&T Clark, 2008.

Mann, C. S. *Mark*. AB 27. Garden City: Doubleday, 1986.
Manson, T. W. *The Sayings of Jesus*. 1937. Repr., Grand Rapids: Eerdmans, 1979.
—. *The Servant-Messiah: A Study of the Public Ministry of Jesus*. 1953. Repr., Grand Rapids: Baker, 1977.
Marcus, Joel. *Mark 1–8*. AB 27. New York: Doubleday, 2000.
Marshall, I. Howard. *New Testament Theology: Many Witnesses, One Gospel*. Downers Grove: InterVarsity, 2004.
—. *The Origins of New Testament Christology*. Issues in Contemporary Theology. Downers Grove: InterVarsity, 1976.
Martin, Ralph P. *Mark: Evangelist and Theologian*. Grand Rapids: Zondervan, 1972.
Martin, Raymond. *The Elusive Messiah: A Philosophical Overview of the Quest for the Historical Jesus*. Boulder: Westview, 1999.
Mason, Steve. *Josephus and the New Testament*. Peabody: Hendrickson, 1992.
Meeks, Wayne A. *The Prophet-King. Moses Traditions and the Johannine Christology*. NovTSup 14. Leiden: Brill, 1967.
Meier, John P. *Companions and Competitors*. Vol. 3 of *A Marginal Jew: Rethinking the Historical Jesus*. ABRL. New York: Doubleday, 2001.
—. *The Roots of the Problem and the Person*. Vol. 1 of *A Marginal Jew: Rethinking the Historical Jesus*. ABRL. New York: Doubleday, 1991.
Meyer, Ben F. *The Aims of Jesus*. London: SCM, 1979.
—. "Jesus Christ." Pages 773–96 in vol. 3 of *Anchor Bible Dictionary*. 6 vols. Edited by David N. Freedman. New York: Doubleday, 1992.
Moloney, Francis J. "The Fourth Gospel and the Jesus of History." *NTS* 46 (2000): 42–58.
—. *The Gospel of Mark: A Commentary*. Peabody: Hendrickson, 2002.
Morris, Leon. *The Gospel According to John*. NICNT. Grand Rapids: Eerdmans, 1995.
—. *The Gospel According to Matthew*. Pillar New Testament Commentary. Grand Rapids: Eerdmans, 1992.
Moule, C. F. D. *The Origin of Christology*. Cambridge: Cambridge University Press, 1977.
Mowinckel, Sigmund. *He That Cometh: The Messiah Concept in the Old Testament and Later Judaism*. 1956. Repr., Grand Rapids: Eerdmans, 2005.
Müller, Mogens. *The Expression "Son of Man" and the Development of Christology: A History of Interpretation*. Copenhagen International Seminar. London: Equinox, 2008.
Myers, Ched, Marie Dennis, Cynthia Moe-Lobeda, Joseph Nangle, Karen Lattea, and Stuart Taylor. *"Say to This Mountain": Mark's Story of Discipleship*. Maryknoll: Orbis, 1996.
Neusner, Jacob. *Messiah in Context: Israel's History and Destiny in Formative Judaism*. Philadelphia: Fortress, 1984.
Neusner, Jacob, William Scott Green, and Ernest S. Frerichs, eds. *Judaisms and Their Messiahs at the Turn of the Christian Era*. Cambridge: Cambridge University Press, 1987.
Nickelsburg, George W. E. "Enoch, Levi, and Peter: Recipients of Revelation in Upper Galilee." *JBL* 100 (1981): 575–600.

O'Day, Gail R. "The Gospel of John: Introduction, Commentary, and Reflections." Pages 491–865 in vol. 9 of *The New Interpreter's Bible*. 12 vols. Nashville: Abingdon, 1995.
Perkins, Pheme. "The Gospel of Mark: Introduction, Commentary, and Reflections." Pages 507–733 in vol. 8 of *The New Interpreter's Bible*. 12 vols. Nashville: Abingdon, 1995.
—. *Peter: Apostle for the Whole Church*. Minneapolis: Fortress, 2000.
Perrin, Norman. *Rediscovering the Teaching of Jesus*. New York: Harper & Row, 1967.
Pesch, Rudolf. *Das Markusevangelium*. 2 vols. HTKNT 2. Freiburg im Breisgau: Herder, 1977.
Pokorný, Petr. *The Genesis of Christology: Foundations for a Theology of the New Testament*. Translated by Marcus Lefébure. Edinburgh: T&T Clark, 1987.
Polkow, Dennis. "Method and Criteria for Historical Research." Pages 336–56 in *SBL Seminar Papers, 1987*. SBLSP 26. Atlanta: Scholars, 1987.
Porter, Stanley E. *The Criteria for Authenticity in Historical-Jesus Research: Previous Discussion and New Proposals*. JSNTSup 191. Sheffield: Sheffield Academic Press, 2000.
Quast, Kevin. *Peter and the Beloved Disciple: Figures for a Community in Crisis*. JSNTSup 32. Sheffield: JSOT Press, 1989.
Rajak, Tessa. *Josephus: The Historian and His Society*. London: Duckworth, 1983.
Räisänen, Heikki. *The "Messianic Secret" in Mark's Gospel*. Translated by Christopher Tuckett. Studies of the New Testament and Its World. Edinburgh: T&T Clark, 1990.
Rousseau, John J., and Rami Arav. *Jesus and His World: An Archaeological and Cultural Dictionary*. Minneapolis: Fortress, 1995.
Rowland, Christopher. *Christian Origins: An Account of the Setting and Character of the Most Important Messianic Sect of Judaism*. 2nd ed. London: SPCK, 2002.
Safrai, Shemuel, and Menahem Stern, eds. *The Jewish People in the First Century: Historical Geography, Political History, Social, Cultural and Religious Life and Institutions*. Vol. 1, section 1 of *Compendia Rerum Iudaicarum ad Novum Testamentum*. Edited by Shemuel Safrai and Menahem Stern. Assen: Van Gorcum, 1974.
Sanders, E. P. *Jesus and Judaism*. Philadelphia: Fortress, 1985.
Santos, Narry F. *Slave of All: The Paradox of Authority and Servanthood in the Gospel of Mark*. JSNTSup 237. London: Sheffield, 2003.
Sänger, Dieter. *Gottessohn und Menschensohn: exegetische Studien zu zwei Paradigmen biblischer Intertextualität*. Biblisch-theologische Studien, 67. Neukirchen-Vluyn: Neukirchener, 2004.
Schalit, Abraham. "Josephus Flavius." Pages 11:435–42 in *Encyclopaedia Judaica*. 2nd ed. 22 vols. Edited by Fred Skolnik and Michael Berenbaum. Detroit: Macmillan; Jerusalem: Keter, 2007.
Schnabel, Eckhard J. "The Silence of Jesus: The Galilean Rabbi Who Was More Than a Prophet." Pages 203–57 in *Authenticating the Words of Jesus*. Edited by Bruce D. Chilton and Craig A. Evans. NTTS 28.1. Leiden: Brill, 1999.
Schnackenburg, Rudolf. *The Gospel According to John*. 3 vols. New York: Seabury, 1980–82.

Schürer, Emil. *The History of the Jewish People in the Age of Jesus Christ (175 B. C. – A. D. 135)*. New English ed. 3 vols. Edited by Geza Vermes, Fergus Millar, and Matthew Black. Edinburgh: T&T Clark, 1973–87.

Schwartz, Seth. *Josephus and Judaean Politics*. Columbia Studies in the Classical Tradition, 18. Leiden: Brill, 1990.

Schwemer, Anna Maria. "Jesus Christus als Prophet, König und Priester: Das *munus triplex* und die frühe Christologie." Pages 165–230 in *Der messianische Anspruch Jesu und die Anfänge der Christologie: Vier Studien*. By Martin Hengel and Anna Maria Schwemer. WUNT 2.138. Tübingen: Mohr Siebeck, 2001.

Smith, Morton. *Jesus the Magician*. San Francisco: Harper & Row, 1978.

Stein, Robert H. "The 'Criteria' for Authenticity." Pages 225–63 in *Studies of History and Tradition in the Four Gospels*. Edited by R.T. France and David Wenham. Gospel Perspectives, 1. Sheffield: JSOT Press, 1980.

–. *Mark*. BECNT. Grand Rapids: Baker, 2008.

–. *The Method and Message of Jesus' Teachings*. Rev. ed. Louisville: Westminster John Knox, 1994.

Strecker, Georg. "The Pseudo-Clementines: Kerygmata Petrou." Pages 531–40 in vol. 2 of *New Testament Apocrypha*. Rev. ed. 2 vols. Edited by Wilhelm Schneemelcher and R. McL. Wilson. Louisville: Westminster John Knox, 1990–91.

Stuhlmacher, Peter. "The Messianic Son of Man: Jesus' Claim to Deity." Pages 325–44 in *The Historical Jesus in Recent Research*. Edited by James D.G. Dunn and Scot McKnight. Sources for Biblical and Theological Study. Winona Lake: Eisenbrauns, 2005.

–. "My Experience with Biblical Theology." Pages 174–91 in *Biblical Theology: Retrospect and Prospect*. Edited by Scott J. Hafemann. Downers Grove: InterVarsity, 2002.

Tabor, James D. "'Are You the One?': The Textual Dynamics of Messianic Self-Identity." Pages 179–89 in *Knowing the End from the Beginning: The Prophetic, the Apocalyptic and Their Relationship*. Lester L. Grabbe and Robert D. Haak. JSPSup 46. London: T&T Clark, 2003.

Talmon, S. "The Concepts of *Māšîaḥ* and Messianism in Early Judaism." Pages 79–115 in *The Messiah: Developments in Earliest Judaism and Christianity*. Edited by Charlesworth. James H. Minneapolis: Fortress, 1992.

Taylor, Vincent. *The Gospel According to St. Mark*. 2nd ed. London: Macmillan, 1966.

Theissen, Gerd, and Annette Merz. *The Historical Jesus: A Comprehensive Guide*. Translated by John Bowden. Minneapolis: Fortress, 1998.

Theissen, Gerd, and Dagmar Winter. *The Quest for the Plausible Jesus: The Question of Criteria*. Translated by M. Eugene Boring. Louisville: Westminster John Knox, 2002.

Tuckett, Christopher M., ed. *The Messianic Secret*. IRT, 1. Philadelphia: Fortress, 1983.

–. "The Son of Man and Daniel 7: Inclusive Aspects of Early Christologies." Pages 164–90 in *Christian Origins: Worship, Belief, and Society*. Edited by Kieran J. O'Mahony. JSNTSup 241. London: Sheffield, 2003.

–. *Christology and the New Testament: Jesus and His Earliest Followers*. Louisville: Westminster John Knox, 2001.

Tzaferis, Vassilios. "Cults and Deities Worshipped at Caesarea Philippi-Banias." Pages 190–201 in *Priests, Prophets, and Scribes: Essays on the Formation and Heritage of Second Temple Judaism in Honour of Joseph Blenkinsopp*. Edited by Eugene Ulrich, John W. Wright, Robert P. Carroll, and Philip R. Davies. JSOTSup 149. Sheffield: JSOT Press, 1992.
Vermès, Géza. *Jesus the Jew: A Historian's Reading of the Gospels*. London: Collins, 1973.
–. "The Use of בר נשא/בר נש in Jewish Aramaic." Pages 310–30 in *An Aramaic Approach to the Gospels and Acts*. 3rd ed. Edited by Matthew Black. Oxford: Clarendon, 1967.
Vögtle, Anton. *Die "Gretchenfrage" des Menschensohn-Problems: Bilanz und Perspektive*. QD, 152. Freiburg im Breisgau: Herder, 1994.
Webb, Robert L. "Jesus' Baptism: Its Historicity and Implications." *BBR* 10 (2000): 261–309.
–. *John the Baptizer and Prophet: A Socio-Historical Study*. JSNTSup 62. Sheffield: JSOT Press, 1991.
Weeden, Theodore J. *Mark-Traditions in Conflict*. Philadelphia: Fortress, 1971.
Wiarda, Timothy. *Peter in the Gospels: Pattern, Personality, and Relationship*. WUNT 2.127. Tübingen: Mohr Siebeck, 2000.
Wilckens, Ulrich. *Geschichte des Wirkens Jesu in Galiläa*. Vol. 1, Part 1 of *Theologie des Neuen Testaments*. 2nd ed. Neukirchen-Vluyn: Neukirchener Verlag, 2005.
Wilkins, Michael J. *The Concept of Disciple in Matthew's Gospel: As Reflected in the Use of the Term Μαθητής*. NovTSup 59; Leiden: Brill, 1988.
Willitts, Joel. "Presuppositions and Procedures in the Study of the 'Historical Jesus': Or, Why I Decided Not to be a 'Historical Jesus' Scholar." *JSHJ* 3 (2005): 61–108.
Wink, Walter. *Engaging the Powers: Discernment and Resistance in a World of Domination*. Minneapolis: Fortress, 1992.
Witherington, Ben, III. *The Christology of Jesus*. Minneapolis: Fortress, 1990.
–. *The Gospel of Mark: A Socio-Rhetorical Commentary*. Grand Rapids: Eerdmans, 2001.
–. *The Many Faces of the Christ: The Christologies of the New Testament and Beyond*. Crossroad Companions to the New Testament. New York: Crossroad, 1998.
Wrede, William. *The Messianic Secret*. Translated by J. C. G. Greig. London: Clarke, 1971.
Wright, N. T. *Jesus and the Victory of God*. Vol. 2 of *Christian Origins and the Question of God*. Minneapolis: Fortress, 1996.
–. "Theology, History and Jesus: A Response to Maurice Casey and Clive Marsh." *JSNT* 69 (1998): 105–12.
Xeravits, Géza G. *King, Priest, Prophet: Positive Eschatological Protagonists of the Qumran Library*. STDJ, 47. Leiden: Brill, 2003.

Chapter 9

Jesus' Royal Entry into Jerusalem[1]

BRENT KINMAN

1. Introduction

The image is familiar: enthusiastic crowds welcome Jesus into Jerusalem and hail him as the one who comes "in the name of the Lord" as he humbly approaches the city on a donkey's colt. Days later, the crowd's enthusiasm turns out to have been short lived, for they also demand his death by crucifixion (Mark 15:13; Luke 23:21; John 19:6). This image could be culled from any one of several movies that depict the last days of Jesus – but is it the image of the Gospel records; and, more critically, is it a fair depiction of the historical Jesus?

Jesus' Entry into Jerusalem is noteworthy in several ways: (1) it is one of a handful of narratives to appear in each of the four Gospels (Matt 21:1–11; Mark 11:1–10; Luke 19:28–40; John 12:12–15); (2) it signals the beginning of Jesus' final week in Jerusalem; and, (3) it was an act open to great misunderstanding by early witnesses to the event. Such misunderstanding could come from friends, enemies, or merely detached onlookers, as well as from early readers of the Gospels. These points would seem to make the Entry an ideal candidate for careful scrutiny by members of the Jesus Seminar (hereafter JS), and by historical Jesus scholars more generally, yet such careful attention has rarely materialized. The Entry is excluded without comment from the JS's recent book about what events the JS regards as authentic.[2] This omission cannot be taken to suggest there is a consensus of critical opinion on the subject, for many critical scholars regard as authentic the Entry described in the Gospels – including at least one prominent member of the Seminar itself![3]

---

[1] This essay is a revised and expanded version of that published as Brent Kinman, "Jesus' Royal Entry Into Jerusalem," *BBR* 15 (2005): 223–60.

[2] Robert W. Funk and The Jesus Seminar, *The Acts of Jesus: The Search for the Authentic Deeds of Jesus* (San Francisco: HarperSanFrancisco, 1998). The core event of the Entry can only manage a "gray" score, while the individual Gospel accounts of it all score "black."

[3] So Marcus J. Borg, *Jesus, A New Vision: Spirit, Culture, and the Life of Discipleship*

It is nevertheless important to ask and understand why so many critical scholars doubt the event's authenticity that seems, on its face, to be so well attested. The objections generally fall along two lines. The first we might label the "christological objection." Jesus could not have selected the colt and ridden it into Jerusalem as the Gospels[4] describe because, it is thought, to do so would have been out of character. He seems consistently to eschew messianic identification in the earliest traditions found in the Gospels – but choosing to ride on a colt into Jerusalem is clearly a messianic act, so this action is inconsistent with the overall picture of Jesus we possess. Rudolf Bultmann long ago anticipated this objection to historicity when he formulated the classic statement: "… die Voraussetzungen, die man machen müßte, um den Bericht als geschichtlich anzusehen – daß Jesus die Erfüllung von Sach 9,9 inszenieren wollte, und daß die Menge den Esel sogleich als messianisches Reittier erkannte – , sind absurd."[5] It may be stipulated from the outset that very few historians who raise this particular objection doubt Jesus came to Jerusalem at the outset of his final week. Instead, they question the particular details of the biblical accounts of his arrival, details which, they assert, are more "christological" than "historical."[6] Upon closer

---

(San Francisco: Harper & Row, 1987), 173–75. For examples of others who accept the Entry as authentic, see also C. H. Dodd, *The Founder of Christianity* (London: Collins, 1971), 141–44. More recently see A. E. Harvey, *Jesus and the Constraints of History* (The Bampton Lectures, 1980; London: Duckworth, 1982), 120–28, and Paula Fredriksen, *Jesus of Nazareth, King of the Jews: A Jewish Life and the Emergence of Christianity* (New York: Knopf, 1999), 243–55.

[4] Strictly speaking, only the Synoptic Gospels have Jesus arranging to ride the colt beforehand; John appears to view Jesus' riding as spontaneous – there will be more to say about this below.

[5] Rudolf Bultmann, *Die Geschichte der synoptischen Tradition* (2nd ed.; Göttingen: Vandenhoeck & Ruprecht, 1931), 281. Eng: "The presuppositions, which one must make in order to view the report as historical – that Jesus wanted to produce the fulfillment of Zech. 9:9, and that the masses immediately recognized the donkey as a messianic mount – are absurd" (my translation). He does not go so far as to say that Jesus did not come to Jerusalem, only that the elements of the story that make it notable were probably missing.

[6] Of course, this assertion immediately brings into play the issue of presuppositions and criteria because it is not immediately obvious why a regal or messianic self-affirmation on the part of Jesus cannot be "historical" (apart from the *Voraussetzungen*, as Bultmann might say, that require the distinction *a priori*). Indeed, the penetrating arguments set forward years ago by Morna D. Hooker concerning method ("Christology and Methodology," *NTS* 17 [1970–71]: 480–87) and I. Howard Marshall concerning the relationship between history and theology (*Luke: Historian and Theologian* [Grand Rapids: Zondervan, 1970]) have rarely been engaged by skeptics, much less answered satisfactorily. This is not the place to examine the methodological flaws that characterize some JS scholarship; others have done that well enough and at length. See, for example, Ben Witherington, III, *The Jesus Quest: The Third Search for the Jew of Nazareth* (Downers Grove, Ill.: InterVarsity, 1995), 42–57; also Stanley E. Porter, *The Criteria for Authenticity in Historical-Jesus Research: Previous Discussion and New Proposals* (JSNTSup 191; Sheffield:

examination we discover that this objection to authenticity has typically not so much been argued as asserted.[7]

Sheffield Academic Press, 2000); Craig L. Blomberg, *The Historical Reliability of John's Gospel* (Downers Grove: InterVarsity, 2001), 63–66; and, perhaps most provocatively, Luke Timothy Johnson, *The Real Jesus: The Misguided Quest for the Historical Jesus and the Truth of the Traditional Gospels* (San Francisco: HarperSanFrancisco, 1996). In addition to these, see the helpful background essay "The Problem of Historical Knowledge" in William Lane Craig, *Reasonable Faith: Christian Truth and Apologetics* (Wheaton: Crossway, 1994), 157–91. Having said that, for the purpose of this study, it may be stipulated that when consistently and conscientiously employed, the criteria for authenticity of (i) multiple attestation, (ii) embarrassment, (iii) dissimilarity, (iv) effect (or "explanation"), (v) memorable content or form, (vi) language and environment, and (vii) coherence are both valid and useful. These criteria are ably summarized by Mark Allen Powell, *Jesus as a Figure in History: How Modern Historians View the Man from Galilee* (Louisville: Westminster John Knox, 1998), 46–50. See also in this volume ch. 2, § 4.1. In my view the Gospels represent the attempts of various first century Christians to chronicle important features of the Jesus story for particular but not insular audiences. This would certainly be the case for Luke, who specifies that he is writing for "Theophilus" (Luke 1:3; Acts 1:1); it may well be true for others, but on this note see the caution sounded by Richard Bauckham, "For Whom Were Gospels Written?" in *The Gospels for All Christians: Rethinking the Gospel Audiences* (ed. Richard Bauckham; Grand Rapids: Eerdmans, 1998), 9–48. As such, there was a genuine interest to know and preserve what Jesus said and did as well as to highlight those features of his life adjudged to be most salient to the first readers/hearers of the Gospels by the Gospel writers. The Gospels were written by Christians, that is, by those with a faith commitment at the time of writing to the veracity and personal relevance of the Jesus story (e.g., Luke 1:1–4; John 20:30–31), but while this undoubtedly influenced the selection and/or exclusion of material, it does not necessarily follow that a faith commitment produces historical error and distortion. To be sure, many people, including some scholars, believe that it does, but that assertion lies in the realm of opinion, not fact nor logical necessity. I realize this last statement, included as it is in a paper that arguably is part of the "Third Quest," may well leave me open to Robert W. Funk's charge of engaging in an "apologetic ploy" (*Honest to Jesus: Jesus for a New Millennium* [San Francisco: HarperSanFrancisco, 1996], 65; so be it – I intend to go where the evidence leads me. Craig A. Evans pointedly suggests that religious bias does not necessarily "invalidate historical Jesus research [any more] than the love of art invalidates the work of an art critic or the love of science invalidates the research of a scientist" ("The Need for the 'Historical Jesus': A Response to Jacob Neusner's Review of Crossan and Meier," *BBR* 4 [1994]: 133).

[7] Jürgen Becker (*Jesus of Nazareth* [trans. James E. Crouch; Berlin: De Gruyter, 1998]) supplies a good contemporary example of this. Early in the book he attempts to lay out for the reader in an even-handed fashion the criteria by which he will judge authentic Jesus material. He says on p. 15, "There is an increasingly positive attitude today about the trustworthiness of the synoptic tradition, especially when compared with the early days of Form Criticism. This change is due in part to the fact that today we recognize two false judgments that earlier fed historical skepticism: the assumption that only ideally formed, simple traditions can be original, and an exaggerated view of the creative power of the church to which everything was attributed at the slightest suspicion that something might not be authentic. While it is true that we needed to move beyond the earlier skepticism, today's more positive attitude unfortunately reveals a wholesale assertion within a general milieu, which for historical scholarship simply is not adequate. Therefore, we conclude this section on methodology by emphasizing again that we must submit both general skepticism and general trust to trial by fire and that we can do that only in the analysis of each individual tradition."

The second category of objection to the Entry's historicity we might call the "historical anomaly objection." E.P. Sanders raises the question with customary flair: "If the entry was what we are told it was, why did it take so long for the Romans to execute Jesus? Why were the disciples not rounded up and killed? ... The Romans were not slow to act when sedition threatened ..."[8] Sanders's skepticism rests on the assumption that a demonstration of the sort found, or, to anticipate a later conclusion, *thought* to be found in the Gospels would have provoked a swift Roman response. But is Sanders's assumption of the likelihood of Roman intervention warranted? Equally important, what does he mean by "if the entry was what we are told it was" – what *are* we told? How many of the assumptions built into the objection of Sanders and others are open to question?

Yet when it comes to Jesus' Entry, Becker's fire seems to have run out of gas. He writes, "In its present form the account is heavily christological. If it preserves any historical recollection at all, it might be that Jesus was so well known among the pilgrims from Galilee that they surrounded him wherever he appeared" (p. 345). Becker does not identify those features of the account he finds historically troublesome, nor does he explain precisely what about them requires a critical historian to regard the account as historically problematic. A notable exception to this lack of argumentation is David Catchpole ("The 'Triumphal' Entry," in *Jesus and the Politics of His Day* [ed. E. Bammel and C. F. D. Moule; Cambridge: Cambridge University Press, 1984], 319–34). He argues that Mark's entry narrative is built on the model of other entry stories from antiquity where a great leader enters a town to acclaim after achieving victory or receiving kingly authority. For Catchpole, since Jesus' victories and putative kingship are features of Markan redaction, the historical basis for the Entry narrative is undercut and with it the historicity of the Entry itself. But Catchpole's arguments are flawed. In the first place, his conclusions rely on Mark as the sole primary source for information about the Entry and, as J. F. Coakley observes, "it may be noticed how hasty is his [Catchpole's] pronouncement against the possibility that there was any account of the messianic entry independent of Mark's" ("Jesus' Messianic Entry Into Jerusalem [John 12:12–19 Par]," *JTS* 46 [1995]: 466). As we shall see, there is a persuasive case for John containing tradition independent of Mark in the matter of Jesus' Entry. A second obstacle to accepting Catchpole's argument is that he implies Jesus' Entry is messianic (as we shall see, this characterization is also open to question), but its messianism is built on prior healings and his identification as a son of David (both of which are historically unreliable, in his view). But even if the healings and so on were proved historically untenable, Jesus could yet have made a distinctive Entry into Jerusalem; that is to say, there is nothing to make the features that make the Entry most noteworthy impossible – Jesus' ride on a colt to the acclaim of witnesses – save the *a priori* assumptions that a prior recognition of kingship based on observation of Jesus' miracles is necessary to the Entry to have occurred. Put somewhat differently, Ben Witherington (*The Christology of Jesus* [Minneapolis: Fortress, 1990], 104) notes that "Catchpole appears to be guilty of a common fallacy when pursuing a *formgeschichtliche* approach to a narrative: he assumes that because the narrative seem to fit a particular formal pattern, one can therefore draw conclusions about the historical authenticity of the narrative's essential content."

[8] E. P. Sanders, *Jesus and Judaism* (Philadelphia: Fortress, 1985), 306. Sanders contends that the Gospel accounts of Jesus' Entry into Jerusalem are, historically speaking, merely "probable" (p. 307). His views may have changed over the years; see his more recent *The Historical Figure of Jesus* (London: Penguin, 1993), 253–54, 272.

Related to but somewhat beyond the question of authenticity or historicity is the matter of what meaning Jesus intended to convey through the event (assuming, for the moment, that it bore some resemblance to the Gospel accounts of it). Was the Entry, as many think, designed to identify him as a particularly humble king?[9] Conversely, perhaps (as S. G. F. Brandon argues) it was deliberately provocative: an act designed to "challenge both the Jewish leaders and the Romans."[10]

In this essay I assess the historical trustworthiness of the Gospel accounts of Jesus' Entry into Jerusalem by (1) examining them in the light of various critical criteria for authenticity, and (2) giving a plausible sketch of "what *really* happened." In the course of doing this I will address the two objections against authenticity just raised and explore the issue of Jesus' intentions. I propose to argue that the Entry is best understood as a deliberately provocative – indeed, *royal* – act on the part of Jesus, one that represented a shift in his self-presentation to Israel. I further argue that despite its implicitly provocative nature, it was in reality a relatively modest affair – one easily overlooked by the Roman authorities charged with maintaining order at the Passover season.

2. The Historicity of Jesus' Royal Entry

Several criteria traditionally employed by Jesus scholars to assess historical reliability argue for a preliminary verdict in favor of the Entry's historicity.

2.1. The Criterion of Multiple Attestation

The Entry is not mentioned in extra-biblical sources such as the *Gospel of Thomas*. This is not surprising, since that and similar works are dedicated to the words (as over against the acts) of Jesus. This being the case, the possibility for multiple attestation is greatly reduced. Each canonical gospel has Jesus coming to Jerusalem on a colt to the royal acclaim of his disciples (Matt 21:1–11; Mark 11:1–10; Luke 21:28–40; John 12:12–15). The Synoptic Question easily explains the narrative's appearance in Mark, Matthew, and Luke (pointing to a Marcan tradition)[11] – but John's account differs from

---

[9] For example, J. M. Creed, *The Gospel According to St. Luke* (London: Macmillan, 1930), 240; Willem Adolf Visser't Hooft, "Triumphalism in the Gospels," *SJT* 38 (1985): 491–504; Witherington, *The Christology of Jesus*, 104–7; Markus Bockmuehl, *This Jesus: Martyr, Lord, Messiah* (Edinburgh: T&T Clark, 1994), 91.

[10] S. G. F. Brandon, *Jesus and the Zealots: A Study of the Political Factor in Primitive Christianity* (Manchester: Manchester University Press, 1967), 349–50.

[11] While acknowledging the usefulness of "Q" as a designation for material common to Matthew and Luke (but not Mark), the often heterogeneous nature of the material as to

them in some notable ways, thus raising the possibility that the Johannine account preserves independent tradition concerning Jesus' Entry. In fact, three features of John's account vis-à-vis the Synoptic Gospels point to John's instead being dependent on non-Synoptic tradition.

First, every Synoptic Gospel devotes several lines of text to depicting Jesus as engineering the whole episode – *he* sends disciples with explicit instructions to fetch a special colt and bring it to him, so that readers are not surprised when he rides it into Jerusalem. From John, however, we form a different impression: without apparent provocation from Jesus, his enthusiastic followers acclaim him "king." Later, he locates a colt and sits on it (John 12:12–13). Since considerable space is given in each of the Synoptics to the fact that it was *Jesus'* plan to arrange for a ride, the complete absence of his arranging the ride beforehand in John suggests an independent tradition may be at work.

Second, in each of the Synoptic Gospels the Entry narrative is introduced by the story of Jesus' encounter with a blind man (Mark 10:46–52; Luke 18:35–43) or blind men (Matt 20:29–34) at Bethany. It is important to note that John, too, introduces the Entry account with a mention of Bethany, but for him, Bethany is not significant on account of any healing of a blind man but rather because it is the home of Mary, Martha, and Lazarus (John 11:1). Again, this incidental detail concerning Bethany corroborates the Synoptic accounts but in such a way as to suggest the presence of an independent tradition in John.[12]

Third, there is significant disparity between Mark and John in the size and composition of the crowds attending the Entry. Mark makes no mention of Lazarus, nor does he leave the impression that any crowd other than

---

its form, order, and function casts doubt to my mind on its existence as an independent, unitary, and documentary source of material for Matthew and Luke. If one grants that a documentary source underlies some of the Q material (see, for example, the long sections of verbatim agreement in Matt 3:7-10 = Luke 3:7-9; Matt 4:1-11 = Luke 4:1-13), the Entry narrative does not show the kind of agreement between Matthew and Luke (and divergence from Mark) that one finds in the other sections. Thus, it is improbable that a documentary Q is behind the variations in the Entry accounts. In an extensive treatment of Q, Siegfried Schulz (*Q: Die Spruchquelle der Evangelisten* [Zürich: Theologischer Verlag, 1972]) does not count this section in Luke as Q material. With respect to Luke's knowledge of Matthew, see Christopher M. Tuckett, "On the Relationship Between Matthew and Luke," *NTS* 30 (1984): 130–42.

[12] In addition, Coakley ("Jesus' Messianic Entry," 466–77) argues that significant differences between John and Mark exist in the matters of the crowds' actions, in their acclamation of Jesus, and in the use of the Hebrew Bible in the account. D. Moody Smith, Jr. ("John 12:12ff and the Question of John's Use of the Synoptics," *JBL* 82 [1963]: 58–64) also argues that John here is an independent source. Smith is especially concerned to demonstrate that the apparent similarity in the Jewish scriptural quotations used in the Entry narratives by John and the Synoptics need not favor the dependence of the former on the latter.

the disciples attended Jesus until he neared the city (11:1–10). By contrast, according to John's Gospel the crowds that accompany Jesus were drawn to him both from Bethany, where Jesus had reappeared at Lazarus's house (11:38–12:2), and from the crowds that had descended on Jerusalem for the Passover feast (12:12). Other criteria, to which we now turn, also point to the authenticity of the accounts.

2.2. The Criterion of Embarrassment

By invoking the criterion of embarrassment, I mean that the Entry accounts preserve details that we might have expected the Gospel writers to exclude or downplay because they could have been problematic or "embarrassing" for the nascent church in some way or other.[13] In particular, the sorts of embarrassment envisioned here concern the relationship of Jesus and the early church to Rome and the internal coherence of the Gospels' depictions of Jesus.

Early Christians were suspected and sometimes accused of disloyalty to Caesar and the Empire. The evidence for this is early, widespread, and virtually undisputed. That Christians should fall under suspicion is entirely comprehensible in the social-cultural milieu of the first century on two counts. First, their founder had suffered a criminal's death – indeed, a *seditious* criminal's death – at the hands of a duly appointed Roman governor.[14] Second, as the Christian movement began to be viewed not merely as a Jewish sect but as a distinct and new religion, it would have been subject to the apprehension that seemed typically to accompany religious novelty.[15]

---

[13] For further discussion of this criterion, see in this volume ch. 2, § 4.1.

[14] On crucifixion as punishment for sedition, see Martin Hengel, *Crucifixion in the Ancient World and the Folly of the Message of the Cross* (Philadelphia: Fortress, 1977), 33–38, 46–50. See also in this volume ch. 13, § 2.

[15] In the past, it was common to find writers who admired the capacity of Rome to accommodate various religions and sects, but recent studies have indicated that this accommodation was made reluctantly. The growth of a new sect or religion caused concern among Roman authorities, who disliked change in religion, inasmuch as novelty, whether in religion or politics, was often viewed as a challenge to the stability of the Empire. This perspective is illustrated, for example, where Dio Cassius puts in the mouth of Maecenas the extended discourse to Augustus Caesar: "Those who attempt to distort our religion with strange rites you should abhor and punish, not merely for the sake of the gods ... but because such men, by bringing in new divinities in place of the old, persuade many to adopt foreign practices, from which spring up conspiracies, factions, and cabals ..." (Dio Cassius 52.36.2 [Cary, LCL]). See further J.A. North, "Conservatism and Change in Roman Religion," *Papers of the British School at Rome* 44 (1976): 1–12; J.H.W.G. Liebeschuetz, *Continuity and Change in Roman Religion* (Oxford: Clarendon, 1979); and Peter Garnsey, "Religious Toleration in Classical Antiquity," in *Persecution and Toleration: Papers Read at the Twenty-Second Summer Meeting and the Twenty-Third Winter Meeting of the Ecclesiastical History Society* (ed. W.J. Sheils; SCH 21; Oxford: Blackwell, 1984), 1–27.

The Christian movement thus encountered formidable cultural and political obstacles as it sought to spread the gospel message throughout the ancient world (and, as we shall see, the Gospel accounts of Jesus' Entry would not necessarily have made him a more benign figure to those troubled by his putative relationship to Rome).

There is evidence, of course, that Christians were sensitive to these kinds of "political" accusations. For example, Luke repeatedly shows his awareness of political issues by editing material taken over from Mark in such a way as to distance Jesus and the early Christian movement from revolutionary leaders and seditious movements of the first century. To cite but one example, at Luke 9:23 he appears to clarify the metaphorical nature of Jesus' comments in Mark 8:34 about "taking up the cross" by inserting the phrase καθ' ἡμέραν ("daily"). Luke does not want Theophilus (Luke 1:1–4) to think Jesus was in the habit of encouraging his followers to actions that would *literally* result in crucifixion, since these would almost invariably have been seditious acts.[16]

The Romans did not separate religion from politics nor would they have expected to find such a dichotomy among their subjects. In a world where subject peoples typically continued to worship their own gods, and proselytism for the sake of religious ideology was rare, the link between local gods and local / nationalistic interests was natural. Two pre-Christian exceptions to this lack of emphasis on proselytism were the Bacchanalia and the Jews. The Roman historian Livy explains that the newness of the former along with its deplorable orgiastic initiation rites and cultic practices were the reasons for its official suppression. J. A. North argues that the cult was probably not new to Rome per se but that it represented the first step in the evolution of the nature of religious organizations, namely, "the creation for the first time of groups of specifically religious function" ("Religious Toleration in Republican Rome," *Proceedings of the Cambridge Philological Society* 25 [1979]: 95). With its emphasis on joining by free choice (and, perhaps, on concomitant proselytizing), it subverted state control of religious practices and was viewed as a threat. The Jews faced expulsion from Rome at various times owing to their proselytizing (cf. Valerius Maximus 1.3.3; Dio Cassius 57.18.5). Josephus recognized the sensitive nature of Jewish proselytizing (Louis H. Feldman, "A Selective Critical Bibliography of Josephus," in *Josephus, the Bible, and History* [ed. Louis H. Feldman and Gohei Hata; Leiden: Brill, 1989], 373–74), although he attributes the expulsion under Tiberius to four Jewish swindlers who took advantage of Tiberius's friend (*Ant* 18.81–84); see also E. Mary Smallwood, *The Jews Under Roman Rule. From Pompey to Diocletian: A Study in Political Relations* (SJLA 20; Leiden: Brill, 1981), 128–32, 201–16. If the Romans were inclined to be tolerant of foreign religions prior to the establishment of emperor worship, that religious liberalism probably had more to do with the resistance that would have been engendered by the quashing of local customs than with a regard for what we moderns call "toleration"; see Robert M. Grant, *Augustus to Constantine: The Thrust of the Christian Movement Into the Roman World* (London: Collins, 1971), and Garnsey, "Religious Toleration in Classical Antiquity." The newness of Christianity surely produced concern among the authorities. Martin Goodman (*The Ruling Class of Judaea: The Origins of the Jewish Revolt Against Rome, A.D. 66–70* [London: Cambridge University Press, 1988]) has suggested that the Druids of Gaul and Britain provide a NT era example of the difficulties that could be posed by foreign religions.

[16] Hengel, *Crucifixion*, 46–50. See also Brent Kinman, "Luke's Exoneration of John the

As to the Entry narratives, the Greco-Roman background of παρουσία would have figured prominently in the evaluation of Jesus' Entry by eyewitnesses to the event and by the first readers of the Gospels.[17] In the Hellenistic world a παρουσία most often signaled the coming of a ruler or royal figure. It began to be a notable feature of imperial practice during the Principate.[18] Numerous extant sources, including literary, epigraphic, numismatic and archaeological materials, provide information about celebratory welcomes (here παρουσία) in the ancient world, and from these data basic patterns of behavior emerge.[19] The conventions revealed in the

---

Baptist," *JTS* 44 (1993): 595–98, along with the NT admonitions to Christian to submit to imperial authorities in Romans 13 and 1 Pet 2:13–17.

[17] For more on this, see Brent Kinman, *Jesus' Entry Into Jerusalem: In the Context of Lukan Theology and the Politics of His Day* (AGJU 28; Leiden: Brill, 1995), 25–65. While "victory" is surely the main thrust of the well-known Roman Triumph, the Triumph itself is the least likely precedent for Jesus' Entry. The Roman Triumph is one of the background motifs that scholars sometimes appeal to when discussing Jesus' Entry (e.g., Helmut Flender, *Heil und Geschichte in der Theologie des Lukas* [BEvT 41; Munich: Kaiser, 1965], 85; Josef Ernst, *Das Evangelium nach Lukas* [5th ed.; RNT; Regensburg: Pustet, 1977], 526). The most exhaustive classical treatment of the Triumph is H. S. Versnel, *Triumphs: An Inquiry Into the Origin, Development and Meaning of the Roman Triumph* (Leiden: Brill, 1970). The traditional label for the event, the "Triumphal Entry," naturally invites comparison between Jesus' Entry and the Roman Triumph proper. Such a comparison can have only limited value, however, for several reasons. First, the ideology of the Triumph is not likely to have been as relevant to Jesus' Entry as the ideology of the παρουσία. The Triumph in the first centuries B.C.E. and C.E. was fundamentally a military honor and did not essentially involve notions of kingship or the "divinity" of the magistrate/emperor being celebrated. True enough, Caligula sought divine honors and Augustus and others accepted them (though primarily when abroad and explicitly not in Rome). But regarding the Triumph held at Rome, emperors in and around the NT era were not eager to be viewed as kings in the traditional sense of the term (in fact, they clearly avoided the label). On the other hand, the παρουσία typically did involve the coming of a royal figure (without necessarily celebrating his military prowess). This is not to say there is no comparison at all between Jesus' coming and the advent of emperors for, as we know, the Hellenistic παρουσία imagery was often incorporated into imperial ceremonies (beginning with the Principate), particularly in the provinces. Second, the traditional Triumph could only be held at the city of Rome and the first witnesses to the event are not likely to have drawn comparisons between a Triumph at Rome and Jesus' Entry at Jerusalem. Third, the Triumph was given to an eligible Roman magistrate and on this count Jesus hardly qualifies.

[18] For example, Augustus was regularly welcomed on his travels, both within and outside Rome (Dio Cassius 51.20.2–4; Suetonius *Augustus* 53.1). Caligula was fêted despite the fact that he was accompanying the body of Tiberius for burial (Suetonius *Caligula* 4.1). Similarly, Nero received grandiose welcomes in his travels (Suetonius *Nero* 25.1–3). Trajan, too, was splendidly welcomed (Pliny the Younger *Pan.* 22.1–5).

[19] See Albrecht Oepke, "παρουσία, πάρειμι," *TDNT* 5:859–60; Adolf Deissmann, *Light from the Ancient East* (trans. Lionel R. M. Strachan; New York: Doran, 1927), 368–73; see also H. Cohen, ed., *Description historique des monnaies frappées sous l'Empire Romain*, Vol. I: *Néron* (Paris: Rollin & Feuardent, 1880), § 391, 403 and B. V. Head and R. S. Poole, eds., *A Catalogue of the Greek Coins in the British Museum: Corinth, Colonies of Corinth, etc.* (London: Longmans, 1889), § 567.

inscriptions and literary accounts are broadly consistent, whether an entry occurs in Asia Minor, Palestine, or Egypt.[20] It is hard to overestimate the importance of the breadth of these data, for it indicates the extent to which society at large would have been aware of the phenomena associated with celebratory welcomes and, as a result, provides an illuminating background to Jesus' Entry.

For now, we can summarize that παρουσίαι tended to be highly politicized events. No Gospel writer could have been unaware this fact – and yet, when it comes to the Entry narrative, its appearance in Mark opens both Jesus and the disciples to charges of political unrest. Such charges could have been made because the Entry as depicted by Mark was planned by Jesus, regal in nature, and participated in by disciples. The Entry is perhaps the only action in Mark (as opposed to "saying") that could plausibly leave Jesus open to the charge of making himself "king" (Mark 15:2, 9; cf. Luke 23:2) – and it was this charge that was not only partly responsible for getting Jesus crucified (an event whose historicity is well established) – but was also one that Christians subsequently had to defend themselves against (e.g., Acts 17:7). And still the narrative appears in Mark.

Similarly, John's inclusion of the Entry account is potentially embarrassing in that it introduces an apparent contradiction in Jesus' attitude about kingship. While Jesus privately accepts the label "son of God" as tantamount to "king" according to John 1:49, in a more public venue Jesus is alarmed by the prospect of being "made king" (ποιήσωσιν βασιλέα) and withdraws from the crowds (John 6:1–15). Yet at his Entry in John 12:12–15, Jesus is lauded as king (ὡσαννά· εὐλογημένος ὁ ἐρχόμενος ἐν ὀνόματι κυρίου, καὶ ὁ βασιλεὺς τοῦ Ἰσραήλ, v. 13), but he makes *no* attempt to avoid the crowds or suppress the acclaim.

Luke, too, has Jesus instigating his own royal entry into Jerusalem and refusing to concede that the disciples were misguided in acclaiming him "king" (Luke 19:28–40).[21] It has been observed that certain features of Luke's redaction of the Entry narrative itself can best be traced to Luke's political apologetic concerning Jesus (thus the Entry narrative was not preserved uncritically). Nevertheless, his retention of the basic outline of Mark's Entry narrative suggests that it was considered to have been helpful, in Luke's mind, to convey to Theophilus his "carefully investigated" story (Luke 1:1–4) in spite of the fact the entry could have been "politically embarrassing."

---

[20] E.g., Josephus *Ant.* 11.329; Plutarch *Vit. Luc.* 2.5; Philostratus *VA* 5.27; Cicero *Pis.* 51–52; *Sest.* 63; Dionysius of Halicarnassus 2.60.2–3; Diodorus Siculus 37.26.1. In addition, see W. Weber, *Untersuchungen zur Geschichte des Kaisers Hadrianus* (Leipzig: Teubner, 1907), 92, n. 310.

[21] On this, see Brent Kinman, "'The Stones Will Cry Out' (Luke 19,40) – Joy or Judgment?" *Bib* 75 (1994): 232–35.

To sum up: when set against the dual backgrounds of the commonly understood political nature of an entry and the early church's concern not to be viewed as seditious or anti-Roman, the criterion of embarrassment suggests that the Entry narratives in the Gospels are authentic and historically reliable. In them we find the sort of clear political overtones that would appear to be at odds with the apologetic and redactional interests of early Christians. This brings us to the criterion of "effect."

2.3. The Criterion of Effect

Assuming for a moment the historicity of the basic contours of the Entry narratives – what consequences flowed from the event, and are they, in turn, historically reliable? The criterion of effect argues that a later effect must have adequate antecedent causes, and along these lines I suggest the Entry supplies a key ingredient to the charges made by the Jewish authorities against Jesus before the Roman governor, Pilate. How so?

We know that the Roman governor Pontius Pilate sentenced Jesus to death.[22] We further know that Jesus was crucified, a form of execution consistent with a charge of sedition.[23] According to the Gospel trial narratives, Pilate understood that Jesus was being accused of a political crime (Mark 15:1–15; Matt 27:11–23; Luke 23:1–7,13–24; John 18:33–19:16), and the appearance of the *titulus* on his cross, while conceivably exaggerated or sarcastic in its wording,[24] nevertheless accords well with a charge rooted in

---

[22] Acknowledged as authentic (i.e., it is colored "red") by the JS itself (so Funk and Seminar, *The Acts of Jesus*, 567). See also Harvey (*Jesus and the Constraints of History*, 11–35), who writes: "*He was crucified under Pontius Pilate.* It would be no exaggeration to say that this event is better attested, and supported by a more impressive array of evidence, than any other event of comparable importance of which we have knowledge from the ancient world" (p. 11). See also in this volume ch. 13.

[23] Jesus' crucifixion is mentioned in the earliest Christian writings (Gal 3:1; 6:14; 1 Cor 1:23; 2:2, 8; 2 Cor 13:4; Phil 2:8; Eph 2:16; Col 1:20; Rev 11:8) and is there acknowledged as a potential hindrance to faith. The tradition of Jesus as crucified is also found outside the NT (Tacitus, *Ann.* 15.44; perhaps also Josephus, *Ant.* 18.63–64); for a discussion of the Josephus passage, see John P. Meier, *The Roots of the Problem and the Person* (vol. 1 of *A Marginal Jew: Rethinking the Historical Jesus*; ABRL; New York: Doubleday, 1991–2009), 59–69. For crucifixion as the supreme penalty for sedition, see Hengel, *Crucifixion*. These data along with the argument to follow constitute a reply to Gerd Thiessen's comment that "Apart from the rarely doubted fact that Jesus was crucified under Pontius Pilate, there are no clear views about who provoked Jesus' condemnation and on what grounds he was executed" (Gerd Theissen and Annette Merz, *The Historical Jesus: A Comprehensive Guide* [trans. John Bowden; Minneapolis: Fortress, 1998], 442). For further discussion, see in this volume ch. 13, § 2.

[24] For this, see especially Ernst Bammel, "The *Titulus*," in *Jesus and the Politics of His Day* (ed. Ernst Bammel and C. F. D. Moule; Cambridge: Cambridge University Press, 1984), 353–64.

the perception of political agitation.²⁵ The question is, what action or statement of Jesus could warrant this charge, or, at the least, make it plausible when represented to the governor?

While the mention of Jesus as king is found in each of the Gospel trial narratives,²⁶ there is only one event in the Synoptics prior to his trial where Jesus is called "king" – the Entry into Jerusalem, which, according to the Gospels, occurred just a few days before his arrest and trial.²⁷ Because certain anti-Roman Jewish figures had made royal claims in the years just prior to Jesus' ministry, Pilate would at least have had some grounds for regarding Jesus with suspicion had the Entry occurred as the Gospels suggest. A handful of significant disturbances involving would-be royal figures erupted in Roman Palestine in the period between the death of Herod the Great (4 B. C. E.) and Jesus' trial (ca. 30–33 C. E.).²⁸ In the first instance, Josephus refers to the activities of Judas, the son of Ezekias (the latter was said to be an ἀρχιληστής, *Ant.* 17.271) shortly after the death of Herod the Great (ca. 4 B. C. E.).²⁹ Josephus credits him with two dominant attributes: greed and an "ambition for royal rank."³⁰ Judas assembled a band of desperados in

---

²⁵ Paul Winter, *On the Trial of Jesus* (SJ 1; Berlin: De Gruyter, 1961), 108; Ben F. Meyer, *The Aims of Jesus* (London: SCM, 1979), 176–78; Gerhard Schneider, "The Political Charge Against Jesus (Luke 23:2)," in *Jesus and the Politics of His Day* (ed. E. Bammel and C. F. D. Moule; Cambridge: Cambridge University Press, 1984), 403–14. Again, see further in this volume ch. 13, § 3.4.2.

²⁶ Darrell L. Bock (*Blasphemy and Exaltation in Judaism and the Final Examination of Jesus* [WUNT 2.106; Tübingen: Mohr Siebeck, 1998]) observes that the charges made before the Jewish council are considerably different than the ones made before Pilate. My reference here is to the trial before Pilate.

²⁷ Craig A. Evans ("From Public Ministry to the Passion: Can a Link Be Found Between the [Galilean] Life and the [Judean] Death of Jesus?" in *SBL Seminar Papers, 1993* [SBLSP 32; Atlanta: Scholars, 1993], 460–72) outlines the link between Jesus' teaching about the kingdom of God in Galilee and the later political charges he faced in Judea. Evans's arguments provide an additional background against which to view the charges made before Pilate, particularly if the charges directly involved a "royal entry."

²⁸ While acknowledging that the issue is disputed, I take the view that Jesus was crucified in 33 C. E. For differing views and reviews, see Harold W. Hoehner, *Chronological Aspects of the Life of Christ* (Grand Rapids: Zondervan, 1977), and Meier, *The Roots of the Problem and the Person*, 386–433.

²⁹ As Richard A. Horsley ("Josephus and the Bandits," *JSJ* 10 [1979]: 39) notes, this Judas is not himself called a ληστής by Josephus, though one could argue that in this context the implication is "like father, like son." Clearly, his activities are bandit-like, as even Horsley admits.

³⁰ This account appears anachronistic in Josephus, inasmuch as the very next book of the *Antiquities* refers to a rebel leader named Judas, also from the region of Galilee. He is not identified as the first Judas (*Ant.* 18.4–9, 23). Scholarly opinion is divided as to whether or not Josephus is referring to one or two men. Support for the view that Josephus refers to the same person is found in Emil Schürer, *The History of the Jewish People in the Age of Jesus Christ (175 B. C. – A. D. 135)* (new English ed.; 3 vols.; ed. Geza Vermes, et al.; Edinburgh: T&T Clark, 1973–87), 2:600; J. S. Kennard, "Judas of Galilee and His Clan,"

Galilee, assaulted a palace, took arms and other valuables, and embarked on a career of thievery. It is noteworthy that, in Judas, royal aspirations were linked to armed resistance to Rome.[31] Later, Simon, a slave of Herod the Great, was able to attract many followers, who acknowledged him as king by placing a diadem on his head (*Ant.* 17.273). He plundered, then burned, Herod's royal palace in Jericho. This was followed by other similar acts. He was eventually caught and executed (*Ant.* 17.276–77). Finally, Athronges crowned himself and organized his armed followers into companies under the command of his four brothers, who "applied themselves vigorously to slaughtering the Romans and the king's men ..." *(Ant.* 17.278–81).

This brief survey of royal pretenders supplies a useful background for thinking about the criterion of "effect": because Jewish royal claimants had repeatedly been associated with sedition and other unlawful activities, the royal claims implicit in Jesus' Entry could have been used against him at trial, should it have proven convenient for his accusers to do so. Once we recognize the Entry narratives as basically authentic, we have grounds for understanding how someone plausibly could bring political charges against Jesus to Pilate.

Of course, one may well ask, "If the Entry was such a politically charged event, why did the Romans not arrest Jesus as he made his royal procession?" This question touches on the issue of "what really happened" at the Entry and will be dealt with below. For now it is important to recognize that I am not suggesting the Entry *necessarily* resulted in Jesus' arrest and crucifixion on political charges. Rather, I am saying the Entry, unique among Jesus' actions (excluding, possibly, the so-called temple cleansing), provided Jesus' opponents a way of exploiting a Roman governor's concern with sedition. Such an approach to Pilate by the Jewish leadership sought to achieve their own aims because of the political associations that were often attached to such events. The Entry left Jesus open to a charge of sedition,

---

JQR 36 (1945): 281–86; and Martin Hengel, *The Zealots: Investigations Into the Freedom Movement in the Period from Herod I Until 70 A.D.* (2d ed.; Edinburgh: T&T Clark, 1989), 331. Those who distinguish the two include F. J. Foakes Jackson and Kirsopp Lake, *Prolegomena I: The Jewish, Gentile and Christian Backgrounds* (vol. 1 of *The Beginnings of Christianity*; 5 vols.; London: Macmillan, 1933), 424; Smallwood, *The Jews Under Roman Rule. From Pompey to Diocletian: A Study in Political Relations*, 153, n. 40; and Horsley, "Josephus and the Bandits," 39–40. On the whole, the arguments against identifying the two are to be preferred.

[31] Richard A. Horsley ("Popular Messianic Movements Around the Time of Jesus," *CBQ* 46 [1984]: 485) has argued that Judas became the focus of a popular messianism which had its political support from the peasant classes and an ideological framework derived from the Scriptures. He recognizes the difficulty of supposing there to have been unequivocal messianic expectations, yet nonetheless draws attention to regal imagery from the OT to illuminate popular ideas of "anointed" kingship (see pp. 473–80).

even if such a charge was a distortion of what really happened or what Jesus really intended.

It is preferable to consider other criteria for authenticity in a later section. For now, we can conclude that at the very least the criteria considered thus far make the story of Jesus' Entry historically plausible. Indeed, the data surveyed up to now strongly point to a verdict in favor of historicity, though the survey is admittedly incomplete.

3. The Background, Context, and the Event of Jesus' Entry

Historical Jesus scholars endeavor to reconstruct a picture of Jesus' life and ministry. If a convincing reconstruction emerges through the fires of critical studies, it will be commended as such, not because it provides an uncontestable or exhaustive picture of Jesus, but rather because it accounts for more of the data about Jesus than competing theories. When it comes to reconstructing a particular event, such as his entry into Jerusalem, the task is all the more daunting on account of the relative paucity of data and the need to make certain assumptions as the data are incorporated into the larger study of Jesus' life. Having said that, we now turn to the Gospel narratives to explore the question of how Jesus' Entry and related events might have appeared to eyewitnesses, and what can be inferred from these actions about Jesus' intentions.

3.1. Jesus' Actions

In each Gospel, the narrative of Jesus' Entry occurs at the outset of his final week and gives the impression, at least, of taking place at the Passover season.[32] Every Gospel account of Jesus' Entry recalls that he rode into Jerusalem on a colt and was, either explicitly or implicitly, acclaimed king. Mark's story of Jesus' Entry is shorter than its Matthean and Lukan counterparts. Mark (along with Matthew, Luke and John) locates the Entry's beginning near the small villages of Bethphage and Bethany (11:1), the former being identified as a suburb of Jerusalem and inhabited from the second-century B.C.E.[33] In Mark Jesus gives explicit instructions to the disciples to assist them in finding a colt (11:1–6); afterward, he is placed on it and rides to the city as people supply a royal welcome (11:7–10). The Markan narrative

---

[32] For years scholars have debated the season or festal time at which Jesus entered Jerusalem. Those who favor Tabernacles include T. W. Manson, "The Cleansing of the Temple," *BJRL* 33 (1951): 271–82; C. W. F. Smith, "No Time for Figs," *JBL* 79 (1960): 315–27; and C. W. F. Smith, "Tabernacles in the Fourth Gospel and Mark," *NTS* 9 (1963): 130–46. The majority of commentators view Passover as the time of Jesus' Entry.

[33] Scott T. Carroll, "Bethphage," *ABD* 1:715.

seems to credit Jesus with unusual, one might almost infer *supernatural*, prescience in knowing where the colt would be located and the response of bystanders who witness the disciples fetching it (Mark 11:1–3 and parallels). But the account does not *have* to be read in this way. It may simply be the case that Jesus arranged beforehand with the colt's owner for it to be picked up (roughly the same thing appears in Mark 14:12–16, where arrangements for the last supper have apparently been made in advance by Jesus). With respect to the Johannine account of preparations for Jesus' Entry, J. F. Coakley takes John's deliberate ambiguity concerning the finding of the colt as a mark of authenticity, for, he notes, John is not reluctant to credit Jesus with special foreknowledge or insight elsewhere (1:48; 4:17–18; 6:6), so the failure to mention it here likely means the colt was procured in a rather pedestrian way.[34]

Mark's Jesus specifies that the πῶλος is unridden (ἐφ' ὃν οὐδεὶς οὔπω ἀνθρώπων ἐκάθισεν, Mark 11:2). Before asking what an unridden animal might signify, we should clarify what sort of animal Mark envisions. W. Bauer argued that the "colt" in view must have been that of a horse, since when the term πῶλος appeared without further qualification (i.e., "of a camel," "of an ass"), it normally had equine associations.[35] This was denied in subsequent essays by H. W. Kuhn and O. Michel.[36] Michel in particular persuasively showed that πῶλος was easily exchanged for the Hebrew עיר and often denoted a young, strong ass – even when no further qualification appeared. Mark's use of the ambiguous πῶλος is, it seems, clarified by other writers who, for political or theological reasons, note that Jesus was astride the colt of an "ass" (Matt 21:2; John 12:15).[37] The fact that the animal had not been ridden before could have suggested to eyewitnesses and early Gospel readers that it was preserved for royal use. In several other ancient Near

---

[34] Coakley, "Jesus' Messianic Entry," 477.

[35] Walter Bauer, "The 'Colt' of Palm Sunday (Der Palmesel)," *JBL* 72 (1953): 220–29.

[36] H. W. Kuhn, "Das Reittier Jesu in der Einzugsgeschichte des Markusevangeliums," *ZNW* 50 (1959): 82–91; Otto Michel, "Eine philologische Frage zur Einzugsgeschichte," *NTS* 6 (1959–60): 81–82.

[37] Matthew's clarification of Mark might have stemmed from a desire to show that Jesus' ride was in fulfillment of prophecy, for example, Zech 9:9, or perhaps to indicate that Jesus was not riding a horse, an act that would surely have been viewed as politically suspicious. One occasionally finds a scholarly comment to the effect that Matthew was so preoccupied with depicting the event as fulfillment that he has Jesus seated on the *two* animals mentioned in Zech 9:9. This theory might stem from a misreading of Matt 21:5–7. In v. 7 we learn that the disciples "brought the donkey and the colt and put on them their cloaks, and he sat on them" (ESV; so also NIV, NKJV; Greek: ἤγαγον τὴν ὄνον καὶ τὸν πῶλον καὶ ἐπέθηκαν ἐπ' αὐτῶν τὰ ἱμάτια, καὶ ἐπεκάθισεν ἐπάνω αὐτῶν). The nearest antecedent to the αὐτῶν at the end of verse is τὰ ἱμάτια ("the garments"); thus when we read Jesus sat on "them," we should probably understand that he sat on "the garments" (not the two animals). John explains that the disciples were not aware of any prophetic significance to Jesus' coming (12:16).

Eastern locales it was not uncommon for special animals to be set aside for important persons, including royalty.³⁸

What Jewish precedents may have existed for Jesus' arrival, in particular, his use of a colt to ride on? The wealth of classical material that deals with Greco-Roman entries stands in contrast to the relative lack of information dealing with Jewish celebratory welcomes. The Hebrew Bible and related traditions offer the reader stories about various processions and greetings, yet the sort of formal protocol which characterized the παρουσία, the Roman Triumph, and other ancient entries seems neither to be reflected in the Hebrew Bible nor to have developed in the Second Temple period.³⁹ Given the stress in the Gospel narratives on the fact that Jesus *rode* rather than walked, we should look for Jewish scriptural celebratory welcomes that also contain this feature. There are two: the entry of Solomon in 1 Kgs 1 and the coming of Zion's king in Zech 9.

According to 1 Kgs 1,⁴⁰ as the aged and enfeebled David neared the end of his life, two "parties" vied for Davidic approval and its consequent royal power. One favored Adonijah; the other preferred Solomon. Having de-

---

³⁸ Special animals for important persons to ride on were not uncommon in the ancient Near East (e.g., Gen 41:43; Esth 6:8; Ezek 23:6; Jer 17:25; Appian *Mith.* 27.117; *Pun.* 9.66; Dio Cassius 51.21.9; Dionysius of Halicarnassus 8.67.9; Josephus *J. W.* 7.152; Livy 45.39.8; 45.40.4; Ovid *Tr.* 4.2.54; Plutarch *Aem. Paul.* 34.6). See J. Duncan M. Derrett, "Law in the New Testament: The Palm Sunday Colt," *NovT* 13 (1971): 248–53; but against this, compare Joseph A. Fitzmyer, *The Gospel According to Luke X–XXIV* (AB 28a; Garden City: Doubleday, 1985), 1249. On the debated question regarding the presence here of an allusion in the tethering of the animal to the "oracle of Judah" in Gen 49:10–12, see Joseph Blenkinsopp, "The Oracle of Judah and the Messianic Entry," *JBL* 80 (1961): 55–64; cf. Fitzmyer, *Luke X–XXIV*, 1248–49, who discounts the influence of the oracle here (*contra* I. Howard Marshall, *The Gospel of Luke* [NIGTC 3; Grand Rapids: Eerdmans, 1978], 712, who acknowledges it). It is possible that readers with a Palestinian background would have recognized (developed?) these allusions, since the connections between Messiah and the "Oracle of Judah" are most developed in the Targums (Blenkinsopp, "The Oracle of Judah and the Messianic Entry," 57).

³⁹ An exception to this would be the greeting of Jonathan Maccabaeus into Askalon, probably accounted for by the fact that the city was thoroughly Hellenized (Schürer, *History*, 2:105–8; Martin Hengel, *Judentum und Hellenismus: Studien zu ihrer Begegnung unter besonderer Berücksichtigung Palästinas bis zur Mitte des 2. Jhs. v. Chr.* [3rd ed.; WUNT 10; Tübingen: Mohr Siebeck, 1988], 43, 52). For a more thorough examination of the various "Jewish entries," see Kinman, *Jesus' Entry*, 56–64.

⁴⁰ This chapter of 1 Kings has been the subject of numerous studies (e.g., R. N. Whybray, *The Succession Narrative* [SBT 2.9; London: SCM, 1968]; J. P. Fokkelman, *King David [II Sam. 9–20 & I Kings 1–2]* [vol. 1 of *Narrative Art and Poetry in the Books of Samuel*; SSN 20; Assen, The Netherlands: Van Gorcum, 1981], 345–430; P. K. McCarter, "Plots, True or False," *Int* 35 [1981]: 355–67; P. R. Ackroyd, "The Succession Narrative [So-Called]," *Int* 35 [1981]: 383–96). Form-critical questions concerning the Hebrew text are not an important consideration for the present study. For comments on the slight differences between LXX and Hebrew versions of the story, see John W. Wevers, "A Study in the Exegetical Principles Underlying the Greek Text of 2 Sm 11:2–1 Kings 2:11," *CBQ* 15 (1953): 37.

cided to appoint Solomon to be his heir after hearing the worrying reports of Adonijah's activities, David acted to legitimize and publicize his choice of a successor through a public demonstration (1 Kgs 1:33–40). David himself specifies how the ceremony is to proceed and his instructions are meticulously fulfilled in the narrative (vv. 33–39). The anointing and accompanying celebration for Solomon took place in public (in contrast to the initial anointing of both Saul and David).[41] The choice of the Gihon spring, a water source located between Jerusalem and the Mount of Olives in the Kidron Valley, as the site of the anointing would naturally have been understood as an ideal location at which to present Solomon to the people. The mule (ἡμίονος)[42] is specifically mentioned in connection with the houses of Saul and David,[43] and here Solomon is placed on a mule[44] and rides into Jerusalem

---

[41] 1 Sam 9:25–10:1; 16:13.

[42] According to the LXX, three animals served as royal mounts. In Israel the mule (ἡμίονος) was a gift to celebrated or royal figures (Gen 12:16; 45:23; 1 Kgs 10:25; 18:5; 1 Chr 12:40; 2 Chr 9:24) and a simple beast of burden (Jdt 2:17; 15:11; Isa 66:20; Ezek 27:14). The colt (πῶλος) is ridden by Jair the Gileadite (a "judge") and his sons (Judg 10:4; 12:14) and, significant for the present study, the "coming king" of Zech 9:9 also rides one (taking the καί in καὶ πῶλον νέον as ascensive). Finally, the more generic beast of burden (ὑποζύγιον) was accompanying the animals that the household of king David would ride (τὰ ὑποζύγια τῇ οἰκίᾳ τοῦ βασιλέως τοῦ ἐπικαθῆσθαι) when he was given the inheritance of Mephibosheth (2 Sam 16:2). The horse seems rarely, if ever, to have been used as a royal mount – a clear example of the Jewish king riding a horse is not to be found, though this statement requires qualification. David and Solomon both collected horses (2 Sam 8:4; 1 Kgs 4:26), and it could be inferred that if the kings owned so many horses, they were likely to have ridden them. One may also surmise that horses often pulled chariots in which kings traveled (e.g., 1 Kgs 12:18; 2 Kgs 8:21; 9:16,21; 10:15–16). Amaziah was murdered and brought to Jerusalem for burial ἐφ' ἵππων (2 Kgs 14:20). Jer 17:24–25 and 22:4 speak prophetically of Israel's kings riding though the gates of Jerusalem "in chariots and on horses," if a certain condition is met, namely, observance of the Sabbath. Outside the OT, a possible exception to this is the bronze coin from Palestine minted in C.E. 38/39, which depicts Agrippa II on horseback with the inscription "Agrippa, son of the king" (Ya'akov Meshorer, *Jewish Coins of the Second Temple Period* [trans. I. H. Levine; Tel Aviv: Am Hassefer, 1967], pl. 85 and p. 138). Later commentators seem to envision the Jewish king riding upon a horse, for one admonishes, "None may ride on his [the king's] horse …" (*m. Sanh.* 2:5; this purports to be quotation from R. Simeon, ca. C.E. 140–160). Much later the rabbis refer to the common use of a horse (e.g., *b. Pesaḥ.* 53a). Nevertheless, the observation stands: a clear example of a Jewish king riding a horse is not to be found in the OT.

[43] Doeg the Edomite pastured τὰς ἡμιόνους Σαουλ (1 Sam 21:8; 22:9), that is, the royal flocks. When Absalom held the dinner party at which his brother Amnon was slain, each of his other brothers (i.e., the princes of Israel) fled the scene of the crime ἐπὶ τὴν ἡμίονον αὐτοῦ (2 Sam 13:29). During the crucial military battle in his rebellion against David, Absalom happened to meet his father's soldiers ἐπιβεβηκὼς ἐπὶ τοῦ ἡμιόνου αὐτοῦ (2 Sam 18:9).

[44] In the LXX of 1 Kgs (1 Kgdms) 1:33 the verb ἐπιβιβάζω describes the action of placing Solomon on the mule, and in the context of 1 Kings, the choice of this verb may point to Solomon's passivity – and in so doing highlight the difference between him and his usurping brothers, Absalom and Adonijah (cf. 1 Sam 8:11; 2 Sam 15:1; 1 Kgs 1:5). Another important element in the account of Solomon's accession to the throne is the very obvious

amidst an ostentatious display of public support, including shouts of "Long live King Solomon!"[45] Since this is the first account of dynastic succession in Israel,[46] it might be expected that some of the details found here will reappear in later narratives that deal with kings; this is almost certainly the case with respect to Zech 9:9, to which attention is now turned.[47]

Zechariah 9:9–10 lies in the midst of a more extended oracle of the Lord. Zechariah 9 is the first chapter of the larger complex of writings now most commonly referred to as "Deutero-Zechariah," the dating, authorship, and referents of which are matters of considerable scholarly dispute.[48] The first seven verses of Zechariah 9 speak of God's judgment falling upon the inhabitants of regions and cities to the northwest, west, and southwest of Jerusalem: Hamath, Tyre, Sidon, Askalon, Gaza, and Ekron. Jerusalem itself comes into view in v. 8 where the Lord speaks of establishing a garrison in Jerusalem that will afford the city protection from marauders. The passage continues,

---

association of kingship and anointing: Solomon is anointed king by the high priest. A detailed investigation concerning the use and development of anointing does not fall within the scope of this essay. The studies by Heinrich Weinel ("משׁח und seine Derivate," *ZAW* 18 [1898]: 1–82), Ernst Kutsch (*Salbung als Rechtsakt im Alten Testament und im alten Orient* [BZAW 87; Berlin: Töpelmann, 1963]), Ludwig Schmidt (*Menschlicher, Erfolg und Jahwes Initiative: Studien zu Tradition, Interpretation und Historie in Überlieferungen von Gideon, Saul und David* [WMANT 38; Neukirchen-Vluyn: Neukirchener Verlag, 1970]), and T. N. D. Mettinger (*King and Messiah: The Civil and Sacral Legitimation of the Israelite Kings* [ConBOT 8; Lund: Gleerup, 1976]) would be fundamental for understanding the practice. For helpful summaries, see Mettinger (pp. 185–232) and H. G. M. Williamson, review of *King and Messiah: The Civil and Sacral Legitimation of the Israelite Kings*, *VT* 28 (1978): 499–509.

[45] The phrase "May king [so and so] live!" (1 Kgs 1:39) is also found at 1 Sam 10:24, 2 Kgs 11:12 and 2 Chr 23:11 (where Samuel and Joash are "enthroned") and at 2 Sam 16:16, where Absalom entered Jerusalem and was greeted by Hushai.

[46] That is to say, it would have been first in the minds of readers of the HB, insofar as it describes events prior to those found in Zechariah (i.e., it is not important for the present study to determine when 1 Kings was composed vis-à-vis Zechariah or the Psalms).

[47] Most commentaries on Zechariah do not mention the link between 1 Kgs 1 and Zech 9:9–10 (e.g., Benedikt Otzen, *Studien Über Deuterosacharja* [ATD 6; Copenhagen: Munksgaard, 1964]; Magne Sæbø, *Sacharja 9–14: Untersuchungen von Text und Form* [WMANT 34; Neukirchen-Vluyn: Neukirchener Verlag, 1969]). For an exception, see Paul Lamarche, *Zacharie IX–XIV: Structure littéraire et messianisme* (EBib; Paris: Gabalda, 1961), 115–16. What is perhaps surprising, given the biblical habit of employing the language used to describe crucial early events in the telling of later events (note, for example, the terms shared between the accounts of the plundering of the Egyptians by Israel and Abraham), is that the model of Israel's king riding into Jerusalem is used *only* one other time in the Hebrew Bible, namely, here.

[48] D. E. Sellin (*Das Zwölfprophetenbuch* [KAT 12; Leipzig: Deichert, 1922], 487) remarked, "Die Frage der Zeit des Verf. von Sach 9–13 bzw. 14 kann getrost als eine der schwierigsten und umstrittensten der ganzen alttest. Einleitungswissenschaft bezeichnet werden."

⁹ Rejoice greatly, daughter of Zion; proclaim aloud, daughter of Jerusalem: Behold! Your king comes to you, righteous and bearing salvation, humble and seated upon an ass, even a new colt. ¹⁰ And I will completely destroy the chariots from Ephraim and the horses from Jerusalem and the bow of war will be utterly destroyed and he will speak peace to the nations; and his rule shall be from sea to sea, and from the river to the ends of the earth.

The language employed immediately evokes memories of David as it addresses Jerusalem as the daughter of Zion – the city of David (2 Sam 5:7,9; 6:12,16; 1 Chr 15:1–3).

The description of the coming of Zion's king found here is reminiscent of the arrival of Solomon narrated in 1 Kgs 1. Both stories are set in Jerusalem. In each passage the capital city responds to the king's appearance with joyous celebration. There are linguistic parallels between the verbs used for "mount" in each narrative, both in the MT and in the LXX.[49] There are one or two noteworthy differences, as well. The coming of Zion's king is associated with God's deliverance for Jerusalem, something not mentioned in connection with Solomon's advent.[50] Furthermore, while it is clear Solomon's entry in 1 Kgs 1 is part of an enthronement ceremony, it is not so clear that enthronement is in view in Zech 9. It could be argued that Zech 9 envisages an enthronement, insofar as it is based on 1 Kgs 1. However, owing to the militaristic tone of Zech 9:10, Zech 9 could be understood equally well as describing a victory celebration or an event prior to the beginning of conflict. In fact, it is difficult to characterize precisely what is being pictured in the Zechariah passage. Still, whether it is an enthronement, a victory celebration, or a call to battle, Jerusalem is being summoned to welcome its king.

Against this Scriptural background Jesus arranges to ride a colt into Jerusalem.[51] It is difficult to avoid the conclusion that his actions constitute

---

[49] The Hiphil of רכב is used in 1 Kgs 1:33 and rendered in the LXX by the verb ἐπιβιβάζω. In Zech 9:9, the participle of רכב appears and corresponds to the participle of ἐπιβαίνω (ἐπιβεβηκώς) in the LXX. On the significant differences between the MT and LXX here, see Kinman, *Jesus' Entry*, 54–56.

[50] Modern readers of the NT have undoubtedly grown accustomed to Matthew's citation of Zech 9:9, which mentions the meekness (πραΰς) of the king (Matt 21:5). However, it seems this royal virtue was not necessarily at odds with the idea of a warrior king. While the term *meek* normally refers to people in the Hebrew Bible who, though presently oppressed, can expect God to vindicate them in the future (Job 36:15; LXX: Pss 36:11; 75:9; 146:6; 149:4; Sir 10:14), in at least one instance these same people are enjoined to be warriors and take up the fight (LXX: Joel 4:11). In Zech 9:9 the meekness refers to the king's attitude of contrition and submission to God, not his aversion to battle.

[51] Coakley ("Jesus' Messianic Entry," 479) argues that Jesus did *not* take the initiative to ride; rather, he was forced on the colt by the bystanders. It is true that Jesus' motives are more opaque in the Johannine account, because the details of acquisition found in the Synoptics are missing. Yet Coakley overstates his case here. In John 12:14 it is Jesus, not others, who locates the animal (εὑρὼν δὲ ὁ Ἰησοῦς).

anything but a deliberate attempt to cast himself in the role of Jerusalem's king (it can also be observed that riding a colt would not necessarily signify that he was a nonthreatening or particularly humble king: biblical precedents suggest, or could have suggested to a first-century Jewish mind, that a donkey's colt was precisely the sort of animal a Jewish king might have been expected to ride into Jerusalem). This is not to say Jesus intended his entry be seen as fulfillment of Zech 9:9; the point is, fulfillment or not, the scriptural precedents just mentioned imply that Jesus was following, if not a prophetic prediction, then at the least a royal model in coming on a πῶλος. But this observation naturally gives rise to questions: Was Jesus' Entry not merely royal but also messianic? Could it have been royal but not messianic? What did Jesus intend?

Scholars have often characterized the Entry as obviously messianic – but insofar as *Jesus'* actions are concerned, this characterization of the Entry, when viewed by itself, does not stand up to scrutiny. There was not, from our knowledge of extant evidence, a generally agreed upon "messianic way" to enter Jerusalem. Concerning any messianic associations with Zech 9:9, two points can be made. The first is that there is no clear evidence to support the view that Zech 9:9 was considered a "messianic prediction" within Judaism prior to the writing of the Gospels. The earliest comment on the passage from the rabbis is found in *b. Sanh.* 98a, where R. Joshua b. Levi speculates about how messiah might appear to Israel; this comment was made in the third-century C.E. and thus provides no secure basis for understanding how the passage was understood in the days of Jesus.[52] The second point is this: there seems not to have been any awareness at the time of the Entry that it constituted any sort of "messianic fulfillment." Mark does not depict the entry as "fulfillment," though to be sure, the writing up of the narrative in Matthew and John, especially the introduction of the scriptural quotation and the characterization of the event as "fulfillment," does. J.F. Coakley observes that John, having first quoted Zech 9:9, then adds this caveat, "these things the disciples did not understand at first" (John 12:16a). Coakley writes,

... their significance [the words at 16a] lies precisely in the admission here by the evangelist that the events just narrated did not – except to the eye of faith – obviously conform to the interpretation later placed upon them. If that is true, then it cannot be that the whole narrative is controlled by the commentary.[53]

---

[52] While *Tg. Zech.* 9:9 would be earlier than this, it does not reflect explicit messianism. See Joseph A. Fitzmyer, *The One Who is to Come* (Grand Rapids: Eerdmans, 2007), 172–73. Cf. also n. 65 below.

[53] Coakley, "Jesus' Messianic Entry," 467–68. He further argues that this comment demonstrates John's preservation of historically trustworthy data here.

Thus, while the Entry is clearly messianic at the literary level (given the redaction in Matthew and John), it is not so clear that this was the case on the historical plane, particularly with respect to Jesus' intentions. Having observed that there was not a particularly "messianic way" to enter Jerusalem, I hasten to add that it is obvious that any entry made by messiah would by definition be "messianic." And so the question becomes, "Was Jesus the anticipated Davidic messiah?"

This question implies a particular understanding of "messianic." Unfortunately, a thorough discussion of this question, to which Christian tradition has replied with a resounding "yes," clearly lies outside the scope of the present investigation. But a few observations must be noted. The development of the various forms of first-century Jewish messianism is a fascinating topic; and, while it is not possible to regard first-century Jewish messianic hopes as homogenous, it is fair to conclude that, when the various first-century Judaisms are taken as a whole, the notion of a coming Davidic ruler was not only important and routinely mentioned but also dominant.[54] As John J. Collins summarizes, "This concept of the Davidic messiah as the warrior king who would destroy the enemies of Israel and institute an era of unending peace constitutes the common core of Jewish messianism around the turn of the era."[55] Biblical (2 Sam 7:12–16; 1 Chr 17:11–14; Pss 89:3–4, 19–29, 35–37; 132:10–11; Isa 9:3–9; 11:1–14; Jer 17:24–26; 23:5; Ezek 37:24–25) and extra-biblical texts (*Pss. Sol.* 17; *4 Ezra* 12:32; 4QPBless;

---

[54] For an example of the diversity of expectations, see Jacob Neusner, et al., *Judaisms and Their Messiahs at the Turn of the Christian Era* [Cambridge: Cambridge University Press, 1987]; Andrew Chester, "Jewish Messianic Expectations and Mediatorial Figures and Pauline Christology," in *Paulus und das antike Judentum: Tübingen-Durham-Symposium im Gedenken an den 50. Todestag Adolf Schlatters* [ed. Martin Hengel; WUNT 58; Tübingen: Mohr Siebeck, 1991], 17–89, esp. 17–65); and John J. Collins, *The Scepter and the Star: The Messiahs of the Dead Sea Scrolls and Other Ancient Literature* (ABRL; New York: Doubleday, 1995). For the messianic ideas in the Targums and their relevance to the present discussion, see Chester, "Jewish Messianic Expectations," 39–40, 80–81.

[55] Collins, *The Scepter and the Star*, 68. Collins's work is outstanding. Years earlier Christoph Burger wrote, "Die Beobachtung, daß während der beiden Jahrhunderte vor und nach Christi Geburt in allen jüdischen Texten, die den erwarteten Messias eindeutig als Daviden kennzeichnen, die Terminologie weithin konstant ist und immer wieder dieselben alttestamentlichen Stellen herangezogen werden, ist insofern von Bedeutung, als daraus gefolgert werden kann, daß auch die Vorstellung vom endzeitlichen Davidssproß in ihrem Kern sich gleich bleibt" ("The observation that during the two centuries before and after the birth of Christ the terminology in all the Jewish texts which identify the anticipated Messiah as David is largely unchanging and that the same passages in the Old Testament are drawn on repeatedly is significant, since it leads to the conclusion that the concept of the eschatological son of David remains basically the same.") (*Jesus als Davidssohn: Eine traditionsgeschichtliche Untersuchung* [FRLANT 98; Göttingen: Vandenhoeck & Ruprecht, 1970], 23); Dennis C. Duling agrees; see "Promises to David and Their Entrance Into Christianity: Nailing Down a Likely Hypothesis," *New Testament Studies* 20 (1973): 60. See also, most recently, Fitzmyer, *The One Who is to Come*.

4QFlor 1:10–13; 4QpIsa; *b. Sanh.* 98a; *y. Taʿan.* 4:7) illustrate the repeated connection between a descendant of David and the establishment, or restoration, of Israel's political fortunes. In a few of the biblical texts, the Messiah's imposition of his rule by violence is mentioned or hinted at (e.g., Ps 89:23; Isa 9:3–5; 11:4,13–14). The motif of violence is also present in various extra-biblical texts. For example, *Pss. Sol.* 17 refers to the covenant made with David (v. 4) and implores the Lord: "Raise up for them their king, a son of David, to rule over your servant Israel in the time known to you, O God" (v. 21). The psalmist hopes that this "son of David" will purge Israel and, in particular, Jerusalem, from both its own unrighteous rulers as well as from gentile domination (vv. 22, 28, 30). This longed-for "son of David" is "the Lord Messiah" (v. 32; see also CD 14:18–19; CD 19:10–11; 4QSefM 7:1–6). *4 Ezra* 12 also refers to a coming anointed one from the line of David that arises at the "end of days" (v. 32) and judges the wicked (v. 33) before showing mercy on the "remnant" (v. 34).

As we move from what much of the literature anticipated about a messiah (or messiahs) to what first-century history had offered up, we note that violence had become one criterion for judging any would-be messiah. Richard Horsley argues that the royal pretenders Judas, Simon, and Athronges (mentioned here, above), whose exploits are chronicled by Josephus, emerged as royal and perhaps even messianic figures a few years prior to the time of Jesus precisely because, in addition to their royal claims (Josephus, *Ant.* 17.271–81), they had engaged in the sort of actions that engendered support by the peasantry – they engaged Romans militarily.[56] Thus, at least with respect to one important element of what a messiah was expected to do – fight those perceived to be oppressors of the nation – we can concur with Horsley that some in Israel likely regarded these men as messianic.[57]

---

[56] He notes that Josephus "apparently avoids any suggestion of the distinctive Jewish tradition of an anointed king in his accounts of Judas, Simon, and Athronges" (Horsley, "Popular Messianic Movements," 484). Horsley appears to use the term *anointed* as equivalent to "popular among the people, particularly among the peasant classes" (as opposed to "anointed according to the pattern described in Israel's Scriptures"). Thus for him "messianic" does not necessarily mean messianic according to the expectations reflected in the many biblical and extrabiblical texts cited. While there is no clear evidence these men offered themselves as having a Davidic pedigree, Josephus does comment that one, Athronges, had been a "shepherd" – an allusion, perhaps, to David, though he also says Athronges was not distinguished as to ancestry (*Ant.* 17.278).

[57] Horsley, "Popular Messianic Movements," 471–95. In a rather different vein, William R. Farmer ("Judas, Simon and Athronges," *NTS* 4 [1958]: 147–55) makes the intriguing argument that these men either were or claimed to be of Maccabean descent, thus accounting for the support they enjoyed from Jews who wished to see another purge of Gentile elements from the land. He notes that this Maccabean link was more likely for Judas and Athronges than Simon.

By contrast, as Jesus made his last journey to Jerusalem, he did not approach as one who had taken on Israel's enemies in the popularly anticipated way. He had not engaged the Romans militarily nor encouraged his followers to do so. His wonderworking ministry might have brought to mind certain of the biblical pictures of a new era (e. g., Isa 35:5–6; cf. 4Q521), but he had not fulfilled (or even begun to fulfill) other, more central popular expectations concerning a messiah's role in executing judgment and national liberation prior to his final approach to Jerusalem. Nothing in the manner of Jesus' approach would have encouraged his followers to take up arms and oppose the Romans. As will be noted below, if anything, he tried to discourage that sort of militancy. For now, we can affirm that with respect to *Jesus'* actions, it appears that his coming was above all a "royal" event and not *necessarily* (or at the very least, not unequivocally) a messianic one. However, as we shall see, other elements of the account and other actors at the Entry may well have elevated the mood from merely royal to messianic. What about these other features of his arrival – namely, the actions of those who spread branches as he traveled to Jerusalem and offered him their acclamations?

3.2. The Disciples' Reactions

According to Mark 11:8–10, Jesus' actions to secure a colt are followed by two reactions on the part of the disciples. They make a show of recognizing him as king first by their actions and then by their words.

After Jesus mounts the colt, the disciples spread garments and leafy branches on the road to serve like pavement, so to speak, for his ride into Jerusalem.[58] The spreading of the garments is featured in all the Gospels save John, while the cutting and spreading of branches is found in all but Luke. Such actions were common to celebratory entries in the ancient world whether the entrant was a king or some other important person.[59] There is no clear indication of what prompted this response from the disciples, though the most natural inference from the text is that they recognized the royal connotations of Jesus riding a colt and reacted accordingly to honor him.

Mark's bland depiction of the disciples cutting branches and laying them ahead of Jesus finds interesting confirmation – and greater specificity – in John's account. In Mark the disciples obtain the rather nondescript στιβάδας (branches) from the fields to lay before Jesus. John is more specific, noting

---

[58] There is scriptural precedent for laying garments under a king in 2 Kgs 9:13 where Jehu's fellow army commanders scramble to honor him as king following his impromptu anointing by an unnamed prophet's servant.

[59] E. g., Suetonius *Nero* 6.25.

the crowds cut τῶν φοινίκων (palm branches) from the fields as part of their greeting. John's greater specificity seems not to be readily attributable to any obvious Johannine christological or apologetic motif, and it contributes to the view that Mark's account is based on sound historical footing. How so?

The identification of palm branches as nationalistic symbols is well documented.[60] The mention of palm branches together with royal acclaim for Jesus makes the Johannine version of the Entry somewhat inflammatory because it associates Jesus and his disciples with the sort of nationalistic symbolism easily perceived as seditious. Yet elsewhere, this is precisely the sort of impression John wants to avoid (6:15). Hence, if this feature of the story (the palm branches) is retained in spite of its potential for misinterpretation, there is high probability that it is authentic. This would also mean that Mark's general reference to laying branches before Jesus is doubly attested.

In each of the Gospels the disciples' tacit recognition of Jesus' kingship is followed by explicit statements to that effect. Mark says this: "And those going ahead and those following were crying out, 'Hosanna! Blessed is the one who comes in the name of the Lord! Blessed is the coming kingdom of our father David.'"[61] The first half of the purported acclaim is a quotation from Ps 118:26 (ὡσαννά· εὐλογημένος ὁ ἐρχόμενος ἐν ὀνόματι κυρίου); the second half contains the apparently unprecedented (at least in the extant literature) mention of "David's kingdom" (εὐλογημένη ἡ ἐρχομένη βασιλεία τοῦ πατρὸς ἡμῶν Δαυίδ).

Psalm 118 (LXX 117) is applied to Jesus' Entry by every Gospel writer (Matt 21:9; Mark 11:9; Luke 19:38; John 12:13). There is some evidence that

---

[60] Memories of the Maccabean exploits persisted in Jesus' day. They were especially strong in Roman Palestine, as William R. Farmer demonstrated in *Maccabees, Zealots, and Josephus: An Inquiry Into Jewish Nationalism in the Greco-Roman Period* (New York: Columbia University Press, 1956); see esp. pp. 125–58. Two episodes in Maccabean history are germane to the discussion of "foliage." After Judas Maccabaeus fought the army of Lysia, he went to Jerusalem to cleanse the temple (1 Macc 4:36). Branches and palm fronds were carried by the participants on their way to the temple (2 Macc 10:7). Palm branches were also mentioned prominently in the procession of Simon Maccabaeus to Jerusalem and his rededication of the temple (1 Macc 13:51). Farmer explored the connection between the palm branches taken up by the crowd in John 12:13 and in Maccabean precedents and showed that these branches were distinctive nationalist symbols and easily recognized as such ("Palm Branches in John 12,13," *JTS* 3 [1952]: 62–66). Wayne A. Meeks observes that, though palm branches regularly denoted victory, they had "no necessary connection with royalty" (*The Prophet-King. Moses Traditions and the Johannine Christology* [NovTSup 14; Leiden: Brill, 1967], 86). They appear on various Jewish coins and in the literary accounts of the Maccabees' exploits along with other collections of branches (cf. Paul Romanoff, "Jewish Symbols on Ancient Jewish Coins," *JQR* 34 [1943–44]: 425–40). They originally emerged as symbols in association with the observance of the Feast of Tabernacles (Lev 23:40).

[61] On the meaning of the phrase, see Eduard Lohse, "Hosianna," *NovT* 6 (1963): 115.

the psalm developed in a cultic environment with particular application to a ceremony involving the king.[62] This early, apparently ritualistic use, was recognized and expanded on by later interpreters who delineated the roles of the participants in the antiphonal singing.[63] But the psalm could not have been used in precisely this fashion in the post-exilic era, when no "son of David" occupied the throne of Israel, and the nation was dominated by foreign powers. There is some debate about whether these Hallel Psalms were sung on the way to Jerusalem or were confined to use inside the temple.[64] The Mishnah indicates the Hallel was sung at temple during the sacrifices at Passover (*m. Pesaḥ.* 5:7), while at Tabernacles it was sung by pilgrims approaching Jerusalem (*m. Sukkah* 4:5). This makes its appearance here – outside Jerusalem prior to Passover – seem anachronistic. Having said that, we are hardly in the position to aver that the Hallel could not have been sung at other times; it is not as though there was a proscription against singing it at times other than the "appropriate" feasts. If the Hallel were sung or chanted by pilgrims on the way to Jerusalem, the appearance of the quotation from Ps 118 here in the Gospel narratives would be unremarkable.[65] Yet the Gospel accounts leave the impression that the disciples were not simply reciting pilgrim songs at an auspicious moment – they seem to be directing their acclaim and the words of the psalm toward Jesus: the branches and garments are laid before *him*, onlookers are both preceding and following *him*, and the quotation from the psalm is picked up where an *individual* (εὐλογημένος ὁ ἐρχόμενος) coming to Jerusalem is in view. Given that Jesus has just exercised, as it were, a royal prerogative by having the colt fetched and riding it, and given that the psalm itself was historically understood as featuring Israel's king, its application to Jesus by onlookers is both comprehensible and dramatic.

Yet, in addition to its regal and festal overtones, some scholars have concluded that the particular portion of the psalm cited by Mark (ὡσαννά· εὐλογημένος ὁ ἐρχόμενος ἐν ὀνόματι κυρίου) was recited here by onlookers because the term "the one who comes" (ὁ ἐρχόμενος) had in some quarters

---

[62] Psalms 113–118 formed the Great Hallel and, according to tradition, were sung by pilgrims on the way to Jerusalem. They were typically recited at the major Jewish religious festivals of Passover in the Spring (Unleavened Bread; *m. Pesaḥ.* 5:7) and Tabernacles in the Autumn (*m. Sukkah* 3:9). They were also employed at the celebration of Hanukkah. See Str-B 1:845–850; and Sigmund Mowinckel, *The Psalms in Israel's Worship* (2 vols.; trans. D. R. Ap-Thomas; Oxford: Blackwell, 1962), 1:3, 120–21.

[63] *Tg. Ketab.* Ps 118; *b. Pesah.* 119a; see also Eric Werner, "'Hosanna' in the Gospels," *JBL* 65 (1946): 115.

[64] Lohse ("Hosianna") says they were sung on the way to the festivals; Solomon Zeitlin ("Hallel: A Historical Study of the Canonization of the Hebrew Liturgy," *Jewish Quarterly Review* 53 [1962]: 22–29) believes they were sung *inside* the temple.

[65] Harvey (*Jesus and the Constraints of History*, 127) argues this point.

taken on messianic associations, particularly as reflected in the Targum to Ps 118.⁶⁶ For these onlookers, the "one who comes in the name of the Lord" (v. 26) was not a figure from the past or the current sovereign who was to be fêted as part of a regular national celebration – rather, he was an as yet to be revealed deliverer.⁶⁷ It is impossible to determine how widely this view was held.⁶⁸ Moreover, while the Targum does delineate how the antiphonal singing in the Psalm is to be divided into parts, it is difficult to see how it significantly heightens whatever messianic element might have been already present in the psalm itself. As noted above, the tone of the Entry – at least *as set by Jesus* – is clearly royal but not nearly so clearly messianic or eschatological. So what are we to read into the citation of the psalm here? Were the messianic impulses of the crowd aroused by Jesus riding?

Perhaps. It is not difficult to understand how the crowd accompanying Jesus, or at least, some members of that crowd, would have had eschatological and perhaps even messianic expectations aroused as Jesus came to Jerusalem. After all, he had been preaching about the soon appearance of God's kingdom and performing wonders that not only lent credibility to his teaching but were also themselves signs of the kingdom's presence.⁶⁹ As Sanders and others have noted, Jesus himself expected to occupy a central role in this kingdom, and now, at the religiously and politically charged Passover season, he leads an entourage to Jerusalem.⁷⁰ Moreover, his identification as "son of David" by blind Bartimaeus would have further set the stage for the response of onlookers at the Entry.⁷¹ While it cannot be established be-

---

⁶⁶ Johannes Schneider, "ἔρχομαι," *TDNT* 2:667–71; see also Joachim Jeremias, *The Eucharistic Words of Jesus* (trans. Norman Perrin; NTL; London: SCM, 1966), 256–60.

⁶⁷ Schneider, *TDNT* 2:670; Werner, "'Hosanna' in the Gospels," 97–122. Note in particular the clear but sparing references to an expected figure in the *Sybylline Oracles* and *Psalms of Solomon* (see the discussion in Schürer, *History*, 2:501–13). I adopt the more cautionary approach of Fitzmyer (*The One Who is to Come*, 146–81) in contemplating the extent to which the Targums might reliably be thought to reflect messianic expectations at the time of Jesus.

⁶⁸ John P. Meier (*Mentor, Message, and Miracles* [vol. 2 of *A Marginal Jew: Rethinking the Historical Jesus*; ABRL; New York: Doubleday, 1991–2009], 199) sounds an important, cautionary note: "However, all that these texts [employing the notion or phrase 'coming one'] necessarily show is that the verb 'come' … can take on a solemn eschatological resonance in a given eschatological context. The verb in itself is not attached to any one eschatological figure. Indeed, in an eschatological context, almost everything and anything is said to 'come,' including the days."

⁶⁹ For the timing of the kingdom's appearance as preached by Jesus, see especially Sanders, *Historical Figure*, 169–88; also Witherington, *The Christology of Jesus*, 192–203; and Brent Kinman, *History, Design, and the End of Time: God's Plan for the World* (Nashville: Broadman & Holman, 2000), 49–64.

⁷⁰ On this see, for example, Sanders, *Historical Figure*, 238–48; Witherington, *The Christology of Jesus*, 203–4.

⁷¹ In each Synoptic Gospel Jesus' Entry is bracketed, on one end, by the healing of the blind man outside Jericho (Mark 10:46–52; Matt 20:29–34; Luke 18:35–43) and, on the

yond question that the recitation of Ps 118 here was messianic, when taken together with the other elements of the context just mentioned, the scene surely does take on an eschatological coloring and this, together with the royal one supplied by Jesus, can easily be understood to have led onlookers to regard the whole moment as messianic. Many surely did. Moreover, if Jesus both understood and presented himself as messiah prior to the Entry (with "messiah" understood as a figure who places himself at the center of God's eschatological program and has a unique role in that program), as has been argued elsewhere in this volume, *then the Entry represents a very significant addition to our picture of him in that he now clearly understands and depicts himself to the nation as a royal person, and this presentation corresponds very dramatically to a number of broadly held first-century expectations regarding the coming of God's royal, indeed, Davidic, messiah.*

Having said this, it is worth observing that with respect to the Entry itself, if we can rely on Luke's Gospel there is some evidence that Jesus himself was wary of the nationalistic-messianic overtones that seemed to be emerging at this point in his ministry. What is this evidence?

---

other, by the account of the temple cleansing. The JS regards both of these bracketing episodes as probable ("pink") and many other critical scholars agree; see, for example, Sanders, *Historical Figure*, 254–56; John Dominic Crossan, *The Historical Jesus: The Life of a Mediterranean Jewish Peasant* (San Francisco: HarperSanFrancisco, 1991), 357; Funk and Seminar, *The Acts of Jesus*, 560; Fredriksen, *Jesus of Nazareth*, 207–12. For the most thorough, and to my mind *persuasive* argument in favor of historicity, see Meier, *Mentor, Message, and Miracles*, 686–90. One of the most interesting features of the blind man story is how it raises the "son of David" question as Jesus approaches Jerusalem; to be even more specific, although the label is employed in the appeal of the blind man (in spite of the crowd's desire to quiet him, Mark 10:48), Jesus does not ignore, sidestep, or correct him. The phrase "son of David" would have had messianic connotations for many eyewitnesses; and royal ones, at the least, for all. It is true that according to Mark Jesus distances himself from titles that could be construed as messianic early in his ministry (e.g., "the holy one of God," Mark 1:25, 34; "son of God," Mark 3:12; "the Christ," Mark 8:29–30; "my beloved son," Mark 9:9), but that only makes his apparent embrace of "son of David" here all the more intriguing. His response to the blind man – to listen, grant his request for healing, and commend him with the words "your faith has saved you" (Mark 10:52) – contains not the slightest discomfort or objection to the "son of David" label. If anything, Jesus' actions and words are implicit confirmation that the man has spoken well. On the range of possible connotations of "son of David" in this context, see Chester C. McCown, "The Christian Tradition as to the Magical Wisdom of Solomon," *JPOS* 2 (1922): 1–24; Loren R. Fisher, "'Can This be the Son of David?'," in *Jesus and the Historian: Written in Honor of Ernest Cadman Colwell* (ed. Frederick T. Trotter; Philadelphia: Westminster, 1968), 82–97; Burger, *Jesus als Davidssohn*, 16–24; Klaus Berger, "Die königlichen Messiastraditionen des Neuen Testaments," *NTS* 20 (1973): 3–9; Duling, "Promises to David and Their Entrance Into Christianity: Nailing Down a Likely Hypothesis," esp. 55–69; Dennis C. Duling, "Solomon, Exorcism, and the Son of David," *HTR* 68 (1975): 235–52; and Bruce D. Chilton, "Jesus Ben David: Reflections on the Davidssohnfrage," *JSNT* 14 (1982): 88–112, esp. 92–101. Many of these scholars note that the label "son of David" in a context where healing is sought would have perhaps had more "Solomonic" than "messianic" associations.

Luke claims to have investigated the Jesus story "carefully" (Luke 1:3), and it might therefore be significant that at the Entry narrative he inserts two pericopes that have the effect of demonstrating Jesus' caution about the eschatological and nationalistic hopes that seem to have been aroused as he journeyed to Jerusalem. In the first instance, Luke has inserted the story of Jesus meeting the diminutive chief tax-collector Zacchaeus (19:1–10) between the narratives of the healing of the blind man (Luke 18:35–43 = Mark 10:45–52) and the Entry (Luke 19:28–44 = Mark 11:1–10). If this reflects the actual order of events in Jesus' life (and I see no compelling reason why it could not), it is highly relevant to the issue of how Jesus viewed the whole scene leading up to the Entry, for he embraces Zacchaeus, something the leaders of various first century nationalistic movements would have been reluctant to do given the commonly perceived link between tax-collectors and the Roman oppressors. His embrace of Zacchaeus would likely have dampened (or was at the least intended to dampen) whatever popular nationalistic expectations might have been held among those who witnessed this train of events; at a minimum, it would have given pause to those who embraced the notion that all things touched by the Romans were worthy of destruction. Second, the Zacchaeus episode is followed by Jesus telling the parable of the nobleman going to a far country to receive his kingdom (19:12–27);[72] Luke explains that Jesus told the parable "because he was near to Jerusalem, and because they [his disciples] supposed that the kingdom of God was to appear immediately" (19:11).[73] If, as seems likely, Jesus is the "nobleman" in the parable, it serves to put off expectations that the consummation of the kingdom would come straightaway. The parable demonstrates Jesus' awareness that the time for political expectations to be fulfilled had not come.[74] If these two Lukan additions to Mark's narrative reflect the

---

[72] For a thorough discussion of the parable's meaning, see Kinman, *Jesus' Entry*, 86–87.

[73] Although the parable's source and possible historical referent are debated, it is typically seen to put in the mouth of Jesus a clear warning that expectations of an immediate coming of the kingdom were misguided. Some argue that Luke has combined two separate parables here – the Q-based parable of the talents (cf. Matt 25:14–30) and another one dealing with a "throne-pretender"; see Max Zerwick, "Die Parabel vom Thronanwärter," *Bib* 40 (1959): 654–74; E. Earle Ellis, *The Gospel of Luke* (NCB; London: Marshall, Morgan, & Scott, 1974), 222. Joachim Jeremias suggests the parables were combined in a pre-Lukan tradition (*The Parables of Jesus* [rev. ed.; trans. S. H. Hooke; London: SCM, 1963], 59). Others believe that Luke has edited the parable of Q without combining it with another (Friedrich Hauck, *Das Evangelium des Lukas* [THKNT; Leipzig: Deichert, 1934], 231). Siegfried Schulz (*Q: Die Spruchquelle der Evangelisten*, 288–93) speaks of a "Motiv vom Thronprätendenten" rather than a pre-existing throne pretender parable. Marshall (*Luke*, 701) contends that one parable, which was subjected to a considerable development in its pre-literary form, lies behind the Matthean and Lukan versions; see also C. H. Dodd, *The Parables of the Kingdom* (3rd ed.; London: Nisbet, 1952), 146.

[74] Hans Werner Bartsch suggests that Luke's comments may have been intended to correct the view that "the Passion of Jesus in Jerusalem was already bringing the Parousia"

actual order of events in Jesus' life, they suggest Jesus intended to dampen nationalistic expectations as he approached Jerusalem (his "intention," I submit, was neither entirely discerned nor heeded); if, on the other hand, the two Lukan stories were motivated by Luke's redactional interests, they nevertheless show Luke's perception of the potentially embarrassing nature of Mark's Entry narrative as it stood.

Virtually every element of the Entry story – from its setting at Jerusalem to the riding of the colt to the laying of garments and branches and the giving of acclamations – is, at the least, royal, and thus also potentially understood, when viewed through an eschatological prism, as messianic. The timing of the event, at Passover, when the nation remembered its liberation from foreign oppressors, was an additional, important element in this "prism." But none of these elements is exclusively messianic. Jesus clearly intended his Entry to be seen as "royal"; others recognized and significantly contributed to its eschatological and messianic flavoring, though he could hardly have found this turn of events surprising.[75]

There remain two important backgrounds to the Entry to explore: the size of the crowd that witnessed it, and Pilate's own coming to Jerusalem.

3.3. The Size of the Crowd

In connection with the objections of E. P. Sanders and others (noted earlier), it is appropriate to consider how large the entourage that accompanied Jesus might have been. Was the size of the group itself large enough to raise imperial suspicions? In the Gospel accounts it is easy, at first reading, to suppose that the eyes of everyone in Jerusalem were upon Jesus as he approached the city. But this is hardly the image required by the Gospel texts. Mark 11:8 reports, "And many (πολλοί) spread their garments on the road, and others (ἄλλοι) spread leafy branches which they had cut from the fields." The term πολύς as used in Mark is rather elastic. It can refer to crowds numbering from, at most, several dozen (Mark 2:2, 15; 5:26) to several thousand (6:34). Context normally narrows its range of meaning, but in Mark 11 context supplies little help. Jesus has emerged from Jericho with his disciples and a "great multitude" (ὄχλου ἱκανοῦ), yet by the time we come to the Entry narrative, the story of the colt's acquisition has intervened and disrupted any

---

("Early Christian Eschatology in the Synoptic Gospels: A Contribution to Form-Critical Research," *NTS* 11 [1965]: 393). Luke's parable seems a very oblique way of refuting such a view; more applicable, perhaps, would be Acts 1:6–11, which refers to the return of Jesus.

[75] His failure to quiet the disciples could be understood as tacit approval for their actions, but their actions, as we have seen, are not incontestably "messianic." See, in particular, the sober of assessments of E. P. Sanders (*Historical Figure*, 240–42) and Joseph Fitzmyer (*The One Who is to Come*, 138–40) on the term "messiah" as embraced by Jesus himself.

unambiguous identification of the crowd of people who might be counted among the "many" of 11:8. Matthew's account is comparable to Mark's, although the subject in the first clause of Matt 21:8 is "most of the crowd" (ὁ δὲ πλεῖστος ὄχλος).[76] As in Mark, the identity of this group accompanying Jesus is ambiguous – its size and make-up are unspecified. It might refer to the crowd that witnessed the healing of the blind men outside Jericho, although strictly speaking, the "crowd" in the nearest context is composed of disciples (Matt 21:6). Furthermore, the language hints that only part of the crowd with Jesus joined in the ritual greeting.[77] Luke 19:36 is less specific in identifying those who "spread their garments" (ὑπεστρώννυον τὰ ἱμάτια αὐτῶν), although technically they are the two disciples commissioned to fetch the colt (v. 29).

Similar disparity over the crowd's identification is reflected in the following unit that rehearses the crowds' acclamation based on Ps 118:25–26. Mark 11:9–10 attributes the twofold blessing to "those who went before and those who followed" (οἱ προάγοντες καὶ οἱ ἀκολουθοῦντες), presumably subsets of the "many" mentioned in v. 8. For Matthew, the blessing comes from those "preceding and following," who are later simply called "the crowds" (οἱ ὄχλοι). It is not clear whether this label expands the size of the group mentioned in Matt 21:8. The Lukan account is here more specific. Luke 19:37–38 locates the event "at the descent of the Mount of Olives" and attributes the acclamation to the whole multitude of the disciples (ἅπαν τὸ πλῆθος τῶν μαθητῶν). This latter phrase J. A. Fitzmyer regards as "Lucan hyperbole," and J. Ernst suggests that Luke expressly mentions a large crowd (though not specifically numbered) in order to stress that Jesus had many followers.[78] But by identifying the group as Jesus' disciples, Luke's text conceivably reduces rather than enlarges the size of the crowd: it was indeed "a crowd," but one composed of disciples, not the public at large.[79] We might get some idea of its size by looking ahead to Acts 1:12–15, where Luke gives the impression that most if not all the disciples had assembled in the upper room after Jesus' ascension and that they numbered 120.

As to how the soldiers might have viewed this entourage, Josephus tells us that Roman troops stationed in Jerusalem for the festival were typically housed at the Antonia and were primarily concerned with maintaining or-

---

[76] The RSV, NASB, NLT and ESV translations retain the force of the superlative here; the NIV and NKJV do not.

[77] For this use of the superlative, see Kurt and Barbara Aland, ed., *Griechisch-deutsches Wörterbuch zu den Schriften des Neuen Testaments und der frühchristlichen Literatur von W. Bauer* (6th ed.; Berlin: De Gruyter, 1988), 1382–83.

[78] Fitzmyer, *Luke X–XXIV*, 1250. Similarly, see C. F. Evans, *Saint Luke* (TPINTC; London: SCM; Philadelphia: Trinity, 1990), 680; Ernst, *Das Evangelium nach Lukas*, 526.

[79] For more on how these comments correspond to Luke's redactional interests, see Kinman, *Jesus' Entry*, 120–22, 175–79.

der in the temple precincts.⁸⁰ To revisit Sanders's earlier objection, one need not imagine that the crowd accompanying Jesus outside Jerusalem was so large as to have commanded the attention of soldiers, who were primarily concerned with events inside the city and temple. In fact, one valid way of reading the text is that the lack of military intervention suggests a smaller group accompanied Jesus than is often envisioned.

John's picture is somewhat different and at first reading seems to envision a larger group greeting Jesus than do the Synoptics. He describes the onlookers as a "large crowd" composed not only of those traveling with Jesus but also those inside Jerusalem who had heard of his approach and made their way outside the city to welcome him (John 12:12). A closer examination, however, reveals the crowd need not be perceived as very large. The ὁ ὄχλος πολύς of 12:12 seems to be identical with the group mentioned earlier at 12:9 (ὁ ὄχλος πολύς), which refers to those friends and curiosity seekers who had visited the revived Lazarus. The large crowd may further be traced to the "many Jews" who had consoled Mary and Martha when Lazarus died (11:19–23). Somewhat later, John adds that the crowd was made up of "those who had been with him when he raised Lazarus from the dead" (12:17); this last text hardly contemplates a crowd of thousands, or even hundreds for that that matter, because it refers to those Jews "who were with her in the house" (11:31).

This theory that the crowd that witnessed Jesus' Entry was relatively small is made all the more likely when we consider, by way of comparison, the size of the crowds that would have been ascending to Jerusalem at festival time. The season of Passover attracted large crowds of Jews to Jerusalem from various parts of the world. As Jeremias observed, the population of the city would have been greatly enlarged at this time, and the days prior to the celebration would have witnessed a steady stream of visitors, undoubtedly thousands, to Jerusalem.⁸¹ They would have approached the city from various directions – there were entry points to the city on all sides. If Sanders is correct that the pilgrims would typically arrive several days in advance of the of Passover itself and if he is also correct in thinking some 300,000 might have traveled, it would mean that on average several thousand people per day would have come to the city or loitered in its precincts.⁸² Given this scenario, it is not difficult to imagine that the crowd that accompanied Jesus would have had to have been extremely large for it to be distinguish-

---

⁸⁰ *J. W.* 5.243–45.

⁸¹ Joachim Jeremias, *Jerusalem zur Zeit Jesu: Eine kulturgeschichtliche Untersuchung zur neutestamentlichen Zeitgeschichte* (3rd ed.; Göttingen: Vandenhoeck & Ruprecht, 1962), 66–98. E. P. Sanders (*Judaism: Practice and Belief, 63 BCE–66 CE* [Philadelphia: Trinity, 1992], 125–28) suggests Jerusalem could have held 300,000–400,000 pilgrims!

⁸² Sanders, *Historical Figure*, 249–51.

able from others who were making their way to the city and thus to have attracted Roman attention. It should additionally be noted that the laying of branches under Jesus' feet may well have been beyond the Roman soldiers ability to see. The Synoptics agree that the colt was secured for Jesus in the town of Bethphage, outside Jerusalem. While the acclamations began, according to Luke, at the "descent of the Mount of Olives," at least some of the action took place beforehand: in both John and Luke, the garments and the palm branches are thrown down in front of Jesus before he mounts the colt. While the Roman lookouts would probably have been chosen, at least in part, for their keen eyesight, recognizing the palm branches mentioned in John 12 from a distance of several hundred feet would have been difficult, to say the least.

Furthermore, even if the entourage had been observed, the potentially seditious nature of the event had largely to do with what was said by the disciples. According to the Gospels they hail Jesus as king – but what is the likelihood that what they said would have been heard and understood by the Romans charged with keeping the peace? The soldiers nearest them would have been about 300 yards away, and the human voice is not particularly resonant, even less so at high altitude (i.e., at the altitude as far above sea level as Jerusalem). And yet, even on the assumption that the soldiers could have heard what was being said about Jesus, the question remains: would they have understood its import? For, although the Roman soldiers with Pilate were not regular Italian soldiers (they were largely drawn from Samaria and other nearby regions[83]), it is by no means certain that all of them would have been sufficiently bi- or tri-lingual to understand the words spoken or chanted from a distance, presumably in Hebrew or Aramaic, by Jesus' disciples.

Finally, even if a larger demonstration than the one contemplated here had occurred, it is far from clear that it would have commanded the notice of the Romans. As mentioned earlier, the Roman soldiers' attention would likely have focused on action inside rather than outside the temple, because that was where trouble was most likely to erupt.[84] Moreover, the considerable height of the temple wall in Jesus' day would have meant that only the lookouts that happened to be facing eastward, outside the city, could conceivably have seen Jesus' entourage. But it is unlikely that merely seeing Jesus approach would have caused distress: after all, he was riding a donkey's colt, hardly the sort of animal to raise concern, much less strike fear, into the heart of a Roman soldier. Taken together, the points raised make it

---

[83] Schürer, *History*, 1:362, 365.
[84] Schürer, *History*, 1:366.

likely that the crowd that accompanied Jesus was rather modest in size. No wonder, then, that it failed to raise imperial suspicions.

3.4. The Background of Pilate's Entry

The welcome extended to a royal or other dignitary was designed to court the favor and/or placate the wrath of the visiting celebrity through an ostentatious greeting ceremony. In the Hellenistic world this combination of arrival and greeting was often associated with terms such as παρουσία, ἀπαντάω, and ὑπαντάω (but even if these particular terms were absent, other elements in a description would have made it clear that a special sort of entry was in view). The importance of the occasion in the ancient world is illustrated by the fact that eras were often reckoned from the date of a given παρουσία.[85] There is overwhelming evidence to indicate that the eyewitnesses to Jesus' Entry and the first readers of the Gospels would have been familiar with παρουσίαι, and the protocol of entries would have been familiar to first-century Palestinian Jews not only from the sources just mentioned but also from a recent experience much closer to home – the coming of the Roman governor, Pontius Pilate.

The Gospels agree that Jesus stood trial before Pilate. Because Roman governors headquartered farther north and west, in Caesarea Maritima, Pilate's presence in Jerusalem requires explanation. It is likely that Pilate had come to Jerusalem at the time of Passover not only to ensure civic order in the city but also, in accordance with the custom of Roman governors elsewhere, to conduct trials.[86]

The coming of a Roman governor to a city presented its rulers, merchants and inhabitants with an opportunity to enhance their position in the governor's eyes or, conversely, to risk the retaliation that likely would follow from behavior thought to be curt or insulting.[87] A proper welcome could

---

[85] See Deissmann, *Light from the Ancient East*, 372, and nn. 2–6.

[86] See Brent Kinman, "Pilate's Assize and the Timing of Jesus' Trial," *Tyndale Bulletin* 42 (1991): 282–95. For recent discussions of Pilate, see Jean-Pierre Lémonon, *Pilate et le gouvernement de la Judée: textes et monuments* (EBib; Paris: Gabalda, 1981); Brian C. McGing, "Pontius Pilate and the Sources," *CBQ* 53 (1991): 416–38; and, most recently, Helen Bond, *Pontius Pilate in History and Interpretation* (SNTSMS 100; Cambridge: Cambridge University Press, 1999). Both Josephus and Philo portray him as an eminently dislikeable man. Philo describes Pilate as "naturally inflexible, a blend of self-will and relentlessness ... vindictive and possessed of a furious temper" (*Embassy* 301, 303). He also suggests that Pilate was corrupt, having committed "... briberies, the insults, the robberies, the outrages and wanton injuries ..." (*Embassy* 302). Carl H. Kraeling ("The Episode of the Roman Standards at Jerusalem," *HTR* 35 [1942]: 263–89) tempers Philo's remarks; see also McGing's article.

[87] Examples of a city's failure to welcome its distinguished guests are rare, and with good reason – a city's failure to render the customary regard could have grave consequences and thus was to be avoided. Dio Cassius does mention the notable example of

prove to be a financial and judicial advantage to individual citizens as well as city officials; an improper one could have unpredictable and unfavorable results.[88] These intricate socio-political relationships and expectations were current in the days of Pilate's rule in Judea.[89] Despite his unpopularity, there were arguably several parties interested enough in maintaining the status quo (i.e., their own retention of power) to ensure that he would receive the "welcome" he "deserved" as he approached Jerusalem at the Passover season.

In Judea, Sadducees, Pharisees, and ordinary citizens would probably have been mobilized to greet Pilate as he arrived. These groups would admittedly have formed an ill-at-ease congregation; still, for the purpose of political expediency, it is not impossible to believe they would have co-operated with one another (as seems to have been the case at Jesus' trials; that is, the Council was composed of both Pharisees and Sadducees). The Sadducees had a special interest in placating the governor, for the high priest who was inevitably chosen from among their number was appointed by the prefect;[90] furthermore, according to John's Gospel the Pharisees had vested interests in appeasing Pilate as well (John 11:48).[91] Jerusalem's citizenry could have been encouraged by the prominent religious leaders to greet Pilate – as modern-day events reveal, crowds and demonstrations can always be arranged. Merchants, traders, and other businessmen would have their own reasons for seeing Pilate (as mentioned above).

---

the Roman magistrate T. Virginius Rufus, who besieged the city of Vesontio because it did not receive him properly (Dio Cassius 63.24.1). In a related story, the chief priests at Jerusalem urged the crowds to meet the troops of the Roman governor of Judea, Florus, with customary regard so that he might not have any grounds for further destruction in the city (*J. W.* 2.318–24). The priests' actions show an awareness of appropriate entry customs and the need to observe them.

[88] Fergus Millar, *The Emperor in the Roman World, 31 BC–AD 337* (London: Duckworth, 1977), 28.

[89] As Millar (*The Emperor in the Roman World*, 29) observes, "The various forms of relationship here referred to, which by their very indeterminacy constituted a sensitive area in the contact between subject and governor in the provinces, persisted through the later republic and into the empire." In fact, the possibilities for benefit and harm were sharpened during the time of the emperors when a governor was vested with the power of Rome (which he held by delegation from Caesar), for an insult perceived to be directed toward Caesar (via his appointee) might not be diffused through senatorial interventions, as could have been the case in the republic. Millar adds, "When monarchy was established, all these social and political aspects of a governor's journey reappeared on a larger scale …" (p. 31).

[90] This was true for the time of Pilate in which the Roman prefect governed Judea. Earlier, Herod and Archelaus had appointed high priests. See Schürer, *History*, 2:227–32; also E. Mary Smallwood, "High Priests and Politics in Roman Palestine," *JTS* 13 (1962): 14–34.

[91] See especially Fredriksen, *Jesus of Nazareth*, 253–55, and her discussion of those passages in Josephus that show how Jewish religious leaders faced the wrath of political leaders when insurrection broke out, even without the support of the religious leaders.

Precisely how they would have greeted him is another matter. The coming of a provincial governor often took on the trappings of a stately, if not royal, procession. For example, the Roman magistrate Lucullus received a royal welcome when he visited Egypt in the first century B.C.E.,[92] and a few years later Cicero recorded that at the outset of his judicial tour (in 51 B.C.E.) "extraordinary throngs of people have come to meet me from farms and villages and every homestead."[93] Elsewhere in the Empire, a band of municipal officials and other citizens, including the social, religious, and political élite, typically proceeded some distance from the city in order to meet an approaching dignitary well in advance of the city walls.[94] From the little we know of Pilate, there is no reason to suppose that he, like Roman magistrates elsewhere, would have expected less than a splendid, even if insincere, welcome. Correspondingly, Jewish officials were certainly not strangers to the intricacies of Roman diplomacy; they sent embassies to Caesar and his representatives on more than one occasion (Jos., *Ant.* 17.300–14; *J.W.* 2.280) and greeted other dignitaries at Jerusalem with customary regard (Philo, *Embassy* 297; Jos., *Ant.* 16.12–19; 18.90; *J.W.* 2.297).

While the governor's arrival would have been accompanied by acclamations from the local inhabitants, his appearance would have been staged with an eye toward discouraging those who might have been contemplating a test of Roman power though devious or seditious acts. Although Pilate would not have had the privilege of accompaniment by certain officials,[95] he still would have had an impressive entourage. The largest, most formidable group (from the point of view of intimidation) to travel with a governor would have been the soldiers under his command. It seems probable that both infantry and horsemen would have accompanied Pilate from Caesarea, and the massive increase in Jerusalem's population during the festivals, the Jews' prior record of inciting troubles at festivals, and the Romans' oft-demonstrated intention to maintain order all suggest his retinue would have been large. On the analogy of troops required to put down both previous and later disturbances, it is not unlikely that something on the order of

---

[92] Plutarch, *Vita Luculli* 2.5.

[93] *Ad Atticum* 5.16.

[94] W. Dittenberger, ed., *Sylloge Inscriptionum Graecarum* (3rd ed.; 4 vols.; Leipzig: Hirzel, 1915–42), 332, lines 33–38. The description is comparable to that found in extant literary texts which contain similar language and stock phrases (cf. Polybius 16.25.5–8).

[95] Cicero mentions the following persons as constituents of a consular entourage: an accensus (*QFr.* 1.1.13), lictors (*Fam.* 12.30.7), prefects (*Att.* 6.1), legates and a quaestor (*Att.* 5.16; also Fergus Millar, "The Emperor, the Senate and the Provinces," *JRS* 56 [1966]: 157; and A.H.M. Jones, *Studies in Roman Government and Law* [Oxford: Blackwell, 1960], 119). Not all the officials from Cicero's list would have accompanied Pilate, since he was himself a prefect, functioned as a quaestor (a financial officer), and was subordinate to a legate (the legate of Syria).

one thousand troops would have been with Pilate.[96] Assuming there were one thousand soldiers, their impact would have been considerable. Roman soldiers were impressively fitted with a large shield, breastplates and headpieces, swords, a spear, an axe, and pick-axe. The horsemen also had breastplates and headpieces, a sword, shield, and several spears.[97]

Even though history affords us a look at what was generally true with respect to Roman governors and their treatment by locals, we cannot insist that Pilate's visit to Jerusalem would have conformed in every respect to those of other Roman officials. But it will be instructive, and suggestive for the purpose of this essay, to recognize that Pilate would almost certainly have received a splendid, if not altogether sincere welcome, upon his arrival. Indeed, Marcus Borg suggests that Jesus' Entry on the eastern side of Jerusalem was coincidental with Pilate's arrival on the western side.[98]

The background of Pilate's coming is important for understanding both the Gospel accounts of Jesus' Entry and the apparent lack of response to it on the part of the Roman soldiers. How so? Jesus' Entry was a modest affair compared to the splendid welcome enjoyed by dignitaries generally and by Pilate in particular. One of the reasons Jesus' coming failed to arouse imperial suspicions was that it was not large enough to have done so during festival days. Based on their experience, the soldiers knew when something was large enough or threatening enough in tone to count as sedition or as competing with Rome's governor: Jesus' coming failed to do so on all counts. Moreover, Jesus' Entry also differs from the seditious actions of rebel leaders who came to Jerusalem and did attract imperial attention.[99]

---

[96] For a discussion of troop strength, composition, and location in Syria-Palestine at this time, see T. R. S. Broughton, "The Roman Army," in *Additional Notes* (ed. F. J. Foakes Jackson and Kirsopp Lake; vol. 5 of *The Beginnings of Christianity*; 5 vols.; London: Macmillan, 1933), 427–45, and Schürer, *History*, 1:357–91. The size of this group is admittedly difficult to determine; Josephus says the prefects were accompanied by a cohort, and there is some debate about the precise number of soldiers in a cohort (Schürer, *History*, 1:362).

[97] Josephus, *J. W.* 3.93–96; Polybius 6.22.1–4; 6.23.1–16. See also J. B. Campbell, *The Emperor and the Roman Army, 31 BC–AD 235* (Oxford: Clarendon, 1984), and, by the same author, *The Roman Army, 31 BC–AD 337: A Sourcebook* (London: Routledge, 1994).

[98] Borg, *Jesus, A New Vision: Spirit, Culture, and the Life of Discipleship*, 173–74.

[99] Fredriksen (*Jesus of Nazareth*, 242) makes much the same argument. She suggests that Pilate's familiarity with Jesus' teaching led him to overlook the potentially seditious nature of the scene's "basic historicity": "pilgrim crowds hailed Jesus as messiah as they all coursed into Jerusalem the week preceding his last Passover" (p. 243).

4. Conclusion

Critical examination of the Gospel Entry narratives and the various backgrounds necessary to understand them yields the conclusion that Jesus' Entry, as presented by the Evangelists, is historically plausible, indeed, highly probable, for several reasons. First, there is multiple attestation for the acquisition and ride on the colt, for the event beginning in Bethany near the Mount of Olives, for the crowd's acclaim of Jesus through the use of Ps 118, and for the laying of branches in front of him as he rode. Despite minor discrepancies, these sources place the event at the same point in Jesus' life and describe it in roughly the same way.

Second, the core of the account remains fixed, despite certain features of it that could have been seen as problematic or embarrassing by the Gospel writers. The simple fact that Jesus arranged to ride a colt could arguably, in the eyes of some people in the first century, have made him a self-promoting opponent to Caesar and the imperial order (indeed, this possibility seems to have been exploited by the religious leaders as reflected in the political charges against him at the trial before Pilate; Mark 15:2; Luke 23:2; cf. Acts 17:1–7).

Third, the concept of effect commends the Entry narratives as authentic. If we posit the essential trustworthiness of the narratives, we are able to make sense of other events in Jesus' last week, especially the charge made against him of claiming to be king at his trial before Pilate. Furthermore, by reading the Gospel narratives critically and thereby understanding the Entry as a relatively modest affair, we also can understand why there was no Roman intervention as Jesus came to Jerusalem.

Fourth, when the criterion dealing with language and environment is applied, it does not render a verdict of "inauthentic," for as seen against the background of the OT, Jesus' Entry conformed to the sort of entry we might have expected a Jewish king to make (though there are admittedly few precedents for such).

Beyond the positive case for authenticity, however, lies a particularly penetrating question for the skeptic: Why would an early Christian invent this story? To do so would confer no political advantage for Christians as they sought to spread the story about Jesus. Its politically embarrassing features have already been discussed at length. Nor is the narrative easily interpreted as enhancing our image of Jesus: it shows nothing of his compassion or mercy or wonderworking or teaching. To the sensitive reader of the OT it does indicate Jesus' intention to make a royal entry, but to those not familiar with the Hebrew Bible, his coming is either insipid (alone on a "colt") or liable to be politically misunderstood. The notion that the manner of his coming was christologically important because it constituted an obvious "proof from prophecy" (cf. Zech 9:9) is particularly weak, for riding into town was the sort of thing anyone could conceivably do as opposed to the apologetically stronger and more explicit "evidence" for "Jesus as the Messiah" reflected in healings or exorcisms or resurrection, or, for that matter, Davidic descent (which Jesus had no control over). Moreover, it is not clear that there were any messianic associations connected to Zech 9:9 prior to the time of Jesus' coming.

And so we come to the question of Jesus' intentions. Given that he rode in as a king, and given that he himself was behind the arrangements to do this, we must conclude Jesus intended to present himself as Israel's king and as a central eschatological figure of promise when he came to the city at the Passover season. Does this cohere with our other knowledge of Jesus?

Four strands of secure tradition suggest it does. First, Jesus came preaching about the kingdom of God (ἡ βασιλεία τοῦ θεοῦ) and his words point to his own central role in that kingdom.[100] This gospel proclamation is not inconsistent with a royal self-understanding on his part, an understanding that most clearly emerges at his Entry to Jerusalem.

Second, at his trial before Pilate, Jesus is accused of claiming kingship for himself, and his manner of execution, his crucifixion, fits this political charge – and these two data are entirely consistent with the royal manner of Jesus' Entry.

Third, on two occasions Paul's letters mention Jesus' Davidic descent (Rom 1:3; 2 Tim 2:8; see also Rev 5:5). They were surely (in the case of Romans) or most likely (with respect to 2 Timothy) written before the Gospels. As such, this usage points back to an early, traditional belief that Jesus was a royal person, one that might have roots not only in stories circulating about his genealogy, but also in his own actions and sayings, of which the Entry may be the most pointed example.

Fourth, Jesus appointed twelve disciples with himself as their leader. As Scot McKnight has argued, this "implies a political vision, a vision for the nation, and this in some ecclesial sense." In this vision, Jesus is the leader of the twelve.[101] Again, this coheres with and is certainly not contrary to a royal self-understanding on the part of Jesus reflected at his Entry.

Having noted that the Entry coheres in one way or another with the picture of Jesus as an eschatologically central and unique figure as developed in other, prior studies, it must also be recognized that in two respects the Entry appears to be unique: (1) at last Jesus is identified openly as Israel's king, (2) Jesus himself has encouraged this identification by engineering the acquisi-

---

[100] On this see, for example, Sanders, *Historical Figure*, 238–48; Witherington, *The Christology of Jesus*, 203–4.

[101] See in this volume ch. 5, § 4.2.

tion of the colt, by riding it into Jerusalem, and by implicitly welcoming the acclaim of his disciples. His Entry appears to have signaled a new phase in his mission. It would prove to be a fatal one, as well.

What did Jesus hope to achieve by this remarkable self-presentation? I will conjecture (stipulating that this conjecture has no bearing on the issue of the Entry's historicity): He presented Jerusalem and its leaders with a dilemma – either alter their prior assessments of him and acknowledge him as Israel's king who brings the era he announced, thereby risking not only their reputation and social standing, but also the wrath of imperial Rome; or, conversely, arrest and prosecute him despite his popularity with many of the people in Galilee, Judea, and Jerusalem. Indeed, this dilemma corresponds to the one Jesus later presents to Jewish leaders with respect to John's baptism (Mark 11:27–33 and parallels).

In retrospect, two things are clear. First, Jesus intended to enter Jerusalem as its king and so provoke its people either to embrace or deny him and his message. Second, he was rejected. The Jewish leadership undoubtedly hoped that by subjecting him to the tender mercies of the Roman governor on the political charge of being a king, they could be rid of him and his followers. How wrong they were.

Bibliography

Ackroyd, P. R. "The Succession Narrative (So-Called)." *Int* 35 (1981): 383–96.
Aland, Kurt and Barbara, ed. *Griechisch-deutsches Wörterbuch zu den Schriften des Neuen Testaments und der frühchristlichen Literatur von W. Bauer.* 6th ed. Berlin: De Gruyter, 1988.
Bammel, Ernst. "The *Titulus*." Pages 353–64 in *Jesus and the Politics of His Day*. Edited by Ernst Bammel and C. F. D. Moule. Cambridge: Cambridge University Press, 1984.
Bartsch, Hans Werner. "Early Christian Eschatology in the Synoptic Gospels: A Contribution to Form-Critical Research." *NTS* 11 (1965): 387–97.
Bauckham, Richard. "For Whom Were Gospels Written?" Pages 9–48 in *The Gospels for All Christians: Rethinking the Gospel Audiences*. Edited by Richard Bauckham. Grand Rapids: Eerdmans, 1998.
Bauer, Walter. "The 'Colt' of Palm Sunday (Der Palmesel)." *JBL* 72 (1953): 220–29.
Becker, Jürgen. *Jesus of Nazareth*. Translated by James E. Crouch. Berlin: De Gruyter, 1998.
Berger, Klaus. "Die königlichen Messiastraditionen des Neuen Testaments." *NTS* 20 (1973): 1–44.
Blenkinsopp, Joseph. "The Oracle of Judah and the Messianic Entry." *JBL* 80 (1961): 55–64.
Blomberg, Craig L. *The Historical Reliability of John's Gospel*. Downers Grove: InterVarsity, 2001.

Bock, Darrell L. *Blasphemy and Exaltation in Judaism and the Final Examination of Jesus.* WUNT 2.106. Tübingen: Mohr Siebeck, 1998.
Bockmuehl, Markus. *This Jesus: Martyr, Lord, Messiah.* Edinburgh: T&T Clark, 1994.
Bond, Helen. *Pontius Pilate in History and Interpretation.* SNTSMS 100. Cambridge: Cambridge University Press, 1999.
Borg, Marcus J. *Jesus, A New Vision: Spirit, Culture, and the Life of Discipleship.* San Francisco: Harper & Row, 1987.
Brandon, S. G. F. *Jesus and the Zealots: A Study of the Political Factor in Primitive Christianity.* Manchester: Manchester University Press, 1967.
Broughton, T. R. S. "The Roman Army." Pages 427–45 in *Additional Notes.* Vol. 5 of *The Beginnings of Christianity.* 5 vols. Edited by F. J. Foakes Jackson and Kirsopp Lake. London: Macmillan, 1933.
Bultmann, Rudolf. *Die Geschichte der synoptischen Tradition.* 2nd ed. Göttingen: Vandenhoeck & Ruprecht, 1931.
Burger, Christoph. *Jesus als Davidssohn: Eine traditionsgeschichtliche Untersuchung.* FRLANT 98. Göttingen: Vandenhoeck & Ruprecht, 1970.
Campbell, J. B. *The Emperor and the Roman Army, 31 BC–AD 235.* Oxford: Clarendon, 1984.
–. *The Roman Army, 31 BC–AD 337: A Sourcebook.* London: Routledge, 1994.
Carroll, Scott T. "Bethphage." P. 1:715 in *Anchor Bible Dictionary.* 6 vols. Edited by David N. Freedman. New York: Doubleday, 1992.
Catchpole, David. "The 'Triumphal' Entry." Pages 319–34 in *Jesus and the Politics of His Day.* Edited by Ernst Bammel and C. F. D. Moule. Cambridge: Cambridge University Press, 1984.
Chester, Andrew. "Jewish Messianic Expectations and Mediatorial Figures and Pauline Christology." Pages 17–89 in *Paulus und das antike Judentum: Tübingen-Durham-Symposium im Gedenken an den 50. Todestag Adolf Schlatters.* Edited by Martin Hengel. WUNT 58. Tübingen: Mohr Siebeck, 1991.
Chilton, Bruce D. "Jesus Ben David: Reflections on the Davidssohnfrage." *JSNT* 14 (1982): 88–112.
Coakley, J. F. "Jesus' Messianic Entry Into Jerusalem (John 12:12–19 Par)." *JTS* 46 (1995): 461–82.
Cohen, H., ed. *Description historique des monnaies frappées sous l'Empire Romain,* Vol. I: *Néron.* Paris: Rollin & Feuardent, 1880.
Collins, John J. *The Scepter and the Star: The Messiahs of the Dead Sea Scrolls and Other Ancient Literature.* ABRL. New York: Doubleday, 1995.
Craig, William Lane. *Reasonable Faith: Christian Truth and Apologetics.* Wheaton: Crossway, 1994.
Creed, J. M. *The Gospel According to St. Luke.* London: Macmillan, 1930.
Crossan, John Dominic. *The Historical Jesus: The Life of a Mediterranean Jewish Peasant.* San Francisco: HarperSanFrancisco, 1991.
Deissmann, Adolf. *Light from the Ancient East.* Translated by Lionel R. M. Strachan. New York: Doran, 1927.
Derrett, J. Duncan M. "Law in the New Testament: The Palm Sunday Colt." *NovT* 13 (1971): 248–53.
Dittenberger, W., ed. *Sylloge Inscriptionum Graecarum.* 3rd ed. 4 vols. Leipzig: Hirzel, 1915–42.

Dodd, C.H. *The Founder of Christianity*. London: Collins, 1971.
–. *The Parables of the Kingdom*. 3rd ed. London: Nisbet, 1952.
Duling, Dennis C. "Promises to David and Their Entrance Into Christianity: Nailing Down a Likely Hypothesis." *New Testament Studies* 20 (1973): 55–77.
–. "Solomon, Exorcism, and the Son of David." *HTR* 68 (1975): 235–52.
Ellis, E. Earle. *The Gospel of Luke*. NCB. London: Marshall, Morgan, & Scott, 1974.
Ernst, Josef. *Das Evangelium nach Lukas*. 5th ed. RNT. Regensburg: Pustet, 1977.
Evans, C.F. *Saint Luke*. TPINTC. London: SCM; Philadelphia: Trinity, 1990.
Evans, Craig A. "From Public Ministry to the Passion: Can a Link Be Found Between the (Galilean) Life and the (Judean) Death of Jesus?" Pages 460–72 in *SBL Seminar Papers, 1993*. SBLSP 32. Atlanta: Scholars, 1993.
–. "The Need for the 'Historical Jesus': A Response to Jacob Neusner's Review of Crossan and Meier." *BBR* 4 (1994): 127–33.
Farmer, William R. "Judas, Simon and Athronges." *NTS* 4 (1958): 147–55.
–. *Maccabees, Zealots, and Josephus: An Inquiry Into Jewish Nationalism in the Greco-Roman Period*. New York: Columbia University Press, 1956.
–. "Palm Branches in John 12,13." *JTS* 3 (1952): 62–66.
Feldman, Louis H. "A Selective Critical Bibliography of Josephus." Pages 330–448 in *Josephus, the Bible, and History*. Edited by Louis H. Feldman and Gohei Hata. Leiden: Brill, 1989.
Fisher, Loren R. "'Can This Be the Son of David?'" Pages 82–97 in *Jesus and the Historian: Written in Honor of Ernest Cadman Colwell*. Edited by Frederick T. Trotter. Philadelphia: Westminster, 1968.
Fitzmyer, Joseph A. *The Gospel According to Luke X–XXIV*. AB 28a. Garden City: Doubleday, 1985.
–. *The One Who is to Come*. Grand Rapids: Eerdmans, 2007.
Flender, Helmut. *Heil und Geschichte in der Theologie Des Lukas*. BEvT, 41. Munich: Kaiser, 1965.
Fokkelman, J.P. *King David (II Sam. 9–20 & I Kings 1–2)*. Vol. 1 of *Narrative Art and Poetry in the Books of Samuel*. SSN 20. Assen, The Netherlands: Van Gorcum, 1981.
Fredriksen, Paula. *Jesus of Nazareth, King of the Jews: A Jewish Life and the Emergence of Christianity*. New York: Knopf, 1999.
Funk, Robert W. *Honest to Jesus: Jesus for a New Millennium*. San Francisco: HarperSanFrancisco, 1996.
Funk, Robert W., and The Jesus Seminar. *The Acts of Jesus: The Search for the Authentic Deeds of Jesus*. San Francisco: HarperSanFrancisco, 1998.
Garnsey, Peter. "Religious Toleration in Classical Antiquity." Pages 1–27 in *Persecution and Toleration: Papers Read at the Twenty-Second Summer Meeting and the Twenty-Third Winter Meeting of the Ecclesiastical History Society*. Edited by W.J. Sheils. SCH, 21. Oxford: Blackwell, 1984.
Goodman, Martin. *The Ruling Class of Judaea: The Origins of the Jewish Revolt Against Rome, A.D. 66–70*. London: Cambridge University Press, 1988.
Grant, Robert M. *Augustus to Constantine: The Thrust of the Christian Movement Into the Roman World*. London: Collins, 1971.
Harvey, A.E. *Jesus and the Constraints of History*. The Bampton Lectures, 1980. London: Duckworth, 1982.
Hauck, Friedrich. *Das Evangelium des Lukas*. THKNT. Leipzig: Deichert, 1934.

Head, B.V., and R.S. Poole, eds. *A Catalogue of the Greek Coins in the British Museum: Corinth, Colonies of Corinth, etc.* London: Longmans, 1889.
Hengel, Martin. *Crucifixion in the Ancient World and the Folly of the Message of the Cross.* Philadelphia: Fortress, 1977.
–. *Judentum und Hellenismus: Studien zu ihrer Begegnung unter besonderer Berücksichtigung Palästinas bis zur Mitte des 2. Jhs. v. Chr.* 3rd ed. WUNT 10. Tübingen: Mohr Siebeck, 1988.
–. *The Zealots: Investigations Into the Freedom Movement in the Period from Herod I Until 70 A.D.* 2d ed. Edinburgh: T&T Clark, 1989.
Hoehner, Harold W. *Chronological Aspects of the Life of Christ.* Grand Rapids: Zondervan, 1977.
Hooker, Morna D. "Christology and Methodology." *NTS* 17 (1970–71): 480–87.
Horsley, Richard A. "Josephus and the Bandits." *JSJ* 10 (1979): 37–63.
–. "Popular Messianic Movements Around the Time of Jesus." *CBQ* 46 (1984): 471–95.
Jackson, F.J. Foakes, and Kirsopp Lake. *Prolegomena I: The Jewish, Gentile and Christian Backgrounds.* Vol. 1 of *The Beginnings of Christianity.* 5 vols. London: Macmillan, 1933.
Jeremias, Joachim. *The Eucharistic Words of Jesus.* Translated by Norman Perrin. NTL. London: SCM, 1966.
–. *Jerusalem zur Zeit Jesu: Eine kulturgeschichtliche Untersuchung zur neutestamentlichen Zeitgeschichte.* 3rd ed. Göttingen: Vandenhoeck & Ruprecht, 1962.
–. *The Parables of Jesus.* Rev. ed. Translated by S.H. Hooke. London: SCM, 1963.
Johnson, Luke Timothy. *The Real Jesus: The Misguided Quest for the Historical Jesus and the Truth of the Traditional Gospels.* San Francisco: HarperSanFrancisco, 1996.
Jones, A.H.M. *Studies in Roman Government and Law.* Oxford: Blackwell, 1960.
Kennard, J.S. "Judas of Galilee and His Clan." *JQR* 36 (1945): 281–86.
Kinman, Brent. *History, Design, and the End of Time: God's Plan for the World.* Nashville: Broadman & Holman, 2000.
–. *Jesus' Entry Into Jerusalem: In the Context of Lukan Theology and the Politics of His Day.* AGJU 28. Leiden: Brill, 1995.
–. "Jesus' Royal Entry Into Jerusalem." *BBR* 15 (2005): 223–60.
–. "Luke's Exoneration of John the Baptist." *JTS* 44 (1993): 595–98.
–. "Pilate's Assize and the Timing of Jesus' Trial." *Tyndale Bulletin* 42 (1991): 282–95.
–. "'The Stones Will Cry Out' (Luke 19,40) – Joy or Judgment?" *Bib* 75 (1994): 232–35.
Kraeling, Carl H. "The Episode of the Roman Standards at Jerusalem." *HTR* 35 (1942): 263–89.
Kuhn, H.W. "Das Reittier Jesu in der Einzugsgeschichte des Markusevangeliums." *ZNW* 50 (1959): 82–91.
Kutsch, Ernst. *Salbung als Rechtsakt im Alten Testament und im alten Orient.* BZAW 87. Berlin: Töpelmann, 1963.
Lamarche, Paul. *Zacharie IX–XIV: Structure littéraire et messianisme.* EBib. Paris: Gabalda, 1961.
Lémonon, Jean-Pierre. *Pilate et le gouvernement de la Judée: textes et monuments.* EBib. Paris: Gabalda, 1981.

Liebeschuetz, J. H. W. G. *Continuity and Change in Roman Religion.* Oxford: Clarendon, 1979.
Lohse, Eduard. "Hosianna." *NovT* 6 (1963): 113–19.
McCarter, P. K. "Plots, True or False." *Int* 35 (1981): 355–67.
McCown, Chester C. "The Christian Tradition as to the Magical Wisdom of Solomon." *JPOS* 2 (1922): 1–24.
McGing, Brian C. "Pontius Pilate and the Sources." *CBQ* 53 (1991): 416–38.
Manson, T. W. "The Cleansing of the Temple." *BJRL* 33 (1951): 271–82.
Marshall, I. Howard. *The Gospel of Luke.* NIGTC 3. Grand Rapids: Eerdmans, 1978.
–. *Luke: Historian and Theologian.* Grand Rapids: Zondervan, 1970.
Meeks, Wayne A. *The Prophet-King. Moses Traditions and the Johannine Christology.* NovTSup 14. Leiden: Brill, 1967.
Meier, John P. *Mentor, Message, and Miracles.* Vol. 2 of *A Marginal Jew: Rethinking the Historical Jesus.* ABRL. New York: Doubleday, 1994.
–. *The Roots of the Problem and the Person.* Vol. 1 of *A Marginal Jew: Rethinking the Historical Jesus.* ABRL. New York: Doubleday, 1991.
Meshorer, Ya'akov. *Jewish Coins of the Second Temple Period.* Translated by I. H. Levine. Tel Aviv: Am Hassefer, 1967.
Mettinger, T. N. D. *King and Messiah: The Civil and Sacral Legitimation of the Israelite Kings.* ConBOT, 8. Lund: Gleerup, 1976.
Meyer, Ben F. *The Aims of Jesus.* London: SCM, 1979.
Michel, Otto. "Eine philologische Frage zur Einzugsgeschichte." *NTS* 6 (1959–60): 81–82.
Millar, Fergus. *The Emperor in the Roman World, 31 BC-AD 337.* London: Duckworth, 1977.
–. "The Emperor, the Senate and the Provinces." *JRS* 56 (1966): 156–66.
Mowinckel, Sigmund. *The Psalms in Israel's Worship.* 2 vols. Translated by D. R. Ap-Thomas. Oxford: Blackwell, 1962.
Neusner, Jacob, William Scott Green, and Ernest S. Frerichs, eds. *Judaisms and Their Messiahs at the Turn of the Christian Era.* Cambridge: Cambridge University Press, 1987.
North, J. A. "Conservatism and Change in Roman Religion." *Papers of the British School at Rome* 44 (1976): 1–12.
–. "Religious Toleration in Republican Rome." *Proceedings of the Cambridge Philological Society* 25 (1979): 85–103.
Oepke, Albrecht. "παρουσία, πάρειμι." Pages 858–71 in vol. 5 of *Theological Dictionary of the New Testament.* 10 vols. Edited by G. Kittel and Gerhard Friedrich. Translated by Geoffrey W. Bromiley. Grand Rapids: Eerdmans, 1964–76.
Otzen, Benedikt. *Studien über Deuterosacharja.* ATD, 6. Copenhagen: Munksgaard, 1964.
Porter, Stanley E. *The Criteria for Authenticity in Historical-Jesus Research: Previous Discussion and New Proposals.* JSNTSup 191. Sheffield: Sheffield Academic Press, 2000.
Powell, Mark Allen. *Jesus as a Figure in History: How Modern Historians View the Man from Galilee.* Louisville: Westminster John Knox, 1998.
Romanoff, Paul. "Jewish Symbols on Ancient Jewish Coins." *JQR* 34 (1943–44): 425–40.

Sanders, E. P. *The Historical Figure of Jesus*. London: Penguin, 1993.
—. *Jesus and Judaism*. Philadelphia: Fortress, 1985.
—. *Judaism: Practice and Belief, 63 BCE–66 CE*. Philadelphia: Trinity, 1992.
Sæbø, Magne. *Sacharja 9–14: Untersuchungen von Text und Form*. WMANT 34. Neukirchen-Vluyn: Neukirchener Verlag, 1969.
Schmidt, Ludwig. *Menschlicher, Erfolg und Jahwes Initiative: Studien zu Tradition, Interpretation und Historie in Überlieferungen von Gideon, Saul und David*. WMANT 38. Neukirchen-Vluyn: Neukirchener Verlag, 1970.
Schneider, Gerhard. "The Political Charge Against Jesus (Luke 23:2)." Pages 403–14 in *Jesus and the Politics of His Day*. Edited by Ernst Bammel and C. F. D. Moule. Cambridge: Cambridge University Press, 1984.
Schneider, Johannes. "ἔρχομαι." Pages 666–75 in vol. 2 of *Theological Dictionary of the New Testament*. 10 vols. Edited by G. Kittel and Gerhard Friedrich. Translated by Geoffrey W. Bromiley. Grand Rapids: Eerdmans, 1964–76.
Schulz, Siegfried. *Q: Die Spruchquelle der Evangelisten*. Zürich: Theologischer Verlag, 1972.
Schürer, Emil. *The History of the Jewish People in the Age of Jesus Christ (175 B. C. – A. D. 135)*. New English ed. 3 vols. Edited by Geza Vermes, Fergus Millar, and Matthew Black. Edinburgh: T&T Clark, 1973–87.
Sellin, D. E. *Das Zwölfprophetenbuch*. KAT 12. Leipzig: Deichert, 1922.
Smallwood, E Mary. "High Priests and Politics in Roman Palestine." *JTS* 13 (1962): 14–34.
Smallwood, E. Mary. *The Jews Under Roman Rule. From Pompey to Diocletian: A Study in Political Relations*. SJLA 20. Leiden: Brill, 1981.
Smith, C. W. F. "No Time for Figs." *JBL* 79 (1960): 315–27.
—. "Tabernacles in the Fourth Gospel and Mark." *NTS* 9 (1963): 130–46.
Smith, D. Moody, Jr. "John 12:12ff and the Question of John's Use of the Synoptics." *JBL* 82 (1963): 58–64.
Strack, Hermann L., and Paul Billerbeck. *Kommentar zum Neuen Testament aus Talmud und Midrasch*. 6 vols. Munich: Beck, 1922–61.
Theissen, Gerd, and Annette Merz. *The Historical Jesus: A Comprehensive Guide*. Translated by John Bowden. Minneapolis: Fortress, 1998.
Tuckett, Christopher M. "On the Relationship Between Matthew and Luke." *NTS* 30 (1984): 130–42.
Versnel, H. S. *Triumphs: An Inquiry Into the Origin, Development and Meaning of the Roman Triumph*. Leiden: Brill, 1970.
Visser't Hooft, Willem Adolf. "Triumphalism in the Gospels." *SJT* 38 (1985): 491–504.
Weber, W. *Untersuchungen zur Geschichte des Kaisers Hadrianus*. Leipzig: Teubner, 1907.
Weinel, Heinrich. "משח und seine Derivate." *ZAW* 18 (1898): 1–82.
Werner, Eric. "'Hosanna' in the Gospels." *JBL* 65 (1946): 97–122.
Wevers, John W. "A Study in the Exegetical Principles Underlying the Greek Text of 2 Sm 11:2–1 Kings 2:11." *CBQ* 15 (1953): 30–45.
Whybray, R. N. *The Succession Narrative*. SBT 2.9. London: SCM, 1968.
Williamson, H. G. M. Review of *King and Messiah: The Civil and Sacral Legitimation of the Israelite Kings*. *VT* 28 (1978): 499–509.
Winter, Paul. *On the Trial of Jesus*. SJ 1. Berlin: De Gruyter, 1961.

Witherington, Ben, III. *The Christology of Jesus.* Minneapolis: Fortress, 1990.
–. *The Jesus Quest: The Third Search for the Jew of Nazareth.* Downers Grove: InterVarsity, 1995.
Zeitlin, Solomon. "Hallel: A Historical Study of the Canonization of the Hebrew Liturgy." *Jewish Quarterly Review* 53 (1962): 22–29.
Zerwick, Max. "Die Parabel vom Thronanwärter." *Bib* 40 (1959): 654–74.

Chapter 10

The Temple Incident

KLYNE R. SNODGRASS

1. Introduction

If the issue is the historicity of Jesus' disruption of the commerce in the temple, his driving out buyers and sellers, and his turning over the tables of the money changers, perhaps my task is among the easiest in this volume. Although more deny the historicity of these events than is sometimes recognized, the overwhelming majority of NT scholars assume not only that these events did indeed happen but also that they are the direct cause leading to Jesus' arrest. If, on the other hand, the issue is understanding *why* Jesus performed these acts and the significance they have for comprehending Jesus and his mission, then perhaps my task is among the more difficult, for uncertainty remains for a bewildering number of questions, and a variety of views has been offered. The temple is inherently related to so many important threads of Judaism and Christianity that hypotheses about Jesus' action emerge without difficulty.

2. The Question of Historicity

With regard to historicity, this incident is assessed as one of the most secure in the Jesus material, enough so that E. P. Sanders makes it the starting point and foundation from which to construct his understanding of Jesus.[1] N. T. Wright declares that one of the chief gains of recent Jesus research is that the question of Jesus and the temple is back at the center of the agenda, where it belongs. He finds virtual agreement on two points: that Jesus performed a dramatic action in the temple and that it was one of the main reasons caus-

---

[1] E. P. Sanders, *Jesus and Judaism* (Philadelphia: Fortress, 1985), 11, 61. See also Jostein Ådna, *Jesu Stellung zum Tempel: die Tempelaktion und das Tempelwort als Ausdruck seiner messianischen Sendung* (WUNT 2.119; Tübingen: Mohr Siebeck, 2000), 300–333.

ing the leadership to seek his execution.[2] The decision of the Jesus Seminar was strongly in favor of the authenticity of the event, even though in their estimation exactly what Jesus did was unclear and even though more doubts arose about what he might have said.[3] The authenticity of the event is sufficiently assumed that often no discussion is even offered to substantiate the claim. Two obvious reasons for so much confidence are the multiple attestation of the incident in all four Gospels[4] and the ease with which the incident fits as a causative factor in Jesus' arrest.[5] Without this event, on what grounds was he arrested, and on what grounds would the ruling *priests* be involved?[6] With regard to multiple attestation, while questions will need

---

[2] N. T. Wright, *Jesus and the Victory of God* (vol. 2 of *Christian Origins and the Question of God*; Minneapolis: Fortress, 1996), 405.

[3] Robert W. Funk and The Jesus Seminar, *The Acts of Jesus: The Search for the Authentic Deeds of Jesus* (San Francisco: HarperSanFrancisco, 1998), 121–22, 231–32, 338–39, 373–74. While John 2:13–16a is printed with gray ink and vv. 16b–22 with black, Mark 11:15a is printed with pink ink, 15b with gray, 16 with black, and 17a ("Then he started teaching and would say to them") in pink, with the rest with black. The editors relate that three different times over ten years the fellows affirmed that Jesus performed some act in the temple, even if there was difficulty in knowing exactly what it was. In Robert W. Funk, et al., *The Five Gospels: The Search for the Authentic Words of Jesus* (New York: Macmillan, 1993), 98, we are told that more than two-thirds of the fellows responded affirmatively to the questions whether Jesus performed some anti-temple act and whether he spoke against the temple.

[4] Even if Matthew and Luke are dependent on Mark. Most would see the accounts in Mark and John as independent; the relation of the four accounts is discussed below.

[5] Although criteria for authenticity will be discussed in this essay, I do not think such criteria alone are the key to finding the historical Jesus. Note Dale C. Allison, Jr.'s claim that the criteria are seriously defective and cannot do the job claimed for them ("The Historians' Jesus and the Church," in *Seeking the Identity of Jesus: A Pilgrimage* [ed. Beverly Roberts Gaventa and Richard B. Hays; Grand Rapids: Eerdmans, 2008], 79–95). However, the issue is perhaps more the exclusive dependence on these criteria. See the perspective developed in this volume in ch. 2, § 4.3, in which the criteria are described as fitting within a larger framework for doing history that requires both top-down (i.e., context) as well as a bottom-up (i.e., criteria) approaches to the material.

[6] Craig A. Evans, "Jesus and the 'Cave of Robbers': Toward a Jewish Context for the Temple Action," *BBR* 3 (1993): 93–110. Evans asks, "If Jesus did not protest against temple polity or threaten the temple establishment, then how are we to account for the involvement of the ruling priests, if not the high priest himself, in his arrest and subsequent crucifixion?" He also points to evidence in Josephus (*Ant.* 18.64), usually considered authentic, as validation that Jesus was accused to Pilate by leading Jews. See also Tom Holmén, *Jesus and Jewish Covenant Thinking* (Biblical Interpretation Series 55; Leiden: Brill, 2001), 328. Cf. Richard A. Horsley, *Jesus and the Spiral of Violence: Popular Jewish Resistance in Roman Palestine* (San Francisco: Harper & Row, 1987), 285. At the same time we must note that the temple disruption is *not* explicitly mentioned in the charges brought against Jesus. Of the *many* things of which Jesus is accused (Matt 27:13 = Mark 15:3–4) the only items in Matthew and Mark mentioned specifically are that Jesus claimed he would destroy the temple and the charge of blasphemy. Luke adds the charges that he perverted the nation, forbade paying taxes to the emperor, and claimed to be the Messiah (Luke 23:2).

to be considered below, very few Jesus events or sayings are recorded in all four Gospels. In addition to the temple incident only the following appear in all four: the testimony of the Baptist, the discipleship saying,[7] the feeding of the 5000, the confession of Peter (if you accept that John 6:68–69 is the same event), an anointing by a woman (if Luke 7:36–50 is the same event as the others, which I doubt), the triumphal entry, the foretelling of Judas's betrayal, the foretelling of Peter's denial, the betrayal and arrest, Peter's denial, the questioning by the high priest, the Roman trial, the crucifixion, burial, and resurrection.[8] Two observations are in order: the list is rather basic and forms the foundation of any picture of Jesus, and apart from the temple incident any reason for Jesus' arrest is a mystery.

In addition to multiple attestation and this incident being the causative factor that led to Jesus' arrest, several other factors point to the historicity of the temple incident. To use language typical of authenticity discussions, other indicators of historicity are the brevity and ambiguity of the account, dissimilarity, and embarrassment.

The accounts are all brief and lack indication of the church's stamp or any clear sense of how the church would profit from the account. There is neither exposition of the incident nor motive for creating such a narrative. If the temple incident is not historical, why was it created? What would the church have gained from creating this account, and what theological benefit would early Christians have derived? Neither the evangelists nor the early church make much of the theological significance of the event. The incident is inherently ambiguous, almost a conundrum, as is evidenced by the widely divergent explanations of its intent.[9] If the church had created the event, the theological payout would have been obvious. Even though it was clearly significant in the life of Jesus, there is no indication this event factored into any later conclusions or was significant in the life of the church.

At several levels the temple incident is dissimilar to the concerns of the early church. Negative statements about the temple are rarely the direct focus of the early church's thinking. The temple is not attacked. This is most obvious if we look first at Luke's writings. The temple is viewed positively throughout Luke-Acts. Luke's Gospel begins with a godly priest offering sacrifice in the temple and receiving the promise of the birth of John the Baptist. It ends after the ascension with the disciples praising God *in the*

---

[7] Matt 10:37–39; 16:24–25; Mark 8:34–35; Luke 9:23–24; 14:26–27; 17:33; and John 12:25–26.

[8] There are, of course, shared themes in all four Gospels: the kingdom, the focus on the Spirit, love, judgment, and God as Father, just to name the most obvious.

[9] Note that Alexander J. M. Wedderburn ("Jesus' Action in the Temple: A Key or a Puzzle?" *ZNW* 97 [2006]: 1–22) thinks the event is more a puzzle than a key. See the section of this essay below on significance. See also the discussion of the criterion of inherent ambiguity discussed in this volume in ch. 2, § 4.1.

temple. In Acts, even if the Pentecost event did not take place in the temple precincts,[10] immediately after that we are told the Christians were continuing to meet in the temple (2:46), which is confirmed by their going to the temple to pray, by the healing of the man at the "Beautiful Gate" and Peter's speech in Solomon's portico (Acts 3:1–26), and by the apostles continuing every day to teach in the temple (Acts 5:42). In Acts 6–7 Stephen is accused of saying Jesus will destroy "this place" and is asked by the high priest if this is so (7:1), which Stephen does *not* affirm. He does say God does not live in temples made by hands, a point made before him by Solomon (1 Kgs 8:27) and after him by Paul in his speech at Athens (Acts 17:24), but such a realization is not a rejection of the temple.[11] Elsewhere it is reported that Paul after his conversion was praying *in the temple*, that he was eager to be in Jerusalem for Pentecost, and that he went through a purification rite in the temple (Acts 22:17; 20:16; 21:26–27). Luke's reporting of the temple incident is the briefest of all, almost cryptic, with Jesus after the incident teaching every day in the temple as if nothing had happened (Luke 19:45–47).

Elsewhere in the NT, writers do spiritualize temple language (1 Cor 3:16–17; 6:19; Eph 2:20–22; and 1 Pet 2:4–9), but Jewish writers did the same both before and after the destruction of the temple without any thought that the temple was being rejected (e.g., 1 Sam 15:22; Mic 6:6–8; Ps 51:16–19; Hos 14:2 [3, Hebrew: "bulls of our lips"]; 1QS 8:4–10; 9:1–6; and *'Abot R. Nat.* 4, the last both with regard to studying Torah and acts of loving kindness). Only in Hebrews 5–10 do we find that the temple order is now obsolete, not because it was wrong, but because it was temporary and something better has come, and in Rev 22:22, in a book full of temple language, is it explicit that a temple is not needed, but that is in the eschaton.

Jesus in all of the Synoptics, of course, speaks of the destruction of the temple, even if John is not so direct, and we will have to assess the relation of Jesus' action in the temple to his comments about destruction, but the announcement of the destruction is not based in a negative view of the temple as an institution. No early Christian suggests the temple is a bad place and should be torn down. Also, in all the Gospels Jesus teaches in the temple.[12]

Matthew, like Luke, seems to have a positive attitude toward the temple, as is evidenced by the mention of sacrifice in 5:23–24, the discussion of oaths in 23:16–22, and by the fact that Jesus heals in the temple and is acclaimed

---

[10] It well may have.

[11] It is in *Sib. Or.* 4:5. Interestingly, in Acts the word ναός occurs only at 17:24 and 19:24 – of pagan temples. References to the temple in Jerusalem use ἱερόν, even when speaking of Paul's purification rite, which would have taken place in the inner court. Νάος is used in Luke 1:9, 21, 22, and 23:45, where the focus is on the inner court.

[12] Matthew does not mention this in his narrative, unlike the other evangelists, but in 26:55 Jesus reminds those arresting him that he sat daily teaching in the temple and they did not seize him.

as son of David in the temple. The repetition of ἐν τῷ ἱερῷ in 21:14 and 15 underscores the importance of the place. The lament over the destruction of Jerusalem and the temple is indeed a *lament* (Matt 23:37–39 = Luke 13:34–35).

Mark is viewed by some as anti-temple,[13] but that is an assessment that should at least be questioned. Is Mark anti-temple or opposed to the temple officials? If Mark were anti-temple, why would he create or use the words of 11:16, words which he alone has about Jesus not permitting anyone to carry vessels through the temple? If Jesus or Mark has rejected the temple, why bother with this effort to ensure sanctity?[14] This does not fit with the agenda of the church in any way.[15] Like Luke, Mark 12:41–44 reports the widow's offering in the temple as a legitimate and appropriate gift, even though she is poor. The attempt to turn this event into a complaint against the temple does not derive from the text of Mark or Luke.[16]

One could conclude John comes closest to suggesting the temple is unimportant because of the statement in John 4:21 that neither on Mount Gerizim nor in Jerusalem is the place where it is necessary to worship. There is a temple-replacement theme in the Fourth Gospel,[17] but even so, the temple is still the place where Jesus teaches regularly, and the explanation from the evangelist for the temple incident is that zeal *for* the temple caused Jesus to act.[18] In fact, we must conclude that none of the Gospels portrays the temple negatively via the temple incident. On the contrary, in all of them the event is a positive act for the good of the temple, which does not match the agendas of the church. Further, rarely are priests and levites the target

---

[13] E. g., Burton L. Mack, *A Myth of Innocence: Mark and Christian Origins* (Philadelphia: Fortress, 1988), 292; and Paula Fredriksen, "Jesus and the Temple, Mark and the War," in *SBL Seminar Papers, 1990* (SBLSP 29; Atlanta: Scholars, 1990), 293–310, 297.

[14] See the discussion of v. 16 below.

[15] See Maurice Casey, "Culture and Historicity: The Cleansing of the Temple," *CBQ* 59 (1997): 321–23, 331–32.

[16] Despite Joseph A. Fitzmyer, *The Gospel According to Luke X–XXIV* (AB 28a; Garden City: Doubleday, 1985), 1321; and Craig A. Evans, "Jesus' Action in the Temple: Cleansing or Portent of Destruction?" in *Jesus in Context: Temple, Purity, and Restoration* (by Bruce Chilton and Craig A. Evans; AGJU 39; Leiden: Brill, 1997), 405.

[17] Among many see Bertil E. Gärtner, *The Temple and the Community in Qumran and the New Testament: A Comparative Study in the Temple Symbolism of the Qumran Texts and the New Testament* (SNTSMS 1; Cambridge: Cambridge University Press, 1965), 119–22; Alan R. Kerr, *The Temple of Jesus' Body: The Temple Theme in the Gospel of John* (JSNTSup 220; London: Sheffield Academic Press, 2002); and Ådna, *Jesu Stellung zum Tempel*, 286, 368, 429–33, 439–48.

[18] This interpretation understands οἴκου as an objective genitive. Judith Lieu ("Temple and Synagogue in John," *NTS* 45 [1999]: 53, 66–68) goes so far as to say that in John the temple is the primary location where Jesus claims authority to speak for and represent God. She argues that in John Jesus says nothing judgmental about the temple, does not speak about the temple, and does not teach anywhere but in the temple or in a synagogue. However, this does not seem to do justice to the teaching in John 3 and 4.

of Jesus' complaints. Other than the temple incident, only the parable of the Good Samaritan suggests anything clearly negative about temple personnel.

I do not want to overstate the case. Baptism for the forgiveness of sins by John and Jesus and Jesus' declarations of forgiveness (Matt 9:2–8 = Mark 2:2–12 = Luke 5:17–26; Luke 7:47–50) mitigate the focus on the temple as the exclusive place of forgiveness, cleansing, and purity. The church seems to have been slow to draw conclusions we think are obvious, but the temple was for the evangelists and other early Christians a symbol of the presence of the God of Israel.[19] They did not set out an agenda for abandoning – and certainly not for destroying – the temple.

With regard to the criterion of embarrassment, early Christian writers were concerned to avoid being seen or having Jesus be seen as seditious. Rome viewed itself as a defender of temples and proper proceedings in temples.[20] If that is true, the church would hardly have created the one event that made Jesus seem seditious and thereby created embarrassment for themselves.[21]

Two other items pertaining to historicity should be mentioned. First, the action against the money changers makes little sense if it were a creation of the church. Again the criteria of inherent ambiguity and dissimilarity are both evidenced. No teaching is drawn from the action, and the money changers are not an issue for the church. Elsewhere Jesus advises Peter to pay the temple tax for the two of them to avoid offence (Matt 17:24–27), and Paul directs Christians to pay their taxes (Rom 13:6–7). This event does not fit with the church, but we will see that it fits well in the ministry of Jesus.[22] Second, the relation of the temple incident to the question of the authority by which Jesus does "these things" (Matt 21:23 = Mark 11:28 = Luke 20:2 = John 2:18 ["What sign are you showing us?"]) is a strong support of authenticity. The connection of the event and the question from Jewish leaders in all four accounts cannot be ignored. The question from the leaders refers primarily, if not exclusively, to the temple incident. The question of authority does not likely stem from the church since it seems to place Jesus on a

---

[19] Note Paul's positive reference to the temple service in Rom 9:4.

[20] E. g., see Josephus, *J. W.* 1.27; 5.402; *Ant.* 14.309–10; 15.357; 18.65–84; 19.1–8 (temples defiled by the madness of Gaius), 160; and 20.131.

[21] See Richard Hiers, "Purification of the Temple: Preparation for the Kingdom of God," *JBL* 91 (1971): 82, who points to Mark 12:13–17; 15:5, 10, 14–15, and 39 as evidence of Mark's concern to avoid a charge of sedition. See also Ben Witherington, III, *The Christology of Jesus* (Minneapolis: Fortress, 1990), 109; and Wedderburn, "Jesus' Action," 6–7, 19, who suggests the evangelists may have suppressed the true reason for Jesus' condemnation – the temple incident – because it was an embarrassing and politically subversive act.

[22] See the discussion by Casey, "The Cleansing of the Temple," 311, 313–16, 323. However, as we will see, there are additional reasons why Jesus may have objected to the money changers that Casey does not treat.

level with John the Baptist, but the question of authority makes no sense without the incident to which it refers.[23]

Issues of historicity will continue to surface as individual aspects of the temple incident and its significance are discussed.

Given the certainty so many have about the historicity of the temple incident, why do some decide the Gospel accounts of the incident are fabrications? Here too, people often state their opinions without giving cogent argument or evidence. Among those rejecting the incident are George Buchanan, Ernst Haenchen, Burton Mack, Robert Miller, and David Seeley.[24] The reasons offered to substantiate this doubt include:

1. The temple act belonged to a basic Markan plot as an inaugural event of provocation. The four elements (the driving out, the teaching of Isa 56:7 and Jer 7:11, the response of the chief priests, and the amazement of the crowd) reflect the first "teaching" of Jesus in the synagogue at Capernaum (with the exorcism there paralleling the casting out of the temple). Jesus was crucified as one who desecrated the temple, but if one deletes the themes essential to the Markan plots, there is nothing left over for historical reminiscence. The anti-temple theme is clearly Markan, and there is no evidence for an anti-temple attitude in the Jesus traditions prior to Mark. "Nothing happens ... [The] temple act is a Markan fabrication."[25]

2. The word λῃστής refers, not to robbers, but to violent people, brigands, or zealots. It does not describe the priests unless it is metaphorical, but more likely it refers to the persons and events of 68–70 C.E. The zealots in control of the temple at that time could justly be called a "cave of brigands."[26]

---

[23] See Casey, "The Cleansing of the Temple," 327. The decision of the Jesus Seminar was that the question of authority is secondary, partly because the sayings in this incident are neither a parable nor an aphorism, which is odd. See Funk and Seminar, *The Acts of Jesus*, 124. Why should a statement connected to an event necessarily be an aphorism or a parable?

[24] George Wesley Buchanan, "Mark 11.15–19: Brigands in the Temple," *HUCA* 30 (1959): 169–77; George Wesley Buchanan, "Symbolic Money-Changers in the Temple?" *NTS* 37 (1991): 280–89; Ernst Haenchen, *Der Weg Jesu: Eine Erklärung des Markus-Evangeliums und der kanonischen Parallelen* (Berlin: Töpelmann, 1966), 382–89; Mack, *Myth*, 266, 270, 291–92; Robert J. Miller, "The (A)Historicity of Jesus' Temple Demonstration: A Test Case in Methodology," in *SBL Seminar Papers, 1991* (SBLSP 30; Atlanta: Scholars, 1991), 235–52; David Seeley, "Jesus' Temple Act," *CBQ* 55 (1993): 263–83; and David Seeley, "Jesus' Temple Act Revisited: A Response to P. M. Casey," *CBQ* 62 (2000): 55–63.

[25] Mack, *Myth*, 266, 270, 291–92; followed by Miller, "The (A)Historicity of Jesus' Temple Demonstration," 246–52.

[26] Especially Buchanan, "Brigands," 175–77. Seeley ("Jesus' Temple Act," 273–83) thinks the temple incident was conceived in light of the temple's destruction in 70 C.E., obviously assuming, as many do, that Mark was written later than this date. Such a date needs rethinking. Further, the assumption that the destruction of the city leads to the creation of the temple incident can offer little for justification.

3. The "cleansing" fits a pattern of cleansings by such kings as Hezekiah (2 Kgs 18:1–6; 2 Chr 29:3–19) and Judas Maccabeus (Josephus, *Ant.* 12.316–322), so Christians would have thought something like this occurred, especially to fulfill Zech 14:21. After the fall of Jerusalem some Christian who opposed the action of the zealots in Jerusalem formed the midrash in Mark 11:16–17 to prove that the zealotic action was wrong and deserved to be punished.[27]

4. Several aspects of this account do not fit what we know of Jesus elsewhere. The incident is an exercise of raw power that does not fit with the Jesus of the parables and sayings. The concern for ritual purity in Mark 11:16 does not fit with Jesus' teachings. Jesus does not seem concerned about Gentiles elsewhere, and it seems awkward for him to stress the temple as a place to pray.[28]

5. Since Jesus' motivation is unclear, it is hard to consider the event historical.[29]

6. The reported incident is difficult to imagine from several standpoints, a problem already recognized by Origen.[30] The area of the temple mount covered approximately thirty-five acres and was a noisy market place. One person could hardly take over all the money changers and animal sellers, if indeed animals were even present, and could not police the whole area to prevent people from carrying vessels through, as Mark reports. Since the temple was the national treasury and a heavily fortified fortress, with the Roman guard increased during festival times when trouble was feared,[31] it is difficult to imagine how any disturbance could happen without repercussions from both temple guards and Roman soldiers stationed in the nearby Antonia fortress.[32] At other times the authorities reacted quickly to temple

---

[27] Buchanan, "Symbolic Money-Changers?" 283, 289; Miller, "The (A)Historicity of Jesus' Temple Demonstration," 242, following David Catchpole, "The 'Triumphal' Entry," in *Jesus and the Politics of His Day* (ed. E. Bammel and C. F. D. Moule; Cambridge: Cambridge University Press, 1984), 319–21. Catchpole is concerned with patterns of a triumphal entry and lists twelve incidents, some of which concern other cities, not all of which end in a temple, and none of which is really pertinent to the temple incident of Jesus. Some would add accounts of Apollonius of Tyana correcting temple rituals. See *Life of Apollonius* 1.16 and 4.40. Such parallels are remote. Another rejecting the historicity of the event is Henk Jan de Jonge ("The Cleansing of the Temple in Mark 11:15 and Zechariah 14:21," in *The Book of Zechariah and Its Influence* [ed. Christopher Tuckett; Hampshire: Ashgate, 2003], 87–99), but he more assumes his conclusion than argues it. He thinks the event is improbable and was created in response to the prophetic vision of Zech 14:21 by someone who valued the person of Jesus.

[28] Haenchen, *Der Weg Jesu*; Seeley, "Jesus' Temple Act," 269.

[29] Seeley, "Jesus' Temple Act," 270.

[30] Origen commented on the difficulties in *Comm. Jo.* 10:16 (*ANF* 9:393–395).

[31] Josephus, *Ant.* 15.247–248; 20.106–107.

[32] Buchanan, "Symbolic Money-Changers?" 281–85; Haenchen, *Der Weg Jesu*, 382–89.

disturbances.³³ One cannot argue it all happened too quickly for the authorities to react, for Mark 11:16 presumes control for some time. Nor can one think that pilgrims who had come to the temple to pay their taxes and offer sacrifices would have looked favorably on Jesus' action and would have assisted him, especially since Jesus would not have been well-known to the crowds.³⁴

The force of these items varies, but the first five objections carry rather little persuasive power. The sixth raises issues that every interpreter must face, even if the phrasing of the objection already makes interpretive decisions.

To be more specific, the first objection, which is from Burton Mack, assumes a parallel between Mark 1:21–28 and 11:15–19 that does not exist and does not assess adequately either Mark's or Jesus' attitude toward the temple. Further, on what grounds should anyone deny the themes essential to Mark's plot, especially when those themes are present as well in the Johannine account?³⁵ Mack has asserted a view rather than made a case. I would argue that neither Jesus nor Mark is against the temple. The claim that Mark is anti-temple is difficult to accept when he alone has 11:16, the comment about Jesus not permitting vessels to be carried through the temple. This verse assumes a concern for the sanctity of the temple.

Concerning the second objection, λῃστής does mean "violent one," "brigand," or "insurrectionist," not merely "swindler" or "thief," but brigands often were robbers (e.g., Luke 10:30; John 10:1, 8). The meaning of the word is not in question. At issue is whether the application of Jer 7:11 to the temple incident emerged as Mark's literal description of the zealots who took over the temple in 68 C.E. or whether it is a metaphorical description or adaptation of the Jeremiah text to describe the failure of the ruling priests in the temple in Jesus' day. The latter is much more likely for three reasons. First, Jeremiah's own use was a metaphorical description of the priests in his day. Second, Josephus reports that Jesus ben Ananias four years before the war voiced condemnation of the temple *with language from Jer 7:34* but

---

³³ Josephus, *Ant.* 17.155–163, *J. W.* 1.651–653; Acts 21:30–33. Some of the instances listed by Catchpole ("The 'Triumphal' Entry," 332–33) to demonstrate quick reaction by authorities are of dubious relevance since they are very unlike Jesus' temple incident. Most do not occur in the temple, and the ones that do involve acts of violence or desecration.

³⁴ Haenchen, *Der Weg Jesu*, 386–89. He also argued the Gospels use Isa 56:7 and Jer 7:11 in ways contrary to their intent. Seeley ("Jesus' Temple Act Revisited," 58–59) is the one who suggests Jesus was not well-known.

³⁵ It is not likely that John is dependent on Mark. For a critique of Mack's rather brief treatment, see Evans, "Jesus and the 'Cave of Robbers'," 93–100; for a critique of Miller see Jerome Murphy-O'Connor, "Jesus and the Money Changers (Mark 11:15–17; John 2:13–17)," *RB* 107 (2000): 42–55, esp. 43–46.

with no mention of zealots.³⁶ Third, if the term λῃστής were derived from the situation of the Jewish War, it would hardly be applied to the ruling priests and temple management, for they are the ones the zealots opposed.³⁷

The third objection, the supposed pattern of cleansing to which the account has been made to conform, is highly speculative and without substantiation. The supposed parallels are very *unlike* the incident recorded in the Gospels. In the case of both Hezekiah (2 Kgs 18:1–6 and 2 Chr 29:1–19) and Judas Maccabeus (Josephus, *Ant.* 12.316–322) the temple had fallen into disuse. In the case of the former idols polluted the temple, and in the case of the latter it is the priests who cleanse the temple. Rather than Jesus' temple incident being conformed to an expectation, the theory has forced the text into an assumption about its origin. Furthermore, it is difficult to think of any leader coming to Jerusalem and having any impact without involvement in the temple. Where else would a religious teacher or a prophet go in Jerusalem, especially if that person had any reformist, eschatological, or messianic expectations?

The fourth objection claims some items in the accounts do not fit what is known about Jesus, but these claims are unjustified. Neither Jesus nor anyone else could have thought it awkward to go to the temple to pray. The parable of the Pharisee and the Tax Collector describes two men precisely going up to the temple to pray, the temple was referred to as a house of prayer or the place from which prayers ascend,³⁸ and the early Christians still went to the temple to pray after Pentecost. Jesus *did* display concern for cultic issues when he directed lepers to show themselves to the priests (Matt 8:4 = Mark 1:44; Luke 17:14) and in his comments about the attitude with which one brings a sacrifice (Matt 5:23–24). With regard to the "Gentiles" (ἔθνη), the concern is not for the church's mission to the *Gentiles* but the eschatological vision in the Jewish scriptures that all *nations* would come to the temple to worship God (e.g., Isa 2:2–4; Mic 4:1–3; Zech 14:16; see also Mal 1:11), a vision already expressed at the dedication of Solomon's temple (1 Kgs 8:41–43). Surely this concern stems from Jesus' restoration eschatology, which I will argue is a major factor in understanding the temple incident.

As for "raw power" being something unsuitable for the Jesus we know, perhaps we have settled too quickly for a Jesus "meek and mild" that is a distortion. Mark reports Jesus getting angry (3:5), and the Jesus of the para-

---

³⁶ See Josephus, *J. W.* 6.301–309 and the discussion of this passage by Craig A. Evans, *Mark 8:27–16:20* (WBC 34b; Nashville: Nelson, 2001), 177.

³⁷ See Robert H. Gundry, *Mark: A Commentary on His Apology for the Cross* (Grand Rapids: Eerdmans, 1993), 645.

³⁸ 1 Macc 7:37; Josephus, *Ant.* 8.108; Philo, *Moses* 2.133; *b. Ber.* 7a; 32b = *b. B. Meṣiʿa* 59a; *b. Meg.* 18a; *b. Yoma* 87b.

bles, like all prophets,[39] uses extremely violent – even offensive – language (e.g., Matt 18:34; 24:51 = Luke 12:46; Luke 19:27), and he does not hesitate to denounce Pharisees and other religious types. Jesus commits no physical violence on people in the temple, even though he does act forcefully. If he thought the most sacred symbol of God's presence was being mismanaged, is it really a surprise that he took forceful action?

The fifth objection, that unclear motivation renders historicity suspect, hardly merits attention.[40] If that were the case, a good deal of the history we know would be suspect. Our inability to explain an event fully does not make the event less real.

One piece of the sixth objection is misguided – the suggestion that Jesus was not well-known. Everything about the Gospels suggests otherwise,[41] but this issue is of less importance in dealing with the questions in the sixth objection. The issues involved in understanding how this event could have taken place are real and must be addressed, regardless of the view one takes. Clearly though, the difficulty of imagining how and to what extent Jesus drove out the money-changers and merchants is not a sufficient basis for rejecting the historicity of the event. The very people – like E. P. Sanders – who see the temple incident as one of the most certain acts of Jesus are the ones who wrestle with the problems of scale. These items will be discussed below.

3. The Relationship between the Accounts

3.1. Examining the Various Accounts

The following is a table comparing the four accounts found in the NT.

Matthew 21:12–16	Mark 11:15–18	Luke 19:45–48	John 2:13–22
¹² Καὶ εἰσῆλθεν Ἰησοῦς εἰς τὸ ἱερὸν καὶ ἐξέβαλεν πάντας τοὺς πωλοῦντας καὶ ἀγοράζοντας ἐν τῷ ἱερῷ, καὶ τὰς	¹⁵ Καὶ ἔρχονται εἰς Ἰεροσόλυμα. Καὶ εἰσελθὼν εἰς τὸ ἱερὸν ἤρξατο ἐκβάλλειν τοὺς πωλοῦντας καὶ τοὺς ἀγοράζοντας ἐν τῷ ἱερῷ, καὶ	⁴⁵ Καὶ εἰσελθὼν εἰς τὸ ἱερὸν ἤρξατο ἐκβάλλειν τοὺς πωλοῦντας ⁴⁶ λέγων αὐτοῖς· γέγραπται· καὶ ἔσται ὁ οἶκός μου οἶκος προσευχῆς,	¹³ Καὶ ἐγγὺς ἦν τὸ πάσχα τῶν Ἰουδαίων, καὶ ἀνέβη εἰς Ἱεροσόλυμα ὁ Ἰησοῦς. ¹⁴ Καὶ εὗρεν ἐν τῷ ἱερῷ

---

[39] See Scot McKnight, "Jesus and Prophetic Actions," *BBR* 10 (2000): 197–232.
[40] For a critique of Seeley's first article see Casey, "The Cleansing of the Temple," 324–31.
[41] Josephus' reference to Jesus (*Ant*. 18.63–64) has suffered interpolation, but most accept there is an authentic core from Josephus giving evidence of Jesus. See in this volume ch. 13 § 2.1.2.

Matthew 21:12–16	Mark 11:15–18	Luke 19:45–48	John 2:13–22
τραπέζας τῶν κολλυβιστῶν κατέστρεψεν καὶ τὰς καθέδρας τῶν πωλούντων τὰς περιστεράς, ¹³ καὶ λέγει αὐτοῖς· γέγραπται· ὁ οἶκός μου οἶκος προσευχῆς κληθήσεται, ὑμεῖς δὲ αὐτὸν ποιεῖτε σπήλαιον λῃστῶν. ¹⁴ καὶ προσῆλθον αὐτῷ τυφλοὶ καὶ χωλοὶ ἐν τῷ ἱερῷ, καὶ ἐθεράπευσεν αὐτούς. ¹⁵ ἰδόντες δὲ οἱ ἀρχιερεῖς καὶ οἱ γραμματεῖς τὰ θαυμάσια ἃ ἐποίησεν καὶ τοὺς παῖδας τοὺς κράζοντας ἐν τῷ ἱερῷ καὶ λέγοντας· ὡσαννὰ τῷ υἱῷ Δαυίδ, ἠγανάκτησαν ¹⁶ καὶ εἶπαν αὐτῷ· ἀκούεις τί οὗτοι λέγουσιν; ὁ δὲ Ἰησοῦς λέγει αὐτοῖς· ναί. οὐδέποτε ἀνέγνωτε ὅτι ἐκ στόματος νηπίων καὶ θηλαζόντων κατηρτίσω αἶνον;	τὰς τραπέζας τῶν κολλυβιστῶν καὶ τὰς καθέδρας τῶν πωλούντων τὰς περιστεράς κατέστρεψεν, ¹⁶ καὶ οὐκ ἤφιεν ἵνα τις διενέγκῃ σκεῦος διὰ τοῦ ἱεροῦ. ¹⁷ καὶ ἐδίδασκεν καὶ ἔλεγεν αὐτοῖς· οὐ γέγραπται ὅτι ὁ οἶκός μου οἶκος προσευχῆς κληθήσεται πᾶσιν τοῖς ἔθνεσιν; ὑμεῖς δὲ πεποιήκατε αὐτὸν σπήλαιον λῃστῶν. ¹⁸ Καὶ ἤκουσαν οἱ ἀρχιερεῖς καὶ οἱ γραμματεῖς καὶ ἐζήτουν πῶς αὐτὸν ἀπολέσωσιν· ἐφοβοῦντο γὰρ αὐτόν, πᾶς γὰρ ὁ ὄχλος ἐξεπλήσσετο ἐπὶ τῇ διδαχῇ αὐτοῦ.	ὑμεῖς δὲ αὐτὸν ἐποιήσατε σπήλαιον λῃστῶν. ⁴⁷ Καὶ ἦν διδάσκων τὸ καθ' ἡμέραν ἐν τῷ ἱερῷ. οἱ δὲ ἀρχιερεῖς καὶ οἱ γραμματεῖς ἐζήτουν αὐτὸν ἀπολέσαι καὶ οἱ πρῶτοι τοῦ λαοῦ, ⁴⁸ καὶ οὐχ εὕρισκον τὸ τί ποιήσωσιν, ὁ λαὸς γὰρ ἅπας ἐξεκρέματο αὐτοῦ ἀκούων.	τοὺς πωλοῦντας βόας καὶ πρόβατα καὶ περιστεράς καὶ τοὺς κερματιστὰς καθημένους, ¹⁵ καὶ ποιήσας φραγέλλιον ἐκ σχοινίων πάντας ἐξέβαλεν ἐκ τοῦ ἱεροῦ τά τε πρόβατα καὶ τοὺς βόας, καὶ τῶν κολλυβιστῶν ἐξέχεεν τὸ κέρμα καὶ τὰς τραπέζας ἀνέτρεψεν, ¹⁶ καὶ τοῖς τὰς περιστεράς πωλοῦσιν εἶπεν· ἄρατε ταῦτα ἐντεῦθεν, μὴ ποιεῖτε τὸν οἶκον τοῦ πατρός μου οἶκον ἐμπορίου. ¹⁷ ἐμνήσθησαν οἱ μαθηταὶ αὐτοῦ ὅτι γεγραμμένον ἐστίν· ὁ ζῆλος τοῦ οἴκου σου καταφάγεταί με. ¹⁸ Ἀπεκρίθησαν οὖν οἱ Ἰουδαῖοι καὶ εἶπαν αὐτῷ· τί σημεῖον δεικνύεις ἡμῖν ὅτι ταῦτα ποιεῖς; ¹⁹ ἀπεκρίθη Ἰησοῦς καὶ εἶπεν αὐτοῖς· λύσατε τὸν ναὸν τοῦτον καὶ ἐν τρισὶν ἡμέραις ἐγερῶ αὐτόν. ²⁰ εἶπαν οὖν οἱ Ἰουδαῖοι· τεσσεράκοντα καὶ ἓξ ἔτεσιν οἰκοδομήθη ὁ ναὸς

The Temple Incident

Matthew 21:12–16	Mark 11:15–18	Luke 19:45–48	John 2:13–22
			οὗτος, καὶ σὺ ἐν τρισὶν ἡμέραις ἐγερεῖς αὐτόν; ²¹ ἐκεῖνος δὲ ἔλεγεν περὶ τοῦ ναοῦ τοῦ σώματος αὐτοῦ. ²² ὅτε οὖν ἠγέρθη ἐκ νεκρῶν, ἐμνήσθησαν οἱ μαθηταὶ αὐτοῦ ὅτι τοῦτο ἔλεγεν, καὶ ἐπίστευσαν τῇ γραφῇ καὶ τῷ λόγῳ ὃν εἶπεν ὁ Ἰησοῦς.
¹² Then Jesus entered the temple and drove out all who were selling and buying in the temple, and he overturned the tables of the money changers and the seats of those who sold doves. ¹³ He said to them, "It is written, 'My house shall be called a house of prayer'; but you are making it a den of robbers." ¹⁴ The blind and the lame came to him in the temple, and he cured them. ¹⁵ But when the chief priests and the scribes saw the amazing things that he did, and heard the children crying out in the temple, "Hosanna to the Son of	¹⁵ Then they came to Jerusalem. And he entered the temple and began to drive out those who were selling and those who were buying in the temple, and he overturned the tables of the money changers and the seats of those who sold doves; ¹⁶ and he would not allow anyone to carry anything through the temple. ¹⁷ He was teaching and saying, "Is it not written, 'My house shall be called a house of prayer for all the nations'? But you have made it a den of robbers." ¹⁸ And when the chief priests and the scribes heard it, they kept looking	⁴⁵ Then he entered the temple and began to drive out those who were selling things there; ⁴⁶ and he said, "It is written, 'My house shall be a house of prayer'; but you have made it a den of robbers." ⁴⁷ Every day he was teaching in the temple. The chief priests, the scribes, and the leaders of the people kept looking for a way to kill him; ⁴⁸ but they did not find anything they could do, for all the people were spellbound by what they heard.	¹³ The Passover of the Jews was near, and Jesus went up to Jerusalem. ¹⁴ In the temple he found people selling cattle, sheep, and doves, and the money changers seated at their tables. ¹⁵ Making a whip of cords, he drove all of them out of the temple, both the sheep and the cattle. He also poured out the coins of the money changers and overturned their tables. ¹⁶ He told those who were selling the doves, "Take these things out of here! Stop making my Father's house a marketplace!" ¹⁷ His disciples remembered that it was written, "Zeal

Matthew 21:12–16	Mark 11:15–18	Luke 19:45–48	John 2:13–22
David," they became angry ¹⁶ and said to him, "Do you hear what these are saying?" Jesus said to them, "Yes; have you never read, 'Out of the mouths of infants and nursing babies you have prepared praise for yourself'?"	for a way to kill him; for they were afraid of him, because the whole crowd was spellbound by his teaching.		for your house will consume me." ¹⁸ The Jews then said to him, "What sign can you show us for doing this?" ¹⁹ Jesus answered them, "Destroy this temple, and in three days I will raise it up." ²⁰ The Jews then said, "This temple has been under construction for forty-six years, and will you raise it up in three days?" ²¹ But he was speaking of the temple of his body. ²² After he was raised from the dead, his disciples remembered that he had said this; and they believed the scripture and the word that Jesus had spoken.

The claim of multiple attestation and treatment of the significance of each account requires a closer analysis of the various accounts. As indicated above, Luke's account is quite abbreviated, but it follows the story line and placement of Matthew and Mark. Luke 19:45, at least as far as it goes, agrees with Mark 11:15 verbatim. Except for the opening line of Mark 11:15, Matt 21:12 agrees with Mark except that Matthew has two finite verbs instead of Mark's participle and infinitive (εἰσελθὼν ... ἐκβάλλειν), does not have the article before ἀγοράζοντας, and has the verb κατέστρεψεν after κολλυβιστῶν rather than at the end of the verse. Neither Matthew nor Luke has the statement in Mark 11:16 about carrying vessels through the temple. Unlike the others, in 11:17 Mark specifies that Jesus was teaching. Also in 11:17 and parallels each of the three has a different form of the verb λέγειν. Luke 19:46 and Matt 21:13 agree against Mark in rendering the words of Isa 56:7 as a statement, whereas Mark 11:17 has a question, and unlike Mark neither of the other evangelists has the words "for all the nations" (πᾶσιν τοῖς ἔθνεσιν). Matthew and Mark both use κληθήσεται in the quotation, but Luke has ἔσται. Except for each having a different form of the verb ποιεῖν (ποιεῖτε, πεποιήκατε, ἐποιήσατε) and Mark's placing the pronoun αὐτὸν after this verb instead of before, the second half of the quotation is the same in all three. Matthew 21:14–17 includes material that is in neither Mark nor Luke concerning the blind and the lame coming to Jesus for healing, and Jesus receiving acclamations in the temple that he is the son of David. This results in a complaint from the ruling priests and scribes to which Jesus responds with words from Ps 8:3. Matthew does not indicate that the ruling priests and scribes seek to destroy Jesus but could not for fear of the crowd, which both Mark and Luke do with some variation, and both emphasize the positive response of the people.

A difference exists in the framing of the incident as well. Neither Luke nor John has the account of the cursing of the fig tree, but Mark, in keeping with his tendency to use bracketing to convey implicit commentary, has bracketed the temple incident with the cursing of the fig tree before the event and after with the fig tree being withered the next day. Matthew has the cursing after the temple incident, but the withering takes place immediately. The result is that Matthew has the temple incident the same day as the entry into Jerusalem, whereas for Mark it is a day later. Mark's bracketing is usually viewed as his redactional work,[42] but for both Matthew and Mark the cursing of the fig tree is something of an acted parable and has implications for their understanding of the temple incident. Whether the target is the temple itself, the temple rulers, or the nation more generally is not clear. Further, unexpectedly both evangelists interpret the cursing, not in relation to the temple, but in relation to praying with faith. I do not think that the mention of "this mountain" (Matt 21:21 = Mark 11:23) is a reference to the temple mount[43] or that the mention of forgiving others while praying (Mark 11:25) has anything to do with the temple.

John's account, of course, is considerably different. Whereas the Synoptics have this event just after the triumphal entry, John places it near the beginning of his Gospel (2:13–22) as the second public act Jesus performs. The event is essentially the same except that Jesus makes and uses a whip and that cattle and sheep are also driven out. In John, Jesus does not use Isa

---

[42] E.g., Robert H. Stein, *Gospels and Tradition: Studies on Redaction Criticism of the Synoptic Gospels* (Grand Rapids: Baker, 1991), 124, suggests that the pre-Marcan tradition did not connect the cleansing and the cursing and that originally there existed no vital connection between the two. See the discussion and cautions by Adela Yarbro Collins, *Mark* (Hermeneia; Minneapolis: Fortress, 2007), 523–25.

[43] As Wright, *Jesus and the Victory of God*, 334–35, 494.

56:7 and Jer 7:11 as in the Synoptics, but John reports an indirect allusion to Zech 14:21 with the admonition that people should not make "the house of my Father a house of business." The sellers of doves are treated differently. In Matthew and Mark their seats are overturned, but in John they are only instructed to remove the doves. A Johannine note is added in 2:17 explaining that the disciples later remembered the words of Ps 69:9 [10]: "Zeal for your house will consume me." The wording in John for this incident is not close to the other accounts and coincides only at the most essential words: ἱερῷ, πωλοῦντας, ἐξέβαλεν, κολλυβιστῶν, τραπέζας, and περιστεράς. Of major importance is the agreement of all four accounts that the temple incident is followed by the ruling priests, scribes, and elders – in John just "the Jews" – questioning Jesus about the basis of his action. In the Synoptics they ask "By what authority," and in John they ask "What sign are you demonstrating to us because you are doing these things?" In the Synoptics the focus is Jesus' counter question about the Baptist; in John the focus is his statement about destroying the temple. John's account is so different that it cannot merely be written off as secondary[44] or seen as dependent on the Synoptic tradition.[45] As the overwhelming majority of scholars conclude, the Johannine account must be seen as an independent witness to the event.[46] Given the recent focus on oral tradition, it bears repeating that it is myopic for scholars to operate only with a literary model in discussing Synoptic relations. We should not assume we have only two sources for the temple incident, that of Mark and John. Rather, Synoptic relations are not so simple as the four source hypothesis would suggest, as is evidenced by frequent recourse to deutero-Markan hypotheses.[47] Can we believe that the first time Matthew and Luke learned of the temple incident is when they read it in Mark, if they did? The brevity of Luke's account does not allow one to draw conclusions, but Matthew seems to have independent tradition. There is a good chance that we have at least three different traditions of the temple incident, that of Matthew, that of Mark, and that of John.

---

[44] As Casey, "The Cleansing of the Temple," 324.

[45] As Seeley, "Jesus' Temple Act," 272–73; and J. Duncan M. Derrett, "No Stone Upon Another: Leprosy and the Temple," *JSNT* 30 (1987): 3.

[46] Among many see Raymond E. Brown, *The Gospel According to John I–XII* (AB 29; New York: Doubleday, 1966), 116–20; Mark A. Matson, "The Contribution to the Temple Cleansing by the Fourth Gospel," in *SBL Seminar Papers, 1992* (SBLSP 31; Atlanta: Scholars, 1992), 496; Kim Huat Tan, *The Zion Traditions and the Aims of Jesus* (SNTSMS 91; Cambridge: Cambridge University Press, 1997), 163; and John P. Meier, *Mentor, Message, and Miracles* (vol. 2 of *A Marginal Jew: Rethinking the Historical Jesus*; ABRL; New York: Doubleday, 1991–2009), 892–94.

[47] Witness Ulrich Luz, *Matthew 21–28* (trans. James E. Crouch; Hermeneia; Minneapolis: Fortress, 2005), 6, who, because of numerous minor agreements, is uncertain which changes in Matthew come from him and which from a deutero-Markan source.

Some might mention *Gos. Thom.* 64 ("The buyers and the merchants [shall] not [come] into the places of my Father") and 71 ("I shall destroy [this] house, and no one will be able to [re]build it"). In fact, John Dominic Crossan thinks saying 71 is the most original version of the saying about destruction,[48] which seems unlikely to me. Saying 64 stems from Thomas's rejection of materialism and is not related to the temple incident. The sayings in *Gos. Thom.* are not pertinent for understanding the temple incident.

3.2. The Synoptic vs. the Johannine Chronology

The difference between the Synoptics and John on the chronology of the temple incident leads some to conclude there were two cleansings.[49] While this cannot be absolutely precluded,[50] it is not likely.[51] Not only are the accounts very close in what happened, both traditions have the temple incident followed by questioning from the religious leaders. Most assume as well that such an incident would have brought a quick response, not a delay until the act was repeated two to three years later. Would the second temple event have led to Jesus' death while an earlier, similar event merely raised questions?

Whether the Synoptic or the Johannine chronology is to be preferred is not easily determined. People frequently assume the Synoptic version is correct partly because it presumes an established popularity of Jesus and because it leads directly to Jesus' arrest.[52] The more one views the temple incident as the cause of the arrest the more one will be inclined to think the Synoptic sequence is correct. John then would be viewed as bringing the incident to the beginning of his Gospel because he viewed the raising of

---

[48] John Dominic Crossan, *The Historical Jesus: The Life of a Mediterranean Jewish Peasant* (San Francisco: HarperSanFrancisco, 1991), 356.

[49] E. g., Leon Morris, *The Gospel According to John* (NICNT; Grand Rapids: Eerdmans, 1995), 189–91. For a recent discussion of the issues see E. Randolph Richards, "An Honor/Shame Argument for Two Temple Cleansings," *TJ* 29 (2008): 19–43. Richards argues for two cleansings because he thinks John's account is a claim for honor by Jesus, a claim that was challenged and in which Jesus was shamed. The Synoptics did not include this first temple incident, a cleansing, because they did not understand it. The second incident was a symbolic cursing or closing of the temple. This explanation is hardly convincing. The evidence for an honor/shame focus is nonexistent, and the claim that the Synoptic incident is about cursing or closing the temple does no justice to Jesus' healing in the temple in Matthew or his refusal to allow anyone to carry items through the temple in Mark.

[50] See the discussion by Craig L. Blomberg, *The Historical Reliability of John's Gospel* (Downers Grove: InterVarsity, 2001), 87–91.

[51] See Brown, *John I–XII*, 117; Tan, *Zion Traditions*, 161; and Ådna, *Jesu Stellung zum Tempel*, 309–12.

[52] E. g., Ådna, *Jesu Stellung zum Tempel*, 311–12.

Lazarus as the primary reason for Jesus' arrest,[53] to show the new beginnings occurring with Jesus,[54] or as an exegesis of the statement "He came to his own but his own did not receive him."[55] Admittedly, none of these explanations is totally convincing.[56]

Those who argue the Johannine chronology is better raise several significant points.[57] First, the Synoptics record only one trip of Jesus to Jerusalem.[58] They have no other alternative at which they could place the temple incident. Both the discussions concerning John the Baptist and the charge that Jesus said he would destroy the temple would make more sense on the Johannine chronology. On the Synoptic positioning John the Baptist probably has been dead a year or more; would a question about him still be so pertinent or threatening if answered wrongly?[59] The false witnesses were unable to agree or to get the complaint straight; is that likely if the statement were made just a few days earlier? Further, the Johannine account brings the destruction theme directly into relation with the event.[60] More relevant perhaps is the date marker in the Johannine account that the temple had

---

[53] Brown, *John I–XII*, 118; see John Ashton, *Understanding the Fourth Gospel* (Oxford: Clarendon, 1991), 414, who suggests John moved the account earlier to show that the whole of Jesus' career would be lived under the shadow of the cross.

[54] E. g., Kerr, *The Temple of Jesus' Body*, 69–77. Included in such a statement is the assumption the temple replacement motif in John in which Jesus takes over the functions and role of the temple. Obviously this motif is evident in 2:19. See n. 17 above.

[55] Bruce D. Chilton, *The Temple of Jesus: His Sacrificial Program Within a Cultural History of Sacrifice* (University Park: Pennsylvania State University, 1992), 117. John 1:11 would also fit well with Ps 69:8 [9]: "I have become a stranger to my kindred, an alien to my mother's children."

[56] Lieu ("Temple and Synagogue in John," 63–64) points out that the explanation John moved the incident forward to symbolize the replacement of the Jewish system faces serious difficulties since there is no judgment expressed on the temple and no splitting of the veil in John.

[57] See John A. T. Robinson, *The Priority of John* (ed. J. F. Coakley; London: SCM, 1985), 127–31.

[58] Although they contain hints that Jesus was in Jerusalem more frequently or at least longer than they suggest. See Mark 3:7–8; 11:19; Luke 4:44; 19:47–20:1; 21:37–38. The money-changers set up tables in the temple to collect the temple tax on the twenty-fifth of Adar according to *m. Šeqal.* 1:3. No mention is made of the time they were removed. If they were removed on the first of Nisan, the date prescribed for payment, then the temple incident would have taken place prior to the so-called passion week. See Victor Eppstein, "The Historicity of the Gospel Account of the Cleansing of the Temple," *ZNW* 55 (1964): 45.

[59] Murphy-O'Connor, "Jesus and the Money Changers," 53–54, places the incident early in Jesus' life while he was still aligned with the ministry of John the Baptist. If there was still a movement centered around John the Baptist, which is probable, the question would still be relevant.

[60] This is significant enough that it leads Brown (*John I–XII*, 118) to suggest the unlikely reconstruction that on his first journey to Jerusalem Jesus uttered the prophetic warning about the destruction of the temple and on a subsequent visit he cleansed the temple. On this view John gives us the correct sequence for the first visit but not the other.

been in the process of being built for 46 years. If Herod's temple building effort began in 20 or 19 B.C.E., then forty-six years later would be 27 or 28 C. E., the time usually designated as the beginning of Jesus' ministry, not its end, and the time which would coincide with the fifteenth year of Tiberius Caesar.[61]

I lean toward the Synoptic chronology because of the incident's logical connection with Jesus' arrest, but in the end I do not think either option may be excluded. If John's chronology were accurate, the incident would still be a causative factor in Jesus' arrest, as the quotation of Ps 69:9 in John 2:17 attests, but it would not be the climactic, motivating factor it is in the Synoptics.

4. What Happened, Where, and under What Circumstances?

As mentioned above, one of the problems for all interpreters of this text is understanding what really happened since the temple mount covered about thirty-five acres. How could one person take charge of all the proceedings and control such a large area? For this reason many suggest this was a minor incident, a relatively obscure event, hardly noticed, or only a gesture.[62] The problem is that those same people often see this event as leading to Jesus' death, but they cannot have it both ways. The more one makes the event a minor incident, the more difficult it is to see it as causing Jesus' arrest.

Another problem is that far too little is known about the specifics of the temple or the event. Were animals other than doves for sale in the temple, as in John's account, and where would any selling of animals and/or doves take place? Where were the money changers, and why were they needed? Was there corruption in the way the temple was being run? What vessels or objects[63] did Jesus prohibit being carried through the temple, as Mark 11:16 has it? Just what was the problem that Jesus reacted against? Despite all that we do not know, the point is obvious that the business of the temple *required* money changers and the purchase of sacrificial animals.[64] People

---

[61] Robinson, *The Priority of John*, 130–31.

[62] Among many see Sanders, *Jesus and Judaism*, 69–70, 304; Luz, *Matthew 21–28*, 11; Witherington, *The Christology of Jesus*, 110–15; Martin Hengel, *Was Jesus a Revolutionist?* (trans. William Klassen; Philadelphia: Fortress, 1971), 16–17; and Marcus J. Borg, *Conflict, Holiness & Politics in the Teachings of Jesus* (Studies in the Bible and Early Christianity 5; New York: Mellen, 1984), 171–72 (who says it would take scores of people to control the area). As Borg points out, Origen (*Comm. Jo.* 10:16 [*ANF* 9:395]) compared the event to Jesus' miracles.

[63] σκεῦος can be used of an object, a thing, or property as well as a container. See Matt 12:29 = Mark 3:27; Luke 17:31; Acts 10:11, 16; and 11:5.

[64] A point made repeatedly; see e.g., Sanders, *Jesus and Judaism*, 63–65.

had only two options: they could bring animals from their homes, which was not easy and carried the risk that the animal might be rejected, or they could acquire an animal at the temple or on the Mount of Olives.

4.1. The Scale of the Event

The picture in our minds of what happened is determined by what we think we know about the temple and Jesus. It could be that Jesus' temple action was a minor, symbolic event, but there is reason to rethink the issue.

The original temple mount was 500 cubits by 500 cubits,[65] or approximately 250 meters square comprising about 62,500 sq. meters. Herod more than doubled the area by adding an outer court resulting in a trapezoid measuring 480 meters on the west, 470 on the east, 315 on the north, and 280 on the south, approximately 150,000 sq. meters.[66] If the thought was about clearing this whole area, the task would be enormous. However, the layout of the temple mount both creates questions and reduces the area. First, we must recognize the different words that the evangelists and others used in referring to the temple. A distinction is made between ἱερόν, which is used for the whole temple mount, and ναός, which is used for the sanctuary, the inner court.[67] Of major importance is the fact that all four canonical accounts use ἱερόν, not ναός, of the temple incident, and ἱερόν, when reporting Jesus' prediction of the destruction of the temple (Matt 24:1–2; Mark 13:1–2; and Luke 21:5–6). However, ναός appears in the charge of the false witnesses that Jesus said he would destroy the temple (Matt 26:61 = Mark 14:58) and in the mocking during the crucifixion (Matt 27:40; Mark 15:29). Only John uses ναός in *any* connection with the temple incident, but it is in

---

[65] *m. Mid.* 2:1. The cubit is usually figured to be about 20.5 inches.

[66] The figures are from Shemuel Safrai, "The Temple," in *The Jewish People in the First Century: Historical Geography, Political History, Social, Cultural and Religious Life and Institutions* (ed. Shemuel Safrai and Menahem Stern; vol. 2, section 1 of *Compendia Rerum Iudaicarum ad Novum Testamentum*; Assen: Van Gorcum, 1976), 865, and G. Foerster, "Art and Architecture in Palestine," in *The Jewish People in the First Century: Historical Geography, Political History, Social, Cultural and Religious Life and Institutions* (ed. Shemuel Safrai and Menahem Stern; vol. 2, section 1 of *Compendia Rerum Iudaicarum ad Novum Testamentum*; Assen: Van Gorcum, 1976), 977. M. Ben-Dov gives the measurements as 1595 feet on the west, 1020 on the north, 1562 on the east, and 921 on the south. See M. Ben-Dov, "Temple of Herod," *IDB* 870. See also E. P. Sanders, *Judaism: Practice and Belief, 63 BCE–66 CE* (Philadelphia: Trinity, 1992), 57–58, who has slightly different figures.

[67] People do not always use language the same way. Peter Richardson uses *temenos* for the whole enclosed structure on the temple mount, restricts *hieron* to the area between the *soreg* and the *naos*, and *naos* to the sanctuary itself beyond the altar. See Peter Richardson, *Building Jewish in the Roman East* (Supplements to the Journal for the Study of Judaism 92; Waco: Baylor University Press, 2004), 272–73, 284–97. The NT does not use the word τέμενος, but Josephus uses it both to refer to the altar on which Uzziah offered sacrifice illegitimately (*Ant.* 9.223) and in 15.298 of a larger sacred area distinguished from a ναός.

the ensuing discussion about the sign Jewish leaders ask from Jesus. In John 2:19–21 ναός appears three times: in Jesus' statement "Destroy this temple ..." and in the ensuing comments from the Jewish leaders and the evangelist.

The ἱερόν was changed considerably by Herod's extension.[68] In the descriptions of temples in the Hebrew Bible (Solomon's, Zerrubabel's, and Ezekiel's vision) and in Hasmonean alterations, at least as far as is known, there was no outer court which served as a lesser place for Gentiles and no restriction on Gentiles coming into the area of sacrifice.[69] Nor was there a court of the women. With the idealized picture in 11Q Temple there is an outer court for daughters, strangers (i.e., proselytes), and children, but non-Israelites and the impure were excluded.[70] Herod's reconstruction changed things both for non-Israelites and for women. His enlargement created an outer court to which Gentiles had access. It is misleading to call this outer court "the court of the Gentiles." This is a modern label, not used in early sources, and this outer court was used by everyone, not just Gentiles. It was the area beyond which Gentiles and impure persons could not go. Herod also created the court of the women within the inner court and allowed them to see through the court of the Israelites to the altar where sacrifices were carried out. Women could go beyond the court of the women if they were presenting a sacrifice.

As is well-known, there was a low stone wall, the *soreg*, that marked out the area where non-Israelites and the impure were not allowed. Signs in both Greek and Latin warned of death for Gentiles violating the restriction.[71] Beyond the *soreg* was the *ḥel*, the rampart or terrace with twelve steps leading up to it.[72] There were steps at each new level of restriction. From the court of the women to the court of the Israelites there were fifteen steps, and five more from there to the court of the priests, and then twelve from the court of the priests to the porch leading into the Inner Sanctuary and the Holy of Holies. One kept ascending the closer one came to the divine presence.

---

[68] For descriptions of Herod's rebuilding the temple see Josephus, *Ant.* 15.380–425 and *J. W.* 5.184–227.

[69] Numbers 15:14–16 affirms the right of Gentiles to offer sacrifices. Sanders, *Judaism: Practice and Belief, 63 BCE–66 CE*, 57, on the basis of Josephus, *Ant.* 12.145, thinks there was a small outer court for Gentiles in the pre-Herodian temple, but I see no basis for the conclusion.

[70] See 11Q Temple 39:7 and 40:5–6. See the discussion by Richardson, *Building Jewish*, 287, and notice his chart (pp. 272–273) of the sources providing information on the various components of the temple.

[71] Josephus, *J. W.* 5.193; 6.124–128; *Ant.* 15.417; cf. *m. Mid.* 2:3; *m. Kelim* 1:8.

[72] *m. Mid.* 2:3; fourteen steps according to Josephus, *J. W.* 5.195.

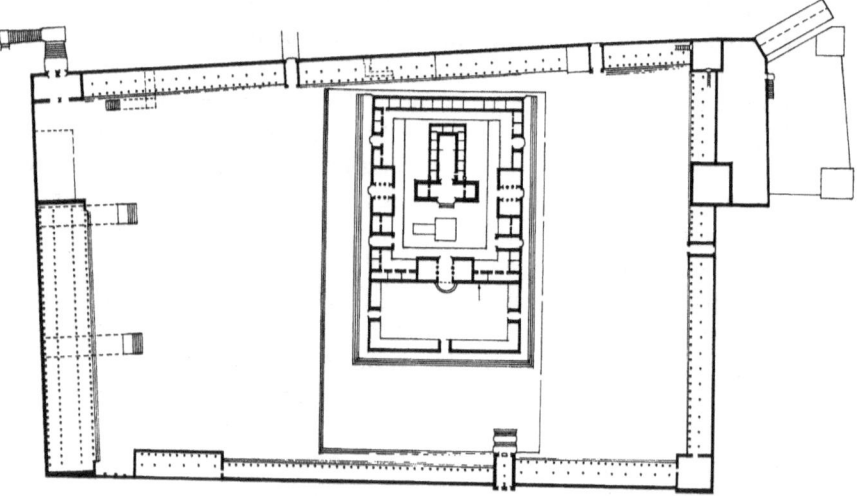

Fig. 1: Busink's Diagram[73]

A glance at any diagram of the temple shows that the rampart and its buildings are situated in the middle of the temple mount and take up approximately one-third of the whole.

The passage on the west between the *soreg* and the colonnade from the northern part of the temple mount to the southern part is rather narrow, and the passage on the east is not large either. Further, considerable uncertainty exists, not only about where the sanctuary was, but also over the relation of the *soreg* and the rampart. Did the *soreg* enclose the whole area of the original temple mount as it existed before Herod's extension? Dan Bahat sees this as likely,[74] and if this were true, the space of the outer court is considerably reduced. Note his diagram on the next page and the changed perspective it gives. It seems likely that the holiness of the original temple mount would not be diminished and the whole would be enclosed by the *soreg*.

From this perspective the *soreg* would have marked off almost two-thirds of the total area of Herod's temple. The most frequented space was the southern section with its royal portico. Almost certainly the money changers and dove sellers would be in the portico or adjacent to it, which means

---

[73] The diagram above is adapted from Theodor A. Busink, *Der Tempel von Jerusalem von Salomo bis Herodes: Eine archäologisch-historische Studie unter Berücksichtigung des westsemitischen Tempelbaus* (2 vols.; Leiden: Brill, 1980), 2:1179.

[74] Dan Bahat, "Jesus and the Herodian Temple Mount," in *Jesus and Archaeology* (ed. James H. Charlesworth; Grand Rapids: Eerdmans, 2006), 304. See also the discussion by F. J. Hollis, *The Archaeology of Herod's Temple* (London: Dent, 1934), 153–57.

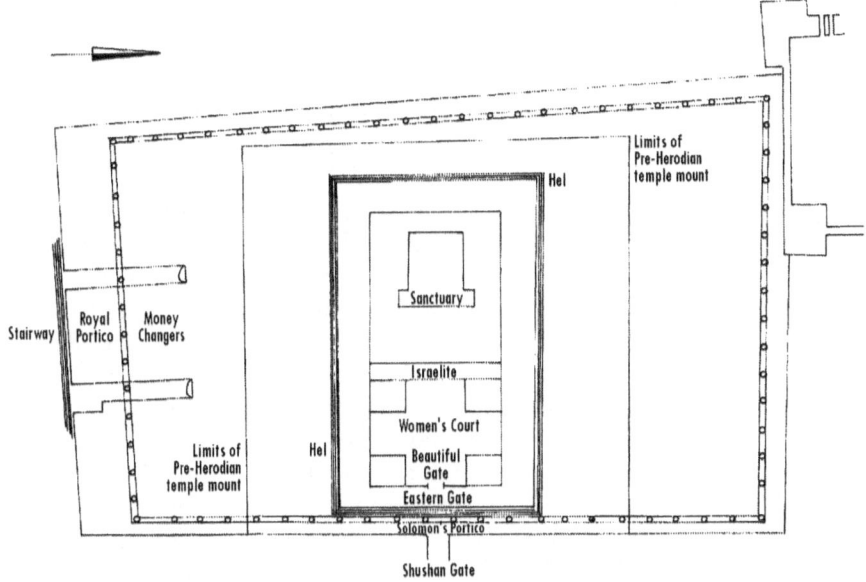

Fig. 2: Bahat's Diagram

Jesus' temple action took place in the southern portion of the outer court and probably in or near the royal portico.[75] We do not have to think of the whole temple mount. The temporary tables of the money changers could not have taken so much room that Jesus' action was impossible. In Bahat's diagram the money changers are actually located between the openings onto the temple mount from the two Huldah gates, which, however, cannot be proven, but the action against the money changers and dove sellers is not the least implausible if the issue is the space involved.

Shops for supplies for temple worship were also set up on the Mount of Olives. Were animals sold in the temple as well?[76] The primary source evi-

---

[75] That the Royal portico is the most likely place see Jostein Ådna, "Jesus' Symbolic Act in the Temple (Mark 11:15-17): The Replacement of the Sacrificial Cult by His Atoning Death," in *Gemeinde ohne Tempel, Community without Temple: zur Substituierung und Transformation des Jerusalemer Tempels und seines Kults im Alten Testament, antiken Judentum und frühen Christentum* (ed. Beate Ego, et al.; Tübingen: Mohr Siebeck, 1999), 463; Ådna, *Jesu Stellung zum Tempel*, 250–52; Bahat, "Jesus and the Herodian Temple Mount," 306–7; Casey, "The Cleansing of the Temple," 309–10; and Murphy-O'Connor, "Jesus and the Money Changers," 44 (but he thinks any animals being sold would be at the north end of the temple complex).

[76] W. D. Davies and Dale C. Allison, Jr., *A Critical and Exegetical Commentary on the Gospel According to Saint Matthew* (3 vols.; ICC; Edinburgh: T&T Clark, 1988–97), 3:138, suggest those buying were not people buying sacrificial animals but temple

dence detailing the process of acquiring and bringing animals to slaughter in the temple is surprisingly sparse. People often assume animals were not in the temple,[77] but some evidence suggests they were. Zechariah 14:21 may be an early complaint against traders, but does not mention animals specifically. In a dispute over the necessity of laying hands on a sacrifical animal, Baba ben Buta is reported to have brought "the whole Qedar flock" into the temple and made them available for anyone who wanted to lay hands on them.[78] Enough animals were present during the siege by Pompey that the daily sacrifice was continued until the capture[79] and during the siege of the Jewish War until August of 70 C.E.[80] The Mishnah refers to seals labeled "calf," "ram," "kid," and "sinner" which could be purchased.[81] V. Eppstein noted that the Sanhedrin was removed from the chamber of hewn stone in the temple to Hanuth on the Mount of Olives, the place for shops for purchasing ritually pure animals and objects for sacrifice.[82] He suggests Caiaphas allowed animals to be sold in the temple at the time of the expulsion of the Sanhedrin.[83] This may be, but the evidence is insufficient, and the suggestion is often – and fairly – viewed as speculative.[84] A number of people have suggested that "Solomon's Stables," the vaulted section under the Royal Portico, could have been a place for corralling animals.[85] The discussion of animals, of course, pertains only to the Gospel of John, but it is at least possible that animals would have been present. Given that animals were also available on the Mount of Olives, their numbers may not have

---

staff buying supplies. That certainly is not clear and would not help in dealing with the Johannine account.

[77] E.g., Sanders, *Judaism: Practice and Belief, 63 BCE–66 CE*, 87. He worries over excrement and urine fouling the area, but that is an issue with all the animals for sacrifice, and at Passover the number of lambs would have been so large that his worries are clearly misplaced.

[78] *y. Ḥag.* 2.3; *y. Beṣah* 2.4; *t. Ḥag.* 2.11 and *b. Beṣah* 20a.

[79] Josephus, *J. W.* 1.148, which Haenchen (*Der Weg Jesu*, 382) suggests required at least 200 sheep.

[80] Josephus, *J. W.* 6.94, although *y. Taʿan.* 4:5 reports people letting down two baskets with gold to bribe the besiegers to send up two sheep.

[81] *m. Šeqal.* 5:1–5.

[82] See *b. Roš Haš.* 31a; *b. Šabb.* 15a; *b. ʿAbod. Zar.* 8b. See *y. Taʿan.* 4:7.4.

[83] Eppstein, "The Cleansing of the Temple," 54–55. See also Chilton, *The Temple of Jesus*, 108–9; and his "[ὡς] φραγέλλιον ἐκ σχοινίων (John 2.15)," in *Templum Amicitiae: Essays on the Second Temple Presented to Ernst Bammel* (ed. William Horbury; JSNTSup 48; Sheffield: JSOT Press, 1991), 330–44, especially 337–338. Chilton points out the advantage of a decision by Caiaphas to have animals sold in the temple. Nothing could happen to the animal between Hanuth and the temple. See also Hans D. Betz, "Jesus and the Purity of the Temple (Mark 11:15–18): A Comparative Religion Approach," *JBL* 116 (1997): 461–67.

[84] E.g., Evans, "Jesus' Action in the Temple," 432; Murphy-O'Connor, "Jesus and the Money Changers," 49, n. 25.

[85] E.g., Tan, *Zion Traditions*, 49, n. 25.

been large. If animals were present, it would not take much to get a flock / herd moving.

We should also ask what was being sold and bought. Is reference merely to wine, flour, and oil – items needed for worship, or should we think more of items unrelated to worship, which might include items for sale that had been donated to the temple,[86] items associated with the temple and priests that might have significance for worshippers,[87] or possibly even food or crafts? The text gives us no hint, but it seems we are dealing with items unrelated to worship.

Several other issues of scale must be considered. Did Jesus act alone? The Gospels often focus so fully on Jesus it appears he is the only one in the scene. Some people assume he acted alone and some that he was accompanied by his disciples, or even that others in the outer court would have been sympathetic with his action. The text gives no indication either way, but I see no reason why we should assume Jesus went to the temple by himself that day or was the only person upset with what he saw. The passage *m. Mid.* 1:1 indicates that priests and levites were stationed at various places to keep watch, with one levite being stationed at each of the five gates of the temple mount and one at each of its four corners. The Antonia fortress is at the opposite end of the temple mount and fairly removed from the southern portico, and if Jesus had any support at all,[88] a few levites would not be a lot of resistance, assuming that they would have been upset with Jesus' action. Further, Jesus' action would not be viewed as revolutionary or inciting a riot as far as the Romans were concerned.[89] However, it is not true that there was no reaction from the Jewish authorities. Each of the Gospels, especially Matthew, tells of the authorities confronting Jesus about why he did what he did. There are two possible reasons why no immediate action was taken. First, *if* Jesus' action were communicated in time for immediate reaction, those in authority may have delayed to avoid making the situation worse.[90] Second, as several people argue and as Mark 11:18 = Luke 19:47–48 attest,

---

[86] John Nolland, *The Gospel of Matthew* (NIGTC; Grand Rapids: Eerdmans, 2005), 843.

[87] Certainly such items were sold in pagan temples.

[88] Chilton, *The Temple of Jesus*, 108, suggests that Pharisees may have viewed trade in the southern side of the temple mount as anathema. A significant number of Jews may have objected to temple proceedings for a variety of reasons and, if so, they would have been supportive of Jesus' action.

[89] Gundry, *Mark*, 646. He notes that there was no agitation of the crowd.

[90] Horsley, *Jesus and the Spiral of Violence*, 298, assumes Jesus' act was of considerable size and seriousness and that restraint accords with behavior of authorities in preindustrial cities. He points out that neither Archelaus in 4 B.C.E. nor Cumanus in the 50s sent in troops at the first sign of a disturbance.

there was no reaction against Jesus because of fear of the people.[91] The authorities took no action against him because they felt it would be dangerous to do so. This accords with an undeniable fact: Jesus was arrested *at night*, presumably at a time when his supporters would not be a threat. Passover (or any festival) would be a time of heightened tension, large crowds, and increased eschatological hopes.[92] This would have been both an opportune time and a dangerous time for Jesus' action.

Another fact is relevant. Most people coming to the temple would have come from the south and would have entered through one of the Huldah gates,[93] probably the eastern entrance of the double Huldah gate, gone through a tunnel under the Royal Portico, and emerged at the level of the temple mount. They would have moved around the ναός in a counter-clockwise direction and back to the southern end where they would exit through the western entrance of the double Huldah gate. The exception to this procedure was that, if one was in mourning, he or she would move in the opposite direction to be greeted by people coming in the normal direction.[94] If one were going to prevent people from carrying an illegitimate object through the temple, it would be fairly easy to do so in either of two places: most likely at the opening used by people to come up to the temple court after entering through the Huldah gate, or alternatively at the space between the eastern portico and the ναός. Mark 11:16 is not difficult to imagine at all.

Therefore, the issue of scale has been overplayed, and I do not think we must see Jesus' action as limited in scope, that is, *merely a symbolic gesture*.[95] Certainly the act was symbolic, but to think no one noticed is unreasonable. The act was a bold move, required significant effort, and carried some risk. Most important, the event is a plausible action.

---

[91] See Ådna, *Jesu Stellung zum Tempel*, 304–5; Casey, "The Cleansing of the Temple," 319–26; Eppstein, "The Cleansing of the Temple," 56–57. Eppstein assumes Jesus was accompanied by the twelve and perhaps partisans of Hanuth and that the temple guard may also have opposed what Caiaphas was doing or may have feared the people. Tan, *Zion Traditions*, 187, suggests the populace probably sympathized with Jesus, and Evans, *Mark*, 167 and 182 assumes the presence of many supportive pilgrims. Gundry, *Mark*, 646, speaks of an admiring crowd.

[92] Note the catastrophe that occurred just after Herod's death (*Ant.* 17.207–218 = *J. W.* 2.2–13). The suggestion of some (e. g., Chilton, "[ὡς] φραγέλλιον ἐκ σχοινίων [John 2.15]," 338) that the event took place during Sukkoth has little in its favor.

[93] Some presume they would have entered through the triple gate and exited through the double gate, but others conclude the triple gate was primarily for temple officials and that most people would have entered and exited through the double Huldah gate.

[94] See *m. Mid.* 1:3; 2:2.

[95] Cf. Gundry, *Mark*, 646.

4.2. The Reason for Money Changers

As is well known, Jewish men twenty and older had to pay a half shekel temple tax to support the temple's functions, but they were required to use Tyrian shekels. The money changers would have been appointed to make this possible, and they would have received a small commission. Some think Tyrian coinage was used to avoid offensive images on the coins, but that is not the case. Tyrian coins had two offensive symbols on them: an image of the god Melkart on one side and an eagle on the other with the inscription "Tyre the holy and inviolable."[96] Especially when we remember the uproar near the time of Herod's death in 4 B.C.E., at which students were persuaded to cut down the eagle Herod had installed above a temple gate,[97] we have some idea how offensive these coins would be to many. They were used because they were the best of bad choices. While under foreign domination Jews were not allowed to mint their own coins. (During both revolts Jews quickly minted their own coins, apparently to provide aniconic coins for use in the temple.) The Tyrian coins were of the highest quality and highest silver content, and they were less offensive than the coins of the Roman oppressors.[98]

Not everyone agreed with the interpretation that the temple tax was to be paid each year. The men at Qumran interpreted Exod 30:11–16 to mean that one should pay the tax only once in his life (4Q159 f1 2:6–7). That Jesus at least sat loosely with regard to the temple tax is evident in Matt 17:24–27.

Jesus may have overturned the money changers' tables both because the coins were offensive and the tax itself was being taken every year.[99] He may also have objected to the burden it placed on the poor. We will return to this question below.

4.3. Corruption in the Temple Practice

Sometimes people doubt corruption was much of a factor in the administration of the temple or downplay evidence for it,[100] but the evidence is

---

[96] Richardson, *Building Jewish*, 246, and plate 35. See David Hendin, *Guide to Biblical Coins* (4th ed.; New York: Amphora, 2001), no. 917 and the treatment on pp. 420–28.
[97] Josephus, *J. W.* 1.648–655.
[98] See the discussions of Richardson, *Building Jewish*, 246–47; and Murphy-O'Connor, "Jesus and the Money Changers," 46–50.
[99] This is the position of both Richardson, *Building Jewish*, 246–51; and Murphy-O'Connor, "Jesus and the Money Changers," 46–50.
[100] E. g., Sanders, *Jesus and Judaism*, 62–67; Ådna, *Jesu Stellung zum Tempel*, 339–40; Adela Yarbro Collins, "Jesus' Action in Herod's Temple," in *Antiquity and Humanity: Essays on Ancient Religion and Philosophy* (ed. Adela Yarbro Collins and Margaret M. Mitchell; Tübingen: Mohr Siebeck, 2001), 53. Collins thinks the evidence points to problems later than the time of Jesus.

overwhelming that corruption of various sorts was a very real problem. No one has done more to highlight the corruption than Craig Evans in a series of articles.[101] Several lines of evidence indicate temple corruption.

First, the biblical prophets complained against the temple and warned of its destruction because of bribery, theft, murder, and a variety of other sins, including idolatry (which was not a problem in the first century). Among many texts see Isa 28:7; 66:3; Jer 6:13; 7:9–15; 23:11–12; Lam 4:13; Hos 4:4–9; 6:9; Mic 3:9–12; Zeph 3:1–4; Mal 1:6–14; 2:7–8; 3:1–5. While this evidence has no direct relevance to Jesus' temple action, it does point to corruption as a perennial problem.

Second, the evidence from Qumran is particularly poignant.[102] 1QpHab 8:7–13 interprets the one who amasses the wealth of others (Hab 2:5–6) as "the wicked priest," apparently a reference to the high priest, who deserted God, betrayed the laws for riches, robbed and hoarded wealth from violent men, seized public money, and performed repulsive acts of every type of filthy licentiousness. In 9:2–16 the complaint continues. The words of Hab 2:8–11 concerning one who pillaged many countries is interpreted of the last priests of Jerusalem who will accumulate riches and loot from plundering the peoples. The reference to violence and bloodshed on land, city, and inhabitants (2:8b) is understood of the wicked priest, for his wickedness against the Teacher of Righteousness and the members of his council (cf. 10:5–6). In 11:2–15 the woe to the one who makes his companion drunk is also interpreted of the wicked priest, who pursued the Teacher of Righteousness and whose disgrace will exceed his glory. Then in 12:1–10 the violence and bloodshed of 2:17 is understood of the wicked priest for what he did to the poor and his intent to destroy the poor. He has performed repulsive acts and defiled the sanctuary of God, and he has plundered the possessions of the poor.

4QpNah [4Q 169] f3 and 4 1:10 interprets "your throng" (Nah 2:14) as his gangs of soldiers, and "his cubs" as his nobles, and "his spoils" as the wealth which [the pries]ts of Jerusalem accu[mulated].[103]

---

[101] Craig A. Evans, "Jesus' Action in the Temple and Evidence of Corruption in the First-Century Temple," in *SBL Seminar Papers, 1989* (SBLSP 28; Atlanta: Scholars, 1989), 522–39; Craig A. Evans, "Opposition to the Temple: Jesus and the Dead Sea Scrolls," in *Jesus and the Dead Sea Scrolls* (ed. James H. Charlesworth; ABRL; New York: Doubleday, 1992), 235–53; Craig A. Evans, "Predictions of the Destruction of the Herodian Temple in the Pseudepigrapha, Qumran Scrolls, and Related Texts," *JSP* 10 (1992): 89–147; Evans, "Jesus and the 'Cave of Robbers'"; Evans, "Jesus' Action in the Temple."

[102] The summaries of the texts from Qumran are based on Florentino García Martínez and Eibert J. C. Tigchelaar, *The Dead Sea Scrolls Study Edition* (2 vols.; Grand Rapids: Eerdmans, 1997).

[103] 4Q 390, frag. 2, 1.10 also refers to violence of priests.

CD A 6:14–17 instructs covenanters to abstain from the wicked wealth of the temple and from stealing from the poor of the people, from making their widows their spoils, and from murdering orphans.[104]

4QPs 37 2:14 and 3:6 and 12 interpret the wicked of Ps 37:12–13, 20–22 of the ruthless ones of the covenant who are in the House of Judah, the wicked princes who oppress his holy people. 4:8 interprets Ps 37:32–33 of the wicked priest who spies on and wants to kill the just man.

4QMMT 82–83 [of the composite text] complains that some of the priests and the peo[ple mingle], squeeze each other and defile the [holy] seed with fornications.

Third, several other early Jewish documents make the same kinds of charges. *1 Enoch* 89:72–73 describes the rebuilding of the temple and a table before it with polluted and impure food. The eyes of the "sheep" are dim-sighted, and they are delivered to shepherds who trample them and eat them.

Testament of Levi 14:1–15:1[105] draws on "the writings of Enoch" to describe endtime impiety, but asserts that "your father, Israel, is pure with respect to all the impieties of the chief priests." The accusation is made that "You plunder the Lord's offerings ... steal choice parts, contemptuously eating them with whores ... teach the Lord's commands out of greed for gain; married women you profane; you have intercourse with whores and adulteresses. You take gentile women for your wives ... You will be inflated with pride over your priesthood ... With contempt and laughter you will deride the sacred things. Therefore the sanctuary which the Lord chose shall become desolate through your uncleanness, and you will be captives in all the nations" (Kee, OTP).

Testament of Levi 17:8–11 describes the seventh priesthood in which pollution is so heinous that it cannot be declared in the presence of humans. In the seventh week priests will come who are idolators, adulterers, money lovers, arrogant, lawless, voluptuaries, pederasts, and those who practice bestiality.

Testament of Judah 23:1–3 describes the destruction of God's sanctuary by fire because of licentiousness, witchcraft, and idolatry.

The *Testament of Moses* is perhaps the most important witness because it usually is dated about 30 C.E. In 5.3f.–6.1 we are told that the word was fulfilled that they will avoid justice and approach iniquity and they will pollute the house of their worship with the customs of the nations and idolatry. Certain of them will pollute the high altar by their offerings; "They are not

---

[104] See also 4:17 and 5:5–8. Cf. 11Q Temple [11Q 19] 57:9, which says the king will appoint people who are enemies of bribery.

[105] Although Christian interpolations occur in this section, none affect the argument.

(truly) priests (at all), but slaves, yea sons of slaves." Leaders will admire avaricious persons who accept polluted offerings, and sell justice by accepting bribes. Powerful kings will be called priests of the Most High God, but they will perform great impiety in the Holy of Holies.

In 7:1–10 we are told that the times will quickly come to an end when destructive and corrupt people will rule and consume the goods of the poor. They will feast continually. "They, with hand and mind, will touch impure things, yet their mouths will speak enormous things, and they will even say, 'Do not touch me, lest you pollute me in the position I occupy'" (Priest, OTP), surely a reference to priests.

Jubilees 23:21 says of the future evil generation "They will pollute the holy of holies with their pollution and with the corruption of their contamination" (Wintermute, OTP).

Psalms of Solomon 1:8 says that Solomon's children surpassed the gentiles in lawlessness and completely profaned the sanctuary of the Lord, and 2:3 adds that the sons of Jerusalem defiled the sanctuary, profaning offerings with lawless acts. The description of sin in 8:9–13 includes stealing from the sanctuary of God, walking on the place of sacrifice of the Lord, and defiling the sacrifices.

Fourth, what is known about high priests also gives evidence of corruption. High priests were regularly deposed and replaced because of bribery or for political or other gains, which does not create a context for integrity. High priests were in effect retainers of the elite rulers.[106] Herod at one point replaced the high priest with another man so that he could marry the latter's daughter.[107] *Pesiqta Rabbati* 47:4 provides a convenient picture in contrasting the eighteen priests of the first temple with the eighty that served the Second, the former viewed positively and the latter negatively because in the time of the Second Temple priests used to outbid each other for the office.[108] Josephus himself reports being a victim of such bribery to the high priest.[109]

Even with such a high turnover, between 37 B.C.E. and 70 C.E. all but two of the twenty-eight high priests came from four power-hungry, ille-

---

[106] See Josephus, *Ant.* 18.33–35 and 20.203.

[107] Josephus, *Ant.* 15.320–322. See *b. Yebam.* 61a; *b. Yoma* 18a. The passage *t. Yoma* 1:6–8 points to the religious duty of high priests to be greater than their brethren in beauty, strength, wealth, wisdom, and good looks, and 1:7 says, "When [unacceptable] kings became many, they ordained the practice of regularly appointing priests, and they appointed high priests every single year" (Neusner, *The Tosefta*).

[108] The passage interprets "With this" (בזאת) in Lev 16:3 numerically as 410, the exact years of the first temple. It applies the first half of Prov 10:27 ("The fear of the Lord prolongs days") to the priests of the first temple and the second half to the priests of the second ("The years of the wicked shall be shortened"). The passage is also in *Lev. Rab.* 21:9. Whether the number "eighty" is correct is debated.

[109] *Life*, 193–196.

gitimate non-Zadokite families.[110] Nearly all the evidence we have suggests corruption. Josephus reports that Ananias, an earlier high priest, daily paid court with gifts to Albinus and to the current high priest and that he had servants who were utter rascals and would take by force the tithes of the priests, beating those who refused to give. The ruling priests were guilty of the same practices and could not be stopped. Older priests who had been maintained by tithes starved.[111] Josephus describes this violence under two different high priests and also tells of class "warfare" among priestly factions pelting each other with stones.[112] When insurgents took the upper city, the wealthy district, they burned the home of the high priest, the palaces of Agrippa and Bernice, and the public archives with its record of debts. The high priest escaped only to be caught later and killed.[113]

These passages from Josephus pertain to the last decade of the temple, but *t. Menaḥ.* 13:18–23 reports something similar for an earlier time. Powerful men of the priesthood would come and take the hides from sacrifices by force, and from the money for these hides the temple porch was covered with gold, which hardly applies to the last decade. Likewise, strong-fisted men would come and take sycamore beams in Jericho by force. About such representatives of the high priests it was said, "Woe is me because of the House of Boethus. Woe is me because of their staves. Woe is me because of the house of Qadros. Woe is me because of their pen. Woe is me because of the house of Elḥanan. Woe is me because of their whispering. Woe is me because of the house of Ishmael ben Phiabi. For they are high priests, and their sons, treasurers, and their sons-in-law, supervisors, and their servants come and beat us with staves" (Neusner, *The Tosefta*). An assessment follows of the reason for the first temple's destruction being because of idolatry and licentiousness and bloodshed, but the destruction of the second resulted from love of money and hate for one another.[114]

Fifth, evidence from the targums is instructive as well. The most significant is the targum at Isa 28:1–4 which pronounces a woe on the person who gives a turban to the wicked one of the sanctuary, who along with the prince, is overcome with wine. The charge of drunkenness is repeated alongside charges of polluted food, oppression, not doing the law, and viewing service

---

[110] Markus Bockmuehl, *This Jesus: Martyr, Lord, Messiah* (Edinburgh: T&T Clark, 1994), 69. For a history of the high priests see James C. VanderKam, *From Joshua to Caiaphas: High Priests After the Exile* (Minneapolis: Fortress, 2004).
[111] *Ant.* 20.205–207.
[112] *Ant.* 20.179–181.
[113] Josephus, *J. W.* 2.426–427, 441.
[114] The same complaint against the priestly houses appears in *b. Pesaḥ.* 57a. Further evidence for the debate over hides and powerful men of the priesthood taking them by force apears in *t. Zebaḥ.* 11:8, 16–17 and *y. Maʿaś. Š.* 5:5.

to the sanctuary as a small thing (vv. 7–13), and woe is pronounced on the altar (29:1).

The targum on 1 Sam 2:17–32 describes the sons of Eli as corrupt, but on the basis of *b. Pesaḥ.* 57a that may be a lens through which to view the priesthood of the Second Temple.[115]

Sixth, in addition to rabbinic evidence cited above a few other passages deserve attention as evidence of corruption and distrust of priests at the same time that they reverence the temple itself. In *m. Bek.* 5:4 we find concerning blemishes caused to a sacrificial animal that herdsmen who are priests are not considered trustworthy.[116] One of the few passages explicit about overcharging is *m. Ker.* 1:7, which reports a pair of doves in Jerusalem at one golden denar. This led to a ruling of R. Simeon ben Gamaliel which allowed one offering for multiple instances of uncleanness, and the price fell to a quarter denar. In *m. Šeqal.* 1:3 we read that the temple tax was exacted from levites, Israelites, proselytes, and freed slaves, but not from priests in the interests of peace. The passage *Sipre Deut.* 105 (on 14:22) reports that the stores of the house of Hanan (Annas) were destroyed three years before the rest of Jerusalem because they did not tithe their produce.

ʾAbot de Rabbi Nathan 4 interprets Zech 11:1 ("Open thy doors, O Lebanon, that the fire may devour thy cedar") as referring to the high priests who threw the keys for the temple to the sky, saying, "Master of the Universe, here are Thy keys which Thou didst hand over to us, for we have not been trustworthy custodians to do the King's work and to eat of the King's table" (Goldin, *The Fathers According to Rabbi Nathan*).

Given that so much power and wealth was associated with the temple administration, corruption should be no surprise. Apart from the *Testament of Moses*, not much of the evidence is an explicit condemnation of the temple in Jesus' day, but virtually every period for which we do have evidence points to corruption. It would be naive to argue corruption was not a factor. However, this does not prove that corruption was the *motivating* factor for Jesus. The same can be said for the offensive coins of the money changers.

4.4. *The intention of prohibiting carrying vessels or objects*[117] *through the temple*

I consider the determination of the significance of this prohibition to be a difficult question. The first problem is knowing how σκεῦος should be taken. Is it generic, an object (e.g., Luke 17:31), or is it specifically a con-

---

[115] See Evans, "Jesus' Action in the Temple and Evidence of Corruption in the First-Century Temple," 527–28, for this and treatment of other possibly relevant targumic texts.
[116] *y. Peʾah* 1.5 prevent priests from hoarding agricultural offerings.
[117] See n. 63.

tainer (e.g., Luke 8:16)? The NRSV translates the word as "anything" and the NIV as "merchandise." The passage *m. Ber.* 9:5 prohibits entering the temple mount with staff, sandal, wallet, or dust on one's feet, or to take a shortcut, which shows a concern for the sanctity of the area.[118] Jesus in Mark is clearly concerned with purity of some sort.[119] Some suggest that Jesus intended to create the conditions of the new age as set out in Zech 14:21, which excludes traders from God's house, and if all vessels are holy, they must not be taken out of the temple. On this view Jesus prohibited people taking from the temple common vessels they had brought in so that they could be retained for sacred use.[120] Bruce Chilton likewise thinks Jesus' sacrificial program is an enactment of Zechariah's and concludes that God will prepare his own people and vessels for eschatological worship.[121] Zechariah is particularly relevant for Jesus' actions, but it is difficult to see how Zech 14:20–21, which says every pot in Jerusalem and Judah will be holy, relates to Jesus' prohibition. Adela Collins thinks Jesus taught that it was improper to carry an ordinary, profane container or implement from outside the temple mount through the temple area and out again.[122] William Telford argues that the natural meaning of σκεῦος is a sacred vessel for carrying materials used for offering and concludes Jesus was forbidding sacrifice.[123] Similarly Kim Tan argues that Jesus was prohibiting temple staff from carrying vessels with sacred supplies (flour, oil, wine) to storehouses in the court of women, items that would later be sold for sacrifice.[124] The conclusions Telford and Tan draw are not convincing, for I do not think Jesus was forbidding sacrifice, and sacred supplies would have to be available. Josephus mentions that no vessel should be carried into the temple, specifically the inner sanctuary,[125] which suggests Jesus might have been concerned with items that did not

---

[118] Joachim Jeremias ("Zwei Miszellen: 1. Antik-Jüdische Münzdeutungen. 2. Zur Geschichtlichkeit der Tempelreinigung," *NTS* 23 [1976]: 179) thought this passage does not relate to normal temple visitors but to pilgrims entering Jerusalem.

[119] Chilton (*The Temple of Jesus*, 125–26) thinks Matt 10:9–10; Luke 9:3; 10:4 show Jesus considered all of Israel as pure.

[120] Cecil Roth, "The Cleansing of the Temple and Zechariah xiv 21," *NovT* 4 (1960): 178; and Christopher M. Tuckett, *The Contemporary Revival of the Griesbach Hypothesis* (SNTSMS 44; Cambridge: Cambridge University Press, 1983), 114.

[121] Chilton, *The Temple of Jesus*, 136.

[122] Collins, "Jesus' Action in Herod's Temple," 47. She also suggests (p. 49) that Jesus' prohibition may have been in his teaching rather than in any enforcement.

[123] William R. Telford, *The Barren Temple and the Withered Tree* (JSNTSup 1; Sheffield: JSOT Press, 1980), 92–93, n. 102. See also Ådna, *Jesu Stellung zum Tempel*, 256–65, who focuses more on vessels used to carry money, as does J. Massyngberd Ford, "Money 'Bags' in the Temple (Mk 11,16)," *Bib* 57 (1976): 249–53.

[124] Tan, *Zion Traditions*, 180–81. He points to *m. Šeqal.* 4:3; 5:4. It is worth noting in 4:3 that R. Akiba declared, "They may not traffick with what belongs to the Temple, nor with what belongs to the poor" (Danby, *The Mishnah*).

[125] *Ag. Ap.* 2.106.

belong in sacred space. P. M. Casey suggests Jesus extended his prohibition to the whole temple mount and explains that this would include cages for birds, containers for priests to carry joints of large animals, and containers for money, which would mean the receptacles for offensive coins would be placed outside.[126] While certainty is not possible, what is certain is that according to this text Jesus was concerned with purity issues pertaining to the outer court. It seems most likely that Jesus prohibited people carrying containers not directly related to sacrifice, i.e., containers related to the commercialism of v. 15. It is obvious that the inherent ambiguity of the purpose of the prohibition speaks in favor of its historicity, but the level of certainty here is less than for the larger temple incident.

By way of summary, Jesus disrupted the usual proceedings at the southern end of the temple mount where worshippers would have entered and where buying and selling could take place and coins be exchanged. He took offence at the *place* where the action was happening. It was a sanctity issue. The actions themselves, except to the extent they may have taken advantage of the poor, could be practiced elsewhere. While the area in and around the southern portico was large, it was not so large that Jesus' action is unthinkable.

5. The Significance of Jesus' Action in the Temple

What Jesus sought to accomplish with this event is murky at best. The evangelists give little commentary, and each has something a bit (or a lot) different from the others. At one level they all show Jesus in control of the temple; the center of gravity shifts from the focus on sacrifice in the inner court to Jesus' activity in the outer court. With Matthew Jesus "holds court" and heals the blind and the lame in keeping with themes from Isa 61 (cf. 11:5 and 15:30) and is acclaimed "son of David." Mark has Jesus teaching and controlling what takes place. Luke immediately focuses attention on Jesus the teacher, and John emphasizes Jesus' zeal for the temple and his close association with – even substitution for – the temple.

The options suggested for understanding the significance of the temple incident include:[127]

---

[126] Casey, "The Cleansing of the Temple," 310–11. He sees the prohibition of carrying vessels through the temple as central to the event.

[127] For a history of interpretation see Christina Metzdorf, *Die Tempelaktion Jesu* (WUNT 2.168; Tübingen: Mohr Siebeck, 2003). I do not think J. Duncan M. Derrett's suggestion that Jesus cleansed the temple and then predicted its destruction resulted from his viewing the temple as a leprous house. See his "No Stone Upon Another."

1. Jesus' act was an over-confident attempt to start a revolution, but people did not follow him. He failed as a world deliverer, and the Gospels have de-emphasized his violence and his goal.[128]

2. With this act Jesus objected to any distinction between profane and holy.[129]

3. This was a symbolic act pointing to the coming destruction of Jerusalem and its temple.[130] Usually assumed with this position is that destruction is preparation for rebuilding.

4. Jesus' act was an attack on the sacrificial system itself and, therefore, meant the cessation of sacrifice.[131] Some would see Jesus attacking external worship, but most scholars would not. Bruce Chilton argues Jesus was protesting the sacrifice of animals which did not belong to those who offered them, much like Hillel.[132] For J. Neusner and B. Chilton the Eucharist was to be substituted for the temple worship.[133]

5. Jesus' act was an objection to Herod's turning the extended temple mount into a civic center. Jesus sought to extend the holiness of the inner court to the outer court.[134]

6. The incident is a "cleansing" of commercialism and corruption. This could include reaction against the offensive Tyrian coins. For some the

---

[128] Charles H. Talbert, ed., *Reimarus: Fragments* (trans. Ralph S. Fraser; Lives of Jesus Series; Philadelphia: Fortress, 1970), 146–50; S. G. F. Brandon, *Jesus and the Zealots: A Study of the Political Factor in Primitive Christianity* (Manchester: Manchester University Press, 1967), 331–36.

[129] Borg, *Conflict, Holiness & Politics*, 176.

[130] E. g., Sanders, *Jesus and Judaism*, 61–76; Holmén, *Jesus and Jewish Covenant Thinking*, 323–29; Matson, "Contribution," 489–506; Gerd Theissen and Annette Merz, *The Historical Jesus: A Comprehensive Guide* (trans. John Bowden; Minneapolis: Fortress, 1998), 433; William R. Herzog, II, *Jesus, Justice, and the Reign of God* (Louisville: Westminster John Knox, 2000), 128, 142; and Wright, *Jesus and the Victory of God*, 334.

[131] Ådna, *Jesu Stellung zum Tempel*, 383–87, 412–13, 429–48; Jostein Ådna, "The Attitude of Jesus to the Temple," *Mishkan* 17/18 (1992–93): 65–80; Jacob Neusner, "Money-Changers in the Temple: The Mishnah's Explanation," *NTS* 35 (1989): 287–90; Holmén, *Jesus and Jewish Covenant Thinking*, 326–27; Herzog, *Jesus, Justice, and the Reign of God*, 142; Tuckett, *The Contemporary Revival of the Griesbach Hypothesis*, 116; Theissen and Merz, *The Historical Jesus*, 433.

[132] Chilton, *The Temple of Jesus*, 101–3, 111, 133. This is part of his view that Jesus assumed that the whole land is pure, in which "Forgiveness is the condition in which sacrifice is rightly offered, rather than the condition of which sacrifice is a remedy" (p. 133). See also his *A Feast of Meanings: Eucharistic Theologies from Jesus Through Johannine Circles* (NovTSup 72; Leiden: Brill, 1994), 57–74. See *t. Ḥag.* 2:11 and *b. Beṣah* 20a–b.

[133] Neusner, "Money-Changers in the Temple: The Mishnah's Explanation," 290; Chilton, *The Temple of Jesus*, 150–54. Chilton thinks Jesus' program of purity led to the predictive and catastrophic temple incident, after which a change occurred. Jesus' meals assumed a character they did not have before. The food and drink consumed are the sacrifice. This new, alternative cult led to his arrest.

[134] Collins, "Jesus' Action in Herod's Temple," esp. 57–61.

cleansing is so that the Gentiles may have a proper place to worship, but most scholars holding this view would not emphasize Gentile worship.[135]

7. The action was a prophetic protest that pointed to future eschtological hope.[136] Often this approach emphasizes the expectation that the Messiah would be a temple builder.

All the options except maybe the first assume something was wrong with the temple or its administrative leadership. Just how wrong and its consequences are the issues of debate. Did Jesus think the temple was hopeless or that it still had a future? The options are not necessarily mutually exclusive, and various representatives include two or more of the options in their views. Any acceptable conclusion must be able to bring together Jesus' action with his teaching in other contexts. An interpretation of the temple incident that has no support from Jesus' sayings and actions elsewhere is in my opinion virtually excluded.[137] I will suggest a combination of options five, six, and seven with emphasis placed on the seventh, the eschatological role expected for the temple.

The *first option* is the easiest to set aside. Almost no one now would accept that Jesus wanted to start a revolution. The temple incident is the only real evidence pointing in that direction, but that is to assume the conclusion. Hardly anything else in Jesus' statements or actions in any of the Gospels supports such a view, and a great deal contradicts it. The command to love one's enemies hardly fits with violence and revolution against Rome.[138] Further, the theory is rendered exceedingly difficult in that it requires a wholesale change by Jesus' disciples in a more positive direction and a wholesale rewriting of the Jesus tradition.

The *second option*, Marcus Borg's explanation that Jesus was obliterating any distinction between the profane and the holy, is not adequate either. Disgreements about purity were important in Jesus' relation to his contemporaries, and his view of holiness was clearly different from that of the Pharisees. At times Jesus does not seem to have been concerned about

---

[135] Among others see Evans, "Jesus' Action in the Temple"; Evans, "Jesus and the 'Cave of Robbers'"; Betz, "Jesus and the Purity of the Temple," 455–72; Bockmuehl, *This Jesus*, 72–76; and Casey, "The Cleansing of the Temple," 331.

[136] E.g., Ben F. Meyer, *The Aims of Jesus* (Princeton Theological Monograph Series 48; San Jose: Pickwick, 2002), 170, 209, 214; Tan, *Zion Traditions*, 190–93; and see n. 179.

[137] Cf. Sanders, *Jesus and Judaism*, 57.

[138] See the critiques of James D. G. Dunn, *Jesus Remembered* (vol. 1 of *Christianity in the Making*; Grand Rapids: Eerdmans, 2003–xx), 622–24; and Luz, *Matthew 21–28*, 10–11. For a more susbstantive discussion of Brandon's view, see Ernst Bammel, "The Revolution Theory from Reimarus to Brandon," in *Jesus and the Politics of His Day* (ed. Ernst Bammel and C. F. D. Moule; Cambridge: Cambridge University Press, 1984), 11–68.

purity issues at all,[139] but the temple incident is *directly* about the sanctity of the holiest place in Jewish life.[140] Borg's emphasis on Jesus' substituting the mercy code for the holiness code[141] is an exaggeration, even if a helpful exaggeration. When it comes to the temple, however, nothing suggests the concern is to do away with holiness issues. If that were the concern, the action of driving out makes no sense. It would have been easier to leave the merchants there and to teach the money changers that coinage did not matter. Further, Borg's view implies that Jesus did not consider the temple a special place, which is contrary to every indication we have.

The *third option*, viewing the incident as a symbolic act pointing to the future destruction of the temple, has been popular and has in its favor Jesus' prediction of Jerusalem's, and specifically the temple's, dismantling.[142] That Jesus spoke of the temple's destruction is rarely doubted, but was his *action in the temple* an acted parable signaling destruction,[143] or is that jumping to unwarranted conclusions? Just what is it about the *temple incident* that is a symbol of destruction? Sanders claims that turning over even one table points toward destruction,[144] but that is hard to imagine. Turning over tables is a weak symbol of destruction,[145] if one at all. Chilton's complaint that Sanders' Jesus looks more like the lemon throwers (who pelted Alexander Jannaeus) than the Gospel portrait is apt.[146] Two other factors also make destruction less likely. No evidence exists that the Messiah was expected to be a temple destroyer. If Jesus was making a claim to messiahship, how were people supposed to draw the conclusion about destruction? Further, all the treatments of the temple incident refer to the ἱερόν, but the discussion of destruction in John 2:19–21, the charge of the false witnesses, and the mocking at the cross refer to the ναός. (The prediction of destruction in Matt 24:1–2; Mark 13:1–2; and Luke 21:5–6 does use ἱερόν.) The temple

---

[139] E. g., Matt 8:1–8, 18–26; 15:10–20.

[140] See James D. G. Dunn, "Jesus and Purity: An Ongoing Debate," *NTS* 48 (2002): 449–67, esp. 466–467.

[141] Borg, *Conflict, Holiness & Politics*, 123–43.

[142] See Matt 23:37–39 =Luke 13:34–35; Matt 24:1–2 = Mark 13:1–2 = Luke 21:5–6; Matt 26:61 = Mark 14:58; Matt 27:40 = Mark 15:29; John 2:19.

[143] Holmén, *Jesus and Jewish Covenant Thinking*, 313; Wright, *Jesus and the Victory of God*, 334.

[144] Sanders, *Jesus and Judaism*, 70. He reports C. F. D. Moule's doubt and Moule's suggestion that a broken pot would have been a better symbol, but Sanders escapes the problem by leaving that decision to others.

[145] Cf. Richardson, *Building Jewish*, 242, who stated his doubt even more strongly in an earlier version of his discussion, Peter Richardson, "Why Turn the Tables? Jesus' Protest in the Temple Precincts," in *SBL Seminar Papers, 1992* (SBLSP 31; Atlanta: Scholars, 1992), 508. See also Tan, *Zion Traditions*, 167.

[146] Chilton, *The Temple of Jesus*, 100. See Josephus, *Ant.* 13.372–373, and *m. Sukkah* 4:9.

incident and temple destruction are closely related in John, but caution is in order at least.[147]

The close association of the cursing of the fig tree and the temple incident by Matthew and Mark does provide implicit commentary on the temple, especially so with Mark's bracketing the temple incident with the cursing and later withering of the tree. The clear message is that the current temple practice – or at least Israel[148] – is fruitless, but when both evangelists explain the event, they focus on prayer and say nothing about destruction. Whether the temple act and the cursing were originally connected is debated.[149] Stopping traffic and being concerned about proper worship do not fit with destruction either.[150]

There are two main arguments for seeing destruction as the aim. One is the use of Jer 7:11, for the context of this biblical passage is a warning of the destruction of the temple. The words actually used from Jer 7:11, however, say nothing of destruction. The other argument is Jesus' challenge to the authorities to destroy the temple and he would raise it in three days (John 2:19). This requires us, though, to take the statement not as meaning what it says, but what it becomes in the mouth of false witnesses in Matt 26:61; 27:40; and Mark 14:58; 15:29. In John the statement is understood of Jesus' body and does not reappear in the passion narrative. It is fair to say that Jesus must have uttered some such saying of judgment on the temple, for the church would not have created something so awkward,[151] but is it fair to interpret the temple incident on the basis of John 2:19 but against its intent? Further, one can judge the temple without necessarily destroying it.

I do think a close connection exists between the temple incident and the prediction of destruction. Jesus' act demonstrates something was wrong in the temple and with Israel, which if not rectified would lead to ruin. Further, it is wrong to oppose cleansing and destruction,[152] but that does not explain the significance of Jesus' act nor make it primarily a symbol of destruction.

The *fourth option*, that Jesus' act was an attack on the sacrificial system itself or some aspect of it, is also quite popular. This view does not usually focus on sacrifice merely as ritual and external religion, which would not be a fair assessment of temple worship. The claim is that Jesus' attack on money

---

[147] Cf. Donald Juel, *Messiah and Temple: The Trial of Jesus in the Gospel of Mark* (SBLDS 31; Missoula, Mont.: Scholars, 1977), 128–29.

[148] Gundry, *Mark*, 672, points out that the fig tree is a symbol for the nation, not the temple.

[149] See above n. 42.

[150] For argument against destruction being the focus, see Gundry, *Mark*, 671–82; and cf. Chilton, *The Temple of Jesus*, 116–19.

[151] Horsley, *Jesus and the Spiral of Violence*, 292–93.

[152] See Bockmuehl, *This Jesus*, 75–76; Matson, "Contribution," 489; Davies and Allison, *Matthew*, 3:136, and Evans, "Jesus' Action in the Temple," 434.

changers and those selling prohibited the very acts needed for temple worship to continue. His action is intended to signal the cessation of sacrifice.[153]

Several aspects of this argument are problematic. To start first with the suggestion of Neusner and Chilton that the Eucharist is intended to be a substitute for temple service,[154] there is no bridge to take one from the text to the theory. Neusner believes no Jew of the time could have understood Jesus' action and also that Christianity in its early stages is utterly incomprehensible in the context of Judaism. Perhaps he has made a move that is incomprehensible. The Eucharist is intended to express a new covenant and a new means of forgiveness,[155] which fits with the ideas of replacement of the temple, but any line from the temple incident to the Eucharist is missing. Buchanan quips that, if the concern were the Eucharist, Jesus could have told his disciples in private without taking any risk.[156]

Jesus' other teachings do not attack the temple or its prescribed activities at all.[157] He does take a prophetic view that obedience is better than sacrifice,[158] but that does not mean a rejection of the temple. His other comments and acts seem to affirm the legitimate role of temple worship, notably the advice to one sacrificing with a wrong attitude (Matt 5:23–24), the advice for the leper to show himself to the priest and offer the gift Moses commanded (Matt 8:4 = Mark 1:44 = Luke 5:14), his instructions to Peter concerning payment of the temple tax (Matt 17:24–27), and the parable of the Pharisee and the Tax Collector, which speaks of two men who go up to the temple to pray (Luke 18:9–14). If Jesus really wanted to reject the temple and its practice, he missed a number of good opportunities. If other sayings or actions of Jesus express value for the temple, on what grounds do we think he suddenly rejected it? And, how would the expression "my Father's house" square with a negative view?

Further, if Jesus were going to reject the temple outright, would he have received any hearing or following from Jews at all,[159] and, as Casey argues,

---

[153] See n. 131 above. It is hard to argue for the cessation of sacrifice from Jer 7:11 when Jer 17:26 and 33:18 anticipate future sacrifices.

[154] Neusner, "Money-Changers in the Temple: The Mishnah's Explanation," 290; Chilton, *The Temple of Jesus*, 150–54.

[155] See in this volume ch. 11.

[156] Buchanan, "Symbolic Money-Changers?" 285.

[157] Only the parable of the Good Samaritan views priests and levites as negative characters. There is the statement that one greater than the temple is here (Matt 12:6), but that does not express a rejection of the temple. The parable of the Wicked Tenants is sometimes read as targeting the temple authorities (see n. 172), which is possible, but the parable could also be directed against all Jewish authorities.

[158] Matt 9:13; 12:7; Mark 12:32–34.

[159] Evans comments ("Jesus' Action in the Temple," 397) that rabbinic tradition viewed threats of violence against the temple as warranting capital punishment. Actually the threat is of punishment in Gehenna or perpetual sleep even if the person repents. See *t. Sanh.*

would he not have needed a campaign and a theology articulating reasons for this rejection?[160] Would he have been allowed to continue teaching in the temple? Even more, would action in or near the southern portico have had any effect on the sacrifices going on in the ναός, especially when the elements needed for sacrifice were available on the Mount of Olives, which would be accessed through the eastern gate?[161] The temple incident cannot have been intended to bring about the cessation of sacrifice. Nor can one point to Isa 56:7 to contrast sacrifice with prayer and spiritual worship, for the double mention of "house of prayer" in the verse brackets the promise that God will accept *their burnt offerings and their sacrifices on his altar*. Finally, one must ask, if the intent was the abolition of the temple system, why is there not more evidence in the Gospels and the life of the early church that this is the case?[162]

The *fifth option* sees Jesus' act as an objection to Herod's turning the extended temple mount into a civic center and an attempt to extend the holiness of the inner court to the outer court.[163] This is closely related to the view, considered next, that the incident was a "cleansing" of commercialism and corruption. It deserves consideration in its own right, for Herod's reconstruction of the temple mount had plenty against which some Jews would take offence. The reconstruction was patterned after an Egyptian Hellenistic enclosed-portico type of architecture, one evidenced in the *Kaisareion*, a complex devoted to the worship of Caesar in Alexandria. The southern portico, the Royal Stoa, was modeled after Roman basilicas, which served important communal and commercial purposes.[164] If there were memories of the Herodian "messianism" attached to the rebuilding efforts,[165] the objections would be even stronger. Clearly Jesus found the activities in the southern end of the temple mount objectionable; both this fact and the prohibition in Mark 11:16 of carrying things through the temple arena

---

13:5; *b. Roš Haš.* 17a. That the temple remained in ruins was viewed as the cause of disasters; see *y. Ber.* 9.2.3.

[160] Casey, "The Cleansing of the Temple," 322.

[161] See Gundry, *Mark*, 642; and Evans, *Mark*, 182.

[162] There is, of course, evidence from the Ebionites preserved by Epiphanius, *Pan.* 30.16.5, 7. See Seán Freyne, *Galilee, from Alexander the Great to Hadrian, 323 B. C. E. to 135 C. E.: A Study of Second Temple Judaism* (Studies in Judaism and Christianity in Antiquity 5; Wilmington: Glazier, 1980), 276.

[163] Collins, "Jesus' Action in Herod's Temple," esp. 57–61.

[164] See Collins, "Jesus' Action in Herod's Temple," esp. 57–58; William Horbury, "Herod's Temple and 'Herod's Days'," in *Templum Amicitiae: Essays on the Second Temple Presented to Ernst Bammel* (ed. William Horbury; JSNTSup 48; Sheffield: JSOT Press, 1991), 103–49, especially 104, 108–115, and 147; and Jostein Ådna, *Jerusalemer Tempel und Tempelmarkt im 1. Jahrhundert n. Chr.* (Abhandlungen des deutschen Palästina-Vereins 25; Wiesbaden: Harrassowitz, 1999), 32–71.

[165] See especially Horbury, "Herod's Temple and 'Herod's Days'," 104–15, 147.

suggest that indeed he expected a higher level of purity and respect for the temple mount than people were showing.

The *sixth option*, to view the incident as a "cleansing" of commercialism and corruption, has to be given serious attention. Even if one decides for some other option, commercialism and corruption may well still be motivating factors, as the evidence on corruption above demonstrates. We may set aside the idea that the concern was to create or preserve a worship space for Gentiles. This is a lofty motive, but it is not in focus with this incident or with Jesus' ministry. As indicated above, "Court of the Gentiles" is a modern label, and most of the people using the outer court would not have been Gentiles. At the same time, E. P. Sanders' comment that the place of trade and Jesus' action are coincidental[166] is extreme. As I will argue below, the nations are quite important in understanding Jesus' concern, but it is an eschatological concern, not merely one dealing with worship.

The evidence for corruption listed above points to problems many Jews would have felt.[167] The protests from Qumran, Hillel, Simeon ben Gamaliel, *Testament of Levi*, and *Testament of Moses* are all significant, but a few other protests should be mentioned: the ridicule of Alexander Jannaeus for his suspicious heritage and his incorrect exercise of the Tabernacles ritual, the cutting down of the eagle over a temple gate near the time of Herod's death, and especially the protest of Jesus ben Ananias, a protest which has some similiarity to Jesus' protest.[168] Jesus ben Ananias was a rude peasant who at Tabernacles four years before the outbreak of the war started crying out in the temple, "A voice from the east, a voice from the west, a voice from the four winds; a voice against Jerusalem and the sanctuary, a voice against the bridegroom and the bride [an allusion to Jer 7:34], a voice against all the people" (Thackeray, LCL). He was arrested by "leading citizens," turned over to the Romans, and beaten, but with each stroke he responded "Woe to Jerusalem." Josephus records this as a portent of the fall of Jerusalem.[169]

To return to the Jesus of the Gospels, whatever else the temple incident was, it was a protest against the temple leadership and the way temple affairs were being conducted. Several factors are behind the protest. One has to be the temple's abuse of the poor. The temple was an instrument of Rome's control of a subjected people, evidenced nowhere so much as in the control of the high priest's vestments and in the high priests' collusion with Rome's

---

[166] Sanders, *Jesus and Judaism*, 86.
[167] See § 4.3 above.
[168] See Josephus, *Ant.* 13.291–296 and 372–373; *J. W.* 1.648–655 and *Ant.* 17.149–167; and *J. W.* 6.300–309, respectively.
[169] For comparison of the parallels to Jesus' protest see Evans, *Mark*, 177.

concerns.[170] The opulence of the temple,[171] the greed of the ruling priests,[172] and the evidence of overcharging for doves all point in the direction of the abuse of the poor, but the text is not explicit about the poor being the motivating factor unless one reads in implications from the widow's offering. Mark and Luke both want the reader to see those implications, for in both the account of the widow's offering is juxtaposed to the disciples' awe at the grandeur of the buildings and Jesus' prediction of the temple's destruction (Mark 12:41–13:2 = Luke 21:1–6).

Another factor could have been the offensive coins being used. Several people correctly point out that Tyrian coins required for the half shekel temple tax would be offensive to sensitive Jews.[173] Again, however, the text is not explicit, and questions quickly arise. Would Jesus have viewed a coin as a recognition of foreign gods the way some Jews would? Perhaps, but if that were the motivation, with what coinage would he expect the temple tax to be paid, even if it is to be paid only once in one's lifetime? Would any coin be without offence? The suggestion has been made that Jesus rejected the whole idea of a tax and in doing so challenged the priestly aristocracy who benefited from the tax.[174] Jesus seems to "sit loose" with regard to the tax (Matt 17:24–27), but no evidence validates the suggestion of a total rejection.

What seems to be clear is that Jesus cared very much for what went on in the temple precincts. His own activity there in attendance at feasts, his teaching – and in Matthew healing – in the temple shows something of the temple's proper use. The temple is about worship of God, not about making money. Whether we call it a demonstration, an occupation, a disruption, or confrontation, Jesus' action was intended to reorder how people viewed the temple and its proceedings, and it was a critique of the ruling priests.

---

[170] Horsley, *Jesus and the Spiral of Violence*, 287. See Josephus, *Ant.* 15.248 and, concerning the high priest's vestments, 15.404–408. Tiberius granted Jews themselves the right to control the vestments for a period.

[171] *t. Menaḥ.* 13:18–23 and *b. Pesaḥ.* 57a both point to gold covering the temple edifice as a result of the violence of priests. See Josephus, *J. W.* 5.222.

[172] Randall Buth and Brian Kvasnica go so far as to use the word "mafia" to describe the ruling priests and suggest that Ananias's refusal to pay tithes, while at the same time using the tithes of others for themselves, stands behind Jesus' parable of the Wicked Tenants. See their "Temple Authorities and Tithe-Evasion: The Linguistic Background and Impact of the Parable of *the Vineyard, the Tenants and the Son*," in *Jesus' Last Week: Jerusalem Studies in the Synoptic Gospels – Volume One* (R. Steven Notley, et al.; Leiden: Brill, 2006), 67–72.

[173] Richardson, *Building Jewish*, 241–51; Murphy-O'Connor, "Jesus and the Money Changers," 46–50; and Collins, "Jesus' Action in Herod's Temple," 60.

[174] Richard Bauckham, "Jesus' Demonstration in the Temple," in *Law and Religion: Essays on the Place of the Law in Israel and Early Christianity* (ed. Barnabas Lindars; Cambridge: Clarke, 1988), 72–89. In his view Jesus protested the temple tax on the grounds that, since God is Father, theocratic taxation was illegitimate. Bauckham thinks Jesus also opposed temple profit-making schemes. See also Tan, *Zion Traditions*, 174–77.

Another question must be raised at this point. If Jesus' concern was the mismanagement of the temple by the ruling priests, why did he not confront the priests more directly? We could say he struck at the place they were most vulnerable and most affected – the financial concerns, but that is less than convincing. Some offer another suggestion having to do with purity issues. People coming to the feast were to purify themselves for seven days.[175] Did Jesus take part in such purification rites, as Paul did (Acts 21:26–27)? V. Eppstein and E. P. Sanders assume he did;[176] G. Theissen and Annette Merz and W. Herzog assume he did not, with Theissen and Merz concluding Jesus was detached from the temple and Herzog concluding he had no inclination for ritual purification and, therefore, was confined to the outer court.[177] Certainly the rest of the Gospel accounts do not suggest this kind of *detachment* from the temple. The NT texts do not give enough evidence to say whether Jesus participated in purification rites, but this discussion assumes that every worshipper would have to undergo seven days purification, and that is not necessarily the case. Sanders assumes local priests could purify the family and house prior to the pilgrimage to Jerusalem.[178] Without better evidence elaborate conclusions ought not be drawn about purification rites, but if Mark 11:16 is given any attention, Jesus *did* care about the purity of the temple.

Regarding the question why Jesus did not attack the ruling priests more directly, it would seem that his concern was more commercialism than corruption, and the former would be most obvious at the southern end of the temple complex.

The *seventh option*, that the temple incident was a prophetic protest that pointed to future eschatological hope, is the most compelling option.[179] This approach can incorporate elements of cleansing and possibly of destruction as well.[180] Often this approach emphasizes the expectation that the Mes-

---

[175] See John 11:55–56 and Num 19. Cf. Philo, *Spec. Laws* 1.261.

[176] Eppstein, "The Cleansing of the Temple," 148; E. P. Sanders, *The Historical Figure of Jesus* (London: Penguin, 1993), 250–52.

[177] Theissen and Merz, *The Historical Jesus*, 432; Herzog, *Jesus, Justice, and the Reign of God*, 141.

[178] See Sanders, *Judaism: Practice and Belief, 63 BCE–66 CE*, 113, 134; Sanders, *Historical Figure*, 250.

[179] In addition to the items mentioned in n. 136, see Ernst Lohmeyer, *Lord of the Temple: A Study of the Relation Between Cult and Gospel* (trans. Stewart Todd; Richmond: John Knox, 1962), 34–44; Ben F. Meyer, *Christus Faber: The Master Builder and the House of God* (Princeton Theological Monograph Series 29; Allison Park: Pickwick, 1992); Hiers, "Purification of the Temple"; Donna Runnalls, "The King as Temple Builder: A Messianic Typology," in *Spirit Within Structure: Essays in Honor of George Johnston on the Occasion of His 70th Birthday* (ed. Edward J. Furcha; Allison Park: Pickwick, 1983), 15–38; and Catchpole, "The 'Triumphal' Entry," 333–34.

[180] The relevant texts do not focus much on destruction.

siah would be a temple builder, but the focus of the evidence is less on who would build than on the fact that a future, glorious temple would be built. Clearly there was dissatisfaction with the Herodian temple, if for no other reason than that Herod, someone not from a Davidic line, built it.[181] The corruption and mismanagement and the control of Herod and later the Romans were also obvious factors leading people to hope for a temple as God intended. Such hopes had strong support from the Jewish scriptures. The prophets were especially concerned with the temple and its failures and the malpractice in it. Sometimes this is expressed as strongly as in Isa 65–66, but most often it is expressed in the hope that one day the temple would be what it should be and the nations will flow to it (Isa 2:1–4 = Mic 4:1–4). The hope for a pure temple was a constituent part of God's promises for the future and certainly of any restoration eschatology. God or God's agent would come and rebuild or restore the temple.[182] It would have been almost impossible for a Jew to think about God's promises apart from the future temple. A variety of texts describe nations coming to Jerusalem to worship God, the temple being rebuilt, and justice administered. Several of these texts merit attention:[183]

1. Perhaps the most important for our purposes is 4Q174, which is extremely concerned with the temple and interprets the promises to David in 2 Sam 7:10–14 and Amos 9:11 (with its reference to the "hut" of David) of the "branch of David" who will arise in the last days and will build the temple of the Lord. This fits with the expectation in Zech 6:12–13, a text, however, which is not cited in the NT.

2. 11Q Temple 29:8–10 speaks of God's future temple, which God will sanctify and create, establishing it forever. 46:1–18 underscores the purity of the temple, which will be separated from the city so that no one enters quickly and defiles it. 47:1–11 again focuses on the purity of the future temple God will establish.

3. *1 Enoch* 90:28–29 speaks of the future transformation of the temple when the "Lord of the sheep" brings about a new and loftier house. *1 Enoch* 91:13 also refers to a house built for the Great King in glory for evermore.

4. Tobit 13:16–17 points to the time when "Jerusalem will be built as his house for all ages," and 14:4–7 tells of a time when the temple will be destroyed, but God will bring people back to the land, and "they will rebuild the temple of God, but not like the first one until the period when the times of fulfillment shall come. After this they all will return from their exile and will rebuild Jerusalem in splendor; and in it the temple of God will be

---

[181] Evans, "Predictions of the Destruction," 134–46.
[182] See also Isa 56:1–8; Ezek 37:21–28; 40–46; Zeph 3:8–20; Zech 6:9–15; 14:4–21; and Mal 3:1–4.
[183] See also *T. Benj.* 9:2; *Pss. Sol.* 17:26–30; *Sib. Or.* 3:657, 663, 702–720, and *y. Taʿan.* 4:7.

rebuilt, just as the prophets of Israel have said concerning it. Then the nations in the whole world will all be converted and worship God in truth" (NRSV).

5. *Jubilees* 1:15–17 speaks of God gathering his people and building his sanctuary, and 1:27 points to the same idea.

6. *Sibylline Oracles* 3:286–294 (second century B.C.E.) tells of God sending a king and a royal family that will have dominion and will raise up a new shrine of God, and then the temple will be as it was before. People from every land will bring incense and gifts to the house of God (3:772–774). Similar ideas appear in 5:414–432 (perhaps late first century).

7. *2 Baruch* 68:5–6 points to the time Zion will be rebuilt, the offerings restored, priests return to their ministry, and all nations come to honor it.

8. *y. Taʿan.* 3:9–3:14 explains that when the temple is rebuilt people will sing using various Jewish scriptural texts and adds that all who mourn for Jerusalem in this world will rejoice with her in the next. The text quotes Isa 66:10–11 as proof.[184]

9. Benediction 14 of *Shemoneh Esreh* asks God to have compassion on Jerusalem and on the temple and concludes, "Blessed are you Lord, God of David, builder of Jerusalem." The material within quotation marks is in the Geniza fragments, and the Palestinian version of this fourteenth benediction, in the estimation of David Instone-Brewer, presupposes that the temple is still standing.[185] The Babylonian version assumes the temple has been destroyed and asks God to return in compassion and build Jerusalem "soon in our days." Both versions assume the sanctity of Jerusalem in God's kingdom and that God is the builder of the city.[186]

These texts show that for many Jews any thought of the future kingdom involved reform and, in many cases, rebuilding of the temple. The hope and expectation was that one day the temple worship would be what it should be and people from many nations would stream to Jerusalem to worship God on his holy mountain. The kingdom could not be present if it did not involve the temple. It could not be proleptically present if it did not point in this direction. Jesus' action in the temple is a prophetic, parabolic act, one that for a brief time enacts the reform expected in God's future kingdom.

---

[184] This text and *2 Bar.* 68:5–6 are, of course, later than the time of Jesus, but they still provide evidence of Jewish attitudes.

[185] David Instone-Brewer, "The Eighteen Benedictions and the Minim Before 70 CE," *JTS* 54 (2003): 32–35. Like others he concludes that the Eighteen Benedictions existed prior to 70 C.E. See p. 27.

[186] Some texts speak of God as the one building the end time temple, and some of people who will build it. For God as builder, in addition to this text, see *Jub.* 1:15–17; 11Q Temple 29:8–10; *1 En.* 90:28–29; *Sib. Or.* 5:420, 432; and for the people as builders see Tob 14:5; *Sib. Or.* 3:290.

As has been noted often, Jesus' actions in Jerusalem seem intentionally to enact elements from Zechariah. The triumphal entry obviously reflects Zech 9:9, and it appears that the ideals presented in Zech 14 provided the impetus for Jesus' temple action, which is granted by people taking quite diverse approaches to the event. If Jesus was enacting a restoration eschatology for the nation, which for me is a given, then what better place, what more necessary place to effect restoration than the temple? Most of the essays in this volume point to this background. The temple incident is not just preparation for the coming of the kingdom. It is an *enactment* of the kingdom.[187] Jesus' action expressed an authority, enough so that the basis of this authority is sought by the religious leaders. The event is a symbolic, messianic act.

There are two indications that with this event the eschatological hopes for the temple were being implemented. Matthew points to this meaning by focusing on Jesus in the temple healing the blind and the lame and being hailed as son of David. The healing of the blind and the lame is evidence of the presence of the kingdom in Matt 11:5 = Luke 7:22 and shows Isa 61 is being accomplished. Matthew, at least, wants us to understand the event eschatologically. Second, the use of Isa 56 points in the same direction, for it is a passage about God gathering the outcasts, setting things right in his temple, and admitting foreigners and eunuchs.

6. Concluding Reflections

Whatever else is said, the temple incident shows Jesus' concern for the spiritual health of the nation Israel and the validity / purity of the center of Israelite worship, the temple. Even if we do not understand all the details, clearly Jesus thought something was woefully wrong in the most sacred place in Israel. In driving out sellers and taking control for however long, Jesus issued a call for reform. He *was* concerned with purity issues. More importantly, this act was also an unparalleled and unexpected expression of the authority of Jesus,[188] like so many other incidents treated in this volume. Although lacking priestly jurisdiction,[189] Jesus was claiming and exercising

---

[187] Note Tan, *Zion Traditions*, 190: "... Jesus viewed this particular phase of his ministry not only as the climax of his vocation but also as the fulfilment of what Yahweh had promised regarding the temple on Zion through the prophets. In this light the presence and activities of Jesus in Jerusalem could be said to be a hinge moment in the eschatological scenario."

[188] See Lieu, "Temple and Synagogue in John," 68; Wright, *Jesus and the Victory of God*, 490; and Chilton, *The Temple of Jesus*, 100, 122.

[189] Although some argue Jesus presented himself in a priestly role. See Crispin H. T. Fletcher-Louis, "Jesus as the High Priestly Messiah: Part 1," *JSHJ* 4 (2006): 155–75; Crispin H. T. Fletcher-Louis, "Jesus as the High Priestly Messiah: Part 2," *JSHJ* 5 (2007): 57–79;

a surprising authority over the temple and its workings, an authority which carried with it messianic associations.[190] No matter whether this is in anticipation of the end time role the temple has as the place to which all nations will come or merely a call for reform in view of the kingdom preached by Jesus, the event is eschatological.[191] However one sorts out the significance of the event, this symbolic act was designed to bring to mind the expectations of God's restored temple and to stop people in their tracks so that they had to reconsider what was going on in the temple, reconsider their own worship, and ascertain who Jesus really was. The question of authority naturally follows. In effect the authorities ask, "Just who do you think you are?"[192]

The temple incident leaves a lot of loose ends. How long did Jesus exercise control over the traders and money changers? Did he come back the next day to enforce his strictures? Apparently not, but no matter how we answer such questions, in the end Jesus' temple action viewed by itself, at least as far as we can determine, had no lasting effect on temple worship, which again is an indication that the church did not create the story. Nor did the event and Jesus' words reveal all that needed to be said. Considerable development took place in the life of the early church before it hammered out conclusions about sacrifice and temple worship. Further, what is the relation of the temple incident to Jesus' intent to form a community? The choosing of the twelve, the words to Peter, and several other sayings point to Jesus' desire to form a community. Does this incident relate to any thought of a new temple embodied in the relation of Jesus and his followers, as is evident in other expressions of a spiritualized temple? There is a huge gap between the temple incident and later Christian theology. It is important for us to allow the event to be what it is and not force it to convey all one might like about Christian worship, but the event was still highly significant as an enactment of restoration eschatology in the most important place in all Judaism and as an expression of the role Jesus felt he played in God's purposes.[193]

---

and Anna Maria Schwemer, "Jesus Christus als Prophet, König und Priester: Das *munus triplex* und die frühe Christologie," in *Der messianische Anspruch Jesu und die Anfänge der Christologie: Vier Studien* (by Martin Hengel and Anna Maria Schwemer; WUNT 2.138; Tübingen: Mohr Siebeck, 2001), 226–30.

[190] Cf. Wright, *Jesus and the Victory of God*, 417: "Furthermore, Jesus, by making this claim in this way, perceived himself to be not merely a prophet like Jeremiah, announcing the Temple's doom, but the true king, who had the authority which both the Hasmoneans and Herod had thought to claim."

[191] See Ådna, *Jesu Stellung zum Tempel*, 286–87, 349, 368, 382–87; and Matson, "Contribution," 489, 500–506.

[192] Jesus' response appeals to the role of John the Baptist because the ministry of John the Baptist was eschatological and operated independently of any sanction by the Jewish leadership.

[193] The event demonstrates a shift in the center of gravity from the temple to Jesus. The criterion of double dissimilarity applies to what I have just described.

Bibliography

Ådna, Jostein. "The Attitude of Jesus to the Temple." *Mishkan* 17/18 (1992–93): 65–80.

—. *Jerusalemer Tempel und Tempelmarkt im 1. Jahrhundert n. Chr.* Abhandlungen des deutschen Palästina-Vereins, 25. Wiesbaden: Harrassowitz, 1999.

—. *Jesu Stellung zum Tempel: die Tempelaktion und das Tempelwort als Ausdruck seiner messianischen Sendung.* WUNT 2.119. Tübingen: Mohr Siebeck, 2000.

—. "Jesus' Symbolic Act in the Temple (Mark 11:15–17): The Replacement of the Sacrificial Cult by His Atoning Death." Pages 461–75 in *Gemeinde ohne Tempel, Community without Temple: zur Substituierung und Transformation des Jerusalemer Tempels und seines Kults im Alten Testament, antiken Judentum und frühen Christentum.* Edited by Beate Ego, Armin Lange, and Peter Pilhofer. Tübingen: Mohr Siebeck, 1999.

Allison, Dale C., Jr. "The Historians' Jesus and the Church." Pages 79–95 in *Seeking the Identity of Jesus: A Pilgrimage.* Edited by Beverly Roberts Gaventa and Richard B. Hays. Grand Rapids: Eerdmans, 2008.

Ashton, John. *Understanding the Fourth Gospel.* Oxford: Clarendon, 1991.

Bahat, Dan. "Jesus and the Herodian Temple Mount." Pages 300–308 in *Jesus and Archaeology.* Edited by James H. Charlesworth. Grand Rapids: Eerdmans, 2006.

Bammel, Ernst. "The Revolution Theory from Reimarus to Brandon." Pages 11–68 in *Jesus and the Politics of His Day.* Edited by Ernst Bammel and C. F. D. Moule. Cambridge: Cambridge University Press, 1984.

Bauckham, Richard. "Jesus' Demonstration in the Temple." Pages 72–89 in *Law and Religion: Essays on the Place of the Law in Israel and Early Christianity.* Edited by Barnabas Lindars. Cambridge: Clarke, 1988.

Ben-Dov, M. "Temple of Herod." Pages 870–72 in vol. 5 of *The Interpreter's Dictionary of the Bible.* 5 vols. Nashville: Abingdon, 1962.

Betz, Hans D. "Jesus and the Purity of the Temple (Mark 11:15–18): A Comparative Religion Approach." *JBL* 116 (1997): 455–72.

Blomberg, Craig L. *The Historical Reliability of John's Gospel.* Downers Grove: InterVarsity, 2001.

Bockmuehl, Markus. *This Jesus: Martyr, Lord, Messiah.* Edinburgh: T&T Clark, 1994.

Borg, Marcus J. *Conflict, Holiness & Politics in the Teachings of Jesus.* Studies in the Bible and Early Christianity, 5. New York: Mellen, 1984.

Brandon, S. G. F. *Jesus and the Zealots: A Study of the Political Factor in Primitive Christianity.* Manchester: Manchester University Press, 1967.

Brown, Raymond E. *The Gospel According to John I–XII.* AB 29. New York: Doubleday, 1966.

Buchanan, George Wesley. "Mark 11.15–19: Brigands in the Temple." *HUCA* 30 (1959): 169–77.

—. "Symbolic Money-Changers in the Temple?" *NTS* 37 (1991): 280–89.

Busink, Theodor A. *Der Tempel von Jerusalem von Salomo bis Herodes: Eine archäologisch-historische Studie unter Berücksichtigung des westsemitischen Tempelbaus.* 2 vols. Leiden: Brill, 1980.

Buth, Randall, and Brian Kvasnica. "Temple Authorities and Tithe-Evasion: The Linguistic Background and Impact of the Parable of *the Vineyard, the Tenants and the Son.*" Pages 53–80 in *Jesus' Last Week: Jerusalem Studies in the Synoptic Gospels – Volume One*. Edited by R. Steven Notley, Marc Turnage, and Brian Becker. Leiden: Brill, 2006.

Casey, Maurice. "Culture and Historicity: The Cleansing of the Temple." *CBQ* 59 (1997): 306–32.

Catchpole, David. "The 'Triumphal' Entry." Pages 319–34 in *Jesus and the Politics of His Day*. Edited by Ernst Bammel and C. F. D. Moule. Cambridge: Cambridge University Press, 1984.

Chilton, Bruce D. *A Feast of Meanings: Eucharistic Theologies from Jesus Through Johannine Circles*. NovTSup 72. Leiden: Brill, 1994.

–. *The Temple of Jesus: His Sacrificial Program Within a Cultural History of Sacrifice*. University Park: Pennsylvania State University, 1992.

–. "[ὡς] φραγέλλιον ἐκ σχοινίων (John 2.15)." Pages 330–44 in *Templum Amicitiae: Essays on the Second Temple Presented to Ernst Bammel*. Edited by William Horbury. JSNTSup 48. Sheffield: JSOT Press, 1991.

Collins, Adela Yarbro. "Jesus' Action in Herod's Temple." Pages 45–61 in *Antiquity and Humanity: Essays on Ancient Religion and Philosophy*. Edited by Adela Yarbro Collins and Margaret M. Mitchell. Tübingen: Mohr Siebeck, 2001.

–. *Mark*. Hermeneia. Minneapolis: Fortress, 2007.

Crossan, John Dominic. *The Historical Jesus: The Life of a Mediterranean Jewish Peasant*. San Francisco: HarperSanFrancisco, 1991.

Davies, W. D., and Dale C. Allison, Jr. *A Critical and Exegetical Commentary on the Gospel According to Saint Matthew*. 3 vols. ICC. Edinburgh: T&T Clark, 1988–97.

de Jonge, Henk Jan. "The Cleansing of the Temple in Mark 11:15 and Zechariah 14:21." Pages 87–99 in *The Book of Zechariah and Its Influence*. Edited by Christopher Tuckett. Hampshire: Ashgate, 2003.

Derrett, J. Duncan M. "No Stone Upon Another: Leprosy and the Temple." *JSNT* 30 (1987): 3–20.

Dunn, James D. G. "Jesus and Purity: An Ongoing Debate." *NTS* 48 (2002): 449–67.

–. *Jesus Remembered*. Vol. 1 of *Christianity in the Making*. Grand Rapids: Eerdmans, 2003–.

Eppstein, Victor. "The Historicity of the Gospel Account of the Cleansing of the Temple." *ZNW* 55 (1964): 42–58.

Evans, Craig A. "Jesus and the 'Cave of Robbers': Toward a Jewish Context for the Temple Action." *BBR* 3 (1993): 93–110.

–. "Jesus' Action in the Temple and Evidence of Corruption in the First-Century Temple." Pages 522–39 in *SBL Seminar Papers, 1989*. SBLSP 28. Atlanta: Scholars, 1989.

–. "Jesus' Action in the Temple: Cleansing or Portent of Destruction?" Pages 395–439 in *Jesus in Context: Temple, Purity, and Restoration*. By Bruce Chilton and Craig A. Evans. AGJU 39. Leiden: Brill, 1997.

–. *Mark 8:27–16:20*. WBC 34b. Nashville: Nelson, 2001.

–. "Opposition to the Temple: Jesus and the Dead Sea Scrolls." Pages 235–53 in *Jesus and the Dead Sea Scrolls*. Edited by James H. Charlesworth. ABRL. New York: Doubleday, 1992.

–. "Predictions of the Destruction of the Herodian Temple in the Pseudepigrapha, Qumran Scrolls, and Related Texts." *JSP* 10 (1992): 89–147.

Fitzmyer, Joseph A. *The Gospel According to Luke X–XXIV*. AB 28a. Garden City: Doubleday, 1985.

Fletcher-Louis, Crispin H. T. "Jesus as the High Priestly Messiah: Part 1." *JSHJ* 4 (2006): 155–75.

–. "Jesus as the High Priestly Messiah: Part 2." *JSHJ* 5 (2007): 57–79.

Foerster, G. "Art and Architecture in Palestine." Pages 971–1006 in *The Jewish People in the First Century: Historical Geography, Political History, Social, Cultural and Religious Life and Institutions*. Vol. 2, section 1 of *Compendia Rerum Iudaicarum ad Novum Testamentum*. Edited by Shemuel Safrai and Menahem Stern. Assen: Van Gorcum, 1976.

Ford, J. Massyngberd. "Money 'Bags' in the Temple (Mk 11,16)." *Bib* 57 (1976): 249–53.

Fredriksen, Paula. "Jesus and the Temple, Mark and the War." Pages 460–72 in *SBL Seminar Papers, 1990*. SBLSP 29. Atlanta: Scholars, 1990.

Freyne, Seán. *Galilee, from Alexander the Great to Hadrian, 323 B.C.E. to 135 C.E.: A Study of Second Temple Judaism*. Studies in Judaism and Christianity in Antiquity 5. Wilmington: Glazier, 1980.

Funk, Robert W., and The Jesus Seminar. *The Acts of Jesus: The Search for the Authentic Deeds of Jesus*. San Francisco: HarperSanFrancisco, 1998.

Funk, Robert W., Roy W. Hoover, and The Jesus Seminar. *The Five Gospels: The Search for the Authentic Words of Jesus*. New York: Macmillan, 1993.

García Martínez, Florentino, and Eibert J. C. Tigchelaar. *The Dead Sea Scrolls Study Edition*. 2 vols. Grand Rapids: Eerdmans, 1997.

Gärtner, Bertil E. *The Temple and the Community in Qumran and the New Testament: A Comparative Study in the Temple Symbolism of the Qumran Texts and the New Testament*. SNTSMS 1. Cambridge: Cambridge University Press, 1965.

Gundry, Robert H. *Mark: A Commentary on His Apology for the Cross*. Grand Rapids: Eerdmans, 1993.

Haenchen, Ernst. *Der Weg Jesu: Eine Erklärung des Markus-Evangeliums und der kanonischen Parallelen*. Berlin: Töpelmann, 1966.

Hendin, David. *Guide to Biblical Coins*. 4th ed. New York: Amphora, 2001.

Hengel, Martin. *Was Jesus a Revolutionist?* Translated by William Klassen. Philadelphia: Fortress, 1971.

Herzog, William R., II. *Jesus, Justice, and the Reign of God*. Louisville: Westminster John Knox, 2000.

Hiers, Richard. "Purification of the Temple: Preparation for the Kingdom of God." *JBL* 91 (1971): 82–90.

Hollis, F. J. *The Archaeology of Herod's Temple*. London: Dent, 1934.

Holmén, Tom. *Jesus and Jewish Covenant Thinking*. Biblical Interpretation Series, 55. Leiden: Brill, 2001.

Horbury, William. "Herod's Temple and 'Herod's Days.'" Pages 103–49 in *Templum Amicitiae: Essays on the Second Temple Presented to Ernst Bammel*. Edited by William Horbury. JSNTSup 48. Sheffield: JSOT Press, 1991.

Horsley, Richard A. *Jesus and the Spiral of Violence: Popular Jewish Resistance in Roman Palestine*. San Francisco: Harper & Row, 1987.

Instone-Brewer, David. "The Eighteen Benedictions and the Minim Before 70 CE." *JTS* 54 (2003): 25–44.
Jeremias, Joachim. "Zwei Miszellen: 1. Antik-Jüdische Münzdeutungen. 2. Zur Geschichtlichkeit der Tempelreinigung." *NTS* 23 (1976): 177–80.
Juel, Donald. *Messiah and Temple: The Trial of Jesus in the Gospel of Mark.* SBLDS 31. Missoula, Mont.: Scholars, 1977.
Kerr, Alan R. *The Temple of Jesus' Body: The Temple Theme in the Gospel of John.* JSNTSup 220. London: Sheffield Academic Press, 2002.
Lieu, Judith. "Temple and Synagogue in John." *NTS* 45 (1999): 51–69.
Lohmeyer, Ernst. *Lord of the Temple: A Study of the Relation Between Cult and Gospel.* Translated by Stewart Todd. Richmond: John Knox, 1962.
Luz, Ulrich. *Matthew 21–28.* Translated by James E. Crouch. Hermeneia. Minneapolis: Fortress, 2005.
Mack, Burton L. *A Myth of Innocence: Mark and Christian Origins.* Philadelphia: Fortress, 1988.
Matson, Mark A. "The Contribution to the Temple Cleansing by the Fourth Gospel." Pages 489–506 in *SBL Seminar Papers, 1992.* SBLSP 31. Atlanta: Scholars, 1992.
McKnight, Scot. "Jesus and Prophetic Actions." *BBR* 10 (2000): 197–232.
Meier, John P. *Mentor, Message, and Miracles.* Vol. 2 of *A Marginal Jew: Rethinking the Historical Jesus.* ABRL. New York: Doubleday, 1994.
Metzdorf, Christina. *Die Tempelaktion Jesu.* WUNT 2.168. Tübingen: Mohr Siebeck, 2003.
Meyer, Ben F. *The Aims of Jesus.* Princeton Theological Monograph Series, 48. San Jose: Pickwick, 2002.
–. *Christus Faber: The Master Builder and the House of God.* Princeton Theological Monograph Series, 29. Allison Park: Pickwick, 1992.
Miller, Robert J. "The (A)Historicity of Jesus' Temple Demonstration: A Test Case in Methodology." Pages 235–52 in *SBL Seminar Papers, 1991.* SBLSP 30. Atlanta: Scholars, 1991.
Morris, Leon. *The Gospel According to John.* NICNT. Grand Rapids: Eerdmans, 1995.
Murphy-O'Connor, Jerome. "Jesus and the Money Changers (Mark 11:15–17; John 2:13–17)." *RB* 107 (2000): 42–55.
Neusner, Jacob. "Money-Changers in the Temple: The Mishnah's Explanation." *NTS* 35 (1989): 287–90.
Nolland, John. *The Gospel of Matthew.* NIGTC. Grand Rapids: Eerdmans, 2005.
Richards, E. Randolph. "An Honor/Shame Argument for Two Temple Cleansings." *TJ* 29 (2008): 19–43.
Richardson, Peter. *Building Jewish in the Roman East.* Supplements to the Journal for the Study of Judaism, 92. Waco: Baylor University Press, 2004.
–. "Why Turn the Tables? Jesus' Protest in the Temple Precincts." Pages 507–23 in *SBL Seminar Papers, 1992.* SBLSP 31. Atlanta: Scholars, 1992.
Roberts, Alexander, and James Donaldson, eds. *The Ante-Nicene Fathers.* 10 vols. 1885–1887. Repr., Peabody: Hendrickson, 1994.
Robinson, John A. T. *The Priority of John.* Edited by J. F. Coakley. London: SCM, 1985.

Roth, Cecil. "The Cleansing of the Temple and Zechariah xiv 21." *NovT* 4 (1960): 174–81.
Runnalls, Donna. "The King as Temple Builder: A Messianic Typology." Pages 15–38 in *Spirit Within Structure: Essays in Honor of George Johnston on the Occasion of His 70th Birthday*. Edited by Edward J. Furcha. Allison Park: Pickwick, 1983.
Safrai, Shemuel. "The Temple." Pages 865–907 in *The Jewish People in the First Century: Historical Geography, Political History, Social, Cultural and Religious Life and Institutions*. Vol. 2, section 1 of *Compendia Rerum Iudaicarum ad Novum Testamentum*. Edited by Shemuel Safrai and Menahem Stern. Assen: Van Gorcum, 1976.
Sanders, E. P. *The Historical Figure of Jesus*. London: Penguin, 1993.
–. *Jesus and Judaism*. Philadelphia: Fortress, 1985.
–. *Judaism: Practice and Belief, 63 BCE–66 CE*. Philadelphia: Trinity, 1992.
Schwemer, Anna Maria. "Jesus Christus als Prophet, König und Priester: Das *munus triplex* und die frühe Christologie." Pages 165–230 in *Der messianische Anspruch Jesu und die Anfänge der Christologie: Vier Studien*. By Martin Hengel and Anna Maria Schwemer. WUNT 2.138. Tübingen: Mohr Siebeck, 2001.
Seeley, David. "Jesus' Temple Act." *CBQ* 55 (1993): 263–83.
–. "Jesus' Temple Act Revisited: A Response to P. M. Casey." *CBQ* 62 (2000): 55–63.
Stein, Robert H. *Gospels and Tradition: Studies on Redaction Criticism of the Synoptic Gospels*. Grand Rapids: Baker, 1991.
Talbert, Charles H., ed. *Reimarus: Fragments*. Translated by Ralph S. Fraser. Lives of Jesus Series. Philadelphia: Fortress, 1970.
Tan, Kim Huat. *The Zion Traditions and the Aims of Jesus*. SNTSMS 91. Cambridge: Cambridge University Press, 1997.
Telford, William R. *The Barren Temple and the Withered Tree*. JSNTSup 1. Sheffield: JSOT Press, 1980.
Theissen, Gerd, and Annette Merz. *The Historical Jesus: A Comprehensive Guide*. Translated by John Bowden. Minneapolis: Fortress, 1998.
Tuckett, Christopher M. *The Contemporary Revival of the Griesbach Hypothesis*. SNTSMS 44. Cambridge: Cambridge University Press, 1983.
VanderKam, James C. *From Joshua to Caiaphas: High Priests After the Exile*. Minneapolis: Fortress, 2004.
Wedderburn, Alexander J. M. "Jesus' Action in the Temple: A Key or a Puzzle?" *ZNW* 97 (2006): 1–22.
Witherington, Ben, III. *The Christology of Jesus*. Minneapolis: Fortress, 1990.
Wright, N. T. *Jesus and the Victory of God*. Vol. 2 of *Christian Origins and the Question of God*. Minneapolis: Fortress, 1996.

Chapter 11

The Last Supper

I. HOWARD MARSHALL

1. Introduction: The Challenge of the Last Supper[1]

One of the most common practices in the church is the celebration of the Lord's Supper. Traditionally, this rite is associated with Jesus' Last Supper, where he prepared his disciples for his death and explained what his coming death meant through the symbols of the bread and the cup. But what are the roots of such symbolism in the church's meal, and in particular is it rooted in the ministry of Jesus? Today that association is not a given. So this essay takes a careful look at the historicity of the Last Supper and its significance for understanding Jesus.

In his review of John Koenig's work *The Feast of the World's Redemption*, Dennis E. Smith comments:

> ... the weakest argument of the book ... is the idea that the historical Jesus started it all. K[oenig] argues for a historical Last Supper at which Jesus uttered basically what Mark records ... Koenig uses the Jesus Seminar as a straw man, identifying with this group the view that the Last Supper was not historical, whereas this view is widespread in NT scholarship.[2]

Smith goes on to suggest that Koenig does not really engage with the arguments of the Jesus Seminar in its own publications (though admitting that he does interact with members of the Seminar individually, specifically M. Borg, J.D. Crossan and B. Chilton).[3]

Similar views are expressed by other scholars:

---

[1] I am grateful to my colleagues in the group for their helpful comments, and also to various others including Dr Ruth B. Edwards, Dr David Instone-Brewer and Dr Peter J. Williams.

[2] Dennis E. Smith, review of John Koenig, *The Feast of the World's Redemption: Eucharistic Origins and Christian Mission*, *CBQ* 64 (2002): 168–69. For Smith's own views see Dennis E. Smith, *From Symposium to Eucharist: The Banquet in the Early Christian World* (Minneapolis: Fortress, 2003). He himself is a member of the Jesus Seminar.

[3] Other works presenting a generally skeptical attitude to the traditions in the Gospels include Ron Cameron and Merrill P. Miller, eds., *Redescribing Christian Origins* (SBLSymS 28; Atlanta: Society of Biblical Literature, 2004); see the trenchant response,

That which eventually became the sacrament which is variously called the Lord's Supper, Holy Communion, the Eucharist and the mass does not have its origins in any putative last supper that Jesus shared with his disciples. There was no last supper of Jesus such as that which is portrayed in Paul's letter to Corinth or in the gospels. This view, which has been argued cogently in recent years, cannot be dismissed as merely the opinion of a few overly-skeptical (German) NT scholars ... The passion narratives of the gospels, which include the last supper scenes, are ecclesial compositions.[4]

However, Smith's comment that this view is widely held in NT scholarship is something of an exaggeration. There is certainly a skeptical attitude among some scholars,[5] but the view of the Jesus Seminar can hardly be called "widespread." So cautious and critical a scholar as O. Hofius could write:

There is no sufficient scientific basis for doubting the reliability of this information and hence the historicity of the establishment of the Lord's Supper by the earthly Jesus himself.[6]

S. McKnight can say: "Most scholars today, the Jesus Seminar included, attribute some historical core to the last supper."[7] He cites E. P. Sanders[8]

James D. G. Dunn, review of Ron Cameron and Merrill P. Miller, eds., *Redescribing Christian Origins, JBL* 124 (2005): 760–64.

[4] John W. Riggs, "The Sacred Food of Didache 9–10 and Second-Century Ecclesiologies," in *The Didache in Context: Essays on Its Text, History, and Transmission* (ed. Clayton N. Jefford; NovTSup 77; Leiden: Brill, 1995), 257; cf. Huub van de Sandt and David Flusser, *The Didache: Its Jewish Sources and Its Place in Early Judaism and Christianity* (CRINT 5; Assen: Royal Van Gorcum; Minneapolis: Fortress, 2002), 306–7. Gerd Lüdemann, *Jesus After 2000 Years: What He Really Said and Did* (Amherst: Prometheus, 2001), 94–97, holds that Jesus held a supper and that Mark 14:25 is probably authentic, but there is a lack of Passover symbolism and the meal did not institute the Lord's Supper.

[5] "Die historische Ausbeute einer gewissenhaften Analyse der Leidensgeschichte im einzelnen nicht sehr ergiebig ist." ("The historical findings of an assiduous analysis of Christ's passion in detail are not very rewarding.") So Gerhard Schneider, *Die Passion Jesu nach den drei älteren Evangelien* (Biblische Handbibliothek 11; Munich: Kösel, 1973), as cited by Rudolf Pesch, *Das Markusevangelium* (2 vols.; HTKNT 2; Freiburg im Breisgau: Herder, 1977), 2:23. Walter Schmithals, *Das Evangelium nach Markus Kapitel 9,2–16,18* (ÖTK 2; Gütersloh: Gütersloher Verlagshaus; Würzburg: Echter Verlag, 1979), 586–625, ascribes most of the Lord's Supper narrative to the invention of "Mark" himself; cf. Walter Schmithals, *Theologiegeschichte des Urchristentums: eine problemgeschichtliche Darstellung* (Stuttgart: Kohlhammer, 1994), 206.

[6] Otfried Hofius, *Neutestamentliche Studien* (WUNT 132; Tübingen: Mohr Siebeck, 2000), 283, n. 20 (my translation).

[7] He is presumably referring to the opinions of individual scholars who are members of the Seminar and not to the publications of the Seminar itself; Scot McKnight, *Jesus and His Death: Historiography, the Historical Jesus, and Atonement Theory* (Waco: Baylor University Press, 2005), 276. As an example of a scholar in the Seminar he could have cited Marcus J. Borg, who cautiously says: "It is difficult to make any historical judgment about the details of the 'last supper', including the words actually spoken by Jesus, simply because the remembrance and celebration of it were so central in the worship of the early

and J. D. G. Dunn.⁹ A fuller list of representative scholars who hold that it is probable that Jesus held a meal that substantially accorded with the basic description of it given by NT writers would include: G. R. Beasley-Murray; M. Bockmuehl; M. Hengel and A. M. Schwemer; J. Klawans; H.-J. Klauck; H. Patsch; R. Pesch; H. Schürmann; P. Stuhlmacher; G. Theissen and A. Merz; and N. T. Wright.¹⁰

church. Thus the details of the story have been affected by the liturgical practice of the church. That Jesus held such a final meal does seem historically likely, however" (*Jesus, A New Vision: Spirit, Culture, and the Life of Discipleship* [San Francisco: Harper & Row, 1987], 187–88).

A mediating position is held by Jens Schröter, *Das Abendmahl: frühchristliche Deutungen und Impulse für die Gegenwart* (SBS 210; Stuttgart: Katholisches Bibelwerk, 2006), 132–34, who accepts the historicity of a last meal at which Jesus refrained from sharing in the cup and made the statement which is the basis of Mark 14:25, but the sayings about the bread and cup stem from the aetiological myth developed in the early church and can throw no light on the historical course of events at the meal. Somewhat more conservative is Gerhard Friedrich, *Die Verkündigung des Todes Jesu im Neuen Testament* (Neukirchen-Vluyn: Neukirchener Verlag, 1982), 13, who accepts the historicity of the meal but thinks that Jesus merely said "This is my body (i. e., it represents me)" and "This is my blood (i. e., I must die)." Yet another possibility is advanced by W. D. Stacey, "The Lord's Supper as Prophetic Drama," *Epworth Review* 21 (1994): 65–74: the Last Supper contained the symbolism of the bread as representing Jesus himself who is distributed among his disciples as a body to continue his existence and activity through them, but the identification of the wine as his blood is a later development.

⁸ E. P. Sanders, *Jesus and Judaism* (Philadelphia: Fortress, 1985), 307, lists three gestures by Jesus symbolizing the coming kingdom: "a. the temple (certain); b. the supper (almost equally certain); c. the entry (probable)." Unfortunately he does not go into detail on the supper, although it seems clear that for him Jesus did not have a view of his death as atoning (see pp. 331–33).

⁹ James D. G. Dunn, *Jesus Remembered* (vol. 1 of *Christianity in the Making*; Grand Rapids: Eerdmans, 2003–xx), 229–31, 427–28, 771–73, 795–96, 804–05, 815–18; cf. James D. G. Dunn, *The Theology of Paul the Apostle* (Grand Rapids: Eerdmans, 1998), 606–8.

¹⁰ George R. Beasley-Murray, *Jesus and the Kingdom of God* (Grand Rapids: Eerdmans, 1986), 258–73; Markus Bockmuehl, *This Jesus: Martyr, Lord, Messiah* (Edinburgh: T&T Clark, 1994); Martin Hengel and Anna Maria Schwemer, *Jesus und das Judentum* (vol. 1 of *Geschichte des frühen Christentums*; 4 vols.; Tübingen: Mohr Siebeck, 2007–xx); Jonathan Klawans, "Interpreting the Last Supper: Sacrifice, Spiritualization, and Anti-Sacrifice," *NTS* 48 (2002): 1–17; Hans-Josef Klauck, *Herrenmahl und hellenistischer Kult: eine religionsgeschichtliche Untersuchung zum ersten Korintherbrief* (NTAbh 15; Münster: Aschendorff, 1982); Hans-Josef Klauck, "Lord's Supper," *ABD* 4:362–372; Hermann Patsch, *Abendmahl und historischer Jesus* (Calwer Theologische Monographien 1; Stuttgart: Calwer Verlag, 1972); Rudolf Pesch, *Das Abendmahl und Jesu Todesverständnis* (QD 80; Freiburg: Herder, 1978); Heinz Schürmann, *Der Paschamahlbericht, Lk xxii. (7–14) 15–18* (Münster: Aschendorff, 1953); Heinz Schürmann, *Der Einsetzungsbericht, Lk 22, 19–20* (Münster: Aschendorff, 1955); Heinz Schürmann, *Jesu Abschiedsrede, Lk 22, 21–38* (Münster: Aschendorff, 1957); Heinz Schürmann, *Jesu ureigener Tod* (Freiburg: Herder, 1975); Peter Stuhlmacher, *Biblische Theologie des Neuen Testaments* (2 vols.; Göttingen: Vandenhoeck & Ruprecht, 1992), 1:139–43; N. T. Wright, *Jesus and the Victory of God* (vol. 2 of *Christian Origins and the Question of God*; Minneapolis: Fortress, 1996).

To this list could be added those scholars who hold firmly to the historicity of the meal but are skeptical about the bread and cup sayings. For example, Ferdinand Hahn

Nevertheless, the existence of a whole series of debatable historical problems concerning what actually happened cannot be denied, and a responsible approach must take account of these. Following Smith's nudge in its direction and because of the widespread publicity given to its findings, we shall shape our study around the findings of the Jesus Seminar. The proceedings of the Seminar are summed up in a volume that goes through each of the Gospels to search for the historical deeds of Jesus.[11] They start with the hypothetical sayings source "Q" and then move on to the Gospel of Mark, assumed to be the source on which Matthew and Luke are dependent. Since their book is concerned with actions of Jesus and the source Q consists almost entirely of teaching of Jesus, the heart of the last meal is passed over very quickly.[12] Q apparently did not contain an account of the passion of

---

(*Die Einheit des Neuen Testaments: Thematische Darstellung* [vol. 2 of *Theologie des Neuen Testaments*; Tübingen: Mohr Siebeck, 2002], 534–36) accepts the authenticity of Mark 14:22b ("This is my body") and 14:25 (but not of 14:24). Schröter, *Das Abendmahl*, 132–34, accepts only Mark 14:25. Most recently Hengel and Schwemer, *Jesus und das Judentum*, 582–86, assume the historicity of the meal and argue for its paschal character; the precise original wording of Jesus' statements is beyond our reach, but Mark 14:25 is "historisches Urgestein" (p. 585).

John P. Meier, *Mentor, Message, and Miracles* (vol. 2 of *A Marginal Jew: Rethinking the Historical Jesus*; ABRL; New York: Doubleday, 1991–2009), 302–9, briefly argues for the historicity of "a final farewell meal held by Jesus" and the authenticity of Mark 14:25, but does not examine the eucharistic actions and sayings. His earlier article (John P. Meier, "The Eucharist at the Last Supper: Did It Happen?" *TD* 42 [1995]: 335–51), as summarized in *NTA* 40 (1996) § 1426 "concludes that Jesus did and said certain things regarding bread and wine that form the basis of the later Christian celebration of the Eucharist."

[11] Robert W. Funk and The Jesus Seminar, *The Acts of Jesus: The Search for the Authentic Deeds of Jesus* (San Francisco: HarperSanFrancisco, 1998).

[12] An earlier publication of the Seminar is devoted to the question "What did Jesus really say?" (Robert W. Funk, et al., *The Five Gospels: The Search for the Authentic Words of Jesus* [New York: Macmillan, 1993]). However, it contains scarcely any discussion of the material that interests us here. Mark 14:10–16 is assumed to be a Marcan composition and it contains nothing that could be isolated as an aphorism used by Mark (p. 116; cf. p. 259). Mark 14:22–26 is a composition related to previous material in the Gospel (the feeding stories, the anointing and Mark's own interpretation of the death of Jesus). But the supper tradition is so overlaid with Christian elements that it is impossible to recover any original event, let along original words of Jesus; Even Mark 14:25 is dubious. This is not to deny that Jesus may have done symbolical actions at some of his meals (pp. 117–18). For discussion of the prophecy of betrayal see pp. 259–60; here the saying in Matt 26:24 is seen to be something that Jesus could have said, but "it is so general that it would have been suited to any number of special occasions" (p. 260). The words of institution are taken to be Christian theological interpretation (p. 386). Luke 22:8 is cited as "irrefragable evidence that the evangelists do not hesitate to create words for Jesus to speak in their narratives" (p. 387). One might have expected Jesus to celebrate a Passover meal, but none of the Evangelists describes a Passover celebration; only Luke 22:15 suggests it; the meal has already been turned "into a cultic meal by Christian practice and theological interpretation" (p. 388). Luke seems to have combined two meals into one story. He is not dependent on Paul despite some phrases in common. He creates a symposium with the following sayings. The condemnation of the betrayer contains part of a saying from Mark. "Since the proverb

Jesus (and hence of the last meal), but that, of course, is no reason for assuming that people associated with its compilation were ignorant of it or disinterested in it. Our procedure, after some preliminary remarks, will be to go through the constituent parts of the story one by one.

2. The Historicity and Background of the Meal

2.1. Approaching the Issue

This essay is concerned with the problem of whether there was a historical Last Supper and, if so, what can be known historically about it.[13] We should remind ourselves that what can be established as probable or very probable by a historian is not necessarily what actually happened. Again, if there were several people at some particular event, their memories of what took place would probably not be identical and their perceptions of the significance of what happened could well be different. Moreover, the understanding of an ancient event by modern writers is affected by their own interests and perceptions. There may, therefore, be gaps between what happened and what historians can establish with reasonable probability.

---

assumes that the betrayal has already taken place, they concluded that the storyteller more likely fabricated Jesus" prediction of his own betrayal, including the proverb" (p. 388). The material in John is all seen as Johannine creation with no historical basis (p. 444–48).

[13] Our primary written sources are the Synoptic Gospels and 1 Corinthians. The latter records what Paul says had been handed down to him, and is the earliest that can be reliably dated. The Synoptic accounts are often thought to rest on at least two sources, as seen in the Luke/Mark differences (although some scholars explain the text of Luke as redaction of Mark with Pauline influence). John records a final meal but says nothing about the "eucharistic" character and content of it, although John 6 contains material which appears to reflect eucharistic language. We may thus well have multiple attestation for the event.

There are no other significant primary sources. The preserved fragment of the *Gospel of Peter* begins after the Jewish trial of Jesus. There is nothing in the other apocryphal gospels except for the *Gospel of the Ebionites*, fragment 7, which has: "But they abandon the proper sequence of the words and pervert the saying, as is plain to all from the readings attached, and have let the disciples say: Where wilt thou that we prepare for thee the passover? and him to answer to that: Do I desire with desire at this Passover to eat flesh with you?" (ποῦ θέλεις ἑτοιμάσωμέν σοι τὸ πασχα φαγεῖν; ... μὴ ἐπιθυμίᾳ ἐπεθύμησα κρέας τοῦτο τὸ πασχα φαγεῖν μεθ᾽ ὑμῶν; Philipp Vielhauer and Georg Strecker, "Jewish-Christian Gospels," in *New Testament Apocrypha* [rev. ed.; 2 vols.; ed. Wilhelm Schneemelcher and R. McL. Wilson; Louisville: Westminster John Knox, 1990–91], 1:170; A. Huck, *Synopse der drei ersten Evangelien* [ed. H. Greeven; Tübingen: Mohr Siebeck, 1981], 238).

Justin 1:66:3 ("Having taken bread and given thanks Jesus said: Do this in remembrance of me; this is my body; and likewise having taken the cup and given thanks he said: This is my blood") claims to be dependent on the Gospels, and his wording is a free combination from them.

Further, the presence in a narrative of some details that may appear not to be historically correct is not necessarily proof that the narrative as a whole is substantially unhistorical. This needs to be affirmed against the claim that, if writers can be shown to make some errors (just how many is not stated), then they cannot be trusted not to make other errors, and the existence of some errors in an account calls the reliability of the whole narrative into question. There is a logical fallacy here, and common sense suggests that such skepticism is often unwarranted. I may not remember accurately the color of the car that knocked me over in the street yesterday and say that it was dark blue, whereas in fact it was black, but the slip of memory certainly does not imply that it is doubtful whether I was knocked over: why else am I lying in a hospital bed with my leg in plaster? Of course, the number and nature of palpably unhistorical details in a narrative may be sufficient to require the hypothesis that the narrator is making it all up; if a writer makes a substantial number of major errors, it may be best to regard the whole narrative with some suspicion.[14]

Historians must also be careful to distinguish between two situations: (1) the insufficiency of the evidence to enable a decision for or against historicity to be made, and (2) the sufficiency of the evidence to rule out the possibility of historicity. Critics of biblical narratives sometimes seem to think that they have argued that something never happened when the evidence does not permit a conclusion stronger than that there is no compelling proof that it did happen. Some of the scholars cited above (e.g., Riggs) actually deny that there was a last meal of Jesus that corresponded with the description of it in the Gospels and Paul rather than simply claiming that we cannot prove its historicity. At the end of our own investigation, therefore, we may not be able to affirm more than that the evidence against the substantial historicity of what is recorded of the Last Supper is not persuasive without being able to adduce evidence that absolutely compels acceptance of its historicity.

Another very important point that should be carefully noted is that, whereas in some areas of human study the simplest solution is the best (cf. Occam's Razor), this is a highly dubious principle to adopt in historical studies where, for example, a whole range of motives may be at work in a person's coming to a particular decision. Complexity is the name of the game, and the simplest solution is not necessarily the right one. "There is always a well-known solution to every human problem – neat, plausible, and wrong."[15]

---

[14] Similarly, the fact that the story of my accident is similar to that of other pedestrians being knocked over might be thought to give grounds for supposing that my story is made up on the basis of theirs. Common sense suggests that this is unconvincing.

[15] H. L. Mencken, *Prejudices (Second Series) "The Divine Afflatus"* (New York: Knopf, 1920), 158.

Finally, the strange belief that, if a narrative has a function such as providing a basis for some current practice and so is a "cult legend" or "aetiological story," then it is *ipso facto* to be regarded as an unhistorical invention dies hard.[16] There is no reason in the world why a story told to account for a particular practice should not be capable of being a reliable historical report.[17] And, of course, details in the narrative that do not have aetiological significance are all the more likely to be historical.[18] Function and origin (or historicity) are two different categories that should be clearly distinguished in any analysis. Even if a plausible motive can be found for the invention of a story by an author, this is not an adequate reason for assuming that it is unhistorical unless there are other grounds for this hypothesis, such as the presence of significant improbabilities in the story.

2.2. An Analysis of the Pericopae preceding the Meal

The historicity issues tied to the Last Supper are multiple and complex. In addition, the scene is actually composed of several distinct units. So this study proceeds one unit at a time and treats more comprehensive issues as they arise within that sequence.

2.2.1. The Plot against Jesus and the Role of Judas (Mark 14:1–2, 10–11)

The account of the Last Supper includes the foretelling by Jesus of his betrayal. A consideration of its historicity is partly dependent upon an evaluation of the earlier material about the intention of the Jewish leaders and the role of Judas.

The Jesus Seminar adopts a generally skeptical attitude to much of the passion narrative. This emerges right at the beginning of the story with the account of the Jewish leaders' decision to get rid of Jesus, which they regard

---

[16] Thus Smith (*From Symposium to Eucharist*, 188) says of the Last Supper narrative: "The text is more likely to be etiological than historical in both form and content. That is to say, it functions as a story that arose to explain a practice in the church." Cf. the apodictic dismissal of the account by Schmithals, *Theologiegeschichte des Urchristentums*, 206: "eine Kultlegende, kein historischer Bericht" ("a cult legend, not an historical report"); to be sure, there are also other reasons why Schmithals finds it hard to imagine the account of the Last Supper being historically plausible.

[17] Contrast the view of Dunn, *Jesus Remembered*, 226: "tradition functioning as 'sacred words' within a cult or liturgy is generally more conservative in character; the transmission ... is in the nature of sacred repetition in celebration and affirmation of a community's identity-forming tradition." In this case, "it was tradition remembered as begun by Jesus himself, and remembered thus from as early as we can tell" (Dunn, *Jesus Remembered*, 230). Similarly, Robert F. O'Toole, "Last Supper," *ABD* 4:237: "[the] correct literary form is 'etiology', which as such says nothing about the historical question."

[18] Cf. the criterion of "strongly against the grain; too much with the grain," developed by E. P. Sanders and Margaret Davies, *Studying the Synoptic Gospels* (London: SCM, 1989), 304–15.

as a Markan invention reflecting a Christian tendency to blacken the Jews and exonerate the Romans in the post-70 C.E. period. All that remains is that some Jewish leaders probably urged Pilate to execute Jesus.[19] Almost inevitably, therefore, the account of the contract by Judas to betray Jesus is likewise regarded as unhistorical, and some of the Seminar regarded Judas himself as an unhistorical figure.[20]

No argument is offered for this rejection of the story of the "plot" against Jesus.[21] Similarly, no argument is offered for denying the action of Judas.[22] Here is a prime example of a critique that simply asserts that a story is a fiction whereas no compelling argument has been offered to demonstrate that it could not have happened.[23]

The additional detail given by Matthew that a price of 30 silver coins was agreed is regarded as embellishment of the fictitious story in the light of Exod 21:28–32 (the value of a slave) and Zech 11:12 (the wages of the shep-

---

[19] It is arguable that if there was no plot against Jesus by the Jewish leaders (with or without Judas's complicity), then there would have been no basis for Jesus to hold a meal that had a farewell character. Hence the existence of the Jewish plot is a necessary basis for the holding of a professedly farewell meal.

[20] Funk and Seminar, *The Acts of Jesus*, 134–35, 136–37. For a strong defense of the historicity see John P. Meier, *Companions and Competitors* (vol. 3 of *A Marginal Jew: Rethinking the Historical Jesus*; ABRL; New York: Doubleday, 1991–2009), 141–46, 208–11.

[21] There is no reason why the Romans would have wanted to take an initiative against Jesus. Most of his activity took place in Galilee which (being ruled by Antipas) was outside their jurisdiction at this time. When he came to Jerusalem, his debates were with the Jewish leaders and nothing is reported which could be construed as anti-Roman. The "triumphal entry" was probably a small affair (see in this volume ch. 9). As the Seminar admits, it is likely that some Jewish leaders urged Pilate to execute Jesus. If this were not the case, the whole of the story in the Gospels is fictitious, and we are left totally in the dark as to what happened except for the crucifixion itself.

[22] Rudolf Bultmann, *Die Geschichte der synoptischen Tradition* (4th ed.; Göttingen: Vandenhoeck & Ruprecht, 1958), 282–83, states without argument that the story has the form of a "legend" and that nobody could have learned about the decision of the authorities. The decision has been deduced from what happened subsequently. But this is to confuse "form" and historicity. Contrast Vincent Taylor: "The historical value of Mark's account is beyond question. The earliest tradition would never have ascribed the betrayal of Jesus to 'one of the Twelve' if the facts had been otherwise" (*The Gospel According to St. Mark* [2nd ed.; London: Macmillan, 1966], 534); similarly, Dunn, *Jesus Remembered*, 510, 770–71; Hengel and Schwemer, *Jesus und das Judentum*, 579–80.

[23] Burton L. Mack, *A Myth of Innocence: Mark and Christian Origins* (Philadelphia: Fortress, 1988), 299, 304–5, holds that the story and the motif of betrayal did not exist before Mark invented it. A motif of handing over/betrayal runs through the Gospel. The motif developed both for narrative reasons and to deal with a problem in Mark's community. Similarly, Ludger Schenke, *Studien zur Passionsgeschichte des Markus: Tradition und Redaktion in Markus 14, 1–42* (FB 4; Würzburg: Echter Verlag, 1971), 12–66. However, Detlev Dormeyer, *Die Passion Jesu als Verhaltensmodell: literarische und theologische Analyse der Traditions- und Redaktionsgeschichte der Markuspassion* (NTAbh 11; Münster: Aschendorff, 1974), 82–85, analyses the narrative to separate tradition and Marcan redaction; he argues that vv. 10–11a are tradition.

herd who threw them to the potter at the house of the Lord). This part of the story hangs together with Matthew's version of the fate of Judas which refers to the text in Zechariah. Zechariah may well be the source of the precise sum of money, but the actual sum can presumably have been in that region, and Matthew's readers would be able to recognize the symbolical, allusive nature of the reference which forms part of the chain of Zechariah references in the passion narrative. "It cannot be finally determined whether the exact sum is an accommodation to the prophecy or an element in the tradition which helped direct Matthew's attention to Zech. 11."[24] In any case, it does not affect the historicity of the basic narrative.

This discussion highlights another important methodological factor. This is the common assumption that Mark recorded everything that was handed down regarding the incidents that he records and left out no further details for subsequent storytellers to include; it can then be postulated that anything extra that is found in the later Evangelists must be regarded as fictitious embellishment. But there is ample evidence that oral tradition continued to operate after the writing of the Gospels (and not least when only one Gospel was in existence and in use within a limited geographical area), and there is no good reason to suppose that the later Evangelists were not able to conclude further items from tradition.[25] Whether the tradition was reliable in each and every detail is a different question, but this possibility certainly cannot be ruled out a priori.[26]

2.2.2. Preparation for the Passover Meal (Mark 14:12–16)

The Seminar offers four arguments against the historicity of this account. First, Mark created the story of the events leading up to the crucifixion out of his imagination. It is assumed that this narrative too stems from his pen. Second, the narrative cannot have existed on its own as an isolated tale told as an anecdote. It must owe its existence to the creator of the passion story. Third, since the Seminar doubt whether Jesus celebrated a Passover meal at

---

[24] Douglas J. Moo, *The Old Testament in the Gospel Passion Narratives* (Sheffield: Almond, 1983), 199.

[25] This question arises particularly with the "extra" cup in Luke. See below.

[26] These remarks about the probability of reliable tradition being available to the later Evangelists do not of course apply to the recently publicized *Gospel of Judas*, which is generally held to be a second-century heavily Gnosticised composition. This work refers very briefly at the end to the scribes approaching Judas when they were seeking an opportunity arrest Jesus. "Judas answered them as they wished. And he received some money and handed him over to them" (codex p. 58). If this were independent of the canonical Gospels, it could be part of a case for multiple attestation of the bare fact of the betrayal for money, but its independence is very unlikely; at the very least, the document does not contradict the basic point that Judas betrayed Jesus. Cf. Simon J. Gathercole, "The Gospel of Judas," *Expository Times* 118 (2007): 209–15.

all (in view of the chronological problems to be discussed), it follows that a story about preparations for the meal must be equally unhistorical. Fourth, the formation of the narrative can be explained as imitation of a scriptural example. This story and the earlier one of the finding of the colt (which is similar in style and structure) are both thought to be suggested by 1 Sam 10:1–8. Saul, having been anointed by Samuel, will meet two men who will advise him that the donkeys he was seeking have been found (by his father); then he will meet three men carrying goats, bread and wine, and will give the bread to Saul. Then Saul will meet prophets and join them, sharing their inspiration. He will then go to Gilgal and must wait for Samuel to come and offer sacrifices. The story of the fulfillment says that all these signs were fulfilled but gives no description of what happened before Saul met the prophets. The story is similar with Jesus. In Mark Jesus enters Jerusalem twice, once for the entry and once on the day of preparation for the meal. "Like Saul, Jesus was anointed, after which he acquired a donkey (under strange circumstances), and then found a place to eat Passover, which involved bread and wine (on equally mysterious terms). The acquisition of donkey and upper room were also in their way a kind of 'sign.'"[27]

2.2.2.1. A Basis in the Hebrew Bible?

Sometimes when a scriptural parallel or anticipation of an event that has not been noticed before is pointed out to us, we say "Of course, why didn't I see it before?" because the correspondences are manifest. This is hardly so in this case. The contrasts are great:

– The parallel between Saul being anointed (χρίω) with *oil* as *king* and Jesus being "anointed" (μυρίζω) with *myrrh* as part of a *burial* rite is not exactly close.[28]

– Saul *meets* two men who tell him about the donkey; Jesus *sends* two men.

– Saul *does not find* the donkey, but it returns somehow to his father; Jesus' disciples *do* find and bring the donkey to him.

– Saul meets three men with *goats, bread and wine*, although he is only said to *receive some of the bread*. Jesus sends two disciples to arrange for a room, and nothing is said about finding or bringing any provisions in the story.

– *No meal* is described in the Saul story. The Jesus story centers on the meal.

---

[27] Funk and Seminar, *The Acts of Jesus*, 137–38. According to the Seminar, Matthew may have missed the significance of the biblical account of anointing of Saul that has influenced Mark. Luke's version embellishes the story by identifying the two anonymous disciples.

[28] The verb μυρίζω is not found here or anywhere else in the LXX.

– The *goats* play no role in the Jesus story; nor is a lamb overtly mentioned in Mark's version.
– Bread and wine are such normal items of food and drink that there is nothing remarkable about the mention of them in the Saul story.

The real similarity is that in both stories somebody (Samuel, Jesus) tells another person (Saul) or persons (the two disciples) what is going to happen and then it happens, and in each case what is going to happen involves meeting somebody who will behave in a certain way. In the Saul story, the event serves to give divine confirmation of the anointing. In the Jesus story, the function of confirmation is not present. In both cases, however, it could be argued that there is a miraculous element in the giving of a prophecy that is then fulfilled. Certainly that element is not emphasized in the Jesus story.

The resemblances between the Saul story and the preparation for the meal story are so few that it is very hard to envisage the former being the source or model for the latter. There is perhaps a better case in respect of the story of the finding of the animal in Mark 11. However, the animal in Mark is a πῶλος, not an ὄνος as in 1 Samuel; true, it is accompanied by an ὄνος in Matthew, but that is due to the perception of the link with Zech 9:9. And the functions of the animals are quite different. To see one story as the origin for the other is quite fanciful. How did a story about lost donkeys being *found* become the basis for a story about Jesus *riding* one into Jerusalem?

There is, in any case, the probable explanation that in both cases Jesus had made a prior arrangement with friends so that what he wanted to do could be done.[29]

The only conceivable hypothesis regarding the arrangement for the room that remains requires the two-stage process that (1) the story of the donkey is modelled on the Saul story, and then (2) the story of the room is modelled on the donkey story. For there is nothing in common between the Saul story and the room story. Regardless of the Samuel connection, the two Marcan stories do have a similar shape that is adequately explained by their coming from the hand of the same narrator. The motif of sending two disciples is

---

[29] Joseph A. Fitzmyer, *The Gospel According to Luke X–XXIV* (AB 28a; Garden City: Doubleday, 1985), 1383 ("clearly implies prearrangement"). Schmithals (*Markus*, 605) criticizes Pesch for adopting this explanation, which he regards as a piece of modern rationalism that does not explain the story (when understood as making a theological point); cf. also Dieter Lührmann, *Das Markusevangelium* [HNT 3; Tübingen: Mohr Siebeck, 1987], 236. Likewise, Robert H. Gundry, *Mark: A Commentary on His Apology for the Cross* [Grand Rapids: Eerdmans, 1993], 821, rejects the explanation on the grounds that Mark's main concern in this narrative is to stress the (supernatural) predictive power of Jesus, a trait that he also discovers in the eucharistic sayings. The motif that Jesus is in control of the situation and is not taken by surprise can be present on either reading of the story.

adequately explained by the practice of *paarweise Sendung* that was characteristic of Jesus[30] and does not require the Saul story to explain it.

I conclude that the preparation for Passover story was not spun out of the Saul story. There is no evidence to indicate that it was the inspiration for the room story, nor that it contributed to it.

2.2.2.2. The Question of a Pre-Marcan Passion Narrative

The negative verdict on this incident appears to have been based on a negative attitude to this whole section of Mark. The Seminar makes three points.[31] First, the disciples fled at the arrest of Jesus, and so there were no eye-witnesses to what happened. However, the Seminar does not explain why they are so certain about the former point. In any case any such flight is irrelevant to preservation of eye-witness testimony to the Last Supper, since it preceded the arrest! Even if the disciples did flee, are we forced to assume that they displayed no interest or curiosity whatever in finding out what happened to Jesus after the arrest?

Second, the Seminar views the original passion story as an extended composition, and it originated in searching the Scriptures for an explanation of why Jesus was crucified. The former of these observations is correct, in that the passion story does show signs of continuity that are lacking in some other parts of the Gospels. The latter is open to serious questioning, since it has been shown that it is more likely that the individual incidents were seen to have links to Scripture rather than that they were created on the basis of Scripture.[32]

Third, for the Seminar there appears to have been one basic account of the passion reflected in the five versions (i. e., including the Gospel of Peter) that have survived. The Seminar agreed by a solid majority that "the first *written* passion story"[33] was created by Mark probably in the 70s.[34]

The hypothesis of a connected passion narrative that preceded the composition of the Gospels has been around for some time; the earlier form-

---

[30] Joachim Jeremias, "Paarweise Sendung im Neuen Testament," in *New Testament Essays. Studies in Memory of Thomas Walter Manson, 1893–1958* (ed. A. J. B. Higgins; Manchester: Manchester University Press, 1959), 136–43.

[31] Funk and Seminar, *The Acts of Jesus*, 132–33.

[32] See Moo, *The Old Testament in the Gospel Passion Narratives*.

[33] Their italics; Funk and Seminar, *The Acts of Jesus*, 133.

[34] Skepticism regarding the existence of a passion narrative is expressed by Smith, *From Symposium to Eucharist*, 225; cf. Werner H. Kelber, "Conclusion: From Passion Narrative to Gospel," in *The Passion in Mark: Studies in Mark 14–16* (ed. Werner H. Kelber; Philadelphia: Fortress, 1976), 153–59; Vernon K. Robbins, "Last Meal: Preparation, Betrayal, and Absence (Mark 14:12–25)," in *The Passion in Mark: Studies in Mark 14–16* (ed. Werner H. Kelber; Philadelphia: Fortress, 1976), 21–40; Gundry, *Mark*, 806. See further below.

critics recognized the cohesion of the material.³⁵ The hypothesis was taken up by J. Jeremias, who identified a short account that was then expanded to a longer account (including the Last Supper, the announcement of the betrayal and the prophecy of the denial).³⁶ If the theory is tenable, the basic passion story is not the creation of Mark in the 70s but may date back considerably earlier.

The existence of a lengthy and full pre-Marcan narrative has been most strongly defended by Pesch.³⁷ He notes the wide variations between previous scholars in identifying traditional and redactional material, so much so that one may well despair of coming to any kind of firm conclusion. His own analysis, which takes a maximalist position, depends upon various arguments regarding content and form. Even if Pesch's work is to be regarded as making the existence of a pre-Markan narrative very likely,³⁸ it cannot be established conclusively in detail what was in this narrative and what was added to it. There is enormous variation between scholarly views of the matter, with some hypotheses postulating the existence of different, parallel accounts.³⁹ Thus, for example, Jeremias excluded the preparation for the meal from his longer version, whereas Pesch includes it.

Unfortunately the detailed treatment of the passion by R. E. Brown begins after the Last Supper narrative, and consequently he does not discuss whether this was included within the pre-Marcan narrative or not. He concludes that Mark was using an existing narrative but that the problem

---

[35] Cf. Craig A. Evans, *Mark 8:27–16:20* (WBC 34b; Nashville: Nelson, 2001), 352 (with references to the classical works of R. Bultmann, M. Dibelius, K. L. Schmidt, and V. Taylor).

[36] Joachim Jeremias, *The Eucharistic Words of Jesus* (trans. Norman Perrin; NTL; London: SCM, 1966), 89–96.

[37] Pesch, *Das Markusevangelium*, 2:1–27, building on various previous studies. Current scholarship is divided on the issue; see the scholars listed by Evans, *Mark*, 352, and summarized by Pesch, *Das Markusevangelium*, 2:7–10. In keeping with the general practice in their book, the Jesus Seminar neither mentions nor (apparently) interacts with these works of scholarship, so that the reader is left quite unaware of the substantial weight of scholarship taking the opposite position from their own (and, in fairness, the weight of scholarship in favor of their own position).

[38] A major point advocated by Pesch is the difference in narrative techniques between the first part of the Gospel and the second, making it unlikely that Mark himself was responsible for the change in the passion story. Pesch discovers various linguistic characteristics of the source together with matters of content including the remarkable amount of allusions to the Hebrew Bible.

[39] See Kelber, "From Passion Narrative"; Evans, *Mark*, 351–52, lists recent attacks on the hypothesis but also says that generally one or even two passion sources are accepted by scholars. Even if such a narrative existed, there is considerable uncertainty over what was and what was not included in it; see the survey by M. L. Soards, "Appendix IX: the Question of a Premarcan Passion Narrative," in Raymond E. Brown, *The Death of the Messiah* (2 vols.; ABRL; New York: Doubleday, 1994), 2:1492–1524.

of isolating different layers of tradition and separating them from Marcan redaction is probably insoluble.[40]

The hypothesis of some kind of pre-Marcan narrative, at least in oral form, is plausible.[41] The Seminar's hypothesis that the narrative was first written down by Mark is less likely. Once it is recognized that certain elements in Mark's story are distinguishable as probably redactional additions to a basic account, Marcan authorship of the basic account becomes less likely.[42]

Certainly the absence of a passion narrative from Q is no argument against a pre-Marcan narrative. The proposal that there was a single "Q" source containing all that its compilers knew about Jesus is a dubious hypothesis. And if Q was what it appears to be, namely primarily a compilation of sayings of Jesus, the absence of a passion narrative from it is not strange. In fact, one might turn the argument on its head and claim that, if a separate passion narrative did exist, this could be one reason why it was not thought necessary to include a passion narrative in Q.

But there is a crucial "give away" by the Seminar in the emphasized word "written." This leaves open the possibility that the Seminar is prepared to allow that there were earlier oral traditions, even a connected basic account. It should be remembered that the common form-critical assumption that the tradition was handed down in discrete units (especially short sayings rather than connected discourses and single narrative pericopae rather than connected stories) is precisely that, an *assumption* that flies in the face of what we know about oral story-telling (cf. the obvious examples of the Iliad and Odyssey). Consequently, even if Mark were the first person to put the passion narrative into writing, this by no means indicates that there was not an earlier unwritten passion narrative.

---

[40] Brown, *The Death of the Messiah*, 1:46–57.

[41] There may, of course, have been more than one account of the story as a whole or of parts of it. There is a continuing debate as to whether Luke possessed a special source (or sources) for parts of his passion narrative; this view is accepted by Hans Klein, *Das Lukasevangelium* (KEK 1.3; Göttingen: Vandenhoeck & Ruprecht, 2006), 46. The fact that Paul knew traditions about the Last Supper, crucifixion, burial and resurrection appearances of Jesus strengthens the case for an oral passion narrative. See further Lührmann, *Das Markusevangelium*, 227–31, who argues from the common matter in Mark and John (which he regards as independent of each other) that the underlying passion narrative included a last meal of Jesus with his disciples that was bound up with the announcement of the denial by Peter. Gundry, *Mark*, 806, adopts a skeptical attitude towards such theories on the grounds (a). that it is impossible to define the contents of such a narrative and (b). that it is unnecessary on the assumption that Peter was Mark's chief informant. But hypotheses can be true without being "necessary," and it is likely that Peter would have told the story as a story and that his telling would have enabled an oral tradition to crystallize.

[42] Unless it is suggested that Mark himself composed the account and then redacted it later. It is certainly the case that authors may revise their original accounts over time, but is this the kind of revision that is being detected here?

The point is important for our estimate of the passion stories generally, especially the accounts of the trials and crucifixion However, in view of the uncertainties that must remain about the original contents of the passion narrative, it may be wise not to attach too much weight to it. It would be rash to be dogmatic one way or the other on this particular pericope, but the over-all conclusion that the substance of the passion narrative is pre-Marcan is significant for the question of the historicity of the story as a whole, including the Last Supper itself.

Consequently, while it may therefore be wise not to make its existence foundational for a discussion of the Last Supper narrative, it can be said with considerable confidence that the criticisms offered by the Jesus Seminar fall well short of proving that such a source did not exist.[43]

Finally, to return to the present pericope, it should be noted that, if we take away the account of the preparation, we are left with a somewhat unmotivated and unexplained meal whose character is not apparent without the account of the preparation that establishes that (for the narrator) it was a Passover meal. There is thus a case that the account of the preparation forms an integral part of a larger unit.

2.2.2.3. The Content of the Narrative

From these general considerations we turn to the content of the story. Why is this particular narrative included? It makes clear that the meal that is about to be described is a Passover meal and shows that the correct procedure was followed. There would normally be two parts to this: the slaughter of a lamb and the preparation of a room in the city.

Mark 14:12 can be understood in two different ways. First, the clause "when they were slaughtering the Passover (sc. lamb)" can be taken to refer to the disciples themselves actually doing this and, while doing so, asking Jesus where the meal was to be held.[44] The more usual interpretation is that the clause refers to people in general and simply explains what customarily happened on the day for the benefit of the readers.[45] Even if this latter view is taken, the unavoidable implication would still be that the disciples attended to this matter.[46] To say that the disciples went to prepare the Passo-

---

[43] Ultimately the question regarding the date at which it acquired written form is not that important, given the basic broad reliability of traditions handed down orally. Cf. generally Dunn, *Jesus Remembered*, 229–31.

[44] Maurice Casey, *Aramaic Sources of Mark's Gospel* (SNTSMS 102; Cambridge: Cambridge University Press, 1998), 222–23; Evans, *Mark*, 373.

[45] So Taylor, *St. Mark*, 537, who notes that Luke so understood it; Gundry, *Mark*, 820–21; Pesch, *Das Markusevangelium*, 2:341–42; R. T. France, *The Gospel of Mark* (NIGTC; Grand Rapids: Eerdmans, 2002), 564 (because he places the action earlier on the day before the slaughter).

[46] It was not necessary for Jesus to participate personally.

ver, and that it was the custom as part of the preparations to slaughter a Passover lamb, clearly implies that the disciples did so; otherwise, the failure to prepare the meal properly would have had to be indicated. It is thus part of a deliberate presentation of the meal as a Passover meal.

The narrative is regarded by R. Bultmann as a variant to Mark 11:2–6. The motif of foreknowledge reminds him of 1 Sam 10 where Samuel tells Saul whom he will meet on the way. But the ultimate basis for regarding it as unhistorical is its alleged resemblance to the fairy-tale motif of a person (or an animal) who precedes a traveler and shows him the way to his destination. The story here is not an independent tradition but presumes the following story of meal. Bultmann also claims that the formulation of the date in v. 12 is completely impossible for Judaism and comes from Mark, unless the whole story is an early creation in the Hellenistic church; that, however, is hardly possible because the narrative presupposes that it was a Passover festival, an element that was ousted by the Hellenistic eucharist.[47]

Bultmann's description of the story as a "variant" of the other one, when unpacked, means simply that both of them develop in different ways the motif of Jesus supernaturally knowing beforehand what will happen.[48] The alternative explanation is that in both cases Jesus has made a prior arrangement, and it is plausible that he did so to avoid the meal being interrupted or simply because it would have been impossible to hold a meal at this time in Jerusalem without a prior arrangement. The story thus fits the background. Bultmann's problem is that he starts from the presupposition that the account of the meal is unhistorical, and therefore he has to offer a non-historical explanation of the preparation for it.[49]

The date given is "the first day of unleavened bread." The festival of unleavened bread was normally understood to begin on Nisan 15. The added description as the day when Passover sacrifices were made shows that the reference must be to Nisan 14.[50] An equivalent expression is used by Josephus, thus demonstrating that this was a possible way of referring

---

[47] Bultmann, *Geschichte*, 283–84.

[48] Normally to describe two stories as "variants" would mean that they were different accounts of the same incident. Bultmann, however, means that they use the same motif in describing two different events.

[49] In fairness to Bultmann, it should be pointed out that there is a historical problem concerning the date of the meal, with the possibility that the meal was held before the Passover meal was normally held, in which case the historical question arises as to whether it was possible to slaughter a lamb before the appointed time for doing so arises. There is also the problem that Mark apparently describes what the disciples are supposed to have done at the appointed time for doing so.

[50] Cf. Martin Hengel, "Das Mahl in der Nacht, 'in der Jesus ausgeliefert wurde' (1 Kor 11,23)," in *Le Repas de Dieu: Das Mahl Gottes* (ed. Christian Grappe; Tübingen: Mohr Siebeck, 2004), 138.

to Nisan 14.⁵¹ In any case the second, defining phrase shows plainly what Mark meant.⁵²

Positively, the narrative fits in perfectly with the Jewish customs of the time.⁵³

The objections to the historicity of this part of the story thus fall to the ground, provided that the problem of the dating of the meal can be solved.

2.2.3. The Betrayer (Mark 14:17–21)

The account of the meal itself begins with a reference to the time, which again fits in with the Passover custom of holding the meal in the evening, and to the arrival of Jesus and the Twelve.⁵⁴ But now comes a surprise, although one for which the readers (but not the original hearers) have been prepared. The meal has begun and is proceeding: the company are reclining at table and eating. The mention of eating is essential because the enormity of the betrayal is that it is a breaking of a fellowship sealed by eating together and takes place in the closest temporal proximity to the meal. "One

---

⁵¹ See especially Pesch, *Das Markusevangelium*, 2:341–42, citing Josephus, *J. W.* 5.99 (*contra* Jeremias, *Eucharistic Words*, 16–19). A general identification of the two festivals of Passover and unleavened bread probably lies behind the usage. Cf. Robert H. Gundry, *Matthew: A Commentary on His Handbook for a Mixed Church Under Persecution* (2nd ed.; Grand Rapids: Eerdmans, 1994), 524; Casey, *Aramaic Sources*, 221–22.

⁵² See below for a more detailed discussion of the dating problem.

⁵³ Certainly there are problems in knowing how far later Jewish practices were in existence in the first century. What can be said is that the story in the Gospels fits in with these later accounts and may even be regarded as earlier testimony to the practices. Current Jewish scholarship tends to regard the extant post-70 C.E. sources as giving evidence only for that period and argues that we cannot safely extrapolate to the period before 70 C.E. A different position is adopted by E.P. Sanders, *Judaism: Practice and Belief, 63 BCE–66 CE* (Philadelphia: Trinity, 1992), 132–38, who discusses in detail the mechanics of slaughtering so many animals in the short time and limited space available (cf. the earlier calculations by Joachim Jeremias, *Jerusalem in the Time of Jesus* [London: SCM, 1969], 77–84). There is pre-70 C.E. evidence from 1 Esd 1, Philo, Josephus, *Jub.* 49 and the Qumran Temple Scroll which justifies a less skeptical attitude to the later evidence. One problem is whether the meal was eaten in the temple area or in homes. Sanders discusses the number of people involved and shows how difficult it was even to get all the animals slaughtered in the temple: this suggests that cooking and eating the meal must have taken place elsewhere.

⁵⁴ This last detail has been questioned by skeptics who point out pedantically that two of the disciples had been sent on ahead of the others (Lührmann, *Das Markusevangelium*, 236). Lührmann also suggests that it is not clear in Mark whether Judas himself was actually present (he goes away in v. 10 and returns in v. 43). Of course, it is possible that the two disciples finished their task earlier and had returned to Jesus. The question whether others were present in addition to the Twelve is variously answered. Evans, *Mark*, 374, argues for a larger number; Gundry, *Mark*, 837, limits to the Twelve in view of v. 17. Evans' arguments (he assumes that the two sent to make the arrangements are not members of the Twelve and that women were present in the light of Luke 10:38–42) are not forceful, but a firm decision one way or the other is difficult.

of you will hand me over." Nothing is said in the context about what "hand over" means: but the word is used in the second and third of the passion sayings earlier in the Gospel, and therefore Mark probably presumes that the disciples should have been able to grasp the point; in any case the reader will do so in view of vv. 10–11. The thought of treachery alarms and saddens the disciples, a natural human reaction. When they ask, "Is it I?" this probably means: "It is not me that you suspect, is it?";[55] the thought may be of Jesus' foreknowledge of something that they might find themselves doing even though it is not their present intention. Jesus responds, "It is one of the Twelve," which may mean "it is one of the Twelve as opposed to the larger number of other disciples present at the meal."[56] On the other hand, the reference to "one who dips into the bowl with me" would presumably apply to the whole company present. The statement does not identify the offender but emphasizes the enormity of the offence.[57] No further reference is made to dipping into the bowl; it is assumed that readers recognize this as a normal happening at such a meal.[58]

The response of Jesus is followed by a longer saying in which he states that the Son of Man "goes" (sc. to death),[59] as is laid down in Scripture (and therefore by the will of God) but it is a grievous thing for the person who is responsible for causing this to happen. The implication is that this person stands under divine judgment. Even though a divine purpose is carried out, nevertheless it is a sinner who brings it about.[60]

The pericope is consistently rejected by the Jesus Seminar, in line with their rejection of the previous references to the betrayer in Mark 14:1–2,

---

[55] Cf. Gundry, *Mark*, 836, for the view that μήτι ἐγώ "suggests a possibility only to negate it."

[56] Evans, *Mark*, 376–77.

[57] Taylor, *St. Mark*, 541.

[58] The question of how Jesus knows about the intention of Judas is not one that can be certainly answered. One possibility is supernatural knowledge, and probably this was the view of some of the early story-tellers, particularly when the story is coupled to that of the prediction of Peter's denial. But acute psychological insight coupled with observations of Judas's behavior over some time is a perfectly possible explanation. There are insightful people who are far more sensitive to how others are thinking than the general run of us.

[59] The use of the verb אזל in this euphemistic sense is attested in the rabbinic material cited by Casey, *Aramaic Sources*, 233–36; see also the earlier discussion (utilizing the notes of A. J. Wensinck) by Matthew Black, *An Aramaic Approach to the Gospels and Acts* (Oxford: Clarendon, 1954), 237–38.

[60] The point is that it was God's will that Jesus should suffer as a result of human sin in order to atone for it, but this does not diminish the sinfulness of this particular sin. Had not Judas acted, others would have done so, and indeed other sinful actions took place in the process of trial and execution. Even if Judas had not betrayed him, they would have found another way to get him. Hence the prediction by Jesus leaves open the possibility that Judas could respond to it with repentance. Even the entry of Satan into Judas (John 13:27) may not have been an irreversible stage in the process.

10–11, as unhistorical.⁶¹ They make several points: First, the name Judas was not introduced into the Gospel tradition until its appearance in Mark. This assertion is said to be confirmed by, or based on, the fact that Paul mentions the tradition of betrayal but does not name anybody. Second, the name may be explained as a personification of "the Jews." (But, they add, even if there was a real Judas, the stories about him are not historical). Third, the story could be based on the betrayal of Joseph by his brothers in Genesis for silver. Fourth, Ps 41:9 may also have been influential.

Further arguments were already provided by Bultmann. He claimed that the Psalm provided the motif for a legend and this was then embedded in a meal scene. He held that there is a more primitive account in Luke 22:21.⁶² Whether the meal in question was originally thought of as the last meal is not sure, since Mark 14:17–21 is an independent tradition. The meal is not thought of as a paschal meal, since at the latter each guest had his own dish. The betrayal prophecy originally made no mention of a specific disciple, reference to Judas not being made until Matthew and John. The mention of "12" is a further sign of legend. The announcement of betrayal does not lead to any appropriate action but to a woe that stems from the community. John was the first to notice that Judas's departure on his errand must be mentioned.⁶³

We can now turn to an evaluation of these arguments. The final three points made by the Seminar are not strictly arguments against historicity, but attempts to provide explanations that would be compatible with an assumption of non-historicity, or rather explanations that would account for

---

⁶¹ Funk and Seminar, *The Acts of Jesus*, 138–39.

⁶² In Luke the prophecy of the betrayal follows the meal and introduces the lengthier set of sayings of Jesus. In John's Gospel the eucharistic elements are missing, leaving open the question at what stage in the Johannine meal the incident occurred. If we are correct in identifying the sharing of the bowl with the preliminary course in the meal, then the incident will have occurred at the same relative position in the meal. However, in John Judas goes out immediately after receiving the piece of bread and presumably before the actual main course, which would be very surprising (but may have been necessitated by the need to get the arresting force mobilized in time). A significant part of the Last Supper tradition was teaching given by Jesus at this time. Doubtless the tendency to attach particular importance to a person's last words may have led to the development of this feature. Once a brief core had been established, the tendency to include material from other traditions would have been strong. It may have been this tendency which led to the alternative placement of the betrayal prophecy in Luke. In Mark and Matthew the prophecy of Peter's denial takes place after departure from the guest room on the Mount of Olives, whereas in Luke and John it takes place in the guest room. Cf. Darrell L. Bock, *Luke* (2 vols.; Baker Exegetical Commentary on the New Testament 3a–b; Grand Rapids: Baker, 1994–96), 2:1733–34.

⁶³ Bultmann, *Geschichte*, 284–85. Cf. *inter alios* Schmithals, *Markus*, 597–603, 608–13 (as part of his broader hypothesis that the group of Twelve did not exist during the lifetime of Jesus); Mack, *Myth*, 299, 304–5.

the creation of a story that is deemed on other grounds to be unhistorical. This procedure raises again the methodological question: if one can give a plausible account of how what looks like a historical story could be shown to have been created as a fictitious story, how does one balance the probabilities of the historical explanation against the fictitious one?

First, the fact that the name of the betrayer is not attested before Mark is no proof that it was unknown. The non-mention by Paul says nothing about whether Paul knew the name or not; there was no reason why he should mention it in 1 Cor 11 (and in any case Paul may be referring to being handed over by God). The claim that the name was not introduced earlier into the gospel tradition is absurd and unprovable because we do not possess a copy of that tradition to check its presence or absence. This is an unsubstantiated argument from silence.

Second, it is a long stretch from Jesus being "handed over" by the Jews to the fictitious creation of a story of a specific betrayal by an individual. There was no need to invent the betrayer, when the Jewish leaders were themselves active characters in the story. From a fictional perspective, had they wished to take action, it would have been perfectly simple to have spies note where Jesus was staying and carry out a dawn raid. The story of the betrayal is not a necessary item in such a process of invention.

Third, in both stories, it is true, a brother or companion is treated in a way that is inconsistent with the relationship by being handed over to people who were not his friends. The term "betrayal" could perhaps be broadly used in both cases, although Joseph was simply sold as a slave and the sale is seen as an improvement on killing him, which was his brothers' original intention. The sums of money (20 shekels and 30 pieces of silver) do not correspond. Thus the thrusts of the two stories are rather different and there are no textual hints to suggest an association.[64]

Fourth, an echo of Ps 41:9 is present; but the whole theory that such verses were the basis of the creation of the stories is not sustainable. The proverbial nature of the allusion is seen from its use in 1QH 13:23–25.[65]

We are therefore being asked to suppose that once the story of the arrest in the garden had been created, it was thought necessary to explain how the arresting party knew where to go, and therefore the idea that one of Jesus' friends told them was dreamt up, and the details concocted on the basis of these scriptural allusions. This is stretching credulity to the limit.

We now turn to Bultmann's objections. If, as he claims, there is a more primitive account in Luke, this could be seen rather as providing additional

---

[64] The issue is clouded somewhat by the debate over whether the action of Judas is to be seen as "handing over" or "betrayal." While the verb ($\pi\alpha\rho\alpha\delta\acute{\iota}\delta\omega\mu\iota$) can be used neutrally, the negative sense here is clear enough.

[65] Cf. Moo, *The Old Testament in the Gospel Passion Narratives*, 239.

evidence for the story;⁶⁶ however, this hypothesis is too uncertain to be a firm basis for argument either way.⁶⁷ His claim that the pericope was originally independent of the Last Supper narrative rests on the assumptions (a) that the early church was incapable of handing down anything other than single pericopae; (b) that the tradition was incapable of assigning incidents to their right historical settings. Neither of these claims is self-evident or plausible. Bultmann's uncertainty about whether the meal was paschal is used to cast doubt on whether a common dish was used. The question of whether multiple dishes or a single dish were used at the Passover is discussed by Jeremias who shows that the evidence for the former practice can be presumed to go back to the first century.⁶⁸ The use of a reference to the Twelve as a sign of non-historicity rests on a general theory about the creation of that group that cannot be followed up here.⁶⁹ In any case, even if the phrase itself is a later embellishment of the saying, it says nothing about the general historicity of the scene.⁷⁰

Bultmann is on stronger ground when he asks why no action was taken by the other disciples against the betrayer. As Mark tells the story, the answer is simply that none of them knew to whom Jesus was referring.⁷¹ The same may be true for the other Synoptic Gospels. In Matthew Judas himself is singled out as asking "Is it I?" like the other disciples, and Jesus says "You said it." This shows the reader that Jesus knew who it was, which is surely implicit in Mark, but says nothing about whether the other disciples saw

---

⁶⁶ William Klassen, *Judas: Betrayer or Friend of Jesus?* (Minneapolis: Fortress, 1996), 93, n. 21, picks up from A. Suhl the point that, if the Lucan version is the most primitive, it is surprising that it lacks the Hebrew Bible reference that is said to have started off the process of creation of the story.

⁶⁷ The general opinion is that Luke is redacting Mark (so Schürmann, *Jesu Abschiedsrede*, 3–21); the possibility of a parallel, independent source was defended by Friedrich Rehkopf, *Die lukanische Sonderquelle: Ihr Umfang und Sprachgebrauch* (WUNT 5; Tübingen: Mohr Siebeck, 1959), 7–30; but apart from my own cautious support in I. Howard Marshall, *The Gospel of Luke* (NIGTC 3; Grand Rapids: Eerdmans, 1978), 807–08, it seems to have found no supporters, and it would be unwise to depend upon it (cf. Klein, *Das Lukasevangelium*, 667–68).

⁶⁸ Jeremias, *Eucharistic Words*, 70–71.

⁶⁹ The objection presumably rests on the assumption that the creation of the "Twelve" lies outside the lifetime of Jesus. For a defense of the historicity of the Twelve, see in this volume ch. 5.

⁷⁰ One possibility is that the phrase differentiates the close disciples from other persons who may have been present at the meal (so Evans, *Mark*, 377; *contra* Gundry, *Mark*, 837). As it stands, the point of the description is not so much to narrow down the identification of the betrayer as to indicate the enormity of the act.

⁷¹ We might compare how in the contemporary world the motif of a group of people, one of whom is a murderer, who take no action because they do not know which of them it is, is so commonplace in the "house party" type of whodunnit crime fiction that no reader would think this absence of action to be significant. Nothing that Jesus says indicates that he was thinking of an immediate act of betrayal.

anything noteworthy about this particular individual. In Luke the disciples are said to debate with one another which of them it was. This different formulation of the incident, which is placed after the meal, conveys essentially the same general sense.

There is, however, a more detailed story in John where the beloved disciple asks Jesus, "Who is it?," and Jesus replies by saying that it is the particular disciple to whom he then gives a morsel dipped in the bowl. In this form of the story it would seem that, if anybody, only the beloved disciple (and presumably Peter) got the message.[72] John in fact states that none of the disciples understood the real reason why Judas left the room. On John's view the beloved disciple and Peter did nothing, possibly because they did not realize that the betrayal was so imminent.[73] Whatever view we take of the historical nature of John's narrative, the doubts it raises are not sufficient to call in question the historicity of the basic act of betrayal by Judas.

A further question concerns the historicity of the actual sayings ascribed to Jesus. Pesch holds that the sayings in Mark 14:18, 21 are "scarcely authentic." In v. 18 the "Amen" form could be an imitation of the style of Jesus, and the use of Scripture here and in v. 21 is a possible sign of creation by the early church. He holds that a better case might be made for v. 20. Pesch grants the original Semitic form of the pericope (extending to the narrative as well as the sayings).[74]

Pesch's argument raises the general question concerning Jesus' use of Scripture. R.T. France makes a detailed case against the general principle that we cannot accept many of the scriptural allusions in the Gospels as

---

[72] Cf. John 13:27–30 for the ignorance of the other disciples regarding Judas' action. The point is left open by C.H. Dodd, *Historical Tradition in the Fourth Gospel* (Cambridge: Cambridge University Press, 1963), 52–53.

[73] The fact that the beloved disciple takes no action is a sign of the unhistorical nature of the Johannine version of the story for some commentators (C.K. Barrett, *The Gospel According to St. John: An Introduction with Commentary and Notes on the Greek Text* [London: SPCK, 1955], 373). Rudolf Schnackenburg, *The Gospel According to John* (3 vols.; New York: Seabury, 1980–82), 3:30–31, holds that John is simply making the christological point that Jesus foreknew what would happen, and has not considered the problem that arises from his narrative. Leon Morris, *The Gospel According to John* (Grand Rapids: Eerdmans, 1971), 628, suggests a combination of possible reasons: "there is nothing in the narrative to show that Jesus meant that betrayal was imminent"; the disciples may have been thinking that Jesus was talking about some kind of involuntary action of betrayal that any of them might commit rather than an act of calculated betrayal; and "it must have seemed incredible that Jesus should urge Judas to do his work of betrayal quickly." Cf. D.A. Carson, *The Gospel According to John* (Grand Rapids: Eerdmans, 1991), 474.

[74] Pesch, *Das Markusevangelium*, 2:352. Cf. his later rejection of the sayings in vv. 27–31.

coming from Jesus himself, and nothing needs to be added here to France's careful discussion.[75]

In the present case there is no cogent reason why Jesus should not have appropriated the language of Ps 41:9. If the early church could have seen the career of Jesus in light of the *passio-iusti* motif, there is no reason to suppose that he himself could not have done likewise.

As for Mark 14:21 this is a Son of Man saying. The historicity of the saying is defended by M. Casey but on his understanding of the saying as a general comment applicable to anybody in the appropriate circumstances that Jesus applies to himself.[76] On this view, the saying is a condemnation of anybody who acts as the betrayer of a friend. The weakness of Casey's understanding is the inclusion of the phrase "as it is written of him" which appears to demand a specific reference. It is just possible that Casey's interpretation could stand if we assume that "as it is written of him" applies to Jesus as a person who knows that his death is foretold, and then adds that he is a man who is being betrayed by a fellow who will come under judgment for this act of betrayal. Those who are doubtful of Casey's interpretation find no real difficulty in assuming that Jesus was making a self-reference and uttering a statement that is more in the nature of a specific prediction concerning this particular betrayer.[77]

I conclude that there is nothing in this pericope itself that speaks decisively against historicity.[78] If the Seminar agrees (as they do) that some high

---

[75] R. T. France, *Jesus and the Old Testament: His Application of Old Testament Passages to Himself and His Mission* (London: Tyndale, 1971); cf. Moo, *The Old Testament in the Gospel Passion Narratives*, 387.

[76] Schmithals, *Markus*, 610–13, holds that Mark 14:21 was created on the basis of Luke 17:1 (Q) which was known to Mark who developed his saying in light of the tradition that Judas came to a dreadful end. On the contrary, it is arguable that the parallelism in structure between the two sayings is an indication that they come from the same speaker.

[77] Cf. Gundry, *Mark*, 838.

[78] See Klassen, *Judas: Betrayer or Friend of Jesus?* (cf. also William Klassen, "Judas Iscariot," *ABD* 3:1091–1096), who despite his attempts to give a different picture of Judas from that of the NT and subsequent writers, has no doubts about his historicity and his making of an arrangement to bring Jesus into contact with the high priest. See also Brown, *The Death of the Messiah*, 2:1394–1418. However, Wolfgang Trilling, "Zur Entstehung des Zwölferkreises: Eine geschichtskritische Überlegung," in *Die Kirche des Anfangs: Festschrift für Heinz Schürmann zum 65. Geburtstag* (ed. Rudolf Schnackenburg, et al.; Leipzig: St Benno-Verlag, 1977), 201–22, regards the historicity of Judas as the major argument for the pre-Easter existence of the Twelve. For the use of this criterion of "embarrassment" see further Meier, *Companions and Competitors*, 125–97. After the careful discussion by Meier, *Companions and Competitors*, 141–46, 208–11, there should remain no basis for disputing the historicity of Judas and his act of betrayal: "There is no cogent reason why the early church should have gone out of its way to invent such a troubling tradition as Jesus' betrayal by Judas, one of his chosen Twelve" (p. 142). "None of the Old Testament texts cited, taken by itself, could have given rise to the idea of the betrayal of Jesus by one of the Twelve" (p. 143).

Jewish officials handed Jesus over to Pilate, what was to stop a Judas, knowing of their enmity, from going to them and easing their task?[79]

2.3. The Core Narrative of the Meal Itself (Mark 14:22–25)

The account of the central feature in the meal, as the tradition saw it, faces a complex of critical questions. It will be convenient to begin with the general objections to its historicity voiced by the Seminar. Many of these rest on work by Burton L. Mack that will be considered in more detail below.

2.3.1. General Objections to the Historicity of the Meal

2.3.1.1. The Seminar's Critical Comments on Mark's Version

The Seminar's basic argument against historicity rests on the fact that the earliest mention of the meal held by Jesus comes from Paul some twenty years or so before the writing of the earliest Gospel. Likewise, Paul provides the earliest mention of the church's meal. It is then argued that the church meal described by Paul originated in Asia Minor and Greece, not in Jerusalem. Two background points are advanced in support of this conclusion.[80]

First, Jews did not drink blood as a matter of religious principle; even the thought of drinking the blood of Jesus symbolically would have been offensive, an attitude that is accurately reported in John 6:48–66. This symbolism of drinking the blood of a god cannot have arisen in a Jewish context and probably developed in a pagan context.[81]

---

[79] There is, of course, the historical question of whether Judas's motives can be made credible. Treachery and the lure of money are well-attested human sins. The investigation is complicated by the desire of some scholars to paint a different picture of Judas in which he is no longer a treacherous friend. But there is no good historical reason for disputing that Judas could have been motivated so to act. Cf. Casey, *Aramaic Sources*, 232. William Klassen, "The Authenticity of Judas' Participation in the Arrest of Jesus," in *Authenticating the Activities of Jesus* (ed. Bruce D. Chilton and Craig A. Evans; Leiden: Brill, 1999), 389–410, disputes strongly that the action was one of betrayal and holds that it was a "handing over" carried out in obedience to Christ himself; nevertheless, he does not question the historicity of the handing over in some form. It is not clear to me how Klassen can make this alternative motivation credible.

[80] Funk and Seminar, *The Acts of Jesus*, 139–42.

[81] In passing, we may observe that the suggestion (by a member of the Seminar) that "Jesus was himself interpreting what went on in the sacrificial cult in the temple in terms of his own body and blood" is rejected without any reason being given (Funk and Seminar, *The Acts of Jesus*, 139). The reference here is presumably to various works by Bruce D. Chilton in which he develops the view that, having failed to achieve purity in the temple, Jesus substituted for it bread as his "body," i. e., sacrificial victim (cf. Heb 10:5; Gen 15:11), and wine as his "blood," i. e., sacrificial offering (Bruce D. Chilton, *The Temple of Jesus: His Sacrificial Program Within a Cultural History of Sacrifice* [University Park: Pennsylvania State University, 1992]; Bruce D. Chilton, *A Feast of Meanings: Eucharistic Theologies from Jesus Through Johannine Circles* [NovTSup 72; Leiden: Brill, 1994]; Bruce Chilton,

Second, a better background is found in the Hellenistic customs of celebrating a meal in memory of a dead person and drinking a cup in honor of some god. When the jailer gives Socrates the fatal cup of hemlock, the latter says "What do you say about making a libation out of this cup to some god?" (i.e., pouring out some of the contents as an offering to the god. Plato, *Phaedo* 117).

From this background developed the story told by Paul (1 Cor 11:23–26). Mark then modified the Pauline interpretation. He transferred the "in memory of me" motif to the preceding story (Mark 14:9), and he connected the meal to the celebration of the arrival of the future kingdom beyond time (Mark 14:25).

The Seminar admits that Jesus did have meals with his disciples that had symbolical significance in terms of egalitarianism, at which he taught,[82] and that sometimes they were criticized as scenes of scandalous over-indulgence. Therefore there was a last meal, but what purports to be a historical narrative of it in Mark is most probably fictitious.[83]

2.3.1.2. The Seminar's Critical Comments on Matthew's Version

The other Gospel accounts naturally fare no better. Further evidence relating to the story is offered in the comments on Matthew's version; these could equally well have been gathered together into the section on Mark.[84] The Seminar now enlarges on the argument against Paul's version of the church's meal by arguing that what Paul saw as a memorial meal was originally a meal celebrating the arrival of the kingdom. The evidence adduced for this is the material in the *Didache*.[85] We are reminded that neither Q nor

---

Jesus' Prayer and Jesus' Eucharist: His Personal Practice of Spirituality [Valley Forge: Trinity, 1997]). So far as I can see, on this view Jesus was not identifying the bread and wine with himself (Chilton, *Feast of Meanings*, 63–74; Chilton, *The Temple of Jesus*, 152–53). It would appear, therefore, that the summary by the Seminar is at least misleading. Chilton holds that Jesus may have made this kind of statement at several meals after his failed action in the temple, and that what Judas betrayed was this rejection of the temple system. Against Chilton see Klawans, "Interpreting the Last Supper," 9–17, who argues from the lack of anti-temple attitudes in the early church.

[82] It is quite extraordinary that, if Jesus "undoubtedly taught at meals," virtually nothing of what he actually said was actually remembered by anybody. He must have been a very poor teacher! On Jesus' fellowship at meals see in this volume ch. 6.

[83] Nevertheless, it just scraped into the "grey" category, presumably because of voices such as Chilton's.

[84] Funk and Seminar, *The Acts of Jesus*, 250–51. The only comment referring specifically to Matthew is to note the addition of the phrase "for the forgiveness of sins," which is generally held to be an (appropriate) interpretive comment by Matthew.

[85] Possibly the decision to include the evidence of the *Didache* at this point in the exposition (rather than in the discussion of the basic Marcan narrative) was because of the links that have often been seen between it and Matthew. But this point is not mentioned, and the account in the *Didache* is not significantly closer to Matthew than to the other Gospels.

the Gospel of Thomas refer to a last supper, and told that Jesus did not focus on his own actions or death.[86]

These objections all focus on the question of a Jewish or pagan background and origin for the meal. Other difficulties arise with the dating of the meal and the consequent problem of its nature; the establishment of what actually happened; and the interpretation of what was said and done.

2.3.1.3. *The Seminar's Critical Comments on Luke's Version*

A further installment of the argument is included in the Seminar's reflections on Luke's version.[87]

An obvious variation here is the fact that the order of the bread and cup is different. Or rather, in the generally accepted text of Luke there are two cups, one before and one after the bread. In some textual authorities Luke 22:19b–20 is missing, and if this is original there is a simple inversion of the order. This order coincides with that in the *Didache*, which may suggest that there was no fixed practice; or possibly Luke has expanded the narrative to imitate Jewish practice at the Passover with two cups, one to sanctify the occasion, and one in memory of the events of Exodus.

Only at this point does the Seminar introduce the problem of the apparent variation in the dating of Jesus' meal between the Synoptics and John. They note that in John Jesus apparently has his meal the night before the Passover.[88] The two different datings cannot both be right (although both might be wrong). The Seminar concluded from the description of the meal that it was not a normal Passover meal and therefore the Synoptic date must be erroneous. They back up this statement by reference to the lack of paschal features in Paul and the *Didache*. "In view of the discrepancies in date and description of the meal, the Seminar concluded that the synoptic account was not the report of an actual event."[89]. A typical Jesus meal came

---

[86] One might observe somewhat cynically that this last remark is not surprising after the way in which all such references to Jesus speaking about himself or his fate have been carefully edited out of the Gospels. The broader issue of whether Jesus foresaw his death should be mentioned. Denial of this possibility may well be suspected to lie behind much of the skepticism regarding the Last Supper narratives. That at least by this point Jesus did expect to die is widely affirmed by contemporary scholarship.

[87] Funk and Seminar, *The Acts of Jesus*, 347–48.

[88] Some of this material is repeated in the Seminar's discussion of John (Funk and Seminar, *The Acts of Jesus*, 417–21). They note that John's account omits any reference to the bread and cup and the action described is purely the feet-washing. There is no meal involving bread and wine. The date of the meal is different. Nevertheless, they observe that the narrative has the same kind of structure as in Luke (prophecy of betrayal followed by extensive teaching, but on different themes). They conclude that the whole account in John is imaginary.

[89] Funk and Seminar, *The Acts of Jesus*, 348.

to be identified with a hypothetical Passover meal and then the bread and wine were interpreted theologically.

2.3.1.4. Bultmann's objections

The account given by the Seminar is very similar to that of Bultmann. He states that the account of the inauguration of the meal is a "cult legend," as others had previously claimed; by this he means a story created to give a rationale for a ritual. Comparing Mark 14:18 and 22 (with their double mention of the occasion) shows that we have two traditions side by side. But vv. 22–25 hardly record what followed on from vv. 12–16 since there is no mention of at this point of the Passover; thus Mark refers to "bread" and not to unleavened bread; the participants drink from one cup (contrary to Passover custom); no reader would see the beginning of a meal in 22 and its end in 23; and there is no mention of a lamb. In vv. 22–25 a Hellenistic cult legend has displaced an original account of Passover meal. There is some older material in Luke, but Luke's narrative has the (unhistorical) character of a biographical legend.[90]

Putting these points together the following areas of discussion arise: the question of pagan or Jewish origins for the NT accounts; and the particular form of this hypothesis proposed by Burton L. Mack; the relevance of the *Didache*; the evolution of early church meals; the text of Luke's version of the narrative; the question of the paschal nature and setting of the meal, and the reported sayings of Jesus at the meal. Each of these will be discussed in turn.

2.3.2. Jewish or Pagan Origins and Background of the Meal

The Pauline evidence is certainly significant, but not in the way that it is used in the critical comments made by the Seminar.[91]

First, like most if not virtually all early Christian congregations, the church in Corinth was evangelized by Jewish Christians and consisted of a mix of Jewish and Gentile Christians. The postulation of Gentile congregations that would have followed purely pagan Hellenistic models without any restraining Jewish influence goes against all the evidence. Neither Acts

---

[90] Bultmann, *Geschichte*, 285–87; cf. Rudolf Bultmann, *Theology of the New Testament* (trans. Kendrick Grobel; 2 vols.; New York: Scribner, 1951–55), 1:57–58, 144–52.

[91] For a full description of the different types of Graeco-Roman and Jewish meals see most conveniently Smith, *From Symposium to Eucharist*; cf. Klauck, *Herrenmahl und Hellenistischer Kult*; Matthias Klinghardt, *Gemeinschaftsmahl und Mahlgemeinschaft: Soziologie und Liturgie frühchristlicher Mahlfeiern* (Texte und Arbeiten zum neutestamentlichen Zeitalter; Tübingen: Francke Verlag, 1996). At a more popular level see Ben Witherington, III, *Making a Meal of It: Rethinking the Theology of the Lord's Supper* (Waco: Baylor University Press, 2007).

nor Paul know of purely Gentile congregations. A Jewish presence of some kind is clearly attested for the congregations in Rome, Corinth, Thessalonica, Philippi, Ephesus, Colossae, Galatia, Antioch, and the congregations reflected in the Pastoral Epistles.[92] If so, it is highly likely that the memory of the meals held by Jesus with his disciples and the meals held from the earliest days of the church in Jerusalem would have had a strong influence on the practices of the Pauline churches.[93]

Second, whatever some of the Greek members of the congregation in Corinth may have got up to in terms of over-eating and drinking, their practice was not in line with Paul's own ideas, and he corrected them strenuously. In particular, he attacked those who ate meals in pagan temples (1 Cor 8–10). Paul can hardly have taken over practices that were so compromised.

To say this is not to deny that Jewish meals were already Hellenized to some extent by this time, but they were still governed by Jewish conventions. Consequently the distinction that is being drawn between Hellenistic meals and Jewish meals in the Christian congregations is a false one, and the fact that the Corinthian meal had degenerated into a rowdy Hellenistic party is not an argument against its having its origin in a more seemly Jewish type of meal.

Third, the Seminar bundles together the practices of holding memorial meals and offering libations, which were regarded as offerings to a deity. The term libation strictly referred to the pouring out of part of the contents of a cup in honor of a god before the consumption of the remainder, but it came to refer to the whole action.[94] The example of a libation offered by the Seminar is, as we have seen, that of Socrates, but this obviously did not take place at a memorial meal, and Socrates did not drink the cup of hemlock in honor of "some god" (it does not seem to matter which one!). The libation is a red herring in this enquiry.[95] There is nothing in any of the accounts of the Christian meals to suggest that a libation took place.

Fourth, what about the practice of memorial meals? The Pauline (and the [longer] Lucan) narratives are concerned with the setting up of a meal that will remember Jesus. The Last Supper itself is clearly not a memorial meal, since it occurs before the death of Jesus, but is at best the basis for holding one. The question is then: did the concept of a memorial Lord's Supper

---

[92] Even in Lystra there is Timothy's Jewish mother; we have no information about Derbe.

[93] Cf. Hahn, *Die Einheit*, 533–34.

[94] Smith, *From Symposium to Eucharist*, 28–30.

[95] The metaphor is used in a totally different context of Paul's possible death seen as an accompaniment to the sacrificial service of the readers (Phil 2:17; cf. 2 Tim 4:6). Nothing here suggests a reference to any kind of church ritual. The use of the language no more permits the conclusion that Christians offered libations than does the use of the language of wagers ("you can bet your life on it") imply gambling by modern Christians.

develop against a background of similar meals, whether Jewish or Graeco-Roman, and/or on the basis of a putative Last Supper?

Jeremias investigated the language of remembering the dead person used in the narratives and concluded that it could not be accounted for as a development from practices in ancient commemorative meals. The lack of evidence for dependence in respect of the feature that might be regarded as most characteristic of the remembrance motif speaks strongly against the form of the meal as a whole being derived from such a source.[96] Of course, the practice of having such a meal could be influenced by the knowledge that such events took place, but once again the characteristic content of the Christian meal cannot be explained from this background.[97] Nor must it be forgotten that for early Christians the Lord who died is the Lord who was raised from the dead, and therefore a memorial meal, in the sense of remembering somebody whose life and activity came to an end with his death, is excluded.[98]

Fifth, drinking the blood of a god is not the same thing as pouring a libation as an offering to a god. Consequently, the latter does not provide any parallel to the concept of drinking blood if that is what is meant by the symbolism of the cup in the Lord's Supper.[99] I do not know of any evidence from Graeco-Roman sources for wine being drunk to symbolize drinking the blood of a deity.[100] Nor is it easy to see how a meal involving the symbolism of a loaf could have developed out of this.

---

[96] Jeremias, *Eucharistic Words*, 237–43.

[97] Cf. I. Howard Marshall, *Last Supper and Lord's Supper* (Exeter: Paternoster, 1980), 27–29, and the authorities cited there. I am not aware that subsequent research has altered the situation.

[98] Cf. Gordon D. Fee, *The First Epistle to the Corinthians* (NICNT; Grand Rapids: Eerdmans, 1987), 552.

[99] Within a Jewish context with its abhorrence of drinking blood, "the symbolic context is too strong for the disciples to have felt seriously that they had drunk blood" (Casey, *Aramaic Sources*, 241). Consequently, there is no need for the hypothesis that the use of the cup can only have arisen in a non-Jewish context. The description of (red) wine as "the blood of the grape" is found in Gen 49:11; Deut 32:14; Sir 39:26; 50:15; 1 Macc 6:34, and the symbolism of the wine press for slaughter and shedding of blood occurs in Isa 63:1–6; Jer 25:15–31 (see O. Böcher, "αἷμα," *EDNT* 1:39). There is thus no need for any non-Jewish background to account for the choice of wine as a symbol of blood and especially of blood shed in slaughter or sacrifice. From there the path to understanding the drinking of the wine that is a symbol of the shed blood as a symbol of sharing in the benefits conveyed by the death would seem to be natural enough. It is striking, however, that none of the eucharistic texts in the NT actually refers to wine but only to the cup.

[100] In the taurobolium it was actual blood that was drunk, not something symbolizing it. R. B. Edwards reminds me that the Dionysiac rites included eating the raw flesh of an animal, presumably complete with its blood, but, although Dionysius was the god of wine, there is no indication that the rite was specifically linked to drinking wine.

Sixth, one of the early designations of the congregational meal is "breaking of bread" (Acts 2:42; *Did.* 14:1; cf. Luke 24:35). The verbal form, found in Acts 2:46; 20:7, 11; 27:35–36 (cf. Ign. *Eph.* 20:4), was known to Paul (1 Cor 10:16). This phrase is hardly an appropriate designation for a rite whose central element was a libation or some other form of drink, and it makes it extremely unlikely that the occasion developed from any such rite. If it is correct to interpret the Pauline phrase "as often as you drink it" (1 Cor 11:25) to imply that there were occasions at which wine was not available and only bread was shared,[101] this would strengthen the point: such wine-less occasions are hardly likely to have developed out of a rite in which the use of a libation was basic. However, this point is less certain.[102] The household setting may also be relevant, pointing away from anything resembling the meeting of an association to a more family-oriented situation. Even though wine appears to have been plentiful for rich people in the Corinthian situation, it cannot be assumed that this was so everywhere else in the early church.

Seventh, Paul developed his case against malpractices at the congregational meal by reference to a tradition. The wording is a citation, not Paul's own. The most plausible source for it is the same as that from which he gained his summary of the kerygma (1 Cor 15:3–5), but the latter is clearly of Jewish-Christian origin.[103] Paul emphasized his unity on all essential points with other Jewish Christians including those associated with Jerusalem. It is utterly impossible that he got his tradition about the Lord's Supper from any other source than a Jewish-Christian one. Moreover, the traditions are most plausibly connected with the time of his conversion and his early associations with believers in Jerusalem and Antioch. Stuhlmacher asserts that the tradition would have come from the circle around Stephen, who got it from the apostles, and so it can be traced back to Jesus.[104] Had Paul differed significantly from the Jerusalem church, he could not have penned what he says in Galatians 2 about the essential agreement between them, sealed with the right hand of fellowship. Unless we accuse Paul of being

---

[101] Schröter, *Das Abendmahl*, 36 (n. 51), 51 (n. 67). Similarly, Hahn, *Die Einheit*, 545.

[102] Schürmann, *Der Einsetzungsbericht*, 70, 72, rejected it on the grounds that there is no evidence for wine-less celebrations in the apostolic congregations. However, Schröter, *Das Abendmahl*, 36 (n. 51), 51 (n. 67), 102–110, notes the use of bread only (or bread and water) in the *Acts of John* and *Acts of Thomas*, apparently for ascetic reasons. In any case, the extended repetition in v. 26, which applies the corresponding phrase to the bread, makes this interpretation uncertain.

[103] See Hengel, "Das Mahl in der Nacht". Klein, *Das Lukasevangelium*, 732, notes evidence suggesting that Paul and Luke used the same early traditions about the mission and sayings of Jesus.

[104] Stuhlmacher, *Theologie*, 1:364.

economical with the truth[105] or incompetent,[106] he got his understanding of the meal from Jewish Christians.[107]

Eighth, when Paul relates the narrative of the Last Supper in 1 Cor 11, he states that he had already shared it with the readers, and the obvious conclusion is that he did so during his lengthy founding visit to Corinth. What he is attacking in the letter are subsequent practices that had developed on the part of some in the congregation, not practices that he himself had introduced; they are perversions of the rite, not fundamental parts of it from the beginning. That is to say, there is no evidence for any earlier form of the Corinthian meal than the form introduced by Paul, which was subsequently subjected to some malpractice; the hypothesis that the Corinthians created their own church meal on the analogy of Hellenistic meals and Paul only later corrected it by reference to an existing Jewish-Christian tradition (or the fabrication of such a tradition) has no sound basis.

Ninth, the actual content of this tradition is plainly Jewish, or rather Jewish Christian. This is immediately evident from the references to the new covenant and to the coming of the Lord. It is also clear from the reference in 1 Cor 10:16 to the "cup of blessing."[108] The tradition is traced back to "the Lord," which in this case will be a reference to a tradition relating what the Lord said and did that gives the church its instructions and authority for

---

[105] This raises the question of whether early Christians might have fabricated "historical" items. For example, Andrew T. Lincoln, *The Gospel According to Saint John* (BNTC; London: Continuum; Peabody: Hendrickson, 2005), 15–17, writes: "such historians would mix more factual reporting with accounts of incidents that might or could have happened. What was important to them was that this elaborated material might be plausible and illustrate the general truths they wanted to draw out about their subject. In ancient biography there was even less of a distinction between what we would call 'factual' and 'fictional' elements ... what we know of this genre should lead us to expect, as ancient readers would also have done, a narrative which contained a substratum of core events from the tradition with substantial correspondence to what happened in the past but which was now shaped by an interpretive superstructure with varying amounts of embellishment, including some legendary or what we would call 'fictive' elements." Here, however, we are not dealing with a historian but with a transmitter of tradition. In view of what we know about the nature of early Christian traditions this is not the context in which a purely fictive account would be developed; cf. Richard Bauckham, *Jesus and the Eyewitnesses: The Gospels as Eyewitness Testimony* (Grand Rapids: Eerdmans, 2006); Dunn, *Jesus Remembered*; Hengel and Schwemer, *Jesus und das Judentum*, 244–62.

[106] The criticism may, of course, apply to the person who fabricated the tradition if this was not Paul himself.

[107] Hahn, *Die Einheit*, 556, urges that the development of a common meal in Antioch involving both Jews and Gentiles is inconceivable if it did not have a basis in Palestinian (i. e., Jewish-Christian) tradition.

[108] The phraseology is Jewish (*Jos. Asen.* 8:5; 19:5; Leonhard Goppelt, "ποτήριον," *TDNT* 6:154–58); cf. Anthony C. Thiselton, *The First Epistle to the Corinthians: A Commentary on the Greek Text* (NIGTC; Grand Rapids: Eerdmans; Carlisle: Paternoster, 2000), 756–60.

what it is to do. But it is surely wildly improbable that some practice derived from pagan practices could be described in this way.

Tenth, a contrast is sometimes made between a type of meal celebrating the coming of the kingdom and the Pauline meal remembering the death of Jesus. This is a mistake.[109] As regards the eschatological expectation, if the last meal of Jesus with his disciples was one celebrating the arrival of God's kingdom (Mark 14:25; Luke 22:15-18),[110] this one looks forward with anticipation to the point when he comes. Also, if the cry of Maranatha is rightly connected to the Pauline meal, then it expresses the longing for the coming of the Lord. The Maranatha cry is also part of the formal prayer in *Did.* 10:6, and for the early church the prayer for the coming of the Lord is functionally equivalent to the longing for the coming of the Kingdom: the King (Messiah and Lord) and the Kingdom are one. Consequently, the contrast drawn between the meal of Jesus and the Pauline meal is false.

Eleventh, the other part of the contrast is the allegation that the Pauline meal introduces the element of memorializing of the death of Jesus which was not part of any meal held by Jesus. Certainly, there is no mention of his death in the other meal scenes in the Gospels,[111] but this is not surprising. Nevertheless, throughout the Gospels there is an undercurrent of allusion to Jesus' suffering and death that forms a solid basis for the view that he expected to be put to death and referred to this in his teaching to his closest disciples.[112] A meal held at the point of crisis when everything was closing in on Jesus would surely be colored by it.

Finally, we have already noted that the absence of the last meal from such a putative collection of sayings as Q and the late compilation in the Gospel of Thomas is in no way remarkable, given the genre of these collections. It cannot be used as evidence that the meal did not happen.

The arguments so far against the Jewish character of the church's meal and its links to a putative Last Supper are accordingly to be rejected as uncon-

---

[109] This is an example of the failure to recognize the complexity of historical realities and the way in which motifs can be readily combined without any feeling of incompatability.

[110] This interpretation is often applied to other meals of Jesus. Cf. Meier, *Mentor, Message, and Miracles*, 302–9.

[111] An exception might be the meal at Bethany where Jesus interprets the anointing with ointment as an anointing for his burial (Mark 14:1-9), and in John the feeding miracle becomes the occasion for a subsequent discourse in which the significance of the death of Jesus is discussed (John 6).

[112] The case made by Vincent Taylor, *Jesus and His Sacrifice: A Study of the Passion-Sayings in the Gospels* (London: Macmillan, 1937), has been powerfully developed and restated by such scholars as Joachim Jeremias, "παῖς θεοῦ," *TDNT* 5:712-17, and McKnight, *Jesus and His Death*; cf. Joachim Gnilka, *Jesus of Nazareth: Message and History* (trans. Siegfried S. Schatzmann; Peabody, Mass.: Hendrickson, 1997), 282–84, and references cited there.

vincing. The Seminar invites us to postulate the existence of an imaginary meal for which there is no positive evidence.

2.3.3. Burton L. Mack's Reconstruction of a Hellenistic Origin

Against the background of these general considerations we now focus on the hypothesis propounded by Burton L. Mack that forms the basis for the Seminar's attempt to find a Hellenistic origin for the church's meal and for the Lord's Supper narrative that came to be associated with it.[113]

2.3.3.1. Paul's Aetiological Myth

Without any attempt at argument, Mack rejects the attempt of Jeremias to reconstruct the original wording of the narrative. He regards the traditions in the Pauline texts as older than those in the Synoptic texts.[114] According to his interpretation of the Pauline evidence, Christians followed the pattern of Hellenistic association meals. At such pagan meals "the pattern was to gather, eat together, then sing a hymn and pour out a libation to the patron deity in preparation for the party or meeting to follow."[115] The Christians adapted this by including appropriate after-dinner discourse. Two special moments were given symbolical value. "Eating bread and drinking wine" is a shorthand reference to a meal. The Christians substituted thanksgiving for the bread for the Jewish blessing over it.[116] The meal was ritualized as they worked out the Christ myth. Body and blood are motifs taken from the martyrological tradition. Paul uses the idea of the new covenant to relate the death of Christ to the establishment of the new community. "The etiological features ... that imagine the Lord Jesus presiding and saying the words must be recognized as cult legend." Similarly, "do this in remembrance of me" must be set aside. What is left is a connection between the two special moments of the meal and the death of the martyr. The wine would be more easily associated with the death, especially if the earliest practice was a libation. The breaking of bread would start the dining occasion. "One could imagine an early thanksgiving to the effect that Christ handed his body over 'for' the gathered community."[117] The breaking of the bread could have been linked to this. The formula "this is my body" could then arise, evoking various associations. The meal was not sacrificial, memorializing Jesus' death as a sacrifice by re-enacting

---

[113] Mack, *Myth*, 114–20, 298–304.
[114] Mack, *Myth*, 298.
[115] Mack, *Myth*, 114.
[116] Note in passing that this fails to recognize that thanksgiving and blessing are in fact identical. The blessing is a blessing (or thanking) of God for his provision, not something that is done to the food. See further n. 300.
[117] Mack, *Myth*, 119.

the Last Supper. Early Christian meals functioned in various ways, one example being found in the *Didache* where there is no influence from the Hellenistic martyr myth.[118] But the Pauline text is "evidence for an early social formation as a strictly religious society, complete with myth, ritual, and symbol system, that makes the Hellenistic Christ cult distinctively different from the groups formed by the Jesus movements." [119]

2.3.3.1. Mark's "Historical" Narrative

At a later stage, according to Mack, Mark turned this aetiological myth found in Paul into a historical narrative: First, Mark took the reference to Jesus being handed over (sc. by God) and from it developed the narrative of betrayal by Judas. Second, whereas the meal intervenes between the symbols in the Pauline text, Mark linked the bread and cup together as a narrative requirement. He also included Judas as a partaker of the meal. Third, there is no mention of a memorial in Mark. His account was not meant to serve as an "institution" of the church's meal but as a narrative of a final meal of Jesus with his disciples. Finally, there is more stress on the cup. Mark added "poured out for many," deleted "new" and produced an infelicitous phrase ("my blood of the covenant"). In this way he gained an allusion to Exod 24:8 and possibly also to martyrdom (blood "poured out" as in Luke 11:50–51).

In Mack's reconstruction, in these ways Mark de-emphasized the cultic nuances of the Hellenistic meal and strengthened the martyrological identifications by linking the narrative to the motif of the persecuted righteous One as a martyr.

2.3.3.2. An Exercise in Imagination

What is happening here? We start from a well-attested account of a narrative known to Paul and purporting to go back to earlier Christians – an account that refers to an event whose historicity there is no inherent reason to disbelieve. We are then invited to accept in its place what is frankly an imaginary reconstruction of a process of forming an aetiological myth that has no basis in history. But why should we prefer trusting the imagination of Mack to giving some credence to Paul?[120] We should remember that Paul's account is dated within 25 years at most, probably less, of the event,

---

[118] Mack, *Myth*, 120, n. 15.

[119] Mack, *Myth*, 120.

[120] Clearly Paul's account, if it is false, was not the product of a "mistake" by whoever was responsible for devising it. It was a deliberate attempt to mislead, and the goodness of the motive does not alter the verdict on the means used. Even if Paul claimed to have had a revelation of something previously unknown, the Twelve would have been able to "test the Spirit" and reject it.

and persons who would have been present at the event, were still alive and in contact with Paul and the congregation at Corinth, specifically including Peter, James and John. How is it even remotely conceivable that this group hatched a plan to delude their followers with a story that had no historical basis? Wright is justified in commenting:

> I find it simply incredible that so central and early a tradition as Paul recounts in 1 Cor. 11.23–6 would have been invented wholesale by the early church without a firm basis in Jesus' own actions.[121]

Further, Paul and his apostolic colleagues were Jews, and all the language that is used is Jewish. We have seen the possibility of Gentile Christians being infected by Hellenistic Graeco-Roman practices, but what Paul is doing is reminding them of Jewish roots and doing all he can to avoid contamination of the congregation by pagan customs.

The key stages in Mack's argument are appeals to imagination. Thus the proposal that the Christian meetings originally included the pouring out of a libation[122] is sheer unfounded and improbable speculation. The notion that the Christians somehow came to see a loaf as a symbol of a martyr's body likewise must presumably rest on imagination, since no evidence is provided. Although the term "body" is found in the Jewish martyrological texts, it is more because of its being the locus of physical pain and maltreatment; it is the identification of the body of the sufferer with a loaf of bread that is lacking. The suggestion that the breaking of bread and the libation were combined at the start of the Hellenistic symposium seems to be unfounded; the former action is, however, well-attested for Jewish meals.[123]

Whatever does not fit the proposed development is simply cast aside by Mack. In his explanations of what is left the crucial phrase is "one could imagine." But what basis is there for such a feat of imagination other than the postulate that the account cannot be historical?

2.3.3.3. Conclusion

The effect of these considerations is to show that the kind of meal held in Corinth was essentially Jewish rather than pagan, although it was perhaps inevitable that a Christian meal would be compared with pagan ones and be in danger of contamination from them since many of the converts were former pagans and brought with them pagan standards of morality from which Paul had to wean them away. But the hypothesis that would derive

---

[121] Wright, *Jesus and the Victory of God*, 558, n. 81.
[122] The inclusion of a libation in the Christian meal as the bridge between Hellenistic meals and Christian ones is clearly implied in Mack's treatment.
[123] The phrase "break bread" is said not to be found in secular Greek, Philo, or Josephus (Johannes Behm, "κλάω, κτλ," *TDNT* 3:728). It is Jewish.

the origin of the Christian meal from pagan ones simply founders on the facts of the Jewish background and the lack of pagan characteristics other than the basic similarities that would be found in formal meals of any kind.

There is no need to place the Jewish-Christian type of meal and Hellenistic meals in an either/or relationship. Witherington has rightly emphasized that Hellenistic influences affected Jewish meals.[124] Therefore drawing attention to the Hellenistic influences that could have gone into the development of Christian meals is not an argument against the presence of Jewish features and the influence of early Christian traditions going back to Jesus. This fact is recognized by scholars who want to find a background to the church's meals in Jesus' fellowship meals with his disciples but not in the specific event of the last supper.

2.3.4. The Evidence of the Didache

One particular document, the *Didache*, has been thought to gives us a window into the existence of an ongoing early practice of meals that bore little resemblance to the Pauline ones. The argument is that the *Didache* is a reasonably early document that "makes no mention of a last supper, of Passover, nor does it connect eucharist with the passion of Jesus."[125] The Seminar picks up the claim by J. D. Crossan that the *Didache* reflects Jesus' frequent meals with his disciples at open table; these were then ritualized to give initially the kind of meal described in the *Didache*. Then it was developed in a different manner by Paul and finally formalized in the account in Mark.[126] Crossan finds six stages in the development of the motif:

– Stage 1: Commensality with a *deipnon* followed by a *symposion*.
– Stage 2: Open commensality, where Jesus and his friends have a meal which in the light of events turns out to have been a last meal.
– Stage 3: The meal(s) described in the *Didache*.

---

[124] Witherington, *Making a Meal of It*, 32. However, this is a far cry from arguing that any of the meals in the Gospels are described redactionally as, or were historically, similar to Greco-Roman symposia; see in this volume ch. 6.

[125] Funk and Seminar, *The Acts of Jesus*, 250.

[126] John Dominic Crossan, *The Historical Jesus: The Life of a Mediterranean Jewish Peasant* (San Francisco: HarperSanFrancisco, 1991), 360–67. A similar view is taken by Riggs, "Sacred Food," 256–62; see further Mack, *Myth*, 120, n. 15. Schmithals, *Theologiegeschichte des Urchristentums*, 208–10, finds an eschatological meal that is not in continuity with the meals of Jesus with his disciples and friends but is nevertheless a survival from the earliest church. See also Klaus Berger, *Theologiegeschichte des Urchristentums: Theologie des Neuen Testaments* (Tübingen: Francke Verlag, 1994), 282–87; Bernd Kollmann, *Ursprung und Gestalten der frühchristlichen Mahlfeier* (GTA 43; Göttingen: Vandenhoeck & Ruprecht, 1990), 79–101; Klinghardt, *Gemeinschaftsmahl und Mahlgemeinschaft*, 373–492.

- Stage 4: The pre-Pauline tradition in 1 Cor 11.[127]
- Stage 5: The meal in Mark 14 and parallels.
- Stage 6: John 6:51–58.

According to Crossan, the account in the *Didache* combines two originally separate accounts of celebrations, *Did.* 10 (the earlier one) and *Did.* 9, each containing four parts: the introductory command, the double thanksgiving, the apocalyptic prayer, and the warning concerning worthiness.[128] There is no ritualization of the bread or cup and no reference to the passion. Crossan cannot believe that the community reflected here knew about the eucharistic elements and yet deliberately ignored them; they must have been ignorant of them. This silence is held to be original. The existence of this pattern alongside or prior to the pre-Pauline form is held to show that the latter cannot go back to Jesus. In the latter the references to body and blood indicate a martyrological tradition. Mark's Passover meal is interpreted as

---

[127] At this point Crossan's scheme is similar to that of Mack and is open to the same objections.

[128] The texts are as follows in J.B. Lightfoot and J.R. Harmer, *The Apostolic Fathers: Revised Greek Texts with Introductions and English Translations* (Grand Rapids: Baker, 1984), 232–34, with the English updated:

9:1 But as regards the eucharistic thanksgiving give thanks thus. ² First, as regards the cup: We give you thanks, our Father, for the holy vine of your son David, which you made known to us through your Son Jesus; yours is the glory for ever and ever.

9:3 Then as regards the broken bread: We give you thanks, our Father, for the life and knowledge which you made known to us through your Son Jesus; yours is the glory for ever and ever. ⁴ As this broken bread was scattered upon the mountains and being gathered together became one, so may your church be gathered together from the ends of the earth into your kingdom; for yours is the glory and the power through Jesus Christ for ever and ever.

9:5 But let no one eat or drink of this eucharistic thanksgiving except those that have been baptized into the name of the Lord; for concerning this also the Lord said: "Give not that which is holy to the dogs."

10:1 And after you are satisfied, give thanks thus: ² We give you thanks, holy Father, for your holy name, which you have made to tabernacle in our hearts, and for the knowledge and faith and immortality, which you have made known to us through your Son Jesus; yours is the glory for ever and ever. ³ You, almighty Master, created all things for your name's sake and gave food and drink to human beings for enjoyment, that they might render thanks to you; but you bestowed upon us spiritual food and drink and eternal life through your Son. ⁴ Before all things we give you thanks that you are powerful; yours is the glory for ever and ever. ⁵ Remember, Lord, your church to deliver it from all evil and to perfect it in your love; and "gather it together from the four winds" – even the church which has been sanctified – into your kingdom which you have prepared for it; for yours is the power and glory for ever and ever. ⁶ May grace come and may this world pass away. Hosanna to the God of David. If any one is holy, let them come; if any one is not, let them repent. Maranatha. Amen.

10:7 But permit the prophets to offer thanksgiving as much as they desire.

14:1 And on the Lord's own day gather yourselves together and break bread and give thanks, first confessing your transgression, that your sacrifice may be pure.

an anti-ritualization of the meal (by comparison with Paul). The command to repeat is dropped, and within the structure of Mark the meal shows the disciples' failure to understand Jesus (the betrayal).[129]

2.3.4.1. The Uncertainty Surrounding the Interpretation of the Didache

Various factors indicate that the evidence of the *Didache* must be handled with great caution and not regarded as a firm basis for far-reaching hypotheses.

First, the sources and interpretation of the material in the *Didache* are much disputed. For example, K. Niederwimmer lists some seven different interpretations of the instructions for the meal and himself argues that the description in *Did.* 9–10:5 is that of an ordinary church meal, with prayers before and after the meal, followed after 10:6 by the Lord's Supper (which is not actually described); he has to admit that there is an unsolved problem as regards explaining the absence of any distinctively eucharistic material at this point.[130] If this particular theory were sound, then the differences between the meal described here and the Pauline type of Lord's Supper would be of little or no significance since two different occasions are being described. However, the arguments for such a reconstruction as this are not necessarily any stronger than those for Crossan's hypothesis.

It follows that at the present state of research differences in interpretation regarding the *Didache* are so great that it would be very unsafe to use any particular interpretation of it as a solid basis for wider hypotheses regarding the celebration of the Lord's Supper. With this *caveat* we shall consider the matter on the fairly widely accepted basis that what is described is a church meal that can be regarded as the local example of a "eucharist."

Second, further uncertainty arises because the choice of actual topics covered in the document as a whole is limited and selective. Much is left unmentioned, for example, in the teaching concerning baptism (who may be baptized?). Hence it is not surprising if the congregational meal is dealt with in a fragmentary manner.

Third, a document that does not mention (though it implies) the resurrection and exaltation of Jesus is not a full exposition of the belief and practice of an early Christian church. Neither is anything said about sins in connection with baptism nor about the gift of the Spirit.[131] We may well wonder if

---

[129] There is a fair amount of sheer assertion here with some reference for support to Mack, *Myth*, 118, 298–306.

[130] Kurt Niederwimmer, *The Didache: A Commentary* (trans. Linda M. Maloney; Hermeneia; Minneapolis: Fortress, 1998), 139–43. For arguments against this view see Schröter, *Das Abendmahl*, 68–69.

[131] The use of the trinitarian form does not necessarily imply this.

there is any good reason why the testimony of so fragmentary a representative of Christianity should be preferred to that of the NT documents.

Some of these omissions have been cited as indications of the primitive nature of the contents. For example, it has been argued that the christology of the *Didache* represents Jesus as the Davidic Messiah and nothing more: "the only really tangible Christology identifiable in the *Didache* is a Davidic Christology of Jesus as the heir of David and restorer of the Kingdom of Israel, the Kingdom of God."[132] While this kind of christology is seen by some scholars as being a very early primitive form, this does nothing to date the occurrence in the *Didache*.[133] Ebionitism appears to have continued well into the first century and represents a Jewish form of Christianity that did not reflect higher views of Jesus that may have existed alongside it from the beginning. In any case, alongside this messianic understanding of Jesus as God's servant, we should also note the use of the "Maranatha" prayer which is to be taken as a reference to the coming of Jesus.[134]

The conclusion to be drawn from these comments is that we are dealing with a document whose origins and development are so obscure that it may be a case of *obscurum per obscurius* if we try to reconstruct from it a stage in the early church's meals prior to that reflected in the NT documents.

2.3.4.2. The Meal in the Didache

In the present space it is not possible to enter in any detail into the interpretation of the material and the disputes over this. The position that seems to command most support is that *Did.* 9 and 10 give instructions for a church meal which has come to be known as "thanksgiving" (εὐχαριστία).[135] This was a full meal which was presumably "eucharistic," since we do not know of any other kind of early church meal at this stage (such as an agape meal).

---

[132] Jonathan A. Draper, "Do the Didache and Matthew Reflect an 'Irrevocable Parting of the Ways' with Judaism?" in *Matthew and the Didache: Two Documents from the Same Jewish-Christian Milieu?* (ed. Huub van de Sandt; Assen: Van Gorcum, 2005), 238–39.

[133] Enrico Mazza, "Didache 9–10: Elements of a Eucharistic Interpretation," in *The Didache in Modern Research* (ed. Jonathan A. Draper; Leiden: Brill, 1996), 279–83, argues that the christology in the eucharistic prayers with its references to the house and vine of David must precede the Council of Jerusalem. I find this claim quite unpersuasive. It ignores the recognition of Christ as Lord elsewhere in the *Didache* and in the early church generally.

[134] Cf. Larry W. Hurtado, *Lord Jesus Christ: Devotion to Jesus in Earliest Christianity* (Grand Rapids: Eerdmans, 2003), 617.

[135] The noun εὐχαριστία can mean "that for which thanks has been given, namely the cup and broken [bread]" and hence the food/drink served at the meal and so, by a natural extension the meal (or the event of the meal) as such. The verb εὐχαριστέω clearly means "to give thanks" in *Did.* 9:1 and all the other references. The term εὐχαριστία is found with this sense in Ignatius and Justin but not in the NT.

Whether this meal was a memorial of the death of Jesus with significance attached to his body and blood is a key point of debate.

The view of Crossan that *Did.* 9 and 10 give us two parallel accounts of the same occasion with one account being earlier than the other is speculative and does not appear to be supported by current scholarship on the *Didache*. Nothing can be firmly based upon it.[136]

The absence of the words of institution does not have the significance assigned to it by some scholars as testifying to a form of meal which had developed independently of them. One possibility is that, if words of institution were to be said, they were known from the Gospel and did not need to be included.[137] More probably, however, the words were not actually in use for this purpose at this point (nor indeed in many places for quite some time). There is good evidence that the recital of the words was not constitutive of the meal at this stage; the words functioned in 1 Corinthians as teaching for the congregation, reminding them of what they had forgotten, and 1 Cor 11 provides no proof that they were regularly recited at the meal. Paul presumes familiarity with the words, and this implies that the account was (or should have been) read or recited regularly at Corinth, but he does not say that it ought to be read as an integral part of the memorial meal. On the contrary, it was used to teach the church what Jesus did and to command the church to do what he did.[138] In fact, the practice of reading the account does not seem to have become widespread until very considerably later; a significant number of later liturgical documents do not include the account.[139]

---

[136] A survey of different interpretations is given by Paul F. Bradshaw, *Eucharistic Origins* (London: SPCK, 2004), 24–32: (1) A church meal ancillary to the eucharist proper; (2) A different kind of eucharist from the Pauline eucharist; (3) An Agape meal as opposed to a eucharist; (4) An early form of eucharist. Bradshaw rejects views 1 and 3. He wants to propose that there were several different patterns side by side in the church without placing them in a single evolutionary order. The *Didache* appears to represent one primitive survival still in use at a later date. In particular, Bradshaw hunts for evidence of a rite in which the cup preceded the bread.

[137] The *Didache* knows the Gospel of Matthew (or some of the traditions incorporated in it). However, the fact that the words of the Lord's Prayer are cited in *Did.* 8 suggests that known material could nevertheless be cited.

[138] Paul's citation of a narrative account of what happened at the Last Supper with its command to "do this" does not necessitate that this was actually recited at the congregational meal. The narrative was already known at Corinth and was on a par with the tradition in 1 Cor 15:3–5. This parallel strengthens the case that what Paul records in 1 Cor 11 was not a unique revelation made to himself. The language rather implies that this is church tradition. Cf. the further reference to "traditions" in 1 Cor 11:2. The language and syntax reveal no features that could be said to point clearly either to composition by Paul himself or to use of a tradition.

[139] Cf. Andrew Brian McGowan, "Is There a Liturgical Text in This Gospel?': The Institution Narratives and Their Early Interpretive Communities," *JBL* 118 (1999): 73–87. Various liturgical sources do not include the words. See, for example, Gerard Rouwhorst, "Didache 9–10: A Litmus Test For the Research on Early Christian Liturgy Eucharist," in

Hence, if it was not normal or necessary to repeat the "words of institution" at the meal, their absence is not surprising.

The real issue is whether, even when this account is not cited, the theology that it expresses is present explicitly or implicitly. Within the NT, and for whatever reason, the Gospel of John does not include the account in its description of the Last Supper,[140] even though some familiarity with it must be presupposed on the part of the author in view of the teaching about a feeding upon Christ that brings eternal life in John 6. Thus in 1 Cor 10:14–22, although Paul reflects knowledge of the significance of the cup and bread as symbolizing the blood and body of Christ, he develops the thought in other ways (i. e., without reference to the death of Christ) in terms of participation in the blood and body and then in terms of the unity between those who share in the bread.

One specific thing that the words of institution do not do is to give guidance on what to say in the prayers of thanksgiving. The *Didache* fills this gap by providing a form of words, but this instruction is for those who do not know what to say; where prophets are present, they may pray as they are led by the Spirit (*Did.* 10:7).[141] Where there are no prophets (or alongside them), members of the congregation needed to be given a pattern to follow, and this may well have been the basis for extemporization. Christians would want to give a Christian content and form appropriate to the occasion rather than simply repeating Jewish prayers, and so the *Didache* provides the missing element. That is all that it is seeking to do. Therefore, it may not be so surprising that this is in fact all that it does.[142]

Thus what the Didachist does is to provide the needed information for various points on which guidance was needed. The prayers come first; then the statement about the condition of baptism. Then there is the concluding prayer and the comment on the freedom given to prophets. In a separate section the need for purity on the part of the congregation was emphasized, the reason being added that otherwise their sacrifices will not be pure. The

---

Matthew and the Didache: Two Documents from the Same Jewish-Christian Milieu? (ed. Huub van de Sandt; Assen: Van Gorcum, 2005), 147. W. D. Davies and Dale C. Allison, Jr., *A Critical and Exegetical Commentary on the Gospel According to Saint Matthew* (3 vols.; ICC; Edinburgh: T&T Clark, 1988–97), 3:467, n. 88, comment that this is so in the later *Anaphora of Addai and Mari*, and even in the Gospel of John which betrays knowledge of the significance of body and blood elsewhere. See further Mazza, "Didache 9–10," 289–91.

[140] Witherington, *Making a Meal of It*, 63–85, argues that John's meal is a different occasion from the meal described in the Synoptics, although some material from the latter has been included in his account.

[141] Cf. Niedernwimmer, *The Didache*, 164.

[142] The *Didache*, says Dunn, *Jesus Remembered*, 230, n. 242, may assume the traditional core and simply adds appropriate prayers for the liturgical occasion. Cf. Schröter, *Das Abendmahl*, 66, for the view that the *Didache*'s main concern is to establish the wording of the prayers.

sacrifices consist of thanksgiving, and the purity lies in the purity of those who give thanks, which is achieved by confession of sin prior to taking part (*Did.* 14).

2.3.4.3. Comparing the Didache with Paul's Writing

Does this set of instructions witness to a kind of occasion (and theology) different from that implied and described by Paul? There is a strong case that very similar occasions are being described. The *Didache* shows numerous points in common with the Pauline material: First, the implication that the meal takes place on Sunday is common to both (*Did.* 14:1; 1 Cor 16). Second, in both cases baptism and the meal are paired and treated alongside each other. In the *Didache* the meal is specifically for the baptized (*Did.* 9:5). This is implied in 1 Cor 10 where the analogy with the Israelites who were "all" baptized into Moses and "all" (the same group) participated in the heavenly food must be determinative. Third, the need for the participants to be "pure" in order to participate is found in both accounts (1 Cor 11:28). The motif of exclusion of the unworthy is already present in 1 Corinthians. In 1 Cor 10 it is present in the injunction not to share in pagan feasts as well as the Lord's Supper. The warning against food offered to idols recurs in *Did.* 6:3 The meal fellowship brings about or symbolizes a fellowship with the deity, whether God/the Lord or demonic forces. In 1 Cor 11 the unworthy are also excluded for fear of their experiencing condemnation and its consequences.

Fourth, in 1 Cor 16 we have a curse pronounced upon those who do not love the Lord accompanied by the call to the Lord to come (here probably to judgment).[143] The force is probably the same in the *Didache*.[144] Fifth, the basic practice of having a full meal is reflected. Sixth, the meal includes a cup and a loaf accompanied by some form of "ritual." Seventh, the use of a cup and a loaf of bread and the breaking of the bread and giving thanks are common to both writers. Thanksgiving is made for the cup; the bread is broken and shared among those present.

The eighth point in common is that the order of cup followed by loaf found in *Didache* also appears in 1 Cor 10:16–17.[145] The significance of this is debatable. J. Schröter argues that this reflects the order of events in pagan cultic meals that began with a drink offering.[146] P. F. Bradshaw argues that

---

[143] Thiselton, *First Corinthians*, 1347–53.
[144] Niederwimmer, *The Didache*, 163–64.
[145] For the view that this represents the actual order in Corinth, see van de Sandt and Flusser, *The Didache*, 307–9. They also refer to Luke 22:15–19a as an example of the same order in the early church. See further Bradshaw, *Eucharistic Origins*, 44–48, following Enrico Mazza, *The Origins of the Eucharistic Prayer* (trans. Ronald E. Lane; Collegeville: Liturgical, 1995).
[146] Schröter, *Das Abendmahl*, 30–31. He also argues that the order of events in 1 Cor

the order is also seen in other sources and that there is no evidence that the Corinthian celebration followed the order given in the narrative in 1 Cor 11:23–25.[147]

However, Paul is more probably using a rhetorical inversion in order to allow him to develop the crucial point of the unity of the members of the congregation which is more obviously represented by the loaf.[148] The order of food and cup is found both in 1 Cor 10:3–4 and also repeatedly in 11:21, 22, 23–24, 25, 26, 27, 28, 29.[149] The use of the bread-cup order is the natural inference from 1 Cor 11, and this inference should be accepted as valid in the absence of compelling evidence to the contrary. In the *Didache* the order of thanksgiving strongly suggests the order cup – bread,[150] but the closing prayer reverts to the more normal order (*Did.* 10:3; cf. 9:5).[151]

Ninth, the background in Paul is Jewish with the use of the characteristic Jewish term "cup of blessing" and with the analogy being drawn with the food and drink in the desert. The prayers in the *Didache* are clearly based on Jewish motifs and vocabulary, although the precise relationship is a matter of debate. Peculiar to the *Didache* is the prayer after the meal, which bears resemblances to the Jewish prayer known as the Birkat Ha-Mazon ("blessing for the nourishment").[152]

Tenth, the bread and wine are seen as spiritual food and drink (*Did.* 10:3). This is certainly implied by 1 Cor 10:3, 4, where the spiritual (πνευματικός)

---

11 is that of the Last Supper in the tradition, and not necessarily the order followed in Corinth.

[147] Bradshaw, *Eucharistic Origins*, 44–48.

[148] This is the generally accepted view of the matter. For example: Hahn, *Die Einheit*, 549.

[149] The order of "cup" and "table" in 1 Cor 10:21 probably reflects what went on in pagan temples rather than in the Christian meeting. It reflects the concern over drinking which was doubtless the prime stimulant to the idolatrous and immoral behavior in Corinth.

[150] If this order corresponds in any way to the sequence of events, then it suggests that there is no foundation for the concept of a meal followed by a symposium.

[151] As for the order in Luke 22:15–20: (1) If the longer text is followed, we have cup – loaf – cup, with the second of these two cups clearly identified as the one associated with the blood of Christ. The former cup is explained as what the disciples share apparently without Jesus and belongs to the story, not to the subsequent practice. (2) If the shorter text is followed, then this is a shortening of the longer account in Mark and the material is either drawn from a different source or it is a Lucan creation based on Mark. Either way, there is no indication that it rests on a cup – loaf pattern followed in some congregation known to Luke.

[152] Cf. Jeremias, *Eucharistic Words*, 110, for the wording. For discussion see van de Sandt and Flusser, *The Didache*, 310–25; Oskar Skarsaune, *In the Shadow of the Temple: Jewish Influences on Early Christianity* (Downers Grove: InterVarsity, 2002), 406–13; Bradshaw, *Eucharistic Origins*, 32–35, questions whether Jewish meal-prayers are reflected, but does not deny the generally Jewish character of the material.

drink in the wilderness is seen as proceeding from Christ: nothing less can be true of the cup and the loaf.

In the *Didache* the cup signifies the holy vine of God's Son, David, made known through Jesus. This suggests that the contents of the cup symbolize the fruit of the vine understood as spiritual nourishment, particularly since it is referred to as spiritual drink. The bread signifies life in the same kind of way as in John 6 where Jesus is the bread of life and the giver of bread, and this is clearly spiritual nourishment that supports life.

In Paul the cup signifies participation in the blood of Christ and the bread signifies participation in the body of Christ. The implication is that pagan feasts also involve sharing with the demons in the food and the drink. The thought is not of consuming the deity but of a communion brought about by a meal. But the idea that the cup represents the blood of Christ or the bread represents the body of Christ can arise only if the identification has somehow been made.

Eleventh, the motif of the oneness of the disciples in the church is common to 1 Cor 10 and the *Didache*.[153] In the latter it takes on the special form of an eschatological hope. What the *Didache* prays for is seen by Paul as already taking place (at least partially) in the present gathering of the congregation. In both cases the company who sit down consists of both Jewish and Gentile Christians.[154]

The twelfth and final point in common is that the Christian meal is seen as bearing some similarity to the eating of sacrifices in 1 Cor 10:18–20. Paul parallels the eating of food consecrated to idols through having been offered in sacrifice to a god with the Christian cup and loaf. It is probable that the Pauline meal is regarded as similar to the Jewish meal after a communion or peace offering has been made; the meal itself is not sacrificial, but follows the sacrifice made by Christ on the cross.[155] However, when the Christian thanksgiving in *Did.* 14:1–3 is said to be "your sacrifice," this means nothing more than that the believers offer praise and thanksgiving to God, as in Hebrews 13. The thought of offering a sacrifice to take away sin is completely absent. This idea of a sacrifice could be due to use of Matt 5 where the need for reconciliation with a brother before presenting an offering is taught; this is then linked by word association with Mal 1:11, 14. Thus, although sacrificial language is used by both Paul and the *Didache*, the senses in which it is used are different.

---

[153] Cf. Schmithals, *Markus*, 620–22; Schmithals, *Theologiegeschichte des Urchristentums*, 208–18; he holds that in the earliest meal, celebrated only with bread, the bread refers to the church which consists of all who partake of the one loaf.

[154] Cf. Michelle Slee, *The Church in Antioch in the First Century CE: Communion and Conflict* (JSNTSup 244; London: Sheffield Academic Press, 2003), 94–100.

[155] Marshall, *Last Supper and Lord's Supper*, 122–23.

The result of these considerations is to demonstrate the very considerable and close similarities between Paul's and the Didachist's accounts of congregational meals, specifically between 1 Cor 10 and *Did.* 9–10.[156] There is, of course, no reason to suppose that the meal in 1 Cor 10 is a different occasion from that in 1 Cor 11; the separate treatments arise from the two different problems that are being discussed, and they indicate the different ways in which the symbolism could be developed to deal with different matters. Nevertheless, the treatment in 1 Corinthians emphasizes the significance for Paul of the loaf and cup symbolizing the body and blood of Christ and so proclaiming his death, and this is the point that is missing from the *Didache*. The *Didache* makes no overt reference to the body and blood of Christ or indeed to his death "for you" at any point in the document; nor does it refer explicitly to his resurrection, although it does mention his future coming (*Did.* 10:6; 16:6–7).

But the *Didache* does have the following: First, the spiritualization of the cup: the fruit of the vine which it contains symbolizes the fruit of the holy vine of David,[157] and this will refer to the kingdom of God ruled by the Messiah that is now made known through Jesus. The Jewish motif of the vine as a symbol for Israel is the basis for this new understanding of the cup, which fits in with what we know of the symbolism of the vine and the vineyard used by Jesus; there may well be an echo of the saying in Mark 14:25 (Cf. Luke 22:18). Second, it has the spiritualization of the broken bread:[158] it symbolizes the life and knowledge made known through Jesus. This is more distinctly Christian (and Johannine); the thought of Jesus as the bread of life would appear to be present. It is noteworthy that this christological, soteriological element comes first in the prayer before the application of the broken loaf to the regathering of God's people into one. Third, this point is confirmed by the prayer after the meal; the language is loose, but it indicates that believers have been graciously granted spiritual food and drink and eternal life through Jesus. This suggests that the spiritual food and drink consist in eternal life, the former nourishing the latter. God's name has been placed in their hearts (*Did.* 10:2, an unparalleled motif); the knowledge, faith and immortality have been made known by Jesus. In the

---

[156] Cf. Schröter, *Das Abendmahl*, 30, 60–72. In unpublished work J. Spivak has championed the view that *Did.* 9–10 records a frequent (possibly even daily) communal banquet on the lines of a Jewish ritual meal (cf. Acts 2) but ch. 14 describes a completely different event, namely a sacrificial eucharist held on Sundays. This hypothesis seems dubious to me in view of the close parallels between the former meal and the Corinthian meals.

[157] Probably the term "vine" here stands for the vine and its fruit.

[158] The reading with κλάσμα in vv. 3 and 4 is rejected by Niederwimmer, *The Didache*, 148, and some other scholars on the grounds that the word cannot mean "the broken bread" and is not found in later liturgies. This does not seem to me to be adequate evidence for abandoning the MS.

context of the food, this cannot do other than signify that the food symbolizes the spiritual gifts given through Jesus. The separation of the earthly food and drink (v. 3a) from the spiritual food and drink (v. 3b) indicates that the former is symbolical of the latter and is not to be identified with it. But the crucial point is that this indicates that the food is seen to symbolize the reception of Jesus who is life and knowledge; hence the identification of the cup with his blood and the loaf with his body is tacit.

Fourth and finally, the language of spiritual food and drink presupposes a meal that is more than simply a celebration of the arrival of God's kingdom, whether now or in the future. It goes beyond simple celebration and looking towards the future and has more in common with 1 Cor 10 (spiritual food and drink; avoid food sacrificed to idols). This combination of motifs may suggest a more developed theology rather than a primitive one that precedes the NT developments in Paul and John. Although the language of the prayers is determined to a considerable extent by the Jewish models on which they are based, the theology has developed in a Johannine direction with the references to the vine, life and knowledge, as well as spiritual food and drink and the eschatological references to gathering together the church from all over the earth into the kingdom.

The identification of the cup and loaf as giving spiritual food most probably implies the tacit understanding that they symbolize the blood and body of Christ, as is clear in the Gospel of John despite its lack of the institution narrative. When we bear in mind the lack of attention to the significance of baptism in relation to the forgiveness of sins and the reception of the gift of the Holy Spirit, it may not be so surprising that the symbolism of the Lord's Supper is likewise not developed. The Johannine echoes may well suggest that the thought in the *Didache* is not as primitive as it is often made out to be, and the very strong list of parallels to Pauline teaching may strengthen the case that the absence of specific reference to the bread and cup as symbolizing the body and blood of Jesus should not be over-emphasized.

2.3.4.4. The Didache *and the History of Christian Meals*

Crossan and others have interpreted the *Didache* as evidence for a more primitive type of meal than the Pauline one, closer to the meals held by Jesus earlier in his mission. It has been argued that the absence of references to Jesus' death and his body and blood point to such a meal-practice in the early church, and this can be strengthened by reference to the Lucan account of "breaking of bread." Hence it is concluded that at this stage the early church was not influenced by the kind of last meal reported in Paul and the Gospels because no such meal (and no such report) existed. But the precise way in which this happened is far from clear, and this is seen in the different theories of what was going on: One theory is an early stage with the kind of meal described in the *Didache* being followed by a later stage modelled on the Last Supper account. On this view the Didachist's account is an archaic survival. Alternatively, two parallel forms of meal, the table fellowship version and the Pauline "Last Supper" version, existed side by side for a considerable period of time. A third theory is that the original table-fellowship type of meal was uninfluenced by the traditions regarding the Last Supper. On this view the Last Supper narrative existed as a historical report, but it did not influence the early church.[159] Very gradually the latter began to influence practice. One theory is that this began with the celebration of an annual (quarto-deciman) Passover.[160] Finally, what the Didachist describes is the meal that preceded the Eucharist proper; the latter, which he has not described, was along conventional lines.[161]

In assessing these possibilities it is important that Paul's account can be dated in terms of its *terminus ante quem* with great precision to ca. 53–55 CE, i.e., within 20–25 years of the crucifixion. But the kind of church meal that Paul envisages depends on what had been passed on to Paul, and it is plausible that this goes back to his time in Antioch or even earlier, thus narrowing the time gap even further. The church there existed from shortly after the death of Stephen and the conversion of Paul and therefore began within a very short time of the death of Jesus. The date of the *Didache* is considerably later, and what is described there is contemporary practice. Either we have an archaic survival of a meal in which there is no reference to the Lord's death (nor to his risen presence), or the account is selective (and the actual eucharistic part is not directly mentioned) or we should interpret the account as presupposing the Last Supper pattern.

What we have seen is the practice of a meal that shows considerable similarities with the Pauline meal, and specifically includes an understanding of the cup and bread as spiritual food, just as in 1 Cor 10; this is not a far cry from identifying the cup and bread with the blood and body of Christ, although that step is not explicit in the *Didache*; we have further seen that the *Didache* may have known the Last Supper narrative even though it (like much else) is not explicitly mentioned. Thus to find a fundamental difference or even incompatibility between the Pauline and *Didache* meals is unjustified.[162] There is no evidence here to suggest the unhistorical nature of the Last Supper narrative or its non-existence in the early years of

---

[159] An alternative possibility is that the account of the Last Supper was unknown until it was either given to Paul by special revelation or was fictively created by him (cf. Mack's account above).

[160] For these possibilities see the summary in Rouwhorst, "Litmus Test," 153–56.

[161] Cf. Niederwimmer, *The Didache*, 142–43.

[162] Cf. Schröter, *Das Abendmahl*, 67, who proposes that a common tradition lies behind 1 Cor 10 and the *Didache*.

the church. At the very least the *Didache* does not furnish any compelling evidence for the late origin of the Lord's Supper tradition.

2.3.5. Other Possible Origins of the Church Meals

Other possibilities regarding the background of the church meals have been suggested and some of them still have supporters.[163] One is that it was an Essene meal. The Qumran sect held meals at which bread and wine were taken after thanks or a blessing had been said by a priest (1QS 6:2–5). There is also reference to a meal at which two anointed people, a priest and a royal figure, are present (1QSa 2:17–27). It has been suggested that the former meal anticipates an eschatological meal, and that it replaced the temple cult for the Qumran community. K. G. Kuhn, who proposed the theory, saw the Qumran meal as the model for the church's meal, but did not draw conclusions for Jesus' own action.[164]

A second alternative is derived from *Joseph and Aseneth*. G.D. Kilpatrick drew attention to the way in which Joseph is described as a man who "worships God, blesses with his mouth the living God, eats the blessed bread of life, drinks the blessed cup of immortality, and is anointed with the blessed oil of incorruption." The relevance of this meal to the Lord's Supper has been discussed by C. Burchard; he dismisses it, noting that the theory has had no supporters since it was first put forward by G.D. Kilpatrick. The analogy is too remote both geographically and conceptually.[165]

A third alternative is Hellenistic fellowship meals. It has been argued that the church's fellowship meals do not need any particular explanation; such meals were commonplace in social associations.[166] But the church's meal was one at which unusual things were done, and some explanation is needed for these.

---

[163] See Schürmann, *Jesu ureigener Tod*, 75–76. In the present context these proposals are concerned with the background of church meals and not with the ways in which they might possibly provide a background to a Last Supper held by Jesus; for this latter type of proposal see below.

[164] K.G. Kuhn, "The Lord's Supper and the Communal Meal at Qumran," in *The Scrolls and the New Testament* (ed. Krister Stendahl; London: SCM, 1958), 65–93; cf. the discussion by Gerd Theissen and Annette Merz, *The Historical Jesus: A Comprehensive Guide* (trans. John Bowden; Minneapolis: Fortress, 1998), 412–13. Heinz-Wolfgang Kuhn, "The Qumran Meal and the Lord's Supper in Paul in the Context of the Graeco-Roman World," in *Paul, Luke and the Graeco-Roman World: Essays in Honour of Alexander J.M. Wedderburn* (ed. A. Christophersen; JSNTSup 217; London: Sheffield, 2002), 229, finds scarcely any influence from the Hellenistic world on the Qumran meal.

[165] Christoph Burchard, "The Importance of Joseph and Aseneth for the Study of the New Testament: A General Survey and a Fresh Look at the Lord's Supper," *NTS* 33 (1987): 118–19.

[166] Klinghardt, *Gemeinschaftsmahl und Mahlgemeinschaft*.

A fourth proposal is that it was a sacrificial thanksgiving meal. H. Gese referred to the meal of thanksgiving in Ps 22:26 in which somebody gives thanks for deliverance from death. Since Ps 22 is associated with the passion, the early church picked up the allusion and held a meal in thanksgiving for Jesus' deliverance from death. Again, nothing is said about a meal held by Jesus himself.[167]

Despite the continuing support for some of them, none of these suggested origins appears plausible.[168] All of them have in common the attempt to explain the character of the congregational meals without recourse to their institution by Jesus at his last meal and thus implicitly to argue that the latter did not influence the church or simply never happened. The dominical basis is thought not to be needed because another basis can be provided. Hence not only can we say nothing about a meal held by Jesus, but its existence becomes superfluous and unlikely, since it did not in fact influence the church (who would surely have been influenced by such a meal if it had happened.)

It cannot be entirely ruled out that occasions of this kind (particularly fellowship meals) could have contributed to the earliest establishment of the church meal. But the meal's unique development that is presupposed in the traditions Paul cites in 1 Corinthians does rest on an appeal to what Jesus did at his last meal, and therefore these proposals are irrelevant to the quest for the historical Last Supper.[169]

Critics are in some danger of confusing the two questions of (1) the fact that early Christians met together in the context of a meal (like many other religious and secular groups), and (2) the particular form that their meals took with their focus on Christ and his death. The former question can be answered in sociological terms, but the latter requires a different kind of answer.

With this matter behind us we can now proceed to look at the account of the "eucharistic" part of the meal with a view to assessing its historicity. Here a preliminary matter regarding the sources requires attention.

2.3.6. The Text of Luke concerning the Meal

The difficulty concerns the extent of one of the major witnesses to the meal. There is a well-known problem with the text of the Lucan version, as to whether Luke 22:19b–20 (containing the latter part of the bread saying and the cup saying) is integral to it or not. These verses are omitted in a number

---

[167] Hartmut Gese, *Essays on Biblical Theology* (trans. Keith Crim; Minneapolis: Augsburg, 1981), 117–40.
[168] Cf. Hengel, "Das Mahl in der Nacht," 141.
[169] Mention must also be made of the possibility that the earliest form of church meal had bread but no wine (H. Lietzmann, followed by Schmithals, *Markus*, 619–20).

of manuscripts, including D a d ff² i l. Various other manuscripts and versions (b e sy^(c s p)) appear to presuppose this shorter text and make what are sometimes regarded as attempts to improve it.[170] After the identification by Westcott and Hort of what they regarded as non-western interpolations in the text of the Gospel, it was common to prefer the shorter text in this pericope and elsewhere. A change of attitude, reflected in the differences between the RSV and the NRSV, set in from the 1950s thanks to powerful defenses of the longer text from J. Jeremias and H. Schürmann.[171] But the shorter text has never been without its defenders, including especially M. Rese and C. F. Evans.[172] A major recent contribution is that of B.D. Ehrman, who argues that Luke inherited the long reading from Mark but shortened it for his own theological reasons; then scribes, in effect, restored it in the interests of orthodoxy. Scot McKnight accepts his case, stating that "Ehrman's presentation has not received an adequate answer" and therefore currently holds the field.[173]

More recently M.W. Martin has argued that the nine western non-interpolations all occur in Luke 23–24 and are probably the work of a single

---

[170] So far as the Syriac evidence is concerned, John Nolland, *Luke 18:35–24:53* (WBC 35c; Dallas: Word, 1993), 1041, followed by Bradly S. Billings, *Do This in Remembrance of Me: The Disputed Works in the Lukan Institution Narrative (Luke 22:19b–20): An Historico-Exegetical, Theological, and Sociological Analysis* (Library of Biblical Studies; London: T&T Clark, 2006), 8, holds that it is not clear whether b e sy^(c s p) are attempting to deal with the problem caused by the shorter text or with the anomalous cup-bread-cup sequence in the longer text. P.J. Williams (personal communication) likewise notes that some of the early Syriac witnesses may presuppose both the shorter and the longer texts and do not necessarily favor the former. In the case of sy^p vv. 17–18 are omitted simply by homoeoarcton between vv. 17 and 19 (or homoeoteleuton between vv. 16 and 18). The Syriac evidence should therefore be treated with considerable caution.

[171] Jeremias, *Eucharistic Words*, 138–59; Heinz Schürmann, *Traditionsgeschichtliche Untersuchungen zu den synoptischen Evangelien* (KBANT; Düsseldorf: Patmos-Verlag, 1968), 159–92; cf. Bruce M. Metzger, *A Textual Commentary on the Greek New Testament* (2nd ed.; Stuttgart: Deutsche Bibelgesellschaft, 1994), 148–51, 164–66; Marshall, *Luke*, 799–801; Marshall, *Last Supper and Lord's Supper*, 36–38. The longer reading is supported by major commentaries: Bock, *Luke*, 2:1721–22; Fitzmyer, *Luke X–XXIV*, 1387–88; Nolland, *Luke 18:35–24:53*, 1041; Klein, *Das Lukasevangelium*, 664–65. Likewise Lührmann, *Das Markusevangelium*, 238, assumes the longer reading. Beasley-Murray, *Jesus and the Kingdom of God*, 260, describes his conversion to acceptance of the longer reading. See also Schröter, *Das Abendmahl*, 50 ("vermutlich mit Recht").

[172] Bultmann, *Geschichte*, 286, n. 1; Martin Rese, "Zur Problematik von Kurz- und Langtext in Luk 22:17ff," *NTS* 22 (1975): 15–31; C. F. Evans, *Saint Luke* (TPINTC; London: SCM; Philadelphia: Trinity, 1990), 786–91. Cf. also Mikeal C. Parsons, *The Departure of Jesus in Luke-Acts: The Ascension Narratives in Context* (JSNTSup 21; Sheffield: JSOT Press, 1987), 29–52.

[173] McKnight, *Jesus and His Death*, 260–61; Bart D. Ehrman, *The Orthodox Corruption of Scripture: The Effect of Early Christological Controversies on the Text of the New Testament* (New York: Oxford University Press, 1993), 197–227; D. C. Parker, *The Living Text of the Gospels* (Cambridge: Cambridge University Press, 1997), 150–57. The same position is maintained by M. Holmes (personal communication).

scribe who was defending an anti-separationist christology against those who held that the divine Christ departed from the human Jesus before his passion; the scribe emphasized the presence of the deity in Jesus right through his death and resurrection as the Lord who is worthy to be worshipped.[174]

The matter is of some importance since it concerns the existence of an independent source for multiple attestation of the so-called eucharistic words that may possibly be more original in places than the Marcan and Pauline accounts; the question of the relationship of the first (only) cup mentioned by Luke to the course of the meal also arises.

2.3.6.1. In Favor of the Shorter Text

Bart Ehrman offers the following seven arguments in defense of the shorter reading. First, the omission in D a d ff² i l is an example of a western omission or so-called non-interpolation. Since the western text is normally expansionist, such uncharacteristic omissions must be taken all the more seriously. Ehrman argues that the group of omissions by the western text in Luke 24 should be regarded as original.[175] The effect is to destroy the myth of the reliable "neutral" text and require us to consider each case individually on its own merits.

Second, not only does the expansion itself contain non-Lucan features, but also it is surprising that these are not taken up elsewhere by Luke.

Third, the concept of Jesus dying for others or as an atonement for sins is not found elsewhere in Luke-Acts. Rather, Luke deliberately suppresses it.[176] He omits Mark 10:45, and in effect replaces it by the "neutral" wording in Luke 22:24–27. In Acts 8:32–33 he uses Isaiah 53:7–8a to paint a picture of Jesus as an innocent victim who is vindicated (cf Acts 3:13) and stops short of quoting Isaiah 53:8b. In the account of the crucifixion he moves the incident of the rent veil of the temple to before the death of Jesus with the result that it no longer symbolizes the opening up of the way to God through the death of Jesus. And he also changes the centurion's confession to indicate the innocence of Jesus rather than his divine sonship (Luke 23:47). This is part of making the death to be that of a righteous martyr.

Fourth, Acts 20:28 does not refer to an atoning act for sin; rather "the blood of Jesus produces the church because it brings the cognizance of guilt

---

[174] Michael W. Martin, "Defending the 'Western Non-Interpolations': The Case for an Anti-Separationist *Tendenz* in the Longer Alexandrian Readings," *JBL* 124 (2005): 269–94.

[175] Earlier, Parsons, *The Departure of Jesus*, 29–52, argued the same case. Ehrman holds that if there is no specific reason to assume that an omission took place during copying, we should conclude that it has not occurred; P. J. Williams thinks it probable, however, that many omissions took place for no specific describable reason.

[176] Similarly, McKnight, *Jesus and His Death*, 260, n. 4.

that leads to repentance,"[177] that is, presumably the "cost" of producing repentance was letting Jesus be put to death. Elsewhere in Luke-Acts "blood" refers to the fate of the persecuted. There is no Pauline doctrine of the atonement here. Only the shorter text of Luke 22:19 fits in with this soteriology.

Fifth, the structure of the text favors omission. Although J.H. Petzer has attempted to show that the literary structure is ruined if the passage is omitted, Ehrman argues that this is not so.[178] For Petzer the longer text gives two sets of sayings, each containing two pairs of signs and explanations in parallelism. However, Ehrman responds that omission of the final pair leaves three pairs of signs and explanations standing in the literary form of a chiasmus. He argues that without the longer text we have in fact a better, contrasting relationship of v. 19a to the saying about the betrayal in v. 21.

Sixth, the most potent argument is that of transcriptional probability. For Ehrman all attempts to explain how the longer text could have been shortened – whether by *disciplina arcani* or by accidental omission – are unconvincing.

Seventh, by contrast, it is easy to see how scribes would have extended the shorter text to conform with the other Gospels. The longer reading is a case of scribal insertion that harmonizes Luke with Mark but does so in the light of the Pauline material.[179] For Ehrman the chief motivation in doing so was the desire of orthodox Christians to make the shorter text more strongly anti-docetic by emphasizing that Christ's human body was broken and his blood shed.

It is not of first importance for our purpose to solve this question. This is because the scholars who take this view argue that Luke's shorter text is one that was produced by shortening and editing an existing text, namely that of Luke's source at this point (Mark), and was produced for theological reasons. Luke 22:14–19a is thus not a testimony to a primitive type of Lord's Supper. Consequently, it cannot be used to argue against the age and authenticity of the Marcan and Pauline versions of the Last Supper narrative. Nevertheless, there is a case that Luke 22:15–19a (*or* –20) was not formed by redaction of Mark but is based on a separate source.[180]

---

[177] Ehrman, *Orthodox Corruption*, 202.

[178] J.H. Petzer, "Luke 22:19b–20 and the Structure of the Passage," *NovT* 26 (1984): 249–52.

[179] For Pesch, *Das Markusevangelium*, 2:368–69, the (genuine) longer text is the result of Lucan redaction of Mark and 1 Corinthians (cf. McKnight, *Jesus and His Death*, 64, 263–64, who adopts this as a fall-back position if the shorter text is not original). Hence, whether they adopt the longer or the shorter text, some scholars hold that Luke 22:19b–20 is not based on tradition and is therefore without value for reconstructing the original account.

[180] Joel B. Green, *The Gospel of Luke* (NICNT; Grand Rapids: Eerdmans, 1997), 761; more fully in Joel B. Green, *The Death of Jesus: Tradition and Interpretation in the Pas-*

2.3.6.2. In Favor of the Longer Text

However, there are seven arguments that can be raised in support of the longer text in Luke. First, the western non-interpolations: As Ehrman recognizes, the presence of other western non-interpolations in Luke whose originality he defends cannot by itself be a conclusive argument for the originality of this or any other particular instance. At most the other instances create a context in which the phenomenon of an original western non-interpolation is credible and even (on his view) likely.[181]

Second, non-Lucan style: Any non-Lucan linguistic characteristics in Luke 22:19b–20 can be explained as due to the tradition that Luke has taken over. They are not necessarily the result of *later* scribal activity. However, it has been argued that the style of these verses is no more non-Lucan than is the surrounding material.[182] This would not be surprising if Luke were dependent on source material.[183]

Third, the lack of traces elsewhere: The additional argument that significant features found in the longer text ("for you"; "remembrance"; "new covenant in my blood") do not figure elsewhere in Luke-Acts has no

---

sion Narrative (WUNT 2.33; Tübingen: Mohr Siebeck, 1988), 35–42. Bultmann, *Geschichte*, 286, appears to regard Luke 22:14–18 as "older tradition," but in *Theology* I, 146, he claims that none of Luke 22:14–20 has the value of independent tradition.

[181] Each major case of a western shorter text was examined on its merits by Jeremias, *Eucharistic Words*, 148–52, who came to a negative conclusion in each case. Although the committee responsible for the NA text was divided in its opinion in seven cases (including the present one), in every single case (except the special case of Luke 12:39), the NA text adopts the longer reading. Billings, *Do This in Remembrance of Me*, 28, n. 14, draws attention to Luke 9:26 as a further example where essentially the same group of witnesses as in Luke 22:19b–20 have an omission that is clearly harmonizing and secondary. P. J. Williams notes that the textual evidence varies for the different cases and thinks that this may be an indicator that they did not all originate simultaneously.

[182] J. H. Petzer, "Style and Text in the Lucan Narrative of the Institution of the Lord's Supper (Luke 22:19b–20)," *NTS* 37 (1991): 113–29.

[183] Schürmann, *Der Einsetzungsbericht*, 15–81, argued that the Lucan version shows signs of primitiveness compared with Paul. A difficult question is whether it contains Semitisms that would establish it as more primitive than Paul's version. "Pre-Lucan" could of course be a mistaken categorization of elements that are simply "non-Lucan" and are the result of later scribal activity. The question of whether they show Semitic features could be significant. Luke has μου after σῶμα contrary to the Greek word order in Paul; the result is more Semitic, but could reflect influence from Mark. Similarly with ἐν τῷ αἵματί μου. The omission of the copula ἐστι in the cup saying (diff. Paul) could also be Semitic. Pesch holds that the omission was because of the addition of the participial phrase, but this is dubious: cf. the inclusion of the copula in every other version of the sayings with the participial phrase. See Pesch, *Das Markusevangelium*, 2:368–69; B. D. Smith, "The More Original Form of the Words of Institution," *ZNW* 83 (1992): 166–86. The argument is too finely balanced to be decisive but offers some support for the originality of the longer text if this is probable on other grounds.

strength;[184] in Acts Luke does not include any teaching regarding the celebration of the Lord's Supper, and therefore the absence of the remembrance and new covenant motifs is not in any way surprising.[185] "Blood" occurs in Acts 20:28 (see further below). The absence of "for you" from the preaching admittedly remains as a problem, which is partly explicable from the way in which the first thing that needed to be done in the preaching was to establish the messiahship of Jesus and the wickedness of putting him to death.

Two minor observations by Schürmann on possible influence from the longer text elsewhere in Luke may have some force. The word order τοῦτο τὸ ποτήριον in Luke 22:42a (diff. Mark 14:36a) could be influenced by the order in Luke 22:20. He also argues that the start of v. 21 assumes the existence of v. 20, and that the use of διατίθημι in v. 29 presupposes the covenant reference in v. 20.[186]

Fourth, Luke's alleged aversion to atonement theology: Luke's omission of Mark 10:45 is the result of his omission of the whole pericope Mark 10:35-45, which in turn is explained at least in part by his substitution of other material elsewhere (Luke 12:50; 22:25-27), in both cases using material that is from other sources rather than the fruit of his own creativity.[187] If the longer text is original, the "ransom" saying would have been redundant. It is also probable that Luke 19:10 and Acts 20:28 function as replacements for the omitted "Son of Man" saying.

In Acts 8 the crucial initial point that needed to be dealt with was the identity of the Servant as Jesus, just as in other speeches the main theme was the identification of the Messiah as Jesus (or, put otherwise, the confirmation of Jesus as the Messiah). It is sufficient for the purpose that the identification be made. Luke 22:37 also cites Isaiah 53, where the possibility of identification of Jesus with sinners should not be excluded.[188]

At the crucifixion the incident of the veil has become part of a general account of cosmic signs. Ehrman's understanding of its function in Mark is only one of various possibilities. There is no way to be sure that Luke perceived the symbolism of the rending in Mark to be an indication that

---

[184] In any case, where Luke is citing source-material, there is the lesser expectation that he will repeat it later than is the case with material that forms part of his own theological vocabulary.

[185] It may be worth observing that, apart from teaching to correct the problems at Corinth, Paul also lacks these motifs.

[186] Schürmann, *Traditionsgeschichtliche Untersuchungen*, 174-75, 193-97; cf. E. Earle Ellis, *The Gospel of Luke* (London: Nelson, 1966), 253-55; Bock, *Luke*, 2:1722.

[187] This is a familiar Lucan procedure and seems to rest largely on a desire to incorporate the material he has gathered from other sources rather than from an aversion to the Marcan material which is displaced.

[188] Leon Morris, *Luke: An Introduction and Commentary* (rev. ed.; TNTC; Leicester: InterVarsity, 1988), 339. Other commentators tend to deny that there is any explicit substitutionary reference here.

the way into God's presence or the coming of God to human beings was brought about by the death of Jesus and therefore deliberately suppressed it.

That Jesus is portrayed as a martyr by Luke is generally accepted, but the belief that the martyrs were suffering for the sins of Israel rather than their own sins was current at the time, and the possibility that Luke knew and shared this belief should not be dismissed.[189]

Ehrman argues that Acts 20:28 does not refer to something positively achieved by the death of Jesus. But his suggestion that "the blood of Jesus produces the church because it brings the cognizance of guilt that leads to repentance" is an extraordinary way of understanding the concept of divine "purchase" of the church. The saying is not so much concerned with the way in which people respond to the death of Jesus, but rather with the high responsibility of those called to shepherd the church in view of its high value in the sight of God who did not spare his own Son but gave him up to death as the cost to be paid. The verb περιεποιήσατο implies some kind of purchase by God[190] rather than bringing about a sense of guilt and repentance. Thus the case that Luke has "deliberately suppressed" atonement theology is open to strong criticism.[191]

We are thus brought to the conclusion that there is no evidence elsewhere that indicates that Luke is likely to have suppressed the atonement theology that is expressed in Luke 22:19b–20. Granted that, if Luke's account had concluded at 22:19a, it is easy to understand that scribes would have completed it, we are left with the problem that no convincing reason has been adduced for Luke's creation of the shorter text, given that he knew Mark's account.

Fifth, arguments from structure: As they stand, neither Petzer's nor Ehrman's arguments from structure strike me as particularly convincing, and certainly Ehrman's is no stronger than Petzer's.[192] Petzer is right to the extent that he sees two sets each consisting of two two-part statements. Where he is not persuasive is in seeing the two sets as parallel to each other. But if we allow the two sets to function separately, we have a care-

---

[189] On the minor point of the translation of δίκαιος, Peter Doble, *The Paradox of Salvation: Luke's Theology of the Cross* (SNTSMS 87; Cambridge: Cambridge University Press, 1996), has demonstrated conclusively that the word does not mean "innocent" but "righteous."

[190] This is all the more the case if Acts 20:28 is to be regarded as Luke's equivalent for his omission of Mark 10:45. It has been argued that Luke often provides equivalents both in the Gospel and in Acts for Marcan statements that he has omitted in the appropriate places in his narrative. See, for example, Klein, *Das Lukasevangelium*, 692, n. 1.

[191] Billings, *Do This in Remembrance of Me*, 40, argues that Luke is working to a different agenda rather than carrying out "a wholesale rejection of the atonement theology."

[192] Petzer assumes that "to eat the Passover" corresponds to "this is my body," whereas it is arguable that "Passover" means either the meal as a whole (of which the bread is only one part) or the Passover lamb. Cf. Ehrman, *Orthodox Corruption*, 253, n. 107.

ful structure. Ehrman argues that vv. 15–18 stand together, and that vv. 19a functions to open the next pericope and provide a contrast to the forecast of betrayal in vv. 21; vv. 21a and 21b then provide further explanation in clauses that parallel vv. 19a and 21 respectively. The weakness in this view is that it leaves v. 19a completely enigmatic; by itself "this is my body" is opaque, and it needs either the Pauline supplement ("which is for you") or the context provided by the cup-word to render it intelligible. C. Böttrich also comments that Luke's presentation gives a fuller and better picture of a meal that Jesus longed to have rather than reducing the actual meal almost to vanishing point.[193]

Sixth, explaining the motives for interpolation: The main point in Ehrman's argument (and of those who share his view) is that the difficulty of explaining how the omission of the longer text (if original) could have taken place is far greater than overcoming the obstacles to the originality of the shorter reading. Ehrman thinks that he can account more easily for the shorter text as original (a) because it fits in with his understanding of Luke's theology in which Luke has systematically eradicated all references that might be construed as supporting an understanding of the cross as a saving event and (b) because the addition can be easily explained as a harmonization to the longer account in the other Gospels and Paul and as congenial to the "proto-orthodox heresiologists of the second century."[194]

So far as Ehrman's broader thesis of "orthodox corruption" is concerned, doubts have been expressed regarding its cogency.[195] In the present case, if the shorter text were original, the urge to harmonize it with the fuller text in the other Synoptic Gospels seems to me to be fully adequate to explain

---

[193] Christfried Böttrich, "Proexistenz im Leben und Sterben: Jesu Tod bei Lukas," in *Deutungen des Todes Jesu im Neuen Testament* (ed. Jörg Frey and Jens Schröter; WUNT 181; Tübingen: Mohr Siebeck, 2005), 421–22.

[194] Ehrman, *Orthodox Corruption*, 209.

[195] See further Ulrich Schmid, "Eklektische Textkonstitution als theologische Rekonstruktion: Zur Heilsbedeutung des Todes Jesu bei Lukas (Lk 22,15–20 und Apg 20,28)," in *The Unity of Luke-Acts* (ed. Joseph Verheyden; Leuven: Leuven University Press, 1999), 577–84. For Schmid, Ehrman's procedures are eclectic and hence arbitrary. He does not take sufficiently into account the possibility of other reasons than theological ones for textual variations. He fails to observe that D goes its own way in Luke 23:45–46, retaining the word-order that retains the atoning sense of the passage that Ehrman postulates for Mark, and his interpretation of Acts 20:28 is inconsistent with it. The discussion is complicated by the possibility of two types of heresy. Docetism regarded Christ as completely divine and not as a flesh and blood human being; he only seemed to be the latter. Presumably what people saw being crucified was in fact a phantasy (or the person of Simon of Cyrene swapping identities with Jesus). Separationism regarded the (human) Jesus and the (divine) Christ as separate entities, with the latter withdrawing from Jesus before the crucifixion so that it was only the human figure who died (Ehrman, *Orthodox Corruption*, 181, cited by Martin, "Defending the 'Western Non-Interpolations'," 289, n. 75). Thus for Ehrman the purpose of the interpolation was to stress that the divine Christ truly died.

the addition by the scribes. Such harmonizations are rife throughout the Gospels.

The puzzling fact in this case is that there would also have been some influence from Paul. H. Klein notes that the longer text is a combination of Pauline and Marcan material, and argues that a copyist would be more likely to conform the text simply to Mark/Matthew. He therefore rejects the originality of the shorter text.[196] Against him it might be urged that for this pericope (and this pericope alone) 1 Cor 11 ranks as a further "synoptic" source alongside Mark and Matthew.[197]

Ehrman argues that the insertion was made by scribes who "wanted to stress, in direct opposition to certain groups of docetic opponents, that Christ experienced a real passion in which his body was broken and his blood was shed for the sins of the world."[198] He claims that this theological point was not necessary to Luke's understanding of the death of Jesus. But what is there about the alleged insertion that is specifically anti-docetic? And in any case the danger posed by docetism was already prevalent in the first century (cf. 1 John), and the motif is obvious enough in Luke 24:37–43 (with or without v. 40).[199] Moreover, it remains very odd that the anti-docetic tendency should have operated only in the case of Luke and left no trace in the transmission of the other accounts of the Last Supper. Docetism is irrelevant to the Supper narrative. It is much more plausible that, if the longer text is an interpolation it could be explained simply in terms of scribal harmonization to Mark and Paul. That would be an entirely adequate explanation.

Seventh, accounting for the text as scribal omission: For defenders of the shorter text the puzzle is how one particular narrow line of evidence can preserve the original text. Jeremias notes in this case that *only one Greek MS* would contain the original text.[200] Further, Schürmann observes that

---

[196] Klein, *Das Lukasevangelium*, 664–65.

[197] This is due to the sparsity of references to the Jesus-tradition in the epistles (one example is the assimilation in some MSS of Matt 5:37 to Jas 5:12).

[198] Ehrman, *Orthodox Corruption*, 209.

[199] The fact that the passage is concerned with an anti-docetic understanding of the resurrected Jesus rather than the earthly Jesus does not affect the point.

[200] Jeremias, *Eucharistic Words*, 144. This point is weakened by the possibility of other singular readings of D being original, and by any examples of other singular readings of Greek MSS being adopted as original (e.g., Luke 14:17). More recently, in unpublished material C.-B. Amphoux holds that the original text of Luke was preserved in D. It simply described a paschal meal which began like a Greek symposium. The text was altered by Marcion, who suppressed the "paschal" element in vv. 16–18 (because of his rejection of the Hebrew Bible) and replaced it with vv. 19–20 (taken, naturally, from Paul). The various other texts that we have can then all be understood as corrections of Marcion's text. In particular, the Alexandrian recension combined the two forms of the text to produce the long reading at the cost of doubling the number of cups. The *Didache* testifies to the original order of cup and bread in D, as does 1 Cor 10:16, and it was Paul who introduced

the total evidence for omission is confined to only a limited number of witnesses within the western tradition, the longer text being probably attested in Marcion, Justin and Tatian.[201]

From the opposite angle one might ask how all the rest of the witnesses came to produce the same expansion to the text and whether this coincidence is more probable than the omission in one small area of the transmission.[202]

There have been numerous attempts to explain how a scribal omission could have arisen. F. G. Kenyon and S. C. E. Legge argued that scribes understood the mention of the cup in vv. 17–18 as a reference to the sacramental cup and then proceeded to put the text "right" by omitting mention of the second cup.[203] However, the first cup would surely have been a likelier choice for omission than the one that persisted in church practice. And why was the interpretation of the bread also omitted?

Jeremias argued for omission in the interests of *disciplina arcani*, but this explanation has been universally rejected.[204] The motif of conforming to a liturgical practice of communion in one kind or a communion in which the cup preceded the bread is listed and rejected by Schürmann.[205] C. Böt-

---

the bread-cup order in 1 Cor 11. This is part of a wider theory concerning the use of a Bezan type of text by Marcion, which in turn is part of a much broader discussion of the composition of the Gospels, but this section of it could presumably stand on its own. It may seem to offer a cogent explanation of the creation of the longer text of Luke. Luke, however, appears to be describing a meal and not simply a symposium. One important weakness is that it does not explain the origin of the Pauline account. And does it satisfactorily account for the absence of any influence of the text of D on other Greek MSS? (I am grateful to Professor Amphoux for a summary of his theory and to Dr J. Read-Heimerdinger for alerting me to his work and sharing with me her own broader studies on the text of Luke 23–24).

[201] Schürmann, *Traditionsgeschichtliche Untersuchungen*, 160–63.

[202] Jeremias, *Eucharistic Words*, 144; Böttrich, "Proexistenz," 421. It may be significant that there are virtually no significant variants in the longer form of the text, with the exception of a reversal of "and the cup likewise" (assimilation to 1 Corinthians). If the longer text were a later addition, variation would be expected (unless we can trace all occurrences of it back to a common ancestor).

[203] Cited by Metzger, *A Textual Commentary on the Greek New Testament*, 150. The weaknesses of this view are that the scribes also omitted the second part of v. 19, and that scribes who knew the text of the other Gospels would have known that the cup after the bread saying was the sacramental cup; however, they might have wished to retain the peculiarly Lucan material. The omission of v. 19b could, of course, be accounted for as an assimilation of the text to that of Mark/Matthew.

[204] See the discussion in Billings, *Do This in Remembrance of Me*, 91–133. Nolland, *Luke 18:35–24:53*, 1041, favors the view that we have the abbreviation of a liturgical text but not for reasons of secrecy; everybody by this time knew what followed. But this is no explanation of why the abbreviation took place!

[205] Bock, *Luke*, 2:1722, n. 13, speaks of "a scribal reduction for liturgical reasons," but does not explain what such reasons might be. A similar view is taken by Hahn (*Die Einheit*, 555), who holds that a restriction to the bread saying was current in the area reflected

trich offers the improbable hypothesis that a scribe could have created the shorter text to get rid of the atonement motif for which the longer text is the sole evidence in the theology of Luke-Acts.[206] The possibility of accidental scribal omission has been raised. This should not be regarded as impossible, given the erratic behavior of scribes,[207] but it is less likely if this omission is seen as part of a set of western readings.

Schürmann argues that Luke 22:15–18 gives an account of the Passover meal followed in vv. 19–20 by the actual eucharistic meal. For Schürmann this Jewish-Christian meal originally began with breaking of bread after the preliminary course and concluded with thanksgiving for the wine (the third cup in the series) after the main course.[208] At a second stage in the early church there was a move to put the breaking of bread and the thanksgiving for the cup together at the end of the main course. A third stage is attested by the time of Justin when the eucharist was separated from the meal and associated with a verbal service in the morning. Schürmann claims that the longer text in Luke could correspond to stage one or stage two, but the shorter text can only reflect stage three when the eucharistic ritual was celebrated on its own. Hence the shorter text arose as a result of a desire to bring the text into harmony with church practice.[209]

B. S. Billings proposes that:

the shorter reading is an intentionally abbreviated text that serves to safeguard the community *cultus* against misinterpretation and misunderstanding by outsiders, not for esoteric reasons, but to avoid socially and politically destructive allegations.[210]

He reminds his readers how the early church was exposed to allegations and accusations of various crimes including infanticide, cannibalism (including

---

in the text of D it. But the shorter text does not testify to communion in bread only, but rather to the order cup → bread.

[206] Böttrich, "Proexistenz," 421. But why should someone in the second-century church have been so motivated?

[207] It is rejected by Ehrman, *Orthodox Corruption*, 208, on the grounds that there was nothing in the text that could lead to such an accident. Billings (*Do This in Remembrance of Me*, 87–88) notes that D has the disputed words as a single colophon (το σωμα μου πλην ιδου η χειρ του), showing that the scribe took them as expressing "a continuous unit of thought," thus making accidental omission a less likely explanation; cf. Bradly S. Billings, "The Disputed Words in the Lukan Institution Narrative (Luke 22:19b–20): A Sociological Answer to a Textual Problem," *JBL* 125 (2006): 511, n. 12. Despite Ehrman's comment, scribal accidents are not necessarily to be accounted for rationally. Might it be significant that the longer text begins and ends with parallel phrases τὸ ὑπὲρ ὑμῶν ἐκχυννόμενον? Is there the possibility of a kind of homoioteleuton where the scribe was confused and omitted both instances of the phrase?

[208] Consequently, there is nothing improbable about Luke's account, and it fits in with the paschal meal ritual.

[209] Schürmann, *Traditionsgeschichtliche Untersuchungen*, 185–91.

[210] Billings, *Do This in Remembrance of Me*, 136.

the drinking of human blood) and orgiastic sex. The Last Supper narratives were particularly open to supporting such misinterpretation, and therefore the omission of the misleading words could have been carried out at a point in the transmission of Luke when its western text still circulated separately from that of the other Gospels. This could have occurred at Lyons, where such accusations were circulating. The identification of this point in time for the omission would explain why nothing similar was done in the texts of the other Last Supper narratives (or John 6).[211]

A possible weakness in this proposal is that the identification of the bread as "my body" could still be thought to imply cannibalism, but Billings holds that this part of the wording would have been unclear, and that the other omissions took away the most offensive items, the identification of the contents of the cup with the blood of Jesus and the terminology indicative of a *sacramentum*.[212]

One significant merit of this solution is that it gives an explanation of why the shorter text is found only in the case of Luke's Gospel and is not found in MSS of Mark or Matthew. It gives a cogent explanation of the abbreviation as being due to local circumstances.

Billings has produced a possible explanation of the development of the shorter text which is sufficiently robust.

Finally, O. Skarsaune says:

The decisive argument ... is the simple fact that the long text is the only one that does *not* conform to any known liturgical practice in the later church. It therefore cannot be explained as an attempt to streamline the account of the last supper into conformity with later liturgical practice, whereas the short version of Luke's text makes it agree with the liturgy of *Didache* 9. If Luke 22:19–20 were a literary interpolation from 1 Cor 11, we would have the strange situation that a purely literary operation resulted in a text which makes excellent sense within the sequence of the Passover meal![213]

This explanation fits in with the fact that some of the indirect evidence for the shorter text is found in "western" authorities which seem to have some relationship to Syria.

---

[211] Billings, *Do This in Remembrance of Me*, 165–74; Billings, "Disputed Words".

[212] Billings, *Do This in Remembrance of Me*, 160, refers to another possible objection raised by McGowan who questions the connection between the accusations against the Christians and possible misunderstanding of the Lord's Supper. See Andrew McGowan, "Eating People: Accusations of Cannibalism Against Christians in the Second Century," *JECS* 2 (1994): 413–42.

[213] Skarsaune, *In the Shadow of the Temple*, 403, n. 8. According to Skarsaune (following Mazza), Luke 22:14–20 gives the original sequence of cup, bread, meal and cup. But this left one cup without explanation, so the result was that different groups simplified to cup → bread before meal (Didache; ? 1 Cor 10) or to bread → (meal) → cup (Mark; 1 Cor 11).

The proposals by Billings and Skarsaune are both plausible and deserve further examination. I conclude that the case for the shorter text is not irrefutable. If the longer text is authentic, then it is possible that we have another partly independent witness to the eucharistic sayings which stands alongside the Pauline evidence. In what follows we shall endeavor to avoid basing an argument on the uncertainties affecting either solution.

If the shorter text is not original, then there is no argument for the very early existence of a Lord's Supper celebration that took a different shape from that attested by our other NT sources. The earlier part of Luke's account appears to be a different tradition concerning the course of the earlier part of the meal. The shorter text is then an abbreviation of Luke's original text at a fairly early date for one or other of the reasons suggested above.

2.3.7. The Nature and Date of the Meal: Paschal or Otherwise

Uncertainty and debate regarding the precise date of an occurrence is not necessarily an indication of unhistoricity.[214] The various traditions agree that the events took place around the time of the Jewish Passover, but they differ as to whether the crucifixion took place after the Passover sacrifices had been offered on the previous day (so apparently the Synoptic Gospels) or at the same time (so apparently John's Gospel). The point is important not only for determining the nature of the meal but also because a discrepancy between the witnesses on so important a point could affect the question of whether a paschal meal was held at all. In addition, uncertainty on what might be regarded as a key feature in the story might be thought to threaten the historicity of the event.

As regards the year of the crucifixion and hence of the meal, the NT authors offer no information, and therefore none of them can be faulted for making any error in this matter. Astronomical considerations have reduced the possibilities to 30 or 33 C.E., and nothing significant for our present purposes hangs on the choice between them.[215]

The key question is rather the nature and timing of the meal held by Jesus. There are four main possibilities.[216] It may have been a meal that had no spe-

---

[214] Compare the vast number of people in earlier times who did not know their own date of birth.

[215] For 30 C.E.: John P. Meier, *The Roots of the Problem and the Person* (vol. 1 of *A Marginal Jew: Rethinking the Historical Jesus*; ABRL; New York: Doubleday, 1991–2009), 401–2; for 33 C.E.: Harold W. Hoehner, *Chronological Aspects of the Life of Christ* (Grand Rapids: Zondervan, 1977). Brown, *The Death of the Messiah*, 2:1373–76, sees no way of settling between 30 and 33, and clearly does not think that it matters.

[216] There is, of course, the possibility that the question is insoluble. So, for example, Fitzmyer, *Luke X–XXIV*, 1382.

cifically paschal features,[217] or a Passover meal held at the normal time for doing so in accordance with the [official] Jewish calendar. A third alternative is that it was a meal held at an earlier date which could nevertheless have had a broadly paschal character, since it was being held at some point in the "Passover season." (One might compare a "birthday" meal held for some reason on a date close to the anniversary rather than on the actual day.) A fourth possibility is that it was a meal held at an earlier date or time which was in fact regarded by those who celebrated it as a paschal meal (with or without a lamb) in accordance with some alternative calendar or timetable.

2.3.7.1. Jeremias's Arguments concerning the Nature of the Meal

The Synoptic Gospels say that the meal was a Passover meal. This is the unavoidable implication of the story of the preparation for the meal (Mark 14:12–16); Luke records that at the meal Jesus spoke of eating "this Passover" (Luke 22:15). We have already seen that there is no intrinsic reason for disputing the historicity of the story of the preparation. It should also be noted, as an argument from silence, that there are no features of the meal in the Synoptic accounts which would be inappropriate in a paschal meal.[218]

Paul's so-called silence on the matter is not an issue, since there is no reason why he should have been expected to mention it. The problem is the apparent denial by John whose account contains not only no "eucharistic" features but also no paschal features.[219].

McKnight proposes that it was Mark who fashioned the meal of Jesus into a Passover meal, in other words that "Mark 'Passoverised' a Passover week meal into the *Pesah* meal itself." The meal was a celebration of the Passover although it was apparently not a Passover meal in the technical sense of the term.[220] But McKnight furnishes no real argument as to why Mark should have done so.

The classic study of Jeremias listed fourteen points which either are compatible with a Passover meal or are better explained on that assump-

---

[217] Presumably such a meal would not have taken place on the usual date and time for a Passover meal. If a meal was held at that time, it could hardly have been other than a paschal meal.

[218] The one point that might be raised is the alleged lack of reference to a paschal lamb. But this is an argument from silence, and it is countered by the argument that the description of the meal is limited to those features which were important for the church's meal. The claim that Luke 22:15 refers to the lamb is justified in my opinion. See C. K. Barrett, "Luke XXII.15: To Eat the Passover," *JTS* 9 (1958): 305–7.

[219] Apart from some possible hints that have been detected beneath the surface of the narrative. Note Witherington's view (*Making a Meal of It*, 63–85) that it is a different meal that is being described in John. See n. 140.

[220] McKnight, *Jesus and His Death*, 271–73. I call this a proposal because it is difficult to find evidence for or against it. The best that might be done is to provide a convincing reason why Mark should have wanted to make the identification.

tion.²²¹ We need to distinguish carefully as far as possible between these two categories and also (as noted above) to look for any features that may be inconsistent with a paschal meal. Moreover, in view of the ambiguity of the dating, we should distinguish features that belong inherently to the pattern and content of the meal from those features that may belong rather to the impression given by the Evangelists. Some scholars regard the paschal account of the meal as a framework created by the evangelists into which a non-paschal "statement" has been incorporated. But, since such a statement could have been focused on describing what was significant for the early church's practice, we might not expect paschal features to be necessarily preserved. Certainly by the time of Paul the Lord's Supper was celebrated frequently and not just annually as a form of Christian Passover.

First, the Passover meal had to be held in Jerusalem. Despite lodging at Bethany, it is stated that Jesus and his disciples came into Jerusalem for the meal; it is assumed that Bethany was outside the boundary. Clearly they could have held a meal in Jerusalem for some other reason, and so this statement by itself is not a proof that the meal was a Passover meal. However, it gains considerably in force in the light of the comment that Jesus stayed in Jerusalem for it is contrary to his custom on other nights (Luke 21:37).

Second, a room was readily made available for him in Jerusalem. Jeremias attaches no weight to this.

Third, the meal was held at night (Paul!), contrary to usual practice. It seems that other, festive or formal meals were not normally held so late. Jeremias mentions as exceptions circumcision and weddings, but clearly this meal was not of that kind. McKnight argues that the meal could have been late in the day for any number of plausible but hypothetical reasons.

Fourth, the number of persons present was ten-plus, but not larger than a family gathering. This has no force.²²²

Fifth, the guests reclined. This was a Rabbinic requirement for the Passover, but it also seems to have been the practice at other formal and festive meals.²²³

---

²²¹ Cf. Hengel, "Das Mahl in der Nacht," 141–56; Casey, *Aramaic Sources*, 229, makes the important point that Mark does not go out of his way to stress the paschal features of the meal because he has already made it clear to his readers that it was a paschal meal and assumed that they would understand it accordingly.

²²² See n. 54 for the question whether others besides the Twelve were present. Gnilka, *Jesus of Nazareth*, 279, allows the possibility that women were present. McKnight, *Jesus and His Death*, 254–55, argues that Mary was present, since she was in Jerusalem at and after the crucifixion.

²²³ It was certainly normal at Graeco-Roman formal meals. It is not clear whether Jeremias, *Eucharistic Words*, 48–49, has eliminated the possibility of reclining at other meals. He notes that people naturally reclined at meals in the open air. He holds that at ordinary indoor meals people sat at the table. He has to allow that Luke 12:37; 22:27 refer to special occasions. The Gospels, however, refer to various meals at which Jesus and

Sixth, the guests were in a state of levitical purity, if this is a correct deduction from John 13:10. How far this was necessary for Passover in the first century is not clear, but it is a possible pointer to the occasion's sacred nature.

Seventh, the reported order of events corresponds with a Passover meal. Eating of the bread was not the first item on the menu, and this fits the Passover seder but appears to be contrary to Jewish custom otherwise. It has been objected that formal meals might include a preliminary course before entry to the dining room; but just how formal was this occasion (and how lavish the facilities)? McKnight objects that bread could surely be eaten at any time in a meal; but what is described is not just eating bread but a significant act of giving thanks for it.

Skarsaune notes how Luke 22:14–20 matches the Passover sequence; the thanks for the first cup and the bread corresponds to the introductory *qiddush* (blessing) before the meal and the thanks for a further cup comes at the end of the meal and corresponds to the *birkat ha-mazon*.[224] There is general agreement that, if this is a Passover meal, the cup in question would be the third cup in the sequence, "the cup of blessing."[225]

Unfortunately there is uncertainty surrounding the order of the meal before 70 C.E. B.M. Bokser claims that the so-called seder meal, as we know it from the Mishnah, did not develop until after that date. It may be unwise, therefore, to attach too much significance to coincidences with

---

others reclined (e.g., Mark 2:15; 14:3; Luke 7:36, 49). These were meals at which guests were present, and the Last Supper could be seen as such a meal. Smith, *From Symposium to Eucharist*, 349, n. 8, proposes that the Gospel references generally to people "reclining" at meals with Jesus are (fictitious) attempts "at presenting Jesus in a table setting corresponding to the conventions of the Greco-Roman banquet as it was practiced and represented in literature throughout the Greco-Roman world." This is historical skepticism running riot. We cannot rule out the possibility of Hellenistic influence on Jewish practice (cf. Hengel and Schwemer, *Jesus und das Judentum*, 583, n. 57; Witherington, *Making a Meal of It*, 13). In any case, the simple fact is that no other verb expressing posture seems to have been in use. The verb καθίζω was evidently not preferred for posture at a meal; it is used only once in the NT in an LXX citation for sitting down to eat and drink. It would seem more likely that the "recline" verbs had come to mean simply "to have a meal" or "to adopt the appropriate posture for a meal" without specifying what particular posture was adopted (other than a change from standing). See Jeremias, *Eucharistic Words*, 48, n. 5.

[224] Skarsaune, *In the Shadow of the Temple*, 402–3.

[225] The identification depends on how the synoptic accounts are to be interpreted in the light of the seder (cf. *m. Pesaḥ*. 10:7; *b. Pesaḥ*. 118a). A case for the fourth cup was offered by D. M. Cohn-Sherbok, "A Jewish Note on τὸ ποτήριον τῆς εὐλογίας," *NTS* 27 (1981): 704–9, and for the second by Phillip Sigal, "Another Note to 1 Corinthians 10:16," *NTS* 29 (1983): 134–39. If the course of the meal did not follow the seder, the problem does not arise.

the seder, although the traditional account is supported by R. Routledge's recent treatment.[226]

Jeremias' eighth and ninth points are that wine was drunk, specifically red wine,[227] which was a Passover requirement. But clearly red wine could have been drunk on other festive occasions.

Tenth, Judas went out and was thought to be buying something for the feast or to give alms; this makes sense if there would be no opportunity for purchases thereafter. On any other occasion purchases could be made the next day.

Eleventh, concern for the poor seems to have been associated with Passover, and there is no obvious reason why alms should have been given on any other night.

Twelfth, the meal ended with singing. This was characteristic of the Passover meal and not of other meals.[228] But church practice might have been

---

[226] A general outline of the Passover meal, based on the material in Pesahim and later Jewish sources, is given by Str-B 4.1:41–76; cf. Jeremias, *Eucharistic Words*, 84–88; Gordon J. Bahr, "Seder of Passover and the Eucharistic Words," *NovT* 12 (1970): 181–202. Various scholars note, but without elaborating on the point, that the liturgy underwent significant changes after the destruction of the temple; see Peter J. Tomson, "Jesus and His Judaism," in *The Cambridge Companion to Jesus* (ed. Markus Bockmuehl; Cambridge ; New York: Cambridge University Press, 2001), 39; Davies and Allison, *Matthew*, 3:469, n. 98. For details of current Jewish scholarship see Baruch M. Bokser, *The Origins of the Seder: The Passover Rite and Early Rabbinic Judaism* (Berkeley: University of California Press, 1984); Baruch M. Bokser, "Unleavened Bread and Passover, Feasts Of," *ABD* 6:763–64. The subsequent account given by Robin Routledge, "Passover and Last Supper," *TynBul* 53 (2002): 203–21, although referring to Bokser, does not show any fundamental differences from earlier accounts, and McKnight, *Jesus and His Death*, 264, n. 16, criticizes him for failing to take recent scholarship into account. It is argued that the Passover seder was created after 70 C. E. to provide a basis for continuing observation of Passover without the possibility of offering the sacrifice in the temple. Apparently the Passover lamb was no longer part of the meal and did not feature in the interpretation of the elements. Consequently, we cannot read back from the seder to pre-70 practice, and instead of regarding the NT as a first-century witness to Jewish practice, it is said to be more likely that Jewish practice, specifically the recital of the Haggadah, developed in reaction to the Christian observance of the Lord's Supper. See further Christine Schlund, "Deutungen des Todes Jesu im Rahmen der Pesach-Tradition," in *Deutungen des Todes Jesu im Neuen Testament* (ed. Jörg Frey and Jens Schröter; WUNT 181; Tübingen: Mohr Siebeck, 2005), 398–99, following Joseph Tabory, "Towards a History of the Paschal Meal," in *Passover and Easter: Origin and History to Modern Times* (ed. Paul F. Bradshaw and Lawrence A. Hoffman; Notre Dame: University of Notre Dame Press, 1999), 62–80, and Israel J. Yuval, "Easter and Passover As Early Jewish-Christian Dialogue," in *Passover and Easter: Origin and History to Modern Times* (ed. Paul F. Bradshaw and Lawrence A. Hoffman; Notre Dame: University of Notre Dame Press, 1999), 98–124.

[227] The assumption is that the symbolism with blood would have been odd otherwise.

[228] If a Passover meal, this would be the second part of the *hallel*. Presumably this custom is open to the same skepticism regarding the content of the first-century Passover celebration as the other elements. See Gundry, *Mark*, 846, for support, pointing out that LXX usage of the verb supports a reference to the singing of Jewish Psalms. Hengel and

read back. We cannot exclude the possibility that other meals concluded with singing.[229]

Thirteenth, Jesus followed Passover practice in staying in Jerusalem after the meal and not attempting to return to Bethany.[230]

Jeremias' fourteenth and final point is that the provision of an interpretation of the special elements (in this case the bread and cup) fits in with a custom at the Passover meal, but not at any other that is known to us.[231] The motif of remembrance is written into the Passover celebration at its foundation: "This day shall be [a day of] remembrance for you" (Exod 12:14 NRSV).[232] To be more precise, the paschal lamb, bread and bitter herbs were interpreted in the Passover meal, whereas Jesus interpreted the bread and the cup. Although Jesus interpreted the bread, he did not do so with respect to its unleavened nature, although Paul as a Jew was aware of its character and in a different context employed this symbolism. (Wine would not have been interpreted in the Passover meal because it was not an integral part of the Passover in the Hebrew Scriptures[233]). Jesus did not interpret the lamb typologically either because there was none or because he chose not to interpret it. Consequently, the understanding of the meal as one for remembering

---

Schwemer, *Jesus und das Judentum*, 583, note that the Hallel concluded with Ps 118, and argues that the early church cry *Maranatha* at the end of the Lord's Supper developed from this use of Ps 118:26 (with Dan 7:13). (One might trace "till he comes," 1 Cor 11:26, to the same source.)

[229] Singing at Hellenistic meals is well attested. But citation of Athenaeus as evidence for what pious Jews in Jerusalem might have done seems quite anachronistic! One might as well use a rowdy night at a sleazy downtown pub as shedding light on a contemporary church meal.

[230] Mention should be made of the argument in Kevin O'Brien, *But the Gates Were Shut* (San Francisco: International Scholars Publications, 1996), that the gates of Jerusalem were shut every night at sunset, even during festivals, and therefore the various goings in and out described in the Gospels cannot have taken place. Against his assertions see the earlier work of Jeremias, *Eucharistic Words*, 55; he observes that, although Passover pilgrims had to eat the Passover meal within the city itself, they nevertheless encamped around Jerusalem (Jos. *Ant.* 17:217; *J. W.* 2:12; cf. 11Q 17:9), and therefore means of access in and out must have been available for them.

[231] McKnight, *Jesus and His Death*, 256, claims that it is doubtful whether the *Haggadah* was a liturgical custom at this time. He is not clear on the point, since he also states that "*Pesah* was an official meal followed by instruction consisting of reciting the exodus and some psalms as well as an explanation of the events of the exodus for the family" (p. 249). The reason for doubt appears to be the hypothesis that the development of the Haggadah was due to the desire to provide a substitute for the act of sacrifice, along the same lines as the Mishnah generally provides a substitute for temple worship. It is an argument from silence, omitting the possibility that the development was of an existing feature rather than something with no precedent. It must be emphasized that "the closest parallel to the words interpreting the elements of the Supper is above all the Passover Meal" (Kuhn, "The Qumran Meal," 233).

[232] Hengel, "Das Mahl in der Nacht," 147–48.

[233] Skarsaune, *In the Shadow of the Temple*, 402.

God's mighty act of salvation fits in very neatly into a meal which already had this purpose in the first century.[234]

Jesus thus did not re-interpret those three elements which already had a Jewish interpretation. The effects of this, intended or unintended, are that the church's meal was not celebrated as a paschal meal and tied down to a Passover setting (whether in character or in dating).[235] Furthermore, the church's meal did not retain a fundamentally Jewish character but became open to a non-Jewish setting.

2.3.7.2. Objections to the Paschal Character of the Meal Itself

Before weighing this evidence, account must be taken of possible objections to the paschal character of the meal. These are of two kinds. The first group consists of problems with the description of the course of the actual meal. The second is a set of problems associated with the time and date of the meal held by Jesus.

First, a fundamental problem is the point already noted that recent scholarship doubts that our sources give us a reliable picture of the Passover meal before 70 C. E.; consequently, it is argued, similarities between the reports of Jesus' meal in the Gospels and the later picture of the Passover cannot count for much, and the state of the sources may be such as to make the attempt in principle impossible.

Clearly this argument can be used both ways. If it is said to forbid showing that the meal was a paschal meal, equally any differences between the meal and later paschal practice cannot be used as evidence that the meal was not conducted in accordance with pre-70 paschal practice. And if accounts of Jesus' meal, found in first-century documents, contain elements that belong to later paschal practice, this testimony could be regarded as contemporary evidence for the existence of these elements already before 70.[236]

Second, it has been argued that it would have been difficult, if not impossible to find a free room in Jerusalem on Passover night. But this is pure speculation and, in any case, the story suggests a pre-booking with somebody already known to Jesus.[237]

---

[234] The recounting of the Lord's death in the church's meal (1 Cor 11:26) will rest on this Passover practice; cf. Hengel and Schwemer, *Jesus und das Judentum*, 583.

[235] Unless this happened when the meal coincided with the Jewish Passover.

[236] Schlund, "Deutungen des Todes Jesu," 398, appears to assume that the early Christian reports of the Last Supper represent ecclesiastical attempts to create roots for the Lord's Supper celebration in a hypothetical last meal of Jesus, and that these attempts were concurrent with the Jewish developments.

[237] Presumably there would have been no difficulty with a meal 24 hours earlier.

Third, an old objection is that the term "bread" does not signify "unleavened bread."[238] This argument has been refuted in detail and can be confidently set aside.[239]

Fourth, it is often remarked that there is no mention of going to the temple to slaughter a lamb. One possibility is that this did not need to be said because it was an accepted part of the preparations. Another possibility is that Mark 14:12 means "when they (sc. the disciples) were sacrificing the lamb," they asked Jesus where the meal was to be held.[240] This interpretation is certainly possible for Mark, but Luke 22:7 may suggest that Luke understood Mark to be referring to the day when "they" (sc. people in general) sacrificed their lambs. Either way, there would not seem to be a substantial objection.

Fifth, it is said that there is no mention of other items in the Passover meal; specifically, the lamb and bitter herbs are passed over in silence. Why did Jesus not compare himself with the lamb?

It is a sufficient answer that the account tends to focus on the elements that were significant from a Christian standpoint and carried over into the Christian meal.[241] More positively, however, the bowl of bitter herbs is implicit in Mark 14:20, and the provision of a lamb may well be implied in Mark 14:12 and probably mentioned in Luke 22:15. The Gospel of the Ebionites inserts the word "meat" before "this Passover," showing that the phrase was understood to mean "this Passover lamb"; the word is a gloss to make clear what the ambiguous phrase signifies.[242]

Sixth, the objection that at Passover the breaking of bread preceded the blessing, contrary to the description of Jesus blessing and then breaking the bread, has been shown to be erroneous. Passover was like any other meal in this respect.[243]

Seventh, according to P. Billerbeck's interpretation of the evidence individual cups were used at Passover, not a common one. However, according to Jeremias this objection rests on an erroneous misreading of late Jewish sources.[244] We simply do not know for certain what first-century practice was, compared with that of the second century. And we certainly cannot

---

[238] J. Wellhausen, "Ἄρτον ἔκλασεν Mc 14,22," *ZNW* 7 (1906): 182. Bultmann, *Geschichte*, 285, n. 4, admits that this could simply be carelessness.

[239] Jeremias, *Eucharistic Words*, 62–66. Nevertheless, Schmithals, *Markus*, 606, still holds to this view without supplying any evidence for it (he does the same with regard to the use of the common or individual cups).

[240] Casey, *Aramaic Sources*, 222–23.

[241] It does not have to be a "cultic formula" (as Jeremias, *Eucharistic Words*, 67, supposes) for this to be the case.

[242] Cited above, n. 7.

[243] Jeremias, *Eucharistic Words*, 68–69.

[244] Jeremias, *Eucharistic Words*, 69–70; the Jewish sources are in Str-B 4.1:58–61.

rule out Jesus doing something unusual. Schürmann claims strongly that Jeremias's interpretation is mistaken, that individual cups were most probably in use at a formal meal, and that Jesus was in fact doing something highly unusual.[245] At the very least, Schürmann's interpretation must be said to be possible, but it may be best to admit our ignorance of first-century practice.

Eighth, it is also said that each guest had his own dish of bitter herbs (contrast Mark 14:20 where bread is dipped "in the bowl"). However, this custom is only known from late Jewish sources.[246]

2.3.7.3. The Issue of the Date of the Meal

A further group of problems for the paschal character of the meal arises from the question of when it was held.

First, Mark 14:2 speaks of a plan to avoid the arrest of Jesus "during the feast"(so TNIV; NRSV). If the meal was a regular Passover meal, this plan was not carried out. Jeremias argued that the phrase means "in the presence of the festal crowd."[247] But one could also interpret the story to mean that Judas provided the authorities with an opportunity to arrest Jesus at a place and time when there would be no crowds of supporters, and therefore they were able to proceed to arrest him even though the feast was still on.[248]

Second, one possible interpretation of the offer to release Barabbas (Mark 15:6) is based on the Jewish custom of allowing prisoners to celebrate the Passover (as per *m. Pesaḥ* 8:6),[249] but this action would have come too late for him to be able to eat the Passover. Certainly the narrative links the release with the fact that there was a festival in progress, and it makes best sense for the release to be in time for the main point in the celebration.[250] There is, however, some dispute whether the Jewish regulation is relevant to this action, particularly as we are concerned here with a Roman action.

Third, the argument that 1 Cor 5:7 states that Christ died at the same time as the slaughter of the lambs rests on the dubious assumption that Paul's statement implies a specific time for his death.

Fourth, similarly, 1 Cor 15:20 has been interpreted to mean that Christ rose on the same day as the first fruits were dedicated, i.e., on the morrow after the sabbath, Nisan 16; therefore (in order to be raised on the third day) he cannot have died later than Nisan 14, the day of preparation for

---

[245] Schürmann, *Der Paschamahlbericht*, 60–61; cf. Schürmann, *Jesu ureigener Tod*, 76–77.

[246] Jeremias, *Eucharistic Words*, 70–71.

[247] Jeremias, *Eucharistic Words*, 71–73; similarly Schmithals, *Markus*, 588.

[248] Cf. Hengel and Schwemer, *Jesus und das Judentum*, 584, for the argument that the time immediately after the Feast was ideal for the arrest, since most of Jerusalem would have been celebrating the meal or sleeping off the aftereffects.

[249] Evans, *Mark*, 479–80, gives a full summary of the debate on this point.

[250] If Jesus' own meal was before the "official" date, this objection would lose its force.

the Passover. But it is questionable whether Paul is making a chronological statement here.

Fifth, it is said that the Quarto-Deciman practice of celebrating the meal on the afternoon of Nisan 14 developed on the basis of the belief that this was when they believed that Christ had died. Jeremias has shown this to be erroneous.[251]

Sixth, if the last supper was a Passover meal, then the following unlikely, if not impossible, events took place on a feast day: (1) The Sanhedrin met to try Jesus on the feast day. Whatever happened seems to have been irregular. (2) The Roman trial took place on a feast day, an action that would have been insensitive to Jewish feelings. (3) Not only Jesus (a special case) but also two ordinary criminals were executed the same day. (4) The burial and purchases for it could not have happened on the evening of the day of Passover which was a Sabbath. Exceptions were possible. (5) Simon came in to Jerusalem from the fields.

Some of these objections have little weight (particularly 3 and 4), but the others are more forceful. What is sometimes overlooked is that they could well apply to a dating on the day of preparation for the Passover as well. But none of them is sufficiently substantial to affect the argument.

Seventh and finally, it is urged that the early church's daily (or weekly) rite cannot have been derived from a kind of meal that happened only annually. It is an adequate reply to this point that the early church meals were also related to the everyday meals of Jesus with his disciples. Jeremias states that originally the disciples' post-Easter meals were repetitions and continuations of the daily table fellowship that they had had together when Jesus was with them.[252] and that only gradually, but still in the very early pre-Pauline period, were they linked with and influenced by the Last Supper.[253] It is quite feasible that originally the memorial of the Lord's death was associated with the Easter season and then came to be incorporated in the regular congregational meals. [254] We do not know how soon these meals took on the pattern of the meals attested by Paul. Manifestly we are dealing with a very short time span of a few years at most. It is not inconceivable (to put it no stronger) that the pattern of the Last Supper began to be adopted as an annual meal practice,[255] and then influenced the weekly meals. But this was not

---

[251] Jeremias, *Eucharistic Words*, 83–85, 122–25.

[252] Jeremias, *Eucharistic Words*, 66.

[253] Cf. Jeremias, *Eucharistic Words*, 66, 204–7.

[254] Some such explanation is generally accepted by scholars who believe that the church's meal was shaped from an early date by the Last Supper.

[255] This could be the case whether or not the Last Supper was itself a paschal meal; it is clear that the association of the death of Jesus with the Passover season was early. Attention has been directed to the annual Christian paschal meals of the Quarto-Decimans as evidence pointing in this direction. Cf. Hengel, "Das Mahl in der Nacht," 119, n. 16;

necessarily the case. More probably the frequency of the daily gatherings described in Acts belonged to the early days of the church in Jerusalem and a less frequent practice developed as time went on. There is no incompatability between frequent meals and special annual occasion.

These considerations show that the actual meal was understood by the Synoptic Evangelists to be a Passover meal, and the objections made to features of the meal itself as being incompatible with this can be answered. There are greater difficulties with the surrounding events. And, of course, there is the *prima facie* interpretation of John as placing the meal a day earlier. However, it is a moot point whether the evidence is adequate to demonstrate beyond all doubt that it was a Passover meal rather than any other kind. Here we are hindered by the uncertainties regarding paschal practice in the first century and by the indecisiveness of the evidence in providing points that require it could only have been a Passover meal. One thing at least is abundantly clear: to deny that it could have been a Passover meal goes well beyond the evidence.

If the meal was not a Passover meal, it could have been either a quasi-Passover meal (in the sense of being held in the context of the imminent Passover festival) or an ordinary meal that was specially remembered in the light of what followed or perhaps some other kind of Jewish meal[256]. The various possibilities noted above for the origin of the church's meal, namely a kiddush meal,[257] a haburah meal, and an Essene meal, were also suggested by earlier scholars as models for Jesus' meal, but they have been discounted by Jeremias.[258] Gese's more recent suggestion of a thanksgiving meal in anticipation of his own death has not found favor.[259] A further possibility is that it was a Passover meal but one held at a time other than that appointed by the "official" calendar.

2.3.7.4. Alternative Proposals concerning the Date of the Meal

In the light of these points we consider the various types of explanation concerning the date of the meal.

First, was it a non-paschal meal? From some points of view the easiest hypothesis to adopt would be that the meal held by Jesus was not a paschal

---

Anna Maria Schwemer, "Das Problem der *Mahlgemeinschaft* mit dem Auferstandenen," in *Le Repas de Dieu: Das Mahl Gottes* (ed. Christian Grappe; Tübingen: Mohr Siebeck, 2004), 208–17.

[256] See the critical survey by Paul F. Bradshaw, *The Search for the Origins of Christian Worship: Sources and Methods for the Study of Early Liturgy* (New York: Oxford University Press, 1992), 49–51.

[257] Cf. Bo Reicke, *The New Testament Era: The World of the Bible from 500 B.C. to A.D. 100* (trans. David E. Green; Philadelphia: Fortress, 1968), 178, 181.

[258] Jeremias, *Eucharistic Words*, 26–36.

[259] Gese, *Essays on Biblical Theology*, 125.

meal in any sense (except that it fell within the Passover time of year), and the synoptic presentation of it as such is mistaken. If this view is adopted, then the problem of the chronological discrepancy disappears, and elaborate hypotheses to account for the two different dates are unnecessary. The Johannine dating may be taken as a genuine possibility, unless it is regarded as theologically motivated and therefore historically useless.[260]

It should be emphasized that acceptance of this view does not require that the actual description of the meal itself be treated as fictitious. If we did not have the Synoptic Gospels and were dependent solely on the Pauline narrative, the nature of the meal would remain an open question,[261] and the paschal problems simply would not arise.[262]

Second, was it a paschal meal at the "official" time? If the meal was a proper Passover meal, we have to offer some cogent explanation of the apparently different calendar of events in John. This has been done in three ways.

The first is to argue that for theological reasons John has synchronized the death of Jesus with the slaughter of the paschal lambs so that an appropriate typology could be traced.[263] The identification of Christ as "our Passover" (1 Cor 5:7) is early and could lie at the root of such a development. John has (on this view) dropped all paschal (and indeed all eucharistic) features from the meal, placed it before the Passover and told the story as if everything happened 24 hours earlier.

There are difficulties with this proposal. One is that Passover typology is not so highly developed elsewhere in John as to make this theological move likely. Another is that, if the tradition reflected in the other Gospels was well-known at this time, it is difficult to see how John could have "got away" with such a fictitious re-dating.[264] But against this argument it could be noted that John at least gives the impression that the cleansing of the

---

[260] So Schmithals, *Markus*, 605–7; Theissen and Merz, *The Historical Jesus*, 426–27. According to Schmithals the date of the passion of Jesus cannot be ascertained, although it is not unlikely that Jesus was in Jerusalem at the Passover season. Paul N. Anderson, *The Fourth Gospel and the Quest for Jesus: Modern Foundations Reconsidered* (LNTS 321; London: T&T Clark, 2006), argues that John's dating is not theologically motivated and that his presentation of the meal as a common meal rather than a Passover meal is plausible; the words of institution ("cultic innocence") were not used (information from author). Cf. Witherington, *Making a Meal of It*, 63–65.

[261] However, the question of the nature of a meal at which the bread and cup have symbolical value could arise, and the simplest answer is a paschal meal.

[262] The difference between this interpretation and that which sees the meal as a kind of substitute for a proper Passover meal and hence celebrated in a paschal mood is not great; cf. McKnight, *Jesus and His Death*, 264–73.

[263] So Gnilka, *Jesus of Nazareth*, 280; Gundry, *Mark*, 823; Hengel, "Das Mahl in der Nacht," 140; Hengel and Schwemer, *Jesus und das Judentum*, 582–86.

[264] This would be particularly the case if not only John but also his readers had some familiarity with Mark's Gospel.

temple took place early in Jesus' mission rather than later; could he not then in the same way have rearranged the passion events?

The second route is to argue that the impression given by John that everything took place 24 hours later than in the Synoptics is a mistaken one: the passages that seem to support this scenario can and should be interpreted otherwise. Thus it is claimed that John 13:1 does not refer to the time of the meal in v. 2 but to the knowledge and love of Jesus, and the meal itself can be understood as a Passover meal at the right time. John 18:28 refers to the desire of the Jewish leaders not to be ritually prevented from eating the various other meals that occurred during the rest of the Passover / leavened festival. John 19:14 is taken to mean not the day of preparation for the Passover (Nisan 14) but the day of preparation for the sabbath in Passover week (Friday, Nisan 15), as is also meant in John 19:31.[265]

These interpretations of the Johannine material have been strongly defended by a number of scholars, most fully by B. D. Smith.[266] Nevertheless, in my view they are not the most plausible reading of John.[267]

---

[265] See Jeremias, *Eucharistic Words*, 81–82, for the view that the Synoptic dating appears to be that of the tradition *behind* John. Thus John 19:14 and 31 refer to Friday in Passover week, not to Nisan 14. Further he notes that according to Bultmann, if the high sabbath of John 19:31 was the day of the sheaf offering, this would be Nisan 16, with the implication that Jesus was crucified on Nisan 15 (as in the Synoptics). But according to John's representation in 18:28 the Jewish leaders have evidently not yet eaten the Passover meal. Similarly, Beasley-Murray, *Jesus and the Kingdom of God*, 259 (repeated in George R. Beasley-Murray, *John* [WBC 36; Waco, Tex.: Word, 1987], 225); Nolland, *Luke 18:35–24:53*, 1024. Cf. Cullen I. K. Story, "The Bearing of Old Testament Terminology on the Johannine Chronology of the Final Passover of Jesus," *NovT* 31 (1989): 322–23, for the view that the leaders had sacrificed their lambs but had not yet been able to eat them because they had been interrupted by the need to arrest Jesus.

[266] See especially D. A. Carson, "Matthew," in *The Expositor's Bible Commentary* (ed. Frank E. Gaebelein; Grand Rapids: Zondervan, 1984), 8:528–32; Carson, *John*, 455–58, 460, 475, 589–90, 603–04, 622; Craig L. Blomberg, *The Historical Reliability of John's Gospel* (Downers Grove: InterVarsity, 2001), 187–88, 237–39, 246–47, 254.

[267] Donald A. Hagner, *Matthew 14–28* (WBC 33b; Dallas: Word, 1995), 764, states, "Any of these [other] possibilities seems preferable to the Herculean attempt to harmonize the discordant chronologies (as, e. g., by Carson, 528–32)." Cf. Leon Morris, *The Gospel According to John* (NICNT; Grand Rapids: Eerdmans, 1995), 774–86; Marshall, *Last Supper and Lord's Supper*, 68–70. Of the three points mentioned in the text, the first appears to be an unnatural reading of the text; the double reference to Jesus' knowledge in John 13:1 and 3 strengthens the case that "before the feast of the Passover" refers to the pericope as a whole; the attempt to distinguish the foot-washing (before the meal, on Nisan 14) from the meal itself (on Nisan 15) is not persuasive. The second point rests on an unnatural reading of the text, and is open to the objection by Morris, *The Gospel According to John*, 778–79, that the phrase is not attested in the sense of "the feast of unleavened bread without the Passover" (Carson, "Matthew," 531, claims that the objection is irrelevant, but I am not altogether convinced; cf. Jeremias, *Eucharistic Words*, 19–21). The third point is valid (cf. Jeremias, *Eucharistic Words*, 80–81).

A third route is taken by J. Nolland.[268] Noting the difficulties caused by the crowding of events following the meal on the assumption that the crucifixion took place that same day, he argues that Mark has produced "an artistic and theological day rather than a historical and chronological day."[269] In fact, the Passover could have been earlier in the week (cf. the Tuesday evening of the solar Qumran calendar) and Jesus was crucified on the Friday, with sufficient time in between to allow the various events (and incidentally to avoid the problems caused by the trial and crucifixion on the day of the festival).[270] Where John has given a theological dating of the death of Jesus, Mark has given a theological day for the events of last meal and crucifixion.

Third, was it a quasi-paschal meal before the "official" time? The view that Jesus held a meal earlier than the official time for the Passover meal, but one that had a paschal character has been developed in various different forms.[271] A very weak argument from silence in favor of this hypothesis is the non-mention of a paschal timing in the Pauline account. One late external source places the crucifixion before the Passover (*b. Sanh.* 43a), but it is not clear that much reliance can be placed on it.[272] M. Bockmuehl draws attention to Synoptic evidence that favors this dating: the report of the intention of his adversaries to avoid a crisis during the festival and the possible interpretation of Luke 22:15–16 to indicate a desire to take part in the celebration that he would not live to see.[273]

The principal difficulty with this view is that Mark 14:12 appears to place the preparation for the meal on the actual day when the Jews made their

---

[268] Nolland, *Luke 18:35–24:53*, 1023–26; John Nolland, *The Gospel of Matthew* (NIGTC; Grand Rapids: Eerdmans, 2005), 1044–46.

[269] He might have cited the possible parallel in Luke 24 which gives the impression that all the resurrection appearances and the final departure of Jesus took place on one day. Nolland's proposal is very similar to that of McKnight.

[270] On this view we are not limited to 30 and 33 C.E. as the only possible years for the crucifixion (since only in these years was Nisan 15 a Friday).

[271] Bockmuehl, *This Jesus*, 92–94; Wright, *Jesus and the Victory of God*, 555–56; Thiselton, *First Corinthians*, 871–74; McKnight, *Jesus and His Death*, 264–73. Cf. Evans, *Mark*, 370–72, who thinks that the Markan tradition is "confused and edited."

[272] The reference is to a baraita in *b. Sanh.* 43a, but the reliability of this reference is said to be too doubtful to allow any weight to be placed on it (in favor of it see Josef Blinzler, *The Trial of Jesus* [Westminster: Newman, 1959], 76, who says that the text is "tendentious, biased and unreliable in its other particulars ... but in the remark concerning the day of execution one seeks in vain for any bias"). According to Jeremias, *Eucharistic Words*, 19, n. 7, the baraita does not refer to Jesus of Nazareth but to an earlier namesake. Cf. Gnilka, *Jesus of Nazareth*, 280, n. 34, who refers to Johann Maier, *Jesus von Nazareth in der Talmudischen Überlieferung* (EdF 82; Darmstadt: Wissenschaftliche Buchgesellschaft, 1978), 219–37. See further L. H. Silberman, "Once Again: The Use of Rabbinic Material," *NTS* 42 (1996): 153–55. The same date is found in *Gos. Pet.* 2:5.

[273] Bockmuehl, *This Jesus*, 93.

sacrifices (Nisan 14), so that the meal itself would have taken place on Nisan 15. Various suggestions have been made to deal with the problem.

R. T. France argues that Jesus could have made his preparations and held his Supper after sunset in the evening of Thursday. This was in fact the earlier part of the day of preparation (Nisan 14, which ran from sunset on Thursday evening to sunset on Friday evening), i. e., the evening before the slaughter of the lambs. He was then crucified on the Friday which was still the same day of preparation before the official Jewish Passover was held on Friday evening (the beginning of Nisan 15).[274]. On this view, previous scholars have been misled into thinking that Mark 14:12 must refer to an event in the afternoon of Nisan 14, whereas it could refer to an event in the evening that formed the earlier, first part of that day.

The question arises whether such a meal would have included a paschal lamb. France assumes that serving a paschal lamb would not have been possible, but that this did not matter for Jesus since the lamb played no significant part in his meal.[275]

The critical question is whether this new proposal gives a natural reading of Mark 14:12 where the mention of making the sacrifice would seem to place the preparation at that time instead of some 18 hours earlier![276] Mark's account of the preparation for the meal appears to describe it clearly as a Passover meal, prepared at the time when people were sacrificing their lambs. Likewise, in Luke 22:15 Jesus is presented as referring to the meal as a Passover meal, although it was not one.[277] If Mark is not simply in error, it is arguable that he is referring loosely to the meal held by Jesus as a Passover meal since that it is to all intents and purposes what it was, even though it was held at an earlier time. I am not persuaded that France has offered a natural reading of the crucial text.

---

[274] France, *Mark*, 559–64; R. T. France, "Chronological Aspects of 'Gospel Harmony'," *VE* 16 (1986): 43–54. Similarly, Reicke, *New Testament Era*, 176–84, who identifies the occasion as a Qiddush meal at the beginning of Nisan 14. On this view the day of preparation for the Passover and the day of preparation for the weekly sabbath coincide; cf. Mark 15:42 and John 19:31. Reicke argues that this is the view of the Synoptic evangelists, but they use ambiguous language.

[275] He also has to take Luke 22:15 to refer to the meal as a whole, understood as a paschal meal. As noted above, the reference could be specifically to the Passover [lamb]. See n. 217. However, if the hypothesis proposed by Instone-Brewer (see below) is tenable, this difficulty can be overcome.

[276] Presumably if Mark was writing for a community which already believed that Jesus died at the same time as the Passover lambs, they could have interpreted his statement accordingly.

[277] Unless "this Passover" in Luke 22:15 refers not to the meal on the table but to the still future official Passover meal which Jesus knew that he would not be able to celebrate (as in Bockmuehl's view above). But this is an unnatural interpretation of the passage which refers either to the meal as a whole or the principal item on the menu.

Fourth, Can matters be explained by different reckonings of a "day"? This hypothesis works with different methods of regarding the new day as beginning in the evening (the Jewish method) or from midnight or from dawn.

H. Hoehner argues that the official calendar used the sunset-to-sunset method of calculation, but Galileans and Pharisees used the sunrise-to-sunrise method. Hence Jesus made his Passover preparations in the afternoon of Thursday (Nisan 14) and had his meal that same day in the evening (still Nisan 14 by this reckoning), whereas official Judaism had its preparations on the afternoon of Friday (Nisan 14) and its meal in the evening (now Nisan 15).[278] Again this hypothesis would require that Jesus did not have a lamb or that sacrifices were allowed on two days (which we have seen above to be a possibility), and there is no actual evidence for the different method of reckoning when days began.

Fifth, was it a paschal meal on a different calendar or timetable? A more promising scenario is that what Jesus celebrated was a paschal meal with a lamb, but one held 24 hours earlier than the "official" time. Various hypotheses have been developed to explain how this might have been possible. They have to overcome the two problems of explaining how a sacrificial lamb could be obtained ahead of the official period for slaughter and why people would have held an earlier celebration.

One possibility is an extended period for slaughter. M. Casey drew attention to a rabbinic dispute which makes the assumption that some sacrificing of Passover animals was done on the morning of Nisan 14 and also earlier in the afternoon of Nisan 13 (*m. Zebaḥ.* 1:3). This slaughter was carried on under some other name (peace offerings), since the temple authorities would not have permitted Passover offerings so-called to be sacrificed outside the statutory period. This dispute thus implies that sacrifices took place on two days, just as Billerbeck had earlier suggested as a possibility but without any evidence to show how it might have been possible.

Although Casey himself does not use this evidence to support the view that the disciples could have slaughtered their lamb on the 13th, it is so used by D. Instone-Brewer who argues that Jesus in the Synoptics held his meal on the 14th, whereas John records what the priests did on the appointed day.[279] Thus on this view Jesus held a Passover meal 24 hours before the official time. The advantage of this solution is that it allows Jesus to prepare

---

[278] Harold W. Hoehner, "Chronology," *DJG* 120–121.

[279] Maurice Casey, "The Date of the Passover Sacrifices and Mark 14:12," *TynBul* 48 (1997): 245–48; Casey, *Aramaic Sources*, 223–26; David Instone-Brewer, "Jesus's Last Passover: The Synoptics and John," *ExpTim* 112 (2001): 122–23.

his lamb at a time that was officially recognized for doing so, and the information given in Mark 14:12 can be interpreted in a way that permits this.[280]

While this proposal allows us to date the slaughter twenty-four hours earlier, it does not specifically show that having the Passover meal earlier was also permissible. However, it can be taken for granted that a sacrificial meal would not be held over until a day later than the sacrifice itself.[281]

This hypothesis enables supporters of France's or Hoehner's theories to have a meal with a lamb, but leaves open the question whether their calendrical proposals are viable.

A second possibility is the use of two calendars. We now consider the related hypothesis that alongside the official calendar there existed some other calendar which was one day (or more) out of step with it. Could it be that some Jews thought that the 13th of Nisan (on the official calendar) was actually the 14th in terms of their different reckoning of the beginning of the month and that the dating given in Mark 14:12, referring to the first day of unleavened bread (i.e., Nisan 14) is in fact based on a different calendar from the official one? There are various different proposals.

It is known that the Qumran sect followed a solar calendar which led to different dates from the official lunar one. A. Jaubert proposed that Jesus followed this calendar. However, this hypothesis requires that the difference was as great as three days, which does not fit with Jesus being crucified on a Friday, a date which is consistently present in the various accounts that we have. This particular calendrical theory should be set aside.[282]

J. Pickl hypothesized that the reason why (some) Galileans did not work on the day before Passover (*m. Pesaḥ.* 4:5) was because they celebrated the

---

[280] If this view can be sustained, then the comment (typical of many scholars) made by McKnight that there is no evidence for the priests sacrificing on two days, is no longer valid. The interpretation is questioned by Nolland, *Matthew*, 1044, n. 15. He holds that the rabbinic opinions cited between them rule out the practice since the sacrifices are offered under the wrong name and at the wrong time. D. Instone-Brewer (private correspondence) has defended his view.

[281] Presumably there would have been the danger of food poisoning if meat was not consumed soon after preparation.

[282] A. Jaubert, *La date de la Cène* (Paris: Gabalda, 1957). The Qumran calendar followed by Jesus and the Synoptic Evangelists placed the last meal of Jesus on the evening of Tuesday; the official" one was followed by John. John Meier (*The Roots of the Problem and the Person*, 386–401) identified as major problems the lack of any indication as to why Jesus should have followed the Qumran calendar, the difficulty of sacrificing Passover lambs before the official day, and the fact that Jaubert has to admit errors in the Synoptic presentation to make the theory work. The consensus continues to be against Jaubert's theory (cf. Gnilka, *Jesus of Nazareth*, 280). Nevertheless, its possibility is affirmed by Tomson, "Jesus and His Judaism," 38–39. McKnight, *Jesus and His Death*, 265, n. 22, mistakenly lists me as a follower of Jaubert's theory; I did favor some theory of differing calendars but not this one.

Passover a day earlier in order to avoid the enormous crowds sacrificing on Nisan 14.

Billerbeck suggested that different groups may have dated the beginning of the month (which depended on observations of the new moon) differently. On his view there were occasions when the Pharisees commenced the month a day earlier than the Sadducees, so that the 13th of the month on the Sadducean calendar was the day that they regarded as the 14th on the Pharisaic calendar.

In a refinement of this theory Instone-Brewer proposes that this discrepancy could have arisen in an effort to avoid Nisan 14 falling on a sabbath (cf. the debate in *t. Pesaḥ.* 4:13–14). In order to celebrate the Passover on this calendar, it was necessary for participants to have their lambs slaughtered under the designation of "peace offerings," a practice which was regarded by some later rabbinic authorities as legitimate though for different reasons (*m. Zebaḥ.* 1:3).

The proposal is then that Jesus and his disciples followed the Pharisaic calendar, and the dating given in the Synoptic Gospels is given accordingly. John's Gospel used the Sadducean calendar and so has the meal of Jesus before the "official" day observed by the Sadducees.

2.3.7.5. *Evaluating the Alternative Proposals*

The view that the meal described by Paul and the Evangelists was non-paschal in any meaningful sense runs foul of the combination of features that are better understood against a paschal background.[283] While it can be asserted that none of them individually requires a paschal background to account for their presence, the cumulative effect of the arguments that favor, or are consistent with, the Passover *character* of the meal (whether or not it was celebrated with a lamb and on Nisan 15 by the "official" calendar) is sufficiently strong. This is particularly the case with the interpretation of the bread and cup, for which the Passover custom of interpreting the lamb and other items still offers the best precedent.[284]

Admittedly in Paul there is nothing more than exodus and Passover typology. For Paul's typology ("Christ our Passover") to "work" it is sufficient that Christ died in close proximity to Passover (which nobody denies). However, once Christ had been identified by his followers as the Passover lamb (1 Cor 5:7), it is less probable that the meal *before* his death should be turned into a Passover meal (with the result that his death comes after the death of the lambs). If the historical Jesus had reinterpreted some of the ele-

---

[283] Some scholars argue that they are redactional rather than traditional, but it is hard to separate out the elements; some at least belong to the basic account.
[284] Jeremias, *Eucharistic Words*, 55–61.

ments at his last meal, then the identification of him as the Passover lamb in his death could easily have suggested itself. If Jesus had drawn on Passover typology at the Last Supper (or if this typology developed very soon in the early church), this would help to account for Paul's theologizing.

As for the *timing*, the Johannine dating is easier to accept historically since it at least reduces the problems that arise if the trial and death of Jesus take place on the actual day of the Passover festival. In addition, no over-riding theological grounds for John's re-dating of an event that had previously been placed a day later have been given.[285] Finally, the attempt to re-interpret the Johannine material to make it agree with the Synoptic dating involves a somewhat artificial reading of the crucial texts.

If the Johannine dating of the meal before the official time is accepted, it follows either that the Synoptic understanding of the meal as a paschal meal is mistaken or that the evidence has been misunderstood. Either Jesus held an ordinary meal (presumably without a lamb) with a paschal coloring (sufficient for it to be loosely called a Passover), or there was the possibility of following a variant calendar and of sacrificing lambs earlier than the official time of slaughter.

If we follow the first possibility then we have to say either that Mark 14:12 is mistaken in stating that a proper Passover meal was held on the proper day, or that its ambiguity has allowed modern readers to gain an erroneous impression.[286]

If we follow the second possibility, either Mark 14:12 is mistaken in terms of the official calendar or Mark is silently following a different Jewish calendar from that in John. The latter is a perfectly credible scenario. The explanation can only be hypothetical, but so far it makes the best sense of the evidence. The rabbinic evidence shows that such calendrical disparities did exist and that some people did sacrifice early. Admittedly we do not have any firm evidence for Jesus (and the Synoptic Evangelists) knowing and following a Pharisaic calendar, but it is arguable that he stood closer to the Pharisees than to any other Jewish group.[287]

---

[285] There is nothing explicit in John about the coincidence of the death of Jesus and the slaughter of the lambs.

[286] Cf. Evans, *Mark*, 370–72.

[287] Brown's discussion (*The Death of the Messiah*, 2:1350–78) concludes with an agnostic attitude. First Corinthians suggests that Paul knew that Jesus died around Passover time, reflected in the comparison of Jesus with a Passover lamb. This much is historical (since in effect there is no other plausible alternative). Mark appears to have taken over a description of the meal as paschal (rather than inventing it himself), but like the other Synoptic Evangelists he does not specify a particular date for the crucifixion. He has not thought about the consequences of this. John develops the concept of Jesus as paschal lamb and has woven this into his narrative. But John's dating of the passion does not include any paschal references to Jesus himself. Hence Jesus appears to have died on Nisan 14 (which fits in with resurrection on Nisan 16 as day of firstfruits) because there is no

In any case it does not seem that the lingering uncertainty over the date and the precise character of the meal is sufficient to raise historical doubts about the actual content of the narrative (which is not dependent upon the answers to these questions).

If the meal was a Passover meal, it will have been colored by the theological associations of the event. It was essentially a commemoration of the redemption from Egypt that inaugurated the exodus leading to the possession of the promised land. This may have been linked with hopes of future redemption, probably understood in terms of deliverance from Gentile dominion over the land. In some sources the binding of Isaac is brought into the picture.[288]

2.3.8. The Account of the Meal

We now face the question of the nature of the narrative. Scholars have detected various motifs in the narratives which raise the question of sources. Thus there is said to be a difference between the motif of Jesus' abstinence and the eschatological hope of eating and drinking in the kingdom of God on the one hand and the interpretation of the bread and cup in terms of Jesus' body and blood on the other. Linked to this difference is that between a Passover focus and a Christian, eucharistic focus. This is most obvious in Luke's account where Luke 22:15–18 focuses on the Passover and Luke 22:19–20 on the eucharist, but it may also be seen in Mark 14:22–24/25. It is easy to understand how an original "historical" account of the meal could be trimmed down to focus on those aspects that were most relevant to the later practice of the church. It is also arguable that an original account of a Passover meal was either expanded in the light of early church practice or combined with a separate account of a eucharistic type of meal. This kind of hypothesis is developed by Bradshaw following hints by X. Léon-Dufour.[289] It is then tied in with suggestions that there were different early Christian

---

plausible alternative. Meier (*The Roots of the Problem and the Person*, 386–401), forced to choose between the two accounts, accepts the Johannine chronology like Brown. He argues that the references to Passover in the Synoptic accounts belong to later stages of development of the tradition and that the original tradition simply recorded "a solemn farewell meal." These formalities account for the features that Jeremias identifies as typical of a Passover meal, but which could have been part of any formal meal. See also Beasley-Murray, *Jesus and the Kingdom of God*, 259–60, who notes that most scholars think that Jesus probably held a Passover meal, but that it is impossible to come to a firm decision on this point; nevertheless "Passover associations ... are presupposed in *all* the traditions concerning it" (p. 259; he means "all the Gospel traditions"). A forthcoming work by C. Humphreys will argue for yet another calendrical solution, utilizing fresh evidence.

[288] See briefly Barry D. Smith, "Last Supper, Words of Institution," in *Encyclopedia of the Historical Jesus* (ed. Craig A. Evans; London: Routledge, 2008), 365–68.

[289] Bradshaw, *Eucharistic Origins*, 6–10.

groups that celebrated different kinds of meals. Thus Bradshaw suggests that Paul connected the eucharistic sayings with the night when Jesus was handed over but not with a Passover meal held by him, and suggests that other Christians may have held a meal that was more like a Passover meal. He insists that we have no evidence that any early Christians actually followed the pattern of a "Last Supper, with a bread ritual before the meal and a cup ritual afterwards."[290] A further difference may have been that some groups had a ritual which placed the cup before the bread, as may perhaps be seen in the *Didache*.

The problem arises because the tradition related by Paul, which appears in a variant form in Mark, is essentially an account of those features of the meal which provide a rationale and pattern for what should happen in the church meal. Paul's account suggests that this tradition was handed down as a discrete narrative. The Gospels recount the story of Jesus' last meal as a whole. One possibility is that an original account of a Passover meal was enlarged by the addition of the separate "liturgical" account, as Bultmann and others have argued. I have argued elsewhere that this proposal will not stand.[291] Paul's discussion of the congregational meal included an allusion to the Passover cup known as "the cup of blessing" (1 Cor 10:16) and the tradition reflects the "eschatological outlook" in the phrase "until he comes." In the Gospels the alleged "stitch" between two accounts, "as they were eating,"[292] may be better explained as a historical comment on the progress of the meal, indicating what Jesus did at a specific point in the Passover meal.[293] The Lucan account is best interpreted as an integrated account rather than as a clumsy collocation of separate traditions. The stories in the Gospels do not give the impression of being basically liturgical accounts, but are rather historical reports with significance for the church's practice.

---

[290] Bradshaw, *Eucharistic Origins*, 13.
[291] Marshall, *Last Supper and Lord's Supper*, 34–35.
[292] Taylor, *St. Mark*, 543.
[293] In Mark 14:18 the reference to reclining and eating indicates that the meal is envisaged as already in progress. It is precisely at this significant juncture of close fellowship and celebration that Jesus announces the betrayal and thus heightens the enormity of the prophesied action. The statement thus serves a literary function. The second reference in Mark 14:22 may function to indicate a short gap from the previous episode prophesying the betrayal and/or to indicate that the taking of the bread took place during the meal rather than right at its outset or at its conclusion. Compare how in 1 Cor 11:25 the cup is expressly placed "after the meal" and forms a climax to it. Matthew retains the phrase both times, indicating that he did not find it awkward or redundant. The Pauline citation of the account as a tradition suggests that at some stage the "eucharistic" part of the story was a tradition handed down by itself and this could have affected the wording. There is also the possibility that the prophesying of the betrayal took place after the words of institution (though John 13:26 might be thought to suggest otherwise), as in Luke, and that the duplication of the wording is connected with the rearrangement. For similar connective genitive absolute constructions see Mark 5:35; 14:43.

2.3.8.1. Some General Considerations

We now come to the heart of the account, the "eucharistic" actions and sayings of Jesus. Common to all the accounts are the actions of Jesus in taking a loaf of bread and a cup of wine and giving thanks for them and sharing them with his companions to the accompaniment of explanatory words. With the exception of the explanatory words the sharing of bread and a cup correspond to normal Jewish practice at meals, and consequently no historical problems arise. The prayers of thanksgiving that Jesus is said to have given are not recorded, possibly because they were not considered relevant to the needs of the readers, and perhaps more probably because the wording would have been based on Jewish models well-known at least to the original Jewish tradents and their audience.[294] The traditions of the sayings of Jesus show variations on a common core, and there is an unsettled debate regarding what the original wording might have been.

The historicity of the sayings continues to be questioned. Schröter lists three general arguments against their authenticity: First, the parallelism in the bread and cup sayings is more easily explained as part of an aetiological explanation of the origin and meaning of the church's meal. Second, the form of the sayings is focused on the contemporization of the meal that is explicit in the Lucan/Pauline command to remember Jesus. This is easier to understand in the church situation than in Jesus' meal. Third, the content of the sayings is hard to reconcile with the other teaching of Jesus. In particular, the covenant theme is absent from Jesus' other teaching and it is unlikely that Jesus interpreted his death as the completion of a covenant. Again it is more likely that the church was anchoring its meal in the last meal of Jesus.[295]

In response to Schröter, several points may be made. First, although the parallelism between the two sayings is undeniable, the Luke/Pauline form is less developed than the Marcan form. There was thus a tendency to heighten the parallelism, but this does not rule out an original parallelism along the lines of "This is my body/This cup is the new covenant in my blood." If we reject the historicity of the alleged sayings of Jesus, we are left with the problem of explaining why there was a parallelism of bread and cup as significant elements at the origin of the church's meal. In other words, we are left without an adequate explanation of the origin of the actions at the church's meal.[296]

Second, the hypothesis that the sayings may have been contemporized to meet the needs of the church's meal surely requires that there were some

---

[294] Hence the *Didache* supplies the gap by offering appropriate Christian wording.

[295] Schröter, *Das Abendmahl*, 132–33. Other scholars cited by him are K. C. Felmy and M. Theobald.

[296] See above for Mack's attempt at an explanation and reasons for not accepting it.

sayings that formed the basis of the contemporization rather than that they were created *ex nihilo*. But the contemporization surely may go back earlier. As the accounts stand, the urge to contemporization arose precisely because Jesus wanted his disciples to meet together in the time of his absence. Schröter allows that a meal was held at which Jesus distinguished between this last meal and the future Passover or meal in the kingdom of God; if so, his focus on future meetings before this future meal is comprehensible.

Third, Schröter's doubts over the originality of the covenant theme in the cup saying are independently developed by McKnight.[297] In his case he argues that (1) Jesus uses the term "covenant" only in this saying about blood. (2) His central category is kingdom, and he is unlikely to have shifted from it on his last night. (3) Nowhere does Jesus connect kingdom and covenant. (4) The last supper shows few signs of a covenant reestablishment (and Passover theology was not concerned with covenant or forgiveness), and no trace of appropriate conditions. (5) Thus the covenant would have been foreign to the mission of Jesus.

Some aspects of this argument are reminiscent of the failed attack on Jesus' use of Son of Man based on the claim that this term never occurs in company with kingdom language. In the present case, kingdom language is securely anchored in the last supper tradition, so there is no shift away from it.

The presence of the covenant motif in the teaching of Jesus is not dependent simply upon one occurrence of the key word.[298] We may compare the fact that the language "a ransom for many" is found only in one saying, and yet this is not a decisive reason for rejecting its authenticity; there are in fact strong grounds for accepting the authenticity of Mark 10:45.[299] Even stronger is the motif of forgiveness which is firmly rooted in the tradition. Forgiveness is linked to the new covenant in Jer 31:34, although it is more generally part of the good news (Isa 61:1–2), and is appropriately introduced in Matt 26:28. McKnight notes how the restoration of the twelve tribes is associated with the new covenant, although this is explicit only in Ezek

---

[297] McKnight, *Jesus and His Death*, 304–12.

[298] Elsewhere in the Gospels the nearest that we get to overtly covenantal language is in Luke 22:29–30 = Matt 19:28 where Jesus confers (διατίθεμαι) kingship on his disciples, just as his Father has conferred it on him. But it is questionable whether the use of this verb would arouse covenantal associations. The specific wording in Luke 22:29 is not found in Matt 19:28 and is often considered secondary.

[299] Admittedly the authenticity of Mark 10:45b is still debated. Hesitation is voiced by McKnight, *Jesus and His Death*, passim. Cf. Ferdinand Hahn, *Die Vielfalt des Neuen Testaments: Theologiegeschichte des Urchristentums* (vol. 1 of *Theologie des Neuen Testaments*; Tübingen: Mohr Siebeck, 2002), 153. Recent defenders include Stuhlmacher, *Theologie*, 1:120–22, 127–30; followed by Hengel and Schwemer, *Jesus und das Judentum*, 355; cf. Donald A. Hagner, "Ransom Saying," in *Encyclopedia of the Historical Jesus* (ed. Craig A. Evans; London: Routledge, 2008), 488–91.

47–48. This motif recurs in the early days of the church according to Acts. But this motif is firmly grounded in the mission of Jesus with his choice of the Twelve. Accordingly some covenantal motifs are to be found in Jesus' own conception, and it is possible that these were then taken up in the early church. Perhaps the most that can be said is that the evidence is quite insufficient to justify denying that Jesus could have spoken in this manner, but also insufficient to prove that he did.

The account opens with Jesus giving thanks for the bread. Despite the way in which some scholars distinguish between "blessing" and "thanking," it is clear that "blessing" refers to praising and thanking God for his gifts.[300] Nothing is said about the words that Jesus would have used, and we have to assume that he used the typical Jewish forms of prayer, although he may have had his own form of words.

The breaking of the bread into smaller pieces so that he might distribute a piece to each person present is followed by a statement given in various different wordings, and similarly with the sharing of the cup. The two sets of wording are here placed alongside one another for ease of analysis.

Mark:	λάβετε· τοῦτό ἐστιν τὸ σῶμά μου	Take; this is my body.
Matt:	λάβετε φάγετε· τοῦτό ἐστιν τὸ σῶμά μου	Take, eat; this is my body.
Luke:	τοῦτό ἐστιν τὸ σῶμά μου τὸ ὑπὲρ ὑμῶν διδόμενον· τοῦτο ποιεῖτε εἰς τὴν ἐμὴν ἀνάμνησιν	This is my body, which is given for you. Do this in remembrance of me.
Paul:	τοῦτό μού ἐστιν τὸ σῶμα τὸ ὑπὲρ ὑμῶν· τοῦτο ποιεῖτε εἰς τὴν ἐμὴν ἀνάμνησιν	This is my body that is for you. Do this in remembrance of me.
Mark:	τοῦτό ἐστιν τὸ αἷμά μου τῆς διαθήκης τὸ ἐκχυννόμενον ὑπὲρ πολλῶν	This is my blood of the covenant, which is poured out for many.
Matt:	πίετε ἐξ αὐτοῦ πάντες· τοῦτο γάρ ἐστιν τὸ αἷμά μου τῆς διαθήκης τὸ περὶ πολλῶν ἐκχυννόμενον εἰς ἄφεσιν ἁμαρτιῶν	Drink from it, all of you; for this is my blood of the covenant, which is poured out for many for the forgiveness of sins.

---

[300] Bradshaw, *Search for the Origins of Christian Worship*, 15–17, wants to make a difference between the Jewish *berakah* (blessing) and *hodayah* (thanksgiving), but in both cases God is the object and there does not seem to have been any kind of consecration of the material gifts which he has bestowed (despite Schürmann, *Jesu ureigener Tod*, 79–80, who thinks that the effect was to make the bread a means of conveying blessing). Blessing God for his gift of food is different from uttering a prayer for God to bless children.

Luke:	τοῦτο τὸ ποτήριον ἡ καινὴ διαθήκη ἐν τῷ αἵματί μου,	This cup ... is the new covenant in my blood
	τὸ ὑπὲρ ὑμῶν ἐκχυννόμενον	that is poured out for you
Paul:	τοῦτο τὸ ποτήριον ἡ καινὴ διαθήκη ἐστιν ἐν τῷ ἐμῷ αἵματί,	This cup is the new covenant in my blood.
	τοῦτο ποιεῖτε, ὁσάκις ἐὰν πίνητε,	Do this, as often as you drink it,
	εἰς τὴν ἐμὴν ἀνάμνησιν	in remembrance of me.

The inter-relationship between these sets of variations is a matter of continuing uncertainty.[301] Scholars tend to fall into three groups: (1) those supporting the relative originality of the Marcan account;[302] (2) those supporting the relative originality of the Pauline/Lucan account,[303] And (3) those taking an eclectic approach: that any of the accounts may be more original at different points (just as happens in textual criticism).[304]

Two points may be relevant to a comparative evaluation of the accounts. First, Stuhlmacher proposes as a working principle that the shortest and most difficult form of the words should be taken as original, since it most easily accounts for the variants.[305] Second, Paul's account in 1 Cor 11 was in all probability put in writing before the dates generally assigned to any of the Gospels, and therefore it is arguable that there was less time for, and hence less likelihood of, changes in the wording of the oral traditions on which it depends than would be the case with oral material incorporated in the Gospels. Nevertheless, it is not impossible that the later account might preserve an earlier form of the tradition.

---

[301] Some points are reasonably clear: The Matthaean "eat" is a simple addition to make it quite clear that the symbolical bread is to be eaten. The Matthaean "drink from it all of you" is a transposition of the Marcan "they all drank from it" into a command, and the addition of "for" in the next clause is to provide a suitable connective.

[302] Bultmann, *Theology*, 1:146; Jeremias, *Eucharistic Words*, 173; Kollmann, *Ursprung und Gestalten*, 171-76; Pesch, *Das Markusevangelium*, 2:369-71; Patsch, *Abendmahl und historischer Jesus*, 87; Schmithals, *Markus*, 615; Stuhlmacher, *Theologie*, 1:132-33; Hengel, "Das Mahl in der Nacht," 145-46; McKnight, *Jesus and His Death*, 262, n. 10; Casey, *Aramaic Sources*, 248-50.

[303] Schürmann, *Der Einsetzungsbericht*; Helmut Merklein, "Erwägungen zur Überlieferungsgeschichte der neutestamentlichen Abendmahlstraditionen," *BZ* 21 (1977): 88-101, 235-44; Smith, "More Original Form"; Gundry, *Mark*, 829-34; Dunn, *The Theology of Paul the Apostle*, 607-8, slightly prefers the Pauline version, though noting that each form contains development.

[304] Cf. Marshall, *Last Supper and Lord's Supper*, 40-53 (but tending towards preference for the Lucan/Pauline version); Hofius, *Neutestamentliche Studien*, 282-83. Davies and Allison, *Matthew*, 3:466-67, prefer Mark for the bread and eschatological sayings, and Luke/Paul for the cup saying. Cf. Klauck, *Herrenmahl und Hellenistischer Kult*, 304-18.

[305] Stuhlmacher, *Theologie*, 1:132-33.

2.3.8.2. The Bread Saying

The bread saying in Mark begins with the imperative "take," not found in Paul and the shorter text of Luke (but cf. Luke 22:17).[306] Jeremias held that the command was necessary since Jesus himself was bound by his vow of abstinence not to partake.[307]

All the sources agree on the basic clause "this is my body."[308] The addition "which is for you" is found in Luke and Paul (the longer text of Luke adds "being given").[309] Such an addition (with or without the participle) has been shown to be entirely possible in both Hebrew and Aramaic, and therefore there are no linguistic grounds for questioning its originality.[310] The absence of the words from Mark has been thought to place a question mark against them, and it has been argued that they were a later addition formed by parallelism with the similar phrase in the cup saying found in both Mark and (the longer version of) Luke.[311] The question is whether the enigmatic nature of the bread saying led to expansion of it either in the light of the cup saying (longer text of Luke) or by transferring the phrase from the cup saying (Pauline version), or whether the saying without a further explanation is too enigmatic to be original in that form.[312] In Mark, as we have it, the bread saying can be understood in the context of the cup saying,[313] whereas, if the bread and cup sayings were originally separated by the meal, some kind of interpretation of the bread saying would appear to have been necessary.[314]

---

[306] Cf. Smith, "More Original Form," 174, n. 33, who inclines to omission.

[307] Jeremias, *Eucharistic Words*, 165–66.

[308] The Marcan form with the possessive after the noun is more Semitic and likely to be original. Cf. Smith, "More Original Form," 174.

[309] The tense is to be understood as future; Jeremias, *Eucharistic Words*, 178–79; Lynne Courter Boughton, "'Being Shed for You/Many': Time-Sense and Consequences in the Synoptic Cup Citations," *TynBul* 48 (1997): 249–70, discusses the translation of the participle in the cup saying and comes to the same conclusion.

[310] It has been shown conclusively that there are no unsurmountable difficulties in retro-translating the words of institution in their Lucan/Pauline or Marcan forms into Aramaic; cf. Fitzmyer, *Luke X–XXIV*, 1394–95; Casey, *Aramaic Sources*, 219–52.

[311] On the other side, it is noteworthy that the phrase is reflected in John 6:51 (Kollmann, *Ursprung und Gestalten*, 172).

[312] If the explanation is original, the problem is how it ever came to be omitted, whether by Mark or by the tradition that he used. A possible answer is that the presence of similar words in the cup saying could have made them seem redundant in the bread saying.

[313] Cf. Schmithals, *Markus*, 616, who states that, as the words stand in Mark, the interpretation in the cup saying naturally applies also to the bread.

[314] That the original account of the meal had the breaking of bread and the thanksgiving prayer (in conjunction with the final cup of wine) separated from each other by the main part of the meal (cf. Paul: "likewise after supper") is surely correct. Whether this custom was still followed by the time of 1 Corinthians is debated (so Hofius, *Neutestamentliche Studien*, 284, n. 26; Gerd Theissen, "Soziale Integration und sakramentales Handeln: Eine Analyse von 1 Cor. XI.17-24," *NovT* 16 [1974]: 179–206). I have claimed elsewhere that bread and wine were both taken at the beginning of the meal (Marshall, *Last Supper*

This consideration inclines me to acceptance of the longer form in Paul and the longer text of Luke.³¹⁵

2.3.8.3. The Cup Saying

The position regarding the cup saying is more difficult. There exist two different forms of its basic core: "This is my blood of the covenant" (Mark) or "This cup is the new covenant in my blood" (Paul; longer text of Luke).³¹⁶ The old argument against the originality of the Marcan version that it is linguistically difficult if not impossible in Aramaic can no longer be sustained.³¹⁷ In favor of the originality of the Pauline form is the tendency that there could have been in the early church to bring the bread and cup sayings into closer parallelism with each other. In the Pauline form there is no direct equation of the contents of the cup with the blood of Jesus, and this can be taken in two ways. Either it represents a later change to avoid the offence that could possibly be caused by the implications of drinking something symbolical of blood,³¹⁸ or it can be argued that the change from the Pauline version was made at a later stage when the Marcan form of statement was not thought to be offensive and the desire for parallelism with the bread

---

and Lord's Supper, 111). In any case, the problem in the congregation seems to have been people over-eating before the congregational meal proper.

³¹⁵ Klauck, *Herrenmahl und Hellenistischer Kult*, 306–9; Theissen and Merz, *The Historical Jesus*, 421; cf. Smith, "Last Supper," 366–67. Contra: Fee, *First Corinthians*, 551.

³¹⁶ The Pauline version is favored by Gnilka, *Jesus of Nazareth*, 286–87, who goes so far as to speak of a consensus in its favor. He himself holds that two interpretative categories are present in the sayings: (a). atonement and substitution and (b). the idea of covenant. He thinks that the latter in its Pauline form is original and that the concept of atonement was added secondarily. He notes, however, that some scholars argue for the reverse process. See below the discussion of McKnight on the covenant motif. Cf. Merklein, "Erwägungen"; similarly Klauck, *Herrenmahl und Hellenistischer Kult*, 308–09, 321.

³¹⁷ So, finally, Maurice Casey, "The Original Aramaic Form of Jesus' Interpretation of the Cup," *JTS* 41 (1990): 1–12; Casey, *Aramaic Sources*, 241. Cf. n. 310 above. Smith, "Last Supper," 367, appears to be unaware of Casey's work.

³¹⁸ It should be emphasized, however, that there is a considerable difference between drinking blood and drinking wine that symbolizes blood. It is the former that would be abhorrent, not the latter. Consequently, there may have been little or no offence caused, even in Jewish Christian circles, by the symbolizing of blood as wine (cf. Klawans, "Interpreting the Last Supper," 4–7). The point can be made even more strongly if we are right to claim that thinking in terms of substances is inappropriate and that in a Jewish context "body and blood stand for the *event* on the cross, for the *death* of the Lord, as Paul expressly explains in 1 Cor 11:26" (Schmithals, *Markus*, 616). Being sprinkled with blood and drinking blood was part of the taurobolium described by Prudentius which was regarded with utter abhorrence by later Christians at a time when the use of wine in the Lord's Supper was quite normal. Prudentius, *Peristephanon* x. 1011–50, cited by C. K. Barrett, ed., *The New Testament Background: Selected Documents* (rev. ed.; London: SPCK, 1987), 126–27, § 109.

saying was uppermost.[319] We have to ask whether an original close parallelism that was lost in later developments is more likely than an original lack of parallelism which was supplied at a later date. It is possible to explain the Marcan wording as a development from the Pauline by deletion of "cup" and turning "blood" into a predicate.[320] On the other hand, it is simpler to identify the contents of the cup with blood rather than to identify them with a covenant (brought about through the death of Christ).

I suspect that one's conclusions on this matter depend on how you are feeling on any given day; neither side appears to me to have an over-riding argument.[321]

The originality of the term "new" is a moot point. It is arguable that it fits neatly enough into the Pauline wording and is necessary, since "the covenant in my blood" is an obscure phrase. The inclusion of the word in the Marcan form would have overloaded the phrase, although it is not impossible, and the phrase "the blood of the covenant" gives a clear enough allusion to Exod 24:8 (cf. Zech 9:11[322]) without any addition.

The phrase "which is shed for many" (longer text of Luke "for you") fits naturally into the Marcan wording. Nevertheless, because of its absence from the Pauline version, McKnight regards it as a later theological interpretation (and with it the possible allusion to Isa 53 disappears from the earliest form of the words).[323] It is arguable that it represents a different realm of ideas from the preceding reference to covenant blood, but this is not necessarily a barrier to its inclusion.

If anything were to be omitted, it would perhaps rather be "of the covenant" which could be regarded as a secondary explanation despite its being firmly in place in both versions of the saying.[324] This is the route followed by McKnight, on the broad grounds that Passover and covenant "are countries and ideas apart."[325] Rather Jesus simply said, "This is my blood" in parallelism with "This is my body."[326]

---

[319] Cf. Stacey, "The Lord's Supper," 71. Stacey, however, thinks that interpretation of the cup was not part of the original Last Supper.

[320] Smith, "More Original Form," 182–83.

[321] Theissen and Merz, *The Historical Jesus*, 421–23, again prefer the Pauline wording.

[322] Bockmuehl, *This Jesus*, 205, n. 32, notes the proximity of this text to Zech 9:9, which might suggest that it would readily come to the mind of those who were aware of the latter text.

[323] McKnight, *Jesus and His Death*, 291–92. But he is not self-consistent, in that he allows that the expression "poured out," which occurs in Mark (but not in Paul) could possibly go back to Jesus, although he thinks that "for many" could be a Marcan addition (cf. pp. 323–25).

[324] For scholars omitting the phrase see Smith, "More Original Form," 183, n. 72. Cf. Klauck, *Herrenmahl und Hellenistischer Kult*, 329.

[325] See above.

[326] Similarly, Chilton, *Feast of Meanings*, 71–72, holds that the most original form of

The variations in wording between Mark and Paul at this point are not a problem, since variation is part of the total picture; moreover, the saying has been shown to be possible in Aramaic in both its forms.[327].

2.3.8.4. The Command(s) To "Do This"

The command to "do this" is absent from the Marcan tradition and is probably regarded as inauthentic by the majority of scholars.[328] It is not primarily a command to repeat the rite (as it is popularly taken to be)[329] but rather a command that it should be carried out in memory of Jesus, as the Pauline explanation ("you show forth the Lord's death) makes clear.[330] The absence from Mark forced Jeremias to admit that it was not part of the oldest tradition but could be a special tradition preserved in another line of transmission.[331]

This defense should not necessarily be regarded as special pleading; rather it rests on the important fact that reliable oral traditions continued over many years in the early church and are from time to time reflected in the variations between the Gospels, in particular in the materials found in Matthew and Luke that are not in Mark and in some of the changes made by the later Evangelists in editing Mark.

Admission of this possibility is not, of course, proof that this is what is happening here. Certainly the Evangelists picture Jesus as being aware of the likelihood of impending death, and therefore a call to do something after he is no longer physically present in order to remember him makes perfectly good sense. It may be easier to see this command as original to the tradition rather than as a later addition. This would leave the question as to how it came to be omitted or not present in the Marcan tradition. The reason may simply be that it is a separate saying from the explanations of the bread and the cup, and this is what P. Benoit was saying in his famous remark "On ne récite pas une rubrique, on l'exécute": it was not part of the explanation and

---

wording is that found in Justin, *Apol.* I:66: "This is my body; this is my blood." But this conclusion rests on his unusual interpretation of what Jesus was doing.

[327] Casey, *Aramaic Sources*, 220, opts for the Marcan wording "This (is / was) my blood, it (is) of the covenant, shed for many."

[328] Kuhn, "The Qumran Meal," 238–39, cites 1QSa 2:21–22 ("and according to this ruling they shall proceed at every preparation …") as a parallel to the command to repeat the act.

[329] It seems to be universally assumed that the verb is an imperative, and this may well be so in light of the surrounding imperatives. But it could function equally well as an indicative: "what you are doing when you do this is remembering me."

[330] The need for repetition is, of course, implicit. The point is that the saying is more focused on remembering Jesus.

[331] Jeremias, *Eucharistic Words*, 237–38, 255.

therefore it could be dropped. This strengthens the case for its originality.[332] Whether it occurred one or two times is perhaps impossible to determine. If the Passover setting is historical, this was an occasion which was essentially repetitive, and this context would affect the meal held by Jesus.[333]

We can summarize the above discussion by saying that there is a set of core statements which are attested in both forms of the tradition:

- A statement which explains "this" (the loaf) as symbolizing the body of Jesus.[334]
- A statement which explains "this" ([the contents of] the cup) as symbolizing either his blood or something brought about in relation to his blood.
- A statement that the body (Paul; longer text of Luke; not Mark) or the blood (Mark; longer text of Luke; not Paul) is "for" the benefit of certain people. A clarifying participle may be present (longer text of Luke with body and blood; Mark with blood only).
- A reference to the [new] covenant.
- A command or statement about "this" being done in memory of Jesus (Paul [twice]; the longer text of Luke [once]).[335]

The variations and textual uncertainties affect the following motifs:

- The explanatory phrase associating the blood of Jesus with the *forgiveness* of sins is peculiar to Matthew.
- The *breaking* of the body of Jesus (as opposed to the breaking of the bread) is found only in a textual variant.

---

[332] Cf. Smith, "More Original Form," 184–85. Contrast McKnight, *Jesus and His Death*, 334.

[333] McKnight, *Jesus and His Death*, 334.

[334] Mention should be made of the theory of D. Daube that a small piece of unleavened bread known as the "aphikoman" was kept until the end of the meal and then consumed by all present; this was taken to signify what the Messiah would eat when he comes, and by identifying his body with it Jesus was making a messianic claim. The theory is summarized and developed by Deborah Bleicher Carmichael, "David Daube on the Eucharist and the Passover Seder," *JSNT* 42 (1991): 45–67, and discussed positively by Evans, *Mark*, 390–91; Davies and Allison, *Matthew*, 3:468–69; Stacey, "The Lord's Supper," 68. The idea is treated negatively by McKnight, *Jesus and His Death*, 251, n. 19 (with additional references), 281, n. 24. Carmichael argues that the use of wine and the application to the death of Jesus are secondary.

[335] Dunn (*Jesus Remembered*, 229–31) comments that the variations are due to "two slightly variant liturgical practices." Liturgical shaping brought out more clearly the parallelism in Mark. The Pauline (and Lucan) version maintained the framework of a meal with sayings at the beginning and end. In both cases there was "a concern to maintain the key elements of the words used by Jesus as carefully as necessary, with a flexibility (including elaboration) which in this case no doubt reflects the developing liturgical practices of different churches" (p. 231). What Maccoby referred to as verbal "glaring contradictions" Dunn rightly sees as "performance variation." Cf. Hyam Maccoby, "Paul and the Eucharist," *NTS* 37 (1991): 247–67.

- It is uncertain whether the phrase "which is for many / you" goes with the bread or the cup, or both of them.
- There is variation between "you" (the disciples present) and "many" (the people generally insofar as they respond positively to Jesus).[336]
- If the longer Lucan text is not original, the specific reference to *"pouring out"* the blood of Jesus is peculiar to Mark (and Matt).[337]
- The variation in wording of the reference to the *covenant* might be regarded as a sign of secondary insertion. In particular, the word *"new"* is open to some suspicion.
- The command to *remember Jesus* is peculiar to Paul (and the longer text of Luke).[338] Parallels to this kind of statement can be found in Hellenistic sources, and Barrett comments that its formulation may owe much to Hellenistic custom.[339] Such an origin is, however, vigorously rejected by Jeremias, and it is hard to believe that Hellenistic commemorative meals for the dead lie at the origin of the Christian meal.[340]

The reconstruction of the original sayings of Jesus thus leads to a set of statements of varying probability. The core of the development is to be found in the two parallel sayings "This is my body; this is my blood." Each of these demands further explanation, whether by Jesus himself or by his followers. We have two lines of transmission. Each contains the element of "for you / many." Each also contains reference to covenant. These elements are minimal. Although I have argued elsewhere for the greater originality of the Lucan / Pauline tradition, it may be wiser to recognize that certainty is impossible.

---

[336] Cf. Schmithals, *Markus*, 616–17, who rightly notes that "many" can refer to "all" in general or specifically *"die* Vielen meinen, die das Heilswerk des Kreuzes an sich geschehen lassen," ("means the many who affirm the effects of the salvation on the Cross") i. e., "you."

[337] Dunn, *Jesus Remembered*, 815–16, rejects any allusion to Isa 53:12 in Mark 14:24, preferring the Pauline version which does not have "poured out." Similarly Heinz Schürmann, *Gottes Reich – Jesu Geschick: Jesu ureigener Tod im Licht seiner Basileia-Verkündigung* (Freiburg: Herder, 1983), 220–21. The status of the other verbal link with Isaiah 53 "for many" is also problematic; it is a moot point whether an original "for many" was particularized to "for you" or whether the latter was universalized by including the echo of Isaianic language. Despite the weight of scholarly opinion to the contrary I am inclined to think with Jeremias, *Eucharistic Words*, 179–82, that the former development is the more probable.

[338] It is not clear whether Mark's introductory "take" should be seen as an alternative to it; it does not look like the source from which the more theological command developed.

[339] C. K. Barrett, *The First Epistle to the Corinthians* (London: Black, 1968), 267.

[340] Jeremias, *Eucharistic Words*, 238–43.

2.3.8.5. The Statements about Future [Eating and] Drinking

Absent from Paul is any comment by Jesus about his own relationship to future eating and drinking. Mark 14:25 contains a statement introduced by the emphatic "Amen, I say to you," that Jesus will not drink again of the fruit of the vine[341] until he drinks it new in the kingdom of God. This saying has met with far less critical skepticism than the other sayings at the meal, partly because it fits in with the central element in the teaching of Jesus[342] and partly because there is considerable difficulty in attributing it to the later creativity of the church.[343] The fact that it is not present in Paul is not an argument against its originality, since it was not relevant to Paul's purpose (and it has in any case left a trace in Paul's "until he comes").

However, there is a problem in that Luke 22:15–18 contains some similar statements, placed before the eucharistic sayings, in which Jesus says two things. First, he says that he has greatly longed to eat this Passover because he will not eat it until it is fulfilled in the kingdom of God. Second, he gives thanks for a cup of wine and tells the disciples to divide it among themselves, because he will not drink from now (textual variant, "no more") of the fruit of the vine until the kingdom of God comes. The significance of this variant account is debated. Thus it is not clear whether Luke 22:17 is to be interpreted to mean that Jesus abstained from wine (and food) at this meal.[344] It is highly improbable that Jesus said essentially similar things concerning the wine twice (i.e., both before and after the eucharistic words). The alternatives are either that Luke has followed a source other than Mark or that he has rewritten Mark 14:25. There are other passages in the passion narrative (and elsewhere in the Gospel) where Luke has material that varies significantly in wording from Mark or has no Marcan parallel at the same point, and there is no agreement among critics regarding the origin of such matter.[345] Use of a non-Marcan source is strongly defended by J. A. Fitzmyer: "It is impossible that vv. 15–18 are a mere reworking of Mark 14:25."[346] Gundry

---

[341] This Jewish form of reference is naturally occasioned by the wording of the Jewish prayer of thanksgiving for the wine.

[342] Schröter, *Das Abendmahl*, 47–48.

[343] For a full-scale discussion see Meier, *Mentor, Message, and Miracles*, 302–9. Hengel and Schwemer, *Jesus und das Judentum*, 585, rightly affirm that the saying is meaningless as a community-creation. Schmithals, *Markus*, 624–25, raises the question whether it was composed by the narrator, but in the end leaves the question open. Klauck, *Herrenmahl und Hellenistischer Kult*, 329, regards it as the original conclusion of the cup saying.

[344] Schürmann, *Der Paschamahlbericht*, 63–65, argued that Jesus did take part in the meal. Beasley-Murray, *Jesus and the Kingdom of God*, 262, argues that Luke 22:17 expresses an intention to abstain and the same must be presumed for Luke 22:16.

[345] That Luke has spun the pericope out of basically Marcan material is the view of Walter Schmithals, *Das Evangelium nach Lukas* (Zürich: Theologische Verlag, 1980), 208.

[346] Fitzmyer, *Luke X–XXIV*, 1386–87; similarly, Green, *The Death of Jesus*, 30–35; Beasley-Murray, *Jesus and the Kingdom of God*, 260–61; Nolland, *Luke 18:35–*

asserts that Mark in fact delayed the saying of Jesus from its position before the eucharistic sayings so as to follow them.[347]

It should be noted, however, that the establishment of use of an earlier source by Luke does not necessarily mean that this source gives a reliable account of what happened.[348]

The matter is not unimportant. One proposal is that there was an account of a farewell meal by Jesus which did not contain the "eucharistic" material; this account is found in Luke 22:[14]15–18, 24–30 and 35–38 and in fragmentary form in Mark 14:25; the "eucharistic" material came from a separate tradition handed down by itself (1 Cor 11) and then incorporated in the Gospels. This theory has been elaborated by Schürmann who in effect sees Luke 22:15–18 and 19–20 as two accounts of the same events from different points of view. Jeremias also recognized the fact of two independent traditions, but held that they represented two stages in the description of the same meal. More recent scholars have been less inclined to see the "eucharistic" section as an addition by Mark to a passion narrative that originally did not contain it, and prefer to see it as something that had already been included in the earlier form of the passion narrative.[349] The co-existence of a passion narrative containing an account of the Last Supper and an excerpt from it used to give teaching about the conduct of the Lord's Supper is perfectly possible, just as in congregations today we read passages from the Gospels rather than the Gospels as a whole.

Whether the Lucan wording is a midrash on the Marcan account or is based on an independent account, the saying (or sayings) attribute to Jesus the consciousness of approaching death and the fact that despite this there will nevertheless be a banquet in the consummation when there will be a new partaking. In addition to statements about the kingdom as a present reality the NT writers speak somewhat indifferently about the kingdom both as a future state and as a state of affairs that will come. These two latter conceptions are regarded by E. Grässer as belonging to different strands of

---

24:53, 1041–44. Nolland notes the difficulty of isolating sources with Luke's tendency to rewrite them in his own style, but contends that his editorial procedures are such as to favor a wider traditional base than that given by Mark. This verdict is contrary to that argued by Pesch, *Das Markusevangelium*, 2:364–77, who holds that Luke 22:15–18 is spun out of Mark 14:25, and accepted by McKnight, *Jesus and His Death*, 262–64.

[347] Gundry, *Mark*, 829–30.

[348] There are two different questions here. The one is whether the Lucan account has been created by the Evangelist out of Mark. The other is whether, granted that the Lucan account rests on a special source, the source is a traditional development beyond an earlier form reflected in Mark. In other words, even if the Lucan account rests on a source and not on Mark, this does not prove that it is tradition-historically earlier. The majority opinion is that the Lucan tradition is secondary to Mark's (so, for example, Schröter, *Das Abendmahl*, 49; *pace* Schürmann).

[349] Pesch, *Das Markusevangelium*, 2:354.

apocalyptic imagery found in different sources, and he thinks that they are distinct from one another, the one more "Jewish apocalyptic" and the other more "Platonic."[350] It seems more likely that both could co-exist in the same sources, and it is not too difficult to conceive of a heavenly "state" that can become an earthly reality when God brings the Messiah to the world. In Luke we have this combination of fulfillment in the Kingdom of God and when the Kingdom of God comes. The language of coming implies an interval before things come to pass. It is for this period that Jesus instructs his disciples to remember him.

This "eschatological outlook" is reflected in the Pauline narrative with its reference to showing forth the death of the Lord "until he comes." It is essentially the same motif as in the Gospels. It is not clear whether the Pauline comment is part of the cited tradition[351] or his own comment on it,[352] but the latter has wider scholarly support and is more likely, with Paul explaining the significance of the tradition in v. 26 and then drawing the inference from the interpreted tradition in v. 27. In any case, it is a comment on the action and not a saying of Jesus himself at the Last Supper (cf. the shift from first person to third, and the use of κύριος). It is thus to be understood as a theological interpretation of the saying(s) of Jesus. Either way, the Pauline narrative testifies to the originality of this motif in the Supper narrative.[353]

Comparison of the Lucan and Marcan forms of words leads most to argue that Mark is original and Luke is editing Mark, contra Schürmann who argued that Luke was editing a different source.[354]

We are not claiming that every part of the account be seen as authentic verbatim teaching of Jesus; this is indeed excluded by the fact of the variations between the different forms of wording, and a naive harmonization is not possible. The recognition that these variations developed is not in itself an argument against basic historicity. Various elements may have developed

---

[350] Erich Grässer, *Aufbruch und Verheissung: Gesammelte Aufsätze Zum Hebräerbrief* [ed. Martin Evang and Otto Merk; Berlin: De Gruyter, 1992], 233–38. The concept of a future place of rest is found in *4 Ezra*; the similitudes of *1 Enoch*; *T. Dan*; *2 Baruch*; et al.); the concept of a heavenly place is in *Joseph and Aseneth*; *2 Enoch*; Apocalypse of Sedrach; Sentences of Syriac Menander.

[351] So apparently Richard B. Hays, *First Corinthians* (Int; Louisville: John Knox, 1997), 197.

[352] Barrett, *First Corinthians*, 270; Fee, *First Corinthians*, 556; Thiselton, *First Corinthians*, 886.

[353] I suppose it could be argued that Mark 14:25 is a late development from the Pauline comment, turning the Pauline wording into a saying of Jesus; with Mack one might say "one could imagine" (Mack, *Myth*, 118, 119). But this does not look very likely since the content of the saying of Jesus is in the appropriate idiom of the kingdom and is concerned with his own behavior, not with that of the disciples.

[354] On the interpretation of the saying, see McKnight, *Jesus and His Death*, 328–34.

as the church explored the implications of shorter statements by Jesus in the light of its fuller understanding after Easter, but the fact that something developed and changed is not an argument that it did not exist in the first place. Scholarly uncertainty on the precise wording will continue to exist, but the different accounts testify to a basic core of motifs that persisted in varied wording.

2.3.9. After the Meal

2.3.9.1. Other Sayings

The accounts of the meal in the Gospels vary considerably in the after-meal dialogue. After Jesus' statement that he would not drink again until the kingdom of God, Mark and Matthew record nothing further in the upper room. In Luke the foretelling of the betrayal is postponed to this point and is then followed by other sayings: greatness in the Kingdom, a prophecy of Peter's denial (which in Mark and Matthew is delayed until after departure from the upper room), and the saying about the two swords (Luke 22:21–38). All of this material (except the last item) has parallels elsewhere in the other Gospels, but the Lucan version of it is generally quite distinctive. Similarly, after the meal there is the prophecy of Peter's denial and then the first part of the lengthy farewell discourse in John.

A detailed discussion of this material is not possible here. We may well have a tendency, similar to that generally recognized in the lengthy discourses in Matthew, to gather together sayings of Jesus that may have been spoken on this or on other occasions and so to produce an extended discourse. None of this material is so integrally tied to the account of the Last Supper that its historicity or otherwise affects the central account of the meal. There are also sayings attributed to Jesus elsewhere in the Gospels whose original setting may well have been the meal, such as Mark 10:45.[355]

2.3.9.2. The Hallel

The singing of a hymn before leaving the upper room is recorded by Mark and Matthew but omitted by Luke. The singing of the Great Hallel was a part of the Passover meal, and singing at the end of other Jewish meals is not attested (though presumably not impossible).

2.3.9.3. The Prediction of Peter's Denial

Since this pericope is included by Luke in his account of the meal, it deserves brief mention. The Seminar argue for the unhistorical nature of this pericope. Mark is said to like to make predictions followed by their fulfillment,

---

[355] Hengel and Schwemer, *Jesus und das Judentum*, 585–86.

and this passage is part of such a series. The facts that there is a three-fold denial (a folklore type of motif) and that the fulfillment story is nested in the trial scene (another frequent Marcan type of structure) leads Mack to hold that the story as a whole is invented. Since the story does not have the shape of an anecdote, it cannot have been handed down in the oral tradition. Mark invented it on the basis of: Peter's confession and subsequent rebuke; the teaching ascribed to Jesus that discipleship requires denial and fortitude; possible influence of Zech 13:7 where sheep are scattered; the oath of loyalty by Ittai to David in 2 Sam 15:21.[356]

Behind this assessment there seems to lie the principle that "this story is intercalated, therefore it was created for the purpose." The assumption about stories that do not have the shape of anecdotes not being part of oral tradition is precisely that – an *assumption* that turns a certain amount of observable phenomena into a basis for immutable laws that those who handed down of tradition must have obeyed.[357] The general question as to the manufacture of details of stories and whole incidents out of Jewish scriptural material has already been discussed, and we have seen good reason to be skeptical concerning it. As regards Zech 13:7, this is cited as part of the story, and the only possible reason for rejecting it is the doctrinaire assumption that Jesus himself did not quote Scripture directly. But how could the rest of the story concerning Peter have been spun out of that text? How did desertion turn into denial? As for the oath by Ittai, this is an oath that is kept, not one that is broken, and the wording is quite different. The theory that the picture of the disciples in Mark is a deliberate, imaginative attempt to blacken their character by the early church attributes an inexplicable sordid motive to it that is without basis. There is some difference between honestly recounting stories which may not be to somebody's credit but are factual[358] and deliberately creating smear and slander.

---

[356] Funk and Seminar, *The Acts of Jesus*, 142–43; Mack, *Myth*, 305–6. Similarly, Pesch, *Das Markusevangelium*, 2:383–84. *Contra*: Moo, *The Old Testament in the Gospel Passion Narratives*, 186–87, on Mark 14:25; Taylor, *St. Mark*, 548; Evans, *Mark*, 399.

[357] I would again draw attention to the criticism made by A. M. Ramsey of a scholar who asserted that certain sayings in the Gospels "must be judged by the rules of traditio-historical criticism to be reflections of the church's Christology": "What rules?" said Ramsey, "Historical science does not have rules, and the suspicion arises that the rules here may be more those of a game than a science" ("History and the Gospel," in *Studia Evangelica IV* [ed. F. L. Cross; Berlin: De Gruyter, 1968], 78).

[358] Material of this kind is in any case likely to be historical according to the criterion of embarrassment.

3. Historical and Theological Significance of the Last Supper

The extended discussion that constitutes the main part of this essay has been necessitated by the detailed criticism of the Last Supper narrative by members of the Jesus Seminar and other scholars. The present essay has hopefully at least shown that their denials of the historicity of the essential elements in that narrative are untenable. It is one thing to cast doubt on details of the story; it is another thing to rule out any possibility of basic historicity. By contrast this essay has aimed to show that what is presented to us in historical form in the Gospels has a right to be treated as historical unless there are solid grounds for a different conclusion. The suspicions that may attach to some parts of the story and the historical difficulties created by others are not on such a scale as to call in question the essential historicity of what is recorded.

First, we noted the arguments for the existence of a connected passion narrative, originally oral in form, and, while recognizing that there is some scholarly doubt concerning its existence and extent, we saw that on the whole the positive evidence is stronger, and the likelihood is that the early Christians did remember this centrally significant element in the story of Jesus. This would, of course, tie in with the renewed claim of Bauckham and others that eyewitness memories and testimonies strongly influenced the early church in its proclamation and teaching.

Second, we examined the introductory narratives concerning the plot against Jesus, the role of Judas and the preparations for a meal in an apparently secret location, and saw that the attempts to understand these accounts as being largely midrashic developments from Jewish scriptural texts were not persuasive, even though the narrators certainly identified elements in the story that could be regarded as foreshadowed in the Hebrew Bible.

Third, we discussed the nature of congregational meals in the early church, in particular the claim that the origins of these are to be found in Hellenistic symposia involving libations and memorials of the dead, which were secondarily transformed by Paul and others into the celebrations of a Hellenistic Christ cult which were foreign to the practices of the earlier Jesus movements. The *Didache* in particular was seen as evidence for one type of meal with no trace of the distinctive interpretation of the bread and the cup that came into being through the influence of the myth of the Last Supper developed in Pauline circles. On this theory the accounts of the Last Supper in 1 Corinthians and the Gospels have no historical basis and are unnecessary to account for the rise of the earliest Christian practices but rather are later aetological myths. We were able to show that this proposed explanation is not only sheer speculation but also that it goes against the evidence that establishes clearly the Pauline type of meal, which recalls the

Last Supper, as the earliest form known to us, and that shows the remoteness of the possibility that the origins of the Christian meal are to be found in Hellenistic symposia. The evidence of the *Didache* is too uncertain to make it the basis for wide-ranging hypotheses regarding the Lord's Supper in the earliest church, and the meal there in fact bears strong resemblances to the Pauline meal.

Fourth, the accounts of the meal in the Synoptic Gospels and 1 Corinthians agree in their broad outlines. A possible exception is the account in Luke if we follow the western text in omitting Luke 22:19b–20 from the original account, but this omission is on balance secondary.

Fifth, a major argument against the historicity of these accounts derives from the *prima facie* evidence for a different dating of the meal (and the crucifixion) in John: if the date of so important an event was not known for sure, what are the implications of this for the historicity of the meal? (The same argument might of course be applied to the historicity of the crucifixion itself, but I am not aware of any responsible scholars going down this route.) The possibilities that John is giving a theological dating for the death of Jesus as a paschal lamb or that different calendars were in use arise, and in a situation where there is still no agreed solution (but an increasingly strong likelihood that a calendrical solution is possible) the objection can certainly not be regarded as fatal. The odds are increasing that the meal was in some sense a paschal meal, and therefore should be interpreted against that background. Scholarly opinion is divided as to whether the later detailed and precise Jewish rubrics for the paschal meal were observed at this time; if so, the agreements and disagreements between the Last Supper and Jewish practice cannot be used as a criterion for or against its historicity.

Sixth, the heart of the account consists in the actions and sayings of Jesus with the bread and the cup. The minute differences in wording between the versions in the four sources that we have (the Synoptic accounts and 1 Cor 11) can be partly accounted for redactionally, but the quest for a single 'original' wording from which the existing versions can be derived continues to lead to uncertain conclusions. Even if the end-result is a set of statements whose wording can be ascertained only with varying degrees of probability, the main elements are not in any real doubt. There is a basic core of motifs that persisted in varied wording.

In light of its essential historicity, we can, finally, draw some conclusions concerning the significance of the Last Supper.

First, from this narrative we gain some important insight into the historical Jesus and the way in which he approached his death. In particular the narrative anchors the significance of death in his own understanding of it.

In his helpful discussion Beasley-Murray mentions that followers of Bultmann's position are forced to the view that there is insufficient evidence that "on the occasion of his last meal Jesus interpreted his death in the sense of a service to his own, and so as the fulfillment of his work."[359] One of the merits of Beasley-Murray's own presentation is that he is able to relate the Last Supper traditions coherently to the teaching and mission of Jesus regarding the Kingdom of God. Some scholars find the view that Jesus saw his death as necessary for the achievement of his purpose to be incompatible with the free offer of forgiveness to sinners that was at the heart of his mission. Against this Beasley-Murray argues at length on the solid basis of the eschatological saying(s) in Luke 22:15–18; Mark 14:25 that Jesus was not simply confident that the Kingdom of God would come despite his death but rather he saw "his death as part and parcel of the process whereby the kingdom of God comes."[360] He draws attention to Schürmann's important argument that the *ipsissima facta* of Jesus' actions with the bread and cup show him offering salvation based on his death. The reported sayings of Jesus "provide a testimony that is consistent and harmonious with the acts of Jesus in the giving of the bread and wine, viewed in the context of his total ministry, and with the eschatological prospect of the messianic feast."[361] At the same time the Passover setting places the death of Jesus over against the redemption out of Egypt and sees it as a corresponding new act of God.

These eschatological and soteriological dimensions to Jesus' self understanding of his death cohere well with the emphases of the other essays that Jesus' presentation of the kingdom had clear eschatological implications and show him to be central to all that is happening in God's program. They also cohere nicely with the theme of Jesus' authority seen in most of the events treated in these essays. In particular, we have Jesus altering significant symbolism, not merely to enhance the understanding of the past event of the Exodus, but also to characterize an approaching event involving him as its equivalent. Such an act underscores the importance and centrality of Jesus' approaching death as he saw it.

Second, we have found a historical dominical basis for the Lord's Supper that gives a coherent basis for the subsequent developments. The Lord's Supper lies at the heart of Christian practice. It would be wrong to overemphasize its role over against the reading and exposition of Scriptures and fellowship with God in prayer and praise. Nevertheless, its centrality, as the event in which believers proclaim the death of their Lord and express their sharing in salvation through the symbols of his body and blood, stands beyond question. It is, therefore, of considerable importance that this oc-

---

[359] Beasley-Murray, *Jesus and the Kingdom of God*, 268, citing Jürgen Roloff, "Anfänge der soteriologischen Deutung des Todes Jesu: Mk. X.45 und Lk. XXII.27," *NTS* 19 (1972): 62.
[360] Beasley-Murray, *Jesus and the Kingdom of God*, 269; cf. 267–73.
[361] Beasley-Murray, *Jesus and the Kingdom of God*, 273.

casion should be capable of being seen as fully in line with the purpose of Jesus himself.

Not only so, but there are some contemporary understandings of the Supper which see it more as an occasion for fellowship between believers, almost indeed as little more than an act of commensality, and which ignore the decisive relationship of the meal to the death of Jesus as the basis for salvation: "you are proclaiming the Lord's death until he comes." A liberal type of theology which plays down the centrality and significance of the death of Jesus as God's intended act of sacrificial redemption for sinners and sees it as essentially an act of self-identification with suffering humanity is likely to be embarrassed by the symbolism in the story. And a Christianity which places more stress on belonging to the community of the people of God and attaches less importance to belief in Jesus as the Savior who died on behalf of us all is likewise going to find a stumbling block in this interpretation of the passion that goes back to Jesus himself. Rooting the Lord's Supper in the interpretation placed by Jesus on his death requires us to place the emphasis in the right place, namely as a memorial of his death for us by which we are forgiven and accepted as his covenanted people.

Bibliography

Anderson, Paul N. *The Fourth Gospel and the Quest for Jesus: Modern Foundations Reconsidered*. LNTS 321. London: T&T Clark, 2006.

Bahr, Gordon J. "Seder of Passover and the Eucharistic Words." *NovT* 12 (1970): 181–202.

Barrett, C. K., ed. *The New Testament Background: Selected Documents*. Rev. ed. London: SPCK, 1987.

–. *The First Epistle to the Corinthians*. London: Black, 1968.

–. *The Gospel According to St. John: An Introduction with Commentary and Notes on the Greek Text*. London: SPCK, 1955.

–. "Luke XXII.15: To Eat the Passover." *JTS* 9 (1958): 305–7.

Bauckham, Richard. *Jesus and the Eyewitnesses: The Gospels as Eyewitness Testimony*. Grand Rapids: Eerdmans, 2006.

Beasley-Murray, George R. *Jesus and the Kingdom of God*. Grand Rapids: Eerdmans, 1986.

–. *John*. WBC 36. Waco, Tex.: Word, 1987.

Behm, Johannes. "κλάω, κτλ." Pages 726–43 in vol. 3 of *Theological Dictionary of the New Testament*. 10 vols. Edited by G. Kittel and Gerhard Friedrich. Translated by Geoffrey W. Bromiley. Grand Rapids: Eerdmans, 1964–76.

Berger, Klaus. *Theologiegeschichte des Urchristentums: Theologie des Neuen Testaments*. Tübingen: Francke Verlag, 1994.

Billings, Bradly S. "The Disputed Words in the Lukan Institution Narrative (Luke 22:19b–20): A Sociological Answer to a Textual Problem." *JBL* 125 (2006): 507–26.

–. *Do This in Remembrance of Me: The Disputed Works in the Lukan Institution Narrative (Luke 22:19b–20): An Historico-Exegetical, Theological, and Sociological Analysis*. Library of Biblical Studies. London: T&T Clark, 2006.

Black, Matthew. *An Aramaic Approach to the Gospels and Acts*. Oxford: Clarendon, 1954.

Blinzler, Josef. *The Trial of Jesus*. Westminster: Newman, 1959.

Blomberg, Craig L. *The Historical Reliability of John's Gospel*. Downers Grove: InterVarsity, 2001.

Bock, Darrell L. *Luke*. 2 vols. Baker Exegetical Commentary on the New Testament, 3a–b. Grand Rapids: Baker, 1994–96.

Bockmuehl, Markus. *This Jesus: Martyr, Lord, Messiah*. Edinburgh: T&T Clark, 1994.

Bokser, Baruch M. *The Origins of the Seder: The Passover Rite and Early Rabbinic Judaism*. Berkeley: University of California Press, 1984.

–. "Unleavened Bread and Passover, Feasts Of." Pages 755–65 in vol. 6 of *Anchor Bible Dictionary*. 6 vols. Edited by David N. Freedman. New York: Doubleday, 1992.

Borg, Marcus J. *Jesus, A New Vision: Spirit, Culture, and the Life of Discipleship*. San Francisco: Harper & Row, 1987.

Boughton, Lynne Courter. "'Being Shed for You/Many': Time-Sense and Consequences in the Synoptic Cup Citations." *TynBul* 48 (1997): 249–70.

Böcher, O. "αἷμα." Pages 37–39 in vol. 1 of *Exegetical Dictionary of the New Testament*. 3 vols. Edited by Horst Balz and Gerhard Schneider. Grand Rapids: Eerdmans, 1990–93.

Böttrich, Christfried. "Proexistenz im Leben und Sterben: Jesu Tod bei Lukas." Pages 413–36 in *Deutungen des Todes Jesu im Neuen Testament*. Edited by Jörg Frey and Jens Schröter. WUNT 181. Tübingen: Mohr Siebeck, 2005.

Bradshaw, Paul F. *Eucharistic Origins*. London: SPCK, 2004.

–. *The Search for the Origins of Christian Worship: Sources and Methods for the Study of Early Liturgy*. New York: Oxford University Press, 1992.

Brown, Raymond E. *The Death of the Messiah*. 2 vols. ABRL. New York: Doubleday, 1994.

Bultmann, Rudolf. *Die Geschichte der synoptischen Tradition*. 4th ed. Göttingen: Vandenhoeck & Ruprecht, 1958.

–. *Theology of the New Testament*. Translated by Kendrick Grobel. 2 vols. New York: Scribner, 1951–55.

Burchard, Christoph. "The Importance of Joseph and Aseneth for the Study of the New Testament: A General Survey and a Fresh Look at the Lord's Supper." *NTS* 33 (1987): 102–34.

Cameron, Ron, and Merrill P. Miller, eds. *Redescribing Christian Origins*. SBLSymS 28. Atlanta: Society of Biblical Literature, 2004.

Carmichael, Deborah Bleicher. "David Daube on the Eucharist and the Passover Seder." *JSNT* 42 (1991): 45–67.

Carson, D. A. *The Gospel According to John*. Grand Rapids: Eerdmans, 1991.

–. "Matthew." Pages 1–599 in vol. 8 of *The Expositor's Bible Commentary*. Edited by Frank E. Gaebelein. Grand Rapids: Zondervan, 1984.

Casey, Maurice. *Aramaic Sources of Mark's Gospel*. SNTSMS 102. Cambridge: Cambridge University Press, 1998.

Casey, Maurice. "The Date of the Passover Sacrifices and Mark 14:12." *TynBul* 48 (1997): 245–48.
Casey, Maurice. "The Original Aramaic Form of Jesus' Interpretation of the Cup." *JTS* 41 (1990): 1–12.
Chilton, Bruce. *Jesus' Prayer and Jesus' Eucharist: His Personal Practice of Spirituality*. Valley Forge: Trinity, 1997.
Chilton, Bruce D. *A Feast of Meanings: Eucharistic Theologies from Jesus Through Johannine Circles*. NovTSup 72. Leiden: Brill, 1994.
–. *The Temple of Jesus: His Sacrificial Program Within a Cultural History of Sacrifice*. University Park: Pennsylvania State University, 1992.
Cohn-Sherbok, D. M. "A Jewish Note on τὸ ποτήριον τῆς εὐλογίας." *NTS* 27 (1981): 704–9.
Crossan, John Dominic. *The Historical Jesus: The Life of a Mediterranean Jewish Peasant*. San Francisco: HarperSanFrancisco, 1991.
Davies, W. D., and Dale C. Allison, Jr. *A Critical and Exegetical Commentary on the Gospel According to Saint Matthew*. 3 vols. ICC. Edinburgh: T&T Clark, 1988–97.
Doble, Peter. *The Paradox of Salvation: Luke's Theology of the Cross*. SNTSMS 87. Cambridge: Cambridge University Press, 1996.
Dodd, C. H. *Historical Tradition in the Fourth Gospel*. Cambridge: Cambridge University Press, 1963.
Dormeyer, Detlev. *Die Passion Jesu als Verhaltensmodell: Literarische und theologische Analyse der Traditions- und Redaktionsgeschichte der Markuspassion*. NTAbh 11. Münster: Aschendorff, 1974.
Draper, Jonathan A. "Do the Didache and Matthew Reflect an 'Irrevocable Parting of the Ways' with Judaism?" Pages 217–41 in *Matthew and the Didache: Two Documents from the Same Jewish-Christian Milieu?* Edited by Huub van de Sandt. Assen: Van Gorcum, 2005.
Dunn, James D. G. *Jesus Remembered*. Vol. 1 of *Christianity in the Making*. Grand Rapids: Eerdmans, 2003–.
–. Review of Ron Cameron and Merrill P. Miller, eds., *Redescribing Christian Origins*. *JBL* 124 (2005): 760–64.
–. *The Theology of Paul the Apostle*. Grand Rapids: Eerdmans, 1998.
Ehrman, Bart D. *The Orthodox Corruption of Scripture: The Effect of Early Christological Controversies on the Text of the New Testament*. New York: Oxford University Press, 1993.
Ellis, E. Earle. *The Gospel of Luke*. London: Nelson, 1966.
Evans, C. F. *Saint Luke*. TPINTC. London: SCM; Philadelphia: Trinity, 1990.
Evans, Craig A. *Mark 8:27–16:20*. WBC 34b. Nashville: Nelson, 2001.
Fee, Gordon D. *The First Epistle to the Corinthians*. NICNT. Grand Rapids: Eerdmans, 1987.
Fitzmyer, Joseph A. *The Gospel According to Luke X–XXIV*. AB 28a. Garden City: Doubleday, 1985.
France, R. T. "Chronological Aspects of 'Gospel Harmony.'" *VE* 16 (1986): 33–59.
–. *The Gospel of Mark*. NIGTC. Grand Rapids: Eerdmans, 2002.
–. *Jesus and the Old Testament: His Application of Old Testament Passages to Himself and His Mission*. London: Tyndale, 1971.

Friedrich, Gerhard. *Die Verkündigung des Todes Jesu im Neuen Testament.* Neukirchen-Vluyn: Neukirchener Verlag, 1982.
Funk, Robert W., and The Jesus Seminar. *The Acts of Jesus: The Search for the Authentic Deeds of Jesus.* San Francisco: HarperSanFrancisco, 1998.
Funk, Robert W., Roy W. Hoover, and The Jesus Seminar. *The Five Gospels: The Search for the Authentic Words of Jesus.* New York: Macmillan, 1993.
Gathercole, Simon J. "The Gospel of Judas." *Expository Times* 118 (2007): 209–15.
Gese, Hartmut. *Essays on Biblical Theology.* Translated by Keith Crim. Minneapolis: Augsburg, 1981.
Gnilka, Joachim. *Jesus of Nazareth: Message and History.* Translated by Siegfried S. Schatzmann. Peabody, Mass.: Hendrickson, 1997.
Goppelt, Leonhard. "ποτήριον." Pages 148–58 in vol. 6 of *Theological Dictionary of the New Testament.* 10 vols. Edited by G. Kittel and Gerhard Friedrich. Translated by Geoffrey W. Bromiley. Grand Rapids: Eerdmans, 1964–76.
Grässer, Erich. *Aufbruch und Verheißung: Gesammelte Aufsätze zum Hebräerbrief.* Edited by Martin Evang and Otto Merk. Berlin: De Gruyter, 1992.
Green, Joel B. *The Death of Jesus: Tradition and Interpretation in the Passion Narrative.* WUNT 2.33. Tübingen: Mohr Siebeck, 1988.
–. *The Gospel of Luke.* NICNT. Grand Rapids: Eerdmans, 1997.
Gundry, Robert H. *Mark: A Commentary on His Apology for the Cross.* Grand Rapids: Eerdmans, 1993.
–. *Matthew: A Commentary on His Handbook for a Mixed Church Under Persecution.* 2nd ed. Grand Rapids: Eerdmans, 1994.
Hagner, Donald A. *Matthew 14–28.* WBC 33b. Dallas: Word, 1995.
–. "Ransom Saying." Pages 488–91 in *Encyclopedia of the Historical Jesus.* Edited by Craig A. Evans. London: Routledge, 2008.
Hahn, Ferdinand. *Die Einheit des Neuen Testaments: Thematische Darstellung.* Vol. 2 of *Theologie des Neuen Testaments.* Tübingen: Mohr Siebeck, 2002.
–. *Die Vielfalt des Neuen Testaments: Theologiegeschichte des Urchristentums.* Vol. 1 of *Theologie des Neuen Testaments.* Tübingen: Mohr Siebeck, 2002.
Hays, Richard B. *First Corinthians.* Int. Louisville: John Knox, 1997.
Hengel, Martin. "Das Mahl in der Nacht, 'in der Jesus ausgeliefert wurde' (1 Kor 11,23)." Pages 115–60 in *Le Repas de Dieu: Das Mahl Gottes.* Edited by Christian Grappe. Tübingen: Mohr Siebeck, 2004.
Hengel, Martin, and Anna Maria Schwemer. *Jesus und das Judentum.* Vol. 1 of *Geschichte des frühen Christentums.* 4 vols. Tübingen: Mohr Siebeck, 2007–.
Hoehner, Harold W. *Chronological Aspects of the Life of Christ.* Grand Rapids: Zondervan, 1977.
–. "Chronology." Pages 118–22 in *Dictionary of Jesus and the Gospels.* Edited by Joel B. Green and Scot McKnight. Downers Grove: InterVarsity, 1992.
Hofius, Otfried. *Neutestamentliche Studien.* WUNT 132. Tübingen: Mohr Siebeck, 2000.
Huck, A. *Synopse der drei ersten Evangelien.* Edited by H. Greeven. Tübingen: Mohr Siebeck, 1981.
Hurtado, Larry W. *Lord Jesus Christ: Devotion to Jesus in Earliest Christianity.* Grand Rapids: Eerdmans, 2003.
Instone-Brewer, David. "Jesus's Last Passover: The Synoptics and John." *ExpTim* 112 (2001): 122–23.

Jaubert, A. *La date de la Cène*. Paris: Gabalda, 1957.
Jeremias, Joachim. *The Eucharistic Words of Jesus*. Translated by Norman Perrin. NTL. London: SCM, 1966.
–. *Jerusalem in the Time of Jesus*. London: SCM, 1969.
–. "Paarweise Sendung im Neuen Testament." Pages 136–43 in *New Testament Essays. Studies in Memory of Thomas Walter Manson, 1893–1958*. Edited by A. J. B. Higgins. Manchester: Manchester University Press, 1959.
–. "παῖς θεοῦ." Pages 654–717 in vol. 5 of *Theological Dictionary of the New Testament*. 10 vols. Edited by G. Kittel and Gerhard Friedrich. Translated by Geoffrey W. Bromiley. Grand Rapids: Eerdmans, 1964–76.
Kelber, Werner H. "Conclusion: From Passion Narrative to Gospel." Pages 153–80 in *The Passion in Mark: Studies in Mark 14–16*. Edited by Werner H. Kelber. Philadelphia: Fortress, 1976.
Klassen, William. "The Authenticity of Judas' Participation in the Arrest of Jesus." Pages 389–410 in *Authenticating the Activities of Jesus*. Edited by Bruce D. Chilton and Craig A. Evans. Leiden: Brill, 1999.
–. *Judas: Betrayer or Friend of Jesus?* Minneapolis: Fortress, 1996.
–. "Judas Iscariot." Pages 1091–96 in vol. 3 of *Anchor Bible Dictionary*. 6 vols. Edited by David N. Freedman. New York: Doubleday, 1992.
Klauck, Hans-Josef. *Herrenmahl und hellenistischer Kult: eine religionsgeschichtliche Untersuchung zum ersten Korintherbrief*. NTAbh 15. Münster: Aschendorff, 1982.
–. "Lord's Supper." Pages 362–72 in vol. 4 of *Anchor Bible Dictionary*. 6 vols. Edited by David N. Freedman. New York: Doubleday, 1992.
Klawans, Jonathan. "Interpreting the Last Supper: Sacrifice, Spiritualization, and Anti-Sacrifice." *NTS* 48 (2002): 1–17.
Klein, Hans. *Das Lukasevangelium*. KEK 1.3. Göttingen: Vandenhoeck & Ruprecht, 2006.
Klinghardt, Matthias. *Gemeinschaftsmahl und Mahlgemeinschaft: Soziologie und Liturgie frühchristlicher Mahlfeiern*. Texte und Arbeiten zum neutestamentlichen Zeitalter. Tübingen: Francke Verlag, 1996.
Kollmann, Bernd. *Ursprung und Gestalten der frühchristlichen Mahlfeier*. GTA, 43. Göttingen: Vandenhoeck & Ruprecht, 1990.
Kuhn, Heinz-Wolfgang. "The Qumran Meal and the Lord's Supper in Paul in the Context of the Graeco-Roman World." Pages 221–48 in *Paul, Luke and the Graeco-Roman World: Essays in Honour of Alexander J. M. Wedderburn*. Edited by A. Christophersen. JSNTSup 217. London: Sheffield, 2002.
Kuhn, K. G. "The Lord's Supper and the Communal Meal at Qumran." Pages 65–93 in *The Scrolls and the New Testament*. Edited by Krister Stendahl. London: SCM, 1958.
Lightfoot, J. B., and J. R. Harmer. *The Apostolic Fathers: Revised Greek Texts with Introductions and English Translations*. Grand Rapids: Baker, 1984.
Lincoln, Andrew T. *The Gospel According to Saint John*. BNTC. London: Continuum; Peabody: Hendrickson, 2005.
Lüdemann, Gerd. *Jesus After 2000 Years: What He Really Said and Did*. Amherst: Prometheus, 2001.
Lührmann, Dieter. *Das Markusevangelium*. HNT, 3. Tübingen: Mohr Siebeck, 1987.
Maccoby, Hyam. "Paul and the Eucharist." *NTS* 37 (1991): 247–67.

McGowan, Andrew. "Eating People: Accusations of Cannibalism Against Christians in the Second Century." *JECS* 2 (1994): 413–42.
McGowan, Andrew Brian. "Is There a Liturgical Text in This Gospel?': The Institution Narratives and Their Early Interpretive Communities." *JBL* 118 (1999): 73–87.
Mack, Burton L. *A Myth of Innocence: Mark and Christian Origins*. Philadelphia: Fortress, 1988.
McKnight, Scot. *Jesus and His Death: Historiography, the Historical Jesus, and Atonement Theory*. Waco: Baylor University Press, 2005.
Maier, Johann. *Jesus von Nazareth in der Talmudischen Überlieferung*. EdF, 82. Darmstadt: Wissenschaftliche Buchgesellschaft, 1978.
Marshall, I. Howard. *The Gospel of Luke*. NIGTC 3. Grand Rapids: Eerdmans, 1978.
–. *Last Supper and Lord's Supper*. Exeter: Paternoster, 1980.
Martin, Michael W. "Defending the 'Western Non-Interpolations': The Case for an Anti-Separationist *Tendenz* in the Longer Alexandrian Readings." *JBL* 124 (2005): 269–94.
Mazza, Enrico. "Didache 9–10: Elements of a Eucharistic Interpretation." Pages 276–99 in *The Didache in Modern Research*. Edited by Jonathan A. Draper. Leiden: Brill, 1996.
–. *The Origins of the Eucharistic Prayer*. Translated by Ronald E. Lane. Collegeville: Liturgical, 1995.
Meier, John P. *Companions and Competitors*. Vol. 3 of *A Marginal Jew: Rethinking the Historical Jesus*. ABRL. New York: Doubleday, 1991–2009.
–. "The Eucharist at the Last Supper: Did It Happen?" *TD* 42 (1995): 335–51.
–. *Mentor, Message, and Miracles*. Vol. 2 of *A Marginal Jew: Rethinking the Historical Jesus*. ABRL. New York: Doubleday, 1991–2009.
–. *The Roots of the Problem and the Person*. Vol. 1 of *A Marginal Jew: Rethinking the Historical Jesus*. ABRL. New York: Doubleday, 1991–2009.
Mencken, H. L. *Prejudices (Second Series) "The Divine Afflatus"*. New York: Knopf, 1920.
Merklein, Helmut. "Erwägungen zur Überlieferungsgeschichte der neutestamentlichen Abendmahlstraditionen." *BZ* 21 (1977): 88–101, 235–44.
Metzger, Bruce M. *A Textual Commentary on the Greek New Testament*. 2nd ed. Stuttgart: Deutsche Bibelgesellschaft, 1994.
Moo, Douglas J. *The Old Testament in the Gospel Passion Narratives*. Sheffield: Almond, 1983.
Morris, Leon. *The Gospel According to John*. Grand Rapids: Eerdmans, 1971.
–. *The Gospel According to John*. NICNT. Grand Rapids: Eerdmans, 1995.
–. *Luke: An Introduction and Commentary*. Rev. ed. TNTC. Leicester: InterVarsity, 1988.
Niederwimmer, Kurt. *The Didache: A Commentary*. Translated by Linda M. Maloney. Hermeneia. Minneapolis: Fortress, 1998.
Nolland, John. *The Gospel of Matthew*. NIGTC. Grand Rapids: Eerdmans, 2005.
–. *Luke 18:35–24:53*. WBC 35c. Dallas: Word, 1993.
O'Toole, Robert F. "Last Supper." Pages 234–41 in vol. 4 of *Anchor Bible Dictionary*. 6 vols. Edited by David N. Freedman. New York: Doubleday, 1992.
O'Brien, Kevin. *But the Gates Were Shut*. San Francisco: International Scholars Publications, 1996.

Parker, D.C. *The Living Text of the Gospels.* Cambridge: Cambridge University Press, 1997.
Parsons, Mikeal C. *The Departure of Jesus in Luke-Acts: The Ascension Narratives in Context.* JSNTSup 21. Sheffield: JSOT Press, 1987.
Patsch, Hermann. *Abendmahl und historischer Jesus.* Calwer Theologische Monographien, 1. Stuttgart: Calwer Verlag, 1972.
Pesch, Rudolf. *Das Abendmahl und Jesu Todesverständnis.* QD, 80. Freiburg: Herder, 1978.
–. *Das Markusevangelium.* 2 vols. HTKNT 2. Freiburg im Breisgau: Herder, 1977.
Petzer, J.H. "Luke 22:19b–20 and the Structure of the Passage." *NovT* 26 (1984): 249–52.
–. "Style and Text in the Lucan Narrative of the Institution of the Lord's Supper (Luke 22:19b–20)." *NTS* 37 (1991): 113–29.
Ramsey, A.M. "History and the Gospel." Pages 75–85 in *Studia Evangelica IV.* Edited by F.L. Cross. Berlin: de Gruyter, 1968.
Rehkopf, Friedrich. *Die lukanische Sonderquelle: ihr Umfang und Sprachgebrauch.* WUNT 5. Tübingen: Mohr Siebeck, 1959.
Reicke, Bo. *The New Testament Era: The World of the Bible from 500 B.C. to A.D. 100.* Translated by David E. Green. Philadelphia: Fortress, 1968.
Rese, Martin. "Zur Problematik von Kurz- und Langtext in Luk 22:17ff." *NTS* 22 (1975): 15–31.
Riggs, John W. "The Sacred Food of Didache 9–10 and Second-Century Ecclesiologies." Pages 256–83 in *The Didache in Context: Essays on Its Text, History, and Transmission.* Edited by Clayton N. Jefford. NovTSup 77. Leiden: Brill, 1995.
Robbins, Vernon K. "Last Meal: Preparation, Betrayal, and Absence (Mark 14:12–25)." Pages 21–40 in *The Passion in Mark: Studies in Mark 14–16.* Edited by Werner H. Kelber. Philadelphia: Fortress, 1976.
Roloff, Jürgen. "Anfänge der soteriologischen Deutung des Todes Jesu: Mk. X.45 und Lk. XXII.27." *NTS* 19 (1972): 38–64.
Routledge, Robin. "Passover and Last Supper." *TynBul* 53 (2002): 203–21.
Rouwhorst, Gerard. "Didache 9–10: A Litmus Test For the Research on Early Christian Liturgy Eucharist." Pages 143–56 in *Matthew and the Didache: Two Documents from the Same Jewish-Christian Milieu?* Edited by Huub van de Sandt. Assen: Van Gorcum, 2005.
Sanders, E.P. *Jesus and Judaism.* Philadelphia: Fortress, 1985.
–. *Judaism: Practice and Belief, 63 BCE–66 CE.* Philadelphia: Trinity, 1992.
Sanders, E.P., and Margaret Davies. *Studying the Synoptic Gospels.* London: SCM, 1989.
Schenke, Ludger. *Studien zur Passionsgeschichte des Markus: Tradition und Redaktion in Markus 14, 1–42.* FB, 4. Würzburg: Echter Verlag, 1971.
Schlund, Christine. "Deutungen des Todes Jesu im Rahmen der Pesach-Tradition." Pages 397–411 in *Deutungen des Todes Jesu im Neuen Testament.* Edited by Jörg Frey and Jens Schröter. WUNT 181. Tübingen: Mohr Siebeck, 2005.
Schmid, Ulrich. "Eklektische Textkonstitution als theologische Rekonstruktion: Zur Heilsbedeutung des Todes Jesu bei Lukas (Lk 22,15–20 und Apg 20,28)." Pages 577–84 in *The Unity of Luke-Acts.* Edited by Joseph Verheyden. Leuven: Leuven University Press, 1999.
Schmithals, Walter. *Das Evangelium nach Lukas.* Zürich: Theologischer Verlag, 1980.

–. *Das Evangelium nach Markus Kapitel 9,2–16,18.* ÖTK, 2. Gütersloh: Gütersloher Verlagshaus; Würzburg: Echter Verlag, 1979.
–. *Theologiegeschichte des Urchristentums: Eine problemgeschichtliche Darstellung.* Stuttgart: Kohlhammer, 1994.
Schnackenburg, Rudolf. *The Gospel According to John.* 3 vols. New York: Seabury, 1980–82.
Schneider, Gerhard. *Die Passion Jesu nach den drei älteren Evangelien.* Biblische Handbibliothek, 11. Munich: Kösel, 1973.
Schröter, Jens. *Das Abendmahl: Frühchristliche Deutungen und Impulse für die Gegenwart.* SBS, 210. Stuttgart: Katholisches Bibelwerk, 2006.
Schürmann, Heinz. *Der Einsetzungsbericht, Lk 22, 19–20.* Münster: Aschendorff, 1955.
–. *Gottes Reich – Jesu Geschick: Jesu ureigener Tod im Licht seiner Basileia-Verkündigung.* Freiburg: Herder, 1983.
–. *Jesu Abschiedsrede, Lk 22, 21–38.* Münster: Aschendorff, 1957.
–. *Jesu ureigener Tod.* Freiburg: Herder, 1975.
–. *Der Paschamahlbericht, Lk xxii. (7–14) 15–18.* Münster: Aschendorff, 1953.
–. *Traditionsgeschichtliche Untersuchungen zu den synoptischen Evangelien.* KBANT. Düsseldorf: Patmos-Verlag, 1968.
Schwemer, Anna Maria. "Das Problem der *Mahlgemeinschaft* mit dem Auferstandenen." Pages 187–226 in *Le Repas de Dieu: Das Mahl Gottes.* Edited by Christian Grappe. Tübingen: Mohr Siebeck, 2004.
Sigal, Phillip. "Another Note to 1 Corinthians 10:16." *NTS* 29 (1983): 134–39.
Silberman, L. H. "Once Again: The Use of Rabbinic Material." *NTS* 42 (1996): 153–55.
Skarsaune, Oskar. *In the Shadow of the Temple: Jewish Influences on Early Christianity.* Downers Grove: InterVarsity, 2002.
Slee, Michelle. *The Church in Antioch in the First Century CE: Communion and Conflict.* JSNTSup 244. London: Sheffield Academic Press, 2003.
Smith, B. D. "The More Original Form of the Words of Institution." *ZNW* 83 (1992): 166–86.
Smith, Barry D. "Last Supper, Words of Institution." Pages 365–68 in *Encyclopedia of the Historical Jesus.* Edited by Craig A. Evans. London: Routledge, 2008.
Smith, Dennis E. *From Symposium to Eucharist: The Banquet in the Early Christian World.* Minneapolis: Fortress, 2003.
–. Review of John Koenig, *The Feast of the World's Redemption: Eucharistic Origins and Christian Mission. CBQ* 64 (2002): 168–69.
Stacey, W. D. "The Lord's Supper as Prophetic Drama." *Epworth Review* 21 (1994): 65–74.
Story, Cullen I. K. "The Bearing of Old Testament Terminology on the Johannine Chronology of the Final Passover of Jesus." *NovT* 31 (1989): 316–24.
Strack, Hermann L., and Paul Billerbeck. *Kommentar zum Neuen Testament aus Talmud und Midrasch.* 6 vols. Munich: Beck, 1922–61.
Stuhlmacher, Peter. *Biblische Theologie des Neuen Testaments.* 2 vols. Göttingen: Vandenhoeck & Ruprecht, 1992.
Tabory, Joseph. "Towards a History of the Paschal Meal." Pages 62–80 in *Passover and Easter: Origin and History to Modern Times.* Edited by Paul F. Bradshaw and Lawrence A. Hoffman. Notre Dame: University of Notre Dame Press, 1999.

Taylor, Vincent. *The Gospel According to St. Mark*. 2nd ed. London: Macmillan, 1966.
–. *Jesus and His Sacrifice: A Study of the Passion-Sayings in the Gospels*. London: Macmillan, 1937.
Theissen, Gerd. "Soziale Integration und sakramentales Handeln: Eine Analyse von 1 Cor. XI.17–24." *NovT* 16 (1974): 179–206.
Theissen, Gerd, and Annette Merz. *The Historical Jesus: A Comprehensive Guide*. Translated by John Bowden. Minneapolis: Fortress, 1998.
Thiselton, Anthony C. *The First Epistle to the Corinthians: A Commentary on the Greek Text*. NIGTC. Grand Rapids: Eerdmans; Carlisle: Paternoster, 2000.
Tomson, Peter J. "Jesus and His Judaism." Pages 25–40 in *The Cambridge Companion to Jesus*. Edited by Markus Bockmuehl. Cambridge; New York: Cambridge University Press, 2001.
Trilling, Wolfgang. "Zur Entstehung des Zwölferkreises: Eine geschichtskritische Überlegung." Pages 201–22 in *Die Kirche des Anfangs: Festschrift für Heinz Schürmann zum 65. Geburtstag*. Edited by Rudolf Schnackenburg, Josef Ernst, and Joachim Wanke. Leipzig: St Benno-Verlag, 1977.
van de Sandt, Huub, and David Flusser. *The Didache: Its Jewish Sources and Its Place in Early Judaism and Christianity*. CRINT, 5. Assen: Royal Van Gorcum; Minneapolis: Fortress, 2002.
Vielhauer, Philipp, and Georg Strecker. "Jewish-Christian Gospels." Pages 134–78 in vol. 1 of *New Testament Apocrypha*. Rev. ed. 2 vols. Edited by Wilhelm Schneemelcher and R. McL. Wilson. Louisville: Westminster John Knox, 1990–91.
Wellhausen, J. "Ἄρτον ἔκλασεν Mc 14,22." *ZNW* 7 (1906): 182.
Witherington, Ben, III. *Making a Meal of It: Rethinking the Theology of the Lord's Supper*. Waco: Baylor University Press, 2007.
Wright, N. T. *Jesus and the Victory of God*. Vol. 2 of *Christian Origins and the Question of God*. Minneapolis: Fortress, 1996.
Yuval, Israel J. "Easter and Passover As Early Jewish-Christian Dialogue." Pages 98–124 in *Passover and Easter: Origin and History to Modern Times*. Edited by Paul F. Bradshaw and Lawrence A. Hoffman. Notre Dame: University of Notre Dame Press, 1999.

Chapter 12

Blasphemy and the Jewish Examination of Jesus[1]

DARRELL L. BOCK

1. Introduction: The Authenticity of the Event of Jesus' Examination by Jewish Temple Authorities

There is little doubt that if one is to treat the historical Jesus, then one must consider Jesus' relationship to the Jewish temple leadership in Jerusalem and the issues that led him to be crucified. No scene is more important for this topic than the Jewish leadership's examination of Jesus. In fact, this scene is of such importance that John Meier argues that the criterion of rejection and execution is a category one can appeal to for examining authenticity, even as he notes that it cannot authenticate a specific saying or deed. That the Jewish leadership had a role in Jesus' death is something Josephus implies as well in his *Ant.* 18.64, where "the principal men among us" (τῶν πρώτων ἀνδρῶν παρ' ἡμῖν) gave the suggestion to Pilate that Jesus be condemned.[2] The Jewish examination of Jesus is the topic of this essay in this introductory section, I will explain why the nature of our sources leads us to concentrate on the event as it is presented in Mark. Second, I shall consider the factors one must consider in looking at the event's historicity and defend the scene's essential historicity. Third, I will consider, given its historicity, what the event's significance is: how the trial scene contributes to an understanding of Jesus' work and ministry.

---

[1] This essay is a revised and expanded version of that published as Darrell L. Bock, "Blasphemy and the Jewish Examination of Jesus," *BBR* 17 (2007): 53–114.

[2] There is a significant debate about the exact wording of this section of Josephus, but this phrase about the Jewish leadership is likely to be present. As John Meier notes, the unit is present in all Greek manuscripts and in numerous manuscripts of the Latin translation, a tradition whose preservation predates our Greek manuscripts. One issue often raised here is the silence of the Fathers on this unit before Eusebius. Meier argues that this is not surprising given the fact that without the now famous likely interpolations, this unit "hardly support mainline Christian belief in Jesus as the Son of God who rose from the dead." John P. Meier, *The Roots of the Problem and the Person* (vol. 1 of *A Marginal Jew: Rethinking the Historical Jesus*; ABRL; New York: Doubleday, 1991–2009), 56–88, esp. 59–69 and notes 37–38. The citation is from n. 38 on p. 79. See also the discussion in this volume in ch. 13, § 2.1.2.

Jesus' examination by the Jewish leadership appears in the Synoptic tradition in Mark 14:53–65, Matt 26:57–68, and Luke 22:54–71. There is no real parallel to the Jewish examination in John's Gospel, because the fourth evangelist merely presents a short exchange between Jesus and the high priest in John 18:19–23. This exchange in John has no corroboration and merely records Jesus' statement that he taught openly, not in secret. As such, this uniquely attested exchange would offer little of significance to the discussion of the historical Jesus and the significance of his death. So we shall not consider the Johannine scene. However, one should also note implications in other texts that suggest a Jewish role in Jesus' death. Here texts such as Acts 4:23–26 and 1 Thess 2:14–15 offer a generic charge against the Jews, likely as an allusion to the leadership's role. Then there is the parable of the vineyard in Matt 21:33–45 and the *Gos. Thom.* 66. It points to the recognition of this role for the leadership. Any claim that the leadership of the Jews had no role in Jesus' death must ignore multiple independent references that even go beyond Christian and biblical texts (i.e., strong multiple attestation), and thus such a claim is not credible.

When one looks at other gospels that we possess, there is not much additional information to be found. The *Gospel of Peter* begins with the Roman examination. It mentions that the Jewish leadership was involved, saying "none of the Jews washed their hands," but this type of summary statement also adds little, even if we could establish that it had roots in historically based tradition. In 1:2, Herod orders Jesus sent to the cross. The likely mid-second-century text, which alludes to Pilate's washing of his hands from Matt 27:24, places more blame on the Jewish leadership.[3] The remark could simply reflect the generally held belief that the Jewish leadership was involved in Jesus' death, as well as increasing tension between Christians and Jews, while trying to stay out of trouble with the Romans. So it also has little to add. However, if the tradition it reflects is independent of Matthew, then we have multiple attestation for Pilate's hesitation to crucify Jesus, which means the pressure to do away with him came from elsewhere.[4]

---

[3] Christian Maurer and Wilhelm Schneemelcher, "The Gospel of Peter," in *New Testament Apocrypha* (rev. ed.; 2 vols.; ed. Wilhelm Schneemelcher and R. McL. Wilson; Louisville: Westminster John Knox, 1990–91), 1:216–22. Raymond E. Brown (*The Death of the Messiah* [2 vols.; ABRL; New York: Doubleday, 1994], *The Death of the Messiah* [2 vols) notes this *Tendenz* in commenting on this passage. He goes on to note on p. 382 that the Christian apocryphal writings on this scene "have no independent historical value" but does not discuss their contents in any detail.

[4] The roots of this gospel are difficult to establish. The gospel fragment was published in 1892, having been found in Akhmim in Upper Egypt in 1886/87. Since then, two of the Oxyrhynchus papyri published in 1972 were found to contain portions of the gospel. The gospel's mention by Serpion places its date before 200 (*Eccles. Hist.* 5.22.1). The tradition history has been variously assessed with the early view being that it was dependent on the four Gospels. The current status is summarized in Helmut Koester, *Ancient*

The *Gospel of Nicodemus* (also known as the *Acts of Pilate*) also assigns a major role to the Jewish leadership when it begins with the trial before Pilate. This is the appeal of yet another source, pointing to multiple attestation for the generic scene. The account opens with the accusations the leadership brings against Jesus in terms of his self-claims as Son of God and a king, as well as his healing of "the lame, the bent, the withered, the blind, the paralytic, and the possessed" on the Sabbath, which it interprets as acts of sorcery in association with the authority of Beelzebul, as well as wishing "to destroy the law of our fathers" (1:1).[5] The leaders note that healing on the Sabbath is a violation of their law. These remarks about sorcery echo Synoptic charges that appear in another context (Mark 3:22, Matt 12:24, Luke 11:15) and echo the kind of summary of the charges we see in Luke 23:3. The leaders are named: "Annas and Caiaphas, Semes, Dathes and Gamaliel, Judas, Levi, and Nephthalim, Alexander and Jairus and the rest of the Jews." Pilate responds, "This is not to cast out demons by an unclean spirit, but by the god Asclepius." Pilate's reply appeals to the Roman god of healing, while the list of Sabbath healings looks like a summary of the Gospel tradition. The fact that Pilate is present means that the scene does not belong to the same tradition strand or event as the Synoptics, being set at a time when Rome is considering what to do with Jesus.

So when we come to the actual sayings of the scene versus the generic event, we are left with the material in the Synoptic tradition. One should recall that this kind of scene would likely have been much discussed and circulating in an oral context (that is, even Mark's version is likely not the only form of this scene in circulation). However, it also should be noted that the traditions we do have are fairly close to each other in what this scene entails, supporting the suggestion of James Dunn that the tradition reflects a desire to remember Jesus presented as "stable themes and flexibility, of fixed and variable elements in oral retelling."[6] The role of the twelve in being

---

Christian Gospels: Their History and Development (London: SCM; Philadelphia: Trinity, 1990), 216–20, where he questions the theory on this gospel of John Dominic Crossan that this was the earliest passion source. On pp. 220–22, Koester argues that the washing of hands tradition, although rooted in Deut 21:6–8, goes in different directions in the two Gospels and so reflects independent traditions. If so, there is an element of multiple attestation for the Jewish leaders' role implied for Jesus' death. See also in this volume the discussion of this text in ch. 13, § 2.1.1.

[5] Citations are from Felix Scheidweiler, "The Gospel of Nicodemus, Acts of Pilate and Christ's Descent Into Hell," in *New Testament Apocrypha* (rev. ed.; 2 vols.; ed. Wilhelm Schneemelcher and R. McL. Wilson; Louisville: Westminster John Knox, 1990–91), 1:501–36. Scheidweiler notes how the gospel reflects Matthew at many points.

[6] Here we are appealing to the basic claim of what oral tradition of the time did, as James D. G. Dunn, *Jesus Remembered* (vol. 1 of *Christianity in the Making*; Grand Rapids: Eerdmans, 2003–xx), 238–54. The phrase cited is on p. 253. He goes on to note that there would have been a concern to maintain "core or key features."

involved in bearing this church tradition is also worth noting, although as we shall see the potential sources for this scene are actually more extensive than this specific group.

These accounts are quite similar with regard to the key exchange involving the high priest and Jesus. All three parallels have this exchange. I shall focus on this portion of the account, especially as it appears in what is likely to be the earliest form of this tradition, namely, Mark 14:61–64, if the two-document hypothesis is correct. The key part of the scene involves a question by the high priest as to whether Jesus is the Christ, a question all three Synoptics raise. Mark and Matthew have a descriptive addition to the question about the Christ. Matthew has the high priest ask, "If you are the Christ, the Son of God" (εἰ σὺ ὁ χριστὸς ὁ υἱὸς τοῦ θεοῦ), while Mark has "Are you the Christ, the Son of the Blessed?" (σὺ εἶ ὁ χριστὸς ὁ υἱὸς τοῦ εὐλογητοῦ). It is this question from the account and Jesus' response that have always garnered the most intense debate as to its potential value for understanding one element contributing to Jesus' death. It is this exchange and its result that I am considering in this essay: namely, can we determine if Jesus was seen by the Jewish leadership as a blasphemer and as a result took Jesus on to Pilate? Mark 14:64 and Matt 26:65 describe the leadership's response to Jesus as being based on blasphemy, while Luke 22:71 simply speaks of testimony adequate to indict.

In sum, we have the generic scene meeting two criteria: that of rejection and execution (from Meier) and that of multiple attestation (as we see it reflected not only in the Synoptic tradition but also in the acceptance of a rejection coming from the Jewish leadership as portrayed in *Gospel of Thomas*, *Gospel of Peter*, and the *Gospel of Nicodemus*).[7] However, none of this can give us evidence of the authenticity of any details about the scene. Can we go further than a mere declaration that Jesus was examined and condemned in some way that led to his crucifixion and caused him to be tried by Rome? What about the evidence for and against the authenticity of the blasphemy remark?

2. The Historicity of the Blasphemy Remark in Jesus' Examination by the Jewish Temple Authorities

The core event involves a query by the High Priest concerning whether Jesus is the Son of the Almighty. Jesus responds positively in Mark 14:62 and

---

[7] For discussion of the use of criteria for authenticity, see the discussion in ch. 2, § 4.1. Whether one sees these other gospels as independent strands, as influenced by the tradition of the four gospels, or as a mix of such features (which is also possible), the retention of this theme widens the witnesses that affirm the presence of this aspect of the event.

in a qualified manner in Matt 26:64 and Luke 22:70. The answer invokes the images of the Son of Man and this figure's locale at God's right hand (appealing to Ps 110:1) in all the synoptics. In Mark and Matthew the imagery includes a reference to riding the clouds (imagery from Dan 7:13). In all the gospels this response leads to the sending of Jesus to Pilate. Mark 14:63 and Matt 26:65 have the High Priest tear his garments and refers directly to his reading of Jesus' remarks as blasphemy. Luke's account (22:71) simply reports that there was no need to gather any further testimony (also Matt 27:65; Mark 14:63) and does not mention blasphemy explicitly.

2.1. The Issue of Blasphemy in Overview

Donald Juel states the problem and the current state of the discussion most clearly and succinctly as he reflects on the Jewish background. The mishnaic charge of blasphemy as recorded in *m. Sanh.* 7:5 requires pronunciation of the divine name for blasphemy to be present, and so Juel observes:

If this second-century conception of blasphemy is an appropriate reflection of early first-century legal standards, it is impossible that Jesus could have been legally condemned for this offence. In fact, his response to the question of the high priest contains clear indications of respectful avoidance of the name of God ("The right hand of power"). Most scholars insist, therefore, that the legal definition of blasphemy must have been considerably broader in the first century. The difficulty with such proposals is the lack of source material for reconstructing legal practice prior to A.D. 70 ... Even if the broadest definition of blasphemy be accepted, however, the problem is far from solved. It is still unclear precisely what in the question of the high priest or Jesus' response would constitute a blasphemous statement or claim.[8]

Juel's remark is stated with care. What we lack are sources that give us details of the *legal* practice before 70 C.E. However, we do have, as my earlier full monograph on the subject of blasphemy shows, a significant amount of material that describes Jewish views of blasphemy in this period as a *cultural* matter and with a consistency that suggests it was a widely held view, even among Judaism's religious leaders.[9] This chapter will contend that this

---

[8] Donald Juel, *Messiah and Temple: The Trial of Jesus in the Gospel of Mark* (SBLDS 31; Missoula, Mont.: Scholars, 1977), 97–98. In fact, little changes as far as the impact on historical questions, if one accepts Matthean priority, because Mark and Matthew run very close together in terms of content.

[9] Darrell L. Bock, *Blasphemy and Exaltation in Judaism and the Final Examination of Jesus* (WUNT 2.106; Tübingen: Mohr Siebeck, 1998), 30–112. The first chapter reviews the state of the debate regarding the blasphemy passage before 1995, evaluating studies by Hans Lietzmann (1931), Paul Winter (1961, 1974), Josef Blinzler (1969), David Catchpole (1971), August Strobel (1980), Otto Betz (1982), E.P. Sanders (1985), Martin Hengel (1991, 1995), Robert Gundry (1993), Raymond Brown (1994), J.C. O'Neill (1995), and Craig Evans (1995). These works are cited individually at the relevant places in this essay. Lietzmann questioned the Jewish involvement in Jesus' death because he regarded the

cultural background is pervasive enough to indicate what in Jesus' response "would constitute a blasphemous statement or claim" for his distinguished inquisitors. In doing so, it will appeal to a criterion similar to Theissen and Winter's "historical plausibility."[10] However the lack of multiple attestation for this exchange plus its specific nature means that we shall need to proceed very carefully piece by piece. The exchange is basically Markan, so it is with this version that I will be most concerned. This event is instructive, because it shows that even in texts where multiple attestation is lacking there can be grounds for making a case for the credibility of the Gospel tradition. Single attestation need not preclude authenticity.

The consideration of Mark's account proceeds in five major steps, though the first is in many ways a prolegomena. First, I consider the general function of the account in Mark's Gospel, apart from issues of detailed historicity. This is to get at the claim, sometimes made, that this scene is only theologically motivated. By showing what Mark is doing, we can begin to see what these concerns are and ask if the trial scene is only addressed to these pastoral concerns. I pursue this question because for some this is the key value of the event, namely, what it does for Mark theologically and pastorally, *not historically*. I argue that Mark has two major concerns. The nature of at least one of these concerns suggests a need for a historical base to his account.

(1) There is Marcan interest in detailing how Jesus came to be executed. What issues were at the center of the storm between him and the Jewish officials? Mark does have a broad historical concern in his account to show both Jesus' innocence and the basis of his execution. Mark has traced these concerns in his gospel. This is a macro concern for Mark. The theme represents his attempt to detail the various disputes that undergirded the ongoing tension between Jesus and the leadership during his ministry. Issues such

---

crucifixion as evidence of both Roman responsibility and Jewish noninvolvement. He also rejected the high priest's question as reflecting a Jewish concern; nor did Jesus' answer reflect a blasphemous response (Lietzmann mostly appealing to *m. Sanh.* 7:5). Most who reject this scene do so on this basis or by rejecting the possibility of an early juxtaposition of Ps 110:1 and Dan 7 going back to Jesus, partly on the basis that there were no disciples present at this examination to know what Jesus said. This chapter will examine all of these issues in turn, plus some others that are mentioned against historicity. Little has changed in this basic debate over historicity in the last ten years, as is shown by the updated discussion from Anna Maria Schwemer, "Die Passion des Messias nach Markus und der Vorwurf des Antijudaismus," in *Der messianische Anspruch Jesu und die Anfänge der Christologie: Vier Studien* (by Martin Hengel and Anna Maria Schwemer; WUNT 2.138; Tübingen: Mohr Siebeck, 2001), 133–63.

[10] Gerd Theissen and Dagmar Winter, *The Quest for the Plausible Jesus: The Question of Criteria* (trans. M. Eugene Boring; Louisville: Westminster John Knox, 2002). This work discusses the criteria of authenticity and develops the idea of a criterion tied to plausibility in some detail. See also the discussion of this criterion and others in ch. 2, § 4.1.

as the authority to heal and forgive sins, purity, legal disputes, the tensions surrounding the temple, and the disputes of the last days in Jerusalem fit in here.[11] Even viewed from the standpoint of a narrative, they set the stage for this decisive meeting. There is even an interesting kind of "Son of Man / blasphemy" *inclusio* in Mark. It binds the first Jewish dispute with Jesus in Mark 2:1–12, which leads to a charge of blasphemy against him for claiming to forgive sin, to the final dispute here in the examination scene of 14:60–64. In this final text, the claim concerning the Son of Man, among other terms, reappears with fresh force in terms that speak of heavenly exaltation. But the very fact that the narrative slows down to a crawl at this key point indicates Mark's concern to communicate some detail about these events. I will not develop this point, because it becomes a burden of the rest of this chapter. How careful Mark's work was in more detail is something that requires careful examination. Mark's pastoral concerns, which certainly also exist, do not necessarily rule out the possibility that he possessed some historical concern. Too often the two themes of pastoral theology and history are assumed to be in a kind of exclusive competition, where the presence of one precludes the other. Could the consistent narrative tension also reflect a historical concern? I hope in this chapter to make a case for their union, at least in this section of Mark.

(2) Nevertheless, Mark was also interested in an important pastoral point, portraying Jesus as the model disciple who is unjustly persecuted while trusting God.[12] Disciples can study his experience to see how they should

---

[11] Many of these particular concerns are also topics addressed in the other chapters, namely, healing-Sabbath disputes, the temple scene, and other last week disputes. The fact that such concerns are touched upon in Mark's version rather obliquely versus being injected as a summarizing literary theme in fact may well support a historical concern. The indirect nature of allusions of this sort at an examination scene may be another indicator of historicity.

[12] A specific determination about the date and setting of Mark is part of a long, complex debate that I cannot resolve here. The preponderance of the evidence, mostly external in nature, does suggest that the Gospel was written by a companion of Peter, John Mark, in Rome because the largely Gentile community was undergoing the threat of significant persecution sometime in the sixties. The external evidence could support any date from the outbreak of the Neronian persecution. For a date of 65–67 C. E., see C. E. B. Cranfield, *The Gospel According to Saint Mark* (CGTC; Cambridge: Cambridge University Press, 1959), 3–9; for a date of 68–69 C. E., Martin Hengel (*Studies in the Gospel of Mark* [trans. John Bowden; Philadelphia: Fortress, 1985], 1–30) has a full discussion of the ancient sources. D. A. Carson and Douglas J. Moo, *An Introduction to the New Testament* (2nd ed.; Grand Rapids: Zondervan, 2005), 179–82, survey dates for Mark ranging from the forties to the seventies. Those supporting a date in the forties include C. Torrey and J. Wenham. Traditions that tie the gospel to Peter and Rome make this view unlikely. Those supporting the fifties include Harnack, Reicke, and Mann. The key to this view is that Luke–Acts dates to the early sixties, which is debatable. We have already noted those who support a date in the sixties. In support of it are the traditions that suggest Peter was near death or had died, that the context is one of persecution pointing to a time around Nero's

walk and what they might face. Jesus is one who simply offers his powerful confession when asked. In the content, tone, and strength of Jesus' response lies the example. Both points, history and pastoral theology, are important to Mark's portrayal of these key events. What has produced skepticism about the scene is the way in which christological designations pile up in the interrogation. For many, Mark is simply reflecting the christology of his own time, not the christology of Jesus at the examination. This issue will be addressed directly when questions related to possible sources of transmission and authenticity are directly treated below.

With the backdrop of Marcan narrative and pastoral concerns noted, I move to consider the historical elements of Mark's presentation more closely in the following four subsections. Second, I criticize an assumption

---

rule, and details surrounding the manner in which Mark 13 is presented, which seems to point to a period before the fall of Jerusalem. However, none of these three points is unassailable. Those who date Mark after seventy see it as coming after the fall of Jerusalem because of the way they read Mark 13. This basis for dating is "seriously flawed" according to Carson and Moo. An important feature here is the lack of reference to the fulfillment of this prediction, if it had already taken place (a point that applies especially if one sees Mark 13 as created by the church, since if the community can create a prophecy after the fact *ex nihilo*, then they certainly can take one more step and note its realization just as he claimed). They opt for a date in the late fifties or sixties, which is a likely range for the origin of this gospel. A good argument also exists for the Mark-Peter connection being trustworthy. It is that if one were choosing simply to make a connection to Peter to get to apostolic authority or to name an author that one really did not know, Mark would not be the most obvious choice for such a connection, since his ministry record was quite spotty and his connections to Peter are not transparent. Again if the church was in the habit of creatively making such connections, then why not just connect the text directly to Peter? That would give the work more credibility in assigning an author than an appeal to Mark, who possessed a troubled resume. Yet the tradition seems consistent here about this connection. Where did this consistency credibly come from if not from a likely genuine connection passed on within the tradition? Traditions existed that John Mark had not been the most persistent and faithful of ministry companions as Acts 13–14 make clear. Mark also was responsible for a split between Paul and Barnabas (Acts 15:36–41). So he is hardly a stellar candidate to be randomly selected for this Petrine connection. For the case against Marcan authorship which also often assumes a post-70 date, see M. Eugene Boring, *Mark* (NTL; Louisville: Westminster John Knox, 2006), 9–14, and C. Clifton Black, *Mark: Images of an Apostolic Interpreter* (Studies on Personalities of the New Testament; Columbia: University of South Carolina Press, 1994). I find Boring's argument about how Mark came to be linked to Peter to be quite speculative in light of the realities of the tradition about Mark noted above. However, for our purposes, what is important is not fixing the date, but rather providing the general setting as the context of persecution, a point about which there is little dispute. *This context applies to Mark's gospel, whether one dates him early or late and regardless of whether Mark as a follower of Peter is an author of this gospel.* So, regardless of the date chosen, Mark treats a persecution context. As Cranfield states: "The purposes which are special to Mark would seem to be to supply the catechetical and liturgical needs of the church in Rome, to support its faith in the face of the threat of martyrdom and to provide material for missionary preachers" (p. 14). That some things in Mark only tangentially touch on these catechetical themes points in the direction of additional historical concerns.

that has clouded the way in which many have examined this scene, namely that the scene reports a Jewish capital trial. Third, I consider potential sources for the saying and the blasphemy itself. Here I only ask if it is possible that the saying could reflect knowledge of the Jewish examination of Jesus. Could there exist a chain of transmission for the saying? Fourth, I consider the saying itself and the issue of blasphemy in it. An attempt will be made to define the various elements of the perceived blasphemy in Jesus' reply. It is here that I apply the historical background of my monograph. At the least, the study should indicate what cultural assumptions Mark's presentation of the blasphemy involved and how he saw this key dispute. It would seem clear that this is how Mark framed his argument, whether he got the actual history right or not. Was he playing off cultural considerations that make some sense of the dispute as he saw it at the time he wrote? If such sensitivities reflect a careful reading of Jewish cultural and theological perspective, then might that suggest Mark's framing is rooted in knowledge of the dispute from an earlier time? These represent key elements of background that must be assembled before the saying itself can be fully assessed. Finally, I treat the consideration of the saying as a whole and the nature of its historical character. It is at this point that various issues that are a part of the saying's analysis must be considered: the role and sensibility of the temple charge, the "Jewish" expressions in the scene, the use of Ps 110:1 and Dan 7:13, the apocalyptic Son of Man and Jesus, and the combination and relationship of titles present in the question and the reply. Only within a consideration of these final questions can one evaluate the issue of the actual historicity of the scene as an event in the life of Jesus.

2.2. *The Pastoral Function of the Examination Scene within Mark*

The Jewish examination of Jesus performs a major function in the Marcan narrative.[13] G.B. Caird has put the Marcan question in terms of the purpose of the entire Gospel this way: "Why must the followers of Jesus suffer? Why, if he was the promised Messiah, did he suffer, and why should Gentiles believe in him if his own people have rejected him?"[14] Put in this light, the question of the Jewish examination serves to explain the path to suffering and the cross. Jesus as the model disciple is a theme developed by

---

[13] Most commentaries do not consider the Marcan account from the standpoint of its narration, being more consumed with questions of the scene's historical detail or the meaning of the scene itself for Mark, especially for his christology. These approaches to the scene were discussed in the opening chapter of Bock, *Blasphemy and Exaltation*. Only recently has attention been focused on the Gospels as narratives, which seeks to place the scene more significantly into the whole of Mark's presentation.

[14] G.B. Caird, *New Testament Theology* (ed. L.D. Hurst; Oxford: Clarendon Press, 1994), 53.

Philip Davis, as he compares what Mark contains versus the omissions in Matthew and Luke.[15] Davis argues that the absence of an infancy account or a detailed presentation of the resurrection leaves the predictions of resurrection in Mark 8:31; 9:9, 31; 10:34; and 14:28 as resolved in the declared accomplishment of resurrection noted in 16:6–7. The effect is a story starting with baptism that moves through various scenes of temptation and opposition and that "culminates in suffering and death toward an as yet unseen vindication."[16] If God kept his promise for Jesus, he will keep it for the disciple who follows Jesus' path.

The Marcan contrast between Jesus and Peter during the time of the examination in 14:53–72 also underscores this theme, as Jesus refuses to wilt under the pressure of trial as Peter does (esp. vv. 66–72).[17] The disciples should be prepared to follow him in suffering (10:39, 13:9, 14:36). The Spirit will give utterance to what one must say when brought before the tribunal (13:9–12). So Jesus' confession in 14:62 is his only statement of defense as he endures his unjust suffering. Larry Hurtado develops this point:

Mark writes this passage not only to show Jesus openly affirming who he is, but also to provide the readers with a shining example of how they were to react when put to trial on account of their faith in Jesus. The false witnesses show that this is really a trial based solely on the claim that Jesus is the Son of God and has nothing to do with any illegal behavior of Jesus. By this account, the readers are implicitly instructed to be certain that any trial they undergo stems from their faith and not from any wrongdoing on their part (cf. 1 Pet 3:13–16; 4:12–16). Jesus' forthright acknowledgment of his claim ("I am," v. 62) exemplifies the unhesitating courage the readers are to show in confessing their faith in Jesus as the Son of God.[18]

These remarks provide a clear description of Mark's pastoral purpose, especially when combined with another note of irony in the passage, which also reflects narrative concerns. There is an interesting interplay within Mark surrounding the charge of blasphemy. For Mark, the blasphemy would involve those who reject the one his Gospel has presented as the Son of God

---

[15] Philip Davis, "Christology, Discipleship, and Self-Understanding in the Gospel of Mark," in *Self-Definition and Self-Discovery in Early Christianity: A Case of Shifting Horizons: Essays in Appreciation of Ben F. Meyer from His Former Students* (ed. David J. Hawkin and Tom Robinson; Studies in the Bible and Early Christianity 26; Lewiston: Edwin Mellen, 1990), 101–19.

[16] Davis, "Christology, Discipleship, and Self-Understanding in the Gospel of Mark," 109. He notes that the omissions tend to involve events that are not subject to imitation.

[17] For a fuller development of how the theme of Peter's failure fits into Marcan teaching on discipleship and the example of the twelve in failing to get things right during Jesus' ministry, see Larry W. Hurtado, "Following Jesus in the Gospel of Mark – and Beyond," in *Patterns of Discipleship in the New Testament* (ed. Richard N. Longenecker; Grand Rapids: Eerdmans, 1996), 9–29.

[18] Larry W. Hurtado, *Mark* (NIBCNT; Peabody, Mass.: Hendrickson, 1989), 249, bold highlight replaced with quote marks.

(1:1 perhaps, depending on how the textual problem is read in the verse; 3:11; 15:39). That offense against the program and plan of God took place in the leadership's rejection of a claim Jesus makes that his entire ministry has substantiated. A tracing of this ironic theme shows where the remark from the examination fits.

The first major controversy surrounding Jesus in Mark appears in 2:7, where he is charged with blasphemy for claiming to forgive sin. The charge seems to revolve around Jesus' taking up an exclusively divine prerogative with such directness based on his own authority. The offense appears to revolve around the fact that forgiveness comes outside any cultic requirements in a mere declaration, an approach that points to Jesus' own authority.[19] But two other relevant blasphemy texts appear in Mark. In each of these cases, it is others who blaspheme or risk blaspheming. In 3:29, Jesus warns about blaspheming the Spirit, as opposed to the other sins and blasphemies that the "sons of men" might perform. Those who blaspheme the Spirit are guilty of a sin that cannot be forgiven, for it is an "eternal sin." The remark comes in response to the claim that Jesus casts out demons by Beelzebul in 3:22 or by an unclean spirit in 3:30, texts that form a bracket around the remark. The combination of 2:7 with 3:29 sets up a "battle of the blasphemies" in Mark, with each side accusing the other of offending God by their appraisal of Jesus.[20] Jesus meets the accusation of the Jewish leadership in 2:7 and in 3:22 with a reciprocal warning. Mark puts at the top of the list of sins an improper assessment of Jesus.

Putting this backdrop next to the examination, we see that, while the leadership accuses Jesus of blasphemy in 14:64, he has already warned of the theological danger of doing so with reference to him. This is later reinforced in 15:29. Those onlookers who insult Jesus are said to blaspheme him, when they deride him for his claim to raise up the temple in three days and as they call for him to save himself.[21] For Mark, the answer to this derision is not only his narrative description of their remarks here but the vindication that

---

[19] For this reading of Mark 2, see James D. G. Dunn, *The Parting of the Ways: Between Christianity and Judaism and Their Significance for the Character of Christianity* (London: SCM, 2005), 46–47. Forgiveness was possible without recourse to priests or rabbis. The implications for religious authority structures are huge, since these authorities would believe that the way they bestowed forgiveness was in line with divine instruction. See also Bruce D. Chilton, *The Temple of Jesus: His Sacrificial Program Within a Cultural History of Sacrifice* (University Park: Pennsylvania State University, 1992), 130–33, on Jesus and forgiveness.

[20] I thank David Capes for pointing out this connection to me during a response he gave to a section of my work during the national meeting of the SBL in 1997.

[21] The only other Marcan text to use the term βλασφημέω or βλασφημία is 7:22, where it appears in a list of those who sin from "the inside." This remark also occurs in the midst of a controversy scene and has implications about how those who followed Jesus related to questions of the Law and purity, but it is not as christologically significant as these

comes in the report of the resurrection in 16:6–7, a divine act that answers their retort. Here is Mark's judgment about which option God sees as blasphemy as indicated in the battle over who blasphemes. The entire narrative exercise is designed to give those confessing Jesus confidence that their confession is valid, even in the face of those who would accuse them because of their association with Jesus. Thus, the "blasphemy" theme in Mark, viewed strictly from a narrative standpoint, is an important one to which the trial scene contributes significantly. At the very minimum, then, this is how the scene functions for Mark. But the difference of opinion about Jesus raises the question whether there is more to the account than mere narratological and pastoral-theological framing of the examination. A narrative reading shows its value in helping us to see Mark's concerns, but is that all the passage is doing?[22] Does a detailed consideration of the text and its cultural background allow us to say anything more?

2.3. The Setting and the Appeal to Jewish Irregularities: A Capital Case with Multiple Violations?

Perhaps one of the most prominent features in the critical examination of the trial scene is the noting of its supposed, many legal "irregularities" in terms of Jewish legal custom. This feature has been common to the examination of the passage since Hans Lietzmann's study. Lietzmann's examination focused on one complex issue, the right to perform capital execution, and the fact that a Jewish execution would involve stoning.[23] With this focus, something crept into the discussion that was often assumed by others as well – namely, that this scene involves a Jewish capital case before the Sanhedrin. More recent studies indicated how the scene does not correspond at all to mishnaic prescriptions. Not only does Jesus fail to utter the divine name, though blasphemy is charged, but also the Mishnah is violated in several other matters. This element of assessment has been quite stable as can be shown by comparing the essay on the trial of Lohse (1973) to the discus-

---

other texts using the term. In fact, in this context, given the range of the vices mentioned, it might only mean "slander."

[22] For all the important attention that a narrative reading of the Gospels is receiving these days, these readings often do not exhaust how a passage should be examined. If there is a flaw in such reading, it is that not paying careful attention to cultural backgrounds can lead to missing key cultural scripts an author is using that point to his meaning.

[23] Hans Lietzmann, *Der Prozeß Jesu* (SPAW 14; Berlin: de Gruyter, 1931). What is important for us here is that Lietzmann's study emphasized the capital nature of the trial and questioned the scene on that basis. See my examination of Lietzmann and his impact on subsequent study of this scene in Bock, *Blasphemy and Exaltation*, 7–29. Subsequent scholarly discussion and my own work have raised questions about reading the text as full of such illegalities.

sion of the Marcan scene in Reinbold (1994).[24] Lohse's list of irregularities includes: (1) a capital trial can only be held in the day (*m. Sanh.* 4:1); (2) it cannot be held on a Sabbath or feast day (*m. Sanh.* 4:1, *m. Beṣah* 5:2); (3) no judgment on the day of the trial (*m. Sanh.* 4:1); (4) blasphemy requires use of the divine name (*m. Sanh.* 7:5), and (5) the trial should not be held in the high priest's house but in a gathering room for the council (*m. Sanh.* 11:2). Reinbold's list is similar except that he adds the additional note that capital cases are to begin with a defense of the one charged (*m. Sanh.* 4:1), a detail totally lacking in the Marcan scene. He also omits mentioning what blasphemy requires. These irregularities are seen as one basis for rejecting the scene and viewing it as Mark's own creation. The claim is that the scene does not fit Jewish practice and so is not authentic.

A significant side discussion has developed as a result of these claims with some arguing that the Mishnah reflects Pharisaic, not Sadducean practice, a solution made famous by Blinzler.[25] Others have suggested that the more informal scene of Luke, something less than a trial, may be the more original account.[26] Others, like Strobel, have argued that the presence of a "deceiver" required an exceptional and more public kind of examination. Such an examination could include an inquiry that started and finished on the same day or that could run into or from the night (*m. Sanh.* 11:3 [Danby = 11.4]; *t. Sanh.* 7:11; 10:11).[27] It may be that Strobel's approach explains the matter, but this is not the only possibility. One could well argue that the entire discussion has contained a false assumption; namely, that the procedures

---

[24] Eduard Lohse, "Der Prozeß Jesu Christi," in *Die Einheit des Neuen Testaments: Exegetische Studien zur Theologie des Neuen Testaments* (ed. Eduard Lohse; Göttingen: Vandenhoeck & Ruprecht, 1973), 96–97; Wolfgang Reinbold, *Der älteste Bericht über den Tod Jesu: Literarische Analyse und historische Kritik der Passionsdarstellungen der Evangelien* (BZNW 69; Berlin: de Gruyter, 1994), 252.

[25] Josef Blinzler, *Der Prozeß Jesu* (4th ed.; Regensburg: Pustet, 1969), 216–29.

[26] David R. Catchpole, *The Trial of Jesus: A Study in the Gospels and Jewish Historiography from 1770 to the Present Day* (StPB 18; Leiden: Brill, 1971), 153–220.

[27] August Strobel, *Die Stunde der Wahrheit: Untersuchungen zum Strafverfahren gegen Jesus* (WUNT 21; Tübingen: Mohr Siebeck, 1980), 85. Since Danby includes as 11:3 a paragraph not in the Naples 1492 printed edition of the Mishnah, this tractate is alternately numbered as 11:3 or 11:4. The remark in 11:3 notes a feast day execution in Jerusalem for a deceiver. Such a person is to be "put to death at once" with a public announcement of his crime. Other elements in support of Strobel's view have been taken up in subsequent studies by D. Neale, "Was Jesus a *Mesith*? Public Response to Jesus and His Ministry," *TynBul* 44 (1993): 89–101; Graham N. Stanton, "Jesus of Nazareth: A Magician and a False Prophet Who Deceived God's People?" in *Jesus of Nazareth: Lord and Christ: Essays on the Historical Jesus and New Testament Christology* (ed. Joel P. Green and Max Turner; Grand Rapids: Eerdmans, 1994), 164–80; N. T. Wright, *Jesus and the Victory of God* (vol. 2 of *Christian Origins and the Question of God*; Minneapolis: Fortress, 1996), 149–474, esp. 439–42. These later studies deal with some of the significant objections others have raised about Strobel's approach. See my discussion of Strobel in Bock, *Blasphemy and Exaltation*, 13–15, esp. n. 23.

used were those of a formal Jewish capital trial, since a Jewish trial is what Mark portrays. What if this examination was never intended to be seen as a Jewish capital case or a Jewish trial? Then the entire debate over mishnaic procedure may very well be superfluous. Commenting on the legal status of Jews in the Roman province, Betz proposes,

> The Jews did not have the *ius gladii* under the Roman administration; it was reserved for the prefect (*War* 2.117; *Ant* 18.2; John 18:31; 19:10). In the provinces, however, the local courts were kept intact and often cooperated with the Roman prefect. Therefore, in the trial of Jesus the Sanhedrin of Jerusalem may have formed a kind of *consilium iudicum* which did the investigation of the case (*cognitio*) and prepared the accusation (*accusatio*) for the court of the prefect. That is why the nocturnal hearing of Jesus, carried through by a commission of the Sanhedrin under the high priest (Mark 14:53–65), and the morning session of the Sanhedrin (Mark 15:1) should not be treated as unhistorical creations of the Christian community; these events fit the legal situation in a Roman province of that time.[28]

In other words, one must reckon with the real possibility that this gathering was never seen or intended as a formal Jewish capital case but a kind of preliminary hearing to determine if Jesus was as dangerous as the leadership sensed and whether he could be sent credibly for judgment by Rome. In turn, a possible false premise has led the discussion of this scene down a distracting path. But a claim for a hearing does not show that a hearing is necessarily present. Is there evidence that the Jewish leadership's intended goal for Jesus was to present him to Pilate as Rome's representative who could execute him?

Four strands of evidence point to this conclusion. First, the description of the decision in Mark is that Jesus is worthy of death (ἔνοχον εἶναι θανάτου, 14:64).[29] The question is whether Jesus is worthy to die, or if he qualifies for such a fate. This is described as a condemning judgment (κατέκριναν) in response to a question about how it seems to the council (τί ὑμῖν φαίνεται). This evaluation can function as a statement of an opinion to pass on to Pilate, an indictment to continue the process – rather than a final decisive formal legal judgment of guilt. If the text had said, "they condemned him

---

[28] Otto Betz, "Jesus and the Temple Scroll," in *Jesus and the Dead Sea Scrolls* (ed. James H. Charlesworth; ABRL; New York: Doubleday, 1992), 87–88. Betz notes the work of A. N. Sherwin-White, *Roman Society and Roman Law in the New Testament* (The Sarum Lectures, 1960–1961; Oxford: Clarendon, 1963); and S. A. Fusco, "Il dramma del Golgota, nei suoi aspetti processuali," *Rassegna Pugliese* 7 (1972): 4–30. See also the discussion in this volume in ch. 13, § 3.

[29] Some later manuscripts, like A, W, Θ, families 1 and 13, and the Byzantine tradition have a different word order, placing the infinitive first in the phrase, but this makes no difference to the point. Also noting this as a possibility is Ferdinand Hahn, *Christologische Hoheitstitel: ihre Geschichte im frühen Christentum* (5th ed.; Göttingen: Vandenhoeck & Ruprecht, 1995), 177. These remarks derive from the 1963 edition.

to death," then the statement might have been evidence of a formal, decisive verdict. For example, Luke's account (Luke 23:14) has Pilate using the term αἴτιος, which is the legal technical term for guilt,[30] and its variation αἰτία does not appear in the Marcan scene. These terms are reserved for formal Roman judgment or descriptions of procedures associated with Rome (Luke 23:4; John 18:38; 19:4, 6; Matt 27:37; Mark 15:26; Acts 13:28; 28:18). The one place where the term is used of the Jewish perspective is in Acts 13:28, but even here it is said that they "could not find anything deserving death (μηδεμίαν αἰτίαν θανάτου εὑρόντες), yet they asked Pilate to have him killed." All of this language fits well with the possibility of an examination for cause, rather than a more formal trial.

The Acts 13 text is important, because v. 27 notes that the people in Jerusalem and their leaders "condemned" (κρίναντες) him in fulfillment of Scripture. This term looks like the verb in Mark 14:64 and could appear to represent a formal condemnation at a trial, yet it sets up the remarks already noted from Acts 13:28, where the actual condemning procedure is described in terms of seeking death from Pilate. Thus the remarks also fit an examination of Jesus, rather than a formal capital trial. This fits with traditional remarks that describe Jesus as rejected (Luke 9:22, Mark 8:31) or given over to a death sentence (Luke 24:20) or Stephen's charge that the leaders betrayed and killed "the Just One" (Acts 7:52). There is a causative thrust to all of this language, but all of it reflects the awareness that Pilate is the ultimate goal. Brown speaks of "the impression of a trial" in Mark and Matthew, citing the convening of authorities, witnesses with specific testimony, interrogation by the high priest, an admission of a messianic claim by Jesus, an indication that blasphemy has been uttered, and a condemnation of the remark as making Jesus worthy of death.[31] But it must be noted that none of these elements or their combination precludes what would take place at a hearing looking for cause. In fact, it is preferable to argue that the high priest's direct involvement points more to such a hearing than a formal case, where he would likely be silent as chief of the court.[32] Of course, this language could also apply to a formal judgment, as well. It is ambiguous. The problem is that such a hearing, if held, would still be a legal procedure, just not the ultimate one. Now my point is that the rules for examination might differ when someone with authority for a sentence is present. The kind of hearing can affect the nature of the examination.

---

[30] BDAG 31.
[31] Brown, *The Death of the Messiah*, 423–24. In his discussion, he suggests a less formal feel to both Luke and John, which is the case, but this may be influenced by the fact that causative language has been read as having a more decisive legal thrust of finality.
[32] Rudolf Pesch, *Das Markusevangelium* (2 vols.; HTKNT 2; Freiburg im Breisgau: Herder, 1977), 2:416–17.

The second strand of evidence is the presence of the temple charge itself in Mark 14:55–59. What was being examined was whether there were grounds to bring Jesus before Rome on political charges, as the Romans would not be interested in a Jewish religious dispute unless it impacted Roman interests or the public peace. One of the things the Romans worked hard to protect was the *pax Romana*. These remarks about the temple, if they could be proved to the Roman governor, would have made Jesus appear as a serious disturber of the peace in a socially sensitive locale. As a serious threat to provincial peace, Jesus would have to be dealt with as a matter of appropriate Roman stewardship. What on the surface looks like a nonsensical section of the examination scene – the presentation of planned false witnesses who cannot agree on their testimony – is, in fact, quite an important element. The witnesses' testimony needed to be solid enough and credible enough to eventually present to Pilate as Rome's representative. Such a charge need not necessarily reflect all the concerns of the Jewish leadership. They needed only to make a case for the dangerous prospect of political instability. That charge needed to be able to stand up to scrutiny to those outside the Jewish leadership. It is a sign of the strength of the presentation and its lack of anti-Jewish *Tendenz*, when considered as part of a hearing, that these witnesses were judged to be inadequate.[33] In fact, there is no good explanation for why this detail would be created by the community, only to be dropped as inadequate.[34] It does not fit the claim that Mark portrays the trial as unfair, because the charges are seemingly acknowledged by the examiners as being insufficient to make a case. What the council was investigating was legal cause, a charge that had a real chance of being convincing to outsiders and that had a political tinge to it. So the very way in which this temple charge is handled and dropped indicates concern for an outside audience that also will need sufficient cause to convict. This dropped element fits better in a hearing context than as an element in a strictly Jewish capital case, because the pursuit of the temple charge was not merely for internal Jewish purposes but had to be able to work its political effect outside the council. Something

---

[33] So quite correctly, Renatus Kempthorne, "Anti-Christian Tendency in Pre-Marcan Traditions of the Sanhedrin Trial," *TU* 126 (1982): 283–85. For a discussion of the likely background involved in the temple act itself, see Chilton, *The Temple of Jesus*, 91–111.

[34] The inadequacy of the testimony is seen in the fact that the high priest steps in and takes over the questioning, while pushing the discussion in a new but related direction. The argument that what one has here is early church polemic fails to explain why this charge is never picked up again after this scene. It clearly becomes irrelevant in light of subsequent events. Thus its subordinate role argues for its trustworthiness. This detail runs against the redactional tendencies to make the leadership look bad, even in this scene where the witnesses are called false witnesses. The dropping of the charge appears to serve as an example of the Jewish leadership's attempting to be careful about whether they have real evidence or not. The detail runs against the *Tendenz* to see the examination as an attempt to frame Jesus.

was needed that indicated that Jesus was a political threat to Judea, Rome and its emperor. The lack of development of the temple charge suggests that there was little or no confidence that a case could be made on this basis alone. There is one other advantage to this argument. If Jesus were convicted and executed by Rome, then the blame for his removal could always be placed on Rome's doorstep. The Jewish leadership would be "covered" on both ends. Judas, one of his own, said Jesus was a threat, and Rome concurred. The role the leadership had was simply responsibility for investigating a charge and passing the judgment on to Rome to make the final, fatal call.

The third trace of evidence is that there was no attempt at a defense with witnesses – a requirement in a formal trial (*m. Sanh.* 4:1 required that a capital case begin with reasons for acquittal). Now this could simply be the result of a condensation of the scene, but it also would fit with a hearing. Once sufficient evidence existed to bring a charge and ask for death, then any issue of a full defense would be deferred until a later, formal trial. In fact, it should not be overlooked that Jesus was asked if he had any reply in Mark 14:60. He simply remained silent in Mark's account, a version Matthew follows. Jesus responds in Luke 22:67 that his public statements were enough, so that to respond now is useless. The result of the Lucan response could be understood as the equivalent of not responding. As a result, there is not much that can be made of this absence of a defense, but it does cohere better with a hearing scene.

The last point of evidence looks to earlier motive. The sequence of Mark 12:12–16 shows that the plan to arrest Jesus had Rome in mind, potentially, beginning with an earlier moment. The question about the payment of taxes to Rome was the first controversy after the note about the desire to arrest him (Mark 12:12). It is an initial effort to "entrap" Jesus after he came to Jerusalem (ἀγρεύσωσιν, Mark 12:13). It shows that an eye was already turned toward Pilate and Rome. Now the "taxes" saying is one of the few in Mark that is seen as authentic by most, though some dispute the setting.[35] But the setting in Jerusalem should not be doubted. The question of this tax is appropriate for a locale in Jerusalem, because it was here that taxes were paid to Caesar through Pilate, as his representative, and through his collectors. When someone was in Galilee, it was Herod Antipas, as a Jewish leader,

---

[35] For example, Rudolf Bultmann (*The History of the Synoptic Tradition* [trans. John Marsh; New York: Harper & Row, 1963], 26) treats the scene as genuine. The Jesus Seminar accepts the saying as authentic, rating the remark in v. 17 as the only saying in Mark that they see as totally authentic, though they prefer the version of the account in the Egerton Gospel 3:1–6, which means that they regard the rest of the context as inauthentic; see Robert W. Funk, et al., *The Five Gospels: The Search for the Authentic Words of Jesus* (New York: Macmillan, 1993), 102. What they cannot explain is why v. 17 would circulate on its own, without some context. By itself, the saying makes no sense at all.

who collected the tax. Herod's role could be defended because at least he was partially Jewish. The offense in Judea was paying tax to a Gentile, or better, to Rome who were seen as exacting a high level of tax (Josephus, *Ant* 15.109 [of Herod]; 17.27–28 [of the Romans]). The question is only relevant to someone who lived in the Jerusalem area. The account itself shows that there was an attempt to see if the prophetic Jesus might be as hostile toward Rome as other prophets had been to outside nations. On the other hand, should the sequence reflect the tumultuous events in Jerusalem, and given the presence of the Herodians and the recent temple controversy this is quite possible, then we have a case of attempting to see if Jesus could be seen as a threat to Rome.[36]

These four elements suggest that the examination was only an attempt to gather charges so that a case could be made before Rome and Pilate. The haste of the examination, which also indicates this desire, was fueled by three other considerations: (1) the short-term presence of Pilate in the city and (2) the danger the leaders would have felt had events dragged out too long or had they taken place in too public a forum. The city was filled with Galilean pilgrims celebrating Passover. The night arrest, examination, and early morning sentence lessened the risk of a reaction, because the pilgrims had to journey outside the town overnight (compare with Jesus' own practice, Luke 21:37). By getting the events to Pilate by daylight and making the legal issue his, security became his problem. (3) A third advantage resulted from an immediate resolution. Once security was no longer a concern, there was also the advantage of making Jesus a public example among all those present, should the execution come quickly, while pilgrims were still present. Not only was this something that was legally allowed, it was even advised for a figure perceived to be a major deceiver.[37]

2.4. *Potential Sources for the Debate in the Examination*

But what of the key saying then? Before considering it, we need to give attention to the potential sources for such a report. Of course, we do not know the source, and none of Jesus' disciples at the time would have been present at whatever examination took place. This reality has led some to argue that there is no potential source for this scene or that, at least, there is no great likelihood of a train of transmission for it.[38] This view is clearly

---

[36] As Pesch (*Das Markusevangelium*, 226) notes, "Die Alternativfrage, die Jesus gestellt ist, ist eine Falle: Entweder würde Jesus Steuerverweigerung und damit politischen Aufruhr oder Steuerzahlung und damit Götzendienst predigen."

[37] On the case for Jesus' being perceived as a deceiver, see text with n. 27 above.

[38] For example, one of the claims of Lietzmann's work is that, although the source for Peter's denials was likely to be the disciple himself, this could not be claimed for the trial scene, for he was in the courtyard and remained there, so he could not have heard the

articulated by E. P. Sanders when he claims, "It is hard, though not impossible, to imagine a chain of transmission which would have passed on the exchanges of the supposed trial."[39]

This hesitation to consider sources for the scene seems strongly overdrawn. Numerous potential candidates exist. For example, prominent Jews, who would have had access either to the examination itself or to reports about it, also would have had close contact with the Christian community. Prominent among such figures would be Joseph of Arimathea, who is connected with the burial of Jesus and who apparently had official access to the decision (Mark 15:43).[40] A figure such as Nicodemus also comes to mind. Any prominent, official Jewish leaders who subsequently became Christians would have had access to knowledge about these events. Surely the persecutor Saul fits in this category. His violent opposition to the new sect would have meant he would have known what the Jewish involvement and position on Jesus would have been. Other priests also became a part of the community in Jerusalem (Acts 6:7).

The possible chain of transmission could also have emerged quite naturally out of the flow of everyday events in Jerusalem. What took place with Jesus reflected a heated polemical debate within Judaism that raged in the city because of disputes about Christians' "breaking the law," with intense public debate until at least 70 C. E.[41] It is hard, if not impossible, to imag-

---

testimony and there are no other witnesses (Lietzmann, *Der Prozeß Jesu*, 314–15). On p. 315, Lietzmann argued that "daß uns keine Quelle für diesen Bericht glaubhaft wird. Petrus ist nicht der Gewährsmann, denn er ist, wie zweimal (14, 54.66) ausdrücklich betont wird, nur bis in den Hof des hohenpriesterlichen Palastes vorgedrungen und unten im Hof geblieben. Er kann also von der Verhandlung nichts gehört haben, und einen anderen Zeugen sehen wir nicht."

[39] E. P. Sanders, *Jesus and Judaism* (Philadelphia: Fortress, 1985), 298.

[40] It is highly unlikely that Joseph is a figure created by the Church. The portrayal of a member of the Sanhedrin as sympathetic to Jesus in the midst of traditions that highlighted the animosity of the leadership and in the face of the polemical environment in the early church makes the description of his office quite credible. See Brown, *The Death of the Messiah*, 1240. William John Lyons has also defended a historical Joseph who was retained in the tradition: "On the Life and Death of Joseph of Arimathea," *JSHJ* 2 (2004): 29–53. Lyons challenges Brown's idea that Joseph became a believer, seeing it as a "harmonizing" reading of the evidence. For Lyons, Joseph died a pious Jew. However, it seems unlikely that such a sympathetic portrait of a Sanhedrin member would be preserved in the tradition had its root description not been true. Even in the cases of Caiaphas in John and Gamaliel in Acts, their position with regard to the gospel is clear. So the tradition can preserve a picture of a Jewish member who opposes the gospel and yet acts in a circumspect way with regard to the new movement. This background also explains how the subsequent tradition about Joseph works. It is not that the original portrait of Joseph is "swept aside" but that it was the natural consequence of what happened to Joseph, something the new movement was quite aware of because of Joseph's previous social and religious status.

[41] See Josephus, *Ant.* 20.200. The case of James, slain by Annas the Younger in 62 C. E. is especially revealing. Josephus tells us that he was given over to be stoned "for having

ine that a Jewish view of the trial did not emerge in the midst of this quite public debate. It is virtually impossible to believe that the Jewish position on Jesus was never made public. The Annas clan would have justified its role in sending Jesus to Rome as a matter of ensuring an understanding of the priesthood's policy concerning the newly emerging, socially disturbing movement. Included in this would have been the reasons Jesus was taken before Pilate. Moreover these debates would have involved the family of the high priest, including the powerful patriarch of the family, Annas. It is significant to note that the center of this controversy involved the same priestly family from the time of Jesus until the stoning of James, Jesus' brother in 62 C.E., a period of around 30 years.[42] Josephus seems to have had access to reports about the trial of James and the reaction to it. The example of letters like that of Claudias Lysias to Felix shows that sometimes a legal examination came with an explanation from the examiner sending the prisoner to a leader (Acts 23:26–30). But the issue of how these records were generally kept is not clear.[43] However, if there were some records of a situation such as James's, then should we think it was any different from the trial of the

---

transgressed the Law" (παρανομησάντων κατηγορίαν ποιησάμενος παρέδωκε λευσθησομένους). What law was it that James broke, given his reputation within Christian circles as a Jewish-Christian leader who was careful about keeping the Law? It seems likely that the law had to relate to his Christological allegiances and a charge of blasphemy. This would fit the fact that he was stoned, which was the penalty for such a crime, and parallels how Stephen was handled as well. There is a pattern of treatment that runs through the Jewish-Christians' relationship to the Jewish leadership. This public commotion surely also produced public discussion of the original event. The verb for transgression, παρανομέω, which appears 42 times in Josephus, is a very broad term because it can refer to acts against another person (*Ant.* 12.288). However, many serious transgressions against God by numerous kings of Israel are singled out by use of this term; many are said to have followed in the footsteps of Jeroboam (*Ant.* 8.245 – Jeroboam; 8.253 – Rehoboam; 9.168, 170 – Joash; 9.18 – Ahab like Jeroboam; 9.95 – Joram like Jeroboam).

[42] Josephus, *Ant* 20.197–203. I thank Martin Hengel for pointing out this argument to me. A similar position with regard to Annas's family's animosity toward Christians is noted by Brown, *The Death of the Messiah*, 409. As he says, "every famous Christian who died violently in Judea before the Jewish Revolt suffered in a tenure of a priest related to Annas." Annas and his five sons all served as high priests at one time or another in this period, as did one son-in-law (Caiaphas, the high priest during the time of Jesus; John 18:13; Josephus, *Ant.* 20.198; 18.34–35). This family had considerable power for much of a 50-year period and engaged in a constant battle with the Jewish Christians in Jerusalem during this time. It should also not be overlooked that when Josephus describes this incident (*Ant.* 20.199) he describes the Sadducees as "more heartless in judging offenders than any of the rest of the Jews" (εἰσὶ περὶ τὰς κρίσεις ὠμοὶ παρὰ πάντας τοὺς Ἰουδαίους). This standard evaluation may mean that Blinzler (*Der Prozeß Jesu*, 197–98, 227) is right to suggest that the rules of judgment under Sadducean authority were more strict than those that emerged under the Pharisees as reflected in the Mishnah.

[43] Sherwin-White (*Roman Society and Roman Law*, 105–6) notes that in Pliny's letters to Trajan most of the materials for the trial came from the participants. Only once is an official document used, and another time there is a request to check an official document for information. This indicates that records were probably kept but that if they existed

one whose movement was at the center of the controversy? And given the continuity within the Jewish leadership during this period, would it be too much to argue that the two sides would have known the views and rationale for opposition much as the leaders of opposing political parties might today? This means that numerous potential (and some quite public) chains of transmission for this scene existed. Surely the events associated with the public spectacle of a trial circulated widely in the city.

The possibility of the saying reflecting the real debate does not, however, mean that it came from this event. This requires a careful examination of the key saying itself. Can one specify the nature of the blasphemy as it is reflected in this saying? At the least, one should be able to describe from Mark's (and the early church's) point of view what the nature of the blasphemy was and the cultural assumptions that this remark drew upon for this conclusion. Once this is done, then consideration can be given to the question of whether or not the saying has roots in the actual trial scene.

2.5 The "Blasphemy" in the Jewish Examination of Jesus

The Greek text where Jesus' controversial replay appears in Mark 14:62 is as follows: ἐγώ εἰμι, καὶ ὄψεσθε τὸν υἱὸν τοῦ ἀνθρώπου ἐκ δεξιῶν καθήμενον τῆς δυνάμεως καὶ ἐρχόμενον μετὰ τῶν νεφελῶν τοῦ οὐρανοῦ (I am, and you shall see the Son of Man seated at the right hand of power and coming with the cloud of heaven). Of course, the original discussion would have likely taken place in Aramaic. There are three general options for the nature of the blasphemy: (1) pronunciation of the divine name is blasphemous; (2) something is blasphemous about being at the right hand of God; and (3) the blasphemy involves how the leaders are addressed.[44] After reviewing these options, we will look at the details of how the blasphemy was most probably seen.

There are three potential elements in the report of Mark 14:61–62 that could have led to the Jewish view that Jesus had blasphemed and that match the three options just noted: the mention of God's name in a blasphemous manner, an offense against God's unique honor, and an offense against the leadership. As will be made clear, the second and third elements serve as

---

Rome would have been the likely locale. In sum, the nature of such records and how they might have been kept is a question that could use some detailed study.

[44] Robert H. Gundry (*The Old is Better: New Testament Essays in Support of Traditional Interpretations* [WUNT 178; Tübingen: Mohr Siebeck, 2005], 102) notes a fourth view that the Sadducean standard was not limited to the pronunciation of the divine name. This view does not directly address what was said as much as could be allowed to count for blasphemy. The remark appears in an essay entitled "Jesus' Blasphemy according to Mark 14:61b–64 and Mishnah Sanhedrin 7:5," Gundry's fullest examination of this question. It is restated in his article "Jesus' Supposed Blasphemy (Mark 14:61b–64)," *BBR* 18 (2008): 131–33.

the more likely sources of the evaluation against Jesus. The combination of these elements is important to note, because often the charge is seen to stem from a single factor only. Yet one must consider the possibility that the reply challenges an array of Jewish cultural assumptions, making the remarks particularly offensive for the leadership. Might it be possible that Jesus' reply was offensive at multiple levels, making the offense even greater in the leadership's view?

2.5.1. Option 1: Pronunciation of the Divine Name

The first option is the view of Robert Gundry that a key element in the blasphemy was that Jesus pronounced the divine name in violation of *m. Sanh.* 7:5 when he alluded to Ps 110:1. However this citation was suppressed in the public reports of the scene, including Mark's, so as not to repeat the blasphemy and compound the offense.[45] This procedure would reflect practice noted in the Mishnah (also in *m. Sanh.* 7:5), where report of the exact wording of the blasphemy is only repeated in the privacy of a hearing and not in a public report, so as to avoid repeating the sin.[46] Thus, Jesus said, "I am, and you will see the Son of Man sitting at the right hand of Yahweh," but it was reported publicly as "seated at the right hand of power," as Mark 14 has it. The key to this view is that the utterance repeating the divine name strengthens the case for historicity of a charge of capital blasphemy by reflecting the violation noted in the Mishnah. Gundry claims that this idea of blasphemy is rooted in old Jewish texts: Sus 44–59; 11QTemple[a] 61:9; Lev 24:15–16 LXX; Philo, *Moses* 2.203–8; and Josephus, *Ant.* 4.202. He argues that the tearing of the garments for a verbal blasphemy of this sort fits the mishnaic background.

This explanation is possible, but only with certain additional assumptions that are not at all a given.[47] It must be noted that it was common for

---

[45] Robert H. Gundry, *Mark: A Commentary on His Apology for the Cross* (Grand Rapids: Eerdmans, 1993), 915–18. Craig A. Evans (*Jesus and His Contemporaries: Comparative Studies* [AGJU 25; Leiden: Brill, 1995], 412–13) discusses this option. Evans also argues that this fact alone cannot explain the blasphemy in the scene, a point with which I agree for reasons I am about to show. Gundry's updated essay (*The Old is Better*, 98–110) challenges the view argued for here and in Bock, *Blasphemy and Exaltation*.

[46] For a citation and more discussion of this mishnaic text, see the section on it in Bock, *Blasphemy and Exaltation*, 67–68.

[47] Gundry (*The Old is Better*, 105) claims that the goal of my arguments in the monograph involved having "disposed" of his verbal blasphemy through the divine name view. However, my goal was simply to suggest that a pronunciation of the divine name alone cannot explain the charge, nor would pronouncing the name have been absolutely necessary to produce such a charge. There was no disposal of the view, only the claim that pronouncing the name by itself cannot explain everything. In Gundry's most recent article ("Jesus' Supposed Blasphemy [Mark 14:61b–64]," 131–33) he notes his agreement with my view that more than pronunciation of the name from Ps 110:1 was needed here,

biblical texts to be pronounced with a substitute for the divine name, as also was the case for benedictions, with the exception of a few specified cases. One of the situations with benedictions is noted in *m. Soṭah* 7:6. This text describes how the common priestly benediction of Num 6:24–26 was given to the people. So here we have a scriptural text and a benediction. In the provinces, each verse was read by itself, and the crowd would respond with amen in each case, while at the temple it was read as a whole and treated as a single verse. But the more important consideration for us comes next when the issue of the pronunciation of the name is treated. The text reads, "in the temple they pronounced the name as written, but in the provinces by a substituted word." So it is no guarantee that the presence of the divine name in Scripture meant that it would be read or spoken in public.[48]

Another text is *m. Yoma* 6:2. This text records the confession of the high priest over the lamb for the nation's sins on the Day of Atonement. Included in the saying is the citation of Lev 16:30. This verse includes a reference to the divine name, which the high priest did read, and the crowd bowed and fell on their faces when "the people which stood in the temple court heard the expressed name come forth from the mouth of the high priest." In addition, they responded to the confession and the use of the name with a euphemism, "Blessed be the name of the glory of his kingdom forever and ever."[49]

These two texts show that using Scripture in the temple and pronouncing the divine name is not blasphemy because (1) one is quoting Scripture, and (2) one is doing it in the temple precincts. So Jesus quoting or alluding directly to the language of a passage would not have been seen as blasphemous in itself because he was simply citing Scripture. Something else about what was said or the manner in which Jesus did this had to be the basis for the blasphemy, a point on which Gundry and I agree.[50]

---

something he has argued as early as his commentary on Mark (*Mark*, 916–17), as well as more recently (*The Old is Better*, 101–2). He is correct to make a point of this because it is a point I had missed and did not note in my earlier discussions of his view as I should have.

[48] This possibility may well challenge the claim of Gundry (*The Old is Better*, 104) that Jesus likely used the divine name rather than the circumlocution reflected in Mark 12:36. In fact, the argument over the term "Lord" works better there, if there was a verbal substitute for the divine name.

[49] The command is also noted in exactly the same way in *m. Yoma* 3:8.

[50] It is this point that Gundry's treatment of blasphemy may understate. The Name could have been pronounced, but it would have been done in allusion to Scripture, and as such would not have been seen as a blasphemous offense on its own or in itself as a problem. The use of the divine name, if it was used, might have been viewed as insensitive to temple-public discourse distinctions. Gundry speaks of a solemn setting making pronunciation of the name likely and perhaps offensive, but I point to the temple settings of these examples to which the examination scene does not belong. However, for Jesus to cite the name in citing Scripture would not in itself have been a problem. This means something else had to be key. It is the conceptual manner of Jesus' use that makes the remark an offense, not the use of Scripture. So I still question whether *m. Sanh.* 7.5 is in

Still a third example appears at Qumran, though it is not consistent.[51] In the *Isaiah Scroll*, יהוה is occasionally altered to אדני, or the dual phrase (יהוה אדני) is reduced to only אדני (1QIsa\u1d43 glosses the name in 28:16, 30:15, 65:13, by writing above it אדוני; and reduces it in 49:22, 52:4, 61:1).[52] In 1QIsa\u1d43 50:5, it is replaced with אלוהים. The name is omitted from 1QIsa\u1d43 45:8, while in 1QIsa\u1d43 52:5 and 59:21, it is omitted once when it appears twice in the MT. In 1QIsa\u1d43 3:17, ואדוני appears for the name, while 3:15 writes אדוני א over the name. In 1QIsa\u1d43 40:7 and 42:6, a row of dots appears where the name would be expected, while in 42:5 the term האלוהים appears instead of the name. The same occurs in other texts from Qumran as well.[53] These changes show that some Jews were careful to avoid writing the divine name in Scripture, which in turn would prevent its being pronounced as well. These examples show it is not clear whether the name would have been pronounced or avoided.

---

play here, even if Jesus cited the divine name when he read the Psalm. I am arguing that pronouncing the divine Name was not necessary or even crucial for a charge of blasphemy. The distinction is a small one. Either of us could be right about what may have been said. Either way, in my view, the scene possesses historical credibility.

[51] Steven T. Byington, "יהוה and אדני," *Journal of Biblical Literature* 76 (1957): 58–59.

[52] Contra Siegfried Schulz ("Maranatha und Kyrios Jesus," *ZNW* 53 [1962]: 133), there is evidence of this type of change in early material. On pp. 132–33 he notes that a shortened form of the divine name (יהו) appears in the Elephantine papyri of the fifth century B.C.E. (ιαω), but he raises questions about how much can be drawn from this practice. However, the very presence of an alternate and *abbreviated* form of the name shows that the name is being treated with respect by not being reproduced exactly. The texts at Elephantine can be found in A. Cowley, ed., *Aramaic Papyri of the Fifth Century B. C.* (Oxford: Clarendon, 1923). The passages where יהו appears are: 6.4, 6, 11; 22.1, 123; 25.6; 27.15; 30.6, 15, 24–27 (3x); 31.7, 24–25 (2x); 33.8; 38.1; 45.3–4; and 56.2. Care with regard to speaking the divine name is also noted in Josephus, *Ant* 2.275–76; and in Philo, *Moses* 2.114. For evidence of a substitution of the name with Lord, one can note the LXX and the examples at Qumran; see next note below. On the use of ιαω, see R. Ganschinietz, "Iao," *PW* 9:698–721; Menahem Stern, *Greek and Latin Authors on Jews and Judaism: Edited with Introductions, Translations and Commentary* (3 vols.; Jerusalem: Israel Academy of Sciences and Humanities, 1976–81), 1:98, 171–72, 211–12; 2:140–41, 410–12, 673; and David Aune, "'Ιαο ('Ιαώ)," *RAC* 129:1–12.

[53] Michael A. Knibb, *The Qumran Community* (Cambridge Commentaries on Writings of the Jewish and Christian World, 200 BC to AD 200 2; Cambridge: Cambridge University Press, 1987), 134, 170, 232–33, 250. He notes how the name is written in old script in 1QpHab vi 14, while in 1QS 8:14, the citation of Isa 40:3 leaves only four dots where the name Yahweh appeared. Interestingly, in 4QpPsa ii 13 the reverse is the case, as Yahweh appears where "Lord" was present. Joseph A. Fitzmyer has criticized Schulz at this point in "Contribution of Qumran Aramaic to the Study of the New Testament," *NTS* 20 (1974): 386–91. He notes in 11QTgJob the absolute use of מרא and comments on: (1) the construct chains Schulz mentioned in the Elephantine papyri at 30:15, (2) the use of אלהא for the tetragrammaton in 11QTgJob 37:3, 38:2 (2x), 38:3, and 38:7, and (3) the rendering of שדי twice by מרא in 11QTgJob 34:5, 7, as well as its likely presence in 36:8. In 34:6–7 he is confident it appears for the divine name. For another probable absolute use of the term Lord (מרי), see also 1QapGen 20:12–13.

What these examples mean is that it is not certain that even if Jesus cited Ps 110:1 he would have read the divine name as written, given the possible variations permitted within oral delivery. This raises doubts about whether Jesus pronounced the divine name. Regardless, it also is not certain that the reading of the name from Scripture would have been considered uttering the name "unseasonably," which is a type of blasphemy noted by Philo as worthy of death (*Mos.* 2.206, 208). As Evans notes, "Uttering the Divine Name, especially in the context of quoting Scripture and if with all proper reverence, is not blasphemous."[54] The just-noted examples of Scripture read in the temple are examples of Evans's point. Thus, this suggestion of pronouncing the divine name is not central to the offense, unless one argues that what created the charge was a lack of "proper reverence" in the way it was cited. What is agreed about here is that other, more fundamental and conceptual grounds must have been present to form the essence of the blasphemy – which is possible for this scene, as the following options will show.[55]

Nonetheless, this option is important to work through, because the above ambiguity in practice raises the possibility that the reported circumlocution of "the power of the blessed One" is sensitive to Jewish practice. Does the reference to "the power of the blessed One" reflect a Marcan rendering, pre-Marcan Christian tradition, a Jewish report of the trial where the allusion to the divine name is reported in an indirect way, or is it a report of Jesus' words? The move could have been made at any stage. Someone was aware of potential Jewish sensitivities here. This question concerning "Jewish" expressions in vv. 61–62 is resumed in more detail below.

2.5.2. Option 2: Being at the Right Hand of God

The second option argues that the major feature of what was seen as blasphemous in the view of the leadership came within Jesus' reply about the

---

[54] Evans, *Jesus and His Contemporaries*, 413.

[55] Gundry (*The Old is Better*, 101) raises an objection against my exclusively conceptual view; it is that Jesus' earlier claim to forgive sin should have evoked a charge of capital blasphemy if a conceptual view of blasphemy is in play where the divine name is not pronounced. It is a very fair problem to raise. Two observations are important here. (1) The text *does raise* the issue of blasphemy. However, because Jesus introduces the concept indirectly and ties the authority to an otherwise undefined "Son of Man" figure, the reaction is one of raising the question, not being able really to pin Jesus down as having made a clear claim about himself. Matthew's version indicates some confusion because such authority was given to a human. (2) A second feature is that in the case of verbal blasphemy it often was the case that one might be warned first and then a second violation would result in culpability (*y. Sanh.* 7.25a–b = Neusner 7.8–9). Now, it is the case that the entire series of controversies did lead some leaders to seek to remove Jesus (Mark 3:6). This event of claiming the right to forgive sins was the beginning of these concerns. However, the event itself was not a clear enough example to warrant an immediate action. What this earlier event did do was to raise eyebrows.

Son of Man. After Jesus responds positively to the question whether he is the Christ, the Son of the Blessed, he goes on to speak of the council's seeing the Son of Man seated at the right hand of power and coming on the clouds. Again the key reply reads, ἐγω εἰμι, καί ὄψεσθε τὸν υἱὸν τοῦ ἀνθρώπου ἐκ δεξιῶν καθήμενον τῆς δυνάμεως καὶ ερχόμενον μετὰ τῶν νεφελῶν τοῦ οὐρανοῦ.[56] Now, it is contextually plain that within the account the reference to the Son of Man is a self-reference to Jesus.[57] The reply combines an allusion to the enthroned authority of a regal figure from Ps 110:1 with the authoritative figure of one like a Son of Man from Dan 7:13.[58]

There has been some debate on what it is that Jesus promises the council will see. Some argue that the entire remark is a description only of Jesus' exaltation, an allusion to resurrection to the right hand, a going to God.[59] Jesus promises that the council will see his vindication by God and the effects of his installment into authority. The case for this is grounded in three points. (1) There is the original meaning of Dan 7:13, which portrays one like a Son of Man "going to God" and thus serves as the interpretation of the remark. (2) In addition, Matthew and Luke highlight an instantaneous seeing, with Matthew's ἀπ ἄρτι (26:64) and Luke's ἀπὸ τοῦ νῦν (22:69). Only a resurrection can fit this near setting. (3) There is the grammatical tightness of a verb controlling two participles, which one would normally expect to refer to simultaneous events.

However, it is unlikely that resurrection alone is what is meant. Mark 14:28 shows that Mark is not hesitant about alluding directly to resurrection in reporting what Jesus says. What is amazing about this trial scene is the total absence of reference to resurrection. Only an indirect reference to exaltation is present. This could suggest the use of old tradition, and yet mention

---

[56] There are no major text-critical problems here. A few manuscripts (Θ, family 13, 565, 700) add "you say that" (σὺ εἶπας ὅτι) before the reply, while D omits καὶ ερχόμενον. Both these readings are clearly secondary.

[57] I treat only the issue of the passage's meaning here and the nature of the blasphemy charge in the account as it is presented. The discussion of authenticity follows in a section called "The Potential Authenticity of the Saying," after a description of how the blasphemy is presented in this text.

[58] For a careful study of the background of these two texts, one reflecting messianic enthronement discourse (Ps 110:1) and the other a judicial throne discourse, see Timo Eskola, *Messiah and the Throne: Jewish Merkabah Mysticism and Early Christian Exaltation Discourse* (WUNT 2.142; Tübingen: Mohr Siebeck, 2001). His analysis does not discuss historical Jesus questions but notes that this combination is a Christian innovation that belonged to the "first" Christians, with the judicial strain appearing to derive from Jesus himself (pp. 283, 333–35, 366–70). Its roots are both related to and distinct from Jewish Throne teaching often discussed in relationship to Merkabah mysticism.

[59] Thomas Francis Glasson, "Reply to Caiaphas (Mark 14:62)," *NTS* 7 (1960): 88–93. This view is also vigorously defended by Morna D. Hooker, *The Son of Man in Mark: A Study of the Background of the Term "Son of Man" and Its Use in St. Mark's Gospel* (London: SPCK, 1967), 166–71.

of exaltation alone seems not to be the only emphasis here. For example, the riding on the clouds, though it is a heavenly, theomorphic image, is not about heavenly activity but portrays a vindication that involves figures on earth, as even Dan 7 shows. There it is the saints on earth who benefit from the work of the Son of Man.[60] As Müller states of the Dan 7 scene,

> Dabei will bedacht sein, daß nirgends in der alttestamentlichen, frühjüdischen und talmudischen Literatur jemals "Wolken" eine Rolle spielen, solange es darum geht, den Verkehr und die Bewegung der Himmlischen untereinander im Raum ihrer den Augen der Menschen entzogenen Transzendenz ins Wort zu rücken. Erst wenn einer von ihnen aus deren Verborgenheit *heraustritt*, werden Epiphaniewolken und Wolkenvehikel bemüht. Diese Beobachtung legt es nahe, das anhand einer Partizipialkonstruktion pointierte "Kommen" des Menschensohnes als *Abstieg* vom Himmel *zur Erde* zu begreifen.[61]

Now it might be objected that Dan 7:9–13 itself is a heavenly scene, so that Müller is wrong. But this fails to appreciate the fact that the reason for the heavenly installation of the Son of Man who is on the clouds is to vindicate the saints on earth (vv. 21–27). In other words, the reason one is given a glimpse of what is happening in heaven is because it impacts what will happen on earth. Seen in this light, Müller's remarks are appropriate. The allusion, then, anticipates a return to rule and vindicate the saints (in this case, Jesus also is including himself as among the vindicated!).

One can debate whether what is affirmed here by Jesus is a return to judge as a result of vindication, as I have claimed earlier, or a dominion that is given after God judges in vindication of the saints, as Adela Yarbo Collins argues is the point in Dan 7.[62] In Dan 7, the Ancient of Days judges and then gives the resultant authority to the Son of Man. The problem here is that Jesus so identifies in his approaching exaltation with the Father that judgment and dominion appear to be shared in his view. Jesus' teaching about the work of the returning and judging Son of Man elsewhere suggests this

---

[60] George R. Beasley-Murray, *Jesus and the Kingdom of God* (Grand Rapids: Eerdmans, 1986), 301; Karlheinz Müller, "Der Menschensohn im Danielzyklus," in *Jesus und der Menschensohn: für Anton Vögtle* (ed. Rudolf Pesch and Rudolf Schnackenburg; Freiburg im Breisgau: Herder, 1975), 37–80, esp. 45.

[61] Müller, "Der Menschensohn im Danielzyklus," 45. The emphasis is his. In English the citation states, "At the same time, it will be carefully noted that nowhere in the Old Testament, early Jewish, or Talmudic literature do 'clouds' ever play a role, if it is about the transport and movement of the heavenly beings to be closer together in their sphere of withdrawn transcendence from before the eyes of men. When one of them emerges from seclusion, he or she calls upon the service of clouds of epiphany and clouds as vehicles. This observation leads to the obvious conclusion that the example of a participial construction points to the 'coming' of the Son of Man being understood as a *descent* from heaven *to earth*" (author's translation).

[62] Adela Yarbro Collins, "The Charge of Blasphemy in Mark 14.6," *JSNT* 26 (2004): 379–401.

linkage in his thought, if those texts are authentic. These nuances are not the key to what is heard as offensive by the leaders. Jesus' bold affirmation of his presence at the side of God and coming authority (whether as judge, ruler, or merely as a vindicated person) is what they found offensive. This language is not speaking about taking a cloud to heaven as part of an apocalyptic vision in order to see what the future holds. Rather, the one taking the cloud rides that cloud to meet with God and receive authority. The point of the ride is to participate in events. Any claims that riding the clouds is simply an apocalyptic vision motif and thus does not point to divinity misses the setting of this scene. So, not only will God vindicate Jesus, but he will exalt him to a place of honor that is shared with God. This position is what the saying indicates the leadership heard as blasphemous.

In fact, the claim to come on the clouds is a significant claim, not only alluding to Dan 7:13, but also using imagery that claims a right only some form of deity possesses. Everywhere else in the Hebrew Scriptures, only God or the gods ride the clouds (Exod 14:20, Num 10:34, Ps 104:3, Isa 19:1).[63] Thus, comprehensive heavenly authority is present in the image. The picture is of a sovereign, divinely related exercise of power.

As for the claim that, grammatically, one would expect simultaneous events when there is a verb linked with two participles, we must remember that this is a prophetic allusion using metaphorical language, so a combination of events may be placed in proximity that, in fact, are quite distant from one another. In addition, the order of these events with seating first and then a mention of coming on the clouds speaks against a reference only to exaltation, as does the earlier allusion to Dan 7 in Mark 13:26, which clearly alludes to a later *parousia*. If exaltation were meant and the clouds alluded to exaltation, then one would expect the ascension into the clouds to God to lead to the seating. The order of the participles would be reversed. The changes by Matthew and Luke, which move the participle "being seated" to before the right hand, only make explicit what this remark assumes, that a vindication of Jesus is the presupposition for his return, because evidence of his exaltation is seen not only in his return but in the activity among his people that precedes it. The redactional changes by the other evangelists only highlight this additional implied emphasis in the remark. Mark has not stated the point quite strongly enough for them, so they develop the implications more fully. Thus the combined allusion is a declaration of total vindication by God that allows Jesus to share authority with God and return, functioning with final judgment on behalf of God's saints. When he returns, it will probably be as eschatological judge, exercising the judicial power of God on behalf of the righteous. At the least, he returns as one

---

[63] John A. Emerton, "The Origin of the Son of Man Imagery," *JTS* n.s. 9 (1958): 225–42.

whom God has designated to rule over the world. By implication, part of this vindication comes on his own behalf in reaction to the judgment that the leaders are contemplating against him.

The problem that the Jewish leaders at Jesus' examination would have seen with his remark is probably not that such a figure existed. The portrait in *1 Enoch* of the Son of Man shows that this category was contemplated within Judaism, somewhere by the middle of the first century.[64] To expect such a glorious figure in the future was possible. What would have caused the offense was that Jesus was making this identification with himself in his *claim* to share authority with God. He – as a Galilean preacher or a wonder worker or an eschatological prophet, or even as one making a messianic claim – was extending the claim to the right to share in God's final judgment as the sent *heavenly* ruler and possibly even the final judge from heaven. It is the juxtaposition of seating and coming on the clouds that makes clear the transcendent function that Jesus gives himself here, with the reference to clouds making it apparent that more than a pure human and earthly messianic claim is present.[65] There is an implication in this remark as well. If

---

[64] On the disputed date of *1 Enoch*, see E. Isaac, "1 (Ethiopic Apocalypse of) Enoch," in *Old Testament Pseudepigrapha* (2 vols.; ed. James H. Charlesworth; New York: Doubleday, 1983–85), 1:6–7, who argues for a first century date; and Siebert Uhlig, *Das Äthiopische Henochbuch* (vol. 5.6 of *Jüdische Schriften aus hellenistisch-römischer Zeit*; Gütersloh: Gütersloher Verlaghaus, 1984), 574–75, who considers dates ranging from the end of the Hasmonean period into the first century and sees roots extending back into the first century B.C.E. A fresh discussion of the date debate appears in Gabriele Boccaccini, ed., *Enoch and the Messiah Son of Man: Revisiting the Book of Parables* (Grand Rapids: Eerdmans, 2007), 415–96. A full review of this discussion about dating the Parables of Enoch is found in my forthcoming, "The Date of Enoch's Parables: A *Forschungsbericht*," in a yet to be titled book edited by James Charlesworth and myself. It will argue for a late first century B.C.E. or early first century C.E. date, given the latest allusion in the material is to conflict with the Parthians in ca. 40 B.C.E. (see *1 En.* 56:6–8).

[65] Another possible reading exists, if one does not see a self-claim by Jesus in the allusion to the Son of Man. It would be a claim that a vindicating judgment is coming in the eschaton through such a figure, who remains enigmatically unidentified, and that Jesus is so closely identified with what the Son of Man represents that Jesus will be vindicated in that judgment on behalf of the righteous. Seen in this light, there is still blasphemy, because the insight and spiritual discernment of the leadership are still being directly and seriously challenged. So they would be regarded as being among the judged. This remark then could be read as a violation of Exod 22:27[28]. Jesus would be seen as cursing the leaders by implying their judgment, since the leaders would be excluded from being among the righteous at the end. In Exodus, the verb for "curse" stands in parallelism to blaspheming God, showing a close relationship between the two. Goliath and Sennacherib are seen as violating this prohibition (1 Sam 17, 2 Kgs 19:3, Isa 37:3, Ezek 35:12 – of Edom). On the roots of this idea, see Bock, *Blasphemy and Exaltation*, 32–36, 41–42. The remark would be seen as a subtle anathema against the leadership. I think this option is less likely, for reasons I shall consider in discussing the apocalyptic Son of Man; it is another way in which the tradition could be read and seen as essentially authentic. For this view, see the remarks of Carsten Colpe, "ὁ υἱὸς τοῦ ἀνθρώπου," *TDNT* 8:435–41. He says, "In this respect there is a parallel to what he says about His perfecting to various hearers and also

they are contemplating judging him now, he will eventually rule or judge them later.

The self-made claim to sit at the right hand and ride the clouds would be understood as a blasphemous utterance, a false claim that equates Jesus in a unique way with God and that reflects an arrogant disrespect toward the one true God. As an examination of Jewish exaltation shows, a proximate seating next to God might be considered for a privileged few, either a few universally acknowledged greats of the past (such as Moses in *Exagoge to Ezekiel*) or the future eschatological figure of judgment (such as Son of Man in *1 Enoch*). But this honor would never be contemplated by the leadership for a humble, rural Galilean preacher like Jesus. The crux of Jesus' claim is tied to his being seated at the right hand. He will share the throne with the Shekinah and sit next to him at his right hand.[66] Jesus is not only near to God and working with him, he is seated in a way that shares the highest honor with him. Only the figure of Enoch–Son of Man seems close to this imagery, and even his access to God in this way was controversial, despite his translation by God according to Gen 5:24. Jesus' remarks would have been read as blasphemous along the lines that Philo described in *Dreams* 2.130–31 or *Decalogue* 61–64.[67] In *On Dreams*, Philo had said that a man

---

to His proclamation of God's kingdom to the whole people of Israel. Just as the kingdom of God and the Son of Man could not be in competition in this respect, so it is with Jesus and the Son of Man. The apocalyptic Son of Man is a symbol of Jesus' assurance of perfecting. With a shift from the assurance to the one who has it, the whole process may be interpreted as a dynamic and functional equating of Jesus and the coming Son of Man with the future perfecting of Jesus in view. On this view the primitive community then made of it a static personal identification accomplished already in the present Jesus." For Colpe, future perfecting is another way to speak of vindication. He regards Luke 22:69 as authentic, while arguing that the appearance of Dan 7 in Mark 14:62 is a reflection of the early church (see p. 435).

[66] As Martin Hengel has argued (*Studies in Early Christology* [Edinburgh: T&T Clark, 1995], 185–203), this claim was unique, though some exaltation imagery comes conceptually close to this. Jesus has chosen to state the point uniquely in the most emphatic way possible.

[67] Bock, *Blasphemy and Exaltation*, 30–112, esp. 110–12. This detailed portrait is largely supported in a recent essay by Adela Yarbo Collins ("The Charge of Blasphemy in Mark 14.6"), who went back over these Jewish texts up to Josephus. One key conclusion was that Philo's concept of blasphemy was "a specific kind of insult to God, namely, speech that compromises the Jewish affirmation that only the God of Israel is divine." She cites the (already noted above) *Embassy* 166–70 and *Dreams* 2.125–32. The second text involves an unnamed Egyptian governor who did away with the Sabbath and asked that he be served on that day, claiming he (among other things) was the whirlwind and controlled destiny. Philo reacts, asking what one should think of someone who thinks or utter such things. Philo calls him "an evil thing hitherto unknown," "he who likened to the All-Blessed his miserable self," and one who would not hesitate "to utter blasphemies (βλασφημεῖν) against the sun, and the moon, and the rest of the stars," if they made him too hot or too cold or did not bear fruit. She correctly notes on p. 388, in a critique of my chapter, that *Decalogue* 61–69 condemns those who worship the sun, moon, and

claiming the prerogatives of God is a person who possesses "evil of an extraordinary nature," "a man miserable in every respect," who "has dared to compare himself to the all-blessed God" (2.130–31). Such a man utters blasphemies against the creation, when it does not treat him right. In *Decalogue*, he argued that those who give those in the heavens (sun, moon, and stars) the same honors as those of the creator are "the most foolish and most unjust" of men. Those who think to ascribe to themselves honor like that given to God are possessed with "an insolent and free-spoken madness," as they "make an open display of the impiety which dwells in their hearts, and venture to blaspheme the deity, whetting an evil tongue, and desiring to vex the pious, who immediately feel an indescribable and irreconcilable affliction" (61–64) Philo's attitude, even as a heavily hellenized Jew, describes his perception of pagan arrogance, especially against any form of ruler cult. How much more the council would have been offended by Jesus' remarks, made as they were by a Jew. Philo's commentary could explain why the response to this remark was the priest's ripping of his clothes. Afflicted by

---

stars – not rulers, as I had earlier suggested. However, the point of the text changes little about how cultural blasphemy was seen with this change of referent. It is a slander against God to regard anything else as sharing his unique honor. Her summary is from pp. 395–96. On p. 396, she says that Mark's use of blasphemy is like that of Philo (and Josephus). Her view is reprinted in Geert van Oyen and Tom Shepherd, eds., *The Trial and Death of Jesus: Essays on the Passion Narrative in Mark* (CBET 45; Leuven: Peeters, 2006), 149–70. Another view moving away from a historical reading is raised by Jeffrey Gibson in the same volume in his study "The Function of the Charge of Blasphemy in Mark 14:64," 171–87. He dismisses the pursuit of a historical reading on the basis of "the observation, grounded in both narrow and wide studies of the idea of 'blasphemy' in first century Judaism, that nothing Mark reports Jesus as saying at Mark 14:62 would or could have been characterized as Mark says it was" (p. 172). He then goes on to cite Raymond Brown in support, despite the fact that in the scene as a whole Brown takes precisely the historical position Gibson refuses to pursue on this basis, as I indicate below. In fact, the evidence of Second Temple Judaism, as Collins and my works shows, is split on whether Jews would see such a claim of exaltation as blasphemous. Some Jews contemplated the types of things Jesus claimed without seeing blasphemy, but other Jews, camps like those of the leadership, rejected such possibilities and would have seen them as blasphemous. Gibson claims Mark's portrayal makes the point not that the blasphemy is not what Jesus claims about himself, but that Jesus makes such a claim. This distinction only works if the leadership belongs to Jewish circles that shared apocalyptic hope like that expressed in *1 Enoch*, but this is not a given. The Sadducees disliked apocalyptic, and the Pharisees in leadership may also have cast a skeptical eye on views like those out of the Enochic school. The Pharisaic tradition warns rabbi Akiba that claiming that someone can sit next to the Shekinah profanes the Shekinah. This rebuke makes the point with historical evidence (*b. Hag.* 14a; *b. Sanh.* 38b). Gibson is correct to note that part of the equation is that a Galilean teacher made such claims, when the possibility of such was reserved for Jewish greats like Moses, Enoch and Son of Man in such speculations. However, it is not at all certain that the first century Jewish leadership in Jerusalem would have embraced the plausibility of such an exaltation. Other aspects of Gibson's reading of Mark are also problematic, such as his view that Mark completely rejects Peter's confession at Caesarea Philippi. For a refutation of that reading, see in this volume ch. 8, § 2.4.2.2.

what he had heard, he gave the clear sign that blasphemy had been uttered (Mark 14:63; *m. Sanh.* 7:5).

In Jewish perception, what Jesus claims here is like, if not worse than, what other traditional blasphemers of Jewish lore said or did. What the actions of Sisera, Goliath, Sennacherib, Belshazzar, Manasseh, and Titus shared was a disregard for God's unique power and honor. An examination of blasphemy in Judaism shows how each of these figures was described and condemned. The midrashim supply particularly interesting additional examples when one considers how Isa 14:12–14 is handled by later rabbis. In these texts, Nebuchadnezzar becomes the illustration of arrogance, though in one major discussion he shares the stage with Pharaoh; Hiram; Joash, king of Judah; and Sennacherib (*Exod. Rab.* 8.2). In this midrash, Hiram is condemned, as Ezek 28:2 is related to him, while Isa 14 is applied to Nebuchadnezzar, who "claimed deity." According to the text, Pharaoh also made such a claim, as the midrash appeals to Ezek 29:3. Joash also fails because he received worship, with 2 Chr 24:17–25 being the key text supplying the evidence. The last example is Sennacherib, noting 2 Kgs 19:35. In the midst of this developed exposition, comes this emotional note. In discussing Zech 4:10, the midrash says, "this refers, however, says R. Berekiah (ca. 340 C.E.), to the haughty who declare themselves to be gods, but whom God makes abominations in the world." Here we see a later rabbi's reactions to those who were perceived to have portrayed themselves as too much like God. One can note, in addition, the tradition involving a son of man claim in *y. Ta*ᶜ*an.* 2:65b (Neusner 2:1). Here Rabbi Abbahu (ca. 300 C.E.) makes two statements: "If a man should tell you, 'I am God,' he is lying. If he says, 'I am the son of man,' in the end he will regret it: 'I will ascend to heaven,' he said it but he will not carry it out." This tradition is like what is seen in the rabbinic handling of Isa 14.[68] Such statements are to be rejected and subject one to judgment.

---

[68] Nebuchadnezzar is the example in reference to Isa 14:12–14 in several texts, such as *Exod. Rab.* 15:6 and 21:3; *Lev. Rab.* 18:2; and *Num. Rab.* 9:24 and 20:1. In this last text, Solomon is contrasted with Nebuchadnezzar: "the former built the Temple and uttered numerous songs and supplications, while the latter destroyed it and reviled and blasphemed, saying, "I will ascend above the height of the clouds; I will be like the Most High (Isa 14:14)." This is one of the few texts to actually speak of Nebuchadnezzar's blasphemy while making a point from Isa 14, but the key is not only his action against the temple, which would be seen as a direct attack against God's presence, but the attribution through the application of Isaiah of a heart attitude that is condemned. If someone was perceived as having made a claim that brought one too close to God or made oneself to be too much like him, these texts help show how such a claim would have been viewed. These Isa 14 texts parallel what is seen in the Jewish blasphemy texts in general, indicating how consistently these portraits are, as well as the reaction to them. The views of the later rabbis are like those of Philo. This may well point to the age of the view. The feeling is centuries old. The translation of the Son of Man text in *y. Ta*ᶜ*an.* 2:65b can be

The Jewish leadership believed that Jesus' remarks fell into this class. The consistency of these illustrative portraits of the blasphemer reveals a commonly held view of how blasphemy could be perceived in remarks or actions that appeared to reduce God's unique stature. The Jewish reaction to a sense of violation of God's presence, as seen in *Ant.* 12.406 or in 1 Macc 2:6, shows how important the protection of the uniqueness of God's presence was. In *Antiquities*, the priests pray after Nicanor's blasphemy, and he is defeated by Judas. In 1 Macc 2, Judas slays those who sacrifice a pig on an altar independent from the one in Jerusalem, an act he considered blasphemous. As our earlier study of figures going into God's presence showed, respect for God's unique presence was jealously guarded. Those who enter gain access by his invitation only. Access of this sort is rarely contemplated. Jesus' remarks possess a frankness that dissolves these formalities.

In considering Jesus' remarks, some have argued for a type of precedent in texts declaring the vindication of the righteous, such as *T. Job* 33:2–4, *Apoc. El. (c)* 37:3–4, and *T. Benj.* 10:5–6.[69] Here are descriptions of figures who receive thrones with imagery that mentions God's right hand. However, these texts speak of honor coming *from* the right hand of God or of a privilege shared *with others*, so that the *Testament of Job* speaks of a throne from above whose "splendor and majesty are from the right hand," while the Coptic *Apocalypse of Elijah* speaks of a host of righteous Christian martyrs set "at God's right hand." These martyrs render thanks for others as they conquer the Son of Iniquity, see the destruction of heaven and earth, and receive the thrones of glory and crowns. In the *Testament of Benjamin*, the patriarchs Enoch, Noah, Shem, Abraham, Isaac, and Jacob are raised up (not seated!) "at the right hand in great joy." But Jesus' claim is not to be among the righteous but to lead them as God's vice-regent, a ruling figure like that mentioned in Ps 110:1. There is more in his claim than what we see in these texts about the vindication of the righteous, though what these texts show is a background that parallels to a lesser degree what Jesus claims. If such honor goes to the righteous, how much more honor can be contemplated for the one who brings their vindication. Perhaps this kind of expectation fueled an element of the development of this view within Jesus. Jesus, as eschatological leader of the yet-to-be vindicated righteous, was to possess a special position in heaven.

Morna Hooker summarizes well the leadership's view of the blasphemy charge, a charge that fits the appropriate Jewish religious and cultural background. As she says, "*To claim for oneself* a seat at the right hand of power,

---

found in Jacob Neusner, ed., *Talmud of the Land of Israel* (25 vols.; Atlanta: Scholars, 1998–99), 18:183; or Str-B 1:486. On the Son of Man text, see Hengel, *Studies in Early Christology*, 181 and n. 130.

[69] See, for example, Beasley-Murray, *Jesus and the Kingdom of God*, 297–98.

however, is to claim a share in the authority of God; *to appropriate to oneself* such authority and *to bestow on oneself* this unique status in the sight of God and man would almost certainly have been regarded as blasphemy."[70] The dispute surrounding Jesus was a debate about his authority as it related to his person and mission. The Marcan text presents this as the essence of the dispute and as central to his conviction to crucifixion.

The leaders handed Jesus over to Roman officials, because they saw in him a dangerous blasphemer and deceiver. But they presented the accusation in political terms – in a form that Pilate could understand and feel enough threatened by to act.[71] Someone like Jesus with such a comprehensive view of his own authority could be portrayed not only as a threat to Israel but also as a potentially serious problem for Rome. In addition, by subjecting Jesus to crucifixion, the Jewish leadership was making an additional public statement that explicitly turned Jesus' death into one cursed by God, because the contemporary reading of Deut 21:23 would have seen a crucifixion in these terms.[72] In fact, God would be seen as the source of the judgment of "accursed" by permitting a crucifixion to take place.

At the very least, this is how the church, as reflected by Mark, portrayed the dispute from the Jewish side. But it is significant to note that this portrayal would have been done at great risk to the church, when Mark's Gospel emerged in Rome. To blame both the Jewish leadership and the Romans as having a role in Jesus' death meant that two major, powerful forces in the early Christians' world would share responsibility for the death. To admit that Jesus was charged as a political subversive and was executed for such a crime put Rome on notice about the Christians, even though the church would have regarded the charge against Jesus as false. To present the account this way suggests that at its base must be roots that motivated this broad sweep of responsibility. The story had to be told, even if there was risk for the church in terms of who got blamed.

2.5.3. Option 3: Blasphemy involves how the leaders are addressed

There is a third option concerning the blasphemy that one ought to note, because it serves as a second feature that adds to the sense of offense. Two elements of potential background illuminate this aspect of the blasphemy. First, when Jesus claims to be a judging figure and claims that the council

---

[70] Hooker, *The Son of Man in Mark: A Study of the Background of the Term "Son of Man" and Its Use in St. Mark's Gospel*, 173, emphasis added.

[71] For discussion, see in this volume ch. 13, § 3.4.

[72] On this first-century view of crucifixion, see my discussion of the work of Otto Betz in Bock, *Blasphemy and Exaltation*, 15–17, my discussion of 11QTemple 64:6–13, and n. 66 there.

will see this exercise of authority, he may well be appealing to martyrdom language that has already been noted in the expectation of vindication. But the point here is more specific. The idea of "seeing" has been discussed as an allusion to Zech 12:10, "they will look upon (ἐπιβλέψονται) him whom they have pierced ... and will mourn over him."[73] But there is really nothing in this context to suggest an allusion to this text.[74] There is no allusion to "piercing" or to the need for repentance. Rather, the concept of "seeing" emerging out of the martyrdom tradition provides a more likely background. Three texts show the theme. Wisdom 5:2 reads, "When the unrighteous see (ἰδόντες) them, they will be shaken with dreadful fear and they will be amazed at the unexpected salvation of the righteous." *Apocalypse of Elijah* 35:17 (= 5:28 in Charlesworth, *OTP*) reads, "Then the sinners in torment will see the place of the righteous. And thus grace will occur." This is a composite text, mixing Jewish and Christian elements, but again in an eschatological context, those who see are those who are judged and what they see is the vindication of the righteous. A Christian text with a similar motif is Luke 16:23. The third text is perhaps the most important. It is *1 En.* 62:3–5.[75] The text reads, "On the day of judgment, all the kings, governors, the high officials, and landlords, *shall see* and recognize him – how he sits on the throne of his glory and righteousness is judged before him ... They shall be terrified and dejected; and pain shall seize them when *they see* that Son of Man sitting on the throne of glory."[76] Not only does this text repeat the theme of the seeing of vindication, but it includes a reference to the seen Son of Man. As Borsch noted, the three themes of (1) they "see," (2) the "Son of Man," and (3) "sitting" are all parallel. These three concepts appear in the same order in both texts and reflect "indications of the influence of older common conceptions."[77] The background means that Jesus challenges and warns his accusers that the real authority is not the Jewish council but himself, who will preside over them one day. This future prospect makes their examination a sham.

---

[73] Norman Perrin, *Rediscovering the Teaching of Jesus* (New York: Harper & Row, 1967), 181–85.

[74] Correctly Joel Marcus, *The Way of the Lord: Christological Exegesis of the Old Testament in the Gospel of Mark* (Louisville: Westminster John Knox, 1992), 166–67. The following discussion of martyrdom background follows his treatment. See also Pesch, *Das Markusevangelium*, 2:438.

[75] This connection was made by Frederick Houk Borsch, "Mark XIV.62 and 1 Enoch LXII.5," *NTS* 14 (1968): 565–67. See also Hengel, *Studies in Early Christology*, 185–89. He notes that the seating here is something a little less than being seated at the right hand.

[76] Emphasis added.

[77] Borsch, "Mark XIV.62 and 1 Enoch LXII.5," 567. For an alternative reading of this emphasis, which also would be seen as blasphemous, see the discussion surrounding n. 45 above.

Jesus' remark about what will be seen is made in such a vague manner, however, that it is unlikely to be a creation of the church. It lacks the kind of directness one might expect from a saying formulated by the church after Jesus' vindication.

Second, this aspect of the remark represents an attack on the "divinely appointed" leadership of the nation – at least this is how the leadership would have seen themselves. This attack would be read as a violation of Exod 22:27, which is one of the Torah's prominent blasphemy texts. For example Hyrcanus expected the Pharisees to judge a figure named Eleazar for casting blasphemous insults upon him as the leader. He was disappointed when they preferred a whipping over death (Josephus, *Ant.* 13.293–96).[78] This violation makes Jesus both a political and a religious threat. In the leader's view, not only was Jesus making a false and religiously dangerous claim by evaporating the distance between himself and God, but he was also challenging the authority of those who had responsibility for the spiritual well-being of the nation, suggesting that they would be reckoned among those judged in the end. As such, he raised the prospect of intense political-social unrest, as the temple incident had already suggested. Now anyone who threatened the well-being of the people and their political stability before Rome was also subject to reaction by the Jewish authorities, because presenting oneself as a person who might cause the nation to fall into Gentile hands was viewed as a dangerous political act. An act of this sort could be seen as a criminal offense that carried a penalty of death. Here the key text informing the cultural background is 11Q*Temple* 64:6–13.[79] This text in the key lines, 7–9, reads: "(7) If a man slanders his [God's] people and delivers his people up to a foreign nation and does evil to his people (8) you shall hang him on a tree, and he shall die. According to the mouth [= testimony] of two witnesses and the mouth of three witnesses (9) he shall be put to death, and they shall hang him on a tree." Two features of the passage are important. The first is that slandering the people and putting them at risk is what leads to the sentence. Second, the text mentions hanging by a tree, the first-century cultural equivalent of which was crucifixion. The allusion is to Deut 21:22–23, which described the public display of an offender *after* he was executed on a tree. In the first century, crucifixion was seen as an equivalent of this text, even though the death came simultaneously with the public hanging.[80]

Jesus' remarks were a provocation of the strongest kind. The judges are being threatened with being judged by the accused, while he functions as

---

[78] Schwemer, "Die Passion des Messias," 133–63.

[79] Betz, "Jesus and the Temple Scroll," 80–81, 87–89. The brackets in the translation clarify the pronoun's antecedent, while the parentheses explain an idiom.

[80] David J. Halperin, "Crucifixion, the Nahum Pesher, and the Rabbinic Penalty of Strangulation," *JJS* 32 (1981): 32–46.

God's intimate representative. His threatening of the leadership with his claim to be eschatological judge and the remark suggesting that the council was unrighteous in having him stand before them were blasphemous at this second, social level. It seriously challenged their claims of divinely appointed leadership and responsibility for Israel. This element of the charge provided the political grounds that the leadership needed to take him to Rome and present him as a threat to public order. So Jesus' claims would not only have been perceived as false – a premise that could allow a very public process, as Strobel has noted – but the claims would be seen as potentially dangerous.[81] It is the combination that caused the leadership to act according to Mark.

2.5.4 Conclusion on the Nature of the Blasphemy

Thus, Jesus' remark was perceived as blasphemous on two levels. First, his claim to have the prerogative of final judgment and sit next to God in heaven represented a claim to comprehensive authority, a function that the leadership could never contemplate or accept for one of such humble background. Such prerogatives, even when they were contemplated, were reserved only in the most rare of cases, for an exceptional luminary like Moses or the Son of Man. His direct claim to possess such a position would have been automatically offensive. Second, his claim was also an attack on the leadership in violation of the spirit of Exod 22:27 and an attitude that could put the social structure of the nation at risk before Rome. Jesus was different from a later object of messianic honor, Bar Kochba, as the latter figure at least had the support of some of the social-political leadership in the nation (for example, Akiba). Jesus' claim of authority went beyond political messianic claims in the view of the leadership, because it held them eschatologically accountable for what they would do with him. Such a challenge would not go uncontested. Not only had Jesus made himself too close to God, he had also created a great, irreversible gap between himself and the leadership. At least, this is how Mark portrays the event. What one must conclude about this saying is that much within it fits well in the cultural thought world of first-century Judaism.

3. The Potential Authenticity of the Saying

The background of the Jewish perception of Jesus' blasphemy has been examined. The exchange makes sense in a Jewish context. It has "historical

---

[81] See the discussion above and n. 27.

plausibility," to name a criterion suggested by some as a way to validate such material. In this section, I will apply the criteria of historical plausibility, dissimilarity, ambiguity, and Jewishness to different features of the saying to see if it meets such standards.[82] Does this saying and its background possess the potential to be regarded as an authentic summary of the real scene? This question is stated carefully, for not only are we dealing with a Greek translation but a text that is about 35 to 40 years removed from the original scene. This section treats various elements that have been considered in the past to make the scene a questionable one: (1) the temple charge, (2) the "Jewish" expressions in vv. 61–62 – namely, the circumlocutions of God involving εὐλογητός and δύναμις, (3) the use of Ps 110:1 and Dan 7:13, (4) the possibility of Jesus' calling himself the apocalyptic Son of Man, and (5) the combination of christological titles that appear in the question and reply. Only after all of the first four subtopics are treated can we consider the presence and relationship of the titles to one another and assess the likelihood of the saying's authenticity.

3.1. A Lack of Coherence between the Temple Charge and the Rest of the Scene

The movement from the temple charge directly into the christological issue has been seen by many as a problem for the passage. It is argued that the transition into christology is too abrupt to be credible and thus reflects Mark's work. The scene is designed to heighten the drama, not portray reality. Mark's goal is to get to the theme of Jesus' theologically loaded definition of who he is. The redactional effort is often seen as reflecting a combination of traditional material and material from Mark. For example, Hugh Anderson writes in his comments on vv. 60–65 that "the question that the 'high priest' now puts to Jesus, 'Are you the Christ, the Son of the Blessed?' is introduced somewhat abruptly in so far as it has no obvious connection with the foregoing proceedings, certainly not with the alleged prediction of Jesus' part of the destruction of the Temple."[83] Anderson suggests that perhaps the temple charge goes back to the trial, but the juxtaposition of temple and christology is not credible.[84]

---

[82] For further discussion of critical of authenticity, see in this volume ch. 2, § 4.1. The appeal to ambiguity is that a detail is so ambiguous that it gives evidence of not being made up, since if it were created, it would be clearer. The appeal to Jewishness is that the detail in question is both so obscure and so reflective of a Jewish setting that it must come from an early part of the tradition.

[83] Hugh Anderson, *The Gospel of Mark* (NCB; London: Oliphants, 1976), 330–31, bold highlight replaced with quote marks.

[84] Anderson (*The Gospel of Mark*, 329) argues that Matt 26:60 may reflect history in that a temple saying of Jesus was used at the trial. However, on p. 331, he argues that the

Now the question is whether such a transition is unconnected and abrupt from a historical perspective. In making literary or form judgments about what Mark has done or how he might have summarized what he may have been aware of from tradition, it is important that we do not under develop historical background questions or ignore possibilities for showing the text's unity. A striking illustration of this problem is the criticism of Otto Betz in the recent study by W. Reinbold.[85] As he examines the passage historically, he dismisses the entire work of Betz's study by questioning Betz's suggestion that a morning trial took place in its traditional, temple locale.[86] But questioning this detail of Betz's view does not represent a careful assessment of the overall argument from historical background but merely criticizes one minor point. Nor is his rejection of Strobel entirely compelling.[87] He rejects Strobel's work primarily on the premises that idolatry, which is allegedly the key to a Jewish deceiver charge, is nowhere in view for Jesus, and that the charge of deception is nowhere raised in the NT tradition (a point that is not true when one considers Luke 23:2 with its important reference to Jesus' distorting custom in the context of a religion steeped in a commitment to revelation and tradition).

In fact, Reinbold's assessment is inadequate in a variety of ways. First, there are NT texts indicating that Jesus was seen as a deceiver explicitly using terms such as πλάνος and πλανᾶ (Matt 27:63–64; John 7:12, 47).

Second, this testimony about Jesus' deception also appears in Jewish sources. There is a key text in the Jewish tradition that makes a similar point, saying that Jesus was stoned because he "practiced sorcery and enticed Israel to apostasy" (*b. Sanh.* 43a, על שכישף והסית והדיח את ישראל). That such a crime was punishable with execution is shown in the list of capital crimes from *m. Sanh.* 7:4, because the המסית is a crime subject to the death penalty of stoning. It seems likely that the reference to stoning is a figurative way to refer to a capital execution by means of biblical language. Another, less well-known set of texts from Qumran discuss how the high priest is to test for a

---

high priest's question is a case that "here the church has put its own language on the lips of the high priest." When it comes to Jesus' reply, Anderson argues that, "for Mark, the speaker here, the harried and persecuted one, is the very one inseparably connected with God's ultimate triumph." Similar in thrust are Eta Linnemann, *Studien zur Passionsgeschichte* (FRLANT 102; Göttingen: Vandenhoeck & Ruprecht, 1970), 129–30; and Lohse, "Der Prozeß Jesu Christi," 99–100, who notes that the view of a disjunction is also found in Bultmann and Dibelius. See Lohse's n. 42.

[85] Reinbold, *Der älteste Bericht über den Tod Jesu: Literarische Analyse und historische Kritik der Passionsdarstellungen der Evangelien*, 256.
[86] Otto Betz, "Probleme des Prozesses Jesu," *ANRW* 2.25.1.613–644.
[87] Strobel, *Die Stunde der Wahrheit*, 81–92.

false prophet and deceiver, using the Urim and Thummin (4Q375, 4Q376).[88] Other passages also develop this deceiver theme.[89]

In the texts in the Fathers where there is contention with Jews, the charge against Jesus is consistently that he was a magician or a deceiver, a person subject to the evil arts. For example, there is a long discussion in Justin Martyr, *Dial.* 69:7, where Justin's Jewish opponent attributes Jesus' abilities in magical arts to his being "a magician and a deceiver of the people" (μάγον ... καὶ λαοπλάνον). In 108:2, he is called "a Galilean deceiver" (Γαλιλαίου πλάνου). Origen also dealt with such a claim. In *Cels.* 1:68, there is a long discussion over Jesus' works and ministry. Celsus charges that he is an evil and godless man, while in 1:71, he is a God-hating and unworthy magician (θεομισοῦς ἦν τινος καὶ μοχθηροῦ γόητος GCS 1, 22). Eusebius repeats the charge in his *Dem. ev.* 3, 3, 1–4 and 3, 6, 1, where he considers the deceiver (πλάνος) charge (GCS 23, pp. 108–9). The consistent testimony of Christians, Jews, and the Christians who were reporting about the Jewish view is that he was put to death, in part, for deceiving Israel. Thus, the tradition of the Talmud has old roots.

Third, Reinbold's assessment also ignores both the relationship and the distinction between idolatry and blasphemy in the Jewish materials. In Judaism, idolatry and blasphemy were comparable and sometimes were seen as interrelated offenses, but they did not have to be.[90] The punishments

---

[88] On this passage, which calls for sacrifices and a test using the Urim and Thummin, see John Strugnell, "Moses-Pseudepigrapha at Qumran: 4Q375, 4Q376, and Similar Works," in *Archaeology and History in the Dead Sea Scrolls: The New York University Conference in Memory of Yigael Yadin* (ed. Lawrence H. Schiffman; JSPSup 8; Sheffield: Sheffield Academic Press, 1990), 221–56; and Johannes Zimmermann, "Messianische Vorstellungen in den Schriftfunden von Qumran," Ph.D. diss. (Tübingen: Tübingen University, 1996), 204–16. This work is now available as Johannes Zimmermann, *Messianische Texte aus Qumran: königliche, priesterliche und prophetische Messiasvorstellungen in den Schriftfunden von Qumran* (WUNT 2.104; Tübingen: Mohr Siebeck, 1998), 233–43. The text is fragmentary and seems to be an apocryphon of Moses. It has uncertain origins, though it appears not to be from the Qumran community itself. Josephus discusses a similar process in *Ant* 3.214–18, though the two sets of passages disagree whether the stone on the left (4Q376) or the right (Josephus) shines to give the signal. According to Nehemiah, these stones went out of use by the time of Ezra (Neh 7:65), but Josephus dates their non-use later, at ca. 120 B.C.E.; see Strugnell, "Moses-Pseudepigrapha at Qumran," 243. The text is significant because it shows that concern for these issues remained alive to the extent that how examinations should take place was contemplated. The resultant view was that the penalty for the crime for being a false prophet or deceiver was death.

[89] Martin Hengel, *Nachfolge und Charisma: Eine exegetisch-religionsgeschichtliche Studie zu Mt 8,21f. und Jesu Ruf in die Nachfolge* (BZNW 34; Berlin: Töpelmann, 1968), 44–45, n. 14.

[90] See my discussion in Bock, *Blasphemy and Exaltation*, 110–12, which distinguishes between acts of blasphemy that *can be* idolatrous acts *and/or* acts of arrogance, from the category of blasphemous utterances. For example, the already-discussed criticism of God's leaders is not idolatrous but is seen as a blasphemous attack on God's honor reflect-

for them were often viewed as similar, and the way they were assessed was often paralleled.

A fourth point that Reinhold fails to consider is the difference in Betz's position from Strobel's argument. Betz tightened Strobel's argument at the places where Strobel's links were the weakest by adding additional background.[91] Whereas Strobel emphasized Jesus the deceiver, Betz highlights how Jesus in his messianic claim is seen as a deceiver. The difference is significant, because it fills in a gap in Strobel's argument, which Reinhold rightly notes but overplays. In sum, Reinhold's critique thoroughly fails to come to grips with the historical evidence on all sides of the controversy that Jesus was slain as a deceiver, a point that lends credibility to the careful historical background work of Strobel and Betz.

From a careful consideration of Betz's work there emerges a credible unity to the summarized flow of events that reflects not abruptness but rather a careful understanding of the conceptual connections that existed at the time. This is part of what meets the demands of Theissen and Winter's "historical plausibility" criterion. The connection shows a nuanced awareness of the cultural background. Betz showed how the temple threat could have been interpreted as putting the nation at risk before Rome in a way that demanded response. Here the already-cited 11Q*Temple* 64:6–13 reflects sensitivity to the political realities that a temple disruption could cause with Rome. There existed in the view of the leadership the need to deal severely with such a challenge, including the prospect of crucifixion for one found guilty of the charge. Betz also noted a temple-king connection in Jewish tradition, stretching back to 2 Sam 7 and appearing as well in the 14th petition of the *Shemoneh Esreh*, in which the hope of a cleansed, everlasting Jerusalem where God again dwells and the raising up of David's throne are placed side by side. The 14th petition reads, "And to Jerusalem, your city, return with mercy and dwell in its midst as you have spoken; and build it soon in our days to be an everlasting building; and raise up quickly in its midst the throne of David. Blessed are you, Lord, who builds Jerusalem." The concerns here would be Jewish, of course, not Roman.

But there still could be a minor problem with the argument in this form. It is found in the view that Messiah is possibly not explicitly said to be the builder or destroyer of the temple in these early Jewish texts.[92] The con-

---

ing criticism of the divine choice. Acts dishonoring God's temple are another example (1 Macc 2:6).

[91] See the works of Strobel (*Die Stunde der Wahrheit*) and Betz ("Jesus and the Temple Scroll") and notes 27 and 28 above.

[92] Gundry, *Mark*, 898–901. He notes that it is God who builds the temple in the early key text of 4QFlor 1–2, 10, where it is also a question whether the temple is meant, the dynasty of regal Davidic rule, or probably both (temple in vv. 1–2, dynasty in v. 10). For views on what Jesus' saying in Mark might have meant, see Gundry's discussion.

nection may not be an explicit one, but rather an implicit one. Nonetheless, the key to the high priest's transition in the question is not in this detail of building or destroying a temple, in my view; it is rather in the authority, the claim of social and structural restoration, and the arrival of the era that this restorative claim implies is present. Even though this temple charge apparently was dropped as unproved, what the potential but unproved claim did was raise Jesus' association with some type of golden age restoration from God. Jesus did look for a restoration of the nation in which he would have a key role. Now a figure from Judaism that this type of association would suggest was a messianic one – especially if one thinks about the *Shemoneh Esreh*. This association with Messiah also made it possible to raise a political question in relationship to Rome. Thus, the transition is a quite natural one and can make good historical sense in the context, whether one takes the more explicit approach of Betz or sees only a conceptual move based on Jesus' claim of bringing restoration here.

As I will argue, it is almost irrelevant what the exact meaning here is, because it was the association related to authority and restoration that led to the more-focused personal question that the high priest asked. Gundry's view could be slightly overstated if, at this time, texts such as Zech 6:12 were read in the way that *Tg. Zech.* 6:12 and *Tg. Isa.* 53:5 suggest. Both these later targums suggest that Messiah will build the temple, for the *Isaiah Targum* says that Messiah "will build the sanctuary which was profaned for our sins," and the *Targum to Zechariah* speaks of the Anointed, who will be revealed, be raised up, and "shall build the temple of the Lord." Of course, the problem with these texts is that they are late. However, if this understanding of Messiah's role existed in this earlier period, then Betz's case is more direct, because the suggestion of a messianic building of the temple would then be explicit. But my point is that, even if the connection is more implied, the connection still easily comes to the surface. For other discussions of the relation of the temple to Messiah, see E. Earle Ellis, "Deity-Christology in Mark 14:58," in *Jesus of Nazareth: Lord and Christ: Essays on the Historical Jesus and New Testament Christology* (ed. Joel P. Green and Max Turner; Grand Rapids: Eerdmans, 1994), 200 and nn. 44–45; David Darnell Edwards, "Jesus and the Temple: A Historico-Theological Study of Temple Motifs in the Ministry of Jesus (Synoptic Gospels)," Ph.D. diss. (Fort Worth: Southwestern Baptist Theological Seminary, 1992), 204–7; Dunn, *The Parting of the Ways*, 51–53, who stresses the involvement of the key priests in sending Jesus to his death as part of a dispute over religious authority; and Volker Hampel, *Menschensohn und historischer Jesus: ein Rätselwort als Schlüssel zum messianischen Selbstverständnis Jesu* (Neukirchen-Vluyn: Neukirchener Verlag, 1990), 174–75, who also notes *Lev. Rab.* 9:6 (111a) for this theme. They see a connection between Messiah and temple as possible for this era. The entire temple pericope as raising the authority question is fully developed by Jostein Ådna, "Jesu Kritik am Tempel: Eine Untersuchung zum Verlauf und Sinn der sogenannten Tempelreinigung Jesu, Markus 11,15–17 und Parallelen," Ph.D. diss. (Tübingen: Stavanger, 1993); see esp. pp. 565–79. This work has now been published as Jostein Ådna, *Jesu Stellung zum Tempel: die Tempelaktion und das Tempelwort als Ausdruck seiner messianischen Sendung* (WUNT 2.119; Tübingen: Mohr Siebeck, 2000); see esp. pp. 381–448.

3.2. The Issue of "Jewish" Expressions in Mark 14:61–62

According to Mark, Jesus' silence on the temple charge leads the high priest to step in and ask, σὺ εἶ ὁ χριστὸς ὁ υἱὸς τοῦ εὐλογητοῦ ("Are you the Christ, the Son of the Blessed One?").[93] The phrase "the Son of the Blessed One" is an indirect reference to God. "The Blessed One" is a circumlocution that avoids speaking directly of God out of respect for the deity.[94] In turn, Jesus' reply refers to ἐκ δεξιῶν καθήμενον τῆς δυνάμεως ("seated at the right hand of power"). The reference to "the Power" or "the Almighty" is another circumlocution that describes God through his attributes of power and authority, just as the English name "the Almighty" would. The avoidance of pronouncing God's name is a Jewish custom, but whether these phrases could reflect roots in an authentic tradition has been disputed.

Two examples summarize the reasons raised for questioning the expression's authenticity and regarding it as the work of Mark or the early church. Hugh Anderson writes,

> Although the description 'Son of the Blessed' is a typically Jewish reverential circumlocution for 'Son of God', it is quite improbable that a high priest of the Sadducean party would have used this language in collocation with the term 'Christ' or 'Messiah'. The semblance of verisimilitude barely disguises the fact, therefore, that here the Church has put its own language on the lips of the high priest.[95]

Though it is not entirely clear from Anderson's remarks why it is improbable that a high priest of the Sadducees would use such an expression, an explanation is provided by the remarks of Donald Juel as a part of his judgment that "the best explanation of the phrase in Mark is that it is a pseudo-Jewish expression created by the author as appropriate in the mouth of the high priest."[96] Earlier he had noted that (1) the term "'the Blessed One' as a circumlocution for the name of God is almost completely unattested" and

---

[93] This is the Greek text. A few manuscripts (G, F, and *pc* in apparatus) lack the reference to the Christ.

[94] This wording is changed from the wording in Bock, *Blasphemy and Exaltation*, 214, where I mistakenly spoke of a circumlocution for the divine name, where only a generic reference to God was present, not a use of the divine name. The error was pointed out by Maurice Casey, review of Darrell L. Bock, *Blasphemy and Exaltation in Judaism and the Final Examination of Jesus*, *JTS* 52 (2001): 245–47. This review was highly critical of my work. I have responded to him in detail and updated the discussion of this theme in Darrell L. Bock, "Jewish Expressions in Mark 14.61–62 and the Authenticity of the Jewish Examination of Jesus," *JSHJ* 1 (2003): 147–59. Schwemer ("Die Passion des Messias") called the review "völlig ungerechtfertigt" ("completely unjustified").

[95] Anderson, *The Gospel of Mark*, 331, bold highlight replaced with quote marks. I noted in the discussion surrounding n. 83 above the concluding part of this citation earlier in connection with the claim that the shift to christology was abrupt after the temple discussion.

[96] Juel, *Messiah and Temple*, 79.

(2) that the title "'Son of God' is rarely used as a messianic designation in extant Jewish literature."[97]

The tendency of the scholars discussing this problem is to isolate the example of "Son of the Blessed One" from a discussion of the "right hand of Power," since the "Son" phrase is the more rare and disputed usage. But it could be argued that it is the pair of references taken together that is revealing. The care of the high priest to be reverential is respected and repeated by Jesus even as he replies.[98] The detail and the paired response add notes of solemnity to the report. The fact that the two expressions play off one another should be noted before we look at each expression separately.

It is important to summarize the key linguistic data for both expressions.[99] Traces of a similar expression, "the Blessed One," can be found in *m. Ber.* 7:3 and in *1 En.* 77:2.[100] In other words, the concept is common, while the exact expression is not. The usage in *1 Enoch* is potentially significant because it refers to "the eternally Blessed." However, the Aramaic fragments we have of *1 Enoch* from Qumran unfortunately do not include this text,

---

[97] Juel, *Messiah and Temple*, 78.

[98] This point only applies if the report of the trial did not alter a direct reference to God by Jesus to match the priest's question in order to remove an element of potential blasphemy by naming God directly, a view noted above and held by Robert Gundry (see discussion surrounding nn. 42–53). My contention is that this is one of the reasons Gundry's suggestion is less than likely at this point. I view the pairing as significant, at least for Mark's portrayal of the event. Though Jesus is making bold claims, he is portrayed as doing so while showing respect for God that the high priest introduced. Only Mark's version has this pair of circumlocutions, because Matt 26:63 ("Are you the Christ, the Son of God?") and Luke 22:67 ("If you are the Christ, tell us") alter the question slightly. The variation means that we are dealing with summaries of the scene here, as opposed to the actual wording in at least two of the synoptic gospel portrayals, but a movement away from an almost liturgical-like circumlocution is more likely than the reverse, since a circumlocution is more indirect. Nonetheless, the question remains whether even these summaries are a good general reflection of what took place.

[99] Gustaf Dalman, *Die Worte Jesu* (2nd ed.; Darmstadt: Wissenschaftliche Buchgesellschaft, 1965), 163–65; Str-B 2:51; and Evans, *Jesus and His Contemporaries*, 421–22.

[100] The key expression in the Mishnah is המבורך. See especially Joseph Heinemann, *Prayer in the Talmud: Forms and Patterns* (SJ 9; Berlin: de Gruyter, 1977), 100–111, 314; esp. p. 105, n. 1. His index contains 37 different blessing formulas involving God. Judaism was in the habit of showering blessings upon God in its worship. See also *Sifre Deut.* 306 (Finkelstein, p. 342, line 6). This account has both the blessing ("Bless you the Lord who is to be blessed") and a response that uses the phrase "Bless you the Lord who is to be blessed forever." The two phrases here are ברכו את ה' המבורך for the blessing and ברוך ה' המבורך לעולם for the response. Though the expression "the eternally Blessed" has not been found in Aramaic fragments of this *1 Enoch* passage, a parallel expression is found in 4Q209 as it reflects *1 En.* 23:3–4 (see also Maier's translation, vol. 2, p. 161). The connection to 23:3–4 is noted in Michael A. Knibb, *The Ethiopic Book of Enoch: A New Edition in the Light of the Aramaic Dead Sea Fragments* (2 vols.; in collaboration with Edward Ullendorff; Oxford: Clarendon, 1978), 179. The Yerushalmi text noted below can be found in Peter Schäfer and Hans-Jürgen Becker, eds., *Synopse zum Talmud Yerushalmi: Band I/1–2* (Texte und Studien zum Antiken Judentum 31; Tübingen: Mohr Siebeck, 1991), 188–91.

because Qumran only has about one-fifth of this book in Aramaic.[101] The other Jewish uses of "Blessed One" reveal that this phrase is an old synagogue expression used in prayer, a common respectful way to refer to what God does by the context of its consistent usage, though it is in a dependent, adjectival construction and is not used independently as an isolated name.

In fact, there is a long string of traditional discussions about this blessing that invokes God as the one who is to be blessed (המבורך), a phrase tied to a remark by Rabbi Ishmael (ca. 120 C.E.), who said that the blessing in the synagogue should be, "Bless the Lord who is blessed." The remark concludes a long discussion about the proper benedictions for a variety of situations and audience sizes (*m. Ber.* 7:3). The development of the discussion on proper blessing formulas continues in texts such as *b. Ber.* 49b–50a (2x), *Mek. Pisḥa* 16 on Exod 13:3 (lines 130–40, Lauterbach), and *y. Ber.* 11b–c (3x, though the first reference in 11b is only in the London and Paris mss). The benediction comes to expression in the very old Jewish prayer known as the *Qaddish*.[102] It also was associated with a morning invitation to worship with the call, "Bless you the Lord the one to whom blessing is due.[103] Another Jewish text alludes to this prayer without using the specific benediction (*t. Ber.* 5:18). So this description of God as a Blessed One is part of the central prayer life of the nation – an old synagogue prayer. It has overtones of appreciation, prayer, and worship. Its widespread use in the liturgical tradition suggests an old practice. It shows that it is perfectly appropriate to speak of God as the "Blessed One."[104]

---

[101] Knibb, *The Ethiopic Book of Enoch*, 6–15.

[102] Ismar Elbogen, *Der jüdische Gottesdienst in seiner geschichtlichen Entwicklung* (3rd ed; 1931; repr., Hildesheim: Olms, 1962), 92–98. The prayer comes at the end of the reading of the Torah or at the end of a public sermon. In *Sop.* 21:6, 10:7, and 19:1, the prayer is associated with the conclusion of the reading of Torah and comes at the end of the sequence of prayers. These connections appear to be a little more recent in origin. The oldest named rabbi who is tied to the prayer's use is Jose b. Ḥalafta (ca. 150 C.E.). See *Sifre Deut.* 306 and *b. Ber.* 3a. The expression is יהא שמה רבא מברך לעלם. D. W. Staerk, *Altjüdische liturgische Gebete* (Kleine Texte für Vorlesungen und Übungen 58; Berlin: de Gruyter, 1930), 30–31.

[103] Heinemann, *Prayer in the Talmud*, 25.

[104] In my article "Jewish Expressions in Mark 14.61–62" I have added the evidence of numerous texts from Qumran and the Mishnah for the expressions that look to God as one to be blessed. In the conclusion of that section, I said, "So as unprecedented as the expression 'Son of the Blessed One' is, the concept of God as the one who is blessed is not rare at all. It is this combination of similarity and dissimilarity that speaks to the likelihood that what we have in Mark 14 is a trace of Jewish expression, not made up by Mark or the church, but retained from the Jewish roots and serious nature of the examination of Jesus" (p. 153). The use of the expression underscores the serious, even solemn nature of the query, rooted as it is in prayer and worship. In expressing myself this way, I am appealing to Tom Wright's variation of the criterion of dissimilarity, what has come to be called double dissimilarity, which means close to but not quite like Judaism or early church expression. The NT reflects such usage in Eph 1:3 and 1 Pet 1:3.

However, there is a difference in Mark's usage that points to the criterion of dissimilarity, if we can apply it in this case to something the high priest says. The high priest uses the term "Blessed" as part of the description of God's son (Son of the Blessed One) as opposed to the normal way of using it as part of a blessing one offers for what God has done. In other words, the usage is a variation on a common Jewish idea but does not match that common usage as a created saying likely would. More than that, Mark does not use the verb "to bless" (εὐλογέω) to refer to God in his other uses (6:44, 8:7, 14:22 – in prayer with a request that God bless, 11:9–10 – where the entering Jesus and the kingdom to come are said to be blessed; 8:7, 11:10 are uses unique to Mark). Nowhere else in a gospel is this name used for God. It is used of God in a qualified manner like the Jewish practice in Rom 1:25; 9:5; 2 Cor 11:31, where it describes God as blessed. It is interesting that these NT uses are limited to the most scribally trained Jew of the NT writers, Paul. It also is unlikely that this expression and its Jewish-like character were created by Mark, because his audience was not savvy on Jewish cultural themes, as his explanation of terms in a passage such as Mark 7:1–4 shows. When we add the fact that Mark uses "Son of God" with ease elsewhere (1:1, 3:11, 5:7 – in a vocative, 15:39), then this expression looks like one that came to Mark through the tradition.

If the Semitic expression was used at Jesus' examination in a way that the Greek reflects, then the priest is speaking of God with great respect as he introduces the question, a point that adds solemnity to its import. Now what is also important in the *1 Enoch* 77:2 text is that it appears next to a parallel reference to "the Most High," showing that Jews could pile up titles or solemn ideas in proximity to one another when discussing a significant figure. This point is important for the later consideration of the proximity of titles in the Mark 14 setting.

In the Mishnah, the reference to God as blessed comes, as was already noted, from Rabbi Ishmael (ca. 120 C.E.), who reports one of the congregational blessings to be, "Bless you the Lord who is to be blessed." Here the expression is adjectival, a reading that also could be applied to the Marcan text as an alternative way to translate what the Semitic could have been behind the text of Mark. So, although the exact phrase "Son of the blessed One" is not attested, all of the elements for it are present and parallels of this type of expression do exist in Judaism, such as the expression "Son of the Most High" in 4QpsDanA^a shows.[105] In responding to Juel's claim that

---

[105] For a recent discussion of this Qumran text, see Émile Puech, "Fragment d'une Apocalypse en Araméen (4Q246=Pseudo-Dand) et le 'Royaume de Dieu'," *RB* 99 (1992): 98–131. For discussion of its significance for NT studies, see Fitzmyer, "Contribution of Qumran Aramaic to the Study of the New Testament," 382–401; and his article "4Q246: The 'Son of God' Document from Qumran," *Bib* 74 (1993): 153–74; as well as Evans (*Jesus*

this is a "pseudo-Jewish" expression, Marcus cautions, "The fragmentary nature of our sources for first-century Judaism, however, casts doubt on the appropriateness of the prefix 'pseudo-.'"[106] Even the fragmentary sources show a series of examples that are quite similar to what we have in Mark. Although all of this falls short of clear proof that the expression itself is ultimately rooted in Jesus and the trial, it does suggest that what we have is more likely to have come to Mark through the tradition than to have been his own creative expression. So one can ask, is there more evidence from the context that might tip the balance even further?

When it comes to the reference to power, things are a little clearer.[107] *1 Enoch* 62:7 has a figurative reference to power, though not as a name, when it says, "For the Son of Man was concealed from the beginning, and the Most High One preserved him in the presence of his power." The expression itself appears throughout the Jewish tradition in *Sipre Num.* 112 [on 15:31], where Rabbi Ishmael (ca. 120 C.E.) refers to the mouth of "the Power" (הגבורה). Similar are references to "from the mouth of the Power" in *b. Jer.* 54b (מפי הגבורה, 2x); *b. Yebam.* 105b (מפי הגבורה); and *Tg. Job* 5:8 and its reference to "from the Power [תקיפא]." The two talmudic texts describe how Moses received the Law from the Almighty. Similar is *b. Šabb.* 88b, where the giving of the Law to Moses meant "every single word that went forth from the mouth of the Almighty (מפי הגבורה) was split up into seventy languages." In *b. Meg.* 31b, Rabbi Abaye (ca. 335 C.E.) notes that the curses in Leviticus need to be read one verse at a time because "Moses uttered them from the mouth of the Almighty" (מפי הגבורה). We will see below that this theme appears in other texts as well and is tied to the prohibition to idolatry – an important connection for our topic. A variation on the phrase is "the Power that is above" in *Sipre Deut.* 319 [on 32:18], while "from the mouth of the Power" appears again in *ʾAbot R. Nat.* [A] 37:12. An alternate text to *Sipre Deut.* 9 on Deut 1:9 says, "Moses said to Israel, 'I did not speak to you on my own, but out of the mouth

---

and His Contemporaries, 107–11), who rightly defends a probable messianic reading for this text, noting parallels between it, Isa 10:20–11:16, and Ps 89:27–28[26–27] against Fitzmyer's nonmessianic reading. This messianic reading is argued in detail by Zimmermann, *Messianische Texte aus Qumran*, 128–70. He sees a link between the Son of Man of Dan 7 and the use of this title here. This text has been alternately numbered 4Q246 and 4Q243 (how Fitzmyer numbered the text in 1974). The recognized designation now is 4Q246.

[106] Joel Marcus, "Mark 14:61: 'Are You the Messiah-Son-of-God?'," *NovT* 31 (1989): 127, n. 6.

[107] For brief discussions of these texts, see Arthur Marmorstein, *The Names and Attributes of God* (vol. 1 of *The Old Rabbinic Doctrine of God*; 2 vols.; Jews' College Publications 10 and 14; London: Oxford University Press, 1927–37), 82; Dalman, *Die Worte Jesu*, 164–65; Str-B 1:1006–7; 2:308.

of the Almighty.'" *Mekilta* also has several examples invoking Moses.[108] *Mek. Beshallah* 2 (26a) on Exod 14:2 has Moses report on the freedom of the Israelites that came from "the mouth of the Almighty" (מפי הגבורה). *Mek. Amalek* 4 (59b) on Exod 18:19 calls Moses to seek counsel "with the Power" (בגבורה). *Mek. Ba'odesh* 9 (71a) on Exod 20:18 has Ishmael (ca. 120 C. E.) report the words of Akiba (ca. 120 C. E.) that speak of the people hearing the fiery word coming out of the "mouth of the Power" (מפי הגבורה). *Mek. Amalek* 1 on Exod 17:13 (54b) has Rabbi Eleazar (ca. 130 C. E.) speak of the war being by "the order of the Power" (מפי הגבורה). *Mek. Vayassa* 1 on Exod 15:22 has two references coming from Rabbi Eleazar that Moses got the command for the journey "from the mouth of the Almighty" (מפי הגבורה). Later in the same passage in the discussion on Exod 15:24, the remark is made that when Israelites spoke against Moses they were "speaking against the Almighty" (על הגבורה). Both refer to the time of the Exodus and God directing the journey. The term is especially suited to the authority of God and the events associated with the Exodus. This usage is well enough distributed to be seen as common, even though these texts are later than the time of Jesus.

In fact the *Sipre Num.* 112 text was noted in the discussion on blasphemy and is a significant text.[109] Here the reference to Moses comes through the teaching of Ishmael (ca. 120 C. E.). Idolatry associated with blasphemy is the topic. The act is seen as a violation of the first commandment, which "Moses had spoken from the mouth of the Almighty" (מפי הגבורה). Similar in force is *b. Mak.* 24a, where the command not to have other gods is said by R. Hamnuna (ca. 290 C. E.) to have come "from the mouth of the Almighty" (מפי הגבורה). Parallel to that is a reference in *b. Hor.* 8a, where Ishmael again is the source and again the word about idolatry is "I [am the Lord your God] and you shall not have [any other gods before me]," which was heard from the "mouth of the Almighty" (מפי הגבורה; the context makes it clear that idolatry is the topic). This phrase shows up consistently as an expression for the revelation to Moses and in a wide range of materials. The association of the term with the authority of God in establishing the nation and giving the

---

[108] The following *Mekilta* references are keyed to Lauterbach's English translation edition and the numbering system of Finkelstein. See Lauterbach, 26a on 1:190; 54b on 2:147; 59b on 2:182, and 71a on 2:266. For a discussion of this theme, see Ephraim E. Urbach, *The Sages, Their Concepts and Beliefs* (2 vols.; trans. Israel Abrahams; Jerusalem: Magnes, 1975), 80–96 and 722–24, esp. 84–86. On p. 86, he closes his survey with this remark, "Without doubt, this epithet corresponds to the term δύναμις that occurs also in Matthew xxvi 6. Jesus declares: 'Hereafter shall ye see the Son of Man sitting on the right hand of the *Gevûra-* (ἐκ δεξιῶν τῆς δυνάμεως).'" He notes that it is found by the end of the first century with this force.

[109] Karl G. Kuhn, *Sipre zu Numeri*, RT 2, vol. 3, p. 330, esp. n. 74, and the edition of Horowitz, p. 121, line 9.

Law is significant background information. It is a title associated with the salvific power and revelation of the one true God.

The expression is almost an idiom. *'Abot R. Nat.* 37 elaborates when it notes in comparing Moses and Aaron as recipients of God's revelation that "Moses heard the words from the mouth of the Almighty, while Aaron heard them from the mouth of Moses" (משה שמשה שמע מפי הגבורה ואהרן שמע מפי משה).[110] Thus, to invoke "the Power" is to speak of the God of the nation, who speaks with authority. The expression is so widely attested in the early midrashim that it has a good claim to early roots. The consistency of the usage shows that the expression is full of subtlety and significance. Jesus claims he will sit next to this Almighty One, serving beside the true God with full authority as his unique representative. To allude to a description of God that may have been associated with Moses, the Exodus, and the nation's origin surely makes the claim of Jesus even stronger – and more provocative. This kind of involved Jewish expression is unlikely to have its origin in the early church, particularly in a gospel that is written with Gentile concerns in mind.

All of this evidence shows that both expressions fit this setting exceedingly well (*contra* Anderson). One can speak of the exchange fitting the cultural context, being plausible as an expression of very nuanced Jewish ideas. The juxtaposition of the two expressions, echoing the solemnity of the scene, helps to suggest that the evidence for the less well-attested expression of the Blessed One is strengthened by the evidence for the "power" or "Almighty."

However, because the argument is not clear-cut, it is also important to consider what arguments exist for the likelihood that Mark did not create the wording of this exchange. First, as I just noted, Mark has no hesitation in using "Son of God." He does so at various key points, including possibly 1:1 (introduction), 3:11, 5:7, 15:39 (centurion). The middle two cases involve unclean spirits. Interestingly in 5:7, there is the complex expression "Jesus, Son of God, the Most High" (υἱὲ τοῦ θεοῦ τοῦ ὑψίστου). So the expression without a direct reference to God is unusual for Mark. As Kazmierski notes, to attribute its origin to Mark "would be strange in light of his redactional interest in the Hellenistic form of the confession of Sonship."[111] Though I would hesitate to characterize "Son of God" as a Hellenistic title in light of Qumran texts (such as 4QFlor 1:10–11) and the tighter interrelationship

---

[110] For the text, see Salomon Schechter, ed., *Aboth de Rabbi Nathan* (3rd ed.; Vienna: Lippe, 1887), 110. I thank Martin Hengel again for putting me on the trail of many of these texts both for blessing and for power.

[111] Carl R. Kazmierski, *Jesus, the Son of God: A Study of the Markan Tradition and Its Redaction by the Evangelist* (FB 33; Würzburg: Echter Verlag, 1979), 171. He prefers to argue that Mark got it from Jewish-Christian tradition.

between the various cultures, Kazmierski's point about Marcan preferred expressions is correct and speaks against Marcan creation.

Second, the very dissimilarity of the expression to Christian titles speaks for "Son of the Blessed One" as a non-Christian use, for it requires not only the use of the circumlocution but an appreciation by Mark's audience of the fact that it substitutes for "Son of God." His audience might not appreciate the subtlety of the indirect reference, regardless of whether "Son of God" should be read in messianic or in more exalted terms. In other words, the liturgical and respectful background of the term is not appreciated by a Gentile audience. Significantly, Matthew, writing for a Jewish audience, opts for the more direct "Son of God" here in 26:63, even doubling the reference by including before the question an oath to the "living God." This indicates that Mark is far less likely to have created the phrase. Not only was it not his style, it was a difficult expression for his audience.

Third, power is not a substitute for God elsewhere in the NT, despite the numerous uses of Ps 110:1 in these texts (Acts 2:34–35; Rom 8:34; Eph 1:20; Col 3:1; Heb 1:3, 13; 8:1; 10:12; 12:2). All of this points to the exceptional usage as being exactly that, exceptional, and not contrived. Something motivated Mark to write in this indirect style. Neither is it clear that the source would be a creative attempt to echo Jewish tradition perhaps through Jewish-Christian sources, because the evangelist Matthew, writing for that setting, lacks such a reference, though he does retain the reference to power in 26:64 (as does Luke 22:69). When these circumlocutions appear, the evangelists seem motivated by something present in their tradition that causes them to use them. The respect shown to God by the high priest in asking his key question in this sensitive trial setting and the reciprocal response by Jesus are very appropriate for this setting. It is a subtle, detailed touch that by its unique character likely points to authenticity at the root of the trial tradition.

3.3. The Use of Ps 110:1 and Dan 7:13

This topic and the next one are closely bound together. One could discuss them together, but the availability of these images from the Jewish scriptures is still a separate discussion from Jesus' use of the Son of Man title. So I will consider issues tied to the question of the apocalyptic Son of Man separately. First, I discuss the use of Ps 110:1, especially as it appears in Mark 12. Then I take up the question of Dan 7 and the debate over the Son of Man.

In considering authenticity issues associated with the use of Ps 110:1, our key text is Mark 12:35–37, because it sets the backdrop to the examination scene. In that passage, Jesus raised the question why David calls the Christ Lord, if he is supposed to be David's son.[112] If this passage raising the issue

---

[112] For a full treatment of Ps 110:1 and its suitability to this setting, see my discussion

of what Messiah should be called is authentic, then there is nothing unusual about its presence in the trial scene.

Now the major objection to the authenticity of this Mark 12 text and its use of Ps 110:1 is its alleged dependence on the LXX to make its argument. It is claimed that the wordplay involving the title "Lord" is only possible in the LXX, so this text must be a later christological reflection of the post-Easter, Hellenistic Christian community.[113] Ferdinand Hahn also rejects any attempt to suggest how this text may have been read in Hebrew or Aramaic had there been an attempt to avoid pronunciation of the divine name, a view Gustaf Dalman noted years ago.[114]

Two points need to be made here. First, one cannot exclude by mere declaration the possibility that the divine name was not pronounced in an oral setting. The evidence for this likelihood was considered above in the discussion of whether the blasphemy might have entailed pronunciation in the reading of the divine name.[115] There it was noted as possible but not certain that the divine name was not pronounced. The minute such a substitution was made, the ambiguity would exist in Aramaic (אמר מריא למראי). In Hebrew, a substitution revolving around the reuse of אדני is also a possibility.

Second, even if the substitution was *not* made, the problem that the Mark 12 text introduces remains, though with slightly less of an edge. The problem of the Mark 12 text is not that the divine title Lord is used but that David, an ancestor in a patriarchal society, calls a descendant his Lord.[116] This problem exists in the text in its Hebrew form as well. In the entire dispute over the later christological significance emerging from this text, it has been forgotten that the dilemma originally rotated around the honor that David gives to the proposed Messiah, who also is his descendant, a fact that is ironic in a culture that gives honor to the elder, not the younger. Thus it is quite possible that the text in an unaltered Semitic form could raise the dilemma that Jesus points out is present in the text. Why would David call his descendant Lord? These two considerations mean that Ps 110:1 could be used as a way of probing the authority of the Messiah from the perspective of the one to whom the royal promise, according to Jewish tradition, was given.[117] Nothing in this understanding or the tension it raises requires a post-Easter reading of this passage.

---

in Darrell L. Bock, *Luke* (2 vols.; Baker Exegetical Commentary on the New Testament 3a–b; Grand Rapids: Baker, 1994–96), 2:1630–41.

[113] This argument is clearly summarized by Hahn, *Christologische Hoheitstitel: ihre Geschichte im frühen Christentum*, 112–15.

[114] Dalman, *Die Worte Jesu*, 270.

[115] See the discussion above surrounding Byington's work and n. 51.

[116] Jesus' argument appears to assume that David is the speaker of the utterance.

[117] The one assumption that Jesus and his audience share about the psalm is that David is the speaker, a view that would fit the first-century setting. Given that the text is royal

But there is a final consideration as well that speaks for the authenticity of Jesus' use of Ps 110:1 in Mark 12. It is the very ambiguity and Jewishness of the way Jesus makes his point. The playing down of the Davidic sonship of the messianic figure is counter to the normal post-Easter emphasis, as Acts 2:30–36, 13:23–39; Rom 1:2–4; and Heb 1:3–14 show. Those who see a post-Easter creation must deal with this question: would the later, post-Easter community have expressed its conviction about Jesus as Lord in a way that is so ambiguous and that at the same time gives an impression that the long-established and quite traditional and widely used Son of David title is not really an important designation? The form of Jesus' query has long been noted to parallel the Jewish style of putting two remarks in opposition to one another. The point is not to deny one remark or the other but to relate them to each other.[118] Jesus is simply affirming that David's calling Messiah "Lord" is more important than his being called Son of David. The query, which is unanswered in the Mark 12 context, serves to underscore the Messiah's authority and the ancestor's respect for his anticipated great descendant. At a narrative level, the unanswered question looks for a resolution. The trial scene does that for Mark. The coming exaltation of the One to be crucified explains the passage, and the passage explains the significance of that exaltation.

Now this issue of Messiah's authority as an abstract theological topic is not a post-Easter question. It had been raised by the very nature of the Jerusalem events in which this dispute appears. An earlier query about Jesus' authority came after he cleansed the temple (Mark 11:27–33). Jesus' query here is an answer to the question the leadership posed to him earlier but with a critical and reflective edge. If David, the one who received the promise, responds to Messiah as Lord, how should others (including you leaders!) view him? Jesus does not make an identification of himself with Messiah in Mark 12 but merely sets forth the question theoretically and leaves the conclusions to his listeners, as Mark does for his readers. Would a post-Easter creation be so subtle? Here is a good example of what many of the essays in our collection have called the criteria of inherent ambiguity.

James Dunn in treating the Messiah issue and Jesus' self-understanding argues that Jesus rejected the messianic title and its linkage to the "long-hoped-for David's royal son" with a qualified no.[119] We prefer to argue that the reply is a qualified yes. The category of David's son is at work, but

---

and that Israel lacks a king in Jesus' time, it is also likely that the text would be seen as applying to a king in a restored monarchy, a restoration that could easily conjure up messianic implications.

[118] David Daube, *The New Testament and Rabbinic Judaism* (JLCRS 2; London: University of London, Athlone Press, 1956), 158–63.

[119] Dunn, *Jesus Remembered*, 652.

its role is not as central as others wish to make it. The messianic role Jesus undertakes is more comprehensive in its authority than the Davidic son category suggests. This scene is like Peter's confession at Caesarea Philippi in representing a reprioritizing of how Christ is seen. At Peter's declaration, Christ is affirmed as the better confession than prophet, but lacks the note of suffering it is to bear, so that silence for a time is urged.[120] With the query over Ps 110:1 here, Jesus points out that the Messiah is David's Son, but far more importantly he is David's (i.e., his ancestor's!) Lord, another qualified yes on the confession developing the authority Jesus saw in the role. In agreement with Dunn, I would argue that Jesus rejected the understanding of Christ as currently seen by many in Judaism, but in the end Jesus embraced the association once it was related to other realities of his divinely anointed call. The events of the final week were helping to reveal the fresh points of association. Where Dunn argues that the early church "emptied the title of its traditional content and filled it with new content provided by the law and the prophets and the psalms"[121] after Good Friday, I contend it was Jesus who started them on this road to reconfiguration by his acts as well as words like those present here. What gives the appearance that this creative work was from the early church was that Jesus did not push hard to express these points until the end of his ministry as he faced the events that he saw as disclosing what God was doing through him. So while Dunn sees little of value tied to Christ for getting to Jesus' self-understanding, I would contend it was a base from which he built in such a way as to be able to connect other titles and concepts to the idea. By using it as he did, Jesus avoided using the title too extensively (and thus enhancing the potential for misunderstanding its common use and his distinctive use might generate). He also hesitated to use it too early without clearer definition for his disciples as to prevent a similar kind of possible confusion. However, as we move into the decisive confrontation in Jerusalem, Jesus pushes such acts and remarks more to the fore as he fills out the portrait he sees himself representing.

In sum, the evidence of Mark 12:35–37 indicates that it is far more likely that Ps 110:1 goes back to a period when the issues surrounding Jesus' identity were surfacing than to roots in a community that was openly confessing him in the midst of dispute. For this likelihood is the very ambiguity of the presentation in the face of the common affirmation in the early church tradition that Jesus is the Christ, even to the point of naming him Jesus Christ. A later created statement likely would have been more direct and emphatic. As it stands, this saying's claims to authenticity are strong. This means that

---

[120] See in this volume the discussion in ch. 8, § 2.4.2.3.2.
[121] Dunn, *Jesus Remembered*, 653.

the roots of the well-attested NT use of Ps 110:1 go back, in all likelihood, to Jesus himself, and so this was a text he could use in his defense later, particularly if he contemplated a vindication by God for what was currently taking place. But to show that Ps 110:1 could be used by Jesus, or even was used by him on one occasion, does not indicate that it was used as shown in Mark 14:62. This requires consideration of the text to which Ps 110:1 is paired, Dan 7, along with some reflection on the Son of Man concept that also is present within the examination scene.

So I turn to Dan 7 as a way into the discussion about the Son of Man. The question of the possibility of Jesus' use of Dan 7:13–14 is closely tied to the issue of the apocalyptic Son of Man. This question is examined here in two steps. First we consider the conceptual parallels that indicate that, during the time of Jesus, speculation about an exalted figure like the Son of Man existed in Judaism. If this is the case, then it can be seriously questioned whether such reflection would have taken place only in a post- Easter context. Then we consider the issue of the apocalyptic Son of Man and Jesus by looking at the evidence of these sayings themselves, regardless of whether the evidence discussed in this section is deemed persuasive or not.[122]

It has been a hotly debated question whether one should speak of a Son of Man figure in Judaism, because (1) the expression in Dan 7 is not a title but a metaphor ("one like a son of man"), and (2) it was argued that there is no clear evidence in early Jewish texts that such a figure was ever the subject of intense Jewish speculation.[123] More recently the debate has been renewed in a more cautiously stated form. Whether there was *a* Son of Man concept might be debated, but there certainly was speculation about an exalted figure whose roots lie in Dan 7.[124]

The summary evidence involves a wide array of sources from Judaism of varying strength. For example, in 11QMelch 2:18, there is reference to the bearer of good tidings, who is "the messiah of the spirit of whom Dan[iel] spoke." Now, the allusion in the context is probably to Dan 9:25 because seven weeks are mentioned, but William Horbury notes that this text was often associated with Dan 2 and 7 in Jewish thinking, so the same figure may

---

[122] This two-tiered division of the discussion reflects the way the issue is carefully discussed by Brown, *The Death of the Messiah*, 509–15.

[123] Ragnar Leivestad, "Exit the Apocalyptic Son of Man," *NTS* 18 (1972): 243–67. His argument is that only *1 Enoch* gives potential early Jewish evidence for such a title, that it is too late to count, that a title is not certain in the Similitudes, and that a title is not present in Dan 7. One can certainly challenge Leivestad's view of the date of *1 Enoch*. Other points that he raises will be addressed shortly.

[124] John J. Collins, "The Son of Man in First-Century Judaism," *NTS* 38 (1992): 448–66; William Horbury, "The Messianic Associations of 'The Son of Man'," *JTS* 36 (1985): 34–55.

be in view.¹²⁵ In *Ezekiel the Tragedian*, a text where in a dream Moses gets to sit on God's throne, note that the throne of exaltation on which Moses sat was associated with the plural expression "thrones," language from Dan 7:9.

Other slightly later texts have even clearer points of contact. *1 Enoch* is filled with Son of Man references (46:2–4; 48:2; 62:5, 7, 9, 14; 63:11; 69:27, 29 [2x]; 70:1; 71:14, 17). His enthronement in 62:2–14 is clearly connected to Dan 7, with its reference to a seat on the "throne of glory."¹²⁶ *1 Enoch* 46:1 and 47:3 also seem to allude to Dan 7, as do 63:11; 69:27, 29. The three variations in the way "Son of Man" is referred to here do not alter the point that it is Dan 7 that is the point of departure for the imagery here.¹²⁷ *4 Ezra* 13 is another, later text that also reflects speculation about the figure of Daniel. A rabbinic dispute attributed to the late first century involves Akiba's claim that the "thrones" are reserved for David. It suggests an interesting regal, Dan 7 connection (*b. Ḥag.* 14a; *b. Sanh.* 38b).¹²⁸ Some have compared the Melchizedek figure to aspects of Son of Man speculation.¹²⁹ Finally, there is the image of the exalted figure in 4Q491, who also echoes themes of Dan 7.¹³⁰ The variety of passages indicates that Dan 7 imagery was a part of first-century Jewish eschatological and apocalyptic speculation, apart from the question of the presence of a defined Son of Man figure. This means that Dan 7 was a text that was present in the theologically reflective thinking of Judaism, and thus was quite available to Jesus once he started thinking in terms of eschatological vindication. There is nothing here that requires a post-Easter scenario. The moment Jesus contemplated the possibility of vindication of a divinely given authority, this text would become a prime candidate for consideration. Everything about Jesus' ministry and the essays up to this point show that Jesus had such an eschatological focus. Once he also contemplated official rejection, something he was used to experiencing by now, a theological means for expressing vindication likely would

---

¹²⁵ Horbury, "The Messianic Associations of 'The Son of Man'," 42. Among the texts he notes are *Num. Rab.* 13:14 on Num 7:13 and *Tanḥ.* (Buber) Gen, *Toledoth* 20, with the second text including a reference to Isa 52:7 as well.

¹²⁶ For issues tied to the dating of this material, see the discussion of Enoch tied to n. 64 above. It is probably a first-century text. On the differences between the Enoch imagery and Ps 110:1–Dan 7, see Hengel, *Studies in Early Christology*, 185–89; Enoch lacks explicit reference to the intimate right-hand imagery. However, it must be noted that Enoch's imagery otherwise is very close to these older texts. The issue in all of them is judging authority carried out as the exclusive representative of God from a heavenly throne. The throne and authority are associated directly with God.

¹²⁷ *Contra* Leivestad, "Exit the Apocalyptic Son of Man," 247–48.

¹²⁸ These talmudic texts were also discussed in Bock, *Blasphemy and Exaltation*, 145–54, under David with mention of *4 Ezra* in a separate subsection.

¹²⁹ Paul J. Kobelski, *Melchizedek and Melchiresa* (CBQMS 10; Washington, D.C.: Catholic Biblical Association of America, 1981), 136.

¹³⁰ Hengel, *Studies in Early Christology*, 202.

have been sought. So the availability of Dan 7 for reflection about the end, authority, and vindication seems clear enough. In fact, one can argue that the use of the title to point to vindication and authority lies closest to its explicit sense in Daniel.

Only two questions remain with regard to the use of these texts. (1) Did Jesus speak of himself as the apocalyptic Son of Man? (2) Is the kind of stitching together of Hebrew Bible allusions such as the combination in Mark 14:62 possible for Jesus? It is to those questions I now turn, but it must be said before considering them that there is nothing in the evidence about the use and availability of Ps 110:1 or Dan 7:13 that demands that the usage here be seen as post-Easter. When Perrin wrote arguing that Mark 14:62 reflected a Christian pesher tradition, he did not note any of the Jewish texts alluding to Dan 7 texts already cited, a collection of passages showing how alive these ideas were in first century Judaism.[131] Little has changed since Perrin wrote for many commentators of Mark, who think Mark has given us only a carefully crafted narrative that has historical verisimilitude. Boring says it like this, "However, such historical verisimilitude is almost incidental to Mark's purpose, and should not divert attention from the primary meaning at the Markan level of the text."[132] Boring sees this as Jesus' climactic words that he is the Christ, pointing to an affirmation of what he regards as a later Christian confession placed into Jesus' mouth, as Jesus definitively dissolves the messianic secret by his answer (although all the acts Jesus has performed in this last week have already done as much as the essays in our collection show). Later he says, "Thus the reason for Jesus' condemnation and death in Mark is not to be explained in political and juridicial terms, but is a matter of Markan Christology and discipleship."[133] The only question such views have is to question whether Jesus would have portrayed himself as the authoritative figure described in these texts, whether Mark would be interested in such questions and how such affirmations fit early Christian confession.[134] Boring's view argues that the fact that these remarks fit into

---

[131] Norman Perrin, "Mark XIV.62: The End Product of a Christian Pesher Tradition?" *NTS* 12 (1966): 150–55.

[132] Boring, *Mark*, 413.

[133] Boring, *Mark*, 414. It is important to note that Boring later argues Mark presents the blasphemy as "an affront to God, the temple, and the Torah, which qualified as blasphemy in Jewish eyes, and his declaring himself to be the Christ could be represented to Pilate as claiming to be king" (pp. 414–15), precisely the view I am defending Mark is interested in showing as historically tied to Jesus. Earlier he called the scene rooted in a historical core and historically plausible (p. 410). So why is one forced to choose between history and Christological confession here? Surely Jesus gave thought to who he was and why he was in this situation, including what in God's program could help to explain what he was doing.

[134] The respective answers to these questions for such views are: (1) that Jesus would not be so explicit or did not make such connections, (2) that Mark was not interested in

the church's confession and the confession sublimates everything under the idea of the Son of Man disqualifies the remark from being historical because that association is the work of the later church. But is it really clear that the Son of Man title is late so that one must choose between only one of three options: (1) the Christ confession, (2) the use of the Son of Man, or (3) the absence of either of these ideas with Jesus? This kind of either/or thinking really does not consider seriously the issue of whether there might be a real cause-effect between Jesus' teaching and the church's confession, as well as rejecting the option of a both-and linking at work here that could go back to Jesus. Our reading seeks to challenge such a one-sided reading of Mark, which does not take seriously the historical possibilities and connections raised by the ancient evidence. We have already argued the case for Jesus' use of Ps 110:1 above in discussing Mark 12:35–37, but what of the apocalyptic Son of Man?

3.4. Jesus and Apocalyptic Son of Man

The Son of Man title has been the object of intense debate for years and shows no signs of abating.[135] In this essay, we can only treat where the discussion stands and develop the points most relevant to our concern.

Numerous issues surround the discussion, including an intense debate over whether the expression is representative of a title (like the form of its consistent NT use) or is an idiom. If it is an idiom, then it has been argued that the meaning is either a circumlocution for "I" (Vermes) or an indirect expression with the force of "some person" (Fitzmyer).[136] It seems that, for most students of the problem today, a formal title, or at least a unified

---

such questions, and (3) that Mark was solely concerned with an affirmation of pastoral Christology for discipleship.

[135] Representative of a host of recent monographs since 1980 are A. J. B. Higgins, *The Son of Man in the Teaching of Jesus* (SNTSMS 39; Cambridge: Cambridge University Press, 1980); Seyoon Kim, *The "Son of Man" as the Son of God* (WUNT 30; Tübingen: Mohr Siebeck, 1983); Barnabas Lindars, *Jesus, Son of Man: A Fresh Examination of the Son of Man Sayings in the Gospels in the Light of Recent Research* (Grand Rapids: Eerdmans, 1983); Chrys C. Caragounis, *The Son of Man: Vision and Interpretation* (WUNT 38; Tübingen: Mohr Siebeck, 1986); Hampel, *Menschensohn und Historischer Jesus*; Anton Vögtle, *Die "Gretchenfrage" des Menschensohn-Problems: Bilanz und Perspektive* (QD 152; Freiburg im Breisgau: Herder, 1994); Delbert Burkett, *The Son of Man Debate: A History and Evaluation* (SNTSMS 107; Cambridge: Cambridge University Press, 1999).

[136] See my comments on this issue in a special excursus entitled "The Son of Man in Aramaic and Luke (5:24)," in Bock, *Luke*, 1:924–30; and in Darrell L. Bock, "The Son of Man in Luke 5:24," *BBR* 1 (1991): 109–21. For other arguments, see Géza Vermès, "The Use of בר נש / בר נשא in Jewish Aramaic," in *An Aramaic Approach to the Gospels and Acts* (3rd ed.; ed. Matthew Black; Oxford: Clarendon, 1967), 310–30; Joseph A. Fitzmyer, "Another View of the 'Son of Man' Debate," *JSNT* 4 (1979): 58–68; Joseph A. Fitzmyer, *A Wandering Aramean: Collected Aramaic Essays* (SBLMS 25; Missoula, Mont.: Scholars, 1979), 143–61.

Son of Man concept, did not yet exist in the early first century, and that Fitzmyer has more evidence available for his view on the idiom. It is the idiomatic element in the Aramaic expression and the lack of a fixed concept in Judaism that allow any "son of man" remark to be ambiguous unless it is tied to a specific passage or context. This means the term could be an effective vehicle as a cipher for Jesus that he could fill with content and also define as he used it. One can argue that Jesus used the term ambiguously initially and drew out its force as he continued to use it, eventually associating it with Dan 7.[137]

But as was shown above, it is one thing to say that the Son of Man figure was neither a unified term nor a clearly defined concept in Judaism and quite another to say that Dan 7 was not the object of reflection in that period. Even if a fixed portrait and title did not exist, the outlines of such a figure were emerging and were available for reflection and development.

So what is the evidence in the Gospels themselves concerning the apocalyptic Son of Man? The designation Son of Man appears 82 times in the Gospels and is a self-designation of Jesus in all but one case, where it reports a claim of Jesus (John 12:34).[138] When one sorts out the parallels, it looks as though 51 sayings are involved, of which 14 appear to come from Mark and 10 from the sayings source, Q.[139] Of the four uses outside the Gospels, only one (Act 7:56) has the full phrase with the definite article as it appears in the Gospels (Heb 2:6; Rev 1:13, 14:14). In other words, the term is very much one associated with Jesus' own speech. So in texts where the early church is clearly speaking, the term is rare, and the full form of the title almost never appears. The nature of its usage by Jesus and the oddity of the term as a Greek expression is the probable reason that the expression appears in this limited way. Other titles such as Son of God, Messiah, and Lord were more functional. Joachim Jeremias makes the following observation about the pattern of usage:

How did it come about that at a very early stage the community avoided the title ὁ υἱὸς τοῦ ἀνθρώπου because it was liable to be misunderstood, did not use it in a single confession, yet at the same time handed it down in the sayings of Jesus, in the synoptic gospels virtually as the only title used by Jesus of himself? How is it that the instances of it increase, but the usage is still strictly limited to the sayings of Jesus? There can only be one answer; the title was rooted in the tradition of the

---

[137] I have made this argument elsewhere already in Bock, "The Son of Man in Luke 5:24" and in Excursus 6, "The Son of Man in Aramaic and in Luke (5:24)" in Bock, *Luke*, 1:924–30.

[138] Mark 2:10 is sometimes seen as an editorial aside by Mark, but the syntax of the verse makes the case for this awkward and quite unlikely. The breakdown is 69 times in the Synoptics (Matt 30, Mark 14, Luke 25) and 13 times in John.

[139] Brown, *The Death of the Messiah*, 507.

sayings of Jesus right from the beginning; as a result, it was sacrosanct, and no-one dared to eliminate it.[140]

These factors make a good case for seeing the expression as having roots in Jesus' own use. But such observations only defend the general use of the term. What can be said about the apocalyptic Son of Man sayings in particular? Apocalyptic Son of Man sayings appeal to a role in the final rule for this figure or picture him as exercising judgment.

It is significant to note how well-attested the apocalyptic Son of Man is within the tradition:[141]

Markan texts:	Mark 8:38; 13:26; 14:62
Q texts:	Q 17:24 (Matt 24:27 = Luke 17:24); 17:26 (Matt 24:37 = Luke 17:26); 7:30 (Matt 24:39 = Luke 17:30); 12:8 (Matt 10:32 = Luke 12:8, though Matt 10:32 lacks the title)
Matthean texts:	Matt 10:23; 13:41; 19:28 (= Luke 22:30 lacks the title; this could be Q); 24:44; 25:31
Lukan texts:	Luke 17:22

What the list clearly shows is that the apocalyptic Son of Man shows up in every level of the Synoptic Gospel tradition. If the criterion of multiple attestation means anything or has any useful purpose, then the idea that Jesus spoke of himself in these terms should not be doubted. The text that a few of these sayings most naturally reflect is Dan 7:13–14 (triple tradition: Mark 13:26 = Matt 24:30 = Luke 21:27; Mark 14:62 = Matt 26:64 [though Luke 22:69 lacks an allusion to Dan 7]; M: Matt 13:41; Matt 19:28; Matt 25:31; Q: possibly Luke 12:8 [though the parallel in Matthew lacks the title, it does have a vindication-judgment setting]). Though the association with Dan 7 is less widely attested, it is the only named biblical text that supplies the elements for the texts that do treat vindication. Once the category of apocalyptic Son of Man is associated with Jesus, then a connection with Dan 7 cannot be very far away.

The idea that this expression was the sole product of the early church faces two significant questions that bring the early church view into doubt. (1) Why was this title so massively retrojected, seemingly being placed on Jesus' lips in an exclusive way unlike any other major title, such as "Lord," "Son of God," and "Messiah"? (2) If this title was fashioned by the early church and was created as the self-designation of Jesus, why has it left almost no trace in non-Gospel NT literature, also unlike the other titles?[142] All of this

---

[140] Joachim Jeremias, *New Testament Theology: The Proclamation of Jesus* (trans. John Bowden; New York: Scribner, 1971), 266. These variations may be a clue that oral tradition is at work as to the randomness of these uses.

[141] The following list is part of a longer discussion in Bock, *Luke*, 2:1171–72.

[142] These two penetrating questions are raised by Brown (*The Death of the Messiah*, 507). If the identification of Jesus with the apocalyptic Son of Man is not correct, one

makes it inherently much more likely that Jesus referred to himself as Son of Man in an apocalyptic sense than that the church was responsible for this identification. The evidence suggests that this text was a significant feature of his thinking by the end of his ministry, because most of the explicit references to Dan 7 appear as Jesus drew near to Jerusalem.

One other strand of evidence also makes a connection between king and Son of Man. The combination of Son of Man imagery and the imagery of a royal figure, the very combination appearing in Mark 14:62, also has traces in the NT and in Jewish tradition. In the NT the other such text is Mark 2:23–27, where the authority of David appears side by side with an appeal to the authority of the Son of Man, because the famous king is the prototype and justification for Jesus' exceptional activity with his disciples on the Sabbath.[143] In Judaism, it has been noted how the Danielic figure has elements of authority that other texts from the Jewish Scriptures attribute to the great expected king.[144] Bittner notes how the themes of rule, kingdom, and power reflect the presentation of a regal figure, not a prophetic figure: "Das Wortfeld von Herrschaft, Königtum, und Macht ist in der altorientalischen Königsvorstellung, wie sie sich in der davidischen Königstradition widerspiegelt, verwurzelt, hat aber mit Prophetenberufungen nichts zu tun."[145] He also notes that such authority, when it involves vindication or the subordination of the nations, points to the royal office (Mic 5:3–4; Zech 9:10; Pss 2, 89). When the issue of duration surfaces, it is kingship that is present (2 Sam 7:16, Isa 9:5 [6–7]). The description of the king as Son and the closeness of the Son of Man to God is paralleled most closely by the image of the king as son (2 Sam 7:14, Ps 2:6, Isa 9:5 [6–7]). As such, the parallels, all of which are a part of the Jewish Scripture and so were available to Jesus, suggest the possibility of making the association present in this text between Messiah and Son of Man. Thus, the old attempt to separate kingdom from Son of Man will not work.

Another challenge to the use of these two texts together comes from James Dunn.[146] Dunn argues that Ps 110:1 was not likely originally present.

---

can still defend the authenticity of the saying by appeal to a close, enigmatic use by Jesus, a view I discuss below in n. 154.

[143] This example is noted in Evans (*Jesus and His Contemporaries*, 452). One must be careful here. There is no direct reference to Daniel; only the title is present. Nonetheless, the issue of authority in a major area, the Law, leads one to see the usage as descriptive of a person with some form of judicial or discerning authority.

[144] Wolfgang Bittner, "Gott-Menschensohn-Davidsohn: Eine Untersuchung zur Traditionsgeschichte von Daniel 7,13f," *FZPhTh* 32 (1985): 357–64.

[145] Bittner, "Gott-Menschensohn-Davidsohn," 358. Bittner's quotation observes that sonship language is associated with kingship in the ancient Near East and in Israel is associated with the Davidic House, not with the prophetic office.

[146] Dunn, *Jesus Remembered*, 749–54.

So he sees Dan 7 as original, the early church adding awkwardly the Ps 110:1 reference and then Luke resimplifying the reference by dropping the Dan 7 allusion in this scene.[147] He goes on to suggest the possibility that Jesus did appeal to the representation in Dan 7 as a way of declaring his own vindication, a move that he sees just as possible for Jesus as the early church. This was then heard as a self-claim of Jesus. Each of these suggestions, though possible, seems unduly complicated. The tradition historical sequence requires three changes,[148] while the use of Dan 7 requires a move from a vague allusion to a more direct reference to Jesus. The key problem is that Dan 7 is never entirely absent from the citation, since the title that remains in Luke's version is from Dan 7, which by the time of the gospels would have been seen as an appeal to Dan 7. This retention of Son of Man does show Dan 7 is rooted deeply in the saying's tradition. This is reinforced by the fact that Son of Man is Jesus' key self-designation. I have already argued above that the use of Ps 110:1 also makes sense as a text Jesus used by the ambiguous way he appeals to it in Mark 12:35-37. So both texts are available to Jesus. In my view, the "at-the-right-hand" text points to near-term vindication, while Dan 7 points to long-term vindication. But then what of another key difference: why does Luke lack a reference to riding on the clouds that Mark and Matthew have? Luke's lack of a use of the coming on the clouds is simple to explain. To establish his point about divine vindication, Jesus' allusion to the right hand of God makes the key point. It is all that is required. Even harder to see is how a vague reference to the Son of Man would be seen as blasphemous, *unless* it was a reference to Jesus, not merely heard as such. Had Jesus merely desired to point to some vague future divine vindication outside of himself for his mission, he could have made such a point clearly enough. However, Jesus' own consistent use of Son of Man in the tradition is against such a vague association.

Although I am challenging Dunn's reading here, one other point needs to be made. Had Jesus used only one of these texts in his reply (arguing that Son of Man referred to Jesus), then either one of them by themselves could

---

[147] Dunn claims an awkward syntax because Son of Man is interrupted by the at the right hand reference. He sees this as pointing to an insertion and a shift from coming *to* the Ancient of Days to coming *from* him. Dunn fails to see that if one is going to combine these references and speak of judging the leaders one day, then the point of the clouds is not merely a vindication in exaltation, but a reception of authority that will one day be exercised on the earth. This point is correctly made by C.F.D. Moule, not as a finesse move as Dunn claims, but because it encapsulates a key point from Jesus, namely, that his vindication by God means that this Jewish examination is not the last, or even the key, examination about who Jesus is. Moule's point is in *The Origin of Christology* (Cambridge: Cambridge University Press, 1977), 18.

[148] The three fold sequence is no use of Ps 110, then Ps 110 added, and then Dan 7 removed.

have generated the leadership's charge of blasphemy. Ps 110:1 would have said Jesus had the right to share God's rule, presence, *and* glory in heaven, pointing in the direction of something Richard Bauckham has called monolotry.[149] Dan 7 argued that Jesus would execute a judgment against the leadership with an authority that used the imagery of a divine act in the riding of the clouds. So, although I am contending for the use of both texts, the case for core historicity only requires one of these texts to generate the central charge of blasphemy.

A look at the nature of the use of Dan 7 and Ps 110 suggests that both texts were passages Jesus was aware of and could have used. Each passage contributes to the argument Jesus made as presented in Mark in ways that do not require later christology. In terms of content, nothing in the use or argument from these passages prevents the allusions to them from having been made here. However, an argument from content alone does not make the full case.

A formal question remains. Is there evidence that Jesus may have combined texts from the Jewish Scriptures in a way like that found in this passage? Objection is often made that Jesus does not combine texts from the Scripture in the way Mark 14:62 does.[150] Yet two texts point to the potential of Jesus' conceptually linking texts together like this, side by side. In Mark 7:6–10 = Matt 15:4–9, Jesus ties together references to the honoring of parents and the honoring with lips (Isa 29:13; Exod 20:12 [Deut 5:16]; Exod 21:17 [Lev 20:9]) in a way that recalls Jewish midrashic reflection. The concepts of "honor" and "father and mother" appear here. In a second text, Matt 22:33–39 (like Mark 12:29–31), there is a linkage involving the concept of love (Deut 6:4–5, Lev 19:18), resulting in a text on the great commandments of love.[151] This kind of linkage was a very Jewish way to argue, rooted in the hermeneutical rules associated with Hillel. These texts touch on ethical themes often seen as reflective of Jesus' social emphases. Their form of presentation indicates that the style of linking two themes from the Scriptures together could be reflective of Jesus.[152] So, there is nothing in

---

[149] Richard Bauckham, *God Crucified: Monotheism and Christology in the New Testament* (Grand Rapids: Eerdmans, 1999), 13–16.

[150] So, for example, Hampel, *Menschensohn und Historischer Jesus*, 179–80. He argues that this form of the combination reflects the early church, as does discussion of a returning Son of Man. Against the second point, see above. In fact, this is probably the most common argument for inauthenticity. The claim is that the linkage of Ps 110:1 and Dan 7:13–14 reflects an early church midrashic teaching about Jesus.

[151] A similar teaching appears in the response of the scribe in Luke 10:25–29 to introduce the parable of the Good Samaritan, but the context is distinct enough that this may well reflect a distinct tradition, not a true parallel. See my discussion of the Lucan pericope in Bock, *Luke*, 2:1018–21.

[152] Another example is Luke 4:16–20, where Isa 61 and 58 are combined (but it is singly attested).

terms of content or form that prevents this kind of association of texts from reaching back to Jesus. In many cases the evidence that the expression goes back to him is stronger than that the church created it.

Because he has said it so clearly, I cite two of Raymond Brown's remarks about Mark 14:62.[153] One full citation involves one of his key observations as he assesses Perrin's claim that Mark 14:62 is Christian midrash, a common view paralleled by Hampel and Boring. The second citation comes from his conclusion on the Son of Man in Mark 14:

> First, if it seems quite likely that the Gospel picture is developed beyond any single OT or known intertestamental passage or expectation, and that this development probably took place through the interpretative combination of several passages, any affirmation that all this development *must have* come from early Christians and none of it from Jesus reflects one of the peculiar prejudices of modern scholarship. A Jesus who did not reflect on the OT and use the interpretative techniques of his time is an unrealistic projection who surely never existed. *The perception that OT passages were interpreted to give a christological insight does not date the process.* To prove that this could not have been done by Jesus, at least inchoatively, is surely no less difficult than to prove that it was done by him. Hidden behind the attribution to the early church is often the assumption that Jesus had no christology even by way of reading the Scriptures to discern in what anticipated way he fitted into God's plan. Can one really think that credible?

Later he concludes,

> Jesus could have spoken of the "Son of Man" as his understanding of his role in God's plan precisely when he was faced with hostile challenges reflecting the expectations of his contemporaries. Inevitably the Christian record would have crossed the *t*'s and dotted the *i*'s of the scriptural background of his words. Even though *all* of Mark 14:61–62 and par. is phrased in Christian language of the 60s (language *not* unrelated to issues of AD 30/33), there is reason to believe that in 14:62 we may be close to the mindset and style of Jesus himself.[154]

---

[153] Brown, *The Death of the Messiah*, 513–14, is the first citation, and the second appears on pp. 514–15. The emphasis in the citation is his.

[154] Brown (*The Death of the Messiah*, 515, n. 55) adds one more point for authenticity in this Marcan text. He notes that the phrase "you will see" is difficult and may favor authenticity, because "post factum, Christians producing such a statement might have been clearer." A variation on this kind of defense of authenticity, which I believe is less likely is advocated by Bruce Chilton, who suggests that Jesus taught about the Son of Man as an angel of advocacy in the divine court, who would defend and vindicate the accused because Jesus' mission represented the program of God. In this view, the Son of Man, though distinct from Jesus, is inseparably bound with his mission. Thus, at the trial, the remark would still reflect some authenticity and would still be seen by the leadership as a blasphemous rebuke of the leadership's rejection of Jesus' divinely directed announcement of God's program. The Synoptics transform this close association into a purely christological identity. See Bruce D. Chilton, "Son of Man: Human and Heavenly," in *The Four Gospels 1992: Festschrift Frans Neirynck* (3 vols.; ed. F. Van Segbroeck, et al.; BETL 100; Leuven: Leuven University Press, 1992), 1:203–18. This reading does defend the remark's essential historicity but construes its force differently. Such a view, though possible, seems

I agree and would like to push Brown's point. There is a far greater likelihood that this text, with all of its sensitivity to Jewish background, goes back to Jesus. One of those elements of sensitivity is present in the way the charge of blasphemy coheres with perceptions that would have belonged to the Jewish leadership, a point to which I now return as I examine one final argument against authenticity.

3.5. The Meaning and Relationship of the Titles

It has been claimed that the stacking up of titles, as in this text, is an argument against authenticity.[155] But on formal and conceptual grounds, this claim can be rejected as based on questionable logic, as well as understating the likelihood of a stack of titles appearing in certain contexts. I take these shortcomings one at a time. With respect to logic, in discussing the Son of Man, I noted that development is not the private domain of the early church and that combining allusions does not date when such combinations took place. Jesus was capable of formulating an association between Ps 110:1 and Dan 7:13. But this response only deals with the nature of Jesus' reply. What about the way the high priest forms his question with multiple titles? Is the stacking up of titles in his question necessarily artificial?

That the high priest would be concerned about Jesus as Messiah is natural, because a charge is being considered that the leadership feels makes Jesus a candidate to be taken to the Roman authorities. As also was noted, the temple incident and sayings might suggest that Jesus had associated himself with events tied to the return of the Messiah. The Son of Man title is Jesus'

---

to leave the issue of the person of Jesus understated and unanswered as the reply in effect becomes, "I am who I claimed, whoever that is, and God will vindicate me through his agent, showing this examination to be in grave error." Chilton argues that Jesus' appeal to the witness of heaven is like an appeal he engages in Mark 9:1, where the idiomatic phrase "to taste death" refers to the immortality of the witnesses Moses and Elijah, to whom Jesus appeals through an oath in the midst of the transfiguration scene. My problem with this view of Mark 9 is that, despite the important linguistic evidence for the possibility of an idiom, it is not clear that Moses was seen in Jewish tradition as one who was taken up while never experiencing death. See the dispute over this in the Moses discussion in Bock, *Blasphemy and Exaltation*, 133–37. For this view, see Bruce D. Chilton, "'Not to Taste Death': A Jewish, Christian and Gnostic Usage," in *Studia Biblica 1978, II: Papers on the Gospels, Sixth International Congress on Biblical Studies, Oxford, 3–7 April 1978* (E. A. Livingston; JSNTSup 2; Sheffield: JSOT Press, 1980), 29–36. For reasons I am arguing, I think a more direct, personally focused reply from Jesus is slightly more likely.

[155] As Donald Juel states about the Mark 14 combination, "The combination of allusions presumes a developed stage of reflection." This is similar to Perrin's midrashic argument in another form, only here titles, not texts are in view. See Donald Juel, *Messianic Exegesis: Christological Interpretation of the Old Testament in Early Christianity* (Philadelphia: Fortress, 1987), 146. As a result, many of the reasons for this view have been noted in the previous section above.

way to refer to himself, so both of these elements fit. The only potentially extraneous element is the allusion to the Son of the Blessed.

So what about the stacking up of titles? Is it artificial? It must be observed that on formal grounds it is not unusual in Judaism for titles to be piled on one another when one is emphasizing a point. I already noted in an earlier discussion that two names were given for God in *1 En.* 77:2, namely, "Most High" and "eternally Blessed." One can point to *1 En.* 48:2 with its reference to "the Lord of Spirits, the Before-time," a construction much like the one seen in Mark 14. Similar is *Pss. Sol.* 17:21 with its reference to "their king, the son of David." Of course, the outstanding biblical example of the piling up of names is Isa 9:6 [Eng.], and here also it is a royal figure being named. When this takes place, there is something solemn about what is being said. So there is nothing formally odd about the high priest's questioning Jesus and doing so with a combined set of titles that suggests the moment's seriousness.

Read in this light, it appears that the high priest is asking Jesus to confirm his messianic status. Now this point in the question has been challenged in the past because it is not a capital crime in Judaism to claim to be Messiah – that is, a messianic claim is not blasphemous.[156] The point that messianic confession is not inherently blasphemous is a correct one, as the examination of blasphemy within Judaism shows. But this objection makes an assumption about the sequence of questions that should be criticized. The incorrect assumption is that what the examination was seeking and what resulted from the examination were exactly the same thing. It assumes that Jesus' affirmative reply to the high priest's messianic question makes the blasphemous remark revolve around messiahship. But my contention is that this is not the relationship between the priest's question and Jesus' answer. The examination was about messiahship, so that a sociopolitical issue could be taken to Rome. The threat that Jesus represented to the people in the leadership's view, in a view much as 11QTemple 64:6–13 expresses, meant that he should be stopped and brought before Rome as a socio-political threat. If a messianic claim and danger could be proven, then Jesus could be taken to Rome. The leadership could have developed real concern about this threat when Jesus uttered the parable of the wicked tenants, which was clearly an attack on the leadership and suggested that Jesus was a "son," whose rejection would be vindicated by God.[157] The threat to Jewish leadership could be translated into a threat to Rome's leadership as well. Jesus

---

[156] See the remarks in Marcus, "Mark 14:61," 127–29.

[157] This is perceptively noted by Jack Dean Kingsbury, *The Christology of Mark's Gospel* (Philadelphia: Fortress, 1983), 118–19. On this parable, see Klyne Snodgrass, *The Parable of the Wicked Tenants: An Inquiry Into Parable Interpretation* (WUNT 27; Tübingen: Mohr Siebeck, 1983).

believed that he represented God and had authority from above. This could be represented as possessing a claim to independent authority, a risk to all current sociopolitical structures and a potential source of public instability. This is what the priest's question sought to determine.

But Jesus' reply responds to this messianic query *and yet does even more*. It represents a severe assault on the sensibilities of the Jewish leaders on two levels. First, the reply speaks of an exalted Jesus, who sees himself as too close to God in the leadership's view. Second, he makes claims as a ruler or judge who one day will render a verdict and/or experience a vindication against the very leadership that sees itself as appointed by God. In the first element of Jesus' affirmation, the leadership sees a dangerous claim to independent authority that they can take to Rome. In both aspects of Jesus' reply there is, in their view, cause for seeing the highest of religious offenses possible – namely, blasphemy. The high priest's ripping of his garments says as much (Num 14:6, Judg 11:35, 2 Sam 1:11, 1 Macc 2:14; *y. Mo'ed Qat.* 3.83b [= Neusner 3.7]; *b. Sanh.* 60a). What started out as an investigation about Messiah becomes more than that because of the way Ps 110:1 and Dan 7:13 are woven together. This does not mean that the messianic charge is wrong or even that it is "corrected." It means that Jesus defines who the Messiah is in terms of the totality of the authority he possesses. This figure is so close to God that he possesses authority even over the nation's highest religious authorities. That is Jesus' claim. It parallels the claim he made earlier in the parable, except that now God's vindication is to be carried out by and/or on behalf of the very person they are trying to condemn. Jesus claims total independence from the authorities of the day. He can be taken to Pilate.

This point has a corollary for those who try to argue that Mark's concern is strictly pastoral and not historical. In this narrative theological view, Jesus is a model in how to face charges of blasphemy for the early church, which is facing such charges.[158] Mark's pastoral lesson is that, in suffering as Jesus did, they follow his way and example. The point is true enough about Mark's pastoral goal, but in separating history and pastoral theology, the significance of the uniqueness of Jesus' reply about himself is understated. Jesus is an example in how he faces the charge, but the reply he gives applies uniquely to him and is not in its content an example to be followed. In fact, the reply explains the unique vindication that Jesus receives at God's right hand. Now the question begs, if Jesus is only an example in how he faces the charge of blasphemy and the scene is Mark's or the early church's creation, why create an exemplary reply that does

---

[158] Helen K. Bond, *Caiaphas: Friend of Rome and Judge of Jesus?* (Louisville: Westminster John Knox, 2004), 106–7.

not help Mark's members know how they should reply? The difference suggests that portraying Jesus as an example and making a point about historical christology are both addressed.

One final point needs attention. Recent scholarly debate has surfaced over whether the two titles in the phrase "Christ, Son of the Blessed [of God]" are synonymous and what their relationship is within Jesus' Son of Man reply. Some have argued the case that Son of the Blessed or Son of Man limits the Christ title or operates in a distinct way from it.[159] The difference may be summarized in four different options, two for the question and two for the reply: (1) Did the high priest ask about Jesus as the royal messiah (synonyms)? (2) Was he asking about a "Son of God"-type Messiah (second title restricts the first)? (3) Was Jesus replying in terms of public function, not making a titular confession (son of man as "this man")? (4) Was Jesus replying by using a title referring to the figure he preferred to highlight (Son of Man = apocalyptic Son of Man).

I contend that arguing for these differences in force is too subtle for the trial setting. Distinctions such as these would not be present in the original setting. To grasp this point, let us take each option one grouping at a time. It certainly would not be present in the question of the high priest. Although it is likely that Mark's readers, given subsequent events, could have raised important distinctions and implications from the terms and may even have read this scene as containing such implications in the titles (i.e., option 2), the original setting is unlikely to have been a confrontation with this level of distinction. The temple-Messiah connection, where the examination starts in the pericope, argues for an earthly figure as the issue, a royal messianic figure of some kind (option 1). And the Jewish use of the expression "Son of God," as in texts such as 4QFlor 1:10–11 with its connection to 2 Sam 7, does not suggest such a distinction for Son of God. What about the replies? With regard to the "Son of Man," the use of Dan 7 points attention immediately to the figure of that text (option 4) and suggests an additional

---

[159] Though the phrase "Christ, Son of the Blessed" is usually considered synonymous so that Jesus' reference to the Son of Man is seen as saying the same thing in a more precise way, recently various ways of arguing for a distinction have been presented. Marcus ("Mark 14:61," 125–41) prefers a sense of Messiah, that is, the Son of God type of Messiah. But there is no sense in the text that the high priest is pursuing a fresh line of questioning or that "Son of God" *to Jewish ears* would suggest an exalted, transcendent image in distinction to a royal one, unless something else in addition was said to show it was taken as such. Kingsbury (*The Christology of Mark's Gospel*, 118–23, 160–67) argues that "Son of God" is a confessional title, while "Son of Man" is a "public" title, showing what Jesus does rather than identifying who he is. So the priest asks who Jesus is, while Jesus replies what he will do as "this man" (= Son of Man). Marcus's distinction is designed to question the use of "Son of Man" as a title. But it is hard, given the allusion to Dan 7, not to see an identification with that figure as present in Jesus' remarks. In fact, the response makes an equation of that Son of Man figure with the Son of God figure about whom he is asked.

identification with the messianic figure about which the priest asks. Jesus' highlighting a vindication from heaven including judgment allows him to use what is his favorite self designation. In this event the high priest merely queried Jesus if he was the central figure of deliverance who was called to challenge Israel and lead her into a new era. Jesus answered positively but, beyond the question, also noted that God would vindicate him both now and in the future with a cloak of total heavenly authority. The Jewish leadership heard Jesus' claim of divine exaltation and vindication as blasphemy.

In sum, Jesus' reply is what led to his conviction on a blasphemy charge. This reply had sociopolitical elements in it, as well as a religious dimension that constituted blasphemy. None of the objections to the historicity of this scene have persuasive substance. Though one cannot prove absolutely that the dialogue goes back to Jesus and the high priest, the evidence makes it likely that the Marcan summary is reflective of what took place or is a reasonable representation of the fundamental conflict of views at this crucial examination. The scene has great historical plausibility, fitting the background that would apply to such a scene. Moreover, the scene possesses clear indications that make it far more likely that it goes back to the examination and not to Mark.

4. The Significance of Jesus' Examination by the Jewish Temple Authorities

The significance of this analysis can be summarized in two points. One summarizes what the background on blasphemy and exaltation bring to the event. The second focuses on what a historical reading of this event tells us about the historical Jesus. Because most of the details of these two points have been treated in the examination of historicity, I summarize the implications for significance.

4.1 *Implications for Method: Importance of Historical Background Work*

A careful study of the historical background of Jewish views on blasphemy and exaltation does help bring new light to a passage that stands near the center of the description of the final events of Jesus' life. In an era when literary study and various exclusively textual approaches to the Gospels are on the rise, it is important to recall that such studies cannot replace the need for careful work in the socio-cultural environment of these texts. Literary and formal studies can tell us much about the author and how he tells his story, but they often cannot answer the historical questions the text raises. To assume that they can without a careful philological and conceptual examination of the historical background risks making literary and formal studies roam into an area for which they are not equipped. In addition, to flee the discussion of history for a treatment of the text only on a narrative level is to bifurcate something the Gospels do not present themselves as being. They are not narrative only but also claim to present the tradition about Jesus so as to make him known. When it comes to history, the text must be placed in a broader context than mere form and literary analysis. Much recent study of Jesus has moved exclusively in a literary direction. There is much to be said for the study of the Gospels as a historical query and what these important and related disciplines can contribute to each other. There also is much that the sources can tell us about Jesus as a result.

Another problem has been that too much historical Jesus study has looked for historical parallels in the wrong milieu – a Hellenistic one. There will always be a need for detailed work in the Jewish environment in which these texts and the events associated with them operated.[160] Studies like these from the IBR Jesus Group show that there is room for careful historical work in the sources. In a time when there is renewed interest in the Jewish background of the Gospels, a study like this essay shows that there is still much to be gained by a careful pursuit of the roots to concepts in these historically significant texts. Some concepts give evidence of a wide distribution in the many sources that explain Judaism. Such distribution indicates that the ideas they possess may have ancient roots in Jewish belief. Both blasphemy and exaltation give evidence of such a wide distribution. Though both areas were debated and discussed, there are fundamental elements of belief that appear alongside the more disputed points.

I offer the following two conclusions about blasphemy and exaltation in Judaism and in the life of Jesus:[161]

First, blasphemy certainly included the use of the divine name in an inappropriate way (*m. Sanh.* 6.4, 7.5; Philo, *Moses* 2.203–6). This is blasphemy defined in its most narrow sense. Some suggest that the use of alternate names also constituted verbal blasphemy, though this was heavily debated (*m. Šeb.* 4:13; *b. Šeb.* 35a; *b. Sanh.* 55b–57a, 60a). Such alternate utterances did produce warnings. Unheeded warnings produced violations and possible full culpability. But there are also acts of blasphemy that might or might not include a narrow blasphemous utterance. Acts of idolatry and of arrogant disrespect for God or toward his chosen leaders were seen as blasphemous. Judgment, whether from God or through intermediate agents, was the appropriate response. Numerous examples fit in this category.

---

[160] This point has recently been emphatically made by James H. Charlesworth, *The Historical Jesus: An Essential Guide* (Nashville: Abingdon, 2008), 8–14.

[161] This summary covers texts that I discussed in *Blasphemy and Exaltation* so that the context for evaluating the scene of the trial is evident in its full range of evidence.

They include: Sisera (*Num. Rab.* 10.2), Goliath (Josephus, *Ant.* 6.183), Sennacherib (2 Kgs 18–19 = Isa 37:6, 23), Belshazzar (Josephus, *Ant.* 10.233, 242), Manasseh (*Sipre Num.* 112), and Titus (*b. Giṭ.* 56; *ʾAbot R. Nat.* 7[B]). Defaming the temple is also seen in such a light. Significant for this study is the view that comparing oneself or another person to God is blasphemous and is like the other arrogant acts condemned as an affront to God (Philo, *Dreams* 2.130–31 – of self claims; *Decalogue* 61–64 – of exalting the sun, moon, and stars).

Second, God's presence is unique and so glorious that only a few are contemplated as being able to approach him directly. Such figures are great luminaries of the past or anticipated luminaries of the future. Those who sit in his presence constitute an even smaller group. They are directed to do so by God and often sit for a short time.

Of the angels, only Gabriel is said to sit and that is merely as an escort to Enoch (*2 En.* 24). In fact, in general, angels do not sit before God. Even Michael, the great archangel, is never portrayed as seated before God. This honor, if it is considered to exist at all, is left to some made "in the image of God." In fact, Metatron-Enoch is punished when he sits in a way that allows him to be confused with God (*3 En.* 16).

The list of humans who sit is longer: Adam, Abel, Enoch, Abraham, Moses, David, Job, the Messiah, Enoch–Son of Man, and Enoch-Metatron. Some sit for a time merely to record revelation (Enoch: *Jub.* 4:20; *T. Ab.* 10–12; *2 En.* 24:1–3). Adam and Abraham sit as witnesses to the final judgment (*T. Ab.* 10–13), while Abel sits for a time and exercises an initial stage of judgment. Adam is returned to the position he had before the fall (*L. A. E.* 47:3; *Apoc. Mos.* 39:2–3 [= later version of *Life of Adam and Eve*; *OTP* 2:259]). Job argues that he will be restored to a heavenly seat of honor (*T. Job* 33). It is possibly a messianic seating that appears in 4Q491 1:13–17, though it is not certain (an honoring of the Teacher of Righteousness, the end-time prophet, or the Eschatological High Priest are other options). What is excluded is an angelic figure. David sits before God on Israel's throne in 4Q504 frag. 2 IV 6. Messiah sits on the right, with Abraham on the left in *Midr. Ps.* 18:29, while David sits by God in heaven according to Akiba (*b. Ḥag.* 14a; *b. Sanh.* 38b). None of these seatings in God's presence look like the full vice-regency that other Jewish texts suggest. Only a few texts describe a seating that suggests a significant sharing of authority with heaven.

More-exalted portraits appear with Moses (*Exagoge*, 68–89), but this dream scene looks to portray symbolically his Exodus ministry and is not eschatological. Enoch-Metatron is given extensive authority, only to have it removed when it appears that he has claimed to share power with God (*3 En.* 3–16). The unique picture in the Jewish material is Enoch–Son of

Man (*1 En.* 45:3, 46:1–3, 51:3, 61:8, 62:2–8, 70:2, 71:1–17). This figure appears to possess full eschatological power. But the portrait was not without controversy, because other traditions strongly counter this portrait, suggesting discomfort among some in Judaism with the extensive authority attributed to Enoch (*T. Ab.* B 11:3–8; *b. Sanh.* 38b, where reference is to Metatron, who is often associated with Enoch, as *3 En.* 4:2–3 with 16:1–5 show).

Some Jews seemed willing to consider the possibility of being seated next to God for a select few great figures and under very limited conditions. Except for perhaps the Enoch–Son of Man portrait, none of these images appears to portray a figure seated at God's right hand or sharing the merkabah throne at the same time God is seated there. To sit at God's right hand on the same throne, as opposed to sitting on a separate throne next to God or somewhere else in heaven, is a higher form of exaltation than merely sitting in heaven. This kind of explicit language never appears concerning any of these figures, although Akiba's remarks about David are close (*b. Ḥag.* 14a; *b. Sanh.* 38b). Other Jewish material challenges all such forms of exaltation (*3 En.* 3–16). In the exceptionally rare cases of those who get to go into God's presence, those who go there are divinely directed there. It is not a role one claims for oneself.

4.2. *Implications for the Historical Jesus from the Jewish Examination of Jesus*

Here I note four key implications.

First, the examination of Jesus was never intended as a Jewish capital trial. Rome was always the goal. Though we do not know the exact legal procedures for the time of Caiaphas, the discussion of capital authority and procedures for the period of Roman rule would have been an idealized discussion, since Jews did not possess this authority under the Romans. Rules recorded for the Mishnah over a century later may share an idealized quality as well. Nevertheless, the fact that a hearing and not a final, decisive capital trial was undertaken with Jesus might explain why the procedure of Jesus' examination looks so different from a capital trial as it is portrayed in the Mishnah. In fact, cases in which a figure is seen as a deceiver call for a quick and ultimately public procedure (*m. Sanh.* 11:3 [Danby = 11.4]; *t. Sanh.* 7.11, 10.11).

Second, numerous potential sources for the trial scene would have existed from people who were present to people who would have known what took place. Note that I do not mean only people who were present but also people who had access to those present. Among the candidates who could have been sources of information are Joseph of Arimathea, Nicodemus, Saul, and the very public polemic against Jewish Christians directed by Annas's family, a battle that ran for more than 30 years. Some could have been present such as Joseph and a beloved disciple mentioned as present who knew the high priest in John 18:15. Others had access to people who were present, such as Saul. Jesus' trial scene does not lack for sources, even though no disciples of Jesus were present in the examination room.

Third, Jesus' blasphemy operated at two levels. It is these findings that are so important for assessing the historical Jesus. (1) Jesus' claimed to possess comprehensive authority from God. Though Judaism might contemplate such a position for a few, the teacher from Galilee was not among the luminaries the Jewish leaders would have seen as a candidate. As a result, his remark would have been seen as a self-claim that was an affront to God. To claim to be able to share God's glory in a Jewish context would mean pointing to an exalted status that was even more than a prophet or any typical view of the Jewish Messiah. That is how the Jewish leadership would have seen the claim. What Jesus' statement means is that he saw his mission in terms of messianic kingdom work that also involved his inseparable association and intimacy with God. His coming vindication by God would indicate all of this. Ps 110:1 and Dan 7:13–14 taken together explain it. Jesus was Christ, Son of the Blessed One, and Son of Man in one package, and the right hand of God awaited him after his unjust death. That coming vindication and the position it reveals him to possess at God's right hand helps all to see and the church to explain who Jesus was and is. (2) Jesus also attacked the leadership by implicitly claiming to be their future judge and/or by claiming his vindication by God for the leadership's anticipated act. This would be seen by the Jewish leadership as a violation of Exod 22:27, where God's leaders are not to be cursed. A claim that their authority was nonexistent and that they would be accounted among the wicked is a total rejection of their authority. To the leadership, this was an affront to God, because they were, in their own view, God's established chosen leadership. Jesus' claim to possess comprehensive, independent authority would serve as the basis of taking Jesus before Rome on a sociopolitical charge, as well as constituting a religious offense of blasphemy that would be seen as worthy of the pursuit of the death penalty. In the leadership's view, the sociopolitical threat to the stability of the Jewish people was the underlying reason why this claim had to be dealt with so comprehensively. Jesus' reply, in his own view, simply grew out of the implications of who he saw himself to be.

Fourth, the scene as a summary of trial events has a strong claim to authenticity, a stronger claim than the alternative, that the scene was created by Mark or by the early church. This means that this examination is a core event for understanding the historical Jesus. It is a hub from which one can work backward to some degree into the significance of his prior ministry or forward into how these events were the catalyst for the more developed expressions and explanations of who Jesus was and is. These explanations are found in the works of the early church, the works of the apostolic testimony that is reflected in much of the rest of the NT, as well as in other works that clearly saw the implications of the unique claims Jesus made for himself.

The conflict between Jesus and the Jewish leadership two millennia ago was grounded in fundamentally different perceptions of who he was and the authority he possessed for what he was doing. Either he was a blasphemer or the agent of God destined for a unique exaltation / vindication. Either he was a deceiver of the people or the Son of the Blessed One. The claims Jesus apparently made were so significant and the following he gathered was so great that a judgment about him could not be avoided.

This essay has sought to understand how those who examined Jesus saw his claims in light of their legal and theological categories. Why did the leadership seek to deal decisively with Jesus? The checkered trail of history since these events, especially between Jews and Christians, requires that every effort be made to understand what caused a segment of Judaism's leadership to send Jesus to face capital examination by Rome's representative. Especially important is to consider what claims Jesus made that they saw as so disturbing. Every generation will surely assess these events afresh in light of new data and methods that may emerge, but it is important that these assessments appreciate how the issues were seen and framed at the time. A study of Jewish views of blasphemy and exaltation illumines the ways in which the Jewish leadership perceived Jesus' claims. They saw in Jesus' claim of exaltation an affront to God's unique honor and to their position as representatives of God's people. Jesus saw in his anticipated exaltation a vindication of his calling, ministry, and claims, so that one day he would be seen by all as Son of Man seated at God's right hand. In other words, the ancient sources and their cultural scripts reveal how blasphemy and exaltation clashed during this examination in ways that changed the course of history. I have argued that the case for the authenticity of this historic clash is strong.

Bibliography

Anderson, Hugh. *The Gospel of Mark*. NCB. London: Oliphants, 1976.

Ådna, Jostein. "Jesu Kritik am Tempel: Eine Untersuchung zum Verlauf und Sinn der sogenannten Tempelreinigung Jesu, Markus 11,15–17 und Parallelen." Ph.D. diss. Tübingen: Stavanger, 1993.

—. *Jesu Stellung zum Tempel: die Tempelaktion und das Tempelwort als Ausdruck seiner messianischen Sendung*. WUNT 2.119. Tübingen: Mohr Siebeck, 2000.

Bauckham, Richard. *God Crucified: Monotheism and Christology in the New Testament*. Grand Rapids: Eerdmans, 1999.

Bauer, Walter. *A Greek-English Lexicon of the New Testament and Other Early Christian Literature*. 3rd ed. Revised and edited by Frederick William Danker. Chicago: University of Chicago Press, 2000.

Beasley-Murray, George R. *Jesus and the Kingdom of God*. Grand Rapids: Eerdmans, 1986.

Betz, Otto. "Jesus and the Temple Scroll." Pages 75–103 in *Jesus and the Dead Sea Scrolls*. Edited by James H. Charlesworth. ABRL. New York: Doubleday, 1992.

–. "Probleme Des Prozesses Jesu." Pages 565–647 in *Aufstieg und Niedergang der römischen Welt: Geschichte und Kultur Roms im Spiegel der neueren Forschung*, Part 2, *Principat*, 25.1. Edited by Hildegard Temporini and Wolfgang Haase. Berlin: De Gruyter, 1982.

Bittner, Wolfgang. "Gott-Menschensohn-Davidsohn: Eine Untersuchung zur Traditionsgeschichte von Daniel 7,13 f." *FZPhTh* 32 (1985): 343–72.

Black, C. Clifton. *Mark: Images of an Apostolic Interpreter*. Studies on Personalities of the New Testament. Columbia: University of South Carolina Press, 1994.

Blinzler, Josef. *Der Prozeß Jesu*. 4th ed. Regensburg: Pustet, 1969.

Boccaccini, Gabriele, ed. *Enoch and the Messiah Son of Man: Revisiting the Book of Parables*. Grand Rapids: Eerdmans, 2007.

Bock, Darrell L. *Blasphemy and Exaltation in Judaism and the Final Examination of Jesus*. WUNT 2.106. Tübingen: Mohr Siebeck, 1998.

–. "Blasphemy and the Jewish Examination of Jesus." *BBR* 17 (2007): 53–114.

–. "Jewish Expressions in Mark 14.61–62 and the Authenticity of the Jewish Examination of Jesus." *JSHJ* 1 (2003): 147–59.

–. *Luke*. 2 vols. Baker Exegetical Commentary on the New Testament, 3a–b. Grand Rapids: Baker, 1994–96.

–. "The Son of Man in Luke 5:24." *BBR* 1 (1991): 109–21.

Bond, Helen K. *Caiaphas: Friend of Rome and Judge of Jesus?* Louisville: Westminster John Knox, 2004.

Boring, M. Eugene. *Mark*. NTL. Louisville: Westminster John Knox, 2006.

Borsch, Frederick Houk. "Mark XIV.62 and 1 Enoch LXII.5." *NTS* 14 (1968): 565–67.

Brown, Raymond E. *The Death of the Messiah*. 2 vols. ABRL. New York: Doubleday, 1994.

Bultmann, Rudolf. *The History of the Synoptic Tradition*. Translated by John Marsh. New York: Harper & Row, 1963.

Burkett, Delbert. *The Son of Man Debate: A History and Evaluation*. SNTSMS 107. Cambridge: Cambridge University Press, 1999.

Byington, Steven T. "יהוה and אדני." *Journal of Biblical Literature* 76 (1957): 58–59.

Caird, G. B. *New Testament Theology*. Edited by L. D. Hurst. Oxford: Clarendon Press, 1994.

Caragounis, Chrys C. *The Son of Man: Vision and Interpretation*. WUNT 38. Tübingen: Mohr Siebeck, 1986.

Carson, D. A., and Douglas J. Moo. *An Introduction to the New Testament*. 2nd ed. Grand Rapids: Zondervan, 2005.

Casey, Maurice. Review of Darrell L. Bock, *Blasphemy and Exaltation in Judaism and the Final Examination of Jesus*. *JTS* 52 (2001): 245–47.

Catchpole, David R. *The Trial of Jesus: A Study in the Gospels and Jewish Historiography from 1770 to the Present Day*. StPB, 18. Leiden: Brill, 1971.

Charlesworth, James H. *The Historical Jesus: An Essential Guide*. Nashville: Abingdon, 2008.
Chilton, Bruce D. "'Not to Taste Death': A Jewish, Christian and Gnostic Usage." Pages 29–36 in *Studia Biblica 1978, II: Papers on the Gospels, Sixth International Congress on Biblical Studies, Oxford, 3–7 April 1978*. E. A. Livingston. JSNTSup 2. Sheffield: JSOT Press, 1980.
–. "Son of Man: Human and Heavenly." Pages 203–18 in vol. 1 of *The Four Gospels 1992: Festschrift Frans Neirynck*. 3 vols. Edited by F. Van Segbroeck, C. M. Tuckett, G. Van Belle, and J. Verheyden. BETL 100. Leuven: Leuven University Press, 1992.
–. *The Temple of Jesus: His Sacrificial Program Within a Cultural History of Sacrifice*. University Park: Pennsylvania State University, 1992.
Collins, Adela Yarbro. "The Charge of Blasphemy in Mark 14.6." *JSNT* 26 (2004): 379–401.
Collins, John J. "The Son of Man in First-Century Judaism." *NTS* 38 (1992): 448–66.
Colpe, Carsten. "ὁ υἱὸς τοῦ ἀνθρώπου." Pages 400–477 in vol. 8 of *Theological Dictionary of the New Testament*. 10 vols. Edited by G. Kittel and Gerhard Friedrich. Translated by Geoffrey W. Bromiley. Grand Rapids: Eerdmans, 1964–76.
Cowley, A., ed. *Aramaic Papyri of the Fifth Century B. C.* Oxford: Clarendon, 1923.
Cranfield, C. E. B. *The Gospel According to Saint Mark*. CGTC. Cambridge: Cambridge University Press, 1959.
Dalman, Gustaf. *Die Worte Jesu*. 2nd ed. Darmstadt: Wissenschaftliche Buchgesellschaft, 1965.
Daube, David. *The New Testament and Rabbinic Judaism*. JLCRS 2. London: University of London, Athlone Press, 1956.
Davis, Philip. "Christology, Discipleship, and Self-Understanding in the Gospel of Mark." Pages 101–19 in *Self-Definition and Self-Discovery in Early Christianity: A Case of Shifting Horizons: Essays in Appreciation of Ben F. Meyer from His Former Students*. Edited by David J. Hawkin and Tom Robinson. Studies in the Bible and Early Christianity, 26. Lewiston: Edwin Mellen, 1990.
Dunn, James D. G. *Jesus Remembered*. Vol. 1 of *Christianity in the Making*. Grand Rapids: Eerdmans, 2003–.
–. *The Parting of the Ways: Between Christianity and Judaism and Their Significance for the Character of Christianity*. London: SCM, 2005.
Edwards, David Darnell. "Jesus and the Temple: A Historico-Theological Study of Temple Motifs in the Ministry of Jesus (Synoptic Gospels)." Ph.D. diss. Fort Worth: Southwestern Baptist Theological Seminary, 1992.
Elbogen, Ismar. *Der jüdische Gottesdienst in seiner geschichtlichen Entwicklung*. 3rd ed. 1931. Repr., Hildesheim: Olms, 1962.
Ellis, E. Earle. "Deity-Christology in Mark 14:58." Pages 192–203 in *Jesus of Nazareth: Lord and Christ: Essays on the Historical Jesus and New Testament Christology*. Edited by Joel P. Green and Max Turner. Grand Rapids: Eerdmans, 1994.
Emerton, John A. "The Origin of the Son of Man Imagery." *JTS* n. s. 9 (1958): 225–42.
Eskola, Timo. *Messiah and the Throne: Jewish Merkabah Mysticism and Early Christian Exaltation Discourse*. WUNT 2.142. Tübingen: Mohr Siebeck, 2001.
Evans, Craig A. *Jesus and His Contemporaries: Comparative Studies*. AGJU 25. Leiden: Brill, 1995.

Fitzmyer, Joseph A. "4Q246: The 'Son of God' Document from Qumran." *Bib* 74 (1993): 153–74.

—. "Another View of the 'Son of Man' Debate." *JSNT* 4 (1979): 58–68.

—. "Contribution of Qumran Aramaic to the Study of the New Testament." *NTS* 20 (1974): 382–407.

—. *A Wandering Aramean: Collected Aramaic Essays.* SBLMS 25. Missoula, Mont.: Scholars, 1979.

Funk, Robert W., Roy W. Hoover, and The Jesus Seminar. *The Five Gospels: The Search for the Authentic Words of Jesus.* New York: Macmillan, 1993.

Fusco, S. A. "Il dramma del Golgota, nei suoi aspetti processuali." *Rassegna Pugliese* 7 (1972): 4–30.

Glasson, Thomas Francis. "Reply to Caiaphas (Mark 14:62)." *NTS* 7 (1960): 88–93.

Gundry, Robert H. "Jesus' Supposed Blasphemy (Mark 14:61b–64)." *BBR* 18 (2008): 131–33.

—. *Mark: A Commentary on His Apology for the Cross.* Grand Rapids: Eerdmans, 1993.

—. *The Old is Better: New Testament Essays in Support of Traditional Interpretations.* WUNT 178. Tübingen: Mohr Siebeck, 2005.

Hahn, Ferdinand. *Christologische Hoheitstitel: Ihre Geschichte im frühen Christentum.* 5th ed. Göttingen: Vandenhoeck & Ruprecht, 1995.

Halperin, David J. "Crucifixion, the Nahum Pesher, and the Rabbinic Penalty of Strangulation." *JJS* 32 (1981): 32–46.

Hampel, Volker. *Menschensohn und historischer Jesus: ein Rätselwort als Schlüssel zum messianischen Selbstverständnis Jesu.* Neukirchen-Vluyn: Neukirchener Verlag, 1990.

Heinemann, Joseph. *Prayer in the Talmud: Forms and Patterns.* SJ 9. Berlin: de Gruyter, 1977.

Hengel, Martin. *Studies in Early Christology.* Edinburgh: T&T Clark, 1995.

—. *Studies in the Gospel of Mark.* Translated by John Bowden. Philadelphia: Fortress, 1985.

—. *Nachfolge und Charisma: Eine exegetisch-religionsgeschichtliche Studie zu Mt 8,21f. und Jesu Ruf in die Nachfolge.* BZNW 34. Berlin: de Gruyter, 1968.

Higgins, A. J. B. *The Son of Man in the Teaching of Jesus.* SNTSMS 39. Cambridge: Cambridge University Press, 1980.

Hooker, Morna D. *The Son of Man in Mark: A Study of the Background of the Term "Son of Man" and Its Use in St. Mark's Gospel.* London: SPCK, 1967.

Horbury, William. "The Messianic Associations of 'The Son of Man.'" *JTS* 36 (1985): 34–55.

Hurtado, Larry W. "Following Jesus in the Gospel of Mark – and Beyond." Pages 9–29 in *Patterns of Discipleship in the New Testament.* Edited by Richard N. Longenecker. Grand Rapids: Eerdmans, 1996.

Hurtado, Larry W. *Mark.* NIBCNT. Peabody, Mass.: Hendrickson, 1989.

Isaac, E. "1 (Ethiopic Apocalypse of) Enoch." Pages 5–89 in vol. 1 of *Old Testament Pseudepigrapha.* 2 vols. Edited by James H. Charlesworth. New York: Doubleday, 1983–85.

Jeremias, Joachim. *New Testament Theology: The Proclamation of Jesus.* Translated by John Bowden. New York: Scribner, 1971.

Juel, Donald. *Messiah and Temple: The Trial of Jesus in the Gospel of Mark*. SBLDS 31. Missoula, Mont.: Scholars, 1977.

—. *Messianic Exegesis: Christological Interpretation of the Old Testament in Early Christianity*. Philadelphia: Fortress, 1987.

Kazmierski, Carl R. *Jesus, the Son of God: A Study of the Markan Tradition and Its Redaction by the Evangelist*. FB, 33. Würzburg: Echter Verlag, 1979.

Kempthorne, Renatus. "Anti-Christian Tendency in Pre-Marcan Traditions of the Sanhedrin Trial." *TU* 126 (1982): 283–85.

Kim, Seyoon. *The "Son of Man" as the Son of God*. WUNT 30. Tübingen: Mohr Siebeck, 1983.

Kingsbury, Jack Dean. *The Christology of Mark's Gospel*. Philadelphia: Fortress, 1983.

Klauser, Theodor, ed. *Reallexikon für Antike und Christentum*. Stuttgart: Hiersemann, 1950–.

Knibb, Michael A. *The Ethiopic Book of Enoch: A New Edition in the Light of the Aramaic Dead Sea Fragments*. 2 vols. In collaboration with Edward Ullendorff. Oxford: Clarendon, 1978.

—. *The Qumran Community*. Cambridge Commentaries on Writings of the Jewish and Christian World, 200 BC to AD 200, 2. Cambridge: Cambridge University Press, 1987.

Kobelski, Paul J. *Melchizedek and Melchiresa*. CBQMS 10. Washington, D.C.: Catholic Biblical Association of America, 1981.

Koester, Helmut. *Ancient Christian Gospels: Their History and Development*. London: SCM; Philadelphia: Trinity, 1990.

Leivestad, Ragnar. "Exit the Apocalyptic Son of Man." *NTS* 18 (1972): 243–67.

Lietzmann, Hans. *Der Prozeß Jesu*. SPAW 14. Berlin: de Gruyter, 1931.

Lindars, Barnabas. *Jesus, Son of Man: A Fresh Examination of the Son of Man Sayings in the Gospels in the Light of Recent Research*. Grand Rapids: Eerdmans, 1983.

Linnemann, Eta. *Studien zur Passionsgeschichte*. FRLANT 102. Göttingen: Vandenhoeck & Ruprecht, 1970.

Lohse, Eduard. "Der Prozeß Jesu Christi." Pages 88–103 in *Die Einheit des Neuen Testaments: Exegetische Studien zur Theologie des Neuen Testaments*. Edited by Eduard Lohse. Göttingen: Vandenhoeck & Ruprecht, 1973.

Lyons, William John. "On the Life and Death of Joseph of Arimathea." *JSHJ* 2 (2004): 29–53.

Marcus, Joel. "Mark 14:61: 'Are You the Messiah-Son-of-God?'" *NovT* 31 (1989): 125–41.

—. *The Way of the Lord: Christological Exegesis of the Old Testament in the Gospel of Mark*. Louisville: Westminster John Knox, 1992.

Marmorstein, Arthur. *The Names and Attributes of God*. Vol. 1 of *The Old Rabbinic Doctrine of God*. 2 vols. Jews' College Publications 10 and 14. London: Oxford University Press, 1927–37.

Maurer, Christian, and Wilhelm Schneemelcher. "The Gospel of Peter." Pages 216–22 in vol. 1 of *New Testament Apocrypha*. Rev. ed. 2 vols. Edited by Wilhelm Schneemelcher and R. McL. Wilson. Louisville: Westminster John Knox, 1990–91.

Meier, John P. *The Roots of the Problem and the Person*. Vol. 1 of *A Marginal Jew: Rethinking the Historical Jesus*. ABRL. New York: Doubleday, 1991.

Moule, C. F. D. *The Origin of Christology.* Cambridge: Cambridge University Press, 1977.
Müller, Karlheinz. "Der Menschensohn im Danielzyklus." Pages 37–80 in *Jesus und der Menschensohn: für Anton Vögtle.* Edited by Rudolf Pesch and Rudolf Schnackenburg. Freiburg im Breisgau: Herder, 1975.
Neale, D. "Was Jesus a *Mesith*? Public Response to Jesus and His Ministry." *TynBul* 44 (1993): 89–101.
Neusner, Jacob, ed. *Talmud of the Land of Israel.* 25 vols. Atlanta: Scholars, 1998–99.
Oyen, Geert van, and Tom Shepherd, eds. *The Trial and Death of Jesus: Essays on the Passion Narrative in Mark.* CBET 45. Leuven: Peeters, 2006.
Pauly, A. F., ed. *Paulys Realencyclopädie der classischen Altertumswissenschaft.* 49 vols. New ed. Edited by Georg Wissowa. Munich: Druckenmüller, 1980.
Perrin, Norman. "Mark XIV.62: The End Product of a Christian Pesher Tradition?" *NTS* 12 (1966): 150–55.
–. *Rediscovering the Teaching of Jesus.* New York: Harper & Row, 1967.
Pesch, Rudolf. *Das Markusevangelium.* 2 vols. HTKNT 2. Freiburg im Breisgau: Herder, 1977.
Puech, Émile. "Fragment d'une Apocalypse en Araméen (4Q246=Pseudo-Dand) et le 'Royaume de Dieu.'" *RB* 99 (1992): 98–131.
Reinbold, Wolfgang. *Der älteste Bericht über den Tod Jesu: Literarische Analyse und historische Kritik der Passionsdarstellungen der Evangelien.* BZNW 69. Berlin: de Gruyter, 1994.
Sanders, E. P. *Jesus and Judaism.* Philadelphia: Fortress, 1985.
Schäfer, Peter, and Hans-Jürgen Becker, eds. *Synopse zum Talmud Yerushalmi: Band I/1–2.* Texte und Studien zum Antiken Judentum, 31. Tübingen: Mohr Siebeck, 1991.
Schechter, Salomon, ed. *Aboth de Rabbi Nathan.* 3rd ed. Vienna: Lippe, 1887.
Scheidweiler, Felix. "The Gospel of Nicodemus, Acts of Pilate and Christ's Descent Into Hell." Pages 501–36 in vol. 1 of *New Testament Apocrypha.* Rev. ed. 2 vols. Edited by Wilhelm Schneemelcher and R. McL. Wilson. Louisville: Westminster John Knox, 1990–91.
Schulz, Siegfried. "Maranatha und Kyrios Jesus." *ZNW* 53 (1962): 125–44.
Schwemer, Anna Maria. "Die Passion des Messias nach Markus und der Vorwurf des Antijudaismus." Pages 133–63 in *Der messianische Anspruch Jesu und die Anfänge der Christologie: Vier Studien.* By Martin Hengel and Anna Maria Schwemer. WUNT 2.138. Tübingen: Mohr Siebeck, 2001.
Sherwin-White, A. N. *Roman Society and Roman Law in the New Testament.* The Sarum Lectures, 1960–1961. Oxford: Clarendon, 1963.
Snodgrass, Klyne. *The Parable of the Wicked Tenants: An Inquiry Into Parable Interpretation.* WUNT 27. Tübingen: Mohr Siebeck, 1983.
Staerk, D. W. *Altjüdische liturgische Gebete.* Kleine Texte für Vorlesungen und Übungen 58. Berlin: de Gruyter, 1930.
Stanton, Graham N. "Jesus of Nazareth: A Magician and a False Prophet Who Deceived God's People?" Pages 164–80 in *Jesus of Nazareth: Lord and Christ: Essays on the Historical Jesus and New Testament Christology.* Edited by Joel P. Green and Max Turner. Grand Rapids: Eerdmans, 1994.

Stern, Menahem. *Greek and Latin Authors on Jews and Judaism: Edited with Introductions, Translations and Commentary*. 3 vols. Jerusalem: Israel Academy of Sciences and Humanities, 1976–81.

Strack, Hermann L., and Paul Billerbeck. *Kommentar zum Neuen Testament aus Talmud und Midrasch*. 6 vols. Munich: Beck, 1922–61.

Strobel, August. *Die Stunde der Wahrheit: Untersuchungen zum Strafverfahren gegen Jesus*. WUNT 21. Tübingen: Mohr Siebeck, 1980.

Strugnell, John. "Moses-Pseudepigrapha at Qumran: 4Q375, 4Q376, and Similar Works." Pages 221–56 in *Archaeology and History in the Dead Sea Scrolls: The New York University Conference in Memory of Yigael Yadin*. Edited by Lawrence H. Schiffman. JSPSup 8. Sheffield: Sheffield Academic Press, 1990.

Theissen, Gerd, and Winter, Dagmar. *The Quest for the Plausible Jesus: The Question of Criteria*. Translated by M. Eugene Boring. Louisville: Westminster John Knox, 2002.

Uhlig, Siebert. *Das Äthiopische Henochbuch*. Vol. 5.6 of *Jüdische Schriften aus hellenistisch-römischer Zeit*. Gütersloh: Gütersloher Verlagshaus, 1984.

Urbach, Ephraim E. *The Sages, Their Concepts and Beliefs*. 2 vols. Translated by Israel Abrahams. Jerusalem: Magnes, 1975.

Vermès, Géza. "The Use of נשא בר / בר נש in Jewish Aramaic." Pages 310–30 in *An Aramaic Approach to the Gospels and Acts*. 3rd ed. Edited by Matthew Black. Oxford: Clarendon, 1967.

Vögtle, Anton. *Die "Gretchenfrage" des Menschensohn-Problems: Bilanz und Perspektive*. QD, 152. Freiburg im Breisgau: Herder, 1994.

Wright, N. T. *Jesus and the Victory of God*. Vol. 2 of *Christian Origins and the Question of God*. Minneapolis: Fortress, 1996.

Zimmermann, Johannes. *Messianische Texte aus Qumran: königliche, priesterliche und prophetische Messiasvorstellungen in den Schriftfunden von Qumran*. WUNT 2.104. Tübingen: Mohr Siebeck, 1998.

–. "Messianische Vorstellungen in den Schriftfunden von Qumran." Ph.D. diss. Tübingen: Tübingen University, 1996.

Chapter 13

The Roman Examination and Crucifixion of Jesus: Their Historicity and Implications

ROBERT L. WEBB

1. Introduction

For people today, the crucifixion of Jesus is one of the more widely known events from ancient times. It has shaped Western thought, history, and culture in ways far to numerous to list. It has been explored from many directions, from history and theology to art and film. Given the vastness of the perspectives and literature on the subject, this essay must of necessity be narrow and focused if it is to make any contribution at all.

Most historical discussions of Jesus' crucifixion are an attempt to explain Jesus' death (i.e., "why was he executed?") or to apportion blame for Jesus' death (i.e., "who was responsible?"). In other words, the discussion proceeds from elements in Jesus' life as a means of exploring and explaining Jesus' death. In this essay, however, I proceed in the reverse. I examine the death of Jesus itself along with its manner and circumstances in order to explore their significance for understanding Jesus' life. In particular, the questions addressed in this essay are: (1) What can be established with greatest historical probability concerning the manner of Jesus' death? (2) How do we understand these elements within their historical and cultural context? (3) What are the historical implications of the manner of Jesus' death for understanding his life? While the narratives of Jesus' death include numerous details and events, many of these, while interesting, do not really have historical significance for understanding Jesus' earlier ministry. Furthermore, the historicity of some of these details are debated and cannot be corroborated with any probability using generally-accepted principles of historical method. Discussing whether they are historical or not produces little of value in terms of their contribution to understanding Jesus' life and ministry. Examples would include Barabbas being released, Simon of Cyrene carrying Jesus' cross, and various details associated with the crucifixion. Therefore, to address the question raised in this essay the focus of attention is upon the specific elements that have the greatest potential for addressing the question at hand:

– Jesus was executed by means of crucifixion;
– Jesus was executed at the direction of Rome's governor, Pontius Pilate;
– Jesus was executed for the charge of claiming to be "the king of the Jews."

These elements are explored in the order stated above – the reverse of the order of the events themselves. The reasons for this order are methodological. First, it allows for building a case based on that for which the most evidence exists (Jesus was executed by crucifixion) and thus is most sure historically to that for which less evidence exists. Second, it allows for developing a case in which the implications build upon each other. Jesus being executed by crucifixion has implications for understanding the role of Pontius Pilate in the matter, and the involvement of Pilate has implications for understanding the charge that was brought against Jesus. Building an understanding of the circumstances surrounding Jesus' death in this manner provides us with the material needed to consider their implications for understanding Jesus' life and ministry.

2. Jesus' Execution by Means of Crucifixion

We begin our study with the particular means by which Jesus was executed, not only because it is the most sure datum we have concerning this historical figure, but also because the use of this particular means of execution has significant implications for understanding other elements surrounding his death as well as his life and ministry. While this event is widely known among people today, for many it may fall in the popular equivalent of ancient myth or folk tale, rather than historical event.[1] Thus, I lay out the evidence in more detail than might normally be done, and I do so in order that the extent of the historical evidence might be fully appreciated.

---

[1] The results of an Ipsos Reid poll were released on April 16, 2006, indicating that a significant minority of people in North America (13% of Americans and 17% of Canadians) think that Jesus' crucifixion was faked. The report speculated that this may be as a result of Dan Brown's popular book, *The Da Vinci Code*. For a newspaper article based on the poll, see Janice Tibbets, "Many Canadians believe Da Vinci theory." Online: http://www.canada.com/nationalpost/news/story.html?id=f97e6516-8ffe-48f6-8d81-81a5f607e2de [cited 18 April 2006]. For the poll itself, see http://www.ipsos-na.com/news/pressrelease.cfm?id=3045 [cited 18 April 2006].

2.1. The Historicity of Jesus' Execution by Crucifixion

It is sometimes observed that our historical knowledge of ancient events is actually far more tenuous than we might first imagine. This is partially due to the limited quantity and nature of the evidence that has survived for us to use. Much ancient history must be based upon one or perhaps two sources, for that is all we have. By contrast, the ancient sources with reference to the death of Jesus are numerous and varied – not only that he was executed, but that the means of execution was crucifixion. We begin by laying out this ancient evidence before proceeding to explore its implications in light of the ancient Mediterranean world. This evidence will be laid out according to the approximate date of the sources, beginning with the earliest. The focus here is on the evidence that can be dated to within approximately 100 years of the event, and thus our cut-off point will be mid-second century. One point of interest concerning this particular event is that there are references to it in both early Christian literature as well as contemporaneous ancient non-Christian literature.

2.1.1. Early Christian references to Jesus' crucifixion

The earliest evidence for Jesus' crucifixion is found in a number of early Christian texts, and the earliest of these are the letters of Paul. Most references by Paul to the death of Jesus are without specific reference to its means, and their intent is to make assertions about the theological significance of his death (e. g., Rom 5:10). But Paul does make a number of specific references to crucifixion. The earliest of these are in his letter to the Galatians, which may be dated either 53–54 C.E. or as early as 49 C.E.[2] Thus the earliest extant references to Jesus' crucifixion are less than 25 years after the event. Paul's statements in Galatians include:[3]

---

[2] The dating of Galatians and the order of Paul's letters is a notoriously knotty problem in Pauline studies. The later date of 53–54 C.E. has Paul writing Galatians during what is known as his "third missionary journey," and thus 1 Thessalonians would be Paul's earliest letter. Whereas the earlier date of 49 C.E. has Paul writing Galatians after his "first missionary journey" and prior to the Jerusalem Council, and thus Galatians would be Paul's earliest letter. Whether 1 Thessalonians or Galatians is Paul's earliest letter is irrelevant to the matter at hand, for Paul does not mention crucifixion in the Thessalonian correspondence. Thus either way, Galatians is Paul's earliest reference to crucifixion. For support of the later date, see Hans Dieter Betz, *Galatians* (Hermeneia; Philadelphia: Fortress, 1979), 9–12; for support of the earlier date, see Richard N. Longenecker, *Galatians* (WBC 41; Dallas: Word, 1990), lxii–lxxxviii; for more detailed discussion of the issues, see Robert Jewett, *Dating Paul's Life* (Philadelphia: Fortress, 1979); Loveday C. A. Alexander, "Chronology of Paul," in *Dictionary of Paul and His Letters* (ed. Gerald F. Hawthorne, et al.; Downers Grove, IL: InterVarsity, 1993), 115–23; Hans Dieter Betz, "Paul," in *The Anchor Bible Dictionary*, vol. 5 (ed. David N. Freedman; New York: Doubleday, 1992), 186–201, esp. 190–92.

[3] Unless otherwise indicated, all biblical translations are taken from the NRSV.

> You foolish Galatians! Who has bewitched you? It was before your eyes that Jesus Christ was publicly exhibited as crucified (ἐσταυρωμένος)! (Gal 3:1)

> But my friends, why am I still being persecuted if I am still preaching circumcision? In that case the offense of the cross (τὸ σκάνδαλον τοῦ σταυροῦ) has been removed. (Gal 5:11)

> It is those who want to make a good showing in the flesh that try to compel you to be circumcised – only that they may not be persecuted for the cross (σταυρῷ) of Christ ... May I never boast of anything except the cross (σταυρῷ) of our Lord Jesus Christ, by which the world has been crucified (ἐσταύρωται) to me, and I to the world. (Gal 6:12, 14)[4]

In these Galatian texts, Paul's references to Jesus' death are part of his proclamation of the gospel, and he includes in this proclamation that Jesus' death was by means of crucifixion (3:1). His crucifixion was perceived as offensive (5:11), and it was a reason for persecuting those who were his followers (6:12). For Paul, however, while crucifixion was apparently a difficulty for those to whom he proclaimed his gospel, he considered it integral to the gospel, so much so that it led to something of an "in-your-face" boasting in the cross (6:14).

Similar references to Jesus' crucifixion are made by Paul in his Corinthian correspondence, which may be dated to the mid-50s C. E.:

> For Christ did not send me to baptize but to proclaim the gospel, and not with eloquent wisdom, so that the cross (σταυρός) of Christ might not be emptied of its power. For the message about the cross (σταυροῦ) is foolishness to those who are perishing, but to us who are being saved it is the power of God. (1 Cor 1:17–18)

> For the Jews demand signs and Greeks desire wisdom, but we proclaim Christ crucified (ἐσταυρωμένον), a stumbling block to Jews and foolishness to Gentiles. (1 Cor 1:22–23)

> When I came to you, brothers and sisters, I did not come proclaiming the mystery of God to you in lofty words of wisdom. For I decided to know nothing among you except Jesus Christ, and him crucified (ἐσταυρωμένον). (1 Cor 2:1–2)[5]

In these texts the offense of the cross noted in Galatians is clarified, for the proclamation of "Christ crucified" is problematic for Paul's audience, whether it be Jews or Gentiles – to the former "a stumbling block" and to the latter "foolishness" (1:22–23). Paul evidently felt the temptation to give

---

[4] In Gal 6:14 Paul refers to the cross of Christ as an event in which he "boasts," but then moves from this allusion to the past event to using the language of crucifixion to describe the present transformation brought about through Christian faith. Elsewhere in Galatians Paul also uses the language of cross/crucifixion to affirm matters of Christian theology rather than past historical event; see not only Gal 6:14b but also Gal 2:19; 5:24.

[5] Other Corinthian texts include 1 Cor 2:8; 2 Cor 13:4. Cf. 1 Cor 1:13 in which the language of cross/crucifixion is used rhetorically without reference to Jesus' death.

his audience what they wanted – something that sounded eloquent and wise (1:17; 2:1) – something that avoided mentioning Jesus' crucifixion. But within his theological framework the crucifixion was integral to the gospel. To downplay the crucifixion was to sap it of its power (1:17–18).

A slightly later text[6] is Paul's letter to the Philippians. What is significant about this reference is that, while we find it in one of Paul's later letters, it is citing an early Christian hymn (Phil 2:6–11).[7] If, as is likely that this is a piece of pre-Pauline tradition, then it could be argued that this text is in fact the earliest reference to Jesus' crucifixion. However, the specific line in this hymn that refers to crucifixion (v. 8c) is often understood to be a Pauline gloss,[8] and thus I have cited this text here in chronological order, according to the date of Paul's letter, rather than placing it earlier, according to an earlier date for the traditional material.

7a [Christ Jesus] ... emptied himself,
7b taking the form of a slave,
7c being born in human likeness.
7d And being found in human form,
8a he humbled himself
8b and became obedient to the point of death –
8c even death on a cross (σταυροῦ). (Phil 2:7–8)[9]

Whether v. 8c was part of an earlier, pre-Pauline hymn or was added by Paul, the clause "even death on a cross" needs to be understood within this hymn's context as it now stands. While it may not fit well from a hymnic perspective, nevertheless it contributes admirably to the rhetoric of the

---

[6] Dating Philippians is difficult due to the ambiguity over where Paul is imprisoned at the time of writing. If in Rome, then the letter can be dated to 60–62 C. E., but if one of Paul's other imprisonments, particularly the Caesarean imprisonment then it could be dated a little earlier, 57–59 C.E. For discussion see John T. Fitzgerald, "Philippians, Epistle to The," in *The Anchor Bible Dictionary*, vol. 5 (ed. David N. Freedman; New York: Doubleday, 1992), 322–23. For support of the earlier, Caesarean imprisonment, see Gerald F. Hawthorne, *Philippians* (WBC 43; Waco, TX: Word Books, 1983), xxxvi–xliv; for support of the later, Roman imprisonment, see Gordon D. Fee, *Paul's Letter to the Philippians* (NICNT; Grand Rapids: Eerdmans, 1995), 34–37. Robert Jewett (*Dating Paul's Life*, 103–4, 165) dates it even earlier to 55 C. E.

[7] Most scholars view most of Phil 2:6–11 as a pre-Pauline hymn. For a classic study of this text, see Ralph P. Martin, *Carmen Christi: Philippians 2:5–11 in Recent Interpretation and in the Setting of Early Christian Worship* (2 ed.; Grand Rapids: Eerdmans, 1983). Martin (43) states: "The verdict which sees the hymn as a separate composition, inserted into the epistolary prose of Paul's writing, commands almost universal assent in these days." See also the brief survey in Fitzgerald, "Philippians," 323–24. For a recent statement of the minority position against this view, see Fee, *Philippians*, 39–46, and for a more recent discussion of the majority position, see Peter T. O'Brien, *Commentary on Philippians* (NIGTC; Grand Rapids: Eerdmans, 1991), 186–202.

[8] See the discussions by the authors cited in n. 7.

[9] See also Phil 3:18. Other texts within the Pauline tradition that refer to Jesus' crucifixion include Eph 2:16; Col 1:20; 2:14.

point that Paul is making in citing the hymn, and could even be considered the rhetorical climax of its first half.[10] His death by means of crucifixion exemplifies not only Jesus' humility but also the lowliness of having "taken the form of a slave."[11]

The next ancient source to consider that makes reference to Jesus' death by crucifixion is the *Sayings Gospel* Q. Whether Q should be dated as earlier than Paul's letter to Galatians (i.e., the 40s C.E.) or perhaps contemporaneous with the later date for Philippians (i.e., early 60s C.E.) is a matter of debate. This issue is further complicated by the hypothesis that Q may have been a composite document with later material being added to earlier material. This debate is far beyond the confines of this essay. Thus I will be conservative and place Q just after the Pauline traditions – probably early-to mid-60s – though it could be argued that certain specific traditions are much earlier, and thus I note that this Q tradition could be from the 40s or 50s.[12]

It is an often-stated truism that the *Sayings Gospel* Q does not contain a passion narrative. This is not surprising given the rather obvious fact that Q is a *sayings* Gospel and not a *narrative* Gospel.[13] This truism is sometimes stated in a way that implies that Q had no interest in the death of Jesus. But this is incorrect. Q is both aware of, and interested in, the death of Jesus. Several Q texts (Q 6:22–23; 7:31–35; 11:47–51; 13:34–35; 14:27)[14] deal with "persecution and death in a way that could readily have been applied to [Jesus'] demise."[15] Q 14:27 is the most relevant of these texts for our purposes here, due to its explicit reference to "cross."

---

[10] Fee, *Philippians*, 217.

[11] The relationship of humiliation and slavery to crucifixion is developed below in § 2.2.

[12] Gerd Theissen (*The Gospels in Context: Social and Political History in the Synoptic Tradition* [trans. Linda M. Maloney; Minneapolis: Fortress, 1991], 206–21) argues for an early date of shortly after 41 C.E. Similarly, Dale C. Allison (*The Jesus Tradition in Q* [Valley Forge, PA: Trinity Press International, 1997], 49–54) argues for the earliest stage of Q in the 30s, with the final form in the 40s or 50s. On the other hand, Paul Hoffmann ("The Redaction of Q and the Son of Man: A Preliminary Sketch," in *The Gospel Behind the Gospels: Current Studies on Q* [ed. Ronald A. Piper; NovTSup 75; Leiden: E.J. Brill, 1995], 159–98) dates Q to near the end of the First Jewish Revolt, approximately 70 C.E. John S. Kloppenborg's view (*Excavating Q: The History and Setting of the Sayings Gospel* [Edinburgh: T & T Clark, 2000], 87) is to place the bulk of Q in the period of calm prior to the Revolt, in the late 50s to early 60s, though the final form may not have taken shape until just after 70 C.E. For a helpful discussion of the alternative views, see Kloppenborg, *Excavating Q*, 80–87.

[13] This distinction between a sayings Gospel and a narrative Gospel is a modern descriptive distinction used to observe the difference in the content of different collections of Jesus material. But they are not mutually exclusive, for narrative Gospels contain sayings material, and Q, a sayings Gospel, does contain some narrative material.

[14] I follow the convention of citing Q texts by their Lukan reference; e.g., Q 3:16 = Matt 3:11 = Luke 3:16.

[15] David Seeley, "Blessings and Boundaries: Interpretations of Jesus' Death in Q," *Semeia* 55 (1991): 131.

ὅς οὐ λαμβάνει τὸν σταυρὸν αὐτοῦ καὶ ἀκολουθεῖ ὀπίσω μου, οὐ δύναται εἶναί μου μαθητής.

The one who does not take one's cross and follow after me cannot be my disciple. (Q 14:27)[16]

In this text a connection is made between the possible suffering and death of Jesus' followers with Jesus' own shameful death by crucifixion. This text implies that those responsible for the Q tradition knew of Jesus' death, knew that it was a death by crucifixion, and they considered this significant for understanding how they functioned as Jesus' disciples.[17]

A somewhat different form to that in the *Sayings Gospel Q* of this saying concerning the cross and discipleship is also found in the *Gospel of Thomas*, another sayings Gospel. The dating of this text is notoriously difficult, with scholarly proposals from mid-first century to late-second century, with the date of 140 C. E. often being cited, usually without evidence.[18] The complete

---

[16] This reconstruction of Q14:27 is slightly different from each of its later forms found in Matt 16:24 = Luke 14:27. The text and translation reproduced here is that produced by James M. Robinson, et al., *The Critical Edition of Q* (Hermeneia; Minneapolis: Fortress, 2000), 454. While a form of this saying is also found in Mark 8:34, there are sufficient Matthew / Luke parallels to support the view that this is a Mark / Q overlap and Matt 10:38 = Luke 14:27 should be considered a Q text.

[17] Cf. David Seeley ("Jesus' Death in Q," *NTS* 38 [1992]: 226) who states concerning the presence of σταυρός ("cross") in Q 14:27: "The term could hardly be cited without calling to mind Jesus' death. However uninterested members of the Q community (or communities) may have been in Jesus' death, it is difficult to believe that they were unaware he had suffered crucifixion." Arland J. Hultgren (*The Rise of Normative Christianity* [Minneapolis: Fortress, 1994], 31–41) goes so far as to argue that Q is aware of several elements that also are found in the passion narratives. He argues that Q 14:27 reveals knowledge of either Jesus or Simon of Cyrene carrying the cross. John S. Kloppenborg (*Excavating Q*, 369–70) however questions the specificity of this knowledge, but he does agree that "... Q14:27 would inevitably be interpreted with Jesus' death in view. More than this, the saying suggests that discipleship be seen as inextricably connected with the willingness to undergo the same shameful death as Jesus." Cf. also Seeley, "Blessings and Boundaries," 131–46. For a brief history of the interpretation of Jesus' death in Q, see Daniel A. Smith, *The Post-Mortem Vindication of Jesus in the Sayings Gospel Q* (LNTS 338; London: T&T Clark, 2006), 5–21.

[18] The date of 140 C. E. is frequently used, usually based upon the work of Grenfell and Hunt, the two scholars responsible for the original publication of the Greek papyrus fragment, P. Oxy. 1. But they actually propose 140 C. E. as the *terminus ad quem* (Bernard P. Grenfell and Arthur S. Hunt, *ΛΟΓΙΑ ΙΗΣΟΥ: Sayings of Our Lord from an Early Greek Papyrus* [London: Henry Frowde [for the Egypt Exploration Fund], 1897], 16), and argue for a compilation of the collection "... not later than the end of the first or the beginning of the second century ..." (p. 18). Francis T. Fallon and Ron Cameron ("The Gospel of Thomas: A Forschungsbericht and Analysis," in *ANRW*, vol. 2.25.6 [ed. H. Temporini and W. Haase; Berlin: Walter de Gruyter, 1988], 4224–25) complain that in later discussion Grenfell and Hunt's date of 140 C. E. "... is still repeatedly asserted in the literature today, without any evidence or argumentation." For surveys of recent research on the *Gospel of Thomas*, see Gregory J. Riley, "The Gospel of Thomas in Recent Research," *CurBS* 2 (1994): 227–52; Philip H. Sellew, "The Gospel of Thomas: Prospects for Future Research,"

text of the *Gospel of Thomas* is only extant in Coptic (part of the collection of predominantly Coptic texts discovered at Nag Hammadi), and this may be dated to the fourth century. But, the existence of Greek fragments (P. Oxy. 1, 654, and 655), which may be dated to approximately 200 C.E., indicate that the Coptic is probably translated from an earlier Greek text.[19] The linguistic evidence in the *Gospel of Thomas* has been variously interpreted. April DeConick, for example, has argued that numerous Semitisms point to the possibility of an Aramaic origin for at least some of the *Gospel of Thomas*. She proposes an early "Kernel Gospel" was composed in Aramaic, arising out of oral traditions gathered in Jerusalem from 30–50 C.E., which were subsequently taken to Syria where three sets of accretions were added between 30–50 C.E. and 120 C.E. (which helps to explain the Syriac influence).[20] This Kernel *Gospel of Thomas* is independent of the Synoptic Gospels, and the parallels with the Synoptics in the accretions material may be due to the influence of the oral performance of Synoptic material on the oral performance of Thomasine material.[21] Nicholas Perrin, on the other hand, has recently argued that this same linguistic evidence points to the *Gospel of Thomas* being originally composed in Syriac and was dependent upon Tatian's *Diatessaron* (written approximately 175 C.E.). Thus, according to Perrin's reconstruction, the *Gospel of Thomas* should be dated no earlier than around 180 C.E.[22] The issues are notoriously complex and

---

in *The Nag Hammadi Library After Fifty Years: Proceedings of the 1995 Society of Biblical Literature Commemoration* (ed. John D Turner and Anne McGuire; NHS 44; Leiden: Brill, 1997), 327–46.

[19] See the discussion by Helmut Koester (*Ancient Christian Gospels: Their History and Development* [Philadelphia: Trinity Press International, 1990], 75–77) and the literature he cites.

[20] See her discussion in April D. DeConick, *Recovering the Original* Gospel of Thomas*: A History of the Gospel and Its Growth* (LNTS 286; London: T&T Clark, 2005), and the summary charts (pp. 97–98 and 99–110).

[21] See the discussion in April D. DeConick, *The Original* Gospel of Thomas *in Translation: With a Commentary and New English Translation of the Complete Gospel* (LNTS 287; London: T&T Clark, 2006), 13–24. Also arguing for an early date for Thomas is Stephen J. Patterson, *The Gospel of Thomas and Jesus* (Foundations & Facets; Sonoma, CA: Polebridge Press, 1993), esp. 113–18. Patterson's forthcoming commentary on the *Gospel of Thomas* in the Hermeneia series will also be helpful on this issue. I thank him for his willingness to share with me a pre-publication section on the question of *Thomas*' date. See also the earlier discussion by Koester, *Ancient Christian Gospels*, 84–124.

[22] See Nicholas Perrin, *Thomas and Tatian: The Relationship Between the* Gospel of Thomas *and the* Diatessaron (SBLABib 5; Atlanta: Society of Biblical Literature, 2002); Nicholas Perrin, *Thomas, The Other Gospel* (Louisville: Westminster John Knox, 2007). DeConick has critiqued Perrin, for which see *Original Gospel of Thomas*, esp. 48–49. Perrin attempts a response in Nicholas Perrin, "The Aramaic Origins of the *Gospel of Thomas* – Revisited," in *Das Thomasevangelium: Entstehung – Rezeption – Theologie* (ed. Jörg Frey, et al.; BZNW 157; Berlin: De Gruyter, 2008), 50–59. Others have, of course, argued for the *Gospel of Thomas* being secondary and dependent upon the Synoptic

beyond the limits of this essay. While I find DeConick's approach slightly more convincing, I do not wish to use this controversial early date to support the case being built here, and so I grant that the final form of the *Gospel of Thomas* is relatively late (120/180 C.E., depending upon one's arguments), and only if one accepts some form of stratification as proposed by DeConick and others, then there is the possibility that certain sayings in the *Gospel of Thomas* may be earlier, with the earliest being from the 30s–40s C.E., with each saying needing to be evaluated individually.[23]

The relevant text is *Gos. Thom.* 55b, which is quite similar to the early Christian tradition also found in Q 14:27 discussed above:

ⲁⲩⲱ ⲛ̄ϥⲙⲉⲥⲧⲉ ⲛⲉϥⲥⲛⲏⲩ ⲙⲛ̄ ⲛⲉϥⲥⲱⲛⲉ ⲛ̄ϥϥⲉⲓ ⲙ̄ⲡⲉϥⲥ̄ⲧⲟⲥ ⲛ̄ⲧⲁϩⲉ ϥⲛⲁϣⲱⲡⲉ ⲁⲛ ⲉϥⲱ ⲛ̄ⲁⲝⲓⲟⲥ ⲛⲁⲉⲓ

And whoever does not hate his brothers and sisters and take up his cross in my way will not be worthy of me. (*Gos. Thom.* 55b)[24]

Knowledge of Jesus' death is also suggested by *Gos. Thom.* 12, 65, and possibly 56 as well. But the means of death is not mentioned, nor are any other historical details. The same conclusions made above can also be made here, namely that this text's author knew of Jesus' death by crucifixion. In DeConick's analysis, this saying forms part of the Kernel *Gospel of Thomas*, and thus it may be dated very early (30s–40s C.E.) and viewed as independent witness to the saying.[25] I will, however, grant that others will differ on the matter of this text's date, and so I am willing to date it according to *Gospel of Thomas*' final form (i.e., 120/180 C.E.) with a notation that the saying itself may be much earlier.

Other early Christian texts also specify that the death of Jesus was by crucifixion. These texts are probably later than Paul's letters and, depend-

---

Gospels. See for example, Christopher Tuckett, *Nag Hammadi and the Gospel Tradition: Synoptic Tradition in the Nag Hammadi Library* (SNTW; Edinburgh: T&T Clark, 1986), and Klyne R. Snodgrass, "The Gospel of Thomas: A Secondary Gospel," *SecCent* 7 (1989): 19–38. Also arguing in support of Perrin is Craig A. Evans, *Fabricating Jesus: How Modern Scholars Distort the Gospels* (Downers Grove, IL: InterVarsity, 2006), 52–77.

[23] DeConick does this in both *Original Gospel of Thomas*, and *Gospel of Thomas in Translation*. See this approach also in Reinhard Nordsieck, *Das Thomas-Evangelium: Einleitung – Zur Frage des historischen Jesus – Kommentierung aller 114 Logien* (3 ed.; Neukirchen-Vluyn: Neukirchener, 2006), and Uwe-Karsten Plisch, *The Gospel of Thomas: Original Text with Commentary* (trans. Gesine Schenke Robinson; Stuttgart: Deutsche Bibelgesellschaft, 2008).

[24] *Gospel of Thomas* 55 is not one of the sayings found in the Greek fragments of this Gospel. The translation reproduced here is that by Thomas O. Lambdin in James M. Robinson, ed., *The Nag Hammadi Library in English* (3d ed.; San Francisco: Harper and Row, 1988), 132.

[25] See her commentary on this logion in DeConick, *Gospel of Thomas in Translation*, 189–91; see also Nordsieck, *Das Thomas-Evangelium*, 223–27; Plisch, *Gospel of Thomas*, 138–39.

ing upon a number of factors, a variety of dates could be assigned to them in the range of mid-60s (especially Hebrews) to mid-90s (for Revelation), and 1 Peter may be dated to the 60s to the 80s depending upon one's view of authorship.[26]

... looking to Jesus the pioneer and perfecter of our faith, who for the sake of the joy that was set before him endured the cross (σταυρόν), disregarding its shame, and has taken his seat at the right hand of the throne of God. (Heb 12:2)[27]

He himself bore our sins in his body on the cross (ξύλον, lit. "tree"), so that, free from sins, we might live for righteousness; by his wounds you have been healed. (1 Pet 2:24)

... and their dead bodies will lie in the street of the great city that is prophetically called Sodom and Egypt, where also their Lord was crucified (ἐσταυρώθη). (Rev 11:8)

The significance of these texts is not that they add anything to our understanding per se, but rather that they are, once again, witnesses to Jesus' death by means of crucifixion – witnesses that are independent of the other early Christian sources already cited. It should also be noted that each of these texts is slightly different in its witness. Heb 12:2 alludes to crucifixion as a shameful death – a theme also noted in some of the earlier Christian texts above. 1 Pet 2:24 uses different terminology to refer to death by crucifixion. And Rev. 11:8 is concerned with the place where the crucifixion took place.

In contrast to the NT letters and the sayings Gospels, which only make reference to the datum of crucifixion itself, the narrative Gospels, as we would expect due to the nature of their literary genre, provide a narrative account of the crucifixion and a variety of events that accompanied it. A chart outlining 25 pericopae associated with the crucifixion narrative is provided in § 5: "Appendix A: Accounts of Jesus' Roman Examination and Crucifixion in Narrative Gospels" below. All five narrative Gospels (Matthew, Mark, Luke, John, and Peter) state in briefest terms that Jesus was crucified, and each Gospel provides additional descriptions of several accompanying events, including, for example, the location of Golgotha, the offer of wine mixed with myrrh, and the soldiers casting lots for his garments.

The dates of the first four of these narrative Gospel witnesses are widely discussed within scholarly literature. If one takes the commonly held view of the two-document hypothesis,[28] then commonly accepted dates for these witnesses would be to date Mark around 70 C.E., Matthew and

---

[26] For discussion of the issues, see appropriate critical commentaries and NT introductions.

[27] Hebrews 5:7–8 refers to Jesus death involving suffering, but it does not reference crucifixion specifically.

[28] See the brief discussion in ch. 2, § 4.1.

Luke in the 80s C.E., and John in the 90s C.E.[29] And the two-document hypothesis also leads to the conclusion that these are not all independent witnesses, for if Matthew and Luke are dependent upon Mark's account, then Matthew and Luke's accounts are secondary to Mark's testimony.[30] Matthew and Luke each have a few pericopae that do not draw upon Mark.[31] But most of these pericopae are not relevant to this investigation; for those that are, whether they indicate the availability of additional sources or redactional interests of the Gospel writers will be discussed at the appropriate place in this essay. Finally, whether John is an independent witness to the passion narrative or is dependent upon Mark is also an issue, with worthy advocates on both sides of it.[32] With respect to John's passion narrative, I conclude that it is probably independent of the Synoptics, for their differences are significant and difficult to explain if dependent, and the similarities may be equally explained as their common usage of widespread early Christian tradition.[33] Furthermore, the Fourth Gospel's

---

[29] For discussion see introductions and commentaries on the Gospels. A classic discussion may be found in Werner Georg Kümmel, *Introduction to the New Testament* (rev. ed.; trans. Howard Clark Kee; Nashville: Abingdon, 1975), and for a more recent discussion, see Paul J. Achtemeier, et al., *Introducing the New Testament: Its Literature and Theology* (Grand Rapids: Eerdmans, 2001). I realize that scholarly debates might want to tweak these dates a little. For example, whether Mark is pre-70 C.E. or post-70 C.E. is widely discussed. But for the purposes of argument here such nuancing is irrelevant. Some conservative scholars do argue for earlier dates, for which see, e.g., D.A. Carson, et al., *An Introduction to the New Testament* (Grand Rapids: Zondervan, 1992).

[30] It is debated whether or not Mark was dependent upon a pre-Markan passion narrative. In the context of the oral culture of early Christianity, it is likely that there were numerous different preached accounts or oral performances of Jesus' passion. For discussion, see how this is developed by James D.G. Dunn, *Jesus Remembered* (vol. 1 of *Christianity in the Making*; Grand Rapids: Eerdmans, 2003), 173–254, 765–69. Whether Mark used a pre-existing passion narrative is very difficult to determine with any confidence, and the reconstruction of such, if it did exist, is virtually impossible. See the judicious discussion by Raymond E. Brown, *The Death of the Messiah: From Gethsemane to the Grave: A Commentary on the Passion Narratives in the Four Gospels* (2 vols; ABRL; New York: Doubleday, 1994), 53–57. See also Marion L. Soards, "Appendix IX: The Question of a PreMarcan Passion Narrative," in *The Death of the Messiah: From Gethsemane to the Grave: A Commentary on the Passion Narratives in the Four Gospels* (2 vols; Raymond E. Brown; Anchor Bible Reference Library; New York: Doubleday, 1994), 1492–1524.

[31] Matthew reports Judas returning the blood money and committing suicide (27:7–10), Pilate washing his hands of Jesus (Matt 27:24–25), and the chief priests posting a guard at the tomb (27:62–66). Luke reports Herod Antipas also examining Jesus (23:6–12), Pilate declaring Jesus innocent to the chief priests (23:13–16), the women wailing and Jesus' response (23:27–32), and the crowd returning home beating their breasts (23:48).

[32] See the lists provided by Brown, *Death of the Messiah*, 84 n. 91, n. 92.

[33] For discussion see Brown, *Death of the Messiah*, 75–93. Classic statements of the independence of the Fourth Gospel may be found in C.H. Dodd, *Historical Tradition in the Fourth Gospel* (Cambridge: Cambridge University Press, 1965), and Raymond E. Brown, *The Gospel According to John* (AB 29; New York: Doubleday, 1966–70). A classic

passion narrative contains knowledge of independent traditions (e.g., the spear at the crucifixion, John 19:34). Thus, with reference to the canonical narrative Gospels, the net result is that we probably have two independent sources, Mark and John, with Mark being dated earlier, around 70 C.E., and John being dated later, probably in the 90s C.E., as well as a few additional traditions in Matthew and Luke.

With reference to Mark and John as independent witnesses to Jesus' death by crucifixion, we note the following texts in particular:

And they crucify (σταυροῦσιν) him ... (Mark 15:24a)[34]
There they crucified (ἐσταύρωσαν) him ... (John 18:18a)

The passion narratives are quite lengthy, contributing extensively to the length of each Gospel. And these passion narratives are quite theological in their reflections on the significance of Jesus' passion. It is interesting to observe just how sparse the narrative is precisely at this point. Given the prominence of the Jesus' cross in later Christian piety (whether theological or artistic), it is noteworthy just how brief are the accounts of the action of crucifixion itself.[35]

These same issues of date and sources are more problematic with respect to the extra-canonical narrative Gospel, the *Gospel of Peter*. This Gospel, mentioned a number of times by the early church fathers, was discovered in Akhmîm, Egypt in 1886–87 in fragmentary form, and another fragment was later discovered at Oxyrhynchus (P. Oxy. 2949). These fragments contain

---

statement of the Fourth Gospel's dependence on the Synoptics may be found in C. K. Barrett, *The Gospel According to St. John: An Introduction with Commentary and Notes on the Greek Text* (2 ed.; London: SPCK, 1978), and more recently, Andrew T. Lincoln, *The Gospel According to Saint John* (BNTC; London: Continuum, 2005). An alternative possibility proposed by some is that the Fourth Evangelist knew of Mark's Gospel, but did not draw upon it as a source, for which see J. N. Sanders and B. A. Mastin, *A Commentary on the Gospel According to St. John* (1968; repr., HNTC; Peabody, MA: Hendrickson, 1988).

[34] Mark's verb is in the present tense (lit. "and they crucify him ..."), and is translated that way here to point out the small difference between Mark and John. Most translations, however, translate this more idiomatically as a simple past ("and they crucified him"). This form of the present tense is sometimes called the "historical present," being frequently used in narrative texts (particularly Mark in the NT) to describe a past event. It may have been done to make the narrative particularly vivid and dramatic. For discussion of the historical present, see Daniel B. Wallace, *Greek Grammar Beyond the Basics: An Exegetical Syntax of the New Testament* (Grand Rapids: Zondervan, 1996), 526–32.

[35] John Dominic Crossan (*The Historical Jesus: The Life of a Mediterranean Jewish Peasant* [San Francisco: HarperSanFrancisco, 1991], 372) questions the historicity of much of the passion narratives, calling them "the historicization of prophecy." But the crucifixion itself he does acknowledge to be historical (pp. 372–91). For a critical review of Crossan's provocative thesis, see Craig A. Evans, "The Passion of Jesus: History Remembered or Prophecy Historicized?" *BBR* 6 (1996): 159–65; Mark Goodacre, "Scripturalization in Mark's Crucifixion Narrative," in *The Trial and Death of Jesus: Essays on the Passion in Mark* (ed. Geert van Oyen and Tom Shepherd; Leuven: Peeters, 2006), 33–47.

an account of Jesus' passion, from the end of his examination before Pilate to his resurrection.[36] At numerous points the account is similar to that in the other narrative Gospels, but at other points its account provides additional episodes and details that differ from those in the other Gospels. Since its discovery, the relationship of the *Gospel of Peter* to the other narrative Gospels has been a matter of considerable debate.[37] Since this text is not as widely known as the other narrative Gospels, it behooves us to consider it in more detail. The opening pericope of the extant fragment can provide an example of the issues involved:[38]

---

[36] For a description of this text and its discovery, see Wilhelm Schneemelcher, *Gospels and Related Writings* (vol. 1 of *New Testament Apocrypha*; trans. R. McL. Wilson; Louisville: Westminster John Knox, 1991), 216–18; James K. Elliott, *The Apocryphal New Testament: A Collection of Apocryphal Christian Literature in an English Translation* (Oxford: Oxford University Press, 1993), 150–54.

It has been debated recently whether the Akhmîm fragments should, in fact, be identified as part of the *Gospel of Peter*. See the discussion between Paul Foster, "Are There Any Early Fragments of the So-Called *Gospel of Peter*?" *NTS* 52 (2006): 1–28; Dieter Lührmann, "Kann es wirklich keine frühe Handschrift des Petrusevangeliums geben? Corrigenda zu einem Aufsatz von Paul Foster," *NovT* 48 (2006): 379–83; Paul Foster, "The Disputed Early Fragments of the So-Called *Gospel of Peter* – Once Again," *NovT* 49 (2007): 402–5. I will follow most scholars and call these fragments the *Gospel of Peter*. Whether this label is correct or not, is really secondary to the question of the traditions contained within the extant text, whatever we might call this text.

[37] For summaries of the debate, see Schneemelcher, *Gospels and Related Writings*, 218–20; Alan Kirk, "Examining Priorities: Another Look at the *Gospel of Peter*'s Relationship to the New Testament Gospels," *NTS* 40 (1994): 572–75.

Most recently, John Dominic Crossan has argued that a primitive stratum in the *Gospel of Peter*, the "Cross Gospel," predates the other narrative Gospels and is their source for the passion and resurrection narratives, first in John Dominic Crossan, *Four Other Gospels: Shadows on the Contours of Canon* (San Francisco: Harper & Row, 1985), 132–35, and then most extensively in John Dominic Crossan, *The Cross That Spoke: The Origins of the Passion Narrative* (San Francisco: Harper & Row, 1988). Similarly, Helmut Koester argued that the *Gospel of Peter* contained primitive traditions, pre-dating the canonical Gospels in Helmut Koester, "Apocryphal and Canonical Gospels," *HTR* 73 (1980): 105–30. He later expanded upon this in Koester, *Ancient Christian Gospels*, 213–38. It should be noted that Koester (pp. 219–20) disagreed with a number of elements in Crossan's view. Initial responses to Crossan's and Koester's theses were made by Raymond E. Brown, "The *Gospel of Peter* and Canonical Gospel Priority," *NTS* 33 (1987): 321–43, and Frans Neirynck, "The Apocryphal Gospels and the Gospel of Mark," in *The New Testament in Early Christianity* (ed. Jean-Marie Sevrin; BETL 86; Leuven: Leuven University Press, 1989), 140–57. In particular, Brown argued that the *Gospel of Peter* is not literarily dependent on the canonical Gospels, but it does show an oral knowledge of them. But these responses were made prior to the publication of Crossan's and Koester's later works. A more recent response to Crossan and Koester is by Kirk, "Examining Priorities," 572–95, who argues that in pericopae that Crossan and / or Koester claim are prior to the narrative Gospels, they actually show literary dependence on these Gospels.

[38] The Greek text cited here is from Maria Grazia Mara, *Évangile de Pierre: Introduction, texte critique, traduction, commentaire et index* (Sources Chrétiennes 201; Paris: Éditions du Cerf, 1973), 40–67. An older edition of the text may be found in J. Armitage Robinson and Montague Rhodes James, *The Gospel According to Peter and the Revela-*

1:1 ... τ[ῶν] δὲ Ἰουδαίων οὐδεὶς ἐνίψατο τὰς χεῖρας, οὐδὲ Ἡρῴδης οὐδὲ [ε]ἷς [τ]ῶν κριτῶν αὐτοῦ. Κ[αὶ μὴ] βουληθέντων νίψασθαι ἀνέσ[τ]η Πειλᾶτος· 1:2 καὶ τότε κελεύει Ἡρῴδης ὁ βασιλεὺς παρ[απη]μφθῆναι τὸν Κύριον, εἰπὼν αὐτοῖς ὅτι ὅσα ἐκέλευσα ὑμῖν ποιῆσαι αὐτῷ ποιήσατε.

1:1 ... But of the Jews none washed their hands, neither Herod nor any of his judges. And as they would not wash, Pilate stood up. 1:2 And then Herod the king commanded that the Lord should be marched off, saying to them, "What I have commanded you to do to him, do."

Comparing this with the other narrative Gospels, we note several similarities and differences, though the differences are more prominent. First, Matt 27:24 reports that Pilate did wash his hands (only found in Matthew), while *Gos. Pet.* 1:1 reports that neither the Jews nor Herod washed their hands – something not stated in any other Gospel. It is quite possible (indeed likely?) that the text preceding *Gos. Pet.* 1:1 stated that Pilate washed his hands and the refusal of the Jews and Herod is in contrast to Pilate's action, but this text is no longer extant. Either way, this refusal is a narrative element that is distinct from the other accounts. Second, in the other Gospels Pilate is the one primarily responsible for examining Jesus (Mark 15:2–5 = Matt 27:11–14 = Luke 23:2–5; John 18:29–38), and it is only Luke that reports Pilate sending Jesus to Herod Antipas (at which Pilate is not present; Luke 23:6–12). In *Gos. Pet.* 1:1 it is Herod and "his judges" who examine Jesus, and Pilate is primarily an observer of the proceedings. Third, in the other Gospels it is Pilate who condemns Jesus to his flogging and crucifixion (Mark 15:15 = Matt 27:26 = Luke 23:24–25; John 19:16), whereas in *Gos. Pet.* 1:2 it is Herod who gives the command for Jesus to be taken away for his scourging and crucifixion (which follows in *Gos. Pet.* 3:6–4:10). Finally, we note that *Gos. Pet.* 1:2 gives Herod the title of "king" – a title

---

tion of Peter: Two Lectures on the Newly Recovered Fragments Together with the Greek Texts (2 ed.; London: C.J. Clay & Sons, 1892), 83–88, and H.B. Swete, *The Gospel of Peter: The Text in Greek and English with Introduction, Notes, and Indices* (1893; repr., Ancient Texts and Translations; Eugene, OR: Wipf & Stock, 2005). See also the recent study Thomas J. Kraus and Tobias Nicklas, eds., *Das Petrusevangelium und die Petrusapokalypse: Die griechischen Fragmente mit deutscher und englischer Übersetzung* (GCS 11; Berlin: Walter de Gruyter, 2004). The translation is my own, but it follows closely that of Elliott, *Apocryphal New Testament*, 154–58, in consultation with Schneemelcher, *Gospels and Related Writings*, 223–27.

Particular points in the *Gospel of Peter* are not identified by chapter and verse. Two different numbering systems were employed early in the study of the *Gospel of Peter*: J.A. Robinson divided the text into 14 units and A. Harnack divided it into 60 units. It has since become customary to identify a text using both Robinson's and Harnack's numeration, and to place a colon or a period between them. For example, *Gos. Pet.* 5:15 identifies the first part of Robinson's unit 5 and Harnack's unit 15. Thus, there is no 5:1–14; rather Robinson's unit 5 consists of Harnack's 15–20, and Robinson's unit 6 begins at Harnack's unit 21.

which Herod Antipas never actually had (he was a "tetrarch"). This suggests a confusion of Herod Antipas with his father, Herod the Great, who did possess this title. This brief examination of the opening pericope leads to four conclusions that are equally borne out by a complete comparison of the entire text of the *Gospel of Peter* in comparison with the other narrative Gospels: (1) The wording in the *Gospel of Peter* shows surprisingly little explicit verbal similarity to that of the other Gospels.[39] (2) At numerous points the descriptions of events in the *Gospel of Peter* differ from those in the other Gospels. (3) The *Gospel of Peter* contains several pericopae and data that are not found in the other Gospels. (4) The author of the *Gospel of Peter* demonstrates a lack of understanding at several points of the socio-

---

[39] Raymond E. Brown ("The *Gospel of Peter* and Canonical Gospel Priority," 333) admits that "[a]lthough *GP* and the canonical Gospels share many scenes, there is remarkably little exact verbal identity in word or form." Brown (p. 333) identifies the two closest parallels as *Gos. Pet.* 8:30 = Matt 27:64 and *Gos. Pet.* 12:53–54a = Mark 16:3. These texts, with their exact verbal parallels indicated by double underlining and verbal similarities indicated by single underlining, are as follows:
Gos. Pet. 8:30:
Παράδος ἡμῖν στρατιώτας, ἵνα φυλάξωμεν τὸ μνῆμα αὐτοῦ ἐπὶ τρεῖς ἡμ[έρας], μήποτε ἐλθόντες οἱ μαθηταὶ αὐτοῦ κλέψωσιν αὐτὸν καὶ ὑπολάβῃ ὁ λαὸς ὅτι ἐκ νεκρῶν ἀνέστη, καὶ ποιήσωσιν ἡμῖν κακά.
"Give us soldiers so that we may guard his tomb for three days, lest his disciples come and steal him, and the people suppose that he is risen from the dead, and do us harm."
Matt 27:64:
κέλευσον οὖν ἀσφαλισθῆναι τὸν τάφον ἕως τῆς τρίτης ἡμέρας, μήποτε ἐλθόντες οἱ μαθηταὶ αὐτοῦ κλέψωσιν αὐτὸν καὶ εἴπωσιν τῷ λαῷ· ἠγέρθη ἀπὸ τῶν νεκρῶν, καὶ ἔσται ἡ ἐσχάτη πλάνη χείρων τῆς πρώτης.
"Therefore command the tomb to be made secure until the third day; lest his disciples come and steal him, and tell the people, 'He has been raised from the dead,' and the last deception would be worse than the first."
Gos. Pet. 12:53–54a:
Τίς δὲ ἀποκυλίσει ἡμῖν καὶ τὸν λίθον τὸν τεθέντα ἐπὶ τῆς θύρας τοῦ μνημείου, ἵνα εἰσελθοῦσαι παρακαθεσθῶμεν αὐτῷ καὶ ποιήσωμεν τὰ ὀφειλόμενα; 12.54αΜέγας γὰρ ἦν ὁ λίθος, ...
"But who will roll away for us even the stone that is across the door of the tomb, so that we may go in and sit beside him and do what is due?" For the stone was great, ...
Mark 16:3–4:
καὶ ἔλεγον πρὸς ἑαυτάς· τίς ἀποκυλίσει ἡμῖν τὸν λίθον ἐκ τῆς θύρας τοῦ μνημείου; 16:4καὶ ἀναβλέψασαι θεωροῦσιν ὅτι ἀποκεκύλισται ὁ λίθος· ἦν γὰρ μέγας σφόδρα.
They had been saying to one another, "Who will roll away for us the stone from the door of the tomb?" When they looked up, they saw that the stone had already been rolled back, for it was very great.
It is interesting to note that these two closest parallels comprise verbal statements made by characters in the narrative, rather than descriptive statements in of the narrative itself (apart from Mark 16:4). It is sometimes observed that in the oral tradition process of early Christianity statements by Jesus were treated more conservatively than descriptive material. I do not know of a study that has examined this feature with reference to other statements made by characters in the Jesus tradition, but it is interesting to note it here.

political realities of life in the Palestine of Jesus' day.[40] This evidence leads me to the conclusion that the *Gospel of Peter* is largely dependent upon the other narrative Gospels, but this dependence is more likely based on an oral knowledge of these Gospels rather than a direct literary dependence. It is also probable that the *Gospel of Peter* has access to other oral traditions not found in the other narrative Gospels.[41] The date for composition of this Gospel is probably during the first half of the second century.[42] For those traditions also found in the other Gospels, it provides no independent attestation. For traditions that differ from, or are in addition to, the other Gospels, any possible historical value needs to be weighed on a case by case basis. With reference to Jesus' death by crucifixion, the subject of this section, the *Gospel of Peter* states:

Καὶ ἔνεγκον δύο κακούργους καὶ ἐσταύρωσαν ἀνὰ μέσον αὐτῶν τὸν Κύριον·

And they brought two criminals and crucified the Lord in the middle between them. (*Gos. Pet.* 4:10a)

In light of the preceding discussion, since this adds nothing distinctive in addition to what is known from the other Gospels, *Gos. Pet.* 4:10a is most likely dependent on a knowledge of the canonical passion narratives at this point, and probably Luke 23:33b in particular.[43]

---

[40] For example, *Gos. Pet.* 1:1–2; 2:4–5 portray Herod as having authority in Judea, which he did not. *Gos. Pet.* 8:28–33; 10:38 portray the Jewish leadership spending the night in a cemetery, guarding the tomb of Jesus – an act that is culturally implausible.

[41] Thus I concur with Kirk's ("Examining Priorities," 572–95) to Crossan and Koester: the *Gospel of Peter* is dependent upon the canonical Gospels, but I think he has gone too far in claiming literary dependency. I find Brown's view ("The *Gospel of Peter* and Canonical Gospel Priority," 335, 337) more adequately explains the data as he prefers the "... oral dependence of *GP* on some or all of the canonical Gospels" as well as "... ongoing non-canonical material ..." See most recently the contribution by Martha K. Stillman, "The Gospel of Peter: A Case for Oral-Only Dependency?" *ETL* 73 (1997): 114–20. Her study leads her to conclude concerning the vocabulary substituted in the *Gospel of Peter* for that in the canonical Gospels "... the substitutions occurred during the process of oral transmission – oral transmission without written texts – and are the written traces left behind in this process" (p. 120).

[42] Brown, "The *Gospel of Peter* and Canonical Gospel Priority," 339–40. See also the introductory discussion of this Gospel by Schneemelcher, *Gospels and Related Writings*, 216–22.

[43] The statement of crucifixion is found in all four canonical Gospels. In Mark and Matthew the statement of Jesus' crucifixion and the mention of two thieves are separate from one another (Mark 15:24, 27 = Matt 27:35, 38), and the the other subjects of crucifixion are identified as λῃσταί ("robbers"). In John's Gospel the statement of Jesus' crucifixion is combined with that of the crucifixion of two others, but they are otherwise not labelled (John 19:18). In Luke 23:33b the statement of Jesus' crucifixion is associated with that of the crucifixion of two others, and they are identified as κακούργους ("criminals"), as in *Gos. Pet.* 4:10a.

There are several other references to Jesus' crucifixion in early Christian literature, but these all are dependent on earlier Christian traditions, including those already cited above.[44]

2.1.2. Ancient non-Christian references to Jesus' crucifixion

The execution of Jesus by crucifixion is not only reported in a number of early Christian traditions, it is also found in early non-Christian sources as well. The most significant of these is by Josephus (ca. 37–100 C.E.) in his work, *Jewish Antiquities*, dating from the 90s C.E.,[45] in a passage which has become known by the name, *Testimonium Flavianum* (i.e., a Latin phrase referring to the testimony by Flavius Josephus concerning Jesus).[46] The received text of *Ant.* 18.63–64 contains a short description of Jesus' life and ministry, death, as well as a reference to his resurrection. Several of the statements in the *Testimonium* are quite obviously not from the hand of Josephus, for it is highly unlikely that a non-Christian Jewish historian would make descriptive statements that would require a Christian's faith perspective. These Christianized statements include three statements in particular: "if indeed one should call him a man," as well as "he was the Messiah," and "he appeared to them on the third day, alive again, as the divine prophets had spoken about these and countless other marvelous things concerning him." These Christian features have led some scholars to reject the entire text of the *Testimonium* as an insertion by Christian scribes. However, many scholars conclude that the text probably did originally contain a description of Jesus, but that it was explicitly Christianized by early Christian scribes.[47]

That a non-Christianized version of the *Testimonium Flavianum* was originally present in Josephus' text is confirmed by two points: First, there exists Arabic and Syriac versions of the *Testimonium* that lack these Christianized elements.[48] Second, Origen, a Church Father of the third

---

[44] Cf. *Barn.* 7:3; Ign. *Trall.* 9:1.

[45] Louis H. Feldman, "Josephus," in *The Anchor Bible Dictionary*, vol. 3 (ed. David N. Freedman; New York: Doubleday, 1992), 985.

[46] Jesus is also referred to in an incidental manner in Josephus, *Ant.* 20.200–201.

[47] For discussion of the current state of the debate with respect to the issues and the literature, see Zvi Baras, "*Testimonium Flavianum*: The State of Recent Scholarship," in *Society and Religion in the Second Temple Period* (ed. Michael Avi-Yonah and Zvi Baras; vol. 8 of *The World History of the Jewish People*; Jerusalem: Masada, 1977), 303–13, 378–85; Louis H. Feldman, "The *Testimonium Flavianum*: The State of the Question," in *Christological Perspectives: Essays in Honor of Harvey K. McArthur* (R. F. Berkey and S. A. Edwards; New York: Pilgrim, 1982), 179–99, 288–93. For a history of scholarship, see Alice Whealey, *Josephus on Jesus: The Testimonium Flavianum Controversy from Late Antiquity to Modern Times* (Studies in Biblical Literature 36; New York: Peter Lang, 2003).

[48] See Shlomo Pines, *An Arabic Version of the Testimonium Flavianum and Its Implications* (Jerusalem: The Israel Academy of Sciences and Humanities, 1971); Whealey,

century (185–254 C.E.), states that Josephus did not believe that Jesus was the Messiah. In *Contra Celsum* 1.47 Origen states explicitly concerning Josephus that "[t]he same author, although he did not believe in Jesus Christ ..." Similarly, in *Comm. Matt.* 10.17 he states, "... and wonderful it is that, while he [i.e., Josephus] did not receive Jesus for Christ, he did nevertheless bear witness that James was so righteous a man" (alluding to the reference to James in Josephus, *Ant.* 20.200). This indicates that Origen's text of Josephus' *Antiquities* most likely had a form of the *Testimonium* in it, but that it lacked the Christianized elements. Thus Origen was able to state what Josephus thought about Jesus. The first known citation of the Christianized version of the *Testimonium* is by Eusebius (260–338 C.E.) in his *Eccl. Hist.* 1.11.7–8. Eusebius was the successor to Origen at the school in Caesarea. He knew Origen's works and was dependent upon them (cf. *Eccl. Hist.* 6.36.3). It is possible that Eusebius may have been responsible for the Christianizing of the *Testimonium*.[49]

A variety of proposals have been made concerning the original, non-Christianized form of the *Testimonium*, from affirming that it is impossible to reconstruct, to highly edited and speculative reconstructions, to simply removing the explicit Christianized clauses to produce a coherent text. I find this last alternative the most convincing because it results not only in a smooth-flowing text, but also a text that is consistent with Josephus' style.[50] In other words, the Christianizing of the text was accomplished by a Christian (possibly Eusebius) simply by inserting three clauses to alter its meaning and thus provide explicit Christian apologetic material in support of their claims about Jesus. The following is the received text of the *Testimonium* (*Ant.* 18:63–64) but with the three Christianized clauses struck through:[51]

Josephus on Jesus, and the recent literature on the *Testimonium* that discusses this evidence.

[49] For discussion of the relationship between Origen and Eusebius in their use of Josephus' account of the martyrdom of James and the *Testimonium*, see Zvi Baras, "The Testimonium Flavianum and the Martyrdom of James," in *Josephus, Judaism, and Christianity* (ed. Louis Feldman, H. and Gohei Hata; Detroit: Wayne State University Press, 1987), 338–48. See also Whealey, *Josephus on Jesus*, 12–29.

[50] For defense of this alternative see John P. Meier, "Josephus on Jesus: A Modest Proposal," *CBQ* 52 (1990): 72–103; John P. Meier, *The Roots of the Problem and the Person* (vol. 1 of *A Marginal Jew: Rethinking the Historical Jesus*; New York: Doubleday, 1991), 57–88; cf. also C. Martin, "Le 'Testimonium Flavianum'. Vers une solution définitive?" *Revue Belge de Philologie et d'Histoire* 20 (1941): 409–65; Joseph Klausner, *Jesus of Nazareth: His Life, Times, and Teaching* (trans. Herbert Danby; New York: Macmillan, 1925), 55–60; Meier, "Josephus on Jesus," 72–103.

[51] The following is my own translation, which in an attempt to render the Greek in a somewhat literal fashion, and thus differs slightly from that of L.H. Feldman (LCL) and Meier (*Roots of the Problem*, 60–62).

⁶³ Γίνεται δὲ κατὰ τοῦτον τὸν χρόνον Ἰησοῦς σοφὸς ἀνήρ, ~~εἴγε ἄνδρα αὐτὸν λέγειν χρή·~~ ἦν γὰρ παραδόξων ἔργων ποιητής, διδάσκαλος ἀνθρώπων τῶν ἡδονῇ τἀληθῆ δεχομένων, καὶ πολλοὺς μὲν Ἰουδαίους, πολλοὺς δὲ καὶ τοῦ Ἑλληνικοῦ ἐπηγάγετο· ~~ὁ χριστὸς οὗτος ἦν.~~ ⁶⁴ καὶ αὐτὸν ἐνδείξει τῶν πρώτων ἀνδρῶν παρ' ἡμῖν σταυρῷ ἐπιτετιμηκότος Πιλάτου οὐκ ἐπαύσαντο οἱ τὸ πρῶτον ἀγαπήσαντες· ~~ἐφάνη γὰρ αὐτοῖς τρίτην ἔχων ἡμέραν πάλιν ζῶν τῶν θείων προφητῶν ταῦτά τε καὶ ἄλλα μυρία περὶ αὐτοῦ θαυμάσια εἰρηκότων.~~ εἰς ἔτι τε νῦν τῶν Χριστιανῶν ἀπὸ τοῦδε ὠνομασμένον οὐκ ἐπέλιπε τὸ φῦλον.

⁶³ At this time there lived Jesus, a wise man, ~~if indeed one should call him a man~~. For he was a doer of remarkable deeds, a teacher of people who receive truth agreeably, and many Jews as well as many Greeks were persuaded. ~~He was the Messiah.~~ ⁶⁴ And when Pilate, due to an accusation by the leading men among us, condemned him to the cross, those who loved him before did not stop doing so. ~~For he appeared to them on the third day, alive again, as the divine prophets had spoken about these and countless other marvelous things concerning him.~~ And still until now the tribe of Christians, named after him, has not failed.

As a first-century Jewish author with access to Jewish and Roman sources, Josephus' description provides independent corroboration of Jesus' execution by crucifixion.

A second non-Christian source is Cornelius Tacitus (ca. 56–117 C.E.), a public Roman figure (e.g., proconsul of Asia, 112–113 C.E.) and historian responsible for the *Annals* as well as the *Histories*. In *Annals* 15.44, his final work and thus dated in the 110s C.E., Tacitus explains that Nero deflected the rumors that he was responsible for ordering the burning of Rome by blaming it on Christians:

Ergo abolendo rumori Nero subdidit reos et quaesitissimis poenis adfecit, quos per flagitia invisos vulgus Christianos appellabat. Auctor nominis eius Christus Tiberio imperitante per procuratorem Pontium Pilatum supplicio adfectus erat; repressaque in praesens exitiabilis superstitio rursum erumpebat, non modo per Iudaeam, originem eius mali, sed per urbem etiam.

Therefore, to scotch the rumour, Nero substituted as culprits, and punished with the utmost refinements of cruelty, a class of men, loathed for their vices, whom the crowd styled Christians. Christus, the founder of the name, had undergone the death penalty in the reign of Tiberius, by sentence of the procurator Pontius Pilatus, and the pernicious superstition was checked for a moment, only to break out once more, not merely in Judaea, the home of the disease, but in the capital itself (Annals 15.44; Jackson, LCL).

The view that Tacitus presents of the early Christian movement is extremely negative. While it is possible that his statements concerning Jesus may be merely reiterating what he has heard of Christian claims, he does not present it as such. It is more likely that, as a Roman official and historian, Tacitus may have had access to non-Christian sources for his statement – certainly his opinion of the movement is anti-Christian. While Tacitus is not explicit in stating that Jesus was crucified, he does affirm that Jesus was executed by the Roman authorities in Judea. The term he uses (*supplicium*, "death penalty") is specifically used for those forms of capital punishment involving suffering, like crucifixion, and thus Tacitus' description is consistent with what we know elsewhere concerning the mode of Jesus' execution.[52]

Another interesting source – though not a text, nor even an inscription – is the Alexamenos graffito scratched on a stone used on Palatine Hill in Rome. Discovered in 1857 and now housed in the Palatine Antiquarium in Rome, this graffito portrays a man with the head of an ass and with his hands outstretched on a cross. Looking up at this figure is another man. The scratching below is Αλεξαμενος σεβετε θεον which is literally "Alexamenos, worship God!," but it is possible that the imperative form could be understood as a mis-spelling of the indicative, and thus is "Alexamenos worships [his] God."[53] This graffito, which has been dated from late first century to third century, conveys a sense of how the idea of venerating a crucified person could be mocked as contemptible, as indicated by the ass's head.[54] For our purposes here, it also corroborates the widespread understanding among common people that Jesus had been crucified.[55]

A few other non-Christian Roman texts do make reference to Jesus or the early Christian movement, but they make no reference to the mode of Jesus' death.[56] There are also references to Jesus in later Rabbinic literature as well as the Qur'an, but there is nothing in these to suggest that we have

---

[52] See P. G. W. Glare, ed., *Oxford Latin Dictionary* (Oxford: Oxford University Press, 1992), 1882–83, and the discussion below in § 2.2.

[53] For discussion and a reproduction of the image, see Everett Ferguson, *Backgrounds of Early Christianity* (3d ed.; Grand Rapids: Eerdmans, 2003), 596–97. Reproductions may also be seen on the internet.

[54] The Jewish people were vilified in the Mediterranean world for worshipping an ass, for which see Tacitus, *Hist.* 5.3–4; Josephus, *Ag. Ap.* 2.80. This accusation was later applied to Christians as well, for which see Tertullian, *Apology* 16.2. This graffito is evidence of such mockery among common people of the period. For other examples, see G. H. R. Horsley, *New Documents Illustrating Early Christianity*, vol. 4 (North Ryde, Australia: Ancient History Documentary Research Centre, Macquarie University, 1987), 137, § 34 "A Crucified Donkey."

[55] While commenting on this graffito, B. Hudson MacLean states (B. Hudson MacLean, *An Introduction to Greek Epigraphy of the Hellenistic and Roman Periods from Alexander the Great Down to the Reign of Constantine [323 B. C.–A. D. 337]* [Ann Arbor, MI: University of Michigan Press, 2002], 208): "Graffiti provide invaluable information concerning the popular language, thoughts, ideas, and religious beliefs of common people."

[56] E.g. Suetonius, *Claudius* 25.4; Pliny, *Epistles* 10.96. The Mara bar Serapion letter (late first century C. E.) refers to the Jews "executing their wise king," but the method of execution is unstated. For discussion of this letter, see F. F. Bruce, *Jesus and Christian Origins Outside the New Testament* (Grand Rapids: Eerdmans, 1974), 31; Craig A. Evans, "Jesus in Non-Christian Sources," in *Studying the Historical Jesus: Evaluations of the State of Current Research* (ed. Bruce Chilton and Craig A. Evans; NTTS 19; Leiden: E. J. Brill, 1994), 455–57; Robert E. Van Voorst, *Jesus Outside the New Testament: An Introduction to the Ancient Evidence* (Grand Rapids: Eerdmans, 2000), 53–58.

access to historical traditions relevant to Jesus. Though they are, of course, very important for understanding later views of Jesus.[57]

2.1.3. The criteria of historicity applied to Jesus' execution by crucifixion

Applying the criteria used in historical Jesus research to the evidence gathered in the preceding two sections, it is evident that some of these criteria are relevant.[58] First of all, the criterion of multiple attestation is applicable, for Jesus' execution specifically by means of crucifixion is attested in a significant number of independent sources. On the matter of the independence of these sources, I do recognize, however, that the weight of evidence for independence is greater for some sources than others, so in the chart below I also provide a weighting of their independence:

Date Range (C.E.)	Text / Author	Reference	Independence
50s–60s	Paul	Gal 3:1; 5:11; 6:12, 14; 1 Cor 1:17–18, 22–23; 2:1–2; Phil 2:7–8	certain
60s (or 40s–50s)	Sayings Gospel Q	Q 14:27	certain
60s	Hebrews	Heb 12:2	probable
68–72	Gospel of Mark	Mark 15:24 (etc.)	certain
80s (or 60s)	First Peter	1 Pet 2:24	probable
90s	Revelation	Rev 11:8	probable
90s	Gospel of John	John 19:18 (etc.)	probable
90s	Josephus	*Ant.* 18.63–64	certain
110s	Tacitus	*Annals* 15.44	certain
120s/180s (or 30s–40s)	*Gospel of Thomas*	*Gos. Thom.* 55b	probable
late first or second century	Alexamenos	graffito	certain

Thus, within approximately the first 100 years after Jesus' death there are six witnesses that are certainly independent and another five that are probably independent. And of these witnesses, three of them are non-Christian, and of these three, two of them are explicitly anti-Christian. These are witnesses to the specific fact of Jesus' execution by crucifixion. If one were to broaden

---

[57] For discussion of these later traditions, see Bruce, *Jesus and Christian Origins Outside the New Testament*; Evans, "Jesus in Non-Christian Sources," 443–78. With reference to later Jewish authorities, see William Horbury, "The Trial of Jesus in Jewish Tradition," in *The Trial of Jesus: Cambridge Studies in Honour of C. F. D. Moule* (ed. Ernst Bammel; SBT 2.13; London: SCM, 1970), 103–21.

[58] For a discussion of these criteria, see in this volume ch. 2, § 4.1.

the scope to include references to Jesus' death more generally, the number of independent witnesses, both Christian and non-Christian would increase. Thus, of all the events and/or sayings of Jesus, there is probably no other that has such an extensive collection of witnesses that meets the criterion of multiple attestation.

The second criterion that is relevant is the criterion of embarrassment, for Jesus' execution by crucifixion was highly problematic and a potential source of shame for the early Christian movement. The criterion of embarrassment, when fully considered, plays a weighty role, for there are three distinct strands to the embarrassment. Two of these arise from specific Jewish religious issues, and the third arises from broader Mediterranean views. First, early Christian proclamation included the claim that Jesus was the Christ, the Messiah – the one anointed and sent by Israel's God to fulfill Israel's scriptures and meet Jewish eschatological expectations. The difficulty (i.e., the embarrassment) was that Jewish expectation concerning its Messiah did not include one that had died. Yes, Jewish eschatological expectation in the first century was quite diverse,[59] but whatever type of messianic figure that was expected, the expectation was for a *living* messianic figure – one that had not yet died. It was a living Messiah who would provide the leadership necessary to free God's people.[60] Yes, the early Christian proclamation also included the resurrection of Jesus, but resurrection in Jewish categories was a transformation to life in a new sphere of existence and not a resuscitation to life in this same, mundane sphere of existence.[61] Jesus had died – this fundamentally precluded him from meeting traditional

---

[59] For discussion see James H. Charlesworth, ed., *The Messiah: Development in Earliest Judaism and Christianity* (Minneapolis: Fortress, 1992); John J. Collins, *The Scepter and the Star: The Messiahs of the Dead Sea Scrolls and Other Ancient Literature* (New York: Doubleday, 1994). For a more recent survey, see Craig A. Evans, "Messianic Hopes and Messianic Figures in Late Antiquity," *JGRChJ* 3 (2006): 9–40.

[60] Some later Jewish texts (*4 Ezra* 7:29–30; *2 Bar.* 30:1) do make reference to a Messiah dying, but the messianic figure does so only after having brought about the blessings of the messianic age. Furthermore, these texts can be dated to the end of the first century C.E. and beginning of the second, 90–120 C.E.

It is sometimes claimed that the Qumran scroll, 4Q541, makes reference to a suffering Messiah who makes atonement. While the text does state that a figure "… will atone for all the children of his generation …" (4Q541 fr.9 1:2; García Martínez) and then goes on to describe this figure suffering, there is no explicit identification of who this figure is. Collins' conclusion (*The Scepter and the Star*, 124–26) is the most probable when he states that the person "… is a priest and makes atonement by means of the sacrificial cult" (p. 125).

[61] This definition is somewhat simplistic but nevertheless adequate for making the point here. The literature on resurrection is immense. See the recent survey on resurrection in the Hebrew Bible and later Jewish literature by N.T. Wright, *The Resurrection of the Son of God* (vol. 3 of *Christian Origins and the Question of God*; Minneapolis: Fortress, 2003), 85–206. See also the discussion by Dale C. Allison, *Resurrecting Jesus: The Earliest Christian Tradition and Its Interpreters* (London: T&T Clark, 2005), 198–375, and the discussion in this volume ch. 14.

Jewish expectations for a messianic figure, and the Christian claim that he had been resurrected did not really alleviate this problem. Paul, the earliest extant source referring to Jesus' crucifixion noted above, alludes to this problem in his statement that "we proclaim Christ crucified, a stumbling block to Jews ..." (1 Cor 1:23).[62]

A second way that Jesus' death by crucifixion was a potential source of embarrassment arises out of a particular view of crucifixion held within Second Temple Judaism. Deut 21:22–23 refers to an ancient practice of hanging the body of an already-executed person on a tree (evidently as a warning). This text does not require the practice, but rather regulates it by insisting that the corpse not be left overnight but rather taken down and buried the same day. The reason given is, "for anyone hung on a tree is under God's curse. You must not defile the land that the Lord your God is giving you for possession" (v. 23b). The Qumran literature reveals that some Jews during the Second Temple period considered this text to also reference crucifixion.[63] In particular, 4QpNah fr.3–4 1:6–8 alludes to the language of Deut 21:22 to describe the horror of crucifixion:[64]

[6] ... פשרו על כפיר החרון [7] [אשר ימלא חורה רוב פגרי לעשות נק]מות בדורשי החלקות אשר יתלה אנשים חיים [8] [על העץ לפעול תועבה אשר לוא יעשה] בישראל מלפנים כי לתלוי חי על העץ ...

[6] ... Its interpretation concerns the Angry Lion [7] [who filled his cave with a mass of corpses, carrying our rev]enge against those looking for easy interpretations, who hanged living men [8] [from the tree, committing an atrocity which had not been committed] in Israel since ancient times, for it is [hor]rible for the one hanged alive from the tree ... (4QpNah fr.3–4 1:6–8, García Martínez)

This action by the "Angry Lion" evidently alludes to the Sadducean high priest Alexander Jannaeus. His enemies, the Pharisees ("those looking for easy interpretations") had attempted to overthrow him, but they failed. Alexander Janneus, upon returning to Jerusalem, had 800 of these enemies crucified and killed their wives and children while they watched (cf. Josephus, *J. W.* 1.96–98; *Ant.* 13.380). The language in 4QpNah of "hanged alive from the tree" picks up the language from Deut 21:23, except for the addition of "alive" which reinterprets the Deuteronomic text as a reference to crucifixion. 4QpNah assumes that the practice of hanging corpses had been practiced in ancient Israel, and it interprets Alexander Janneus' actions

---

[62] See also Gal 5:11.

[63] For discussion see Yigael Yadin, "Pesher Nahum (4QpNahum) Reconsidered," *IEJ* 21 (1971): 1–12, plate 1; Joseph A. Fitzmyer, "Crucifixion in Ancient Palestine, Qumran Literature, and the New Testament," *CBQ* 40 (1978): 493–513; Max Wilcox, "Upon the Tree – Deut. 21:22–23 in the New Testament," *JBL* 96 (1977): 85–99.

[64] The text and translation of Qumran texts is taken from Florentino García Martínez and Eibert J. C. Tigchelaar, eds., *The Dead Sea Scrolls: Study Edition* (2 vols; Grand Rapids: Eerdmans, 1997–98). The lacunae are their conjectures.

as in continuity with that ancient "horrible" practice "… which had not been committed] in Israel since ancient times" (1:8). Thus, Deut 21:22–23 is being reinterpreted as reference to crucifixion.

A similar interpretation is found in a regulation provided in the Temple Scroll which also interprets Deut 21:22–23 as referring to crucifixion. 11QT^a 64:9–13 states:

⁹ ... כי יהיה באיש חטא משפט מות ויברח אל ¹⁰ תוך הגואים ויקלל את עמו ואת בני ישראל ותליתמה גם
אותו על העץ ¹¹ וימות ולוא תלין נבלתמה על העץ כי קבור תקוברם{ה} ביום ההוא כי ¹² מקוללי אלוהים
ואנשים תלוי על העץ ולוא תטמא את האדמה אשר אנוכי ¹³ נותן לכה נחלה ...

⁹ ... If it happens that a man has committed a capital offence and he escapes ¹⁰ amongst the nations and curses his people / and / the children of Israel, you also shall hang on the tree ¹¹ and he will die. And their corpse shall not spend the night on the tree; instead you shall bury them that day because ¹² those hanged on a tree are cursed by God and man; thus you shall not defile the land which I ¹³ give you for an inheritance. (11QT^a 64:9–13, García Martínez)

The word order in 64:10–11 indicates that "hang on the tree" is the means of execution that results in "he will die." Thus, Deut 21:22–23 is being reinterpreted to apply to crucifixion.⁶⁵ It is also interesting to note the reason for removing the body on the same day is expanded so that the executed person is not only cursed by God but also viewed as cursed by humans as well. This interpretation of Deut 21:22–23 is not limited to the Qumran literature, for it is also found in Philo who explains in *Spec. Laws* 3.151–52:

¹⁵¹ ... ἐπεὶ δὲ τοῦτ' οὐκ ἐνεδέχετο, τιμωρίαν ἄλλην προσδιατάττεται κελεύων τοὺς ἀνελόντας ἀνασκολοπίζεσθαι. ¹⁵² καὶ τοῦτο προστάξας ἀνατρέχει πάλιν ἐπὶ τὴν αὐτοῦ φιλανθρωπίαν, ἡμερούμενος πρὸς τοὺς ἀνήμερα εἰργασμένους, καί φησι· μὴ ἐπιδυέτω ὁ ἥλιος ἀνεσκολοπισμένοις, ἀλλ' ἐπικρυπτέσθωσαν γῇ πρὸ δύσεως καθαιρεθέντες ...

¹⁵¹ ... But since this was impossible he [i. e., God] ordained another penalty as an addition and ordered the murderers to be crucified. ¹⁵² Yet after giving this injunction he hastened to revert to his natural humanity and shows mercy to those whose deeds were merciless when he says, "Let not the sun go down upon the crucified but let them be buried in the earth before sundown." (Philo, *Spec. Laws* 3.151–152; adapted from Colson, LCL)⁶⁶

---

⁶⁵ Most scholars do interpret this as a reference to crucifixion. An exception is J. M. Baumgarten, "Does *TLH* in the Temple Scroll Refer to Crucifixion?" *JBL* 91 (1972): 472–81. He argues that the text is a reference to strangulation. But see the response by Fitzmyer, "Crucifixion in Ancient Palestine," 504–5 and Joe Zias and James H. Charlesworth, "Crucifixion: Archaeology, Jesus, and the Dead Sea Scrolls," in *Jesus and the Dead Sea Scrolls* (ed. James H. Charlesworth; ABRL; New York: Doubleday, 1992), 273–89, esp. 277–79.

⁶⁶ Philo uses the verb ἀνασκολοπίζω twice in this text. It could be more literally translated as "fixed to a stake." Philo uses this term two other times (*Post.* 61; *Somn.* 2.213) and in both instances it is used in association with the imagery of nailing to a tree (e.g., ὕλαις προσήλωνται, *Post.* 61), which indicates he uses the term for crucifixion. This term is used in other literature for crucifixion as well; see the next section.

These texts indicate that within Second Temple Judaism Deut 21:22–23 was interpreted to refer to crucifixion. In particular, this interpretation indicates that those crucified were understood to be cursed by God and by extension cursed by humans as well – at least those for whom this text functioned as scripture and so informed their understanding of those crucified. For Jewish Christians in particular, that Jesus had been crucified compounded the potential embarrassment of claiming that Jesus was the Messiah. Not only was it problematic in Jewish terms that their claimed Messiah was dead, but having been executed by crucifixion meant that he was under a divine curse and was to be viewed that way by faithful Jews as well! Paul's exegetical exercise in Gal 3:10–14 is his attempt to address this problem by incorporating Jesus being divinely cursed according to Deut 21:22–23 into his understanding of the gospel, with the result that Christ "becoming a curse for us" is the means by which "Christ redeemed us from the curse of the law" (Gal 3:13).

The first two strands for the criterion of embarrassment focus on Jewish sensibilities. The third strand broaden, to include the entire ancient Mediterranean world. Third, crucifixion was viewed as a shameful death, not only because of the public display of its horrors but also because it was reserved for the lower strata of society and the worst of criminals.[67] Thus the death of Jesus by crucifixion brought with it a social stigma of shame. Paul alludes to this in Phil 2:7–8 when Jesus' humility is described as "taking the form of a slave" which culminates in his "death on a cross" (Phil 4:7–8). Similarly Heb 12:2 states that Jesus "endured the cross, disregarding its shame." The shame of death by crucifixion was a broad Mediterranean perspective, and it is the "embarrassment" of this to which Paul probably is alluding when he states "we proclaim Christ crucified, ... foolishness to Gentiles (1 Cor 1:23). It is this shame that made Alexamenos the butt of mockery by his peers who scratched a picture of him worshiping a crucified man with an ass's head.

Therefore, on the basis of the diverse multiple attestation to this event and the actual evidence that this event was a source of embarrassment for the early Christian movement, it is reasonable to conclude that Jesus' execution by crucifixion is one of the more probable events that can be established in ancient history, and it is certainly the most probable that can be established concerning Jesus. In fact, it is so probable that it forms the basis of its own criterion: the criterion of rejection and execution. This criterion is used by some historical Jesus scholars to evaluate other Jesus traditions: that which contributes to understanding why Jesus was rejected by certain Jewish authorities and executed by Roman authorities is more likely to be authentic.[68] Other criteria could also be mentioned, such as the criterion of multiple

---

[67] See the discussion of crucifixion in § 2.2 below.
[68] For further discussion of this criterion, see ch. 2, § 4.1.

forms and the criterion of Palestinian environment, but the historicity of Jesus' execution by crucifixion stands or falls upon the two primary criteria explored here, namely, multiple attestation and embarrassment.

To many readers, it may seem that the discussion up to this point has been overkill. For during the first 100 years after this event, there is no evidence that this event was ever called into question, and there is no evidence of any attempt to explain Jesus' death in any other way. Centuries later, some Jewish discussions would refer to the method of Jesus' execution as death either by hanging or stoning.[69] Still later, the Qur'an would state in Surah 4.155–58 that the "People of the Book," that is, the Jews, claimed, "'We slew the Messiah, Jesus son of Mary, the Messenger of God' – yet they did not slay him, neither crucified him, only a likeness of that was shown to them … [N]o indeed; God raised him up to Him."[70] The ambiguity of the statement about "only a likeness …" gives rise to the view in later Islamic tradition that it was someone else, who looked like Jesus, who was actually crucified, and Jesus himself was raised up to God.[71] A similar view had been expressed earlier, for Irenaeus in *Haer.* 1.24.4 attributes to Basilides the view that: Jesus transfigured Simon of Cyrene to look like him, so "that he might be thought to be Jesus, was crucified, through ignorance and error, while Jesus himself received the form of Simon, and, standing by, laughed at them."[72]

Alternate claims are proposed in modern times. For example, Tom Harpur in *The Pagan Christ* (2004) denies the existence of Jesus, claiming that the early Christian beliefs drew upon much earlier myths and legends.[73] Or Michael Baigent in *The Jesus Papers* (2006) proposes that Pilate, "while he condemned Jesus and had to go through with the required sentence of crucifixion, he could not dare have it reported to Rome that Jesus had actually died. So Pilate took steps to ensure that Jesus would survive."[74] Thus Jesus

---

[69] See *b. Sanh.* 43a; cf. *b. Sanh.* 67a. But for crucifixion, see *t. Sanh.* 9:7.

[70] Translation by Arthur J. Arberry, trans., *The Koran* (The World's Classics; Oxford: Oxford University Press, 1983), 95.

[71] For discussion of Jesus in the Qur'an, see Bruce, *Jesus and Christian Origins Outside the New Testament*, 167–77; Muhammad Ata ur-Rahim, *Jesus: A Prophet of Islam* (Karachi: Begum Aisha Bawany Waqf, 1981); Michael G. Fonner, "Jesus' Death by Crucifixion in the Qur'an: An Issue for Interpretation and Muslim-Christian Relations," *JES* 29 (1992): 432–50.

Translation from Alexander Roberts and James Donaldson, eds., *The Apostolic Fathers – Justin Martyr – Irenaeus* (vol. 1 of *The Ante-Nicene Fathers*; 1885; repr., Grand Rapids: Eerdmans, 1979), 349.

[72] See also the Coptic Nag Hammadi text, *Apoc. Pet.* (NHC VII,3) 81–83.

[73] Tom Harpur, *The Pagan Christ: Recovering the Lost Light* (Toronto: Thomas Allen, 2004). For a critique of Harpur's proposals, see Stanley E. Porter and Stephen J. Bedard, *Unmasking the Pagan Christ: An Evangelical Response to the Cosmic Christ Idea* (Toronto: Clements Publishing, 2006).

[74] Michael Baigent, *The Jesus Papers: Exposing the Greatest Cover-Up in History*

only appeared to die, surviving the cross by being drugged,[75] returning to Egypt where he had been raised. The problem with all these theories, whether ancient or modern, is that, while *theoretically* possible, they fly in the face of all of the evidence from the first 100 years after the event, and this evidence from friend and foe alike is consistent in its basic witness: Jesus was executed by crucifixion.[76]

2.2. Crucifixion in the Ancient Mediterranean World[77]

The term "cross" and visual representations in religious art and jewelry evoke images of two pieces of wood *cross*-ing each other. But neither the Greek term σταυρός nor the Latin term *crux* actually have this sense.[78] They both refer to an upright stake or pole which has been embedded in the ground. The terms could function as posts for a foundation (e.g., Herodotus 5.16) or together as a fence (e.g., Thucydides 4.90.2) or barrier (e.g., Thucydides 7.25.5). And this upright stake could also serve as an instrument of torture, humiliation, and execution. Since the basic item needed for a crucifixion was a vertical piece of wood, other terms were also used for the instrument of crucifixion. In Greek, for example, such terms include σκόλοψ ("stake" or something having a "point") and ξύλον ("tree" or "wood," i.e., a piece of wood). The related verbs for crucifying usually involve the act of attaching the person to the upright piece of wood, including σταυρόω / ἀνασταυρόω, ἀνασταυρίζω ("to fasten to a pole / cross," i.e., "to crucify"), ἀνασκολοπίζω ("to fasten to a stake," i.e., "to crucify"), προσηλόω ("to nail"), and κρεμάννυμι ("to hang"). Similarly, the Latin verb *crucifigo* also has this sense as it combines the verb *figo* ("to nail, fasten") and *crux* ("cross") to mean "to attach to a cross, to crucify."[79] Thus crucifixion used an upright

---

(New York: HarperCollins, 2006), 126, cf. 115–32. For a critique, see Evans, *Fabricating Jesus*, 207–17, esp. 213–17.

[75] For this last hypothesis, Baigent is dependent upon Hugh Schonfield, *The Passover Plot: New Light on the History of Jesus* (London: Hutchinson, 1965).

[76] Just how flimsy is the theoretical nature of Baigent's case in *Jesus Papers*, may be observed in the repeated use of clauses like "it is not hard to imagine ..." (p. 124), or "it is not hard to suppose that ..." (p. 125). Imagination and supposition in place of evidence is the hallmark of fiction.

[77] For classic discussions of this subject, see Martin Hengel, *Crucifixion in the Ancient World and the Folly of the Message of the Cross* (trans. John Bowden; Philadelphia: Fortress, 1977); Heinz-Wolfgang Kuhn, "Die Kreuzesstrafe während der frühen Kaiserzeit. Ihre Wirklichkeit und Wertung in der Umwelt des Urchristentums," in *ANRW*, vol. 2.25.1 (ed. H. Temporini and W. Haase; Berlin: Walter de Gruyter, 1982), 648–793.

[78] So Brown, *Death of the Messiah*, 945.

[79] See the discussions in the various entries in LSJ and Glare, *Oxford Latin Dictionary*. The verb *crucifigo* is also related to the verb *crucio*, "to inflict torture" and other words of this root. The Hebrew vocabulary related to crucifixion includes the roots תלה ("hang"), זקף ("raise up"), and צלב ("impale, hang").

pole as a means of torture, humiliation, and execution to which the victim was attached by tying, nailing, hanging, or impaling. At times the terms were used for victims who were crucified after they had been executed by some other means, while more frequently they refer to crucifixion as the means of torture and execution itself. The results varied as well, for a victim impaled on a stake would die instantly or at least relatively quickly, whereas a victim attached to a stake could experience a slow and lingering death. At times the victim was attached simply to the vertical post itself, whereas at other times a horizontal crossbeam was used as well, and the victim was attached to it.

This language of crucifixion indicates that the terms were usually used interchangeably to refer to a variety of related practices.[80] This is exemplified in the description by Seneca:

Video istic cruces non unius quidem generis sed aliter ab aliis fabricatas: capite quidam conversos in terram suspendere, alii per obscena stipitem egerunt, alii brachia patibulo explicuerunt.

Yonder I see crosses, not indeed of a single kind, but differently contrived by different peoples; some hang their victims with head toward the ground, some impale their private parts, others stretch out their arms on a fork-shaped gibbet. (Seneca, *Dial.* 6.20.3; adapted from Basore, LCL)

Thus, the particular elements in Jesus' crucifixion are but a subset of a variety of ancient practices. To attempt to distinguish Jesus' form of crucifixion from others would probably be a futile exercise. Rather, it is more helpful to understand Jesus' execution as one type of these varied crucifixion practices in general, and to interpret it in that light.

While crucifixion practices may have been quite diverse, when viewed from the perspective of the executioners, crucifixion served several related functions that were relatively simple and clear. First, the process of crucifixion was designed to humiliate the victim and thus bring shame upon the person. Whether the victim was dead or alive, the public exposure in this fashion stripped the person of the last vestiges of honor, leaving the person totally shamed.[81] This applies to the degrading practices which preceded the crucifixion to the public exposure on the cross itself accompanied by the mockery of the crowd. With reference to a public execution in a manner

---

[80] Martin Hengel (*Crucifixion*, 24) points out that Herodotus used ἀνασκολοπίζω for crucifying living persons and ἀνασταυρόω for the crucifixion of the dead, but that after Herodotus, these two terms are used synonymously.

[81] Cf. Heb 12:2 which describes Jesus' crucifixion in terms of shame. For discussion of crucifixion from the perspective of the honor/shame paradigm, see Jerome H. Neyrey, "Despising the Shame of the Cross: Honor and Shame in the Johannine Passion Narrative," *Semeia* 68 (1994): 113–15. See also Peter J. Scaer, *The Lukan Passion and the Praiseworthy Death* (New Testament Monographs 10; Sheffield: Sheffield Phoenix Press, 2005), 1–2.

similar to crucifixion, Philo describes the effects of "... the cruel stress of the accumulated punishments, the wind, the sun, [as well as] the shame of being seen by the passers-by (καὶ τῇ ἀπὸ τῶν παριόντων αἰχύνῃ) ..." (Philo, *Spec. Laws* 3.160; Colson, LCL). Elsewhere Philo describes the practice of Flaccus (the prefect of Egypt, 32–38 C.E.) who even incorporated crucifixion and its accompanying tortures with the festival celebrating the birthday of the emperor. The festival included "... the crucifixion of the living ..." followed by "... dancers and mimes and flute players and all the other amusements of theatrical competitions" (Philo, *Flaccus* 84–85; Colson, LCL).

Second, if the victim were still alive, then crucifixion functioned as a means of capital punishment. For example, Cicero considered crucifixion to be "that cruel and disgusting penalty" (*crudelissimi taeterrimique supplicci*) which was "the worst extreme of tortures" (*extremo summoque supplicio*; Cicero, *Verr.* 2.5.64, 66, § 165, 169; Greenwood, LCL).[82] As a means of execution, however, it served as such in two somewhat distinct ways. During times of war or unrest it was used quite indiscriminately against the enemy or rebel forces, but during times of relative peace it was used to execute certain types of criminals.

Whether peace-time execution of criminals or war-time execution of the enemy, in either case crucifixion served a third function, and this with reference to its audience. Crucifixion was a public execution – the horrors and humiliation of this suffering and death were intended to serve as a deterrent to those who observed it. Quintilian explains the principle of deterrence:

Quotiens noxios cruci figimus, celeberrimae eliguntur viae, ubi plurimi intueri, plurimi commoveri hoc metu possint. Omnis enim poena non tam ad delictum pertinet quam ad exemplum.

When we crucify criminals the most frequently used roads are chosen, where the greatest number of people can look and be seized by this fear. For every punishment has less to do with the offence than with the example. (Quintilian, *Decl.* 274.13; Shackleton Bailey, LCL)

Similarly, the *Digest*, written much later, also explains this rationale in similar fashion, indicating how widespread was this thinking:

---

[82] In *Digest* 48.19.28 the *furca* is described as the "extreme penalty" (*summum supplicium*), beyond that of being burnt alive. The *furca* is sometimes translated "gallows," but this may be misleading for it is not a reference to hanging. A *furca* was a forked instrument to which a person's arms were tied and then the person was scourged to death as a means of capital punishment (Suetonius, *Nero* 49). The *furca* also functioned like a cross in that a person was "hung" or suspended on the *furca*; e.g., *Digest* 28.13.7, "hanged on the gallows" (*in furca suspendisse*); cf. *Digest* 48.19.38.2: "Those who are responsible for sedition and disturbance when a mob has been excited are, according to their social standing, either hanged on the gallows (*in furcam tolluntur*; note: Paulus [a noted Roman jurist] reads *crucem* here instead of *furcam*) or thrown to the beasts or deported to an island."

Famosos latrones in his locis, ubi grassati sunt, furca[83] *figendos compluribus placuit, ut et conspectu deterreantur alii ab isdem facinoribus et solacio sit cognatis et adfinibus interemptorum eodem loco poena redita, in quo latrones homicidia fecissent.*

The practice approved by most authorities has been to hang notorious brigands on a gallows in the place which they used to haunt, so that by the spectacle others may be deterred from the same crimes, and so that it may, when the penalty has been carried out, bring comfort to the relatives and kin of those killed in that place where the brigands committed their murders. (*Digest* 48.19.28.15; Mommsen)

We can observe this principle being put into practice in Josephus' description of the Roman crucifixion of Jews attempting to escape the siege of Jerusalem during the First Jewish War:

[449] ... μαστιγούμενοι δὴ καὶ προβασανιζόμενοι τοῦ θανάγου πᾶσαν αἰκίαν ἀνεσταυροῦντο τοῦ τείχους ἀντικρύ. [450] Τίτῳ μὲν οὖν οἰκτρὸν τὸ πάθος κατεφαίνετο πεντακοσίων ἑκάστης ἡμέρας ἔστι δ' ὅτε καὶ πλειόνων ἁλισκομένων, οὔτε δὲ τοὺς βίᾳ ληφθέντας ἀφεῖναι ἀσφαλὲς καὶ φυλάττειν τοσούτους φρουρὰν τῶν φυλαξόντων ἑώρα· τό γε μὴν πλέον οὐκ ἐκώλυεν τάχ' ἂν ἐνδοῦναι πρὸς τὴν ὄψιν ἐλπίσας αὐτοὺς <ὡς>, εἰ μὴ παραδοῖεν, ὅμοια πεισομένους·

[449] ... They were accordingly scourged and subjected to torture of every description, before being killed, and then crucified opposite the walls. [450] Titus indeed commiserated their fate, five hundred or sometimes more being captured daily; on the other hand, he recognized the risk of dismissing prisoners of war, and that the custody of such numbers would amount to the imprisonment of their custodians. But his main reason for not stopping the crucifixions was the hope that the spectacle might perhaps induce the Jews to surrender, for fear that continued resistance would involve them in a similar fate. (Josephus, *J. W.* 5.449–450; adapted from Thackeray, LCL)

When crucifixion was used in times of war, those crucified among the enemy might be of any class. For example, Cassius Dio describes the execution of the Hasmonean king Antigonus as taking place in multiple stages, including crucifixion:

... τὸν δ' Ἀντίγονον ἐμαστίγωσε σταυρῷ προσδήσας, ὃ μηδεὶς βασιλεὺς ἄλλος ὑπὸ τῶν Ῥωμαίων ἐπεπόνθει, καὶ μετὰ τοῦτο καὶ ἀπέσφαξεν

... but Antigonus he [i.e., Antony] bound to a cross and flogged, – a punishment no other king had suffered at the hands of the Romans, – and afterwards cut his throat. (Cassius Dio, *Hist. Rom.* 49.22.6; adapted from Gary, LCL)

But when used during times of peace as a means of executing criminals, crucifixion was generally reserved for those of the lower class (i.e., *humiliores*, the "low-born;" these constituted the majority of the population).[84] Taci-

---

[83] On the *furca* as a crucifixion-related device of capital punishment, see the note above.
[84] On the status distinction between the *honestiores* and the *humiliores* as those of higher and lower status in Roman society, see Peter Garnsey, *Social Status and Legal Privilege in the Roman Empire* (Oxford: Oxford University Press, 1970), 221–23. With

tus, for example, alludes to the crucifixion of a runaway slave, Geta, who passed himself off as a noble person (i.e., a *honestior*, "well-born"). When his deception was discovered, "he suffered the punishment usually inflicted on slaves" (Tacitus, *Hist.* 2.72; Moore, LCL). For Cicero it was the "worst extreme of the tortures inflicted upon slaves" (Cicero, *Verr.* 2.5.66, § 169; Greenwood, LCL). Cicero makes this comment while describing how terrible it would be if a Roman citizen were to be crucified.[85] Elsewhere he states:

... *et nomen ipsum crucis absit non modo a corpore civium Romanorum sed etiam a cogitatione, oculis, auribus. Harum enim omnium rerum non solum eventus atque perpessio sed etiam condicio, exspectatio, mentio ipsa denique indigna cive Romano atque homine libero est.*

... [A]nd the very word "cross" should be far removed not only from the person of a Roman citizen but from his thoughts, his eyes and his ears. For it is not only the actual occurrence of these things or the endurance of them, but liability to them, the expectation, nay, the mere mention of them, that is unworthy of a Roman citizen and a free man. (Cicero, *Rab. Perd.* 5.16; Hodge, LCL)

Tacitus alludes to crucifixion when describing a man who impersonated a *honestior* who was thought to have been killed by Nero, but the impersonator was discovered to have been a runaway slave, and so "he suffered the punishment usually inflicted on slaves" (Tacitus, *Hist.* 2.72; Moore, LCL). While Rome's general practice was to exempt its citizens from the humiliation of being executed by crucifixion, at times citizens were crucified.[86] Occasionally a citizen might be crucified,[87] but in other circumstances a citizen could be crucified if they were deemed to have behaved in a way that in effect forfeited their citizenship, such as through treason.[88] For example, Livy reports that at the end of the Second Punic War the Carthaginians returned Roman deserters to the Roman forces. Publius Cornelius Scipio, the consular leader of the Roman forces, executed them for desertion:

---

reference to the use of crucifixion for both slaves and *humiliores*, see Garnsey, *Social Status and Legal Privilege*, 126–27.

[85] Cicero goes on to state in this same context: "To bind a Roman citizen is a crime, to flog him is an abomination, to slay him is almost an act of murder: to crucify him is – what? There is no fitting word that can possibly describe so horrible a deed" (*Verr.* 2.5.66, § 170; Greenwood, LCL).

[86] There evidently was no law, *per se*, which prohibited the crucifixion of citizens. Rather, it was assumed due to the prevailing view that crucifixion was for the execution of slaves. For further discussion, see Garnsey, *Social Status and Legal Privilege*, 126–27; Hengel, *Crucifixion*, 39–45; A.H.M. Jones, *Studies in Roman Government and Law* (New York: Frederick A. Praeger, 1960), 53–65.

[87] E.g., Suetonius, *Galba* 9.1.

[88] This is apparently related to an ancient practice of hanging those found guilty of treason on the *arbor infelix* ("gallows," lit. "barren tree"). Later this was interpreted to be crucifixion. Cf. Hengel, *Crucifixion*, 39–40.

De perfugis gravius quam de fugitivis consultum; nominis Latini qui erant securi percussi, Romani in crucem sublati.

The deserters were more severely treated than the runaway slaves, Latin citizens being beheaded, Romans crucified. (Livy 30.43.13; Moore, LCL)

While Livy does report the crucifixion of Roman citizens, the language of his contrast between citizens and slaves reveals the prevalent attitude that crucifixion was generally reserved for slaves and the lower class.

2.3. *The Historical Significance of Jesus' Execution by Crucifixion*

The preceding discussion leads to a few observations that may be made concerning Jesus' execution by crucifixion. First of all, Jesus was executed during a time of relative peace in Palestine, rather than during a time of war. The period of Roman rule from 6–41 C.E. under seven Roman prefects was largely a period of political calm. Yes, there were movements that needed to be quelled, but the overall scene was one of relative peace, at least on the surface of Palestinian society. This pre-Agrippa period (Agrippa I ruled Palestine from 41–44 C.E.) should be distinguished from the post-Agrippa period of 44–66 C.E. when seven Roman procurators ruled over Palestine.[89] During this later period there was increasing unrest leading up to the first Jewish Revolt. Thus Jesus being executed by crucifixion should be understood in a context in which crucifixion was used to deal with serious criminals rather than to deal with enemy forces during a time of war. Jesus' execution as a criminal is consistent with the portrayal in the NT that he was crucified with two other men that Mark 15:27 identifies as "bandits" (λῃστής, "robber, highwayman, bandit;" also Matt 27:38) and Luke 23:33, 39 as "criminals" (κακοῦργος, "evil-doer, criminal;" also *Gos. Pet.* 4:10).[90] And in Mark 14:48 Jesus challenges those coming to arrest him, "Have you come out with swords and clubs to arrest me as though I were a bandit (λῃστήν)?" Whether one can determine more precisely the nature of Jesus' criminal charge is discussed below.

Second, the decision to crucify Jesus implies that there was something about Jesus that made it beneficial to the Roman authorities to use his public execution by crucifixion as a message to the Jewish population. There were other ways to silence or do away with Jesus. By choosing public crucifixion, Rome was issuing a warning: popular movements among commoners and peasants that had the potential to lead to unrest were not tolerated. By cru-

---

[89] From 41–44 C.E. Herod Agrippa ruled over Judea as well as the territory of Antipas (Galilee and Perea). When direct Roman rule was reintroduced in 44 C.E. the province included this expanded region of Palestine.

[90] John 19:18 also mentions Jesus being crucified with two others, but does not provide a label for them.

cifying the leader of one such movement was not only a message to possible members of that movement, it was also a message to the populace at large, whatever their allegiances. This also is explored further in the next section.

3. Jesus' Examination before Rome's Prefect, Pontius Pilate

We are able to glean more specific elements with reference to our understanding of Jesus' death beyond just the datum *that* he was executed by means of crucifixion. For this we turn to the immediate historical circumstances that led to his crucifixion – his examination before Rome's governor of Judea, Pontius Pilate. Here we proceed in several steps. First, we consider the historical evidence for this event, evaluating the probability of its historicity. Then we turn to several elements that provide contextual information for understanding the event. In particular, second, we explore the nature of Pilate's prefecture of Judea, and third, we consider Roman rule and its procedures with reference to capital crimes in Roman provinces. Finally, we pull this material together to reconstruct the core elements in Jesus' examination by Pilate and then conclude with the significance of this event for understanding the life of Jesus.[91]

---

[91] There are numerous studies of this material. The most important study in the past century must be the two-volume work by Brown, *Death of the Messiah*, which also contains extensive bibliographies. In addition to more general studies of the historical Jesus which do discuss his trial, some of the other more important studies that focus on Jesus' trial from the past century include Giovanni Rosadi, *The Trial of Jesus* (translated and edited by Emil Reich; New York: Dodd, Mead & Co., 1905); Friedrich Doerr, *Der Prozess Jesu in rechtsgeschichtlicher Beleuchtung ein Beitrag zur Kenntnis des jüd-röm. Provinzialstrafrechts* (Berlin: W. Kohlhammer, 1920); Max Radin, *The Trial of Jesus of Nazareth* (Chicago: University of Chicago Press, 1931); Solomon Zeitlin, *Who Crucified Jesus?* (2 ed.; New York: Harper, 1947); Josef Blinzler, *The Trial of Jesus: The Jewish and Roman Proceedings Against Jesus Christ Described and Assessed from the Oldest Accounts* (2 ed.; trans. Isabel McHugh and Florence McHugh; Cork, Ireland / Westminster, MD: Mercier / Newman, 1959); Paul Winter, *On the Trial of Jesus* (2 ed.; revised by T. A. Burkill and Geza Vermes; SJ 1; Berlin: Walter de Gruyter, 1974); J. Duncan M. Derrett, *An Oriental Lawyer Looks at the Trial of Jesus and the Doctrine of the Redemption* (London: School of Oriental and African Studies, 1966); S. G. F. Brandon, *The Trial of Jesus of Nazareth* (London: Batsford, 1968); Ernst Bammel, ed., *The Trial of Jesus: Cambridge Studies in Honour of C. F. D. Moule* (SBT 2.13; London: SCM, 1970); David R. Catchpole, *The Trial of Jesus: A Study of the Gospels and Jewish Historiography from 1770 to the Present Day* (SPB 18; Leiden: E. J. Brill, 1971); Haim Cohn, *The Trial and Death of Jesus* (London: Wiedenfeld & Nicolson, 1972); Otto Betz, "Probleme de Prozesses Jesu," in *ANRW*, vol. 2.25.1 (ed. H. Temporini and W. Haase; Berlin: Walter de Gruyter, 1982), 565–647; Ellis Rivkin, *What Crucified Jesus?* (London: SCM, 1984); K. Kertelge, ed., *Der Prozess gegen Jesus. Historische Rückfrage und theologische Deutung* (QD 112; Freiberg: Herder, 1988); John Dominic Crossan, *Who Killed Jesus? Exposing the Roots of Anti-Semitism in the Gospel Story of the Death of Jesus* (San Francisco: Harper Collins, 1995); Gerard S. Sloyan, *The Crucifixion of Jesus: History, Myth, Faith* (Minneapolis: Fortress, 1995); Alan Watson, *The*

3.1. The Historicity of Jesus' Trial before Pontius Pilate

As with references to Jesus' crucifixion, so also the evidence for Jesus' examination before Pilate is found in both Christian and non-Christian sources.

3.1.1. Early Christian references to Jesus' examination by Pilate

This discussion of the evidence for Jesus' examination before Pilate assumes the discussion above concerning the dating and relationship of these sources.

The earliest extant source referring to Pilate examining Jesus is the account in Mark 15:1–15. This account portrays Jesus being handed over to Pilate by certain Jewish leaders and Pilate examining him with the question "Are you the King of the Jews?" (vv. 1–5). Pilate offers to release either Barabbas or this King of the Jews (vv. 6–10), but the chief priests and the crowd cry out that Pilate should "crucify him!" (vv. 11–14). So Pilate releases Barabbas and, "after flogging Jesus, he handed him over to be crucified" (v. 15).[92]

The second extant text recounting Pilate's examination of Jesus that is probably an independent source is the Fourth Gospel. In John 18:28–19:16 the same basic set of events are portrayed as found in Mark, except that the language is significantly different, and a number of the features of Pilate's examination are different. For example, in Mark's Gospel, Pilate's examination of Jesus takes place in public, before his accusers and the crowd (Mark 15:2–5, 8–9), whereas in John's Gospel, Pilate's examination of Jesus takes place inside the praetorium, while his interaction with the chief priests and the crowd takes place outside, with Pilate moving back and forth between

---

Trial of Jesus (Athens, GA: University of Georgia Press, 1995); Simon Légasse, *The Trial of Jesus* (trans. John Bowden; London: SCM Press, 1997); Gerard S. Sloyan, *Jesus on Trial: A Study of the Gospels* (Minneapolis: Fortress, 2006); Wolfgang Reinbold, *Der Prozess Jesu* (BThS 28; Göttingen: Vandenhoeck & Ruprecht, 2006).

[92] Luke has used Mark as a source for much of his Gospel. But in this part of the passion narrative Luke also has several additional pericopae, and this may indicate that he had access to additional material, or potentially an alternate source for this portion of the passion narrative. With respect to the section of the Roman examination and crucifixion, Luke has the following additional pericopae: (1) Pilate sends Jesus to be examined by Herod, who does so and returns him to Pilate (23:6–12); (2) Pilate declares Jesus innocent before the chief priests and the people (23:13–16); (3) on the way to crucifixion, the women follow wailing, and Jesus addresses them (23:27–32), and (4) the crowds return home from the crucifixion beating their breasts (23:48). For viewing this material largely as a result of Lukan redaction, see Jerome H. Neyrey, *The Passion According to Luke: A Redactional Study of Luke's Soteriology* (Mahwah, NJ: Paulist, 1985). For arguments viewing this material as largely historical, see the relevant sections and further literature in John Nolland, *Luke* (3 vols; WBC 35; Dallas: Word Books, 1989–93); Darrell L. Bock, *Luke* (2 vols; BECNT 3; Grand Rapids: Baker, 1994–96). See also the helpful discussion on these units by Brown, *Death of the Messiah*. While this is an interesting question for the details concerning the Roman examination and crucifixion, it does not make a material difference with respect to the core elements that are the primary focus in this essay.

these two locations (e.g., John 18:28–29, 33). As well, the order of some of the event details are different in the two accounts.[93]

There are a few other early Christian references to Pilate's examination of Jesus. In the conclusion of 1 Timothy, the author begins his charge to the reader:

In the presence of God, who gives life to all things, and of Christ Jesus, who in his testimony before Pontius Pilate made the good confession, I charge you ... (1 Tim 6:13)

This letter is notoriously difficult to date, the issue being wrapped up in the question of its authorship. If it was composed after Paul's death, it is probably to be dated in the latter part of the first century, somewhere 70s–90s C.E.[94] What is perhaps more interesting about this source is that it not only makes reference to Pilate's examination of Jesus, it also claims that, in this examination Jesus "made the good confession." This could be understood to be in some tension with the Gospel narrative. Mark, for example, has Jesus replying somewhat ambiguously, "You say so (σὺ λέγεις)" to Pilate's question, "Are you King of the Jews" (15:2), after which Jesus is silent (15:5; cf. John 19:9).[95] This might suggest that this author, while aware that Pilate examined Jesus, is unaware of the details contained in Mark's Gospel. Alternatively, the author may simply be alluding to Jesus' willingness to face death.

In three of the letters of Ignatius, reference is made to Jesus' life and death "in the time of Pontius Pilate," including Jesus being crucified (Ign. *Magn.* 11; Ign. *Trall.* 9:1; Ign. *Smyrn.* 1:2), but no explicit reference is made to Pilate's active involvement.

3.1.2. *Ancient non-Christian references to Jesus' examination by Pilate*

In addition to these early Christian references to Pilate's examination, there are two early non-Christian sources that also make explicit reference to

---

[93] For a chart comparing the ordering of events, see the appendix to this essay, § 5. It is sometimes claimed that there is an increasing tendency from earlier traditions (Mark) to later traditions (Luke, John; cf. Acts 4:27) to downplay Pilate's responsibility and to highlight the role of the Jewish leaders. See, for example, Winter, *On the Trial of Jesus*, 85–88. However, the recent work by Helen Bond has demonstrated that this is, in fact, not the case. Each source has its own rhetorical purpose, but this tendency is not in evidence. See Helen K. Bond, *Pontius Pilate in History and Interpretation* (SNTSMS 100; Cambridge: Cambridge University Press, 1998).

[94] The issues are complex and the literature is voluminous. In my estimation a recent, balanced review of the evidence and discussion may be found in I. Howard Marshall and Philip H. Towner, *A Critical and Exegetical Commentary on the Pastoral Epistles* (ICC; Edinburgh: T&T Clark, 1999), 57–92. Those who hold to Pauline authorship, would date this letter in the mid-60s, for which see Carson, et al., *Introduction*, 367–71, 377–78.

[95] Though in John's account Jesus has more extended interaction with Pilate (18:33–38), though much of the language is Johannine. And Jesus still ends up being silent before Pilate (19:9).

an examination of Jesus by Pilate. Both of these sources have already been discussed above with reference to Jesus' crucifixion. It remains to note explicitly their description of Pilate's involvement.

First of all, in the *Testimonium Flavianum*, already discussed in some detail above (§ 2.1.2), Josephus' statement is quite explicit that Jesus' execution is at the behest of Pilate (*Ant.* 18.64):

⁶⁴ καὶ αὐτὸν ἐνδείξει τῶν πρώτων ἀνδρῶν παρ* ἡμῖν σταυρῷ ἐπιτετιμηκότος Πιλάτου οὐκ ἐπαύσαντο ...

⁶⁴ And when Pilate, due to an accusation by the leading men among us, condemned him to the cross ...

This statement may be dated to the 90s C. E. It is interesting for two reasons. First, it provides independent corroboration to the basic Gospel narrative that has Pilate acting in response to an accusation brought by Jewish leaders. Second, it is Pilate who makes the decision to have Jesus executed by means of crucifixion.

A second non-Christian reference to Pilate's involvement is also found in the *Annals* by the Roman historian Tacitus already discussed above (§ 2.1.2). The relevant portion of the text is:

Auctor nominis eius Christus Tiberio imperitante per procuratorem Pontium Pilatum supplicio adfectus erat ...

Christus, the founder of the name [i. e., Christians], had undergone the death penalty in the reign of Tiberius, by sentence of the procurator Pontius Pilatus ... (*Annals* 15.44; Jackson, LCL)

As noted above, Tacitus' description of the early Christian movement is very negative, calling it a "pernicious superstition" and a "disease" in this text. Tacitus certainly had no reason to create anything that might portray Jesus in a positive manner. Yet he still described the execution of Jesus as being done explicitly "by sentence of the procurator Pontius Pilatus."

As an aside, it should be noted that there exists a much later text, the *Acts of Pilate*, which provides a detailed account of Jesus' trial, crucifixion, and resurrection, focusing on Pilate's involvement in the affairs. It may have a link to other, later legends that portray Pilate as exonerating Jesus and even becoming a Christian. These later texts and traditions have no historical value for the purposes of this essay, though they do shed much light on later Christian perspectives concerning Pilate, suggesting a polemical attempt to limit Roman liability for Jesus' death.[96]

---

[96] For discussion, see Winter, *On the Trial of Jesus*, 87–89; Clayton N. Jefford, "Pilate, Acts Of," in *The Anchor Bible Dictionary*, vol. 5 (ed. David N. Freedman; New York: Doubleday, 1992), 371–72. For an introduction and translation, see Ron Cameron, ed., *The Other Gospels: Non-Canonical Gospel Texts* (Cambridge: Lutterworth, 1982), 163–

3.1.3. The criteria of historicity applied to Pilate's examination of Jesus

Once again we can apply the criteria of historicity used in historical Jesus research to the evidence gathered above. First of all, the criterion of multiple attestation is applicable here as well, for Jesus' examination by Pilate is attested in a number of independent sources. On the matter of the independence of these sources, I do recognize, however, that the weight of evidence for independence is greater for some sources than others, so in the chart below I also provide a weighting of their independence:

Date Range (C.E.)	Text/Author	Reference	Independence
68–72	Gospel of Mark	Mark 15:1–15	certain
70s–90s	First Timothy	1 Tim 6:13	possible/probable
90s	Gospel of John	John 19:18 (etc.)	probable
90s	Josephus	*Ant.* 18.64	certain
110s	Tacitus	*Annals* 15.44	certain

Thus, within approximately the first 100 years after Jesus' death there are three extant sources that are certainly independent and another two that are probably independent. And of these witnesses, two of them are non-Christian sources. Other texts also made mention of Pilate, but do not explicitly reference his examination of Jesus.

Second, the criterion of embarrassment also applies in this situation, though not perhaps quite as strongly as with reference to Jesus' crucifixion. To be examined by a Roman governor and executed as a result of the charges – regardless of whether the charges were true or not (more on this below) – raises all kinds of questions about the movement that sprang up following this Jesus called Christ: "Are they troublemakers? Do they pose a threat to peace and stability? Regardless of how they might explain it, their leader was crucified by Rome's governor, after all!" Thus, to be examined by Pilate and condemned to death as a consequence, would be something that the early Christian movement would find embarrassing, and for which they would need to provide explanations for what happened that would exonerate Jesus and defend the legitimacy of the early Christian movement. It is hard to conceive of a reason why the early Christian movement might create such an embarrassing event as this. But it does explain why they might shape the particular narratives of the event to provide a response to this embarrassment.

82; E. Hennecke and W. Schneemelcher, eds., *Gospels and Related Writings* (vol. 1 of *New Testament Apocrypha*; rev. ed.; trans. R. McL. Wilson; Louisville: Westminster/John Knox, 1991), 501–36.

Third, the criterion of rejection and execution is also relevant to this event. As we will see below, the principles of Roman law are quite explicit about capital punishment. It is only the governor of the province who holds the *imperium*, and thus the power to execute a criminal lies with him alone. To claim, therefore, that Jesus might have been crucified, but Pilate was not involved in examining Jesus, is to propose something that not only flies in the face of both Christian and non-Christian evidence, it also violates Roman principles for governing their provinces.[97]

In light of this evidence and these criteria, it is reasonable to conclude that the event of Pilate's examination of Jesus is to be judged highly probable as historical. It should be noted with care, however, what I am claiming here: it is very probable *that* Pilate examined Jesus in some fashion and was responsible for the decision to have him executed by means of crucifixion, but the *details* and *actions* by those involved is another matter not yet addressed – some of these are examined below.

3.2. The Character of Pontius Pilate's Rule as Prefect of Judea

To help us understand and evaluate Pilate's functioning at Jesus' examination, it is necessary to place this one event into a larger framework of how Pilate functioned in other situations while he was Judea's prefect (26–36 C.E.).[98] By observing how Pilate functioned in a number of different incidents, we can understand something of his character and mode of behavior, particularly as he related as Roman governor with his Jewish subjects and their distinctive social and religious sensitivities.

The primary texts for developing a picture of Pilate include narratives contained in the early Christian Gospels and the Jewish writings of Josephus and Philo. It is widely recognized that the Gospels as well as the writings of Josephus and Philo are rhetorical in nature – by that I mean that they shape their narratives to convince their readers to take a particular point of view about what is narrated. Thus, in examining these narratives and in making historical judgments about them, their rhetoric must be taken into account.[99] One cannot, therefore, take these texts at face value as has often been done in the past. To aid in understanding Pilate, we survey these sources and the incidents that they report. Other than the execution of Jesus, these sources provide descriptions of several other incidents involving Pilate (albeit two

---

[97] For discussion, see § 3.3 below.

[98] These are the most common dates used for Pilate's prefecture. However, a few scholars argue it may have begun somewhat earlier, in 19 C.E. For discussion see Daniel R. Schwartz, "Pontius Pilate," in *The Anchor Bible Dictionary*, vol. 5 (ed. David N. Freedman; New York: Doubleday, 1992), 396–97.

[99] This point about the rhetorical point of each text about Pilate is one of the significant contributions made by Bond, *Pontius Pilate*.

are very brief allusions). It is interesting to note that we know of a number of these incidents – doubtless there were others of greater or lesser magnitude about which we know nothing. We examine these known incidents in their probable historical order.

But I begin this analysis, not with these events, but rather with an "event" of another type – one which is both "event" as well as a form of "text." In fact, it could be claimed that Pilate himself has left us with "texts" that he is responsible for composing. I refer to the coins he had minted. The discipline of numismatics provides evidence from the material remains of Pilate's prefecture.

3.2.1. The Coins Minted by Pilate

Coins are usually minted by those who hold the political and economic power in a region. Their basic functions are to facilitate commerce and the collection of taxes. The symbols and text used on coins usually promote the ideology of those holding power. They are virtually a "text" intended to communicate a socio-political message by the ruling elite, and thus coins function as "propaganda."[100] This holds true, whether for modern coins or those minted in ancient civilizations – whether it is an American quarter with the words "Liberty" and "In God We Trust" on one side and on the other an eagle with outstretched wings, or it is a Roman sestertius with the inscription *"Mars Victor"* with an image of Mars, the god of war, and Victoria, the goddess of victory, intended to celebrate the *pax Romana* that Rome's armies had produced throughout the Empire.[101]

What do we learn when we examine Pilate's coins? In the Hasmonean period, various rulers minted bronze coins using the Seleucid monetary system – a practice followed by the early Herodians, including Herod I, Archelaus, and Antipas, as well as the early Judean prefects. In the early years of the Principate, the minting of gold and silver coins was under the control

---

[100] For recent discussions of propaganda with reference to coins in the ancient Mediterranean world, see for example, Jane DeRose Evans, *The Art of Persuasion: Political Propaganda from Aeneas to Brutus* (Ann Arbor, MI: University of Michigan Press, 1992), 1–34; Garth S. Jowett and Victoria O'Donnell, *Propaganda and Persuasion* (4 ed.; Thousand Oaks, CA: Sage, 2006), 53–55. On the use of images in general, see Paul Zanker, *The Power of Images in the Age of Augustus* (trans. Alan Shapiro; Jerome Lectures 16; Ann Arbor, MI: University of Michigan Press, 1988).

[101] For discussion of this coin, see Klaus Wengst, *Pax Romana and the Peace of Jesus Christ* (trans. John Bowden; London: SCM, 1987), 11–12. For other essays on the relationship between Roman coins and the NT world, see Larry J. Kreitzer, *Striking New Images: Roman Imperial Coinage and the New Testament World* (Sheffield: Sheffield Academic Press, 1996).

of the emperor,[102] but the minting of bronze or copper coins was permitted in the provinces and was under the control of the local governor. As had the preceding Roman prefects of Judea, Pilate also minted coins, for which examples exist from three successive years. These bronze perutahs measure between 13.5 mm and 17 mm in diameter and may be described as follows:[103]

29/30 C.E. (16th year of Tiberius):
   Obverse: three ears of grain, in which the outer two ears droop while the centre one stands upright; the stalks are bound twice or else are held in a frame
      surrounded by text: ΙΟΥΛΙΑ ΚΑΙΣΑΡΟΣ[104] (i.e., "Julia, of Caesar")[105]
   Reverse: a *simpulum* with an upright handle
      the date: LIϚ (i.e., "year 16")[106]
      surrounded by text: ΤΙΒΕΡΙΟΥ ΚΑΙΣΑΡΟΣ (i.e., "of Tiberius Caesar")

30/31 C.E. (17th year of Tiberius):
   Obverse: a *lituus* with the crook facing right
      surrounded by text: ΤΙΒΕΡΙΟΥ ΚΑΙΣΑΡΟΣ (i.e., "of Tiberius Caesar")
   Reverse: a wreath, open at one end and intertwined at the other
      the date: LIZ (i.e., "year 17")

---

[102] The responsibility to mint silver coins was at times delegated to certain cities, such as, for example, the silver Tyrian shekel used by Jews to pay the temple tax was minted in Tyre.

[103] Descriptions and drawings of these coins may be found in Helen K. Bond, "The Coins of Pontius Pilate: Part of an Attempt to Provoke the People or Integrate Them Into the Empire?" *JSJ* 27 (1996): 243–44; David Hendin, *Guide to Biblical Coins* (4 ed.; Dix Hills, NY: Amphora, 2001), nos. 648–50; Joan E. Taylor, "Pontius Pilate and the Imperial Cult in Roman Judaea," *NTS* 52 (2006): 557. Descriptions and photographs of these coins may be found in Hendin, *Biblical Coins*, nos. 648–50; A. Reifenberg, *Ancient Jewish Coins* (6 ed.; Jerusalem: Rubin Mass, 1973), 56, nos. 131–33. See also the study by Jean-Philippe Fontanille and Sheldon Lee Gosline, *The Coins of Pontius Pilate* (Marco Polo Monographs 4; Warren Center, PA: Shangri-La Publications, 2001). For online photographs, see www.menorahcoinproject.org.

[104] The wording on the coins is in Greek. The formation of the letters are similar to the capital Greek font used here, except for the sigma which is shaped more like a C rather than a Σ. The shape of a sigma as C rather than Σ is referred to as a "lunate sigma," and is found in eastern forms of the Greek alphabet.

[105] According to Bond ("Coins of Pontius Pilate," 245) this is probably a reference to Tiberius' mother, Livia Drusilla who, when adopted into the Julian *gens*, was given the name Julia Augusta. It was dropped from the two succeeding years of Pilate's coin because she died in 29 C.E., the year this coin was minted.

[106] The Latin "L" was used as an abbreviation for the Greek λύκαβας or "year." The numbering of the years used the letters of the Greek alphabet to represent them. Α–Θ = 1–9, Ι = 10, Κ = 20, etc. (in case you are counting numbers one through nine, note that the Greek letter *stigma*, between *epsilon* and *zēta*, represents the number six).

31/32 C.E. (18th year of Tiberius):[107]
   Obverse: a *lituus* with a crook facing right
           surrounded by text: ΤΙΒΕΡΙΟΥ ΚΑΙΣΑΡΟΣ (i.e., "of Tiberius Caesar")
   Reverse: a wreath, open at one end and intertwined at the other
           the date: LIH (i.e., "year 18")

The following is a pictorial representation of these features:[108]

©Joan E. Taylor.

Certain aspects concerning the identification and interpretation of these symbols is reasonably clear, while other elements are debated. The obverse of the first coin (16th year) has three ears of grain (barley or wheat) which have evidently been cut because the two ears on the outside are bending over while the centre one stands straight, or else this is intended to suggest bending forward in the direction of the viewer (an attempt at three-dimensional representation). The stalks of the grain are depicted as either bound twice, one binding lower than the other,[109] or else they are being held in a display frame or tripod.[110] Ears of grain had been used in the coins minted by two previous prefects, Coponius and Marcus Ambibulus,[111] and would also be used shortly after Pilate's time by Agrippa I.[112] In these other coins the

---

[107] This coin is essentially the same as the previous year's coin, except that the date has been changed.
[108] I am indebted to Joan E. Taylor for allowing me to reproduce her drawings, which I found to be the clearest of several that I have seen.
[109] So Bond, "Coins of Pontius Pilate," 243.
[110] Taylor, "Pontius Pilate and the Imperial Cult," 560. Taylor proposes a "tripod," but I don't see how the two parallel bands holding the stalks depict a tripod. Thus I use the more generic term "display frame."
[111] Hendin, *Biblical Coins*, nos. 635–38.
[112] Hendin, *Biblical Coins*, no. 553.

single or triple heads of grain are standing upright with nothing binding them (thus appearing as if they are still growing). Pilate's depiction could be interpreted in two different ways: as with the depiction of grain in the other coins of the era, the grain could symbolize the agricultural produce of the land of Israel.[113] However, Taylor proposes that the distinctiveness of Pilate's depiction, with the bent heads and being held, is better interpreted as being held in a display frame for ritual or cultic use, possibly in honor of Ceres, the goddess of grain.[114] In support of this interpretation, this side of the coin honors Julia, the mother of Tiberius, who in sculpture and coinage is frequently associated with Ceres, and thus the symbolism of the grain should be interpreted in conjunction with the person honored on the coin.[115] While the Israelite agricultural interpretation is possible, the Roman cultic interpretation is more likely in light of the evidence presented by Taylor. We should note, however, that the interpretation of a symbol is determined not only by the one using the symbol initially, but also by the culture of the viewer. So while Pilate probably intended a Roman cultic portrayal in this symbol, it is possible that the average Jewish common person using the coin might have (mis-)interpreted it as an Israelite agricultural symbol, particularly as it had be used similarly in earlier coins of the period.

The reverse of the first coin (16th year) is most often understood to depict a *simpulum*.[116] This utensil was a ladle with a long handle that was

---

[113] So, e.g., Bond, "Coins of Pontius Pilate," 250.

[114] Taylor ("Pontius Pilate and the Imperial Cult," 560) states: "... the ears droop. This draws attention to the fact that they are in Pilate's coinage cut and positioned in a tripod, as if they are being used in a ritual (which would explain their drooped appearance, because they are no longer growing). This practice of cutting wheat to place it on display in a metal tripod is still maintained in parts of southern Europe to this day in summer celebrations of cereal crops. In Roman times one would naturally associate cut ears of wheat or barley with some veneration of Ceres (Greek Demeter), the Roman goddess of grain and marriage."

[115] See the considerable evidence discussed by Taylor, "Pontius Pilate and the Imperial Cult," 560–61, who states (p. 561) for example, "Already by 18 CE there were dedications to Livia [Julia's prior name as husband of Augustus; she received the name Julia Augusta upon the death of Augustus] as Ceres Augusta within Italy, symbolism that was not intended to deify Livia, but designed as a form of symbolic honour whereby the maternal and generous attributes of Ceres are applied to the empress, the mother of the emperor."
Taylor ("Pontius Pilate and the Imperial Cult," 561) also suggests that the harvested, drooping ears of grain may be linked to Julia Augusta in another way. As the grain has been cut down and is thus dead, so Julia died in the year this coin was minted. If minted later in the year, after her death, then this coin would be a commemorative one. Her death would also explain why she did not appear on the coins of subsequent years. For descriptions of Julia's death and the Roman response to it, see Cassius Dio, *Hist.* 58.2.1–6; Tacitus, *Ann.* 5.1–3.

[116] Virtually all scholars understand this to depict a *simpulum* (ladle). But Taylor ("Pontius Pilate and the Imperial Cult," 559) suggests the possibility that it might be a *culullus* (cup) instead. I prefer the *simpulum* interpretation due to the vertical length of the handle

used specifically within Roman cult by a priest for tasting the wine used in a libation before pouring it out on the head of a sacrificial animal. It was a symbol widely used on Roman coins and engravings to portray the Roman cult, frequently along with other cultic objects. In particular, it was a symbol for the *pontifex* or the college of *pontifices*; that is, the college of priests who controlled Roman public religion. The office of high priest, or *pontifex maximus*, gradually became politicized, so that by the time of Augustus the role of emperor included serving in the priestly role of *pontifex maximus*. Thus, on this coin the *simpulum* surrounded by the text, ΤΙΒΕΡΙΟΥ ΚΑΙ-ΣΑΡΟΣ (i.e., "of Tiberius Caesar") is being used by Pilate to symbolically honor Tiberius in his role as *pontifex maximus*, and thus this is an explicit expression of the imperial cult.[117]

The obverse of the second and third coins (17th and 18th years) depicts a *lituus* which is a staff made of wood or metal that ended in the shape of a spiral or crook. It was an identifying symbol of an *augur*, a particular type of priest in the Roman cult who held it in their right hand and used it in cultic rituals for dividing the heavens into regions for determining sacred space, or for raising it to the sky for divination, or for invoking the gods and making predictions. This symbol is also found widely on Roman coins and engravings. As with *pontifex maximus*, so also the role of emperor came to include that of *augur*, and the symbol of the *lituus* was used to indicate the emperor's role as *augur* in the imperial cult. Thus, on these coins the *lituus* surrounded by ΤΙΒΕΡΙΟΥ ΚΑΙΣΑΡΟΣ (i.e., "of Tiberius Caesar") is honoring Tiberius in his role as *augur*, and thus this also is an explicit expression of the imperial cult.[118]

The reverse of these coins (17th and 18th years) depicts a wreath joined at one end and open at the other. It was used as a symbol of victory and power in a wide variety of cultural contexts. It appears as a symbol on Roman coins as well as a variety of Jewish coins, including Hasmonean and Herodian coins. In almost all instances it surrounds the name of the one in power. For example, on one of the earliest Hasmonean coins the wreath sur-

---

which, to my untrained eye, looks more like a ladle as portrayed on other coins. Whichever is the case, the cultic significance is essentially the same.

[117] Ya'akov Meshorer, *Ancient Jewish Coinage* (2 vols; Dix Hills, NY: Amphora Books, 1982), 2.180. Cf. the discussion by Bond, "Coins of Pontius Pilate," 251; Taylor, "Pontius Pilate and the Imperial Cult," 558–59. For a discussion of the role of *pontifex maximus* as well as the emperor having this title, see Mary Beard, et al., *Religions of Rome* (2 vols; Cambridge: Cambridge University Press, 1998), 1.55–58, 186–89, and for pictures and description of Roman coins depicting the role of *pontifex maximus* using the symbols of the *lituus* and the *simpulum*, see Beard, et al., *Religions of Rome*, 2.204–5.

[118] Anne V. Siebert, "Lituus," in *Brill's New Pauly: Encyclopedia of the Ancient World*, vol. 7 (Leiden: Brill, 2002), 737; Bond, "Coins of Pontius Pilate," 252; Taylor, "Pontius Pilate and the Imperial Cult," 559; Beard, et al., *Religions of Rome*, 1.182–86, 2.205.

rounds יהוחנן הכה גד יהם (abbreviation for "Johannan the High priest and the Council of the Jews), and on several of the coins minted by Herod Antipas the wreath surrounds ΤΙΒΕΡΙΑΣ ("Tiberius").[119] While the coins issued by the first two Roman prefects did not have a wreath, most of the coins issued by Valerius Gratus, Pilate's predecessor (16–26 C.E.) did have it. On some of his coins it surrounds the words ΚΑΙΣΑΡ ("Caesar"), in the others it surrounds ΙΟΥΛΙΑ ("Julia," the mother of the emperor[120]), and on the rest it surrounds ΤΙΒ ΚΑΙΣΑΡ (abbreviation for "Tiberius Caesar").[121] In a few instances when Jewish coins depict the head of the emperor, the head is depicted wearing a laurel wreath, which strengthens the symbolic association of the wreath with power. For example, some coins of Herod Philip depict Augustus wearing a wreath, and later coins depict Tiberius wearing a wreath.[122] Thus, the symbolism of the wreath is to honor the person who has ultimate political power over the region.[123]

The coins issued by the Roman prefects of Judea prior to Pilate depict agricultural imagery, including upright ears of grain, palm trees with dates, cornucopias, lilies, vine leaves, and amphoras. All these symbolize the agricultural bounty of the land. The only imagery that might be viewed as problematic by some Jews was the use by Pilate's predecessor, Gratus, of the laurel wreath surrounding either "Caesar," "Julia," or "Tiberius Caesar."[124] With such, Gratus was making a statement that celebrated Rome's political control over Judea, whereas to some within the Jewish population, it could be viewed as a symbol of political oppression. Pilate continued to use the laurel wreath, but his innovation was to also use explicit symbols from the Roman imperial cult to honor Tiberius, and initially his mother Julia as well, in their roles in the imperial cult.

---

[119] For examples of Hasmonean coins, see Hendin, *Biblical Coins*, nos. 452, 453, 455, 457, 459, 465, 466, 473, 475, 478, 479; the one cited is no. 452. For examples of Herodian coins, see Hendin, *Biblical Coins*, nos. 506, 507, 509, 511, 512, 513, 515, 517, 522, 524, 525, 526, 527, 541.

[120] On the possible significance of these references to Julia, see Taylor, "Pontius Pilate and the Imperial Cult," 560–61.

[121] Hendin, *Biblical Coins*, nos. 639–42, 645–47.

[122] Hendin, *Biblical Coins*, nos. 531, 533, 534, 537, 538. Bond ("Coins of Pontius Pilate," 251) observes that it also reappeared on coins of the first Jewish revolt. She cites George F. Hill, ed., *Catalogue of the Greek Coins of Palestine in the British Museum* (London: British Museum, 1914), 271, no. 21.

[123] On this point, then, I think Bond ("Coins of Pontius Pilate," 251) is incorrect when she claims that, because the wreath was widely used on Jewish coins, it was "... acceptable to the people of Judaea." If one was in support of the one in power, then it would be acceptable, but if one did not, then such a depiction could equally symbolize the power of the oppressor. Thus, in this instance I think Taylor ("Pontius Pilate and the Imperial Cult," 561–62) doesn't take the symbolism of the wreath far enough.

[124] Hendin, *Biblical Coins*, nos. 639–42, 645–47.

The implications this has for understanding Pilate in his role as prefect has been variously interpreted. Ethelbert Stauffer, as part of his Sejanus hypothesis,[125] claimed that these coins were "a deliberate provocation," intended to cause the Jewish people to rise up in revolt so that they could be destroyed.[126] But, if Pilate's intent and motive was to cause the greatest possible offense, it would have been better accomplished by depicting the actual image of the emperor's head himself.[127] Helen Bond on the other hand, notes that the Tyrian shekel made of silver, that was used by Jews to pay the Temple tax in the first century C.E. had images of the either Tyche, the goddess of luck, or else the head of the Tyrian god Melquarth.[128] Thus, there may have been distaste or disdain for coins bearing such images, but they hardly were viewed as a reason to revolt. Bond proposes that Pilate was placing a "purely Jewish design" on one side and a symbol of the Roman imperial cult on the other "in an attempt to continue the attempt of Herod I and his successors to integrate Judaea into the empire."[129] But, as has been demonstrated above, neither the ears of bent grain associated with Julia, nor the laurel wreath associated with Tiberius are "purely Jewish designs" at all. They may have incorporated elements that were similar to those used on other Jewish coins, but their associations were either with Roman imperial cult or Roman political power.

I would suggest that these coins are better interpreted as suggesting three interrelated things about Pilate: First, as a Roman prefect of a Roman province where the population was largely non-Roman, he sought to honor the Roman emperor and his family. Second, he explicitly wanted to honor Tiberius in his religious roles within the imperial cult.[130] The imperial cult had already been introduced to Judea by Herod. Now Pilate was taking it one step further. Third, he sought to make explicit that it was Rome and Rome's emperor that had political power over Judea. These demonstrate that, rather

---

[125] For further discussion, see § 3.2.7 below.

[126] Ethelbert Stauffer, *Christ and the Caesars: Historical Sketches* (London: SCM, 1955), 119. His interpretation of Pilate's coins is followed by a few others, e.g., E. Mary Smallwood, *The Jews Under Roman Rule from Pompey to Diocletian: A Study in Political Relations* (SJLA 20; Leiden: E.J. Brill, 1981), 167. Stauffer (pp. 119–20) also argues that Pilate's ceasing to mint coins in 31 C.E. is tied to the death of Sejanus. But a better explanation may be that the production was taken over by the mint in Syrian Antioch with the arrival of a new governor in the province of Syria in 32 C.E. See the discussion by Ernst Bammel, "Syrian Coinage and Pilate," *JJS* 2 (1951): 108–10; Brown, *Death of the Messiah*, 700; Jean-Pierre Lémonon, *Pilate et le gouvernement de la Judée: textes et monuments* (EBib; Paris: Gabalda, 1981), 114–15.

[127] Brown (*Death of the Messiah*, 700) also notes that there is no record of any disturbance caused by these coins. While true, this argument from silence holds little weight in light of our incomplete evidence of the period.

[128] Bond, "Coins of Pontius Pilate," 259. Cf. Hendin, *Biblical Coins*, no. 917.

[129] Bond, "Coins of Pontius Pilate," 260.

[130] Taylor, "Pontius Pilate and the Imperial Cult," 562–63.

than being anti-Jewish, Pilate was being pro-Roman, and that he was being more aggressively pro-Roman than the previous prefects. In so doing, he was manifesting not only a lack of sensitivity for Jewish issues,[131] but also a more blatant lack of concern, for by the time he minted these coins he had been prefect for three or more years – a long enough time to learn what some of the Jewish sensitivities were. After all, these coins were minted after the iconic standards incident – the incident to which we now turn.

3.2.2. The Iconic Standards Incident (ca. 26 C.E.)

The earliest known event in Pilate's prefecture is an incident that took place shortly after his arrival in Judea (26 C.E.),[132] in which he introduced iconic[133] standards into Jerusalem (Josephus, *J. W.* 2.169–74; *Ant.* 18.55–59).[134] Josephus reports that Pilate "took a bold step in subversion of the Jewish practices, by introducing into the city the busts of the emperor that were attached to the military standards" (*Ant.* 18.55; Feldman, LCL). This action involved Pilate bringing a new cohort to Jerusalem under the cover of night – a cohort that had not been there previously, for Roman standards always travelled with the troops as an expression of their allegiance to Rome and its religion.[135] In contrast to previous cohorts in Jerusalem (cf.

---

[131] Cf. the "lack of sensitivity" views expressed by Lémonon, *Pilate et le Gouvernement de la Judée*, 114–15; Brown, *Death of the Messiah*, 700; Bond, "Coins of Pontius Pilate," 261.

[132] This date is implied by the wording of Josephus, *J. W.* 2.169; cf. *Ant.* 18.55 (Feldman, LCL, 42 n. e).

[133] The term "iconic" here refers to these standards having an "icon" or "image" on them. This is in contrast to a later incident in Pilate's prefecture that involves "aniconic" standards – standards that did *not* bear an image.

[134] On the differences between the two accounts in *Jewish War* and *Jewish Antiquities*, and the roles they play in the differing rhetoric of each text, see Bond, *Pontius Pilate*, 49–57, 62–70.

This incident manifests certain similarities to the aniconic shields incident reported by Philo in *Embassy* 299–305 (see the discussion below in § 3.2.5), which has led a few scholars to propose that they are, in fact, different accounts of the same incident. For a recent example of such argumentation, see Daniel R. Schwartz, "Josephus and Philo on Pontius Pilate," in *The Jerusalem Cathedra: Studies in the History, Archaeology, Geography, and Ethnography of the Land of Israel*, vol. 3 (ed. Lee I. Levine; Jerusalem / Detroit: Yad Izhak Ben-Zvi Institute / Wayne State University Press, 1983), 26–45. However, most scholars view these as two distinct incidents (see the bibliographic list in Schwartz, 37–39). The difference of Josephus' iconic standards vs. Philo's aniconic shields makes it difficult to equate the two accounts, especially in light of how each serves the differing rhetoric of their texts. On viewing these two incidents as distinct, see Paul L. Maier, "The Episode of the Golden Roman Shields at Jerusalem," *HTR* 62 (1969): 111–14; Smallwood, *The Jews Under Roman Rule*, 165–67; Brown, *Death of the Messiah*, 702–3.

[135] On this incident see the helpful analysis by Carl H. Kraeling, "The Episode of the Roman Standards at Jerusalem," *HTR* 35 (1942): 263–89. The link between the standards and the religion of the soldiers is intimated by the account in Josephus, *J. W.* 6.316 in which

Ant. 18.56, this one's standards had embossed images (εἰκόνας) of the emperor. Some of the Jewish people travelled to Caesarea (where the prefect's primary residence was located) and requested that Pilate withdraw these standards from Jerusalem, for the images were viewed as a violation of the biblical commandment against images. Pilate refused, for "to do so would be an outrage (ὕβριν) to the emperor" (*Ant.* 18.57; Feldman, LCL). The Jews continued their petitions for five days, and on the sixth Pilate prepared to address them in the stadium, but he had his soldiers hidden and surrounded the crowd. When the soldiers revealed themselves, the Jews expressed their willingness to die rather than allow their law to be broken. Observing their commitment to the law, Pilate withdrew the cohort with the standards.

In this incident Pilate appears to have been a prefect who wanted to start his governorship with a clear statement of Rome's presence and authority. This interpretation is supported by our discussion of Pilate's coins – he was being more blatantly pro-Roman than his predecessors. The statement by Josephus in *Ant.* 18.55 that Pilate's motive was to "subvert Jewish practices"(missing in *Jewish War*) is part of Josephus' rhetoric in *Antiquities* that seeks to explain factors that led to the later Jewish revolt.[136] That the incident began at night suggests that Pilate was aware of its potential offense. But it would appear that Pilate used the cover of darkness with a view to avoiding a crowd while entering Jerusalem in order to have the standards already in place for the next morning. He thought that, if they were already installed, the inhabitants would probably accept their presence, as they evidently did when the cohort with these same standards was garrisoned in Caesarea. His later actions in Caesarea suggest his resolve, and in turn his willingness to test the resolve of the protesters. But Pilate evidently underestimated the sentiments of the people, so to avoid a massacre he judiciously chose to withdraw the troops.[137] Thus, Josephus' statement that Pilate's motive was to "subvert Jewish practices" communicates a Jewish perspective on the matter. But viewed from Pilate's perspective, it was an attempt to stamp more clearly the presence and authority of Rome in Jerusalem – it was not so much a matter of being anti-Jewish as being pro-Roman.[138] This

---

the Roman soldiers celebrated their victory over the Jerusalem's temple (and its God) by setting up their standards in the temple court and sacrificing to them. Cf. also 1QpHab 6.3–5 which describes the Kittim (i. e., the Romans) offering "sacrifices to their standards."

[136] See especially Bond, *Pontius Pilate*, 69–78.

[137] See the judicious historical evaluation of this incident by Bond, *Pontius Pilate*, 78–85. She also points out (85) that "[s]elf-interested motives may also have played a part: it would not have looked good in Rome if one of Pilate's first acts as governor was to massacre unarmed people."

[138] Bond (*Pontius Pilate*, 81) states: "Offending the Jewish Law, then, was not Pilate's prime intention, though his actions do show arrogance and contempt towards the people and their customs, linked with an underestimation of the strengths of their religious feel-

would explain the action, the matter of its execution, as well as his willingness ultimately to back down. Thus, backing down was neither a sign of weakness nor of vacillation, but rather of being politically savvy.

3.2.3. The Aqueduct Protest Incident (ca. 27–29 C. E.)

A second incident that Josephus narrates is Pilate's response to the aqueduct protest (Josephus, *J. W.* 2.175–77; *Ant.* 18.60–62).[139] Pilate had used money from the temple treasury to fund the construction of an aqueduct to Jerusalem. How Pilate got the money is not stated. It might have been by force or intimidation, or it may have been with the agreement of the chief priests and the temple treasurer – we do not know.[140] If it was the former, then a protest would probably be immediate. But this protest by the Jewish crowd appears to have taken place after the construction was well under way, or perhaps even finished. The protesters also waited until Pilate is in Jerusalem. Thus the issue was probably not simply the use of money from the temple treasury but some perceived abuse of it.[141] In contrast to the iconic stand-

---

ing. Anxious to take no nonsense from the people, Pilate's actions seem designed to establish from the start both his own superior position in the province and that of the Empire which he served." Similarly, Smallwood (*The Jews Under Roman Rule*, 161) concurs with this view, noting that "... though his action was disrespectful towards it [i.e., the Law], he was not demanding emperor-worship of the Jews."

[139] The date of this incident is unknown, but in *Antiquities* Josephus places it after the iconic standards incident but before the *Testimonium Flavianum*, and thus, if he is following a chronological order, it is relatively early in Pilate's prefecture, probably somewhere between 27 and 29 C.E.

[140] On the finances of the temple treasury, see Emil Schürer, *The History of the Jewish People in the Age of Jesus Christ* (ed. Geza Vermes, et al.; Edinburgh: T & T Clark, 1973–87), 2.279–84. He comments (2.283–84) that the priestly and political authorities often worked together in ways that used the funds of the temple treasury, and that the political authorities may have had some authority over these funds as well.

[141] In *J. W.* 2.175 Josephus states that this "sacred treasury" was "known as *corbonas* (κορβωνᾶς)," whereas in *Ant.* 18.60 it was simply the "sacred treasury." Scholars differ over what was the offense perceived by the Jewish people. Feldman (*Ant.* 18.60; LCL, 46–47, n. b) states that "Pilate was expropriating for his own secular purposes the shekalim which had been contributed by Jews everywhere for the purchase of sacrificial animals" and cites *m. Šeqal.* 3:2, though it is not clear why this mishnaic text is cited. If *m. Šeqal.* 4:2 was intended, this latter text actually does specify the purchase of sacrificial animals from the temple treasury, but it also states that "... the wall of the city [of Jerusalem] and its towers, and all the requirements of the city were purchased from the surplus of the Temple Treasury-chamber" (Blackman, *Mishnah*). Brown on the other hand (*Death of the Messiah*, 700) states that "... the money was destined for social welfare and public works to maintain Jerusalem ..., so Pilate was not simply being greedy." Bond (*Pontius Pilate*, 86–87) suggests the use of these funds may have been legitimate (citing *m. Šeqal.* 4:2), but the use of the verb ἐξαναλίσκω ("to use up") might imply that the project required more funds than initially thought, and that Pilate used up more than the surplus, thus threatening the purchasing of the daily sacrifices. It is also possible that Pilate also began to take the temple treasury for granted, expecting to use it for a variety of his own purposes.

ards episode, this crowd is described as more unruly by Josephus: "tens of thousands of men assembled and cried out against him ... Some too even hurled insults and abuse ..." (*Ant.* 18.60; Feldman, LCL; cf. *J. W.* 2.175: "angry clamour ... tumult"; Thackeray, LCL). Pilate's response is also more violent. In a manner similar to that of the iconic standards episode, he had disguised soldiers scattered throughout the crowd with orders to use cudgels rather than their swords. This time on his signal the soldiers beat the protesters, with the result that many were injured, and many were killed either by the beating or by being trampled to death. And thus the protest (στάσις) was put down.[142]

In contrast to the iconic standards incident, this aqueduct protest reveals the Jewish people demonstrating a more "belligerent attitude" and Pilate in turn manifesting "greater impatience."[143] Pilate considered himself to be acting appropriately in using this money to construct something that would benefit the people of Jerusalem and the temple. Since the construction was well on its way or perhaps even completed, there was little for him to back down from (in contrast to the iconic standards episode). If he perceived the protest as στάσις ("unrest, revolt") as Josephus described it, then he had the obligation as the Roman prefect to quell this protest, for his job was, first and foremost, to maintain peace. In disguising his soldiers and having them infiltrate the crowd, instructing them to use cudgels rather than swords, Pilate was attempting a measured response rather than an action that might result in a wholesale massacre.[144]

3.2.4. The Galilean Pilgrims Incident (ca. 28–29 C. E.)

Luke 13:1 makes reference to "... some present who told him [i.e., Jesus] about the Galileans whose blood Pilate had mingled with their sacrifices." This is a report brought to Jesus in Galilee which initially would probably

---

Bond (*Pontius Pilate*, 55) points out that Josephus does not explain to his non-Jewish audience how Pilate's action of using the funds was offensive (as he has elsewhere explained matters of Jewish practice), and this suggests that it is not Pilate's initial perceived offense that was important, but rather the Jewish reaction and how Pilate responded.

[142] In *J. W.* 2.177 Josephus gives the result as "the multitude was reduced to silence" (Thackeray, LCL), but in *Ant.* 18.62 Josephus uses the Greek term στάσις ("unrest, revolt"): "Thus ended the uprising (στάσις)" (Feldman, LCL).

[143] Smallwood, *The Jews Under Roman Rule*, 162. This characterization is accurate, but Smallwood attributes this "mutual distrust" to what each learned from the iconic standards incident. But this is unlikely, at least as a direct cause, for there is considerable time between the incidents, and Pilate no doubt did other things in the intervening period. To link the two incidents causally simply because Josephus narrates them back to back goes beyond the evidence.

[144] S. G. F. Brandon (*Jesus and the Zealots: A Study of the Political Factor in Primitive Christianity* [New York: Charles Scribner's Sons, 1967], 76 n. 3) suggests that this indicates that "Pilate planned a police, not a military, operation."

have come from pilgrims returning from Jerusalem.[145] Since these were Galileans, they had evidently made a pilgrimage to Jerusalem for one of the festivals, which is confirmed by the reference to mingling blood with their sacrifices. This descriptive phrase also suggests that the most probable festival is Passover, for this is only time when the people were involved in killing their own sacrifices.[146] It is impossible to know whether this incident involved soldiers entering the temple itself to kill these pilgrims or whether the language is more a metaphorical expression alluding to their status as pilgrims.[147] While it is possible that this might be an ambiguous allusion to one of the incidents also mentioned by Josephus or Philo, they are sufficiently different to make such a conclusion unlikely.[148] Furthermore, we do know that Josephus was certainly not exhaustive in listing all such incidents, for he does not mention the aniconic shields incident described by Philo (see below). It does not appear to have been a major episode, and those killed were probably few in number, for within this pericope (Luke 13:1–5) Jesus compares this incident with "eighteen who were killed when the tower of Siloam fell on them ..." (13:4).

In the allusion to this incident no explanation is provided for Pilate's action, but the description implies an immediate, military response to some form of unrest,[149] rather than execution after a trial process. Thus, while

---

[145] The brief nature of this reference makes it difficult to date. But if Jesus' death is placed at 30 C. E., then this incident probably took place at some point earlier than that. Less likely though still possible is that a later incident has been retrojected back into this sayings complex.

[146] Cf. *m.Pesaḥ.* 5:6; E. P. Sanders, *Judaism: Practice and Belief 63 BCE – 66 CE* (Philadelphia: Trinity Press International, 1992), 135–38.

[147] Smallwood (*The Jews Under Roman Rule*, 163) considers it possible that the bloodshed was in the temple, whereas Winter (*On the Trial of Jesus*, 75 n. 9) considers this "oriental picturesque language" that does not need to imply violation of the temple. He presumes that if Pilate's soldiers had violated the temple, Josephus would have mentioned the incident. But this assumption is unwarranted.

[148] For a survey of the variety of proposals, see Bond, *Pontius Pilate*, 194–95; Joseph A. Fitzmyer, *The Gospel According to Luke* (2 vols; AB 28; Garden City, NY: Doubleday, 1981–85), 1006–7; Bock, *Luke*, 1204–5. See also the discussion by Josef Blinzler, "Die Niedermetzelung von Galiläern Durch Pilatus," *NovT* 2 (1957–58): 24–49; Bond concludes (p. 195) that "Luke 13.1 refers to an otherwise unknown event."

The brevity of the account provides limited data on which to make a judgment concerning historicity. But given the variety of other actions by Pilate that are described in our sources, there would be no need to create one when other historical events lay close at hand. Cf. the judgment of Fitzmyer, *Luke*, 1007.

[149] Geza Vermes (*Jesus the Jew: A Historian's Reading of the Gospels* [Philadelphia: Fortress, 1973], 47) states that these "must have been Galilean revolutionaries" along the lines of Judas the Galilean. Such a claim goes beyond the evidence, but it is certainly possible. For Judean prefects were known to bring extra soldiers to Jerusalem during Passover (when the Israelite people celebrated their God freeing them from oppression in Egypt) because it was often a time of unrest.

this incident tells us little about Pilate, it does suggest his willingness to use his power to keep peace in Jerusalem during festivals, including putting to death persons who were not his subjects but were rather the subjects of Herod Antipas.[150]

3.2.5. The Aniconic Shields Incident (ca. 31–32 C.E.)

A later incident, narrated by Philo, involves Pilate introducing aniconic shields into Jerusalem (*Embassy* 299–305).[151] Philo's *On the Embassy to Gaius* is a polemic account of the Emperor Gaius Caligula's hostility to Jews and in particular his treatment of a delegation of Jews from Alexandria. It was probably written at the beginning of Claudius' reign (which was 41–54 C.E.) as "... an attempt to persuade the new Emperor not to follow Gaius' policies with respect to the Jewish people but those of his predecessors, Augustus and Tiberius."[152] Part of Philo's account is a citation of an earlier letter, supposedly from Agrippa I to Gaius,[153] attempting to convince Gaius not to set up a statue of himself in the Jerusalem Temple. It is in this letter that reference is made to an incident involving Pilate: He set up in the Herodian palace in Jerusalem gold-covered shields in honor of Tiberius, but according to Philo, he did so "not so much to honour Tiberius as to annoy the multitude" (*Embassy* 299; Colson, LCL). Philo admitted that there was no image on the shields except the names of the one being honored and the one honoring.[154] But the Jewish people objected that this was against Tiberius' policies and threatened to send a delegation to him. Pilate appeared ready to withdraw them, but he also didn't want to appear to back down, so Jewish officials wrote to Tiberius arguing their case. Tiberius wrote in response ordering Pilate to withdraw the shields and set them up in the Temple of Augustus in Caesarea. The account concludes, "So both objects

---

[150] Smallwood (*The Jews Under Roman Rule*, 163) suggests that Pilate's responsibility "for the death of subjects of an independent tetrarch may have caused the hostility recorded between Pilate and Antipas at the time of the Crucifixion."

[151] While it is difficult to date this incident, Bond (*Pontius Pilate*, 45–46) argues for the plausibility of it taking place shortly after the death of Sejanus in October, 31 C.E.
On the scholarly discussion of whether or not this incident is the same as the iconic standards incident reported by Josephus (see § 3.2.2 above), see the discussion in n. 134.

[152] Bond, *Pontius Pilate*, 33, following Edwin R. Goodenough, *The Politics of Philo Judaeus: Practice and Theory* (New Haven, CT: Yale University Press, 1938), 19–20.

[153] Bond (*Pontius Pilate*, 24) suggests that such a letter is quite feasible, but it is presented in *Legatio ad Gaium* in Philo's own style – as is consistent with historiographic practices of this period. Cf. also Brown, *Death of the Messiah*, 697.

[154] *Embassy* 299; cf. 306. Philo probably mentioned this to downplay somewhat the offense. Nevertheless, from a Jewish perspective, the offense was real, for the inscription probably included a reference to "*divi Augusti*," the "divine Augustus." Thus it was a reference to Tiberius' divinity that was considered offensive. Cf. the helpful discussion by Bond, *Pontius Pilate*, 37–46.

were safeguarded, the honour paid to the emperor and the policy observed from of old in dealing with the city" (*Embassy* 305; Colson, LCL).

Philo's polemical rhetoric can be observed in the motive attributed to Pilate's action: "to annoy the multitude" (*Embassy* 299; Colson, LCL). He also ascribed character qualities to him to explain his initial refusal to remove the shields: "When he, naturally inflexible, a blend of self-will and relentlessness, stubbornly refused ..." (*Embassy* 301; Colson, LCL). Pilate did not want to back down: "So with all his vindictiveness and furious temper, he was in a difficult position. He had not the courage to take down what had been dedicated nor did he wish to do anything which would please his subjects" (*Embassy* 303; Colson, LCL). These are stock character qualities used elsewhere by Philo to describe others who offend Jewish sensibilities, and thus they need to be understood as part of Philo's rhetorical polemic.[155] However, in his explanation of why Pilate feared a delegation going to Rome, Philo blends such stock character qualities with more specific charges: Pilate was afraid they might "... expose the rest of his conduct as governor by stating in full the briberies, the insults, the robberies, the outrages and wonton injuries, the executions without trial constantly repeated, the ceaseless and supremely grievous cruelty" (*Embassy* 302; Colson, LCL). The three specific actions that go beyond the stock rhetorical language include venality, robbery, and executions without trial.

It is probable that the basic elements of this narrative are historical, but Philo's rhetoric attributes motives and character qualities that are unlikely.[156] If this event took place later in Pilate's Judean career – more than likely after the iconic standards incident – then his use of shields without images and his locating them in the praetorium (the centre of his administration in Jerusalem), suggests that he had learned from his past mistakes and that he was attempting to be somewhat sensitive to Jewish sensibilities, but at the same time maintaining his pro-Roman policies and activities. If, as has been suggested, this event takes place in the turbulent period after the death of Sejanus (October, 31 C.E.),[157] then it suggests that Pilate was demonstrating his loyalty to Tiberius, and his reticence to remove the shields was out of concern not to dishonor the emperor.[158] Thus, in a manner similar to the iconic standards incident, this aniconic shields episode also reveals Pilate as a governor intent on maintaining the power and honor of the Roman empire he served and represented. From Pilate's perspective, his actions

---

[155] Cf. the discussion by Bond, *Pontius Pilate*, 27–33. She states (p. 31): "Philo's description of Pilate perfectly conforms to this common picture of the Roman official bent on undermining the Law of his Jewish subjects."

[156] Bond, *Pontius Pilate*, 36–48.

[157] So Bond, *Pontius Pilate*, 45–46; Brown, *Death of the Messiah*, 701.

[158] Bond, *Pontius Pilate*, 46–48.

were legitimate expressions of Roman authority to portray and demonstrate Roman honor. But from the Jewish populace's perspective, the actions were an affront to their religious convictions.

3.2.6. The Samaritan Prophet Incident (36 C. E.)

The final incident in Pilate's prefecture that Josephus reports was his handling of an uprising in Samaria (*Ant.* 18.85–89). Having narrated a variety of disturbances among Jews, Josephus reports this incident as an example that "[t]he Samaritan nation too was not exempt from disturbance" (*Ant.* 18.85a; Feldman, LCL). A Samaritan rallied the people with a promise of leading them to Mount Gerizim where they would unearth sacred vessels buried by Moses. The people gathered in the village of Tirathana in response to this apparent prophetic call, armed themselves, and prepared to climb the mountain. Pilate responded with both cavalry and infantry, which he used to block their route. In the ensuing battle many were killed, others were scattered, and prisoners were taken. The incident ended when "Pilate put to death the principle leaders and those who were most influential among the fugitives" (*Ant.* 18.87b; Feldman, LCL).[159] According to Josephus, the Samaritan council appealed to Vitellius, the governor of Syria,[160] claiming that the group Pilate attacked were not rebels but rather refugees fleeing Pilate's persecution. Vitellius ordered Pilate to return to Rome, and replaced him with a temporary prefect. Thus, Pilate's prefecture was ended (36 C. E.), but he did not actually arrive back in Rome until after the Emperor Tiberius had died in March, 37 C. E. (*Ant.* 18.88–89).

Josephus portrays the Samaritans in *Antiquities* quite consistently in a negative light. Thus, his description of the Samaritan prophet is explicitly negative, as is his portrayal of other prophetic movements. He describes the movement as effectively being an armed rebellion. The way Josephus describes Pilate's military response is that it was an appropriate display of force against unrest (Josephus twice refers to it as an "uprising" (θόρυβος, "disturbance, uproar;" *Ant.* 18.85a, 88a). Josephus describes the response of the Samaritan council as being their claim about the event rather than an accurate account of it.[161] Thus, Josephus portrays Pilate relatively positively in this particular incident. Yet, from Josephus' perspective, Pilate must an-

---

[159] For a discussion of this incident, see Richard A. Horsley and John S. Hanson, *Bandits, Prophets, and Messiahs: Popular Movements at the Time of Jesus* (Minneapolis: Winston, 1985), 162–64; Marilyn F. Collins, "The Hidden Vessels in Samaritan Traditions," *JSJ* 3 (1972): 97–116; Robert L. Webb, *John the Baptizer and Prophet: A Socio-Historical Study* (JSNTSup 62; Sheffield: Sheffield Academic Press, 1991), 333–34.

[160] On the relationship of the Roman provinces of Judea and Syria, see the discussion below § 3.3.1.

[161] Bond, *Pontius Pilate*, 71–73.

swer for his "hubris" (ὕβρις, "insult, mistreatment;" *Ant.* 18.88b) as prefect of Judea.[162]

3.2.7. Pilate and the Influence of Sejanus

This final element is neither a historical incident, nor material remains, but is rather the need to address the question of the possible influence that Sejanus may have had on Pilate and the character of his prefecture. To understand this issue, a little background may be helpful. The emperor Tiberius, who reigned from 14 to 37 C.E., had a difficult relationship with the Roman senate, due in part to him having been away for the previous thirty years leading his army. During the early years of his Principate he thus came to depend upon the Praetorian Guard. An equestrian (a rank of lower nobility), Lucius Aelius Sejanus, gained Tiberius' confidence and eventually became the only praetorian prefect. In 26 or 27 C.E. Tiberius left Rome to reside on the island of Capri, leaving the administration of the empire in the hands of Sejanus who also now controlled governmental communication with the absent Tiberius. Sejanus' rise however had been manipulative, and now with effective power, his aims became treasonous. Tiberius discovered Sejanus' plotting in 31 C.E., and he had him arrested and executed on October 18, 31 C.E. At this point Tiberius took back the direct reins of power.

Two questions arise with reference to Sejanus that are relevant here. First, was Sejanus anti-Jewish as reported by Philo? And second, what was the relationship between Sejanus and Pilate, and more particularly, had Sejanus appointed Pilate and was thus his patron? If the answers are positive, then it would be possible to interpret certain of Pilate's actions as taking an aggressive anti-Jewish stance. Also, if positive, Pilate's sense of security in his position would be different depending upon what date is used for Jesus' crucifixion: whether 30 C.E., when Sejanus was at the height of his power, or 33 C.E., after Sejanus had been exposed and executed. The view of Ethelbert Stauffer has been quite influential on these questions. He argued that Sejanus had an explicitly anti-Jewish policy, and that he personally appointed Pilate as prefect in Judea with the intent to rule in such a way as to provoke the Jewish people to rebellion and thus provide an opportunity to crush the revolt and annihilate them. However, Sejanus' premature death in 31 C.E. prevented their plan coming to fruition, leaving Pilate in a precarious position. According to Stauffer, this explains the tension between the portrayal in Jewish sources (Josephus and Philo) of the harsh, unyielding

---

[162] Smallwood (*The Jews Under Roman Rule*, 171) suggests that the prompt removal of Pilate by Vitellius may not have been so much in response to this incident in particular, but may also have been in response to other, earlier incidents as well. Vitellius simply took the opportunity occasioned by the Samaritan complaint.

and provocative Pilate and the portrayal in the Gospels of the vacillating and weak Pilate: before 31 C.E. he was provocative because he had the support of Sejanus and his anti-Jewish policy, but in 33 C.E. (the date of the crucifixion in this view, rather than 30 C.E.) he no longer had Roman support for such an anti-Jewish policy.[163]

Stauffer's view has been quite influential in subsequent 50 years of scholarship,[164] but more recently this view has increasingly been called into question.[165] The portrayal of Sejanus as plotting against the Jews is found in Philo's *On the Embassy to Gaius* (159–61),[166] but it has no corroboration in any other source concerning Sejanus, who is otherwise usually portrayed quite negatively for his treasonous plotting against Tacitus.[167] It is more likely that Philo has portrayed Sejanus in this manner to suit his rhetorical purposes in *On the Embassy to Gaius*. Writing to persuade the new emperor Claudius to reject the policy of his predecessor Gaius towards the Jews and to follow the policies of the preceding emperors, Augustus and Tiberius, Philo attributes to the now disgraced and executed Sejanus the negative quality of anti-Judaism in order to highlight the positive qualities and policies of Tiberius towards the Jews. In contrast to Sejanus, Tiberius is described by Philo as knowing that accusations against the Jews in Rome were false, and issuing an edict to his procurators to reassure their Jewish inhabitants that they may dwell in their cities in peace and that none of their customs would be disturbed.[168] Thus it is unlikely that Philo's portrayal of an anti-Jewish Sejanus is historical. Furthermore, no evidence exists of a relationship between Pilate and Sejanus. Therefore, the use of the Sejanus hypothesis to explain Pilate's actions should be rejected.[169]

---

[163] Stauffer, *Christ and the Caesars*, 118–20.

[164] Followed by, for example, Maier, "Episode," 114–15; Cohn, *The Trial and Death of Jesus*, 15–17; Smallwood, *The Jews Under Roman Rule*, 165–70, 201–10; Harold W. Hoehner, "Pontius Pilate," in *Dictionary of Jesus and the Gospels* (ed. Joel B. Green, et al.; Downers Grove, IL: InterVarsity, 1992), 615–17.

[165] For a survey of the scholarship on this issue, see Bond, *Pontius Pilate*, xiii–xvi. Examples of recent rejections of the Sejanus hypothesis include Schwartz, "Josephus and Philo on Pontius Pilate," 35–36; Lémonon, *Pilate et le Gouvernement de la Judée*, 275–77; Brown, *Death of the Messiah*, 693–94.

[166] Philo also alludes to it in *Flaccus* 1. Eusebius (*Hist. eccl.* 2.5) also refers to this, but this is not an independent corroboration for he explicitly cites Philo as his source.

[167] Cf. the extensive descriptions of Sejanus in Cassius Dio, *Hist. Rom.*, 57.22–58.16; Suetonius, *Tib.* 61–65; Tacitus, *Ann.* 6; Juvenal, *Sat.* 10; Josephus, *Ant.* 18.181–82.

[168] This contrast is very explicit in Philo, *Embassy* 160–61. Cf. the discussion in § 3.2.5 above concerning Philo's description of the aniconic shields incident.

[169] Those who reject the Sejanus hypothesis with reference to Pilate include H.E.W. Turner, "The Chronological Framework of the Ministry," in *Historicity and Chronology in the New Testament* (ed. D.E. Nineham, et al.; London: SPCK, 1965), 59–74, esp. 68–74; Lémonon, *Pilate et le Gouvernement de la Judée*, 223–25, 275–76; Schwartz, "Josephus

3.2.8. Conclusion: The Prefecture of Pontius Pilate

This examination of his coins and the accounts of various incidents during his prefecture of Judea, allows us to draw a number of conclusions about Pilate. The evidence from numismatics and from these events show certain common themes or trends. As noted in the beginning of this section, these known incidents are almost certainly not the only that took place during his rule. Philo's description, while no doubt showing rhetorical excess, does also point to the likelihood of numerous other incidents in "the rest of his conduct as governor by stating in full the briberies, the insults, the robberies, the outrages and wonton injuries, the executions without trial constantly repeated, the ceaseless and supremely grievous cruelty" (*Embassy* 302; Colson, LCL). But from the evidence we do have, several conclusions can be reached concerning Pilate.

First, Pilate followed a more aggressive pro-Roman policy than the prefects that had ruled prior to him. He sought to put more forcefully the stamp of Rome on Judea. From his point of view, Judea was now a Roman province – it was now ruled by Rome and was the beneficiary of the peace that Rome brought to the world – and so it should display its Roman character.

Second, Pilate was not really anti-Jewish (as in some kind of Sejanus plot). Rather, from Pilate's point of view, he saw Jewish sensibilities as secondary and subservient to his aggressive pro-Roman stance. He might acknowledge an awareness of Jewish issues, and this might shape how he would advance his pro-Roman agenda, but it would not ultimately hinder that agenda. After all, Judea was now a Roman province. From the point of view of his Jewish subjects, however, Pilate's actions were seen as showing disdain for their Jewish distinctives, and thus they were perceived as being anti-Jewish.

Third, Pilate was politically astute and was guided primarily by how his Roman masters would perceive his actions, rather than by how they might affect or be perceived by his Jewish subjects. Thus, he was willing at times to change his plans, depending upon how their potential consequences would be perceived by Rome. This was not being weak-willed or vacillating on his part; rather, he was being politically astute.

3.3. Roman Rule and Capital Crimes in a Roman Province

Having concluded that it is highly probable historically that Pilate did examine Jesus in some fashion, and having examined what we can know about Pilate, we can now turn to place this within the larger historical context of

---

and Philo on Pontius Pilate," 35–36; Schwartz, "Pontius Pilate," 399; Brown, *Death of the Messiah*, 693–94; Bond, *Pontius Pilate*, xv–xvi, 22–23.

how Roman provinces functioned, particularly in terms of how it handled cases involving capital crimes.

3.3.1. Roman rule of the Province of Judea

Judea (including Samaria and Idumea) became a Roman province in 6 C. E.[170] when Herod Archelaus was exiled and his territory was transferred into the hands of a Roman prefect who ruled directly over Judea as a Roman province. Though relatively small, Judea was an imperial province and thus was under the Emperor's control with its prefect responsible directly to him.[171] Judea did not, however, have Roman legions garrisoned within its borders – the close proximity of the four legions in the province of Syria to the north was considered sufficient. Thus, while Judea was an independent province, the legate of Syria had some oversight of its affairs.[172] Most provinces were ruled by men of senatorial rank. The larger provinces were ruled by former consuls, and thus had the title of proconsul, while the smaller provinces were ruled by former praetors with the title of propraetor.[173] A few smaller provinces, however, were ruled by men of lower, equestrian rank. This was particularly done with a region that had been recently assimilated and its people were considered rebellious or semi-barbaric – situations which perhaps required military rule, and thus men drawn from the

---

[170] Judea and Samaria were ruled by a Roman prefect from 6 to 41 C. E. Agrippa I had been granted by Caligula the territory of Herod Antipas (Galilee and Perea) in 40 C. E. In 41 C. E. Claudius extended Agrippa's territory to include Judea and Samaria. Thus Agrippa ruled for a brief time over the same territory as his grandfather, Herod the Great, had. But Agrippa I died in 44 C. E., and at that time all of Palestine was returned to provincial status and ruled directly by a Roman procurator.

[171] This stands in contrast to senatorial provinces, whose governors were appointed by the Roman Senate. The governors of these provinces were responsible to the Senate. The Emperor had direct control of the army, and thus the imperial provinces were those where the Roman legions were located. G. H. Stevenson, *Roman Provincial Administratation: Till the Age of the Antonines* (New York: G. E. Stechert & Co., 1939), 101–5; Maurice Sartre, *The Middle East Under Rome* (trans. Porter, et al.; Cambridge, MA: Belknap Press of Harvard University Press, 2005), 31–87.

[172] Josephus' statement (*Ant.* 17.355) that Judea was added to the province of Syria after the deposition of Archelaus is probably incorrect or at least too simplistic a comment. Contrast the statement by Tacitus (*Ann.* 2.42) recognizing Judea and Syria as separate provinces. See the discussion by Theodor Mommsen, *The Provinces of the Roman Empire* (2 vols.; rev. ed.; trans. William P. Dickson; 1909; repr., New York: Barnes & Noble, 1996), 2.185 n. 1. Smallwood, *The Jews Under Roman Rule*, 144–45. That some oversight was exercised in exceptional circumstances may be seen in the appeal by Samaritan residents of Judea to Vitellius, the legate of Syria, over what they perceived as Pilate's oppressive rule. Vitellius responded by removing Pilate from office, ordering him to return to Rome. See Josephus, *Ant.* 18.88–89.

[173] John Richardson, *Roman Provincial Administration 227 BC to AD 117* (1976; repr., Inside the Ancient World; London: Bristol Classical Press, 1984), 85; Schürer, *History of the Jewish People*, 1:357.

equestrian rank would be particularly well-suited because of their military experience.[174] Prior to Claudius' reign (41–54 C.E.) the title for these equestrian-ranked governors was prefect (*praefectus*, ἔπαρχος).[175]

While a prefect did not come from the senatorial ranks of someone who governed as a proconsul, he nevertheless held the *imperium* ("power") – the independent power and control over his province, just as a proconsul did.[176] Whether proconsul or prefect, having the *imperium* meant that he was responsible for, and had the power over, the administration (especially the collection of taxes), criminal jurisdiction, defense, and the general maintenance of the *pax Romana* ("the peace of Rome," i.e., public order).[177] One difference, however, between a prefect and a proconsul what the type of military under their command. A proconsul usually had one or more Roman legions

---

[174] A. N. Sherwin-White, *Roman Society and Roman Law in the New Testament* (Oxford University Press, 1963; repr., Grand Rapids: Baker, 1978), 6; Schürer, *History of the Jewish People*, 1:357–58, 360.

[175] From the time of Claudius onwards the title *procurator* (ἐπίτροπος) was used instead. Thus, Tacitus (e.g., *Ann.* 15.44), writing in a later period anachronistically uses the title *procurator* for Pontius Pilate, but during Pilate's day his title was actually *praefectus*. Similarly, Josephus (e.g., *J. W.* 2.169) and Philo (*Embassy* 299) use the Greek equivalent, ἐπίτροπος anachronistically for Pilate. That Pilate's actual title was *praefectus* has been confirmed by an inscription discovered in Caesarea Maritima by Antonio Frova in 1961 which identifies Pilate's title as such. Antonio Frova, "L'iscrizione di Ponzio Pilato a Cesarea," *Rendiconti dell'Istituto Lombardo, Academia di Scienze e Lettere, Classe di Lettre* 95 (1961): 419–34; Schürer, *History of the Jewish People*, 1:358–59. For a broader discussion of the issues, see Jones, *Studies in Roman Government and Law*, 117–25. The NT does not use either ἐπίτροπος ("procurator") or ἔπαρχος ("prefect") for Pilate; rather it uses the generic ἡγεμών ("governor"; Matt 27:2, 11, 14; Luke 20:20), as does Josephus also for Pilate (*Ant.* 18.55).

[176] Tacitus explains that "... the emperor was heard to remark that judgments given by his procurators ought to have as much validity as if the ruling had come from himself" (*Ann.* 12.60; Jackson, LCL). See also Josephus, *Ant.* 18.2; *J. W.* 2:117. The *Digest* states that the prefect of Egypt's "... command (*imperium*) ... during Augustus's reign was given to him by statute on the model of the proconsulship ..." (*Digest* 17.1). For a defense of a prefect having the same power as a proconsul see Sherwin-White, *Roman Society and Roman Law*, 5–11.

The *imperium* ("power") granted to Augustus at the beginning of the Principate was a recognition of his authority over the imperial provinces. His authority was recognized by the Senate as "greater" (*maius*) and thus was *maius imperium*. The Emperor could, however, delegate his *imperium* to the proconsuls and prefects who ruled in the imperial provinces on his behalf. See Mary T. Boatwright, et al., *The Romans from Village to Empire: A History of Ancient Rome from Earliest Times to Constantine* (Oxford: Oxford University Press, 2004), 292–93. The term *imperium* may be defined as "[t]he power of the higher republican magistrates ... and later the emperor to issue orders and enforce them, in particular the right to administer justice and to give military commands." See Theodor Mommsen, et al., *The Digest of Justinian* (4 vols; Philadelphia: University of Pennsylvania Press, 1985), 1:xx.

[177] Sherwin-White, *Roman Society and Roman Law*, 2.

under their control, whereas a prefect only had auxiliary troops.[178] So if the situation in a prefect's province degenerated into significant unrest or was attacked by an external large force, then the legions from the neighboring proconsul's province could be sent in to address the problem. Thus, the Roman province of Syria to the north had four legions posted there,[179] but in Judea there were only five cohorts and one cavalry unit, comprising a little more than 3,000 men.[180] The prefect in Judea still held the *imperium* in his own province, but if the situation warranted, the Syrian proconsul could step in with Rome's legions.[181]

3.3.2. Responsibility for capital crimes in a Roman Province

Holding the *imperium* just like a proconsul, a prefect's power was quite independent and virtually absolute, being only limited by a few laws, particularly the laws of extortion and of treason.[182] But, he did still answer to the emperor for his actions. One area of a prefect's authority was criminal jurisdiction, and this authority included the power of capital punishment. Holding the *imperium* meant that the power resided in the prefect. It is important to note at this point that the prefect could not delegate it to anyone else, particularly with reference to capital crimes. This is demonstrated by the later text, *The Digest of Justinian* (hereafter *Digest*):[183]

---

[178] Each legion was comprised of 5,000 to 6,000 men, and these were were Roman citizens (or provincials who received citizenship upon recruitment). Auxiliary troops were drawn from the provincials and did not receive citizenship rights. These auxiliary forces were organized into cohorts of 500 to 1,000 men each. Generally the armour and weaponry of auxiliary forces was lighter than that of the legionnaires. Schürer, *History of the Jewish People*, 1:362.

[179] Tacitus, *Ann.* 4.5. Though prior to Tiberius there were only three legions in Syria; Josephus, *J. W.* 2.40.

[180] Josephus, *J. W.* 2.52; Josephus, *Ant.* 19.364–65. Cf. the discussion by Smallwood, *The Jews Under Roman Rule*, 146–47; Schürer, *History of the Jewish People*, 1:362–64.

[181] This probably explains what Josephus meant when he described Archelaus' former territory becoming the province of Judea in 6 C.E. as being "assigned to Syria" (προσνεμηθείσης τῇ Σύρων; *Ant.* 17.355) and then almost immediately as having been "annexed to Syria" (προσθήκην τῆς Συρίας, *Ant.* 18.2). Josephus describes Quirinius being sent to Syria as proconsul while Coponius is sent to Judea to be its first prefect. Though Josephus does not use the title prefect, he describes Coponius' task as "to rule over the Jews with full authority" (ἡγησόμενος Ἰουδαίων τῇ ἐπὶ πᾶσιν ἐξουσίᾳ, *Ant.* 18.2).

[182] Sherwin-White (*Roman Society and Roman Law*, 1, 3) explains the law of extortion: "A proconsul could be as harsh and arbitrary as he liked, so long as he did not take money or property, 'things', *res*, from a provincial, even with the provincial's consent" (3).

[183] The use of *The Digest of Justinian* with reference to Roman practice in the period of the early Empire is problematic, for it reflects a collection of Roman jurisprudence covering several centuries. Thus, it is possible that something in the *Digest* reflects later practice and cannot be attributed to the early Empire of the first century C.E. The issues are not dissimilar to the use of Rabbinic material for NT studies. I would point out, however, two things about my use of the *Digest* here. First, Roman jurisprudence was quite conserva-

Ulpianus libro primo de officio proconsulis. Solent etiam custodiarum cognitionem mandare legatis, scilicet ut praeauditas custodias ad se remittant, ut innocentem ipse liberet. sed hoc genus mandati extraordinarium est: nec enim potest quis gladii potestatem sibi datam uel cuius alterius coercitionis ad alium transferre.

Ulpian, *Duties of Proconsul, book 1:* Proconsuls commonly delegate to their legates the examination of prisoners also, that is, on the principle that they remit cases to the proconsul after a preliminary hearing of the prisoners, freeing by themselves those who are innocent. But this type of delegation is irregular; for no one indeed can transfer to another a power of the sword or of coercing other people granted to himself. (Digest 1.16.6)

More explicitly with respect to capital punishment, the *Digest* also states:

Uenuleius Saturninus libro secundo de officio proconsulis. Si quid erit quod maiorem animaduersionem exigat, reicere legatus apud proconsulem debet: neque enim animaduertendi coercendi uel atrociter uerberandi ius habet.

Venuleius Saturninus, *Duties of Proconsul, book 2:* If a matter should arise which calls for one of the heavier punishments, the legate must refer it to the proconsul's court. For he [i.e., the legate] has no right to apply the death sentence or a sentence of imprisonment or of severe flogging. (*Digest* 1.16.11)

This principle – that a governor cannot delegate to another person the examination for severe punishments and particularly for capital crimes – is here clearly explained from the later Roman law gathered in the *Digest*. But this same principle of Roman governance is also valid much earlier, virtually the same time period of concern here. In correspondence between Pliny the Younger and Trajan, Trajan responds to a question from Pliny (*Ep.* 10.29.1–2) concerning two slaves discovered by Caelianus among some army recruits. Caelianus has sent them to Pliny, and Pliny asks the advice of Trajan as to a suitable punishment. Trajan responds:

Secundum mandata mea fecit Sempronius Caelianus mittendo ad te eos, de quibus cognosci oportebit, an capitale supplicium meruisse videantur.

Sempronius Caelianus was carrying out my instructions in sending you the slaves. Whether they deserve capital punishment will need investigation. (Pliny, *Ep.* 10.30.1a; Radice, LCL)

Caelianus had been instructed by Trajan to send the slaves to Pliny as the governor of the province Bithynia-Pontus (approx. 103–105 C.E.) because only someone who held the *imperium* was able to conduct a trial involving

---

tive in its developments. Second, in most instances of my use of the *Digest*, I use it for the purposes of summary and illustration, but I also demonstrate that what the *Digest* summarizes may also be found in earlier Roman texts – ones closer to the time period under consideration here. For discussion of these matters with reference to the use of the *Digest*, see e.g., Garnsey, *Social Status and Legal Privilege*, 7–10; John A. Crook, *Law and Life of Rome* (Ithaca, NY: Cornell University Press, 1967), 13–15.

capital punishment. The instructions that follow in the rest of the letter (*Ep.* 10.30.1b–2) guide Pliny in deciding the extent of their guilt, and whether or not "they will have to be executed" (*Ep.* 10.30.2; Radice, LCL) – a decision only he could make as governor.

And this same principle of Roman governance can be traced to an even earlier text, one preceding the time period of Pilate's rule. In the fourth of the Cyrene Edicts (7–6 B.C.E.), Caesar Augustus instructs the proconsul of Cyrene that criminal jurisdiction may be delegated to local courts *except* in cases involving capital punishment – these must be tried by the proconsul himself, though he may choose to involve a panel of jurors to assist him:[184]

⁶² αὐτοκράτωρ Καῖσαρ Σεβαστὸς ἀρχιε- ⁶³ ρεὺς δημαρχικῆς ἐξουσίας τὸ ἑπτακαιδέκατον λέγει· αἵτινες ⁶⁴ ἀμφισβητής<ε>ις ἀνὰ μέσον Ἑλλήνων ἔσονται κατὰ τὴν Κυρηναικὴν ἐπαρχήαν, ⁶⁵ ὑπεξειρημένων τῶν ὑποδίκων κεφαλῆς, ὑπὲρ ὧν ὅς ἂν τὴν ἐπαρχήαν διακατέχῃ ⁶⁶ αὐτὸς διαγεινώσκειν κ[αὶ] ἱστάναι ἢ συμβούλιον κριτῶν παρέχειν ὀφείλει, ⁶⁷ ὑπὲρ δὲ τῶν λοιπῶν πραγμάτων πάντων Ἕλληνας κριτὰς δίδοσθαι ἀρέσκει, ...[185]

The Emperor Caesar Augustus, *pontifex maximus*, holding the tribunician power for the seventeenth year, declares:

Regarding disputes which occur henceforth between Greeks within the province of Cyrene, excluding indictments for capital crimes, where the governor of the province must himself conduct the inquiry and render a decision or else set up a panel of jurors – for all other cases it is my pleasure that Greek jurors shall be assigned ...[186]

These texts (which both precede as well as follow our time period) lead to the conclusion that within the early Roman Empire a small province like Judea would only have a prefect as governor, and yet this prefect would still have held the *imperium*. One element of this *imperium* was that he had the right as well as the responsibility to render judgment in capital cases – a responsibility that rested on his shoulders alone, for he could not delegate it.[187]

---

[184] For further discussion of this text, see Sherwin-White, *Roman Society and Roman Law*, 15–16. He notes that this jury system appears to have been limited to the reign of Augustus, and perhaps to Cyrene only; it evidently disappeared afterwards.

[185] The Greek text is taken from Victor Ehrenberg and A. H. M. Jones, eds., *Documents Illustrating the Reigns of Augustus and Tiberius* (2 ed.; Oxford: Oxford University Press, 1955), 141.

[186] The translation is taken from Naphtali Lewis and Meyer Reinhold, eds., *The Empire*, in *Roman Civilization Sourcebook* (vol 2; New York: Harper & Row, 1966), 39.

[187] One of the questions that sometimes is raised in discussions of the death of Jesus, is whether or not the Jewish authorities had the power to put someone to death. In John 18:31 the Jewish authorities state, "We are not permitted to put anyone to death." This statement reflects the legal situation in a first-century Roman province, though it has, of course, been debated. For a brief history of the debate and bibliographic citations, see G. R. Beasley-Murray, *John* (2 ed.; WBC 36; Nashville: Thomas Nelson, 1999), 308–10. Classic statements in its defense may be found in Blinzler, *Trial of Jesus*, 157–63; Sherwin-White, *Roman Society and Roman Law*, 1–23.

That this was the situation in Judea under the Roman prefects is confirmed by Josephus in his description of Coponius, Judea's first prefect (6–9 C. E.):

Τῆς δὲ Ἀρχελάου χώρας εἰς ἐπαρχίαν περιγραφείσης ἐπίτροπος τῆς ἱππικῆς παρὰ Ῥωμαίοις τάξεως Κωπώνιος πέμπεται, μέχρι τοῦ κτείνειν λαβὼν παρὰ Καίσαρος ἐξουσίαν.

The territory of Archelaus was defined as a province, and Coponius, of the equestrian order among the Romans, was sent as a procurator with the power to put to death[188] received from Caesar. (*J. W.* 2.117)[189]

Thus 20 years later, when Pontius Pilate became prefect (26–36 C. E.), he governed Judea holding the *imperium*, and so he was responsible – and he alone – for making judicial decisions involving capital punishment.[190]

3.3.3. Roman procedure in a capital situation

In the late Republican period and early Principate, Rome was formalizing its criminal judicial system with a detailed series of statutes covering major crimes, whether against the state, society, or individual persons. This system was the *ordo iudiciorum publicorum* (lit. "List of State Judgments"). This system was designed, however, primarily to address the crimes committed by the *honestiores* (the "more honorable" or "well-born" persons) – Rome's upper class who governed the Empire. Trials for serious crimes committed by *honestiores* were conducted before *quaestiones* ("tribunals") and involved *iudicia publica*, or trials before a magistrate and jury.[191] On the

---

[188] The sense of the clause μέχρι τοῦ κτείνειν ... ἐξουσίαν could perhaps be more fully translated as "having full power even up to (and including) execution." Thackeray (LCL) translates the clause, "with full powers, including the infliction of capital punishment."

[189] Josephus' account immediately proceeds with an allusion to Judas of Galilee and his inciting of fellow Jews to revolt (*J. W.* 2.118). The implication is perhaps that Coponius used his power of capital punishment to deal with Judas. Josephus does not make this explicit, but Acts 5:37 does refer to Judas' death and his followers being scattered.

[190] While it has sometimes been argued that the Sanhedrin had the power to execute (e. g., Smallwood, *The Jews Under Roman Rule*, 149–50), it is generally accepted now that the death penalty was a power reserved for Rome's authority, and that the Jewish authorities did not possess such power. See the discussion by Légasse, *The Trial of Jesus*, 51–56; Christopher Bryan, *Render to Caesar: Jesus, the Early Church, and the Roman Superpower* (Oxford: Oxford University Press, 2005), 71–75. It is also on this point that Ernst Bammel's thesis ("The Trial Before Pilate," in *Jesus and the Politics of His Day* [ed. Ernst Bammel and C. F. D. Moule; Cambridge: Cambridge University Press, 1984], 415–51) about the Jewish authorities being largely responsible for crucifying Jesus falls down.

[191] For discussion see Richard A. Bauman, *Crime and Punishment in Ancient Rome* (London and New York: Routledge, 1996), 5, 21–34; Olga Tellegen-Couperus, *A Short History of Roman Law* (London and New York: Routledge, 1993), 88; A. H. M. Jones, *The Criminal Courts of the Roman Republic and Principate* (Oxford: Blackwell, 1972), 45–85. The *iudicium publicum* began in the latter part of the Republic and continued into the early Principate. Prior to the *iudicium publicum*, the procedure in the early Republic was the *iudicium populi*, or trial by magistrate and people; on which see Bauman, *Crime and Punishment in Ancient Rome*, 5, 9–20; Jones, *Criminal Courts*, 1–39.

other hand, crimes by the *humiliores* (the "more lowly" or "low-born" persons), the common people, whether freeborn or slaves, were judged more summarily by the *praefectus urbi* (a type of "police-court magistrate"[192] or "urban chief of police"[193]). Since these judgments were not according to the *ordo iudiciorum publicorum*, they were considered *extra ordinem* ("outside the List"). With the expansion of the Empire's provinces, the emperors of the early Principate formalized a new judicial procedure, *cognitio* ("judicial inquiry") which was *extra ordinem*.[194] Peter Garnsey explains:

> Jury-court procedure was accusatorial. The praetor simply presided over the contest between accuser and accused and pronounced the verdict of the jury. The cognitio procedure, on the other hand, was inquisitorial, and gave immense power to the judge. He sought and questioned witnesses, and interrogated the accused. Before passing sentence he regularly consulted his advisers, but was not bound by their counsel ... The judge was able to vary the penalty according to his own social prejudices.[195]

In the Roman provinces, it was the proconsul or prefect, by virtue of holding the *imperium*, who examined capital cases of the average *peregrinus* (i. e., "provincial;" lit. "foreigner") by personal *cognitio*, and the punishments were *extra ordinem*.[196]

In a *iudicium publicum* (trial by jury) someone had to function as a *delator* ("accuser, denouncer") to bring an accusation and provide a *nominus delatio* ("grounds for accusation").[197] "Trials depended on private initiative. There was no official prosecutor, and if no member of the public came forward as an accuser there was no prosecution."[198] Upon a successful prosecution, the accuser was rewarded, often with a portion of the condemned person's property, but if the person was acquitted, the accuser could face penalties.[199]

---

[192] Sherwin-White, *Roman Society and Roman Law*, 14.

[193] Garnsey, *Social Status and Legal Privilege*, 91. Cf. the description in Tacitus, *Ann.* 6.11. Garnsey (p. 95) also explains that the *praefectus vigilum* or the "prefect of the watch" could be responsible for the punishment of lesser crimes, but more serious cases would be referred to the *praefectus urbi*. Cf. *Digest* 26.10.3.15. On this role of city prefect, see *Digest* 1.12.

[194] For further discussion of the *ordo* and *extra ordinem* judgment, see Garnsey, *Social Status and Legal Privilege*, 90–98; Sherwin-White, *Roman Society and Roman Law*, 13–15. See also the discussion of "criminal courts under the Principate" in James Leigh Strachan-Davidson, *Problems of the Roman Criminal Law* (2 vols; Oxford: Clarendon Press, 1969), 2.153–75. See also Bauman, *Crime and Punishment in Ancient Rome*, 50–76; Jones, *Criminal Courts*, 91–118.

[195] Garnsey, *Social Status and Legal Privilege*, 6.

[196] Sherwin-White, *Roman Society and Roman Law*, 15–16.

[197] Bauman, *Crime and Punishment in Ancient Rome*, 23; Jones, *Criminal Courts*, 110–14.

[198] Bauman, *Crime and Punishment in Ancient Rome*, 23.

[199] On rewards for the accuser, see Tacitus, *Ann.* 4.20; on penalties for the accuser, see Tacitus, *Ann.* 6.30; cf. also *Digest* 48.2.7 explains that "... no one should readily leap to

In the situation of a *cognitio* (judicial inquiry) a *delator* or accuser could still bring an accusation, but in other situations a *cognitio* could go forward without a formal *delator* if the accusation was made by the police or some other type of official, or by an informer.[200] Even though in the *cognitio* the role of a *delator* was optional and less formal, those bringing the accusation were still held responsible.[201]

In the correspondence between Pliny the Younger and Trajan already examined above (Pliny, *Ep.* 10.29–30), concerning two slaves discovered among army recruits, Trajan's instruction to Pliny was, "whether they deserve capital punishment will need investigation (*cognosci*) …" (Pliny, *Ep.* 10.30.1). Trajan uses the verb *cognosco* which means "to investigate judicially,"[202] the verbal form of the noun *cognitio*. Trajan is pointing out that, even though they are slaves, if they are to be executed, Pliny will need to investigate the matter by means of a *cognitio*.

3.4. Reconstructing Core Elements in Jesus' Examination by Pontius Pilate

Given the discussion above, it may be judged as virtually certain that Pontius Pilate, as prefect of Judea, examined Jesus and was responsible for the verdict of death by crucifixion. While widely accepted, such a conclusion is not universally held. Crossan, for example, questions whether Pilate was directly involved at all. He states: "I doubt very much if Jewish police and Roman soldiery needed to go too far up the chain of command in handling a Galilean peasant like Jesus."[203] Such a view might appear plausible to modern people at first glance. But it really must be rejected, for it not only flies in the face of the multiple independent sources, both Christian and non-Christian, as well as the other criteria for historicity, it also ignores both Roman law and Roman practice in the provinces. Thus, in light of the evidence gathered above, the historicity of an examination by Pilate himself examination is virtually certain.

However, particular details that were involved in the process are somewhat more difficult to corroborate. Once we move to examining these de-

---

an accusation since he knows that his accusation will not be brought without risk to himself." Jones, *Criminal Courts*, 111; Strachan-Davidson, *Problems of the Roman Criminal Law*, 2.164–65.

[200] Jones, *Criminal Courts*, 113–14; Strachan-Davidson, *Problems of the Roman Criminal Law*, 2.164–65.

[201] Strachan-Davidson, *Problems of the Roman Criminal Law*, 2.164.

[202] Glare, *Oxford Latin Dictionary*, 346.

[203] John Dominic Crossan, *Jesus: A Revolutionary Biography* (San Francisco: HarperSanFrancisco, 1994), 152. It is possible that he has subsequently changed his opinion, for in a recent co-authored work, Pilate's direct involvement is implied, for which see Marcus J. Borg and John Dominic Crossan, *The Last Week: A Day-by-Day Account of Jesus's Final Week in Jerusalem* (New York: HarperCollins, 2006), 143–44.

tails, our sources become more limited, for we are chiefly dependent upon the narrative Gospels, and this leads to several issues with reference to answering many of the historical questions that we might want to ask of these texts concerning these particular details. First, while there are five narrative Gospels, they are not five independent sources. As discussed above, if Matthew and Luke are dependent upon Mark, then the basic synoptic source for Jesus' trial before Pilate is Mark 15:1–15. Matthew, however, does add a few details to Mark's account, notably the warning by Pilate's wife (Matt 27:19) and Pilate washing his hands, declaring Jesus innocent, and the Jewish audience taking responsibility for Jesus' blood (Matt 27:24–25). Luke has more extensive additions to Mark's account: a statement of the charge by the Jewish authorities (Luke 23:2), Pilate's three statements that he finds no basis for a charge against Jesus (Luke 23:4, 13–16, 22), and sending Jesus the Galilean to Herod Antipas (Luke 23:6–12). It has been a matter of scholarly debate whether Luke's distinctive elements in the Roman examination are based on his having access to additional traditions rather than his own redactional interests. While this is possible, there does not appear to be evidence for a single coherent source for Luke's distinctive elements, and thus any weighing of the evidence for such must be evaluated on a case-by-case basis.[204] The Gospel of John, which is probably independent of the Synoptic Gospels,[205] does provide a second, independent testimony to Jesus' trial. At numerous points the Fourth Gospel's account contains material that is similar to that found in the Synoptics, but it is structured and ordered quite differently.[206] At other points the Fourth Gospel contributes material that is different from the Synoptics, including the discussion about whether the Jews had the authority to execute (John 18:31–32), Jesus' defense before Pilate (John 18:34–38), Pilate's conversation with the Jewish leaders after Jesus is scourged (John 19:4–7), Pilate's conversation with Jesus (John 19:8–12) and then presenting Jesus to the crowd as their king (John 19:13–15). The *Gospel of Peter*, though probably dependent on an oral knowledge of the other Gospels (cf. the discussion above), portrays Jesus' trial somewhat differently, by having Pilate and Herod together try Jesus and it is Herod who sends Jesus to his crucifixion (*Gos. Pet.* 1:1–2). It should be noted that this Gospel's text is fragmentary, with the extant text beginning at this point near the end of Jesus' trial.

The second issue is that, at times, these Gospel narratives exhibit differences when compared with each other. For example, Mark portrays the charge brought against Jesus as claiming to be king of the Jews (Mark

---

[204] Cf. the discussion below concerning the possibility that there is a source for the additional charges brought by the Jewish authorities to Pilate in Luke 23:2.

[205] See the discussion in § 2.1.1 above.

[206] Cf. the discussion in Brown, *Death of the Messiah*, 757–59.

15:2; cf. Matt 27:11), whereas Luke refers to additional charges, including perverting the nation and forbidding paying tribute to Caesar (Luke 23:2). John, on the other hand, alludes to the Jewish leaders discussing more Jewish-oriented charges with Pilate, such as being an evil-doer, and claiming to be the Son of God (John 18:30; 19:7) in addition to the charge of being King of the Jews (John 18:33). While Mark and Matthew only narrate the single charge of being King of the Jews, both texts do make reference to "many charges" being made against Jesus (Mark 15:3, 4; Matt 27:13). We already noted above that *Gos. Pet.* 1:1–2 portrays Herod as the one who delivered Jesus up to be crucified while in the other narrative Gospels it was Pilate. This is an example of a larger tension among the narrative Gospels over their portrayal of Pilate. For example, Helen Bond's careful study of the portrayals of Pilate observes that in Mark "... he is a skillful politician, manipulating the crowd to avoid a potentially difficult situation, and is a strong representative of imperial interests."[207] However, in Luke "Pilate seems in control as he summons Jewish representatives to his tribunal but soon shows signs of weakness. Eventually he convicts a man whom he has declared innocent and releases a rebel and murderer because of the demand of the people. Bowing to Jewish pressure he undermines not only his own judgement but also that of Herod."[208] Another difference concerns chronology of events, for Mark and Matthew place Jesus being mocked by the soldiers scourging after he has been condemned and scourged, but John places the mockery in the midst of the examination, well before Jesus has been condemned and scourged (Mark 15:15, 16–20 = Matt 27:26, 27–31; John 19:16; 19:2–3). These different portrayals are due, at least in part, to the rhetorical distinctives of the different Gospels, which is a matter we will return to in a moment. A final example of the differences among the Gospels is that the Synoptics portray Jesus as silent before Pilate and his accusers (Mark 15:5 = Matt 27:12, 14; cf. Luke 23:12) apart from the enigmatic response of "You have said so" (Mark 15:2 = Matt 27:11 = Luke 23:3) to Pilate's question about being king of the Jews. Whereas in the Fourth Gospel Jesus responds with explanations to Pilate's questions twice (John 18:33–38; 19:10–11), including in particular a defense against the charge of being king of the Jews (John 18:34–37). These tensions can be understood, at least in part, as the result of the rhetorical and theological emphases of each Gospel, but it does complicate matters when we seek historical answers to address our own questions from these texts.

---

[207] Bond, *Pontius Pilate*, 117.
[208] Bond, *Pontius Pilate*, 159. It is possible, however, to read Luke's portrayal of Pilate as responding to leaders he has had a long-term relationship with. He is also concerned not to have an adverse public response, and so operates in a manner that tries not to add to the tension. This may be viewed, not as a sign of weakness, but as political calculation.

A third issue relates to the possibility of witnesses to be the source(s) for the various details in these narratives of Jesus' examination before Pilate. The narrative Gospels make quite clear that Jesus' disciples had fled at Jesus' arrest (Mark 14:50 = Matt 26:56; cf. Mark 14:27 = Matt 26:31; John 16:32). While Peter is reported to have followed Jesus to his examination by the Jewish authorities (Mark 15:53–54 = Matt 26:57–58 = Luke 22:54–55; John 18:13–16), it is at this point that all Gospels report Peter's denials of Jesus, at which point he also leaves (Matt 26:75 = Luke 22:62; cf. Mark 14:72). No Gospel account gives any intimation that any of Jesus' followers were present at his Roman examination. It is only at the crucifixion itself where reference is made to women followers being present (Mark 15:40–41 = Matt 27:55–56 = Luke 23:49; John 19:25). Furthermore, while later claims were made that there existed written court documents, this is part of the pious fiction that arose later around the figure of Pilate – the *cognitio* and execution *extra ordinem* of a Jewish person who was both a *humilior* ("low-born") and a *peregrinus* ("foreigner") required no documentation. Thus, every indication is that, if Jesus' followers were to have any knowledge of what transpired at Jesus' Roman examination, it could only come either from later inquiries made of those who might have been present – none of whom were followers of Jesus and thus not inclined to observe it from his point of view,[209] or from a general knowledge (whether accurate or not) of what might typically transpire at such a Roman examination, or later public disclosures about the examination in subsequent public debates.[210] These are possibilities, but there is no explicit evidence for any of them.[211]

---

[209] Thus even the recent thesis proposed by Richard Bauckham (*Jesus and the Eyewitnesses: The Gospels as Eyewitness Testimony* [Grand Rapids: Eerdmans, 2006]) that the Gospel's are based on eyewitness testimony fails with respect to this particular event. Bauckham's discussion of "Anonymous Persons in Mark's Passion Narrative" (ch. 8) largely ends with Jesus' arrest.

[210] Brown (*Death of the Messiah*, 712) comments that "[w]hatever historical information they [i.e., the Evangelists] had about the trial would have ultimately been derived from hearsay, from explanations offered post factum by the Roman and Jewish authorities, and from shrewd guesses as to likelihood."

[211] One might point to contacts in Herod's court (e.g., Luke 8:3) and with the Sanhedrin (e.g., Mark 15:43), which suggest that some persons in the Jesus movement had contacts with those in positions of influence and power. But neither of these provide *explicit* evidence of access to Pilate's examination. Of the alternatives listed here, perhaps the last is possible, for at least there is evidence of public debate in Jerusalem between Christian leaders and opponents. There is no *explicit* evidence, however, of the Roman examination being a point of debate where new information might have been gleaned. For a similar discussion with reference to the Jewish examination of Jesus, see Darrell L. Bock, *Blasphemy and Exaltation in Judaism and the Final Examination of Jesus: A Philological-Historical Study of the Key Jewish Themes Impacting Mark 14:61–64* (WUNT 2.106; Tübingen: Mohr Siebeck, 1998), 195–97 who observes greater possibility for access by persons in the Jesus movement to the Jewish examination. See also the discussion in this volume in ch. 12, § 2.4.

A fourth issue concerns the intent of these narrative accounts. These Gospels use narrative for rhetorical purposes.[212] This rhetorical intent is not only to address theological and pastoral issues, it is also intended to shape the perceptions of the readers / hearers with respect to the events being narrated. Thus those who initially composed the narrative of the events and those who passed on these narratives to others communicated their rhetorical intent by selecting what they narrated and shaping how they expressed the narrative. With reference to the narrative of Jesus' Roman examination, this rhetorical shaping may be observed in statements concerning Pilate's private emotions, thoughts, and motives. Pilate's emotions, for example, are found in the narration of Jesus' silence before his accusers: Mark 15:5 states that "Pilate was amazed." Later the narrator comments on his thoughts in explaining Pilate's offer to release Jesus or Barabbas: Pilate "realized that it was out of jealousy that the chief priests handed him over" (Mark 15:10). Similarly, the narrator claims that Pilate's motives in releasing Barabbas and delivering Jesus to be crucified were that he did so "wishing to satisfy the crowd" (Mark 15:15). Such statements make quite evident how the narrator wished the reader / hearer to perceive and evaluate the narrative. But it should also be quite evident that the narrator actually had no direct access to Pilate's private emotions, thoughts, and motives, let alone someone who might have been present having that access. From a rhetorical perspective, such comments are intended to guide the reader / hearer to view Jesus as the innocent, suffering victim, and to perceive Pilate as going against his better judgment and handing Jesus over to crucifixion only under pressure from the Jewish authorities.

This observation concerning the general rhetorical thrust of the Gospels' narrative of Pilate's examination is strengthened by observing the rhetorical intent of the actual wording of much of the dialogue reported and the precise actions taken by the parties involved, particularly in Matthew and Luke as they reshape and add to the traditions they are drawing from Mark. For example, Luke reports that Pilate three times declared Jesus innocent in reported statements such as, "I find no guilt in this man" (Luke 23:4 cf. vv. 14, 22). Similarly, Matthew reports that Pilate washed his hands and then records the dialogue between Pilate and the crowd: "'I am innocent of this man's blood; see to it yourselves.' Then the people as a whole answered,

---

[212] For a careful analysis of each Gospel's narrative, see Joel B. Green, *The Death of Jesus: Tradition and Interpretation in the Passion Narrative* (WUNT 2.33; Tübingen: J. C. B. Mohr (Paul Siebeck), 1988); John T. Carroll and Joel B. Green, *The Death of Jesus in Early Christianity* (Peabody, MA: Hendrickson, 1995), 3–109. With reference to Luke's account, see Alexandru Neagoe, *The Trial of the Gospel: An Apologetic Reading of Luke's Trial Narratives* (SNTSMS 116; Cambridge: Cambridge University Press, 2002). On the genre of the narrative Gospels see the study by Richard A. Burridge, *What Are the Gospels? A Comparison with Graeco-Roman Biography* (2 ed.; Grand Rapids: Eerdmans, 2004).

'His blood be on us and our children!'" (Matt 27:24b–25). Such dialogue and actions have a sense of verisimilitude, but given how they fit the rhetorical perspective of the Gospel narrators, it is difficult to move beyond these being possibilities and make judgments of probability about the details of what happened.[213]

These four issues explain why it is more difficult to reconstruct the details of what happened historically at Pilate's examination of Jesus and the accompanying events with the same degree of probability that can be established for the basic core elements. Yes, possible scenarios can be proposed, and the verisimilitude of certain details can be argued. But possibility and verisimilitude must be recognized for what they are. Historical judgments and reconstructions should first and foremost be built upon that which can be demonstrated with greater levels of probability.[214]

All this being said, the focus of this essay is not a historical study of all the details of the trial and death of Jesus, and so we do not need to engage in an evaluation of all these details.[215] Rather, this is a more limited examination of only those core elements of his trial and death that have historical significance for understanding the life of Jesus, and these other details, while interesting, do not really contribute to this larger question. Thus our attention will focus on those elements that can be established with greater probability as well as contribute to this end. These include: (1) the Jewish priestly authorities as Jesus' accusers; (2) the nature of the charge(s) against Jesus, and (3) Pilate's verdict concerning Jesus.

As we turn to examine these core elements that can be established with greater probability, we should note a similar event that took place about 30 years later in Judea, as reported by Josephus in *J. W.* 6.300–305. In 62 C. E., a peasant named Jesus, son of Ananias, stood in the temple and repeatedly proclaimed a woe oracle against Jerusalem and the temple. After

---

[213] On features that characterize Gospels as Greco-Roman biographies (βίοι), see Burridge, *What Are the Gospels?*. On authors having some license in composing speeches in historical narratives, see Thucydides, *Pel. War* 1.22.1; Lucian, *Hist.* 58. A helpful introduction to Greco-Roman history may be found in David E. Aune, *The New Testament in Its Literary Environment* (Library of Early Christianity 8; Philadelphia: Westminster, 1987), 77–157.

[214] This is an issue discussed by numerous historical-Jesus scholars; e.g., E. P. Sanders, *Jesus and Judaism* (Philadelphia: Fortress, 1985), 294–309; Dunn, *Jesus Remembered*, 765–81.

[215] For which see the exhaustive work done by Brown, *Death of the Messiah*, and especially what he labels as "Act III: Jesus before Pilate, the Roman Governor," – an examination that takes more than 200 pages (pp. 661–877). He concludes that there is "a historical kernel in the Roman trial: Pilate sentenced Jesus to die on the cross on the charge of being 'the King of the Jews.' The evangelists, however, are interested in making that drammatically effective as a vehicle of proclaiming who Jesus is, not in telling readers how Pilate got his information, why he phrased it the way he did, or with what legal formalities he conducted the trial" (p. 725).

doing this for some days, he was arrested by "leading men" and examined by "magistrates" who eventually turned him over to Albinus, the Roman governor of Judea at the time. Albinus examined this Jesus, upon which he "pronounced him a maniac and let him go" (*J. W.* 6.305; Thackeray, LCL). The parallels are instructive: Jewish authorities arrest a Jewish commoner who is perceived as a threat; after examining him they turn him over to the Roman governor; it is the Roman governor who conducts a *cognitio* and renders the verdict.[216]

3.4.1. *The Jewish priestly authorities as the accusers of Jesus*

The first element that is significant for the focus of this essay is that Pontius Pilate did not initiate the proceedings against Jesus.[217] Rather, it was the Jewish priestly authorities who, having arrested Jesus, examined him and determined his guilt, and then they took him to Pilate. The historical probability and significance of the Jewish examination of Jesus has been discussed elsewhere, and it is outside the scope of this essay.[218] What is important to note here is that these priestly authorities did not hand Jesus over and go their own way. Rather, they continued in the role of Jesus' accusers at the Roman examination.

The historical probability that these Jewish authorities were involved in the Roman examination may be established on two grounds. First, given the historical probability that the proceedings against Jesus began with an arrest and examination by the Jewish priestly authorities[219] before handing him over to Pilate, it is not unreasonable to presume that they would continue

---

[216] For further discussion of this event and its parallels to the last days of Jesus, see Craig A. Evans, *Jesus and His Contemporaries: Comparative Studies* (AGJU 25; Leiden: E.J. Brill, 1995), 359–61. The parallels are instructive, but it is going too far to argue influence of one upon the other, as Theodore J. Weeden has done ("Two Jesuses, Jesus of Jerusalem and Jesus of Nazareth: Provocative Parallels and Imaginative Imitation," *Forum* n.s. 6.2 [2003]: 135–341), arguing that Josephus' account influenced the Gospel writers. This essay was originally presented to the Jesus Seminar, and their subsequent voting on Weeden's thesis was uniformly "grey," indicating that they were largely unpersuaded. The comments by Evans (*Jesus and His Contemporaries*, 361 n. 48) on this matter are more judicious.

[217] It has occasionally been proposed that there was no involvement by Jewish authorities in Jesus' arrest, but this view has not found widespread support. See the literature cited and discussion by Ingo Broer, "The Death of Jesus from a Historical Perspective," in *Jesus from Judaism to Christianity: Continuum Approaches to the Historical Jesus* (ed. Tom Holmén; LNTS 352; London: T&T Clark, 2007), 145–68.

[218] See the discussion, for example, in this volume in ch. 12, § 1. See also his more extensive development in Bock, *Blasphemy and Exaltation in Judaism and the Final Examination of Jesus: A Philological-Historical Study of the Key Jewish Themes Impacting Mark 14:61–64*.

[219] For support of this, see n. 218 above.

to follow the proceedings, for it allowed them to continue to pursue the agenda they had initiated at their own examination.

Second, the involvement of Jewish authorities at the Roman examination is affirmed by independent sources. Mark's account affirms that they handed Jesus over to Pilate: "... the chief priests held a consultation with the elders and scribes and the whole council. They bound Jesus, led him away, and handed him over to Pilate" (Mark 15:1). They also remained present in order to make accusations against him: "and the chief priests accused him of many things" (15:3). Matthew and Luke follow Mark in affirming their presence and role as accusers (Mark 15:1 = Matt 27:1–2 = Luke 23:1; Mark 15:3 = Matt 27:12 = Luke 23:2, 10).[220] The Fourth Gospel, while quite different in the details, also affirms the same scenario: "Then they took Jesus from Caiaphas to Pilate's headquarters. It was early in the morning. They themselves did not enter the headquarters, so as to avoid ritual defilement and to be able to eat the Passover" (John 18:28). While the Synoptic Gospels portray the chief priests as present where the examination is taking place, the Fourth Gospel portrays them as remaining outside (to avoid defilement) and thus Pilate must shuttle back and forth between the praetorium and these leaders outside. But the basic role of the priestly authorities is the same in John's Gospel: "So Pilate went out to them and said, 'What accusation do you bring against this man?' They answered him, 'If this man were not an evildoer, we would not have handed him over'" (John 18:29–30). Thus, while the details are different, due to the different traditions being used as well as the rhetorical points being made, these two independent sources both affirm that the priestly authorities are at Jesus' Roman examination, and they function as his accusers. A third independent witness is provided by Josephus who stated that, "when Pilate, due to an accusation by the leading men among us, condemned him ..." (*Ant.*18.64).[221] Josephus' account does not specify that the "leading men" were the priestly authorities, but it does make clear that Jesus' accusers where Jewish. Thus these multiple sources support the historical probability of the presence of priestly authorities at Jesus' Roman examination in the role of accusers.

---

[220] The extant portion of the fragmentary *Gospel of Peter* only begins at the end of Jesus' Roman examination: "... But of the Jews (Ἰουδαίων) none washed their hands ..." (*Gos. Pet.* 1:1; Elliott). The refusal to wash their hands implies the active involvement of Jews in the Roman examination, but neither their identity as priestly authorities, nor their role as accusers is specified. Their identity and function at the examination is, however, implied later in the *Gospel of Peter* when, after Jesus is buried, "... the Jews and the elders and the priests (οἱ ἱερεῖς), perceiving what great evil they had done to themselves, began to lament ..." (*Gos. Pet.* 7:25; Elliott).

[221] On the issues surrounding the authenticity of this Josephus text, see the discussion in § 2.1.2 above.

In light of discussion in the preceding section concerning the role of *delatores* (accusers) as well as their responsibilities, it is significant that the Jewish authorities do remain active in Jesus' Roman examination as his accusers. If this had been a formal Roman trial, then their continued presence and involvement would have been required. But this was not a formal Roman trial by jury, for Jesus was only a *humilior* ("low-born") and a *peregrinus* ("foreigner") and thus a *cognitio* was sufficient. In a *cognitio* the presence of accusers was not necessary; it was sufficient that an accusation had been made or there was the suspicion of wrongdoing that led to the arrest. Thus, the Jewish authorities could have simply handed Jesus over to Pilate and left. But they did not. From their point of view, they needed Pilate to make the right decision with respect to Jesus. Having arrested Jesus, examined him and found him guilty of blasphemy and being a threat to their own position and the temple, it would have been a public-relations nightmare for them to have Jesus be found not guilty and be released. Thus, it was in their interests to see the matter through to the end. However, as was also noted above, in a *cognitio* it was the magistrate – in this instance, the prefect Pontius Pilate – who was responsible to take the lead and move the investigation forward, functioning as prosecuting attorney, judge, and jury single-handedly (as distinct from the procedure in a *iudicium publicum*, or trial by jury).

3.4.2. The nature of the charge(s) against Jesus

We already noted above that the narrative Gospels express the charges brought against Jesus in different ways. A careful examination of each Gospel's report does allow us to come to a historical judgment concerning these charges.

The narrative in Mark 15:1–3, our earliest report, states that the Jewish authorities bound Jesus and "handed him over (παρέδωκαν) to Pilate" (v. 1), and then it describes Pilate beginning to examine Jesus, "Are you king of the Jews?" (v. 2). The brevity of Mark's account does not make explicit that it was the Jewish authorities that brought the charge of claiming to be king of the Jews to Pilate, and the language of "handed him over" might imply they were distancing themselves from the process. However, the narrative flow makes clear that the Jewish authorities remained engaged, and it also implies that "king of the Jews" is their charge, for v. 3 does make explicit that the chief priests are present in an accusatory role: "And the chief priests accused him repeatedly."[222] Throughout the rest of the Roman examination scene in Mark it is "king of the Jews" that is the focus (15:9, 12, 18).

---

[222] In Mark 15:3 the word πολύς could be functioning as a direct object and have the sense of "many (things)," or it could be functioning adverbially and have the sense of

Matthew's account of the charges follows Mark's narrative closely: in Matt 27:1–2 they "hand him over to Pilate" which is followed in 27:11[223] with Pilate asking Jesus, "Are you king of the Jews?" Again, it is not explicit that this is the charge brought by the Jewish authorities, but Matthew also follows Mark in reporting that "he was accused by the chief priests and elders" (27:12). In Matthew's later narrative of the Roman examination, twice he replaces Mark's "king of the Jews" with "Jesus who is called Christ" (27:17, 22 = Mark 15:9, 12). This is not an introduction of another charge, but rather a Matthean redaction intended to highlight Jesus' messianic status at this point and to distinguish this Jesus from Jesus Barabbas (for Barabbas is also named "Jesus" only in Matthew's Gospel, 27:16–17).[224] However, in narrating the soldiers' mockery, Matthew retains Mark's "Hail, king of the Jews" (27:29 = Mark 15:18). Thus, in Matthew as in Mark, the charge laid against Jesus is the singular charge of claiming to be king of the Jews.

In contrast to Matthew, Luke does not follow Mark as closely. Instead of Mark's "they handed him over (παρέδωκαν) to Pilate," Luke states that "they brought him (ἤγαγον) to Pilate"(23:1). The change of verbs perhaps makes a little more explicit that the Jewish authorities remained engaged in the process. In 23:3 Luke follows Mark 15:2 closely by reporting that Pilate examined Jesus with exactly the same question, "Are you the king of the Jews?" But Luke inserts prior to this a statement making explicit what Mark and Luke left implicit, namely that the Jewish authorities brought the charge against Jesus: "And they began to accuse him saying, 'We found this man subverting (διαστρέφοντα) our nation, forbidding us to pay taxes to Caesar, and saying that he himself is the Messiah, a king'" (23:2). Thus Luke makes explicit that the Jewish authorities have provided the charge of being, in effect, "king of the Jews," but he also reports other, related charges being brought by them. Also, in 23:5 the Jewish authorities are reported to have expressed these charges in slightly different terms: "He incites (ἀνασείει) the people, teaching throughout all Judea, starting from

---

"repeatedly." In Mark's narrative there is nothing to imply that the chief priests have a variety of charges. Therefore, the latter sense is probably preferable, and so translated here as "repeatedly." Similarly, πόσος in 15:4 could be translated "how much." Matthew's parallel (27:12) simply states that they "accused him." Cf. Craig A. Evans, *Mark 8:27–16:20* (WBC 24B; Nashville, TN: Thomas Nelson, 2001), 478–79.

[223] Matthew inserted between Mark 15:1 and 2 the account of Judas returning the thirty pieces of silver and his suicide (Matt 27:3–10).

[224] Robert H. Gundry, *Matthew: A Commentary on His Literary and Theological Art* (Grand Rapids: Eerdmans, 1982), 561–62. Davies and Allison point out (*Commentary on Matthew XIX–XXVIII* [vol. 3 of *A Critical and Exegetical Commentary on the Gospel According to Saint Matthew*; ICC; Edinburgh: T&T Clark, 1997], 585) the irony that Jesus Barabbas (in Aramaic, "son of the father") and Jesus Messiah are both "Jesus, son of the father." This irony is one which Matthew's Jewish readers would be most likely to pick up.

Galilee even to this place." Later, Luke's narrative reports Pilate conversing with the Jewish authorities which reiterates, "You brought me this man as one who was misleading (ἀποστρέφοντα) the people, and behold I, having examined him before you, have found no guilt in this man of anything you accuse him" (23:14).

Scholars are divided over whether Luke has used additional sources in 23:1–5 for his distinctive presentation of the charges against Jesus,[225] or whether Luke is dependent only on Mark and the distinctive features are the result of his redactional interests.[226] While it is possible that Luke had access to another source at this point, the material can equally, perhaps even better, be explained as Lukan redaction,[227] particularly in light of the political apologetic in Luke-Acts defending Christians to a Roman audience. Luke's additional charges do, however, give an air of verisimilitude, for it is quite possible that various charges and evidence would have been discussed in support of the overall charge of claiming to be king of the Jews. Whether derived from a source, or based on redactional interests, or perhaps a deduction based upon an understanding of the implications of the key charge, one can still inquire of the historical value of this material, and in particular the charges brought against Jesus. It is possible that Luke 23:2 is intended to be one general charge ("subverting the nation") which is followed by two more specific sub-charges ("forbidding us to pay taxes to Caesar, and saying that he himself is the Messiah, a king") that are intended to be evidence to substantiate the general charge of subversion.[228] This is suggested by Luke's use in the subsequent narrative of similar language: "he incites (ἀνασείει) the people" (23:5), and "misleading (ἀποστρέφοντα) the people" (23:14). While this language may be Lukan, it does provide an explanation of the historical implications of the more specific charge of being "king of the Jews." In other words, Luke is explaining to a Roman audience that Jesus' accusers were using the language of "king of the Jews" to imply a challenge to Rome's rule and that there was the danger of such ideas creating *stasis* (unrest) among the people. Similarly, by working the charge as "saying that

---

[225] So, e.g., Vincent Taylor, *The Passion Narrative of St. Luke: A Critical and Historical Investigation* (SNTSMS 19; Cambridge: Cambridge University Press, 1972), esp. 86–87; I. Howard Marshall, *The Gospel of Luke* (NIGTC; Grand Rapids: Eerdmans, 1978), 852. More recently see Bock, *Luke*, 1806–8, and the other scholars cited there.

[226] So, e.g., Fitzmyer, *Luke*, 1472; Nolland, *Luke*, 1114–14; More recently, see Brown, *Death of the Messiah*, 736–43 and the other scholars cited there.

[227] I find the arguments by the following to be most convincing on this matter: Gerhard Schneider, "The Political Charge Against Jesus (Luke 23:2)," in *Jesus and the Politics of His Day* (ed. Ernst Bammel and C. F. D. Moule; Cambridge: Cambridge University Press, 1984), 403–14; Brown, *Death of the Messiah*, 736–43.

[228] This is argued by Schneider ("Political Charge," 407–8) on grammatical grounds as well, but his grammatical evidence is questionable.

he himself is the Messiah, a king" would explain to a Gentile audience the link of the later emphasis on "king of the Jews" in the Roman examination and crucifixion with the earlier allusions to Jesus as "the Messiah" in Luke's Gospel (e.g., 2:11, 26; 4:41; 9:20) and to Jesus being "the Messiah" at the Jewish examination (22:67).[229]

The account of Pilate's examination in John's Gospel (18:28–19:16a) is a carefully constructed dramatic narrative consisting of seven episodes.[230] The account begins with Jesus being led from Caiaphas' house to Pilate's praetorium. It is not specified who is leading Jesus, but it is implied by the narrative sequence that it is the priestly authorities who have just completed their examination, and they are so identified later as Jesus' accusers (18:35). These accusers remain outside the praetorium, while Jesus is inside. In the narrative episodes Pilate moves back and forth: from inside where he examines Jesus, to outside where he talks with these "chief priests" (18:35; cf. 19:6) or simply "the Jews" (18:31, 38b; 19:7). Initially Pilate goes out to inquire, "What accusation (κατηγορίαν) do you bring against this man?" (18:29). Their response is, "If this man were not an evildoer (κακὸν ποιῶν), we would not have handed him over to you" (18:30). Thus, no specific charge is reported in John's narrative at this point, and yet in the next episode, when Pilate goes inside the praetorium to examine Jesus, his question is "Are you the king of the Jews?" (18:33) – using exactly the same phrase as is found in all three Synoptic Gospels. Their ensuing discussion revolves around the nature of Jesus' kingship being "not of this world" (18:36–38). In the subsequent episodes the term "king of the Jews" is used twice more: the offer to release Jesus or Barabbas (18:39) and the mocking by the soldiers (19:3). General references to "king" are also found in 19:12, 14–15 in contrasting Jesus being "a / your king" over against "Caesar" as king. The one addition to the charges that are made against Jesus in the Fourth Gospel is in the exchange between Pilate and the chief priests. In this exchange, Pilate's response to their cries to "Crucify him" is an invitation to "Take him yourselves and crucify him, for I find no charge against him" (19:6). Their response is an explanation by "the Jews" that "We have a law, and according to that law he ought to die, because he claimed to be the Son of God" (19:7).

---

[229] For further discussion of the Messiah concept in this volume, see ch. 8, § 3.1.

[230] Brown (*John*, 2.858–59) demonstrates that these seven episodes are a carefully constructed chaiasm:
A. Jesus is accused by the chief priests before Pilate, 18:28–32
  B. Pilate's first interrogation of Jesus, about his kingship, vv. 33–38a
    C. Pilate declares to the Jews that Jesus is innocent, offers to release him, vv. 38b–40
      D. Pilate has Jesus flogged and mocked by the soldiers, 19:1–3
    C' Pilate presents Jesus as a mock king and declares that Jesus is innocent, vv. 4–8
  B' Pilate's second interrogation of Jesus, about his authority, vv. 9–11
A' Pilate hands Jesus over to crucifixion at the insistence of the Jews, vv. 12–16a

This provides a Jewish orientation to the authorities' claims against Jesus. It is interesting that in the Fourth Gospel's account of the Jewish examination no explicit charge is discussed (18:19), while in the synoptic accounts of the Jewish examination, Jesus is asked whether he is "the Son of God" (Mark 14:61 ["Son of the Blessed"] = Matt 26:63 = Luke 22:70). That this Jewish issue is raised in the Johannine account of the Roman examination indicates that the Johannine community is aware of this tradition, and that the question was a matter of debate between the Johannine community and its opponents (e.g., 5:18; 10:33).

The fragmentary *Gospel of Peter* does not begin until towards the end of the Roman examination, and thus if there was an account of any charges being brought initially, it is no longer extant. However, the extant text does report the royal mockery and scourging of Jesus after the examination. In response to being dressed in a purple robe and placed on the judgment seat, the verbal abuse was "Judge justly, king of Israel (βασιλεῦ τοῦ Ἰσραήλ)" (*Gos. Pet.* 3:7), and the verbal abuse accompanying the scourging was "With this honour let us honour the Son of God (τὸν υἱὸν τοῦ θ[εο]ῦ)" (*Gos. Pet.* 3:9; cf. also 3.6).[231] In all other narrative Gospels it is "king of the Jews" and not "king of Israel" that is used either as a charge against Jesus or in the royal mockery scene. Though in two other narrative Gospels in the crucifixion scene Jesus is mocked using this term, "Let the Messiah, the king of Israel, come down from the cross now ..." (Mark 15:32 = Matt 27:42).[232] Thus, while the *Gospel of Peter* does not make explicit the charges against Jesus, it does allude to the issues as being claims to kingship and to being the Son of God.

This examination of the accounts of the Roman examination indicates that at all levels of the tradition the primary charge brought by the priestly authorities against Jesus was that he claimed to be "king of the Jews," though the *Gospel of Peter* diverges slightly with "king of Israel."[233] While the addition of other charges by Luke may be due to his own redaction, the general charge of "subverting the nation" does give some insight into how "king of the Jews" might be explained to a Roman audience, as does Luke's phrasing of the charge that Jesus claimed to be "the Messiah, a king." The addition of "Son of God" in the Fourth Gospel and the *Gospel of Peter* is most likely due to the introduction of concepts from the Jewish examina-

---

[231] The Greek text is from *P.Cair.* 10759; cited from Andrew E. Bernhard, *Other Early Christian Gospels: A Critical Edition of the Surviving Greek Manuscripts* (LNTS 315; London: T&T Clark, 2006).

[232] Identifying Jesus as "king of Israel" is only found elsewhere in the Gospels in John 1:49; 12:13.

[233] On the use of the terms "Jew" and "Israel" in the first century, see the interesting article by John H. Elliott, "Jesus the Israelite Was Neither a 'Jew' Nor a 'Christian': On Correcting Misleading Nomenclature," *JSHJ* 5 (2007): 119–54.

tion into the Roman examination. From an historical point of view, it is certainly possible that the actual Roman examination of Jesus might have included the more general issues of *stasis* (unrest) and subversion, and that the Jewish authorities might have tried to explain how Jesus offended their Jewish law – such issues are theoretically possible and do have verisimilitude. But their presence at the individual points in the narrative Gospels do not appear to be the result of drawing upon other historical sources. They may better be explained as due to the redactional interests of their authors, or their exploration of the implications of the key charge. The same cannot be said of the charge of claiming to be "king of the Jews." This is found at all levels of the tradition, and it is multiply attested, being found in both Mark and John.[234]

The narrative Gospels focus on "king of the Jews" as either the implied or explicit charge brought before Pilate by the Jewish authorities, and they also report that Pilate's prime interest was in querying Jesus, "Are you the king of the Jews?" That this is also the charge for which Jesus was actually executed is strengthened by the reports of the *titulus* posted on his cross. While this is, strictly speaking, part of the crucifixion rather than the Roman examination, it is discussed here because its presence is as a result of the Roman examination. Mark 15:26 refers to this as an "inscription of the charge (ἐπιγραφὴ τῆς αἰτίας)."[235] Matthew's account does not use any term, but rather refers to putting "above his head his charge (αἰτίαν) which read …" (27:37). Luke drops the reference to the charge, stating simply that "there was an inscription (ἐπιγραφή) over him" (23:38). John uses a different term and states more explicitly that "Pilate wrote a title (τίτλον) and put it on the cross" (19:19). In *Gos. Pet.* 4:11 the verbal form of "inscription" is used: "they inscribed (ἐπέγραψαν)."[236]

The use of the Greek term ἐπιγραφή ("inscription") is a broad term for a public notice of identification, often inscribed into the material,[237] but the verbal form could also be used as a legal term indicating to "set down the penalty or damages in the title of an indictment."[238] The Greek term τίτλος also means "inscription,"[239] but is a loanword from the Latin *titulus*, referring to "a flat piece of wood, stone, or other material inscribed with a notice, identification, or other information, a placard, tablet, label, etc.," or it could

---

[234] On the independence of John from Mark, see the discussion above, § 2.1.1.

[235] The term αἰτία generally means "cause, reason," but it is also a technical term in legal texts to refer to a "charge" or "a basis for legal action." See BDAG 31.

[236] *P.Cair.* 10759.

[237] BDAG 369 comments that ἐπιγραφή was used "ordinarily of a document incised on stone, but also of identifying notices on any kind of material." Cf. Mark 12:16 where the term is used for an inscription on a coin; cf. Acts 17:23 for the verbal form of the word.

[238] LSJ 628.

[239] BDAG 1009; LSJ 1799.

refer to the inscription itself, often "giving details of a person's ancestry, career, etc."[240] These terms and others were used for the occasional practice of identifying the crime for which a person was executed. For example, in *Cal.* 32.2, Suetonius reports concerning Caligula:

> At a public banquet in Rome he immediately handed over a slave to the executioners for stealing a strip of silver from the couches, with orders that his hands be cut off and hung from his neck upon his breast, and that he be led about among the guests, preceded by a placard (*titulo*) giving the reason (*causam*) for his punishment. (Rolfe, LCL)

Similarly, in *Dom.* 10.1 Suetonius reports concerning Domitian:

> A householder who said that a Thracian gladiator was a match for the *murmillo*,[241] but not for the giver of the games, he caused to be dragged from his seat and throne into the arena to dogs, with this placard (*titulo*), "A favourer of the Thracians who spoke impiously." (Rolfe, LCL)

In *Hist. Rom.* 54.3.7, Cassius Dio explains that Augustus frequently acted in the public good (cf. 54.3.1, 6) and provides the following as an example:

> [W]hen Caepio's father freed one of the two slaves who had accompanied his son in his flight because this slave had wished to defend his young master when he met his death, but in the case of the second slave, who had deserted his son, led him through the midst of the Forum with an inscription making known the reason (γραμμάτων τὴν αἰτίαν) why he was to be put to death, and afterwards crucified him, the emperor was not vexed. (Carey, LCL)

It should also be noted that later Christian authors also report similar practices. For example,[242] Eusebius in *Hist. Eccl.* 5.1.44 similarly describes a Christian, named Attalus, who suffered for his faith:

> He was led around the amphitheatre and a placard (πίναχος[243]) was carried before him on which was written in Latin, "This is Attalus, the Christian." (Lake, LCL)[244]

It is often claimed that the use of a *titulus* at executions and crucifixions was a widespread if not universal practice.[245] However, the evidence provided

---

[240] Glare, *Oxford Latin Dictionary*, 1944–45.

[241] A *murmillo* is another type of gladiator. Rolfe (LCL, 340 n. b) explains that this person's comment implied "unfairness on the part of Domitian, who favoured the Thracians."

[242] See also Tertullian, *Apol.* 2.20.

[243] On πίναξ LSJ (1405) comments that this is a board or plate on which something could be drawn or written. Cf. the variant form of the word in Luke 1:63.

[244] It should be noted that, in this instance, the governor found out that Attalus was a Roman, and thus he was returned to jail, awaiting the response of the emperor to whom the governor had written (Eusebius, *Hist. eccl.* 5.1.44).

[245] For example, Blinzler (*Trial of Jesus*, 251) states: "When anyone was crucified, the tablet was displayed on the cross after the execution." No evidence for this claim is provided.

above[246] indicates that it was only used on an *ad hoc* basis. It is evident that the practice was not a legal procedure, and the *titulus* itself was not a formal statement of the actual crime. Rather, it was intended to humiliate the person being executed, or to warn the audience about the person's crime. When the text identified the manner in which the *titulus* was displayed to the audience, it was paraded before the person as they proceeded to the execution. There is no explicit mention of it being attached to a cross[247] (but crucifixion is only mentioned in one example), though if the *titulus* was intentionally displayed beforehand, there would be no reason for it not to continue being displayed during the public execution itself.

The historicity of the *titulus* at Jesus' execution is quite probable on several grounds. If, as discussed earlier, the Fourth Gospel provides an independent witness, then this element has multiple attestation. Secondly, this particular title does not reflect the early church's christological understanding of Jesus. For example, the earliest account containing the *titulus* is Mark's Gospel, in which the clear christological emphasis is to present Jesus as the Son of God – "king of the Jews" plays no role in Mark's portrayal. Within the passion narratives of the Gospels, many details are explored as having theological significance, but this is not the case with reference to the *titulus*.[248] In the Mark, Matthew, and the *Gospel of Peter* the statement of

---

[246] Another possible allusion may be found in *b.Sanh*. 43a where a reference is made to "Jeshu" being hanged on the eve of the Passover. This is taken by most scholars as an allusion to the death of Jesus, but instead of crucifixion, he is executed by a means recognized by the rabbis. The account goes on to report that for the 40 days prior to the hanging "a herald went forth and cried, 'He is going forth to be stoned because he practiced sorcery and enticed Israel to apostasy. Anyone who can say anything in his favour, let him come forward and plead on his behalf'" (Soncino). At one level the herald functions in a similar way as the *titulus*, in that Jesus' crime is reported. But in another sense the rhetorical intent is very different: the herald is, ostensibly at least, an inquiry for information, whereas the *titulus* is quite different. Cf. the discussion by Ernst Bammel, "The *titulus*," in *Jesus and the Politics of His Day* (ed. Ernst Bammel and C.F.D. Moule; Cambridge: Cambridge University Press, 1984), 360–63. See also the references to Jesus' death in the *Toledot Yeshu*. For discussion see Hillel I. Newman, "The Death of Jesus in the *Toledot Yeshu* Literature," *JTS* 50 (1999): 59–79.

[247] A.E. Harvey (*Jesus and the Constraints of History* [Philadelphia: Westminster, 1982], 13 n. 11) notes a later reference in Hesychius, but suggests it "may derive from the gospels."

[248] Craig A. Evans ("Authenticating the Activities of Jesus," in *Authenticating the Activities of Jesus* [ed. Bruce Chilton and Craig A. Evans; Leiden: Brill, 1999], 23 n. 50) comments in the regard that W. Bousset "... viewed the *titulus* as unhistorical, an 'erbauliche Betrachtung der gläubigen Jesusgemeinde.' But in what sense could the *titulus*, which for early Christians inadequately described Jesus, serve as an 'edifying meditation'?" For other examples of those rejecting the historicity of the *titulus*, see Ernst Haenchen, *Der Weg Jesu: Eine Erklärung des Markus-Evangeliums und der kanonischen Parallelen* (Berlin: Töpelmann, 1966), 536; David R. Catchpole, "The Triumphal Entry," in *Jesus and the Politics of His Day* (ed. Ernst Bammel and C.F.D. Moule; Cambridge: Cambridge University Press, 1984), 328.

the *titulus* is left as a bare detail in the crucifixion account. In Luke's Gospel the *titulus* is associated more directly with the mocking by the soldiers who use the same language. It is only in John's Gospel that an attempt is made to comment on the *titulus*: the Jewish leaders call into question Pilate's wording of the *titulus*, requesting that it be changed from a statement that Jesus was king of the Jews, into a claim, "This man said, I am king of the Jews" (19:21). Also, it is in John's Gospel that Pilate and Jesus have a conversation about the nature of Jesus' kingship being "not of this world" (19:33–37). These additions in the Fourth Gospel probably arise out of the Johannine community's embracing the embarrassing reality of the *titulus* – diffusing its problematic nature by spiritualizing it. And this leads to the third criterion in support of this traditions' authenticity: embarrassment. The early church in the first couple of centuries repeatedly had to maintain that they were not a threat to Rome's authority; thus, to create a *titulus* that supported a claim that they had to deny is quite unlikely.[249] Fourth, in terms of historical plausibility, it would make sense that if the Romans wished to use this crucifixion as a warning to Jewish onlookers about how they perceived what Jesus had done, then clarifying the charge in this manner made the impact of the crucifixion far more effective. Thus, I conclude that the *titulus* is historically quite probable.[250]

The content of the *titulus* is variously reported in the Gospels:

Mark 15:26: ὁ βασιλεὺς τῶν Ἰουδαίων
Matt 27:37: οὗτός ἐστιν Ἰησοῦς ὁ βασιλεὺς τῶν Ἰουδαίων
Luke 22:38: ὁ βασιλεὺς τῶν Ἰουδαίων οὗτός
John 19:19: Ἰησοῦς ὁ Ναζωραῖος ὁ βασιλεὺς τῶν Ἰουδαίων
Gos. Pet. 4:11: οὗτός ἐστιν ὁ βασιλεὺς τοῦ Ἰσραήλ

Mark 15:26: The king of the Jews
Matt 27:37: This is Jesus, the king of the Jews
Luke 22:38: The king of the Jews [is] this [man]
John 19:19: Jesus of Nazareth, the king of the Jews
Gos. Pet. 4:11: This is the king of Israel

---

[249] Cf. Acts 17:7. Harvey (*Jesus and the Constraints of History*, 13) notes: "It was precisely the suggestion that Jesus represented some kind of political threat to the Roman authorities that Christians of the early centuries had most strenuously to deny. It is hard to believe that they would have fabricated a piece of evidence which could so easily be turned against them."

[250] While most scholars do accept the historicity of the *titulus*, the following provide argumentation to support the claim: Winter, *On the Trial of Jesus*, 153–57; Harvey, *Jesus and the Constraints of History*, 13–14; Bammel, "The *titulus*," 353–64; Brown, *Death of the Messiah*, 962–68; Evans, "Authenticating the Activities of Jesus," 23–24; Lynn H. Cohick, "Jesus as King of the Jews," in *Who Do My Opponents Say That I Am?: An Investigation of the Accusations Against the Historical Jesus* (ed. Scot McKnight and Joseph B. Modica; LNTS 358; London: T&T Clark, 2008), 112–14.

While the existence of a titulus is historically quite probable, to determine the precise wording is somewhat more difficult, for each source reports it slightly differently. For our purposes here, what can be concluded is that the titulus contained at minimum the expression "the king of the Jews." If the rhetorical functions of the titulus were to mock and humiliate Jesus and his followers as well as to warn the Jewish onlookers, then the wording of the titulus would most probably have been in Aramaic. Thus, the Greek texts reported in the narrative Gospels are various attempts to translate whatever the Aramaic stated.[251]

We have established the high historical probability that the charge that was brought against Jesus by the Jewish authorities, that was the basis of Pilate's examination of Jesus, and that was on the titulus at the crucifixion was that Jesus was "king of the Jews." But what was this expression intended to communicate? The term "king of the Jews" was known in both Jewish and Roman circles, for most recently, Herod the Great had been known as "king of the Jews." Josephus, in *J. W.* 1.282–83, states that Herod had initially been given the title of tetrarch, but the Roman Senate, with the influence of Antony, granted him the title of "king of the Jews" (βασιλέα ... Ἰουδαίων) because of his loyalty to Rome. It is interesting to note that Josephus' account describes Antony's motivation for influencing the Senate's decision was "his aversion for Antigonus, whom he regarded as a promoter of sedition (στασιώδη; related to στάσις, "unrest") and an enemy (ἐχθρόν) of Rome" (14.283, Thackeray, LCL).[252] Herod as "king" is stamped on the coins he minted to use in his kingdom: ΗΡΩΔΟΥ ΒΑΣΙΛΕΩΣ, "of king Herod."[253] When the kingdom was turned over to his sons, they were not given the title of "king" by Rome, though Herod had wanted Archaelaus to be made king. Augustus decided to give Archelaus, who ruled over Judea, Samaria, and Idumea, the title of "ethnarch," and "he promised to reward him with the title of king if he really proved able to act in that capacity" (Josephus, *Ant.* 17.317; Marcus, LCL). Antipas and Philip were given the title of "tetrarch."[254] Archelaus, of

---

[251] Only the Fourth Gospel reports that the text was in three languages: Greek, Latin, and Hebrew. While possible, this is more likely the result of the Fourth Gospel's distinctive handling of the charge, giving it a sense of formality and solemnity such as would be found on formal, multi-lingual inscriptions honouring a person in the Mediterranean world. For discussion see Bammel, "The *titulus*," 359, esp. n. 43; Brown, *Death of the Messiah*, 964–66. Brown's judgment (p. 965) is that "... we can be reasonably sure that soldiers would not have taken care to transcribe a criminal charge in three languages." It is possible, however, due to the mixed nature of the crowds in Jerusalem who have come there as pilgrims at Passover, which might have led the Roman authorities to seek maximum impact.

[252] See the full expression ὁ τῶν Ἰουδαίων βασιλεὺς Ἡρώδης, "Herod, king of the Jews," in Josephus, *Ant.* 15.409; cf. *Ant.* 14.9, 280; 15.373; 16:292, 311.

[253] See Hendin, *Biblical Coins*, no. 486–502.

[254] Cf. *Josephus, Ant.* 17.318–20; *J. W.* 2.93–97. For their coins with these respective titles, see Hendin, *Biblical Coins*, no. 503–44. For a discussion on Herod Antipas' coins,

course, never became king because he never met the criterion Augustus had established in his promise ("if he really proved able to act in that capacity"). His brief rule was market by cruelty, and so he was removed and exiled by Rome in 6 C.E. for being a despot. He was replaced by direct Roman rule through a succession of Roman prefects – two decades later, that prefect was Pontius Pilate.

The title of "king of the Jews" was also associated with some of the Hasmonean rulers prior to Herod. For example, Josephus describes a gift sent to Rome with the inscription, "From Alexander [Jannaeus], the king of the Jews (τοῦ τῶν Ἰουδαίων Βασιλέως)" (*Ant.* 14.36; Marcus, LCL).[255] Similarly, Josephus in *Ant.* 17.92 uses the title "king of the Jews" for Antigonus, the last of the Hasmonaean kings prior to Herod.[256] This title is also reflected in the coins issued by these rulers.

Going back further in time, the title "king" was used throughout Israel's pre-exilic history narrated in the books of the former prophets in the Hebrew Bible (1 Samuel through 2 Chronicles) for Saul and David through to Zedekiah. Josephus does refer to David as "king of the Jews" (*Ant.* 7.72),[257] though the use of the term "Jews" in this context is quite anachronistic.[258]

To trace "king of the Jews" from Herod back through to Israel's earliest kings shows how the term was used for those with the political power to rule, usually over an independent state. Herod was granted the title of "king of the Jews," though he ruled as Rome's client king. He was granted this seemingly rare and privileged title by Rome because he had demonstrated his unswerving loyalty to Rome and its rulers. Rome appeared to recognize that there were potential hazards with this title, for it had possible implications for independence of the region and people so ruled.

But tracing the line from Herod back to Israel's earliest kings provides only half of the picture with reference to this title. For from king David comes another line that provides the other half of the picture. David's rule as king was later viewed as Israel's ideal state. As the nation's prospects de-

---

see Morten Hørning Jensen, *Herod Antipas in Galilee: The Literary and Archaeological Sources on the Reign of Herod Antipas and Its Socio-Economic Impact on Galilee* (WUNT 2.215; Tübingen: Mohr Siebeck, 2006), 187–217.

[255] Cf. Josephus, *J. W.* 1.85; 7.171. A number of Alexander's coins bear the Greek inscription, ΒΑΣΙΛΕΩΣ ΑΛΕΞΑΝΔΡΟΥ ("of king Alexander") and others the Hebrew יהונתן המלך ("Yehonatan the king"), for which see, Hendin, *Biblical Coins*, no. 467–77.

[256] For the use of the title "king" on Antigonus' coins, see Hendin, *Biblical Coins*, no. 481–85.

[257] For David as "king of the Jews" see also Josephus, *J. W.* 6.439. In Josephus, *Ant.* 6.98 there is a textual problem over whether Saul is referred to as "king of the Jews" or "king of the Hebrews." With reference to other Israelite kings, see also Josephus, *J. W.* 6.104.

[258] For the development of the term "Jew" and its use in our literature, see the recent essays by Elliott, "Jesus the Israelite," 119–54; Steve Mason, "Jews, Judeans, Judaizing, Judaism: Problems of Categorization in Ancient History," *JSJ* 38 (2007): 457–512.

clined with Israel and then Judah going into exile, there arose the prophetic hope for a return to Israel's former glory under another king like David.²⁵⁹ In Second Temple Jewish literature, this developed into the eschatological hope for a Davidic Messiah.²⁶⁰ This may be seen most clearly in the first century B.C.E. text *Pss. Sol.* 17–18, of which a few verses are cited here to exemplify this point:

^{17.21} See, Lord, and raise up for them their king,
   the son of David, to rule over your servant Israel
   in the time known to you, O God.
²² Undergird him with the strength to destroy the unrighteous rulers,
   to purge Jerusalem from gentiles
   who trample her to destruction; ...
³² And he will be a righteous king over them, taught by God.
There will be no unrighteousness among them in his days,
   for all shall be holy,
   and their king shall be the Lord Messiah. (*Pss. Sol.* 17.21–22,32; Wright, OTP)

The complex issue of messianic expectation in the Second Temple period along with other types of expected eschatological figures is far beyond the confines of this essay.²⁶¹ For our purposes here it is sufficient to note the line of development from king David in the narrative of the former prophets of the Hebrew Bible through the expectation of a king like David in the latter prophets to the eschatological expectation of a Davidic Messiah in the Second Temple literature.

This second half of the picture is not yet complete, for in Jesus' day there was not only eschatological expectation of a Davidic messiah, there were also several persons who, in one form or another, laid claim to being that messiah. In other words, there was in Jesus' day both the ideological and the historical – the ideals expressed in messianic expectation and the realities borne out in a variety of messianic figures and movements. Our knowledge

---

²⁵⁹ In the Hebrew Bible and later Jewish literature, see Isa 9:1–7; Jer 23:3–8; 30:9; Ezek 34:23–24; 37:24–25; Hos 3:5; Mic 5:1–4; Hab 2:20–23; Zech 12:7–13:1; Sir. 47:11, 22; *Pss. Sol.* 17:4; 4Q504 fr. 1–2 4.6–8; 4QPBless 1–4.

²⁶⁰ That the expectation of a Davidic king in the Hebrew Bible came to be interpreted in terms of a Davidic Messiah may be seen in texts like 4QFlor, 4QTest, 4QPBless, as well as frequently throughout the NT. For a study of the messianic texts in the Qumran literature, see Craig A. Evans, *Jesus and His Contemporaries: Comparative Studies* (AGJU 25; Leiden: E.J. Brill, 1995), 83–154.

²⁶¹ For my own discussion of the variety of expected figures, along with the Davidic messiah, see the primary texts and secondary literature cited in the chapter, "Judgment/Restoration Figures in the Old Testament and Second Temple Jewish Literature" in Robert L. Webb, *John the Baptizer and Prophet: A Socio-Historical Study* (1991; repr., JSNTSup 62; Eugene, OR: Wipf & Stock, 2006), 219–60. For recent discussions, see Jacob Neusner, et al., *Judaisms and Their Messiahs at the Turn of the Christian Era* (Cambridge: Cambridge University Press, 1987); Charlesworth, *The Messiah*; Collins, *The Scepter and the Star*.

is largely dependent upon Josephus, who describes a number of these messianic figures. But it should be noted that his description is uniformly very negative, for he laid partial blame for the Jewish War of 66–70 C.E. upon them. Nevertheless, we can see in his description of them that there was a royal / messianic element to them.²⁶² Particularly interesting are Josephus' description of three messianic movements that arose shortly after the death of Herod. First, in *Ant.* 17.271–72, Josephus describes the movement led by Judas, son of Ezekias, who attacked Herod's royal palace in Sepphoris to seize the weapons stored there. Josephus describes him as having "ambition for royal rank (βασιλείου τιμῆς)" (Marcus, LCL).²⁶³ Similarly, Josephus describes Simon, a former servant of Herod, who "was bold enough to place the diadem (διάδημ on his head, and having got together a body of men, he was himself also proclaimed king (αὐτὸς βασιλεὺς ἀναγγελθείς) by them in their madness ..." (*Ant.* 17.273–74; Marcus, LCL).²⁶⁴ Another example is Athronges, an otherwise unknown shepherd who, with his brothers, gathered a large movement among the peasants. Josephus states that "he had the temerity to aspire to the kingship (βασιλεία)" and that he "put on the diadem (διάδημα) and held a council to discuss what things were to be done, but everything depended upon his own decision. This man kept his power for a long while, for he had the title of king (βασιλεῖ) and nothing to prevent him from doing as he wished" (*Ant.* 17.278, 280–81; Marcus, LCL).²⁶⁵

Some commonalities may be observed among these messianic movements and their leaders. The participants in the movements were largely drawn from among commoners rather than the elite. The leaders claim some form of popular kingship, probably drawing upon messianic categories, for they had no basis for making such a claim based upon official authority or lineage (perhaps like the early days of king David). These movements were viewed as a threat to Rome's authority in the region. The movements were crushed by those with Roman authority who sought in particular to capture the leaders, whether Gratus with the help of some Roman forces who in a bat-

---

²⁶² For detailed discussion and analysis of these messianic movements and figures, see Horsley and Hanson, *Bandits, Prophets, and Messiahs*, 88–134; and the chapter "Messianic Claimants in the First and Second Centuries" in Evans, *Jesus and His Contemporaries*, 53–81. These messianic movements are to be distinguished from a number of prophetic movements that also arose during this same period. For a description and analysis of them, see Webb, *John the Baptizer*, 307–48.

²⁶³ Cf. Josephus, *J. W.* 2.56.

²⁶⁴ The complete account is Josephus, *Ant.* 17.273–76; cf. *J. W.* 2.57–59. Tacitus also mentions him as a royal claimant: "After Herod's death, a certain Simon assumed the name of king (*regium nomen invaserat*) without waiting for Caesar's decision. He, however, was put to death by Quintilius Varus, governor of Syria" (*Hist.* 5.9; Moore, LCL).

²⁶⁵ The complete account is Josephus, *Ant.* 17.278–284; cf. *J. W.* 2.60–65.

tle captured Simon and beheaded him (*Ant.* 17.276), or the forces of Gratus and Archelaus who captured Athronges and his brothers (*Ant.* 17.284–85).

To summarize, then, we should observe three basic elements that make up the entire picture surrounding the use of the term "king of the Jews" in Jesus' day. The first element is the historical use of the term "king of the Jews." It had most recently been used as a special honor bestowed by Rome upon Herod, their client king over the region. It appears that in normal circumstances Rome preferred to use titles such as ethnarch or tetrarch for such rulers, for these titles lacked the royal element of kingship. This historical use is linked in a thread to other historical figures, going back to some Hasmonaean rulers and then further back to the pre-exilic rulers of Israel and ultimately back to king David. The second element is the ideological thread that leads from king David through the later expectation of a king like David and ultimately to the messianic expectation in the Second Temple period. The third element is the social context in which a variety of Jewish messianic movements around the turn of the era were attempting to bring together the historical and the ideological; that is, there were movements that were attempting to make their eschatological messianic hopes into a historical reality. And in so doing, they were a challenge to Rome's authority, and Rome in turn viewed them as a threat to their power.

This discussion helps us understand the relationship between the issues that arise in the Jewish examination of Jesus and the charge that the Jewish authorities bring to Pilate. At first, there seems to be a disconnect between the issues of blasphemy raised at the Jewish examination and Jesus being "king of the Jews." But, as Darrell Bock explains in his conclusion to the preceding essay, "That is how the Jewish leadership would have seen [Jesus'] claim. What Jesus' statement means is that he saw his mission in terms of messianic kingdom work that also involved his inseparable association and intimacy with God."[266] Jesus' blasphemy at the Jewish examination involved more than just messianic claims, but it did include messianic claims. However, the Jewish authorities knew that Pilate had no interest in the theological issues surrounding blasphemy, but they were able to translate the messianic element of Jesus' claim into terms that Pilate not only understood, but would also be relevant to his sphere of political power.

This charge of being "king of the Jews" also has points of connection with earlier events in Jesus' life that lend plausibility to the charge. First, Jesus proclaimed the "rule/kingdom of God" that stood in explicit contrast to the rule/kingdom of Satan and in implicit contrast to the rule/kingdom of human rulers including Rome.[267] And at times in his proclamation, Jesus

---

[266] See in this volume ch. 12, § 4.2.
[267] See the discussion in this volume in ch. 4.

suggested his own involvement in God's rule. Second, the symbolism of Jesus' entry into Jerusalem has royal implications.[268] Third, Jesus' action in the temple implies a claim to authority.[269] Thus, the charge of claiming to be "king of the Jews" not only translates the concerns of the Jewish authorities into political concerns that would have been relevant to Pilate, it also is made more plausible by its continuity with evidence derived from the teaching and actions of Jesus.[270]

When Pilate heard the charge of claiming to be "king of the Jews" brought against Jesus, he would have been aware of at least some of the contextual information discussed here. He certainly would have known that the last person who officially held that title was king Herod, the ruler of which he was a successor. Though Pilate did not have the title "king," he still was Rome's ruler over the Jews who lived in the province of Judea. Such a charge, then, is a challenge to his own authority as well as that of Rome. Furthermore, there is every likelihood that Pilate knew about the messianic movements that had arisen subsequent to Herod's death – and he would have known how troublesome they were to the Roman authorities and how difficult it was to quell these the movements and to capture their leaders.[271]

The charge of claiming to be king of the Jews would have been viewed as sedition or treason from Pilate's point of view and that of Roman law. In the transition from the Republic to the Empire the *lex maiestatis* ("law concerning majesty / sovereignty") developed in various forms. The term *maiestas* ("dignity, majesty") was used to refer to the majesty of the people or the state and thus its sovereignty. With the rise of the Principate, this *maiestas* was understood to be represented by the emperor in particular as well as others that held the *imperium* (including prefects and procurators who ruled Rome's provinces). The *lex maiestatis* identified as a crime that which lessened or violated that sovereignty, often referred to as *maiestatem minuere* ("to offend against the sovereignty of the people"), so much so that the term *maiestas* came to be a technical term for "treason" or "sedition" (an abbreviation of *maiestas imminuta*, "an offence against the majesty of the state").[272] Tacitus informs us that during the reign of Tiberius (14–37 C.E.,

---

[268] See the discussion in this volume in ch. 9.
[269] See the discussion in this volume in ch. 10.
[270] This has been explored by a number of scholar, e. g., Sanders, *Jesus and Judaism*, 307; N. T. Wright, *Jesus and the Victory of God* (vol. 2 of *Christian Origins and the Question of God*; Minneapolis: Fortress, 1996), 540–611; Cohick, "Jesus as King of the Jews," 119–25.
[271] After all, even Tacitus knew about Simon, the leader of one of these messianic movements.
[272] Glare, *Oxford Latin Dictionary*, 1065. Earlier, the crime was *perduellio* ("treason, crime against the state"), but in the later Republic this was being replaced with *maiestas* due to the development of a variety of *leges de maiestate* ("laws concerning sovereignty"). For discussion of this and *maiestas* in general, see C. W. Chilton, "The Roman Law of

the Emperor during Pilate's tenure in Judea) "the law of treason (*lex maiestatis*) was coming into its strength" (*Ann.* 2.50; Jackson, LCL).[273] The crime of *maiestas* was punishable by death, though in the case of some *honestiores* (i. e., the well-born), exile to a remote region or island was permitted. But by the time of Tiberius exile was less common even for those with high status. Death often faced them, but the difference was in the way the death penalty was performed. *Honestiores* were usually decapitated by the sword (*capitis amputatio*). The *humiliores* (i. e., the low-born), on the other hand, faced the death penalty known as the *summum supplicium* ("ultimate penalty") which referred to death by means that involved extreme suffering, which included being thrown to wild animals (*bestiis dari*), being burnt alive (*vivus exuri*, or *crematio*), or crucifixion (*crux*).[274]

To conclude, it is highly probable that the charge brought against Jesus was for claiming to be "king of the Jews" is historical. It translates the messianic elements that Jesus faced in the Jewish examination into one that Pilate could not only understand, but it was also one that was of concern to him as Rome's ruler of Judea. Furthermore, it was a charge that would have been understood as *maiestas* ("treason") within Rome's legal system, and one that carried with it the penalty of *summum supplicium*, or death involving extreme suffering.

3.4.3. Pontius Pilate's verdict concerning Jesus

Much of the prior discussion has covered the relevant issues, and it need not be repeated here. That Pilate was involved in the decision to execute Jesus is virtually incontrovertible. This datum is established by both Christian and non-Christian sources which have already been discussed. It is also confirmed by the general principle noted above that the governor of a Roman province (whether prefect or proconsul) held the *imperium*, and thus was directly responsible for the judicial process involving capital punishment. This responsibility could not be delegated.

Jesus was not, however, a Roman citizen nor a *honestior* ("well-born"), and thus there was no requirement for a formal trial by jury. As a commoner in a Roman province he was a *humilior* ("low-born") and a *peregrinus* (i. e., "provincial," lit. "foreigner"). In a capital case involving *humiliores*, Pilate, as prefect, was simply required to engage in a personal *cognitio* ("judicial

---

Treason Under the Early Principate," *JRS* 45 (1955): 73–81. Broader discussions may be found in Bauman, *Crime and Punishment in Ancient Rome*. See also Brown, *Death of the Messiah*, 717–19.

[273] In the opinion of Suetonius (*Tib.* 58–59), Tiberius was excessive in his use of it.

[274] Garnsey, *Social Status and Legal Privilege*, 104–5, 125–31. For example, *Digest*, 48.8.3.

inquiry") in which he had considerable flexibility in terms of judgment and punishment because it was considered *extra ordinem* ("outside the List").[275]

That Pilate examined Jesus is the datum that has been established. Since this would have been a *cognitio*, it would have involved Pilate interrogating Jesus about the charge brought against him, as well as questioning his accusers about the nature of the charge and the evidence to support it. Thus, it is inevitable that Pilate would have engaged Jesus about this matter of being "king of the Jews." But here we run into the issues explored in the introduction to this section.[276] It is difficult to establish historically the details of these verbal exchanges beyond asserting a general discussion of the charge. Whether Jesus was largely silent as in the Synoptic Gospels (e.g., Mark 15:2–4) or engaged Pilate with a defense (e.g., John 18:33–38) is difficult to establish historically with any degree of confidence. Furthermore, what Pilate actually thought about the case (e.g., "Pilate wondered," Mark 15:5; or "I find no crime in this man," Luke 23:4) is equally difficult to establish historically. And Pilate's mental musings (e.g., "wishing to satisfy the crowd," Mark 15:15) are beyond historical inquiry.[277] But these details, even if they could be established, would actually contribute little that would further our understanding of the significance of Jesus' examination.

What does contribute to our appreciation of the significance of Jesus' Roman examination is the final element of the event that can be ascertained as historical – Pilate declared Jesus guilty of the charge of claiming to be king of the Jews and sentenced him to execution by crucifixion. Whatever Pilate actually thought and whatever his motivations, Pilate's final action was this verdict and punishment. On the surface, his verdict makes sense from a Roman perspective, especially in light of the *lex maiestatis* and how seriously it viewed the crime of *maiestas* or treason. And in Rome's point of view, the punishment fit the crime, for a *humilior* like Jesus the penalty would naturally be *summum supplicium*, or death involving extreme suffering, and in the Judean context, this most naturally was by crucifixion. His decision here is consistent with what we learned above from what else we know of Pilate: He was a shrewd politician who played various sides of an issue to his own advantage, with an eye of always promoting the good of Rome. If he could do so and continue his working relationship with the priestly aristocracy, so much the better.

Whatever Pilate actually thought about the charges against Jesus, there was enough evidence on the surface of the matter for his verdict to appear reasonable. Did Pilate seriously think that Jesus was a challenge to the Em-

---

[275] See the discussion above in §§ 3.3.2 and 3.3.3.
[276] See the introduction to § 3.4.
[277] For a similar conclusion, see Bond, *Pontius Pilate*, 198. See also Sanders, *Jesus and Judaism*, 300, for a similar judgment.

peror, or did he think Jesus could actually evict the Roman presence from Judea and rule the province independently? From what we know of Pilate, he was a realist, and I don't think he would have viewed these as realistic possibilities. But did he see Jesus as a popular figure who talked about a "kingdom" and that "change was coming," and who had gathered a following among potentially disgruntled Jewish common folk? And did he see the potential for unrest? From Pilate's past experience with his subjects, such a view was very reasonable from his perspective. Thus, whether the charge was really "true" or not, and at whatever level we ask "what is truth?" on the matter, there was enough evidence on the surface from Rome's point of view to render the verdict of guilty and condemn him to be crucified.

It was a matter of perspective.[278] From Rome's point of view, the basic reason Jesus was to be executed is that he was perceived to be a threat to *pax Romana* in Judea. This could be seen in two ways in relation to the two extremes of Judea's Jewish population – the common people and the Jewish priestly leadership. First, Jesus was perceived as a direct threat to *pax Romana* among the common people: The charge "king of the Jews" is essentially a challenge to Rome's direct rule over Judea as a province under the prefects (whether perceived by Rome as a call to return to Herod-style rule or total independence). He was a leader of a movement made up of commoners that had the potential to cause unrest. Pilate had already experienced similar unrest, and he knew that it had also happened in the preceding decades in Judea under other prefects. It is also interesting to note the parallels between this incident with Jesus and the later Samaritan prophet incident (36 C.E.; see § 3.2.6 above): a prophetic figure with influence over a movement among commoners led to unrest to which Pilate responded by executing the leaders. In that incident Pilate responded after the unrest had broken out. But in the case of Jesus, Pilate made a preemptive strike by removing the potential cause before it got out of hand. In doing so, Pilate was acting just like his fellow governor of neighboring Galilee and Perea – Herod Antipas – who handled a similar situation in the same way. With respect to John the baptizer, Josephus explains that

And when others gathered together [around John] (for they were also excited to the utmost by listening to his teachings), Herod, because he feared that his great persuasiveness with the people might lead to some kind of strife (for they seemed as if they would do everything which he counselled), thought it more preferable, before anything radically innovative happened as a result of him, to execute [John], taking action first, rather than when the upheaval happened. (*Ant.* 18.118)

---

[278] On the matter of perspective in evaluation of historical events, see my discussion above in ch. 2, § 2.3.

Thus, from Rome and Pilate's point of view, Jesus' influence over a movement of commoners was a potential threat.

Second, Jesus was perceived as an indirect threat to the *pax Romana* in that this incident could threaten Pilate's working relationship with the Jewish leadership: Pilate evidently had a relatively good working relationship with the Jewish authorities, and in particular with the current high priestly family. Pilate had no interest in their religious concerns; rather, his focus was political. But by working together, each party's interests were served. With the charges being pressed by these Jewish authorities, Pilate's natural desire would have been to maintain the status quo in this working relationship. As such, he was being a shrewd prefect with an eye to Rome's interests.[279]

From the perspective of the Jewish authorities, Jesus did not claim to be "king of the Jews" in the sense in which Pilate understood the term. But the term functioned pragmatically for them, for it translated their concerns into terms that Pilate could both understand and view as a threat. For Jesus had made claims that the Jewish authorities did consider a threat – Jesus' claims were an offense to their religious and theological sensibilities, and they were also a threat to their own authority, for Jesus had influence over a growing movement. Their own power was based upon working with Rome to maintain the *pax Romana* in Judea. Their position of authority was subject to the pleasure of Rome's prefect who had the authority to replace the high priest if he so wished.

From the perspective of his followers watching these events unfold,[280] Jesus certainly should not have been crucified. This horrifying fate suffered by their leader was devastating, crushing their hopes and dreams. From their point of view the punishment was absolutely wrong. But their view of the verdict may have been somewhat different. While Jesus' followers may not have couched their views of Jesus in terms of "king of the Jews," they were evidently looking for the "kingdom" that Jesus taught them about, and they were thinking that both Jesus and they themselves would play some role in that kingdom (e.g., Mark 10:35–40; 11:7–10). They probably would have couched their hopes in more traditional messianic terms rather than the charge that Jesus faced in his Roman examination. But if they did view this kingdom as having implications for their own socio-political situation in addition to their religious beliefs, then from the point of view of Rome's

---

[279] For further discussion, see Bond, *Pontius Pilate*, 203–5. Cf. the conclusion by Légasse, *The Trial of Jesus*, 65: "Pilate was sufficiently impressed by the accusation to conclude that it was necessary to pass the death sentence. At least he was taking a security measure, while wanting to satisfy a hierocracy which was quite devoted to the Roman authorities."

[280] I am commenting here on the perspective of Jesus' followers pre-Easter. Later, of course, the early Christian movement interpreted these events from the perspective of their developing, post-Easter faith.

political control, Pilate's verdict was correct. What Pilate feared might happen was what Jesus' followers hoped would happen: the kingdom that Jesus proclaimed would bring about a change in who ruled as well as the nature and character of that rule.

4. Conclusion: The Historical Significance of Jesus' Execution by Crucifixion at the Behest of Pontius Pilate

There are a number of threads from the preceding discussion that can now be highlighted to identify the historical significance of Jesus' examination by Pilate and subsequent crucifixion. I have a specific focus in the observations made here: this event is significant for the light it can shed on the prior life of Jesus.[281]

First, the mode of execution – crucifixion – identifies Jesus' social status. While Jesus was not a slave (i.e., the lowest status), he was commoner. Crucifixion was one form of *summum supplicium* (execution involving extreme suffering) that was usually reserved for the most serious crimes committed by a *humilior* ("low-born") and a *peregrinus* ("foreigner").

Second, execution by crucifixion implies the serious nature of the crime for which Jesus was examined. And the public nature of the crucifixion, along with the use of a *titulus* specifying the crime, implies that there was something about Jesus' crime that warranted being made a public spectacle as a warning to the Judean populace.

Third, the element linking the crucifixion and the Roman examination is the charge that Jesus claimed to be "the king of the Jews." Depending upon one's perspective, whether Pilate's, the Jewish priestly authorities, or Jesus' followers, one would have a different understanding of (a) the precise meaning of this charge, (b) whether Jesus was actually guilty of it or not, and (c) whether he should actually have been crucified for it. Thus, any answer to the question of whether the charge was "true" and the verdict "just" depended upon the perspective of the person in Jesus' day who was answering the question.

Fourth, from Pilate's point of view, if a person claimed to be "king of the Jews," he was guilty of *maiestas* ("treason, sedition"), for it was a challenge to the authority and majesty of Rome's rule over its province of Judea. The issue was not so much that Pilate saw Jesus as capable of mounting direct challenge to him and the Roman military that backed him, it was rather that

---

[281] In other words, my focus is to look backward and see how it helps us understand Jesus' life. I do not discuss its significance for subsequent historical events, nor its significance in early Christian thought.

a person who made such claims and was at the same time a leader of a movement among commoners could easily cause unrest among the populace. And this was a threat to the *pax Romana*, which was what Pilate was held responsible to maintain as Judea's prefect.

Fifth, the charge of claiming to be "king of the Jews" provides a point of contact between Jesus' death and his earlier ministry, through which runs the theme of the "kingdom of God." Whatever Jesus meant by the kingdom of God, it was implicitly a contrast between God's kingdom and the kingdoms of this world – between rule by God and rule by other authorities. There is, thus, an implicit critique of others who rule, whether that be the priestly authorities or Rome's prefect (as well as the rule of Satan[282]). To proclaim God's rule – whether it was being worked out in the ethics of present village life, or the turning of a heart morally toward God, or being anticipated as imminently consummated in an eschatological event – was a challenge to these other forms of authority. Thus, for those observing Jesus, a charismatic leader of a growing movement among commoners, to be proclaiming the βασιλεία ("kingdom") naturally gives rise to the question of who is to be the βασιλεύς ("king") of this kingdom? The charge against Jesus is the claim to be a "king," which arose in large part due to his earlier ministry of proclaiming the "kingdom."

Sixth, the charge of claiming to be a king was *in large part* due to his proclaiming a kingdom, but it is *not solely* due to this. There was also in Jesus' ministry a thread involving his own authority.[283] The issue of Jesus' authority is implied in a number of key events and characteristic activities in Jesus' earlier ministry, such as the prophetic call experience at the outset of his ministry,[284] or his authority to interpret the Jewish scriptures, or his authority to heal on the Sabbath.[285] But there are also more explicit hints that arise in some events in the final week of Jesus' life, including his entry into Jerusalem,[286] his action in the temple,[287] his last supper with his disciples,[288] and the charges that he addressed at his Jewish examination.[289] It is often said that the shift between pre-Easter and post-Easter is that "the proclaimer became the proclaimed." There is much truth to this statement.

---

[282] See the discussion in this volume in ch. 4.

[283] For a survey of a wide variety of scholars who conclude Jesus made certain claims about himself, see James H. Charlesworth, "The Dead Sea Scrolls and the Historical Jesus," in *Jesus and the Dead Sea Scrolls* (ed. James H. Charlesworth; ABRL; New York: Doubleday, 1992), 14, esp. n. 112.

[284] See the discussion of Jesus' theophanic experience in this volume in ch. 3, § 2.2.

[285] See in this volume ch. 7.

[286] See in this volume ch. 9.

[287] See in this volume ch. 10.

[288] See in this volume ch. 11.

[289] See in this volume ch. 12.

But it is sometimes expressed in a way that implies that the ministry of Jesus was *only* concerned with the kingdom of God, and Jesus' own authority was of no concern. But this black-and-white, either/or, before-and-after view is too simplistic. It is, rather a matter of weight: the *primary focus and concern* of Jesus' ministry was the kingdom, but the issue of his own authority was *implicitly present* from the beginning of his ministry, and it did become *explicitly raised* in certain events in the last week of his life. The predominant weight is on the former, but the latter is still present in Jesus' ministry.

I conclude by pointing out the irony wrapped up in this event that involves Jesus, a Jewish commoner proclaiming God's kingdom, facing off against Pontius Pilate, Rome's prefect who possessed Rome's *imperium* over this province. Pilate thought he was eliminating a potential threat to the *pax Romana*, and that by killing the leader, his movement would simply wither and die. But in fact the opposite happened. The action that should have eliminated the threat actually brought it about, for eventually the movement that arose in his name ultimately replaced Roman rule.[290] How ironic – what Pilate sought to prevent by his actions, he actually contributed to it ultimately taking place.

5. Appendix A: Accounts of Jesus' Roman Examination and Crucifixion in Narrative Gospels

Included here are the four canonical Gospels as well as the *Gospel of Peter*. Since Mark is the earliest Gospel, its order is followed and is presented in the first column. At numerous points the *Gospel of Peter*[291] is significantly different. As much as possible I have placed the *Gospel of Peter* text where it best fits with the other Gospels, but I have placed in the footnotes when there is a significant discrepancy between the *Gospel of Peter* and the other Gospels.

---

[290] Here I am alluding to the Christianizing of the Roman Empire under Constantine (312–337 C.E.), and the subsequent development of the "holy Roman Empire." This replacing of the Roman Empire can be seen, for example, in the title *pontifex maximus*, which identified the high priest in ancient Rome, the head over all the Roman religions. In the Principate, this title belonged to the emperor who not only held political power, but also religious authority as Rome's *pontifex maximus*. With the Christianizing of the Roman Empire, this title was transferred to the Christian pope.

[291] Particular points in the *Gospel of Peter* are not identified by chapter and verse. Two different numbering systems were employed early in the study of the *Gospel of Peter*. J. A. Robinson divided the text into 14 units and A. Harnack divided it into 60 units. It has since become customary to identify a text using both Robinson's and Harnack's numeration, and to place a colon between them. Thus, while 5:15 identifies the first part of Robinson's unit 5 and Harnack's unit 15. Thus, there is no 5:1–14, and Robinson's unit 5 consists of Harnack's 15–20.

Pericope Summary	Mark	Matthew	Luke	John	Gos. Pet.
1. chief priests, council turn Jesus over to Pilate	15:1	27:1–2	22:66–23:1	18:28	
2. Judas returns money, commits suicide		27:3–10			
3. Pilate examines Jesus	15:2–5	27:11–14	23:2–5	18:29–38a	
4. Herod Antipas examines Jesus			23:6–12		1:1[291]
5. Pilate declares Jesus innocent to chief priests			23:13–16 (cf. 23:4, 22)	18:38b	
6. Pilate offers Barabbas or Jesus; crowds choose	15:6–14	27:15–23	23:17–23	18:39–40; 19:4–7,12–15	
7. Pilate converses with Jesus				19:8–11	
8. Pilate washes his hands of Jesus		27:24–25			(cf. 1:1[292])
9. Pilate has Jesus scourged, delivers to crucifixion	15:15	27:26	23:24–25	19:1, 16	1:2[293]; 2:5b
10. soldiers mock Jesus, take him to crucifixion	15:16–20	27:27–31	23:26a	19:2–3, 17a	3:6–9
11. soldiers compel Simon of Cyrene to carry cross	15:21	27:32	23:26b		
12. women wail, Jesus speaks to them			23:27–32		
13. soldiers crucify Jesus, divide his clothes	15:22–25	27:33–36	23:33a, 34	19:17b, 23–25a	4:10b, 12
14. Jesus speaks to Mary, beloved disciple				19:25b–27	
15. charge on *titulus* described	15:26	27:37	23:38	19:19	4:11
16. chief priests object to wording of *titulus*				19:20–22	

---

[292] Herod examines Jesus with Pilate present.
[293] Herod does not wash his hands.
[294] It is Herod who delivers Jesus to crucifixion.

Pericope Summary	Mark	Matthew	Luke	John	Gos. Pet.
17. two others crucified; Jesus mocked	15:27–32[294]	27:38–44	23:33b, 35–37, 39–43	19:18	4:10a, 13–14
18. events during crucifixion until Jesus' death	15:33–39	27:45–54	23:44–47	19:28–30	5:15–20
19. crowds return home beating their breasts			23:48		7:25
20. Jesus' followers witness his crucifixion	15:40–41	27:55–56	23:49	(cf. 19:25b–27)	
21. Peter, disciples sorrowful, in hiding, fasting					7:26–27
22. soldiers pierce Jesus' side				19:31–37	
23. soldiers take out nails, causes earthquake		(cf. 27:51b)			6:21–22
24. Joseph of Arimathea buries Jesus' body	15:42–47	27:57–61	23:50–56	19:38–42	2:3–5a[295]; 6:23–24[296]
25. chief priests post guard at tomb		27:62–66			8:28–9:33[297]

Bibliography

Achtemeier, Paul J., Joel B. Green, and Marianne Meye Thompson. *Introducing the New Testament: Its Literature and Theology*. Grand Rapids: Eerdmans, 2001.

Alexander, Loveday C. A. "Chronology of Paul." Pages 115–23 in *Dictionary of Paul and His Letters*. Edited by Gerald F. Hawthorne, Ralph P. Martin, and Daniel G. Reid. Downers Grove, IL: InterVarsity, 1993.

Allison, Dale C. *The Jesus Tradition in Q*. Valley Forge, PA: Trinity Press International, 1997.

–. *Resurrecting Jesus: The Earliest Christian Tradition and Its Interpreters*. London: T&T Clark, 2005.

---

[295] Mark 15:28 ("And the Scripture was fulfilled that says, 'And he was counted among the lawless'") is probably a secondary addition and not part of the earliest test. It is, therefore, not included here.

[296] Joseph makes the request for the body of Jesus to Pilate, who in turn asks Herod. This is done prior to Jesus' crucifixion.

[297] It is "the Jews" who give Jesus' body to Joseph for burial. Joseph buries Jesus in his own sepulcher.

[298] Pilate appoints Petronius the centurion with other soldiers to secure the tomb.

Arberry, Arthur J., trans. *The Koran*. The World's Classics. Oxford: Oxford University Press, 1983.
Ata ur-Rahim, Muhammad. *Jesus: A Prophet of Islam*. Karachi: Begum Aisha Bawany Waqf, 1981.
Aune, David E. *The New Testament in Its Literary Environment*. Library of Early Christianity 8. Philadelphia: Westminster, 1987.
Baigent, Michael. *The Jesus Papers: Exposing the Greatest Cover-Up in History*. New York: HarperCollins, 2006.
Bammel, Ernst, ed. *The Trial of Jesus: Cambridge Studies in Honour of C. F. D. Moule*. SBT 2.13. London: SCM, 1970.
—. "Syrian Coinage and Pilate." *JJS* 2 (1951): 108–10.
—. "The *titulus*." Pages 353–64 in *Jesus and the Politics of His Day*. Edited by Ernst Bammel and C. F. D. Moule. Cambridge: Cambridge University Press, 1984.
—. "The Trial Before Pilate." Pages 415–51 in *Jesus and the Politics of His Day*. Edited by Ernst Bammel and C. F. D. Moule. Cambridge: Cambridge University Press, 1984.
Baras, Zvi. "The *Testimonium Flavianum* and the Martyrdom of James." Pages 338–48 in *Josephus, Judaism, and Christianity*. Edited by Louis Feldman, H. and Gohei Hata. Detroit: Wayne State University Press, 1987.
—. "*Testimonium Flavianum*: The State of Recent Scholarship." Pages 303–13, 378–85, 405–6 in *Society and Religion in the Second Temple Period*. Vol. 8 of *The World History of the Jewish People*. Edited by Michael Avi-Yonah and Zvi Baras. Jerusalem: Masada, 1977.
Barrett, C. K. *The Gospel According to St. John: An Introduction with Commentary and Notes on the Greek Text*. 2nd ed. London: SPCK, 1978.
Bauckham, Richard. *Jesus and the Eyewitnesses: The Gospels as Eyewitness Testimony*. Grand Rapids: Eerdmans, 2006.
Bauman, Richard A. *Crime and Punishment in Ancient Rome*. London and New York: Routledge, 1996.
Baumgarten, J. M. "Does *TLH* in the Temple Scroll Refer to Crucifixion?" *JBL* 91 (1972): 472–81.
Beard, Mary, John North, and Simon Price. *Religions of Rome*. 2 vols. Cambridge: Cambridge University Press, 1998.
Beasley-Murray, G. R. *John*. 2nd ed. WBC 36. Nashville: Thomas Nelson, 1999.
Bernhard, Andrew E. *Other Early Christian Gospels: A Critical Edition of the Surviving Greek Manuscripts*. LNTS 315. London: T&T Clark, 2006.
Betz, Hans Dieter. *Galatians*. Hermeneia. Philadelphia: Fortress, 1979.
—. "Paul." Pages 186–201 in vol. 5 of *Anchor Bible Dictionary*. Edited by David N. Freedman. New York: Doubleday, 1992.
Betz, Otto. "Probleme des Prozesses Jesu." Pages 565–647 in *ANRW*, vol. 2.25.1. Edited by H. Temporini and W. Haase. Berlin: Walter de Gruyter, 1982.
Blinzler, Josef. "Die Niedermetzelung von Galiläern Durch Pilatus." *NovT* 2 (1957–58): 24–49.
—. *The Trial of Jesus: The Jewish and Roman Proceedings Against Jesus Christ Described and Assessed from the Oldest Accounts*. 2nd ed. Translated by Isabel McHugh and Florence McHugh. Cork, Ireland / Westminster, MD: Mercier / Newman, 1959.

Boatwright, Mary T., Daniel J. Gargola, and Richard J. A. Talbert. *The Romans from Village to Empire: A History of Ancient Rome from Earliest Times to Constantine.* Oxford: Oxford University Press, 2004.

Bock, Darrell L. *Blasphemy and Exaltation in Judaism and the Final Examination of Jesus: A Philological-Historical Study of the Key Jewish Themes Impacting Mark 14:61–64.* WUNT 2.106. Tübingen: Mohr Siebeck, 1998.

–. *Luke.* 2 vols. BECNT 3. Grand Rapids: Baker, 1994–96.

Bond, Helen K. "The Coins of Pontius Pilate: Part of an Attempt to Provoke the People or Integrate Them Into the Empire?" *JSJ* 27 (1996): 241–62.

–. *Pontius Pilate in History and Interpretation.* SNTSMS 100. Cambridge: Cambridge University Press, 1998.

Borg, Marcus J., and John Dominic Crossan. *The Last Week: A Day-by-Day Account of Jesus's Final Week in Jerusalem.* New York: HarperCollins, 2006.

Brandon, S. G. F. *Jesus and the Zealots: A Study of the Political Factor in Primitive Christianity.* New York: Charles Scribner's Sons, 1967.

–. *The Trial of Jesus of Nazareth.* London: Batsford, 1968.

Broer, Ingo. "The Death of Jesus from a Historical Perspective." Pages 145–68 in *Jesus from Judaism to Christianity: Continuum Approaches to the Historical Jesus.* Edited by Tom Holmén. LNTS 352. London: T&T Clark, 2007.

Brown, Raymond E. *The Death of the Messiah: From Gethsemane to the Grave: A Commentary on the Passion Narratives in the Four Gospels.* 2 vols. ABRL. New York: Doubleday, 1994.

–. *The Gospel According to John.* AB 29. New York: Doubleday, 1966–70.

–. "The *Gospel of Peter* and Canonical Gospel Priority." *NTS* 33 (1987): 321–43.

Bruce, F. F. *Jesus and Christian Origins Outside the New Testament.* Grand Rapids: Eerdmans, 1974.

Bryan, Christopher. *Render to Caesar: Jesus, the Early Church, and the Roman Superpower.* Oxford: Oxford University Press, 2005.

Burridge, Richard A. *What Are the Gospels? A Comparison with Graeco-Roman Biography.* 2nd ed. Grand Rapids: Eerdmans, 2004.

Cameron, Ron, ed. *The Other Gospels: Non-Canonical Gospel Texts.* Cambridge: Lutterworth, 1982.

Carroll, John T., and Joel B. Green. *The Death of Jesus in Early Christianity.* Peabody, MA: Hendrickson, 1995.

Carson, D. A., Douglas J. Moo, and Leon Morris. *An Introduction to the New Testament.* Grand Rapids: Zondervan, 1992.

Catchpole, David R. *The Trial of Jesus: A Study of the Gospels and Jewish Historiography from 1770 to the Present Day.* SPB 18. Leiden: E. J. Brill, 1971.

–. "The Triumphal Entry." Pages 319–34 in *Jesus and the Politics of His Day.* Edited by Ernst Bammel and C. F. D. Moule. Cambridge: Cambridge University Press, 1984.

Charlesworth, James H., ed. *The Messiah: Development in Earliest Judaism and Christianity.* Minneapolis: Fortress, 1992.

–. "The Dead Sea Scrolls and the Historical Jesus." Pages 1–74 in *Jesus and the Dead Sea Scrolls.* Edited by James H. Charlesworth. ABRL. New York: Doubleday, 1992.

Chilton, C. W. "The Roman Law of Treason Under the Early Principate." *JRS* 45 (1955): 73–81.

Cohick, Lynn H. "Jesus as King of the Jews." Pages 111–32 in *Who Do My Opponents Say That I Am?: An Investigation of the Accusations Against the Historical Jesus*. Edited by Scot McKnight and Joseph B. Modica. LNTS 358. London: T&T Clark, 2008.
Cohn, Haim. *The Trial and Death of Jesus*. London: Wiedenfeld & Nicolson, 1972.
Collins, John J. *The Scepter and the Star: The Messiahs of the Dead Sea Scrolls and Other Ancient Literature*. New York: Doubleday, 1994.
Collins, Marilyn F. "The Hidden Vessels in Samaritan Traditions." *JSJ* 3 (1972): 97–116.
Crook, John A. *Law and Life of Rome*. Ithaca, NY: Cornell University Press, 1967.
Crossan, John Dominic. *The Cross That Spoke: The Origins of the Passion Narrative*. San Francisco: Harper & Row, 1988.
–. *Four Other Gospels: Shadows on the Contours of Canon*. San Francisco: Harper & Row, 1985.
–. *The Historical Jesus: The Life of a Mediterranean Jewish Peasant*. San Francisco: HarperSanFrancisco, 1991.
–. *Jesus: A Revolutionary Biography*. San Francisco: HarperSanFrancisco, 1994.
–. *Who Killed Jesus? Exposing the Roots of Anti-Semitism in the Gospel Story of the Death of Jesus*. San Francisco: Harper Collins, 1995.
Davies, W. D., and Dale C. Allison. *Commentary on Matthew XIX–XXVIII*. Vol. 3 of *A Critical and Exegetical Commentary on the Gospel According to Saint Matthew*. ICC. Edinburgh: T&T Clark, 1997.
DeConick, April D. *The Original Gospel of Thomas in Translation: With a Commentary and New English Translation of the Complete Gospel*. LNTS 287. London: T&T Clark, 2006.
–. *Recovering the Original Gospel of Thomas: A History of the Gospel and Its Growth*. LNTS 286. London: T&T Clark, 2005.
Derrett, J. Duncan M. *An Oriental Lawyer Looks at the Trial of Jesus and the Doctrine of the Redemption*. London: School of Oriental and African Studies, 1966.
Dodd, C. H. *Historical Tradition in the Fourth Gospel*. Cambridge: Cambridge University Press, 1965.
Doerr, Friedrich. *Der Prozess Jesu in rechtsgeschichtlicher Beleuchtung ein Beitrag zur Kenntnis des jüd-röm. Provinzialstrafrechts*. Berlin: W. Kohlhammer, 1920.
Dunn, James D. G. *Jesus Remembered*. Vol. 1 of *Christianity in the Making*. Grand Rapids: Eerdmans, 2003.
Ehrenberg, Victor, and A. H. M. Jones, eds. *Documents Illustrating the Reigns of Augustus and Tiberius*. 2nd ed. Oxford: Oxford University Press, 1955.
Elliott, James K. *The Apocryphal New Testament: A Collection of Apocryphal Christian Literature in an English Translation*. Oxford: Oxford University Press, 1993.
Elliott, John H. "Jesus the Israelite Was Neither a 'Jew' Nor a 'Christian': On Correcting Misleading Nomenclature." *JSHJ* 5 (2007): 119–54.
Evans, Craig A. "Authenticating the Activities of Jesus." Pages 3–29 in *Authenticating the Activities of Jesus*. Edited by Bruce Chilton and Craig A. Evans. Leiden: Brill, 1999.
–. *Fabricating Jesus: How Modern Scholars Distort the Gospels*. Downers Grove, IL: InterVarsity, 2006.
–. *Jesus and His Contemporaries: Comparative Studies*. AGJU 25. Leiden: E. J. Brill, 1995.

–. "Jesus in Non-Christian Sources." Pages 443–78 in *Studying the Historical Jesus: Evaluations of the State of Current Research*. Edited by Bruce Chilton and Craig A. Evans. NTTS 19. Leiden: E.J. Brill, 1994.
–. *Mark 8:27–16:20*. WBC 24B. Nashville, TN: Thomas Nelson, 2001.
–. "Messianic Hopes and Messianic Figures in Late Antiquity." *JGRChJ* 3 (2006): 9–40.
–. "The Passion of Jesus: History Remembered or Prophecy Historicized?" *BBR* 6 (1996): 159–65.
Evans, Jane DeRose. *The Art of Persuasion: Political Propaganda from Aeneas to Brutus*. Ann Arbor, MI: University of Michigan Press, 1992.
Fallon, Francis T., and Ron Cameron. "The Gospel of Thomas: A Forschungsbericht and Analysis." Pages 4195–4251 in *ANRW*, vol. 2.25.6. Edited by H. Temporini and W. Haase. Berlin: Walter de Gruyter, 1988.
Fee, Gordon D. *Paul's Letter to the Philippians*. NICNT. Grand Rapids: Eerdmans, 1995.
Feldman, Louis H. "Josephus." Pages 981–98 in vol. 3 of *Anchor Bible Dictionary*. Edited by David N. Freedman. New York: Doubleday, 1992.
–. "The *Testimonium Flavianum*: The State of the Question." Pages 179–99, 288–93 in *Christological Perspectives: Essays in Honor of Harvey K. McArthur*. R. F. Berkey and S. A. Edwards. New York: Pilgrim, 1982.
Ferguson, Everett. *Backgrounds of Early Christianity*. 3d ed. Grand Rapids: Eerdmans, 2003.
Fitzgerald, John T. "Philippians, Epistle to The." Pages 318–26 in vol. 5 of *Anchor Bible Dictionary*. Edited by David N. Freedman. New York: Doubleday, 1992.
Fitzmyer, Joseph A. "Crucifixion in Ancient Palestine, Qumran Literature, and the New Testament." *CBQ* 40 (1978): 493–513.
–. *The Gospel According to Luke*. 2 vols. AB 28. Garden City, NY: Doubleday, 1981–85.
Fonner, Michael G. "Jesus' Death by Crucifixion in the Qur'an: An Issue for Interpretation and Muslim-Christian Relations." *JES* 29 (1992): 432–50.
Fontanille, Jean-Philippe, and Sheldon Lee Gosline. *The Coins of Pontius Pilate*. Marco Polo Monographs 4. Warren Center, PA: Shangri-La Publications, 2001.
Foster, Paul. "Are There Any Early Fragments of the So-Called *Gospel of Peter*?" *NTS* 52 (2006): 1–28.
–. "The Disputed Early Fragments of the So-Called *Gospel of Peter* – Once Again." *NovT* 49 (2007): 402–5.
Frova, Antonio. "L'iscrizione di Ponzio Pilato a Cesarea." *Rendiconti dell'Istituto Lombardo, Academia di Scienze e Lettere, Classe di Lettre* 95 (1961): 419–34.
García Martínez, Florentino, and Eibert J. C. Tigchelaar, eds. *The Dead Sea Scrolls: Study Edition*. 2 vols. Grand Rapids: Eerdmans, 1997–98.
Garnsey, Peter. *Social Status and Legal Privilege in the Roman Empire*. Oxford: Oxford University Press, 1970.
Glare, P. G. W., ed. *Oxford Latin Dictionary*. Oxford: Oxford University Press, 1992.
Goodacre, Mark. "Scripturalization in Mark's Crucifixion Narrative." Pages 33–47 in *The Trial and Death of Jesus: Essays on the Passion in Mark*. Edited by Geert van Oyen and Tom Shepherd. Leuven: Peeters, 2006.
Goodenough, Edwin R. *The Politics of Philo Judaeus: Practice and Theory*. New Haven, CT: Yale University Press, 1938.

Green, Joel B. *The Death of Jesus: Tradition and Interpretation in the Passion Narrative*. WUNT 2.33. Tübingen: J. C. B. Mohr (Paul Siebeck), 1988.
Grenfell, Bernard P., and Arthur S. Hunt. *ΛΟΓΙΑ ΙΗΣΟΥ: Sayings of Our Lord from an Early Greek Papyrus*. London: Henry Frowde [for the Egypt Exploration Fund], 1897.
Gundry, Robert H. *Matthew: A Commentary on His Literary and Theological Art*. Grand Rapids: Eerdmans, 1982.
Haenchen, Ernst. *Der Weg Jesu: Eine Erklärung des Markus-Evangeliums und der kanonischen Parallelen*. Berlin: Töpelmann, 1966.
Harpur, Tom. *The Pagan Christ: Recovering the Lost Light*. Toronto: Thomas Allen, 2004.
Harvey, A. E. *Jesus and the Constraints of History*. Philadelphia: Westminster, 1982.
Hawthorne, Gerald F. *Philippians*. WBC 43. Waco, TX: Word Books, 1983.
Hendin, David. *Guide to Biblical Coins*. 4th ed. Dix Hills, NY: Amphora, 2001.
Hengel, Martin. *Crucifixion in the Ancient World and the Folly of the Message of the Cross*. Translated by John Bowden. Philadelphia: Fortress, 1977.
Hennecke, E., and W. Schneemelcher, eds. *Gospels and Related Writings*. Vol. 1 of *New Testament Apocrypha*. Rev. ed. Translated by R. McL. Wilson. Louisville: Westminster / John Knox, 1991.
Hill, George F., ed. *Catalogue of the Greek Coins of Palestine in the British Museum*. London: British Museum, 1914.
Hoehner, Harold W. "Pontius Pilate." Pages 615–17 in *Dictionary of Jesus and the Gospels*. Edited by Joel B. Green, Scot McKnight, and I. Howard Marshall. Downers Grove, IL: InterVarsity, 1992.
Hoffmann, Paul. "The Redaction of Q and the Son of Man: A Preliminary Sketch." Pages 159–98 in *The Gospel Behind the Gospels: Current Studies on Q*. Edited by Ronald A. Piper. NovTSup 75. Leiden: E. J. Brill, 1995.
Horbury, William. "The Trial of Jesus in Jewish Tradition." Pages 103–21 in *The Trial of Jesus: Cambridge Studies in Honour of C. F. D. Moule*. Edited by Ernst Bammel. SBT 2.13. London: SCM, 1970.
Horsley, G. H. R. *New Documents Illustrating Early Christianity*. Vol. 4. North Ryde, Australia: Ancient History Documentary Research Centre, Macquarie University, 1987.
Horsley, Richard A., and John S. Hanson. *Bandits, Prophets, and Messiahs: Popular Movements at the Time of Jesus*. Minneapolis: Winston, 1985.
Hultgren, Arland J. *The Rise of Normative Christianity*. Minneapolis: Fortress, 1994.
Jefford, Clayton N. "Pilate, Acts Of." Pages 371–72 in vol. 5 of *Anchor Bible Dictionary*. Edited by David N. Freedman. New York: Doubleday, 1992.
Jensen, Morten Hørning. *Herod Antipas in Galilee: The Literary and Archaeological Sources on the Reign of Herod Antipas and Its Socio-Economic Impact on Galilee*. WUNT 2.215. Tübingen: Mohr Siebeck, 2006.
Jewett, Robert. *Dating Paul's Life*. Philadelphia: Fortress, 1979.
Jones, A. H. M. *The Criminal Courts of the Roman Republic and Principate*. Oxford: Blackwell, 1972.
–. *Studies in Roman Government and Law*. New York: Frederick A. Praeger, 1960.
Jowett, Garth S., and Victoria O'Donnell. *Propaganda and Persuasion*. 4th ed. Thousand Oaks, CA: Sage, 2006.

Kertelge, K., ed. *Der Prozess gegen Jesus. Historische Rückfrage und theologische Deutung.* QD 112. Freiberg: Herder, 1988.
Kirk, Alan. "Examining Priorities: Another Look at the *Gospel of Peter*'s Relationship to the New Testament Gospels." *NTS* 40 (1994): 572–95.
Klausner, Joseph. *Jesus of Nazareth: His Life, Times, and Teaching.* Translated by Herbert Danby. New York: Macmillan, 1925.
Kloppenborg, John S. *Excavating Q: The History and Setting of the Sayings Gospel.* Edinburgh: T & T Clark, 2000.
Koester, Helmut. *Ancient Christian Gospels: Their History and Development.* Philadelphia: Trinity Press International, 1990.
—. "Apocryphal and Canonical Gospels." *HTR* 73 (1980): 105–30.
Kraeling, Carl H. "The Episode of the Roman Standards at Jerusalem." *HTR* 35 (1942): 263–89.
Kraus, Thomas J., and Tobias Nicklas, eds. *Das Petrusevangelium und die Petrusapokalypse: Die griechischen Fragmente mit deutscher und englischer Übersetzung.* GCS 11. Berlin: Walter de Gruyter, 2004.
Kreitzer, Larry J. *Striking New Images: Roman Imperial Coinage and the New Testament World.* Sheffield: Sheffield Academic Press, 1996.
Kuhn, Heinz-Wolfgang. "Die Kreuzesstrafe während der frühen Kaiserzeit. Ihre Wirklichkeit und Wertung in der Umwelt des Urchristentums." Pages 648–793 in *ANRW*, vol. 2.25.1. Edited by H. Temporini and W. Haase. Berlin: Walter de Gruyter, 1982.
Kümmel, Werner Georg. *Introduction to the New Testament.* Rev. ed. Translated by Howard Clark Kee. Nashville: Abingdon, 1975.
Lewis, Naphtali, and Meyer Reinhold, eds. *The Empire.* In *Roman Civilization Sourcebook.* Vol 2. New York: Harper & Row, 1966.
Légasse, Simon. *The Trial of Jesus.* Translated by John Bowden. London: SCM Press, 1997.
Lémonon, Jean-Pierre. *Pilate et le gouvernement de la Judée: textes et monuments.* EBib. Paris: Gabalda, 1981.
Lincoln, Andrew T. *The Gospel According to Saint John.* BNTC. London: Continuum, 2005.
Longenecker, Richard N. *Galatians.* WBC 41. Dallas: Word, 1990.
Lührmann, Dieter. "Kann es wirklich keine frühe Handschrift des Petrusevangeliums geben? Corrigenda zu einem Aufsatz von Paul Foster." *NovT* 48 (2006): 379–83.
MacLean, B. Hudson. *An Introduction to Greek Epigraphy of the Hellenistic and Roman Periods from Alexander the Great Down to the Reign of Constantine (323 B.C.–A.D. 337).* Ann Arbor, MI: University of Michigan Press, 2002.
Maier, Paul L. "The Episode of the Golden Roman Shields at Jerusalem." *HTR* 62 (1969): 109–21.
Mara, Maria Grazia. *Évangile de Pierre: Introduction, texte critique, traduction, commentaire et index.* Sources Chrétiennes 201. Paris: Éditions du Cerf, 1973.
Marshall, I. Howard. *The Gospel of Luke.* NIGTC. Grand Rapids: Eerdmans, 1978.
Marshall, I. Howard, and Philip H. Towner. *A Critical and Exegetical Commentary on the Pastoral Epistles.* ICC. Edinburgh: T&T Clark, 1999.
Martin, C. "Le 'Testimonium Flavianum'. Vers une solution définitive?" *Revue Belge de Philologie et d'Histoire* 20 (1941): 409–65.

Martin, Ralph P. *Carmen Christi: Philippians 2:5–11 in Recent Interpretation and in the Setting of Early Christian Worship*. 2nd ed. Grand Rapids: Eerdmans, 1983.
Mason, Steve. "Jews, Judeans, Judaizing, Judaism: Problems of Categorization in Ancient History." *JSJ* 38 (2007): 457–512.
Meier, John P. "Josephus on Jesus: A Modest Proposal." *CBQ* 52 (1990): 72–103.
—. *The Roots of the Problem and the Person*. Vol. 1 of *A Marginal Jew: Rethinking the Historical Jesus*. New York: Doubleday, 1991.
Meshorer, Ya'akov. *Ancient Jewish Coinage*. 2 vols. Dix Hills, NY: Amphora Books, 1982.
Mommsen, Theodor. *The Provinces of the Roman Empire*. 2 vols. Rev. ed. Translated by William P. Dickson. New York: Barnes & Noble, 1996.
Mommsen, Theodor, Paul Krueger, and Alan Watson, eds. *The Digest of Justinian*. 4 vols. Philadelphia: University of Pennsylvania Press, 1985.
Neagoe, Alexandru. *The Trial of the Gospel: An Apologetic Reading of Luke's Trial Narratives*. SNTSMS 116. Cambridge: Cambridge University Press, 2002.
Neirynck, Frans. "The Apocryphal Gospels and the Gospel of Mark." Pages 123–75 in *The New Testament in Early Christianity*. Edited by Jean-Marie Sevrin. BETL 86. Leuven: Leuven University Press, 1989.
Neusner, Jacob, William Scott Green, and Ernest S. Frerichs, eds. *Judaisms and Their Messiahs at the Turn of the Christian Era*. Cambridge: Cambridge University Press, 1987.
Newman, Hillel I. "The Death of Jesus in the *Toledot Yeshu* Literature." *JTS* 50 (1999): 59–79.
Neyrey, Jerome H. "Despising the Shame of the Cross: Honor and Shame in the Johannine Passion Narrative." *Semeia* 68 (1994): 113–37.
—. *The Passion According to Luke: A Redactional Study of Luke's Soteriology*. Mahwah, NJ: Paulist, 1985.
Nolland, John. *Luke*. 3 vols. WBC 35. Dallas: Word Books, 1989–93.
Nordsieck, Reinhard. *Das Thomas-Evangelium: Einleitung – Zur Frage des historischen Jesus – Kommentierung aller 114 Logien*. 3rd ed. Neukirchen-Vluyn: Neukirchener, 2006.
O'Brien, Peter T. *Commentary on Philippians*. NIGTC. Grand Rapids: Eerdmans, 1991.
Patterson, Stephen J. *The Gospel of Thomas and Jesus*. Foundations & Facets. Sonoma, CA: Polebridge Press, 1993.
Perrin, Nicholas. "The Aramaic Origins of the *Gospel of Thomas* – Revisited." Pages 50–59 in *Das Thomasevangelium: Entstehung – Rezeption – Theologie*. Edited by Jörg Frey, Enno Edzard Popkes, and Jens Schröter. BZNW 157. Berlin: De Gruyter, 2008.
—. *Thomas and Tatian: The Relationship Between the* Gospel of Thomas *and the* Diatessaron. SBLABib 5. Atlanta: Society of Biblical Literature, 2002.
—. *Thomas, The Other Gospel*. Louisville: Westminster John Knox, 2007.
Pines, Shlomo. *An Arabic Version of the Testimonium Flavianum and Its Implications*. Jerusalem: The Israel Academy of Sciences and Humanities, 1971.
Plisch, Uwe-Karsten. *The Gospel of Thomas: Original Text with Commentary*. Translated by Gesine Schenke Robinson. Stuttgart: Deutsche Bibelgesellschaft, 2008.

Porter, Stanley E., and Stephen J. Bedard. *Unmasking the Pagan Christ: An Evangelical Response to the Cosmic Christ Idea*. Toronto: Clements Publishing, 2006.

Radin, Max. *The Trial of Jesus of Nazareth*. Chicago: University of Chicago Press, 1931.

Reifenberg, A. *Ancient Jewish Coins*. 6 ed. Jerusalem: Rubin Mass, 1973.

Reinbold, Wolfgang. *Der Prozess Jesu*. BThS 28. Göttingen: Vandenhoeck & Ruprecht, 2006.

Richardson, John. *Roman Provincial Administration 227 BC to AD 117*. Inside the Ancient World. London: Bristol Classical Press, 1984.

Riley, Gregory J. "The Gospel of Thomas in Recent Research." *CurBS* 2 (1994): 227–52.

Rivkin, Ellis. *What Crucified Jesus?* London: SCM, 1984.

Roberts, Alexander, and James Donaldson, eds. *The Apostolic Fathers – Justin Martyr – Irenaeus*. Vol. 1 of *The Ante-Nicene Fathers*. Grand Rapids: Eerdmans, 1979.

Robinson, J. Armitage, and Montague Rhodes James. *The Gospel According to Peter and the Revelation of Peter: Two Lectures on the Newly Recovered Fragments Together with the Greek Texts*. 2nd ed. London: C.J. Clay & Sons, 1892.

Robinson, James M., ed. *The Nag Hammadi Library in English*. 3d ed. San Francisco: Harper and Row, 1988.

Robinson, James M., Paul Hoffmann, and John S. Kloppenborg, eds. *The Critical Edition of Q*. Hermeneia. Minneapolis: Fortress, 2000.

Rosadi, Giovanni. *The Trial of Jesus*. Translated and edited by Emil Reich. New York: Dodd, Mead & Co., 1905.

Sanders, E. P. *Jesus and Judaism*. Philadelphia: Fortress, 1985.

–. *Judaism: Practice and Belief 63 BCE – 66 CE*. Philadelphia: Trinity Press International, 1992.

Sanders, J. N., and B. A. Mastin. *A Commentary on the Gospel According to St. John*. HNTC. Peabody, MA: Hendrickson, 1988.

Sartre, Maurice. *The Middle East Under Rome*. Translated by Porter, Catherine, and Elizabeth Rawlings. Cambridge, MA: Belknap Press of Harvard University Press, 2005.

Scaer, Peter J. *The Lukan Passion and the Praiseworthy Death*. New Testament Monographs 10. Sheffield: Sheffield Phoenix Press, 2005.

Schneemelcher, Wilhelm. *Gospels and Related Writings*. Translated by R. McL. Wilson. Vol. 1 of *New Testament Apocrypha*. 2nd ed. Louisville: Westminster John Knox, 1991.

Schneider, Gerhard. "The Political Charge Against Jesus (Luke 23:2)." Pages 403–14 in *Jesus and the Politics of His Day*. Edited by Ernst Bammel and C. F. D. Moule. Cambridge: Cambridge University Press, 1984.

Schonfield, Hugh. *The Passover Plot: New Light on the History of Jesus*. London: Hutchinson, 1965.

Schürer, Emil. *The History of the Jewish People in the Age of Jesus Christ*. Edited by Geza Vermes, Fergus Millar, Matthew Black, and Martin Goodman. Edinburgh: T & T Clark, 1973–87.

Schwartz, Daniel R. "Josephus and Philo on Pontius Pilate." Pages 26–45 in *The Jerusalem Cathedra: Studies in the History, Archaeology, Geography, and Ethnography of the Land of Israel*, vol. 3. Edited by Lee I. Levine. Jerusalem/Detroit: Yad Izhak Ben-Zvi Institute/Wayne State University Press, 1983.

–. "Pontius Pilate." Pages 395–401 in vol. 5 of *Anchor Bible Dictionary*. Edited by David N. Freedman. New York: Doubleday, 1992.
Seeley, David. "Blessings and Boundaries: Interpretations of Jesus' Death in Q." *Semeia* 55 (1991): 131–46.
–. "Jesus' Death in Q." *NTS* 38 (1992): 222–34.
Sellew, Philip H. "The Gospel of Thomas: Prospects for Future Research." Pages 327–46 in *The Nag Hammadi Library After Fifty Years: Proceedings of the 1995 Society of Biblical Literature Commemoration*. Edited by John D Turner and Anne McGuire. NHS 44. Leiden: Brill, 1997.
Sherwin-White, A. N. *Roman Society and Roman Law in the New Testament*. Grand Rapids: Baker, 1978.
Siebert, Anne V. "Lituus." P. 737 in *Brill's New Pauly: Encyclopedia of the Ancient World*, vol. 7. Leiden: Brill, 2002.
Sloyan, Gerard S. *The Crucifixion of Jesus: History, Myth, Faith*. Minneapolis: Fortress, 1995.
–. *Jesus on Trial: A Study of the Gospels*. Minneapolis: Fortress, 2006.
Smallwood, E. Mary. *The Jews Under Roman Rule from Pompey to Diocletian: A Study in Political Relations*. SJLA 20. Leiden: E.J. Brill, 1981.
Smith, Daniel A. *The Post-Mortem Vindication of Jesus in the Sayings Gospel Q*. LNTS 338. London: T&T Clark, 2006.
Snodgrass, Klyne R. "The Gospel of Thomas: A Secondary Gospel." *SecCent* 7 (1989): 19–38.
Soards, Marion L. "Appendix IX: The Question of a PreMarcan Passion Narrative." Pages 1492–1524 in *The Death of the Messiah: From Gethsemane to the Grave: A Commentary on the Passion Narratives in the Four Gospels*. 2 vols. Raymond E. Brown. Anchor Bible Reference Library. New York: Doubleday, 1994.
Stauffer, Ethelbert. *Christ and the Caesars: Historical Sketches*. London: SCM, 1955.
Stevenson, G. H. *Roman Provincial Administratation: Till the Age of the Antonines*. New York: G. E. Stechert & Co., 1939.
Stillman, Martha K. "The Gospel of Peter: A Case for Oral-Only Dependency?" *ETL* 73 (1997): 114–20.
Strachan-Davidson, James Leigh. *Problems of the Roman Criminal Law*. 2 vols. Oxford: Clarendon Press, 1969.
Swete, H. B. *The Gospel of Peter: The Text in Greek and English with Introduction, Notes, and Indices*. Ancient Texts and Translations. Eugene, OR: Wipf & Stock, 2005.
Taylor, Joan E. "Pontius Pilate and the Imperial Cult in Roman Judaea." *NTS* 52 (2006): 555–82.
Taylor, Vincent. *The Passion Narrative of St. Luke: A Critical and Historical Investigation*. SNTSMS 19. Cambridge: Cambridge University Press, 1972.
Tellegen-Couperus, Olga. *A Short History of Roman Law*. London and New York: Routledge, 1993.
Theissen, Gerd. *The Gospels in Context: Social and Political History in the Synoptic Tradition*. Translated by Linda M. Maloney. Minneapolis: Fortress, 1991.
Tuckett, Christopher. *Nag Hammadi and the Gospel Tradition: Synoptic Tradition in the Nag Hammadi Library*. SNTW. Edinburgh: T&T Clark, 1986.

Turner, H. E. W. "The Chronological Framework of the Ministry." Pages 59–74 in *Historicity and Chronology in the New Testament*. Edited by D. E. Nineham, et al. London: SPCK, 1965.
Van Voorst, Robert E. *Jesus Outside the New Testament: An Introduction to the Ancient Evidence*. Grand Rapids: Eerdmans, 2000.
Vermes, Geza. *Jesus the Jew: A Historian's Reading of the Gospels*. Philadelphia: Fortress, 1973.
Wallace, Daniel B. *Greek Grammar Beyond the Basics: An Exegetical Syntax of the New Testament*. Grand Rapids: Zondervan, 1996.
Watson, Alan. *The Trial of Jesus*. Athens, GA: University of Georgia Press, 1995.
Webb, Robert L. *John the Baptizer and Prophet: A Socio-Historical Study*. JSNTSup 62. Sheffield: Sheffield Academic Press, 1991.
–. *John the Baptizer and Prophet: A Socio-Historical Study*. JSNTSup 62. Eugene, OR: Wipf & Stock, 2006.
Weeden, Theodore J. "Two Jesuses, Jesus of Jerusalem and Jesus of Nazareth: Provocative Parallels and Imaginative Imitation." *Forum* n. s. 6.2 (2003): 135–341.
Wengst, Klaus. *Pax Romana and the Peace of Jesus Christ*. Translated by John Bowden. London: SCM, 1987.
Whealey, Alice. *Josephus on Jesus: The Testimonium Flavianum Controversy from Late Antiquity to Modern Times*. Studies in Biblical Literature 36. New York: Peter Lang, 2003.
Wilcox, Max. "Upon the Tree – Deut. 21:22–23 in the New Testament." *JBL* 96 (1977): 85–99.
Winter, Paul. *On the Trial of Jesus*. 2nd ed. Revised by T. A. Burkill and Geza Vermes. SJ 1. Berlin: Walter de Gruyter, 1974.
Wright, N. T. *Jesus and the Victory of God*. Vol. 2 of *Christian Origins and the Question of God*. Minneapolis: Fortress, 1996.
–. *The Resurrection of the Son of God*. Vol. 3 of *Christian Origins and the Question of God*. Minneapolis: Fortress, 2003.
Yadin, Yigael. "Pesher Nahum (4QpNahum) Reconsidered." *IEJ* 21 (1971): 1–12, plate 1.
Zanker, Paul. *The Power of Images in the Age of Augustus*. Translated by Alan Shapiro. Jerome Lectures 16. Ann Arbor, MI: University of Michigan Press, 1988.
Zeitlin, Solomon. *Who Crucified Jesus?* 2nd ed. New York: Harper, 1947.
Zias, Joe, and James H. Charlesworth. "Crucifixion: Archaeology, Jesus, and the Dead Sea Scrolls." Pages 273–89 in *Jesus and the Dead Sea Scrolls*. Edited by James H. Charlesworth. ABRL. New York: Doubleday, 1992.

Chapter 14

Jesus' Empty Tomb and His Appearance in Jerusalem

GRANT R. OSBORNE

1. Introduction

There is no aspect of Christianity more important to its continuing validity than that of the Easter tradition. Paul himself said, "if Christ has not been raised, our preaching is useless and so is your faith" (1 Cor 15:14). In the early Church (and today in Orthodox circles) on Easter morn one would greet travelers with, "He is risen," and the response would be "He is risen indeed!" It is important to recognize that the cross and the empty tomb have always been the core of the Christian faith and the basis of Christian hope. At the same time, Norman Perrin argued that questions of facticity took a back seat to the meaning of the event for the early followers; therefore their theological speculation obviated historical interest and the question regarding "what really happened" was alien to their concerns.[1] Robert Cavin has recently said that "the tiny fraction of New Testament Easter traditions that comprises our bona fide historical evidence – the core empty tomb tradition (Mark 1:1–6, 8) and the appearance list given by Paul (1 Cor 15:3–8) – is woefully inadequate to establish a proposition as bold as the resurrection hypothesis."[2] The purpose of this essay is to address the evidence and ascertain the extent to which the early writers were interested in history and provided a reliable witness. There is no issue in Scripture more important than that of the resurrection of Jesus Messiah. Yet was Paul wrong? This essay is dedicated to answering this question: can the resurrection of Jesus be historically affirmed, and how important is this issue?

---

[1] Norman Perrin, *The Resurrection According to Matthew, Mark, and Luke* (Philadelphia: Fortress, 1977), 78.
[2] Robert G. Cavin, "Is There Sufficient Historical Evidence to Establish the Resurrection of Jesus?" in *The Empty Tomb: Jesus Beyond the Grave* (ed. Robert M. Price and Jeffrey J. Lowder; New York: Prometheus Books, 2005), 36. The entire work attempts to support this hypothesis. In the introductory essay Robert M. Price ("Introduction: The Second Life of Jesus," 11–12) finds it absurd to believe Jesus could still be alive two thousand years later and is both physically present and "awaits one at the cozy hearth of one's heart."

2. The Authenticity of the Resurrection

This essay seeks to answer this question by utilizing the approaches many scholars share but often fail to apply to this event for reasons we shall make clear. Nevertheless, I shall ask the same kinds of questions the other essays in this collection have asked about grounding in history. Can we use the criteria of authenticity to assess the resurrection? Multiple attestation and multiple forms shall be key here, as will arguments related to first century cultural background.

I begin with a look at the earliest creedal expression about the resurrection, which claims to recall what God did in resurrecting Jesus. Now a question might be raised about starting here, since the historical Jesus is not the person "doing" the resurrecting, and usual historical Jesus issues normally treat events or teaching that Jesus is responsible for "doing." However, the idea of vindication by God is something Jesus raised as a point in his teaching as was already established in the essay involving Jesus' meeting with the Jewish leadership. So it was Jesus who raised the issue of divine vindication, making it a relevant topic for our study. In fact what makes the resurrection such an important part of the Jesus story is its function as an event of divine vindication and authentication.

So I look at the case for authenticity tied to the three types of attestation to a resurrection: the earliest creedal statement, the empty tomb and the appearances. In doing so, I appeal to the criterion of multiple forms.

2.1. *The Earliest Resurrection Creedal Statement*

We should begin with an early tradition seen in a widespread (probably) early Aramaic confession ("God [who] raised Christ Jesus from the dead") expressed in Gal 1:1; 1 Thess 1:10; Rom 4:24; 6:4; 8:11; 10:9; Col 2:12; Eph 1:20; 1 Pet 1:21; Pol. *Phil* 2:1; a formula omitting "from the dead" occurs in Acts 3:26; 10:40; 13:33; 1 Cor 6:14; 15:15; 2 Cor 4:14. It is clear that the belief of resurrection is multiply attested. Dale Allison follows Klaus Wengst in arguing that it resembles Jewish confessions like Exod 16:6; Num 15:41; Deut 8:14; Isa 45:6–7 and so represents early worship liturgy.[3] It is generally agreed that 1 Cor 15:3–8 represents the earliest creed in the NT, as Paul uses the rabbinic code-words for the passing on of tradition ("For what I received I passed on to you," cf. 1 Cor 11:23).[4] Paul likely "received" it on

---

[3] Dale C. Allison, Jr., *Resurrecting Jesus: The Earliest Christian Tradition and Its Interpreters* (New York: T&T Clark, 2005), 229–30, following Klaus Wengst, *Christologische Formeln und Lieder des Urchristentums* (SNT 7; Gütersloh: Gütersloher Verlagshaus; Mohn, 1972), 27–48.

[4] In addition, the creedal background is demonstrated by (1) the parallelism exhibited (four ὅτι clauses divided into two sections each on Jesus' death and resurrection) and

his first trip to Jerusalem (Acts 9:26–30) in the mid-30s C.E.,[5] just five years or so after the death and resurrection of Jesus. Moreover, it was already formed by that early date. The parallelism is evident in a series of three ὅτι ... καὶ ὅτι ... καὶ ὅτι conjunctions uniting four finite verbs (ἀπέθανεν ... ἐτάφη ... ἐγήγερται ... ὤφθη) in vv. 3–5a and then this compilation is followed by a series of further conjunctions linking the appearance traditions in vv. 5b–8 (εἶτα ... ἔπειτα ... ἔπειτα ... εἶτα ... ἔσχατον). It is difficult to know whether there was one tradition (vv. 3–8) or two (3b–5, 6–8).[6] Either way we are facing the core of very early Christian belief and a stream of tradition that anchors Christian faith in what Paul believes are historical facts. Thiselton calls this configuration a "self-involving" truth-claim that not only tells what God has done in and through Christ but at the same time demands personal faith and an "oath of loyalty" on the part of the reader.[7]

In vv. 3–5 the empty tomb is not explicit but is presupposed by the further notation, "and was buried." It breaks the rhythm of the parallel "died for our sins according to the Scriptures / was raised on the third day according to the Scriptures" and becomes the swing idea between the two. On one level it emphasizes the reality of Jesus' death, and on another level it combines with "he was raised" to connote the empty tomb.[8] Still, some oppose any connotation of an empty tomb. Adela Yarbro Collins, after examining vv. 3–5, concludes, "for Paul, and presumably for many other early Christians, the resurrection of Jesus did not imply that his tomb was empty."[9]

---

(2) such non-Pauline elements as "for our sins," "according to the Scriptures," "has been raised," "on the third day," "was seen," and "to the Twelve." While it probably had Palestinian origin, the language shows it came to Paul via the Hellenistic Jewish church.

[5] L. C. A. Alexander, "Chronology of Paul," *DPL* 122, places it as 37 C.E.

[6] Alexander J. M. Wedderburn, *Beyond Resurrection* (Peabody: Hendrickson, 1999), 114–15, speaks for many when he opts for two traditions due to the change in language and tenor from v. 5 to v. 6. For the unity of this as a single creed, see Jerome Murphy-O'Connor, "Tradition and Redaction in 1 Cor 15:3–7," *CBQ* 43 (1981): 582–89. However, N. T. Wright, *The Resurrection of the Son of God* (vol. 3 of *Christian Origins and the Question of God*; Minneapolis: Fortress, 2003), 319, says this is ultimately unimportant. "What counts is that the heart of the formula is something Paul knows the Corinthians will have heard from everyone else (Peter and Apollos) as well as himself, and that he can appeal to it as unalterable Christian bedrock."

[7] Anthony C. Thiselton, *The First Epistle to the Corinthians: A Commentary on the Greek Text* (NIGTC; Grand Rapids: Eerdmans; Carlisle: Paternoster, 2000), 1187–88.

[8] For the centrality of this, see especially R. J. Sider, "St. Paul's Understanding of the Nature and Significance of the Resurrection in I Corinthians XV 1–19," *NTS* 19 (1977): 124–41; and W. L. Craig, "The Historicity of the Empty Tomb of Jesus," *NTS* 31 (1985): 39–67, esp. 40–42.

[9] Adela Yarbro Collins, "The Empty Tomb in the Gospel of Mark," in *Hermes and Athena: Biblical Exegesis and Philosophical Theology* (ed. Eleonore Stump and Thomas P. Flint; Notre Dame: University of Notre Dame Press, 1993), 113–14. So also Edward Lynn Bode, *The First Easter Morning: The Gospel Accounts of the Women's Visit to the Tomb of Jesus* (AnBib 45; Rome: Biblical Institute Press, 1970), 98–100.

However, J.D.G. Dunn takes the opposite tack, asserting that "buried" deliberately interrupts the normal movement from death to resurrection and must reflect "the place of the tomb narratives – burial but also empty tomb – in the earliest traditions of Easter."[10] Then in v. 4b we see that the resurrection was accomplished as an act of God (divine passive ἐγήγερται) and that the Scriptures demanded it. "According to the Scriptures," as Thiselton rightly observes, does not so much refer to any specific text (e.g., Ps 2:7, 16:9–10, or Hos 6:2) as to "the witness to a climactic fulfillment of a cumulative tradition of God's promised eschatological act of sovereignty and vindication in grace."[11]

Few doubt some experiential reality behind the appearances listed in 1 Cor 15:6–8, whether they see them as dreams, visions, or physical appearances.[12] A key issue is the meaning of ὤφθη. Many like Michaelis and Marxsen[13] argue that the verb connotes not physical seeing but a "revelation" or "encounter" of the Risen One, with no emphasis on the mode of seeing but rather on the theological consequences which awoke faith in the apostles and legitimated them as the chosen leaders. However, Jacob Kremer translates the verb "appeared / let himself be seen" and says we cannot deny a "visual element" to the verb, since throughout the prophets and the NT it clearly has this function, concluding that this verb signifies "that the power characteristic of Yahweh and the angels to appear visibly is ascribed to the resurrected Christ."[14] However, the verb simply means "to see" and can in some contexts refer to experience but in a context like that of 1 Corinthians 15 must have a sensory component of physical sight. The list refers to witnesses of an event, in this case resurrection appearances of Jesus. As Gordon Fee points out, attempts to make ὤφθη stand for a vision rather than an actual appearance are "either irrelevant or simply prejudicial" since it means Christ visibly "appeared" to people.[15] Alston notes how many generalize

---

[10] James D.G. Dunn, *Jesus Remembered* (vol. 1 of *Christianity in the Making*; Grand Rapids: Eerdmans, 2003–xx), 839.

[11] Thiselton, *First Corinthians*, 1195. Richard Swinburne, *The Resurrection of God Incarnate* (Oxford: Clarendon, 2003), 163–70, argues for the validity of the third day theme on the grounds that the celebration of the eucharist (and meeting of Christians) on the "first day of the week" took place so early and was so widespread (Acts 20:7; 1 Cor 16:2; Rev 1:10) that it can only be explained by the raising of the Lord on Sunday, the "third day."

[12] For the view that they were visionary dreams, see Gerd Lüdemann, *What Really Happened to Jesus: A Historical Approach to the Resurrection* (trans. John Bowden; London: SCM, 1995), 101–3.

[13] Wilhelm Michaelis, "ὁράω, κτλ.," *TDNT* 5:358–61; Willi Marxsen, *The Resurrection of Jesus of Nazareth* (trans. Margaret Hohl; London: SCM, 1970), 98–111.

[14] J. Kremer, "ὁράω, κτλ.," *EDNT* 2:528.

[15] Gordon D. Fee, *The First Epistle to the Corinthians* (NICNT; Grand Rapids: Eerdmans, 1987), 728, n. 73. See also Thiselton, *First Corinthians*, 1197–1203, who after an extensive discussion recognizes that both alternatives are viable (the LXX uses the verb

from Paul's experience enumerated in v. 8 to assume that all the appearances were revelatory visions and concludes, "Why suppose that Paul's putting his own experience in the same list as the others indicates that he took their experiences to be similar to his? ... It would not be unreasonable for him to think it natural that corporeal appearances were limited to the immediate post-resurrection period, whereas at his late date the risen Christ would naturally appear in a different mode, since his situation was different."[16]

It is possible to take the appearance to "Cephas" in v. 5 as a competing tradition to the first appearance to the women in the Gospel tradition,[17] but Paul does not say this was the "first" and is appealing to *apostolic* eye-witness testimony. We have no description of such an appearance elsewhere (though the event is noted in Luke 24:34, while some see it in John 21:15–17), perhaps because it was too intensely personal to Peter.[18] In fact, the brevity of this report is a pointer to history. If any person were creating these stories they would certainly have a detailed account of the appearance to the primary leader of the early Church. And if the early church created stories as easily as it is sometimes portrayed, it is amazing that in the passages that came to be embraced as orthodox we lack any such detailed account from Peter. In fact, the *Gos. Pet.* 60 (probably for this very reason) breaks off where just such an expanded story occurs. The use of "the Twelve"[19] (only here in Paul) rather than the usual Pauline term "the apostles" points to pre-Pauline tradition. This may well be the Jerusalem appearance of Luke 24:36–43 (= John 20:19–23), though it could also refer to Matt 28:16–20 or John 21:11–23. The first may be favored because Luke 24:34, 36f combine the appearances to Peter and the Twelve. Lüdemann believes that a guilt-ridden Peter in deep mourning psychologically dredged up an apparition of Jesus to help him in his mourning process.[20] This seems plausible on the surface, but it is exceedingly difficult to move from this hallucinatory event to the confident cry of the early Christians, "He is risen from the dead!" Hallucinations do not normally make people willing to surrender their lives for a new religion, and they do not create movements that change the world.[21]

---

often of the "appearing" of God's eschatological glory) but states that in this context it must refer to an actual "seeing" within history of the Risen Jesus.

[16] William P. Alston, "Biblical Criticism and the Resurrection," in *The Resurrection: An Interdisciplinary Symposium on the Resurrection of Jesus* (ed. Stephen T. Davis, et al.; New York: Oxford Univ Press, 1997), 160–61.

[17] So Elisabeth Schüssler Fiorenza, *In Memory of Her: A Feminist Theological Reconstruction of Christian Origins* (New York: Crossroad, 1984), 315–34.

[18] For various explanations as to why no account of the visions to Peter and James are recorded, see Grant R. Osborne, *The Resurrection Narratives: A Redactional Study* (Grand Rapids: Baker, 1984), 226–27.

[19] See in this volume ch. 5.

[20] Lüdemann, *What Really Happened*, 93–94.

[21] See the critique of Allison, *Resurrecting Jesus*, 242–43.

It is also difficult to know why no appearances to women are part of this list; the reason may well be apologetic: there were the cultural barriers to such an inclusion; in the Jewish and even more in the Greco-Roman world the idea of women doing such things was not approved in regular society. Such an official list did not seem the place to break such new ground, even though the Gospels themselves consistently do it. It may well be the official nature of the tradition that keeps the focus on the church's leaders since every incident named would have involved at least some of them directly.

The grammar of vv. 6–7 changes (from ὅτι to εἶτα ... ἔπειτα), so these appearances may well have been added by Paul from other traditions. The appearances to "more than 500 at once" and to James in 1 Cor 15:6–7 are not recorded elsewhere. It is pure speculation to inquire where and when the mass appearance took place.[22] But it is clear that when Paul said, "most of whom are still living," he believed it had occurred and was inviting the Corinthians to ask the eyewitnesses about it should they wish.[23] There is a distinct apologetic purpose inherent to vv. 6–8. With this many present at the event, it is difficult to believe it could have been a mass hallucination (ἐφάπαξ stresses "the reality and objectivity of this appearance"[24]), and Paul is suggesting that any of the participants could verify the reality of the event as being the same as the appearance to Peter or James. The appearance to James, like the one to Peter, is never described elsewhere. Yet it is very plausible, for it explains how James, Jesus' brother,[25] who was not a follower during Jesus' life (Mark 3:21, 31–32; 6:4; John 7:5), came to faith and became the leader of the Jerusalem church (Acts 15:13–21). Here there is a parallel with Paul in v. 8, who also was not a believer when Christ "appeared" to him. These two appearance stories counter the suggestion of some that the appearances are improbable because they involved only people who had been followers of Jesus before. In all the narrations, the appearances produced faith rather than being the result of faith (cf. "some doubted" in Matt 28:17). Again, the restraint exercised throughout this list is a marker of authenticity. Paul is not so much trying to prove that the resurrection

---

[22] Reginald H. Fuller, *The Formation of the Resurrection Narratives* (Philadelphia: Fortress, 1980), 36, represents many who believe it a reference to Pentecost, but that is quite speculative, and it is difficult to see how such disparate traditions could have evolved from the same event so quickly (see Thiselton, *First Corinthians*, 1206). Others have thought it to be the appearance of Matt 28:16–20; while possible, it is unlikely because Matthew seems to restrict that appearance to "the Eleven."

[23] Hans Conzelmann, *1 Corinthians* (trans. James W. Leitch; Hermeneia; Philadelphia: Fortress, 1975), 258, takes this in the opposite direction as emphasizing that some of them had already died (on the grounds that Paul in this chapter is interested in the switch from death to life), but this hardly fits the context of vv. 6–8.

[24] Fee, *First Corinthians*, 730.

[25] For the identification with this James, see Osborne, *Resurrection Narratives*, 229–30.

appearances occurred (he presupposes their factuality) as he is expecting the Corinthians to recognize the reality of these events and to apply that to the issue of the future resurrection of believers, the theme of 1 Cor 15 (see further below).

It is hard to know who "all the apostles" in v. 7 are, since Paul has already named an appearance to "the Twelve" in v. 5. It almost sounds as if Paul wishes to distinguish the two groups, but it is more likely that Paul widens the group to others like Barnabas and James. In Acts 1:22, 1 Cor 9:1 it was a requirement for an apostle that he had indeed "seen Jesus our Lord." Some (e. g., Thiselton) believe this is not a single appearance but rather a summary of all the appearances, but this is unlikely since it is part of a list of specific events (like the one to Paul in v. 8). Some believe this refers to the ascension of Luke 24:50–51; Acts 1:6–9, and this may be the best option.

Finally, Paul himself becomes a vital witness for the reality of the Risen Lord. With his "last of all," it is clear Paul believed the appearances were not regular events happening to many Christians but unique events separated from other visions (e. g., his own in 2 Cor 12:1–5) and experiences that would not occur again in this world. As Wright says, the placement of this here, in connection with the "seeing" of Cephas, James, and the other apostles, signifies not just that Paul had the same apostolic authority as they but even more "that he had seen what the other apostles had seen, namely Jesus himself, personally present."[26] There has been a great deal of discussion of the meaning of ἔκτρωμα, a *hapax legomena*, but with the term's background in the idea of a stillborn baby, it is probably best to understand Paul as saying that God in granting him this vision has brought the (spiritually) dead to life as well.[27]

The consensus that vv. 3–11 are an early creed has recently been challenged by Crossan, who believes that the list is not about faith but about authority and power in the early church. These claims set the apostles apart as the divinely chosen leaders of the community.[28] A similar approach is taken by Lüdemann, who says Paul used the list apologetically "to defend

---

[26] Wright, *Resurrection*, 327.
[27] See Thiselton, *First Corinthians*, 1210. He has an excellent discussion of the six options on pp. 1209–10.
[28] John Dominic Crossan, "The Passion, Crucifixion and Resurrection," in *The Search for Jesus: Modern Scholarship Looks at the Gospels* (Hershel Shanks; Washington, D. C.: Biblical Archeological Society, 1994), 123–25. So also Robert M. Price, "Apocryphal Apparitions: 1 Corinthians 15:3–11 As a Post-Pauline Interpolation," in *The Empty Tomb: Jesus Beyond the Grave* (ed. Robert M. Price and Jeffrey J. Lowder; New York: Prometheus Books, 2005), 69–104, who says that this is the result of late post-Pauline Christianity and was interpolated into 1 Corinthians. Originally a list of credentials for key early leaders, it was incorporated into this letter as an apologetic for the resurrection. According to Price the appearance to 500 was an even later apocryphal piece added to the list.

his apostolic authority."²⁹ All three agree that the historical basis was a series of ecstatic "visions," first to Peter then picked up by other leaders. These visionary dreams gave them status in the community and anchored their leadership. On this basis they centered on the fact that Jesus was "alive" to them and concocted a resurrection story. However, is apostolic authority the purpose and tone of the creedal tradition in 1 Cor 15:6–8? On the basis of context that has to be held to be exceedingly doubtful. The whole issue in 1 Corinthians 15 is not about "legitimation formulae" but about the reality and meaning of the resurrection of Christ for the resurrection of the believer. Moreover, the appearance to "others" and to the 500 is hardly indicative of apostolic authority. It is far more likely that vv. 3–8 are a compilation of the events that launched the church, used by Paul especially to anchor his argument regarding the reality of the resurrection. There is no doubt that he at least considered the resurrection a historical fact. As Fee states, this section is not so much attempting to *prove* the resurrection as it is "reasserting the commonly held ground *from which* he will argue against their assertion that there is no resurrection from the dead."³⁰ Either way, the entire purpose is the reality of the resurrection of Jesus for the Christian faith (and not simply to anchor the power and authority of the leaders).³¹ The style of the passage, with its rhythmic phrasing and parallelism, points to a creedal origin, and if anything it is older than Paul rather than later. Moreover, the criterion of multiple attestation applies to one of these appearance stories (to the Twelve = Luke 24:36–43 = John 20:19–23 or Matt 28:16–20), although once one adds this creed to the mix several more also become multiply attested (Cephas, Luke 24:34; all the apostles, Luke 24:50–53, Acts 1:6–9).

2.2. The Empty Tomb

Our discussion regarding 1 Cor 15:1–8 has shown us that we should seriously consider the two lines of evidence it portrays: the empty tomb (vv. 3–5) and the appearance stories (vv. 6–8). So let us examine these one at a time. Before we get to the data on the empty tomb itself, one question must be raised: is it viable to try to reconstruct the disparate accounts? Since any such attempt is artificial and must be done apart from the accounts themselves, I for many years answered "No." Yet as I have reflected on this in recent years, I have changed my mind. Comparing disparate witnesses and sifting them to delineate the original event (often called "harmonizing")

---

[29] Gerd Lüdemann, *The Resurrection of Christ: A Historical Inquiry* (Amherst: Prometheus Books, 2004), 41.

[30] Fee, *First Corinthians*, 718.

[31] Moreover, there is absolutely no basis for Price's contention that vv. 3–11 are a later interpolation; this has had some popularity on the internet but has not been received well by scholars.

is the basic method in historiography as well as in newspaper and police accounts today. It makes perfect sense so long as it is done carefully and explains the data.[32] Moreover, many such attempts have been made. The importance of this point is in showing that differing accounts do not necessarily contradict one another.

Allison calls the empty tomb "a great riddle, a problem presented by Providence to the ingenuity of the historians."[33] However, there is sufficient evidence to give us some confidence in asserting the likelihood of the empty tomb. Let us take the elements of the empty tomb stories one at a time and ask whether they are more likely fictional and late or were based on a historical event. We will begin with the burial itself. Since Mark's account of the burial by Joseph of Arimathea in 15:46 does not mention burial spices (they are found only in John 19:39–40) and since there is no mention of any connection between Joseph's act and the women followers (Mark 15:47), Raymond E. Brown argues that Mark does not depict an honorable burial but rather a criminal burial, with Joseph simply following the command of Deut 21:22–23 ("When someone is convicted of a crime punishable by death and is executed, and you hang him on a tree, his copse must not remain all night upon the tree; you shall bury him that same day").[34] Yet if this were so, Joseph would hardly have buried Jesus in his own newly purchased rock-hewn tomb[35] (cf. Matt 27:60; Luke 23:53[36]). The Roman observance of such Jewish regulations normally meant the body would be thrown in a mass grave with the other executed criminals (see Josephus, *J. W.* 4.317) or in this case be given over for burial (see below). For Joseph to go to the trouble and expense (let alone the approbation he would receive from his colleagues on the Sanhedrin) would seem to call for more than mere piety. Moreover, the description of Joseph as "waiting expectantly for the kingdom of God" in 15:43 could be simply a general statement regarding Joseph's piety, but the use of "kingdom of God" in Mark as a summary of Jesus' message

---

[32] See Craig L. Blomberg, "The Legitimacy and Limits of Harmonization," in *Hermeneutics, Authority, and Canon* (ed. D. A. Carson and John D. Woodbridge; Grand Rapids: Baker, 1995), 139–74.

[33] Allison, *Resurrecting Jesus*, 299.

[34] Raymond E. Brown, "The Burial of Jesus (Mark 15:42–47)," *CBQ* 50 (1988): 233–45.

[35] For details regarding rock-hewn tombs, see Rachel Hachlili, *Jewish Funerary Customs, Practices, and Rites in the Second Temple Period* (JSJSup 94; Leiden: Brill, 2005), 29–74. She points out that entrances were small, and people had to bend down to enter. They had a groove at the entrance and were sealed sometimes with circular stones (e.g., Herod's family tomb near Jerusalem) or a rectangular stone. Mainly, they were heavy and difficult to move from the entrance.

[36] Mark does not mention that it was his own tomb (Matt 27:60, αὐτοῦ), but still Mark notes that it was a rock-hewn tomb, and a crucified criminal would hardly be placed in such a tomb. The passage *m. Sanh.* 6:5 notes that there were special places set aside for burying executed criminals.

(1:14–15) and as the result of his messianic ministry at the least makes him a sympathizer if not a genuine follower of Jesus.[37] At the least, then, Joseph procured a tomb for Jesus. In doing so, it was one he had access to on such short notice is likely.

Yet Robert Funk and the Jesus Seminar declare Joseph "a Markan invention" so as to provide Jesus a proper burial. The details of the story (the rock-hewn tomb, the stone rolled over the opening) serve only to prepare for the empty tomb narrative that follows.[38] Similarly, Crossan argues that crucifixion victims were hardly ever given honorable burials and that Jesus most certainly was thrown into a shallow mass grave.[39] On the other hand, Bultmann calls this story "an historical account which creates no impression of being a legend … It can hardly be shown that the section was devised with the Easter story in mind."[40] Craig Evans disputes the view of Funk and Crossan, arguing that the mass graves were utilized mainly in times of war with a multiplicity of victims, and that evidence exists that it was fairly common to give victims in Jewish lands a burial. For example, Philo comments "I have known cases when on the eve of a holiday of this kind, people who have been crucified have been taken down and their bodies delivered to their kinsfolk, because it was thought well to give them burial and allow them the ordinary rites" (*Flaccus* 83). Similarly, Josephus explains that "the Jews are careful about funeral rites that even malefactors who have been sentenced to crucifixion are taken down and buried before sunset" (*J. W.* 4.377). In light of this ancient evidence, Evans states that it is more plausible to recognize that Jesus would have received a burial like that reported in Mark.[41]

The empty tomb narratives contain several narrative details found in all four Gospels: the women come to the tomb, meet angel(s), the tomb is empty (told to the women by the angels in the synoptics, discovered by the beloved disciple and Peter in John), the women are told to tell the disciples (commanded by the angel in the synoptic tradition, by Jesus in John); the women report the news to the disciples but are not believed (except in

---

[37] See R. T. France, *The Gospel of Mark* (NIGTC; Grand Rapids: Eerdmans, 2002), 666–67. Craig A. Evans, *Mark 8:27–16:20* (WBC 34b; Nashville: Nelson, 2001), 519, believes that Joseph was in basic agreement with Jesus' concerns and may have even thought him a prophet but may not have been an actual follower. He buried Jesus out of pious concern for the law. Yet Matt 27:57 and John 19:38 call him "a disciple of Jesus," and Luke 23:51 says he never "consented to the plan and action" of the Sanhedrin. He was more than just a pious adherent of the law.

[38] Robert W. Funk and The Jesus Seminar, *The Acts of Jesus: The Search for the Authentic Deeds of Jesus* (San Francisco: HarperSanFrancisco, 1998), 159–61.

[39] John Dominic Crossan, *The Historical Jesus: The Life of a Mediterranean Jewish Peasant* (San Francisco: HarperSanFrancisco, 1991), 392–93.

[40] Rudolf Bultmann, *The History of the Synoptic Tradition* (trans. John Marsh; Oxford: Blackwell, 1972), 274.

[41] Evans, *Mark*, 517–18.

Mark). The presence of many of these basic facts found also in 1 Corinthians 15 and the Gospel of Peter (see above) favors the basic authenticity of the story on the basis of the criterion of multiple attestation. Several differing traditions contain elements of the basic story. In addition, the criterion of inherent ambiguity also favors its veracity. No one is portrayed as expecting a resurrection, and it is extremely doubtful that some of these details would have arisen in a church created tradition (more on this later). We have every reason to be quite positive regarding the truth of the empty tomb narratives, at least at the basic level.

Next, let us consider some of the details and look for signs of plausibility or unnecessary contradiction. Two issues can be handled in passing – the time notes and the names of the women. In Matt 28:1 the women start out for the tomb "at dawn"; in Mark 16:2 "just after sunrise"; in Luke 24:1 "very early in the morning"; and in John 20:1 "while it was still dark." It seems clear redactional differences account for the data, and that the event occurring at dawn would allow both emphases. There is no real discrepancy, for John emphasized the darkness in keeping with his darkness motif (1:5; 3:2 etc.) and Mark the coming of light. The time-notes cohere well; they would be fictional only if the whole story is novelistic. Regarding the presence of the women, Bauckham says that "the role of the women as eyewitnesses is crucial" since they are present at his death, burial, and the empty tomb.[42] Yet the names show some divergence. Mark has three (Mary Magdalene, Mary the mother of James, Salome), Matthew two (without Salome), Luke several (without Salome then adding Joanna and "other" women), and John just Mary Magdalene (with "we" in 20:2). Marxsen believes these differences are irreconcilable, and Broer concludes that there is little historical value in these contradictory traditions.[43] Yet one wonders why historians should be so cavalier in dismissing such evidence. The one certain thing is the official nature of the lists. This is actually evidence for historicity, since in the ancient world women could not legally serve as witnesses. No one inventing a story would have added such a detail.[44] Evans calls this "the criterion of embarrassment," for the witnesses would certainly have been male if the

---

[42] Richard Bauckham, *Jesus and the Eyewitnesses: The Gospels as Eyewitness Testimony* (Grand Rapids: Eerdmans, 2006), 48.

[43] Marxsen, *Resurrection*, 41–44; Ingo Broer, *Die Urgemeinde und das Grab Jesu: eine Analyse der Grablegungsgeschichte im Neuen Testament* (SANT 31; Munich: Kösel, 1972), 87–88.

[44] This is challenged by Jeffrey J. Lowder, "Historical Evidence and the Empty Tomb Story," in *The Empty Tomb: Jesus Beyond the Grave* (ed. Robert M. Price and Jeffrey J. Lowder; New York: Prometheus Books, 2005), 283–85, who argues that women could testify if there were no male witnesses, citing *m. Yebam.* 16:7; *m. Ketub.* 2:5; *m. ʿEd.* 3:6. While this is true, it would still be highly unusual for a *created* Jewish novel about the empty tomb to have only women present as official witnesses.

story was invented in any sense.⁴⁵ It is hard to see why the list of names contains actual and irreconcilable discrepancies. Luke notes several "other" women, and none of the lists claim to be exhaustive. Allison also discusses this issue, noting the reluctance of the disciples to believe the women in Luke 24:22–23, the ridicule of Celsus against such a report of "a half-frantic woman" (Origen, *Cels.* 2.59), and the statement of Josephus, "From women let no evidence be accepted, because of the levity and temerity of their sex" (*Ant.* 4.219). In other words, it is highly unlikely this was fictional and extremely probable this story comes from actual memory.⁴⁶ Bauckham goes even further, arguing that the divergences "demonstrate the scrupulous *care* with which the Gospels present the women as witnesses" since each evangelist seems "to name precisely the women who were well known to them as witnesses to these crucial events."⁴⁷ There is no list-fixing taking place.

The motive of the women in coming to the tomb has important differences, with Mark and Luke saying they had come to anoint Jesus' body with spices; Matthew that they "went to look at the tomb"; and John providing no motive at all. Moreover, Mark 16:1 says the spices were purchased "after the Sabbath was over" while Luke 23:56 has them prepare the spices before they rested on the Sabbath. One could not visit a tomb on the Sabbath; Sunday morning at first light would be the earliest they could go. Fitzmyer notes a Jewish tract that allows such Sabbath practices, "They may make ready [on the Sabbath] all that is needful for the dead, and anoint it and wash it ..." (*m. Šabb.* 23:5).⁴⁸ Women often would go to show devotion for seven days after a burial, though for a condemned criminal it could be different (*m. Sanh.* 6:6). The main thing is they were showing private grief. Kirby doubts the historicity of this aspect because there is no parallel for such an anointing on the third day *after* the burial. Such a use of oils and perfumes was done prior to burial, not after.⁴⁹ Yet that is as great a problem for fictional writing, for the person making up such a story would have to be quite ignorant of customs, and that is exceedingly improbable. The best answer is probably provided by France, who points out that the "burial formalities (were) interrupted by the Sabbath," and so the women went to complete their act of devotion. The problem of a badly decomposed body would not be so great given the coolness of the time of year and the body having been

---

⁴⁵ Evans, *Mark*, 531.
⁴⁶ Allison, *Resurrecting Jesus*, 327–31.
⁴⁷ Bauckham, *Jesus and the Eyewitnesses*, 50–51 (italics his); cf. also 129–32.
⁴⁸ Joseph A. Fitzmyer, *The Gospel According to Luke X–XXIV* (AB 28a; Garden City: Doubleday, 1985), 1530.
⁴⁹ Peter Kirby, "The Case Against the Empty Tomb," in *The Empty Tomb: Jesus Beyond the Grave* (ed. Robert M. Price and Jeffrey J. Lowder; New York: Prometheus Books, 2005), 243.

placed in a "rock-cut tomb."⁵⁰ They would identify the tomb by charcoal markings placed by the entrance; the story is very much in keeping with Jewish customs, and the criterion of plausibility makes the story quite tenable. Fitting into such a background is the giving over of the body for a burial, but not in a family tomb (*m. Sanh.* 6:5; *Sem.* 13:7). This is precisely the kind of unique practice that fits with a burial by Joseph of Arimathea. The burial before sundown also fits here (Deut 21:23; 11QT 64:7–13a = 4Q524 frag. 14, lines 2–4– in an execution, not to remain overnight on a tree; *m. Sanh.* 6:4–5). Private grief is permitted, in contrast to any public mourning (*m. Sanh.* 6:6). This is precisely what we see when the women go to the tomb as soon as they can after the burial and after the Sabbath. Their devotion is seen in going there as soon as the sun comes up. Contrast the ignorance of Jewish customs in the *Gospel of Peter*, with sleepovers and a meal in the cemetery. In other words, this restrained account would make sense given the circumstances.

It is logical (again, the criterion of plausibility) that a group of women, concerned that they had not been able to show their devotion to Jesus in his hasty burial by Joseph of Arimathea,⁵¹ would have purchased spices after Jesus died on Friday before the Sabbath had begun. Then at the end of the Sabbath period, Saturday evening, they purchased more spices to make certain they had enough. The next morning they left while it was still dark (between 5 and 6 AM) and arrived at the tomb at first light. If Matt 27:62–66 is correct (see below on the guards), they may not have known about the sealing of the tomb. But even if they did (stones – sometimes circular but usually square [80% of those found] – were normally placed across the small entrance), they would quite naturally have forgotten about it in their desire to show their respect to Jesus. Their anxiety about finding some men to help remove the stone is natural, since the stones were "very large" (Mark 16:4), and a study of skeletons from the first century shows that women were on the average 4'11" or 5' tall and weighed about 95 lbs.

---

⁵⁰ France, *Mark*, 676.
⁵¹ W. D. Davies and Dale C. Allison, Jr., *A Critical and Exegetical Commentary on the Gospel According to Saint Matthew* (3 vols.; ICC; Edinburgh: T&T Clark, 1988–97), 3:647–48, make seven points in favor of the veracity of the burial story: (1) the positive portrayal of a member of the Sanhedrin goes against the tendency of the passion narratives; (2) fictional names are not regular in Mark or the tradition behind him; (3) Acts 13:29, used by Crossan et al. as evidence for the burial of Jesus by hostile forces, implies only burial by Jews and does not of necessity negate Joseph's act; (4) the story of Joseph's action shows little evidence of being legendary (so Bultmann); (5) 1 Cor 15:4 presupposes just such a burial story; (6) Josephus (*J. W.* 4.317) says the Jews regularly gave even crucified victims burial by sunset; (7) there is evidence for crucifixion victims being buried in family tombs (although Jesus was not buried in his own family's tomb, something the Mishnah prohibits to a criminal, as was just noted). In short, the burial story is plausible.

There is nothing in this aspect of the story that is inherently improbable. The stone was rolled away from the tomb not so that Christ could emerge, but so that the women and others could see the tomb was empty. The Jesus Seminar is opposed to this: "The removal of the stone blocking the entrance to the tomb, the appearance of the heavenly messenger" was a major factor in convincing them of the fictive nature of the story.[52] Yet there is nothing inherent in this narration to suggest it was miraculously removed. That is not an emphasis. The story of the women coming to the tomb is a homey touch that is inherently plausible. Note once again the restraint of the account. Contrast the detailed story in *Gospel of Peter*, with its ignorance of Jewish customs (the four Gospels are more culturally realistic here) and such details as the apostles sleeping overnight at the tomb and sharing a meal in the cemetery (neither of which were permitted). Every aspect shows a realistic and carefully understated reliability.

The issues of the guards and the number of angels can also be handled rather quickly. Only Matt 27:65–66 and 28:2–4 mention the guards (temple police rather than Roman guards) at the tomb. Yet there is a great deal of non-Matthean language that likely points to tradition rather than Matthean creation behind the material.[53] Brown goes so far as to posit that 27:62–66, 28:11–15 was originally a single narrative into which Matthew inserted the story of the women at the tomb.[54] Whatever the truth, there is no reason to believe that this is an invented story.[55] It fits the criterion of plausibility. Certainly, it has an apologetic function in refuting the Jewish claim that the disciples stole the body (28:15). Davies and Allison say the story is not compelling as history for this reason,[56] yet such imponderables are the bulwark of history,[57] and it is equally unlikely that a writer making up such a story

---

[52] Funk and Seminar, *The Acts of Jesus*, 467.

[53] Broer, *Die Urgemeinde und das Grab*, 67–68; Fuller, *Formation*, 164; Davies and Allison, *Matthew*, 3:645. There are several *hapax legomena* and stylistic features not common to Matthew.

[54] Raymond E. Brown, *The Death of the Messiah* (2 vols.; ABRL; New York: Doubleday, 1994), 2:1301–5. He also believes *Gos. Pet.* 28–34 provides independent witness to the event, though most take it as based on Matthew. It is even less likely to posit with some that Matthew borrowed his story from the Gospel of Peter.

[55] Contra W. J. C. Weren, "'His Disciples Stole Him Away' (Mt 28,13): A Rival Interpretation of Jesus' Resurrection," in *Resurrection in the New Testament: Festschrift J. Lambrecht* (ed. R. Bieringer, et al.; Leuven: Leuven University Press, 2002), 147–63, who compares this with the guard story in *Gos. Pet.* 8:28–11:49 and concludes Matthew takes a traditional story of the guards as witnesses and invents a new twist not found in the *Gospel of Peter* regarding conscious deception among the leaders. Yet as stated below, there are good reasons to accept the plausibility of the guard story in Matthew. See William L. Craig, "The Guard at the Tomb," *NTS* 30 (1984): 273–81.

[56] Davies and Allison, *Matthew*, 3:653.

[57] See William Lane Craig, *Assessing the New Testament Evidence for the Historicity of*

would present such details with such diversity. The disciples' inability to understand Jesus' resurrection predictions is clear in all the Gospels, so this makes sense (criterion of plausibility). The angels at the tomb also provide several inconsistencies. Mark has one "young man dressed in a white robe," Matthew an "angel of the Lord," Luke "two men in clothes that gleamed like lightning," and John "two angels in white." Though many (Bultmann, Grass, Marxsen, Fuller, Alsup) believe this to be a legendary accretion, one wonders why this is necessarily the case. The whole scene goes far beyond a mere human messenger. The details – sitting on the right side of the tomb, wearing white, the women's fearful reaction, the astounding message – fits a theophanic scene, and the message itself goes way beyond mere human observation. The announcement clearly comes from God himself.[58] Matt 28:2–5 correctly identifies Mark's "young man" as an angel, and thus Mark is using phenomenological language to describe how the women perceived him.

It could be argued that the angels are there for eschatological reasons and highlight the message from God. This is true for the Synoptic Gospels, but in John they play a minor role and simply address Mary's confusion. The difference in the numbers may have a redactional purpose, with the presence of two in Luke and John emphasizing them as divine witnesses, while Mark and Matthew simplify the drama by having only one. Wright asks the valid question why Matthew and the others have not done more if they wished to embellish the existing story. This is a remarkably underplayed scene, and we would expect more in the way of theophanic, apocalyptic details. "The best conclusion we can draw is that, though Matthew felt free to tell the story in his own way, he did not feel free to invent a new one."[59]

The major problem with the angel's command for the disciples to go to Galilee is the fact that they apparently remained in Jerusalem some time (a week in John 20:26). I shall cover this issue in more detail below in discussing the appearances. Yet the disciples remaining initially in Jerusalem makes sense in light of the fact that the Passover celebration lasted eight days, and they would naturally remain until the end of it. Certainly they could have left early and gone to Galilee that same day, but it also makes sense that they stayed. The fact that Jesus appeared to them that same day in the upper room (see the next section) would naturally make them wish to stay on in Jerusalem.

---

the Resurrection of Jesus (Studies in the Bible and Early Christianity 16; Lewiston: Mellen, 1989), 214–15, for further arguments on the reliability of this story.

[58] So France, *Mark*, 678–79. Evans, *Mark*, 536, says angels are often called "young men" (2 Macc 3:26, 33; Josephus, *Ant* 5.277), also often describing angels (2 Macc 5:2; Rev 7:9, 13; 10:1).

[59] Wright, *Resurrection*, 641.

For many critical scholars the empty tomb accounts are not so much history as legend, myth, or creative midrash. The only way to decide these matters is to examine the data and ascertain whether it points to verifiable history or a fictive origin. Peter Kirby finds the evidence in Mark (the basis for the other accounts) singularly ambiguous and improbable, thus a fictional creation of Mark for theological reasons. For him the discrepancies do not point to separate witnesses but rather to creative redactions of a single, fictional account, probably built on the three-day search for Elijah's body in 2 Kgs 2:9–18.[60] Fullmer believes Mark derives it from Hellenistic novels, possibly influenced by Chariton's *Callirhoë* which also has a discovery of an empty tomb.[61] Adela Collins asserts that the focus on the empty tomb in Mark was inspired by stories in the Greco-Roman world regarding heroes (e.g., Ganymedes in the Iliad, Menelaos in the Odyssey, Asclepios) who were translated and made gods and is thus a fictitious presentation of an apocalyptic theme regarding the translation of Jesus to heaven, so immortality rather than resurrection.[62] Funk reports that the Jesus Seminar concluded "that the empty tomb stories represent a later development of the appearance stories that were originally reports of luminous apparitions," and they call the empty tomb "an invention of Mark or some other Christian storyteller before him."[63]

In conclusion, arguments for the historicity of the empty tomb may be summarized from the list provided by Murray Harris:[64] (1) it is recorded in four "independent" strands of tradition (the four Gospels with their differing details). (2) The earliest account (Mark) is "extraordinarily restrained and unadorned." (3) Earliest Christians could not have proclaimed Jesus' resurrection unless the tomb was indeed empty. (4) In their polemic against the Christian claims, the Jews assumed the tomb was in fact empty (see Justin, *Dial.* 108; Tertullian, *De Spectaculis* 30). (5) Early Christians, like Jews, would assume that resurrection meant an empty tomb; (6) If the empty tomb had been a later development, we would expect a "third day" motif as in the appearance stories (1 Cor 15:4), but it occurs on "the first day of the week" (Mark 16:2). (7) The first witnesses were women, and they were named, something that would not have been fabricated in a society where women could not be legal witnesses. Now one might challenge one or two

---

[60] Kirby, "The Case Against the Empty Tomb".

[61] Paul M. Fullmer, *Resurrection in Mark's Literary-Historical Perspective* (LNTS 360; London: T&T Clark, 2007), 83–91.

[62] Collins, "The Empty Tomb in the Gospel of Mark," 124–28, 129–31.

[63] Funk and Seminar, *The Acts of Jesus*, 466–67. On pp. 464–65 the whole of Mark 16:1–8 is in black, indicating the Seminar regards it as improbable and fictive.

[64] Murray J. Harris, *From Grave to Glory: Resurrection in the New Testament* (Grand Rapids: Academie Books, 1990), 107–12.

of these reasons (#1 is questionable in terms of establishing independence and #5 is not clear), but the remaining parts of the list have merit in pointing to a real event, not a fiction, behind the tradition.

To this we might add also an argument based upon effect. Something changed Jesus' followers from defeated, depressed victims hiding for their lives and ready to return to Galilee in defeat (as in the road to Emmaus story in Luke 24) to victorious proclaimers of a religious story that would change the world.

So in thinking about the empty tomb accounts as a whole, there are several features that point to their core credibility and the far greater likelihood that they reflect an event rather than being an early-Christian creation. First, the role of women in the account is not likely for a created event, since the roots of this event involve attestation by witnesses who normally would not be culturally credible, especially in advocating a culturally innovative event. Second, the central leadership figures in the account do not respond in exemplary or heroic ways, which is not how one normally would create a central event that involved a movement's leaders. Third, details tied to the burial fit very well in the culture.

2.3. The Jerusalem Appearance: Luke 24:36–49 = John 20:19–23

There are a total of ten appearances mentioned in the NT accounts: to the women (Mark 16:5–7 and parallels), to Mary (John 20:11–18), to the Eleven in the upper room (Luke 24:36–43; John 20:19–23; 1 Cor 15:5) and then to Thomas a week later (John 20:24–29), to Peter (1 Cor 15:5; Luke 24:34), James, the 500, and "all the apostles" (1 Cor 15:5–7), to the disciples fishing and then the meal scene (John 20:1–23), and in the Great Commission scene (Matt 28:16–20). These appearances narratives place the events over a forty day period (Acts 1:3), so it is quite possible that there were several other appearances as well. One plausible reason for the wide disparity between the appearance stories told in the Gospels stems from the very number of events from which to choose. Each evangelist chose those details that would provide a proper conclusion for their individual Gospel and sum up the major themes that each had developed.

Because of the complexity of the appearance traditions and the limitations of this essay, I will center on one key appearance, believing that to authenticate this one will serve to authenticate the reality of Jesus' resurrection appearances in general, without necessarily claiming based upon this that all are necessarily authentic (each account would have to be examined individually). I have chosen the first group appearance in Jerusalem because it provides a microcosm of the others with many of the themes that permeate them all. The criterion of multiple attestation supports the authenticity of this tradition (Luke 24:36–49; John 20:19–23), but first one has to perform a source-critical study of the Lukan and Johannine story (the fact is that in the Passion narratives John is close to Luke). Few doubt that the two accounts refer to the same event in an multiply attested manner (Synoptic and Johannine traditions), for they have much in common: a first appearance to the disciples; Jesus saying, "Peace be unto you" followed by him showing them his hands and feet; the Risen Lord alleviating their fear[65] followed by their resultant joy; the mission command; and the promise of the Spirit. Yet the question is what kind of relationship lies behind the two. Frans Neirynck argues that John used Luke on the grounds that the shared details in John's story are dependent on Lukan redaction.[66] Bultmann, on the other hand, believes Luke uses a Galilee tradition that has ties with the appearance and mission command in Matt 28:16–20.[67] For a third hypothesis, Alsup believes that this appearance story is a reworking of the "walking on the water" miracle of Mark 6:45–52 and parallel.[68] Yet surely the differences with the mission passage of Matt 28 as well as with the miracle story of Mark 6 are too great. Few others have supported either hypothesis. It is more likely that the Lukan and Johannine accounts demonstrate parallel traditions rather than literary dependence on one or the other and go back to a "shared earlier source."[69] Dunn calls this "shared tradition from the first, having been given its still visible spine, presumably, from the participants talking about it among themselves."[70] In addition to the traditional flavor of the story, multiple attestation also favors authenticity (1 Cor 15:5 as well as Luke and John). Moreover, these are excellent examples of a basic aspect of all the appearance narratives: the authors choose details that will highlight redactional themes that are important to them. Yet these redactional nuances do not evidence fictive creation but rather stem from historical details. Redaction

---

[65] The "Peace be unto you" of v. 36 and v. 40, where Jesus shows his hands and feet, are two of the well-known "western non-interpolations" rejected by Westcott and Hort and many versions. However, the manuscript evidence in favor of their retention is so extensive that most recent scholars accept them as original. See Bruce M. Metzger, *A Textual Commentary on the Greek New Testament* (2nd ed.; Stuttgart: Deutsche Biblegesellschaft, 1994), 160–61.

[66] Frans Neirynck, "Lc 24,36–43: Un récit lucanien," in *À cause de l'Évangile: Études sur les Synoptiques et les Actes* (ed. F. Refoulé; Paris: Cerf, 1985), 655–80.

[67] Bultmann, *The History of the Synoptic Tradition*, 310.

[68] John E. Alsup, *The Post-Resurrection Appearance Stories of the Gospel Tradition: A History-of-Tradition Analysis* (Calwer Theologische Monographien 5; Stuttgart: Calwer-Verlag, 1975), 171–77.

[69] John Nolland, *Luke 18:35–24:53* (WBC 35c; Dallas: Word, 1993), 1211. See also I. Howard Marshall, *The Gospel of Luke* (NIGTC 3; Grand Rapids: Eerdmans, 1978), 900–901.

[70] Dunn, *Jesus Remembered*, 850.

refers to the author's choices of details from the eyewitness tradition they want to highlight. This is one of the primary theories I wish to support in the material that follows.

One issue is the extent of the pericope itself in Luke. Darrell Bock takes Luke 24:50–53 as a "summarizing variation" of the ascension story in Acts 1:6–11 and then vv. 44–49 as part of the meal scene in vv. 36–43.[71] I prefer to restrict the Jerusalem first appearance story to Luke 24:36–43, then place the command to "stay here in this city until you have been clothed with power from on high" (v. 49) near the time of the ascension forty days later in 24:50–53 = Acts 1:9–11 (thematically 24:49 is tied closely to what follows). There is no doubt that Luke 24:44–49 is Lukan redaction and is closely linked to emphases throughout his resurrection narrative. Verses 44–46 summarize themes present in the angels' words in vv. 6–7 and in Jesus' teaching on the road to Emmaus in vv. 25–27, concluding the fulfillment motif so predominant in Luke's resurrection narrative. Verses 47–49 are the Lukan form of the "Great Commission," but there is little verbal similarity with Matt 28:19 (the only phrase common to both is "all nations") and a closer verbal connection with Acts 1:8 ("power," "Holy Spirit," "witnesses," "Jerusalem"). Therefore, it is better to place vv. 47–49 with the ascension of vv. 50–53 than with the meal scene of vv. 36–43. Luke has begun with the first appearance in the upper room of Jerusalem in 24:36–43 then drawn material from other appearances over the next forty days to complete his themes in his resurrection narrative (Jesus fulfilling scriptural expectations in vv. 44–46 and launching the universal mission in 47–49), thereby both concluding his study of Jesus' life and ministry in his Gospel and pointing forward to his presentation of the universal mission of the church in Acts. Anderson agrees with this basic assessment and says,

> He [Luke] telescopes the events of Luke 24 into the time frame of a single day, not because he is ignorant of a protracted elapse of time (viz. forty days between resurrection and ascension, Acts 1:3), but because this allows him to theologically integrate the post-resurrection events ... the empty tomb, post-resurrection appearances, and ascension are characteristics of the fact that Jesus is the first individual to take part in the eschatological resurrection.[72]

One major question is whether all the commission passages (Mark 16:15–16 as a later compilation; Matt 28:18–20; Luke 24:47–49; John 20:21–23) come from a single tradition or from multiple commission traditions. One weak-

---

[71] Darrell L. Bock, *Luke* (2 vols.; Baker Exegetical Commentary on the New Testament 3a–b; Grand Rapids: Baker, 1994–96), 2:1928.

[72] Kevin L. Anderson, *"But God Raised Him from the Dead": The Theology of Jesus' Resurrection in Luke-Acts* (Paternoster Biblical Monographs; Bletchley, U.K.; Waynesboro: Paternoster, 2006), 182.

ness of form and redaction tradition is the assumption that Jesus never did or said anything twice. If there are similar events (e. g., the feeding miracles, the calming of the sea, the miraculous catch of fish miracles) or sayings (the two forms of the Lord's Prayer, the "two ways" sayings in Matt 7:13–14 and Luke 13:23–24), it is presupposed they came from a single original tradition. Yet what itinerant teacher does not use similar material on more than one occasion? Joseph Fitzmyer, for instance, sees in the original tradition a command to "go" (Mark / Matt) / "send" (Luke) the disciples to "preach" (Luke) / "teach" (Mark / Matt) "all I have commanded" (Matt) / "repentance and forgiveness of sins" (Luke) and reach "every creature" (Mark) / "all nations" (Matt / Luke).[73] Yet the language between Matthew, Luke, and John is so different, and second century scribes clearly combined traditions for the commission in the longer ending of Mark. It is preferable to conclude that there was more than one tradition of a commissioning by the Risen Lord, one given in Jerusalem on the first day (John 20:21–23), another in Galilee (Matt 28:18–20), with a third at the ascension (Luke 24:49 = Acts 1:8).

Therefore, once again on the basis of the criterion of multiple attestation (Luke, Paul, John as well as 1 Cor 15 and Acts 9, 22, 26), these commissioning stories are at least early tradition. Let us now look at the details, beginning with those areas that the two accounts hold in common. We will begin with the time of the event. John states it explicitly, "On the evening of that day, the first day of the week." For John the first three episodes of John 20 – the Beloved Disciple, Mary Magdalene, the disciples – occur on the day when Jesus was resurrected, with the first two in the morning and the third in the evening of that day. Luke does not affirm this explicitly, but as we observed earlier, he gives the impression throughout his account of a single day's activities. He begins, "As they were saying this," namely the disciples at the end of the Emmaus account, clearly that first day after the empty tomb was discovered. As Fitzmyer states, the wording in 24:36 "ensures the dating of this appearance of the risen Christ to 'the first day of the week.' See 24:1, 13, 33."[74] Clearly it is an evening appearance in both accounts, as Luke places it after the Emmaus story that concludes "toward evening" (24:29). The agreement between Luke and John demonstrates that this belongs to an early tradition, and it is extremely likely (criterion of plausibility) that Jesus would appear to them at that time in light of their extreme failure (Jesus used the language of apostasy in predicting their desertion in Mark 14:27 and parallels).[75]

---

[73] Fitzmyer, *Luke X–XXIV*, 1580.

[74] Fitzmyer, *Luke X–XXIV*, 1575.

[75] First century Judaism was an honor-shame culture. In this context, it would have been appropriate for one of Jesus' first appearances to have been to Peter (Luke 24:35 =

Jesus suddenly stands among them and promises, "Peace is yours." The wording of the Greek is remarkably the same in Luke 24:36 and John 20:19, pointing to its presence in tradition. Also, the historical present λέγει in both is also traditional and draws the reader into the message, which in a double meaning sense is the normal greeting *shalōm aleikem* and the promise of messianic peace. This is more evident in John where it alludes to John 14:27, "Peace I leave with you, my peace I give to you" (cf. 16:33) as a fulfillment of the divine promise of peace in Ps 29:11; Isa 9:6, 52:7, 57:19. Still, in Luke as well, "the promise of peace associated with the coming of Jesus reaches its fulfillment (2:14, cf. 7:50; Acts 10:36), and the conventional greeting is transformed."[76] Perkins believes that, here as well, Luke is certainly reworking an earlier tradition, as the peace greeting here and in John fits "the general format of appearance stories."[77]

A third common element is the fearful state of the disciples. The details somewhat differ, as Luke 24:37–38 has them "startled and frightened, thinking him a ghost," and they are not only afraid but filled with doubt as well. On the other hand, John 20:19 has them cowering behind closed doors "for fear of the Jews." Nolland finds the presence of fear in Luke strange after the triumphant message of 24:34–35 ("The Lord has risen indeed"). He calls it an adaptation of the fear motif at the angelophany in v. 5.[78] Yet the connection is more theological and social than literary, for their hesitant reaction is not really so unusual, given the unique circumstances. The triumphant message in v. 34 has excited the disciples, but they are unprepared to encounter Jesus himself. They understood little the entire time Jesus was predicting his coming death and resurrection during his ministry,[79] and their lack of comprehension would naturally continue throughout the events to follow. Still, they have the same reaction (ἔμφοβοι) as in v. 5, and this is very natural in both places. Craig Blomberg points out that their fear of the Jewish au-

---

1 Cor 15:6) due to his three denials in order to remove his shame. Another would have between to the other ten disciples to reassure them. The sending of the women by the angels, the action of the two after the Emmaus journey, this first appearance to the ten (Thomas is missing, John 20:24) are all oriented to alleviating the doubts, shame, and crushing fear that were still present with them hiding behind closed doors from the arrest of Jesus in the Garden to this scene.

[76] Marshall, *Luke*, 901.

[77] Pheme Perkins, *Resurrection: New Testament Witness and Contemporary Reflection* (Garden City: Doubleday, 1984), 163.

[78] Nolland, *Luke 18:35–24:53*, 1212.

[79] There is compelling evidence for the veracity of the passion predictions, though the disciples understood only a small part. See Craig A. Evans, "Did Jesus Predict His Death and Resurrection?" in *Resurrection* (ed. Stanley E. Porter, et al.; JSNTSup 186; Sheffield: Sheffield, 1999), 82–97.

thorities is quite natural, given what had happened to Jesus, and in keeping with Mark 14:50–52 (their panic-stricken flight at Jesus' arrest).⁸⁰

The disciples' first thought is that he must be a spirit-apparition (πνεῦμα) like Samuel in 1 Sam 28:2–19 (cf. also Isa 8:19, 19:3, 29:4; Lev 19:31; Dt 18:11). Their shock and incredulity are apparent. In John 20:19 there is a different but similar motif; they are "filled with fear of the Jews." They had spent the last forty-eight hours behind locked doors,⁸¹ clearly afraid of arrest, most likely of suffering the same fate as had their Master.⁸² Still, "fear of the Jews" is a frequent Johannine emphasis (7:13; 9:22; 19:38). As Schnackenburg asserts, the purpose here is redactional: "There was possibly something about (doubt and unbelief) in the source, but John avoids it and keeps this feature for the Thomas pericope."⁸³ The fear and doubt themes are so integral and at the same time so plausible in the resurrection stories (cf. Matt 28:17; Luke 24:38, 41 as well as its presence in the longer ending of Mark 16:11, 13, 14) that it is difficult to deny their authenticity here on the basis of the criterion of multiple attestation. Why would early Christians create a story like this with the apostles looking so ignorant and vulnerable? It is exceedingly doubtful.

Fourth, there is the corporeal demonstration that the one standing before them is indeed the same Jesus as before; this is accomplished by showing them his wounds – not talking about the resurrection hope but about the reality of the resurrection itself. It has been common to see this in both Gospels as an anti-docetic or anti-gnostic polemic against a view that Jesus suffered and died in a pseudo-body. However, this is highly unlikely as the only explanation, for it is questionable whether such a view arose this early, given there is no evidence for such a view this early, and it is far better to recognize this as proof regarding the unity between the earthly Jesus and the risen Christ in line with the Jewish expectation about resurrection (see the next section). If it were a repudiation of such a docetic view, one would

---

⁸⁰ Craig L. Blomberg, *The Historical Reliability of John's Gospel* (Downers Grove: InterVarsity, 2001), 265. He also appeals to Gospel of Peter 7:26 (the search for the disciples that night on the grounds that they were evildoers and had attempted to burn the temple).

⁸¹ There are two themes here: (1) they demonstrate the extent to which the disciples were controlled by their terror at the possibility of being arrested; and (2) the locked doors demonstrate the reality of the resurrection body of Jesus, able to pass through closed doors.

⁸² Ernst Haenchen, *John* (trans. Robert W. Funk; Hermeneia; Philadelphia: Fortress, 1984), 210, thinks this stems from the Jewish/Christian relations at the end of the first century. Yet there is hardly any need for this supposition, since the same relations existed between Jesus and the Jewish leaders by even the most minimal view of the historical Jesus. Very few doubt that Jesus was crucified and that the Romans acted at the instigation of the leaders.

⁸³ Rudolf Schnackenburg, *The Gospel According to John* (3 vols.; New York: Seabury, 1980–82), 3:322.

expect a great deal more detail on the issue. Luke, in particular as the earliest of the versions on the Jerusalem appearance, has no such emphasis in his Gospel. Indeed, Jesus' self presentation is "a means of expressing the deeply significant fact that the same Jesus encounters the disciples as the one with whom they lived before his passion."[84] In fact, this is where we are told he was nailed to the cross,[85] for only here do we learn of the marks on him, certainly those of the nails. In Luke Jesus shows his "hands and feet"[86] (24:39), in John his "hands and side" (20:20), a reference to the soldiers who lanced his side, causing blood and water to pour forth in John 19:34. As Carson says, "others who had been crucified, if somehow they had been raised, could have shown their feet and hands ... only he could show his side."[87] Luke adds to this, "handle me and see," which John omits because he is going to use this theme in the Thomas scene (20:27). Deborah Prince compares Luke's resurrection chapter to contemporary Greco-Roman descriptions of post-mortem appearances, and she concludes that Luke "surpasses all expected modes of post-mortem apparitions by virtue of the fact that it draws upon them all and distinguishes itself from them all" to the extent that it presents the Risen Lord as even more than a "fully palpable, bodily presence." The reality of the disciples' experiences transcends all known categories.[88] This reflects the Second Temple Jewish context of the resurrection as I show in the discussion on the cultural background to these scenes.

The result in both stories is joy (Luke 24:41; John 20:20), an essential part of the resurrection tradition (cf. also Matt 28:8). Yet Luke adds another sense; they "still disbelieved for joy and wondered." It is possible that this refers to unbelief and doubt, a frequent resurrection motif (Matt 28:17 and parallels).[89] However, this more likely refers to incredulous and stupefying joy, an "overwhelming and paralyzing realization" that Jesus is indeed alive.[90] Many believe that this wondrous joy stems from pre-Lukan tradition and that Luke has utilized this in his own way.[91] This theme is a step away from the disbelief of 24:11 and due to the two-fold physical encounter

---

[84] Schnackenburg, *John*, 3:323.
[85] In the crucifixion narratives of Mark 15:24; Matt 27:35; Luke 23:33; John 19:18, we are told only that he was "crucified" and nothing is said of the nails.
[86] This was affirmed in 1968 when an ossuary of a crucified Jew from the first century named "Johanan" was found containing a nail through his ankle-bones.
[87] D. A. Carson, *The Gospel According to John* (Grand Rapids: Eerdmans, 1991), 647.
[88] Deborah Thompson Prince, "The 'Ghost' of Jesus: Luke 24 in Light of Ancient Narratives of Post-Mortem Apparitions," *JSNT* 90 (2007): 289.
[89] This is the view of Richard J. Dillon, *From Eye-Witnesses to Ministers of the Word: Tradition and Composition in Luke 24* (AnBib 82; Rome: Biblical Institute Press, 1978), 192.
[90] Bock, *Luke*, 2:1934.
[91] Marshall, *Luke*, 902; Fitzmyer, *Luke X–XXIV*, 1526; Nolland, *Luke 18:35–24:53*, 1214.

with Jesus (touching him, sharing a meal with him) doubt gradually turns to joy and belief.

The meal scene also occurs often in the resurrection narratives and distinguishes Jesus from a ghost by means of Jewish tradition as well – in Jewish writings ghosts do not eat, so this must be a resurrected body. There are three of these bread and fish meal scenes, Luke 24:30–31 (Emmaus), Luke 24:41–43 (the evening of the day of resurrection), and John 21:9, 12–13 (breakfast after the miraculous catch of fish). They are important because they further anchor and enhance the corporeal dimension of Jesus' resurrection. Crossan believes that the meal scenes stem from a very early eucharistic tradition and metamorphosed from the Eucharistic presence of the risen Lord in the general community as a whole (Luke 24:13–43 to the Eucharistic presence as mediated by a leadership group (Mark 6:33–44; John 6:1–15; John 21:9–13). Therefore, the resurrection meals were composed by the church to ritualize Jesus' post-resurrection presence in the church's Eucharistic celebration.[92] This is an interesting but highly speculative endeavor. For one thing, there is no evidence that fish had a eucharistic connotation until the second century. For another, we have already seen how John saves elements that appear in more than one story for his later appearance accounts (e.g., the doubt and touching aspects in Luke's narration of this appearance). He does so here as well, saving the meal scene for ch. 21.[93] Still, Nolland considers Luke 24:41b–43 to be a Lukan expansion due to the high incidence of Lukan expressions and the connection with the feeding miracle of Luke 9:10–17.[94] However, the presence of Lukan language does not mean free composition. When we tell stories we do so in our own language, and Luke does want to draw the link with the feeding miracle, but does so in order to show that it is the same Jesus as before. The table fellowship (not eucharistic) scene here has a dual purpose: it demonstrates once more the corporeal nature of Jesus' resurrection body (one of the "many proofs" of Acts 1:3), and it signifies a new fellowship instituted between Jesus and his newly established community. This is not Eucharistic but table fellowship, a deepening sharing and unity between the members of the new movement.

A major purpose of the appearance stories is to effect mission. The historical basis of the mission commands (Luke 24:47–49; John 20:21–23) is more complex than previous traditions discussed above. It is assumed by most critical scholars that they are variations of a single earlier command tradition, but the only things they have in common is that they are mission commands and may point forward to Pentecost (I will argue below that this

---

[92] Crossan, *The Historical Jesus*, 399–403.

[93] Dillon, *From Eye-Witnesses to Ministers*, 192, says the meal scene simply does not fit John's needs here, so he omits it.

[94] Nolland, *Luke 18:35–24:53*, 1211, 1214.

is not the case with John). The only linguistic connection would be "forgiveness of sins" in Luke 24:47 = John 20:23, "whatever sins you forgive are forgiven." As stated above, there is a much closer connection of Luke 24:47–49 with Acts 1:8 ("witnesses," "power," "Holy Spirit" [= "power from on high"], "Jerusalem," "all nations" [= "to the end of the earth"]). So it is best to see Luke 24:47–49 (= Acts 1:8) and John 20:21–23 as separate traditions. The Lukan commissioning passage is full of Lukan language and themes. Verse 47 is almost a summary of Lukan soteriology, with "preach" (Luke 3:3; 4:18–19; Acts 8:5; 9:20, et al.), "repentance" (Luke 3:3, 8; 5:32; Acts 5:31; 11:18, et al.), "forgiveness of sins" (Luke 1:77; 3:3; Acts 2:38; 5:31; 10:43 et al.). The passage as a whole is also redactionally connected to Acts 1:8, as noted above.[95] Verses 48–49 are closely related to Acts 1:8 and the rest of that book, with "witnesses" = Acts 1:8, 22; 2:32; 3:15; 5:32; 10:39, 41; 13:31; 22:15; 26:16), "power" = Acts 1:8; 4:7, 33; 6:8; 10:38; "in my name" = Acts 2:38; 3:6, 16; 4:10, 18, 30; 5:40, 41; 8:12; 9:27; 16:18; 19:13, 17. Clearly, there are predominant Lukan motifs throughout this commissioning address.

One of the purposes of Luke's resurrection narrative is to show the continuity between the life of Jesus and the launching of the early church. Luke has chosen scenes that are echoed in the book of Acts, and one of his major themes is the salvation-historical movement in which the church in its mission re-enacts Jesus' life and ministry. But redaction in and of itself does not necessarily signify wholesale creation of new material. It can quite easily be historical. It is better to see it in selection, emphasis, and wording of material.[96] In other words, while Lukan language permeates, there is every reason to believe it stems from traditional material that in all likelihood goes back to the risen Jesus.[97] All the Gospels are in agreement that while Jesus restricted the disciples' mission to Israel (explicit in Matt 10:5–6; 15:24) he himself deliberately exposed the disciples to ministry in Gentile areas (the centurion's servant, the Gadarene demoniac, the Syro-Phoenician woman) and initiated a future Gentile mission. So the commission scenes in the resurrection appearances are very plausible. In Luke 24:47–49 many elements of the commission (repentance, preached, witness, power from on high) are particularly Lukan and intended to provide a bridge from the ministry of Jesus to the launching of the church's mission. At the same time there is a real continuity from one commissioning scene to another, as all involve the risen

---

[95] Fitzmyer, *Luke X–XXIV*, 1580–81, finds eleven examples of Lukan language in vv. 44–49.

[96] See Grant R. Osborne, "Redaction Criticism," in *Interpreting the New Testament: Essays on Methods and Issues* (ed. David Alan Black and David S. Dockery; Nashville: Broadman and Holman, 2001), 128–49; and David Wenham and Steve Walton, *Exploring the New Testament* (Downers Grove: InterVarsity, 2001), 74–79.

[97] See Marshall, *Luke*, 903–4; Bock, *Luke*, 2:1928.

Lord sending his followers into the nations with the gospel proclamation. In short, Luke composed Jesus' commissioning address but did so on the basis of a traditional matrix to which he was faithful. These commissioning scenes are absolutely integral to the whole future of the Christian movement and have the aura of plausibility; nothing could make more sense at the juncture in light of the witnessing that immediately began to happen. Here Wright's criterion on "double similarity and double dissimilarity"[98] is relevant, for this mission was instituted by Jesus in Jewish ministry and yet transcends that setting by moving here to the Gentile mission. The mission command as such provides a bridge from the life of Jesus to the mission of the church.

John's mission statement in 20:21–23 is also heavily redactional. Schneiders call this "a two-member covenant-commission evoking the giving of the Law at Sinai" that reveals "Yahweh's glorious covenant presence (Ezek 34:25 and 37:26–28) in the person of the Risen Lord."[99] "Sent" is a major aspect in John's mission theology. Over thirty times Jesus is described as "sent" from the Father (= *shaliach* or the living representative of the Father, cf. 3:17; 5:23, 30; 8:16, 18), and the Holy Spirit is "sent" by the Father and the Son (14:16; 15:26; 16:7). The cycle is completed here (= 17:18) as the Godhead "sends" Jesus' followers. Yet while this may be Johannine, it is also a traditional Jewish emphasis and most likely stemmed from Jesus himself.[100] When Jesus "breathes on" the disciples and says "Receive the Spirit," this completes the movement from 3:34 (God gives him the Spirit "without limit") to 7:37–39 (the Spirit as "living water" flowing out from Christ's innermost being[101]) to the passages where Jesus sends out the Paraclete (14:16–17, 26; 15:26; 16:7); and this in effect culminates John's theology of the Holy Spirit.[102] The historicity of this "sent" or *shaliach* motif is supported by both the criterion of multiple attestation (it is found in all the Gospels and in Acts) and the criterion of multiple forms (it occurs in

---

[98] See N. T. Wright, *Jesus and the Victory of God* (vol. 2 of *Christian Origins and the Question of God*; Minneapolis: Fortress, 1996), 131–33. He refers to a saying or event that has both similarities to Judaism and the early church as well as dissimilarities to both that point to the historical Jesus.

[99] Sandra M. Schneiders, "The Raising of the New Temple: John 20:19–23 and Johannine Ecclesiology," *NTS* 52 (2006): 344–45.

[100] See Blomberg, *Historical Reliability*, 267; Andreas J. Köstenberger, *The Missions of Jesus and the Disciples According to the Fourth Gospel* (Grand Rapids: Eerdmans, 1998), 10–12.

[101] For the debate regarding the believer or Christ as the source of the living water, see Grant R. Osborne, *The Gospel of John* (Cornerstone; Carol Stream: Tyndale House, 2007), 116.

[102] There is a great debate as to whether this is a symbolic action pointing forward to Pentecost (Carson, Köstenberger) or a separate event, a "Johannine Pentecost" taking place on the first day of the resurrection. This then would be a private infilling of the Spirit with Acts 2 a public empowering for mission (Beasley-Murray, Blomberg, Osborne). This latter best fits the language and scene here.

sayings, narrative, and parables as well as in verbal ["sent"] and substantival ["apostle"]) forms.

The authority to forgive or retain sins (John 20:23) does not have parallels in John, but it does parallel the theme of Jesus as judge (5:22, 30; 8:15–16; 9:39), specifically of Jesus' authority to forgive sins (1:29[103]) and retain them (9:41; 15:21–24). As the disciples are "sent" out in mission by the Father, Son, and Spirit, they partake of the authority of Jesus as dispenser of salvation and as judge of those who reject the encounter. The closest parallel is with Matt 16:19; 18:18 where Jesus gives the "keys of the kingdom" to Peter (18:18) and then likewise gives the church the authority to "bind" (= retain) or "loose" (= forgive) on earth.[104] The presence in both Matthew and John is clear evidence of the origin of this saying in tradition (multiple attestation), but it is impossible to adjudicate whether Jesus gave this saying only once (so the majority, with little attempt to decide if it was pre-resurrection or post-resurrection) or in both settings (my preference, on the grounds of its suitability in both contexts).

The Jesus Seminar places both the Lukan and the Johannine material entirely in black, arguing that Luke for instance constructs this "in a manner consistent with the expectations of his audience and in accordance with his own theological views ... [Thus it] is not history but affirmation, not a rehearsal of facts but an ingredient of his proclamation."[105] Lüdemann recognizes the likelihood that Luke utilizes a tradition in which Jesus appeared in bodily form but takes this as a second generation tradition without any connection to the original witnesses and therefore of no historical worth.[106] However, with all the evidence we have noted above for the historical authenticity of the Jerusalem appearance story, we can confidently attest the great likelihood of its veracity as an event that actually happened. Certainly some of the details can be contested, as we noted, but the basic aspects of Jesus' appearance to the disciples in Jerusalem both to authenticate the reality of his resurrected form and to command them to mission can be affirmed by us with great confidence.

---

[103] I prefer to understand "Behold the Lamb of God who takes away the sin of the world" as a paschal metaphor developing the "lamb led to the slaughter of Isa 53:7, 10 rather than the apocalyptic lamb who triumphs over sin. See Osborne, *John*, 32.

[104] Schneiders, "Raising," 352–54, argues that John 20:23 is not parallel with Matt 18:18 and that κρατέω does not mean "retain sins" but rather "hold fast" and is a covenant promise to forgive sins and then "hold them fast" in the ecclesial community. This is intriguing and provocative but in the final analysis is unconvincing. As Jan Lambrecht says in his "A Note on John 20:23b," *ETL* 83 (2007): 166–68, the two clauses are far more likely to be antithetical than complementary, and as a result the meaning must be that those who are not forgiven remain (are "retained") in a sinful state.

[105] Funk and Seminar, *The Acts of Jesus*, 486–87.

[106] Lüdemann, *What Really Happened*, 45–46.

The debate regarding the Jerusalem appearances vs. the Galilee appearances is also a propos to the issue here. In Mark 16:7 and Matt 28:10 Jesus told the disciples to meet him in Galilee, while in Luke 24:36 and John 20:19 the first appearance was clearly in Jerusalem. We must question why in Matthew and Mark the message to the Eleven would be to meet Jesus in Galilee if Jesus was to meet them that night in the upper room. Two things point the way to reconciling these seemingly contradictory traditions. One is John, who has Jerusalem appearances followed by a Galilee appearance.[107] Second, Acts 1:3 again points to appearances over a forty-day period. It is of course possible that the disciples in their feelings of defeat had been planning to leave the Passover celebration and return home to Galilee, but culturally and religiously all Jews stayed for the whole celebration. Moreover, that first evening Jesus appeared to them in the upper room, thereby alleviating their fears and encouraging them to stay for the seven-day celebration exactly as John 20:26 states it, with Jesus appearing to them a second time with Thomas present. This fits the criterion of plausibility. Then they went to Galilee for some time, where the appearance narrated in John 21 as well as the Great Commission in Matt 28 occurred. Then, in obedience to await their next direction from Jerusalem, they returned to Jerusalem for Pentecost, where the events of Luke 24:44–53 as well as Acts 1:6–11 took place. One should not be overly literal here. Jerusalem is where they will be sent out from into the next phase of what God is doing. The command to go to Galilee would make perfect sense as a fulfillment of Jesus' prophecy at the Last Supper that after the resurrection Jesus would "go ahead of you into Galilee" (Mark 14:28 = Matt 26:32). In addition, Galilee can be identified as the place of revelation (where Jesus gave much of his teaching), so Jesus would naturally have identified this appearance in the upper room. As Davies and Allison say, "not in Jerusalem but in 'Galilee of the Gentiles,' where he first gathered his community, will Jesus reconstitute the flock that has been scattered and then inaugurate the world mission."[108] I would argue that the new community is reconstituted first in Jerusalem (via table fellowship) and then finalized in Galilee. Finally, it is very possible that there was a longer message from the angels at the empty tomb, with Mark and Matthew

---

[107] It is common to argue that ch. 21 is an appendix added later. That was the view I held for many years. However, I have changed my mind because (1) the language and style show it continues the emphases of the rest of the Fourth Gospel and was likely penned at the same time; (2) 20:30–31 does not have to be the final conclusion and was probably paralleled by 21:24–25; (3) ch. 21 centers on mission and would end John the same way as Matthew and Luke; (4) there is no evidence this Gospel ever circulated without ch. 21; (5) this fits the action between Peter and the Beloved Disciple elsewhere in John; (6) the reinstatement of Peter is a natural denouement to Peter's three denials; (7) ch. 21 is in inclusion with 1:1–18 and frames the Fourth Gospel perfectly. See Osborne, *John*, 294.

[108] Davies and Allison, *Matthew*, 3:486.

redactionally centering on the Galilee portion of it (as they do throughout their Gospels). This reconstruction of the scene is of course not certain, but it is highly plausible and fits the sequence found in the Gospels.

In conclusion, the discussion of this early appearance has demonstrated that the basic story is highly probable and goes back to very early tradition, indeed to Jesus himself. On the evening of resurrection day, the disciples were still hiding in the upper room, afraid of arrest. Suddenly Jesus appeared among them, offering his messianic peace. To quell their doubt and fear, he showed them his crucifixion wounds, and thus they knew it was the same Jesus they had deserted two nights before. As further proof of his physical resurrection and to begin the new community that later became the church, he shared a meal with them. At that time he commissioned them with authority to proclaim his gospel to the nations. Theissen and Merz find this so compelling that they "infer a real event behind the accounts" and conclude, "there is no doubt that it really happened."[109]

In conclusion, let us summarize the reasons for accepting the probable historicity of the resurrection events: (1) Paul and James were bitter opponents of Christianity. Paul had even voted for several to be killed (Acts 26:10). Yet on the Damascus Road he "saw" the Lord and had been utterly convinced he had risen from the dead (1 Cor 15:8–10, cf. 9:1). (2) The disciples themselves changed from defeated followers slinking home from the demise of their dreams (Luke 24:13–24) to world-changing proclaimers of the victorious gospel. (3) These followers were willing to give their lives (most of the apostles did so), and that would hardly be for a hallucinatory series of dreams. (4) Women were the recipients of the earliest appearances, and that would never be made up in the chauvinistic world of the first century. (5) Within 3–5 years of Jesus' death and resurrection, Paul "received" a creedal compilation of eye-witness tradition regarding the death, resurrection, and appearances of Jesus, and he challenged the readers to check these truths for themselves (1 Cor 15:3–8). Such would never have been compiled so quickly if they were fictional. (6) The criteria for authenticity[110] support key elements of the empty tomb and appearance narratives. (7) The appearance stories are restrained and filled with plausible details that do not fit a fictive style (women's role; details on burial). (8) The historical value of the empty tomb itself would support the likelihood of appearances. (9) The number of appearances and the different types of reports about appearances fit the criterion of multiple forms (very early creed and narration), and the great variety makes it likely that something really happened, namely the

---

[109] Gerd Theissen and Annette Merz, *The Historical Jesus: A Comprehensive Guide* (trans. John Bowden; Minneapolis: Fortress, 1998), 496.

[110] See the discussion of these criteria in this volume in ch. 2, § 4.1.

risen Jesus appearing to many. It is clear that the disciples were radically changed by these events, and they and the early church believed Jesus had visibly appeared to them after his death. They also presented this material as realistic historical claims and not as fictive legends. So many details (the women as witnesses, their doubt and fear, the misunderstandings) would never have been told this way if they were simply made up. Moreover, if they were only dreams and hallucinations, why would they have abruptly ceased shortly after the events with the ascension, with only Paul's vision after that event? The dreams would have continued for a long time.[111]

So I have made a case for the core likelihood of Jesus' resurrection, but one other important feature needs close attention: the nature of Jewish Second Temple resurrection hope. Does a look at this topic contribute to our understanding of this event? Does it also help us with the claim that the resurrection event was really only some kind of internal private experience. I have questioned this claim already, but the background to resurrection adds to the case. It also points to an innovation in Christian expression that adds to the likelihood that this event brought a change to previous resurrection teaching, underscoring an event that caused the change.

3. The Context of Resurrection in the Hebrew Bible, Second-Temple Judaism, and Hellenism

Where do NT ideas about resurrection come from? How did these views originate? When we begin with the scriptures of Israel, we find sparse evidence for any settled idea of afterlife until Daniel. Several passages give the impression that there is nothing after death. Gen 3:15 says, "for dust you are, and to dust you will return," and Job 7:21 relates, "For I will soon lie down in the dust; you will search for me, but I will be no more" (cf. 3:13–19; 10:9; 33:18, 22; 34:15). Ps 30:9 says, "What gain is there in my destruction, in my going down to the pit. Will the dust praise you?" (cf. 16:10; 88:3–5; 90:3; 116:3). Babylon is warned, "All your pomp has brought you down to the grave ... maggots are spread out beneath you, and worms cover you" (Isa 14:11, cf. 9–20a). The key concept is Sheol, the grave, the pit. The impression is that all life ceases at death, and there is nothing beyond that.

---

[111] For other compilations of reasons for accepting the resurrection appearances as historical, see Wright, *Resurrection*, 679–82, 686–87; Dunn, *Jesus Remembered*, 857–76; Gary R. Habermas, "The Resurrection of Jesus and the Talpiot Tomb," in *Buried Hope or Risen Savior: The Search for the Jesus Tomb* (ed. Charles L. Quarles; Nashville: Broadman & Holman, 2008), 168; William Lane Craig, *The Son Rises: The Historical Evidence for the Resurrection of Jesus* (Chicago: Moody Press, 1981), 100–108.

But does this mean that Israel believed in annihilation after death? Certainly the quotes above mean that death is the cessation of life. While Sheol often means the "grave," it can also mean the "netherworld" (Ezek 32:21, perhaps Ps 86:13), and the dead are often described as dwelling in Sheol as רְפָאִים or shades (Job 26:5; Prov 9:18; Isa 26:14, 19). While in some passages (Ps 88:10) this is a synonym for the dead dwelling in Sheol, the term itself indicates "departed spirits" released from the body upon death. Isa 26:14 says of foreign rulers who lorded it over the nation in the past, "They are now dead, they live no more; those departed spirits do not rise," then says of Israel in v. 19, "But your dead will live; their bodies will rise. You who dwell in the dust, wake up and shout for joy. Your dew is like the dew of the morning. The earth will give birth to her רְפָאִים." This certainly appears to be a clear statement of a Jewish belief in final resurrection.[112] It is part of the so-called "Little Apocalypse" of Isa 24–27. Earlier Isa 25:8 states that God "will swallow up death forever," a verse Paul quotes of resurrection in 1 Cor 15:54. However, some scholars read this section not of physical resurrection but as a poetic paeon to the future glory of Israel.[113] Nevertheless, while these statements could be purely poetic, they appear to be more than that and are at the least part of a burgeoning, even developing, belief in the afterlife.[114]

There are two figures who escaped death in the Jewish scriptures and were "taken up to God": Enoch (Gen 5:24) and Elijah (2 Kgs 2:9–11). Neither of the stories provides any reflection upon the significance of the event. Enoch simply "was no more, for God took him." Still, it is significant that this is the one exception to the common refrain in the genealogical list of the ancestors of Noah in Gen 5, "then he died." While it is true that "was no more" can be a poetic description of death (cf. Ps 39:13; 103:16) and so could depict Enoch simply as an especially pious person, there seems to be a greater contrast with the others in the list, and the phrase "God took him" occurs of Elijah's translation to heaven in 2 Kgs 2:5, 9, 10. Both are depicted as transcending death and being taken up into the presence of God. There

---

[112] See Michael L. Brown, "רְפָאִים," *NIDOTTE* 3:1177–78. Brook W. R. Pearson, "Resurrection and the Judgment of the Titans: ἡ γῆ τῶν ἀσεβῶν in LXX Isaiah 26.19," in *Resurrection* (ed. Stanley E. Porter, et al.; JSNTSup 186; Sheffield: Sheffield, 1999), 33–51, argues that both the MT and LXX assume a resurrection from the dead (perhaps bodily) and that the LXX connects this with the Near Eastern myth regarding the assignment of the Titans to Tartarus.

[113] See C. D. Elledge, "Resurrection of the Dead: Exploring Our Earliest Evidence Today," in *Resurrection: The Origin and Future of a Biblical Doctrine* (ed. James H. Charlesworth; Faith and Scholarship Colloquies; New York: T&T Clark, 2006), 25.

[114] See G. B. Gray, *A Critical and Exegetical Commentary on the Book of Isaiah I–XXVI* (ICC; Edinburgh: T&T Clark, 1912), 446; John N. Oswalt, *Isaiah 1–39* (NICOT; Grand Rapids: Eerdmans, 1986), 488; Grant R. Osborne, "Resurrection," *DJG* 673.

is no developed idea of afterlife in either passage, but at the same time there is seemingly no death.[115]

The event in 1 Sam 28:1–25, when Saul consulted the medium of Endor, who "brought up" the "spirit" (אֱלֹהִים) of Samuel from the ground in order to seek his advice, is another unusual story with implications for ancient Hebrew beliefs. Necromancy (calling up the spirits of the dead) was recognized and forbidden in Israel (Exod 22:18; Lev 19:31; Deut 18:11; Isa 8:19), but it demonstrates a general belief that there were spirits of people that existed after death. James Crenshaw says there were two seed-thoughts that led to this developing view: (1) a "profound sense of community with Yahweh" that gave rise to reflection on an inner נֶפֶשׁ into which God pours his presence, leading to a sense of immortality as God "has swallowed death forever" (Isa 25:8); and (2) a growing conviction that "this object of devotion's power was limitless, leading to the belief that since Yahweh holds the key to death and life, he can enable some like Enoch and Elijah to escape the tentacles of death.[116]

Some passages seem to reflect a belief in the afterlife but are rather metaphorical promises of the corporate preservation or restoration of the nation, such as Hos 6:1–3 ("on the third day he will restore us, that we may live in his presence"), 13:14 ("I will redeem them from death")[117] or the vision of the valley of dry bones in Ezek 37. Other passages are poetic hyperbole depicting divine rescue from life-threatening situations, like Deut 32:39 ("I put to death and I bring to life"), 1 Sam 2:6 ("The Lord brings death and makes alive"), or 2 Sam 5:7 ("Am I God? Can I kill and bring back to life"?).

Still, there seems to be a distinct movement toward a belief that there is something after death. The key question is asked in Job 14:14, "If mortals die, will they live again?" Some see a positive response in Job 19:25–27, where Job replies to Bildad, "I know that my Redeemer lives ... and after my skin has been destroyed, then in my flesh I will see God." Yet elsewhere Job has a consistent view that death is the final end of life, as in 14:10, 12 ("But mortals die and are laid low ... mortals lie down and do not rise again"); 16:22 ("I shall go the way from which I shall not return"). Job ends with his death and no mention of life beyond (42:17). So the thrust of Job is quite disputed.[118] A passage in Ps 49:15 may also hint at existence after

---

[115] To this could be added the death of Moses. In Deut 34:5, 6 his death is recorded, but v. 6 adds that "no one knows his burial place to this day," and later Jewish writers speculated that he too had been translated to heaven.

[116] James L. Crenshaw, "Love Is Stronger Than Death: Intimations of Life Beyond the Grave," in *Resurrection: The Origin and Future of a Biblical Doctrine* (ed. James H. Charlesworth; Faith and Scholarship Colloquies; New York: T&T Clark, 2006), 55–58.

[117] *Tg. Hos.* 6:2 continues this resurrection language. It is possible that emerging ideas of resurrection are behind this metaphor.

[118] Wright, *Resurrection*, 97–98, doubts that Job contains a view of afterlife.

death. This is a wisdom psalm on the vicissitudes of life, especially the mortality of every human being. The two strophes end with "Mortals cannot abide in their pomp; they are like the animals that perish." Yet in v. 15 the author says his fate is different: "But God will ransom my soul from the power of Sheol, for he will receive me." Since the same verb (יִקַּח) is used of Yahweh "receiving" the psalmist and the fools not being able to "take" anything with them beyond the grave (v. 17), there may well be an affirmation of life after death.[119]

The best known, undisputed passage on a belief in resurrection and afterlife is Dan 12:2, "Many of those who sleep in the dust of the earth will awake, some to everlasting life, and some to shame and everlasting contempt." The majority of commentators accept this as a conscious belief in a physical resurrection from the dead.[120] The primary question is the meaning of "many" (רַבִּים). Does this refer only to a portion of humanity, perhaps the faithful who have been martyred vs. those who have hunted them down?[121] Or could "many" be a circumlocution for "all," a frequent use of this pronoun?[122] Either way, it shows a developed view of resurrection by the time Daniel was written (whether in the exilic period [my preference] or in the Maccabean period). It must be said that there was precious little speculation in Israel regarding the afterlife and at best a willingness to accept certain prevalent views regarding existence after death from the surrounding nations. Still, it seems critical that while there is not a great deal of speculation regarding what happens after death, there is also no rejection of views regarding the after-life. Given the prevalence of such views in the surrounding nations and the penchant of Jewish writers in the Hebrew Bible to reject pagan views they find objectionable, the silence of the Hebrew Bible to me seems to indicate a basic acceptance very early of the belief that there is existence after death, unexplored as it was. The major truth is that no matter how one takes the earlier scriptural material, Dan 12 marks a turning point in Jewish beliefs. From this time Jewish ideas on the whole are clearer, and they lay the groundwork for the first-century perspectives that provided the context for interpreting Jesus' resurrection.

---

[119] Crenshaw, "Love Is Stronger," 60. A contrary view is expressed in Peter C. Craigie, *Psalms 1–50* (WBC 19; Waco: Word, 1981), 360, who considers v. 15 an imaginary declaration of self-confidence on the part of the wealthy, who foolishly believe they can "buy their own redemption." While plausible, the context makes Crenshaw's theory more likely. The hope of the righteous will triumph over the folly of the wicked.

[120] See John J. Collins, *Daniel* (Hermeneia; Minneapolis: Fortress, 1993), 391–92.

[121] So Elledge, "Resurrection," 27; Ernest C. Lucas, *Daniel* (Apollos Old Testament Commentary; Downers Grove: InterVarsity, 2002), 295.

[122] See Joachim Jeremias, "πολλοί," *TDNT* 6:536–40. Andrew E. Hill, "רבה," *NIDOTTE* 3:1037–38, shows that the basic root meaning is "multiplicity, increase."

There was a wide disparity of views in Second Temple Jewish literature, with a lot of speculation on what happens after death. Jesus ben Sira states in several places that death leads only to Sheol, the place of unending sleep (Sir 30:17, "before his long sleep") and silence (Sir 17:28, "thanksgiving perishes from the dead"). The only view of immortality that exists in this work centers on the nation or a person's reputation (37:26, a wise man's "name shall be perpetual"; 39:9, "so long as the world endures, [his name] shall not be blotted out"). The group primarily associated with this view, of course, is the Sadducees, reported as rejecting any view of afterlife both in the NT (Mark 12:18 par; Acts 4:1–2; 23:6–10) and Josephus (*Ant.* 18.16; *J. W.* 2.165). In *b. Sanh.* 90b and *m. Ber.* 9:5, the Sadducees are also said to reject the doctrine of the resurrection of the dead. They accepted only the Pentateuch as canon (Josephus, *Ant.* 13.297; 18.17), and since there was no statement of afterlife in those texts, they rejected the doctrine.

Still other texts demonstrate Hellenistic influence in speaking of existence after death as immortality rather than a physical resurrection, i.e. of the soul escaping the body at death. The language of resurrection seems to occur in 2 Macc 7:14 at the martyrdom scene of the seven brothers, relates, "And when he was near death, he said, "One cannot but choose to die at the hands of men and to cherish the hope that God gives of being raised again by him. But for you there will be no resurrection to life!" The language of resurrection dominates. In contrast, the Hellenistic flavor of 4 Macc 10:4 at the martyrdom yields a very different nuance, "Therefore, if you have any means of torture, apply it to my body, but you cannot touch my soul." This is a uniform motif in 4 Maccabees, as in 13:13 ("With all our hearts let us consecrate ourselves to God, who gave us our souls, and let us expend our bodies"), 16:13 ("bringing her brood of sons into immortal life") and in the last verse of the book (18:23, "having received pure and deathless souls from God"). 4 Maccabees seems to reject the view of physical resurrection in 2 Maccabees and substitute its view of the immortality of the soul.[123] Similarly, Hellenistic views dominate *4 Ezra* (7: 75, "every one of us yields up his soul"; and v. 78, "a man shall die, as the spirit leaves the body to return again to him who gave it") and Wisdom of Solomon (2:23, "God created mankind to be immortal"; 3:1–4, "the souls of the righteous belong to God" and "their hope is for immortality"; cf. also 6:19). Finally, as we would expect, the great Alexandrian Jewish thinker Philo believed in the immortality of the soul rather than in physical resurrection. For him the body imprisoned the soul which is set free at death and finds immortality (*Alleg. Interp.* 3.14; *Giants* 14). Clearly, there existed a view that the soul leaves the body upon death and achieves immortality.

---

[123] See Osborne, "Resurrection," *DJG* 674; and also Wright, *Resurrection*, 142–43.

Finally, there was a clear line of texts, indeed a majority, that spoke of physical resurrection in Judaism. The key point here is that when resurrection (as opposed to immortality) is expressed; it has a physical dimension to it. This belief is typified in the second of the Eighteen Benedictions quoted in every synagogue service that celebrated the mighty God who "raise(s) the dead ... bring(s) the dead to life." This view is clear in 2 Macc 12:44, "For if he were not expecting that those who had fallen would rise again, it would have been superfluous and foolish to pray for the dead" (cf. also 7:9, 14, 28–29, 36–38); and in 2 Macc 14:46 there is even a view that missing body parts would be restored ("with his blood now completely drained from him, he tore out his entrails, took them with both hands and hurled them at the crowd, calling upon the Lord of life and spirit to give them back to him again," cf. also 7:10–11, which is quite explicit, for the son offers his body knowing these parts will return).

In Jewish apocalyptic literature there are numerous references to life after death. We must begin with *1 Enoch*, a composite work that was one of the earliest apocalypses, with various parts written in the first two centuries B.C.E. The elect will "inherit the earth" and establish an earthly Paradise (5:7, 10:17–22) with the tree of life in their midst (25:1–5) while the souls of the wicked will spend this period waiting for judgment (22:3–13). In the *Similitudes* (chs. 37–71) a different picture emerges as the righteous have "their dwelling places with the holy angels ... under the wings of the Lord of the Spirits" (39:5–8, cf. 46:6). In 51:1–5 Sheol will return "the deposits which she had received," with the righteous and the Holy Ones taken up and dwelling upon a renewed earth at the arising of "the Elect One." Then in 61:3–9 the Garden of Eden is measured (shades of Rev 22:1–5) and the angelic host rejoices in the "Elect One," while in 62:9–12 the rulers of the earth will be judged, and in 62:8, 13–15 the holy ones will rise and wear "the garments of glory" (cf. 103:4; 1104:1–5; 108:11–15).

Jewish testamentary literature contains several statements reflecting the resurrection doctrine. Let us begin with *The Testaments of the Twelve Patriarchs*, composed sometime in the Maccabean period but with Christian interpolations.[124] In an illuminating article, C. D. Elledge finds four references to resurrection: in *T. Sim.* 6:7 (as part of the eschatological section of 5:4–7:3) he speaks of the destruction of Israel's enemies and states, "Then I shall arise in joy, and I shall bless the Most High." In *T. Jud.* 25 there is an extensive discussion of his coming resurrection; in 25:1 it says "After these things (the messianic king brings a universal reign of peace) Abraham and

---

[124] See Howard C. Kee, "Testaments of the Twelve Patriarchs," in *Old Testament Pseudepigrapha* (2 vols.; ed. James H. Charlesworth; New York: Doubleday, 1983–85), 1:777–78.

Isaac and Jacob shall arise unto life" to participate in the restored Israel and in v. 4 "proclaims the resurrection day as a time for joy, prosperity, nourishment, strength, and life." *T. Zeb.* 10:1–4 concludes a section on eschatological prophecies (9:5–10:4) and speaks of "going away into my rest" and yet proclaims "I shall rise again in your midst." Finally, *T. Benj.* 10:6–10 speaks of Abraham, Isaac, and Jacob "standing on the right hand of gladness" and than adds "we also shall arise, each (of us) over our tribe, worshiping the king of the heavens." [125]

Other Second Temple Jewish texts also attest to a belief in resurrection from the dead. *2 Bar.* 49–52 gives a lengthy description of the "shape" and "splendor" of the resurrected body (49:2) when "the earth ... give(s) back the dead" (50:2). At this time "the shape of those who now act wickedly will be made more evil" (51:2) while the "splendor (of the righteous) will then be glorified by transformations, and the shape of their face will be changed into the light of their beauty so that they may acquire and receive the undying world which is promised to them" (51:3). *4 Ezra* 4:42 says that the chambers of Hades "hasten to give back those things that were committed to them from the beginning," and the vision in ch. 7 speaks of "fire and torments" awaiting the wicked (32–42, 79–87) with the glory awaiting the righteous when "their face is to shine like the sun" and "they are to be made like the light of the stars" (94–99). *Sib. Or.* 4:179–92 concludes with a vision of resurrection and judgment, with Tartarus and Gehenna awaiting the wicked while the saints "will live on earth again when God gives spirit and life and favor to these pious ones." Similarly, *Pss. Sol.* 3:11–12 state that "the destruction of the sinner is forever" while "those who fear the Lord shall rise up to eternal life, and their life shall be in the Lord's sight, and it shall never end." *Pseudo-Phocylides* 97–115 discusses death and the afterlife and says, "we hope that the remains of the departed will soon come to the light (again) out of earth, and afterward they will become gods" (103–4) because "(our) soul is immortal and lives ageless forever" (115). Harrington provides a good summary:

> LAB (Pseudo-Phocylides) envisions two possible punishments for the wicked – annihilation in the case of Korah ... and eternal torment in inextinguishable fire in the case of Doeg. 4 Ezra with its special concern for the very small number of those who will be saved provides a stark contrast to the position of those who look for what approaches universal salvation or who see no need for salvation at all. And the vision

---

[125] C. D. Elledge, "The Resurrection Passages in the *Testaments of the Twelve Patriarchs*: Hope for Israel in Early Judaism and Christianity," in *Resurrection: The Origin and Future of a Biblical Doctrine* (ed. James H. Charlesworth; Faith and Scholarship Colloquies; New York: T&T Clark, 2006), 83–84.

for the world to come for the righteous in 2 Baruch offers striking parallels to the depiction of the New Jerusalem in Rev 21:1–22:5.[126]

George Nickelsburg points out that these texts take place in the context of universal judgment. All the righteous will be rewarded in a universal resurrection, and all the wicked will be punished with a universal judgment.[127]

Next, let us consider the Dead Sea Scrolls at Qumran. It has often been said that there was no doctrine of resurrection in the Essenic sect because they believed they would become like the angels through the presence of the Holy Spirit in the community. This consensus is challenged by James Charlesworth. First, he provides four kinds of passages that are not resurrection texts: (1) the raising of the group from disenfranchisement by the larger Jewish community (e.g., 4QMMT); (2) raising an individual from personal shame to an interpreter of knowledge (1QH^a 10.9–14); (3) the raising of a person from activity to do the will of the Creator (1 QH^a 14:29–30); (4) raising one from meaninglessness to a realized eschatology in a this-worldly sense (1QH 11:19–21).[128] Then he shows three passages that he believes clearly contain a belief in resurrection from death to eternal life: (1) The text *On Resurrection* (4Q521) contains the statement "the Lord (when) he shall come ... will heal those defiled and give life to those dead." (2) Pseudo-Ezekiel (4Q385 frg. 2) interprets the "dry bones" of Ezek 37 as a "large crowd of men" who "will rise and bless the Lord of hosts who causes them to live." (3) *Sapiential Work A* (4Q416 frg. 23.6–8) says "in your death your resemblance will blosso(m foreve)r, and in the end you will inherit joy" (all his translations).[129] Nickelsburg reaches a different conclusion. Recognizing that there is no "certain" text on resurrection at Qumran, he nevertheless finds in the "two ways" theology of Qumran a basic belief in life beyond the grave – every human being is predestined for life or for death, and each person participates in that eternal life or death during this life. He concludes that the Essenes held a view not so much of resurrection as of immortality.[130] N. T. Wright finds a middle ground that seems closer to

---

[126] Daniel J. Harrington, "Afterlife Expectations in Pseudo-Philo, 4 Ezra, and 2 Baruch, and Their Implications for the New Testament," in *Resurrection in the New Testament: Festschrift J. Lambrecht* (ed. R. Bieringer, et al.; BETL 165; Leuven: Leuven University Press, 2002), 34.

[127] George W. E. Nickelsburg, *Resurrection, Immortality, and Eternal Life in Intertestamental Judaism and Early Christianity* (HTS 56; Cambridge: Harvard University Press, 2006), 177–78.

[128] James H. Charlesworth, "Resurrection: The Dead Sea Scrolls and the New Testament," in *Resurrection: The Origin and Future of a Biblical Doctrine* (ed. James H. Charlesworth; New York: T&T Clark, 2006), 145–50.

[129] Charlesworth, "Resurrection: The Dead Sea Scrolls and the New Testament," 150–53.

[130] Nickelsburg, *Resurrection, Immortality, and Eternal Life*, 179–209.

the data. Noting the paucity of interest on the part of Qumran in the issue of resurrection, since their emphasis lay on "present purity rather than future destiny," Wright nevertheless concludes that "the Essenes' future hope was an extension, beyond death and into the future world, of their present religious experience."[131]

Before we close this section we must consider other literature later than the Second Temple period. Rabbinic evidence is quite clear: the rabbis believed that in the end God would restore the righteous dead to life, as argued in Levenson's *Resurrection and the Restoration of Israel*. In a provocative chapter, he explores how extensively the ancient rabbis sought to find the doctrine of resurrection in the Torah, beginning with *Sifre Deut.* 32, "no passage lacks the resurrection of the dead, but we lack the capacity to interpret properly."[132] Building on Isa 60:21 ("your people ... shall possess the land for all time"), *m. Sanh.* 10:1, says, "These are the ones who do not have a share in the World-to-Come: He who says that the resurrection of the dead is not in the Torah, (he who says) that the Torah is not from Heaven, and the skeptic." Rabbi Judah the Patriarch, commenting on Exod 15:1 ("The Moses and the Israelites sang this song to the Lord"), said, "'Then Moses sang (*shar*) is not written here, but rather 'Then Moses will sing (*yashir*). Thus we are instructed that the resurrection of the dead can be derived from the Torah" (*Mek., Shirta* 1). Levenson concludes that while the exegesis is fanciful, it does demonstrate the rabbinic pattern of religion on the after-life.[133]

Kevin Anderson provides a good summary of Hellenistic ideas regarding life after death. The most ancient tradition pictures the tomb as the residence for the dead who maintained an existence around the tomb. Next, there is the Homeric picture of Hades or the underworld with the shades or spirits of the departed dwelling there in a kind of half-life. Heroes and the virtuous had a pleasant existence in the Elysian fields or Isles of the Blessed while the wicked were consigned to the horrors of Tartarus. This evolved to the view that good people ascended to the heavens and dwelt with the divine.[134]

Stanley Porter argues for a strong tradition in the Greco-Roman world that affirms "the soul's destiny in the afterlife, along with examples of bodily resurrection." He goes so far as to argue "that Greek teaching suggested to the Jews, or to some of them, that the dead would be raised from Sheol to live again on the earth, which is what resurrection implied at the

---

[131] Wright, *Resurrection*, 188–89.
[132] Jon D. Levenson, *Resurrection and the Restoration of Israel: The Ultimate Victory of the God of Life* (New Haven: Yale University Press, 2006), 23 (cf. 23–34).
[133] Levenson, *Resurrection*, 24–34.
[134] Anderson, *"But God Raised Him"*, 93–98.

time."¹³⁵ While his statement that Hellenistic ideas lay behind Jewish beliefs is shown wrong by the Jewish evidence noted above, the larger premise regarding some Greek belief in bodily resurrection could be somewhat correct. First, during the ancient period, e.g., in *Odyssey* 11.51–56, at death the soul enters the "realm of the dead" and meets other souls that have died, and in *Iliad* 23 the released soul enters the gates of Hades and wanders about, but for some that time in Hades involves judgment. Others in the ancient period like Herodotus accepted a form of reincarnation where the person could enter different lives including becoming animals. During the classical period this developed into ideas regarding the immortality of the soul. In Plato's *Phaedo* the soul exists before life and goes on after death, indeed is immortal. In his *Gorgias* this involves judgment for evil deeds (Tartarus) and reward for good (the Isles of the blest). The famous Roman practice of placing a coin in the corpse's mouth to pay Charon for transporting the person across the river Styx is found in Lucian's *On Funerals* 1–10.¹³⁶ A movement toward some acceptance of bodily resurrection enters through stories of people taken to the underworld after death and then brought back, especially in Euripides' *Alcetis*, as she is brought back from the dead to her husband Admetus by their friend Heracles. At first glance this seems to be a resuscitation, but in Plato's *Symposium* 179b this is interpreted as a soul returning bodily from the dead; and in Aeschylus' *Eumenides* 723–24 this is also seen as a mortal freed from death and returned to her body.¹³⁷

Anderson finds this especially in Greek novels like Chariton's *Callirhoë*, where the heroine comes back to life (after an apparent death) in her tomb and escapes when grave robbers move the stones blocking the entrance. This is seen also in the reactions to Paul's Areopagus speech in Acts 17: the Epicureans, who believed the soul dissipated at death, mocked; while the Stoics, who were open to a more Platonic view, wanted to hear more (17:32).¹³⁸ In other words, there is some tradition in the Greek world open to the idea of a bodily resurrection. Then D. Zeller sees parallels in the "epiphany of heroes" in Hellenistic literature who in their ascent to life after death approach the Easter appearances in effect.¹³⁹

---

¹³⁵ Stanley Porter, "Resurrection, Greeks and the New Testament," in *Resurrection* (ed. Stanley E. Porter, et al.; JSNTSup 186; Sheffield: Sheffield, 1999), 68. The quote stems from Thomas Francis Glasson, *Greek Influence in Jewish Eschatology: With Special Reference to the Apocalypses and Pseudepigraphs* (London: SPCK, 1961), 30.

¹³⁶ Porter, "Resurrection, Greeks and the New Testament," 68–74.

¹³⁷ Porter, "Resurrection, Greeks and the New Testament," 78–80.

¹³⁸ Anderson, *"But God Raised Him"*, 112–14.

¹³⁹ Dieter Zeller, "Erscheinungen Verstorbener im Griechisch-Römischen Bereich," in *Resurrection in the New Testament: Festschrift J. Lambrecht* (ed. R. Bieringer, et al.; BETL 165; Leuven: Leuven University Press, 2002), 13–14.

Still, there are several who take the opposite approach. Wright argues strongly that the Hellenistic worldview considered death to be a "one-way street" from which no one returned. There was life after death but only in terms of the soul, and it resided in Hades or Tartarus. "The soul was well rid of the body," and though death was a terrible loss, it was also unavoidable. "The ancient world was thus divided into those who said that resurrection couldn't happen, though they might have wanted it to, and those who said they didn't want it to happen, knowing that it couldn't anyway."[140] Wright believes that the so-called resurrection stories alluded to by many like Porter and Anderson are the exception rather than the rule and occur only in myth or fiction. However, such stories still become a recognized alternative and wish in several parts of the pagan world.

In short, there was a lively belief in resurrection from death to eternal life in many segments of Second Temple Judaism and even to a lesser extent (very debated) in the Greco-Roman world, and the NT writers were following a clear tradition stemming from these primarily Jewish developments. Moreover, the movement is not as simple as often predicated. A belief in afterlife did not simply appear out of the blue with Dan 12:2. Basic belief in existence after death began much earlier, exhibited in the stories of the taking up of Enoch and Elijah as well as the appearance of the "spirit" of Samuel to Saul and demonstrated in incipient form in the ideas of the רְפָאִים or "departed spirits" in several texts. Movement from views of some type of existence after death to a distinct belief in resurrection from the dead seems fairly uniform during the biblical period, and the more developed doctrines of the NT are clearly anchored in the dominant tradition of Second Temple Judaism.

Two features here are most relevant for this study. First, resurrection, when held to in contrast to immortality in Second Temple Judaism, is physical. Second, this resurrection in Judaism was seen as part of the closing act of history. In the expression of this hope, no one gets resurrected in the midst of history. The implications of these points are significant. (1) A resurrection in a Jewish context is more than soul immortality – it has a physical dimension. This would add credence to the likelihood that a resurrection from a tomb would yield an empty tomb and some type of material manifestation. (2) Jesus' resurrection in the midst of history is a variation in Jewish belief. Something must have generated this view. Had the early church simply created the story of resurrection on the basis of Jewish precedent, they could have simply argued Jesus would be raised one day according to end-time Jewish resurrection hope, and he would oversee the final judgment. That might have spared them some trouble, but that is not where the accounts go.

---

[140] Wright, *Resurrection*, 82.

Something generated that new view. Most likely it was the event of resurrection that produced the new teaching.

So what does this all mean for the significance of the resurrection? It is to this final crucial question I now turn.

4. The Significance of Jesus' Resurrection

The resurrection narratives were used by each evangelist redactionally to culminate the theological themes each one had developed throughout their narratival development. They carefully chose both stories and the details of those stories to provide a climax to their gospel message. At the same time, however, the resurrection narratives climaxed the story of the historical Jesus. It is not just *Geschichte* but also *Historie* that was reflected in the empty tomb and the appearances.[141] The two sides – redaction and history – were intertwined: the redactional nuances were the result of historical decisions and were not created *de novo* out of the minds of the redactors or the experiences of the early Church. The majority of the essays in this volume have developed the idea that event and significance are tightly tied together in these key events involving Jesus in such a way that certain themes move across these key incidents. The purpose of this section is to draw out several of these significant themes and show how they climaxed the Gospel presentations and led into the themes of the NT letters.

(1) *The empty tomb and appearance stories provided divine vindication for the suffering Jesus and his claims to be at the center of God's realized promise.* Thomas Neufeld sees this as the primary thrust of Easter, saying, "Early followers would have seen Easter as God's final word of approval regarding what Jesus said and did and regarding his willingness to give himself even in death."[142] He points to Jewish martyr theology as background, as exemplified in Wis 5:1, 4–6, 15–16 (cf. also 3:1–4, 7–8; 5:16), "But the righteous one will live forever, and his reward is with the Lord; the Most High takes care of him." Then in 2 Macc 7:9, 22–23, dying martyrs say to their killers, "You accursed wretch, you dismiss us from this present life, but the King of the universe will raise us up to an everlasting renewal of life, because we have died for his laws." He concludes, "Resurrection, vindica-

---

[141] It appears that in 1 Cor 15:3–5, the view of the early church that passed on these traditions was that the death, burial and resurrection of Jesus were similar types of events within history. In other words, it is not just the story's significance (i.e., *Geschichte*), but the event itself (i.e., *Historie*) that was reflected in the early church's concerns.

[142] Thomas R. Yoder Neufeld, *Recovering Jesus: The Witness of the New Testament* (Grand Rapids: Brazos, 2007), 283.

tion, and exaltation are part of one large, encompassing scenario of divine intervention."[143]

Here it is best to begin with the passion predictions that are the cornerstone of the second half of the Synoptic portrayal of Jesus' ministry as it moves upward to Peter's confession of Jesus' as Messiah (Mark 8:29 = Matt 16:16; Luke 9:20) and then downward to his Passion. The plot revolves around the three predictions (Mark 8:31 = Matt 16:21; Luke 9:22; Mark 9:31 = Matt 17:22–23; Luke 9:44; Mark 10:33–34 = Matt 20:18–19; Luke 18:31–33) that set the scene for Jesus' interaction with the disciples.[144] The three predictions regarding his suffering increase in intensity and detail in the three, but all end with the same conclusion, "and after three days he will rise again." This simple yet profound statement means that suffering must lead to vindication, death must be swallowed up in victory (1 Cor 15:54, from Isa 25:8). The "third day theme" is often linked with Hos 6:2 ("on the third day he will restore us," cf. also 2 Kgs 20:5; Jonah 1:17 but probably is even broader, referring to the whole Jewish scriptural tradition of a third day deliverance (Exod 19:11, 16; 2 Kgs 20:5, 8; Est 5:1; John 1:17; cf. also Ps 16:8–11). The divine passive ἐγερθῆναι in the Matthean passages stresses God's sovereign intervention in vindicating Jesus. There is causal agency as God raises Jesus from the dead.

Just as important is the connection of resurrection to the controversies in the ministry of Jesus. This vindication impacts the debate we see in the Gospels over whether Jesus' work was from God or that of a magician-sorcerer empowered by Beelzebul. Jesus' power is from God and shows that "the kingdom of God has overtaken you." As such, it serves to authenticate Jesus' message and ministry, an issue Jesus also raised at the Jewish examination that started the decisive path to the cross. Everything argued here reinforces the central portrait of the essays in this book. Jesus presented himself as standing at the hub of God's salvation activity, at the hub of bringing the promised kingdom to earth. In the array of titles that the Gospels attach to Jesus, this was the reality they were seeking to affirm. The remaining implications represent distinct elements drawn from this central point. In making the points that emerge from resurrection, we show bridges to other parts of the NT that connect to what it shows.

(2) *Jesus has authority over life and death.* The authority of Jesus over death was demonstrated on several occasions when he raised people from the dead (Jairus' daughter, Mark 5:22–42 and parallels; widow's son, Luke

---

[143] Neufeld, *Recovering Jesus*, 283–85.
[144] For a defense of the core authenticity of these sayings, see Hans F. Bayer, *Jesus' Predictions of Vindication and Resurrection: The Provenance, Meaning, and Correlation of the Synoptic Predictions* (WUNT 2.20; Tübingen: Mohr Siebeck, 1986).

7:11–15; Lazarus, John 11:1–44); each was a harbinger of the resurrection and prepared for that event and the authority it represents.

Authority is the issue in several of the events these essays have treated. Jesus has the authority (1) to gather a new community around the kingdom program of God and the Twelve, (2) to determine what is proper on the Sabbath as Lord of the Sabbath, (3) to exorcise demons as part of the evidence that the kingdom is arriving, (4) to re-present liturgy from the Hebrew Scripture at the last supper, (5) to exercise prophetic and messianic power in entering Jerusalem and handling the temple, and (6) in claiming authority as a result of being vindicated by God. The extent and scope of this authority makes the point that God has given Jesus extensive authority, covering wide areas tied to life and well-being.

(3) *The resurrection demonstrates his glory and majesty.* This is stated best in Phil 2:6–11 (often called the "Philippians hymn"), where we are told Jesus in his incarnate state "made himself nothing" and "humbled himself," but in his risen state "God exalted him to the highest place and gave him the name that is above every name." The life of Christ was of the lowest possible estate, born with the animals and laid in a manger (Luke 2:7), then wandering through Galilee as an itinerant prophet with "nowhere to lay his head" (Matt 8:20). He was misunderstood by his own disciples, treated as an entertainment medium by the crowds, and hated and utterly opposed by the leaders, who from the beginning sought his life (Mark 3:6). He died the most ignominious and shameful type of death on the cross – to the Jew to be "hung on a tree" was a "curse" [Gal 3:13, cf. Deut 21:33] and to the Roman it was so demeaning that no citizen could be crucified except by direct edict of Caesar.[145] The resurrection reversed all that, and be became the glorified one, the Risen Lord. The resurrection serves as a hub for themes the church went on to preach as a result of what God did with Jesus here.

(4) *The resurrection constituted the overthrow of the cosmic powers.* Again, this is true via the fact that the early church viewed the cross and the empty tomb as a single event in salvation-history. We saw the anticipation of this idea in the work about overcoming Satan in the essay by Craig Evans. A key, later explanatory text is Col 2:15, "And having disarmed the principalities and powers, he made a public spectacle of them, triumphing over them by the cross." The imagery is that of the Roman triumph when a conquering general would lead his conquered enemy through the streets of Rome to the cheering crowds. This metaphor depicts a procession through the heavens, with Christ after his resurrection triumphantly displaying the "disarmed" and defeated demonic forces in victorious celebration. The res-

---

[145] For further discussion, see in this volume ch. 13, § 2.2.

urrection confirms that Jesus is in a position to bring kingdom benefits to completion and deal with the forces of evil that stand opposed to it.

5. Conclusion

The empty tomb and appearance narratives show a core of history and redactional freedom that is the hallmark of the four Gospels as a whole. The freedom of the evangelists to adapt, rearrange, and highlight individual details is not just found in the resurrection accounts but is the technique used in every part of the Gospels. This does not mean wholesale creation of details but rather selection and adaptation of the details that were there. Many of the essays in this book have testified to such variation within the Gospels, and the resurrection account is no exception. Still among the authorial choices and emphases, there is a core event that drives the presence of the scene. The early church preached a resurrection because its earliest followers believed God had indeed raised Jesus from the dead. The evidence for such a core event behind this event also is strong, rooted in an early creedal statement, descriptions of the empty tomb, and appearance scenes.

The actual event of the resurrection of Jesus, of course, was never witnessed, but its effects dominate the entirety of the Christian movement, and historians have often had to move from effect to cause in determining what is history. As historians, we must treat the resurrection of Jesus like any other purported historical narrative; that is, we examine the data as well as the interpretation of the data by other historians (in this case, Mark, Matthew, Luke, John, and Paul) then determine what explanation best fits the data. In this way we make decisions regarding the viability of both the data and of the interpretation (as we do in the case of the death of Julius Caesar or the defeat of Napoleon at Waterloo).[146] Here we must ask what could account for the rise of early Christianity and the transformation of the disciples into a force that could change the world. What could explain the change from self-centered individuals (Reimarus' theory does accord with the disciples as portrayed in the Gospels!) to the incredible ethical movement that Christianity became? What would cause the core story to highlight women and have its leaders look so unbelieving at the start? Should the post-Enlightenment world-view predominate with its naturalistic bias against supernatural events? It is best to approach the issue with as open a mind as possible, a position supported by the post-Einsteinian view of "natural law." This essay has contended that a genuine resurrection event supplies the best explanation for why we have the creed of a resurrection

---

[146] See the discussion in this volume in ch. 2, § 2.

hope early on, as well as the accounts of the empty tomb and the appearances. This case has been made using the criteria of historical Jesus study and setting these events in their conceptual and historical background. With this perspective, the most natural conclusion would be that there is a personal God who acted that remarkable day and raised Jesus from the dead. Wright's conclusion is *a propos*: Not only does a true bodily resurrection provide a "*sufficient* condition" for an empty tomb and appearances; it provides "a *necessary* condition for these things; in other words, no other explanation could or would do. All the efforts to find alternative explanations fail, and they were bound to do so."[147]

Bibliography

Alexander, L. C. A. "Chronology of Paul." Pages 115–23 in *Dictionary of Paul and His Letters*. Edited by Gerald F. Hawthorne and Ralph P. Martin. Downers Grove: InterVarsity, 1993.

Allison, Dale C., Jr. *Resurrecting Jesus: The Earliest Christian Tradition and Its Interpreters*. New York: T&T Clark, 2005.

Alston, William P. "Biblical Criticism and the Resurrection." Pages 148–83 in *The Resurrection: An Interdisciplinary Symposium on the Resurrection of Jesus*. Edited by Stephen T. Davis, Daniel Kendall, and Gerald O'Collins. New York: Oxford Univ Press, 1997.

Alsup, John E. *The Post-Resurrection Appearance Stories of the Gospel Tradition: A History-of-Tradition Analysis*. Calwer Theologische Monographien, 5. Stuttgart: Calwer-Verlag, 1975.

Anderson, Kevin L. "*But God Raised Him from the Dead*": *The Theology of Jesus' Resurrection in Luke-Acts*. Paternoster Biblical Monographs. Bletchley, U. K.; Waynesboro: Paternoster, 2006.

Bauckham, Richard. *Jesus and the Eyewitnesses: The Gospels as Eyewitness Testimony*. Grand Rapids: Eerdmans, 2006.

Bayer, Hans F. *Jesus' Predictions of Vindication and Resurrection: The Provenance, Meaning, and Correlation of the Synoptic Predictions*. WUNT 2.20. Tübingen: Mohr Siebeck, 1986.

Blomberg, Craig L. *The Historical Reliability of John's Gospel*. Downers Grove: InterVarsity, 2001.

–. "The Legitimacy and Limits of Harmonization." Pages 139–74 in *Hermeneutics, Authority, and Canon*. Edited by D. A. Carson and John D. Woodbridge. Grand Rapids: Baker, 1995.

Bock, Darrell L. *Luke*. 2 vols. Baker Exegetical Commentary on the New Testament, 3a–b. Grand Rapids: Baker, 1994–96.

Bode, Edward Lynn. *The First Easter Morning: The Gospel Accounts of the Women's Visit to the Tomb of Jesus*. AnBib 45. Rome: Biblical Institute Press, 1970.

---

[147] Wright, *Resurrection*, 717.

Broer, Ingo. *Die Urgemeinde und das Grab Jesu: eine Analyse der Grablegungsgeschichte im Neuen Testament.* SANT, 31. Munich: Kösel, 1972.
Brown, Michael L. "רְפָאִים." Pages 1173–80 in vol. 3 of *New International Dictionary of Old Testament Theology and Exegesis.* 5 vols. Edited by Willem A. VanGemeren. Grand Rapids: Zondervan, 1997.
Brown, Raymond E. "The Burial of Jesus (Mark 15:42–47)." *CBQ* 50 (1988): 233–45.
–. *The Death of the Messiah.* 2 vols. ABRL. New York: Doubleday, 1994.
Bultmann, Rudolf. *The History of the Synoptic Tradition.* Translated by John Marsh. Oxford: Blackwell, 1972.
Carson, D. A. *The Gospel According to John.* Grand Rapids: Eerdmans, 1991.
Cavin, Robert G. "Is There Sufficient Historical Evidence to Establish the Resurrection of Jesus?" Pages 19–41 in *The Empty Tomb: Jesus Beyond the Grave.* Edited by Robert M. Price and Jeffrey J. Lowder. New York: Prometheus Books, 2005.
Charlesworth, James H. "Resurrection: The Dead Sea Scrolls and the New Testament." Pages 138–86 in *Resurrection: The Origin and Future of a Biblical Doctrine.* Edited by James H. Charlesworth. New York: T&T Clark, 2006.
Collins, Adela Yarbro. "The Empty Tomb in the Gospel of Mark." Pages 107–37 in *Hermes and Athena: Biblical Exegesis and Philosophical Theology.* Edited by Eleonore Stump and Thomas P. Flint. Notre Dame: University of Notre Dame Press, 1993.
Collins, John J. *Daniel.* Hermeneia. Minneapolis: Fortress, 1993.
Conzelmann, Hans. *1 Corinthians.* Translated by James W. Leitch. Hermeneia. Philadelphia: Fortress, 1975.
Craig, William L. "The Historicity of the Empty Tomb of Jesus." *NTS* 31 (1985): 39–67.
–. "The Guard at the Tomb." *NTS* 30 (1984): 273–81.
–. *Assessing the New Testament Evidence for the Historicity of the Resurrection of Jesus.* Studies in the Bible and Early Christianity, 16. Lewiston: Mellen, 1989.
–. *The Son Rises: The Historical Evidence for the Resurrection of Jesus.* Chicago: Moody Press, 1981.
Craigie, Peter C. *Psalms 1–50.* WBC 19. Waco: Word, 1981.
Crenshaw, James L. "Love Is Stronger Than Death: Intimations of Life Beyond the Grave." Pages 53–78 in *Resurrection: The Origin and Future of a Biblical Doctrine.* Edited by James H. Charlesworth. Faith and Scholarship Colloquies. New York: T&T Clark, 2006.
Crossan, John Dominic. *The Historical Jesus: The Life of a Mediterranean Jewish Peasant.* San Francisco: HarperSanFrancisco, 1991.
–. "The Passion, Crucifixion and Resurrection." Pages 109–26 in *The Search for Jesus: Modern Scholarship Looks at the Gospels.* Hershel Shanks. Washington, D.C.: Biblical Archeological Society, 1994.
Davies, W. D., and Dale C. Allison, Jr. *A Critical and Exegetical Commentary on the Gospel According to Saint Matthew.* 3 vols. ICC. Edinburgh: T&T Clark, 1988–97.
Dillon, Richard J. *From Eye-Witnesses to Ministers of the Word: Tradition and Composition in Luke 24.* AnBib 82. Rome: Biblical Institute Press, 1978.
Dunn, James D. G. *Jesus Remembered.* Vol. 1 of *Christianity in the Making.* Grand Rapids: Eerdmans, 2003–.

Elledge, C. D. "Resurrection of the Dead: Exploring Our Earliest Evidence Today." Pages 22–52 in *Resurrection: The Origin and Future of a Biblical Doctrine*. Edited by James H. Charlesworth. Faith and Scholarship Colloquies. New York: T&T Clark, 2006.

–. "The Resurrection Passages in the *Testaments of the Twelve Patriarchs*: Hope for Israel in Early Judaism and Christianity." Pages 79–103 in *Resurrection: The Origin and Future of a Biblical Doctrine*. Edited by James H. Charlesworth. Faith and Scholarship Colloquies. New York: T&T Clark, 2006.

Evans, Craig A. "Did Jesus Predict His Death and Resurrection?" Pages 82–97 in *Resurrection*. Edited by Stanley E. Porter, Michael A. Hayes, and David Tombs. JSNTSup 186. Sheffield: Sheffield, 1999.

–. *Mark 8:27–16:20*. WBC 34b. Nashville: Nelson, 2001.

Fee, Gordon D. *The First Epistle to the Corinthians*. NICNT. Grand Rapids: Eerdmans, 1987.

Fiorenza, Elisabeth Schüssler. *In Memory of Her: A Feminist Theological Reconstruction of Christian Origins*. New York: Crossroad, 1984.

Fitzmyer, Joseph A. *The Gospel According to Luke X–XXIV*. AB 28a. Garden City: Doubleday, 1985.

France, R. T. *The Gospel of Mark*. NIGTC. Grand Rapids: Eerdmans, 2002.

Fuller, Reginald H. *The Formation of the Resurrection Narratives*. Philadelphia: Fortress, 1980.

Fullmer, Paul M. *Resurrection in Mark's Literary-Historical Perspective*. LNTS 360. London: T&T Clark, 2007.

Funk, Robert W., and The Jesus Seminar. *The Acts of Jesus: The Search for the Authentic Deeds of Jesus*. San Francisco: HarperSanFrancisco, 1998.

Glasson, Thomas Francis. *Greek Influence in Jewish Eschatology: With Special Reference to the Apocalypses and Pseudepigraphs*. London: SPCK, 1961.

Gray, G. B. *A Critical and Exegetical Commentary on the Book of Isaiah I–XXVII*. ICC. Edinburgh: T&T Clark, 1912.

Habermas, Gary R. "The Resurrection of Jesus and the Talpiot Tomb." Pages 152–75 in *Buried Hope or Risen Savior: The Search for the Jesus Tomb*. Edited by Charles L. Quarles. Nashville: Broadman & Holman, 2008.

Hachlili, Rachel. *Jewish Funerary Customs, Practices, and Rites in the Second Temple Period*. JSJSup 94. Leiden: Brill, 2005.

Haenchen, Ernst. *John*. Translated by Robert W. Funk. Hermeneia. Philadelphia: Fortress, 1984.

Harrington, Daniel J. "Afterlife Expectations in Pseudo-Philo, 4 Ezra, and 2 Baruch, and Their Implications for the New Testament." Pages 21–34 in *Resurrection in the New Testament: Festschrift J. Lambrecht*. Edited by R. Bieringer, V. Koperski, and B. Lataire. BETL 165. Leuven: Leuven University Press, 2002.

Harris, Murray J. *From Grave to Glory: Resurrection in the New Testament*. Grand Rapids: Academie Books, 1990.

Hill, Andrew E. "רבה." Pages 1037–41 in vol. 3 of *New International Dictionary of Old Testament Theology and Exegesis*. 5 vols. Edited by Willem A. VanGemeren. Grand Rapids: Zondervan, 1997.

Jeremias, Joachim. "πολλοί." Pages 536–45 in vol. 6 of *Theological Dictionary of the New Testament*. 10 vols. Edited by G. Kittel and Gerhard Friedrich. Translated by Geoffrey W. Bromiley. Grand Rapids: Eerdmans, 1964–76.

Kee, Howard C. "Testaments of the Twelve Patriarchs." Pages 775–828 in vol. 1 of *Old Testament Pseudepigrapha*. 2 vols. Edited by James H. Charlesworth. New York: Doubleday, 1983–85.

Kirby, Peter. "The Case Against the Empty Tomb." Pages 233–60 in *The Empty Tomb: Jesus Beyond the Grave*. Edited by Robert M. Price and Jeffrey J. Lowder. New York: Prometheus Books, 2005.

Köstenberger, Andreas J. *The Missions of Jesus and the Disciples According to the Fourth Gospel*. Grand Rapids: Eerdmans, 1998.

Kremer, J. "ὁράω, κτλ." Pages 526–29 in vol. 2 of *Exegetical Dictionary of the New Testament*. 3 vols. Edited by Horst Balz and Gerhard Schneider. Grand Rapids: Eerdmans, 1990–93.

Lambrecht, Jan. "A Note on John 20:23b." *ETL* 83 (2007): 165–68.

Levenson, Jon D. *Resurrection and the Restoration of Israel: The Ultimate Victory of the God of Life*. New Haven: Yale University Press, 2006.

Lowder, Jeffrey J. "Historical Evidence and the Empty Tomb Story." Pages 261–306 in *The Empty Tomb: Jesus Beyond the Grave*. Edited by Robert M. Price and Jeffrey J. Lowder. New York: Prometheus Books, 2005.

Lucas, Ernest C. *Daniel*. Apollos Old Testament Commentary. Downers Grove: InterVarsity, 2002.

Lüdemann, Gerd. *The Resurrection of Christ: A Historical Inquiry*. Amherst: Prometheus Books, 2004.

–. *What Really Happened to Jesus: A Historical Approach to the Resurrection*. Translated by John Bowden. London: SCM, 1995.

Marshall, I. Howard. *The Gospel of Luke*. NIGTC 3. Grand Rapids: Eerdmans, 1978.

Marxsen, Willi. *The Resurrection of Jesus of Nazareth*. Translated by Margaret Hohl. London: SCM, 1970.

Metzger, Bruce M. *A Textual Commentary on the Greek New Testament*. 2nd ed. Stuttgart: Deutsche Biblegesellschaft, 1994.

Michaelis, Wilhelm. "ὁράω, κτλ." Pages 315–67 in vol. 5 of *Theological Dictionary of the New Testament*. 10 vols. Edited by G. Kittel and Gerhard Friedrich. Translated by Geoffrey W. Bromiley. Grand Rapids: Eerdmans, 1964–76.

Murphy-O'Connor, Jerome. "Tradition and Redaction in 1 Cor 15:3–7." *CBQ* 43 (1981): 582–89.

Neirynck, Frans. "Lc 24,36–43: Un récit lucanien." Pages 655–80 in *À cause de l'Évangile: Études sur les Synoptiques et les Actes*. Edited by F. Refoulé. Paris: Cerf, 1985.

Neufeld, Thomas R. Yoder. *Recovering Jesus: The Witness of the New Testament*. Grand Rapids: Brazos, 2007.

Nickelsburg, George W. E. *Resurrection, Immortality, and Eternal Life in Intertestamental Judaism and Early Christianity*. HTS, 56. Cambridge: Harvard University Press, 2006.

Nolland, John. *Luke 18:35–24:53*. WBC 35c. Dallas: Word, 1993.

Osborne, Grant R. *The Gospel of John*. Cornerstone. Carol Stream: Tyndale House, 2007.

–. "Redaction Criticism." Pages 128–49 in *Interpreting the New Testament: Essays on Methods and Issues*. Edited by David Alan Black and David S. Dockery. Nashville: Broadman and Holman, 2001.

–. "Resurrection." Pages 673–88 in *Dictionary of Jesus and the Gospels*. Edited by Joel B. Green and Scot McKnight. Downers Grove: InterVarsity, 1992.
–. *The Resurrection Narratives: A Redactional Study*. Grand Rapids: Baker, 1984.
Oswalt, John N. *Isaiah 1–39*. NICOT. Grand Rapids: Eerdmans, 1986.
Pearson, Brook W. R. "Resurrection and the Judgment of the Titans: ἡ γῆ τῶν ἀσεβῶν in LXX Isaiah 26.19." Pages 33–51 in *Resurrection*. Edited by Stanley E. Porter, Michael A. Hayes, and David Tombs. JSNTSup 186. Sheffield: Sheffield, 1999.
Perkins, Pheme. *Resurrection: New Testament Witness and Contemporary Reflection*. Garden City: Doubleday, 1984.
Perrin, Norman. *The Resurrection According to Matthew, Mark, and Luke*. Philadelphia: Fortress, 1977.
Porter, Stanley. "Resurrection, Greeks and the New Testament." Pages 52–81 in *Resurrection*. Edited by Stanley E. Porter, Michael A. Hayes, and David Tombs. JSNTSup 186. Sheffield: Sheffield, 1999.
Price, Robert M. "Apocryphal Apparitions: 1 Corinthians 15:3–11 As a Post-Pauline Interpolation." Pages 69–104 in *The Empty Tomb: Jesus Beyond the Grave*. Edited by Robert M. Price and Jeffrey J. Lowder. New York: Prometheus Books, 2005.
Prince, Deborah Thompson. "The 'Ghost' of Jesus: Luke 24 in Light of Ancient Narratives of Post-Mortem Apparitions." *JSNT* 90 (2007): 287–301.
Schnackenburg, Rudolf. *The Gospel According to John*. 3 vols. New York: Seabury, 1980–82.
Schneiders, Sandra M. "The Raising of the New Temple: John 20:19–23 and Johannine Ecclesiology." *NTS* 52 (2006): 337–55.
Sider, R. J. "St. Paul's Understanding of the Nature and Significance of the Resurrection in I Corinthians XV 1–19." *NTS* 19 (1977): 124–41.
Swinburne, Richard. *The Resurrection of God Incarnate*. Oxford: Clarendon, 2003.
Theissen, Gerd, and Annette Merz. *The Historical Jesus: A Comprehensive Guide*. Translated by John Bowden. Minneapolis: Fortress, 1998.
Thiselton, Anthony C. *The First Epistle to the Corinthians: A Commentary on the Greek Text*. NIGTC. Grand Rapids: Eerdmans; Carlisle: Paternoster, 2000.
Wedderburn, Alexander J. M. *Beyond Resurrection*. Peabody: Hendrickson, 1999.
Wengst, Klaus. *Christologische Formeln und Lieder des Urchristentums*. SNT, 7. Gütersloh: Gütersloher Verlagshaus; Mohn, 1972.
Wenham, David, and Steve Walton. *Exploring the New Testament*. Downers Grove: InterVarsity, 2001.
Weren, W. J. C. "'His Disciples Stole Him Away' (Mt 28,13): A Rival Interpretation of Jesus' Resurrection." Pages 147–63 in *Resurrection in the New Testament: Festschrift J. Lambrecht*. Edited by R. Bieringer, V. Koperski, and B. Lataire. Leuven: Leuven University Press, 2002.
Wright, N. T. *Jesus and the Victory of God*. Vol. 2 of *Christian Origins and the Question of God*. Minneapolis: Fortress, 1996.
–. *The Resurrection of the Son of God*. Vol. 3 of *Christian Origins and the Question of God*. Minneapolis: Fortress, 2003.
Zeller, Dieter. "Erscheinungen Verstorbener im Griechisch-Römischen Bereich." Pages 1–19 in *Resurrection in the New Testament: Festschrift J. Lambrecht*. Edited by R. Bieringer, V. Koperski, and B. Lataire. BETL 165. Leuven: Leuven University Press, 2002.

Chapter 15

Key Events in the Life of the Historical Jesus: A Summary

DARRELL L. BOCK

Our study has discussed historical method and presented a dozen key events in the life of Jesus whose core can be credibly defended as going back to him historically. The primary contextual framework used in these essays to interpret these events is that of Second Temple Judaism, and this has resulted in an overall thesis that Jesus operated within the context of Jewish expectation and presented the hoped for kingdom of God as arriving with him as its central eschatological figure. This self-disclosure was complex and involved many interwoven elements that help to paint a unified portrait, some fitting into forms of Jewish expectation and other pieces building in creative directions from them. Jesus set the direction for the unifying of these various elements. The kingdom's disclosure and Jesus' self-revelation emerge primarily through an assessment of the socio-cultural significance of these key actions, as well as the teaching that surrounded these events.

In this final chapter, my responsibility is to summarize the results of the individual essays and their topics by showing a "depth coherence" that this portrait yields. By "depth coherence" I mean that not only do elements cohere, but in such a variety of ways and through such a plethora of themes that the coherence runs deep into the fabric of the presentation.[1] It should

---

[1] We have sought to present the evidence for the likelihood of each of these core events being historical one essay at a time, so we have not treated in detail a discussion of the development of the traditions that surround Jesus in the early church and how the predominantly oral culture worked, as well as issues tied to the formalization of that tradition that leads to our gospels. For such issues, one can now consult Martin Hengel, *Die Vier Evangelien und das eine Evangelium von Jesus Christus: Studien zu ihrer Sammlung und Entstehung* (WUNT 224; Tübingen: Mohr Siebeck, 2008). This work is an updated version of his earlier German and English monograph on this topic that has added forty percent to the original work. Unlike many essays in this volume, Hengel questions the existence of Q and prefers to see Matthew using Luke, a position likely to be among the more discussed points of his volume. Nonetheless, most helpful is his presentation on how early the gospels came to be tied to apostolic roots and began to be seen as four works working in one direction. Our appeal to depth coherence runs parallel to categories Dale C. Allison, Jr. invoked when he argued for recurrent attestation and a focus on key themes

be pointed out, that this depth coherence only gradually began to form for the members of this Study Group as we were part-way through the project, and it emerged more clearly as the final chapters were being completed. Although this concluding essay will have a deductive feel to its presentation, the assembling of this coherence was very much an inductive process that emerged as we proceeded. In spots, I will also suggest potential correlations with other aspects of Jesus' multi-attested teaching that begin to take us toward a more holistic appreciation of his ministry. These potential links, which we have not corroborated with detailed study, may well suggest paths for further development of the initial path these core events reveal.

In constructing a hypothesis about an ancient historical figure, one of the tests is whether the construct treats the variety of data well. The participants' research has concluded that Jesus is best placed in a Jewish prophetic/apocalyptic environment where both the arrival of the kingdom hope and the one who brings it are both important. Historical Jesus studies often highlight the difference in emphases between the evangelists in doing their work. However, a danger is that in rightly pointing to the diversity in the portraits, one might cease to pay attention to an underlying unity in these portraits. We think that these essays show that such a unity is rooted in Jesus' own activity.

We are not claiming a comprehensive treatment of the historical Jesus. Rather, we are arguing that key elements are present around which one can gain a core understanding of Jesus. The dynamic interchange between Jesus' acts, the experiencing of Jesus, his teaching, and the reactions to it reveals this core. These events claim to possess more than mere announcement. They involved authoritative action and an inseparable association with the God of promise. These key actions point to the core of Jesus' ministry. Details in making the case for their historical integrity, as well as their cultural and theological significance, are found in the essays themselves. I do not repeat the detailed cases made there, although in spots I will list key texts that serve as particularly significant pieces of ancient evidence for our synthesis. My goal is to pull together the key strands of what each of these events yields to see if a coherent portrait emerges. The details of how we can see this coherence is my own argument and represents my own way of seeing this synthesis. While the broad strokes of this presentation were discussed in the group and stand affirmed by the group as a whole, we do, as with all these essays, differ on some details and emphases. I shall also review key points that suggest the core of these events do reach back to Jesus. Our

---

that run deep in the Jesus tradition as the way forward. See his "The Historians' Jesus and the Church," in *Seeking the Identity of Jesus: A Pilgrimage* (ed. Beverly Roberts Gaventa and Richard B. Hays; Grand Rapids: Eerdmans, 2008), 79–95. The introductory essay to our volume has commented on his critique of the use of criteria for authenticity.

central question is whether there is a center around which the historical Jesus can be understood.

Jesus' Baptism by John the Baptist

As Robert Webb's essay on John the baptizer shows, several elements are important in setting the backdrop of what Jesus brought. Jesus' involvement with John and what the Baptist's ministry represented places Jesus in a Jewish eschatological framework. John called for spiritual renewal in Israel and the restoration of covenant faithfulness. John's distinctive eschatological baptism for repentance involved a call to people to turn and embrace this renewal. By coming to be baptized by John, Jesus was affirming this message. It means that Jesus was more than a teacher of wisdom and aphorisms. John's placement of this ministry in the wilderness had eschatological overtones. Jesus embraced all of these themes by associating with John.

The case for authenticity relies on the criterion of embarrassment. Jesus' submission to John and his baptism was difficult for the early church as the unique Matt 3:14–15 shows. Nevertheless, all the Gospels note this John-Jesus connection.[2] Jesus even mirrored the structure of John's renewal movement with disciples following a teaching leader. So Jesus shared John's call to the nation for renewal and identified with it. This means that there was more to Jesus than being a religious ethicist, although he also had this element to his teaching.[3] As we shall see, the key events of Jesus' ministry possessed these eschatological-apocalyptic dimensions.

In making this point, we are aware of the debate that has surrounded the use of terms like apocalyptic and eschatological.[4] Our point is that Je-

---

[2] Attempts to suggest Luke 3 lacks a John-Jesus connection because Jesus is baptized after John is arrested reads Luke in too wooden a manner, an irony for what is supposed to be a critical kind of reading. The key reason Luke discussed John's baptism was to set up this baptismal scene. Granted Luke lacks specifically mentioning John in the scene where Jesus was baptized, but the picture of Jesus being baptized as other people were assumes John was doing the baptizing. Luke's removal of John was merely a way to highlight in his presentation that the key to the event's significance was not only that Jesus was baptized but what was said to him.

[3] Some historical Jesus studies want to limit Jesus to being a teacher of wisdom only. The most well known recent effort in this regard is the Jesus Seminar of the nineteen nineties. All eschatological features to his ministry are products of the later community. Even the famous Q source is divided by some into Q^1 and Q^2 (others positing even additional recensions of Q) to reflect this view. I find this unlikely. The eschatological Jesus is too multi-attested in the tradition's sources *and* forms to be excluded from being rooted in Jesus. This case becomes even more established by the other events I shall contend are demonstrably historical. In fairness, it should be noted that this application of the proposed three-fold layer of Q has been opposed even by some who have advocated a layering in Q.

[4] For example, the discussion of the term eschatological in G. B. Caird, *The Language and Imagery of the Bible* (London: Duckworth, 1980), 243–71.

sus identified with John's claim that the time had come for God's decisive salvific act. Israel needed to be spiritually prepared for its arrival. This event involved a long hoped-for expectation of vindication and *shalom* for God's people. With it would come justice and righteousness. Although the details of such expectation took on a variety of distinct details within Judaism, depending on whose vision was embraced,[5] what all these expectations shared was that God would embrace and vindicate the righteous during this special time. John's baptism fits into that kind of expectation. This eschatological starting point is crucial to appreciating all that follows with Jesus. John the Baptist helps us makes sense out of Jesus and his context within Judaism.

Exorcisms and the Kingdom of God Versus Kingdom of Satan

Craig Evans' essay on the kingdom of God teaching builds off of this eschatological-apocalyptic backdrop. The exorcisms Jesus performed fit into this conceptual frame. Jesus' challenge to the spiritual world of destructive forces fits the Second Temple Jewish backdrop that sees kingdom announcement as ultimately involving the defeat of Satan (*T. Mos.* 10:1–2). It also fits with the Jewish polemic against Jesus reported in a variety of sources from the Gospels to Justin Martyr to the Talmud. In these texts, the Jewish sources accept the fact of exorcism and charge Jesus with using power from below. In his opponents' eyes, Jesus is a sorcerer (Mark 3:22; Matt 12:24; Luke 11:15; Justin, *Dial.* 69; *b. Sanh.* 43a).[6]

One of the least disputed facts about Jesus is that he taught about the coming kingdom.[7] Although not a common phrase in the Hebrew Scripture, the idea that God rules is a frequent concept within it. Second Temple Judaism also developed this idea.[8] However, Jesus' use of the kingdom concept

---

[5] One need only look at John J. Collins, *The Scepter and the Star: The Messiahs of the Dead Sea Scrolls and Other Ancient Literature* (ABRL; New York: Doubleday, 1995), and Jacob Neusner, et al., *Judaisms and Their Messiahs at the Turn of the Christian Era* (Cambridge: Cambridge University Press, 1987), to see the variety as applied to messianic hopes.

[6] On this consistent line of response to Jesus in materials giving the Jewish reaction, see Graham N. Stanton, "Jesus of Nazareth: A Magician and a False Prophet Who Deceived God's People?" in *Jesus of Nazareth: Lord and Christ: Essays on the Historical Jesus and New Testament Christology* (ed. Joel P. Green and Max Turner; Grand Rapids: Eerdmans, 1994), 164–80. Stanton also mentions *b. Sanh.* 107b, but it is harder to determine if this text is original to the Talmud. An interesting collection of essays looking at how Jesus' opponents saw him is found in Scot McKnight and Joseph B. Modica, eds., *Who Do My Opponents Say I Am? An Investigation of the Accusations Against Jesus* (LNTS 327; London: T&T Clark, 2008).

[7] James D. G. Dunn, *Jesus Remembered* (vol. 1 of *Christianity in the Making*; Grand Rapids: Eerdmans, 2003–xx), 383.

[8] James H. Charlesworth, *The Historical Jesus: An Essential Guide* (Nashville: Abingdon, 2008), 56. *Pss. Sol.* 17–18 is perhaps the best-known example, but several texts move in this direction as numerous texts at Qumran also show.

is not about the inherent sovereignty God has as Creator, as is often appealed to in the Psalms. Rather it treats the idea of his promised redeeming rule expressed afresh in the world in the arrival of a newly dawning age of *shalom*. This kingdom vindicates the righteous and brings ultimate justice. The defeat of evil was fundamental to this hope. This was a presence that kings and prophets had longed to see (Q: Matt 13:17 = Luke 10:24). Such a defeat involved acts that pointed to the arrival of something God has begun anew to do (Q: Matt 11:2–6 = Luke 7:18–23). This Matt 11 = Luke 7 passage alludes to salvation acts described in Isaiah; something Qumran also affirms in 4Q521. Yet at Qumran it is expectation that is expressed, while with Jesus it is fulfillment that is affirmed. Jesus' claim that the kingdom was coming placed him in a category where either he was a prophet proclaiming God's will in affirming the approach of the kingdom or one who risked being a false prophet. In the first century Jewish world, such claims would either be from God or from the devil. Jesus' exorcisms made the case that God stood behind Jesus' claims. Jesus claimed that the transformation of the possessed to people of sane mind served as evidence for something that was hard to see, the coming of the kingdom. This combination of word and act was central to Jesus' activity. It is present in several of his actions. God's kingdom was coming, so Satan's kingdom stood under attack. It is significant that Q, a source usually seen as lacking such Christological elements, also has this emphasis. Thus, Jesus' exorcisms point to a transcendent act that itself looked to a deeper claim about what came with Jesus. In other words, not only did Jesus announce a time of the arrival of God's promise, much as a prophet would, he helped to bring about the era announced and occupies an indispensable role in that new reality. It is in this link that implications for Christology can be seen.

The Choosing of the Twelve

Scot McKnight's treatment on Jesus' choosing of the Twelve continues to underscore the restoration theme in Jesus' activity. Covenant renewal and eschatological restoration were the point. For McKnight, Joshua and the leaders at Qumran serve as parallels. In addition, one should not miss the critique and authority claimed by such an act. The old structures of Israel were no longer seen as viable on their own terms. This was part of the "new wine skins" that Jesus brought to help accomplish the renewal effort. Thus, this action presupposed a leader, someone worth gathering around and someone who possessed a mission worth undertaking. God's people were being restructured, but that restructuring was based in part on the authority of the person whose teaching and work informed that renewal. The act raised a question: what kind of understanding of one's authority does Jesus' action indicate? Jesus gathered, but he gathered twelve in a manner that mirrored Israel's origins. He sent the twelve out with a message about the coming of God's new era. God's people and nation were being restructured around new leadership. Jesus called on these twelve to help lead the regathering nation in a new era of renewal and discipleship.

Where else do we see this kind of conscious mirroring of the origins of Israel? John the Baptist had disciples and his baptizing ministry was reconstituting the true, remnant Israel. Others, like John the Baptist, had disciples. But we do not see this conscious effort to show a reconstitution of God's people elsewhere. This act is both continuous and discontinuous with the church and with Second Temple Judaism – and it is specifically the feature of the twelve that makes it unique (Qumran had fifteen as McKnight notes).

Often scholars claim that Jesus proclaimed a kingdom, but did not present himself. Special attention should be given to the juxtaposition in the Synoptics between Jesus performing new salvific acts and the frequent lack of explicit discussion and direct declaration about Jesus' person. One of the features of Jesus' teaching, at least as it is seen in the Synoptics, is that he spends much time discussing what he announces (the kingdom of God) and what he brings (the forgiveness and the mercy of God) without making himself an *explicit* object of hope. This feature of his teaching can be misleading because *his actions and other activities* do give hints that he may be at the center of what is coming. In fact in many ways, the kingdom and its benefits implicitly arrive with his presence and activity. A careful eye on the extent of Jesus' authority revealed in this combination of actions actually begins to affirm much about how Jesus saw his role in this ministry. Jesus is believed in for actions, such as the exorcisms and healings, because they point to the time he brings. The lack of direct expression about the person of Jesus actually is evidence for the age of such traditions, because the case is not made as explicitly as it could be if it were created by a confessing church. These are claims *implicit* in the actions Jesus performs, because he is at the center of the benefits of salvation's presence. His disciples, who sometimes perform similar acts, do so by commission from him.

So Jesus opened a door of opportunity from God. The way in came with a call, one to embrace totally and receive without distraction the new reality God was bringing through him. So Jesus taught about a discipleship that demanded all, something other texts develop in a way that coheres with this starting point. The call to the twelve and to those called after them to discipleship in general meant primary allegiance to God, even over one's family. A series of texts, carrying a multiply attested theme, express this idea (Mark: Mark 8:34–9:1; Matt 16:24–28 = Luke 9:23–27; Q: Matt 8:19–22 = Luke 9:57–60; Matt 10:37–38 like Luke 14:25–26; L: Luke 9:61–62).

The uniqueness of how Jesus said and did this is another element of dissimilarity in his teaching. In the tradition, Jesus is the one teacher who people followed and he did the inviting, rather than the students coming to him.[9] In the Gospel tradition, his teaching was the only "teaching" that really counts. We do not see teachers, highlighted within the Jesus tradition, arising alongside Jesus to give their take on the arriving kingdom in the Gospels or even adding a complementary word to what Jesus says. The disciples are very much learners only with a message Jesus gave, not independent teachers with their own distinct access to truth. His word alone was important. Everything else taught, even by theologians such as Paul, is commentary on the way he first established. So Paul called on people to imitate him as he imitated Jesus. These seem to reflect trajectories the historical Jesus set. Jesus called for a total commitment in entering into the way he was introducing. Jesus consistently insisted that his teaching was to be heeded, showing the importance of what he was bringing and announcing. This emphasis on his teaching alone was perhaps best indicated by his familiar multiply attested refrain, "the one who has ears, let him hear" and its variations (Matt 11:15; 13:9, 15–16, 43; Mark 4:9, 23; 8:18; Luke 8:8; 14:35; Marcan, M and L traditions are included here). The twelve had a key role as those closest to Jesus in presenting these themes. However, the relationships Jesus sought out in his ministry raised afresh the question about who can be righteous.

Table Fellowship with Sinners and Outsiders

One of the areas where Jesus aroused opposition and controversy was in the relationships he initiated. He granted acceptance to a wide range of people through table fellowship. Meals played a significant role in Jesus' ministry, and imagery that pictured the eschatological banquet of God are a frequently attested theme in Jesus' teaching. Such passages extend from the Marcan tradition with the feeding of the multitudes to multiple, unique Lucan meal scenes. Craig Blomberg's study works through their importance and social message. Such scenes are distinct from the typical Greek *symposia* that sometimes are a point of scholarly comparison.

Jesus' actions illustrated that God welcomes and initiates relationships with all types of people, including many types that popular piety has excluded from the table. Jesus was neither an elitist nor a separatist. He displayed a special and focused concern for those that society had often made

---

[9] Samuel Byrskog, *Jesus the Only Teacher: Didactic Authority and Transmission in Ancient Israel, Ancient Judaism and the Matthean Community* (ConBNT 24; Stockholm: Almqvist & Wiksell, 1994); Martin Hengel, *The Charismatic Leader and His Followers* (Studies of the New Testament and Its World; Edinburgh: T&T Clark, 1981).

outsiders. So his meals included the poor and those who could not give a banquet in return.

These actions pointed to a kingdom that restructured social and relational concerns. Even the least of those present in society and those cast aside from it could gain his attention. So he took time for children who for this culture had little social value until they could contribute to it. This acceptance indicated a re-priorizing of values and an affirmation that God valued all human beings. Whether one thinks of the call for a different kind of banquet in Luke 14:1–24 or looks to how Jesus treated the sinful woman at the meal in Luke 7:35–50, the teaching is the same. Forgiveness and acceptance pave the way for the pursuit of righteousness. The one who is forgiven much will love much.

Jesus revealed corporate values that differed from much of the social world of his first-century context. Rather than marginalizing what society regarded as fringe people, he pursued and embraced them as an example of those to whom God offered a fresh way through forgiveness and acceptance. This is seen even in how the twelve were structured, for in that group were average people from basic walks of life. Nevertheless, they differed significantly from one another as well. In the same tight fellowship there was a tax collector who labored for Rome as well as a zealot who stood opposed to everything Rome represented. What Jesus brought was bigger than politics even as it sought to reshape how one looked at society and its relationships.

So we see here another key multi-attested element of Jesus' ministry is his reaching out to those on the fringe of society. His association with people regarded as unclean or as likely reprobates was something that created both reaction against him and interest in him .[10] This acceptance was seen in the table fellowship he extended to such people. He also urged those he taught to reach out in a similar manner, showing that the mission he had was to be continued and was to remain focused on people normally excluded as candidates for relationship with God. Jesus engaged with people in ways that led to the criticism of his associations (Q: Matt 11:19 = Luke 7:34; L: Luke 15:1). This was a way of indicating that he intended his message for a wide range of people because Jesus came to seek and save lost sinners (Mark: Mark 2:17 = Matt 9:13 = Luke 5:32; L: Luke 5:8; 15:1–32; Luke 19:10).

---

[10] E. g., tax collectors: Mark: Mark 2:15–16 = Matt 9:10–11 = Luke 5:30; Q: Matt 11:19 = Luke 7:34; M: Matt 21:31; L: Luke 15:1; lepers: Mark 1:40 = Matt 8:2; 10:8; Mark 14:3 = Matt 26:6; Q: Matt 11:4–5 = Luke 7:22–23: L: Luke 17:10–17; the poor: Q: Matt 5:3 = Luke 6:20; Matt 11:4–5 = Luke 7:22–23; Mark: Mark 10:21 = Matt 19:21; Mark 12:41–42 = Luke 21:2–3; L: Luke 4:16–19; 14:13–14, 21; 16:19–31; 19:1–10. I list texts by source in order to point out which concepts reflect multiple attestation.

Jesus' actions contrasted starkly with the kind of elaborate piety some Jewish groups expected. One thinks here of the long initiation process required at Qumran. The elaborate discussions of sin, piety and purity were a part of movements within Second Temple Judaism that emerged even more fully after the temple destruction in works like the Mishnah. Before that period, works like *Jubilees* also reflected a concern to be the righteous in ways that could lead to a type of separation from other, more reprobate elements within Israel. Jesus' approach to holiness was different. The kingdom he brought was to be inclusive, inviting participation in it to all layers of society while calling for a renewed pursuit of righteousness. Appreciating being welcomed into the kingdom led to that pursuit of righteousness, rather than being an entry requirement. Exclusion involved a conscious choice not to enter into the forgiveness Jesus offered and demonstrated.

However this kind of social restructuring was not the only area that produced official offense. Jesus' actions roamed in sacred territory beyond defining how righteousness could come. These forays into other areas of Jewish piety brought official reaction as he invoked elements of traditional Second Temple faith in a manner different from the Jewish leadership.

Controversy over the Sabbath with Jewish Leaders

Donald Hagner's essay treats the theme of Jesus and the Sabbath. Jesus' handling of this issue is important, for the Sabbath was a part of the Ten Words, rooted solidly in the Torah. Just as important, by the time of the Second Temple it had come to be seen in many Jewish circles as a pre-Mosaic and even pre-creation institution. The book of *Jubilees* shows this deepened emphasis about the Sabbath. For Jesus to make comprehensive Sabbath pronouncements was yet another act of authority mixed with word.

Jesus' actions on the Sabbath involved him permitting people to be fed or to be healed on the Sabbath. This also pictured restoration and deliverance. Jesus' restorative power pointed to the arrival of rest, a permanent kind of rest as opposed to a one-day-a-week rest. Thus these healings and acts anticipated the *shalom* that comes with the kingdom.

With these acts we again see the fusion of the arrival of a special time and the work of a special person. Who has authority over the day of rest? Jesus' claim to be Lord of the Sabbath (Mark 2:28 = Matt 12:8 = Luke 6:5) says it directly. Here is the beginning of a surfacing of a series of claims about authority that attach to our core events, each in distinctive spheres. This is one of the places where our "depth coherence" begins to surface. These related claims need special attention as we proceed; they are keys to appreciating how these events link together, moving us inductively to deductions about Jesus.

Now I recognize that for many scholars one of the most controversial parts of Jesus' work was his miraculous activity. However, our ancient sources are consistent in not challenging that Jesus performed unusual works. What Jesus' opponents debated with him and his followers was the source of such acts. The Jewish retort that Jesus' power was either a reflection of magic, sorcery, or of satanic power was not a denial that these activities took place but an effort to place their origin in a sphere outside God's benevolent activity.[11] Josephus, certainly no Christian, more neutrally and simply says that what Jesus did was unusual (παραδόξων). Jesus' example through these works was intended to show that God cared. So those who walked in Jesus' footsteps should seek to give themselves to the kind of service (not necessarily miraculous) where word and deed said God reaches out and cares. The Sabbath healings fit here, pointing to what Jesus' action represents as well as exemplifying what his disciples were called to do.

Now some, as Hagner notes, do not see Jesus' words to heal as a Sabbath violation, so that these scenes are treated as artificially creating a tension that would not have historically existed.[12] Such a reading of Jesus' action confuses how Jesus may have intended his word (no violation is present) with how such an effective verbal effort would have been perceived by those whose halachic Sabbath standards had little room for maneuver. It was Jesus using words with the intent to heal that was seen as a violation. Jesus would have been invoking action on a day of rest and acting as an working agent of healing on that day designed for non-activity. So Jesus' action correctly would have been seen as a sovereign act as well as possessing eschatological overtones. No text showed this more clearly than Jesus' retort, when healing a woman, that there is no more appropriate day on which to free one from the bonds of Satan than on the Sabbath (Luke 13:10–17). Jesus is not rejecting the Sabbath here but placing it in its complete context, pointing to its expectation that one day God would give permanent *shalom*. These actions, then not only point to a time, but to a person who brings a special time. Part of what shows the person being in part the issue are the very controversies about Jesus' authority these actions generate. In these acts, again often tied to words, Jesus is shown to bring the new era.

---

[11] See n. 6 above.

[12] Géza Vermès, *The Religion of Jesus the Jew* (Minneapolis: Fortress, 1993), 23, concludes that "The whole debate seems to be, however, a storm in a tea-cup since none of the Sabbath cures of Jesus entailed 'work', but were effected by word of mouth, or at most, by the laying on of hands or other simple physical contact." Eric Eve, *The Jewish Context of Jesus' Miracles* (JSNTSup 231; New York: Sheffield Academic Press, 2002), notes this kind of directness in healing was an unusual characteristic of the presentation of Jesus' healings, since it lacked either an appeal through prayer or the use of various kinds of intermediary means to invoke healing.

Peter's Declaration at Caesarea Philippi

No one who has traveled to this region of the Holy Land can forget seeing the rock cliff at Caesarea Philippi with its many niches. Here is where idols once stood, though some of them do postdate the period when Jesus was there. The setting of this declaration is a surprising one. A created event with such a central Jewish declaration about Messiah might well have been expected in an Israelite setting, in keeping with much of Jesus' ministry. Yet Caesarea Philippi was a region full of the Roman gods' spiritual influence. By Jesus' time, it had been a spot of polytheistic worship for centuries. Peter's statement about Jesus was not one only about Israel. However, a created church statement surely would have been less ambiguous than this text is. Nor would it have ended with a note of silence about making such a confession public. Such factors speak against an event created by the church.

Michael Wilkins argues that Jesus elicited from his disciples a recognition that distinguished between Jesus as a prophetic figure and Jesus as the "anointed one." Peter's declaration affirms that Jesus was the core eschatological figure of promise. The setting is no accident, because in bringing God's kingdom, Jesus was bringing something that transcended the nation of Israel alone. At the center of the kingdom program stood Jesus. His combination activity and teaching had made this evident to Peter.

A careful reading indicates that Jesus accepted the title of Messiah, but with key qualifications. He spent much of the remainder of his ministry developing the nuances of what Peter's declaration really meant. This disciple's idea needed shaping, so there is an aspect of denial in Jesus' response and a call to be silent. Jesus needed to reconfigure Peter's expectations, adding notes of suffering to precede the vindication Peter anticipated. The church surely understood the thrust of Jesus' response as positive because without it, there never would have been the common association of Jesus as "the Christ." The common church name Jesus Christ says as much.

The initial introduction of these themes about suffering caused Jesus to challenge Peter as speaking for Satan at one point. This strong retort points to the authenticity of the entire sequence through an appeal to the criterion of embarrassment. So the full force of Peter's declaration about Jesus as the Christ, though embraced by the disciples he represented, was not yet completely appreciated by those confessing it. A restructuring and reorientation was required.

Alongside hopes of victory and vindication, there would be pain, suffering, and rejection. The road to *shalom* was not paved in an exercise of power or domination. At its core were acts of service and sacrifice. Jesus would be a leader-prophet, delivering much as Moses had, but by means of a route that had not been so anticipated, neither by those opposed to him nor by those now walking with him down this new way.

The hesitation immediately to go forward in public with what Peter said here has been a source of controversy. As was noted in the essay on this event, Wrede made the messianic dilemma famous by initially arguing that the "messianic secret" is something Mark created to make a messianic ministry out of something that was not messianic under Jesus.[13] It is hard to understand why the early church would have gone forward to call Jesus the Christ if the impetus to do so had not come from Jesus. It is even harder to understand how Christ became so quickly and deeply attached to Jesus' name in the early church if he had not accepted the claim that he was the messiah, especially if he explicitly had refused to take on the term in private or public discussion as some claim. In fact in a little-known historical detail, before he died, Wrede renounced his own view of the messianic secret in a private letter to Adolf Harnack.[14] So even Wrede came to see the weakness of this understanding of Jesus. A messianic impulse for understanding Jesus came from Jesus' own acts and responses.

This declaration also develops what we have already seen. First, the presence of the promised one meant that John the Baptist's hope of immanence gets reconfigured, because the new era came through both judgment and service. John anticipated the judgment, but not the service. It also reinforced what was seen in the exorcisms, the claims to defeat Satan in the kingdom's victory. In Sabbath acts, Jesus points to the authority the eschatological figure possesses. He not only heralds the kingdom; he demonstrates the arrival of its authority in his own declarative action. This scene also develops why the twelve were formed. They have come to have access to Jesus and his teaching. Such access placed them in a unique position to appreciate and teach what it was Jesus sought to achieve. Ben Meyer's study, *The Aims of Jesus*, highlights this difference by distinguishing that which Jesus taught publicly from that which he taught the disciples

---

[13] William Wrede, *The Messianic Secret* (trans. J. C. G. Greig; London: Clarke, 1971). This is a translation of his *Das Messiasgeheimnis in den Evangelium*, which in 1901 created quite a stir in Jesus studies arguing that Jesus' call to be silent about his being the Messiah was really a Marcan construction of a ministry that was not intended by Jesus to be seen as messianic. On this issue, see Christopher Tuckett, ed., *The Messianic Secret* (IRT 1; Philadelphia: Fortress, 1983).

[14] Martin Hengel, *Studies in Early Christology* (Edinburgh: T&T Clark, 1995), 17, and with more detail in Martin Hengel and Anna Maria Schwemer, *Jesus und das Judentum* (vol. 1 of *Geschichte des frühen Christentums*; 4 vols.; Tübingen: Mohr Siebeck, 2007–xx), 507–10; also Hans Rollmann and Werner Zager, "Unveröffentliche Briefe William Wredes zur Problematisierung des messianischen Selbstverständnisses Jesu," *Zeitschrift für neuere Theologiegeschichte* 8 (2001): 274–332, esp. 317; Andrew Chester, *Messiah and Exaltation: Jewish Messianic and Visionary Traditions and New Testament Christology* (WUNT 207; Tübingen: Mohr Siebeck, 2007), 309.

privately.¹⁵ The trajectory of these depth linkages is that Jesus intended himself to be seen as the eschatological figure in God's promised program.

Peter's declaration forms the pivot from events in Jesus' earlier ministry to the core events in Jesus' last visit to Jerusalem. It is here that these strands weave together even more tightly and comprehensively.

Jesus' Entry into Jerusalem

Brent Kinman's essay highlights the fact that Jesus' public entry into Jerusalem was a distinctive and public display of his activity. Everything about this entry presented Jesus as a regal figure, but one pointing to humility, not just power. In that sense this entry was a-triumphal. This arrival to Jerusalem provided an opportunity for people to embrace Jesus and his claim to be the central eschatological figure. His disciples embraced the act, but many others did not. As an event involving the approach of many pilgrims, it may have appeared to many, including the Romans, as a the confused throng of activity tied to a massive celebratory migration into the city. This may explain why there was no effort to arrest Jesus at the time.

The idea that Jesus so purposefully entered Jerusalem has raised questions about the event's authenticity. Surely, if Jesus had entered the city in such a bold manner he would have been stopped immediately. However, this challenge to the scene argues for too much. Jesus was one among many pilgrims approaching Jerusalem. The sacred city's population was said to triple during such pilgrim feats, reaching up to 100,000 from tens of thousands. Pilgrims entering the town would have been in a celebratory mood, probably singing among other activities. They might well have chimed in with the act of the disciples, but in Matt 21:11 they did so only seeing Jesus as a prophet, a reputation he had established popularly, but one short of what the actions implicitly represented. Some others may well have joined the disciples in calling out in praise of the entering Son of David (Matt 21:9). This mix of praise makes it likely that the event was more ambiguous than the way the disciples and Jesus had intended it. The kingdom hope Jesus generated up to this point had some wanting to make him king, others seeing him as a prophet. This ambiguity may have led to a mixed response, but how many actually appreciated all that he had been doing here was not clear – it may have been far less than the vast crowd that is often suggested. The Lucan text might be of help by attributing the laying down of palms to disciples. This group of believers is modestly numbered at just over a hundred in Acts. An action like this by an isolated few, during such a commotion, would not necessarily attract a great deal of attention except from those keeping a specific eye on Jesus, namely, the religious leadership. They did challenge Jesus

---

¹⁵ Ben F. Meyer, *The Aims of Jesus* (London: SCM, 1979).

about his entry according to Luke 19:39–40. Even if they had wanted to act, to seize Jesus immediately in this celebratory crowd would have risked really setting off an uproar.

A second feature that raises authenticity issues involves the explicitness of Jesus' act. Is not this kind of public disclosure out of character for his ministry? The answer to that question is certainly yes, but the contrast is the point. Jesus now approached the capital to press the issue of his identity. He entered the city with actions that evoked kingship like Solomon's entry (1 Kgs 1:33–37) and the hope of a coming king like that in Zech 9:9. Yet, unlike the arrival of other dignitaries, the civic leaders of Jerusalem did not come to meet Jesus. There were no speeches for him as there were for other dignitaries who entered ancient cities with pomp. It was a presentation of kingship made in very modest terms. This entry lacked the sense of awe and wonder that most dignitaries received, even though those who appreciated Jesus called out in praise. This is another reason why the entry can be described as a-triumphal.[16]

This event is one of the few told in all four Gospels, underscoring its importance. The variation in the accounts show that more than one source likely is in view. An early church careful about antagonizing Rome would not have created such a story. Why would they create this event if such a potentially provocative act could be denied? Its presence throughout the material suggests it was there because it did occur. Its memory lingered. Its presence also suggests that Jesus entered the city intent on being reckoned with and assessed. His disciples knew he entered the city making kingdom claims and said so. His opponents, if Luke can be accepted, challenged his claim, something their later action confirmed. Jesus' entry set the stage for the decisive confrontation.

This event frames everything that happened later in Jerusalem. The actions and disputes that followed rotate around the authority that this entry suggests Jesus was implicitly claiming. Kingdom hope and a fresh, reprioritized portrait of kingship came together in this entry. As such the event is in line with the themes already traced in the other events.

Jesus' Action in the Temple

Klyne Snodgrass's study of the temple incident shows that this event accomplished several things at once: (1) It served as a prophetic protest against certain temple proceedings. (2) It also was a messianic act of cleansing the temple in an eschatological context, making an implicit claim of authority. (3) As such it represented stepping on priestly toes, directly challenging the

---

[16] Brent Kinman, *Jesus' Entry Into Jerusalem: In the Context of Lukan Theology and the Politics of His Day* (AGJU 28; Leiden: Brill, 1995).

religious leadership's authority in Jerusalem. The action forced the leadership's hand, demanding either a positive or negative response. The incident was eschatological in force. Jesus declared what the temple was designed to be and what it should be. In remarks that appeal to Isa 56, the temple is to be a gathering place for all nations. This public event reinforces who has the right to undertake such a symbolic act on Israel's behalf. Who really speaks for God's chosen people? Jesus makes his claim in Israel's most sacred space, a place all Israel regarded as the earth's most sanctified place.

Few doubt the authenticity of this event. It is multi-attested in at least two distinct versions (Mark: Mark 11:15–19 = Matt 21:12–17 = Luke 19:45–48; John: John 2:13–22).[17] It is one of the few events to appear in all four gospels. It is seen as a catalyst for Jesus' arrest in the Synoptics, a view that makes cultural sense. Moreover it is not clear why this event would have been created had it not taken place. What would have been gained by creating such an event? The early church sought to be careful about being seen as seditious and yet this event plays right into that danger. Thus, its occurrence best explains its presence.

Herod the Great rebuilt the temple mount and expanded the area so that it covered about thirty-five acres. Jesus' action likely took place near the Royal Portico at the southern end of the temple mount, where the money-changers and traders would have been. Temple worship required pure doves and animals. The money-changers allowed men needing to pay the temple tax to purchase the required Tyrian shekels. Although these shekels had symbols on them offensive to Jews, they were of the highest quality and silver content available for this purpose. These were the least offensive, yet suitable, coins available at the time.

Scholars have interpreted Jesus' action in various ways: a protest against the commercialization of the temple, a protest against the temple itself with a prediction of its destruction, or as a call to spiritual reform beginning at the temple. At the least, Jesus' overturning the tables involved a prophetic action. It served as a rebuke of the leadership and the way it ran the temple. As such, Jesus challenged what was regarded as official religious authority, which was why the scene following this event had the leadership pose the question about where Jesus got the authority to do such things.[18]

The reason for Jesus' action may well be complex. Although Jesus did predict the destruction of Jerusalem and although at a later time sacrifices were viewed as unnecessary, Jesus was not pronouncing the destruction of

---

[17] One issue is the chronological difference in these accounts. A few see two distinct cleansings, but those who opt for one cleansing usually see John as moving the account forward to preview the different plane on which Jesus speaks about the temple.

[18] All of what is said here is true regardless of the more contentious question of whether Jesus sought reform or predicted the destruction of the temple here.

Jerusalem or the cessation of sacrifices with *this* incident.[19] The evidence of various sources, especially the Qumran Scrolls, shows that many Jews had concerns about corruption in the temple. Those guilty of corruption were almost exclusively seen as the ruling priestly families, not the regular priests who served daily in the temple.[20] Jesus speaking about what the temple should be in the future argues against a prediction about the temple's destruction. Nothing Jesus said here pointed to a transformation of imagery or perception of the temple as a non-existent place of worship. So we should not read his remarks as anticipating a spiritualizing of the temple developed later in Christian theology. Judgment in the imagery of the withered fig tree was not aimed at the temple, but at the nation.

The confrontation Jesus had with the leadership may well have been an element in play here, but it is unlikely to be all that was at work. So although such corruption might have been a factor, Jesus' purpose was likely more comprehensive. Proclaiming eschatological hope was more important than the replacement of corrupt leadership. Jesus looked to the future in saying the house will be a house of prayer for the nations. Like the prophets before him, Jesus took strategic action *in the temple* to reorder how people viewed the temple and its proceedings. He looked forward, not just back or to current failures. Numerous Jewish texts point to the expectation that at the end time the temple worship would be what it should be. People from many nations would come there to worship (Ezek 40–48; 4Q174, where the house of David arises and the temple is rebuilt, an act pointing to restoration). So Jesus' action was a critique of the current worship and the ruling priests. This critique expressed his conviction about the temple's sanctity. The action implied an unparalleled authority, one that probably carried messianic overtones because this event followed his entry and the eschatological meaning of the series of acts tied to it. The temple challenge also pointed to the fulfillment of promises that God (or the messiah) would set things right in the temple. The juxtaposition of the revived Davidic dynasty and the hope for a restored Jerusalem, expressed in the fourteenth benediction, reflects such a linked hope. Jewish eschatological expectation expressed in regular prayer linked Jerusalem's sanctity with the work of the promised one. This view also appears in the hope of Messiah's transforming Jerusalem into a place of righteousness (*Pss. Sol.* 17–18). In sum, the temple incident was a symbolic messianic act. Jesus had the right to do this not only because he represented God and spoke in his name, but because of his own role within God's program.

---

[19] Part of the evidence suggesting this conclusion is the participation of the new community at the temple after Jesus' death.

[20] 1QpHab 7:7–13; 9:2–16; 11:2–15; 12:1–10; 4QpNah Frag. 3–4, 1:10 [=4Q 169]; CD A 6:134–17; 4Q Ps 37 2:14 and 3:6, 12; 4Q MMT 82–83; also *1 Enoch*; *T. Mos.* 5:3–6:1

Jesus' Last Supper with his Disciples

Our study has been tracing two sets of themes tied to Jesus: one is related to the time he brings, the other treats who brings that time. In many ways, the Last Supper brought these two themes together. In Howard Marshall's study, Jesus took a meal tied to the season, the Passover, and altered its symbolic significance in a way that pointed to his own work and action. Was it a Passover meal? The tradition of the Synoptic Gospels says so (Mark 14:1–2, 12–17), although John leaves another impression (John 18:28). Again, what could be said was that the mood of the Passover season was surely a part of the scene, given the meal at the least came on the edge of Passover, making the association a simple transition.[21] In either chronological setting, Jesus' declaration at this meal pointed to a new covenantal reality coming into existence through what God was about to do through Jesus.

The wording of the event comes down to us in two forms, one seen in Matthew and Mark, the other in Luke and Paul. An allusion to the new covenant, a move the Pauline-Lukan version made specifically (1 Cor 11:25 = Luke 22:20), is clear in either version. The Matthean-Marcan version speaks of the "blood of the covenant" without specifying its character as new (Mark 14:24 = Matt 26:28). However, placed in the eschatological context of all of Jesus' acts, the remark points to a new era of salvation, so a new covenant tied to that new period is invoked. At the least, Jesus' death represented an act of service that cleared the way for others to be blessed. Also likely, in addition, is that this death served as a sacrifice on behalf of others, an act of substitution which God honored in such a way that others could be brought into a new relationship with him. Jesus' suffering would bring a fresh covenantal reality. Jesus memorialized his death as a renewed representative act on behalf of many/you (many: Matt 26:28 = Mark 14:24; you: 1 Cor 11:24 = Luke 22:19 [also in v. 20]). An allusion to Isaiah 53 was possibly intended in the appeal to the "many."[22] Jesus is seen as a righteous sufferer, but his death is more than an example of righteous service. As a sacrifice, it procured a way to forgiveness that participants in the new era are to embrace. Everything about this teaching pointed to the arrival of both an era and of a central figure bringing that era. Jesus both announces and acts.

Jesus' radical altering of sacred Exodus liturgy also points in this direction, because Jesus does not merely harken back and strengthen the links to the Exodus as the old liturgy did; he points exclusively forward to a new

---

[21] One thinks of how today Christmas overtones impact many events in December in many places dominated by Western culture.

[22] The word *many* appears five times in this Isaianic text. It is almost a refrain. It should be noted, however, that some are not convinced this is enough to see an allusion here.

era, distinctively altering the imagery of the old rite. Jewish liturgy was often reworked, but how often was it transformed to refer to a completely separate event? Such an act again raises the question: who has the authority to make such a move and to what kind of authority does it point?

This meal pointed back to the various acts of authority he had already undertaken in Jerusalem. Jesus had already taught a prophet could not die outside of Jerusalem (L: Luke 13:33: Q: Matt 23:37 = Luke 13:34), a claim that cohered with what was taking place here. This act indicated that Jesus saw himself as the center of eschatological activity and the one whose act of suffering brings the new era. At the least, this was an act of *the* eschatological prophet, one who functioned as the expected leader-prophet like Moses. However, Jesus' other acts during this week also frame this event. I speak of his entry, his challenge at the temple and his challenge to understand what Ps 110:1 meant. Taken together these intend to raise messianic implications. Jesus acts as a leader-prophet who delivered in such a way that the eschaton came with him. This sacrifice opened up a covenant. In addition, a call for Israel to turn back to God meant this sacrifice dealt with sin to clear the way for a new relationship to God. So whether Jesus spoke of the sacrifice being for you or for the many, it was the representative feature on behalf of God's responding people that was present in either version. These variations in wording are simply synonymous ways to express the idea. That this meal will be celebrated again in the eschatological future invoked the idea of the messianic banquet. So Jesus saw himself acting as the leader who ushers in the new era.

It is important to note that this event took place among the disciples alone. It was not a public declaration. It served to make clear what Jesus saw himself as facing. It provided the early church with an event for reflection, something the meal certainly quickly became. The scene made it clear that Jesus knew he was facing rejection and death, something subsequent events would prove to be the case.

Jesus' Examination Before the Jewish Leadership

The issue of Jesus' authority is the central point of contention in the scene of the Jewish examination of Jesus. This is not a formal trial, because only the Romans had the authority to put someone to death. The key exchange in this scene treated Jesus' comprehensive claim of vindication and authority. Jesus argued that God would welcome him, not only into heaven as a righteous one, but with a seat by God's side, sharing in divine ruling authority. The remark also suggests that the leadership would be subject to judgment by him one day. The scene involves two distinct judgments about Jesus. One judgment is Jesus' claim of exaltation to come. The other judgment is the leadership's perception that such a claim is blasphemous because it compromises God's unique, sacred glory. The scene permits no middle ground between these two options.

Mark's discussion of the examination begins with Jesus' statement on the temple. This introduction suggests that Jesus' temple act was a key catalyst in Jesus' presence before them. This act was seen as a direct challenge to the leadership's control of the temple. Such a challenge had to be met or else the suggestion would remain that the temple was operating in an unsanctified manner. This scene is also corroborated in a general way by the testimony of Josephus in *Ant.* 18.63–64, which most likely attributes Jesus' death to both the Jewish leadership and Pilate.[23]

An often-made challenge to the authenticity of this event involves the claim of a lack of potential sources from the Christian side who could serve as witnesses. These objections are not persuasive. The lines for possible public disclosure here are multiple. First, we have the potential for witnesses, like Nicodemus or Joseph of Arimathea. Second, another potential source was Paul, who as a one time opponent had access to the leadership during the period when he persecuted the church. Third, there was a decades-long debate between Jesus' followers and the leadership in Jerusalem. In this debate the key issues would surely have surfaced. Annas II, a descendant of Annas and Caiaphas, was responsible for James's death in the early sixties. This event, described by Josephus, shows how long the debate over the new movement lasted (*Ant* 20.200). In the public debate over Jesus, the Jewish leadership surely would have been made their case against Jesus public. The "Jerusalem grapevine" serves as a credible means for the surfacing of what took place.

At the event's core was the exchange between Jesus and the high priest. Jesus was asked to explain who he was. His reply, as recorded in the Synoptic Gospels, invoked Ps 110:1 in all versions (Matt 26:64; Mark 14:62; Luke 22:69) and Dan 7:13 in Matthew and Mark. This was the crux to this scene. In my essay on this event I have argued the likelihood of both citations being linked by Jesus originally, given the likelihood that both texts appeared to have mattered to him.

However, despite what I have argued, it is important to note that all one needed to trigger the offense was that Jesus alluded to one of these two texts. The high priest would have responded with a blasphemy claim had either text been noted.

The appeal to Ps 110:1 with its reference to being seated at God's right hand meant that Jesus anticipated divine vindication and expected to be

---

[23] Issues about the authenticity of the Josephian citation exist and were treated in this volume in ch. 13, § 2.1.2.

ushered into God's very presence, in some way sharing God's presence and glory. This thought of shared glory was controversial to Jews. Some Jews entertained the possibility of something similar for a few potential figures, while other Jews regarded such exaltation as unthinkable. So for the Jewish leadership a Galilean teacher like Jesus did not qualify for such a claim. He lacked the credentials of greatness that the other candidates had, that is, *if* they even accepted such a possibility.[24]

If Jesus had only appealed to Dan 7:13–14 with its image of the Son of Man riding the clouds, then the high priest also would have reacted because such riding of the clouds was something only deity did in the Hebrew Scriptures. The implication in such a reply was that Jesus would return as the Son of Man to exercise judgment. Jesus' response included the idea that one day Jesus would judge his current opponents! So this would be seen as a claim to share divine prerogatives, not to mention functioning as a direct challenge against the leadership. If Jesus uttered both sayings, then the point was that one day he would sit in God's presence and exercise such judgment authority.

In any of these three scenarios (Ps 110:1 alone, Dan 7:13–14 alone, or both texts noted), Jesus' reply either claimed an equality with God, or, at least, a kind of sharing in authority with God, that the leadership would have judged as slander against God's unique glory. Jesus' remark in any form, made it clear that he not only anticipated reception in heaven but far more. With a Danielic allusion, the challenge to the leadership was more direct, as the defendant Jesus claimed that he would become their judge. This role also could have been seen as blasphemous in light of Exod 22:28 [Eng]. A way to contextualize this reply is to think of it as worse than claiming to be able to live in the temple's Holy of Holies, the earthly symbol of God's presence in heaven. Part of what makes the remark so offensive to the leadership was Jesus' placing the locale of vindication so clearly in terms of heaven. Jesus invoked not the symbol or representation of God's presence on earth, but his own presence next to God in glory.

To present Jesus' response as blasphemy was not a charge the leadership could have brought to Rome. The Romans would have refused to enter into a religious dispute among Jews. However, what Jesus' remark permitted the leadership to do was raise the issue of Jesus being disruptive to the *pax Romana* in Judea. If Jesus had claimed to be a figure who bears authority apart from Rome, this claim could be taken to Pilate and presented as a disruptive factor in the province. To translate a heavenly kingship claim as a claim to be a king independent of Rome was all that was needed to merit

---

[24] In fact, the likelihood is that the Sadducean majority would not have entertained such an option for anyone, since the example passages came from outside the Torah.

Pilate's consideration. So the leadership saw itself as having a basis to go to Pilate. They could raise a charge of sedition. Pilate would be forced to act, because he was responsible to protect Caesar's interests. This leads directly into our next key event.

Jesus' Roman Examination by Pilate and his Crucifixion

The essay by Robert Webb focuses on the cultural context that would lead Pilate to get involved. Jesus represented no military threat to Rome. His threat involved social upheaval. The involvement of the Jewish leadership bringing Jesus to Pilate underscored this potential. Here were the Jewish elites with whom Pilate worked the closest alerting him to a figure who in their view was disturbing the peace. These leaders claimed that Jesus easily could destabilize a sensitive, religiously rooted region. Their charge was that Jesus had the potential to be a cause of serious political unrest (στάσις).

Working backwards towards Pilate's examination is the best way to understand its role. Pilate placed the charge that accompanied Jesus' crucifixion on what has become known as the *titulus*. It described Jesus' crime as claiming to be King of the Jews. Since Rome appointed kings, Pilate would see the claim to be king without Roman approval as a form of sedition. Sedition leads to crucifixion, a most horrific form of death. The Romans used it as a deterrent to say if one acts against us, excruciating suffering lies ahead. As such, this kind of death became an opportunity to broadcast to Roman subjects, "Don't act like him or you will end up like this." The fact that Pilate had Jesus crucified meant that it was the claim to be a king that registered with the prefect. Jesus' crucifixion is among the least disputed facts of Jesus' life. Jesus was not crucified merely for being a prophet.

This kingship charge fits closely with where we have seen Jesus' claims leading. It also coheres with the first century context for crucifixion, namely, charges of political upheaval against Rome. It also confirms what we have seen elsewhere. The key perception about Jesus for those opposed to him was that he claimed to be more than a prophet, taking to himself a social-political authority they did not recognize. As we noted already, the Jewish discomfort with Jesus involved a direct challenge to their religious authority. The leadership translated that threat into political terms Pilate could grasp. Jesus' actions in support of his claim to bring a new era also had implications for Roman authority that saw itself as bringing a new era. Jesus' new era claims suggested that Roman authority was not alone. Rome would see this as sedition, something that could not be tolerated. Jesus' movement had already shown it could generate an emotional, popular following, challenging key social institutions. So elements in the Jewish leadership closest to Pilate brought their concern to the prefect. Other examples, such as Theudas and the anonymous Egyptian, show how seriously the Romans handled such situations.

Our earliest sources' core portrait agrees. Pilate became convinced that Jesus and his claims had the potential to disrupt the religiously sensitive Judean province.[25] The Jewish leadership presented the Galilean teacher as a threat to Judean stability. They did so with some insistence. The charges the Jewish leadership brought had to do with Jesus inciting the people, and certainly Pilate could read that the leadership was concerned. The sources consistently argue that the issue was whether Jesus claimed to be a king of the Jews (Mark 15:3 = Matt 27:11, elaborated in Luke 23:2–3). The *titulus* confirms that charge. In my view, another supporting strand of evidence involving Jesus' status in seen in the mocking tied to Jesus' various examinations. They also were directed at regal claims (Mark 15:18 = Matt 27:29; John 19:3). It is unlikely that the early church fabricated such mocking, given how much trouble it would have raised for credibility and social acceptance had it not really been a part of the original story. The scene gives an unflattering portrait of Roman justice and government. So the Jewish leadership notes that Jesus' "appointment" as king had not come from Rome. Pilate had better not allow such a claim to persist. Pilate could not allow such a poor precedent in a potentially unstable region, especially when his top priority was to keep the peace and protect Caesar's interests.

The Jewish leadership appeared to have pressed the point. In many ways, they had to do so. If Jesus had gone before Pilate and been released, Jesus would have received the equivalent of political immunity, since Rome would have examined him and found him no threat. The argument to Pilate became that he should take care of this threat now or else it might grow worse. The Jewish leadership's strategy before Rome was to "nip it in the bud" now before things got worse. One death now might be the end of potential trouble, as often was the case with such movements.

Pilate faced a very practical choice. Option one was to act against Jesus, who clearly had stirred up the leadership in Jerusalem and seemed quite capable of generating popular excitement and religious fervor. Option two was to release him, inciting the anger of those he worked with on religious issues. In addition, it was crucial to act aggressively against Jesus, because the Galilean teacher had raised the specter of independence from Rome in regal-oriented claims. Our knowledge of how Pilate minted coins (the first to mint coins with Roman symbolism in Judea) and how he acted to confirm Roman authority, even to the point of causing religious offense,

---

[25] Pilate had seen this first hand in the Jewish reaction to his effort to place standards in Jerusalem, an act Pilate retreated from when it became clear a bloodbath might result (*Ant* 18.55–59).

shows he was very interested in making Roman authority clear. To have the support of the religious authorities made more palatable what might be seen as an excessive use of force against a non-militaristic Jesus. We need to remind ourselves that this linkage of the Jewish leadership and Pilate was not something limited to early Christian sources. Josephus also makes this association in his brief discussion about Jesus (*Ant* 18.63–64). So we have multiple attestation of dual responsibility for Jesus' death that stretches across ideological lines. Jesus' crime was to act in ways that led others to regard him as king of the Jews, which in turn would have been seen as a threat to Judea's peace and well-being.

This portrait connects with much of what we have seen in the other key events. The idea that Jesus presented a kingdom in which he has a key role sets the backdrop for the kind of charge that is brought before Pilate. The declaration at Caesarea Philippi also moves in this direction. The charges also fit with the events of the entry and temple incident. Those events may well stand behind the leadership's claims that Jesus was challenging Jewish practice in ways that disturbed the peace.

One other feature tied to this title should be noted. It is that the new community quickly came to call Jesus by the name Christ. The question becomes why choose such a name to be the moniker for Jesus if (1) he denied the connection, (2) he did not teach about himself in such a role, and (3) to raise such a title could be seen as a challenge that would bring the reaction of those in authority? It seems far more probable that people made the association so publicly and prominently because the connection came from Jesus. This conclusion is historically likely, even if Jesus gradually disclosed the idea and went more public about it toward the conclusion of his ministry. So assessing the social context for the *titulus* is one of the key ways to gain an appreciation for how people saw Jesus by the end of his ministry. They saw him as a messianic claimant, because what he did and said pointed in this direction. However, from what Jesus also taught his disciples privately it seems quite likely that this category needed refinement in terms of its detailed understanding, something his very death demonstrated. There was more to this messiah than the mere exercise of power; suffering and ultimate divine vindication were a part of his story.

Jesus' Resurrection as Vindication after a Certain Death

In one sense to come to the resurrection is to move beyond historical Jesus study. This is for two reasons: (1) Jesus does nothing here; he is portrayed as the beneficiary of a divine act, and (2) normal historical means can hardly confirm such a claim. All that one can do is to trace the event's impact. Nonetheless, the resurrection is significant to cover because it completed the claim of vindication that Jesus had raised at his Jewish examination. Such vindication became a catalyst for theological reflection in the movement Jesus launched.

So Grant Osborne's essay covers resurrection. One can hardly understand the historical Jesus without looking to the event of vindication that explains Jesus' post-execution impact.

Before getting to the resurrection, we must confirm that it was likely Jesus was dead and buried. Do the details we have of such a burial in our sources fit with Jewish custom?[26] In short, they do. Numerous details of the burial that can be checked fit within the cultural backdrop. In the Mishnah, *Sanh.* 6:5–6, a corpse's burial, even that of a convicted criminal, was to take place before sundown. The Romans were known to permit such burials. However, the family was not permitted to receive the body, nor could they place the criminal's body in the family's tomb. This explains Joseph of Arimethea's involvement. Buried bodies were washed, wrapped, and anointed for seven days after the burial as part of the mourning. So the women went as soon as was permitted, given the late afternoon burial, the Sabbath's having intervened, and their knowledge that an initial anointing had taken place. This means that our sources leading into the scene are completely culturally credible, even down to the details of why the women waited to anoint Jesus and the kind of tomb in which Jesus ended up.

Several features of this event at a historical level suggest that the early church did not invent this event.

First, the first witnesses to the empty tomb were women, according to the gospel sources. In a culture where women did not have the right to be witnesses, would one make up a story to sell a difficult idea (physical resurrection) to a skeptical culture by beginning with people who had no cultural value as witnesses?[27] The detail not only shows the value of women to the movement but also suggests that the women were in the story because they were key to the event's disclosure.[28]

Second, it would have been possible within Judaism to create a vindication story of Jesus that would have been less problematic. Much of Judaism

---

[26] I deal here with claims that Jesus was simply left to rot on the cross in order to further shame him as an executed criminal. This discussion also treats claims or any ideas that Jesus somehow survived his scourging and crucifixion. Everything in all our sources argues that he died. The nature of crucifixion alone is enough to make this certain.

[27] *m. Šebu.* 4:1; *m. Roš Haš.* 1:8; *b. B. Qam.* 88a; Josephus, *Ant.* 4.219. For pagan attitudes consider Plutarch, *Moralia* 142CD; "Advice to Bride and Groom" 32. Accordingly, in light of both Jewish and pagan views of women as witnesses and public speakers, why invent an Easter narrative in which women are witnesses? My thanks to Craig Evans for some of these details.

[28] In fact, it is this cultural problem that may well explain why 1 Cor 15:3–9 lacks their mention.

held that the resurrection would come at the end of history. So why not create a story (if we are to argue the story was created) that simply says the resurrection would come at the end with Jesus leading the judgment? Think how clean an approach this is. It fits Jewish theology. There would be no need to claim an empty tomb. Only appearances would be options. The fact the story did not take this route means that what we have in our sources is a "mutation" on this Jewish expectation.[29] The early Christian sources and preaching claimed that Jesus was raised within history, an unprecedented exception to the expectation. The question is why create a "mutation," when a less problematic alternative existed. More compelling is that something in the experience of the disciples created that change of view. More than that, these early disciples were willing to die for this belief. Is that likely if someone among the disciples had created the claim?

Third, the reaction to the women reflects the criterion of embarrassment. When the women reported their story of the empty tomb, the reaction was not, "Well, of course, it is Jesus!" No, rather these future church leaders saw the women as hysterical and did not initially embrace the women's claims. The new community leadership acted much like one might expect modern, skeptical people to react. Is this likely if one creates the account? Why not have them be in simple awe?

Fourth, if the event's creation is a solid explanation for this teaching, then why are there no detailed stories about Jesus appearing to Peter or James, two of the key leaders of the church? If these stories are so easy to create, then why not have detailed appearance accounts to two of the most important early leaders who the sources suggest saw Jesus?[30]

A resurrection pointing to vindication would lead to the conclusion that God had vindicated the historical Jesus, giving credibility to his claims and mission. To the church such an act would serve as a divine vote for Jesus in the public dispute. Resurrection affirms his claims of bringing the new era promise with him at its center. This helps to explain why the resurrection became so central in the early church's message. It was a heavenly confirmation of all Jesus stood for and affirmed. For all the debate around the details of these accounts, this core theme is something they all share.

---

[29] In my view recent, claims made in 2008 that a Dead Sea Stone Gabriel tablet holds out the possibility of a Jewish belief in a resurrection on the third day require too many gaps to be filled into a partially preserved text and assume an Ephraim-Messiah backdrop that is far less than certain to be credible. This text does show a fascination with the number three, but beyond that the presence of any activity on behalf of vindicated Messiah is not transparent at all from what we have of this text in lines 75–83. For the argument claiming such a connection, see Israel Knohl, "'By Three Days, Live': Resurrection, and Ascent to Heaven in *Hazon Gabriel*," *JR* 88 (2008): 147–58.

[30] James's experience is noted in 1 Cor 15:7, while Peter's is noted in Luke 24:34. Both summaries are told with amazing brevity.

Conclusion

These essays have explored twelve core events. Each presents evidence and arguments for their probable historicity and discusses their significance for understanding the historical Jesus. Jesus' activity centered in a call to Israel to come back to covenant faithfulness and to recognize the arrival of a new era, the promised era of deliverance. His actions supported these claims. In this ministry Jesus extended the work of John the Baptist, working in the same realm of hope rooted in Jewish promise. Eventually the apostles took this message of new covenant deliverance to all the nations.

Jesus presented himself in act and in the words tied to those acts as one who stood at the center of God's program and as the inaugurator of the kingdom. There is an implicit claim of significant authority in virtually all of these core events. Much of this authority is connected to divine prerogatives. Jesus exercises a claim of authority to choose new leaders and reconstitute a people (the Twelve). He claims power over hostile forces (exorcisms), over sin and forgiveness (associations), over sacred space (temple incident), over the Sabbath (healings on the Sabbath), over liturgy (Last Supper), and over judgment (Jewish examination). Such comprehensive authority points to the kingdom's coming. God's rule is at work afresh. Through such a comprehensive, new-era authority, Jesus claimed a role that many Jews would have seen as eschatological and in some sense messianic. The disciples acknowledged this. In his representative confession at Caesarea Philippi, Peter indicated that Jesus was more than a mere prophet; he was the promised anointed one of God. To that portrait at his final meal Jesus added the idea that this deliverer must suffer to initiate the new era's covenant. Jesus revealed these notes of suffering selectively, especially to his disciples.

Jesus' actions showed him consistently reversing the evil present in the world. Such acts could be interpreted as Satan's defeat, and thus pointing to the new age's arrival. He also called for a restructuring of how people related to God and to others. This teaching served as a radical ethical challenge to the way the world tended to see such relationships. Because people could not see demonstrated in an empirical way such comprehensive claims about spiritual relationships, Jesus linked words and deeds together so that what could be seen testified to what could not be seen. If God was acting through Jesus to do the kinds of things he was doing, then there could be no doubt about the kingdom's presence, nor Jesus' role in it. Teaching tied to the exorcisms of Jesus, events we treated, point to this connection.

Such acts of authority were also threatening to many Jewish leaders. They feared a destabilization of what was a tenuous arrangement with Rome. This threatened the largely Sadducean, temple leadership and the comfortable relationship they had with Rome. In addition, the way he handled the law, for example, in his actions tied to the Sabbath, served to undercut the "human traditions" layered on top of the law. This strand of Jesus' activity challenged the most pious of Torah oriented Jews present in Jewish society, mainly the Pharisees. Jesus' values about association and purity as reflected in his reaching out to those outside could be seen as socially destabilizing to those in power and as presenting a serious challenge to a culture built around status, honor, and shame. This threat and Jesus' claims implied in his actions of the last week led those leaders to attempt to stop Jesus. They took the charge to Pilate that Jesus claimed to be a king independent from Rome. In the discussion that followed Pilate could see the potential for destabilization in the leaders' insistence that Jesus must be removed. These were leaders with whom he regularly worked on matters associated with the Jewish faith. So Jesus went to the cross accused of claiming to be King of the Jews, a charge that pointed to sedition and that was recorded on the *titulus* for all to see. Rome was saying, "Do not stir the pot." So Jesus died, and for a brief time all seemed lost. All that was left was a tattered message, severed from the one who had promised to bring it. Then everything changed.

For the new community, the resurrection represented the ultimate example of the divine vindication of Jesus' activity. So they preached Jesus and his divinely vindicated claims through resurrection, vindication that reached back into his earlier activity. Their message was that he was and is the central figure of God's program. As a result of resurrection and consistent with claims Jesus made that led to his death, Jesus now resided at God's side, sharing in the divine mission *and* serving as a part of the authoritative sacred presence. This association with heavenly presence carried with it implications about the person of Jesus. The earliest church claimed that the reality of resurrection disclosed the fullness of who Jesus is and was. The resurrection also explained why Jesus called God his Father, and how he had the authority to define God's will on matters such as the Sabbath, authority over the demonic, the nature of temple practice, and other activities tied to Torah, all events we have treated in detail. In fact, this relationship underscored the source and range of authority he had enacted during his ministry; it was comprehensive authority from above. What emerged from the Jesus of history was the Christ of faith.

Our essays have argued that the linkage between what Jesus announced and who Jesus is was no accident, even at a historical level. Jesus saw himself situated at the center of God's program. He anticipated being completely vindicated as the Son of Man at God's side. The activity tied to this understanding produced a coherent narrative for the early church, where he and the promise he brought became the inseparable message. Such an account of him stands solidly rooted in what the historical Jesus actually said and did.

The gist of these core events provides a coherence working at several levels of the tradition. They point to a historical depth within the early church's tradition about Jesus. The linkage between these events does not have the feel of elements added bit by bit over time. Rather, there is a coherent core around which we get a solid glimpse of the aims of the historical Jesus.

Summing up, the historical Jesus presented the kingdom of God and the opportunity for participation in it. Such participation involved a turning in repentance to reaffirm the covenantal responsibility God originally gave to Israel, something Jesus' participation in John the baptizer's baptism and the selection of the twelve introduced. Jesus' activity called for a restored people of God and a renewed relationship with God that was built upon his own authority. This new relationship, evidenced by the call to outsiders to come in, ultimately would reform the disciples' relationship to others, leading in directions of righteousness and reconciliation. With the privilege of being connected to God's rule came the rest of Jesus' teaching, which we have not sought to corroborate in our study. This teaching called for the pursuit of a challenging personal and societal righteousness that honored God, reconfigured our role as God's creatures, and served as a contrasting paradigm to the world about how to live. This trajectory appears to cohere with what we have established. By acting to show this decisive era's arrival, Jesus affirmed his central role in its coming, calling on people to believe in what God was doing through him and, in doing so, to follow him. In this way, his actions spoke as loud as his words, giving his words presented in conjunction with such acts a context in which they could be illustrated and appreciated.

Understanding the historical Jesus requires appreciating the scope of the significance of his acts and the element of authority implicit in them. Those acts pointed to a new time and an appointed person. Jesus presented himself in his activity with both a demand and an invitation to participate in God's restorative rule. It was a rule that the historical Jesus' ministry in core events and activities sought to illustrate and to inaugurate.

Bibliography

Allison, Dale C., Jr. "The Historians' Jesus and the Church." Pages 79–95 in *Seeking the Identity of Jesus: A Pilgrimage*. Edited by Beverly Roberts Gaventa and Richard B. Hays. Grand Rapids: Eerdmans, 2008.

Byrskog, Samuel. *Jesus the Only Teacher: Didactic Authority and Transmission in Ancient Israel, Ancient Judaism and the Matthean Community*. ConBNT 24. Stockholm: Almqvist & Wiksell, 1994.

Caird, G. B. *The Language and Imagery of the Bible*. London: Duckworth, 1980.

Charlesworth, James H. *The Historical Jesus: An Essential Guide*. Nashville: Abingdon, 2008.

Chester, Andrew. *Messiah and Exaltation: Jewish Messianic and Visionary Traditions and New Testament Christology*. WUNT 207. Tübingen: Mohr Siebeck, 2007.

Collins, John J. *The Scepter and the Star: The Messiahs of the Dead Sea Scrolls and Other Ancient Literature*. ABRL. New York: Doubleday, 1995.

Dunn, James D. G. *Jesus Remembered*. Vol. 1 of *Christianity in the Making*. Grand Rapids: Eerdmans, 2003–.

Eve, Eric. *The Jewish Context of Jesus' Miracles*. JSNTSup 231. New York: Sheffield Academic Press, 2002.

Hengel, Martin. *The Charismatic Leader and His Followers*. Studies of the New Testament and Its World. Edinburgh: T&T Clark, 1981.

–. *Studies in Early Christology*. Edinburgh: T&T Clark, 1995.

–. *Die Vier Evangelien und das eine Evangelium von Jesus Christus: Studien zu ihrer Sammlung und Entstehung*. WUNT 224. Tübingen: Mohr Siebeck, 2008.

Hengel, Martin, and Anna Maria Schwemer. *Jesus und das Judentum*. Vol. 1 of *Geschichte des frühen Christentums*. 4 vols. Tübingen: Mohr Siebeck, 2007–.

Kinman, Brent. *Jesus' Entry Into Jerusalem: In the Context of Lukan Theology and the Politics of His Day*. AGJU 28. Leiden: Brill, 1995.

Knohl, Israel. "'By Three Days, Live': Resurrection, and Ascent to Heaven in *Hazon Gabriel*." *JR* 88 (2008): 147–58.

McKnight, Scot, and Joseph B. Modica, eds. *Who Do My Opponents Say I Am? An Investigation of the Accusations Against Jesus*. LNTS 327. London: T&T Clark, 2008.

Meyer, Ben F. *The Aims of Jesus*. London: SCM, 1979.

Neusner, Jacob, William Scott Green, and Ernest S. Frerichs, eds. *Judaisms and Their Messiahs at the Turn of the Christian Era*. Cambridge: Cambridge University Press, 1987.

Rollmann, Hans, and Werner Zager. "Unveröffentliche Briefe William Wredes zur Problematisierung des messianischen Selbstverständnisses Jesu." *Zeitschrift für neuere Theologiegeschichte* 8 (2001): 274–332.

Stanton, Graham N. "Jesus of Nazareth: A Magician and a False Prophet Who Deceived God's People?" Pages 164–80 in *Jesus of Nazareth: Lord and Christ: Essays on the Historical Jesus and New Testament Christology*. Edited by Joel P. Green and Max Turner. Grand Rapids: Eerdmans, 1994.

Tuckett, Christopher, ed. *The Messianic Secret*. IRT, 1. Philadelphia: Fortress, 1983.

Vermès, Géza. *The Religion of Jesus the Jew*. Minneapolis: Fortress, 1993.

Wrede, William. *The Messianic Secret*. Translated by J. C. G. Greig. London: Clarke, 1971.

List of Contributors

Craig L. Blomberg, Denver Seminary, Denver, Colorado, USA.
Darrell L. Bock, Dallas Theological Seminary, Dallas, Texas, USA.
Craig A. Evans, Acadia Divinity College, Wolfville, Nova Scotia, Canada.
Donald A. Hagner, Fuller Theological Seminary, Pasadena, California, USA.
Brent Kinman, Heritage Evangelical Free Church, Castle Rock, Colorado, USA.
Scot McKnight, North Park University, Chicago, Illinois, USA.
I. Howard Marshall, University of Aberdeen, Aberdeen, Scotland.
Grant R. Osborne, Trinity Evangelical Divinity School, Deerfield, Illinois, USA.
Klyne R. Snodgrass, North Park Theological Seminary, Chicago, Illinois, USA.
Robert L. Webb, McMaster University, Hamilton, Ontario, Canada.
Michael J. Wilkens, Talbot Theological Seminary, La Mirada, California, USA.

Ancient Texts Index

Hebrew Bible

Genesis		Exodus	
1:26	256	2:20	219
2:2–3	271	3–15	39
2:18	199n56	7–10	172
3:15	160, 804	8	172
5	805	8:14–15	172
5:24	618, 805	8:15	172–73
6:1–7	159	8:19	173
12	193	12	219
12:16	399n42	12:14	546
14:18	219	14:20	616
14:18–20	350	15:1	812
15	193	15:3	152
15:11	504n81	15:18	152
17:20	192	16	219
17:21	192	16:6	776
18:1–8	219	18:12	219
24:54	219	18:25	239
25:12–18	192	19:11	816
26:30–31	219	19:16	816
29:22–23	219	20	272
31:54	219	20:8–11	271
35:22–26	192	20:12	650
41:43	398n38	21:17	650
42:13	192	21:28–32	488
42:32	192	22:1	235
43:24–34	219	22:18	806
45:23	399n42	22:27	617n65, 624–25, 660
49:10–12	398n38	22:28	844
49:11	509n99	24:4	192–93
49:28	192	24:8	514, 568
		24:9–11	219
		30:11–16	455

31:14	276n110	13:27	219
31:16–17	272n93	14:6	654
32:6	229n54	15:14–16	449n69
34:21	273	15:30–36	272n93
39:14	193	15:32–36	271
		15:41	776
Leviticus		17:17	193
1–7	219	19	116n64, 471n175
5:5–10	116	19:17	114n50
11	220	23:21b	152
14	116n64	24:15–17	350
14:5–6	114n50	24:17	354, 361, 364
14–15	114n49	31:5	193
14:50–52	114n50	31:14	239
15	116n64	33:54	196
15:13	114n50		
16	159	Deuteronomy	
16:3	458n108	1:13	196
16:4	114n49	1:22–23	192
16:24	114n49	1:23	193, 206
16:30	611	5:12–15	271
18	116n64	5:16	650
18:16	131	5:28–29	350
19:1–2	362n244	6:4–5	650
19:9	260	8:14	776
19:18	650	14:2	220
19:31	796, 806	15:1–8	272
20:9	650	16:18	196
20:21	131	17:6	199n56
23:22	260	18:11	796, 806
23:40	406n60	18:15–18	350
24:9	274	18:18	324n111, 327n121
24:15–16	610	18:18–19	350
25:8–55	233	19:15	199n56
25–26	272	21:4	114n50
		21:6–8	590n4
Numbers		21:22	691
1:5–16	192	21:22–23	624, 691–93, 783
1:44	193, 206	21:23	622, 691, 787
6:24–26	611	21:33	817
7:84	193	23:25	273
7:87	193	32:8–9	156
10:34	616	32:14	509n99

32:17	172n49	8:7	153
32:39	806	8:11	399n44
33:2	153	9:12–24	220
33:5	153, 327n121	9:25–10:1	399n41
33:8–11	350	10	496
33:27	153	10:1–8	490
34:5	806n115	10:19	153
34:6	806n115	10:24	400n45
		12:12	153
Joshua		15:17	196
3:1–4:18	207	15:22	432
3:12	194, 206	16:13	399n41
4	165, 209	17	617n65
4:1	193, 206	21	257, 259
4:1–10	207	21:1–6	274
4:2	192, 194, 206	21:1–7	274
4:3	192–93, 206	21:2–3	259
4:7	193, 206	21:5	274n102
4:8	192, 206	21:8	399n43
4:9	192–93, 206	22:9	399n43
4:20	192–93, 206	28:1–25	806
6	165	28:2–19	796
18:24	192–93		
19:15	192–93	2 Samuel	
21:7	192–93	1:11	654
21:38	193	5:7	401, 806
21:40	192	5:9	401
		6:12	401
Judges		6:16	401
3:10	205	7	629, 655
6:21	220	7:10–14	472
8:23	153	7:11–16	350
10:4	399n42	7:12–16	403
11:35	654	7:14	648
12:14	399n42	7:16	648
14:10	220	8:4	399n42
16:17	330	13:29	399n43
19:29	193	15:1	399n44
		15:21	576
1 Samuel		16:2	399n42
1:3–8	220	16:16	400n45
2:6	806	18:9	399n43
2:17–32	460		

1 Kings		10:15–16	399n42
1	398, 400n47, 401	11:12	400n45
1:5	399n44	14:20	399n42
1:9–10	220	18:1–6	436, 438
1:33	399n44, 401n49	18–19	658
1:33–37	838	19:3	617n65
1:33–39	399	19:22	330
1:33–40	399	19:35	620
1:39	400n45	20:5	816
4:26	399n42	20:8	816
8	220		
8:27	432	**1 Chronicles**	
8:41–43	438	12:40	399n42
10:25	399n42	15:1–3	401
11:30–31	193	17:11–14	403
11:31–32	196		
12:18	399n42	**2 Chronicles**	
13	220	9:24	399n42
17:1–6	220	23:11	400n45
17:7–24	220	24:17–25	620
18:15	399n42	28:8–15	220
18:19	220	29:1–19	438
19:18	190	29:3–19	436
2 Kings		**Ezra**	
2:5	805	6:17	193
2:9	805	9:6–15	134n132
2:9–11	805		
2:10	805	**Nehemiah**	
2:18–19	790	7:65	628n88
4:9	330	9:6–37	134n132
4:38–41	220	13:15–22	272n93
4:42–43	238		
4:42–44	220	**Esther**	
5:10	115n57	5:1	816
5:14–17	115n57	6:8	398n38
6:15–23	220		
6:22	220	**Job**	
6:22–23	222	3:13–19	804
8:21	399n42	6:10	330
9:13	405n58	7:21	804
9:16	399n42	10:9	804
9:21	399n42	14:10	806

14:12	806	47:8	154
14:14	806	48:2	154
16:22	806	49:15	806–7n119
19:25–27	806	49:17	807
26:5	805	51:2	116n64
31:17	222	51:7	116n64
33:2	804	51:16–19	432
33:18	804	60:8	123
34:15	804	68:24	154
36:15	401n50	69:8	446n55
42:17	806	69:9	444, 447
		74:12	154
Psalms		75:9	401n50
2	648	76:9	205
2:6	648	78:55	196
2:7	109, 143n162, 778	82:1–4	205
2:10	205	84:3	154
8:3	443	86:13	805
8:4–8	256	88:3–5	804
8:5	341n171	88:10	805
10:16	154	89	648
10:18	205	89:3–4	403
10:35	205	89:19–29	403
16:8–11	816	89:23	404
16:9–10	778	89:27–28	634n105
16:10	804	89:35–37	403
22	529	90:3	804
22:26	529	91	161
23	221	91:13	160, 169
23:5	222	93:1	154
24:8–10	154	95:3	154
29:10	154	96:10	154
29:11	795	97:1	154
30:9	804	98:6	154
36:11	401n50	99:1	154
37:12–13	457	99:4	154
37:20–22	457	103:6	205
37:32–33	457	103:16	805
39:13	805	104:3	616
41:9	222, 224, 499–500, 503	105[6]:37 (LXX)	172n49
44:4	154	105:15	350n202
47:2	154	106:16	330
47:6–7	154	107:2–3	208

108:9	123	8:19	796, 806
110	649n148, 650	9:1–7	751n259
110:1	593, 597, 610, 613–14n58, 621, 626, 638–42, 643n126, 644–45, 648–50n150, 652, 654, 660, 842–44	9:2–7	124n93
		9:3–5	404
		9:3–9	403
		9:5	648
		9:6	653, 795
110:4	350	10:20–11:16	634n105
113–118	407n62	10:21	190
116:3	804	11:1–14	403
118	406–7, 409, 419, 545n228	11:2	101, 122n86
		11:4	404
118:25–26	412	11:5	462
118:26	406, 408, 545n228	11:11–12	196
132:10–11	403	11:13–14	404
145:1	154	14	620
146	326n118	14:9–20	804
146:6	401n50	14:11	804
146:10	154	14:12	169
149:4	401n50	14:12–14	620
		14:13	169
Proverbs		14:14	620n68
9:18	805	15:30	462
10:27	458n108	19:1	616
25:6–7	242	19:3	796
25:21–22	222	24:21–23	153
27:17	9n1	24:22–23	160
		24:23	205
Ecclesiastes		24–27	805
4:9–12	199n56	25:6	221
8:14	173	25:6–9	221
		25:8	805–6, 816
Isaiah		25:10–12	221
1:4	330	26:14	805
1:16–17	115n57, 116n64	26:19	174, 805
2:1–4	472	26–27	221
2:2–4	438	27:12–13	123n90
3:14	205	27:13	196
4:4	118n68	28:1–4	459
6:5	153	28:1–9	221
7:3	190	28:7	456
7:9	190	28:7–13	460
8:16–20	190	28:16	190

29:1	460	58:7	221
29:4	796	60:21	812
29:13	650	61	204, 326, 462, 474, 650n152
30:15	115n55		
33:22	153	61:1–2	166, 174, 368, 563
35:5–6	174, 325, 368, 405	61:1–11	200n60, 202
37:3	617n65	63:1–6	509n99
37:6	658	63:15–64:1	158n13
37:23	658	63:17	196
37:31	190	65	158
40	166	65:13	158
40:3	155, 166, 612n53	65:20	158
40:9	154, 166	65:25	158
41:10	122n85	65–66	472
41:21	153	66	158
42:1	109, 143n162, 205	66:3	456
42:19	190	66:10–11	473
43:5–6	208	66:14	158
43:10	190	66:15–21	240
43:12	190	66:20	399n42
44:6	153		
45:6–7	776	Jeremiah	
49:4–7	202	3:16	190
49:6	196, 205	3:18	196
52:7	153–54, 166, 643n125, 795	6:13	456
		7:9–15	456
53	534, 568, 571n337, 841	7:11	435, 437, 444, 466, 467n153
53:7	801n103	7:34	437, 469
53:7–8	531	10:6–7a	153
53:8	531	10:7b	153
53:10	801n103	10:8–9	153
53:12	571n337	10:10	153
54:12	195	13:24	123n90
55:7	115	15:7	123n90
56	474, 839	16:5	221
56:1–8	472n182	16:14	300
56:6	272n93	17:24–25	399n42
56:7	435, 437n34, 442–43, 468	17:24–26	403
		17:25	398n38
57:19	795	17:26	467n153
58	650n152	22:4	399n42
58:6–12	221	23:3	190

23:3–4	124n93	36:25–26	118n68
23:3–8	751n259	36:26–27	122n87
23:5	403	37	806, 811
23:5–6	352	37:19	196
23:11–12	456	37:21–24	124n93
25:15–31	509n99	37:21–28	472n182
29:14	196	37:24–25	403, 751n259
30:3	196	37:26–28	800
30:8–9	190	37:40–46	472n182
30:9	751n259	39:17–20	221
31:7–10	196	40–48	840
31:9	196	47:13	197
31:10	190	47:21	197
31:34	563	47–48	563
32:36–41	196	48:1	197
33:18	467n153	48:19	197
		48:23	197
Lamentations		48:29	197
4:13	456	48:31	195, 197
Ezekiel		Daniel	
2:1	341	2	642
2:3	341	2:37	155
2:6	341	2:39–42	155
2:8	341	2:44	156
8:7–13	221	4:21(24)	166n34
16:4	116n64	5:18	155
16:9	116n64	7	159, 166, 342n173, 593n9, 615–16, 617n65, 634n105, 638, 642–44, 646–50, 655
18:30–32	115n55		
23:6	398n38		
27:14	399n42		
28:2	620		
29:3	620	7:9	205, 361, 643
32:21	805	7:9–13	615
32:36–41	197	7:13	122n85, 341n171, 545n228, 593, 597, 614, 616, 626, 638, 644, 652, 654, 843
34:4	161		
34:8	161		
34:15–16	190	7:13–14	341, 642, 647, 650n150, 660, 844
34:22–23	124n93		
34:23–24	751n259	7:14	122n84
34:25	161, 800	7:18	156
35:12	617n65	7:19–28	205
36:8–11	196	7:21–27	615

7:22	157, 166	Micah	
7:27	156	2:12	197
8:11	156	3:9–12	456
8:17	341	4:1–3	438
9:12	205	4:1–4	472
9:21–23	156	4:6–7	191, 197
9:25	642	5:1–4	751n259
10	155	5:2	122n85
10:13	156	5:3–4	648
10:13–14	156	6:6–8	432
12	807	7:18–19	191
12:1	122n85		
12:2	807, 814	Nahum	
12:4	157	2:14	456
12:9	157		
		Habakkuk	
Hosea		2:5–6	456
3:5	751n259	2:8	456
4:4–9	456	2:8–11	456
4:16–19	221	2:17	456
6:1–3	806	2:20–23	751n259
6:2	778, 816		
6:6	262, 275, 279, 283	Zephaniah	
6:9	456	3:1–4	456
7:1–16	221	3:8–20	472n182
13:14	806	3:12	191
14:2	432	3:15	153
		3:16–19	153
Joel		3:17	153
2:28–29	122n87	3:19–20	197
3:18	118n68	9	398, 400
4:11	401n50		
		Zechariah	
Amos		4:10	620
4:1	221	6:9–15	472n182
5:15	191	6:12	629n92
6:4–7	221	6:12–13	472
9:11	472	9	398, 401
9:14	197	9:1–7	400
		9:8	400
Jonah		9:9	122n85, 384, 397n37, 399n42, 400, 401nn49–50, 402, 420,
1:17	816		

	474, 491, 568n322, 838	14:16	153, 438
		14:17	153
9:9–10	400–401	14:20–21	461
9:10	401, 648	14:21	436, 444, 452, 461
9:11	568		
9–13	400n48	Malachi	
10:8–10	197	1:6–14	456
11	489	1:11	438, 524
11:1	460	1:14	524
11:12	488	2:7–8	456
12:7–13:1	751n259	3:1	324n111
12:10	623	3:1–4	472n182
13:1	118n68	3:1–5	456
13:7	576	3:2	122n85
14	400n48, 474	3:2–3	118n68, 122n88
14:4–21	472n182	4:1	123n90
14:8	118n68	4:5	122n85, 324n111
14:9	153		

Apocrypha / LXX

1 Kingdoms		Additions to Esther	
1:33	399n44	14:5	192
		14:17	223
2 Maccabees			
6:18–7:42	223	Judith	
		2:17	399n42
Susanna		10:5	223
44–59	610	10:10–13	223
		12:5–20	223
1 Esdras		13:6–11	223
1	497n53	15:11	399n42
5:1	193–94, 206		
5:4	193–94, 206	1 Maccabees	
7:8	193	1:62–63	223
8:54	193–94, 206	2	621
8:65–66	193	2:6	621, 628n90
		2:14	654
2 Esdras		2:27–38	252
13	341	4:36	406n60
		6:34	509n99
		7:37	438n38

9:27	127n103	36	197
9:73	205	36:13	197
13:51	406n60	36:16	197
14:41	324n111	36:18	197
		36:19	197
2 Maccabees		36:21	197
1:27–28	197	37:26	808
2:18	197	39:9	808
3:26	789n58	39:26	509n99
3:33	789n58	44:23–45:1	192
5:2	789n58	45:11	193
7:9	809, 815	47:11	751n259
7:10–11	809	47:22	751n259
7:14	808–9	48:10	197
7:22–23	815	50:15	509n99
7:28–29	809		
7:36–38	809	Tobit	
10:7	406n60	1:4	192
12:44	809	2:5	114n49
14:46	809	2:9	114n49
		3:17	175
3 Maccabees		4:12	192
3:2–5	223	4:17	223
		5:9–14	192
4 Maccabees		8:3	175
5–18	223	13:16–17	472
10:4	808	14:4–7	472
13:13	808	14:5	473n186
16:13	808	14:7	197
18:23	808		
		Wisdom of Solomon	
Sirach		2:23	808
9:9	223	3:1–4	808, 815
10:14	401n50	3:7–8	815
13:8–13	223	5:1	815
14:10	223	5:2	623
17:17	156	5:4–6	815
17:28	808	5:15–16	815
24:19–23	219	5:16	815
30:17	808	5:23	123n90
31:12–32:2	223	6:19	808
31:25	114n49		
34:25	114n49		

New Testament

Q		3:10	125–26
3:7–9	98–99	3:11	98n5, 113n45, 114,
3:16	98n5, 674n14		115n56, 117, 123–25,
3:16–17	98–99		674n14
3:21–22	99n7, 104	3:11–12	121
4:1–13	98	3:12	117n65, 121n83,
4:3	98		125–26
4:9	98	3:13	98
6:22–23	674	3:13–17	96–97
7:1–10	98n6	3:14–15	103, 108, 133n129,
7:18–23	98n6		827
7:30	647	3:16	111
7:31–35	674	3:17	103
7:31–35	230	4:1–11	159, 167, 387n11
11:14–23	98n6	4:12	136
11:47–51	674	4:17	332n140
12:8	647	4:17–16:20	332n140
13:28–29	236, 239	4:18–22	203
13:34–35	674	5	524
14:27	674–75n17, 677, 689	5:3	832n10
17:24	647	5:13–16	202
17:26	647	5:17	286
22:28–30	185n11	5:17–48	276
		5:19	315n74
Matthew		5:20	369
1:1–4	332n140	5:23–24	432, 438, 467
1:16–19	229	5:37	537n197
1:18	171n45	6:1	369
1:20	171n45	6:11	203, 238
2:6	205	6:25–34	203
2:16–18	364	7:6	202
3:1	130	7:7–9	238
3:2	115	7:11	171n45
3:5	127n108	7:13–14	794
3:5–6	130	8:1–8	465n139
3:6	115	8:1–9:34	203
3:7–10	58n129, 115, 120, 124, 128n113, 387n11	8:2	832n10
		8:4	438, 467
3:7–12	173	8:5–13	202
3:8	115	8:11–12	208–9, 239
3:9	120, 207	8:14–15	58, 174

8:18–26	465n139	11:16–19d	231n65
8:19–22	830	11:18	113n46
8:20	203, 341, 817	11:19	231n66, 832
8:22	65–66	11:25–26	109
8:28–34	201	11:25–27	109
8:33	300	12:1	259, 274
9:2–8	434	12:1–4	262
9:10	231	12:1–8	255, 261n53
9:10–11	832n10	12:1–14	274n101, 284n148
9:12–13	262	12:3–4	262
9:13	467n158, 832	12:5	274n101, 275
9:13a	229	12:5–7	255–56, 262
9:14	135	12:6	275, 284, 467n157
9:35–11:1	199–200	12:7	279, 283, 467n158
10:1	174, 199, 202–3	12:8	256, 284, 833
10:1–4	141	12:9–14	262, 281
10:2–4	181	12:11	266, 281
10:5–6	199n57, 201, 312, 799	12:11–12	263, 265n69, 279
10:7–8	151, 174	12:11–12a	262
10:8	174, 832n10	12:12	279
10:9–10	461n119	12:18	171n45
10:9–15	203	12:22–32	172
10:18	202	12:23	341n171
10:23	647	12:24	591, 828
10:32	647	12:27	170n43
10:37–38	830	12:27–28	109
10:37–39	431n7	12:28	39, 141, 166, 170–71n46, 203, 327
10:38	675n16		
11	829	12:29	447n63
11:1	182	12:31–32	109
11:2	135	12:32	171n45
11:2–3	325	13:9	831
11:2–6	108, 141, 186n15, 202, 207, 325, 368, 829	13:15–16	831
		13:17	829
11:3	123	13:25	315n74
11:4–5	832n10	13:33	238
11:5	166, 171n46, 174, 474	13:41	647
11:7–15	141, 324	13:42	161
11:7–19	208	13:43	831
11:9	121n81	13:50	161
11:9–11	137	13:55	133n128
11:15	831	14:1	338
11:16–19	138	14:1–12	132n124, 328

14:3–4	131	20:18–19	816
14:4	325	20:20–21	205
14:12	135n135	20:29–34	388, 408n71
14:13	328n124	21:1–11	383, 387
14:16–24	238	21:2	397
14:20	199	21:5	401n50
15:4–9	650	21:5–7	397n37
15:10–20	465n139	21:6	412
15:17–20	369	21:7	397n37
15:21	311n56	21:8	412
15:21–28	201	21:9	406, 837
15:24	201n63, 312, 799	21:11	837
16:13	300, 341	21:12	442
16:13–20	294, 296, 300	21:12–13	202
16:16	299–300, 314n72, 816	21:12–16	439, 441
16:17	300	21:12–17	839
16:17–19	66, 314, 318–21	21:13	442
16:17b–19	295n6, 297n7	21:14	433
16:18	65–66, 300	21:14–17	443
16:19	175, 300, 319, 801	21:15	433
16:20	300, 332, 347	21:21	443
16:21	300, 314n72, 332n140, 816	21:23	434
		21:23–27	141
16:21–23	297–98	21:24–27	137
16:21–28:20	332n140	21:25–27	324
16:22	300, 314n72, 332	21:26	121n81, 127n108
16:23	313	21:29	238
16:24	675n16	21:31	832n10
16:24–25	431n7	21:31–32	127n108
16:24–28	830	21:31b–32	237
16:27–28	341	21:32	237
17:11	278n119	21:33–45	590
17:22–23	816	21:33–46	202
17:24–27	434, 455, 467, 470	21:43	208, 327
18:15	65	22:31–32	319
18:18	175, 319, 801	22:33–39	650
18:34	439	23:10	339n162
19:21	832n10	23:16–22	432
19:28	141, 182, 183n5, 185, 188, 190, 204, 205n83, 208–9, 563n298, 647	23:37	842
		23:37–39	433, 465n142
		24:1–2	448, 465
20:17	182	24:14	202
20:17–19	199	24:27	647

24:30	341, 647	27:13	430n6, 734
24:37	647	27:14	726n175, 734
24:39	647	27:15–23	762
24:44	647	27:16–17	741
24:51	439	27:17	741
25:14–30	410n73	27:19	733
25:31	204, 647	27:20–23	344n181
25:31–46	221	27:22	741
26:6	636n108, 832n10	27:24	590, 682
26:6–13	232	27:24–25	679n31, 733, 737, 762
26:13	202	27:26	682, 734, 762
26:14	182	27:27–31	734, 762
26:20	182	27:29	741, 846
26:20–25	199	27:32	762
26:24	484n12	27:33–36	762
26:26–29	62	27:35	684n43, 797n85
26:28	563, 841	27:37	344n181, 345, 603, 745, 748, 762
26:31	735		
26:32	802	27:38	344, 684n43, 700
26:39	109	27:38–44	763
26:55	344, 432n12	27:40	448, 465n142, 466
26:56	735	27:42	744
26:57–58	735	27:45–54	763
26:57–68	590	27:51	763
26:60	626n84	27:55–56	735, 763
26:61	448, 465n142, 466	27:57	784n37
26:63	632n98, 638, 744	27:57–61	763
26:63–68	342	27:60	783
26:64	204, 593, 614, 638, 647, 843	27:62–66	679n31, 763, 787–88
		27:63–64	627
26:65	592–93	27:64	683n39
26:75	735	27:65	593
27:1–2	739, 741, 762	27:65–66	788
27:2	726n175	28	792, 802
27:3–10	741n223, 762	28:1	785
27:7–10	679n31	28:2–4	788
27:9–10	187n19	28:2–5	789
27:11	726n175, 734, 741, 846	28:8	797
		28:10	802
27:11–14	344n181, 682, 762	28:11–15	788
27:11–23	393	28:15	788
27:12	734, 739, 740n222, 741	28:16–20	779, 780n22, 782, 791–92

872   *Ancient Texts Index*

28:17	780, 796–97	1:29–31	58
28:18–20	793–94	1:30–31	174
28:19	793	1:32–34	151
		1:34	174, 334n146, 336, 408n71
Mark			
1:1	599, 634, 637	1:37	258
1:1–6	775	1:40	832n10
1:4	105, 113nn45–47, 115, 130	1:40–45	56n124, 63
		1:44	138n148, 438, 467
1:4b	133	1:45	258
1:5	113n48, 114–15, 127n108, 130, 785	2	599n19
		2:1	264, 310
1:5b	133	2:1–3:6	262n55, 270n89, 284n149
1:6	81		
1:7	123, 125, 168	2:1–12	595
1:7–8	121, 173	2:2	411
1:8	80, 114, 117, 124, 775	2:2–12	434
1:9	95, 98, 105, 106n23, 114	2:7	258, 599
		2:10	646n138
1:9–10	114	2:13–17	227
1:9–10a	105	2:14	230
1:9–11	96–97, 104, 106	2:15	228n51, 229–30, 411, 543n223
1:10	111, 113n48, 171n45		
1:10a	95	2:15–16	832n10
1:10b–11	95, 105	2:15–17	63
1:11	143n162, 168, 336	2:15b	228
1:12	171n45	2:16	63, 230, 258
1:12–13	159, 167	2:17	227, 229–30, 832
1:13	161	2:18	135
1:14	136, 139n153	2:18–19	171n46
1:14–15	59, 165, 168, 784	2:23	274n99, 310
1:15	59–60, 151, 166, 174, 346n193	2:23–3:6	260n43
		2:23–27	648
1:16–20	203	2:23–28	255, 260, 262, 270n89, 279
1:20	228		
1:21	284n149, 310	2:24	257, 273
1:21–28	276, 437	2:25–26	256–58, 261
1:23–27	151	2:27	255, 257, 260–61, 276–77, 283, 287
1:24	330		
1:24–25	301	2:27–28	255, 257–58
1:25	332, 334n146, 408n71	2:28	257, 260–61, 276, 284, 287, 833
1:27	173		
1:28	258	3	170

3:1	310	5:22–42	816
3:1–5	266n72	5:26	411
3:1–6	262–64n66, 268n82, 270, 277, 279	5:35	561n293
		5:41	265
3:1ff	279	5:43	334n146
3:2	263, 277, 785	6	132n124, 792
3:4	263–65, 277	6:1–2	132n124
3:5	438	6:1–6	284
3:6	258, 263–65, 278, 613n55, 817	6:3	133n128
		6:4	326, 366, 780
3:7–8	446n58	6:6b–7	141
3:11	336, 599, 634, 637	6:7	151, 185, 202–3
3:12	332, 334n146, 339, 408n71	6:7–13	174, 199–200
		6:8	207
3:13–15	182	6:8–11	203
3:13–19a	141	6:10	261
3:14	185, 199, 200n61	6:13	174
3:14a	183n5	6:14	312
3:15	202	6:14–16	132n124, 338
3:16–19	181	6:14–29	328
3:16a	183n5	6:14–31	331
3:20	310	6:15	326, 366
3:21	780	6:16	310
3:22	168, 170, 591, 599, 828	6:17–18	131
3:22–27	169	6:17–29	132n124, 207
3:22–30	172	6:18	325
3:23–27	168	6:29	135n135
3:26–27	163	6:30	199
3:27	160, 171, 175, 203, 447n63	6:30–44	220, 238
		6:30ff	201n64
3:28–29	109	6:31–32	328n124
3:29	599	6:32	312
3:30	599	6:33–44	798
3:31–32	780	6:34	411
4:9	831	6:39	239
4:10	182, 185, 198	6:39–40	239
4:23	831	6:40	239
5:1	309–12	6:43	199
5:1–19	312	6:44	634
5:1–20	201	6:45–52	792
5:3	160	7:1–4	634
5:7	336, 634, 637	7:4	113n48
5:17	309, 311	7:6–10	650

7:9	261	9:1	261, 651n154
7:22	599n21	9:2	310
7:24	309–12	9:2–8	302
7:24–29	312	9:7	336
7:24–30	201	9:7–9	336
7:31	309, 311–12	9:9	332, 334n146, 336, 408n71, 598
7:36	334n146		
8:1–10	238	9:12	278n119
8:7	634	9:30	310
8:10	309, 311–12	9:31	598, 816
8:11–13	165, 170	9:33	310
8:18	831	9:35	182, 185, 199
8:22	312	9:41	339n162
8:22–26	311	10:1	310
8:22a	309–10	10:11	199n57
8:26	334n146	10:17	310
8:27	299, 310, 312, 336, 341	10:17–22	283
8:27–9:13	302n16	10:21	832n10
8:27–28	347	10:25	531
8:27–30	294, 296, 299, 302–3	10:32	182, 185, 310
8:27a	310–11	10:32–34	199
8:27b	310–11	10:33–34	816
8:28	299	10:34	598
8:29	299, 314n72, 331, 336, 816	10:35–40	758
		10:35–45	534
8:29–30	301, 408n71	10:39	598
8:29a	336	10:45	535n190, 563, 575
8:30	299, 314n72, 332, 334n146, 347	10:45–52	410
		10:46	310
8:31	299, 313n66, 314n72, 332n140, 336, 341, 348, 598, 603, 816	10:46–52	388, 408n71
		10:48	408n71
		10:52	408n71
8:31–32	365	11	411, 491
8:31–33	297–98	11:1	310, 396
8:32	299, 332, 348	11:1–3	397
8:32b	313n66, 332n140	11:1–6	396
8:33	167n37, 299, 313, 332, 348	11:1–10	71, 383, 387, 389, 410
		11:2	397
8:34	390, 675n16	11:2–6	496
8:34–9:1	830	11:7–10	396, 758
8:34–35	431n7	11:8	411–12
8:38	336, 647	11:8–10	405
9	651n154	11:9	406

11:9–10	412, 634	14	344n184, 517, 610, 633n104, 634, 651, 652n155, 653
11:10	634		
11:11	182, 185, 199		
11:12	310	14:1–2	487, 498, 841
11:15	310, 430n3, 442, 462	14:1–9	512n111
11:15–18	68, 440, 442	14:2	549, 561n293
11:15–19	202, 437, 839	14:3	543n223, 832n10
11:16	430n3, 433, 436–37, 442, 447, 454, 468, 471	14:3–9	232
		14:9	202, 505
11:16–17	436	14:10	182, 185, 497n54
11:17	430n3, 442–43	14:10–11	487, 498–99
11:18	453	14:10–16	484n12
11:19	446n58	14:12	495–96, 548, 554–55, 557, 559
11:23	443		
11:25	443	14:12–16	397, 489, 507, 542
11:27	310	14:12–17	841
11:27–33	141, 324, 421, 640	14:17	182, 185, 497n54
11:28	434	14:17–20	199
11:28–33	137	14:17–21	497, 499
11:32	121n81, 127n108	14:18	502, 507, 561n293
12	638–40	14:20	185, 502, 548–49
12:1–12	202	14:21	502–3n76
12:12	605	14:22	483n10, 507, 634
12:12–16	605	14:22–25	62, 504, 507, 560
12:13	605	14:22–26	484n12
12:13–17	434n21	14:23	507
12:16	745n237	14:24	483n10, 571n337, 841
12:17	605n35	14:25	482nn4, 7, 483n10, 484n12, 505, 512, 525, 572–73, 574n353, 576n356, 579
12:18	808		
12:25–27	261		
12:29–31	650		
12:32–34	467n158	14:26	647–48
12:35–37	638, 641, 645, 649	14:27	735, 794
12:36	611n48	14:27–31	502n74
12:41–13:2	470	14:28	598, 614, 802
12:41–42	832n10	14:36	109, 534, 598
12:41–44	433	14:43	182, 185–86, 497n54, 561n293
13	595n12		
13:1–2	448, 465	14:45	534
13:9	598	14:48	700
13:9–12	598	14:50	735
13:10	202	14:50–52	796
13:26	341, 616, 647	14:50–64	595

14:53–65	590, 602	15:14–15	434n21
14:53–72	598	15:15	682, 702, 734, 736, 756, 762
14:55–59	604		
14:58	448, 465n142, 466	15:16–20	346, 734, 762
14:60	605	15:18	740–41, 846
14:60–65	626	15:21	762
14:61	336, 744	15:22–25	762
14:61–62	342n173, 344, 609, 613, 626, 651	15:24	187n19, 680, 684n43, 689, 797n85
14:61–63	631	15:26	165, 345, 346n193, 603, 745, 748, 762
14:61–64	592		
14:62	592, 598, 609, 617n65, 618n67, 642, 644, 650–51, 843	15:27	344, 684n43, 700
		15:27–32	763
		15:28	763n295
14:63	593, 620	15:29	448, 465n142, 466, 599
14:64	592, 599, 602–3		
14:66–72	598	15:32	336, 346n193, 744
15:1	602, 739–40, 741n223, 762	15:33–39	763
		15:39	336, 434n21, 599, 634, 637
15:1–3	740		
15:1–5	702	15:40–41	735, 763
15:1–15	393, 702, 705, 733	15:42	555n274
15:1–26	344n181	15:42–47	763
15:2	345, 346n193, 392, 419, 703, 733–34, 740–41n223	15:43	607, 735n211, 783
		15:46	783
		15:47	783
15:2–4	756	15:53–54	735
15:2–5	682, 702, 762	16:1	786
15:3	734, 739–40n222, 846	16:1–8	48, 790n63
15:3–4	430n6	16:2	785, 790
15:3–5	345	16:3	683n39
15:4	734, 740n222	16:3–4	683n39
15:5	434n21, 703, 734, 736, 756	16:4	683n39, 787
		16:5–7	791
15:6	549	16:6	48
15:6–10	702	16:6–7	598, 600
15:6–14	762	16:7	802
15:8–9	702	16:11	796
15:9	346, 392, 740–41	16:13	796
15:10	434n21, 736	16:14	796
15:11–14	702	16:15–16	793
15:12	346, 740–41		
15:13	383		

Luke		3:19–20	105, 131
1	129	3:21	103
1:1–4	55, 384n6, 390, 392	3:21–22	96–97, 105
1:3	384n6, 410	3:22	103, 111, 171n45
1:5	116	4:1	167, 171n45
1:5–25	129	4:1–13	159, 167, 387n11
1:9	432n11	4:14	136
1:17	120n77	4:16–19	832n10
1:21	432n11	4:16–20	650n152
1:22	432n11	4:16–21	109
1:23	116	4:16–23	325
1:39–45	129	4:16–30	174, 202
1:57–79	129	4:18–19	799
1:63	746n243	4:18–21	141
1:66	170	4:38–39	58
1:77	799	4:39	174
1:80	129–30	4:41	743
2:7	817	4:44	446n58
2:11	743	5:8	832
2:14	795	5:14	138n148, 467
2:18–20	132n124	5:17–26	434
2:22	138n148	5:24	340n168
2:26	743	5:30	832n10
2:35	241n111	5:32	799, 832
3	827n2	5:33	135
3:2	130, 235	6:1	273
3:3	115, 130, 799	6:1–5	255
3:6	113n47	6:4	271
3:7–9	58n129, 115, 120, 124, 128n113, 173, 387n11	6:5	256, 284, 833
		6:6–11	262–63
3:8	115, 120, 207, 799	6:8	280
3:9	125–26	6:12–16	141
3:10–14	115, 127n108	6:13	182, 199
3:13	235	6:14–16	181, 185
3:15	121, 127n108	6:20	832n10
3:15–17	173	6:20–21	171n46
3:16	98n5, 113n45, 114, 117, 123–25, 674n14	6:21	234
		6:25	234
3:16–17	121	7	829
3:17	117n65, 121nn82–83, 125–26	7:1–10	202
		7:11–15	816
3:18	127n108	7:11–17	220
3:19	136, 325	7:13	234

7:18	135	9:10	199, 300, 312, 328n124
7:18–20	325		
7:18–22	368	9:10–17	798
7:18–23	108, 141, 186n15, 202, 829	9:12	199
		9:17	199
7:19	123	9:18	300, 341
7:21–23	325	9:18–20	299
7:22	166, 174, 474	9:18–21	294, 296
7:22–23	832n10	9:19	300
7:24–30	141, 324	9:20	299–300, 330, 743, 816
7:24–35	208	9:21	300, 347
7:26	121n81	9:22	297–98, 300, 341, 603, 816
7:26–28	137		
7:29–30	127n108	9:23	390
7:31–35	138, 229	9:23–24	431n7
7:32	234	9:23–27	830
7:33	113n46	9:26	533n181
7:34	63, 832	9:44	816
7:35	231n66	9:57–60	830
7:35–50	832	9:58	203, 341
7:36	543n223	9:60	65–66
7:36–50	63, 232, 233nn75–77, 237, 244, 431	9:61–62	830
		10:1	199n57
7:41–43	233	10:1–12	199
7:47	233	10:1–16	200
7:47–50	233, 434	10:4	461n119
7:48	233	10:4–12	203
7:49	543n223	10:5–6	203
7:50	795	10:7	199n57
8:1	182	10:7–8	242n118
8:1–3	185	10:8	199n57
8:3	735n211	10:8–12	199n57
8:4	119n74	10:9	174, 203
8:8	831	10:11	174, 203
8:16	461	10:17–19	169
8:26–39	201	10:17–20	169n39
9:1	174, 202–3	10:18	110n38, 169n39, 203
9:1–2	141, 174	10:19	160
9:1–6	199	10:19–20	162
9:3	461n119	10:21–22	109
9:3–4	242n118	10:23–24	171n46
9:3–5	203	10:24	829
9:7–9	328, 338	10:25–29	650n151

10:25–37	56n124	13:34–35	433, 465n142
10:27–35	220	14:1–6	267–68, 280–81
10:30	437	14:1–24	241, 242n117, 832
10:38–42	242, 497n54	14:2–6	241
11	242	14:3	281
11:1	135	14:4	281
11:3	203	14:5	262, 265n69, 268, 281
11:5–8	238	14:6	281
11:13	171n45	14:7–14	241
11:14–23	172	14:13–14	832n10
11:15	170, 591, 828	14:15–24	63
11:16	170, 172	14:16–24	241
11:19	170	14:17	537n200
11:19–20	109, 169	14:21	832n10
11:20	141, 151, 166, 170–71n46, 203, 327	14:25–27	830
		14:26–27	431n7
11:37–54	240, 241n110	14:27	675n16
11:38	113n48	14:34–35	202
11:50–51	514	14:35	831
12:8	336, 647	15	243
12:10	109	15:1	832
12:22–31	203	15:1–2	242
12:37	543n223	15:1–32	832
12:39	533n181	15:2	63
12:46	439	15:3–32	242
12:50	534	15:11–32	237n90
13:1	717, 718n148	15:26	748
13:1–5	718	16:19–31	832n10
13:4	718	16:23	623
13:10–17	266, 268, 280, 834	17:1	503n76
13:12	175	17:10–17	832n10
13:13	280	17:14	438
13:14	277, 280	17:22	647
13:15	280	17:24	647
13:15–16	266	17:26	647
13:16	160, 174–75, 281	17:30	647
13:23–24	794	17:31	447n63, 460
13:28–29	239	17:33	431n7
13:28–30	208–9	18:9–14	63, 467
13:31–33	207, 331	18:31	182
13:31f	338	18:31–33	816
13:33	842	18:31–34	199
13:34	842	18:35–43	388, 408n71, 410

19:1–10	63, 234, 244, 410, 832n10	22:14–20	532n180, 540n213, 544
19:2	234	22:15	484n12, 542, 548, 555
19:8	235–36	22:15–16	554
19:8b	235	22:15–18	512, 536, 539, 560, 572–73, 579
19:9	236		
19:10	235–36, 534, 832	22:15–19	522n145, 532
19:11	328, 410	22:15–20	62, 523n151, 532
19:12–27	410	22:16	572n344
19:27	439	22:16–18	537n200
19:28–40	383, 392	22:17	566, 572
19:28–44	410	22:17–18	538
19:29	412	22:18	525
19:36	412	22:19	532, 535–36, 538n203, 841
19:37–38	412		
19:38	406	22:19–20	506, 529, 532n179, 533, 535, 537n200, 539–40, 560, 573, 578
19:39–40	838		
19:45	442		
19:45–47	432	22:20	534, 841
19:45–48	202, 440, 442, 839	22:21	499, 532, 534, 536
19:46	442	22:21–23	199, 204n79
19:47–20:1	446n58	22:21–38	575
19:47–48	453	22:24–27	531
20:1–8	141, 324	22:24–30	573
20:2	434	22:25–27	534
20:2–8	137	22:27	543n223
20:6	121n81, 127n108	22:28–30	141, 188, 204
20:9–10	202	22:29	190, 534, 563n298
20:20	726n175	22:29–30	206, 563n298
21:1–6	470	22:30	182, 185, 208–9
21:2–3	832n10	22:35	200
21:5–6	448, 465	22:35–38	573
21:27	341, 647	22:37	534
21:28–40	387	22:42	109, 534
21:37	543, 606	22:54–55	735
21:37–38	446n58	22:54–71	590
22:3	182	22:62	735
22:7	548	22:66–23:1	762
22:8	484n12	22:67	605, 632n98, 743
22:14	199	22:69	614, 617n65, 638, 647, 843
22:14–18	532n180		
22:14–19	532	22:70	593, 744
		22:71	592–93

Ancient Texts Index

23:1	344n181, 739, 741	23:48	679n31, 702n92, 763
23:1–5	742	23:49	735, 763
23:1–7	393	23:50–56	763
23:2	392, 419, 430n6, 627, 733–34, 739, 741–42	23:51	784n37
		23:53	783
23:2–3	846	23:56	786
23:2–5	682, 762	24	531, 554n269, 791, 793
23:3	591, 741		
23:4	603, 733, 736, 756, 762	24:1	785, 794
23:5	741–42	24:5	795
23:6–12	679n31, 682, 702n92, 733, 762	24:6–7	793
		24:7	341n171
23:8	338	24:11	797
23:10	739	24:13	794
23:12	734	24:13–24	803
23:13–16	679n31, 702n92, 733, 762	24:13–32	365
		24:13–35	48
23:13–24	393	24:13–43	798
23:14	603, 736, 742	24:20	603
23:16	530n170	24:21	328
23:17	530n170	24:22–23	786
23:17–18	530n170	24:25–27	793
23:17–23	762	24:29	794
23:18	530n170	24:30–31	798
23:19	530n170	24:33	794
23:21	383	24:34	48, 314, 779, 782, 791, 795, 849n30
23:22	733, 736, 762		
23–24	530, 537n200	24:34–35	795
23:24–25	682, 762	24:35	510, 794n75
23:26	762	24:36	779, 792n65, 794–95, 802
23:27–32	679n31, 702n92, 762		
23:32–38	344n181	24:36–43	779, 782, 791, 793
23:33	684, 700, 762–63, 797n85	24:36–49	791–92
		24:37–38	795
23:34	762	24:37–43	537
23:35	344	24:38	796
23:35–37	763	24:39	797
23:38	345, 745, 762	24:40	537, 792n65
23:39	700	24:41	796–97
23:39–43	763	24:41–43	798
23:45	432n11	24:44–46	793
23:45–46	536n195	24:44–49	793, 799n95
23:47	531	24:44–53	802

24:47	799	3:25	138–39
24:47–49	793, 798–99	3:25–26	135
24:48–49	799	3:26	130, 137–38, 207
24:49	793–94	3:26–30	139
24:50–51	781	3:27	139
24:50–53	782, 793	3:27–30	137, 139
		3:30	142n161
John		3:34	800
1	137	4	433n18
1:1–18	802n107	4:1	139
1:6–9	138n146	4:1–3	137, 139
1:11	446n55	4:2	136n140
1:15	138n146	4:4–42	202n68
1:19–42	138n146	4:17–18	397
1:23	130	4:21	433
1:25	113n45	4:25	299, 323
1:26–27	117	5:1–47	255
1:28	207	5:18	744
1:29	801	5:22	801
1:29–34	99, 104, 108	5:23	800
1:31	100	5:30	800–801
1:32	100, 105, 111	6	316n79, 329, 485n13, 512n111, 521, 524, 540
1:33	100		
1:33–34	106		
1:34b	100	6:1–15	392, 798
1:35	135	6:6	397
1:35–51	137	6:14	326, 366
1:41	299, 323	6:14–15	327–31, 347, 365, 367
1:48	397	6:15	406
1:49	392, 744n232	6:35–58	300
2:6	138	6:48–66	504
2:13–16	430n3	6:51	566n311
2:13–22	440, 442–43, 839	6:51–58	517
2:16–22	430n3	6:59	300, 317
2:17	444, 447	6:60–61	300
2:18	434	6:60–66	329, 331
2:19	446n54, 465n142, 466	6:64	300
2:19–21	449, 465	6:66–69	294, 296
3	135, 433n18	6:66–71	318
3:17	800	6:67	182, 185, 199, 300
3:22	137	6:67–69	300
3:22–24	136	6:67–72	329
3:22b–23a	137		

6:68–69	299–300, 314, 330, 338, 348, 431	12:13	392, 406, 744n232
		12:14	401n51
6:69	317, 330n136	12:15	397
6:70	182, 185, 301	12:16	397n37, 402
6:70–71	297–98, 330	12:17	413
6:71	182, 185, 301	12:25–26	431n7
7:5	780	12:34	646
7:12	627	13:1	553
7:13	796	13:2	553
7:19–24	255	13:3	553n267
7:22–23	275n104	13:10	544
7:37–39	800	13:18	187n19, 222, 224
7:47	627	13:26	561n293
8:15–16	801	13:27	498n60
8:16	800	13:27–30	502n72
8:17	199n56	14:16	800
8:18	800	14:16–17	800
9:1–41	255	14:22	185n14
9:6	280	14:26	800
9:22	796	14:27	795
9:39	801	15:21–24	801
9:41	801	15:26	800
10:1	437	16:7	800
10:8	437	16:32	735
10:23	801n104	16:33	795
10:33	744	17:12	187
10:36	330	17:18	800
10:40	130, 207	18:13	608n42
11:1	388	18:13–16	735
11:1–44	817	18:15	660
11:19–23	413	18:18	680
11:27	314	18:19	744
11:31	413	18:19–23	590
11:38–12:2	389	18:28	553, 739, 762, 841
11:48	416	18:28–19:16	702, 743
11:49–50	346	18:28–29	703
11:55–56	471n175	18:28–32	743n230
12	414	18:29	743
12:1–8	232	18:29–30	739
12:9	413	18:29–38	682, 762
12:12	389, 413	18:30	734, 743
12:12–13	388	18:31	602, 729n187, 743
12:12–15	383, 387, 392	18:31–32	733

18:33	703, 734, 743	19:19–22	346
18:33–19:16	393	19:20–22	762
18:33–37	344n181	19:21	748
18:33–38	703n95, 734, 743n230, 756	19:23–25	762
		19:25	735
18:33ff	346	19:25–27	762–63
18:34–37	734	19:28–30	763
18:34–38	733	19:31	553, 555n274
18:35	743	19:31–37	763
18:36–38	743	19:33–37	748
18:38	603, 743, 762	19:34	680, 797
18:38–40	743n230	19:38	784n37, 796
18:39	743	19:38–42	763
18:39–40	762	19:39–40	783
18:40	344	20	794
19:1	762	20:1	785
19:1–3	346, 743n230	20:1–23	791
19:2–3	734, 762	20:2	785
19:3	743, 846	20:11–18	791
19:4	603	20:19	795–96, 802
19:4–7	733, 762	20:19–23	779, 782, 791–92
19:4–8	743n230	20:20	797
19:6	383, 603, 743	20:21–23	793–94, 798, 799–800
19:7	734, 743	20:23	799, 801
19:8–11	762	20:24	182, 185, 794n75
19:8–12	733	20:24–29	791
19:9	703	20:26	789, 802
19:9–11	743n230	20:27	797
19:10	602	20:30–31	384n6, 802n107
19:10–11	734	21	798, 802
19:12	344n181, 743	21:9	798
19:12–15	346, 762	21:9–13	798
19:12–16	743n230	21:11–23	779
19:13–15	733	21:12–13	798
19:14	553	21:15–17	779
19:14–15	743	21:24–25	802n107
19:16	682, 734, 743, 762		
19:17	762	Acts	
19:18	344, 684n43, 689, 700n90, 705, 763, 797n85	1:1	384n6
		1:3	791, 793, 798, 802
		1:6–9	781–82
19:19	345–46, 745, 748, 762	1:6–11	410n74, 793, 802
		1:8	793–94, 799

1:9–11	793	7:52	603
1:12–15	412	7:56	341n171, 646
1:13	181	8	534
1:16	187n19	8:5	799
1:20	187n19	8:12	799
1:20–26	187n24	8:14	199n56
1:22	781, 799	8:32–33	531
2	525n156, 800n102	8:40	309
2:24	48	9	794
2:30–36	640	9:20	799
2:32	39, 48, 799	9:22	302
2:33	80	9:26–30	777
2:34–35	638	9:27	799
2:38	80, 799	10:1–11:18	218
2:42	218, 510	10:11	447n63
2:46	218, 432, 510	10:16	447n63
3:1–26	432	10:36	795
3:6	799	10:38	799
3:13	531	10:39	799
3:15	799	10:40	776
3:16	799	10:41	799
3:26	776	10:43	799
4:1–2	808	11:5	447n63
4:7	799	11:18	799
4:10	799	12:38	799
4:18	799	13:2	199n56
4:23–26	590	13–14	595n12
4:27	330, 703n93	13:23–29	640
4:28	170	13:27	603
4:30	799	13:28	603
4:33	799	13:29	787n51
5:31	799	13:31	799
5:32	799	13:33	776
5:36	128n110	15:13–21	780
5:37	730n189	15:27	199n56
5:40	799	15:36–40	199n56
5:41	799	15:36–41	595n12
5:42	432	16:18	799
6:2	187	16:34	218
6–7	432	17	813
6:7	607	17:1–7	419
6:8	799	17:7	392, 748n249
7:1	432	17:14	199n56

17:23	745n237	13	390n16
17:24	432	13:6–7	434
17:32	813		
18:25	135n135	1 Corinthians	
19:3–4	135n135	1:13	672n5
19:13	799	1:17–18	672, 689
19:17	799	1:22–23	672, 689
19:22	199n56	1:23	68, 393n23, 691, 693
19:24	432n11	2:1–2	672, 689
20:7	510, 778n11	2:2	393n23
20:7–12	218	2:8	393n23, 672n5
20:11	510	3:16–17	432
20:16	432	5:7	549, 552, 558
20:28	531, 534–35n190, 536n195	6:2–3	204n82
		6:14	776
21:26–27	432, 471	6:19	432
21:30–33	437n33	8–10	508
21:38	128n110	9:1	781, 803
22	794	9:6	199n56
22:15	799	10	522, 524–27n162, 540n213
22:17	432		
23:6–10	808	10:3	523
23:26–30	608	10:3–4	523
26	794	10:4	523
26:10	803	10:7	229n54
26:16	799	10:14–22	219, 521
27:33–36	218	10:16	510–11, 537n200, 561
27:35–36	510	10:16–17	522
28:18	603	10:18–20	524
		10:21	523n149
Romans		11	500, 511, 517, 520, 522–23, 525, 537, 540, 565, 573, 578
1:2–4	640		
1:3	420		
1:3–4	302	11:2	520n138
1:25	634	11:3–11	782n31
4:24	776	11:17–34	219
5:10	671	11:21	523
6:4	776	11:22	523
8:11	776	11:23	776
8:34	638	11:23–24	523
9:4	434n19	11:23–25	62, 523
9:5	634	11:23–26	505, 515
10:9	39, 48, 776	11:24	841

11:25	510, 523, 561n293, 841	Galatians	
		1:1	776
11:26	510n102, 523, 545n228, 547n234, 567n318, 574	1:17	673
		1:17–18	673
		1:22–23	672
11:27	523, 574	2	315, 510
11:27–32	219	2:1	673
11:28	522–23	2:11–15	237n95
11:29	523	2:19	672n4
15	778, 781–82, 785, 794	3:1	393n23, 672, 689
15:1–8	782	3:10–14	693
15:3–5	185–87, 510, 520n138, 777, 782, 815n141	3:13	693, 817
		5:11	672, 689, 691n62
15:3–8	775–77, 782, 803	5:24	672n4
15:3–9	848n28	6:12	672, 689
15:3–11	781	6:14	393n23, 672, 689
15:3b–5	314		
15:4	48, 778, 787n51, 790	Ephesians	
15:4–8	48	1:3	633n104
15:5	183n5, 314, 777n6, 779, 781, 791–92	1:20	638, 776
		2:16	393n23, 673n9
15:5–7	791	2:20–22	432
15:5–8	777		
15:6	777n6, 794n75	Philippians	
15:6–7	780	2:6–11	673, 817
15:6–8	777–78, 780, 782	2:7–8	673, 689, 693
15:7	781, 849n30	2:8	393n23, 673
15:8	779–81	2:17	508n95
15:8–10	803	3:18	673n9
15:14	775	4:7–8	693
15:15	776		
15:20	549	Colossians	
15:54	805, 816	1:13–16	302
16	522	1:20	393n23, 673n9
16:2	778n11	2:12	776
		2:14	673n9
2 Corinthians		2:15	817
4:14	776	3:1	638
6:15	160		
11:31	634	1 Thessalonians	
12:1–5	781	1:10	776
13:1	199n56	2:14–15	590
13:4	393n23, 672n5	2:16	173

1 Timothy
4:1	161	1:21	776
5:19	199n56	2:4–9	432
6:13	703, 705	2:13–17	390n16
		2:24	678, 689
		3:13–16	598

2 Timothy
2:8	420	4:12–16	598
4:6	508n95		

1 John
4:6	161

Titus
3:5	204n78

Jude
12	218

Hebrews
1:3	638
1:3–14	640
1:13	638
2:6	341n171, 646
5:7–8	678n27
5–10	432
8:1	638
9:10	113n48
10:5	504n81
10:12	638
10:28	199n56
12:2	638, 678, 689, 693, 696n81
13	524
13:10	219

Revelation
1:10	778n11
1:13	204n82, 341n171, 646
3:21	204n82
5:5	420
7:9	789n58
7:13	789n58
10:1	789n58
11:8	393n23, 678, 689
12:7	156
14:14	341n171, 646
19:7–9	218
20:4	204n82
20:10	161
20:14	161
21:12–14	195
21:14	187, 205n83
21:19–20	205n83
21:19–21	195
22:1–5	809
22:1–22:5	811
22:22	432

James
4:7	161
5:12	537n197

1 Peter
1:3	633n104

Old Testament Pseudepigrapha

1 Enoch
1:3	330	5:7	809
1:3–4	122n85	6:7	159
1:7–9	122n85	10	158
		10:1	330

10:4–6	158–59	70:1	643
10:17–22	809	70:2	659
13:1–2	159	71:1–17	659
13–15	809	71:14	643
22:3–13	809	71:17	643
23:3–4	632n100	77:2	632, 634, 653
25:1–5	809	89:59	156
37–71	122n84, 159, 809	89:72–73	457
39:5–8	809	90:28–29	472, 473n186
45:3	195, 659	91:13	472
46:1	159, 643	95:3	205
46:1–3	659	103:4	809
46:2–4	643	104:1–5	809
46:6	809	108:11–15	809
47:3	643		
48:2	643, 653	*2 Enoch*	
48:10	349	24	658
49:2–3	122n85	24:1–3	658
51:1–5	809	29:5	169n39
51:3	159, 195, 659	42:5	224
52:4	122n85, 349		
52:9	122n85	*3 Enoch*	
53:5–6	159	3–16	658–59
54:6	122n88	4:2–3	659
55:4	159	16	658
56:6–8	617n64	16:1–5	659
61:3–9	809		
61:8	159, 195, 659	*4 Ezra*	
62:1–2	195	4:42	810
62:2	122n86	7:28	349
62:2–3	159	7:29	349
62:2–8	659	7:29–30	690n60
62:2–14	643	7:32–42	810
62:3–5	623	7:75	808
62:5	204, 643	7:78	808
62:7	635, 643	7:79–87	810
62:8	809	7:94–99	810
62:9	159, 643	12	352
62:9–12	809	12:2	352
62:14	224, 643	12:32	349, 403–4
63:11	643	12:33	404
69:27	643	12:34	404
69:29	122n85, 204, 643	13	341, 643

13:3–14:9	351	*Joseph and Aseneth*	
13:52	336	3:2	199n56
		5:6	193, 197
2 Baruch		8:5	511n108
1:2	196	19:5	511n108
29	243n122		
29:3–4	224	*Jubilees*	
29:5–8	219, 238	1:15	197
30:1	349, 690n60	1:15–17	473
40:72	352	1:23	122n87, 124n97
49:2	810	1:27	473
49–52	810	2:17–21	271
50:2	810	2:25–33	252
51:2	810	4:20	658
51:3	810	10:8	158
62:5	196	17:15–18:13	158
68:5–6	473	21:16a	114n49
70:9	349	22:16	223
72:2–6	240	23	157–58
77:5–6	197	23:21	458
77:19	196	23:23b–31	157
78	197	23:24	157
78:1	196	23:24–25	158n13
78:7	197	23:26	157
		23:27	157
Apocalypse of Abraham		23:28	157
13:8	159	23:28–30a	158
14:3	159	23:29–30a	158
14:4	159	23:30	158n12
23:6–8	159	23:30b	158
		48:2–3	158
Apocalypse of Moses		48:9–12	158
29:11–13	114nn49, 51, 117n66	49	497n53
		50	158
29:12–13	117n67	50:1–13	252
39:2–3	658	50:5	158
Assumption of Moses		*Letter of Aristeas*	
9.4:13	114n49	35–51	194
Coptic Apocalypse of Elijah		*Life of Adam and Eve*	
35:17	623	12:1	169n39
37:3–4	621	47:3	658

Lives of the Prophets

21:3	122n88

Psalms of Solomon

1:8	458
2:3	458
3:11–12	810
8:9–13	458
8:28–32	197
11	197
11:2	197
11:2–3	208
17	324n112, 336, 352, 403
17:1–3	124
17:4	404, 751n259
17–18	352, 751, 828n8, 840
17:21	404, 653
17:21–22	751
17:21–46	124
17:22	404
17:22–31	240
17:26	369
17:26–30	472n183
17:26–34	197
17:28	205, 404
17:30	369, 404
17:32	369, 404, 751
17:37	122n86
17:40	122n85
17:44	197
18	324n112

Pseudo-Phocylides

97–115	810
103–4	810
1115	810

Sibylline Oracles

2:196–97	122n89
2:203–205	122n89
2:252–54	122n89
2:315	122n89
3:286–294	473
3:290	473n186
3:657	472n183
3:663	472n183
3:702–720	472n183
3:772–774	473
4:5	432n11
4:8	120n78
4:27–30	120n78
4:162–170	115n57, 116n59, 117n66, 120n78
4:165	114n49, 117n67
4:165–167	114n51, 117
4:179–192	810
4:188–89	124n97
5:414–432	473
5:420	473n186
5:432	473n186

Testament of Abraham

10–12	658
10–13	658
13:6	195
B 11:3–8	659

Testament of Asher

7:7	197

Testament of Benjamin

5:2	161
9:2	197, 472n183
10:5–6	621
10:6–10	810
10:7	195, 209

Testament of Dan

5:1	161
5:10–11	163
5:12–13	163
5:13b	163

Testament of Job

33	658
33:2–4	621

Testament of Judah

23:1–3	457
24:3	122n87
25	809
25:1	809
25:1–2	163, 195, 209
25:3b	161
25:4	810
25:4–5	164

Testament of Levi

2:3B	115n57, 116n59
2:3B1–2	114n49
2:3B1–14	117n66
2:3B2	114n51, 117n67
2:3B7–8	124n97
6:11	173
14:1–15:1	457
16:6	197
17:8–11	457
18	158n12, 160
18:2–9	350n201
18:11	122n87
18:11b–12	160
18:12	169, 175
18:13–14	164

Testament of Moses

5:3–6:1	457, 840n20
7:1–10	458
10	164n31

10:1	164, 168
10:1–2	828
10:2–3	124n93

Testament of Naphtali

8:3	161
8:4	160
8:4b	167

Testament of Reuben

6:5–12	350n201

Testament of Simeon

5:4–7:3	809
6:7	809

Testament of Solomon

1:14	175n55
3:6	168n38
5:1	175n55
5:6	175n55
13:17	175n55
20:16–17	169n39

Testament of Zebulun

9:1–3	196
9:5–10:4	810
9:7–9	164
9:8	162
10:1–4	810

Dead Sea Scrolls

1Q28a

11–22	194

1Q30

f1:2	301, 330

1QapGen

20:12–13	612n53

1QH

3:28–31	122n89
4:13	162n23
4:18–19	162n23
4:22	205
7:21–23	224
9:22	162n23
10:10–11	224

10:31–36	224	17:5–6	156
11:19–21	811	17:6	122n85
12:7–21	224		
13:23–25	500	1QMelch	
13:23b–24	224	2:18–20	324n111
16:12	124n97		
17:26	124n97	1QpHab	
		6:3–5	714n135
1QHa		6:14	612n53
10.9–14	811	7:7–13	840n20
14:29–30	811	9:2–16	840n20
		11:2–15	840n20
1QIsaª		12:1–10	840n20
3:15	612		
3:17	612	1QS	
28:16	612	1:18	160n17
30:15	612	1:18–2:2	134n132
40:7	612	2:5	160n17
42:5	612	2:19	160n17
42:6	612	2:21–22	239
45:8	612	2:25–3:9	118n71
49:22	612	3:4–9	114n49
50:5	612	3:6–9	116n59, 117n66, 118n68
52:4	612		
52:5	612	3:6–9	115n57
59:21	612	4:9	162n23
61:1	612	4:13	162n23
65:13	612	4:19	118n68
		4:20–21	124n97
1QM	197	4:21	122n87
1:1	160n17	4:25	205n84
1:5	160n17	5:2	224
1:13	160n17	5:7–15	118n71
1:15	160n17	5:10–11	224
2:1–3	195	5:13	224
3:5–6	161n21	5:13–14	117n66
3:14	195n48	5:14–18	224
4:2	160n17	6:2–5	528
5:1–2	195n48	8:1	186n15, 194
8:1	195	8:2	194
11:7–8	350n202	8:4–10	432
11:8	160n17	8:14	612n53
		9:1–6	432

9:11	122n85, 350	4Q252	
10:21	160n17	3:1–14	197
1QSa		4Q257	
2:17–22	225	5:7	162n23
2:17–27	528	5:12	162n23
2:21–22	569n328		
9:10–11	349n200	4Q285	324n112
9.11.1	327n121		
12–13	349n200	4Q385 frag. 2	811
4Q159		4Q390 frag. 2	
2:6–7	455	1:10	456n103
frags. 2–4:3–4	194		
		4Q416 frag. 23	
4Q164		6–8	811
4–6	195		
		4Q429	
4Q174	472	4	162n23
4Q180		4Q451	124n93
1:7	159		
		4Q491	
4Q185		1:13–17	658
1–2	162n23	8–10	162n23
4Q201		4Q504	197
3:9	159		
		4Q504 frag. 1–2	
4Q204		4:6–8	751n259
2:26	159		
		4Q504 frag. 2	
4Q209	632n100	5:6	658
4Q225		4Q508	
2 i 9	156, 158	frg. 2:2	197
2 ii 13	158		
2 ii 13–14	156	4Q513	224
2 ii 14	158		
		4Q514	224
4Q251			
2:5–6	279n123	4Q521	174, 207, 325–26, 368, 405, 811

1–13	326	4QPs37	
2.1	207	2:14	457, 840n20
5	326n118	3:6	457, 840n20
6–8	207	3:12	457, 840n20
7	326n118	4:8	457
12–13	207		
frag. 2, col. 2	204	4QSefM	
frag. 2	207	7:1–6	404
frag. 4	207		
		4QTest	
4Q524 frag. 14		1–8	350
2–4	787	5–8	327n121
		9–13	350
4Q541 frag. 9		14–20	122n85
1:2	690n60	14–22	350
4QFlor		11Q	
1–2	629n92	17:9	546n230
1:10–11	637, 655		
1:10–13	404	11Q13	195
10	629n92	3:7	162n23
4QIsa	404	11Q19	
		18:14–16	197
4QMMT	811	56:20	205
6–11	224	57:5–6	197
82–83	457, 840n20	57:6	195
		57:11–12	195
4QPBless	403	57:11–14	195
1–4	751n259	59:1–13	197
4QpIs	324n112	11Q5	
		19:15	156
4QpNah			
f3, 4	456	11Q6	
		14:16	156
4QpNah frag. 3–4			
1:6–8	691	11QMelch	122n85
1:8	692	2:13	124n93
1:10	840n20	2:18	642
		3:7	122n88
4QpPsa		18	350n202
2:13	612n53		

11QpHab
8:7–13   456
9:2–16   456
10:5–6   456
11:2–15   456
12:1–10   456

11QT
64:7–13   787

11QTemple
29:8–10   472, 473n186
39:7   449n70
40:5–6   449n70
45:7–10   114n49
46:1–18   472
47:1–11   472
57:9   457n104
61:9   610
64:6–13   346, 622n72, 624, 629, 653
64:7–9   624
64:9–13   692
64:10–11   692

11QTgJob
34:5   612n53
34:6–7   612n53
34:7   612n53
36:8   612n53

37:3   612n53
38:2   612n53
38:3   612n53
38:7   612n53

Cairo Genizah copy of the Damascus Document
4:17   457n104
5:5–8   457n104
A 6:14–17   457
A 6:134–17   840n20
14:18–19   404
19:10–11   404

CD
2:12   324n111, 350n202
6:1   301, 330, 350n202
6:14–18   224
7:20–21   349n200
10:10   114n49
10:20–22   258n36
11:13–14   279n123
12:8–10   224
12:22–23   349n200
13:1   239
13:20–22   349n200
19:9–11   349n200
19:10–11   124n93
19:15   124n93
20:1   349n200

Philo

Against Flaccus
1   723n166
83   784
84–85   697

Allegorical Interpretation
3.14   808

On the Change of Names
44–45   219

On the Decalogue
61–64   618–19, 658
61–69   618n67

Ancient Texts Index

On Dreams
2.125–132	618n67
2.130–131	618–19, 658
2.213	692n66

On the Embassy to Gaius
159–161	723
160–161	723n168
166–170	618n67
297	417
299	719–20, 726n175
299–305	714n134
301	415n86, 720
302	415n86, 720, 724
303	415n86, 720
305	720
306	719n154

On Giants
14	808

On the Life of Moses
2.22	273n98
2.114	612n52
2.133	438n38
2.203–206	657
2.203–208	610
2.206	613
2.208	613

On the Posterity of Cain
61	692n66

On the Special Laws
1.119	114n49
1.261	471n175
1.269	114n49
3.151–152	692
3.160	697

That God is Unchangeable
7–8	114n49

Josephus

Against Apion
1.37–41	127n103
2.80	688n54
2.198	114n49
2.203	114n49
2.282	114n49

Jewish Antiquities
2.275–276	612n52
3.214–218	628n88
3.263	114n49
4.202	610
4.219	786, 848n27
4.327	327n121
5.277	789n58
6.98	750n257
6.183	658
7.72	750
8.108	438n38
8.245	607n41
8.253	607n41
9.18	607n41
9.95	607n41
9.168	607n41
9.170	607n41
9.223	448n67
10.233	658
10.242	658
11.66	205n84
11.329	392n20
12.145	449n69
12.277	252
12.288	607n41
12.316–322	436, 438
12.406	621
13.252	258n36

13.282–283	127n105	17.273–274	328, 752
13.291–296	469n168	17.273–276	752n264
13.293–96	624	17.274	359
13.297	808	17.276	360, 753
13.299–300	127n105	17.276–77	395
13.311–313	127n106	17.277	360
13.322	127n105	17.278	404n56, 752
13.372–373	465n146, 469n168	17.278–81	395
13.380	691	17.278–284	752n265
14.9	749n252	17.280–281	752
14.36	750	17.284–85	753
14.63	252	17.300–314	417
14.172–176	127n106	17.317	749
14.280	749n252	17.318–20	749n254
14.309–10	434n20	17.342–44	132n126
15.3–4	127n106	17.345–347	127n106
15.109	606	17.355	725n172, 727n181
15.247–248	436n31	18.2	602, 726n176, 727n181
15.248	470n170		
15.298	448n67	18.4–9	394n30
15.320–322	458n107	18.16	808
15.357	434n20	18.17	808
15:373	749n252	18.23	394n30
15.373–379	127n106	18.28	309n45
15.380–425	449n68	18.33–35	458n106
15.404–408	470n170	18.34–35	608n42
15.409	749n252	18.36–38	114n49
15.417	449n71	18.55	714–15, 726n175
16.12–19	417	18.55–59	714, 846n25
16:292	749n252	18.56	715
16:311	749n252	18.57	715
17.27–28	606	18.60	716n141, 717
17.41–45	127n106	18.60–62	716
17.92	750	18.62	717n142
17.149–167	469n168	18.63–64	393n23, 439n41, 685–86, 689, 843, 847
17.155–163	437n33		
17.207–218	454n92	18.64	430n6, 589, 704–5, 739
17.217	546n230		
17.271	394	18.65–84	434n20
17.271–72	358	18:81–84	389n15
17.271–81	404	18.85	721
17:271–272	752	18.85–87	128n110
17.273	395	18.85–89	721

Ancient Texts Index

18.87	721	1.129	119n75
18.88	721–22	1.148	452n79
18.88–89	721, 725n172	1.282–83	749
18.90	417	1.283	749
18.109–125	131	1.347	128n110
18.116–119	100n9, 131, 207, 325n113, 347	1.648–655	455n97, 469n168
		1.651–653	437n33
18.117	113nn45–47, 115–16n60, 119, 121n81	2.2–13	454n92
		2.12	546n230
18.118	121n81, 127n108, 128, 131, 135, 757	2.40	727n179
		2.52	727n180
18.119	132n124	2.56	752n263
18.181–182	723n167	2.57–59	752n264
18.315	119	2.60–65	752n265
19.1–8	434n20	2.93–97	749n254
19.160	434n20	2.111	132n126
19.364–65	727n180	2.117	602, 726n176, 730
20.97	114n53, 130n120	2.118	730n189
20.97–98	128n110, 165n33, 328	2.120	129
20.106–107	436n31	2.129–32	114n49
20.131	434n20	2.149–50	114n49
20.167–168	128n110	2.159	127n106
20.168	107n29, 114n53, 130n120	2.165	808
		2.168	309n45
20.169–170	165n33	2.169	714n132, 726n175
20.169–171	328	2.169–174	714
20.169–172	128n110	2.175	716n141, 717
20.179–181	459n112	2.175–177	716
20.188	128n110	2.177	717n142
20.197–203	608n42	2.258–260	128n110
20.198	608n42	2.259	107n29, 114n53, 130n120
20.199	608n42		
20.200	607n41, 686, 843	2.261–262	114n53, 130n120
20.200–201	685n46	2.261–263	128n110, 328
20.203	458n106	2.280	417
20.205–207	459n111	2.297	417
		2.318–24	415n87
Jewish War		2.426–427	459n113
1.27	434n20	2.441	459n113
1.68–69	127n105	2.592	311
1.78–80	127n106	3.93–96	418n97
1.85	750n255	3.137–38	356
1.96–98	691	3.341–42	356

3.351	356	6.104	750n257
3.351–354	127n105	6.124–128	449n71
3.354	356	6.285	128n110
3.362–83	356	6.286–288	128n110
3.387–91	356	6.289	354
3.392	356n226	6.300–305	737
3.400	127n105, 356	6.300–309	128n110, 469n168
3.400–403	357	6.301–309	438n36
3.404–407	357	6.305	738
3.406–407	127n105	6.312–314	353
3.515	130n119	6.316	714n135
4.132	119n75	6.439	750n257
4.317	783, 787n51	7.43	311
4.377	784	7.152	398n38
4.655	357	7.164–177	132n124
5.99	497n51	7.171	750n255
5.184–227	449n68	7.186–189	132n124
5.193	449n71		
5.195	449n72	*The Life*	
5.222	470n171	1–6	127n105
5.243–45	413n80	11–12	114n49
5.402	434n20	74–75	311
5.449–450	698	193–196	458n109
6.94	452n80		

Mishnah

ʾAbot		*Beṣah*	
2:8–14	181	5:2	601
Baba Qamma		*ʿEduyyot*	
10:1–2	228n50	3:6	785n44
Bekorot		*ʿErubin*	
5:4	460	2:1–4	281n131
		4:3	258n36
Berakot		10:11–15	275n104
1:5	350		
4:5	203n75	*Ḥagigah*	
6:5	229	1:8	272
7:3	632–33		
9:5	461, 808		

Ancient Texts Index

Ḥallah
4:11   312

Kelim
1:8   449n71

Keritot
1:7   460

Ketubbot
2:5   785n44

Menaḥot
10:1   275n107
11:3   280n130

Middot
1:1   453
1:3   454n94
2:1   448n65
2:2   454n94
2:3   449nn71–72

Miqwa'ot
1:6–8   114n50

Nedarim
3:4   228n50

Negaʿim
13:9   229

Pesaḥim
4:5   557
5:6   718n146
5:7   407
6:1–2   275n104
6:2   280n130
8:6   549
10:7   544n225

Roš Haššanah
1:8   848n27
2:9   203n75

Sanhedrin
1:6   195n50
2:5   399n42
4:1   601, 605
4:3   195n50
6:4   657
6:4–5   787
6:5   783n36, 787
6:5–6   848
6:6   786–87
7:4   627
7:5   593, 601, 610, 611n50,
             620, 657
10:1   812
11:2   601
11:3   601, 659
11:4   601n27

Šabbat
7:1–2   272–73, 274n99
7:2   281n131
18:3   275n104
19:1   280n130
23:5   786

Šebiʿit
4:13   657

Šebuʿot
4:1   848n27

Šeqalim
1:3   446n58, 460
3:2   716n141
4:2   716n141
4:3   461n124
5:1–5   452n81
5:4   461n124

Soṭah
4:3   259n38
7:6   611
9:9–15   350

Sukkah
3:9   407n62
4:5   407
4:9   465n146

Ṭeharot
2:2   231
7:6   228nn49–50

Yebamot
16:7   785n44

Yoma
3:8   611n49
6:2   611
8:6   273, 277

Zebaḥim
1:3   556, 558

Tosefta

Berakot
5:18   633

Demai
2:2   231
2:11   231
2:15   231
2:20–3:10 231
3:4   228

Ḥagigah
2.11   452n78
2:11   463n132

Makkot
3:7   231

Menaḥot
13:18–23   459, 470n171

Pesaḥim
4:13–14   558

Sanhedrin
7:11   601, 659
9:7   694n69
10:11   601, 659
13:2   240
13:5   467n159

Šabbat
15:16   273

Soṭah
13:3   127n103

Yoma
1:6–8   458n107
1:7   458n107

Zebaḥim
11:8   459n114
11:16–17   459n114

Targums

Targum Hosea
6:2   806n117

Targum Isaiah
40:9   166
52:7   166
53:5   629n92

Targum Job
5:8   635

Targum of the Writings
Ps 118   407n63

Targum Yerušalmi I
Exod 20   272

Targum Zechariah
6:12   629n92
9:9   402n52

Jerusalem Talmud

Berakot
9:2:3   467n159
11b–c   633

Beṣah
2:4   452n78

Ḥagigah
2:3   452n78

Maʿaśer Šeni
5:5   459n114

Moʿed Qaṭan
3:83b   654

Peʾah
1:5   460n116

Sanhedrin
7:25a–b   613n55

Taʿanit
2:65b   620
3:9–14   473
4:5   452n80
4:7   404, 472n183
4:7.4   452n82
4:8   361–62n249
68d   361–62n249

Babylonian Talmud

ʿAbodah Zarah
8b   452n82

Baba Meṣiʿa
59a   438n38

Baba Qamma
88a   848n27

Bekorot
31a   228

Berakot
3a   633n102
7a   438n38
32b   438n38

49b–50a 633
54b 635

Beṣah
20a 452n78
20a–b 463n132

Giṭṭin
56 658
56a–b 357

Hagigah
14a 362n244, 618n67, 643, 658–59

Horayot
8a 636

Makkot
24a 636

Megillah
18a 438n38
31b 635

Menaḥot
95b 274n102

Pesaḥim
53a 399n42
57a 459n114, 460, 470n171
118a 544n225
119a 407n63

Roš Haššanah
17a 467n159
31a 452n82

Sanhedrin
38b 362n244, 618n67, 643, 658–59
43a 181, 554, 627, 694n69, 747n246, 828
55b–57a 657
60a 654, 657
67a 694n69
90b 808
98a 402, 404
107b 828n6

Šabbat
1:28a 273n98
15a 452n82
88b 635
118b 272
128b 279n123
132b 275n104

Šebiʿit
35a 657

Soṭah
22a 231

Taʿanit
23ab 228

Yebamot
61a 458n107
105b 635

Yoma
18a 458n107
85b 276n110
87b 438n38

Other Rabbinic Works

'Abot de Rabbi Nathan
4	432, 460
4:5	357
7[B]	658
25	241n113
37	637
[A] 37:12	635

Exagoge of Ezekiel
68–89	658

Exodus Rabbah
8.2	169n40, 620
10.7	172
15:6	620n68

Lamentations Rabbah
2:4	362n249

Leviticus Rabbah
1:5	241n113
9:6	629n92
18:2	620n68
21:9	458n108

Mekilta Amalek 1
54b	636

Mekilta Amalek 4
59b	636

Mekilta Ba'odesh 2
71a	636

Mekilta Bashallah 2
26a	636

Mekilta Exodus
15:1	169n40

Mekilta Pisha
16	633

Mekilta Shirta
1	812

Mekilta Vayassa
1	636

Midrash Psalms
18:29	658

Midrash Tanhuma
B	362n244

Numbers Rabbah
9:24	620n68
10.2	658
13:14	643n125
20:1	620n68

Pesiqta Rabbati
47:4	458

Semahot
13:7	787

Shemoneh Esreh
14	473, 629

Sipre Deuteronomy
9	635
32	812
105	460
306	632n100, 633n102
319	635

Sipre Numbers
112	635, 636, 658

Song Rabbah		Tanḥuma	
8:2	169n40	Gen	643n125
Soperim		Toledoth	
10:7	633n102	20	643n125
19:1	633n102		
21:6	633n102	Yalquṭ	
		1 Sam 21:5	274n102

Apostolic Fathers

Barnabas		14	522, 525n156
7:3	685n44	14:1	510, 517n128, 522
Didache		14:1–3	524
6:3	522	16:6–7	525
8	520n137		
9	517, 519–20, 540	Ignatius, *to the Ephesians*	
9:1	519n135	18:2	104n16
9:1–5	517n128	20:4	510
9:3	525n158	Ignatius, *to the Magnesians*	
9:4	525n158	11	703
9:5	522–23		
9–10	525	Ignatius, *to the Smyrnaeans*	
9–10:5	518	1:1	104n16
10	517, 519–20	1:2	703
10:1–7	517n128	Ignatius, *to the Trallians*	
10:2	525	9:1	685n44, 703
10:3	523, 526		
10:6	512, 518, 525	Polycarp, *to the Philippians*	
10:7	521	2:1	776

Church Fathers

Irenaeus

Against Heresies
1.24.4 694

Jerome

Adversus Pelagianos dialogi III
3.2 103

Commentariorum in Isaiam libri XVIII
11:1–3 101

Justin

Dialogue with Trypho
                    9n2
69   828
69:7   628
108   790
108:2   628

First Apology
31:6   362n251
66   568n326
66:3   485n13

Origen

Against Celsus   9n2
1.47   686
1:68   628
1:71   628
2.59   786

Commentary on John
10:16   436n30, 447n62

Commentary on Matthew
10.17   686

Tertullian

Apology
2.20   746n242
16.2   688n54

On Spectacles
30   790

Other Early Christian Literature

Apocalypse of Peter
81–83   694n72

Egerton Gospel
3:1–6   605n35

Eusebius

Chronicon   362n251

Demonstratio Evangelica
3, 3, 1–4   628
3, 6, 1   628

Ecclesiastical History
1.11.7–8   686
2.5   723n166
5.1.44   746
5.22.1   590n4
6.36.3   686

Gospel of Judas
codex p. 58   489n26

Gospel of Nicodemus
1:1   591

Gospel of Peter
1:1   682, 739n220, 762
1:1–2   682, 684n40, 733–34
1:2   590, 682, 762
2:3–5   763
2:4–5   684n40
2:5   554n272, 762
3.6   744
3:6–4:10   682
3:6–9   762
3:7   744
3:9   744
4:10   684, 700, 762–63
4:11   745, 748, 762
4:12   762
4:13–14   763
5:15   681n38
5:15–20   763
6:21–22   763
6:23–24   763

7:25	739n220, 763	12	677
7:26	796n80	27	100n9, 230n63, 283n141
7:26–27	763		
8:28–9:33	763	46	100n9, 113n46
8:28–11:49	788n55	47	100n9
8:28–33	684n40	51	100n9
8:30	683n39	55	677, 689
10:38	684n40	56	677
12:53–54	683n39	64	445
28–34	788n54	65	677
60	779	66	590
		71	445
		78	100n9
		104	100n9

Gospel of the Ebionites
2–3	100n9
4	103, 105n22, 106
4:1	103, 106
4:2–6	106
4:3	103
4:5	103
4:6	102–3, 106
frag. 7	485n13

Protevangelium of James
8:3	100n9
10:2	100n9
12:2–3	100n9
18:2	229
22:3	100n9
23:1–24:4	100n9

Gospel of the Hebrews
2	101–2, 104, 106

Pseudo-Clementines

Gospel of the Nazarenes
2	103–4, 106

Kerygmata Petrou (H II 16–17)
315

Gospel of Thomas
11	100n9

Greco-Roman Literature

Aeschylus

Eumenides
723–724	813

Appian

The Mithridatic Wars
27.117	398n38

The Punic Wars
9.66	398n38

Aristotle

Rhetoric
1.2.2	23n41
1.2.4	23n41
1.15.1	23n41

Arrian

Campaigns of Alexander (Anabasis)
3.3–4	355n221

Ancient Texts Index

Athenaeus

Deipnosophistae
614a–615a	226

Chariton

Callirhoë 790, 813

Cicero

De inventione rhetorica
1.7.9	23n41

De natura deorum
1.2–3	40n81

Letters to Atticus
5.16	417n93
5:16	417n95
6.1	417n95

Letters to Family
12.30.7	417n95

Letters to Quintus
1.1.13	417n95

In Pisonem
51–52	392n20

Pro Rabirio Perduellionius Reo
5.16	699

Pro Sestio
63	392n20

In Verrem
2.5.64	697
2.5.66	697, 699
2.5.165	697
2.5.169	697
II.1.39.101	237

The Digest of Justinian
1.12	731n193
1.16.6	728
1.16.11	728
17.1	726n176
26.10.3.15	731n193
28.13.7	697n82
48.2.7	731n199
48.8.3	755n274
48.19.28	697n82
48.19.28.15	698
48.19.38.2	697n82

Dio Cassius

Roman History
49.22.6	698
51.20.2–4	391n18
51.21.9	398n38
52.36.2	389n15
54.3.1	746
54.3.6	746
54.3.7	746
57.18.5	389n15
57.22–58.16	723n167
58.2.1–6	710n115
63.24.1	415n87

Dio Chrysostom

Kingship 4
97.98	237

Slavery and Freedom 1
14	237

Diodorus Siculus

Library of History
17.49.2–51	355n221
37.26.1	392n20

Dionysius of Halicarnassus

Roman Antiquities
2.60.2–3	392n20
8.67.9	398n38

Elephantine Papyri
6.4	612n52
6.6	612n52

6.11	612n52
22.1	612n52
22.123	612n52
25.6	612n52
27.15	612n52
30.6	612n52
30.15	612n52
30:15	612n53
30.24–27	612n52
31.7	612n52
31.24–25	612n52
33.8	612n52
33.38	612n52
45.3–4	612n52
56.2	612n52

Epiphanius

Panarion

30.13.7–9	102
30.16.5	468n162
30.16.7	468n162

Herodotus

The Persian Wars

5.16	695

Homer

Iliad

23	813

Odyssey

11.51–56	813

Juvenal

Satirae

5	226
10	723n167

Letters of Alciphron

2.23:1	125n99

Livy

History of Rome

30.43.13	700
45.39.8	398n38
45.40.4	398n38

Lucian

On Funerals

1–10	813

History

39	20n26
58	737n213

Martial

Epigraphy

60	226

Ovid

Sorrows

4.2.54	398n38

Oxyrhynchus Papyri

1	675n18, 676
654	676
655	676
2949	680

Petronius

Satyricon	226

Philostratus

Life of Apollonius

1.16	436n27
4.40	436n27
5.27	392n20

Plato

Phaedo

117	505

Symposium
176E	231
179b	813
233B	226

Pliny the Younger

Letters
10.29.1–2	728
10.29–30	732
10.30.1	728, 732
10.30.1–2	729
10.30.2	729
10.96	688n56

Panegyricus
22.1–5	391n18

Plutarch

Alexander
27.5–11	355n221
27.9	355nn223–24

Apopgthegmata laconica
236B–C	237

Life of Aemilius Paulus
34.6	398n38

Life of Lucillus
2.5	417n92

Life of Lucullus
2.5	392n20

Moralia
142CD	848n27
7.710–11	231

Polybius

Histories
6.22.1–4	418n97
6.23.1–16	418n97
16.25.5–8	417n94

Prudentius

Peristephanon
10.1011–1050	567n318

Quintilian

The Lesser Declamations
274.13	697

Quintus Curtius Rufus

Life of Alexander the Great
4.25–4	355n221

Seneca

Dialogues
6.20.3	696

Strabo

Geographica
17.1.43	355

Suetonius

Augustus
53.1	391n18

Caligula
4.1	391n18
32.2	746

Claudius
25.4	688n56

Domitian
10.1	746

Galba
9.1	699n87

Nero
6.25	405n59
25.1–3	391n18
49	697n82

Tiberius
58–59   755n273
61–65   723n167

Vespasianus
4–5   358
5.7   356n226

Tacitus

Annals
2.42   725n172
2.50   755
4.5   727n179
4.20   731n199
5.1–3   710n115
6   723n167
6.11   731n193
6.30   731n199
12.60   726n176
15.44   393n23, 687, 689, 704–5, 726n175

Histories
2.72   699
5.3–4   688n54
5.9   752n264

Thucydides

History of the Peloponnesian War
1.22.1   737n213
4.90.2   695
7.25.5   695

Valerius Maximus

Memorable Doings and Sayings
1.3.3   389n15

Xenophon

Moralia
1.615   226
1.619   226
4.666   226
5.678   226
7.710   226
7.714   226

Symposium
2.1   231

Other Literature

Qur'an
4.155–158   694

Modern Author Index

Abrahams, Israel 231n64, 258n37, 272n95, 277n114, 285
Achtemeier, Paul J. 679n29
Ackroyd, P. R. 398n40
Agnew, Francis H. 198n54, 200n60
Aland, Barbara 412n77
Aland, Kurt 294n5, 412n77
Alexander, Loveday C. 671n2, 777n5
Allen, Leslie C. 341n169
Allison, Dale C., Jr. 1n1, 3, 4n13, 9n1, 10n3, 50n104, 54n119, 65n146, 69n159, 80n199, 82n204, 111n40, 123n91, 133n129, 140n156, 141n157, 143n162, 171n45, 174n52, 175n54, 185, 199n57, 201n63, 204n79, 205n83, 208n92, 230n63, 240n106, 261n53, 266n73, 311nn56, 58, 315n76, 317n80, 318n85, 320nn94, 96–97, 99, 331n137, 332n140, 338n159, 430n5, 451n76, 466n152, 520n139, 545n226, 565n304, 570n334, 674n12, 690n61, 741n224, 776, 779n21, 783, 786, 787n51, 788, 802, 825n1
Alon, Gedalyahu 222n31
Alston, William P. 778, 779n16
Alsup, John E. 789, 792
Amphoux, C.-B. 537n200
Andersen, Francis I. 197n52
Anderson, Hugh 304n25, 626, 631, 637
Anderson, Kevin L. 793, 812–14
Anderson, Paul N. 316n79, 327nn121–22, 329n129, 552n260
Ankersmit, Frank R. 23–28, 31, 36n70
Anscombe, G. E. M. 200n61

Appleby, Joyce 20n25, 21n33, 30n59, 73n172
Arav, Rami 310n50
Arberry, Arthur J. 694n70
Archer, Margaret 28n55, 29n56
Arens, Eduardo 202n71
Arterbury, Andrew E. 219n20, 242n118
Ashley, Timothy R. 219n21
Ashton, John 446n53
Ata ur-Rahim, Muhammad 694n71
Aune, David E. 127nn105–6, 350n201, 353n217, 355n224, 356n225, 361n241, 362n247, 364n256, 612n52, 737n213
Ådna, Jostein 429n1, 433n17, 445nn51–52, 451n75, 454n91, 455n100, 461n123, 463n131, 468n164, 475n191, 629n92

Badke, William B. 138n147
Bahat, Dan 450–51n75
Bahr, Gordon J. 545n226
Baigent, Michael 694, 695nn75–76
Bailey, Kenneth E. 241n114
Bammel, Ernst 393n24, 464n138, 701n91, 713n126, 730n190, 747n246, 748n250, 749n251
Banks, Robert 284, 285n150, 286
Baras, Zvi 685n47, 686n49
Barrett, C. K. 100n8, 316n78, 502n73, 542n218, 567n318, 571, 574n352, 679n33
Bartsch, Hans Werner 410n74
Bauckham, Richard 56n123, 384n6, 470n174, 511n105, 577, 650, 735n209, 785–86n47

Bauer, David R. 332n140
Bauer, Walter 397
Bauman, Richard A. 730n191, 731nn194, 197–98, 754n272
Baumgarten, Joseph M. 195n49, 692n65
Baur, F.C. 314
Bayer, Hans F. 310n54, 311nn55, 57–58, 816n144
Bäck, Sven-Olav 266n71, 276n111, 278n118, 286
Beard, Mary 711nn117–18
Beards, Andrew 29n58
Beare, Francis Wright 319n86
Beasley-Murray, George R. 100n8, 113n48, 116n61, 151, 204n77, 205nn83–84, 206n87, 301n11, 316n79, 328n126, 329n132, 483, 530n171, 553n265, 559n287, 572nn344, 346, 578–79n361, 615n60, 621n69, 729n187, 800n102
Becker, Hans-Jürgen 632n100
Becker, Jürgen 116n61, 118n71, 119n73, 121n82, 123n91, 126n101, 160n18, 162n26, 163n29, 183n5, 192n42, 203n73, 385n7
Bedard, Stephen J. 694n73
Behm, Johannes 115n55, 515n123
Ben-Dov, M. 448n66
Benoit, P. 569
Bentley, Michael 12n5, 20n25
Berger, Klaus 239n104, 408n71, 516n126
Bermejo Rubio, Fernando 1n1
Bernhard, Andrew E. 744n231
Best, Ernest 121n83
Betz, Hans D. 140n156, 452n83, 464n135, 671n2
Betz, Otto 129n117, 593n9, 602, 622n72, 624n79, 627, 629–30, 701n91
Bhaskar, Roy 28n55
Bilde, Per 358nn227–28
Billerbeck, Paul 548, 558

Billings, Bradly S. 530n170, 533n181, 535n191, 538n204, 539–41
Bird, Michael F. 186n15, 209n95, 240n106
Bittner, Wolfgang 648
Black, C. Clifton 595n12
Black, Matthew 70n161, 120n77, 160n18, 269n85, 498n59
Blackman, Philip 77n189, 716n141
Bleeker, Claas Jouco 118n70
Blenkinsopp, Joseph 398n38
Blevins, James L. 333n144
Blinzler, Josef 554n272, 593n9, 601, 608n42, 701n91, 718n148, 729n187, 746n245
Bloch, Marc 20, 37n73
Blomberg, Craig L. 73n175, 215n2, 216n8, 220n23, 225n39, 227n45, 230n61, 238nn96, 98, 254n17, 384n6, 445n50, 553n266, 783n32, 795, 796n80, 800nn100, 102, 831
Blümner, Hugo 229n55
Boatwright, Mary T. 726n176
Boccaccini, Gabriele 617n64
Bock, Darrell L. 4, 6, 9n1, 142n161, 227n45, 232n71, 239n102, 241n112, 284n149, 285n150, 340n168, 344n184, 394n26, 499n62, 530n171, 534n186, 538n205, 589n1, 593n9, 597n13, 600n23, 601n27, 610nn45–46, 617n65, 618n67, 622n72, 628n90, 631n94, 633n104, 638n112, 643n128, 645n136, 646n137, 647n141, 650n151, 651n154, 702n92, 718n148, 735n211, 738n218, 742n225, 753, 793, 797n90, 799n97
Bockmuehl, Markus 283n142, 312n62, 331n137, 369n266, 387n9, 459n110, 464n135, 466n152, 483, 554, 555n277, 568n322
Bode, Edward Lynn 777n9
Boismard, Marie-Émile 135n136, 136n139

Bokser, Baruch M. 350n204, 544, 545n226
Bolyki, János 215, 216n4, 219n19, 224n35
Bond, Helen K. 360n234, 415n86, 654n158, 703n93, 706n99, 708nn103, 105, 709n109, 710n113, 711nn117–18, 712nn122–23, 713, 714nn131, 134, 715nn136–38, 716n141, 718n148, 719nn151–54, 720nn155–58, 721n161, 723nn165, 169, 734, 756n277, 758n279
Bonnard, Pierre 321
Borg, Marcus J. 69n159, 111n39, 140n155, 184, 383n3, 418, 447n62, 463n129, 464–65n141, 481, 482n7, 732n203
Boring, M. Eugene 63n139, 69n158, 71n167, 230, 305n29, 319n92, 595n12, 644, 651
Bornkamm, Günther 302n16, 319n90
Borsch, Frederick Houk 340n167, 623
Bosch, David 202n68
Bosworth, A. B. 355n222, 356n225
Boughton, Lynne Courter 566n309
Bousset, Wilhelm 747n248
Bovon, François 233n73, 235n86, 243n121, 325n114
Boyd, Gregory A. 53n118
Böcher, O. 509n99
Böttrich, Christfried 536, 538, 539n206
Bradshaw, Paul F. 520n136, 522, 523nn147, 152, 551n256, 560–61n290, 564n300
Brandon, S. G. F. 387, 463n128, 464n138, 701n91, 717n144
Braun, Willi 242
Breisach 20n25
Breisach, Ernst 12n5, 20n25
Bretscher, Paul G. 123n91
Brodie, Thomas L. 316n78
Broer, Ingo 205nn83, 85, 738n217, 785, 788n53

Broughton, T. R. S. 418n96
Brown, Colin 207n90
Brown, Dan 670n1
Brown, Michael L. 203n73, 805n112
Brown, Raymond E. 129n114, 136n140, 138n149, 139n152, 304, 317, 319n89, 328, 330n135, 334n147, 339, 368n262, 370n269, 444n46, 445n51, 446nn53, 60, 493, 494n40, 503n78, 541n215, 559n287, 590n3, 593n9, 603, 607n40, 608n42, 618n67, 642n122, 646n139, 647n142, 651–52, 679nn30, 32–33, 681n37, 683n39, 684nn41–42, 695n78, 701n91, 702n92, 713nn126–27, 714nn131, 134, 716n141, 719n153, 720n157, 723nn165, 169, 733n206, 735n210, 737n215, 742nn226–27, 743n230, 748n250, 749n251, 754n272, 783, 788
Brownlee, William H. 129n117, 221n28
Bruce, F. F. 75n178, 688n56, 689n57, 694n71
Brueggemann, Walter 221n27
Bryan, Christopher 730n190
Buchanan, George Wesley 208, 435, 436nn27, 32, 467
Bultmann, Rudolf 171nn46–47, 227n47, 257n29, 268n82, 302, 305n29, 309, 310n48, 314n71, 320n93, 335n148, 345n190, 384, 488n22, 493n35, 496, 499–501, 507, 530n172, 532n180, 548n238, 553n265, 561, 565n302, 578, 605n35, 626n84, 784, 787n51, 789, 792
Burchard, Christoph 528
Burer, Michael H. 4n16
Burger, Christoph 403n55, 408n71
Burkert, Walter 225
Burkett, Delbert 340nn166–67, 645n135
Burnett, Fred W. 205n84
Burridge, Richard A. 736n212, 737n213

Busink, Theodor A. 450n73
Buth, Randall 470n172
Byington, Steven T. 612n51, 639n115
Byrskog, Samuel 831n9

Caird, George B. 2, 188n25, 190n31, 202n66, 270n89, 597, 827n4
Cameron, Ron 102n11, 103n13, 104n15, 481n3, 675n18, 704n96
Campbell, J. B. 418n97
Campbell, R. Alastair 111n40, 142n160
Capes, David 599n20
Caragounis, Chrys C. 122n84, 340n167, 645n135
Carmichael, Deborah Bleicher 570n334
Carr, Edward H. 20–21n31
Carroll, John T. 736n212
Carroll, Scott T. 396n33
Carson, D. A. 259n39, 278n121, 320n94, 328n126, 329n132, 502n73, 553nn266–67, 595n12, 679n29, 703n94, 797, 800n102
Casey, Maurice 70n166, 260, 266n72, 270, 271n90, 340n167, 341nn170, 172, 433n15, 434n22, 435n23, 439n40, 444n44, 451n75, 454n91, 462, 464n135, 467, 468n160, 495n44, 497n51, 498n59, 503, 504n79, 509n99, 543n221, 548n240, 556, 565n302, 566n310, 567n317, 569n327, 631n94
Catchpole, David R. 314n70, 385n7, 436n27, 437n33, 471n179, 593n9, 601n26, 701n91, 747n248
Cavin, Robert G. 775
Charles, Robert H. 157n11, 158nn12–14, 160n19, 161n20
Charlesworth, James H. 18n19, 76n183, 77n185, 129n117, 166n36, 305n30, 309n43, 323n107, 333n144, 335n148, 336n152, 349n198, 351n208, 617n64, 623, 657n160,
690n59, 692n65, 751n261, 760n283, 811, 828n8
Chester, Andrew 351–52n215, 360n233, 363n254, 403n54, 836n14
Chilton, Bruce D. 126n102, 128n109, 135n133, 151, 153n7, 166n35, 217n10, 409n71, 446n55, 452n83, 453n88, 454n92, 461, 463, 465, 466n150, 467, 474n188, 481, 504n81, 505n83, 568n326, 599n19, 604n33, 651n154
Chilton, C. W. 754n272
Chronis, Harry L. 341n171
Coakley, J. F. 385n7, 388n12, 397, 401n51, 402
Cohen, H. 391n19
Cohen, Shaye J. D. 358n228
Cohick, Lynn H. 346n192, 748n250, 754n270
Cohn, Haim 701n91, 723n164
Cohn-Sherbok, D. M. 261n51, 274n101, 275n106, 544n225
Collier, Andrew 28n55
Collingwood, R. G. 16n14, 17n17, 23n41, 38, 39n79, 40nn80, 82
Collins, Adela Yarbro 228n52, 258n33, 310, 342n175, 443n42, 455n100, 461, 463n134, 468nn163–64, 470n173, 615, 618n67, 777, 790
Collins, John J. 156n9, 323n106, 326, 347n196, 349n198, 350n206, 351n210, 352n212, 360n238, 403, 642n124, 690nn59–60, 751n261, 807n120, 828n5
Collins, Marilyn F. 721n159
Colpe, Carsten 617n65
Conroy, Sherrill A. 29n57
Conzelmann, Hans 302, 319n90, 780n23
Corley, Kathleen E. 216–17, 231, 234n81, 237n94
Cosgrove, Charles H. 233
Cowley, A. 612n52

Craig, William Lane 52n117, 384n6, 777n8, 788nn55, 57, 804n111
Craigie, Peter C. 807n119
Cranfield, C.E.B. 257, 265n68, 276n111, 278, 303, 331n137, 595n12
Crawford, Michael 32n66
Creed, J.M. 387n9
Crenshaw, James L. 806, 807n119
Croce, Benedetto 40n82
Crook, John A. 727n183
Crossan, John Dominic 3, 12n6, 62nn136–37, 95n2, 104n16, 106n23, 108n31, 109, 186n16, 187, 199n56, 202n70, 215n3, 244, 343, 408n71, 445, 481, 516–18, 520, 526, 590n4, 680n35, 681n37, 684n41, 701n91, 732, 781, 784, 787n51, 798
Crossley, James G. 9n1, 24n43
Cullmann, Oscar 118n71, 135n136, 319n88
Culpepper, R. Alan 238n99

D'Amico, Jack 40n82
Dahl, Nils Alstrup 305n29, 344n183, 346
Dalman, Gustaf 70n161, 632n99, 635n107, 639
Danby, Herbert 77n189, 461n124, 601, 659
Dapaah, Daniel S. 135n136
Daube, David 199n56, 273n97, 274n101, 350n204, 570n334, 640n118
Davies, Margaret 35n69, 59n131, 60n134, 63n139, 65nn144–45, 70nn162–64, 73n174, 79nn196, 198, 81n201, 84n205, 487n18
Davies, Philip R. 9n1, 52n118
Davies, W.D. 65n146, 111n40, 123n91, 133n129, 143n162, 171n45, 174n52, 175n54, 201n63, 204n79, 240n106, 261n53, 266n73, 311nn56, 58, 315n76, 317n80, 318n85, 320nn94, 96–97, 99, 331n137, 332n140, 338n159, 451n76, 466n152, 520n139, 545n226, 565n304, 570n334, 741n224, 787n51, 788, 802
Davis, Philip 598
Dawidowicz, Lucy S. 31n64
de Jonge, Henk Jan 436n27
de Jonge, Marinus 160n18, 163, 340n168, 349n199, 351n208, 368n261
DeConick, April D. 676–77n25
Deissmann, Adolf 172n48, 391n19, 415n85
Denton, Donald L. 28n55, 29n58
Derrett, J. Duncan M. 205n84, 242n115, 398n38, 444n45, 462n127, 701n91
Derrida, Jacques 22
Dibelius, Martin 108n30, 237n93, 493n35, 626n84
Dietzfelbinger, Christian 264n66, 265n69, 270n89, 282n137, 284n147
Dillon, Richard J. 797n89, 798n93
Dinkler, Erich 335n148
Dittenberger, W. 417n94
Doble, Peter 535n189
Dodd, C.H. 63n139, 130n119, 135n136, 136n139, 139n151, 317n83, 328n126, 329n132, 383n3, 410n73, 502n72, 679n33
Doering, Lutz 251, 254n18, 257n27, 263n56, 278n120, 281n134, 282–84
Doerr, Friedrich 701n91
Domeris, William R. 330n136
Donaldson, James 77n191, 694n71
Dormeyer, Detlev 488n23
Downing, F. Gerald 107n24
Draper, Jonathan A. 205n83, 519n132
Duguid, Iain 221n28
Duling, Dennis C. 403n55, 408n71
Dunn, James D.G. 2, 12n7, 108n30, 109n35, 110n37, 123n91, 124n96, 141n158, 171n46, 270n89, 303, 304n23, 311nn55, 58–59, 313n67, 316n79, 317, 331n139, 334n147,

340n168, 341n171, 342n173,
348n197, 371n271, 464n138,
465n140, 481n3, 483, 487n17,
488n22, 495n43, 511n105, 521n142,
565n303, 570n335, 571n337, 591,
599n19, 629n92, 640–41n121,
648–49n147, 679n30, 737n214, 778,
792, 804n111, 828n7
Dupont, Jacques 183n5, 200n58

Eddy, Paul Rhodes 53n118, 140n156
Edwards, David Darnell 629n92
Edwards, James R. 228n53, 239n103,
334n147, 339n161
Edwards, Ruth B. 481n1, 509n100
Ehrenberg, Victor 729n185
Ehrman, Bart D. 3, 77n191, 302nn14–15, 530–37n198, 539n207
Elbogen, Ismar 633n102
Elledge, C. D. 805n113, 807n121, 809, 810n125
Elliott, James K. 77n190, 681nn36, 38, 739n220
Elliott, John H. 744n233, 750n258
Ellis, E. Earle 410n73, 534n186, 629n92
Elton, Geoffrey R. 13n8, 15n11, 16n14, 19n24, 21
Emerton, John A. 616n63
Endres, John C. 158n13
Enslin, Morton S. 107–8
Eppstein, Victor 446n58, 452, 454n91, 471
Epstein, I. 77n189
Ernst, Josef 114n53, 115n56, 116n61,
118nn69, 71, 123n91, 129n116,
130n119, 135n136, 136n139, 391n17,
412
Eskola, Timo 614n58
Evans, C. F. 240n108, 412n78, 530
Evans, Craig A. 10n3, 57n127,
60n134, 61n135, 62n137, 63n139, 65,
67n153, 68nn155–56, 69nn158–59,
70, 71nn167–68, 72n170, 75n179,
77n184, 111n41, 120n78, 124n93,
151n1, 152n4, 155n8, 156n10,
164n31, 183n6, 202n65, 254n15,
281n133, 301n10, 305n28, 306–9n43,
311nn57–58, 313nn63, 67, 315n76,
322, 325n113, 330nn133–34,
331n139, 337n155, 338n158,
354n219, 360nn234, 238, 362,
363n253, 369n263, 385n6, 394n27,
430n6, 433n16, 437n35, 438n36,
452n84, 454n91, 456, 460n115,
464n135, 466n152, 467n159,
468n161, 469n169, 472n181,
493nn35, 37, 39, 495n44, 497n54,
498n56, 501n70, 549n249, 554n271,
559n286, 570n334, 576n356, 593n9,
610n45, 613, 632n99, 634n105,
648n143, 676n22, 680n35, 688n56,
689n57, 690n59, 694n74, 738n216,
740n222, 747n248, 748n250,
751n260, 752n262, 784–85, 786n45,
789n58, 795n79, 817, 828, 848n27
Evans, Jane DeRose 707n100
Evans, Richard J. 21nn29, 33, 46n91, 73n172
Eve, Eric 152n5, 281n133, 834n12

Fabry, Heinz-Josef 221n25
Fairburn, Miles 19n23
Fallon, Francis T. 675n18
Farmer, William R. 58n129, 135n136, 404n57, 406n60
Farrer, Austin M. 58n129, 191n36
Febvre, Lucien 20
Fee, Gordon D. 509n98, 567n315, 574n352, 673nn6–7, 674n10, 778, 782
Feldman, Louis H. 325n113, 389n15, 685nn45, 47, 686n51, 714–15, 716n141, 717, 721
Feldmeier, Reinhard 331n138
Felmy, K. C. 562n295
Ferch, Arthur J. 122n84
Ferguson, Duncan S. 33n67

Ferguson, Everett 76n182, 688n53
Fiorenza, Elisabeth Schüssler 779n17
Fisher, Loren R. 408n71
Fisher, Nicholas R. E. 226nn41–42
Fitzgerald, John T. 673nn6–7
Fitzmyer, Joseph A. 69n160, 108n30, 129n116, 170n42, 171n45, 172n48, 241n113, 268, 269n85, 335n151, 340n168, 361n243, 398n38, 402n52, 403n55, 408n67, 411n75, 412, 433n16, 491n29, 530n171, 541n216, 566n310, 572, 612n53, 634n105, 645–46, 691n63, 692n65, 718n148, 742n226, 786, 794, 797n91, 799n95
Fleddermann, Harry T. 58n129, 99n7
Flender, Helmut 391n17
Fletcher-Louis, Crispin H. T. 370n268, 474n189
Flew, R. Newton 191n35
Flusser, David 3, 191n36, 194n46, 205n83, 279, 340n168, 482n4, 522n145, 523n152
Foerster, G. 448n66
Fokkelman, J. P. 398n40
Fonner, Michael G. 694n71
Fontanille, Jean-Philippe 708n103
Ford, J. Massyngberd 461n123
Foster, Paul 681n36
France, R. T. 229, 238n99, 334n145, 338n158, 495n45, 502–3n75, 555, 557, 784n37, 786, 787n50, 789n58
Fredriksen, Paula 3, 183n6, 186n16, 343, 383n3, 408n71, 416n91, 418n99, 433n13
Freedman, David Noel 197n52
Freyne, Sean 209n95, 309n46, 312nn60–61, 327n123, 328n125, 359n231, 364n257, 468n162
Fridrichsen, Anton 137n145
Friedlander, Saul 31n64
Friedrich, Gerhard 482n7
Friedrich, Johannes 204n77
Frova, Antonio 726n175

Fuller, Reginald H. 203n73, 305n29, 335nn148, 150, 780n22, 788n53, 789
Fullmer, Paul M. 790
Funk, Robert W. 3n11, 106n23, 114n52, 130n119, 171n46, 184, 254n13, 256nn19–25, 263nn56–61, 266nn74–75, 267nn76–79, 303, 314nn69–70, 319n87, 333n142, 383n2, 384n6, 393n22, 408n71, 430n3, 435n23, 484nn11–12, 488n20, 490n27, 492nn31, 33, 499n61, 504nn80–81, 505n84, 506nn87–89, 516n125, 576n356, 605n35, 784, 788n52, 790, 801n105
Fusco, S. A. 602n28

Gadamer, Hans-Georg 29, 33, 53, 78
Ganschinietz, R. 612n52
García Martínez, Florentino 77n186, 194n47, 326, 456n102, 690n60, 691–92
Gardiner, Patrick 46n91
Garnet, Paul 111n40
Garnsey, Peter 389n15, 698n84, 699n86, 727n183, 731, 755n274
Gathercole, Simon J. 489n26
Gaventa, Beverly Roberts 1n1
Gärtner, Bertil E. 433n17
Gerhardsson, Birger 342n174
Gero, Stephen 111n40
Gese, Hartmut 529, 551
Geyser, Albert S. 129n117, 204n82
Gibson, J. 235n85, 237n94, 618n67
Glare, P. G. W. 15n12, 688n52, 695n79, 732n202, 746n240, 754n272
Glasson, Thomas Francis 614n59, 813n135
Gnilka, Joachim 132n125, 190n31, 191n35, 196n51, 198n54, 512n112, 543n222, 552n263, 554n272, 557n282, 567n316
Goetz, Stewart C. 73n175, 254n17

Goguel, Maurice 108n30, 118n71, 135n136, 137n144, 139n150
Goldenberg, Robert 278n119
Goodacre, Mark S. 58nn128–29, 680n35
Goodenough, Edwin R. 719n152
Goodman, Martin 390n15
Goppelt, Leonhard 116n61, 118nn69, 71, 203n73, 282n139, 315n76, 316n79, 319n89, 345n185, 511n108
Gorman, Jonathan 17n15, 19n21, 46n93
Gosline, Sheldon Lee 708n103
Goulder, Michael D. 48n97, 58n129, 314nn68, 72, 319n86
Grant, Robert M. 389n15
Gray, G. B. 805n114
Gray, John 153n7
Grässer, Erich 573, 574n350
Green, Joel B. 217n9, 233, 238n100, 240n108, 241n111, 242n116, 532n180, 572n346, 736n212
Greil, Arthur L. 188n27
Grenfell, Bernard P. 675n18
Griesbach, Johann Jacob 58n129
Griffin, Larry J. 19n23
Grobman, Alex 31
Guelich, Robert A. 115n57, 143n162, 238n99, 257n29, 265–66n72, 278n121
Guenther, Heinz O. 183n5
Gundry, Robert H. 228n52, 258, 261, 265nn67–68, 311n58, 313n66, 319n86, 332n140, 338n158, 438n37, 453n89, 454nn91, 95, 466nn148, 150, 468n161, 491n29, 492n34, 494n41, 495n45, 497nn51, 54, 498n55, 501n70, 503n77, 545n228, 552n263, 565n303, 572, 573n347, 593n9, 609n44, 610–11n50, 613n55, 629n92, 632n98, 741n224
Guthrie, Donald 338n158

Haas, N. 18n19
Habermas, Gary R. 804n111
Hachlili, Rachel 783n35
Haenchen, Ernst 107n24, 435, 436nn28, 32, 437n34, 452n79, 747n248, 796n82
Hagner, Donald A. 65n147, 301n12, 315n74, 320nn94, 96–98, 332n140, 553n267, 563n299, 833–34
Hahn, Ferdinand 200n58, 335n148, 483n10, 508n93, 510n101, 511n107, 523n148, 538n205, 563n299, 602n29, 639
Halperin, David J. 624n80
Hampel, Volker 340n167, 629n92, 645n135, 650n150, 651
Hanson, John S. 107n29, 127nn104, 107, 128, 344n182, 354nn219–20, 358n230, 359n231, 360nn233, 236, 238, 362n248, 363n252, 721n159, 752n262
Hare, Douglas R. A. 340n167
Harmer, J. R. 517n128
Harnack, Adolf 4n14, 79n195, 333n143, 595n12, 681n38, 761n291, 836
Harpur, Tom 694
Harrington, Daniel J. 284n148, 810, 811n126
Harris, Murray J. 790
Harrison, R. K. 228n52
Hartley, John E. 220n22
Harvey, A. E. 383n3, 393n22, 407n65, 747n247, 748nn249–50
Harvey, Van A. 38nn74–75
Haskell, Thomas L. 73n172
Hauck, Friedrich 410n73
Hawthorne, Gerald F. 673n6
Hayes, Christine 222n31
Hays, Richard B. 1n1, 574n351
Hägerland, Tobias 134n131
Head, B. V. 391n19
Heath, Malcom 23n41
Hedrick Jr., Charles W. 18n20, 32n66
Heil, John P. 234n80, 240n109, 242n118

Heinemann, Joseph 632n100, 633n103
Hempel, Johannes 203n73
Henderson, Suzanne Watts 338n158
Hendin, David 455n96, 708n103, 709nn111–12, 712nn119, 121–22, 124, 713n128, 749nn253–54, 750nn255–56
Hengel, Martin 2, 65n145, 120n80, 144n164, 171n45, 172n48, 320n94, 322, 323n105, 331n138, 333n143, 334n145, 339, 340n165, 343, 344n180, 346nn191, 194, 354n219, 389n14, 390n16, 393n23, 394n30, 398n39, 447n62, 483, 488n22, 496n50, 510n103, 511n105, 529n168, 543nn221, 223, 545n228, 546n232, 547n234, 549n248, 550n255, 552n263, 563n299, 565n302, 572n343, 575n355, 593n9, 595n12, 608n42, 618n66, 620n68, 623n75, 628n89, 637n110, 643nn126, 130, 695n77, 696n80, 699nn86, 88, 825n1, 831n9, 836n14
Hennecke, E. 75n178, 77n190, 704n96
Herrenbrück, Fritz 228n49, 235n85
Herrmann, Wolfgang 168n38
Herron, Robert W. 200n60
Herzog, William R., II 463nn130–31, 471
Hicks, John Mark 274n101
Hiers, Richard 434n21, 471n179
Higgins, A. J. B. 340n167, 645n135
Hill, George F. 712n122
Hinz, Christoph 283n142, 285n150
Hobbs, T. R. 220n24
Hobsbawm, Eric 73n172
Hoehner, Harold W. 131n121, 132n125, 394n28, 541n215, 556–57, 723n164
Hoffmann, Paul 199n57, 200n59, 674n12
Hofius, Otfried 482, 565n304, 566n314
Holladay, William L. 115n55
Hollenbach, Paul 129n116, 134, 137n143

Hollis, F. J. 450n74
Holmes, Michael 530n173
Holmén, Tom 64n142, 67, 218, 274n100, 279, 282, 305n29, 306n33, 430n6, 463nn130–31, 465n143
Holst, Robert 232n70
Holt, J. C. 183n6
Hooker, Morna D. 64n142, 74, 191n41, 257n30, 264n65, 265n68, 274n99, 277n116, 305n29, 338n158, 340n167, 384n6, 614n59, 621, 622n70
Horbury, William 194, 195n48, 352n214, 468nn164–65, 642, 643n125, 689n57
Horsley, G. H. R. 688n54
Horsley, Richard A. 107n29, 114n53, 127nn104, 107, 128, 129n116, 130n120, 205n83, 208, 327n119, 344n182, 354nn219–20, 358n230, 359n231, 360nn233, 236, 238, 362nn248, 251, 363n252, 365nn258, 260, 394nn29–30, 395n31, 404, 430n6, 453n90, 466n151, 470n170, 721n159, 752n262
Horstmann, Maria 302n16
Hort, F. J. A. 530, 792n65
Howell, Martha 32n66, 36n71, 61n135
Huck, A. 485n13
Hultgren, Arland J. 227n46, 237, 243n120, 675n17
Humphreys, C. 559n287
Hunt, Arthur S. 675n18
Hurtado, Larry W. 337n153, 338n158, 344n183, 345nn186–87, 346, 519n134, 598

Iggers, Georg G. 20nn25–26
Instone-Brewer, David 473, 481n1, 555n275, 556, 557n280, 558
Isaac, E. 617n64

Jackson, F. J. Foakes 394n30
James, Montague Rhodes 681n38

Jastrow, Marcus 172n49
Jaubert, A. 557
Jefford, Clayton N. 704n96
Jenkins, Keith 21n33, 22–24n44
Jensen, Morten Hørning 749n254
Jeremias, Joachim 2, 70nn161, 166, 73n175, 136nn139–40, 186n15, 190, 199n56, 205n85, 237n92, 243n120, 408n66, 410n73, 413, 461n118, 492n30, 493, 497nn51, 53, 501, 509, 512n112, 513, 523n152, 530, 533n181, 537–38n202, 542–51n258, 553nn265, 267, 554n272, 558n284, 559n287, 565n302, 566, 569, 571, 573, 646, 647n140, 807n122
Jesus Seminar 3, 106n23, 171n46, 184–85, 201n63, 254–56n25, 257n27, 262–68, 270, 303, 314n70, 333n142, 383, 384n6, 393n22, 408n71, 430, 435n23, 481–82n7, 484, 487–89, 490n27, 492, 493n37, 494–95, 498–99n61, 503–8, 513, 516, 575, 576n356, 577, 605n35, 738n216, 784, 788, 790, 801, 827n3
Jewett, Robert 671n2, 673n6
Johnson, Luke Timothy 384n6
Johnston, Robert M. 237n91
Jones, A. H. M. 417n95, 699n86, 726n175, 729n185, 730n191, 731nn194, 197, 199, 732n200
Jowett, Garth S. 707n100
Juel, Donald 466n147, 593, 631, 632n97, 634, 652n155

Kant, Immanuel 38n74
Kazen, Thomas 340n168
Kazmierski, Carl R. 128n113, 637–38
Kähler, Christoph 319n89
Kähler, Martin 301n13
Käsemann, Ernst 64n141, 305n29
Keck, Leander E. 111n40
Kee, Howard C. 160n19, 162–63n29, 230n61, 457, 809n124

Keener, Craig S. 327n121, 328n126, 329nn129, 132, 330n133
Kelber, Werner H. 492n34, 493n39
Kelley, Donald R. 20n25
Kellner, Hans 31n64
Kempthorne, Renatus 604n33
Kennard, J. S. 394n30
Kenyon, F. G. 538
Kerr, Alan R. 433n17, 446n54
Kertelge, Karl 230n59, 701n91
Kieweler, Hans V. 223n33
Kilgallen, John J. 233nn76–77
Kilpatrick, G. D. 319n89, 528
Kim, Seyoon 340n167, 645n135
Kingsbury, Jack Dean 332n140, 653n157, 655n159
Kinman, Brent 383n1, 390n16, 391n17, 392n21, 398n39, 401n49, 408n69, 410n72, 412n79, 415n86, 837, 838n16
Kirby, Peter 786, 790
Kirk, Alan 681n37, 684n41
Kissane, E. J. 205nn83, 85
Klassen, William 187n18, 501n66, 503n78, 504n79
Klauck, Hans-Josef 483, 507n91, 565n304, 567nn315–16, 568n324, 572n343
Klausner, Joseph 303, 686n50
Klawans, Jonathan 116n64, 231n68, 483, 504n81, 567n318
Klein, Gunter 183n4, 187n19
Klein, Hans 494n41, 501n67, 510n103, 530n171, 535n190, 537
Klijn, A. F. J. 101n10, 102nn11–12, 103nn13–14, 104n15
Klinghardt, Matthias 216–17, 507n91, 516n126, 528n166
Kloppenborg, John S. 58n129, 99n7, 204n79, 674n12, 675n17
Klumbies, Paul-Gerhard 281nn134, 136
Knackstedt, J. 238n99
Knibb, Michael A. 612n53, 632n100, 633n101

Knohl, Israel 849n29
Kobelski, Paul J. 643n129
Koenig, John 481
Koester, Helmut 302n15, 590n4, 676nn19, 21, 681n37, 684n41
Kollmann, Bernd 516n126, 565n302, 566n311
Köstenberger, Andreas J. 316n79, 800nn100, 102
Kraeling, Carl H. 108n30, 118n71, 120n80, 123nn91–92, 126n101, 129n116, 131n121, 415n86, 714n135
Kraus, Thomas J. 681n38
Kreitzer, Larry J. 707n101
Kremer, Jacob 778
Kuhn, H. W. 397
Kuhn, Heinz-Wolfgang 528n164, 546n231, 569n328, 695n77
Kuhn, K. G. 528n164
Kuhn, Karl G. 528, 636n109
Kuhn, Thomas S. 80n199
Kutsch, Ernst 399n44
Kutsko, John 309n46
Kümmel, Werner Georg 108n30, 191n40, 254, 319n89, 679n29
Kvasnica, Brian 470n172
Ladd, George Eldon 52n118, 151n2

Lake, Kirsopp 394n30
Lamarche, Paul 400n47
Lambdin, Thomas O. 677n24
Lambrecht, Jan 801n104
Lane, William L. 257n29, 265n68, 335n148
Lang, Seán 32n66
Lapham, F. 316n79
Laubach, F. 115n55
Lawrence, Jonathan D. 113n48
Legge, S. C. E. 538
Lehrman, S. M. 172n49
Leivestad, Ragnar 642n123, 643n127
Levenson, Jon D. 812
Levine, Etan 275n107

Lewis, Naphtali 729n186
Légasse, Simon 701n91, 730n190, 758n279
Lémonon, Jean-Pierre 415n86, 713n126, 714n131, 723nn165, 169
Léon-Dufour, X. 560
Liebeschuetz, J. H. W. G. 389n15
Liefeld, Walter Lewis 203n75
Lietzmann, Hans 529n169, 593n9, 600, 606n38
Lieu, Judith 433n18, 446n56, 474n188
Lightfoot, J. B. 517n128
Lincoln, Andrew T. 284n149, 511n105, 679n33
Lindars, Barnabas 316n79, 328n126, 329n130, 340n167, 645n135
Lindberg, David C. 45n90
Lindholm, Lisbet 29n57
Linnemann, Eta 120n80, 136n139, 626n84
Lissarrague, Francois 226n44
Loader, William R. G. 262n55, 274n99, 275n108, 277n117, 283n142, 284n145
Lohmeyer, Ernst 115n56, 123n91, 471n179
Lohse, Eduard 261, 265, 266n72, 268, 269n85, 271n91, 272n92, 276n112, 278n119, 286n154, 406n61, 407n64, 600–601n24, 626n84
Lonergan, Bernard 28n55, 29, 52n118
Longenecker, Richard N. 671n2
Longman, Tremper, III 152n6
Love, Stuart L. 232n72
Lowder, Jeffery Jay 48n97, 785n44
López, José 28n55
Lucas, Ernest C. 807n121
Luz, Ulrich 231n65, 273n98, 319n91, 444n47, 447n62, 464n138
Lüdemann, Gerd 48n97, 482n4, 778n12, 779, 781, 782n29, 801
Lührmann, Dieter 228n53, 491n29, 494n41, 497n54, 530n171, 681n36
Lyons, William John 607n40

Maccoby, Hyam 570n335
Mack, Burton L. 303, 433n13, 435, 437, 488n23, 499n63, 504, 507, 513–15n122, 516n126, 517n127, 518n129, 527n159, 562n296, 574n353, 576
MacLean, B. Hudson 688n55
Macquarrie, John 44, 46
Maier, Johann 554n272
Maier, Paul L. 714n134, 723n164
Malherbe, Abraham J. 189n28
Mann, C. S. 310n52, 311n58, 338n158, 595n12
Manson, T. W. 200, 202, 276n109, 286n154, 319n87, 339n161, 396n32
Manson, W. 203n72
Mara, Maria Grazia 681n38
Marcus, Joel 110n38, 229n57, 238n97, 239n101, 280n128, 334n145, 623n74, 635, 653n156, 655n159
Marmorstein, Arthur 635n107
Marshall, I. Howard 169n40, 232n69, 234nn79, 84, 313n67, 315n76, 337n153, 338n158, 384n6, 398n38, 410n73, 501n67, 509n97, 524n155, 530n171, 553n267, 561n291, 565n304, 566n314, 703n94, 742n225, 792n69, 795n76, 797n91, 799n97, 841
Marshall, Mary J. 230n63
Martin, C. 686n50
Martin, Michael W. 530, 531n174, 536n195
Martin, Ralph P. 339n161, 673n7
Martin, Raymond 302n15
Marwick, Arthur 12n5
Marx, Karl 20–21n31
Marxsen, Willi 130n119, 778, 785, 789
Mason, Steve 358n228, 750n258
Mastin, B. A. 679n33
Matson, Mark A. 444n46, 463n130, 466n152, 475n191
Maurer, Alexander 159n16
May, David M. 228n51

Mazza, Enrico 519n133, 520n139, 522n145, 540n213
McArthur, Harvey K. 237n91
McCarter, P. K. 398n40
McCown, Chester Charlton 130n119, 408n71
McCullagh, C. Behan 46n91
McDonald, Lee Martin 9n1, 53n118
McGing, Brian C. 415n86
McGowan, Andrew 219n19, 520n139, 540n212
McIntire, C. T. 53n118
McKnight, Scot 3, 29n58, 30n60, 173n51, 181n1, 185n10, 191n41, 193n44, 199n57, 201n64, 202n66, 203n72, 204n80, 207nn89–90, 209n95, 219n18, 244n125, 305n30, 327n120, 346n193, 420, 439n39, 482, 512n112, 530, 531n176, 532n179, 542–44, 545n226, 546n231, 552n262, 554nn269, 271, 557nn280, 282, 563, 565n302, 567n316, 568, 570nn332–34, 572n346, 574n354, 828n6, 829–30
McLaren, James 344n183
McLaughlin, John L. 221n26
Mealand, David L. 64n142
Meeks, Wayne A. 327n121, 406n60
Meier, John P. 2, 12n7, 56n123, 60n134, 63n139, 65n144, 67n153, 68, 69n158, 70–71n169, 72n170, 74n177, 95n3, 99n7, 104n18, 106n23, 109n34, 110n38, 134, 141n157, 143n162, 173n51, 182–87n23, 198n54, 200n60, 203n72, 204nn77, 80, 209n95, 217, 244n124, 252–54n12, 257–59n41, 260n42, 264–65, 268, 287–88, 299n8, 304n26, 306–7n40, 309n43, 313, 315, 317n80, 318n84, 322, 334n145, 393n23, 394n28, 408nn68, 71, 444n46, 483n10, 488n20, 503n78, 512n110, 541n215, 557n282, 559n287, 572n343, 589, 592, 686nn50–51
Mencken, H. L. 486n15

Merklein, Helmut 124n95, 565n303, 567n316
Merz, Annette 66n149, 190n31, 217, 258, 269n87, 270n88, 273n98, 278n122, 279, 335n148, 393n23, 463nn130–31, 471, 483, 528n164, 552n260, 567n315, 568n321, 803
Meshorer, Yaʻakov 399n42, 711n117
Mettinger, T. N. D. 399n44
Metzdorf, Christina 462n127
Metzger, Bruce M. 530n171, 538n203, 792n65
Meye, Robert P. 141n157, 183n5
Meyer, Ben F. 2, 29n58, 66n148, 119n72, 136nn138–39, 137nn143, 145, 183n5, 184, 186n16, 190n31, 191n35, 305n28, 320nn95–96, 337, 338n158, 339n161, 348n197, 394n25, 464n136, 471n179, 836, 837n15
Michaelis, Wilhelm 778
Michel, Otto 397
Millar, Fergus 416nn88–89, 417n95
Miller, Merrill P. 481n3
Miller, Robert J. 69n159, 435, 436n27, 437n35
Mills, Mary E. 152n3
Minear, Paul S. 53n118
Mitchell, Alan C. 235n87
Modica, Joseph B. 828n6
Moloney, Francis J. 317n80, 335n148
Mommsen, Theodor 725n172, 726n176
Montefiore, C. G. 192n42, 281, 282n139
Montefiore, Hugh 201n64
Moo, Douglas J. 489n24, 492n32, 500n65, 503n75, 576n356, 595n12
Moore, George Foot 271n91
Moore, Scott 215n1
Moritz, Thorsten 234n83
Morris, Leon 317n83, 338n159, 445n49, 502n73, 534n188, 553n267
Motyer, Stephen 109n32
Moule, C. F. D. 191n37, 203n74, 329n130, 465n144, 649n147

Mowinckel, Sigmund 335, 407n62
Mullen, J. Patrick 232n69
Munslow, Alan 21n33, 24n44
Murphy-O'Connor, Jerome 136n139, 137n143, 139n152, 437n35, 446n59, 451n75, 452n84, 455nn98–99, 470n173, 777n6
Mußner, F. 201n64
Müller, Karlheinz 615
Müller, Mogens 340n167
Myers, Ched 335n150

Naveh, J. 18n19
Neagoe, Alexandru 736n212
Neale, D. 601n27
Neill, Stephen 1n1
Neirynck, Frans 100n8, 257n28, 261n47, 681n37, 792
Neufeld, Thomas R. Yoder 815, 816n143
Neusner, Jacob 77n189, 116n64, 223n32, 231n64, 272n94, 284n146, 285, 349n198, 350n203, 403n54, 458n107, 459, 463, 467, 613n55, 620, 654, 751n261, 828n5
Newman, Hillel I. 747n246
Newton, Michael 224n37
Neyrey, Jerome H. 696n81, 702n92
Ng, Esther Yue L. 242n119
Nickelsburg, George W. E. 158n12, 310n48, 811
Nicklas, Tobias 681n38
Niederwimmer, Kurt 518, 521n141, 522n144, 525n158, 527n161
Nolland, John 65n146, 170nn42, 44, 173, 174n53, 185n13, 204n81, 205n83, 230n62, 232n69, 233, 234n79, 268n81, 269, 453n86, 530nn170–71, 538n204, 553n265, 554, 557n280, 572n346, 702n92, 742n226, 792n69, 795, 797n91, 798
Nordsieck, Reinhard 677nn23, 25
North, J. A. 389n15

Novick, Peter 12n5, 73n172
Noy, David 229n55
Numbers, Ronald L. 45n90

O'Brien, Kevin 546n230
O'Brien, Peter T. 673n7
O'Day, Gail R. 316n79
O'Donnell, Victoria 707n100
O'Neill, J.C. 593n9
O'Toole, Robert F. 487n17
Oepke, Albrecht 113n48, 391n19
Osborne, Grant R. 29n57, 779n18, 780n25, 799n96, 800nn101–2, 801n103, 802n107, 805n114, 808n123, 848
Oswalt, John N. 805n114
Otto, Rudolf 206
Otzen, Benedikt 400n47
Oyen, Geert van 618n67

Pannenberg, Wolfhart 53n118
Park, Eung Chun 199n57
Parker, D.C. 530n173
Parsons, Mikeal C. 530n172, 531n175
Patsch, Hermann 483, 565n302
Patterson, Stephen J. 140n155, 676n21
Pearson, Brook W.R. 805n112
Perkins, Pheme 316, 339n160, 795
Perrin, Nicholas 58n129, 676
Perrin, Norman 59n131, 63, 64nn141–42, 69n158, 74n176, 203n76, 237n93, 305n29, 623n73, 644, 651, 652n155, 775
Pesch, Rudolf 261, 265, 266n70, 310nn53–54, 482n5, 483, 491n29, 493, 495n45, 497n51, 502, 532n179, 533n183, 565n302, 572n346, 573n349, 576n356, 603n32, 606n36, 623n74
Petzer, J.H. 532, 535
Phillips, Thomas E. 231
Pickl, J. 557
Pines, Shlomo 685n48

Plisch, Uwe-Karsten 677nn23, 25
Pokorný, Petr 337n155
Polanyi, Michael 33n67
Polkow, Dennis 63n139, 69n158, 71n167, 305n28
Poole, R.S. 391n19
Poon, Ronnie S. 111n40
Poon, Wilson C.K. 238n100
Pope, Marvin H. 221
Porter, Stanley E. 1n1, 10n3, 53n118, 57n127, 60n134, 64n142, 66n150, 67n153, 68n155, 69nn158, 160, 70n163, 72n171, 218, 236n88, 254n15, 305n28, 307nn39–40, 321n101, 322n104, 384n6, 694n73, 812, 813nn135–37, 814
Potter, Garry 28n55
Powell, Mark Allen 10n3, 384n6
Prevenier, Walter 32n66, 36n71, 61n135
Price, Robert M. 48n97, 775n2, 781n28, 782n31
Priest, J. 164n30, 458
Priest, John F. 224n36
Prince, Deborah Thompson 797
Puech, Émile 634n105

Quast, Kevin 316n78

Radin, Max 701n91
Rajak, Tessa 358n229
Rambo, Lewis R. 188–89
Ramsey, A.M. 576n357
Ranke, Leopold von 20, 21n32
Räisänen, Heikki 333n144, 337n153
Read-Heimerdinger, J. 537n200
Reed, Stephen A. 221n29
Rehkopf, Friedrich 501n67
Reicke, Bo Ivar 118n71, 254n16, 551n257, 555n274, 595n12
Reid, Barbara E. 232n71, 233n73
Reifenberg, A. 708n103
Reinbold, Wolfgang 601, 627–28, 701n91

Reinhold, Meyer 729n186
Reiser, Marius 124n95, 140n156
Rese, Martin 530
Resseguie, James L. 240n107
Richards, E. Randolph 445n49
Richardson, John 725n173
Richardson, Peter 448n67, 449n70, 455nn96, 98–99, 465n145, 470n173
Riesenfeld, Harald 278n119, 283, 286n157
Riesner, Rainer 203n74
Rigaux, Béda 183n5, 187n22, 191n37, 204n79, 206
Riggs, John W. 482n4, 486, 516n126
Riley, Gregory J. 675n18
Ringe, Sharon H. 233n78
Rivkin, Ellis 132n122, 701n91
Robbins, Vernon K. 492n34
Roberts, Alexander 77n191, 694n71
Robinson, J. Armitage 681n38, 761n291
Robinson, James M. 58n129, 77n192, 99n7, 171n45, 190n29, 230n60, 675n16, 677n24
Robinson, John A.T. 123n91, 129n117, 135n136, 136n139, 446n57, 447n61
Rollmann, Hans 836n14
Roloff, Jürgen 187n22, 191, 198nn54–55, 203n74, 204n82, 205n83, 268n83, 579n359
Romanoff, Paul 406n60
Rordorf, Willy 282n139
Rosadi, Giovanni 701n91
Roth, Cecil 461n120
Rousseau, John J. 310n50
Routledge, Robin 545
Rouwhorst, Gerard 520n139, 527n160
Rowland, Christopher 325n114, 337n155, 369n264
Rubio, Fernando Bermejo 10n3
Rudy, David R. 188n27
Runnalls, Donna 471n179
Rusam, Dietrich 169n39

Safrai, Shemuel 229n55, 359nn231–32, 360nn235, 237, 365n259, 448n66
Sanders, E. P. 2, 12n6, 35n69, 49–50n103, 59n131, 60n134, 63n139, 64, 65nn144–45, 66n148, 68nn155–56, 70nn162–64, 73nn173–74, 79nn196, 198, 81n201, 82n204, 84, 95n2, 106n23, 136nn139, 141, 140n156, 141n157, 181n3, 183nn5–6, 184, 186nn15–16, 188, 190, 192n43, 197n53, 200n61, 216–17n10, 228, 262n55, 270, 271n91, 273n96, 279n125, 285, 307–8n41, 343, 386, 408, 411, 413, 420n100, 429, 439, 447nn62, 64, 448n66, 449n69, 452n77, 455n100, 463n130, 464n137, 465, 469, 471, 482, 487n18, 497n53, 593n9, 607, 718n146, 737n214, 754n270, 756n277
Sanders, J. N. 679n33
Santos, Narry F. 338n157
Sartre, Maurice 725n171
Sänger, Dieter 340n167
Sæbø, Magne 400n47
Scaer, Peter J. 696n81
Schalit, Abraham 358n227
Schaller, Berndt 277n115, 278n120, 280n129
Schäfer, Peter 632n100
Schechter, Salomon 637n110
Scheidweiler, Felix 591n5
Schenke, Ludger 488n23
Schiffman, Lawrence H. 224n37, 225n38
Schlund, Christine 545n226, 547n236
Schmid, Ulrich 536n195
Schmidt, Ludwig 399n44
Schmithals, Walter 183n4, 187n19, 482n5, 487n16, 491n29, 499n63, 503n76, 516n126, 524n153, 529n169, 548n239, 549n247, 552n260, 565n302, 566n313, 567n318, 571n336, 572nn343, 345

Schnabel, Eckhard J. 337n155
Schnackenburg, Rudolf 136n141, 139n150, 191n37, 231, 240n105, 316n79, 327n123, 502n73, 796, 797n84
Schneemelcher, Wilhelm 75n178, 77n190, 100n9, 590n3, 681nn36–38, 684n42, 704n96
Schneider, Gerhard 394n25, 482n5, 742nn227–28
Schneider, Johannes 408nn66–67
Schneiders, Sandra M. 800, 801n104
Schonfield, Hugh 695n75
Schorch, Stefan 221n26
Schottroff, Louise 234n82
Schramm, Gene 220
Schröter, Jens 482n7, 483n10, 510nn101–2, 518n130, 521n142, 522, 525n156, 527n162, 530n171, 562–63, 572n342, 573n348
Schulz, Siegfried 387n11, 410n73, 612nn52–53
Schürer, Emil 76n183, 271n91, 361nn239–40, 242, 362nn247, 250–51, 363n252, 394n30, 398n39, 408n67, 414nn83–84, 416n90, 418n96, 716n140, 725n173, 726nn174–75, 727nn178, 180
Schürmann, Heinz 190n30, 191n37, 199n57, 202n70, 206, 207n91, 483, 501n67, 510n102, 528n163, 530, 533n183, 534, 537–39n209, 549, 564n300, 565n303, 571n337, 572n344, 573–74, 579
Schwartz, Daniel R. 706n98, 714n134, 723nn165, 169
Schwartz, Seth 356n226
Schweitzer, Albert 4n14, 10n3, 79n195, 123n91, 190, 258
Schweizer, Eduard 200n61, 257, 258n33, 265n68, 278n121
Schwemer, Anna Maria 2n9, 120n80, 144n164, 333n143, 370n268, 474n189, 483, 488n22, 511n105, 543n223, 545n228, 547n234, 549n248, 550n255, 552n263, 563n299, 572n343, 575n355, 593n9, 624n78, 631n94, 836n14
Scobie, Charles H. H. 116n61, 118n71, 123n91, 129n116, 137n144, 138–39n151
Scott, James M. 164n32, 197n53
Seeley, David 140n156, 435, 436nn28–29, 437n34, 439n40, 444n45, 674n15, 675n17
Sekeles, E. 18n19
Sellew, Philip H. 675n18
Sellin, D. E. 400n48
Shemesh, Aharon 225n38
Shepherd, Tom 618n67
Shermer, Michael 31
Sherwin-White, A. N. 602n28, 608n43, 726nn174, 176–77, 727n182, 729nn184, 187, 731nn192, 194, 196
Shimoff, Sandra R. 223n34
Sider, R. J. 777n8
Siebert, Anne V. 711n118
Sigal, Phillip 283n142, 544n225
Silberman, L. H. 554n272
Sim, David C. 205n84
Skarsaune, Oskar 523n152, 540–41, 544, 546n233
Slee, Michelle 524n154
Slingerland, H. Dixon 160n18
Sloyan, Gerard S. 701n91
Smallwood, E. Mary 389n15, 394n30, 416n90, 713n126, 714n134, 715n138, 717n143, 718n147, 719n150, 722n162, 723n164, 725n172, 727n180, 730n190
Smit, Peter-Ben 239n104
Smith, Barry D. 533n183, 553, 560n288, 565n303, 566nn306, 308, 567nn315, 317, 568nn320, 324, 570n332
Smith, C. W. F. 396n32
Smith, D. Moody, Jr. 388n12

Smith, Daniel A. 675n17
Smith, Dennis E. 216–17, 231, 481–82, 484, 487n16, 492n34, 507n91, 508n94, 543n223
Smith, Derwood C. 118n71
Smith, Morton 307n36
Snodgrass, Anthony 18n20
Snodgrass, Klyne R. 202n67, 653n157, 676n22, 838
Soards, Marion L. 493n39, 679n30
Spivak, J. 525n156
Stacey, W. D. 482n7, 568n319, 570n334
Staerk, D. W. 633n102
Stanton, Graham N. 601n27, 828n6
Stauffer, Ethelbert 123n91, 713, 722–23n163
Steele, E. Springs 241
Stein, Robert H. 58nn128–29, 59n131, 63n139, 69n158, 71n167, 96n4, 217n11, 236n89, 305n28, 313n67, 340n168, 443n42
Stern, David 237n91
Stern, Frank 228n50
Stern, Menahem 359nn231–32, 360nn235, 237, 365n259, 612n52
Stevenson, G. H. 725n171
Stillman, Martha K. 684n41
Stoker, William D. 75n178
Story, Cullen I. K. 553n265
Strachan-Davidson, James Leigh 731nn194, 199, 732nn200–201
Strecker, Georg 102n11, 103n13, 104n15, 315n73, 485n13
Strobel, August 593n9, 601, 625, 627, 629
Strugnell, John 628n88
Stuhlmacher, Peter 254, 323, 371n270, 483, 510, 563n299, 565
Swete, H. B. 681n38

Tabor, James D. 331n137
Tabory, Joseph 545n226
Talbert, Charles H. 463n128

Talmon, Shemaryahu 349nn199–200
Tan, Kim Huat 444n46, 445n51, 452n85, 454n91, 461, 464n136, 465n145, 470n174, 474n187
Tatum, W. B. 106n23
Taylor, Joan E. 107n28, 128n113, 130n118, 132n122, 135n133, 166n36, 708n103, 709nn108, 110, 710, 711nn117–18, 712nn120, 123, 713n130
Taylor, Vincent 171n46, 202n66, 257n29, 265n68, 311n58, 313n67, 315n76, 334n147, 339n161, 488n22, 493n35, 495n45, 498n57, 512n112, 561n292, 576n356, 742n225
Tàrrech, A. P. 169n40
Telford, William R. 461
Tellegen-Couperus, Olga 730n191
Theissen, Gerd 66, 190n31, 191n35, 217–18, 254n15, 258, 269n87, 270n88, 273n98, 278n122, 279, 305, 306nn31–33, 307, 335n148, 393n23, 463nn130–31, 471, 483, 528n164, 552n260, 566n314, 567n315, 568n321, 594, 629, 674n12, 803
Theobald, M. 562n295
Thiselton, Anthony C. 29n57, 33n67, 511n108, 522n143, 554n271, 574n352, 777–78n15, 780n22, 781
Thurber, James 193
Thyen, Hartwig 118n71, 120n80, 123n91
Tibbets, Janice 670n1
Tigchelaar, Eibert J. C. 77n186, 194n47, 456n102, 691n64
Tomson, Peter J. 545n226, 557n282
Torrey, C. 595n12
Tosh, John 32n66
Towner, Philip H. 703n94
Trilling, Wolfgang 183n5, 198n54, 204n79, 205n83, 503n78
Troeltsch, Ernst 43–45, 52n118
Tucker, Aviezer 12n5

Tuckett, Christopher M. 58n128, 96n4, 334n145, 337n153, 342n173, 348n197, 369n267, 370n269, 387n11, 461n120, 463n131, 676n22, 836n13
Turner, H. E. W. 723n169
Twelftree, Graham H. 152n3, 160, 162–63n27, 170, 203n72
Tyrrell, George 4n14, 79n195
Tzaferis, Vassilios 18n19, 310n49

Uhlig, Siebert 617n64
Ulansey, David 109n32
Urbach, Ephraim E. 636n108
Uro, Risto 199n57

Vaage, Leif E. 111n40
van de Sandt, Huub 482n4, 522n145
Van Voorst, Robert E. 75nn178–79, 688n56
VanderKam, James C. 459n110
Vermès, Géza 3, 109n35, 208, 262n55, 279, 285, 335n148, 340n168, 341n170, 645, 718n149, 834n12
Versnel, H. S. 391n17
Vielhauer, Philipp 102n11, 103n13, 104n15, 183n4, 187n19, 485n13
Visser't Hooft, Willem Adolf 387n9
Vögtle, Anton 340n167, 645n135

Waits, Jonathan 215n1
Walker, William O., Jr. 216n8
Wallace, Daniel B. 680n34
Walton, Steve 799n96
Watson, Alan 701n91
Watson, Francis 1n1
Weaver, Dorothy Jean 199n57
Weaver, Walter P. 10n3
Webb, Robert L. 1n1, 4–6, 80nn199–200, 81n202, 95n1, 100n9, 107nn28–29, 108n30, 111n42, 113nn43–44, 48, 114nn51, 53–54, 116nn59–60, 63–64, 117n66, 118n71, 119n75, 120nn76, 79–80, 121nn81, 83, 122nn85, 87, 124nn94, 97, 125n99, 127nn104–7, 128nn110, 113, 130nn118, 120, 131n121, 133n127, 135n134, 136n137, 138n146, 140n154, 141n159, 144n163, 206n88, 207n90, 324, 325n113, 721n159, 751n261, 752n262, 827, 845
Webb, William J. 9n1
Weber, Max 20
Weber, W. 392n20
Wedderburn, Alexander J. M. 431n9, 434n21, 777n6
Weeden, Theodore J. 335n149, 738n216
Weinel, Heinrich 399n44
Weiss, Herold 282n138
Wellhausen, J. 548n238
Wengst, Klaus 707n101, 776
Wenham, David 799n96
Wenham, Gordon J. 116n64
Wenham, J. 595n12
Weren, W. J. C. 788n55
Werner, Eric 407n63, 408n67
Westcott, B. F. 530, 792n65
Westerholm, Stephen 275n103, 283n142
Wevers, John W. 398n40
Whealey, Alice 685nn47–48, 686n49
White, Hayden 22–25n48, 31
Whybray, R. N. 222, 398n40
Wiarda, Timothy 313n66
Wiesel, Elie 31n61
Wigoder, Geoffrey 220n22
Wilckens, Ulrich 329n130
Wilcox, Max 691n63
Wilkins, Michael J. 320n99, 835
Williams, Peter J. 481n1, 530n170, 531n175, 533n181
Williamson, H. G. M. 399n44
Willitts, Joel 305n28
Wink, Walter 108n30, 129n114, 130n118, 135n136, 136n142, 138n146, 237n93, 335n150
Winter, Bruce W. 226n43

Winter, Dagmar 66, 217, 254n15, 305, 306nn31–33, 307, 594, 629
Winter, Paul 394n25, 593n9, 701n91, 703n93, 704n96, 718n147, 748n250
Witherington, Ben, III 111n39, 120n80, 338n158, 353n216, 369n263, 384n6, 385n7, 387n9, 408nn69–70, 420n100, 434n21, 447n62, 507n91, 516, 521n140, 542n219, 543n223, 552n260
Wolff, P. 124n95
Wrede, William 332–33n144, 836
Wright, David P. 116n64
Wright, N. T. 1n1, 2, 12n7, 29n58, 49–52n117, 66–67n151, 109n35, 111n39, 140n156, 151, 181n3, 183n6, 185, 186n16, 190n31, 191n36, 201n62, 215n3, 217–18, 239n101, 304n26, 308n42, 333n144, 337, 338n156, 348n197, 369n265, 429, 430n2, 443n43, 463n130, 465n143, 474n188, 475n190, 483, 515, 554n271, 601n27, 633n104, 690n61, 754n270, 777n6, 781, 789, 800, 804n111, 806n118, 808n123, 811–12n131, 814, 819
Würthwein, E. 115n55

Xeravits, Géza G. 350n205

Yadin, Yigael 691n63
Yang, Yong-Eui 262n54, 275nn105, 107–8, 279n124, 284, 286n156
Yuval, Israel J. 545n226

Zager, Werner 836n14
Zanker, Paul 707n100
Zeitlin, Solomon 407n64, 701n91
Zeller, Dieter 813
Zerwick, Max 410n73
Zias, Joe 18n19, 692n65
Zimmermann, Johannes 628n88, 634n105

www.ingramcontent.com/pod-product-compliance
Lightning Source LLC
Chambersburg PA
CBHW032125010526
44111CB00033B/74